Korea

D0071280

A Historical and Cultural
Dictionary

Durham East Asia Series

Edited from the Department of East Asian Studies,
University of Durham

Already published:

The Book of Changes (Zhouyi): A Bronze Age
document translated with introduction and notes
Richard Rutt (1996)

Strengthen the Country and Enrich the People: the reform writings of Ma
Jianzhong (1845–1900)
Paul Bailey (1998)

China, a Historical and Cultural Dictionary
Michael Dillon, ed. (1998)

Korea, a Historical and Cultural Dictionary
Keith Pratt and Richard Rutt (1999)

In preparation:

Japan, a Historical and Cultural Dictionary
Don Starr, ed.

China's Tibet Policy
Dawa Norbu

Korea
A Historical and Cultural Dictionary

by

Keith Pratt and Richard Rutt

with additional material by

James Hoare

CURZON

First Published in 1999
by Curzon Press
15 The Quadrant, Richmond
Surrey, TW9 1BP

© 1999 Department of East Asian Studies, University of Durham

Typeset in Times New Roman by LaserScript Ltd, Mitcham, Surrey
Printed and bound in Great Britain by
Biddles Ltd, Guildford and King's Lynn

All rights reserved. No part of this book may be reprinted or reproduced or utilised in any form or by any electronic, mechanical, or other means, now known or hereafter invented, including photocopying and recording, or in any information storage or retrieval system, without permission in writing from the publishers.

British Library Cataloguing in Publication Data
A catalogue record of this book is available from the British Library

Library of Congress Cataloguing in Publication Data
A catalogue record for this book has been requested

ISBN 0–7007–0464–7 (Hbk)
ISBN 0–7007–0463–9 (Pbk)

TABLE OF CONTENTS

PREFACE

I

This Dictionary is intended as a quick access handbook, providing factual information about events, people, and topics in the history and culture of Korea. It is not only for specialist use: of course we hope it will prove useful to teachers and students, but we are also anxious to interest a broader readership in the richness and fascination of this small but unique country. Our selection of entries reflects what we have found important and interesting in our study of over two thousand years of Korean history and culture. Others would perhaps have made a different choice, and we are all too conscious of some of our omissions. Nevertheless we believe the overall effect of our entries is properly to reflect Korea's pivotal rôle in the development of the north-east Asian region, the characteristics and qualities that typify its civilisation, and the complexity of its experiences during the twentieth century.

Since this is neither an encyclopaedia nor a text book, we have sometimes been constrained by limitations of space from qualifying or enlarging upon statements which, experts will recognise, can not be as hard and fast as we may make them appear. Where appropriate, therefore, we add titles of books and articles in western languages to which readers may turn for further information and guidance, though we should stress that our entries reflect our own opinions, and not necessarily the judgements of these authors. Books which deserve frequent citation for their widespread relevance are not usually mentioned in this way, but are listed in the General Bibliography on page 542.

II

From end to end Korea measures scarcely six hundred miles. Its people regard themselves as homogeneous, despite the frequent intermixing that has taken place over the centuries with people from outside the peninsula, and although regional variations in spoken dialect and forms of popular entertainment, for example, still reflect the intrusion of mountain and riverine barriers, social habits and cultural preferences have evolved in broadly similar style across the whole peninsula. Korea's history has been subject to just as much division and turmoil as that of any other independently developing nation, both self-inflicted and resulting from a geographical position that makes it the natural prey of neighbours from west, north, and east. The twentieth century has seen perhaps the greatest suffering in the whole of Korean history. Submission to Japan has been followed by the agonising division of the country into North and South which, though a vestige of Cold War rivalry between Eastern and Western political blocs, cannot be blamed any longer on foreigners for its perpetuation. Yet the experience of turbulence and disunity past and present has served only to strengthen the Korean people's sense of nationality and longing for peaceful reunification. When the latter comes, it will create new opportunities for joint archaeological, cultural, and historical research by the foremost scholars of South and North, and for their combined co-operation with colleagues in China, Japan and the West. Then, for the first time, may the rich resources of traditional Korean civilisation be fully subjected to modern critical study, and a better light be shed on its past. Compared with the international research that has advanced understanding of Chinese history during the twentieth century, little has yet been done to penetrate the veil covering Korea. Many topics await illumination; many questions remain unanswered, while others have yet to be asked. The evidence is there to be interpreted. It is to be found in libraries, museums and private collections in North and South Korea and around the world, and much more still lies buried below ground.

III

We have drawn upon both primary and secondary source materials. Any unevenness in our coverage of topics from earliest times to the modern period may be due to our subjective preference for certain cultural fields, but it also reflects the political difficulties that have influenced and limited the unravelling of Korea's past in this century. Before 1945 Japanese specialists – geological, archaeological, ethnographic, and architectural – made an invaluable start and provided a foretaste of the riches waiting to be discovered, but they interpreted and exploited what they found within a preconceived framework of Japanese ethnic and cultural superiority. The basis was thus laid, perhaps unavoidably, for the racial rivalry which continued to dog intellectual discussion of Korean history and culture by scholars from the two countries long after the end of the colonial period.

At the start of the second half of the twentieth century western academic attention was concentrated on China first, Japan second, and on Korea mainly as a perceived bridge for cultural transmission between the two rather than as a civilisation in its own right. The legacy of the Korean War was to reinforce the image of the country's subordinate status and to emphasise its dependence on China (past) and the West (present). Moreover, the new ideological barriers between the two Koreas, China and the West now impeded scholarly co-operation, and even prevented thorough investigation of the peninsula's relationship with the continent as archaeologists unearthed the story of China's prehistory and early civilisation.

Partly under the influence of the *minjung* movement in the 1970s, however, South Koreans rediscovered their pride in their national culture and began to transmit it to the West, which was now developing respect for their country's economic revival. The result, by the end of the millennium, was at last an acknowledgement of Korean political independence and an appreciation of its particular cultural traditions. Nevertheless, the improved intellectual exchange and co-operation between East and West which accompanied the ending of the Cold War were not replicated between South and North Korea, where much historical writing continued to reveal a political agenda. Nor were contentious historical issues quick to be resolved between Korean and Japanese scholars. Only in the 1990s did the exchange of information and ideas between Koreans, Chinese and Japanese begin to show signs of agreement, as on the nature of neolithic culture around the Gulf of Bohai or the identification of Korean works of art preserved in Japan. The eventual removal of communication barriers across the 38th parallel will lead to unprecedented opportunities for all Korean scholars to work together and with foreign experts on the discovery of their history, even if it takes somewhat longer for them to override the effects of the century's ideological scars.

IV

We have tried to present basic information in entries that are concise in themselves but draw the reader's attention to related issues. Cross-references are indicated by the use of bold face.[1] Certain topics may be traced at descending levels from generality to detail.[2] For example, the generic entry on MUSIC will point the reader to a consideration of MUSICAL INSTRUMENTS, then to discussion of musical categories such as COURT MUSIC, *CHŎNGAK*, *NONGAK* and FOLK SONGS. Thereafter may be found entries on musical forms including *KAGOK*, *P'ANSORI* and *SANJO*, and at a subsequent level the names of individual instruments (e.g. *KAYAGŬM, TAEGŬM*), pieces (e.g. *YŎMILLAK*), and persons with musical connections (e.g. PAK YŎN).

We have included two Indices. The presence of an Index in an alphabetically arranged Dictionary may at first appear otiose, but (a) the reader may wish to find references to persons, books, etc., who do not warrant an entry in their own right; and (b) even in the case of those who do have their own entries, location of supplementary mention may help to fill out the necessarily abbreviated synopses.

The dating of events in Korean history before 1894 is bedevilled in Western writing by the discordance between the lunar and solar calendars. We have identified the problems in the Dictionary under the headings *KAPCHA* YEARS, LUNAR MANSIONS, and SOLAR TERMS, with a note also on DATING BY MING LOYALISTS. Within the Dictionary we have aimed at accurate solar-year dating, following the Julian Calendar until 5/15 October 1582 and the Gregorian Calendar thereafter. When the day and month of an event (especially birth and death) cannot be ascertained, we have given the solar year that most nearly coincides with the lunar year in question.

Since the translation of titles given to books, offices, brush-names and terms in Korean often fails to render the flavour of the original, we have frequently given literal equivalents rather than their connotation. For the student, for example, *Haedong yŏksa* is more helpfully interpreted as 'Unravelled Chronicles from East of the Sea' than as 'History of Korea'.

---

1 Exceptions to this rule are the commonly recurring names of dynasties and periods (though not when they occur as names of kingdoms), together with the cities of Seoul and P'yŏngyang and the word 'province/s'.
2 Those that may be pursued in this way include Ceramics; China, relations with; Christianity; Confucianism (including neo-Confucianism); Literature; Music; and Painting

V

Long after the invention of their own alphabet, Koreans continued to write in Chinese characters. Even today they are still in limited use in South Korea and are essential in scholarship, especially for the names of people and places. Since they cannot be guessed with any certainty from romanisation, they are shown where appropriate against entry headwords. *Han'gŭl* transcriptions, however, follow alphabetic principles and are not shown, but the introductory article on page xiii explains the McCune-Reischauer system of romanisation used throughout this book. For all that this is more widely used than any other, it is a system that arouses strong emotions, and it is neither easy nor universally accepted, especially in Korea itself. In April 1997 the South Korean government convened a conference to discuss its official replacement by a new system, which would also be adopted on roadsigns. Foreign scholars, while generally admitting the right of Korean authorities to make such a decision, were unhappy about the aesthetics of many words transliterated according to the proposed alternative rules and remained doubtful that the results were any more accurate than McCune-Reischauer as a representation of Korean sounds.

The devisers of McCune-Reischauer were vague about using the hyphen to divide Sino-Korean words, saying that such division 'is always partially a matter of individual interpretation'. We have followed Korean usage in printing book and institutional titles as phonological units, often dividing them (if at all) by hyphens, preferring *Ch'unhyang-jŏn* to *Ch'unhyang chŏn*, *Sŏnggyun-gwan* to *Sŏnggyun'gwan*. We have also placed hyphens in some Sino-Korean words, to ease the eye, hint at the internal grammar of the word, and suggest the slight syllabic stress that usually follows the hyphen. *Chŏn-hŏmnyun-in* is more reader friendly than *Chŏnbŏmnyunin* ('dharma-cakra-mudra').

Alphabetisation in the body of the Dictionary and the indices is according to the word-by-word system. This has the advantage of keeping all personal names with the same surname together. Thus, CHŎNG YŎRIP precedes CHŎNGAN. We do not differentiate in the alphabetical list between vowels shortened with a breve and those without. However, aspirated consonants are treated separately from the unaspirated. Entries beginning Ch' will be found after those beginning Ch; those beginning K', P', and T' follow K, P, and T.

VI

We have sometimes been confronted by a dilemma about the language in which we should refer to an item. Many of our topics, especially the literary ones, had their origin in China or were closely connected with China. In the past, educated Koreans used Chinese sources, though they read and pronounced them in their own way, and today their descendants are familiar with them in modern Korean transliteration. Many of our own readers, on the other hand, may be more accustomed to the modern Chinese romanisation. Partly for ease of identification, therefore, we have often indicated both Korean and Chinese pronunciation, and in certain cases ('*The Romance of the Three Kingdoms*', for example) we also make use of the commonly used English translation as well. A few key terms, despite being better known in their original Chinese, were yet so important in Korea that we generally refer to them in Korean, while providing cross-reference to their Chinese equivalents. Examples of this are *p'ungsu* (C. *fengshui*) and *ŭm-yang* (C. *yinyang*). Some proper names also demand decisions: Do we refer to the boundary between Korea and Manchuria (itself an imprecise conceptual term until the creation of the Japanese puppet state of Manzhouguo) as the Amnok River, or by its better known Chinese pronunciation Yalu? Do we risk offending either Korean or Chinese sensitivities by calling the military colony of the early centuries AD Lelang (C.) or Nangnang (K.)? And what of Tsushima, which was realistically speaking neither Japanese nor Korean, or of the names for disputed territories such as Tokto? We have found it impossible to be completely consistent, and hope that we do not thereby cause confusion or offence.

We have included plentiful Korean vocabulary, because English-Korean dictionaries are usually inadequate about Korean cultural terms, and because it is often hard to pursue a question further unless one has the Korean words for, say, proverbs or objects. But the Dictionary has been compiled for easy use by western readers. Where possible, therefore, our headwords render Korean terms into English: in an English-language book it makes more sense to entitle an entry 'Four Gentlemen', for example, rather than *Sa-gunja*. However, we admit to some inconsistency on this point. Certain terms are generally left untranslated in usage by western writers, perhaps because – like *p'ansori* for example – they are virtually untranslatable; rather than appear perverse by claiming to find an exact equivalent we have followed the more common practice, simply showing an approximate English rendering. We have tried to avoid the tautology that would arise from both giving and translating common suffixes such as *-sa* ('temple') and *-san* ('mount[ain]'). For an interpretation of common suffixes appearing in the titles of offices, such as *-bu, kwan, -wŏn* etc., the reader is referred to the entry on GOVERNMENT, CENTRAL.

VII

We are deeply indebted to Dr James Hoare for writing the entries on recent political history that have added greatly to the value of this Dictionary. We are grateful too to many people for reading some or all sections of the Dictionary in its draft form, and for patiently answering queries and providing useful comments. Among these are Ed Adams, Stephen Batchelor, Don Clark, Terence Cocks, Gertrude Ferrar, Hong Myoung-hee (Agnita Tennant), Gari Ledyard, Peter Lee, Evelyn McCune, Beth McKillop, Li Kyŏnghŭi, Samuel Moffett, Steve Moore, Ena Neidergang, Susan Pares, Jane Portal, Rob Provine, Johannes Reckel, Joan Rutt, Fr Jeremias Schröder OSB, William Skillend, Roger Tennant and Yu Chaesin. Needless to say, none of them is responsible for any errors remaining in the text. Zhong Hong kindly undertook the laborious task of preparing the Chinese characters, and the Cartography Department of the University of Durham has drawn the maps and diagrams.

Finally, we should like to express our admiration for the skill and patience with which Mark Izard and David McCarthy of LaserScript Ltd have handled an awkward and often complicated text.

Chinson-jae
Summer, 1999

LIST OF ABBREVIATIONS

The following abbreviations are used in the Dictionary and its bibliographic references:

C. Chinese; J. Japanese; K. Korean; S. Sanskrit; b. born; r. reigned; d. died

AA	Asian Affairs (London)
AAS	Arts Asiatiques (Paris)
ACA	Acta Asiatica (Tokyo)
AOA	Arts of Asia (Hong Kong)
AS	Asian Survey (Berkeley)
AST	Asiatic Studies (Tokyo)
BSOAS	Bulletin of the School of Oriental and African Studies (London)
CAJ	Central Asian Journal (Wiesbaden)
CSH	Chinese Studies in History (New York)
CSPSR	Chinese Social and Political Science Review (Peiping)
EAH	East Asian History (Canberra)
HJAS	Harvard Journal of Asiatic Studies (Cambridge, Mass.)
JAOS	Journal of the American Oriental Society (New Haven)
JAS	The Journal of Asian Studies (Ann Arbor)
JCS	Journal of Communist Studies (London)
JKS	Journal of Korean Studies (Seattle)
JSSH	Journal of Social Science and Humanities (Seoul)
KC	Korean Culture (Seoul)
KJ	Korea Journal (Seoul)
KO	Korea Observer (Seoul)
KQ	Korea Quarterly (Seoul)
KS	Korean Studies (Honolulu)
KSF	Korea Studies Forum (Pittsburgh)
MAS	Modern Asian Studies (Cambridge)
MRDTB	Memoirs of the Research Department of the Tōyō Bunko (Tokyo)
MS	Monumenta Serica (Nettetal)
OA	Oriental Art (London)
OE	Oriens Extremus (Wiesbaden)

PA	Pacific Affairs (Honolulu)
PBAKS	Papers of the British Association for Korean Studies (London)
PFEH	Papers on Far Eastern History (Canberra)
SJKS	Seoul Journal of Korean Studies (Seoul)
SKC	Peter H. Lee, ed., *Sourcebook of Korean Civilization*, 2 vols., New York: Columbia University Press, 1993, 1996
TASJ	Transactions of the Asiatic Society of Japan (Tokyo)
TOCS	Transactions of the Oriental Ceramic Society (London)
TP	T'oung Pao (Leiden)
TKBRAS	Transactions of the Korea Branch, Royal Asiatic Society (Seoul 1900–1968)
TRASKB	Transactions of the Royal Asiatic Society, Korea Branch (Seoul 1969 onwards)
WA	World Archaeology (London)
WPQ	Western Political Quarterly (Salt Lake City)

THE McCUNE-REISCHAUER ROMANISATION SYSTEM

Korean-American cooperation produced this, the most widely used system for romanising Korean, published as 'The Romanization of the Korean Language, based upon its phonetic structure' in the *Transactions of the Korea Branch, Royal Asiatic Society* (Volume XXIX, 1939).

George McAfee McCune (1908–48) was born in P'yŏngyang and became the founder of Korean studies in the United States. Edwin Oldfather Reischauer (1910–90) was born in Tokyo, became a leading Japanologist, and was US Ambassador to Japan from 1961 to 1966. They were sons of American Presbyterian missionaries, and friends from boyhood.

In summer 1937 McCune began graduate study at the University of California on *Yijo sillok* (*see* **Chosŏn Wangjo Sillok**) and went to stay in Seoul with his father-in-law, Arthur Becker, at Chōsen Christian College (now Yŏnsei University). At the same time Reischauer was on his way from Harvard University to Peiping for research on **Ennin**, but was delayed in Japan by the aftermath of the Marco Polo Bridge incident. He knew no suitable romanisation for the Korean names in Ennin's work, and filled the time of enforced waiting by visiting Seoul to discuss this problem with McCune.

McCune had spoken, read and written Korean since childhood. Reischauer was trained in linguistics. With the help of three leading Korean phoneticists, Ch'oe Hyŏnbae (1894–1970), Chŏng Insŏp (1905–83) and Kim Sŏn'gi (b. 1907), they worked on a new system. Final details were agreed by correspondence after Reischauer was able to enter China in September.

The system is a phonetic transcription of modern standard Korean, not a transliteration of **han'gŭl**, and not intended for linguistic study. Like Wade-Giles for Chinese and Hepburn for Japanese, it uses consonants as in English and vowels as in Italian, with the breve as its only diacritic. It is simple enough when used, as it most often is, for rendering Sino-Korean proper names, but is capable of rendering any text, and subtle if correctly applied. The devisers pointed out a few ambiguities.

As any transcription, rather than transliteration, is bound to do, it requires users to be well acquainted with Korean pronunciation; and it has to accommodate a wide range of irregularities. Attempts to simplify or change it, by government agencies or individuals, have not so far succeeded, generally because they have ignored its subtleties or confused the principles of transcription and transliteration.

The devisers provided for new Korean spellings that were being introduced in the 1930s, but could not anticipate all the details that were finally standardised in 1946. Doubts may arise in connection with *kyŏngŭmhwa*, the reinforcement of syllabic-initials within certain compound words. This is an important feature of Korean pronunciation, but there are no clear rules for its occurrence. Though noted in good **dictionaries**, it is often not expressed in *han'gŭl* spelling (*munjang*, 'piece of writing', for instance, is spelt the same as *munchang*, 'curtain'). In 1937 it could be shown by writing *sai siot*, 'inserted *s*' before a reinforced consonant, but today this is done only when the previous syllable ends in a vowel, and even then is usually not done when that syllable is Sino-Korean.

The McCune-Reischauer principles for expressing reinforcement are clear.

1) After a vowel (whether written with *sai siot* or not) a reinforced consonant is doubled (as in *haeppit* 'sunshine', where *sai siot* is written, and *chokkŏn* 'item', where it may not be).

2) After a consonant (which is romanised with its final form), a reinforced consonant is romanised with its initial form (as in *munpŏp* 'grammar'). This also applies when final *s* belongs to an originally independent word and is not *sai siot* (as in *satkat*, not *sakkat*, 'reed hat' and *katpŏsŏt*, not *kappŏsŏt*, 'cap fungus').

3) Reinforced syllabic-initial *i* or *y* is romanised as *ni-* or *ny-* and the syllabic-final before it romanised as is usual before *n*: thus *annil* not *anil* 'house-work', *honnibul* not *hot'ibul* 'bedsheet', *puŏngnil* not *puŏgil* 'kitchen work', *nŭnnyŏrum* not *nŭt-yorŭm* 'late summer', *yŏmnyŏp'i* not *yŏp'yŏp'i* 'side by side' and *hwiballyu* not *hwibaryu* 'petrol'.

In the following description the system is applied to the standard orthography and language of the **Republic of Korea**. The table gives all theoretically possible sequences of syllabic final and initial consonants within words. Many of these sequences, especially those with a syllabic final of two letters, are rare. Many may never actually occur.

GENERAL RULES

1) Use a diaresis to show when *aë* and *oë* are dissyllables; and, optionally, when a vowel is repeated (e.g. *noŏng* 'old man').

2) Use an apostrophe to show when *n'g* is not pronounced *ng*.

3) Use hyphens for divisions within words (e.g. Kwanghwa-mun), but not within personal names (e.g. An Sugil, Kim Chonguk).

4) When necessary, indicate long vowels by a macron over *ā*, *ī*, *ō* or *ū*, an acute accent over *é*.

5) Do not romanise syllabic-initial *iŭng*.

6) Do not show euphonic consonant-changes between words.

7) Consult dictionaries for the occurrence of reinforcement.

NOTE 1. The letter *riŭl* occurs as a word initial only in that letter name and in transcriptions of foreign words. The common surname often romanised Lee, Li, Rhee or Ri is romanised Yi, though pronounced *i*.

NOTE 2. The devisers allowed that 'division of Sino-Korean words is partially a matter of individual interpretation.' In this Dictionary Sino-Korean phonological units are given hyphens to indicate internal grammar. This eases the eye and retains euphonic changes. Thus *Hong-Giltong-jŏn* (rather than *Hong Kiltong chŏn*) and *walga-walbu* 'arguing the pros and cons.'

VOWELS

ㅏ	a	ㅕ	yŏ	ㅘ	wa
ㅓ	ŏ	ㅛ	yo	ㅙ	wae
ㅗ	o	ㅠ	yu	ㅚ	oe
ㅜ	u	ㅐ	ae	ㅝ	wŏ
ー	ŭ	ㅒ	yae	ㅞ	we
ㅣ	i	ㅔ	e	ㅟ	wi
ㅑ	ya	ㅖ	ye	ㅢ	ŭi

NOTES TO THE TABLE OF CONSONANTS

Word-initial consonants are shown in the top line and word-final consonants in the left-hand column. Euphonic changes in syllabic finals and initials within words are shown in the body of the table. Reinforcement of a following syllabic initial, whether shown in *han'gŭl* spelling or not, is shown by ^.

Intervocalic finals appear in the three right-hand columns, of which the first is normative and the others are exceptions, as explained in Notes 1 and 2 below. Intervocalic initials are shown in the bottom two lines.

1 Before a verb inflection, a noun suffix or the copula *-i-*.
2 Before *-i* and *-y*, except in verb endings and noun suffixes, *-i* 'person', *-(i)ya* and the copula *-i(da)*.
3 Written *-lch'-* before *-i* and *-y*.
4 Written *-t'-* before a verb inflection or noun suffix not beginning with *-i* or *-y*.
5 Written *-ld-*, *-lj-* in verb stems before endings (*alda, alji*) and when a syllable is repeated (as in *taldal, chŏljŏl*).
6 Before syllabic-initial consonants some speakers may pronounce the *l* and drop the final consonant.
7 Written *-lk-* in *salkwaengi* 'leopard-cat' and sometimes in verb-stems.
8 Written *-th-* when a noun precedes a suffix with initial *-h* (as in *chŏthago* 'with milk').
9 As a syllabic initial, *s-* is replaced by *sh-* before *-wi*.
? Alternative. Pronunciation changes rapidly and speakers of standard Korean do not all say things in the same way.
* Before a suffix, final *-t* of a Korean letter name is treated as *s*, as in *tigŭsŭro, chiŭnman, ch'iŭtto, t'iŭtchŏrŏm, hiŭtpoda*.

TABLE OF CONSONANTS

initial / final		ㄱ k	ㄴ n	ㄷ t	ㄹ r	ㅁ m	ㅂ p	ㅅ s[9]	ㅈ ch	ㅊ ch'	ㅋ k'	ㅌ t'
ㄱ	k	kk	ngn	kt	ngn	ngm	kp	ks	kch	kch'	kk'	kt'
ㄲ	k	kk	ngn	kt	ngn	ngm	kp	ks	kch	kch'	kk'	kt'
ㄳ	k	kk	ngn	kt	ngn	ngm	kp	ks	kch	kch'	kk'	kt'
ㄴ	n	n'g	nn	nd	ll	nm	nb	ns	nj	nch'	nk'	nt'
ㄴ^	n	nk	nn	nt	ll	nm	np	nss	nch	nch'	nk'	nt'
ㄵ	n	nk	nn	nt	ll	nm	np	nss	nch	nch'	nk'	nt'
ㄶ	n	nk'	nn	nt'	ll	nm	np'	nss	nch'	nch'	nk'	nt'
ㄷ	*t	tk	nn	tt	nn	nm	tp	ss	tch	tch'	tk'	tt'
ㄹ	l	lg	ll	[5]lt	ll	lm	lb	ls	[5]lch	lch'	lk'	lt'
ㄹ^	l	lk	ll	lt	ll	lm	lp	lss	lch	lch'	lk'	lt'
ㄺ	[6]k	[7]k	ngn	kt	ngn	ngm	kp	ks	kch	kch'	kk'	kt'
ㄻ noun	m	mg	mn	md	mn	lm	mb	ms	mj	mch'	mk'	mt'
ㄻ verb	[6]m	mk	mn	mt	mn	mm	mp	mss	mch	mch'	mk'	mt'
ㄼ noun	l	lg	ll	lt	ll	lm	lb	lss	lch	lch'	lk'	lt'
ㄼ verb	[6]p	pk	mn	pt	mn	pm	pp	pss	pch	pch'	pk'	pt'
ㄽ	l	lk	ll	lt	ll	lm	lp	lss	lch	lch'	lk'	lt'
ㄾ	l	lk	ll	lt	ll	lm	lp	lss	lch	lch'	lk'	lt'
ㄿ	[6]p	pk	mn	pt	mn	mm	pp	ps	pch	pch'	pk'	pt'
ㅀ	l	lk'	ll	lt'	ll	lm	lp'	lss	lch'	lch'	lk'	lt'
ㅁ	m	mg	mn	md	mn	mm	mb	ms	mj	mch'	mk'	mt'
ㅁ^	m	mk	mn	mt	mn	mm	mp	mss	mch	mch'	mk'	mt'
ㅂ	p	pk	mn	pt	mn	mm	pp	ps	pch	pch'	pk'	pt'
ㅄ	p	pk	mn	pt	mn	mm	pp	ps	pch	pch'	pk'	pt'
ㅅ	t	tk	nn	tt	nn	nm	tp	ss	tch	tch'	tk'	tt'
ㅆ	t	tk	nn	tt	nn	nm	tp	ss	tch	tch'	tk'	tt'
ㅇ	ng	ngg	ngn	ngd	ngn	ngm	ngb	ngs	ngj	ngch'	ngk'	ngt'
ㅇ^	ng	ngk	ngn	ngt	ngn	ngm	ngp	ngss	ngch	ngch'	ngk'	ngt'
ㅈ	*t	tk	nn	tt	nn	nm	tp	ss	tch	tch'	tk'	tt'
ㅊ	*t	tk	nn	tt	nn	nm	tp	ss	tch	tch'	tk'	tt'
ㅋ	k	kk	ngn	kt	ngn	ngm	kp	ks	kch	kch'	kk'	kt'
ㅌ	*t	tk	nn	tt	nn	nm	tp	ss	tch	tch'	tk'	tt'
ㅍ	p	pk	mn	pt	mn	mm	pp	ps	pch	pch'	pk'	pt'
ㅎ	*–	k'	nn	t'	nn	nm	p'	ss	ch'	tch'	tk'	tt'
vowel	–	g	n	d	r	m	b	s	j	ch'	k'	t'
vowel^	–	kk	nn	tt	nn	mm	pp	ss	tch	ch'	k'	t'

TABLE OF CONSONANTS (Continued)

initial / final		ㅍ p'	ㅎ h	ㄲ kk	ㄸ tt	ㅃ pp	ㅆ ss	ㅉ tch	O zero initial —	1	2
ㄱ	k	kp'	kh	kk	ktt	kpp	kss	ktch	g		ngn
ㄲ	k	kp'	kh	kk	ktt	kpp	kss	ktch	g	kk	
ㄳ	k	kp'	kh	kk	ktt	kpp	kss	ktch	g	ks	ngn
ㄴ	n	np'	nh	nkk	ntt	npp	nss	ntch	n		
ㄴ^	n	np'	nh	nkk	ntt	npp	nss	ntch	n		nn
ㄵ	n	np'	nch	nkk	ntt	npp	nss	ntch	nj		
ㄶ	n	np'	nh	nkk	ntt	npp	nss	ntch	n		
ㄷ	*t	tp'	ch'	tkk	tt	tpp	ss	tch	d	j	nn
ㄹ	l	lp'	rh	lkk	ltt	lpp	lss	ltch	r		
ㄹ^	l	lp'	rh	lkk	ltt	lpp	lss	ltch	r		ll
ㄺ	[6]k	kp'	kh	kk	ktt	kpp	kss	ktch	g,?lg		ngn
ㄻ noun	m	mp'	mh	mkk	mtt	mpp	mss	mtch	lm		
ㄻ verb	[6]m	mp'	mh	mkk	mtt	mpp	mss	mtch	lm		
ㄼ noun	l	lp'	rh	lkk	ltt	lpp	lss	ltch	lb		
ㄼ verb	[6]p	pp'	ph	pkk	ptt	pp	pss	ptch	pp		
ㄽ	l	lp'	rh	lkk	ltt	lpp	lss	ltch	r,?ls		
ㄾ	l	lp'	rh	lkk	ltt	lpp	lss	ltch	[3]lt'		
ㄿ	[6]p	pp'	ph	pkk	ptt	pp	pss	ptch	lp'		
ㅀ	l	lp'	rh	lkk	ltt	lpp	lss	ltch	r		
ㅁ	m	mp'	mh	mkk	mtt	mpp	mss	mtch	m		
ㅁ^	m	mp'	mh	mkk	mtt	mpp	mss	mtch	m		mn
ㅂ	p	pp'	ph	pkk	ptt	pp	pss	ptch	b		
ㅄ	p	pp'	ph	pkk	ptt	pp	pss	ptch	b	ps	
ㅅ	t	tp'	th	tkk	tt	tpp	ss	tch	d	s	nn
ㅆ	t	tp'	th	tkk	tt	tpp	ss	tch	ss		
ㅇ	ng	ngp'	ngh	ngkk	ngtt	ngpp	ngss	ngtch	ng		ngn
ㅇ^	ng	ngp'	ngh	ngkk	ngtt	ngpp	ngss	ngtch	ng		ngn
ㅈ	*t	tp'	[8]ch	tkk	tt	tpp	ss	tch	d	j	nn
ㅊ	*t	tp'	th	tkk	tt	tpp	ss	tch	d	ch'	nn
ㅋ	k	kp'	kh	kk	ktt	kpp	kss	ktch	g		ngn
ㅌ	*t	tp'	th	tkk	tt	tpp	ss	tch	[4]d	ch'	nn
ㅍ	p	pp'	ph	pkk	ptt	pp	pss	ptch	b	p'	mn
ㅎ	*–	tp'	th	tkk	tt	tpp	tss	tch	–	–	–
vowel	–	p'	h	kk	tt	pp	ss	tch	–	–	–
vowel^		tp'	th	kk	tt	pp	ss	tch	–	–	–

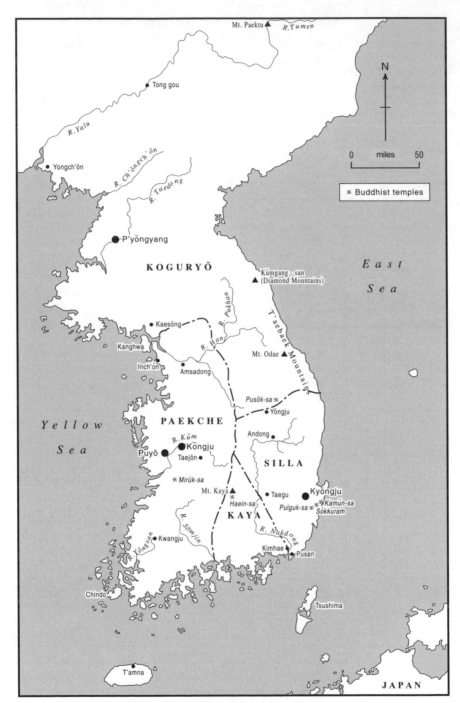

Map 1 The ancient kingdoms of Korea

xviii

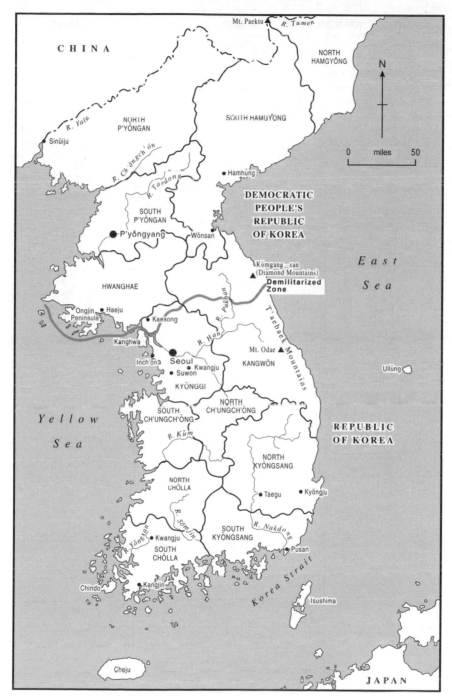

Map 2 The provincial boundaries of modern Korea

xix

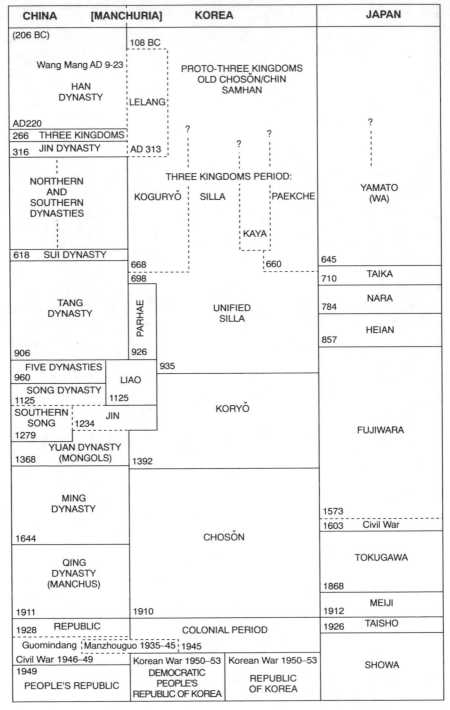

CHINA [MANCHURIA] KOREA			JAPAN
(206 BC)	108 BC		
Wang Mang AD 9-23		PROTO-THREE KINGDOMS OLD CHOSŎN/CHIN SAMHAN	
HAN DYNASTY	LELANG		?
AD220		?	
266 THREE KINGDOMS		?	
316 JIN DYNASTY	AD 313	?	
NORTHERN AND SOUTHERN DYNASTIES		THREE KINGDOMS PERIOD: KOGURYŎ SILLA PAEKCHE	YAMATO (WA)
		KAYA	
618 SUI DYNASTY	668	660	645
	698		710 TAIKA
TANG DYNASTY	PARHAE	UNIFIED SILLA	NARA 784
			HEIAN 857
906	926		
FIVE DYNASTIES 960	LIAO 935		
SONG DYNASTY 1125	1125	KORYŎ	
SOUTHERN SONG	JIN 1234		FUJIWARA
1279			
YUAN DYNASTY 1368 (MONGOLS)	1392		
MING DYNASTY			1573
			1603 Civil War
1644		CHOSŎN	TOKUGAWA
QING DYNASTY (MANCHUS)			1868
1911	1910		1912 MEIJI
1928 REPUBLIC		COLONIAL PERIOD	1926 TAISHO
Guomindang Manzhouguo 1935–45 1945			
Civil War 1946–49	Korean War 1950–53	Korean War 1950–53	SHOWA
1949 PEOPLE'S REPUBLIC	DEMOCRATIC PEOPLE'S REPUBLIC OF KOREA	REPUBLIC OF KOREA	

Chronological chart: the dynastic periods of East Asian history

DICTIONARY

A

AAK 雅樂 'Elegant music'
Music performed exclusively to accompany Confucian **rites and ceremonies** at court. It accompanied both civil (*munmu*) and military (*mumu*) **dances**. The concept of such 'reserved' music was received from China, which first presented the music and instruments for it to the Koryŏ king in 1116 (*see* **Yejong**, King). It made prominent use of certain instruments not normally encountered in other music, notably the *p'yŏnjong* bronze bells and *p'yŏn'gyŏng* stone chimes. Of the twelve Chinese tunes received by the Korean court and revised in the early 15th century, only two now survive, each of 32 notes. Both have been heavily koreanised. At the annual sacrifice to Confucius performed at the *Sŏnggyun-gwan* Confucian Shrine two orchestras, one on the terrace before the shrine, the other in the courtyard below, repeat one of the two in various keys throughout the first six sections of the rite. The other is played for the last section, 'Sending off the Spirits.' The tunes are heptatonic and performed in unison in slow tempo. The beginning of a sequence is marked by three beats from a baton onto the floor of a wooden tub, *ch'uk*, and the end by the sound of a split bamboo brush scraped upwards along the notched spine of a wooden or clay tiger (*ŏ*). Within a piece, the transition from one section to the next is indicated by the ensemble director on the *pak* clappers.
JONATHAN CONDIT, *Music of the Korean Renaissance*, Cambridge University Press, 1983; ROBERT C. PROVINE, *Essays on Sino-Korean Musicology*, Seoul: Il Ji Sa, 1988
See also ***Akhak kwebŏm***; **music, court; musical instruments**

ACADEMY OF SCHOLARS *See Chiphyŏn-jŏn*

ADO (MUKHOJA) 阿道 (墨胡了)
It is generally accepted that **Buddhism** reached **Silla** in the mid-4th or early 5th century and that the first missionary was a monk named Ado (C. Adao), who arrived from **Koguryŏ** and won favour by curing a sick princess, but did not succeed in gaining royal favour for the Dharma. No more is certain. *Samguk sagi* and *Samguk yusa* contain discrepant accounts, and *Haedong kosŭng-jŏn* regrets the lack of clear information. Ado is probably the same man as Mukhoja or Hŭkhoja, 'dark foreigner', a Serindian about whom the same stories are told.

AEGUKKA 愛國歌 'Love country song'
The first western-style national anthem was written by order of King **Kojong** in 1902, when Franz **Eckert** wrote the tune. It began *Sangjenŭn uri Hwangsangŭl tousosŏ*, 'High Lord of Heaven assist our Emperor', and was ordered to be sung in **schools** in 1904. This naturally fell out of use with the abolition of the Empire.

The words officially adopted as the national anthem by the **Republic of Korea** government in 1948 are a *ch'angga* with an obscure history. The words exist in various versions. It has been claimed by some that they were written by **Yun Ch'iho**. A copy signed by him is kept in the New York City Library, dated 1907. The anthem was sung by a Paejae School choir when the corner-stone of the Independence Arch (*Tongnim-mun*; *see* **Yŏngŭn-mun**) was laid in 1896. The tune at first was that of 'Auld Lang Syne', later replaced by that composed by An Ikt'ae (1905–65) in the summer of 1936.

Till the Eastern Sea and Paektu-san
>> dry out and wear away,
Under God's protecting care,
>> our land shall flourish for ay.

(*refrain*)

Thirty thousand leagues of mountains,
>> streams and deathless flowers!*
Taehan people, ever Taehan,
>> we will keep it ours.

Those pines upon the Southern Peak
>> armour and power impart;
Sound of constant wind among them
>> tells the strength of our heart.

* The *mugunghwa* (*Hibiscus syriacus*), **national flower** of Korea

AEGUKTAN 愛國團 'Love country group' *See Ŭibyŏng*

AGE, PERSONAL: KOREAN AND WESTERN RECKONING

By Korean custom, personal age is reckoned by the number of years during which anyone has lived: a new-born child is 1 (i.e. in its 1st year) and another year is added on each lunar **New Year's day**. Westerners count the years completed (described in Korean as *man* 'full'), adding a year on each anniversary of birth. Therefore from the birthday to the next lunar New Year the Korean reckoning is one year older than the western; from the lunar New Year to the birthday the Korean reckoning is two years older than the western.

In the following diagram | = Solar New Year; * = Lunar New Year; x = birthday. Lunar years are known by *kapcha* cyclical names. *See also* **Dates, concordance of lunar and solar**.

SOLAR YEARS	1952	1953		1954		1955		1956
Western age	x0		x1		x2		x3	
LUNAR YEARS	Imjin	Kyesa		Kabo		Ŭlmi		
Korean age	x1	*2		*3		*4		*5
Difference	x <+1>	* <+2>	x <+1>	* <+2>	x <+1>	* <+2>	x <+1>	* <

When year dates only are known, reporting a person's age in western style always involves a 1-year margin of error; converting from Korean to western style involves a 2-year margin of error. For example, **Kojong**'s age on accession is given by Korean writers as twelve. Western historians, knowing that his twelfth birthday came eight months later, give his age as eleven. Had he acceded three weeks later than he did (after lunar New Year's day) Koreans would have said he was thirteen, but westerners would still say eleven. If they did not know the precise days of birth and accession, they could not give his age more accurately than 10–12.

AGRICULTURE

Began in the late **neolithic** period, when millet was cultivated. **Rice** may have been introduced from China by the end of the third millenium BC. Agriculture developed through the **Bronze Age**, practised alongside hunting and fishing. Tools made of **iron** were used from the 4th century BC onwards. Sericulture was introduced from China and clothing was made of **silk** and hempen cloth. An annual harvest **festival** was already celebrated in the state of **Puyŏ**. In the **Samhan,** improvements were made to rice cultivation through the construction of reservoirs. Other crops included millet, maize and beans. Animals such as pigs, horses, oxen, dogs and chickens were domesticated (*see* **animals, domestic**). Among wild crops the value of **ginseng** (*insam*) was already recognised. Pine and walnut trees were grown for their fruit in the Three Kingdoms period, and mulberry for the feeding of silkworms. The ploughing of rice paddy by oxen is said to have been introduced under King Chijŭng (AD 500–514), along with ice-cellar refrigeration.

Cotton cultivation began after the introduction of seeds from China in the 14th century, and the early Chosŏn period saw major advances in agricultural techniques and productivity. The tone was set with the publication in 1429 of *Nongsa-jiksŏl* ('Plain words on agriculture') and given royal impetus by King **Sejong**'s Edict for the Promotion of Agriculture in 1444, urging local officials to support farming families. This was followed in 1451 by an edict from his son, King Munjong, on the importance of irrigation. Better fertilisers were introduced; the square pallet chain pump raised water into ditches; the development of rice seedling transplantation from germination beds into paddy fields led to more economical land use. Through the 17th and 18th centuries agricultural output rose with improved irrigation and the spread of furrowing. **Tobacco** was grown as a cash crop, and sweet **potatoes** as an improvement to the subsistence diet. Nevertheless *sirhak* scholars were aware of the much greater agricultural advances being made in China (*see also* **Pukhak**). Among those who argued, largely in vain, for faster progress in Korea were Yu Hyŏngwŏn (1622–73), **Yi Ik,** and **Pak Chega**.

White potatoes and some chemical fertilisers were brought to Korea in the 19th century, but it was not until the colonial period that major agricultural changes were introduced. Then, to the advantage of the Japanese rather than Korean farmers, rice output rose dramatically as a result of land reclamation schemes, better seed strains, fertilisers, and tools and equipment. More cotton was grown to satisfy Japanese requirements for clothing manufacture, though at the expense of dry cereal crops. Dairy farming remained under-developed, but more varieties of fruit and vegetables were cultivated.

The 1950s saw the beginning of a shift away from an agricultural base in South Korea to a manufacturing one, with resulting changes in the pattern of people's residency and occupations. Agricultural output failed to keep pace, and food imports became necessary. The *Saemaŭl undong,* or New Community Movement, introduced in 1971, aimed to correct this situation and had some success in doing so: self-sufficiency was achieved in rice and barley. But through the 1980s continued migration from the villages into the cities put more pressure on the country's ability to feed itself. Farming was no longer attractive to the young, and by 1985 involved only 20 per cent of the population. Though double-cropping was widely practised in both wet and dry agriculture, only 22 per cent of the land in South Korea is arable, and the rapidly growing population needed more food. The chief crops were rice, cabbage, other fruit and vegetables, and barley. A belated move into dairy farming began to occur. In the late 1980s agricultural output constituted around 11 per cent of the gross domestic product.

3

CHOE CHONG-PIL, 'The Diffusion Route and Chronology of Korean Plant Domestication,' *JAS* 41:3, 1982; CHOE CHONG-PIL, 'Origins of Agriculture in Korea,' *KJ* 30/11, 1990; KOREA DEVELOPMENT INSTITUTE, *Korean Regional Farm Products and Income, 1910–1975*, Seoul: Korean Development Institute, n.d.; SARAH NELSON *et al.*, 'The Origins of Rice Agriculture in Korea: a Symposium,' *JAS* 41.3, 1982; CLARK W. SORENSON, *Over the Mountains are Mountains: Korean Peasant Households and their Adaptation to Rapid Industrialization*, Seattle: University of Washington Press, 1988; YI CH'UN-YONG, 'A Historical Survey of Agricultural Techniques in Korea,' *KJ* 14/1, 1974

AHŬI-WŎLLAM 兒戲原覽 'Primary Survey for Children's Enjoyment'
A short encyclopaedia for children beginning their studies in Chinese characters, arranged in fairly traditional categories from astronomical and meteorological through to the humanities.

AHWANG AND YŎYŎNG 娥皇;女英 (C. Ehuang and Nuying)
Daughters of Yao and wives of the virtuous mythical Chinese ruler Shun. When he died while travelling in the South, near the Xiang River, their tears fell on the **bamboos** and produced the mottled variety *Xiangzhu* (K. *panjuk*). They are known as Sang-buin, (C. *Xiang furen*), and are regarded as emblems of wifely devotion.

AIRING OF BOOKS AND CLOTHES *swaesŏ-p'oŭi* 曬書曝衣
Books and clothes were traditionally put outside in the sun on the 7th day of the 7th moon (about the end of August) to rid them of the pervading damp of the *changma* rainy season. They were watched, and the pages of books were turned from time to time.

AJAENG 牙箏 'rasping zither'
A wooden long zither of Chinese origin used to play both court and folk music. It has seven or eight strings of twisted silk stretched across moveable bridges. Unlike the *kŏmun'go* and the *kayagŭm* it does not rest on the player's knees but is supported at the right-hand end by a wooden stand, and unlike the other two zithers its strings are not plucked but bowed with a resined stick of forsythia wood, which produces a rasping sound. The left hand depresses the strings to vary the pitch and create vibrato. *See also* **music; musical instruments; music, court**

AKCHANG 樂章 'music words'
Akchang as a homogeneous literary genre is still under debate. It refers to the lyrics that accompanied **court music**, but is difficult to define any more closely because it is used to cover *Yongbi-ŏch'ŏn-ga*, *Wŏrin-ch'ŏn'gang-ji-gok*, which are long pure Korean compositions, and 14/15th-century works written in Chinese. It is a useful term, however, in roughly defining the period and purpose of songs written for a developing neo-Confucian court.

AKHAK KWEBŎM 樂學軌範 'Musical Studies Guide'
A great musical encyclopaedia commissioned by King **Sŏngjong**. It was compiled by a team of researchers under the editorship of Sŏng Hyŏn and published in 1493. In its coverage and structural organisation it acknowledged Chinese precedents and indeed cited passages from Chinese musical texts, yet much of the text was newly written and it remained the principal Korean reference work and practical guide on traditional musical matters until the late 20th century. Its nine chapters dealt with (1) music

theory, (2) court orchestras, orchestral music and performance, (3) Chinese (*tangak*) and Korean (*hyangak*) historical dances, (4) Chinese dances of the contemporary Chosŏn period, (5) contemporary Korean dances, (6) **musical instruments** for ritual purposes, (7) other musical instruments, (8) costumes and properties for Chinese and Korean dances, (9) other costumes for entertainers.

ROBERT C. PROVINE, *Essays on Sino-Korean Musicology*, Seoul: Il Ji Sa, 1988
See also **dance; music; music, court; *Yŏngsan hoesang***

ALLEN, HORACE NEWTON 安蓮 (1852–1932)
Born in Delaware, Ohio, Allen studied divinity and medicine before sailing to Shanghai as a doctor in the Northern Presbyterian mission in 1881. He quarrelled with his fellows and was asked to become doctor at the American Legation in Seoul. Barely had he arrived in 1884 when he was summoned to care for those injured in the Post Office *émeute* (*see* **Kapsin Incident**), and saved the life of **Min Yŏngik**. This gained him the king's gratitude, and led to the founding in 1885 of the first royal hospital (**Kwanghye-wŏn**, renamed *Chejung-wŏn* in 1886), which was the prime ancestor of the later Severance and Yŏnsei Hospitals. Allen enjoyed the king's favour even after he transferred to the diplomatic staff of the American legation in 1890, eventually becoming Minister there. He was instrumental in obtaining mining rights and the Seoul-Inch'ŏn **railway** commission for American entrepreneurs. In the troubles of 1895–6 he gave close personal support to the king, and he became increasingly anti-Japanese. After the 1905 accord with the Japanese (*see* **Protectorate Treaty**) he was withdrawn by the US government and spent the rest of his days practising medicine in America.

MARTHA HUNTLEY, *To Start a Work: the Foundations of Protestant Mission in Korea*, Seoul: Presbyterian Church of Korea, 1984; FRED HARVEY HARRINGTON, *God, Mammon and the Japanese: Dr Horace N. Allen and Korean-American Relations 1884–1905*, Madison: University of Wisconsin, 1944

ALTAR OF HEAVEN 圜丘壇 *Wŏn'gu-dan*
When **Kojong** was declared Emperor Kwangmu in October 1897, an imperial Altar of Heaven, *Wŏn'gu-dan*, was built. Modelled on the Altar of Heaven in Beijing, it was a three-tiered circular platform in the open air, with each tier surrounded by a marble balustrade. Imperial sacrifices continued there until the Japanese **annexation** of Korea in 1910, when the Altar was destroyed and the Chosun Hotel built on its site. All that remains is a three-storied subsidiary pavilion, *Hwanggung-u*, commonly known as *p'algak-tang* ('octagonal pavilion'), which enshrined a tablet of Yi T'aejo, founder of the Chosŏn dynasty.

ALTARS OF EARTH AND HARVEST 社稷壇 *Sajik-tan*
The most sacred place in Seoul was established by T'aejo in 1394, in the north-western area of the city. The eastern altar for the spirits of the earth (*sa*) and the western to the spirits of the harvest (*jik*) were two raised earthen areas, about 7 metres square and a metre apart. They stood in the middle of a raised stone platform that had a balustrade round the top, broken by an entrance with steps in the centre of each side. Each entrance once had a *hongsal-mun* (*see* **Red arrow gate**). The king, following the rites of a Chinese vassal king, sacrificed here to the earth in the 2nd moon and to the harvest spirits in the 8th moon, and again on the 12th day after the solar term *Taehan*, 'great cold'. Occasional **sacrifices** were made for crops (*kigok-che*) or for rain (*kiu-je*). The sacrifices were of oxen, sheep (imported from China for the purpose, because

there were none in Korea), pigs and domestic **fowl**, slain by *paekchŏng* butchers. This cultus, of Chinese origin, was begun in Korea during the Three Kingdoms period. On the declaration of the **Great Han Empire** in 1897, the rites were upgraded to those of imperial status.

AMERICA, RELATIONS WITH

The history of relations between Korea and the United States of America falls broadly into two periods, 1866 to 1905 and 1945 to the present. They began inauspiciously with the murder of the crew of the *General Sherman*. This prompted the despatch of a naval expeditionary force in 1871 but only strengthened the anti-foreign inclination of the **Taewŏn'gun**. The conclusion of a treaty between Korea and Japan in 1876 renewed American interest in the peninsula and a Treaty of Amity and Commerce (*see* **Shufeldt Treaty**) was brokered in 1882 by the senior Chinese minister **Li Hongzhang**. This led to the arrival of the first American minister to Seoul, General Lucius Foote, in 1883 and the opening of a Korean legation in Washington in 1887 (*see also* **Dye, William**; **self-strengthening movement**; **Townsend, Walter**). Korea benefited little from any commercial or diplomatic results of the first period relationship. Even during the **Sino-Japanese War** America declared neutrality, and as the prospect of the Japanese **protectorate** loomed this seemed to President Theodore Roosevelt to offer the best chance of checking the Russian advance into East Asia and ensuring the peaceful development of Korea. With the outbreak of the **Russo-Japanese War**, therefore, the United States supported Japan in return for a promise that Japan would not become involved in the Philippines. In 1905 Japan closed down its legation in Seoul. The American **Durham Stevens** became infamous for his pro-Japanese stance while employed as a supposedly independent adviser to the Korean government.

This generally negative experience during the first period of contact was alleviated by the outstanding work of American **protestant** missionaries in Korea, who laid the foundations for a pattern of trust and support that would survive the colonial period and continue into modern times. They instituted important educational and medical work, and became strong advocates of Korean independence. Among them the names of **Horace Allen**, **Horace Underwood**, and **Homer Hulbert** stand out.

The failure of the Western allies to have a plan ready for post-war Korean independence other than Franklin Roosevelt's woolly concept of **trusteeship** was responsible for the unhappy division of the peninsula after 1945. A unit of the US army was hastily despatched to counter the arrival of Soviet troops and an **American Military Government** was set up under Lt-General John **Hodge**. The Americans were welcomed in the south as liberators, but Korean expectations were quickly dashed as the Americans turned for practical administrative assistance to the defeated Japanese colonists. The confused nature of the political scene in Seoul, including the activities of many communist sympathisers, made cooperation difficult, and there was finally an element of desperation in the decision to allow the return of Syngman Rhee (**Yi Sŭngman**) from exile in America in October 1945, where his right-wing nationalism had not won him many supporters, and to recognise his claim to the presidency when the **Republic of Korea** was born.

Fear of Soviet expansionism in the tense post-war world led the United States to take immediate action against communist aggression on the outbreak of the **Korean War** in June 1950. American casualties in the war were very heavy, and their sacrifice was appreciated by South Koreans. The war had immense world-wide effects, deepening the Cold War, instigating hostility between America and the People's

Republic of China, but assisting the recovery of Japan as a result of American aid that now seemed both militarily and politically essential. It forced the United States into an unplanned and costly partnership with South Korea (*see* **US Defense Perimeter**) which brought great benefit to its people, but at the expense of driving their northern neighbours deeper into suffering under the oppressive and isolationist régime of **Kim Ilsŏng**. The United States may not have been primarily to blame for this, though its support for a series of dictatorial governments in the South reinforced political obduracy on both sides of the **DMZ** and hindered the prospect of moves towards reunification even after the ending of the Cold War between the world superpowers. American aid nevertheless underpinned the remarkable economic transformation of South Korea, and American influence is evident in many aspects of Korean life, especially educational. The path towards reconciliation with the North proved difficult, and American adminstrations in the 1990s vacillated over political recognition, their response to the North's continued military and possible nuclear threat, and concern for the physical suffering of its people.

BRUCE CUMINGS, ed., *Child of Conflict: the Korean-American Relationship, 1943–53*, Seattle: University of Washington Press, 1983; CHARLES M. DOBBS, *The Unwanted Symbol: American Foreign Policy, the Cold War, and Korea, 1945–1950*, Kent, Ohio: Kent State University Press, 1981; GEORGE McCUNE, JOHN HARRISON, SPENDER PALMER, SCOTT BURNETT, eds., *Korean-American Relations: Documents Pertaining to the Far East Diplomacy of the United States*, 3 vols, Berkeley: University of California Press, 1951, 1953, Honolulu: University of Hawaii Press, 1989; DONALD MACDONALD, *US-Korea Relations from Liberation to Self-reliance*, Boulder, Colorado: Westview Press, 1992; JAMES MATRAY, *The Reluctant Crusade: American Foreign Policy in Korea, 1941–1950*, Honolulu: University of Hawaii Press, 1985; ANDREW NAHM, ed., *The United States and Korea, American-Korean Relations 1866–1976*, Kalamazoo: Center for Korean Studies, 1979; WILLIAM SANDS, *Undiplomatic Memoirs: The Far East, 1896–1904*, repr. Seoul: Royal Asiatic Society, Korean Branch, 1975

AMERICAN MILITARY GOVERNMENT 美軍政

The United States Army Military Government (USAMGIK) was set up in September 1945 by Lt. Gen. John **Hodge**, commander of the US Eighth Army's XXIV Corps. This army had been drafted into southern Korea at short notice from Okinawa to replace the surrendered Japanese and counter the unexpectedly rapid entry of Soviet troops into the north. It was neither prepared for nor enthusiastic about its task. Washington refused to recognise the **Korean People's Republic** (KPR) as a credible political force because of its left-wing bias, and Hodge was obliged to rely on Japanese officials for assistance in running the country. Major General Arnold succeeded Governor General Abe Nobuyuki as Military Governor, but the Americans incurred Korean scorn and hostility for dealing thus with the enemy. An attempt to persuade **Yŏ Unhyŏng**, the moderate leftist Vice-President of the KPR, to help set up a Democratic Advisory Council was snubbed, and even Syngman Rhee (**Yi Sŭngman**), who was allowed to re-enter Korea from exile in October 1945, was unable to unite many of the feuding political factions. He failed to find common ground with **Kim Ku** and **Kim Kyusik**, returning from China in November (*see* **Provisional Government in Exile**), or with General Hodge. Yi also organised opposition to the terms of the **Moscow Conference** Agreement and the work of the **US-Soviet Joint Commission**. For his part, Hodge had to contend with trouble instigated by both right-wing and left-wing organisations, including communists, and overreacted by imprisoning many independence activists. In 1947 he created a South Korean Interim Legislative

7

Assembly and Interim Government to work with USAMGIK in the hope of satisfying Koreans' political aspirations, but they had no powers and achieved no real level of cooperation with the Americans: Syngman Rhee refused to accept the chairmanship, which was taken by Kim Kyusik. The removal of Japanese restrictions on publishing, religious freedom, and educational and cultural activity had positive effects. In particular, the restored use of the Korean language and teaching about Korean history came as great relief. Japanese-owned land was sold to Korean farmers and a programme for economic recovery defined in May 1946. But conditions were too bad for rapid amelioration and encouraged lawlessness; people remained deeply resentful of their denied liberty.

CHO SOO SUNG, *Korea in World Politics 1940–1950: An Evaluation of American Responsibility*, Berkeley: University of California Press, 1967; BRUCE CUMINGS, ed., *Child of Conflict: American-Korean Relations 1943–1953*, Seattle: University of Washington Press, 1983; E. GRANT MEADE, *American Military Government in Korea*, New York: University of Columbia Press, 1951

See also **Republic of Korea; United Nations Temporary Commission on Korea**

AMHAENG-ŎSA 暗行御史 'secret inspector'
The king occasionally appointed a secret inspector, usually a young man of lower **grade**, to go in disguise to the scene of suspected bad administration or to learn what the common people were saying. The inspector was given a letter marked 'Not to be opened till the Great South Gate has been passed' and severe penalties fell on a man who opened the letter inside the gate or re-entered the city after opening it. He also carried a *ma'pae* and a ruler for measuring cadavers. The letter told him where to go and for what. He was empowered to make judgement on the spot and to dismiss wrong-doers from office, having first shown his *map'ae*. The appointment was temporary and on return to the capital he had to make written reports and return his tokens. The system sometimes worked well, but was open to abuse, especially in times of fierce factional struggle. It is first recorded early in the 16th century and was last used in 1892.
See also **censorate**

AMIDA BUDDHA 阿彌陀佛
Amida Buddha (also called Amitabha and Amitayus), mentioned in the Lotus **Sutra**, is not an historical character. He is an abstraction, the Buddha of Infinite Life, who resides in the Western Paradise of the Pure Land School doctrines. In **Buddhist temple halls** he presides over the *Kŭngnak-chŏn* or *Muryangsu-jŏn*. A common mural painting is the *Kŭngnak-kup'um*,'the nine stages of Paradise'.

AMNOK RIVER 鴨綠江 *See* **Yalu River**

AMSADONG 岩寺洞 *See Chulmun*

AN CHAEHONG 安在鴻 (1891–1968)
As a student in Tokyo in the 1910s he became active in the nationalist movement associated with the Korean **Young Men's Christian Association**. He returned to Korea dedicated to anti-colonialism, and was imprisoned for taking part in the **March First Movement**. He became manager of Sin Sŏgu's *Chosŏn Ilbo*, and in 1927 was one of the founders of the **New Shoot Society**. He served a second term of imprisonment in the late 1930s for sending an agent to Yan'an in China. Prior to the

Japanese surrender in August 1945 he was invited by Governor General Abe Nobuyuki to join with **Yŏ Unhyŏng** and Song Chinu in superintending the transitional period until the arrival of the allied armies, and together they formed a Preparatory Committee for Building the Country (*Kŏn'guk Chunbi Wiwŏnhoe*). An was its vice-chairman, but as the moderate leader of the **Korean Nationalist Party** he disapproved of Yŏ's pro-communist views, and his resignation from the Committee on 1 September opened the way for the formation of the short-lived **Korean People's Republic**. An was nevertheless offered a place on its Central Committee. In the climate of hostility to the **Moscow Conference** agreement on **trusteeship** his cooperation was sought by the head of the **American Military Government**, General **Hodge**. He was an associate of **Kim Kyusik**, and in February 1947 was appointed Civil Governor, the highest post tenable by a Korean under the occupying régime, but like Kim he opposed the **United Nations** plan for **elections** to be held in the South under **UNTCOK** auspices. After the **Korean War** An reappeared in public life in North Korea, holding a post on the Committee for the Peaceful Unification of the Fatherland (*Chaebuk P'yŏnghwa T'ongil Ch'okjin Hyŏpŭihoe*), and calling in 1955 for reunification of the peninsula on communist terms. The Committee was a propagandist organ, and whether he had gone north voluntarily is uncertain.
See also **Korean Democratic Party**

AN CHŎNGBOK 安鼎福 (1712–97)

A *sirhak* scholar, disciple of **Yi Ik**, born at Chech'ŏn. His public career was a long one, though it did not begin until 1751. In the year before he died he was appointed minister-without-portfolio and given the **princely title** Kwangsŏng-gun. He considered himself as carrying on the teaching of **Yi I**, though he patterned his life on **Yi Hwang**, was deeply influenced by the Qing vogue for sifting evidence, and believed that the only proper purpose of study was the common good. He cautioned his friends who were eagerly studying Western ideas against adopting Catholicism because he thought it was individualistic and selfish, as he considered Buddhism also to be. For twenty years he worked at editing *Tongsa gangmok*.

AN CHUNGGŬN 安重根 (1879–1910)

Born at Haeju and early trained in Chinese, horsemanship and archery. He was baptized as a Catholic (Thomas) in 1895. For a while he directed a coal business, but after the Japanese **protectorate treaty** of 1905 he fled in disgust to Vladivostok, where he set up a volunteer army and fought his way back into Korea, reaching Kyŏnghŭng. On 26 October 1909, when the Japanese Resident General in Korea, Prince **Itō Hirobumi**, was on his way to meet Russian representatives, An, disguised as a Japanese, shot and killed him with a pistol at Harbin railway station. He was arrested and executed in Lüshun (Port Arthur) jail.

AN CH'ANGHO 安昌浩 (1878–1938)

Born at Kangsŏ in South P'yŏngan, he went to Seoul in 1895, where he attended a missionary school, became a Presbyterian and joined the **Independence Club**. In 1899 he founded a school in his home town before going to America, where he rallied expatriate Koreans before returning to Korea and taking part in the founding of the secret nationalist society, *Sinminhoe* (*see* **New People's Association**). In 1907 he helped establish **Osan School** at Chŏngju. He worked as a journalist, ran a bookshop in **Taegu** and an earthenware business in P'yŏngyang, and joined **Ch'oe Namsŏn** in founding a student society (*Ch'ŏngnyŏn-hagu-hoe*), before setting off on

a two-year journey to Beijing, Vladivostok, Europe and America, where he again rallied overseas Koreans. In 1913 he started a nationalist club in Los Angeles. After the Independence demonstration of 1 March 1919 he joined the government-in-exile in Shanghai, but soon fled its squabbles and returned to Seoul. In 1925 he was again in the USA; then in 1926 with freedom fighters in **Manchuria**, where he was arrested by the Chinese police, but soon freed. In 1928 he was caught by the Japanese in Shanghai, taken to Korea and imprisoned in Taegu, but released early because of poor health. Arrested again in 1937, he died of cirrhosis of the liver a year later in Seoul University hospital.
See also **March First Movement; Provisional Government in Exile**

AN DAO 安燾
Leader of a substantial Chinese embassy to Korea in 1078. This was the first significant sign of official Chinese amity following a period of diplomatic coolness beginning in 1030. Its two specially built ships carried **textiles**, clothing, belts, **horses**, whips, **tea**, teapots, wine warmers, silver vessels, bowls, candles, and **musical instruments**. The mission was given a rapturous reception in Korea and **tribute** was promptly sent back, including clothing, belts, **horses**, saddles, gold, silver and **rice**.

AN HYANG (AN YU) 安珦(裕) (Hoehŏn, 1243–1396)
His brush name, Hoehŏn 'Twilight Pavilion', was deliberately copied from that of **Zhu Xi**, Huian (K. Hoeam), but his name-character Hyang became tabu in 1545 because it was the personal name of King Myŏngjong, and for the rest of the Chosŏn dynasty he was known as An Yu.

Regarded as the man who first brought neo-Confucianism to Korea, he was a middle-ranker from Kyŏngsang province who entered government service in 1260 at the early age of 17. There is a famous tale of his suppression of *mudang* (shamanesses) at Sangju about 1273. A dozen years later he went with a royal party to Yuan China and brought back pictures of Confucius and Zhu Xi with a copy of Zhu Xi's complete writings. When he re-established the *Sŏnggyun-gwan* in 1303 he obtained more equipment and books from China. In 1304 he established a state fund for Confucian education, though he was in fact a promoter of neo-Confucianism rather than a thinker. For this reason, the first *sŏwŏn* (provincial academy), later called *Sosu Sŏwŏn,* was dedicated to him when it was erected in 1543 at Sunhŭng, near P'unggi, in north Kyŏngsang. He was canonised by the Koryŏ state in 1319.

AN KYŎN 安堅 (Hyŏndongja, 1400–?)
Painter who attained the unusually high status of fourth **grade** in the *Tohwa-sŏ*, and who was patronised by Prince Anp'yŏng (*see* **Yi Yong**). The National Museum in Seoul has his *Eight Views of the Four Seasons*, but his major and only other extant work is *Dream Journey to Peach Blossom Spring* (Tenri Library, Japan; see **Tao Qian**). This long horizontal scroll, inspired by Prince Anp'yŏng's dream of paradise, is a glorious and colourful evocation of an imaginary landscape full of peaks, valleys, trees and blossom.[1] Clearly showing his admiration for the Chinese artist Guo Xi (c.1020–90) and his advice to create an environment that the viewer can imagine himself entering, An paints a complex composition in which finely brushed detail is mixed with ink wash and positive use of empty space to suggest foreground and distance, piling up mountains in rapid succession and leading the viewer deeper and deeper into his idyllic refuge from the present. More than twenty famous contemporary scholars inscribed fine pieces of **calligraphy** at various points along the scroll.

(1) R. WHITFIELD & Y-S PAK, *Korean Art Treasures*, Seoul: Yekyong Publications Co., 1986. AHN HWI-JOON, 'An Kyŏn and 'A Dream Visit to the Peach Blossom Land',' *OA*, XXVI/1, 1980; KUMJA PAIK KIM, 'Two Stylistic Trends in Mid-15th Century Korean Painting,' *OA*, XXIX/4, 1983/4

AN SUGIL 安壽吉 (1911–77)

A novelist born in Hamhŭng, An Sugil was brought up at Longjing in Jiandao (**Kando**), Manchuria. He later went to school in Seoul and was briefly detained by the police at the time of the 1929 **Kwangju Incident**, before he went to Japan to study English at Waseda University in Tokyo. He then returned to **Manchuria**, where his first story was published in 1935. He worked as a teacher and for some years as literary editor of the daily paper *Mansŏn Ilbo* in Changchun, continuing to write fiction. In 1945 he moved to Hŭngnam, and in 1948 reached Seoul, where he worked on the daily *Kyŏnghyang Sinmun* and taught in various **schools** and **universities** for the rest of his life. His output of novels and short stories was immense. The best-known of his works is the five-part novel, *Pukkando* 'North Jiandao', published between 1959 and 1967. It describes the lives and fortunes of a Korean family from their emigration as farmers in the 1880s to their struggles as independence fighters under the Japanese. Jiandao was the most vigorous area of resistance down to 1945, and the novel gives vivid descriptions of the land and the times.

ANAP-CHI 雁鴨池 'Ducks and Geese Lake'

Ornamental lake set amid the pleasure gardens in the Unified Silla capital at **Kyŏngju**, built by King **Munmu** in AD 674 for recuperation after the wars of unification against **Koguryŏ** and **Paekche**. Originally called *Wŏlchi* ('Moon Lake'), it seems to have acquired its subsequent name only in the Chosŏn period. It was drained and excavated in 1975–6, and the archaeological finds have confirmed the luxurious lifestyle led on its shores, as well as providing written evidence of Silla administration. They include a total of 32,587 objects of wood, metal, and stone, including 24,353 decorative tiles, the remains of three boats, and many Buddhist images, suggesting a possible temple site. Unlike the finds from **tombs** of this period all those at Moon Lake were made for practical use. Forming part of the detached palace of the crown prince, it became the focal point for court diplomacy and entertainment, including the reception of visiting foreign embassies. The sites of 28 buildings have been discovered. The largest of the five pavilions overlooking the lake was the *Imhaejŏn* ('Pavilion beside the Sea'), said to have seated a thousand banqueting guests. The gardens were landscaped in imitation of famous Chinese beauty spots and stocked with exotic flora and fauna. Islands in the lake played the part of retreats for Daoist **Immortals**.
ANON., 'Artifacts Excavated in Anapchi Pond,' *KJ*, 21/1, 1981

ANCESTRAL RITES *cherye* 祭禮

Elaborate burial practices and tomb decorations from the Three Kingdoms period reveal early beliefs in an afterlife, and the rites of **shamanism** show how ancestral spirits were thought to take an active interest in human affairs. The strength of the kin group as a political and social unit is shown by the *kolp'um* system of the Silla period, and it is clear that respectful recognition of ancestors was an important function of family heads. Under the influence of neo-Confucianism in the early Chosŏn period it was crystallized into a system of rites which reflected, but did not wholly imitate, Chinese concern for the descent group. These became the legal norm, acting as a powerful unifying force in society. Their purpose was to continue the practice of filial piety after the death of ancestors. Their worship was stressed in the enormously influential works of **Zhu Xi** (1130–1200), especially the editions of his 'Family Rituals' (*Chuja-garye*, C. *Jiali*) edited by **Kwŏn Kŭn** and Yi Chae (1680–1746).

Rites were conducted by the eldest son of the true wife. He enjoyed the sole right to officiate at them, just as he held the principal right of inheritance, even at the expense of an elder son by a secondary wife. Primogeniture and agnatic solidarity were a particular feature of the Korean concept of ancestral worship. The core of the rites was the presentation of wine libations and a banquet before the tablets on which the names of dead ancestors were written. The food was ceremonially tasted by the officiants, and what was left over was eaten afterwards by those present. **Women** did not take part. Ceremonial details were enshrined in the **Confucian Classics**, but because the texts were inconsistent and obscure, many guides and commentaries were needed. Korean literature of this kind proliferated, especially during the 17th century – much of it dealing with who was bound and who was entitled to perform the ceremonies. In principle, rites were performed four times a year and on the anniversaries of death. The more important rites were performed in the ancestral hall *sadang*; others were performed at graves. Men of high rank offered rites for three or four generations back; those of lower rank honoured fewer generations. Commoners had simplified rites, not required by law.

In many families funerary, mourning and commemorative observances reflected Korean priorities rather than Chinese forms and ideas, and ritual manuals showed little evidence of Chinese origin. On the contrary, the influence of **Buddhism** and **shamanism** frequently persisted from the foregoing Koryŏ period.

MARTINA DEUCHLER, *The Confucian Transformation of Korea*, Cambridge, Mass.: Harvard University Press, 1992; R.L. JANELLI & D.Y. JANELLI, *Ancestor Worship and Korean Society*, Stanford University Press, 1982

See also **illegitimate sons; genealogies; lineages; mourning; p'ungsu; rites and ceremonies; ritual studies; women**

ANGLICANS *Sŏnggonghoe* 聖公會

After Chinese and Japanese lay missionaries had been unsuccessful in **Pusan** during the 1880s, Anglican bishops in China and Japan persuaded the Archbishop of Canterbury to found a Korean Mission. Bishop Charles John **Corfe** (1843–1921) arrived in 1890 and established the uniformly Anglo-Catholic tradition of the venture.

It was the only Church of England mission to a country where Britain had no political or commercial interests. Because the Church of England was sensitive about making a bishop 'of' a country outside the British Empire, the title 'Bishop in Korea' was used until a Korean bishop was appointed in 1965. The single diocese had a succession of English bishops, including Mark **Trollope**. They even had a British coat-of-arms – though it was never submitted to the College of Heralds: the same as that of the Bishop in North China, a gold 'cross moline', but on a red ground powdered with golden oak leaves for Korea's wooded hills and set within a wavy white border for the surrounding seas. From 1891 to 1900 the bishopric also included the province of Shengjing (Liaoning) in **Manchuria**, where there was a church in the treaty port of Niuzhuang (now Yingkou).

The mission was always small and underfunded; early medical and educational projects could not be developed. Evangelistic work was concentrated in Kyŏnggi-do and the Ch'ungch'ŏng provinces, extending to P'yŏngan-do in the 1930s. Japanese congregations were served in Seoul, **Inch'ŏn**, **Taegu** and Pusan. An elegant Romanesque cathedral in Seoul, consecrated in 1926, was completed in 1996. Development of Korean leadership was slow until Yi Ch'ŏnhwan (Paul, b. 1926) was made bishop of a new diocese of Seoul in 1965. Thereafter the Anglican Church, though small, began political and social involvement, largely along the same lines as the Catholics. Since 1974 there have been three dioceses (Seoul, Taejŏn and Pusan), which in 1995 became an independent province of the Anglican Communion, known as Taehan Sŏnggonghoe, matching Zhonghua Shenggonghui in China and Nihon Seikokai in Japan. (*Sŏng-gong-hoe* is the translation of 'Holy Catholic Church' used in the Apostles' Creed and was intended to avoid a sectarian title.)

CHARLES JOHN CORFE, *The Anglican Church in Korea*, London, 1906; M. M. MONTGOMERY, *Charles John Corfe*, London, 1927; *Morning Calm*, London, quarterly 1889–1987; MARK NAPIER TROLLOPE, *The Church in Korea*, 1915
See also **Great Britain, relations with; Landis, Eli Barr**

ANGLO-JAPANESE ALLIANCE (1902)

Agreement made on 30 January 1902 between two powers who saw their interests threatened by Russian expansion in Europe and **Manchuria**, exacerbated in Japan's case by a concession obtained by the Russians in April 1901 to develop timber resources on the Korean border at Andong. Japan acknowledged Britain's rights in China, gained under successive unequal treaties, and Britain recognised Japan's special claim to rights in Korea, though the agreement referred to Korean 'independence'. Mutual assistance was promised in the event of war, and indeed Russia's failure to honour a deal made with China (11 April 1902) to withdraw troops from the region was a contributory factor in the subsequent outbreak of the **Russo-Japanese War**.

IAN NISH, *The Anglo-Japanese Alliance: the Diplomacy of Two Island Empires*, London: Athlone Press, 1966; IAN NISH, *Alliance in Decline*, London: Athlone Press, 1972
See also **Anglo-Japanese Treaty**

ANGLO-JAPANESE TREATY (1905)

Revision in April 1905 of the **Anglo-Japanese Alliance**, in which Great Britain recognised Japan's paramount rights in Korea and failed to seek a reiteration of Korean independence. In return, Japan acknowledged British interests in India. Through this and the subsequent **Taft-Katsura Memorandum** the two major western powers, Britain and America, effectively surrendered Korea to Japanese aggression, and many Koreans have seen the Alliance and Treaty as paving the way for the **Protectorate Treaty** of November 1905 and full colonisation in 1910.

IAN NISH, *The Anglo-Japanese Alliance: the Diplomacy of Two Island Empires*, London: Athlone Press, 1966; IAN NISH, *Alliance in Decline*, London: Athlone Press, 1972

ANIMALS, DOMESTIC

The **ox** is known in **neolithic** remains from before 2000 BC. Often pitied, because it worked so hard, it was the normal plough-animal and beast of burden for short distance haulage. Pig, **dog** and **fowl** bones have been found in neolithic remains of similar date. Pigs are kept in every village, signs of prosperity rather than of squalor. The **horse**, **donkey**, and **cat** were later introductions. Sheep are often confused with goats. Neither were very common, and true sheep have rarely flourished in Korea, for want of suitable herbage, though there is passing mention of wool-bearing sheep in Koryŏ times. The meekness of sheep is proverbial. Small herds of little black goats were peddled in Seoul for the sake of their flesh, eaten as a tonic. Camels were foreign, known only because they were seen in Beijing. Their humps occur in place-names, and imported fermented camel-milk was said to have been sold as **medicine** in the part of Seoul called Naktong, 'camel hollow'. **Six domesticated animals** appear in the **zodiac**.

ANIMALS, MYTHIC
The four mystic animals of the cardinal compass points. *Chujak*, the Red Bird of the South, is often called a **phoenix**. Pictures and the Chinese word suggest it is a gallinaceous bird, a pheasant or jungle-fowl from the south of China. (One Song writer suggested a red variety of quail, a summer migrant from the south famed for its pugnacity.) *Ch'ŏngnyong*, the Blue/Green **Dragon**, is a serpentine water spirit, standing for the East, where the great seas lie, east of China and Korea. *Paekho*, the White Tiger of the West, is a dragon-like quadruped, doubtless inspired by the pale North Asian tiger that lives west of the Chinese heartland. *Hyŏnmu*, 'dark warriors', the Black Tortoise of the North, is a tortoise with a snake entwining its shell, reflecting the ancient belief that all tortoises were female and required snakes to fecundate them. Mistaking the embrace for a struggle may underlie the name 'warriors'.

The four names are recorded from later Han, but pictures have been found in late 5th-century BC lacquerware at Leigudun (Suixian, Hubei province, China), where they are connected with astronomical signs. They have always stood for the four quadrants of the ecliptic, given colours related to **Five Elements** theory during the Han period. In Korea they occur first in early 7th-century Koguryŏ **tomb** murals, but became more important after the success of neo-Confucian philosophy, in which the tortoise and tiger were regarded as *yin*, the bird and dragon as *yang*.
See also **five phases; flags, processional; Four Spirits;** *haet'ae*

ANIMALS, WILD
The animals of Korea are essentially temperate forest fauna, largely the same species as in northern China and **Manchuria**, with similar cultural rôles. Apart from the **tiger**, **bear**, and **fox**, other carnivores – leopard (*p'yobŏm*), lynx (*sŭrasoni*) and leopard-cat (*salkwaengi*: *Felis bengalensis*) – had no popular symbolism. The wolf (*iri*, *nŭktae*, or *sŭngnyangi*) was the raider of small livestock and hen-houses. The raccoon-dog *nŏguri* (*Nyctoreutes procyonoides*), whose hair is used for writing-brushes, lacked the ghostly reputation it has in Japan. Pantomime lions in some **masked dance** dramas are not native, but were borrowed from the **lion dances** of Tang China. **Deer** and goral (dark grey *yŏngyang* 'goat-antelopes' or *sanyang* 'wild goats' *Nemorhaedus goral*), existed in all the mountains and were hunted like the wild boar, whose bristles were used in making men's 'horsehair' hats. **Hare**, **rats**, and **bats** were indigenous. There are no native monkeys, though monkeys were sometimes imported as exotic pets in Koryŏ. References to howling gibbons in Korean poetry are stock images for desolation, borrowed from Tang writers.

ANJU 安州
Site of a battle in AD 612 in which a Chinese army sent by Emperor Sui Yangdi was defeated by the **Koguryŏ** general **Ŭlchi Mundŏk**. Having failed to take Liaoyang nearly 300,000 Chinese troops, a third of the total army, headed instead for P'yŏngyang. Here too they were repulsed, and in trying to retreat were ambushed and suffered a calamitous defeat at Anju on the **Ch'ŏngch'ŏn River**. Only 2,700 are said to have returned to the site of the Liaoyang siege, which was then abandoned.
See also **Sui dynasty**

ANNEXATION, TREATY OF (1910) *Hanil-happang choyak* 韓日合邦條約
Signed under duress by Emperor **Sunjong** on 29 August 1910. It had already been signed by the quisling Prime Minister **Yi Wanyong** and the new Resident General Terauchi Masatake, and was followed by an edict from the Japanese emperor

promising benefits to the Korean people as Japanese subjects. In fact, they were never to become equal citizens with their Japanese occupiers. The Treaty of Annexation was the work of Terauchi. Such a move had been opposed by **Itō Hirobumi** and had prompted his resignation, but was the inevitable outcome of the **protectorate** period as Japanese military leaders sought to strengthen their grip on continental territory and to counter continuing Russian influence in **Manchuria**. It had also been the aim of the pro-Japanese *Ilchinhoe* (**United Progress Society**). It promised that Japan, while taking over the full government and administration of Korea, would protect its people's welfare. To discourage popular unrest at news of their subjugation Terauchi had ordered the closure of Korean **newspapers**, and repression and discrimination continued to be the hallmarks of his **Government General**. Many Koreans committed suicide at the national humiliation, and the Treaty of Annexation ushered in a period of military dictatorship.

HILARY CONROY, *The Japanese Seizure of Korea, 1868–1910: a Study of Realism and Idealism in International Relations*, Philadelphia: University of Pennsylvania Press, 1960; PETER DUUS, *The Abacus and the Sword: the Japanese Penetration of Korea, 1895–1910*, Berkeley: University of California Press, 1995; STEWART LONE, 'The Japanese Annexation of Korea 1910: the Failure of East Asian Co-Prosperity,' *MAS*, 25, 1991
See also **Colonial period; Five Traitors; Hwang Hyŏn; Min Yŏngsik; Police system, Japanese; Seven Traitors**

ANP'YŎNG TAEGUN 安平大君 Prince Anp'yŏng *See* **Yi Yŏng**

AŎN-GAKPI 雅言覺非 'Awareness of Errors with Elegant Words'
A collection of common errors in the use of Chinese, arranged under 200 headwords by **Chŏng Yagyong**.

APPENZELLER, HENRY GERHARD (1858–1902)
A Methodist pastor from Pennsylvania who arrived in Seoul in 1885. He established the Methodist Mission and founded Paejae School. For a time editor of *The Korean Repository*, he took a leading part in introducing modern education to Korea. Active in Bible translation, he was drowned when the ship on which he was travelling to a translators' meeting sank off Mokp'o. His daughter Alice Rebecca (1885–1950), born in Seoul, worked at Ihwa Haktang (*see also* **Ewha Women's University**), returning after World War II and dying in Korea.

APRIL 19TH STUDENT UPRISING (1960) *Sasipku ŭigŏ* 四十九義舉
Violent anti-government demonstration staged by **students** in Seoul against the re-election of Syngman Rhee (**Yi Sŭngman**) as president in 1960. It followed riots at Masan on election day, 15 March, in which a student had died. More than 100,000 were estimated to have protested in front of Yi's palace, and in the ensuing battles guards killed 115 and injured up to a thousand more. On 25 April university professors joined the call for Rhee's resignation, and on 26 April, following further pressure from US Ambassador McConaughy and military commander General Magruder, he and his government resigned.

SOHN HAK-KYU, *Authoritarianism and Opposition in South Korea*, London: Routledge, 1989; YANG SUNG-CHUL, 'Student Activism and Activists: A Case of the 1960 April Revolution in Korea,' *KJ*, 12/7, 1972
See also **Pak Chŏnghŭi; South Korea: constitutional changes**

APSARA ch'ŏllyŏ 天女
Also known as *deva*; female spirits, depicted as young women with diadems, clad in filmy veils and floating through the air. They are notable in Buddhist paintings, decorating many a temple ceiling and wall, and on great **bells**. In waiting upon the Buddhas they frequently carry dishes of fruit and play **musical instruments**, especially flutes, **drums**, and the *saeng* mouth organ. They lived in the Devaloka part of the **thirty-three heavens** and were the spouses of the *gandharvas*.

ARCHERY *kungdo* 弓道
A necessary skill for the military *yangban*, with a history of immeasurable antiquity. It was naturally competitive and became a social sport (*see hallyang*). Spring and autumn archery festivals were kept in style, with prepared picnic food and attendant *kisaeng* to encourage the competitors and sing songs of victory when appropriate.

ARCHITECTURE
Korean architecture follows the general East Asian pattern of using a great deal of timber and stone, of raising important buildings above ground level on a platform of packed earth, roofing them with clay tiles, and enclosing building complexes within protective walls. An upper class household might comprise one or more courtyards with separate quarters for the male and female occupants and their servants. Separate rooms were reserved for reception and domestic purposes and for food preparation, and space would be found within the walls for storage jars, domestic animals, and possibly a garden. In the Chinese tradition, the size of buildings was defined in terms of the space between their supporting timber columns. External walls were formed by infilling these spaces with earth, brick or stone; doors were wooden and, like windows, might be decorated with wooden **lattice-work** patterns. Internal room divisions were created by the use of sliding paper doors. Floors were made of timber, except in spaces warmed by the *ondol* system, which had stone floors covered in waxed **paper**. Paper ceilings also covered these rooms, whereas unheated rooms had no ceilings but left the internal roof bracketing visible from below. Timber roof support systems ranged from simple gables to complex hipped constructions with wide overhanging eaves. Painting with bright colours (*tanch'ŏng*) was permitted only on palaces, government buildings, or temples. Peasants' cottages were thatched, until the *Saemaŭl undong* of the 1970s prescribed that they should be roofed with tiles or corrugated iron.

No palace buildings survive from before the **Imjin Wars**, though a small number of temple buildings date from the Koryŏ period, for example at Sudŏk-sa in Yesan (South Ch'ungch'ŏng province) and Pusŏk-sa in Yŏngju (North Kyŏngsang province). However, tomb architecture from the Three Kingdoms period and archaeological evidence from sites such as the **Anap-chi Lake** give some indication of early architectural practices and scale. An idea of early Chosŏn patterns may be obtained from extant palace buildings reconstructed in the 17th century, though many of these have been subject to later alteration and rebuilding.

The outstanding architectural landmark of the early 20th century, the neo-classical Capitol Building erected by the Japanese **Government General** in 1923 in front of the **Kyŏngbok Palace** at the head of Sejong-ro, was demolished in 1997. New Korean architecture of the late 20th century shows a readiness to experiment, albeit with reference to Korean cultural tradition, and includes some distinguished examples such as the National Museum building at Puyŏ (South Ch'ungch'ŏng province), and in Seoul the concert hall of the Seoul City Arts Centre, shaped like a traditional scholar's hat, the Sejong Cultural Centre, and the Olympic Stadium.

AHN KYE-HYON, 'Buddhist Thought and Architectural Design of Temples,' *KJ*, 14/12, 1974; FRANCIS MACOUIN, ed., *Etudes d'Architecture et d'Urbanisme Coréens*, Paris: Collège de France, 1994; SAM Y. PARK, *An Introduction to Korean Architecture*, Seoul: Jugwoo Publishing Co., 1991, 2 vols.
See also **Namdae-mun; pagoda; roof tiles; tombs**

ARIRANG

The best-known Korean folksong. The words now commonly sung tell of lovers parting over a hill, and Arirang is said to be the name of the hill; but there was no such hill until some mountain passes were named after the song in the 20th century. The song is certainly much older and exists in many local versions of both words and melody. The refrain 'A-ri-rang, a-ra-ri-o', is a meaningless melisma of the Fa-la-la, or Fol-di-rol type. All the other words were, and continue to be, improvised. **Hulbert** wrote in *The Korean Repository* in 1896 that Arŭrang could be heard everywhere and incessantly, had become popular about 1883 and had 782 stanzas more or less. The stanza he gave was:

Mun'gyŏng Saejae paktal namu
hongdukkae-bangmang ta naganda.

'The birch trees on the Bird Pass at Mun'gyŏng will all be turned into rollers and paddles.' (The Bird Pass is the great divide between Ch'ungch'ŏng and Kyŏngsang. The sentiment is cynical: the great trees will be used for the little tools of *tadŭmi*.) His musical transcription is so different from today's melody as to suggest it has been sweetened for modern ears.
KIM SHI-OP, *'Arirang*, Modern Korean Folk Song,' *KJ*, 28/7, 1988

ARMISTICE AGREEMENT (1953) 板門店休戰 *P'anmunjŏm hyujŏn*
Truce talks were first held between the United Nations and North Korea and China on 10 July 1951 in **Kaesŏng**. They were transferred to **P'anmunjŏm** on 25 October 1951. While talks continued inconclusively about an armistice and a line of demarcation, the communists fortified their defensive positions across the peninsula and on 27 December a preliminary truce was agreed. Disagreement over the fate of prisoners of war remained the one serious obstacle to a final accord, and occasional outbursts of fighting continued until 1953. In that year the death of Stalin and newly elected President Eisenhower's strong anti-communist stance contributed to a settlement, signed on 27 July. The Demilitarized Zone (*see* **DMZ**) was defined as the temporary line of demarcation pending eventual agreement on peaceful reunification; POWs were either exchanged for repatriation or handed over to the neutral Indian commission (though it is said that 25,000 North Koreans who had not agreed to go home were freed and escaped into the South Korean countryside); and talks were to continue at P'anmunjŏm in pursuit of a peace treaty. They still do. In 1957 the United States moved nuclear weapons to its bases in South Korea in defiance of an Armistice ban on the introduction of new weapon types into the peninsula.
SYDNEY BAILEY, *The Korean Armistice*, London: Macmillan, 1992; ROSEMARY FOOT, *A Substitute for Victory: the Politics of Peacemaking at the Korean Armistice Talks*, Ithaca: Cornell University Press, 1990
See also **Geneva Conference; Thirty-Eighth Parallel; US-ROK Treaty**

ARMOUR
Was made of leather, **paper**, bone, and **iron**. Illustrations of armoured cavalrymen and horses appear on **Koguryŏ** tomb murals at Anak (near P'yŏngyang, late 4th century) and Tonggou (6th century). Rectangular bone plates, bound together with thongs, have been found at Mongch'ŏn T'osŏng, near Seoul, and may come from a **Paekche** tomb of the 5th century. However, the largest number of surviving examples are of iron and come from sites in Yŏngnam, in **Kaya**, with a smaller number from locations in former **Silla** territory. They include helmets and cuirasses. Comparison of these finds with those of contemporary Japanese style from the Yamato state, or the few examples of Yamato armour found in southern Korea, show them to be sufficiently different to counter – though not conclusively – the suggestion that Kaya was a colony of Yamato in the 4th century.
GINA BARNES, 'Discoveries of iron armour on the Korean peninsula', *PBAKS*, 5, 1994

ASAMI LIBRARY
An important collection of over 900 old Korean items made by the Japanese lawyer Asami Rintarō (1869–1943) while he was a judge in Seoul 1906–1918, now at Berkeley, California.
CHAOYING FANG, *The Asami Library: a Descriptive Catalogue*, Berkeley: University of California Press, 1969

ASANA *chwa*, 座 'sitting pose'
A **buddha** or **bodhisattva** is presented as standing (like Sakyamuni at his birth) or lying on his right side (like Sakyamuni at his death). Sitting is described as *yŏnhwa-jwa* (S. *padmasana*) 'lotus pose' or *kabujwa* 'cross-legged pose': either *kyŏl-gabu-jwa* 'twined lotus pose' (each foot placed sole upward on the opposite thigh) or *pan'gabu-jwa* 'half-lotus pose' (one foot above the opposite thigh, the other beneath). Twined-lotus may be *hangma-jwa* 'expelling-demons pose' (left shin over right) or, more often, *kilsang-jwa* 'blessing pose' (right shin over left). *Pan'ga-sayu-jwa* 'half-lotus meditation pose' (S. *ardha-bhadrasana*) is found in Maitreya statues of the Three Kingdoms period: he sits on a stool, left leg pendant in front, right foot on left knee, right elbow on right knee, right hand to chin. This graceful and meditative pose is sometimes called *lalitasana* or *maharaja-lila* 'royal ease', but the latter properly belongs to a pose connected with **Kwanseŭm** or **Manjusri**: sitting on the floor, one knee raised and a hand propped over it in a lordly gesture of consolation. Ç

ASTON, WILLIAM GEORGE (1841–1911)
Born in Derry, Ireland, Aston read classics at Queen's University, Belfast, and joined the British Legation at Tokyo as a translator in 1864. There was no grammar of Japanese, and he had to make his own way in study. He became consul and helped prepare the Korean-British Treaty of 1883, and as consul-general in Seoul 1884–6 was present at the Post Office *émeute* of 1884 (*see Imo* **Incident**). He then returned to Japan, but his health was poor and in 1889 he retired to Beer in Devon. A pioneer Japanese scholar, he published a translation of *Nihon'gi* (1896), and was the first linguist to describe the resemblances between Korean and Japanese, as in 'A Comparative Study of the Japanese and Korean Languages' in *Journal of the Royal Asiatic Society of Great Britain*, XL Pt iii (1879). His collection of Korean books is now in St Petersburg.

ASTRONOMY

Evidence of the importance attached to the study of the heavens in ancient Korea is provided by the survival of the world's oldest observatory (*see Ch'ŏmsŏngdae*), dating from the 7th century AD. In the following century the military commander Kim An established a reputation for his interest in astronomy and natural changes in the universe.

A star map engraved with 5,866 characters and stars on a black stone slab (*Ch'ŏnsang yŏlch'a punya-ji-do*), dating from 1395, is preserved in the **Tŏksu Palace** Museum. It was carved by astronomers headed by **Kwŏn Kŭn**. On its reverse is a second map which may have been carved in 1433. It carries 2,934 characters and stars. King **Sejong** took an active personal interest in astronomy, and under his direction eighteen new instruments were constructed for the Royal Obervatory between the years 1432 and 1442. Astronomy was one of the four specialist topics available to those taking the *chapkwa* **examinations**, and successful candidates might hope to enter the government Office of Astronomy and Geomancy (originally preserving the Koryŏ title *Sŏun-gwan*, but renamed *Kwansang-gam* by King Sejong). In its astronomical sections, Yi Sugwang (1563–1628)'s *Chibong yusŏl* (1614) indicates the contact he had with Matteo Ricci when on an official embassy to Beijing in 1601. A second surviving stone engraved with a star map similar to that of 1395 dates from 1687.

MICHAEL DANIELS, 'Korea's Invaluable Astronomical Records,' *KJ*, 15/7, 1975; KIM YONG-WOON, 'A Study of the Records of Solar Eclipses in Samguk Sagi, I and II,' *KJ*, 16/7, 16/8, 1976; JOSEPH NEEDHAM, *The Hall of Heavenly Records: Korean Astronomical Instruments and Clocks, 1380–1780*, Cambridge University Press, 1986; NHA IL-SUNG & F. RICHARD STEPHENSON, *Oriental Astronomy from Guo Shoujing to King Sejong*, Seoul: Yŏnsei University Press, 1997

AVISON, OLIVER R. 魚丕信 (1860–1956)

A Canadian Presbyterian missionary doctor and educationist, who had no middle name but chose to use the initial R. without a name. He entered Korea and became head of **Kwanghyc-wŏn** in 1893. Two years later he began to reorganise medical work in Korea, using Presbyterian funds. Between 1900 and 1904 he established Severance Hospital (named after Louis H. Severance, the benefactor). In 1917 he established Korea's first medical college in Severance Hospital. He also taught agriculture at Sungsil School in P'yŏngyang and mathematics and science at Yŏnhŭi College. He left Korea in 1935.

ALLEN D. CLARK, *Avison of Korea*, Seoul: Yonsei University Press, 1979

B

BACKGAMMON *ssangnyuk*, 雙六 'double six'

This game, played on a special board with counters or 'stones' and two **dice**, was known in ancient Rome, and came to China by Tang times from India or central Asia. It is mentioned in Koryŏ by **Yi Kyubo**. The name may come from the dice, or from the doubling of the score when two sixes are thrown. The western board has wedge-shaped patterns drawn on the board, pointing away from each player, towards his opponent. On the Korean board these wedges are replaced by half-moons, called *pat* 'fields'. The dice are cast into the largest *pat* each side, the central one. The board has low mortised sides like low fencing, making it into a tray. The moveable pieces (*mal* 'horses') are made of boxwood, shaped like little trumpets standing on their broad ends.

BAI JUYI (K. Paek Kŏi) 白居易 (772–846)
The popular Tang poet, much imitated in Korea, where he is more often known by his *cha* as Paek Nakch'ŏn (C. Letian).

BAIRD, WILLIAM MARTYN (1862–1931)
An American Presbyterian minister who arrived in Korea in February 1891 and in the same year established a mission station in **Pusan**. He prepared the way for James E. Adams to start work in **Taegu** in 1896. A distinguished educator, Baird formulated the educational policy of his mission on **Nevius** principles: to educate in all fields of knowledge, giving priority to Christianity and development of Korean leadership. Thus he founded Sungsil Academy at P'yŏngyang in 1897, and his later foundation there, Sungsil College, in 1908 became the first Korean institution to give college-level degrees. After 1916 he concentrated on literary work with a team of Korean translators. He worked closely with his college classmate, Samuel A. **Moffett**.

BAMBOO
Bamboo, cultivated south of the latitude of Seoul, is one of the **Four Gentlemen**, a symbol of longevity, but even more of fidelity, because it remains green in the snow. Koreans also wonder at the speed with which the shoots grow during the spring rains. (It is possible to see them growing before one's eyes, and a typical story tells of a man who hung his hat on a bamboo while he relieved himself, only to find that when he was ready to go the hat was too high for him to reach.) There are many species and varieties, of which probably only the scrubby *Sasa* species are indigenous. Others include the decorative black-stemmed (*ojuk*) and mottled-stemmed (*panjuk*) varieties of *Phyllostachys nigra* that make excellent flutes (*see* **Ahwang and Yŏyang**). Giant bamboos *wangdae* are grown in Chŏlla and used for scaffolding.

BAMBOO WIFE *chuk-puin* 竹夫人
A long sausage-shaped bolster made of bamboo-strip openwork. It is put under the coverlet on the hottest summer nights to bring cool comfort and calm sleep.

BANKING
The first Korean bank was the Bank of Chosŏn (*Chosŏn Ŭnhaeng*), established in 1896 by Kim Chonghan. But it was the Japanese who first developed modern banking in Korea during the **Protectorate** period. In 1904 Megata Shūtarō had been invited by the Korean government to modernise its financial system, as a result of which six agricultural and industrial banks were set up in 1906 to finance economic development. The Japanese made most deposits and received the most loans. Kim Chonghan also helped found the Hansŏng First Bank of Korea (*Hanil Ŭnhaeng*) in 1906. The Bank of Korea (*Han'guk Ŭnhaeng*) was established in 1909, replacing the Korean branch of the Japanese Daiichi Ginkō as the national central bank. Its founders again included Kim Chonghan, representative of the class of Korean entrepreneurs who had the resources to join in modernizing ventures. In 1911 it was renamed Bank of Chōsen. Throughout the colonial period it was the principal agency for Japanese government financial affairs in Korea, and it also operated in **Manchuria**. In 1918 the six were consolidated by the **Government General** into the single Chōsen Development Bank. Other Japanese banks were opened, including the major Chōsen Development Bank which played a significant part in financing Korea's industrial expansion. The only Korean bank initially authorised was the Hanil Ŭnhaeng. After

1920 six more Korean banks were founded, including the Haedong Bank and the Honam Bank.

YOON-DAE EUH & JAMES C. BAKER, *The Korean Banking System and Foreign Influence*, London: Routledge, 1990; KARL MOSKOWITZ, 'Current assets: the Employees of Japanese Banks in Colonial Korea,' PhD dissertation, Harvard University, 1979

BANNER GATE *chŏngmun* 旌門

A gate of honour granted by the *Ijo*, one of the **Six Boards**, also called *chaksŏl* 'doorposts' or *hongmun* 'red gate'. The door and the pillars supporting the heavy tiled roof of the gate were painted red. Over the lintel was a board inscribed with the reason for the honour and the name of the person honoured. *Chŏngmun* were erected in memory of loyal subjects (*ch'ungsin*), exemplars of filial piety (*hyoja-mun*) and faithful widows (*yŏllyŏ-mun*). They differ from *hongsal-mun* (*see* **Red arrow gate**), which also were painted red.

BATHING

Until the end of Chosŏn baths were taken only in warm weather, when picnic expeditions for bathing were made to suitable places in brooks and streams. Groups were segregated by sex and age-group. The Chinese official Xu Jing (*see* **Xuanhe fengshi Gaoli tujing**) had commented favourably on Korean bathing habits at the beginning of the 12th century. Ritual bathing was required for certain ceremonies, especially of the **kosa** and **tongsin-je** type. The bath-houses that are a feature of all Korea urban areas today are a legacy of the colonial period. Males and females are segregated on the two sides of the building. A bather washes with soap and scrubs his body with a small towel, using water ladled with a bowl, before entering the common bath, which is exceedingly hot. The usual time required for taking a bath is at least an hour and the social aspect of the practice has not completely disappeared.

BATS

Bats are common in Korea and, as in China, are used abundantly in decorative arts as a good-luck rebus, because *pok* (C. *fu*) means both bat and blessings.

BEACONS *pongsu* 烽燧

A system of beacon fires for warning of invasions is mentioned in 1149 when Songdo (**Kaesŏng**) was the capital. It is better known after improvements by **King Sejong** and his successors. The total number of beacons has been estimated at 966, bringing communications to Seoul from all parts of the country. The five main lines and chief branches were approximately as follows:

1) The north-east: Kyŏnghŭng – Tumen valley – Hoeryŏng – Kyŏngsŏng – Kilchu – coast to Yonghŭng (connections from upper **Yalu**) – Anbyŏn – Ch'ŏrwŏn – Seoul.
2) The south-east: **Tongnae** – **Kyŏngju** – Yŏngch'ŏn – Andong (connection from Tongnae by east coast) – Ch'ungju (connections from Kŏje and Kadŏk Islands via Sŏngju and Sangju, and from Namhae Kŭmsan via Ch'ŏngju) – **Kwangju** (Kyŏnggi-do) – Seoul.
3) The north: Kanggye – Yalu valley – Ŭiju – Anju – P'yŏngyang – Hwangju – Kaesŏng – Seoul (the only wholly internal route).
4) The north-west: Ŭiju – west coast, parallel to route 3 – mouth of the Taedong – coast to Haeju – Yŏnp'yŏng Island – Kaesŏng – Seoul.

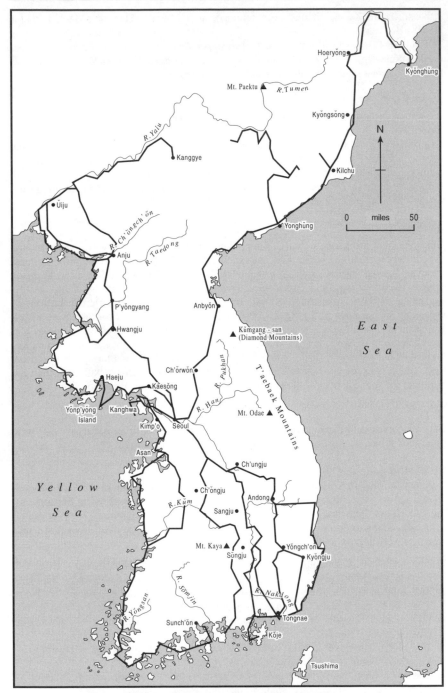

Map 3 The Beacon System of Chosŏn Korea

5) The south-west: Sunch'ŏn – by coast to **Chin-do** – by coast – mouth of the Kŭm – up river – across south Ch'ungch'ŏng to north of Asan Gulf (connnection from the Kŭm estuary by coast) – by coast – Kimp'o – **Kanghwa** – south of the **Han River** valley – Seoul.

The system was well planned and effective. A message was sent on each line every evening: one blaze meant all was quiet; two meant distant threats; three, imminent danger; four, invasion; and five, fighting. The fire-place was a cairn of loose stones about 2·5 m high and 2–3 m across, with a chimney up the middle, ventilated by a horizontal flue at the base. Messages on the longest line took about four hours from Kyŏnghŭng to Seoul, allowing about three minutes for each beacon to be activated. The beacons were tended by *corvée* labour and the workers were socially despised. After the mid-18th century most beacons were served by soldiers. Failures were met by severe punishments.

BEARS
The bear, seemingly a tabu animal, has no place in folklore outside the **Tan'gun** myth, a purely Korean legend that may reflect an ancient totemism. A bear-cub's cry was supposed to sound like a human baby. The black species (*Selenarctos thibetanus*) was common throughout Korea, but Tan'gun's bear will have been the larger brown bear (*Ursus arctos*) of the **Paektu-san** area.

BEIJING, EMBASSIES TO *Yŏnhaeng-sa* 燕行使
Korea sent an annual embassage to Beijing to express her vassal status by offering congratulations to the emperor on **New Year's Day** (conventionally regarded as his birthday, since Chinese and Koreans alike counted another year on their **age** at each new year), keep informed of the calendar (which had to be adjusted by the imperial astronomers) and indulge in a little trade. The 300 or so members of the caravan represented a broad spectrum of Korean society, from high ministers to lowly servants and drivers. They were avid and inquisitive tourists, most of whom conscientiously distinguished between Manchus and Han Chinese. This embassage was called *tongji-sa* 'winter solstice embassy', because it left Seoul about the winter solstice, *hajŏng-sa* 'New Year greetings embassy' or *chŏngsak-sa* 'calendar embassy', because of the calendrical implication. Embassies to Beijing at other times were regarded as occasional or extraordinary, such as *chuch'ŏng-sa* 'petitionary embassies' or, for apologies, *chinju-sa* 'embassy presenting a memorial'.
See also **China, relations with;** *sadae***; tribute;** *Yŏngŭn-mun*
GARI LEDYARD, 'Korean travellers in China,' *Occasional Papers on Korea* 2, Seattle, 1974

BELCHER, EDWARD (1799–1877)
In 1845 Captain Edward Belcher of the Royal Navy surveyed the coasts of **Cheju**, the southwest archipelago and South Chŏlla. His *Narrative of the Voyage of HMS Samarang* (London 1848) contains an account of his visits, including a short Korean vocabulary.

BELLS
Small multi-headed bronze bells first appeared early in the **Bronze Age**. They may have been carriage or horse trappings, they may have been used in the conduct of shamanistic rites, or they may have had some rôle as symbols of authority. A wind bell of solid gold (0·7 cm high) survives from the Silla period. None of these were musical, and there is little evidence that Korea had the sets of tuned percussive hanging bells,

p'yŏnjong, that later formed the most important instrument in the *aak* orchestra, until 1116 (*see* **Yejong,** King).

Korean bronzesmiths, however, were skilled in the casting of exceptionally fine single bells for use in Buddhist temples. Best of all were those of the Unified Silla dynasty. In size and decoration they excelled even those made in **Tang dynasty** China, from which they were distinguished by three features: an elaborate suspension knob, panels of nine studs near the top, and the frequent illustration of pairs of flying *apsaras* on opposite sides of the body. They were clapperless, and were tolled by striking on the side with a wooden beam. The oldest still extant is at Sangwŏn-sa, on Odae-san, dating from AD 725, while the largest is the **Emille** Bell from Pongdŏk-sa (AD 771). It is 3·75 metres tall, 2·27 metres in diameter, and weighs 20 tonnes. It was cast to honour the reign of King **Sŏngdŏk**, and is now in the National Museum at **Kyŏngju**.

In 1346 a 3·2-metre tall, ornately decorated bell was cast for Yŏnbok-sa at **Kaesŏng**. It bears an inscription in six scripts, including Chinese, Sanskrit, Mongolian, and Tibetan, invoking peace between Koryŏ and Yuan China, but it is not clear whether it was made by Chinese bellsmiths, or whether the **Mongols** forced Korean craftsmen to manufacture it to try and enforce the subjugation of the vassal state.

In the belfry at the intersection of Chong-no and Namdaemun-no in Seoul hung a bell cast in 1468, 2·38 metres tall and 6·49 metres in circumference. Originally made for Wŏn'gak-sa it reached its location in Chong-no in 1619 after two earlier moves. It was struck to announce the opening and closing of the city gates, and at every hour. In 1985 it was relocated to the National Museum. The belfry was named *Posin'gak* ('Universal Trust Pavilion') by **King Kojong** in 1895.

E. M. CABLE, 'Old Korean Bells,' *TKBRAS*, XVI, 1925
See also **curfew; musical instruments**

BERNEUX, SIMÉON-FRANÇOIS, SAINT 張敬一 (1814–66)

Arriving in Macao in 1840 as a priest of the Paris Foreign Missions, he met **Kim Taegŏn**. In 1841 he was sent to Tonkin, where he was imprisoned for two years before being rescued in 1843 and, much against his will, made to leave Tonkin. He was sent to **Manchuria**, where he became coadjutor bishop in 1854; in 1856 he was sent to succeed Bishop **Ferréol** as 4th bishop (Vicar-Apostolic) of Korea. With **Daveluy** as his helper he saw great expansion of the Church, the first Korean Christian publications and the first orphanage. When the Hŭngsŏn **Taewŏn-gun** opened his persecution of 1866, Bishop Berneux was his prime target. He was executed at Seoul, aged 52, by all accounts a much loved pastor.
See also **Capsa**

BETHELL, ERNEST THOMAS 裴說 (1872–1909)

Born in Bristol, Bethell went at the age of fifteen to work in a family business in Kobe, exporting Japanese curios. In 1904 he went to Seoul as correspondent for the *London Daily News* in the **Russo-Japanese War**. With the help of **Yang Kit'ak**, he founded two daily newspapers, the *Korea Daily News* in English and *Taehan Maeil Sinbo* in *han'gŭl* with Chinese characters. They were highly critical of Japanese intentions in Korea and Japanese activities in the guerrilla war against volunteer soldiers fighting to maintain Korean independence. In May 1907 Bethell added an edition of *Taehan Maeil Sinmun* in pure *han'gŭl*. The Japanese asked the British to suppress Bethell's papers. He was brought to trial, for breach of public order, before a British consular court in October 1907, but was cleared. Japanese pressure led to a second trial in June 1908 before a judge from Shanghai. This time he was jailed in Shanghai for three months. In May 1909 he died of heart failure brought on by excessive brandy-drinking and smoking. The *Korea Daily News* soon ceased publication; Yang Kit'ak maintained the Korean papers until Japanese bought them in June 1910.

CHONG, C.S., *The Korean Problem in Anglo Japanese Relations 1904–1910: Ernest Thomas Bethell and his Newspapers*, Seoul: Nanam Publishing Co., 1987

BIBLE IN KOREAN, THE 聖經 *Sŏnggyŏng*

The Lord's Prayer in Korean is said to have been brought into the country from China about 1790, but sustained Bible translation began when John **Ross** and **Sŏ Sangnyun** began to work together in 1875, publishing their edition of two gospels in 1882. In 1884 Yi Sujŏng, at the behest of the American Bible Society's agent in Yokohama, printed a revision of Ross's translation of St Mark. In 1887, the year Ross's complete New Testament in Korean was printed at Fengtian, **Underwood** and **Appenzeller** published their version of St Mark in Seoul, and a Permanent Bible Translation Committeee was established. After the British and Foreign Bible Society established its Seoul Bible House in 1893, the committee was reconstituted as the Board of Official Translators: **Underwood, Appenzeller, Gale, Scranton** and **Trollope**. All the gospels and the Acts of the Apostles had been printed by 1900. In 1902 came *Kani-ch'ŏlcha Sinyak-chŏnsŏ*, 'the simplified spelling New Testament', which eliminated the redundant vowel ă and iotised vowels that were beginning to disappear in common usage. This edition was revised in 1905. Work on the Old Testament began in 1900. The complete Bible was printed in 1910, and revised in 1937. All these editions had been in pure *han'gŭl*. A version in *Kukhanmun*, 'mixed script' (including the Chinese characters for all Chinese-derived words), was prepared by Chŏng T'aeyong in 1926 and revised in 1937 and 1939. After 1952 *Kaeyŏk han'gŭl-p'an Sŏnggyŏng chŏnsŏ* in modernised spelling became the only version in general circulation, though there were some Catholic partial versions and several private translations. The language was classical in tone and made its own contribution to Korean writing. Modern language translations began to appear in the 1960s, including the joint Catholic-Protestant *Kongdong pŏnyŏk sŏngsŏ* completed in 1977.

BIBLIOGRAPHY *See* **Four branches of bibliography**

BIRD, ISABELLA LUCY (Mrs Bishop, 1831–1904)

This daughter of an English country clergyman suffered debilitating bad health except when travelling overseas by herself – she regarded herself as eccentric. In 1886 she married an Edinburgh doctor, John Bishop, who died five years later. *Korea and her Neighbours* (1898) is probably the best of the 19 lively books she wrote about her world-wide travels. It describes what she saw on four visits to Korea between January 1894 and March 1897, at a crucial period in the modernisation process. It includes the diary of an exploration of the upper reaches of the Han River in April-May 1894, a vivid account of the **Diamond Mountains**, a report on Seoul immediately after the murder of **Queen Min** and during the **Tonghak** rising, and an early score for the folksong '*Arirang*' (taken from **Hulbert**). Her comments on the Koreans are frank but not unsympathetic.

PAT BARR, *A Curious Life for a Lady*, London, 1970; JAMES GRAYSON, 'Travelling for her Health – the Extraordinary Life of Isabella Bird Bishop,' *TRASKB*, LVIII, 1983

BIRDS

The Chinese passion for caged birds is not common in Korea, though the occasional parrot is known to have been brought to Koryŏ. Native birds are typical of the Eastern Palaearctic region. Their rôle in metaphor and simile is almost the same as in China. Wild geese, migrating to the far north, raise thoughts of solitude and loved ones far away. The swallow is the bird of spring and brings good luck when it nests on a house. Magpies presage the arrival of letters and news. The mandarin duck (*wŏnang-sae*) is the ultimate in conjugal love. The song of the *koekkori*, golden oriole (strictly the 'grey-naped' oriole, *Oriolus chinensis*) is typical of summer, but carries ancient undertones of tragedy, derived from the Chinese *Book of Odes*. The cuckoo's song, too, is a sound of sadness. Cranes, symbols of **longevity**, are seen dancing in the spring and are thus associated with the auspicious but mythical **phoenix**, while the abundant white egrets are a dominant feature of the peaceful landscape. The ring-necked pheasant with plumage in the Five Colours (i.e. multicoloured) is regarded as vain and handsome, while his fawn hen is modest and wise.

M. E. J. GORE & WON PYONG-OH, *The Birds of Korea*, Seoul: Royal Asiatic Society, 1971

BLANK STELAE *paekpi* 白碑

Here and there in the countryside stand stelae without inscriptions. Their explanation is problematical. A fine example at Yŏn'gong-ni, Chinch'ŏn-gun, North Ch'ungch'ŏng, is three metres high, has nine richly carved **dragons** at the top and is thought to be of early Koryŏ date. It may have belonged to a Buddhist statue that was moved before an inscription was carved.

BODHIDHARMA 達磨 (K. Talma)

Korean folklore treasures stories of the Indian monk Bodhidharma coming to China with *Sŏn* doctrine. He arrived in Luoyang about 520 and died before 534, having, it is said, crossed the Yangzi on a floating reed-stem, and spent long years sitting in meditation opposite a blank white wall – some say at Shaolin-si, birth-place of martial arts, near Luoyang. Pictures usually depict him with grotesquely bulging eyeballs, because he cut off his eyelids in order to conquer sleep. (The jettisoned eyelids are supposed to have grown into the first tea-plant.)

BODHISATTVAS 菩薩 *posal*

A bodhisattva is always male, well built and in perfect physical condition, who has reached the threshold of buddhahood but waits a while to help other beings on the Way, without distinguishing between self and not-self. In art bodhisattvas are dressed as Indian princes, crowned, naked to the waist, except for a long delicate scarf, and a girdle, bracelets, armbands and necklace, all richly jewelled. The most important bodhisattvas are **Kwanseŭm** and **Mirŭk**, but there are many others, of whom the following are most commonly seen in Korea.

Munsu (Manjusri), bodhisattva of wisdom, principal character in the Lotus **Sutra**, is shown as a 15-year-old boy, often riding a lion. He brandishes the flaming sword of wisdom that cuts through the irrelevances of existence, and an open book on a fully opened blue lotus flower.

Pohyŏn (Samantabhadra) has an elephant and often accompanies Manjusri. He is the bodhisattva of universal benevolence and figures prominently in the Flower Garland **Sutra**.

Chijang (Kshitigarbha), guardian of the earth till Maitreya returns, patron of departed souls, is the main image in a *Myŏngbu-jŏn* 'hall of the dark regions'. He is often dressed as a shaven-headed priest holding a staff on which hang six rings, used as warning rattles.

Taeseji (Mahasthamaprapta) is a bodhisattva of wisdom and power, right-hand attendant of **Amida Buddha** in the Pure Land, another advocate of departed souls. He often carries a flask of *kamno* 'sweet dew' in his right hand and a lotus flower in his left.

BOOK OF CHANGES *Chuyŏk / Yŏkkyŏng* 周易, 易經

Neo-Confucian philosophy is largely based on the Great Treatise in the *Book of Changes*, which therefore played a dominant rôle in Chosŏn culture. The core text of the *Book of Changes*, properly called *Zhouyi* (K. *Chuyŏk*), is a Chinese collection of 64 prehistoric hexagrams (groups of six lines, each either whole or broken at the centre, traditionally attributed to the mythical Fuxi (K. Pokhŭi-ssi), which were used in royal divinations. The appropriate hexagram for each occasion was chosen by a now forgotten method of counting yarrow wands. At some time in the Western Zhou dynasty, each hexagram was provided with oracular sentences of uncertain origin (traditionally by King Wen and the Duke of Zhou – K. Munwang and Chugong), which came to be treated as a scripture of impenetrable wisdom. Each hexagram is referred to by a one- or two-character tag, usually taken from its oracles, that serves as its name. The first two are Kŏn 'heaven' and Kon 'earth'.

Around the end of the last millennium BC, eight treatises (wrongly attributed to Confucius) were added to *Zhouyi* to form the classic *Yijing* (K. *Yŏkkyŏng*). Because they were edited into ten fascicles, these eight are known as Ten Wings (K. *sib-ik*). Four of the eight (K. *Tanjŏn, Taesang, Sosang* and *Munŏn*) comment sentence by sentence on the hexagrams and are usually split up so that each passage of commentary can be printed beside the line of text to which it refers. The other four are printed as appendixes: the Great Treatise (K. *Taejŏn* or *Kyesa-jŏn*), oldest account of *yin-yang* (*see ŭm-yang*) theory; the 'Trigrams Treatise' (K. *Sŏlgwae*), describing the eight **trigrams** into which the hexagrams can be divided – the basis of much Korean **divination** practice; and two annotated lists of the hexagram tags (K. *Sŏgwae, Chapkwae*). Most Korean editions add the Song period commentaries of **Zhu Xi** (headed *ponŭi*) and Cheng Hao (headed *chŏn*), interspersed throughout the text of *Zhouyi*.

RICHARD RUTT, *The Zhouyi, a New Translation with Commentary*, London: Curzon Press, 1996
See also **Chŏngyŏk**; **Confucian Classics**; **divination**; **Five Sages**

BOOKS *ch'aek, kwŏn, p'yŏn* 册, 卷, 篇

A Korean literary work is described as being in so many *ch'aek* and so many (usually rather more) *kwŏn*.

Ch'aek, translated as 'book', 'volume' or fascicle', was used in China during the later 2nd millennium BC to denote a bound collection of **bamboo** slats on which a document was written in vertical columns. It has survived to mean a physical book.

Kwŏn, also translated as 'book', originally meant a roll of **silk** (later of **paper**) that was more convenient than a bundle of bamboo slats. The same word continued to be used after the long piece of paper began to be folded into 'pages' rather than rolled. (The oldest extant such book, made of paper folded and pasted into seven pages, is a Chinese *Diamond Sutra* of 868, found at Dunhuang in 1907 and now kept in the British Museum.) A very large work, such as Sima Qian's *Shiji*, took up many *kwŏn*, each containing one section or chaper of the whole. When bound volumes of paper with the pages stitched together to form a spine were invented, probably in the 9th century AD, the numbering of the *kwŏn* was retained, and the word *kwŏn* survives with the practical meaning of 'chapter'. Stitched books were known in Korea during the Koryŏ dynasty.

A less ancient term, *p'yŏn*, meaning a flat writing tablet, hence a document, has come to mean a part or section of a literary composition. All three words are also still used colloquially to mean 'book' or 'volume'.

The typical Korean volume varies in size between octavo and duodecimo, and is not thick. The cover is of stiff oiled or waxed paper, yellow in colour, with an embossed **all-over pattern**, produced by the impression of a carved board. The cover is in two separate parts, front and back – there is no spine. Each piece of yellow paper is folded back at the edges like cloth for hemming, and a piece of paper (often waste paper) is pasted over the inner side.

Two pages are printed on one side of a sheet, the first page on the right-hand side, the second on the left. The sheet is folded between the two pages, with the printing outside, so that the fold forms the page edge. (The blank face of the sheet, which is not printed, is hidden by the folding.) All the folded sheets are placed in order between the two cover-pieces and the whole is stitched through from back to front with thread (often red) in five or six places through all the pages. The stitching is done with one length of thread in a simple fashion that leaves visible thread running up and down outside both covers, parallel to the 'spinal' edge (right-hand side of the front cover). This gives rigidity to the 'spine' but prevents the book from lying open quite flat.

On each sheet the text is often bordered by black lines (*pyŏllan*) that define three margins, generous at the top (*sŏmi*), narrower at the bottom and very narrow at the bound edges. Two finer vertical lines within the top and bottom margin-lines border a narrower central column (*p'an'gu*) which when folded makes the outer margin of each page. This column contains the title of the book, the number of the *kwŏn* and the number of the sheet. The central fold runs through these characters, including the sheet number, of which only one half is visible at a time, so that one number serves for two pages. Near the top of this central column is a black rectangle filling the breadth of the column. A triangle, as wide as the column, is cut out at the lower edge of the rectangle, leaving a black *ŏmi* 'fish tail'. The almost invariable mark of a Korean (as distinct from a Chinese) book is that this black fishtail has a white quatrefoil (*hwasim*) or **caltrop** in it.

In traditional **printing**, the block or type (mirror-image of two pages) was set face upwards on a table and the paper pressed on to it. A woodblock was prepared by writing two consecutive pages on a single sheet of thin paper, the first page on the right-hand side, the following page on the left-hand side. The paper was then pasted upside down on a smooth block of jujube or pear or other close-grained wood. The writing showed through in reverse. The white spaces were gouged out, leaving the writing proud for printing. Moveable type, which had to be tied into its forme, was dislodged by every impression taken. Hence moveable type was reserved for special books produced in smaller numbers. Woodblocks, despite the time and cost of preparing blocks, were economical in both time and cost for printing an inexpensive book published in large numbers.

The introduction of **Confucianism** and **Buddhism** from China stimulated the production of books and influenced the respect paid to the written word, which long remained the exclusive preserve of a small educated class. The **Confucian Classics** and Buddhist **sutras**, together with their commentaries, comprised the earliest categories of books. Later references show that in the Unified Silla period the range of titles had broadened to include biographies and **music**. Books were listed as items received from China in return for **tribute** in the Koryŏ and Chosŏn periods, which also saw an outpouring of Korean publications on **poetry** and **prose literature**, philosophy, history, geography, **agriculture**, **law**, **medicine**, **astronomy**, and the compilation of specialist and general compendia. Particular stimulus to book production was given by the great neo Confucian scholar-official **Chŏng ToJŏn**, whose advice encouraged King **T'aejong** to establish a printing press in Seoul early in the 15th century. Later in the dynasty the *sirhak* **movement** was responsible for a further burst of output.

BRIDGE-TREADING *tari-bapki*

A custom, said to date from mid-Koryŏ, of walking over bridges on *Taeborŭm-nal* at night, which was supposed to guard against foot trouble during the coming twelve months. Treading on twelve bridges that night was said to ward off all bad luck for the year. In Seoul the custom centred on Kwangt'ong Bridge (*Kwangt'ong-gyo*). The moonlit streets were crowded, and after the mid-Chosŏn period, **women** postponed their bridge-treading until the night of the 16th, while *yangban* did it on the 13th. By the end of the dynasty women had largely forsaken the custom.

BRONZE AGE

Current evidence suggests that the Korean Bronze Age began early in the first millennium BC, the fully fledged period dating from around 700 BC. The metal culture spread from **Manchuria**, and early artefacts include daggers, swords, spear- and arrowheads, **mirrors** and small **bells**. Bronze possessions indicated tribal leadership and social superiority. They have been found particularly along the Liao and **Taedong** River valleys, the region associated with **Old Chosŏn**, but the significance of the metal was much less marked than in Shang and Zhou China, and the advent of the **iron** age soon effected greater changes on society and the economy. The earliest examples found in the south include a **mirror** and a bracelet from a tomb of the first century BC at **Kyŏngju** and another from a first century AD site in **Kimhae**. During the Three Kingdoms period metal-working skills were finely developed and associated with élite culture. Bronze shoes have been discovered in tombs of **Mahan** and **Paekche** royalty of the 6th century. Fine examples of bronze craftsmanship are to be seen in Buddhist statuary and the casting of decorated temple bells from the Silla period.

In the Koryŏ period bronze was widely used for the manufacture of many everyday objects, including mirrors, bottles, ewers, bowls, chopsticks, cosmetic items, jewellery, and seals.

CHOI MONG-LYONG, 'Bronze Age in Korea,' *KJ*, 24/9, 1984; LEE CHUNG-KYU, 'The Bronze Dagger Culture of Liaoning Province and the Korean Peninsula,' *KJ*, 36/4, 1986; M. RIOTTO, *The Bronze Age in Korea*, Kyoto: Italian School of East Asian Studies, 1989
See also P'yŏnjong

BROUGHTON, WILLIAM ROBERT (1762–1821)

Captain Broughton RN, commanding HMS *Providence*, visited **Tongnae** and surveyed the east coast of Korea in 1797. His book *A Voyage of Discovery to the North Pacific Ocean* (London 1804) describes his experiences and gives a glossary of Korean words. For long afterwards maps showed Wŏnsan Bay as 'Broughton Bay' and the sea between Korea and **Tsushima** as 'Broughton Straits'.

BROWN, JOHN McLEAVEY (1842–1926)

An Irishman who entered the British Consular Service and went to China in 1872. In 1893 he was appointed to the Korean **Maritime Customs Service** and from 1896 was

Chief Financial Adviser to the Korean government. In 1897 he was temporarily displaced by Russian influence, but from 1898 was Head of Customs and Controller of Finances, responsible for all the Treaty Port revenues and curbing the King's expenditure. He was said to be very learned. He was dictatorial and did much to improve the city of Seoul, removing shacks that had intruded on the thoroughfares and designing, among other things, **Pagoda Park**, site of the 1919 **Independence Declaration**. He left in 1906, when the Japanese took over the country, and was later knighted by the King of England.

BROWN, MISS EMILY
In summer 1904 some western newspapers reported that the Emperor of Korea was engaged to marry an American missionary named Emily Brown. **W. F. Sands** says the story was based on reports of Lady Ŏm, who was said by Westerners to be a 'kitchen-maid'. Frustrated American journalists who had been sent to the **Russo-Japanese War,** but were cooped up in Seoul and not allowed to go to the front, amused themselves by inventing Miss Brown.

BRUGUIÈRE, SIMÉON-FRANÇOIS (1792–1835)
The first bishop appointed to Korea. Bruguière worked as a priest of the Paris Foreign Missions in Bangkok from 1825 to 1828, when he was appointed first Vicar-Apostolic of Korea. He was ordained bishop in 1831 and began a long and arduous journey through China to **Manchuria**, preceded by a Chinese priest, Yu Hengde (K. Yŏ Hangdŏk; Pacificus, sometimes wrongly called Francis). When the time to enter Korea seemed right, accompanied by Fr **Maubant**, the bishop set off towards the **Yalu**, but fell ill and died at Majiazi in Liaoning province, Manchuria.
See also **Capsa**

BRUSH-NAMES *ho, aho, tangho* 雅號, 堂號
Names adopted by painters, calligraphers and writers with which they often signed their work. *See* **names, personal**; **painting**

BUDDHAS *pul, pult'a, yŏrae* 佛, 佛陀, 如來
A buddha is a fully enlightened one, who has passed into nirvana. The title *yŏrae* is a translation of the Sanskrit *tathagata* 'he who thus comes'. Some buddhas are historical; some, principally **Vairocana**, **Amida** and **Yaksa-yŏrae**, are personifications or representations of abstract concepts. Others are ambivalent (**Tabo, Mirŭk**).

A buddha is normally portrayed in a monk's robe, very like a toga, leaving the right shoulder uncovered, and often diaphanous. He has a protuberance (S. *usnisa*, K. *yukkye*, 'fleshy topknot') on the crown of his head, which is covered with tight curls. Sakyamuni (K. Sŏkkamoni, Sŏkka-bul or Sŏkka-yŏrae), surnamed Gautama, the historical Buddha (c. 563–483 BC), lived in the 6th century BC in India. Lay people often equate him with **Amida**.

Temples, museums and outdoor sites throughout Korea boast many fine sculptured images of buddhas and **bodhisattvas** dating from the Three Kingdoms to the modern period. Many more are painted on altar reredosses and temple walls, often surrounded by hundreds of attendants. Figures may be recognisable by their *mudra* (hand gestures), their physical attributes, dress and ornaments, or their attendants, but their number is so great that there is often scope for confusion over exact identification. Statues come in all sorts of sizes and materials, from tiny portable votive figures to a huge (27 metres) modern Mirŭk in concrete at Pŏpju-sa, Songni-san, but the finest are those made of bronze to sit on temple altars. The most frequently seen statues and recipients of worship in traditional and modern Korean **Buddhism** are Amida, Avalokitesvara, Bhaisajyaguru (the buddha of healing and ruler of the Eastern Paradise), Kshitigarbha (dedicated to saving the suffering from hell), Maitreya, Sakyamuni, and Vairocana.

See also **Buddhist temple halls; Four Heavenly Kings; Kwanseŭm; Sŏkkuram**

BUDDHISM 佛教 *Pulgyo*

The traditional dates for the reception of this religion at the courts of the Three Kingdoms are AD 372 for **Koguryŏ** (*see* **Sundo**), 384 in **Paekche** (*see* **Malananda**) and 527–35 in **Silla**, where it had to overcome the strongest resistance (*see* **Ich'adon**). In each case its actual introduction from China is likely to have been somewhat earlier (*see* **Ado**). No doubt the encouragement Buddhism received in north China during the Toba Wei dynasty (386–535) assisted the spread of its teachings and cultural forms (notably **sculpture**) across the peninsula, where royal families and the aristocracy patronised it in the hope of benefiting their states. In turn Buddhism was disseminated eastwards to Japan from the early 6th century onwards, initially from Paekche, then also from Silla and Koguryŏ (*see* **Japan, Buddhist missionaries to**).

In Unified Silla Buddhism flourished and dominated culture and society at all levels (*see* bronze **bells; five commandments; sculpture; stupas**). Rich land-owning monasteries dominated the countryside (*see* **Pulguk-sa**) and engaged in **commerce**. Monks became political advisers and were sent to China in search of instruction (*see* **Haedong Kosŭng-jŏn; Hyech'o; nine mountain schools; Wŏnhyo**). **Ennin** found a community of Korean Buddhists in Shandong. Powerful intellectual traditions developed (*see* **O-gyo**), as well as meditative *Sŏn*, usually based on particular **sutras**. Though these traditions originated in China, all came to acquire distinct Korean characteristics. Korea indigenised the Chinese concept of holy mountains: five peaks of Odae in Kangwŏn province were specially worshipped as dwelling places of bodhisattvas.

The Koryŏ court maintained the strong link between state and Buddhism (*see* **Wang Kŏ; Kyunyŏ**). Members of the royal family became monks and were important in developing the intellectual and political rôle of the dharma (*see* **Naong; Chigong**), while Buddhist **rites and ceremonies** were widely observed (*see* *P'algwan-hoe; Yŏndŭng-hoe*). The official printing of the *Tripitaka* failed to save the nation from attacks by the **Khitan** and **Mongols**, but the survival to the present of so many fine **pagodas** and splendidly inscribed and decorated **sutras** illustrates the real cultural strength of Buddhism. Doctrinally the major achievements of the dynasty were **Ŭich'ŏn**'s revitalisation of *Ch'ŏnt'ae-jong*, the integration of *Sŏn* groups with it, and the creation of the *Chogye* sect (*see* **Chinul; T'aego**). Monks became politically and economically powerful, exempt from **taxation** and from **military service** (*see* **Sin Ton**).

With the establishment of the Chosŏn dynasty and the rise of neo-Confucianism in the 15th century, Buddhism enjoyed mixed fortunes. More for political than for religious reasons, it was restrained by King T'aejo and repressed by T'aejong. It was both controlled and supported by **Sejong**, encouraged by **Sejo**, and severely proscribed again under **Sŏngjong**. Under **Yŏnsan-gun** there was persecution and wanton destruction of monasteries, but ground was regained in the next reign, only to be lost again under Myŏngjong (*see* **Pou**). Although there was spiritual vigour in Buddhism in the early 17th century (*see* *Sŏn'ga-gwigam*), its popularity slumped, its literature was declared impious by the ruling literati, and among ordinary people its claims were less and less distinguishable from those of native **shamanism**. It managed to survive, however, and began a revival at the end of the 19th century which has lasted and grown till the end of the 20th (*see* **Han Yongun**). In modern times, despite confusion about its japanisation and modernisation (*see* ***Chogye-jong***; ***Wŏn-Buddhism***) during the colonial period, it has played a prominent part in political affairs, especially by voicing opposition to Japanese oppression and to dictatorship in the post-war republics. Since 1970 westerners have been welcomed as monks in some monasteries.

For the Buddhas and Bodhisattvas most commonly worshipped in Korea, see **Asanas**; **Buddhas**; **Bodhisattvas**

JAMES GRAYSON, *Korea, a Religious History*, Oxford University Press, 1989; KANG WI-JO, 'The Secularisation of Buddhism under the Japanese Colonialism,' *KJ*, 19/7, 1980; KIM TONGHWA, 'The Buddhist Thought in the Paekche Period,' Seoul: *JAS*, 5:1, 1962; LEWIS R. LANCASTER, *Assimilation of Buddhism in Korea, Religious Maturity and Innovation in the Silla Dynasty*, Berkeley: Asian Humanities Press, 1991; LEWIS R. LANCASTER & CHAI-SHIN YU, eds., *Introduction of Buddhism to Korea: New Cultural Patterns*, Berkeley: Asian Humanities Press, 1989; LEWIS R. LANCASTER & CHAI-SHIN YU, eds., *Buddhism in Koryŏ: a Royal Religion*, Berkeley: Institute of East Asian Studies, 1996; LEWIS R. LANCASTER & CHAI-SHIN YU, eds., *Buddhism in the Early Chosŏn: Suppression and Transformation*, Berkeley: Institute of East Asian Studies, 1996; PETER H. LEE, *Lives of Eminent Korean Monks*, Cambridge, Mass.: Harvard University Press, 1969

BUDDHIST TEMPLE HALLS *pŏptang* 法堂

One, three or five principal images are enthroned in a temple hall, representing **Buddhas** or **Bodhisattvas** related to the name of the hall. Identification of the statues is complicated, depending on stance (***asana***), hand-gestures (***mudra***), and accompanying emblems and statue groupings, but some arrangements are common.

In a *Taeung-jŏn* 'hall of the great worthy one', the central image will be the historical Buddha, Sakyamuni. If he is flanked by two Bodhisattvas, they are often Munsu (Manjusri, on his left) and Pohyŏn (Samantabhadra, on his right); or Chijang (Kshitigarbha) and **Mirŭk**; or even by the two *nahan*, Ananda and Kasyapa, though these are likely to be placed at the outside positions in a group of five statues.

A main hall may also have **Vairocana** Buddha in the middle, with Sakyamuni on one side and either Losana Buddha or **Yaksa-yorae** on the other.

In a *Kŭngnak-chŏn* (Sukhavati Hall) 'hall of utmost joy' or *Muryangsu-jŏn* 'hall of infinite life', where the name is derived from *Chŏngt'o* ('Pure Land') teaching, **Amida** Buddha is flanked by Bodhisattvas **Kwanseŭm** on his left and Taeseji on his right.

Subsidiary halls for spirit worship may be *Toksŏng-gak* containing the 'lonely saint' (an obscure hermit, Naban Chonja), *Ch'ilsŏng-gak* for the spirits of the Seven Stars, and *Sansin-gak* for the local mountain spirit. These purely Korean spirits may be regarded as bodhisattvas. They may all be venerated in one building called *Samsin-gak* 'triple spirit shrine', or even reduced to paintings in a *pŏptang*.

BULL-FIGHTING *sossam*

Especially in Kyŏngsang province there was a custom at *Tano* of matching two heavy bulls against one another in a show of strength. They would lower their heads, engage their foreheads and push. Much money was staked on the outcome of the struggle.

C

CAIRO CONFERENCE (1943)

Wartime meeting held in November 1943 between Winston Churchill, Franklin Roosevelt, and Chiang Kai-shek. Chiang spoke on behalf of the Korean Provisional Government in Exile, which sent Chŏng Han'gyŏng to plead the case for Korean independence. The Declaration issued on 1 December considered the future of the Pacific region after a Japanese defeat and referred to the restoration of Korean independence 'in due course', a significant change to the wording of the first draft which had read 'at the earliest possible moment'. The modification enshrined President Roosevelt's belief that former colonial territories of East Asia would need a period of tutelage under allied supervision before gaining their freedom (see Trusteeship).

CALLIGRAPHY sŏye, sŏdo 書藝, 書道

One of the Six Arts that Korean scholars must practise in emulation of their cultured Chinese rôle models. They admired and imitated the styles of Chinese calligraphers, notably Wang Xizhi (307–65), Ouyang Xu (1007–72) and Zhao Mengfu (1254–1322), and developed advanced skills in the major Chinese categories of haesŏ (C. kaishu, regular script), yesŏ (C. lishu, clerical script), haengsŏ (C. xingshu, running script), ch'osŏ (C. caoshu, grass script), and sojŏn (C. xiaozhuan, small seal). Examples of haesŏ, yesŏ, and haengsŏ survive from the Three Kingdoms period, when haesŏ was predominant: it was used, for example, on a stone record of a land deal found in the tomb of King Muryŏng of Paekche. On the other hand, the monument to King Kwanggaet'o erected in AD 414 was carved in yesŏ. Fine calligraphy from the Unified Silla dynasty was promoted by both Confucian and Buddhist scholarship and by the carving of memorials, and there are extant examples by Ch'oe Ch'iwŏn in honour of the Sŏn monk Hyesŏ (or Chin'gam, 744–850), and by Kim Saeng. Ch'osŏ and haengsŏ were increasingly used as the writing of poetry and letters spread, and Korean calligraphers evolved more individual styles of their own. In the Koryŏ period calligraphic art was stimulated by the court patronage of Buddhism and copying of scriptures, and by the development of the examination system. Calligraphy was taught at the Sŏnggyun-gwan. One of the greatest exponents in this period was Yi Am, an admirer of Zhao Mengfu. Adoption of neo-Confucianism by the early Chosŏn court brought a new incentive to practise the scholarly art of calligraphy. Many famous artists flourished. Masters of particular types were Prince Anp'yŏng (see Yi Yong, haesŏ), Kim Ku (1488–1534, yesŏ), and Kim Sangyong (1561–1637, sojŏn). Some artists made reputations as both painters and calligraphers. They included Kang Sehwang and, perhaps the greatest of all Korean calligraphers, Kim Chŏnghŭi.

CALTROP marŭmsoe 菱鐵 (nŭngch'ŏl)

Marŭm 'caltrop', also called water-chestnut or Jesuits' nut, is an aquatic plant. (Its seeds are eaten, but it is not the Chinese 'water-chestnut'). The ripe fruit splits into four hard sepals, which give its name to the caltrop or marŭmsoe and to a motif used in printing. The marŭmsoe consists of a cast-iron four-pointed star, 5 or 6 cm across, two opposite points bent upwards and the other two downwards. The object thus has the outline-points of a tetrahedron and always falls to the ground with one point upwards. Before the advent of barbed wire, it was scattered around buildings to discourage burglars and around camps at war. In the centre of the marŭmsoe is a round hole, so that the objects can be threaded on cord for handling in quantity. The same four marŭm points appear in the white 'water-chestnut' design in the black 'fishtail' at the edge of the page in many printed **books**.

CANDLE-NOTCH POEMS *kakch'ok-pusi* or *kakch'ok-wisi* 刻燭賦(爲)詩
During the 5th and 6th centuries in China there was a great vogue for poetry at the court of the Liang dynasty, when some notable pieces were composed. One of the entertainments of scholars at that time was to compete in writing poems at night, finishing a quatrain in the time taken for a candle to burn to a certain notch. This practice is said to have been popular in Koryŏ.

CANGHAI 滄海
Chinese commandery nominally established by the **Han** government in territory of the former state of **Ye** in 128 BC, replaced by that of **Xuantu** in 107 BC.

CANONISED SAGES *paehyang sŏnsaeng* 配享先生
Eighteen tablets for Koreans stand in the *Sŏnggyun-gwan*, nine on the east side (E), nine on the west (W). The first three were installed in Koryŏ times for the earliest great Korean Confucian scholars: **Ch'oe Ch'iwŏn** (W1) in 1020 and **Sŏl Ch'ong** (E1) in 1022; and for the founder of the *Sŏnggyun-gwan*, **An Hyang** (E2) in 1319. **Chŏng Mongju** (W2), the great loyalist, long honoured as the Father of Korean neo-Confucianism, was canonised when the **Meritorious Subjects** were in power in 1517. About a century later, in 1610, when the Eastern **faction** held sway, the '**Five Sages**' of the Yŏngnam or *sarim* neo-Confucian group, philosophic forebears of the Easterners, were installed: **Kim Koengp'il** (E3), **Chŏng Yŏch'ang** (W3), **Cho Kwangjo** (E4), **Yi Ŏnjŏk** (W4), and **Yi Hwang** (E5). Later in the 17th century, when the Westerners were in power, the first members of the **Kiho** (Kyŏnggi/Ch'ungch'ŏng) grouping were installed, beginning in 1665 with **Cho Hŏn** (W7), who had died in battle for his country, and followed in 1682 by **Yi I** (E6), inspiration of the Westerners, and his friend **Sŏng Hon** (W6). The last two were removed when the Southerners took power in 1689, but restored when they lost control in 1694.

The 18th century saw the addition of four more names, all distinguished in the development of **ritual studies** during the previous century; **Kim Changsaeng** (E7), the first ritualist, in 1717; **Song Siyŏl** (W8) and **Song Chun'gil** (E9) in 1756; and **Pak Sech'ae** (W9) in 1764. **Kim Inhu** (W5), whose scientific interests were no doubt approved by *sirhak* scholars, was installed in 1796. The last to be canonised was **Kim Chip** (E8), a Kiho ritual scholar whose canonisation had been discussed since 1789, but was not carried out until 1883, when factional vigour had waned.

CAOUN, VINCENT (1580–1626)
Among the Koreans taken back to Japan in the Hideyoshi invasions was a 12-year-old boy taken to Kyoto in 1598. His name is recorded as Caoun, which has been taken as a mistake for Kwŏn, but is just as likely to be his given name, Kaun. He was educated in the Jesuit seminary at Arima and destined to return to Korea as a missionary. He spent some years in China, visiting Macao and Beijing, but was arrested and burnt at the stake in Nagasaki on 20 June 1626. He was the second Korean member of the Society of Jesus. He was beatified with his companions in 1867. The first Korean Jesuit was also beatified: Gayo (Gaius, c1572–1624), a former Buddhist monk, martyred at Nagasaki.
JUAN RUIZ DE MEDINA (trans. John Bridges), *The Catholic Church in Korea: its Origins 1566–1784*, Rome: Istituto Storico SI, 1991

CAPITAL CITIES
The following is a list of the modern locations in the vicinity of which earlier capitals were situated. Dates of transfer from one location to another, where known, are shown in square brackets. Alternative contemporary names are shown in round brackets.

OLD CHOSŎN	P'yŏngyang
WIMAN CHOSŎN	P'yŏngyang (Wanggŏmsŏng)
PUYŎ	Nongan, Jilin province, China
KOGURYŎ	Huanren, Liaoning province, China (Cholbon) [AD 3] > Ji'an, Jilin province, China (**Kungnaesŏng**, Hwando) [A.D.427] > P'yŏngyang (Wanggŏmsŏng)
LELANG	P'yŏngyang (T'osŏngni)
PAEKCHE	Seoul (Hansŏng) [475] > Kŏngju (**Ungjin**) [538] > Puyŏ (**Sabi**)
SILLA	**Kyŏngju** (Saro; Kŭmsŏng)
UNIFIED SILLA	Kyŏngju
KORYŎ	**Kaesŏng** (Songak, Kaeju, Kaegyŏng, Songdo); regional capitals at P'yŏngyang and Kyŏngju
CHOSŎN	Seoul (Hanyang, Hansŏng)
COLONIAL KOREA	Seoul (Keijō)
NORTH KOREA (DPRK)	P'yŏngyang
SOUTH KOREA (ROK)	Seoul

See also **P'yŏngyang; Seoul**

CAPPING *kwallye* 冠禮
The Confucian rite of adulthood for boys, which had to be done before **marriage**. The boy's hair, hitherto uncut and worn in a pigtail, was washed and done up into a **topknot** (*sangt'u*). His forehead was bound with a tight band (*man'gŏn*) and the black horsehair hat (*kat*) put on over it. When capped very young, a boy might wear a straw hat until he was about twenty.

CAPSA
According to Catholic custom a bishop must have a diocesan title. If he has no canonically erected diocese, he is given the title of a defunct ancient diocese, usually one now in Muslim territory (formerly called a 'bishopric *in partibus infidelium*'). Bishops **Bruguière**, **Imbert** and **Berneux** were given the title of Capsa (now Gafsa in Tunisia) and were often politely referred to in French as 'Capse'. In English the form 'Capsa' should be used.

CARLETTI, FRANCESCO *See* COREA, ANTONIO

CARTOGRAPHY
The earliest Korean map surviving till the 20th century portrayed Liaodong city (K. Yodong-sŏng) and was drawn in Koguryŏ times (5th-early 7th centuries) on the wall of a **tomb** near Sunch'ŏn in north P'yŏngan province. The skills of cartographers developed during the Koryŏ dynasty. In the second half of the 11th century the Chinese official Su Shi (1037–1101) complained about the risk to national security incurred by the export of Chinese maps to Korea at a time when relations with the **Khitan** were sensitive. Though there are written references to other early maps, none has survived

older than one of 1402, which exists in several copies. Known as *Kangni-do* (short for *Honil kangni yŏktae kukto-chido*, 'Comprehensive territories historical states and cities map'), it is the oldest world map in the East Asian tradition and is thought to have a partly Islamic pedigree. There is also a late 15th-century copy of a map by Yi Hoe and **Kwŏn Kŭn**. No other Korean world map survives from before the Japanese invasion of 1592.

There is reason to believe that maps based on the reports of Central Asia given by the Chinese pilgrim monk Xuan Zang (AD 600–664) were invented in Korea. They are known as 'Buddhist maps' or *Gotenjiku* (K. *O-ch'ŏnch'uk*) 'maps of the five Indian kingdoms', and were popular in Japan from the mid-14th to mid-18th centuries.

The early form of world map called 'wheel map' or *ch'ŏnha-do*, 'map of all under heaven', shows the countries of the Old World, with China in the middle, as a land-mass shaped like a multi-lobed jellyfish, with a circular doughnut-shape land area surrounding the outer seas. All these maps contain similar indications of legendary places, drawn chiefly from *Shanhai jing*.

New approaches came when Ricci's world map arrived in Korea in 1603. Koryŏ University in Seoul possesses a remarkable terrestrial globe (*Sŏn'gi-okhyŏng*), probably dating from the later 18th century, though some claim it was made in Korea in 1669. It is made of wood, covered with oil-painted **paper**, about 9 cm in diameter, and stands in the centre of a clock-driven armillary sphere. Who made it and where have not been established.

Maps of China and Japan, the Chinese ones showing the country as it was administered in Ming times, continued to be made until the end of the 19th century.

Maps of Korea were the responsibility of government, and cartography was superintended by the Hall of **Astronomy** (*Sŏun-gwan*) and Office of Fine Arts (*Tohwa-sŏ*). They were seen as aids in administration and defence, and for the most part they were dominated by concepts drawn from *p'ungsu*, expressed as an arterial network of mountains complemented by a network of rivers. These were *hyŏngse-do*, 'shape and form maps'. In theory the reader could discover how to get from any point to any other without crossing a stream. Copies of such *hyŏngse-do* remain in *Haedong cheguk-ki* (1471) by **Sin Sukchu**. He worked for **Sejong** and **Sejo**, both of whom took personal interest in map-making.

Old maps of Korea can be conveniently considered in four groups.

1) Maps in the style of Chŏng Ch'ŏk (1390–1475, map-maker for Sejo), administrative sketches of the mid-15th to mid-17th centuries. They typically have a flattened horizontal northern boundary to the country.

2) Maps in the style used in *Tongguk yŏji-sŭngnam*, which continued to be made until 1895. They lack the *p'ungsu* interest in mountain arteries, but contain much information about settlements and buildings, often with attractive symbols of mountains and types of building. They are essentially charts to illustrate the written material in historico-geographical texts.

3) Maps in the style of Chŏng Sanggi (1678–1752), who is known for his *Tongguk-chido* ('Map of Korea'). These were the first to take careful cognisance of scale and were a fruit of *sirhak* thinking. They showed the mountain arteries and a more accurate portrayal of the northern boundaries. *Sirhak* scholars took an interest in the realistic depiction of the topography of their country and its communication routes, which was also useful to **merchants** as inter-regional **commerce** developed. Other cartographers of this kind include Chŏng Sun (1676–1759) and Yi Sanggwŏn (late 18th century).

4) The maps of the geologist **Kim Chŏngho** (d. 1864), Korea's great cartographical genius, whose maps of the capital were still the basis for mapmaking in 1900. *Ch'ŏnggu-do*, 'Map of the Green Hills' (see **Korea, names for**) (1834) is a two-album collection of sectional maps, always hand-copied. It was never printed. *Taedong yŏji-do* (1861) is a greatly improved version on folding strips.

There were many maps of Seoul and other local areas to match the *ŭpchi*, usually in the *Yŏji-sŭngnam* style. They include street names for the first time in the 18th century. One very popular map of Seoul is headed *Susŏn-do*, 'Map of the source of all good', after a **Han dynasty** idea of the function of a capital city.

After 1895 western cartography swiftly took over. It is more accurate, but cannot replace the historical information, nor the charm and fascination, of the older maps.
GARI LEDYARD, 'Cartography in Korea', *in* J.B.HARTLEY & DAVID WOODWARD, *The History of Cartography*, Chicago University Press, 1994

CATHOLICISM *Sŏhak* 西學, *Ch'ŏnju-gyo* 天主教 *See* **Roman Catholic Church**

CATS
Domestic cats were house-pets in Koryŏ, probably imported from China, where they were known since Tang times, but are not attested earlier. (Ancient Chinese references to cats are all to wild species). Black-and-white and tabby-and-white kinds were favourites of 18th-century Korean *genre* painters. They were valued as mousers and said to be the only animals allowed indoors, even under the quilt. They were reckoned to be like **women**, quintessentially *yin*, and are still addressed by a coaxing phrase '*Ana nabiya*', reserved for cats alone. There are tales of them saving the *yŏŭiju* 'what-you-will jewel', and they are regarded as fey animals, capable of bestowing a curse. Swallowing a cat-hair may bar entry to the after-life.

CAT'S-CRADLE *silttŭgi*
The universal children's string game in which a loop of yarn about 1·5 metres long is held taut round the thumbs and little fingers of the outstretched hands and manipulated by twisting the fingers and wrists until a pattern appears between the hands. The yarn is then passed to a friend's fingers without collapsing the pattern. Many patterns can be created, including *sangdu-dugi* 'setting up a bier', *padukp'an* '*paduk* board', *chŏtkarak* 'chopsticks', *soe-nunkkal* 'cow's eyeball' and *chŏlgugongi* 'pestle'.

CÉCILLE, JEAN-BAPTISTE THOMAS MÉDÉE (1787–1873)
A French diplomat and administrator with the rank of Admiral, active in east Asia during the 1840s. In 1846 he appeared off the west coast of Korea near Hongju, bringing a letter of complaint from France about the execution of Bishop **Imbert** and his companions in 1839. He promised to return the following year to receive an answer. There is little doubt that the treatment of **Kim Taegŏn** (who had served Cécille earlier as an interpreter) would have been less severe but for Cécille's high-handed approach to the Korean court. In 1849 he was appointed ambassador to London.

CELADON *ch'ŏngja* 青瓷
Céladon, from a Greek word meaning 'the sound of running streams or twittering birds', was the name of the shepherd hero of *Astrée*, a hugely influential French pastoral romance by Honoré d'Urfé (1567–1625). The colour of something in the

shepherd's costume in a stage adaptation of *Astrée* made *céladon* a fashionable French colour-word before 1617. By the first half of the 19th century it was applied in English to Chinese ceramics. At first it probably denoted a bright blue-green, mentioned in *Xuanhe fengshi Gaoli tujing* as *pisaek*, 'kingfisher-colour' or (with different Chinese characters) 'secret colour', and was later extended to the soft grey-greens and light olive-greens of later Koryŏ **stoneware**.

GODFREY GOMPERTZ, 'Korean Inlaid Celadon Wares,' *TOCS*, 28, 1953–4; GODFREY GOMPERTZ, *Korean Celadon and other Wares of the Koryŏ Period*, London: Faber & Faber, 1963; GODFREY GOMPERTZ, 'The Appeal of Korean Celadon,' *OA* XXIII, 1977; I. ITOH, 'Koreanization in Koryŏ Celadon,' *Orientations*, vol.23 no.12, 1982; NIGEL WOOD, 'Technological Parallels between Chinese Yue Wares and Korean Celadons,' *PBAKS*, 5, 1994
See also **ceramics**

CENSORATE
Surveillance branch of the government instituted in imitation of the Chinese model, charged with scrutinising the performance of officials, impeaching the corrupt, guarding against maladministration, preparing reports on the conduct of government, and proposing new measures. In the Koryŏ dynasty it was known as the *Ŏsadae* and in the Chosŏn as the *Sagan-wŏn*, when in the strictly neo-Confucian age it had the important rôle of supervising social policy. Though briefly disbanded by **Prince Yŏnsan** (r.1494–1506), its staff under Kings **Sŏngjong** and Chungjong included members of the highly principled *sarim* literati. One of these, **Cho Kwangjo**, was executed in 1519 for his outspoken criticism of the king's senior **meritorious subjects**.
See also Sahwa

CENSUS REGISTERS
Part of a register dating from AD 755, preserved in the Shōsōin Treasury in Nara, suggests that in the Unified Silla period census counts and land assessments were taken triennially for the purpose of assessing *corvée* and **taxation** dues. Census or household records (*hojŏk*) were continued under the succeeding Koryŏ and Chosŏn dynasties, and a number of copies from the 14th century onwards survive. Records of regular censuses during the 17th and 18th centuries indicate the rate of **population** recovery after the **Imjin Wars**. Separate registers were maintained for *yangban* and lower class families, the former showing detailed genealogical information inappropriate to the **peasantry**. They indicate that the typical household comprised more than one nuclear family under the headship of a grandfather or father, the size perhaps being determined by economic circumstances. The registers were important documents when it came to assessing inheritance, and thus give information on **marriage** arrangements, including the status of primary and secondary wives. They appear to show the development of institutionalised patrilineality from the Koryŏ period onwards.

JIN YOUNG RO, 'Demographic and Social Mobility Trends in Early Eighteenth Century Korea: an Analysis of Samŭn County Census Registers,' *KS*, 7, 1983; JOHN SOMERVILLE, 'Stability in Eighteenth Century Ulsan,' *KSF*, 1, 1976/7; EDWARD WAGNER, 'Social Stratification in Seventeenth-Century Korea: some Observations from a 1663 Seoul Census Register', *Occasional Papers on Korea* 1, Seattle, 1974
See also **genealogies**

CERAMICS
Korean potters developed the art of ceramic manufacture under the influence of their neighbours producing Yue wares in China (*see also* **Chang Pogo**). The earliest **kilns** in

the south-western region of **Kangjin** began production in the mid-9th century. The green and yellow **celadons** and white porcelain produced during the 9th and 10th centuries were not very refined, but standards improved as substantial Chinese imports stimulated home output through the 11th century. Technical innovations included decoration with carved inlay and relief, the use of white slip, and the introduction of copper and iron glaze. Principal kiln sites remained around Kangjin, in Chŏlla Namdo, and at Puan, Chŏlla Pukto. In the first half of the 12th century celadons reached a peak of technical and aesthetic perfection which were unmatched even in China. Semi-transparent jade green pieces (known to the Koreans as 'kingfisher colour' *pisaek*) were unsurpassed, though the range of colour also included yellow, red, brown and near-black. In design, the use of a white and black inlay known as *sanggam* was unique to Korean craftsmen. Favourite patterns depicted cranes, chrysanthemums, peonies, willows, and clouds. The smoothness of the vessel surface, whether plain, painted with slip, or enhanced by underglaze crackling, was supreme. Some of the finest vessels were vases, wine ewers and bowls, but the potential of porcelain was wide and extended to water droppers, figurines, even pillows and drums. On the best pieces, the combination of form, colour, and decoration conferred an almost spiritual character.

The quality of celadons declined through the period of **Mongol** domination, but two subsequent categories of porcelain stand out for their aesthetic virtues, *punch'ŏng* ('powder blue-green') and fine white porcelain (*paekcha*). *Punch'ŏng* was a coarser, bolder style of utilitarian pottery than celadon, less refined in appearance but attractive in its spontaneity as well as its technical mastery. It was popular through the early Chosŏn dynasty. The **Imjin Wars**, which destroyed kilns and forced potters into exile, marked the death-knell of *punch'ŏng*, but the appreciation of plain or simply decorated white porcelain survived and deepened. Like celadon, this was a form of art that Koreans had first learned from the Chinese and then taken to greater levels of perfection. In the early Chosŏn period *paekcha* superseded celadon not only technically and aesthetically in the purity of its style and forms, but symbolically as an indication of the transition in state philosophy from **Buddhism** to neo-Confucianism. Its quality was respected even at the Chinese court, and once the country had recovered from the Japanese invasions it was manufactured again in such quantities that it could be used by both upper and lower classes. It was made of white or grey clay, thickly covered with glaze which sometimes gave it a bluish tint (**ch'ŏngbaek-cha**). The refinement of upper class taste was reflected in simplicity of design. Decoration was sparingly applied and was drawn from nature, such as sprigs of bamboo, *prunus* or chrysanthemum. Outstanding examples followed Chinese style, rather than the indigenous inspiration that typifies *punch'ŏng*, and were painted in underglaze blue cobalt. The first supplies of cobalt came from central Asia via China and were limited, so reinforcing economy in its use, but native deposits from around Kangjin were also used in the 15th century. Artists from the *Tohwa-sŏ* were probably engaged in this kind of work, and in the 16th and 17th centuries the technique was extended to the use of iron- and copper-oxide.

EDWARD ADAMS, *Korea's Pottery Heritage*, Seoul: Seoul International Publishing House 1986; G. AKOBOSHI & H. NAKAMURA, *Five Centuries of Korean Ceramics*, New York & Tokyo: Kodansha Intnl., 1975; G. ST.G. M. GOMPERTZ, *Korean Pottery and Porcelain of the Yi Period*, London: Faber & Faber, 1968; MARGARET MEDLEY, 'Korea, China, and Liao in Koryŏ Ceramics,' *OA*, XXIII, no.1, 1977; NIGEL WOOD & ROSE KERR, 'Graciousness to Wild Austerity: Aesthetic Dimensions of Korean Ceramics Explored through Technology,' *Orientations* 23/12, 1992

See also **pottery**

CHAJANG 慈藏 (7th century)
A monk of **Silla** who went to China in 636 on a pilgrimage to the shrine of the
bodhisattva Manjusri, and returned in 643 to organise the Vinaya school of
Buddhism (one of the *O-gyo*). He is reckoned as one of the great leaders of Silla
Buddhism.

CHANG POGO 張保皋 (d. 846)
A merchant and military garrison commissioner commanding the island of Ch'ŏnghae
(modern Wando, Chŏlla Namdo) from 828 to 846. His navy controlled the seas
between Korea and China and cleared them of Chinese pirates. He had seen military
service in China and later supported a Korean community on the Shandong peninsula
of China (*see* **Ennin**), and with his bases in both countries he monopolised the
international **ceramic** trade. His army assisted Kim Ujing's campaign for the throne
which resulted in an attack on **Kyŏngju** and Ujing's accession as King Sinmu in 839.
Political intrigue led to his assassination.
See also **commerce**

CHANG SŬNGŎP 張承業 (Owŏn, 1843–97)
One of the most renowned painters of the 19th century. Of humble origin and orphaned
early in life, he taught himself to paint by imitating the work of earlier artists, and
despite his lack of professional training or literati education came to be patronised by
the *yangban* and even the king himself. His style developed from an imitation of
Chinese Southern School artists to a more independent, energetic form of brushwork
of his own. Though principally a landscape artist, his scope was much wider, and his
picture of *Eagles* is deservedly well known.[1] He had a reputation for eccentricity, yet
established a basis of rich texture and colour usage on which such orthodox *Tohwa-sŏ*
artists as Cho Sŏkchin (1853–1920) built.
(1) CHOI SUNU, *5000 Years of Korean Art*, Seoul: Hyonam Publishing Co., 1979

CHANGGA 長歌 'long songs'
Changga has two meanings. It can mean *kasa* in distinction from the *tan'ga* 'short
song' or *sijo*, but it is also used for the songs of the Koryŏ period that were precursors
of *kasa* and *sijo*. These songs, chiefly sung by **women** about love or scenery, are part of
an oral tradition and distinguished by their division into stanzas, which may be on
differing subjects, and are divided by meaningless refrains that contribute to the colour
and mood of the piece. The fundamental prosodic element is the 3-word or 4-word
group found in other Korean-language verse. There is a particular form called
kyŏnggi-ch'e ka.
Distinguish **Ch'angga**

CHANGGYE-WON 掌隸院
A group of 8 officials, led by a 3rd **grade** senior, that was responsible for matters
regarding **slaves**.

CHANGHŎN, CROWN PRINCE 莊獻世子 (1735–62)
The second son of **King Yŏngjo**, born to a court lady, not to the Queen. His elder half-
brother died before he was born. Against opposition within the court he was named Crown
Prince while still a toddler and married at the age of ten. In spite of the king's policy of
eliminating **factions**, there were factional efforts to enlist the prince's favour when his
father made him in effect regent. The Queen and others accused him of neglecting his

studies and began to find other causes for complaint. In 1761 he went on an unauthorised pleasure trip to P'yŏngyang. A memorial with ten items was presented to the King, accusing the prince of raping palace women and seducing nuns, murdering **eunuchs** and committing other crimes. The enraged Yŏngjo deprived him of royal status and ordered him to drink **poison**. When he refused to commit suicide in June 1762, the king had him shut up in a great rice-box (*twiju*), where he died after eight days. Hence he is commonly known as *Twiju-daewang*, 'rice-box king' – often called 'coffin king' by foreigners.

His remorseful father very quickly restored him posthumously to royal status and gave him the *siho* Sado Seja (Crown Prince Sado). In 1899 **Emperor Kojong**, who was descended from him, gave him the title King Changjo, which has since been his official name for many Korean writers.

The story of his death (referred to as *Imo-ok* and described in **Hanjung-nok**) has been variously interpreted, since the remaining evidence is all *parti pris*. While it is acknowledged that those who favoured his execution became the Pyŏkp'a and those who sympathized with him became the Sip'a factions, some historians suggest that he was the victim of their struggles.

See also **Chŏngjo, King**

CHANGKKI-JŎN

A fable found as **kodae sosŏl** and as **p'ansori**, known certainly to have existed in the 18th century. A *changkki* (cock pheasant) ignores the warning of his mate (*kkat'uri* or hen pheasant), eats poisoned beans and dies. She then resists offers of marriage by other birds until the proper mourning period has been kept.

CHANGSŬNG (so-called 'devil posts')

Changsŭng (or *changsŏng*) and *susal* are two of the names used for the carved posts that at the end of the Chosŏn period often stood at the entrance to a village and before Buddhist monastery gates. Some of them were boundary posts, others mile-posts, but most had come to be regarded as tutelary gods of the place, related to the sacred **tree**, **sŏnangdang** and **sottae**. Community ceremonies called *changgun-je*, 'generals' sacrifices', were often held in front of them on **Taeborŭm-nal**. At critical times they might be surrounded by tabu ropes (*kŭmtchul*), or receive votive offerings of clothing. A few were of stone, but most were pine-trunks, rather less than 2 metres tall, usually crudely coloured. Because they were crudely carved with human faces, they were often wrongly called 'devil-posts' by foreigners. Typically one was male, with a winged cap (*kwan*) on its head, and inscribed down the front as *Ch'ŏnha Tae-janggun* 'Great general under heaven'; the other was female, had no cap and was inscribed *Chiha Tae-*(or *Yŏ-)janggun* 'Great (or Woman) general under the earth'. Or they might be called *Sangwŏn Tae-janggun* and *Hawŏn Tae-janggun*, 'Great generals', 'first above' and 'first below'. There might five posts in one place: *Tongbang Ch'ŏngje ch'ukkwi changgun* 'devil-repelling general, Blue Ruler of the East'; *Sŏbang Paekche*, White Ruler of the West; *Nambang Chŏkche*, Red Ruler of the South; *Pukpang Hŭkche*, Black Ruler of the North and *Chungbang Hwangje*, Yellow Ruler of the Centre.

See **Five Directions Generals**

CHAOXIAN FU 朝鮮賦 (K. Chosŏn-bu, 'Korea Poem')

A *fu* (K. *pu*) or descriptive poem of 504 verses written by Dong Yue, an envoy of the Ming court, who was sent to Seoul in 1488 to announce the accession of the emperor

Xiaozong. The Korean king was the highly cultured **Sŏngjong**, then 28 years old. The introduction to the *fu* is a brief geographical survey of Korea with compliments on the Confucian correctness of its laws and customs. The journey from the **Yalu** to Seoul is then described, with some details about P'yŏngyang, **Kaesŏng** and Seoul. The reception in Seoul is fully recounted and the account of the banquet rises to rhapsody. The last two-fifths of the work deal with Korean customs, flora, fauna and products. It is all superficial but highly enjoyable.
RICHARD RUTT, '*Ch'ao-hsien fu*', *TRASKB*, XLVIII, 1973

CHAPSANG 雜像 'mixed statues'
Clay figurines in maximum sets of ten to be found along the corner ridges of the roofs of palace buildings, temples, or gateways. They were intended as protection against evil spirits and fire. The first four are said to be characters from the 16th-century Chinese novel *Xiyou ji*: Xuan Zang (K. Hyŏnjang), the monk-hero; Sun Wukong (K. **Son Ogong**), the mythical monkey; the gross Zhu Bajie; and Sha Wujing, the novice-monk. There are other less easily identifiable persons and usually a **dragon**, who is perhaps the dragon-king of the novel.

CHARMS *pyŏlchŏn* 別錢 *See* **Coin-charms**

CHASTAN, JACQUES HONORÉ, SAINT 鄭牙各伯 (1803–39)
A priest of the Paris Foreign Missions Society who went out to Penang in 1827, whence he volunteered to join Bishop **Bruguière** in his mission to Korea and in 1833 began his journey through China. After the bishop's death in **Manchuria**, Chastan finally arrived in Seoul in January 1837. For two and a half years he worked secretly in Kyŏnggi and Ch'ungch'ŏng provinces, until at Bishop **Imbert**'s suggestion he surrendered himself at Hongju in South Ch'ungch'ŏng in June 1839 and was executed with the bishop and Fr **Maubant** at Seoul in September.

CHAT-PEGAE See **pillows**

CHEGAL YANG *See* **Zhuge Liang**

CHEJU REBELLION (1948) *Cheju p'oktong sakkŏn* 濟州島暴動事件
Communist rising led by Kim Talsam which took control of much of **Cheju-do** in anticipation of Syngman Rhee (**Yi Sŭngman**)'s assumption of power in succession to the **American Military Government**. The rebellion broke out on 3 April 1948 and was not subdued for a year. Estimates of deaths range from 15,000 to 30,000 people, between one sixth and a third of the island's population, and the destruction of property was immense. When ordered to recover control of the island, President Rhee's 14th Regiment mutinied (*see* **Yŏsu-Sunch'ŏn Uprising**), and as the threat from the communist North increased with numerous crossings of the **Thirty Eighth Parallel** Korea seemed to be on the verge of following the example of China, where the communists were sweeping to success over Chiang Kai-shek. A ruthless purge of supposed communists and other dissenters accompanied the passing of the **National Security Law** in December 1948 and some 90,000 persons were arrested nationwide. Peace returned to Cheju by April 1949, but communist-inspired incidents continued in other parts of the country throughout the year.
See also **Kim Ku; Korean Independence Party**

CHEJU-DO 濟州島 (Cheju Island)

Sub-tropical island off the south-east corner of the Korean peninsula, dominated by an extinct volcano, Hallam-san. It was a *tamno* feudatory of **Paekche**. In Silla (when it continued as a *sokkuk* tributary state) and Koryŏ times it was known as T'amna. It was first incorporated into the kingdom in 938 by King T'aejo (**Wang Kŏn**), and conquered by the **Mongols** as part of the suppression of the **Sambyŏlch'o** resistance in 1273. Under Mongol control the T'amna commandery became a centre for horse and cattle breeding, and timber from its trees was used to build ships for the ill-fated invasion of Japan. In 1653 a Dutch ship was wrecked on Cheju-do, and the account by one of its crew, **Hendrik Hamel**, of his detention in Seoul provides the earliest western account of Korea. The island was given the name of **Quelpaert**.

Cheju is a place with a distinctive culture and dialect, exercising a strong fascination for other Koreans, to whom it was an island of exile with a warm climate, fine scenery and strange customs and **dialect**. The people are descendants of the *samsŏng* 'three clans': Ko, Pu and Nang; it is the *samda-sammu-do*, 'island of three abundances (women, wind and stones) and three absences (burglars, beggars and water)'; its **horses**, oranges and fish are famous. Polygamy was normal, each wife having her own house, visited by her husband in turn with the other wives' houses. Women were therefore economically dominant, and men easily became idlers. Many women did fieldwork, while others were *haenyŏ*, 'sea-women', who would dive to great depths and for long periods, collecting abalone and edible seaweed. Their boats would migrate northwards seasonally and their mournful whistling as they refilled their lungs on surfacing was a feature of the coasts of Chŏlla and Ch'ungch'ŏng in summertime.

The population of Cheju has a turbulent reputation, which is no doubt related to the use of the island by the Chosŏn authorities as a penal colony and place of exile. Peasants revolted against local government in 1862 (*see also* **Chinju Rising**) and against Japanese influence in 1901, and in 1948 a major communist-inspired rebellion took place against the first South Korean government of Syngman Rhee (**Yi Sŭngman**) (*see* **Cheju Rebellion**).

CHIN SONG-GI, 'Tangsin: Cheju Shamanism,' *KJ*, 17/8, 1977; YOON SOON-YOUNG, 'Magic, Science and Religion on Cheju Island,' *KJ*, 16/3, 1976

CHEMULP'O 濟物浦

Chemulp'o was the old fishing village which served as harbour for the *yamen* of **Inch'ŏn**. It became the most important of the three Treaty Ports which developed through the 1880s (the others being **Pusan** and Wŏnsan), and foreign writers in the 19th century often used 'Chemulp'o' for Inch'ŏn. In the 20th century 'Chemulp'o' survived as a district of the city and the name of a railway station.

CHEMULP'O TREATY   *See Imo* Incident

CHENFAN 辰番

Chinese **commandery**. *See* **Chinbŏn**

CHESS *changgi* 將棋

Chess is believed to have been invented in India or Persia, and has developed different rules in different countries. *Changgi*, 'general's chess', in Korea differs even from the chess of China.

The Korean chess-board, traditionally wider than it is deep, is marked with 10 horizontal lines and 9 vertical. The space between the 5th and 6th horizontal lines represents a river, but has no effect in play. The two sides are regarded as the armies of Liu Bang of Han (K. Han) and Xiang Yu of Chu (K. Ch'o), who fought in 207–202 BC at the founding of the **Han dynasty**. Two diagonal lines through the four squares round the generals' positions form camps for the generals and their aides.

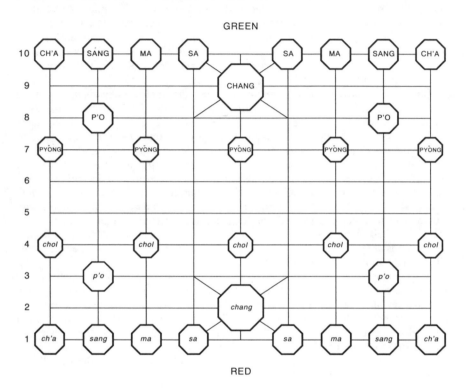

At the start of a game the pieces stand as in the diagram, on the intersections of the lines, not in the squares. The generals (*chang*) and their aides-de-camp (*sa*) stand in the two camps. On the base line behind each general stand two *ma* 'horsemen' (knights), two *sang* 'elephants' (bishops), and two *ch'a* 'chariots' (rooks). One or more of the four horsemen may change places with its neighbouring elephant, as the player wishes. Two *p'o*, 'ballistae' (catapults), are set on the 3rd horizontal. The 4th horizontal has 5 pawns (*chol* for one player and *pyŏng* for the other).

All 32 pieces are thick wooden discs or flat octagonal blocks, with the names of the pieces written as a single Chinese character on each, red for one player, blue or green for the other, one having the characters written in cursive script (*ch'osŏ*). The generals' pieces bear the characters Han and Ch'o or may both be marked *chang*. These two are larger than the others, while the pawns and aides are smaller than all the rest.

The game is won by the checkmate (*oet'ong*) principle. Pieces always move along lines, including the diagonal lines in the camp. The general and aides move one step at a time and cannot leave the camp. A chariot moves vertically or horizontally. A

44

horseman moves one step (provided there is no piece at that intersection) and then crosses a square diagonally. An elephant moves one step and then diagonally across two squares, but, like the horseman, may not vault over another piece. Pawns move one step forward or sideways, but never backwards. (Since there are no queens, pawns cannot become queens.) Any piece coming to rest on an intersection already occupied removes the previous occupant from the game. A ballista moves any distance vertically or horizontally, but only if it can vault another piece, which must not be a ballista. It has the limitations of a siege-engine, and cannot take another ballista.

The game is popular with all ages and classes of people, but is somewhat despised by the well educated.

W.H. WILKINSON, 'Korean chess', *Korean Repository* II, 1895

CHEUNG

A straw mannikin with a coin and a note of a person's name and *saju-p'alcha* stuck into the body. It was prepared on the day before *taeborŭm-nal* for anyone entering on an unlucky year (ages 11, 20, 29, 38, 47, 56 for a male; 10, 19, 28, 37, 46, 55 for a female. See *Nine Palaces*). The mannikin was either thrown down at the roadside or under a bridge, intended to carry away that person's bad luck; or it could be given to boys who went round the houses that evening asking for *cheung*. They picked out the coins and threw the mannikins away.

CHEWANG-UN'GI 帝王韻紀 'Rhymed Record of Emperors and Kings'

Compiled by Yi Sŭnghyu (1224–1300) and published c. 1287. There was a third edition in 1417. It is an annotated history: the first part about China in 7-syllable verse, the second about Korea in 7-syllable verse until the Koryŏ period, for which the style changes to 5-syllable verse. The versions given of ancient Korean history differ from those in *Samguk yusa*. They were the sources of some material in later histories, notably *Tongguk t'onggam*. *Chewang-un'gi* gives, for instance, the 'birch-tree' character, rather than *Samguk yusa*'s 'altar' character, for the first syllable of **Tan'gun**; but some of its versions of history are distorted. Yi Sŭnghyu's accounts of his own period are more valuable. He was employed in several diplomatic missions to the Yuan court, where he made an impression with his poetry. In later life he retired to be a Buddhist *kŏsa* (recluse) in north Kyŏngsang.

CHIBONG YUSŎL 芝峰類說 'Classified essays of Chibong'

An encyclopaedic collection of essays in 25 books by Yi Sugwang (1563–1628), whose brush name was Chibong, 'Immortality-mushroom Peak'. He spent his life in government service, making journeys to China, where he collected much of his material both before and after the 1592 Japanese invasions (*see* **Imjin Wars**). He drew on early collections by such men as **Yi Chehyŏn** and **Sŏ Kŏjŏng**, but *Chibong yusŏl* is divided into topical sections. The principal subject is the art of government. Other sections deal with **astronomy**, the calendar, disasters, geography (especially of the Pacific Rim), art, clothing, **food**, flora and fauna, including notes on etymology and on the Mongol language. There is also information about Catholicism and Western science that he obtained in Beijing.

CHIGE

Literally 'back-carrier'. The common wooden carrying frame of Korea, typical of town and country, called 'jiggy' by the British and 'A-frame' by Americans. It is a simple structure held by two ropes or straps round the shoulders and armpits, designed to hang the weight of a load on the shoulders while the centre of gravity is lower on the back – the optimum disposition for walking and balancing, even on steep gradients. It is not used by **women**, because *nambu-yŏdae* 'men bear loads on the back, women on the head'. The earliest evidence of its use comes from early Silla **ceramic** figures.

CHIGONG 指空 (d. 1363)

A high-caste monk from northern India, named Dhyanabhadra, who went to China at the age of nineteen. In 1328 he visited Korea at the invitation of King Ch'ungsuk, who had met him in Beijing. He stayed awhile in the **Diamond Mountains** before going to Hoeam-sa at Yangju. After he returned to China, he was visited there by the Korean monks Hyegun and **Muhak**, on whom he had great influence. The development of *Sŏn* Buddhism in Korea was largely due to his teaching.

CHILDREN'S DAY *ŏrini-nal*

Pang Chŏnghwan (1899–1931, brush-name Sop'a, 'little wave') was a pioneer in children's literature who campaigned for children to be addressed with polite speech forms. Born in Seoul and well educated, in his teens he worked for the colonial government's Land Survey Office. During the 1919 demonstrations, he was arrested for mimeographing an independence newspaper at home, but soon freed and allowed to go and study English literature in Tokyo. While there in 1922, he proposed the observance of Children's Day on 1 May (changed in 1927 to the first Sunday of May). The idea was popular enough in Korea for the Japanese to suppress it firmly. Pang devoted himself to publishing children's books and magazines until he died from overwork and chronic nephritis in Seoul University Hospital. Children's Day on 5 May was officially adopted in South Korea in 1946.

CHILLYŎNG-GUN 眞靈君 'Prince of the True Spirit'

A *mudang* named Yi, who claimed she was possessed by the spirit of **Guan Yu** (*see Romance of the Three Kingdoms*). During the early 1890s she was favoured by **Queen Min**, whom she had persuaded to build the Kwanwang-myo shrine in Sungin-dong. She was believed to wield much power. In 1893 An Hyoje (1850–1912) memorialised the throne proposing she be executed. (For this he was exiled to the Ch'uja islands near **Cheju**, but later recalled, and eventually tortured by Japanese police at Ch'angnyŏng near **Taegu** for his resistance to the **annexation** of Korea.) Chillyŏng-gun lost her influence after the Queen's assassination in 1895, and attended Yŏnmot-gol Presbyterian church in the 1900s.

CHIN 辰

Ancient state south of the **Han** river which evolved between the second century BC and the first century AD, and out of which the Three Han states (**Samhan**) later developed. It was faced to the north by the state of **Old Chosŏn**, whose ruler Chun fled to Chin when his place was usurped by Wiman (*see* **Wiman Chosŏn**). Its material culture probably benefited from trading contacts with China, but is characterised by distinctive stone **dolmen** burial sites.

See also **iron**

CHINA, RELATIONS WITH

Archaeological remains demonstrate the spread of material culture into the Korean peninsula from **Siberia**, **Manchuria** and China in the **neolithic** era and **Bronze Age**.

The south-eastward movement of tribes from Manchuria helped in the formation of the earliest Korean states (*see* **Old Chosŏn**; **Puyŏ**; **Yemaek**), and in the course of China's Warring States period (c. 481–221 BC) the population of the **Liaodong** region became embroiled in mainland political rivalries (*see* **Wiman Chosŏn**). During the **Han dynasty** Chinese **commanderies** were established on the peninsula and the appreciation of Chinese literary and artistic culture grew (*see* **Lelang**). This developed strongly through the Unified Silla period, encouraging China's proprietorial attitude towards Korea and claim to suzerainty over successive Korean kingdoms until the 20th century, assuming a right to influence their political affairs as part of its tributary system. Conceding the principle of *sadae*, Korean rulers did indeed cooperate in this form of relationship more diligently than those of any other of China's neighbours. Relations between the two countries were often close and friendly, with the frequent exchange of official missions, scholars, monks, **craftsmen**, and **merchants**. Korea benefited greatly from these contacts. Yet the Koreans never resigned their self-perceived independence of China. Though they did sometimes call on Chinese aid when threatened by attack, as for example in the 1590s when the Ming court responded generously to appeals for help against Hideyoshi (*see* **Imjin Wars**), they also showed themselves capable of pursuing policies in their own interests and contrary to those of the Middle Kingdom, and on occasions Chinese armies endeavoured unsuccessfully to enforce their vassals' submission (*see* **Unified Silla dynasty**). In the 18th century the Korean literati, despite a long tradition of imitating Chinese culture, played a significant part in the development of native cultural excellence through the *sirhak* movement. By the second half of the 19th century, however, the country was not strong enough to resist the competing predatory designs of Japan as well as China. China's nomination of **Yuan Shikai** as Resident General, the first time since the 7th century that it had dared to take such a step, was countered by Japan's recommendation of supposedly independent advisers to the Korean government who would in fact advance Japan's interests. Still worse, in 1894–5 Korea found itself the battleground for the two rivals (*see* **Sino-Japanese War**). Chinese claims on Korean allegiance seemed to have gone for good through the Japanese colonial period, but in 1950 the **Korean War** again revived the spectre of Chinese armies fighting to establish mainland dominion over the peninsula. Chinese ideological influence extended over north Korea from 1945 onwards (*see* **Democratic People's Republic of Korea**), and through the 1990s the restoration of diplomatic and commercial relations between China and South Korea once again created conditions in which an independent Korean government heeded Chinese interests as well as its own.

JOHN K. FAIRBANK, ed., *The Chinese World Order*, Cambridge, Mass.: Harvard University Press, 1968; LEE CHAE-JIN, *China and Korea: Dynamic Relations*, Stanford: Hoover Institution Press, 1996; KEITH PRATT, 'Politics and Culture within the Sinic Zone: Chinese Influences on Medieval Korea,' *KJ*, 20/6, 1980; WILLIAM ROCKHILL, *China's Intercourse with Korea from the XVth Century to 1895*, London, 1905, repr. New York: Paragon Book Reprint Co., 1970; MORRIS ROSSABI, *China Among Equals: The Middle Kingdom and its Neighbors, 10th–14th Centuries*, Berkeley: University of California Press, 1984; HUGH D. WALKER, 'Traditional Sino-Korean Diplomatic Relations: A Realistic Historical Appraisal,' *MS*, 24, 1955

See also **Beijing, embassies to**; **Chinbŏn**; **commerce**; **Tang dynasty**; **Ming dynasty**; **Qing dynasty**; **People's Republic of China**; **Sui dynasty**; **Wei, histories of**

CHINA-NORTH KOREA AGREEMENT ON ECONOMIC AND CULTURAL COOPERATION (1953)

Signed on 23 November 1953 in the wake of the **Armistice Agreement** after the **Korean War**. China wrote off the cost of its aid given to North Korea during the war, and promised over 325 million dollars' worth of economic assistance.

CHINBŎN 眞番

Statelet which had developed between the Chabi Pass and the Han River (mainly in the region of modern Hwanghae province) by the 4th century BC. It was subjugated by **Wiman Chosŏn**, which in turn fell to the armies of **Han** China in 108 BC. Chinbŏn was then reconstituted as the Chinese **commandery** of Chenfan. In 82 BC this was absorbed into **Lelang** commandery. It reappeared as a separate commandery established by the rulers of **Liaodong** in the confusion at the end of the Later Han dynasty (early 3rd century AD) when it was known as Taebang (C. Daifang), and was finally conquered by **Paekche** in 314.

H. IKEUCHI, 'A Study of Lo-lang and Tai-fang, Ancient Chinese Prefectures in Korean Peninsula,' *MRDTB*, 5, 1930

CHINDAN HAKHOE 震檀學會 'Eastern land study society'

Chindan was a sobriquet for Korea (*see* **Korea, names for**). The society was founded in 1934 by Yi Pyŏngdo and 23 others, to study the history, language and literature of Korea and publish in the Korean language. Their journal *Chindan hakpo* appeared in November and was published sporadically until closed down by the colonial government in 1940. It was revived after World War II and again after the **Korean War** of 1950. The members became the most distinguished Korean scholars of the 20th century. A 7-volume general history, *Han'guk-sa*, was published 1959–1966.

CHINDO 珍島

A large island off the south-west coast of Korea famous for its its strong attachment to **shamanism** and for its eponymous **dog**, a protected breed. It was briefly held by the **Sambyŏlch'o** loyalists in 1270–1.

CHUN KYUNG-SOO, *Reciprocity and Korean Society: an Ethnography of Hasami*, Seoul National University Press, 1984

CHINDŎK, QUEEN 眞德女王 (r. 647–54) *See* **Silla, Queens of**

CHINESE PEOPLE'S VOLUNTEERS

Name given to units of the Chinese People's Liberation Army involved in the **Korean War**. It was derived from Mao Zedong's order on 8 October, the day after American troops advanced north across the **Thirty-Eighth Parallel**, that the name of the North-East Frontier Force should be changed to 'Chinese People's Volunteers', and should prepare with the XIII Army Group under the command of Marshal Peng Dehuai 'to resist the attacks of U.S. imperialism and its running dogs'. The reason for their intervention in the War is usually explained as fear of an American threat to Chinese territory, but Bruce Cumings (1997) sees it partly as recompense for the aid given to the Chinese communists by 60–90,000 Koreans from Manchuria and North Korea in the anti-Japanese and Chinese civil wars.

The initial force of 200–250,000 men crossed the **Yalu River** into North Korea between 13 and 25 October 1950, mostly on the night of Sunday 19 October, unnoticed by United Nations intelligence. The Soviet Union provided aircraft and trained Chinese pilots to afford air cover. Only when the first Chinese prisoners were taken on 30 October did United States HQ admit that Chinese soldiers were in Korea. It is estimated that 2·3 million Chinese soldiers took part in the war. They achieved notoriety among the allied opposition for their 'human wave' tactics, committing thousands of men to overrun their enemies regardless of losses. Estimates of their casualties vary greatly: figures of almost one million are exaggerated, and a more realistic guess is 360,000 killed and injured and 20,000 taken prisoner.

S.GONCHAROV, J.L.LEWIS, L.XUE, *Uncertain Partners: Stalin, Mao, and the Korean War*, Stanford University Press, 1993; EDWIN HOYT, *The Day the Chinese Attacked: Korea 1950: The Story of the Failure of America's China Policy*, New York: McGraw-Hill, 1990; ALAN WHITING, *China Crosses the Yalu: The Decision to Enter the Korean War*, Stanford University Press, 1960

CHINHAN 辰韓

One of the three tribal federations (**Samhan**) of southern Korea contemporaneous with the northern **commandery** of **Lelang**. Its territory lay to the east of the Naktong river valley. Its strongest clan was that of Saro, with its walled town capital of the same name in the vicinity of modern **Kyŏngju**, and as political consolidation between the clans occurred it developed into the state of **Silla**. Its council of ruling tribal chieftains was the *hwabaek*.

See also **Choyangdong; Mahan; Proto-Three Kingdoms; P'yŏnhan**

CHINJU 晉州

City in South Kyŏngsang province, formerly known as Kangju. It was capital of one of the nine provinces under Unified Silla; the site of peasant risings against Koryŏ local government in 1200; the location for two battles against the Japanese in 1592, after one of which the *kisaeng* Non'gae is said to have lured a Japanese officer to his death; and the centre of the **Chinju Rising** of 1862.

CHINJU RISING (1862)

Peasant rebellion led by Yu Kyech'un against corrupt *yangban* officials and the oppressive local military commander Paek Naksin. It achieved no more than widespread physical damage, but sparked copycat uprisings across southern Korea.

CHINSŎNG, QUEEN 眞聖女王 (r. 887–97) *See* **Silla, Queens of**

CHINUL 知訥 (1158–1210)

'Wise stammerer', also known as Pojo 'universal light' and Mogu-ja 'ox-tender' (after the **ten ox pictures**). He entered a monastery at the age of eight. In his twenties he was enlightened by reading the 'Platform **Sutra**' of Huineng (638–713), the Sixth Patriarch and real founder of *Sŏn* Buddhism. Chinul used the Platform Sutra, the Diamond Sutra and the Flower Garland Sutra in his efforts to unite the two Korean Buddhist schools of *Sŏn* 'meditation' and *Kyo* 'doctrine'. His principle of 'enlightenment followed by self-cultivation' gave primacy to *sŏn*, but admitted *kyo* as a way of life, and accepted also the **mantra** recitation called *yŏmbul* (invoking **Amida** Buddha). This encouraged the mountain monasteries during the **Ch'oe dictatorship**, after a period when court patronage had fostered a less detached Buddhist way of life. Chinul's umbrella for all Korean Buddhists was called **Chogye** Buddhism. He died on the podium, while lecturing.

ROBERT EVANS BUSWELL, *The Korean Approach to Zen: the Collected Works of Chinul*, Honolulu: University of Hawaii Press, 1983

CHIP 集 'personal collections'

When a distinguished man died, or even during his extreme old age, his family would have his surviving manuscripts collected, edited and printed in anything from two to several hundred volumes. Such publications were entitled *chip* 'collection', *yugo* 'remaining manuscripts' or something similar such as *chŏnsŏ* 'complete writings', prefixed by the author's brush-name (*ho*), as in *Wŏlsa-jip*, the works of Wŏlsa (Yi Chŏnggwi 1564–1635), *Tonggo-yugo* (Yi Chun'gyŏng 1499–1572), and *Yulgok-chŏnsŏ* (**Yi I**).

The contents of *chip* are arranged in various ways, but the usual order is:

1) tabular matter, chronologies and lists of contents;
2) poetry, the longer forms (*pu* and *sa*) before the shorter (*si*);
3) prose, (a) records of places and events, (b) literary criticism of the author's own and others' work, (c) treatises, dissertations, essays and notes, (d) memorials to superiors, (e) letters to equals, (f) instructions to inferiors – often drafted for the king, (g) biographies and memoirs, (h) miscellanea – epigrams, admonitions, encomia, eulogies (all on people, animals and objects);
4) ritual compositions – funerary inscriptions, laments, sacrificial prayers, Buddhist and Daoist pieces.

At least 1,500 *chip* are known. The following 45 examples include some of the most famous:

Chibong-jip	'divine fungus peak'	**Yi Sugwang**	1563–1628
Ch'ŏnggang-jip	'clear river'	Yi Chesin	1536–1584
Ch'ŏngŭm-jip	'clear shade'	Kim Sanghŏn	1570–1652
Ch'unjŏng-jip	'springtime pavilion'	Pyŏn Kyeryang	1369–1430
Haeŭn-jip	'sea recluse'	**Kang P'irhyo**	1764–1846
Hanhwŏn-dang-jip	'cold heat'	**Kim Koengp'il**	1454–1504
Hwanjae-jip	'jade baton studio'	Pak Kyusu	1807–1876
Igye-jip	'ear valley'	**Hong Yangho**	1724–1802
Ikchae-jip	'profit studio'	**Yi Chehyŏn**	1287–1367
Kani-jip	'simplicity'	Ch'oe Ip	1539–1612
Kwibong-jip	'tortoise peak'	**Song Ikp'il**	1534–1599
Kyegok-chip	'brook vale'	Chang Yu	1587–1638
Miam-jip	'eyebrow rock'	Yu Hŭich'un	1513–1577
Mogŭn-jip	'pastor recluse'	**Yi Saek**	1328–1396
Mohadang-jip	'longing for Shang'	Kim Ch'ungsŏn	1571–1642
Mongwa-jip	'dream hut'	Kim Ch'angjip	1648–1721
Mun'gok-chip	'literary vale'	**Kim Suhang**	1629–1689
Nammyŏng-jip	'south darkness'	**Cho Sik**	1501–1572
Nogye-jip	'reed valley'	**Pak Illo**	1561–1642
Nosa-jip	'reed sands'	Ki Chŏngjin	1793–1876
Osan-jip	'five mountains'	**Ch'a Ch'ŏllo**	1563–1633
Paekchu-jip	'white islet'	Yi Myŏnghan	1595–1645
Pukhŏn-jip	'north kiosk'	Kim Ch'unt'aek	1670–1717
P'oŭn-jip	'vegetable plot recluse'	**Chŏng Mongju**	1337–1392
P'ungsŏk-chip	'maple stone'	Sŏ Yugu	1764–1845

Sagajŏng-jip	'four excellencies'	Sŏ Kŏjŏng	1489–1546
Sambong-jip	'three peaks'	Chŏng Tojŏn	1345–1392
Samyŏn-jip	'three pools'	Kim Ch'anghŭp	1653–1689
Sinam-jip	'south of market'	Yu Kye	1607–1656
Sindok-chae-jip	'cautious solitude'	Kim Chip	1574–1656
Sŏae-jip	'west cliff'	Yu Sŏngnyong	1542–1607
Sŏgye-jip	'west valley'	Pak Sedang	1629–1703
Sŏkchu-jip	'stone islet'	Kwŏn P'il	1572–1612
Songgang-jip	'pinetree river'	Chŏng Ch'ŏl	1536–1593
Tongch'un-jip	'with springtime'	Song Chun'gil	1606–1673
Tonggang-jip	'east river'	Kim Uong	1540–1603
Tonggye-jip	'east valley'	Pak T'aesun	1653–1704
Tongguk Yi-Sangguk-chip	'Prime Minister Yi'	Yi Kyubo	1168–1241
Toŭn-jip	'pottery recluse'	Yi Sungin	1349–1392
Ubok-chip	'silly prostrate'	Chŏng Kyŏngse	1563–1633
Ugye-jip	'ox valley'	Sŏng Hon	1535–1598
Unyang-jip	'cloud nourish'	Kim Yunsik	1835–1922
Wŏlsa-jip	'moonlight sands'	Yi Chŏnggwi	1564–1635
Yangch'ŏn-jip	'sunlight village'	Kwŏn Kŭn	1352–1409
Yŏnam-jip	'swallow rock'	Pak Chiwŏn	1737–1805

CHIPHYŎN-JŎN 集賢殿 'Hall of Assembled Worthies'
Academy of Confucian scholars first established in the Koryŏ period in imitation of the **Tang dynasty** Chinese Imperial Academy (*Guozi jian*), re-established by King **Sejong** in 1420 to study the intellectual and institutional example of China as a model for the new Chosŏn dynasty. Membership was initially limited to ten leading scholar-officials and later expanded to twenty. They advised the king on the principles and conduct of policy, and pursued literary, historical, cultural and legal research. Their greatest achievement was the invention of the *han'gŭl* alphabet. The nadir of the Hall's fortunes came when some of its members were put to death in 1456 for opposing the accession to the throne of King **Sejo**, who closed it down. It was succeeded by the *Hongmun-gwan*.
See also **Government, central; law**

CHIPSABU 執事部
Silla Chancellery which succeeded the *Hwabaek* as the chief political decision-making body of the state in AD 651. The post of *sangdaedŭng* was perpetuated but was now outranked by the chief minister, *chungsi*.
See also **Government, central**

CHO HŎN 趙憲 (Chungbong, 1544–92)
Sympathetic to the ideas of **Yi I** (whose thought he helped to promulgate) and **Sŏng Hon**, he qualified at 23 and took the brush name 'Double peak'. His long career in government was punctuated with trouble. He irritated the king with contentious memorials and was exiled for a while to Pup'yŏng. He was banished again in 1589 to Kilchu, but during the Japanese invasion of 1592 he raised a guerilla force of volunteers that drove the enemy from Ch'ŏngju and followed them to Okch'ŏn.

Shortly afterwards the Japanese destroyed the whole Korean force at Kŭmsan, where Cho died in the battle. He was canonised in 1665.

CHO KWANGJO 趙光祖 (Chŏngam, 1482–1519)

While he was a boy and his father was serving at Hŭich'on in North P'yŏngan province, he studied under **Kim Koengp'il**, who made him devoted to neo-Confucian philosophy in the tradition of **Kim Chongjik**. He entered government service at 33 as one of the young *sarim* in the **censorate**. He stood for the strictest neo-Confucian probity in government and proposed far-reaching reforms. In the events of 1519 (the *Kimyo sahwa*) it was said that leaves were found in the palace grounds on which the words *chu ch'o wi wang*, 'Cho will be king' were written. They had been written in honey, which insects had eaten away. He was executed by suicide (**poison**) at the age of 37.

The reforms he had advocated, most of which were put in hand, did not last. They included simplifying the **examination** system, abolishing a royal sacrifice he criticised as 'daoist', publishing Korean translations of the **Confucian Classics**, and setting up *hyangyak* (village assemblies with a 'village charter'). He gave himself trouble by interfering in plans for dealing with the **Jurchen** invasion of north Hamgyŏng, and was finally brought down by his attempts to curb the privileges of the *hun'gu* **Meritorious Subjects**. He was canonised in the national shrine in 1610, by which time his orthodoxy was politically correct. His brush name means 'Quiet hermitage'.

CHO MANSIK 曹晚植 (1882–1950)

Christian nationalist who played a prominent part in the **self-strengthening movement** and anti-Japanese movement. He took part in the proclamation of the **Declaration of Independence** by the **Korean Youth Independence Corps** in Tokyo in 1919. He was a moderate member of the **New Shoot Society** (*Sin'ganhoe*), who attempted in vain to protect it from the radicalism which led to its abolition in 1931. In the early 1920s his Korean Products Promotion Society (*Chosŏn Mulsan Ch'angnyŏ-hoe*) led the movement for economic nationalism urging people to buy Korean rather than imported goods. In 1945 he was nominated to a cabinet post in the **Korean People's Republic**, after which he became head of its regional government in P'yŏngyang, the People's Committee for North Korea. There he formed the nationalist Korean (Chosŏn) Democratic Party. He was anti-Soviet, and as a native of P'yŏngyang he enjoyed local popularity. This, together with his moderate views and nationalistic opposition to **trusteeship**, then supported by the Soviet authorities, incurred the enmity of **Kim Ilsŏng**, who purged him with Stalin's approval soon after the beginning of the **Korean War**.

KENNETH WELLS, 'The Rationale of Korean Economic Nationalism under Japanese Colonial Rule, 1922–1932: The Case of Cho Man-sik's Products Promotion Society,' *MAS*, 19:4, 1985

CHO SIK 曹植 (Nammyŏng, 1501–72)

Cho Sik and **Yi Hwang** were contemporaries, the two most influential teachers of the Kyŏngsang *sarim*, each with his own interpretation of neo-Confucian *sŏngni-hak*. The division of the Eastern **faction** into Northerners and Southerners in 1589 was largely based on the loyalty of Northerners to Cho Sik's teaching and of Southerners to Yi Hwang. Inevitably Cho Sik was later criticised by some Southerners, but in his lifetime he was acknowledged as one of the country's most learned men. Repeatedly declining appointments to government office, he spent his time in rural seclusion, studying and teaching disciples to the end of his days. His thought was epitomised as *pan'gung-chehŏm chigyŏng-sirhaeng*: polishing the mind and examining the heart before carefully deciding on action. He was given posthumous honours during the later years of King Sŏnjo and the reign of **Prince Kwanghae**, at times when Northerners were in power.

CHO SOK 趙涑 (Hŭion, 1595–1668)

Artist best known for his **flower and bird** painting, of which – together with **Yi Am** and Kim Sik (1579–1662) – he was regarded as one of the most successful exponents in the mid-Chosŏn period. He particularly excelled at plum and bamboo subjects, and at pictures of birds and branches. His best surviving picture of this kind is thought to be *Magpies in the morning* (Seoul National Museum).[1] He also painted **landscapes** and was a calligrapher. His landscapes show his love of the **Diamond Mountains**, but include a unique Tang-style blue-and-green picture illustrating the **foundation myth** of the Silla kingdom, entitled *Golden box*.[2]

(1)(2) CHOI SUNU, *5000 Years of Korean Art*, Seoul: Hyonam Publishing Co., 1979
See also **calligraphy**; **plum blossom**

CHO YŎNGSŎK 趙榮祏 (Kwanajae, 1686–1761)

A literatus artist whose work included **landscapes** and **flower and bird** subjects. It was for his figure paintings, which are in the style of *genre* paintings soon to be favoured by **Kim Hongdo**, that he attained his reputation in the Chosŏn period.

CHOGYE-JONG 曹溪宗 'Chogye sect'

Chogye was the title adopted by **Chinul** when he unified Korean Buddhists in mid-Koryŏ, taking the name of the monastery of the great *Chan* patriarch Huineng (638–713) at Caoqi (K. Chogye), 'valley of the Cao family', in Guangdong province. The sect combined an emphasis on sudden enlightenment with recognition of the need for intellectual training, but in contrast to the *Ch'ŏnt'ae-jong* of **Ŭich'ŏn** it gave priority to contemplative techniques over those of academic study.

The name was used again to cover all Korean Buddhists under Japanese direction in 1941. When the celibate and married monks formally divided in 1962, the celibate monasteries formed themselves into *Taehan Pulgyo Chogye-jong*, thus claiming themselves as the legitimate heirs of the great Korean Buddhist tradition. The colonial government had encouraged monks to marry – a Japanese practice that had begun surreptitiously in Korea at the end of the 19th century and been asked for by reformers like **Han Yongun**. In 1926 the abbots had formally recognised marriage for monks and it became widespread by 1940. After the Liberation it was seen as japanisation as well as dereliction of the dharma.

In 1955 President Syngman Rhee (**Yi Sŭngman**) demanded the resignation of japanised monks. Public opinion was with him, but struggles for temple property continued until 1962, after which the celibate majority were called *Chogye-jong*, and the diminishing married monks *T'aego-jong* (*see* **T'aego**). In 1986 *Chogye-jong* claimed 1,628 monasteries, many schools and the big Tongguk University in Seoul. It retained the Japanese system of 'main monasteries' called *ponsan*. Its headquarters is at Chogye-sa in Seoul.

CHOKKI

A male garment recently imported, perhaps in the 1890s. It is a loose, straight-cut waistcoat with buttons down the front, worn over the Korean jacket and normally made of the richest fabric in the suit. Modelled on the western vest or waistcoat (the word *chokki* may be derived from *jacket*), it gained ground partly because it has two to four

pockets. Small articles could otherwise be carried only if suspended on cords from the belt.
See also **dress**

CHŎKPYŎK-KA 赤壁歌 'red cliff song'
The Red Cliffs on the Yangzi near Huangzhou were the scene of a great battle between Cao Cao and **Zhuge Liang** in AD 208, as described in *The Romance of the Three Kingdoms*. Cao Cao was defeated. The battle was a popular subject with tellers of *kodae sosŏl* and passed into *p'ansori*. There is also a *chapka* about it.

Two prose-poems (*fu*) called *Chibi fu* (K. *Chŏkpyŏk-pu*), by the great Song poet Su Dongpo, tell of boating picnics at the Red Cliffs in late summer and late autumn 1082. The poet thought he was at the battle site, but in fact he was at different Red Cliffs, further downstream in Huanggang county.

CHŎN HYŎNGP'IL 全鎣弼 (Kansong, 1906–62)
Scion of a landowning family from Chŏngsŏn, Kangwŏn province, who invested his inherited wealth in education and Korean art treasures. Educated in Korea and Japan, he laid the foundations of his great collection of texts, paintings and porcelain during the colonial period. Much of it survived the **Korean War**, and is now preserved in the art museum in Seoul (founded by him in 1938) that bears his brush-name, Kansong. One of the richest collections in Korea, it contains eleven National Treasures.

CHŎN PONGJUN 全琫準 (1854–94) *See* **Tonghak Rebellion**

CHŎN TUHWAN (Chun Doo Hwan) 全斗煥 (b.1932)
President of South Korea from 1980 to 1987. He was born in North Kyŏngsang province in 1932. In 1950, he enrolled in Taegu Technical Middle School, but in 1951 transferred to the (South) Korean Military Academy (KMA). He graduated in 1955 and held various army appointments before becoming a member of Park Chung Hee (**Pak Chŏnghŭi**)'s Supreme Council of National Reconstruction, set up after the 1961 military coup. This was followed by a spell in the Personnel Section of the **Korean Central Intelligence Agency** (KCIA) before he became a battalion commander of the Capital Garrison Command in 1967. Subsequent posts included commander of the 29th Regiment in South Vietnam, and commander of the First Paratrooper Special Force in the early 1970s.

By 1979, Chŏn was commander of the Defence Security Command, a special and somewhat secretive unit in charge of army intelligence. In this rôle, he was charged with investigating the assassination of President Park in October 1979. On 12 December 1979, Chŏn, with the assistance of Roh Tae Woo (**No Taeu**), a fellow member of the KMA class of 1955, staged a coup d'état, arresting the Martial Law administrator, General Chŏng Sŏnghwa, and seizing control of the armed forces. The following year, he made himself acting director of the KCIA and chairman of the Standing Committee for National Security Measures. In this dual rôle, he was responsible for the decision to send special forces to suppress the rebellion known as the 1980 Kwangju Rebellion (*see* **Kwangju Massacre**). Following the resignation of President Ch'oe Kyuha, who had succeeded President Park, Chŏn became acting president in August 1980, and was duly elected president in February 1981 under a modified version of Park's *Yusin constitution*. This limited the presidential term to seven years, and Chŏn made great play of his intention to stand down after his single term. In office, Chŏn was not a popular figure and had few achievements to his credit. He was blamed for events in

Kwangju, for his harsh suppression of former politicians, and his hostility to the media, shown by drastic curbs on journalists and the suppression or forced amalgamation of newspapers and radio and television companies. He also pursued a vendetta against the veteran opposition leaders **Kim Taejung** and **Kim Yŏngsam**. In addition, while Chŏn was himself seen as personally honest, members of his family, including his wife and younger brother, were widely regarded as corrupt.

During his presidency, he devoted much effort to foreign travel and 'summit meetings'. In 1983, he succeeded in negotiating a major aid and loan agreement with Japan, arguing that Japan benefited in security terms from South Korea's rôle as the front line against communism. He made a number of attempts to negotiate with North Korea, but with little success. He was the presumed target of the 1983 Rangoon bomb attack, which was seen as the work of North Korean agents, and which killed several of his closest advisers. Despite this, he accepted the North Korean offer of flood aid in 1984, though it was an initiative which in the end led nowhere. In domestic terms, his period in office was marked by some relaxation of the tight restrictions which had prevailed under the *Yusin* Constitution, but he insisted that the most important development was his pledge to hand over power to his successor in 1987.

Under growing opposition pressure, he agreed in April 1986 that there could be a debate on constitutional revision. When this failed to produce results by April 1987, Chŏn announced that further debate was suspended and that the next presidential election, due at the end of the year, would be based on the electoral college arrangements laid down in the existing **constitution**. There followed much political unrest, including, eventually, middle class demonstrations which attracted world-wide attention. Faced with such bad publicity in the lead-up to the 1988 Seoul **Olympic Games**, Chŏn's preferred successor, Roh Tae Woo, intervened in June 1987. He proposed a package of political reforms, including the direct election of the president, and said that he would not stand for president if Chŏn did not accept them. Chŏn did and the crisis was defused. When he duly stepped down, to be succeeded by Roh in February 1988, he earned little credit for this 'first peaceful transfer of power'. Indeed, so strong was the criticism of the corruption which had surrounded his presidency that he felt compelled to make a public apology, after which he and his wife retired to self-imposed exile in a remote Buddhist monastery.

Following the election of the former dissident Kim Yŏngsam as president in 1992, there were renewed calls for an investigation of Chŏn's presidency and in particular his part in the Kwangju Rebellion. In 1993, former General Chŏng Sŏnghwa brought a case of mutiny to the courts against both Chŏn and Roh for arresting him in 1979. The prosecution agreed that the incident was mutiny, but declined to take action. Popular protest continued, and in December 1995 both Chŏn and Roh were arrested. Treason and mutiny were added to the initial charges of bribery and corruption. Both men were convicted in 1996. Chŏn was sentenced to death and Roh to 22 years and six months' imprisonment, together with heavy fines. Their sentences were reduced on appeal (Chŏn's to life and Roh's to 17 years), and following the 1997 presidential election President Kim Yŏngsam, with the approval of the incoming president, Kim Taejung, released them both from prison, though the heavy fines still stood.

DONALD N. CLARK, ed., *The Kwangju Uprising: Shadows over the Regime in South Korea*, Boulder, Colorado: Westview Press, 1988; ILPYONG KIM, KIHL YOUNG WHAN, eds., *Political Change in South Korea*, New York: The Korean PWPA Inc., 1988.

See also **South Korea: constitutional changes**

CHŎNG CHEDU 鄭齊斗 (Hagok, 1649–1736)

Chŏng was born in Seoul and taught by Yun Chung in the Soron, the less conservative **faction**. A brilliant student, he qualified for an official post at the age of 19 and was many times nominated, but always either declined appointment or withdrew after a very brief spell in office. At the age of 40 he moved to Ansan where he devoted twenty years to studying the thought of the Ming Confucianist, Wang Yangming (1472–1529). For his last twenty-seven years he lived as a recluse on the island of **Kanghwa**, refusing to receive guests. He was both an outstanding scholar-recluse and the leading Korean disciple of Wang Yangming. Like Wang he was depressed by the sterility of the orthodox neo-Confucian intellectuality of his times. He was moved by Wang's preference for intuition, rather than **Zhu Xi**'s rational investigation of things, as the true path to sagehood; by Wang's theory of the inseparability of thought and action; and by Wang's insistence that knowledge and goodness were inherent in all men. Chŏng also discerned that at the deepest level Zhu and Wang were not totally different. In the faction-ridden atmosphere of his days, he managed to avoid condemnation for unorthodoxy by staying out of power. After his death his descendants treated his memory with tact: his collected works were not printed until 1972. His brush name means 'Vale of Haze'.

CHUNG IN-CHAI, 'Chong Chedu', in HAECHANG CHOUNG & HAN HYONG-JO, eds., *Confucian Philosophy in Korea*, Seoul: Academy of Korean Studies, 1996

CHŎNG CHIYONG 奠芝溶 (1903–?1950)

Often described as the finest modern Korean poet, who influenced many others. Son of a Chinese medicine dealer at Okch'ŏn in Ch'ungch'ŏng province, he was married at twelve, before attending Hwimun High School in Seoul. In 1923 he went to study English literature at Doshisha University in Kyoto, and wrote a thesis on William Blake. Returning to Korea, he taught at Hwimun. At about 20 years of age, he began writing poetry full of wonder, affection and nostalgia, culminating in the collection *Paengnok-tam* (White Deer Pool). In 1939–41 he edited the influential magazine *Munjang* (Literature). He was a Catholic and wrote some of the best Korean religious poetry of the 20th century. After 1945 he taught at Seoul National and **Ewha** Universities until he disappeared during the **Korean War**. Publication of his writings was not allowed in the Republic of Korea between 1950 and 1988.

DANIEL A. KISTER, 'The Mature Poetry of Chong Chi-yong' and 'Chong Chi-yong's Night and Mountain Poems', *TRASKB*, LXV, 1990
See also **Kuin-hoe**

CHŎNG CH'ŎL 鄭澈 (Songgang, 1536–94)

One of the foremost Korean-language poets; his brush-name means 'pinetree river'. A brilliant scholar whose political career reached to offices of the 1st **grade**, but included periods of self-imposed banishment and service in the provinces. He was leader of the Western **faction** and was at times exiled by the Easterners. At the time of the Japanese invasion (*see* **Imjin Wars**), he accompanied the king on his journey to the north in 1592, and soon afterwards went to Beijing as envoy to the emperor in 1593. Once again pushed out by the Easterners, he withdrew to **Kanghwa** Island, where he died. His greatest achievement lies in his *kasa* poetry, of which we have five examples, including an allegory of fidelity to the king during his periods of disfavour, expressed as songs of loyalty by a woman parted from her husband. Other themes were the virtues of life in rustic seclusion, praise of wine-drinking and the *kŏmun'go*. Similar themes occur in the large number of *sijo* composed by him.

PETER H. LEE, *Anthology of Korean Literature*, Honolulu: University of Hawaii Press, 1981

CHŎNG CHUNGBU REBELLION 鄭仲夫 (1170)

A move by the Koryŏ military to assert its power against the increasingly dissolute and effete political authority of the court. Rising taxation under King Ŭijong had led to peasant unrest, until in 1170 General Chŏng Chungbu exiled the king to Kŏje Island and the crown prince to **Chindo**, and set his younger brother on the throne as King Myŏngjong. His reign (1171–97) was characterised by violent struggle among military factions and by uprisings of **peasants** and the *ch'ŏnmin* class. Chŏng himself was killed in 1179, but serious disorder continued until the invasion of the **Mongols** in 1231.

EDWARD J. SCHULTZ, 'Military Revolt in Koryŏ: the 1170 Coup d'Etat,' *KS*, 3, 1979
See also **Ch'oe dictatorship**

CHŎNG HASANG, SAINT PAUL 丁夏祥 (1795–1839)

A nephew of **Chŏng Yagyong**. His father and elder brother were martyred for the Catholic faith in 1801. He was brought up in poverty by his mother and sisters, who were typical of the Catholic women in their devotion and courage. At 13 he went to study in Seoul, and then to Hamhŭng, with Catholics who taught him Chinese literature. In 1816, when he was 20, he got a post as servant on the annual embassy to Beijing (*see* **Beijing, embassies to**). On nine other occasions he contrived to join annual embassies, having repeated contact with missionaries in China, but, despite the effort to smuggle in Fr Shen in 1825–6, never succeeded in getting a priest into Korea. Meanwhile he was leader and virtually lay pastor among the Catholics in the country. He and some others sent a letter to the Pope that was influential in gaining the establishment of the Korean Vicariate Apostolic in 1831 and the eventual arrival of Bishop **Imbert** and his two priests in 1835–6. Paul worked with them and took part in arranging the journey of **Kim Taegŏn** to Macao. He was taking first steps toward priesthood himself when the persecution of 1839 engulfed him and the Frenchmen. He was executed, after severe tortures, on 29 December.
See also **Roman Catholic Church**

CHŎNG-GAM-NOK 鄭鑑錄 'The record of Chŏng Kam'

The earliest written evidence of a document called *Chŏng-Gam-nok* dates from 1785, but it is known that ideas from it were circulating at the time of **Chŏng Yŏrip**'s plot of 1589. Other plans from the time of **Prince Kwanghae** onwards had a similar background. Some historians believe that the predictions contained in *Chŏng-Gam-nok* were symptomatic of widespread distress at the state of the government in mid-Chosŏn. No manuscript or early printed edition has survived: only rough manuscript versions appear to have circulated before the 20th century. The core section tells of Chŏng Kam, a supposed ancestor of the Chŏng clans, talking with a supposed ancestor of the Yi in the **Diamond Mountains** and predicting that after some centuries of Yi rule in Hanyang (Seoul), the crown would pass to a Chŏng dynasty, set up on Kyeryong-san in South Ch'ungch'ŏng province. The Chŏng dynasty would be followed in due time by a Cho dynasty, then Pŏm, Wang and other dynasties, all with different capitals. In the version printed in 1923, other elements of a similar prophetic kind have been added.

CHŎNG MONGJU 鄭夢周 (P'oŭn, 1337–1392)

A learned and courageous man of the last days of Koryŏ, who became master of the Confucian college in his twenties. Confucianism was the obvious antidote to the corruption created by the Buddhist influence in Koryŏ state affairs. He set up local

Confucian **schools** and opened a relief granary. **Yi Saek** called him 'Father of Korean *Sŏngnihak*', but it is not clear how interested he was in philosophy: his main effort went into government service. He was employed on exacting diplomatic missions: in 1377 to Kyushu to establish relations with the Ashikaga Shogun, who had recently reasserted his authority in southern Japan, and to negotiate the return of Koreans taken prisoner by **pirates** from Japan; and to China in 1386 to establish relations with the newly founded **Ming dynasty** in Nanjing. He admired **Yi Sŏnggye** and was minded to support him, perhaps because they were both anti-Buddhist, but eventually declared his loyalty to the Koryŏ royal house, hence his assassination at the Sŏnjuk-kyo, 'Good Bamboo Bridge', in **Kaesŏng** by agents of Yi's son Pangwŏn (later King T'aejong) in 1392. Chosŏn was naturally reluctant to give Chŏng posthumous honours at first, but he was admitted to the national shrine early in the 16th century, and is still one of the country's greatest patterns of loyalty. The *sijo* attributed to him is probably a later translation of a poem he is said to have composed in Chinese when supping with Pangwŏn. His brush name means 'Recluse of the Vegetable Plot'.

CHŎNG SŎN 鄭敾(Kyŏmjae, 1676–1759)

Scholar-official who became the most innovative and influential landscape painter in the Chosŏn dynasty. In line with his classical training, he began by painting in the Chinese Zhe and Wu traditions and continued to do so into the 1730s, as can be seen from a *Landscape* preserved in the National Museum of Korea.[1] But by the end of the decade, under the influence of the *Sirhak* **movement**, he had eschewed the Chinese literati tradition of idealised landscapes and evolved a novel style of his own based on real Korean mountain locations and the impression they made on him. It is known as *chin'gyŏng-sansu* ('true view landscape'), and his subjects were frequently drawn from the mountains to the north of Seoul, the east coast, and especially from the **Diamond Mountains**. As a county magistrate and later minister he had frequent cause to travel, and loved the countryside and its sights. His style is characterised by strong areas of dark and light, with overlying layers of ink wash and forceful, sweeping lines. His forests have a heavy, brooding atmosphere, dramatically and mercifully lightened by patches of mist and bisected by rushing waterfalls. Bold shapes of ponderous granite outcrops are sharply interrupted by trees simply yet effectively constructed of vertical trunks and horizontal, axe-cut branch systems. Vegetation grows from dots chopped onto hillsides, a technique adapted perhaps from acquaintance with the rounder dotted style of the great Chinese painter Mi Fei (1052–1107). Mountain peaks soar heavenwards in a forest of thin needles. An excellent example is the painting of a valley in the Diamond Mountains, *Manp'ok-tong Falls* (Seoul National University Museum).[2] It was a style that would influence generations of literati and folk artists alike, and become a source of pride to Korean nationalists in future centuries.

(1) ROGER GOEPPER & RODERICK WHITFIELD, *Treasures from Korea,* London: British Museum Publications, 1984
(2) KEITH PRATT, *Korean Painting*, Hong Kong: Oxford University Press, 1995
KIM YONG-JUN, 'Chŏng Sŏn's Painting Style,' *KJ* 13/12, 1973; LENA KIM-LEE, 'Chong Son: Korean Landscape Painter,' *Apollo*, August 1968

CHŎNG TOJŎN 鄭道傳 (Sambong, d. 1398)

He was a disciple of **Yi Saek**, whose public career began in 1362. In 1375 he was exiled to Naju for two years because he opposed the policy of maintaining Koryŏ's friendship with the Mongol Yuan dynasty. In 1383 he became adviser to the military leader **Yi Sŏnggye**, future founder of the Chosŏn dynasty, and in 1384 accompanied

Chŏng Mongju on an embassy to Ming. Having become Yi's deputy commander, he went on a further embassy to China in 1390. As chief architect of the emerging dynasty's policies, he was embroiled like everyone else in the quarrels of Yi Sŏnggye's son, Pangwŏn (later T'aejong). After the murder of Chŏng Mongju in 1392 he was released from imprisonment, which he suffered because of Pangwŏn's suspicions. When Yi Sŏnggye made himself king in 1392, Chŏng supervised the transfer of the capital from Songdo (**Kaesŏng**) to Hanyang (Seoul) in 1394. He supported the King's designation of Pangwŏn's younger brother Pangsŏk as heir to the throne and in 1398 was beaten to death by Pangwŏn's agents. Chŏng was a soldier, diplomat (expert in drafting delicate documents), strongly anti-Buddhist neo-Confucian philosopher, historian and man of letters: he began the preparation of *Koryŏ-sa*. As an administrator he was keenly interested in **land reform**. His brush name was 'Triple peak', and *Sambong-jip*, his collected works, contains *Chosŏn Kyŏngguk-chŏn*, the basic text of Chosŏn dynasty **law**.
CHAI-SIK CHUNG, 'Chŏng Tojŏn· 'Architect' of Yi Dynasty Government and Ideology,' *in* THEODORE DE BARY & JAHYUN KIM KABOUSH, eds., *The Rise of Neo-Confucianism in Korea*, New York: Columbia University Press, 1985
See also **Kyŏnghok Palace**

CHŎNG YAGYONG 丁若鏞 (Tasan, Yŏyudang, 1762–1836)
His principal brush name, 'tea mountain', referred to the place where he lived in **Kangjin**. He vies with **Yi Hwang** in being called Korea's greatest thinker. He was born at **Kwangju** near Seoul, brother-in-law of **Yi Sŭnghun** the first **Roman Catholic**, and uncle of **Chŏng Hasang** the martyr. His early education was in the Kwangju group interested in western learning. An admirer of **Pak Chiwŏn**, at the age of 15 he read writings of **Yi Ik**, the early exponent of *sirhak* 'practical learning'. By the age of 23 he was probably a baptized Catholic, but he withdrew from the Church over the rites question in 1791. He entered government service and became a favourite secretary of King **Chŏngjo**. In 1794 as Secret Royal Inspector of Kyŏnggi province he submitted a report in verse on rural poverty. His reforming ideas caused him to be sent away to Koksan in Hwanghae province as local magistrate in 1796. In the Catholic persecution of 1801 he was saved by royal favour, but sent into exile for the next 18 years. After 1808 he lived near Kangjin in Chŏlla province. During that period he was astonishingly productive. His most famous works were *Kyŏngse yup'yo*, 'Design for Good Government', proposing a revised administration; *Mongmin simsŏ*, 'Handbook for Tending the People', a guide to agrarian reform and economy; and *Hŭmhŭm sinsŏ*, 'New Work on Sentencing', a treatise on sentencing to capital punishment, in which he pleaded for justice to ordinary folk. In 1818 he retired to his native Kwangju, but whether he returned to the Catholic fold is not clear. His Chinese style was simple and modern for its day. He wrote on a vast array of subjects: language, **proverbs**, **music**, mathematics, Chinese classics, smallpox and civil engineering. He was largely responsible for designing the city **walls** of **Suwŏn** and devising engines to do the work. He had thoroughly absorbed the critical principles of Qing scholarship as well as western learning.
FANG CHAO-YING, *The Asami Library*, Berkeley: University of California Press, 1969

CHŎNG YŎCH'ANG 鄭汝昌 (Iltu, 1450–1504)
Born in Hamyang, he spent three years studying neo-Confucian philosophy with **Kim Chongjik** in the Chiri-san area of South Chŏlla. His brush name means 'Bookworm'. From 1483 onwards he climbed the government ladder, but in the **literati purge** of

1498 was exiled to Chongsŏng, where he died before the purge of 1504, when his corpse was exhumed and mutilated. His widow destroyed most of his writings. He was one of the five scholars canonised in 1610.

CHŎNG YŎRIP 鄭汝立 (d.1589)

A Chŏnju man, choleric and cruel, but a friend of **Yi I** and **Sŏng Hon**. As such he was naturally of the Westerners **faction**, but in 1585 he flattered the ruling Easterners and criticised some Western faction attitudes. The king was displeased and Chŏng was forced to retire to his home area. There he gathered around himself a group dissatisfied with the *status quo*, making deliberate use of prophecies in the popular folk collection ***Chŏng-Gam-nok*** that spoke of the Yi kings being replaced by a royal house called Chŏng. With friends in Hwanghae province he began to plan an attack on the capital during winter, when the Han would be frozen over, but the plan was discovered before any action could be taken. Chŏng fled towards the island of Chukdo, but committed suicide when he was surrounded by troops on the way. The effect of the whole incident was a purge of the Easterners and the reinforcement of court distrust of people from Chŏlla, expressed by reducing appointments of Chŏlla men.

CHŎNGAK 正樂 'Correct music'

Term used to describe a class of native Korean **music** which evolved in the mid-Chosŏn period, and which lay between the most refined ritual Chinese music (*aak* and *tangak*, understood by the literati) and the popular rural tunes (*minyo*) and rhythms of farmers' music (*nongak*). It expresses the musical feelings of both *yangban* and the rising middle class (*chungin*), making use of native styles and tunes, and is particularly associated with the expression of Korean nationalist sentiment foreshadowed in the *sirhak* **movement**. It includes the instrumental suite *Yŏngsan hoesang*, and the vocal forms *kagok*, *kasa*, and *sijo*.

HAHN MAN-YOUNG, trans. Inok Paek and Keith Howard, *Kugak: Studies in Korean Traditional Music*, Seoul: Tamgu Dang, 1990

CHŎNGAN (C. Dingan) 定安

Kingdom founded along the middle reaches of the **Yalu** River by **Malgal** remnants of **Parhae** following its conquest by the **Khitan**. Its existence in the 10th century was brief, and was ended by Khitan conquest when it attempted to negotiate with **Song** China.

CHONGCH'IN-BU 宗親府 'Council of royal kindred'

Chosŏn government department, sometimes called *Chongjŏng-bu*; responsible for the care of the royal pedigree, portraits and robes. Most of the members were royal kindred with **princely titles**. They were aided by fifteen officials.

CHONGGYE-BYŎNMU 宗系辨誣 'Discerning Errors [in royal pedigree]'

Ming records at first gave the wrong name for Yi T'aejo's father (See ***Yonghi-ŏch'ŏn-ga***). For some years the emperor declined Korean requests for correction on the grounds that the 'veritable records' (*sillok*) could not be altered. When Hwang Chŏnguk (1532–1607) went as special envoy in 1584, the alteration was at last promised. The corrected records were received in Seoul in 1588 with great ceremony by **King Sŏnjo**, who greeted them at the *Mohwa-gwan* outside Seoul and immediately reported the fact to his ancestors in the **Chongmyo** shrine. **Meritorious subject** status was granted to the envoys.

CHŎNGJO, KING 正祖 (1752–1800, r. 1777–1800)
Twenty-second king of the Chosŏn dynasty. As a political leader he maintained the policy of his predecessor, his grandfather **Yŏngjo**, of balancing appointments equally among the four main **factions**, thereby achieving a measure of stability and strengthening the reputation of the throne. For the first three years of his reign he was dominated by his wife's relative **Hong Kugyŏng**, the first exponent of *sedo-jŏngch'i*. Amid the atmosphere of intellectual enquiry propagated by the *Sirhak* **movement** he established the *Kyujang-gak* royal library. Despite his dynasty's official preference for neo-Confucianism he showed his support for **Buddhism** by rebuilding and financing many temples. His attitude to Catholicism (*see Sŏhak*) was less open-minded. It was during his reign that the **Rites Controversy** came to a head. This resulted in his proscription of Catholicism in 1785, though it was not followed by widespread persecution during his lifetime. Chŏngjo took a great interest in the arts, especially writing, **painting** and **calligraphy**. His brush name was Hongjae. He paid frequent visits to the **tombs** and shrines of his ancestors, and in 1789 moved the tomb of his father, Crown Prince **Changhŏn**, to **Suwŏn**. He took his responsibilities as a Confucian ruler seriously, mixed with his subjects on the streets of Seoul to learn of their concerns, and encouraged them to submit petitions in cases of hardship. Originally canonised as Chŏngjong, he became Chŏngjo in 1899.
HONGNAM KIM, 'Tragedy and Art at the Eighteenth Century Choson Court,' *Orientations* 25/2, 1994

CHŎNGJU-HAK 程朱學
An alternative name for neo-Confucianism, taken from the names of the Cheng brothers and **Zhu Xi**, three of the **Five Sages of Song**.

CHŎNGMUN See **Banner gate**

CHONGMYO SHRINE 宗廟
The ancestral temple of the Yi clan, founders of the Chosŏn dynasty. Adjacent to the **Ch'angdŏk Palace**, it was originally built in 1395 to house the memorial tablets to the four immediate ancestors of King T'aejo. It was destroyed in the **Imjin Wars** and rebuilt in 1608. Further extensions took place in 1726, 1777 and 1870. Here, on 7 January 1895, King **Kojong** announced the consitutional reforms that followed the *Kapsin* **Coup** to his ancestors. The Shrine is the scene for the Confucian rites still performed to the royal ancestors, twenty-seven kings of the Chosŏn dynasty and their queens. These take place once a year in the *T'aesil*, the two long buildings raised on a terrace above the level of the facing courtyard, in which the tablets of recent and outstanding kings and queens are kept. The slow and stately rites are performed by their surviving descendants to the accompaniment of instrumental and sung music of ancient tradition (*see aak*).
See also **ancestral worship**

CHŎNGŬM 正音
The Korean alphabet. *See Han'gŭl*

CHŎNGYŎK 正易 'Corrected Changes'
A book by Kim Ilbu (1826–1888), a fellow disciple with **Ch'oe Cheu** of Yi Yŏndam. Yi encouraged him to study the *Book of Changes*. About 1880 he published his theory of a third and final (after Fuxi and Wen Wang) arrangement of the eight **trigrams**.

JUNG YOUNG LEE, 'The origin and significance of the Chŏngyŏk', *Journal of Chinese Philosophy* 9 (1982), 211–241

CHŎNSI-GWA 田柴科 'Field and fuel law'
Koryŏ dynasty pattern of land allocation to officials first instituted in 976 under King Kyŏngjong as reward for service to the newly unified state. According to the revised system introduced in 998 under King Mokchong, lands were granted to officials in eighteen **grades**, the income from them being independently assessed and collected, and paid to them as their salary. Lands were returned to the state on the holder's death. Under the law, **peasants** joining the army were allocated *kunin-jŏn*, 'soldiers' fields'. Aristocratic families accumulated private estates which were more profitable to them than their stipendiary lands, and the system was repealed in 1271.
See **land reform; land tenure**

CHŌSEN 朝鮮 (K. Chosŏn)
Japanese name for Korea officially adopted in 1910 as replacement for the nationalist Korean term *Taehan Cheguk* ('Empire of Great Han'), formally proclaimed in 1897 (*see Kabo* **reforms**).
See also **Colonial Period; Korea, names for**

CHŌSEN KOSHO KANKŌKAI 朝鮮古書刊行會
The 'Society for the Publication of Old Korean Books' founded by a group of Japanese bibliophiles in Seoul under the patronage of Prince **Itō Hirobumi**, Resident General in Korea 1905–1909. Other members included Asami Rintarō, **Maema Kyōsaku**, Imanishi Ryū, Ayukai Fusamosuke, **Yi Wanyong** and **Kim Yunsik**. 79 volumes appeared at approximately monthly intervals from November 1909 to June 1916. Some of the editing was careless and most of the editions have now been superseded.
A list is given in RICHARD RUTT, *James Scarth Gale*, Seoul: Royal Asiatic Society, 1972, pp. 357–9.

CHŌSEN SHIMPŌ 朝鮮新報
The first newspaper to be published in Korea. It was produced by a Japanese editor in Pusan, carrying items in both Japanese and Korean. The first issue was printed on 10 December 1881.
ALBERT ALTMAN, 'Korea's First Newspaper: the Japanese *Chōsen Shinpō*,' *JAS*, XLIII/4, 1984

CHOSŎN *See* **Korea, names for**

CHOSŎN DYNASTY 朝鮮 (1392–1910)
Dynasty of the Yi clan, which retained the throne for longer than any of its dynastic predecessors and survived major changes resulting from the Japanese invasions in the 1590s (*see* **Imjin Wars**) and **Manchu invasions** in the 1630s. By the 19th century, however, it was unable to adapt sufficiently to meet the revived challenge from Japan accompanied by that of the West, and inevitably succumbed as Korea became the setting for international great power rivalry. The late Chosŏn rulers are often condemned for their refusal to meet changing times with adequate modernisation and reform programmes, but in contrast to the familiar, self-confident sinocentric world of the 1390s in which their revered ancestors had come to power, the western-orientated world of the late 19th and early 20th centuries offered such different challenges that

they might hardly be expected to have kept pace with them and yet remain filially responsible to their clan traditions.

The rebels of Zhu Yuanzhang in China had done the founder of the dynasty, **Yi Sŏnggye** (King T'aejo), a double service in the 1360s. They had broken the power of the **Mongols** in East Asia, and set up a dynasty – the **Ming** – to which the Confucian literati of Korea could appeal for support on ideological grounds. Yi's revolt against the Koryŏ court was achieved by his own military skill but still more through the determination of a group of scholars to assert the authority of **Confucianism** over the **Buddhism** and **shamanism** which had dominated the Koryŏ court. Though his successors, Kings T'aejong and **Sejong**, were able to exert the power of the monarchy over its officials more effectively, the tone of the dynasty was already set under T'aejo. In seeking the Hongwu Emperor's recognition both for the name of his dynasty, which recalled that of the most ancient state on the peninsula (*see* **Old Chosŏn**), and his own status as king, he pledged a return to Korea's traditional vassaldom to China (*see sadae*). In embracing the values of **Zhu Xi**'s brand of neo-Confucianism as court philosophy, he not only recommended himself to the Chinese emperor but also strengthened the authority of the Korean monarchy over its ministers and of the literati class (the *yangban*) over the rest of society.

The change of dynastic orientation was symbolised by Taejo's choice of site for a new **capital** city, **Hanyang** (even though this was divined by a Buddhist monk, **Muhak**, using *p'ungsu*), and by the court's taste for the purity of white porcelain in preference to the coloured wares formerly preferred in **Kaesŏng** (*see* **ceramics**). A spirit of frugality was deliberately fostered in court **rites and ceremonies** and entertainments, while Buddhism suffered rejection and official persecution which relegated it to the status of a lower class religion. Confucian ideas on social stratification were reinforced, along with the recognition of education in the **Confucian Classics** and the need for success in the **examination system** as the chief criterion for official advancement. The reputation of King Sejong as an inspiration to scholars and innovative thought is pre-eminent in Korean history (*see* **Chiphyŏn-jŏn**), and is symbolised by the invention of the **hunmin chŏngŭm** (**han'gŭl**) alphabet in which he participated. It represented a spirit of Korean independence which was taken up by modernisers and nationalists towards the end of the dynasty, although in the 15th century the primary objective of its inventors was not to set Korea apart from China, but to make reading accessible to a wider public. Other aspects of King Sejong's brilliant reign show a similar concern for his interpretation of the Mencian concept of true kingship. Except for some localised trouble, involving the **Jurchen** led by Yi Chingok in the north-west (1453), and by Yi Siae in the north-east (1467), and recurrent pillaging by **pirates** around the coasts, much of the country enjoyed relative peace and growing prosperity for almost two centuries. Yet for all its monolithic philosophy, unanimity did not long prevail among the literati class, and from the end of the 15th century it was riven by a series of major purges (*see* **sahwa**) and split by **factionalism**.

Political division may have encouraged Toyotomi Hideyoshi to hope for easy success when he launched his attack on Korea in 1592. In using the peninsula as a bridge towards his objective of continental domination he sought to emulate Kublai Khan's imperialistic ambitions from the opposite direction, and met with equal failure. In his case, it was China's suzerain obligation to defend Korea (not to mention a certain perceived self-interest in evicting the presumptuous challenger) that served the Chosŏn court well. The physical destruction caused in the six years of military campaigning was, however, immense, and the deeper effects on politics, society and the economy long lasting. When it found itself all too soon invaded by the Manchus in 1627 and 1636, the dynasty had encountered a watershed which rendered its next three hundred years quite different in character from the first two hundred.

Social changes in the 17th century included more occupational mobility and greater opportunities for those engaged in manufacturing and **commerce**. **Slavery** declined. The superiority of the *yangban* and the power of the landlords remained unchallenged. Adherence to neo-Confucianism continued, but serious questions were asked about the value of an over-subservient attitude towards China, which was given scant credit for resisting Hideyoshi and had failed to keep out the Manchus. The court continued to send **tribute** to Beijing and resumed missions to Japan, but now inclined more towards an isolationist view of foreign policy. This appeared to be justified through the peaceful and relatively prosperous years of the 18th century, but necessitated painful adjustments in the mid-19th century. The literati, while retaining their overwhelming respect for Chinese learning and receptiveness to what it could contribute to their own country, nevertheless began to recognise the qualities inherent in their own native culture, and in the interest of national self-strengthening showed themselves open to new ideas and technologies from whatever source, including the Jesuit missionaries whom some of them encountered in China (*see Sirhak* **movement**). As in China, the 18th century saw the publication of many **books** to broaden the horizons of their readers, although the effect on some was to drive them back into the familiar safety of introspective classicism.

One of the most prominent leaders of the 19th century, the **Taewŏn'gun**, personifies the Korean dilemma which the Chosŏn dynasty was called on to solve, of change versus tradition. In inclining towards the latter he defended Korean nationalism against the assaults of the Japanese but denied his country the benefits of modernisation. Like its neighbour in China, the court in Korea was faced by economic decline which weighed most heavily on the **peasantry** oppressed by the ravages of excessive **taxation**, *corvée* obligations and landlord exploitation. This was not an unfamiliar situation, and might have been treated by familiar methods: the Taewŏn'gun, like earlier leaders in Korea history, admitted the need for **land reform**. Even the prospect of a final, and possibly fatal, **peasant rebellion** was something which could be faced up to as a familiar feature of Korean history. But the economic and psychological cost of coming to terms with foreign-led modernisation was beyond the Chosŏn leadership to manage. So was the associated and equally unprecedented struggle between foreign powers for access to and control over its nation. Relations were only grudgingly established with **America**, **Great Britain**, **France**, **Germany**, **Russia** and other European powers. As the Meiji authorities in Japan sought to extend their influence in Korea (*see* **Kanghwa, Treaty of**), so the *Sirhak* bifurcation of officialdom divided those who admired novel foreign ideas as a source of inspiration against those who looked to traditional Confucianism to defend past glories. The latter naturally looked to China for support and found a powerful ally in **Queen Min**. After the **Shufeldt Treaty** of 1882 their position seemed to have been strengthened, even though it meant the appointment of a Chinese Resident General in Seoul (**Yuan Shikai**). But the pro-Japanese progressives gained a measure of revenge with the *Kapsin* **coup** of December 1884. As the rivalry continued, it intruded into the peasants' rebellion against the government in 1894 (*see* **Tonghak Rebellion**), erupted into war on Korean soil (*see* **Sino-Japanese War**), forced King **Kojong** to initiate radical reforms (*see Kabo* **reforms**), and led to the murder of the Queen. In 1897 Kojong tried to enhance his nation's status by assuming the title of Emperor (*see* **Great Han Empire**). But it was in vain. By the turn of the century Japanese influence, though intense, was widely resented. In an effort to preserve the nation's diplomatic independence the court accepted, ironically, the need for foreign advisers (German, Japanese, Russian, American) within its walls (*see* **Dye, William**; **von Möllendorff**). They were supposedly appointed to defend Korean interests but some sought to advance those of their own embassies (*see also* **Stevens, Durham**).[1] Russia, with which because of its interests in **Manchuria** the court had developed relations as a possible counter to Japanese domination in Korea, proved unable to resist Meiji military might, and its defeat in 1905 opened the way to the Japanese **protectorate** over the Great Han empire. Amid a rising clamour from supporters of Korean independence, including some foreigners (*see* **Hulbert, Homer**), Kojong, his son **Sunjong**, and their governments became puppets of the Japanese, and the **annexation** of the country as a colony in 1910 brought the dynasty to an end in ignominy.

RULERS:

T'aejo	1392–8	Kwanghae-gun (Regent)	1608–23
Chŏngjong	1398–1400	Injo	1623–49
T'aejong	1400–18	Hyojong	1649–59
Sejong	1418–50	Hyŏnjong	1659–74
Munjong	1450–2	Sukchong	1674–1720
Tanjong	1452–5	Kyŏngjong	1720–4
Sejo	1455–68	Yŏngjo	1724–76
Yejong	1468–69	Chŏngjo	1776–1800
Sŏngjong	1469–94	Sunjo	1800–34
Yŏnsan'gun (Regent)	1494–1506	Hŏnjong	1834–49
Chungjong	1506–44	Ch'ŏlchong	1849–63
Injong	1544–5	Kojong	1864–1907
Myŏngjong	1545–67	Sunjong	1907–10
Sŏnjo	1567–1608		

(1) A contemporary account of life at the Chosŏn court by one of these, an American, is W.F.SANDS, *At the Court of Korea*, London: Century Hutchinson Ltd., 1987.
MARTINA DEUCHLER, *Confucian Gentlemen and Barbarian Envoys: the Opening of Korea 1875–1885*, Seattle: University of Washington Press, 1977; MARTINA DEUCHLER, *The Confucian Transformation of Korea: a Study of Society and Ideology*, Cambridge, Mass.: Harvard University Press, 1992; HOMER B. HULBERT, *The Passing of Korea*, New York, 1906, repr. Seoul: Yonsei University Press, 1969; JAMES PALAIS, *Politics and Policy in Traditional Korea*, Cambridge, Mass.: Harvard University Press, 1975

CHOSŎN ILBO 朝鮮日報 'Korea Daily'
Newspaper founded by Sin Sŏgu (1894–1953), first published in March 1920, which quickly changed from being a pro-Japanese organ to an outlet for Korean independence. Like the *Tonga Ilbo* it promoted the use of *han'gŭl* and supported the student anti-illiteracy campaign of the early 1930s. It encouraged the study of traditional Korean culture and sponsored exhibitions of Korean art. Along with other Korean papers it was closed down in 1940, and recommenced publication in 1945.
KIM BONG-GI, *Brief History of the Korean Press*, Seoul: Korean Information Service, 1965
See also **An Chaehong**

CHOSŎN INDEPENDENCE PARTY ARMY *See* ***Ŭibyŏng***

CHOSŎN, OLD; CHOSŎN, WIMAN *See* **Old Chosŏn**; **Wiman Chosŏn**

CHOSŎN WANGJO SILLOK 朝鮮王朝實錄 'Authentic Records of the Chosŏn Dynasty'
Korea followed Chinese precedent in establishing a procedure by which each new reign and new dynasty edited the records of the previous reign or dynasty. The first king of the Chosŏn dynasty thus arranged for editing and printing *Koryŏ-sa*, the official history of the previous dynasty; and each succeeding king appointed special secretaries to keep manuscript records of his own reign, known as *sijŏng-gi*, 'current government records' or *sach'o*, 'historical drafts'.

He also appointed a *sillok-ch'ŏng* 'authentic records office' of about 30 men to edit the manuscript records of his predecessor's reign into a document called *sillok* (or *ilgi*, 'diaries', for the disgraced rulers **Yŏnsan-gun** and **Kwanghae-gun**), of which four copies were printed. When this had been done, the manuscripts were destroyed by washing the ink off the papers. To ensure their preservation, the four printed copies were dispersed one each in the *Ch'unch'u-gwan* and three repositories (*sago*) at Chŏnju, Sŏngju (Kyŏngsang province) and Ch'ungju. Revised versions were added to the *sillok* of three reigns: Sŏnjo (1657), Hyŏnjong (1683) and Kyŏngjong (1781).

Only the set at Chŏnju escaped destruction in the Japanese invasion of 1592 (*see* **Imjin Wars**). It was eventually lodged at Chŏngjok-san on **Kanghwa** Island in 1678, and is now in Seoul National University Library. In 1606 four new copies were made from it. One was kept in the *Ch'unch'u-gwan*, but was destroyed in the rebellion of **Yi Kwal** (1624). The other three were stored in new repositories, staffed by soldiers and Buddhist monks, in remote places. One went to Odae-san, P'yŏngch'ang-gun, Kangwŏn, but was destroyed in the Tokyo earthquake of 1923. The second was settled in 1633 at Chŏksang-san, Muju-gun, north Chŏlla, but was destroyed in the great fire of **Pusan** in 1953. The fourth set went to T'aebaek-san, Ponghwa-gun, Kyŏngsang, and is now in Seoul National University Library.

The colonial government used the T'aebaek-san set to prepare *Yijo sillok*, a facsimile edition limited to some 30-odd copies published in 1933–4. This included the *sijŏng-gi* for the last two reigns (**Kojong** and **Sunjong**, 1863–1910), which were never edited as *sillok*. In 1955–8 the Korean government published a photostat edition in 48 volumes, which was distributed throughout the world.

G. M. McCUNE, 'The Yi Dynasty Annals of Korea', *TKBRAS*, XXIX, 1939

CHOYANG-DONG 朝陽洞
Archaeological site of the **Proto-Three Kingdoms** period excavated outside **Kyŏngju** in 1981–2. It yielded **iron** weapons and Chinese bronze **mirrors**, evidence of contact with the **commandery** at **Lelang**.

CHRISTIAN CONSPIRACY CASE (The *Paego-in* affair, 1912) *See* **Hundred and Five, Case of the**

CHRISTIANITY *See* **Anglicans**; **Bible in Korean, the**; **Protestants**; **Roman Catholic Church**; **Russian Orthodox Mission**
SPENCER PALMER, *Korea and Christianity*, Seoul: Hollym Corporation, 1967

CHU SIGYŎNG 周時經 (1876–1914)
The father of modern Korean language studies. Born at Pongsan in Hwanghae, he studied traditional Chinese letters at home before attending Paejae School in Seoul. A founder member of the **Independence Club**, he taught Korean language, geography, history and mathematics at various schools in Seoul, and was a proof reader on the

Tongnip Sinmun, eventually devoting himself to the study of Korean and promotion of a unified spelling system. He was the inspiration for founding the Korean Language Research Society (*Chosŏnŏ-yŏn'guhoe*) later known as the ***Han'gŭl* Society** (*Han'gŭl Hakhoe*), and worked with **Ch'oe Namsŏn** on his Kwangmunhoe publications. Ch'oe Hyŏnbae and Yi Pyŏnggi were among his disciples. His principal books were *Kugŏ munjŏn ŭmhak* (1908), a study of the history of Korean sounds; *Kungmunpŏp* (1910, reissued in 1911 as *Chosŏnŏ munpŏp*), the first modern grammar of the language, in which he distinguished nine parts of speech and made a seminal study of reduplicated consonants (*toen sori*) and double consonants; and *Marŭi sori* (1914) on Korean phonetics. All three works were reissued as one volume, *Chu Sigyŏng Sŏnsaeng yugo*, in 1933. He also advocated unilinear writing of *han'gŭl* (*see* **han'gŭl, unilinear**). In the wake of the *Paego-in* Incident of 1910–12 (*see* **Hundred and Five, Case of the**), he was preparing to flee the country when he was suddenly taken ill and died at the age of 37.

CHUCH'E 主體 'self-reliance'
From the mid-1950s, as the unity of the communist world broke up in the wake of Khrushchev's de-Stalinisation speech and the Hungarian uprising in 1956, the North Koreans began to stress a doctrine of self-reliance and independence. Eventually, as North Korea faced the dilemma posed by the falling out of its two giant neighbours in the Sino-Soviet dispute, this evolved into the *chuch'e* (always romanised in North Korea as *juche*) doctrine, which has formed the basis of the country's official philosophy ever since. It is not an easy doctrine to pin down. It revolves around two concepts. One is that man is the master of his destiny, the other that he should remain independent of all outside influences. The latter does not mean, as is sometimes claimed in the West, that there should be no outside links or that North Korea should not accept assistance. Rather, there should be no spiritual or psychological dependence in accepting outside assistance. In particular, citizens of North Korea should avoid the traditional practice of *sadae-juŭi*, sometimes translated as 'flunkeyism' or looking up to the great – i.e. China (*see* **sadae**). Although the doctrine stresses the centrality of human beings in the world, people achieve this by their subordination to the leader; it thus supported the rule of **Kim Ilsŏng** and his son's succession. With North Korean funding, but also because it seemed to offer a different way to development, *chuch'e* study groups were established in many third world countries in the 1970s and 1980s; some still continue, but they are dwindling. *Chuch'e* has survived as the basic premise of North Korea's political thought, despite the country's continued clear dependence on outside assistance and the defection to South Korea in 1997 of Hwang Changyŏp, the man widely believed to be the real architect of the doctrine.

It may be noted that neither the term nor the concept of *chuch'e* are exclusive to North Korea: Park Chung Hee (**Pak Chŏnghŭi**) also used it and stressed the value of self-reliance to the South.
ERIC VAN RHEE, 'The Limits of *Juche*: North Korea's Dependence on Soviet Industrial Aid, 1953–76,' *JCS*, vol.5 no.1, 1989; MICHAEL ROBINSON, 'National Identity and the Thought of Shin Ch'ae-ho: *Sadaejuŭi* and *Chuch'e* in History and Politics,' *JKS* 5, 1984

CHUJA-GARYE 朱子家禮 'Zhu Xi's domestic rituals'
A collection of **Zhu Xi**'s writings on the **Four Rites**, originally edited by Qiu Jun in the 14th century and several times reprinted in Korea, where it became a standard handbook.

CHŬLMUN 櫛文 'comb pattern' **CULTURE**
Prehistoric culture of the **neolithic** period dating roughly from the 7th millennium BC
to 700 BC. This long period saw the development from a hunting and gathering
economy into **agriculture**, and the introduction from the Chinese mainland of spinning
and **rice** culture. Stylistic and decorative similarities can be seen in pottery vessels
from Misong, northern P'yŏngan province, and the **Yalu** and **Ch'ŏngch'ŏn** River
valleys and Chinese sites in eastern Liaoning province belonging to the mid-5th
century BC Lower Xiaozhushan culture. Communities were sited close to rivers, as at
Amsadong on the **Han** River to the east of modern Seoul, and along the coast, as at
Osan, Kangwŏn province. Fish was an important part of the diet, together with grain in
the later neolithic period. Dwellings were semi-subterranean, with roofs supported on
posts. Burial practices are marked by the survival of **dolmens** from around 1500 BC.
The characteristic pottery consists of unglazed, reddish brown earthenware, decorated
with incised or stamped geometric designs of short parallel lines usually called 'comb
pattern'. Vessel shapes consist of flat- or round-bottomed bowls, and jugs with narrow
necks and handles appearing late in the period.
SARAH NELSON, *Han River Chulmuntogi: a Study of Early Neolithic Korea*, Occasional Paper
9, Program in East Asian Studies, Western Washington State College, 1975
See also **Mumun**

CHUMONG 朱蒙
The legendary founder of the kingdom of **Koguryŏ**, said to have led one of the tribes
of **Puyŏ** south from northern **Manchuria** into the Tongga River valley; also known as
King Tongmyŏng ('Eastern light').
See **Foundation myths**

CHUNGANG ILBO 中央日報 'Central Daily'
Newspaper founded in October 1931, one of five authorised in the wake of the **March
First Movement** and subject to Japanese censorship. The title was later changed to
Chosŏn Chungang Ilbo ('Korea Central Daily').
See also **Chosŏn Ilbo; Tonga Ilbo**

CHUNGBANG 重房
Military body that formed the supreme ruling council after the military revolt of 1170
against the aristocratic government of the Koryŏ dynasty under King Ŭijong (*see*
Chŏng Chungbu Rebellion). The self-centred ambition of a succession of individual
military rulers such as Chŏng Chungbu, Yi Ŭibang, Kyŏng Taesŭng and Yi Ŭimin
diminished its effectiveness and prepared the way for the dictatorship of Ch'oe
Ch'unghŏn (*see* **Ch'oe Dictatorship**).

CHŬNGBO MUNHŎN PIGO 增補文獻備考 'Expanded Reference Materials'
In 1770 Hong Ponghan (1713–73) compiled an encyclopaedic compendium of extracts
and quotations for use in government, *Tongguk munhŏn pigo*, 'Korean Reference
Materials', arranged in 13 topical sections and based on Ma Duanlin's 13th-century
Wenxian tongkao. A revision with eight further sections, by Yi Manun (b. 1736), was
ordered in 1782 and completed, but never printed. In 1807 it was slightly shortened by
Yi Manun's son. In 1908 a further revision by **Yi Wanyong** appeared in 250 books
with the prefix *chŭngbo* 'expanded'. The 16 sections are: **astronomy** and meteorology,
Korean geography, royal **genealogy**, **rites**, **music**, military affairs, justice, land
revenues, other finances, census, liens and doles, foreign relations, appointments,
education, government departments, literature.

CHUNGCH'U-BU 中樞府

During the Koryŏ dynasty this title was used for a group whose responsibilities included guarding the palace and controlling weaponry. Chosŏn kings modified this rôle and by 1466 *Chungch'u bu* had become a largely honorary body that, because of its origins, remained on the west or military side of the court (*sŏban; see* **yangban**). It gave at least nominal advisory standing to 26 men of high rank who were not in office, and is sometimes referred to as 'a council without portfolios', though in British terms it was strictly more like the Privy Council. It was led by a 1st **grade** senior. During the Japanese colonial period the title was revived as *Chungch'u-wŏn* for an advisory body of senior Korean scholars who published some valuable works and texts. *Ch'u* means 'cardinal, pivotal', and in modern usage *chungch'ugwan* means a cardinal of the Roman Catholic Church.

CHUNGIN 中人 'middle people'

The small hereditary class of petty functionaries who served the **sadaebu** and **yangban** in indispensable ways during the Chosŏn period, principally in central government in Seoul and in rural county towns. They may have derived their name from living in the central part of Seoul. They belonged to **lineages** with genealogies, took their own technical **examinations** (*chapkwa*), and served as clerks, accountants, interpreters, astronomers, doctors, architects and artists. As magistrates' assistants they helped to collect taxes and enforce the law. They could not advance to *yangban* status. Many became wealthy and some showed literary merit, yet their skills went unacknowledged by their social superiors, and though *yangban* men might take *chungin* women as secondary wives (*soja*) and **concubines**, their offspring were not recognised as *yangban*. Inter-marriage between the classes was inadmissible. Not surprisingly, members of the *chungin* played a part in the **Sirhak movement**, and showed interest in westernisation and reform late in the Chosŏn period.

See also **class system; craftsmen;** *yukka chahyŏng*

CHŬNGSAN-GYO 甑山教

A general name for the large number of sects derived from the leadership of **Kang Ilsun**, whose brush name was Chŭngsan. After his death some of his followers rallied and in 1914 renamed their faith *T'aeŭl-gyo*, 'way of the *t'aegŭk*'; but they fought among themselves. Ch'a Kyŏngsŏk (d. 1936) proclaimed *Poch'ŏn-gyo* (first called *Sŏndo-gyo*, 'Daoist way ' or *Pohwa-gyo*, 'way of universal change') in 1921, and called himself Ch'ŏnja, 'Son of Heaven'. Kim Hyŏngnyŏl established a version called Maitreya **Buddhism** at Kŭmsan-sa, later moved to Seoul. Other schisms were called *Samdŏkkyo*, 'three virtues faith', *Yonghwa-gyo*, 'dragon-flower (of Maitreya) faith', *Tonghwa-gyo*, 'Eastern transformation faith', and *Chŭngsan Sŏnbul-gyo*, 'Chŭngsan's Dao-Buddhism'. In 1945 there were some 80 separate groups. Efforts were made to unite them as late as the 1960s, but none was successful. The groups varied as to whether they emphasised Daoist or Buddhist ideas, but lacked coherent doctrines. They saw Korea as the source of the world's salvation, believed they were living in the last days, used **mantras**, charms and amulets (*pujŏk*), and believed in a folksy polytheism with a messianic element. They had no scriptures.

See also **Religions, new**

CHUNGYANG 重陽 'double 9th'

The figure 9, as the largest odd digit, has a strongly *yang* significance, and the 9th day of the 9th moon is a natural choice for festivity – especially since the autumn weather is normally congenial. The date was observed in Silla and became ritualised at the Koryŏ court. During Chosŏn times, in the reign of **Sŏngjong** it was made the occasion of a banquet for old people. *Ch'arye* were offered, *hwach'ae* (prettily cut fruit pieces in honeyed water) was enjoyed and wine flavoured with chrysanthemum flowers was drunk. Outdoor parties (*Chungyang-nori* or *p'unggung-nori* 'maple and chrysanthemum viewing') for the leisured classes were held in beauty spots outside the town, where poems were written and ink paintings made to celebrate the season.

CH'A CH'ŎLLO 車天輅 (Osan, 1556–1615)

A disciple of **Sŏ Kŏjŏng**, born at **Kaesŏng**. Early in his career he was banished for two years to Myŏngch'ŏn for faking a friend's examination papers, but he passed a lifetime in government service, much employed in using his rare skills as a drafter of diplomatic documents to be sent to Ming China. His diplomatic skills were also used on an embassy to Japan, but he is chiefly remembered for his amazing speed in composing Chinese poetry. A favourite anecdote tells how in 1606 he astonished the Chinese envoy Zhu Zhifan with a lengthy composition in praise of P'yŏngyang, written in a fraction of the expected time. Critics, however, generally suggest that his rugged style left many infelicities in his work. His brush name means 'Five mountains'.
See also **Hong Yangho**

CH'ACH'AUNG See **Silla kingly titles**

CH'AEKKŎRI 'books etc.'

A popular category of **folk painting**, often seen on folding **screens**. It shows the contents of a scholar's studio, comprising piles of **books**, writing equipment, and other treasured possessions. These include such things as a hat, pipe, **musical instrument**, incense burner, and **chess**board. Fruit and **flowers** with symbolic meanings may also be present, such as a water melon (longevity) or pomegranate (plentiful offspring). The items are piled on a table or arranged on the shelves of a cabinet, but the style is colourful and decorative rather than realistic, and usually adopts a deliberately flattened perspective.

CH'AMP'AN 參判

The title of the second officer of any of the **Six Boards**, a man of 2nd **grade** junior.

CH'ANGDŎK 'Illustrious Virtue' PALACE 昌德宮

The best preserved of three major Chosŏn dynasty palaces still surviving in modern Seoul (*see also* **Kyŏngbok Palace**; **Tŏksu Palace**). It was first built as a detached palace in 1405 and rebuilt in 1611 after being destroyed by the Japanese invaders in 1592 (*see* **Imjin Wars**). Thirteen kings including the last monarch, **Sunjong**, used it as their official residence. Its furnishings attest to the growth of western influence in the late 19th century (*see* **von Möllendorff**), but it was here that mutinous soldiers broke in in 1882, killed the minister Min Kyŏmho (1839–82), and forced **Queen Min** to flee (*see* *Imo* **Incident**), and here that King **Kojong** struggled for his life and political future two years later (*see* *Kapsin* **Coup**). Its extensive grounds contain the royal family's private *Piwŏn* ('Secret Garden'), and nearby is the Royal Ancestral Shrine (**Chongmyo**) at which the annual sacrifices to the spirits of deceased Yi family ancestors were and still are held (*see* **Confucianism**; *Sŏnggyun-gwan*).
EDWARD B. ADAMS, *Palaces of Seoul: Yi Dynasty Palaces in Korea's Capital City*, Seoul, 1982

CH'ANGGA 唱歌
Songs composed for setting to Western tunes in the late 19th and early 20th centuries.

CH'ARYE 茶禮 'tea rite'
Also pronounced *tarye*. A simple form of food-offering to ancestors, performed in the house or domestic spirit-shrine during the daytime, usually in the early part of the morning. It is typical of new moon and full moon, **New Year's Day**, **Ch'usŏk**, **Tano** and ancestors' birthdays and memorial days. **Tea** is rarely if ever used: here the word indicates a light meal, less than a full sacrificial table, and quite unlike the Japanese tea ceremony.

CH'ILSŎK 七夕 'seventh evening'
A summer **festival** especially liked by women. It is said no crows or magpies can be seen on the 7th day of the 7th moon because they have all gone up to heaven, where they make themselves into a bridge over the Milky Way on which Kyŏnu (C. Chienniu) 'the Herdboy' and Chingnyŏ (C. Chinu) 'the Weaving Maid', who live to east and west of that great river of stars, can meet for an annual tryst. The story came from China. Two small groups of stars are mentioned in the *Book of Odes* 203: the Weaving Women and the Draught Ox. These two asterisms (one in Lyra, the other in Aquila) gave their names to contiguous *xu* (**lunar mansions**) in the northern quadrant. By Han times these names had come to be understood as Weaving Maid and Oxherd Boy, and their romance had been dreamt up. The bridge of birds is probably later. How they came to be associated with a midsummer festival is conjectural, but they provide one of Korea's best-loved folk themes.

CH'ILSŎNG-SIN 七星神 'seven stars spirits'
The spirits of the Great Bear constellation are thought to control personal fate: length of life, success or failure and fulfilment of wishes. They are represented as seven old men like the *sansin* (without **tigers**) and may be given a community celebration, *Ch'ilsŏng-je*, formerly attended by both sexes, but latterly almost restricted to women. If there was no *Ch'ilsŏng-dang* shrine, the sacrifice, perhaps attended by only one or two people, might be made in a secluded place in the hills or by a stream into which **rice** was cast. A shrine for the Seven Stars is to be found in the precincts of most Buddhist temples, symmetrically placed with the *sansin* shrine.

CH'IP'YŎNG YORAM 治平要覽 'Handbook of Good Government'
An anthology of good and bad government decisions, implying admonitions for the future, compiled by the **Chiphyŏn-jŏn** in 1445 and printed in 1516. The examples are taken from Chinese sources from Zhou to Yuan, and Korean sources from **Kija** to Koryŏ.

CH'OE CHEU 崔濟愚 (Ch'oe Poksul, 1824–64)
Born into an unsuccessful *yangban* family in Chŏlla province, Ch'oe was discontented both with the system for literati advancement and the conditions of deprivation and oppression which he saw amongst the **peasantry**. Following a vision he proclaimed the teaching of 'Heaven's Way' (*Ch'ŏndo*) as the principal doctrine of a new religious sect, *Tonghak* ('Eastern learning'). His writings were an amalgam of traditional East Asian religions, **shamanism**, and ironically the Catholicism against which he campaigned. They were circulated in his **Yongdam yusa** ('Hymns from Dragon Pool') and *Tonggyŏng taejŏn* ('Great Compendium of Eastern Scriptures'). His nationalistic creed

might have earned him some upper-class support for its anti-Chinese and anti-Western elements, but by protesting against bureaucratic corruption Ch'oe incurred official wrath. He was accused of misleading the people and, as a result of his teaching about a *Ch'ŏnju* ('Heavenly Lord'), of defying the supreme authority of the king. He was executed in April 1864.

CH'OE TONG-HUI, 'The Life and Thought of Ch'oe Che-u,' *KJ*, 11/9, 1971
See also **Ch'ŏndo-gyo**; **Tonghak Rebellion**

CH'OE CH'IWŎN 崔致遠 (Koŭn, 858–c. 910)

The earliest Korean writer whose work has survived in any quantity, he lived when both Tang and Silla were in terminal decline. When he was 11 years old, he was sent to China to study, and at 18 he received his first official provincial appointment from the Tang court. He took the brush name 'Orphan Cloud'. His compositions were admired, and after he attracted royal attention he was sent on campaign as a secretary during the ten-year warfare with the rebel Huang Chao. Before this struggle eventually brought about the fall of the **Tang dynasty**, he was permitted to return to Silla, aged 27, in 885. Soon he was given a state appointment, and became Vice-Minister of War; but Silla was in as much disarray as Tang. He presented a memorial to Queen Chinsŏng (*see* **Silla, Queens of**) proposing reforms of the administration, but it was not accepted. He withdrew to his native mountains, and is believed to have lived at **Haein-sa**, where he presumably died. His *Kyewŏn-p'ilgyŏng*, 'Brush-pen Ploughings in Gardens of Cinnamon', a collection of pieces written during his stay in China (874–885), was not printed until 1834. He left some lengthy inscriptions on stone and his verse was much anthologised, though it was later criticised in Korea for its late Tang richness of style. Much of his output is in 'parallel prose'. Though he is enshrined in the Confucian temple, he clearly had great respect for **Buddhism** and for Daoist thought.

CH'OE CH'UNG 崔沖 (Sŏngjae, 984–1068)

His brush name Sŏngjae means 'alert study', but he is also known as Haedong Kongja, 'the Confucius of Korea', because of his pioneer teaching programme in mid-Koryŏ times. He was skilled in writing the old-fashioned Chinese 'parallel prose' and realised the value of *Zhong yong* before the Zheng brothers singled it out from *Liji* as a separate book (see **Confucian Classics**). When he retired in 1055 he established the first private Confucian school *Kujae haktang*, 'School of nine studies', so called because the students were divided into nine groups. This was soon followed by other similar **schools**.

CH'OE DICTATORSHIP *Ch'oessi chŏndan chŏngch'i* 崔氏專斷政治

Period of rule under General Ch'oe Ch'unghŏn and his clan from 1196 to 1258, following a long period in the 11th and 12th centuries when civil officials had consistently outdone their military counterparts. In 1196 he killed Chŏng Chungbu (*see* **Chŏng Chungbu Rebellion**), set King Sinjong on the throne in succession to Myŏngjong, and established a ruthless military régime which suppressed peasant unrest and eliminated all possible sources of opposition. After surviving a coup attempt in 1209 Ch'oe created a military caucus (*Kyojŏng Togam*) which effectively ran the government and relegated the king to a subordinate position. On his death in 1218 his son, Ch'oe U, took shrewd steps to placate landowners and Confucian scholars oppressed by his father, but also reorganised the military again so as to retain dictatorial power in his own hands. Risings of **peasants** and **slaves** continued into the 13th century. When the **Mongols** invaded Korea in 1231, Ch'oe U accepted their humiliating demands before leading the court and government to exile on **Kanghwa-**

do. In these beleagured surroundings some support drifted back to the king, Kojong, and in 1258 the fourth and last Ch'oe dictator was assassinated.
EDWARD J. SCHULTZ, 'Ch'oe Ch'unghŏn: His Rise to Power,' *KS*, 8, 1984

CH'OE MUSŎN 崔茂宣 (d. 1395)

In the last decades of the Koryŏ dynasty, Ch'oe Musŏn was eager to learn how to use gunpowder and fire-arms, the existence of which he had learned from China. He did not succeed until 1376, when he persuaded a skilled Chinese to stay with him and teach him. He then argued for the establishment of a government department for firearms and explosives, over which he was given control. Ch'oe mastered the art of making gunpowder, detonating explosives and fashioning both the necessary arms, chiefly forms of cannon, and vessels that could be equipped to deliver bombs, shells, fire-arrows and rockets. His first opportunity to use them in warfare came in 1380 when he was involved in the repulse of a large force of Japanese **pirates** from the mouth of the Kŭm River. He was an old man when his department was closed down in 1389 and he retired to record his knowledge. In the early years of the Chosŏn dynasty he was honoured by the new king, alongside whom he had fought in the service of Koryŏ.

CH'OE NAMSŎN 崔南善 (1890–1957)

A seminal historian and leader of modern literature. Born in Seoul, where his first **newspaper** articles were published when he was eleven, he was educated at Waseda University, from which he returned in 1906 to set himself up as a publisher. In November 1908, at the age of eighteen, he began publication of *Sonyŏn*, 'Young People', Korea's first literary monthly (1908–1911). The first issue contained his epochal free-verse poem *Haeëgesŏ sonyŏnege*, 'From the Sea to the Young', the first poem in colloquial Korean. From 1914 to 1918 he published the magazine *Ch'ŏngch'un*, 'Youth'. Already he had established the Society for Promoting Korean Books (*Chosŏn Kwangmun-hoe*), providing cheap modern editions of old and classic works in *hanmun*, mostly in better texts than appeared in the Japanese **Chōsen kosho kankō-kai** editions. 25 titles appeared between 1911 and 1915. His *Sin chajŏn*, published in 1915, is still a useful Korean dictionary of Chinese characters. In 1919 he drafted, but did not sign, the **Declaration of Independence**, and was imprisoned, but released on parole in 1920. Finding a *modus vivendi* with the Japanese administration, he was appointed to the Government General **Korean History Compilation Committee** in 1927. In 1926 he published a collection of his own *sijo*, *Paekp'al pŏnnoe*, 'The 108 Anxieties' (whose title illustrates his deep interest in **Buddhism**), and in 1928 *Sijo yuch'wi*, an anthology of *sijo* from all periods. His *Asi Chosŏn* (1927) was an important re-evaluation of the **Tan'gun** myth, while his journalism and books on history and travel within Korea did much to form Koreans' consciousness of their history. From 1938 to 1941 he taught in **Manchuria**, making visits to Beijing. In 1949 he was again imprisoned, this time for collaboration with the Japanese during World War II, but was soon bailed out in sickness. In 1954 he edited a new edition of *Samguk yusa*. In November 1955 he was baptized as a Catholic. Two years later he died of a cerebral haemorrhage.
For a list of *Chosŏn Kwangmun-hoe* titles see RICHARD RUTT, *James Scarth Gale*, Seoul: Royal Asiatic Society, 1972, pp. 359–60

CH'ŎKHWA-BI 斥和碑 'Rejection of appeasement' stones

Stones, 1·5 metres high and bearing a warning in twelve Chinese characters, were set up by Hŭngsŏn **Taewŏn'gun** in front of government offices throughout the country in

1871. The inscription read YANGI CH'IMBŎM / PIJŎN CHŬK HWA / CHUHWA MAEGUK, 'Western barbarians are encroaching; failure to resist is appeasement: appeasement means selling our country...' A subscript note in smaller characters added: 'A warning to our descendants for 10,000 years: given in 1866, erected in 1871.'

CH'ŎLCHONG 哲宗 (1831–64, r. 1849–1864)
When **Hŏnjong** died sonless at the age of 22 in 1849, it fell to the senior Queen Dowager, Sunwŏn (1789–1857, widow of **Sunjo**), to nominate his successor, now known as Ch'ŏlchong. Queen Sunwŏn was an Andong Kim, whose family had lost influence during Hŏnjong's reign, and she sought a man who would not hinder her clan's return to power. She chose an 18-year-old great-grandson of Crown Prince **Changhŏn** (the 'coffin king'), Yi Wŏnbŏm, later known as Ch'ŏlchong, who was still a bachelor living as a poor farmer in **Kanghwa**, where his family had been in exile since 1779. The queen soon had him married to an Andong Kim girl (later known as Queen Ch'ŏrin, 1837–78). Utterly unprepared for kingship, he settled down to enjoy himself in the palace while the Kim clan exercised *sedo*, the real power in the land. Widespread corruption and extortion caused riots in **Chinju**, **Cheju** and Hamhŭng. Meanwhile East Asia was increasingly under pressure from Western ideas, and the Catholic Church made great advances in Korea under the relatively sympathetic rule of the Andong Kim. In reaction to all this, the **Tonghak** movement was born during his reign. Ch'ŏlchong fell ill and died in 1864 at the age of 31. He had sired eleven children, but only one daughter survived him.

CH'ŎMJI 僉知
A *Chungch'u-bu* official of 3rd grade senior. The title became a colloquial term for an old man out of office.

CH'ŎMSŎNGDAE 瞻星臺 'Reverently-regarding-stars platform'
The oldest surviving observatory in Asia, built in **Kyŏngju** on the orders of Queen **Sŏndŏk** in AD 634. The circular building is shaped like a flask with a concave neck and is apparently constructed of 365 rectangular stone blocks. It stands on a square base and is 8·8 metres high. Twelve courses of stone are built below and twelve above the single window which faces south, and the whole is surmounted by eight stones forming one square on top of another. Like the rest of the astronomical work of **Silla**, the symbolism and use of this famous landmark are largely unknown, but its significance and observations were undoubtedly of great importance to the court.
JEON SANG-WOON, 'Ch'ŏmsŏngdae and Astronomical Observation,' *KJ*, 12/2, 1972; KIM YONG-WOON, 'Structure of Ch'ŏmsŏngdae in the Light of the Choupei Suanchin,' *KJ*, 14/9, 1974; SONG SANG-YONG, 'A Brief History of the Study of the Ch'ŏmsŏngdae in Kyŏngju,' *KJ*, 23/8, 1983
See also **astronomy**; **Silla, Queens of**

CH'ŎNDO-GYO 天道教 'Heavenly Way Teaching'
The teaching of **Ch'oe Cheu**, which formed the doctrinal basis of the Tonghak cult in the second half of the 19th century. It was in part a Korean reaction against the spread of Christianity, posited upon the presence of God dwelling within man and the resulting equal rights of all men regardless of their social class. The sect assumed the name *Ch'ŏndo-gyo* after the suppression of the **Tonghak Rebellion**, and became deeply involved in anti-Japanese and independence activities. Its third leader, **Son**

Pyŏnghŭi, helped in founding the pro-independence newspaper *Mansebo* ('[Independence]-for-ever Report'), and together with Christian and Buddhist leaders signed the **Declaration of Independence** on 1 March 1919. In 1922 it supported **Cho Mansik**'s Korean Products Promotion Society, and in 1925 it established the Korean Farmers' Association in an attempt to improve living and working conditions in the countryside. It cooperated with the **Korean Communist Party** in forming the *Sin'ganhoe* (**New Shoot Society**). It was still extant in the 1990s, though not as a major religion.

KIM YONG CHOON, *The Ch'ŏndogyo Concept of Man*, Seoul, 1978; BENJAMIN WEEMS, *Reform, Rebellion and the Heavenly Way*, Tucson: University of Arizona Press, 1964

CH'ŎNGBAEK-CHA 青白瓷 'blue-white pottery'
A highly esteemed bluish white porcelain of the Chosŏn period, in fact a white body with a blue glaze.
See also **ceramics**; **pottery**

CH'ŎNGBAENG-NI 清白吏 'pure white official'
A title granted during the Chosŏn dynasty to men of distinguished probity, on nomination by men of 2nd **grade** and above and the **censorate**. Such men were proverbially poor.

CH'ŎNGCH'ŎN RIVER 清川江
Also known as the Salsu River. One of the principal rivers of north-western Korea which formed part of the natural defences of northern Korea against invaders from **Manchuria**, situated mid-way between the **Yalu** and the **Taedong** Rivers. It was here that the invading Chinese army was severely defeated by **Ŭlchi Mundŏk** in 612, and that Koryŏ forces prevented the advance of **Liao** invaders into Korea in 993.

CH'ŎN'GI-DAEYO 天機大要 'Great Digest of Heavenly Indications'
A collection of materials for choosing lucky days for weddings, funerals, house-building and sacrifices, based on **divination** methods derived from various applications of the ***Book of Changes*** and **five phases** theory. It was apparently based on material from Ming China, arranged by Im Soju (or Lin Shaozhou) and edited by Chi Ilbin (otherwise Chi Paegwŏn) in 1737. It is still very popular.
See also ***Kunghap; Nabŭm; nine palaces divination***

CH'ŎNGJU 清州
One of the nine regional capitals of the Unified Silla dynasty (known as Sŏwŏn-gyŏng). Site of the military command HQ for Ch'ungch'ŏng province under the Chosŏn government, it was occupied by the Japanese invaders in 1592 until recovered by **Cho Hŏn**.
See also ***Tanggan chiju***

CH'ŎNGSAN-NI (C. Qingshanli) 青山里
Battle on the Manchurian side of the **Yalu** river that took place in October 1920 between Korean independence armies under Kim Chwajin and Yi Pŏmsŏk and a Japanese army of 20,000 men. Though outnumbered by almost ten to one, the Koreans inflicted heavy casualties and claimed a substantial victory.
See also ***Ŭibyŏng***

75

CH'ŎNJA-MUN 千字文 (C. *Qianziwen*; *The Thousand Character Classic*)
An ingenious composition by Zhou Xingzi of the early 6th century AD. Legend says
the Liang emperor gave him 1,000 characters to be arranged in a poem. Zhou
completed the task in one night, but the effort turned all his hair white – hence the
alternative name *Paektu-mun* 'White-headed Classic'. 125 couplets in 4-character
parallel verse, rhyming in sections of varying length, deal with:

1) Heaven, earth and man (couplets 1–18);
2) Virtue and duties (19–51);
3) The twin capitals, Luoyang and Chang'an (52–65), their memorials to great men
   (66–76) and famous places in the empire (77–81);
4) Life in rural retirement (82–100), domestic simplicity and propriety (101–118),
   memento mori (119–124) and a final flourish of punctuation (125).

The work appealed to neo-Confucians and became popular as a schoolboy primer in
Song China. During the Chosŏn period it filled the same rôle in Korea, usually printed
with only the *saegim* 'definition' and *ŭm* 'pronunciation' in *han'gŭl* under each
character, though an *ŏnhae* 'Korean crib' by **Han Sŏkpong** was printed in 1601. No
book was read by more men, and the opening line *Ch'ŏnji hyŏnhwang*, 'Heaven and
earth, the dark and the dun', is Korea's most hackneyed quotation. *Ch'ŏnja-mun* left its
mark on place-names, **personal names** and **proverbs**, and, as in China, provided an
elegant way of numbering items from 1 to 1,000.

CH'ŎNMA-CH'ONG 天馬塚 *See* **Heavenly Horse Tomb**

CH'ŎNMIN 賤民 'despised people'
Members of the hereditary lowest order of traditional society, virtually outcast though
not untouchable. They may have been descended from the *mujari*. In addition to **slaves**
the class also included those engaged in demeaning occupations such as butchery,
basket-making, entertaining (*see* **kisaeng**; *kwangdae*; *sadang*), and **shamanism**.
Though they were barred from the official **examination system** they became eligible
to enter the **military exams** during the Chosŏn period.
See also **class system**; *paekchang*

CH'ŎNT'AE-JONG 天台宗 (C. *Tiantai zong*)
The principal form of Buddhism in Tang China, established in the Tiantai mountains of
Zhejiang by Zhi Yi (K. Chi Ŭi, 538–597). Centred on the Lotus **Sutra**, it regarded
Sakyamuni as a manifestation of eternal buddhahood, and held that absolute mind
encompassed the whole universe, so that all things partook of Buddha-nature.
　　It was propagated in Korea in the 7th century by the great monk **Wŏnhyo** (617–
686). Its first period of strength came in the 8th century, when as the principal sect in
China it attracted many Korean monks to monasteries there and became a leading
school in the Unified Silla kingdom. Its greatest success, however, came with its
revival after the return of monks Ch'egwan and **Ŭich'ŏn** from China in the 10th and
11th centuries. Because *Ch'ŏnt'ae* teaching allowed for both study (*kyo*) and
meditation (*sŏn*), it was remarkably tolerant. Ŭich'ŏn drew together the two traditions
represented by *Hwaŏm* and *Sŏn* sects so that Ch'ŏnt'ae became the principal form of
Koryŏ Buddhism. Even so, it failed to unite the whole church and a number of *Sŏn*
sects remained outside its umbrella.
YI KI-YONG, 'Wŏnhyo and his Thought,' *KJ*, 11/1, 1971

CH'OP'AIL 初八日 'first eighth day'
The birthday of Sakyamuni **Buddha**, and the greatest festival of the Buddhist year, kept on the 8th day of the 4th moon, as in China and Japan, while Tibet keeps the festival on the 7th. Crowds visit temples, especially in the evening, when long processions, reciting **mantras**, wind their way through the precincts with paper lanterns. In many places householders fill their houses and courts with lanterns, and poles strung with lanterns are erected, a practice that dates back to ***P'algwan-hoe*** in the Koryŏ dynasty.

CH'ŎYONG DANCE 處容舞
Dance performed as part of the popular and national harvest festivities (***P'algwanhoe***) in the Koryŏ period which became formalised into a category of **masked dance** in the Chosŏn dynasty. Despite its probable link with shamanistic exorcism rites it was frequently performed at court and private literati banquets until the early 19th century. It commemorated a Silla story with several variants. According to one of these Ch'ŏyong was a court minstrel who had a vision of four exceptionally ugly men warning the court against its carefree self-indulgence. His masters failed to heed the message and the dynasty fell. The story was immortalised in a dance sequence characterised by five men wearing ugly masks. Ch'ŏyong himself became the patron deity of masked dancers. In the Chosŏn dynasty the five dancers wore robes of red, black, blue, white and yellow respectively, and performed a sequence probably associated with the ancient dance of the Gods of the **Five Directions** (*Obang Changgun*).
See also **Song of Ch'ŏyong**

CH'ŬGU-GI 測雨器 *See* **Rain gauge**

CH'UNCH'U-GWAN 春秋館 'Spring and autumn hall'
The office that kept all Chosŏn state records, comprising twenty officials, presided over by a 1st **grade** senior. It was named after the records of the state of Lu, supposedly kept by Confucius himself and preserved as one of the **Confucian classics**. 'Spring and autumn' was an elegant word for 'years'.

CH'UNGHUN-BU 忠勳府 'Council of loyal merit'
A body concerned with the affairs of **meritorious subjects**. It was also called *Undae* 'cloud terrace', from a portrait gallery of loyal subjects of the **Han dynasty**, and *In'gak* 'unicorn council' from another similar institution of Han times named after the *kirin*, a mythical one-horned animal whose appearance was supposed to signal the advent of a great man.

CH'UNHYANG-JŎN 春香傳
Korea's favourite story of the 'faithful wife' genre. It is set in Namwŏn, south Chŏlla. Ch'unhyang, 'spring fragrance', is 15 years old, the daughter of a *kisaeng*. She secretly marries the governor's son of the same age, Yi Mongnyong, 'dream dragon', usually referred to as Yi Toryŏng, 'bachelor Yi'. Their meeting when she is on a swing at ***Tano*** is a favourite incident. The boy has to go to Seoul when his father is recalled. The new governor tries to make Ch'unhyang live as a *kisaeng* and cruelly imprisons her when she withstands his will. Her husband returns as a Royal Secret Inspector and releases her in a dramatic scene at a banquet. The story is related in the style of a ***kwangdae*** or professional story-teller, with passages of lyric description, exhilarating lists, jokes, word-play, erotic detail and intense excitement. Yi's man-servant or *pangja* offers comic relief and lower-class comment throughout. The oldest known version is a

Chinese poem of 1754. Of the many woodblock printings in Korean, the best is the Chŏnju woodblock called *Wanp'an* (Wanju is a literary name for Chŏnju.) Social criticism is implicit in the tale, but is not its main purpose. It has featured in *ch'anggŭk* (*see **Wŏn'gak-sa***) and **cinema**.
Translated by RICHARD RUTT, in *Virtuous Women*, Seoul: Royal Asiatic Society, Korea Branch, 1974

CH'USŎK 秋夕

Also known as *han'gawi* or *kawi*, the harvest festival held since Silla times at the eighth full moon. It comes when the hot weather is over and there is abundance of ripe grains and fruit. People make offerings (*ch'arye*) to the ancestors in the morning, don new clothes and eat the year's first **rice**. *Songp'yŏn*, half-moon – the shape is fortuitous – rice-cakes filled with sweet beans and steamed with pine-needles, are eaten. Graves are visited and tidied up after the rank growth of summer. Together with New Year this is the most enduring of Korean folk **festivals**.

CINEMA

The first recorded moving picture show in Korea was given in the **Kyŏngbok Palace** by the American, Burton Homes, in 1899. A newsreel of the Japanese naval victory off the Korean coast and an advertisement for Seoul's new tramways were shown in Seoul in 1904. Western films followed. The first Korean film, made in 1921 or 1922, was either *Ch'unhyang* (*see **Ch'unhyang-jŏn***) or Yun Paengnam's *Wŏrhaŭi maengse*, 'Moonlight oath'. There were no subtitles. A *pyŏnsa* (story-teller) would read the dialogue and comment, sometimes with political implications. In 1928 **Na Un'gyu** made *Arirang*. Though it was not considered nationalistic at the time, it is so seen by hindsight. Talking films arrived in 1928 and the first Korean talkie was Yi P'iru's *Ch'unhyang* in 1936, which with Yi Kyuhwan's *Nagŭne* ('Wanderer' 1937) is regarded as pivotal in Korean cinematic history; but no prints of pre-WWII films have survived. Japanese films dominated until 1945. In 1945–50 a score of silent films were made, notably Ch'oe In'gyu's *Chayu manse*, 'Liberation for ever!' (1946). After the **Korean War** the government with U S aid assisted the film industry to revive. Yi Kyuhwan made a notable black-and-white *Ch'unhyang-jŏn* in 1955. Korean music for sound-tracks began to be composed in the early 1960s. The first full-length colour film was *Hong Kiltong* (1967) (*see **Hong-Giltong-jŏn***). Cinemascope was first used in 1968, by which time a star-system for actors was fully developed.

CLANS *See* **Lineages**; **surnames**

CLASS SYSTEM

Through the first millenium AD Korean society was broadly divided into aristocrats and commoners. Aristocracy was defined either on the basis of blood ties (*see kolp'um*) or of land granted by the crown in recognition of political service and its resultant privileges (*chŏnsi-gwa*; *see also* **meritorious subjects**). In the Koryŏ period class distinctions became more sophisticated. Holders of senior political offices were called *munban* (civil class), those of military posts *muban* (military class). Their subordinates were members of the *namban* (south class) and *kunban* (army class) respectively, and beneath them came the **peasantry** (*paeksŏng*) and **slave** class. **Merchants** supplied the commodities sought by the aristocracy, either as government **tribute** agents (*kongin*) or by participation in overseas **commerce**, yet they gained no definable social recognition for doing so. Social mobility was rare, and for most people their occupational and social status was inherited: the skills developed by craft workers in, for example, the **ceramics**, **paper**, **silk**, and precious metal industries, or by such as sculptors, woodworkers and jewellers, were guarded and handed down from father to son.

Chosŏn society grew on the basis of the Koryŏ system and was in all essentials established by the 16th century. There was a clear distinction between educated men, who were eligible to hold public office and owned much of the land, on one hand, and the rest of the people on the other. Upper class men, often called 'literati' in English, were known as *yangban* or *sadaebu*. (The *taebu*, 'great men', were those of **grade** 4 and above, the *sa*, 'knights', were those of grade 5 and below.) The *yangban* who held government posts were divided into the civil and military officialdom; those who could not maintain an appropriate life-style were reduced to becoming small farmers and were known as *chanban*, 'ruined office-holders', but did not lose their social status, which derived from the social class of their mothers.

In the capital and local magistracies there was a small but important class of educated and skilled artisans (*chungin*). All the rest were *sŏmin*, 'the masses', also called *sangmin*, 'the common people', *yangmin*, 'goodmen', or *p'yŏngmin*, 'ordinary people'. The lowest class was that of the *ch'ŏnmin*, 'despicable people', outcasts who performed service occupations such as transport work, water-carrying, butchery, prostitution, and entertainment (including *mudang*). Differences in the life-style and social habits of *yangban* and commoners were marked, and though commoner women might be taken as secondary wives (*ch'ŏp*) by *yangban* men, upward mobility from the lower into the upper class was generally impossible (*see* **concubines**). Within the broader categories sub-classes bore titles such as *sŏri* 'writers,' and *hyangni* 'local scribes' (*see* **provincial administration**).

Non-chattel **slaves** were quite comon until the social reforms instituted in 1894 (*see* **Kabo** **reforms**) abolished slavery along with the hereditary barriers to mobility between *ch'ŏnmin*, *sangmin* and *yangban*, but a strong sense of class distinction persisted into and through the colonial period, and into the society of the Republic of Korea.

JAMES B. PALAIS, 'Confucianism and the Aristocratic/Bureaucratic Balance in Korea,' *HJAS*, 44: 1984; YI T'AE-JIN, 'Social Changes in Late Koryŏ to Early Chosŏn,' *KJ*, 23/5, 1983

See also **craftsmen**; **gentry**; *kwangdae*; **land tenure**; **lineages**; *paekchang*; *samin*

CLASSICS, CONFUCIAN *kyŏng* 經 *See* **Confucian Classics**

CLEAR AND CLOUDY *ch'ŏng-t'ak* 清濁 (C. *qingzhuo*)

A recurrent metaphor of contrast, used in *Zuo zhuan* (Zhao 20; *see* **Confucian Classics**) for an analogy between **music** and cookery, both of which involve harmonious blending. Clarity and thickness in soup correspond to musical *allegro* and *andante*. The same contrast occurs first in a children's rhyme quoted by Confucius in **Mencius** IIa.8: 'When the Canglang river flows clear, I wash my hat-strings; when it is muddy, I wash my feet.' This has been taken as counselling statesmen to assume office when the administration is good and to retire when affairs go badly. The clear and cloudy metaphor extends to plain and modified, wise and foolish, upper and lower (especially in music), peace and disturbance. In Chosŏn political **factions** a clear party is hardline, a cloudy party moderate or compromising. In *Hunmin chŏngŭm* phonetics, unvoiced consonants are called 'clear', voiced consonants 'cloudy'; in discussion of **vowel harmony**, 'clear and cloudy' becomes equivalent to '*yang* and *yin*'.

CLEPSYDRA *nugak* 漏刻

Waterclocks are first recorded for Korea in Silla in 718. They were brought from China, where they were mentioned seven or eight centuries earlier in the **Confucian classic**, *Zhouli*. They seem always to have been public erections and needed periodic adjustment if they were to maintain accuracy. They were called *nuho, nujŏn, nusugi* and *nugak*. The pattern was a framework in which water overflowed through a line of vessels arranged in steps. Under the name of *kyŏngnu*, clepsydras were used especially for counting the **night hours**, when sundials could not be used.

CLOUDS AND RAIN *unu* 雲雨

The most popular Korean literary euphemism for sexual congress. It comes from a story in *Gaotang fu* (K. *Kodang-bu*), attributed to Song Yu who supposedly lived in the 4th-3rd centuries BC (but more probably a **Han dynasty** composition). This *fu* contains the story of a king who took a nap during the daytime and dreamt of a woman who came and shared his couch. She said she lived on the south side of Wu Mountain (K. *Musan*), in the morning as passing clouds, in the evening as passing rain. From this story 'clouds and rain' became a cliché for happy sexual intercourse.

COIN CHARMS *pyŏlchŏn* or *pyŏlton* 別錢

Charm, amulet and talisman are general terms of indistinguishable meaning, all applicable to the metal trinkets that were carried in purses or attached to the clothing of women and children during the Chosŏn dynasty. They were made of silver, bronze, white brass or, most commonly, yellow brass, and might be enamelled with up to three colours: red, yellow and blue. They were intended to bring good luck and to ward off evil, and sometimes used in informal **divination** games (when they were known as *pokchŏn* or *ohaeng-jŏn*). A charm was commonly shaped like a round coin 2·5 to 7·0 cm in diameter, often with a round or square central hole through which a cord or ribbon could be threaded. Others had a tiny ring cast on the edge. The 'coin' might be a simple disc or have a scalloped edge. There were also octagonal and hexagonal shapes, purse shapes, steelyard-weight shapes (*chŏul-ch'u*, quadrilateral with curved edges, the ends convex and the sides concave), shapes such as butterfly, **bat**, fish, **fan**, double-*sŏndong*, forms from the **eight treasures**, and other fancies. Both faces were decorated in relief or openwork with human figures, **flowers**, **birds**, **dragons**, **lunar mansion** constellation diagrams, **swastikas**, the **ten longevity symbols** or other auspicious designs. Auspicious Chinese characters were much used, especially the **five blessings** and other good-luck signs. A poetic couplet might have one line on each face. Several charms might be joined at the edges to form a flat plate. Decorative chatelaines (*yŏlsoe-p'ae* or *kaegŭm-p'ae*, both meaning 'key pendant') were made by mingling charms with coloured ribbons or by linking several charms to one with tiny rings looped into its edge.

FREDERICK STARR, 'Corean coin charms and amulets', *TKBRAS*, VIII, 1917; C. S. HUTCHINS, 'The Five Blessings and Korean Coin Charms', *KJ*, 17/2, 1977

COINAGE

The system of commodity exchange in traditional Korea was based on barter rather than purchase, and official salaries and **taxation** were basically calculated in grain or textiles. Coins minted in 996 (copper and **iron**), 1097 (copper), and 1102 (copper, known as *o*) all imitated the Chinese style of a circular piece of metal with a square central hole, bearing inscriptions such as *haedong t'ongbo*, 'coin from the [land to the] East of the Sea'). These coins had a limited circulation, even though an attempt was made to popularise them in 1102 by the opening of an official tavern in **Kaesŏng**. Small silver bottles shaped like the Korean peninsula, known as *hwalgu* or *ŭnbyŏng* ('silver bottle'), were first made in 1101 and used occasionally until 1331, perhaps more for purposes of investment or bribery than for monetary exchange. Paper money issued in China was used in Kaesŏng by traders dealing with **merchants** from the Middle Kingdom, and a home-made mulberry-bark paper money was used in the 15th century. A further issue of coinage in 1423 was short-lived. Social and commercial changes after the **Imjin Wars** led to the first rapid growth of monetary exchange and usury. The first minting of a successful issue of copper coinage (*sangp'yŏng t'ongbo* 'standard circulating treasure') came in 1678, and thereafter taxation was often commuted into cash payments as a monetary economy developed. It was not stable enough to meet the political and social stresses of the 19th century, however, and respect for the coinage suffered as inflation soared. Both Chinese and Japanese coins were used in Korea by foreign traders, and there was a return to payment in goods, such as quinine. In 1882 a new coinage was issued, *tang-ojŏn* ('five-cent piece'), but was replaced by another, Japanese-designed, in 1892. In 1894 the first major attempted currency reform took place (*see* **Kabo reforms**). Henceforth the system was to be based on silver, with coins of lower denominations in nickel, copper, bronze and brass. Taxation was to be payable in cash, despite the fact that its use had still not penetrated to many rural areas. Only the brass and nickel coins achieved wide circulation, and in 1905, on orders from the government's Japanese-nominated fiscal adviser, these were replaced by a new system of coinage minted by the Daiichi Ginkō Bank. The effect on many Korean businessmen was disastrous, some shutting up shop and others committing suicide.

E.J.MANCE, *Cast Coinage of Korea*, Racine, 1972; SUH RA-SA, 'Coins of Korea,' *AOA*, 2/6, 1972; WON YU-HAN, 'A Study on the Introduction of German Coinage Techniques to Korea,' *KJ*, 14/11, 1974

See also **banking**; **commerce**; **tribute**

COLONIAL PERIOD (1910–45) *Ilche sidae* 日帝時代

Period of Japanese occupation from the **annexation** in 1910 to Japan's defeat by the western allies in 1945. Though Korea was nominally integrated into the Japanese empire, its people did not receive equal treatment with ethnic Japanese, and lasting resentment built up over Koreans' loss of liberties, physical ill-treatment and economic exploitation. Many workers were sent to Japan, while the native population was adversely affected by the **immigration** of Japanese colonisers and the preferential treatment they received. Other Koreans emigrated voluntarily, mostly to **Manchuria**, Japan, **Siberia**, or China. During this time of political subjugation and attempted cultural absorption, Korean **nationalism** was kept alive, despite close supervision from the military police (see **police system, Japanese**) and heavy censorship, by the activities of numerous societies, **newspapers** and periodicals, guerilla armies (*Ŭibyŏng*), and encouragement from Koreans living abroad (*see* **emigration**; **Provisional Government in Exile**). Little interest was shown by foreign governments in Korean pleas for independence, though foreign missionaries (especially **Protestants**) showed their solidarity with Koreans and took part in the resistance movement. Politically, the expression of nationalism ranged from the extreme left-wing views of the **Korean Communist Party** through moderate socialism to the far right-wing policies associated with Korean leaders in exile such as Syngman Rhee (**Yi Sŭngman**). Culturally, it was seen in efforts to promote the use of the Korean language and script (*han'gŭl*) in defiance of Japanese policy, the growth of a new vernacular literature, the promotion of education (*see* **universities**), the formation of intellectual societies, the preservation of traditional Korean **music**, and the organisation of artistic and theatrical events.

Japanese rule was carried out by the **Government General** of Chōsen, as Korea was now officially renamed, and supreme authority vested in the hands of the Governor-General. The first decade of colonial government was marked by Japanese assumption of most positions of authority and responsibility in administration, business, industry, finance, law, and land ownership. Ruthless suppression took place of any Korean attempts to resist, with arrests, school and newspaper closures, and prohibition of meetings. Heavy **taxation**, the effects of the Land Survey (*see* **Land Reform**), the immigration of Japanese farmers, and the operations of Japanese-owned companies such as the **Oriental Development Company** all contributed to Korean subordination.

The second decade was marked by modest success for the Korean independence movement (*see* **March First Movement**). Now in a position of secured authority, Governor-General Admiral Saitō Makoto felt safe in countering the nationalist challenge by introducing a series of measures apparently relaxing some of the earlier anti-Korean discrimination and encouraging racial harmony. These included the learning of Korean language by some Japanese officials, improvements in Korean education, the abolition of Korean-Japanese wage differentials, the restoration of religious freedom, and the re-opening of newspapers. But the changes were not always implemented, and brought no appreciable improvement to Korean living conditions: Japanese secondary **schools**, for example, sometimes refused to accept Korean children as they were supposed to; and while the Japanese government took steps to increase agricultural productivity, mainly in **rice**, its purpose was to boost exports to Japan, and Korean **peasants** continued to sink further into miserable poverty.

The 1930s, when Japan had taken control of Manchuria and its military leaders were already looking forward to even greater continental domination, saw a greater threat from Korean resistance societies. In response came stronger Japanese determination to eradicate Korean cultural traditions and patriotic sentiment, and to emphasise the two peoples' unity with each other and their Manchurian neighbours through their common origins. Under wartime conditions at the end of the decade and in the early 1940s, Korean names were japanised (*see* **Name Creation Order**), the Japanese language alone was used in schools and universities, and children were required to worship at Shinto shrines (*see* **Shrine question**). Korean men were forced to work in Japanese factories and mines both at home and in other parts of the empire, or were drafted into the lowest ranks of the Japanese army and sent to war theatres. Women were forced into prostitution for members of the Japanese forces. The Japanese failed to provide the Koreans with training in modern political procedures, or to give enough of them bureaucratic training, which would have stood the country in good stead on the recovery of independence. In the 1930s fewer than half of all low level official posts were held by Koreans; at a senior level the figure was less than twenty per cent.

Some Koreans did nevertheless manage to exploit entrepreneurial opportunities, especially after Governor-General Saitō's Company Law of 1920 allowed them to develop small companies and a number of manufacturing industries. On the whole Koreans had little capital to invest in large scale industrialisation compared with giant Japanese corporations such as Mitsubishi and Matsui. Some, like the Kims from Chŏlla Namdo province who had owned the Kyŏngsŏng Spinning and Weaving Company (*Kyŏngbang*) since before annexation, trod a careful line between collaboration and support for nationalistic cultural and educational activities; others profited unashamedly from participation in large Japanese enterprises such as **railways**, aircraft, chemicals, petroleum, coal, etc.

Scholars, while resenting false claims that Japan had influenced the early development of the peninsula, nevertheless participated in excellent research undertaken by the Committee for Archaeological Investigation (*Chōsen Koseki Chōsa Iinkai*, established 1916); the Japanese also conducted the most efficient geological mapping ever done of the country. It has been argued that Japanese government systems, industrialisation and expansion of internal communications played an essential rôle in laying the foundations for the modernisation of the Korean economy in the post-war era. It has also been remarked that under colonial rule average Korean life expectancy rose, standards of public health improved, and educational facilities were expanded. These claims can be substantiated, but the cost of any progress during the colonial period was borne by the majority of the people.

GOVERNORS-GENERAL:

TERAUCHI Masatake	1910–6	UGAKI Kazushige	1931–6
HASEGAWA Yoshimichi	1916–9	MINAMI Jirō	1936–42
SAITŌ Makoto	1919–27	KOISO Kuniaki	1942–4
YAMANASHI Hanzō	1927–9	ABE Nobuyuki	1944–5
SAITŌ Makoto	1929–31		

KANG WI JO, *Religion and Politics in Korea under the Japanese Rule*, New York: Edwin Mellen Press, 1987; C.I. EUGENE KIM & D.E. MORTIMORE, *Korea's Response to Japan: the Colonial Period 1910-1915*, Kalamazoo: Western Michigan University, 1975; LEE CHUNG-SIK, *The Politics of Korean Nationalism*, Berkeley: University of California Press, 1965; DAE-YEOL KU, *Korea under Colonialism: the March First Movement and Anglo-Japanese Relations*, Seoul: Royal Asiatic Society Korean Branch, 1985; DENNIS McNAMARA, *The Colonial Origins of Korean Enterprise, 1910–45*, Cambridge University Press, 1990; RAMON MYERS & MARK PEATTIE, *The Japanese Colonial Empire, 1910–1945*, Princeton University Press, 1984; ANDREW NAHM, *Korea under Japanese Colonial Rule: Studies of the Policies and Techniques of Japanese Colonialism*, Kalamazoo: Western Michigan University, 1973; HYUNG IL PAI, 'The Politics of Korea's Past: The Legacy of Japanese Colonial Archaeology in the Korean Peninsula,' *EAH*, 7, 1994; KENNETH ROBINSON, *Cultural Nationalism in Colonial Korea, 1920–1925*, Seattle: University of Washington Press, 1988; SANG-CHUL SUH, *Growth and Structural Changes in the Korean Economy, 1910–1940*, Cambridge, Mass.: Harvard University Press, 1978; KENNETH WELLS, *New God, New Nation: Protestants and Self-reconstruction Nationalism in Korea, 1896–1937*, Sydney: Allen & Unwin, 1990

COLOURS OF COURT DRESS
In the reign of King **Muyŏl** (654–61), Silla adopted the Tang custom of indicating rank by the colour of court dress worn by officers of the **Six Boards**. Details changed over the centuries. In Chosŏn 3rd **grade** senior and above wore red; 3rd grade junior to 6th grade, blue; 7th to 9th grades and local *hyangni*, green.

COMMANDERIES *Han sagun* 漢四郡
Chinese military colonies established in **Manchuria** and northern Korea during the Former **Han dynasty** as a means of extending imperial control. They were ruled by Chinese officials from settlements built and developed as pockets of Chinese

civilisation. The most enduring was that of **Lelang**, which survived until 313. After assisting in the reunification of the peninsula in 668, **Tang** China unsuccessfully attempted to restore Chinese rule over the former lands of **Koguryŏ**, **Paekche** and even its erstwhile ally **Silla** by reviving the system (*see* **Kyerim**).

H. IKEUCHI, 'A Study of Lo-lang and Tai-fang, Ancient Chinese Prefectures in Korean Peninsula,' *MRDTB*, 5, 1930

See also **Canghai**; **Chinbŏn**; **Lintun**; **Xuantu**

COMMERCE

Bartered exchange took place between the peoples of North East Asia from the first millennium BC onwards, resulting in the spread of Chinese goods into the Korean peninsula and across the sea to the Japanese islands. The transmission of key commodities such as **bronze** and **iron** over wide distances assisted the cultural and economic growth of the country at an early date. **Glass** vessels of apparently foreign, perhaps Middle Eastern, origin have been found in tombs of the Silla period in **Kyŏngju**, while for the Unified Silla an Iranian glass bowl was excavated from the Great Hwangnam Tomb (*see* **tombs**). Korean seafarers controlled much of the shipping that plied the China Sea in the 9th century AD (*see* **Chang Pogo**).

In Koryŏ times periodic fairs were held in the capital and throughout the countryside, at which Koreans rubbed shoulders with numerous Chinese merchants. Private **merchants** conducted lucrative trade with China and Japan, the 11th century being a particularly profitable era when the export of Chinese celadon wares stimulated the expansion of the native industry (*see* **ceramics**). Excavation of a ship wrecked in this period has revealed that it was carrying 30,000 pieces of Koryŏ **celadon** from a **kiln** on modern Haenam Island, in south Chŏlla, bound for an unknown destination. Further material evidence of Korean participation in international commerce in the late mediaeval period may come from another wreck raised from the sea at **Sinan**, this time of a Chinese merchant ship sunk in 1323. Though its cargo was probably destined for Japan, the possibility of Korean involvement along this trade route cannot be ruled out. In addition to porcelain, Korean merchants shipped **textiles**, **ginseng**, and animal skins to Japan, and imported metals, minerals, medical and aromatic goods, and dyestuffs. Korean attempts to limit burgeoning trade with Japan to the ports of **Tongnae** (Pusan) and Ungch'ŏn (Naei) were unpopular. Korean coastal waters began to suffer from the activities of **pirates**, usually described as Japanese though some were certainly Chinese and perhaps others Korean. Some were based on **Tsushima** Island, which was attacked by a force led by the recently abdicated King T'aejong in 1419 (*see* **Kyehae Treaty**).

Despite all this, it was not until the 17th century that commerce began to play a significant part in the Korean socio-economy. The Korean literati inherited from China a Confucian antipathy towards trade, but the factors that most inhibited the growth of an active and powerful mercantile class were the ability of the small aristocratic élite in the capital to obtain its needs through the internal **tribute** system, the absence of an extensive communication network of canals and roads, and the inward-looking nature of local rural communities. In the early Chosŏn period, however, the government authorised the establishment in the capital of **six licensed shops** or **markets** with monopolies to trade in **silk**, cotton cloth, ramie, thread, **paper**, and maritime produce, as well as small shops and markets in **Kaesŏng** and P'yŏngyang. After the **Imjin Wars**, changes in the fiscal and economic systems encouraged the development of handicraft production and stimulated the beginnings of a proto-capitalist outlook which broadened commercial opportunities.

Korea's withdrawal from a leading rôle in inter-state affairs and distrust of foreign connections following the **Imjin Wars** and **Manchu invasions** led to an official ban on mercantile trade between Korea and China in the 17th century. The volume of unauthorised trade forced the government to grant official approval again in 1755, but a further ban was imposed in 1787. Commodities exchanged included Korean gold, ginseng, paper, wool and animal skins, and Chinese textiles, **jewellery**, timber, and **medicines**. Continued isolationism in the 19th century made the government unwilling to open Korea up either to trade or diplomacy, but gradually reactionary resistance crumbled, especially as merchants recognised the profits to be made from joining with foreigners in joint venture companies. In the aftermath of the **Sino-Japanese War** the bulk of overseas trade was with Japan, including especially the import of cotton cloth and the export of foodstuffs.

In the colonial period, Korean labour and resources were exploited in the Japanese interest, with most exports of foodstuffs and raw materials going to Japan and most imports coming thence as manufactured goods until the mid-1930s, when Japanese industrial investment in Korea led to a rise in manufactured output in the colony and an accompanying rise in exports to Japan

JUNG CHANG-YOUNG *et al.*, *Economic Life in Korea*, Seoul: Sisa Yongosa, 1982; RAMON H. MYERS & MARK R. PEATTIE, eds., *The Japanese Colonial Empire, 1895–1945*, Princeton University Press, 1984
See also **coinage**

COMMUNISM   *See* **Communist Youth League; Democratic People's Republic of Korea;** *Chuch'e*; **Kim Ilsŏng; Korean Communist Party; Korean War; Koryŏ Communist Party; Pak Hŏnyŏng; People's Assemblies; Yi Tonghwi**
SUH DAE-SOOK, *Korean Communism 1945–1980: A Reference Guide to the Political System*, Honolulu: University of Hawaii Press, 1981

COMMUNIST YOUTH LEAGUE *Chosŏn Ch'ŏngnyŏn Tongmaeng*
Founded in Seoul in January 1946 for men and women between 14 and 30. Its aim was the propagation of communist propaganda among the young, and their incitement to work for the reunification of the country under the leadership of **Kim Ilsŏng**. In 1964, in P'yŏngyang, it was renamed the Korean Socialist Working Youth League.

CONCUBINES *ch'ŏp* 妾
Better called secondary wives. The distinction between primary and secondary wives of *yangban* was legalised in 1413. Taking a secondary wife was a private matter, with no fixed wedding rite. She was a woman of lower social rank (commoner, *kisaeng* or **slave**) and was prohibited from ever rising to primary wife status. She had no legal property rights, and might be dismissed, especially if sonless. Her daughters would probably also become secondary wives. Tensions between primary and secondary wives were proverbial.
HAHM PYONG-CHOON, 'An Historical Study of Discriminatory Legislation against the Descendants of Concubines in Korea, 1415–1894,' *TKBRAS*, XLII, 1966
See also **illegitimate sons**

CONFUCIAN CLASSICS *kyŏng* 經
From the 15th to the 20th centuries Koreans studied Chinese classics before all else, usually in editions prepared and commented on by the great neo-Confucian **Zhu Xi** (K. Chu Hŭi, usually called Chuja, 1130–1200). Editions with Korean cribs were

common. The ordinary curriculum for boys, established by the Song dynasty sages (*see* **Five sages of Song**), was called *Sasŏ-samgyŏng* 'four books and three classics'. The four books were:

(1) *Lunyu* (K. *Nonŏ*), the Analects of Confucius, records conversations with his disciples: it was the best known book in Korea, providing rules for daily life as well as moral attitudes. The Analects introduce the earliest Confucian concepts, including human relationships as the basis of the theory of government, *chŏngmyŏng* (C. *zheng ming*) 'rectification of terms', *dao* 'the Way', Heaven and its mandate, *in* (C. *ren*) 'human goodness' or 'benevolence', and *hyo* (C. *xiao*) 'filial piety'.

(2) *Daxue* (K. *Taehak*), 'Great Learning', a brief treatise on the fundamentals of humanist ethics and government, much beloved by Korean scholars, for whom it was fundamental. It is in fact Chapter 42 of *Liji* ((8) below). It gives three aims for life: *myŏng-myŏng-dŏk* 'refining man's character', *ch'inmin* 'loving the people' and *chi-ŏ-chisŏn* 'striving for the highest goodness'. These are to be obtained by eight steps: *kyŏ'ngmul* investigating all things, *chiji* extending knowledge, *ŭisŏng* sincerity of will, *simjŏng* having a right mind, leading to *susin* personal cultivation, *kaje* regulating the family, *kukch'i* order in the nation and *ch'ŏnha-p'yŏng* peace under heaven.

(3) *Zhong yong* (K. *Chungyong*), 'Doctrine of the Mean', is another treatise, really Chapter 31 of *Liji* ((8) below), but of a more philosophical and even mystical nature. It develops the Confucian doctrine of *dao*, dealing with the unity of nature and man as well as the ideas of moderation and harmony.

(4) *Mengzi* (K. *Maengja*). 'Mencius', the teachings of Mengzi (372–289 BC), is the longest of the four books. It is composed mostly of teachings by the gentle Mencius given in the form of brief conversations with regional rulers during a period of great cruelty. With vivid images and anecdotes, it develops themes from the tradition of Confucius, introducing the idea of *ŭi* 'duty' or 'right behaviour' and the theory that man, though flawed, is fundamentally good.

The three classics, pre-Confucian in origin, were:

(5) *Yijing* (K. *Yŏkkyŏng*), the **Book of Changes**, in Korea usually called *Chuyŏk* (C. *Zhouyi*) 'Changes of Zhou', from its core document, the 64 hexagrams with their oracles. This was always printed with the appendixes called *Sib-i* (C. *Shiyi*) 'Ten Wings', written in the Warring States and Han periods. The whole text was considered a book of wisdom.

(6) *Shijing* (K. *Sigyŏng*) or *Shizhuan* (K. *Sijŏn*), the *Book of Odes*. In Korea it is often called *Mosi*, from a Han dynasty edition by one Mao Heng. It contains 305 ancient, but doubtless much edited, songs: 160 *guofeng* (K. *kukp'ung*), regional folksongs now believed to date from shortly before the time of Confucius (551–479 BC); the rather earlier 31 *daya* (K. *taea*) and 74 *xiaoya* (K. *soa*), more formal compositions; and the 40 even older ritual hymns called *song* (K. *song*) which may date from the end of the second millennium BC. In Korea they were always given a neo-Confucian moralistic interpretation.

(7) *Shujing, Shangshu* or *Shuzhuan* (K. *Sŏgyŏng, Sangsŏ, Sŏjŏn*), the *Book of Documents*, contains speeches and declarations attributed to early Chinese rulers down to the time of Zhou, but now believed to have been written largely in Eastern Zhou (771–221 BC).

For more advanced students the list was expanded to *Sasŏ-ogyŏng* 'four books and five classics'. The two additional classics were:

(8) *Liji* (K. *Yegi*), the *Record of Rites*, a Han dynasty collection, later believed to describe the rites as Confucius knew them. Its details about funeral ceremonies particularly engrossed Koreans.

(9) *Chunqiu* (K. *Ch'unch'u*), the *Spring and Autumn Annals*, the only book said to have been compiled by Confucius himself: a terse, bald chronology of his native state of Lu from 772 to 481 BC. It is always accompanied by three or four Chinese commentaries. Three are pre-Han: *Gongyang zhuan* (K. *Kongyang-jŏn*); *Guliang zhuan* (K. *Kongnyang-jŏn*); *Zuo zhuan* (K. *Chwajŏn*). *Hu Anguo zhuan* (K. *Ho-An'guk-chŏn*) is an 11th-century work used in imperial Ming editions. *Zuo zhuan* is the longest, containing generous and colourful passages of historical narrative that made it Korea's favourite history book. It was probably written in the 4th century BC.

Four other books were regarded as classics by the Song neo-Confucians: (10) *Yili* (K. *Ŭirye*) 'Ceremonies and Rituals' and (11) *Zhouli* (K. *Churye*) 'Rituals of Zhou', both similar in kind to *Liji*; (12) *Xiaojing* (K. *Hyogyŏng*) 'The **Filial Piety Classic**', a Han period essay on themes from *Liji*; and (13) *Erya* (K. *Ia*), a thesaurus of literary glosses, probably from the 3rd century BC.

EDOUARD BIOT, *Le Tcheou-li*, Paris, 1851; JAMES LEGGE, *The Chinese Classics* (5 volumes, 1892, often reprinted; *I Ching* (1882) and *Book of Rites* (1885). All are now outdated, but present the neo-Confucian interpretations accepted in pre-modern Korea); RICHARD RUTT, *The Book of Changes, Zhou Yi*, London: Curzon Press, 1997; JOHN STEELE, *The I-Li*, London, 1917; BURTON WATSON, *Early Chinese Literature*, New York, 1962; BURTON WATSON, *The Tsuo Chuan*, New York, 1989

CONFUCIANISM *Yuga* 儒家

Social and political philosophy imported from China based upon the study and interpretation of a canon of texts (*see* **Confucian Classics**) which profoundly influenced the life and thought of the literate Korean élite and was also absorbed, albeit perhaps unwittingly, by the lower classes in their attitudes and conduct of daily affairs. Together with **Buddhism**, Christianity and Communism it was one of the great ideological invasions experienced by the Korean people. Through the extension of basic human ties of filial piety into the realm of inter-state relations it emphasised the concept of *sadae* ('serving the great'), namely Korea's obligations towards China as a vassal state, but although it contributed substantially to the sinicisation of society and strengthened willing dependence on China politically and culturally, Koreans were nevertheless capable of taking independent action (*see* **China, relations with**; *Sirhak* **movement**) and their own principal belief system, **shamanism**, exerted a hold on all levels of society.

Confucianism was recognised in **Koguryŏ** and **Paekche** by the 4th century, with a Confucian academy established in the former in AD 372, but it can be assumed that the advantages of its orderly approach to state organisation and man-management had first been recognised by Koreans in the Chinese **commanderies**, especially **Lelang**. Its acceptance was indicated both physically and spiritually in the courts' imitation of Chinese-style **rites and ceremonies**, their use of Chinese official dress and sumptuary regulations, and their efforts to understand and practise the principles of the *Book of Rites* (C. *Liji*, K. *Yegi*). The Chinese court paid **Unified Silla** the honour of referring to it as *junzi zhi guo* ('country of gentlemen'), a phrase that had already been heard in earlier times in which the key term *junzi* 'gentleman', taken from the *Analects* of Confucius, recognized Korea's Confucian-ness.

Chinese script was the medium of written communication until and even after the invention of the Korean alphabet in the 15th century (*see* **han'gŭl**). Confucianism was spread through **education** (*see* **Sŏnggyun-gwan**; *T'aehak*), consolidated through the Chinese-style **examination system**, and perpetuated through the arts of literature,

calligraphy, and **painting**. It aided and guided the formation of state bureaucracy in the Three Kingdoms and the Unified Silla periods (*see* **government, central**) through its concepts of loyalty and hierarchical powers, rights and responsibilities. Similarly, it strengthened faith in social harmony by stressing class stratification, clan structure, the principles of duty, trustworthiness and diligence, and respect both for the living and the dead.

Korea produced no major Confucian philosophers of its own until the 14th century (*see* **Chŏng Mongju**; **Yi Saek**; **Yi Sungin**). While China was undergoing the searching re-evaluation of Confucian tradition in the **Song** and Yuan dynasties and formulating neo-Confucianism, Korea was experiencing a period of Buddhist and shamanist popularity at court during which Confucian apologists were sometimes in a minority. Nevertheless, although the founder of the Koryŏ dynasty, **Wang Kŏn**, had proclaimed that the success of the state depended on the favour of Buddha (*see* **Ten Injunctions**), his descendant King **Sŏngjong** issued his own equally firm injunction for the practice of filial piety as the basis of good government, and social structure and behaviour reflected Confucian principles even though the most popular rites and **festivals** were drawn from Buddhism and shamanism.

After the overthrow of the **Mongols** and the divisive end to the Koryŏ dynasty the new Chosŏn rulers were only too glad to restore *sadae* relations with China, and to re-emphasise Confucianism for its political as well as its social value. By now, **Zhu Xi** (K. Chuja)'s version of Confucianism (usually known in modern times as neo-Confucianism) was well on its way to representing orthodoxy in China and was firmly accepted as such in Korea. It put stress on the importance of *samgang oryun,* the **'three bonds and five relationships'** which were centred on the filial obligations of junior to senior members of the family and the state. It particularly underlined social rites (*ye*), rôles and values, including some of those, such as widow chastity, that had attained new emphasis in China and diminished **women**'s status in society. Ironically, the Confucian virtue of loyalty failed to eliminate but rather enhanced the prevalence of political **factions**. Distrustful of this but unable to shake completely free of it, Korea's greatest Confucian thinker, **Yi Hwang**, developed his own interpretation of neo-Confucian metaphysics that has continued to rouse pride among Korean nationalists to modern times.

As in China, 20th-century modernisation challenged the intellectual basis of Confucianism and overthrew many of its outward forms. However, significant vestiges of its attitudes towards people as individuals and as members of social and occupational groups persist. For example, many men and women, as well as children, still perform an annual kowtow to show respect for their parents, while labour relations in companies and factories stress Confucian values of loyalty, mutual responsibility and hard work, and have sometimes been credited with contributing to the rise in Korea's economic fortunes in the latter part of the century.

HAECHANG CHOUNG & HAN HYONG-JO, eds., *Confucian Philosophy in Korea*, Seongnam: The Academy of Korean Studies, 1996; WM. THEODORE DE BARY & JAHYOUN KI HABOUSH, eds., *The Rise of Neo-Confucianism in Korea*, New York: Columbia University Press, 1985; MARTINA DEUCHLER, *The Confucian Transformation of Korea*, Cambridge, Mass.: Harvard University Press, 1992; JOHN DUNCAN, 'Confucianism in the Late Koryŏ and Early Chosŏn,' *KS*, 18, 1994; GREGORY HENDERSON & KEY P. YANG, 'An Outline of Korean Confucianism I and II,' *JAS*, 17, 1958; GILBERT ROZMAN, ed., *The East Asian Region, Confucian Heritage and its Modern Adaptation*, Princeton University Press, 1991

CONFUCIUS, TEMPLE-NAME OF

In Korea Confucius (551–479 BC) is usually called Kongja (C. Kongzi) 'Kong the philosopher'. The posthumous honorific name inscribed on his tablet in a shrine reads *Taesŏng-jisŏng-munsŏnwang*. *Munsŏnwang* (C. *wenxuanwang*) 'illustrious prince of learning' was his first temple name, given by the Tang emperor Xuanzong in 739. *Chisŏng* (C. zhisheng) 'perfect sage', quoted from the panegyric of Confucius in *Zhong yong* 31, was prefixed by the Song emperor Zhenzong in 1012. *Taesŏng* (C. *dacheng*) 'great synthesizer' comes from an orchestral metaphor in *Mencius* Va.2.vi, where Confucius is said to have 'gathered together all that is good.' It was added in 1307, when the Yuan emperor gave the whole name the form that has been retained in Korea, though in China it was emended by Ming.

CONSTITUTION

(1) NORTH KOREA

The **Democratic People's Republic of Korea** (DPRK) adopted its first constitution in 1948. The Chairman was elected by and accountable to the Supreme People's Assembly (SPA) on a four-year basis without limitation of tenure. He was also commander of the armed forces and head of the National Defence Commission. His wide powers included the right to issue decrees on his own account and to ratify decisions of the SPA. Its 655 members were popularly elected from candidates approved by the Communist Party.

In 1972, the new Socialist Constitution was adopted at the first session of the 5th SPA on 27 December. It created the title of President for the head of state and freed him from accountability to the SPA. It also created a set of **People's Committees** parallel to the supreme and regional assemblies, headed by the Central People's Committee (CPC). This was much smaller than the SPA (14 members compared with 541) and constituted a policy-making cabinet of the central govenment superior to the executive Administrative Council. Again, local Committees were established in provinces, counties, cities and towns.

In practice, the powers of the Assemblies and the Committees were circumscribed by the **Korean Workers' Party** (KWP). As in the People's Republic of China, where the National Party Congress has greater real authority than the National People's Congress, so in the DPRK do representatives of the KWP infiltrate and direct all significant government business from the SPA and CPC downwards.

Between its meetings, SPA business is conducted by a Standing Committee, which also elects the Central People's Committee. The CPC directs the National Defence Commission: an amendment to the constitution in 1992 separated supreme military command from the presidency. In September 1998 the SPA abolished the presidency and awarded the title in perpetuity to the late Kim Ilsŏng. The constitution was renamed the Kim Ilsŏng Constitution, and the chairman of the National Defence Committee was once again identified as the head of state.

The constitution defines the limits of state, corporate and private property ownership, lays down systems for socialist management of **agriculture** and industry, and defines people's rights and obligations. Among the former are basic education and medical care. The state's ability to provide these, however, and their content and quality, has been variable according to political and economic circumstances. The people's obligations are based on the application of Marxism-Leninism and the state philosophy of *chuch'e* (socialist self-reliance), and emphasise citizens' collective responsibility to pursue the revolution and submit to collective aims. The judicial system is laid down, with judges of the Central Court and lower courts chosen by the

SPA and equivalent elected bodies at provincial, county and urban level. The constitution stresses the dictatorship of the proletariat and the need to maintain class struggle. It pledges the nation to attain the complete victory of socialism and to achieve the peaceful reunification of the country.

(2) SOUTH KOREA

The original constitution of the **Republic of Korea** (ROK) was adopted in 1948. It was succeeded by new versions in 1960, 1963, 1972, 1980, and 1987, and amended in 1952, 1954, and 1969, reflecting the difficult evolution in leadership concept from the autocratic Confucian style to that of a democratically elected and accountable executive, as well as the effects of continued military threat from the north. Despite the institution of an elected National Assembly in 1948 and the struggle, especially by **students**, to have the views of the people heard, South Korea has frequently been described as a dictatorship or military dictatorship until the presidency (1993–7) of **Kim Yŏngsam**. The communists were banned from the 1948 election. Under the new constitution the president was elected by an electoral college of the National Assembly. In 1952, following his party's drop in representation in that body, Syngman Rhee (**Yi Sŭngman**) decreed that presidential election should be by popular vote, which was rigged to ensure his re-election that year and again in 1956. Despite his enforced resignation in 1960 the system was reconfirmed then. Presidential elections were held in 1963 (October), 1967, and 1971 (April). They were abolished by Park Chung Hee (**Pak Chŏnghŭi**) in 1972 in favour of nomination by an electoral college, restored in 1987 and held again in 1992 and 1997. Meanwhile parliamentary elections were held in 1948, 1950, 1956, 1960, 1963 (November), 1967, 1971 (May), 1973, 1978, 1985, 1988, 1992, and 1996.

Successive presidents have treated the constitution with varying degrees of disregard, especially with regard to the implementation of guaranteed human rights, and prior to 1988 manipulated the National Assembly to serve their interests. Recognition of constitutional obligations began under President Roh Tae Woo (**No Taeu**) and continued under Kim Yŏngsam. The current constitution lays down the structure of central and local government; the rôle of the president as head of state and commander of the armed forces; the operation of the judiciary; the economic powers and duties of the government; the rights and duties of the people. The latter include freedom of movement, association, and speech, and the right to education, work, and collective action. Interests of national security may, however, override these and other rights and freedoms.

INSTITUTE OF NORTH KOREAN STUDIES, *North Korea's Criminal Law*, Seoul, 1991; C.I. EUGENE KIM & KIHL YOUNG WHAN, *Party Politics and Elections in Korea*, Silver Spring, Maryland: the Research Institute on Korean Affairs, 1976; DENNIS McNAMARA, 'State and Concentration in Korea's First Republic, 1948–60,' *MAS*, vol.26 no.4, 1992; PAK CHI YOUNG, 'The Third Republic Constitution of Korea: an Analysis,' *WPQ*, XXI no.1, 1968; SUNG CHUL YANG, *The North and South Korean Political Sytems: a Comparative Analysis*, Boulder, Colorado: Westview Press, 1994; YOON DAE-KYU, *Law and Political Authority in South Korea*, Boulder: Westview Press, 1990
See also **South Korea: constitutional changes**

COREA, ANTONIO

Reportedly the first Korean to live in Europe. He was taken to Japan as a **slave** during the Hideyoshi invasion and bought at Tokyo in 1597–8, together with four other Koreans, by Francesco Carletti, a Florentine merchant. Carletti had them baptised and freed them in Goa, but the one he called Antonio Corea continued with him to Italy, arriving in 1606. Nothing further is known of Antonio, save that he was living in Rome when Carletti wrote.

FRANCESCO CARLETTI, *Ragionamenti del mio viaggio intorno al mondo*, translated by HERBERT WEINSTOCK as *My voyage round the world*, New York, 1964

CORFE, CHARLES JOHN 高要翰 (1843–1921)

A chaplain in the Royal Navy and friend of Queen Victoria's son, Alfred, Duke of Edinburgh, Corfe was ordained 'Bishop in Corea' (it being thought inappropriate for the Queen of England to create a bishopric 'of' another sovereign state) in Westminster Abbey on 1 November 1889. Within a year the province of Shengjing (Liaoning) in **Manchuria** was added to his care. He established the lasting High Church discipline of Korean Anglicanism, telling his staff there should be no baptism of converts for seven years, after which the missionaries should have become competent in the Korean language. In 1901 he personally and anonymously endowed a new diocese of Shandong, so that Shengjing could be detached from the Korean diocese. Always short of men and money, deeply fatigued, and anxious about what he foresaw of Japan's intentions in Korea, he retired in 1904. He then worked as an assistant in a London parish (Kennington) until his last illness; but between 1906 and 1912 he did a year of service in Beijing and three shorter terms in Dalian and Yingkou.

See also **Anglicans**

CORVÉE puyŏk 賦役

Periods of regular labour service owed to the state by men within certain age limits. Together with **taxation** and **military service** they constituted an onerous burden on working class families, especially when those with more influence evaded their obligations and increased the demands on those who were drafted. Some were even forced to abandon their farms to escape excessive *corvée* requirements, and groups of such homeless peasants sometimes took to banditry or even, as in the late 12th century, to revolt.

The system was already practised in the **Samhan** and throughout the Three Kingdoms period and continued through all succeeding dynasties. In early Chosŏn the statutory obligation was for six days *per annum* from males of the *sangmin* class (*see* **class system**) aged between sixteen and sixty, though this was frequently exceeded. The *yangban* were exempt, as were those attached to schools (*sŏwŏn*) and Buddhist temples. Duties included craft manufacture (*see* **craftsmen**), irrigation work, land clearance, mining, building **fortresses** and palaces, services on roads and canals, and labouring for the aristocracy or local officials. By the end of the 15th century the combined demands of military and *corvée* service were impossible for many families to meet, and so many people bought commutation that the system no longer operated effectively. In 1609 it was superseded by the introduction of the *Taedongpŏp* Unified Tax.

COUNTING RODS *sankaji* or *sutkaji*

A Chinese method of counting dating from the 3rd or 2nd millennium BC, which survived in Korean government offices until about AD 1920. Short rods of bone or **bamboo** were laid in squares marked on a graticulated board. For units, hundreds and tens of thousands, rods were set vertically in the appropriate number for 1, 2, 3 and 4. A horizontally placed rod stood for 5, to which vertical rods were added for 6, 7, 8 and 9. For tens and thousands 1 to 4 were set horizontally and 5 vertically. Thus

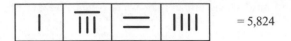

= 5,824

Hamel in the 17th century saw no other form of calculator in use. By the end of the 19th century the use of the abacus was widespread.

COURANT, ROBERT (1865–1925)

Courant studied Chinese in Paris before joining the French Diplomatic Service. He spent two years (1890–1892) in the Seoul Legation, where, helped by Bishop Mutel, he began work on his epochal *Bibliographie Coréenne*, which was published in 1894 after he had visited libraries in China, Japan, America and Europe.

CRAFTSMEN

The award of official ranks to craftsmen in the Three Kingdoms period suggests that the most skilful received recognition for the high degree of artistry that is still visible in the **gold crowns** and **jewellery** found in royal **tombs**, and the social status of the artist was higher than that of common people. In **Paekche** they were known as *changdŏk*, equivalent to official level 7 of **grade** 16, and in **Silla** as *chema*, level 10 of grade 17. The range and quality of their work in the Unified Silla period is exemplified by finds from **Anap-chi** and by surviving examples of fine stone and metal **sculpture**. It is suggested too by the taste for Korean **paper** and ink among the literati in **Tang** China, and the varied list of craft products among the **tribute** sent to China from the courts in **Kyŏngju** and **Kaesŏng**. Nevertheless the adoption of the Chinese **class system** by the Koryŏ court led to a downgrading in the status of all manual workers, despite the court's appreciation of products such as fine **celadon**. Both Koryŏ and Chosŏn governments supervised the manufacture of high quality goods and exercised authority over craftsmen in official workshops in the capital or provincial towns, sometimes as contribution to *corvée* duties. 129 workshops are recorded in Seoul in the early Chosŏn, employing over 2,800 men, and another 27 outside the capital employing more than 3,600. In this way the state was ensured an adequate supply of weaponry, **armour**, carriages, porcelain, **roof tiles**, **textiles**, writing equipment, **furniture**, and goods required in and around the palaces. But the still greater numbers of people employed in making goods to supply homes outside the court are suggested by the importance to the state of the tribute tax (*t'ogong*) and by accounts of hundreds of potters being taken prisoner by Toyotomi Hideyoshi in the **Imjin Wars**. After the wars, the rebuilding that was necessary provided work for many craftsmen. In the 17th century the passing of the Uniform Tax Law (*see Taedongpŏp*) all but removed the obligation for craftsmen to hand their products over to local officials and stimulated commercial demand and supply, first of all through the government's purchasing agents (*kongin*, 'tribute men') and later through the appearance of capitalistic **merchants** (*see* **markets**). Craft guilds were established (*see kye*).

CREMATION *hwajang* 火葬

Cremation of corpses, originally an Indian custom and considered Buddhist, is first recorded from the time of King **Munmu** of Silla (r. 661–681). Although the practice became normative for monks, it has never been popular for others. With the secularisation of the 20th century, however, there has been an increase in the practice.

CROWNS *See* **Gold crowns**

CURFEW *injŏng* or *in'gyŏng* 人定
Saving emergencies, no one but the highest government officials (with their attendants) was allowed to be abroad in city streets during the hours of darkness. The great **bell** of the city (at *Posin-gak* in Seoul) was struck 28 times (for the 28 **lunar mansions**) when the city gates were closed in the evening at the second **watch**, and 33 times (for the **Thirty-three Heavens**) when the gates were opened at the third *chŏm* of the 5th watch. The dawn signal was called *p'aru* 'stopping dripping [of the clepsydra]'. **Drums** and gongs were used for the signals. In late Chosŏn well-born ladies, who were not allowed to appear in the streets during the daytime, could emerge during the first hour of the curfew, accompanied by their servants. The precise times varied slightly with the time of year.

From 1945 to 1982 the South Korean government imposed a curfew between the hours of midnight and 4 a.m as a security measure.

CURRENCY *See* **coinage**

CYCLICAL CHARACTERS 甲子 *See Kapcha*

D

DAGELET ISLAND *See* **Ullŭng-do**

DAIFANG 帶方郡 *See* **Chinbŏn**

DALLET, CLAUDE CHARLES (1829–87)
Born at Langres, Dallet entered the Paris Foreign Missions Society and worked in Canada before returning to Paris, where from 1872 to 1874 he worked on Bishop **Daveluy**'s documents in writing his *Histoire de l'Eglise de Corée* (1874). This is an important source for the early history of Catholicism in Korea, with a long introductory section on the history and culture of the country that is still of great interest. Dallet subsequently travelled to the Society's Asian missions and died of sickness in Saigon.
See also **Roman Catholic Church**

DANCE
Dance was an essential component of much musical performance in both China and Korea. Early evidence for dance in Korea comes from paintings on the walls of **tombs** in former **Koguryŏ** and **Lelang**, and from literary references to Korean dances performed at the **Sui** and **Tang** courts in China. At the Korean court both native dances (*hyangak chŏngjae*) and Chinese dances (*tangak chŏngjae*) were performed as accompaniment to ceremonial and entertainment **rites**. They were performed by teams and single artists, boy dancers being called *mudong* and girls *yŏak*. The *tangak* repertoire ranged from the slow, measured movements on the spot which accompanied Confucian sacrificial rites (*see* **aak**), to carefully choreographed dance games imported from China. *Hyangak chŏngjae* reflected more of the exuberant, uninhibited folk dances of the countryside (*see* **music**; *nongak*), and also included dances of Buddhist origin. An exorcist link may connect the gyrations of the **shaman**'s rites and the original purpose of some forms of **masked dance**, both of which were performed at court in the Koryŏ dynasty. In the Chosŏn dynasty, when

court ceremonial was reformed and purified, strict Confucian protocol governed all aspects of the official dance repertoire and performance, including the choice of music and text appropriate to particular events, the specification of accompanying ensembles, selection and training of male and female dancers, and their dress and props. Extant information comes from the *Akhak kwebŏm* and subsequent encyclopedias, *ŭigwe* texts, and detailed pictures of ceremonies (*kungjung haengsado*) painted on screens from the 17th century onwards. Nevertheless, shamanic influences were not entirely driven out, and the literati continued to be entertained by performances of the *Ch'ŏyong* dance.

Choreographed court dances still performed which have ancient origins include *kŏmgimu*, a sword dance, and two dances of the Koryŏ dynasty, the ball-throwing dance *p'ogurak* and the drum dance *mugo*. Buddhist dances which have achieved modern popularity because of their dramatic qualities include the monk's dance (*sŭngmu*), the butterfly dance (*nabich'um*), the cymbal dance (*parach'um*), the nine-drum dance (*kugomu*), and the dance of the fish (*kogich'um*). One of the most beautiful dances in the repertoire of the modern classical performer is the Spring Nightingale Dance (*ch'unaeng-jŏn*), a solo piece of the utmost elegance and serenity. Dancers wore highly coloured and attractive costumes, often with long sleeves stretching well below the hands, sleeves which they manipulated with skilfully controlled movements.

ALAN HEYMAN, *Dances of the Three-Thousand-League Land*, Seoul: Dong-A Ltd, 1966; CHUNG BYUNG HO, 'The Characteristics of Korean Traditional Dance', *KJ*, 37/3, 1997; ELEANOR KING, 'Reflections on Korean Dance,' *KJ*, 17/8, 1977; PARK JEONGHYE, 'The Court Music and Dance in the Royal Banquet Paintings of the Chosŏn Dynasty, *KJ*, 37/3, 1997
See also **kisaeng**

DAOISM (Taoism) *togyo* 道教
The word 'Daoist' is used in three ways.

(1) 'Daoist' works of pre-Han Chinese philosophy (*Zhuangzi*, *Laozi*, and *Liezi*) have been known in Korea at least since the Koryŏ period, but since 1392 have been regarded as dissident, often mentioned only to be refuted. A moveable metal type edition of *Laozi*, *Noja-jiphae*, was printed about 1600. The rare Korean editions of *Zhuangzi* are usually called *Namhwa-jin'gyŏng*, from Zhuangzi's sobriquet, Nanhua.

(2) Daoism as an organised religion began in China during the 2nd century AD, but was not widely established until the middle of the 6th. A hundred years later King Yŏngnyu of Koguryŏ received Daoist missionaries from Tang in 624. They had some success, but in 643 more teachers and books were requested from Tang. Daoism may then have been more successful, because in 650 the monk Podŏk withdrew to the mountains in protest against the favour shown to it. Attempts to establish it in Koryŏ never reached beyond a restricted band of the élite and were frustrated by the Buddhists. Sogyŏk-sŏ, a minor *maŭl* (**government organ**) for Daoist matters existed in early Chosŏn. **Yi Nŭnghwa** collected historical materials in *Han'guk togyo-sa*, but the whole story remains obscure; Daoism never flourished, and after 1600 was repressed by the neo-Confucian state.

(3) 'Daoist' is often used loosely for anything in Korean culture that is not clearly Buddhist or Confucian, especially in art history or popular belief. Care is needed about this use of the word. Many pre-Han ideas were adopted by Daoism and thus appear to be Daoist; but paper charms (*pujŏk*) and other popular symbols and practices really belong to **shamanism**, though they are possibly influenced by Daoism; while **trigrams**, *t'aegŭk*, *ŭm-yang* theory and other ideas are older than Daoism in China

and came to prominence in Korea as neo-Confucian teachings. In China, too, *fengshui* (K. *p'ungsu*) is older than Daoism. Yet three themes in Chosŏn dynasty culture are truly Daoist: deified star names, **immortals** and *tan*, the pill of immortality. The last two were staples in popular Korean fiction, derived from Chinese fiction of Tang times and later, though with no religious significance.

In general it is wise to be cautious in speaking of 'Daoist' elements in Korean culture without defining one's use of the term, and not to identify things as Daoist if they are older than the 6th century AD in China.

DATES, CONCORDANCE OF LUNAR AND SOLAR

Since the lunar year starts between 20 January and 20 February of the solar year, the years in the two systems are not concurrent. Korean historians customarily number a lunar year with the AD date of the solar year that covers most of the same period. Thus they use 1852 for the lunar year that actually ran from 20 February 1852 to 3 January 1853. Western historians prefer to use the correct Gregorian year date, which for the 1st, 2nd, 11th and 12th lunar month can be discovered only by using a Chinese perpetual calendar and concordance.

King **Kojong**, for example, came to the throne on the 8th day of the 12th moon of the year Kyehae, most of which fell in 1863. Korean historians give his accession year as 1863; but since the solar date was actually 16 January 1864, Western historians give his accession year as 1864. If the days involved were not known, but precision were required, the year could be given as 1863–64.

See also **Lunar mansions; Ming loyalists, dating by;** *Kapcha*; **Solar terms**

DATES OF KINGS

In neo-Confucian dating, Year 1 of a king's reign begins on the first lunar **New Year's Day** after his accession. (For the earlier Korean system see *Tongguk t'onggam.*) Thus **Chŏngjo** came to the throne on the 10th of the 3rd moon of the year Pyŏngsin (27 April 1776) in the 51st year of his predecessor, **Yŏngjo**. The year called Chŏngjo 1 did not begin until New Year's day of the year Chŏngyu (8 February 1776), and the first ten months of Chŏngjo's reign are counted in Yŏngjo 51. Injong, however, acceded on the 20th of the 11th moon of Kapsin (4 December 1544), and New Year's Day of Ŭlsa (13 January 1545) came only six weeks later. He died on the 1st of the 7th moon (7 August 1545), having ruled for only eight months. The year Ŭlsa is nevertheless known as Injong 1.

When a king died before the end of the lunar year in which he came to the throne, one regnal year was intercalated for him, the period from his accession to the end of the year being counted as Year 1 of his reign. Thus King Sunjong of Koryŏ succeeded his father, Munjong, in the 7th moon of Munjong 37 (Kyehae 1083); but Sunjong died in the 10th moon and was succeeded by his brother, Sŏnjong. The Year Munjong 37 is counted as ending in the 7th moon of Kyehae and the six months from the 7th moon to the end of the year are counted as Sunjong Year 1. Sŏnjong 1 begins on New Year's Day of Kapcha (1084).

There were exceptions to these rules. Year 1 of the first king of a new dynasty began on the day of his accession. The 1st year of **Wang Kŏn** as King T'aejo of Koryŏ began on 25 July 918 and lasted only six months until the lunar new year of 4 February 919. In the same way year 1 of **Yi Sŏnggye** as King T'aejo of Chosŏn ran from 8 August 1392 to 12 February 1393.

After the *Kabo* reforms, years were numbered from the foundation (*Kaeguk*) of the Chosŏn dynasty, counting 1392 as the first year. Thus 1894 was called 'Kaeguk 503',

but the Kaeguk sequence was abandoned when the Empire was declared and from 1897 (Kaeguk 506) the **reign title** (Kwangmu) was used.
See also **Dates**; **concidence**; *Kapcha*

DAVELUY, MARIE-NICOLAS-ANTOINE, SAINT 安敦伊 (1818–66)

Daveluy, travelling through Macao and Shanghai, entered Korea at Kanggyŏng with **Kim Taegŏn** and Bishop **Ferréol** in 1845. He was the most scholarly of the early mission priests, had Christian books printed and worked at a Korean-Chinese-French dictionary. His collection of materials on the history of the Korean Church was the basis of **Dallet**'s work. In 1857 **Berneux** consecrated him as coadjutor bishop and after Berneux's death on 8 March 1866, Daveluy was for 22 days the 5th Bishop of the Korean vicariate-general. Arrested at Naep'o in South Ch'ungch'ŏng, he was executed at Poryŏng on 30 March 1866.

DECLARATION OF INDEPENDENCE *See* **Independence, Declaration of**

DEER

The deer that appear in painting as emblems of wealth, because the words for deer and emoluments are homonyms (K. *nok*, C. *lu*), and in poetry as symbols of gentleness, are the spotted Manchurian sika (*Cervus nippon*). They are also regarded as symbols of **longevity**, because of their association in decorative art with pine trees and *yŏngji* 'longevity fungus' (probably *Ganoderma lucidum*, wavy-edged and purplish-black, growing on tree roots). The larger *korani* Red Deer (*Cervus elaphus*) lives only in the furthest north. The proverbially shy roe (*noru*; *Capreolus capreolus*), the hornless 'Chinese' water-deer (*pon-noru*; *Hydropotes inermis*) and the little musk-deer (*sahyang-noru*; *Moschatus moschiferus*) are all colloquially called *noru*. Musk was once marketed. Hunters lured deer by playing a bamboo flute.

DEMOCRATIC LIBERAL PARTY *Chayu Minju-dang* 自由民主黨

In December 1987 Roh Tae Woo (**No Taeu**) (Democratic Justice Party) was elected President, but the clamour to clean up South Korean politics intensified after the Seoul **Olympic Games** in October 1988, and Roh was forced to agree a pact with his main opponents, **Kim Yŏngsam** (Reunification Democratic Party) and **Kim Chongp'il** (New Democratic Republican Party). Their coalition formed the Democratic Liberal Party in 1990. In March 1992 it narrowly failed to win an overall majority in the National Assembly, but in December Kim Yŏngsam was elected President. In 1996 the party was renamed the New Korea Party.
See also **Sixth Republic**

DEMOCRATIC NATIONALIST PARTY *Minju Kungmin-dang* 民主國民黨

Founded in February 1949 from the merging of the **Korea Democratic Party** (*Han'guk Minjudang*) and other opposition parties in the wake of Syngman Rhee (**Yi Sŭngman**)'s manipulation of the 1948 elections. Under Yi Siyŏng, followed by **Kim Sŏngsu**, it formed the principal opposition party to the Liberal Party, but achieved little success in National Assembly or presidential elections. Yi resigned as vice-president in 1951 and Kim in 1952, both in protest against Rhee's repressive measures and apparent scorn for the **constitution**. In 1954 the Party won just 15 of the 203 seats. In 1955 it formed an alliance with independents and became the **Democratic Party**.
CHI-YOUNG PAK, *Political Opposition in Korea 1945–1960*, Seoul National University Press, 1980

DEMOCRATIC PARTY Minju-dang 民主黨

Party formed in 1955 as the principal opposition to President Syngman Rhee (Yi Sŭngman)'s Liberal Party. It fared well in the 1956 presidential election, its candidate for the vice presidency, Chang Myŏn, being elected but awarded no powers by Rhee. In the 1958 National Assembly elections it won 49 seats, against the Liberal Party's 126. In the 1960 elections it won 31 of the 58 seats in the Upper House of the National Assembly and 175 of the 233 in the Lower House, and saw its candidates Yun Posŏn and Chang Myŏn elected President and Prime Minister respectively. But internal disagreements split the party and ruined its success (see Second Republic), some of its members breaking away to found the New Democratic Party.

CHI-YOUNG PAK, Political Opposition in Korea 1945–1960, Seoul National University Press, 1980

DEMOCRATIC PEOPLE'S REPUBLIC OF KOREA (DPRK) Chosŏn Minjujui Inmin Konghwaguk 朝鮮民主主義人民共和國

The Democratic People's Republic of Korea, popularly known as North Korea, formally came into existence on 9 September 1948. On that day, Kim Ilsŏng, who had been head of the government in the Soviet-controlled northern half of the Korean peninsula since 1945, proclaimed the establishment of the new state, declaring that the government of the DPRK represented the entire Korean nation. The DPRK emerged from the confused situation following the Japanese surrender and the establishment of the Korean People's Republic and people's committees throughout the country. The American Military Government in the South refused to recognise these groups, but the Soviet forces in the North worked with them, while at the same time placing their own appointees, including Kim, in important positions. By the spring of 1946 Kim, leader of the North Korean Communist Party since December 1945, was well established on the path which would lead him to supreme control.

When attempts at re-unification failed (see US Soviet Joint Commission), the stage was set for the emergence of separate régimes in the two halves of Korea. The Soviet Union helped Kim to build up large military forces, and in 1950 encouraged him to try to settle the unification by force (see Korean War). The attempt almost succeeded, but the intervention of the United States and the United Nations Organisation halted the DPRK's spectacular advance at the Naktong River near Pusan, and began a counter-offensive which by late October 1950 had taken them to the Yalu River and the border with China. At this point, the Chinese intervened and drove the UN forces back south of the Thirty-Eighth Parallel. Although the war continued until an armistice agreement was signed in July 1953, the battlefront had effectively been stabilised by April 1951, roughly where it had begun (see also DMZ).

Although there seems little doubt that it was Kim Ilsŏng who had begun the war, he emerged from it unscathed, and was able to purge many of his opponents (see Pak Hŏnyŏng). Thereafter, he ruled the DPRK without challenge. An extensive programme of post-war reconstruction began, with much Soviet, East European and Chinese assistance, which turned the DPRK into Asia's second industrialised country (Japan was the first) by the early 1960s. The Sino-Soviet dispute created problems for the DPRK, but by judicious shifts, Kim was able to play the two major powers off against each other, while at the same time, party theoreticians evolved the chuch'e or 'self-reliance' philosophy. This in effect allowed the DPRK to accept assistance while maintaining its spiritual independence. Nevertheless, by the late 1960s the DPRK's economy, though still ahead of the Republic of Korea (ROK)'s, was beginning to falter, as a series of plans after 1961 failed to achieve their aims.

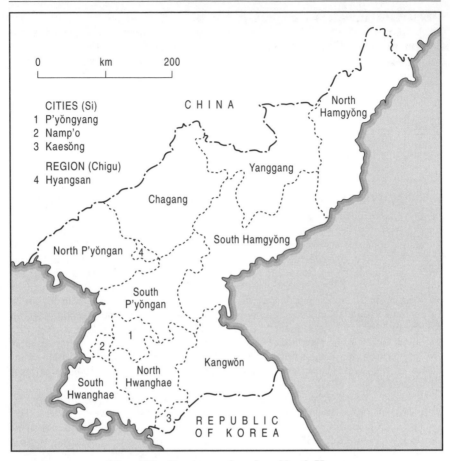

Map 4 The Provinces of modern North Korea

In the political sphere, the DPRK remained firmly under Kim Ilsŏng's control. A constitutional amendment in 1972 transferred executive power from the premier to the president, and Kim Ilsŏng took on this rôle, while remaining secretary-general of the **Korean Workers' Party**. By this stage, Kim was increasingly concerned about the succession; and the appointment of his son, **Kim Chŏngil**, to a series of important posts paved the way for his emergence as the designated successor in the early 1980s. However, it was during this decade that the DPRK steadily lost ground to the ROK, as the former's traditional allies established economic links and eventually diplomatic relations with the ROK. With this loss of international support, the DPRK agreed to joint membership of the United Nations in September 1991, a move which it had hitherto strongly resisted. At the same time, suspicion that the DPRK was developing a nuclear weapons programme led to direct US-DPRK negotiations, culminating in an agreement in 1994 (the Agreed Framework), under which the DPRK abandoned its existing nuclear programme in return for a new nuclear system based on Light Water Reactors, and a series of diplomatic concessions (*see* **North Korean Nuclear Programme**).

The two Koreas had been edging towards closer contact, and in July 1994 were on the point of holding the first ever summit meeting between their two heads of state. At this point, however, Kim Ilsŏng died, and was succeeded in practice, if not in title, by Kim Chŏngil. The ROK president, **Kim Yŏngsam**, declined to send condolences and his government took active measures to suppress any signs of mourning in the ROK. The DPRK showed offence at this attitude and most North-South contacts ceased. A series of natural disasters between 1995 and 1997 badly hit the DPRK's economy, adding to difficulties caused by the collapse of the Soviet Union and the end of the Comecon system, and eventually led P'yŏngyang to appeal for international humanitarian aid. Such aid was forthcoming, both from the West and the ROK, but the DPRK found it difficult to cope with the demands for access and information which tended to be part of western aid relief. Despite many predictions to the contrary, its political structure seemed to remain intact.

Towards the end of 1998 a possible way round the international *impasse* was indicated during a visit to P'yŏngyang by a South Korean 'merchant' (prompting analogies with a mission to Kaesŏng by a Chinese merchant, Huang Zhen, which had thawed frozen Sino-Korean relations in 1069). On 30 October the head of the Hyundai *chaebŏl*, Chŏng Monghun, was received by Kim Chŏngil and it was agreed, (1) to develop Kŭmgang-san (*see* **Diamond Mountains**) for South Korean tourism; (2) to export North Korean oil to South Korea by pipeline following joint undersea exploration off the west coast; (3) to develop an industrial base on the west coast of North Korea over 10 years; (4) to establish a motor assembly plant in North Korea.

CHONG BONG-OK, *A Handbook of North Korea*, Seoul: Naewoo Press, 1996; JOSEPH CHUNG, *The North Korean Economy: Structure and Development*, Stanford: Hoover Institution Press, 1972; KIM YOUN-SOO, ed., *The Economy of the Korean Democratic People's Republic, 1945–77*, Kiel: German-Korea Studies Group, 1979; LEE MUN WOONG, *Rural North Korea under Communism: A Study of Sociocultural Change*, Houston: Rice University, 1976; DON OBERDORFER, *The Two Koreas*, London: Little, Brown and Co., 1998, ANDREA SAVADA, ed., *North Korea: a Country Study*, Washington D.C.: Federal Research Division, Library of Congress, 1994, SUH DAE-SOOK, *Kim Il-sung: The North Korean Leader*, New York: Columbia University Press, 1995; NAM KOON WOO, *The North Korean Communist Leadership, 1945–1965. A Study of Factionalism and Political Consolidation*, University of Alabama Press, 1974
See also **Constitution; Government, central; Hŏ Hŏn**

DEMOCRATIC REPUBLICAN PARTY *Minju Konghwa-dang* 民主共和黨
One of the first parties to be established in 1963 following the lifting of martial law by Park Chung Hee (**Pak Chŏnghŭi**), under his leadership and that of **Kim Chŏngp'il**. It became the ruling party when Park won the presidential election in October and the following month obtained 110 National Assembly seats. In 1969 it supported Park's amendment to the **constitution** permitting an extension to his presidency. In 1978 it lost its majority in the National Assembly to the **New Democratic Party**. Following the assassination of the President in 1979 it became virtually defunct, apart from an unsuccessful attempt at revival by Kim Chŏngp'il in 1987.

DIALECTS 方言
The Korean language has true regional dialects, that is to say, varieties in which the use of grammar and vocabulary identifies the regional background of the user. Regional accents have approximately the same distribution as the dialects and produce typical reactions of amusement or distaste in speakers with other accents. Regional dialects attracted the notice of several *sirhak* writers, such as **Hong Yangho**, in the 18th and

19th centuries, but the first systematic study was published by Ogura Shimpei (1882–1944) in *Chōsen'go Hogen no Kenkyū* (1944). Much further work has been done by Korean scholars and, though there is no firm agreement about the division and naming of the dialects, it is generally agreed that they belong to the main historically defined cultural areas. These shade into one another. The map can nevertheless be broadly sketched: (1) central dialect (the basis of modern standard Korean) in Kyŏnggi, Ch'ungch'ŏng, Kangwŏn, Hwanghae, and part of North Chŏlla; (2) north-east (or Hamgyŏng) dialect in the Hamgyŏng provinces north of Anp'yŏnggun; (3) north-west (or Kwansŏ) dialect in the P'yŏng'an provinces; (4) south-east (or Kyŏngsang) dialect in both Kyŏngsang provinces and the borders of Chŏlla and Ch'ungch'ŏng; (5) south-west (or Chŏlla) dialect in the Chŏllas and parts of South Ch'ungch'ŏng; and (6) **Cheju** (T'amna or Quelpart) dialect, which alone can be unintelligible to speakers of the others. As in other countries, increased social mobility and the growth of national broadcasting now tend to destroy regional dialects.
See also **palace dialect; provinces**

DIAMOND MOUNTAINS *Kŭmgang-san* 金剛山
Korea's most famous scenic district, 160 km² in area and 80 km in circumference, in the main mountain range of the peninsula. It lies between 38·35° and 38·40°N and 128·12° and 128·20°E in Hoeyang-gun and Kosŏng-gun, Kangwŏn province, and has been under communist rule since 1945. South Korean tourists were first admitted in 1998. Biotite granite formations and luxurious vegetation give the region a unique beauty that was renowned in China before the 14th century and in Korea since Silla times. Beloved of travellers, hermits, poets and artists, its scenery prompted analogies with paradise and the dwelling places of the Daoist **Immortals**. 'Diamond' means the Buddhist *kŭmgang* (S. *vajra*), a thunderbolt-sceptre, indestructible as a diamond, that represents the power of the doctrine of emptiness (S. *sunyata*) to destroy all illusion. Like its alternative, *Yŏlban-san* 'Nirvana mountains', the name refers to the many monasteries there, and draws attention to the similarity between the myriad vertical peaks and the shape of the Buddhist thunderbolt.

The western side of the main ridge is called Nae-Gŭmgang, the 'inner' range. Among its peaks are Ch'ŏnghak-pong 'blue crane peak', Paegun-bong 'white cloud peak', and Piro-bong 'Vairocana peak', the highest among the Diamond Mountains. Equally famous are the valleys, Manp'ok-tong 'myriad waterfalls valley' and Paekch'ŏn-dong 'thousand streams valley', Myŏnggyŏng-dae 'bright mirror terrace', and Sambur-am 'three Buddhas rock'. Changan-sa 'monastery of eternal peace', P'yohun-sa 'monastery of universal teaching' and Chŏngyang-sa 'true sunlight monastery' are the principal monasteries. Oe-Gŭmgang, the 'outer' or eastern side is less spectacular, but includes Ongnyu-gye 'jade-flow valley', Kuryong-yŏn 'nine dragons pool' and Sin'gye-sa 'spirit brook monastery'. South of these is Sin'gŭmgang 'new diamond mountains' with Songnim-sa 'pinewoods monastery' and Sibi-p'ok 'the twelve cascades'. Haegŭmgang, the 'sea' range, is an outcrop in the Eastern Sea.

Most Korean writers hymned the Diamond Mountains in prose or verse. **Chŏng Sŏn** painted them many times, and is said to have condensed all twelve thousand peaks onto a single eight-panel **screen**. Pictures of the '12,000 peaks' are favourites for screens, **fans** and scrolls, often illustrating the four seasonal names of the area: Kŭmgang '*vajra*' for spring, Pongnae (C. Penglai) 'luxuriant fairyland' for summer, P'ungak '[crimson] maple peaks' for autumn and Kaegol 'bare bones' for winter. They were interpreted by professional and amateur painters alike, and were especially popular in **folk painting**.

J.S.GALE, 'The Diamond Mountains,' *TKBRAS*, XIII, 1922; ZO ZAYONG, *Diamond Mountain*, 2 vols., Seoul: Emillle Museum, 1975
See also **Bird, Isabella**

DICE *chusawi*
Chinese dice are known since 600 BC. Korean dice were used in pairs (notably in **backgammon**) and usually made of bone. Each die was a cube with spots on each side, arranged so that the sum of the dots on opposite sides is always seven (1–6, 2–5, 3–4). The 1 and the 4 were painted red, and in some other respects too, Korean dice resemble Korean **dominoes**.

DICTIONARIES

The first known Korean dictionary was a Chinese rhyme-list (*unsŏ*), the only book a candidate might carry in state **examinations**. *Tongguk chŏngun* 'Korean rhyming dictionary' (1448) was published by **Sejong**, based on the Ming *Hongwu zhengyun* and using the new *han'gŭl* script. Only the first and last of its six volumes are extant. Ch'oe Sejin revised it in *Sasŏng t'onghae* 'Explanation of the Four Tones' (1517). *Ŏjŏng Kyujang chŏnun* 'Complete Rhymes of the Royal Library' (1796) was an authoritative *unsŏ*, issued in the energetic scholarship programme of King **Chŏngjo**.

Arranging characters by the 214 elements called 'radicals' became normal in China with the great *Kangxi zidian* (1716), containing 49,174 entries. The radicals order was first used in Korea for *Chŏnun okp'yŏn* 'Jade Tablets of all the Rhymes' (1790), which contained about 9,000 characters and remained Korea's standard dictionary, much reprinted during the next hundred years. *Okp'yŏn*, which was originally the title of a dictionary by Gu Yewang in 6th-century China, became the ordinary Korean word for a dictionary arranged by radicals.

The first modern dictionary explaining Chinese characters in Korean was Chi Sŏgyŏng's *Chajŏn sŏgyo* 'Explanation of Characters' (1909), containing demotic as well as literary usage. Others followed, such as **Ch'oe Namsŏn**'s *Sin-chajŏn* 'New Character-dictionary' (1915), with classical references; and Yi Myŏngch'il's *Han-Il-Sŏn-Man sin-sajŏn* 'New Character Dictionary: Chinese, Japanese, Korean and Manchu' (1937).

After the **Korean War** of 1950–3 the most popular character-dictionary was Kim Hyŏkche's *Kukhan myŏngmun-sin-okp'yŏn* 'Korean-Chinese Clear Letter New Okp'yŏn' (1952), which used nostalgic typography and lacked classical references, but gave Chinese pronunciations and a Korean alphabetical index for its roughly 10,000 entries. Kim Minsu's excellent *Sae chajŏn* 'New Dictionary' (1961) contained about 13,000 entries and added further indexes. Chang Samsik, *Tae-Han-Han-sajŏn* 'Great Chinese-Korean Dictionary' (1964), lists 41,388 characters, and includes words as well as single characters.

The first dictionary of the Korean language was the Paris Foreign Missions' *Dictionnaire Coréen-Français* (1880). **J. S. Gale**'s *A Korean-English Dictionary* (1897, 1911/1914, 1931) was the next major work, and *Chōsen'go jiten* (1920), in which Ogura Shimpei (*see* **Dialects**) took part, was published by the colonial **Government General**. The first wholly Korean dictionary was Mun Seyŏng's *Chosŏnŏ sajŏn* (1938), whose title was changed in later editions, finally becoming *Uri mal sajŏn* 'Dictionary of our Language'(1950). Mun's collaborator, Yi Yunjae, published *P'yojun han'gŭl sajŏn* 'Standard Han'gŭl Dictionary' in 1947. The **Han'gŭl** Society had been preparing its *K'ŭn sajŏn* 'Big Dictionary' since 1929. The first three volumes appeared in 1947–1950 and were reprinted in the full six-volume edition of 1957, which set standards for future lexical work, including Yi Hŭisŭng's single- volume *Kugŏ tae-sajŏn* (1961).

A major dictionary has also been published in P'yŏngyang: *Chosŏn-mal sajŏn* (1960).

Middle Korean is covered by Nam Kwangu's *Koŏ-sajŏn* 'Old Language Dictionary' (1960/1979) and Yu Ch'angdon's *Yijo-ŏ sajŏn* 'Dictionary of Yi Dynasty Language' (1964). The best modern Korean-English dictionary is S. E. Martin, Y. H. Lee and S. Chang, *A (New) Korean-English dictionary* (1967). English-Korean dictionaries published in Korea are designed for Korean students of English and give definitions rather than equivalent vocabulary.

DIVINATION *ŭmyang-hak* 陰陽學

Divination or fortune-telling has been important throughout Korean history and is remarkably persistent, too readily dismissed by Westerners as of little interest or value. Most of the methods used originated in China and have roots deep in the amalgam of scientific observation and philosophical speculation that forms the historical bedrock of Chinese thought (*see* **nabŭm**; **Book of Changes**; **kunghap**; **nine palaces divination**; **trigrams**). The most popular divinations are personal, mostly based on the *saju-p'alcha* or numerical signs of the date and hour of birth. Physiognomy (*kwansang*) and palmistry (*susang*) are also of traditional importance. Two important handbooks are **Ch'ŏn'gi-daeyo** and **T'ojŏng pigyŏl**. The *Book of Changes* is referred to, but rarely used with yarrow wands. Related practices, not strictly divinatory, are **p'ungsu** (C. *fengshui*) and the choosing of names. For all these, professionals are required. Interpreting dreams is a homely skill, and domestic divinations are carried out with **yut** sticks and many other devices, not always taken very seriously (*see* **divination with yut sticks**).

Undoubtedly some professional diviners and soothsayers manipulate their material; but behind the older methods lies a noble tradition. Sceptics abound, but they have never succeeded in destroying divinatory practices, which offer psychological comfort and are based on inherited wisdom.

DIVINATION WITH *YUT* STICKS

New Year divinations are made by throwing **yut** sticks three times and noting the scores, 5 counting as 4. Neither board nor counters are used. The three figures scored relate to one of the 64 hexagrams of the **Book of Changes** (here given by number in brackets) and each hexagram is provided with an ambivalent 4-character omen. A book is used for the omens, but interpretation is a matter of joint discussion by the players.

1-1-1 (01)	Baby sees its mother.	1-3-3 (49)	Dragon enters great sea.
1-1-2 (10)	Rat enters granary.	1-3-4 (17)	Tortoise enters bamboo grove.
1-1-3 (13)	Getting lamp on dark night.	1-4-1 (28)	Tree without roots.
1-1-4 (25)	Housefly meets springtime.	1-4-2 (47)	Dead come to life.
1-2-1 (44)	Big stream runs uphill.	1-4-3 (31)	Cold man gets clothed.
1-2-2 (06)	Doing wrong but gaining merit.	1-4-4 (45)	Poor man gets treasure.
1-2-3 (33)	Moth hits lamp.	2-1-1 (14)	Sun enters clouds.
1-2-4 (12)	Metal meets fire.	2-1-2 (38)	Sun seen during monsoon.
1-3-1 (43)	Crane loses feathers.	2-1-3 (30)	Bow loses arrow.
1-3-2 (58)	Hungry man gets food.	2-1-4 (21)	Bird has no pinions.

2-2-1 (50)	Weak horse, heavy load.		3-3-4 (03)	Monk turns layman.
2-2-2 (64)	Crane rises in sky.		3-4-1 (48)	Traveller thinks of home.
2-2-3 (56)	Hungry hawk gets meat.		3-4-2 (29)	No whip for horse.
2-2-4 (35)	Cart has no wheels.		3-4-3 (39)	Traveller finds way.
2-3-1 (34)	Baby gets milk.		3-4-4 (08)	Sun shines on dew.
2-3-2 (54)	Very ill, get medicine.		4-1-1 (26)	Parents gain son.
2-3-3 (55)	Butterfly finds flowers.		4-1-2 (41)	Merit but no reward.
2-3-4 (51)	Bow has arrows.		4-1-3 (22)	Dragon enters deep pool.
2-4-1 (32)	Bowing to guest from afar.		4-1-4 (27)	Blind man goes straight through
2-4-2 (40)	River fish out of water.			gate.
2-4-3 (62)	Patterns on water.		4-2-1 (18)	Light seen in darkness.
2-4-4 (16)	Dragon finds *yŏŭi* jewel.		4-2-2 (04)	Man without hands and feet.
3-1-1 (09)	Big fish enters water,		4-2-3 (52)	Good to see great men.
3-1-2 (61)	Hot weather, get fan.		4-2-4 (23)	Horn bow without string.
3-1-3 (37)	Falcon without talons.		4-3-1 (11)	Wind blows near ear.
3-1-4 (42)	Throw jewel in river.		4-3-2 (19)	Child gets treasure.
3-2-1 (57)	Horns sprout on dragon's head.		4-3-3 (36)	Man found and lost.
3-2-2 (59)	Poor and lowly.		4-3-4 (24)	Disturbed and no luck.
3-2-3 (53)	Poor scholar gets pay.		4-4-1 (46)	Outcome doubtful.
3-2-4 (20)	Cat meets rat.		4-4-2 (07)	Fish bites hook.
3-3-1 (05)	Fish turns into dragon.		4-4-3 (15)	Flying bird meets man.
3-3-2 (60)	Ox gets hay and beans.		4-4-4 (02)	Elder brother finds sibling.
3-3-3 (63)	Blossom turns to fruit.			

DIVORCE

Divorce was ideologically impossible and though men sometimes dismissed their wives, such behaviour was nearly always disapproved. The seven reasons (*ch'ilch'ul*) for divorcing a wife given in *Kungzi jiayu* (K. *Kongja-gaŏ*) were sometimes invoked: disobedience to parents-in-law, failure to bear a son, adultery, theft, jealousy of other wives, incurable illness and undue talkativeness. Three reasons preventing divorce are given in the same place: increased prosperity during the **marriage**, lack of a place for the dismissed wife to go and live, and her having mourned for a parent-in-law. Cases were severely judged and husbands who dismissed their wives were frequently punished.

MARTINA DEUCHLER, *The Confucian Transformation of Korea*, Cambridge, Mass.: Harvard University Press, 1992.

DMZ (De-militarized Zone) *Pimujang chidae* 非武裝地帶

No-man's land created by the **Armistice** Agreement of 1953 as a buffer zone between the **Democratic People's Republic of Korea** and the **Republic of Korea** (*see* **Korean War**). It is approximately three miles in breadth and 150 miles in length across the peninsula. As an artificial border between two countries the DMZ has no topographical, ethnic, linguistic or cultural justification: it simply follows a military cease-fire line. At the western end it skirts the south of the Ongjin peninsula and the north of **Kanghwa** Island. It bisects the **Thirty-Eighth Parallel** near P'anmunjŏm and runs in a generally east-northeasterly direction, reaching the sea a little to the south of Kosŏng, Kangwŏn province. The historic city of **Kaesŏng**, Kyŏnggi province, which had been in South Korea according to the division in 1945, is now in the North, and the more northerly cities of Ch'ŏrwŏn and Kansŏng in the South. The political focal point is the truce village of P'anmunjŏm on the Imjin River, in which South Korean and American negotiators have met regularly with North Koreans since 1953. The South Korean capital of Seoul lies only 35 miles to the south. The DMZ is mined and heavily guarded on both sides and has become a unique wild life sanctuary. In the mid-1970s North Korea, in apparent preparation for military invasion of the South, dug a series of tunnels under it, three of which were discovered.

DOGS

Dog bones occur in **neolithic** remains. Dogs were used for **food** and for **hunting**. Apart from large hunting dogs, varieties included *palbari* of the Pekingese or Shih-tzu type, the shaggy little *sapsari*, and the **Chindo** dog, not unlike the Japanese Akita, a fine breed of stocky spitz endemic to Chindo island. In a few places there are memorial stones and shrines to faithful dogs.

DOLMEN *koindol*

A **Neolithic** or **Bronze Age** burial chamber or pit surmounted by an enormous flat stone. The largest extant stone measures 7·1 by 5·5 metres. This construction system was widespread across the Korean peninsula with regional variations. In the north the stone is generally raised above the ground on supporting stones, while in the south it may lie at ground level above a cist. Some dolmens occur individually but in southern Korea cemeteries of hundreds exist. It is estimated that some 80,000 dolmens and associated standing stones were still in existence following the **Korean War**, but that the number has now fallen to around 25,000 over the whole country. In South Korea they are protected by law. Dolmens are also found on the neighbouring southern Japanese island of Kyushu.

DOMINOES

Dominoes were known in China in the 12th century AD, but in Europe not until the 18th century. In Korea, where they are called *kolp'ae*, 'bone tablets', they were not esteemed by *yangban* and, as in China, had no blank faces. They were rectangular tiles, as small as 19 x 12 x 5 mm, traditionally made of dark hardwood with bone facings in which holes were cut for the spots. There is no dividing line across the middle of a domino. A single spot of large size appears centrally in a half of the face for 1; two side by side for 2; three on the oblique of Z for 3; a square for 4; a quincunx for 5 and two columnns of three for 6. There are 21 values, 11 of which (asterisked in the list below) are duplicated, giving a total of 32 dominoes in a set: **t'ongso* or *soso* 1-1, *paega* (or *chwik'o* 'rat's nose') 1-2, **sosam* 1-3, *paeksa* 1-4, **paego* 1-5, **paengnyuk* 1-6, **china* 2-2, *asam* 2-3, *ŏsa* 2-4, *kwani* 2-5, *aryuk* 2-6, **changsam* 3-3, *samsa* 3-4, *samo* 3-5, *samnyuk* 3-6, **chikhŭng* or *chunhong* 4-4, *sao* 4-5, **saryuk* 4-6, **chuno* 5-5, **oryuk* 5-6, and **chullyuk* 6-6. The 1 and 4 spots may be coloured red.

The best known games with dominoes are *hop'ae* 'Manchu tablets', *tchang-mach'ugi* 'pair-matching' and *kkori-buch'igi* 'tail-joining'.

DONKEY

The donkey, or *Tang-nagwi* 'Tang ass', was the customary mount of a *yangban*, especially the younger gentleman (*saengwŏn*), with proverbial similarities between rider and the slow, stubborn beast. It originated in the Middle East and is first recorded in China in Han times. *Tang* is a conventional adjective for 'Chinese', but the donkey probably did arrive in Tang times. The earliest mention in Korea is the story of a king with ass's ears in *Samguk yusa* (late Koryŏ). Though sometimes used by pedlars, it never became the peasant's beast it was in other regions. Horse-ass hybrids (*pŏsae* 'hinny' and *nosae* 'mule') were known, but were not esteemed.

DOWAGER QUEEN CHANGNYŎL'S MOURNING RITES *Chaŭi Taebi poksang munje* or *Yesong-nonjaeng* 慈懿大妃服喪問題

King Injo (r. 1623–49) had two sons, the princes **Sohyŏn** and Pongnim. Their mother died in 1636 and Injo married again in 1638. His second wife, later known as Queen Changnyŏl (b. 1624), was a teenage member of the Cho family. She bore no sons. In 1645 the Crown Prince, Sohyŏn, died. When Injo died in summer 1649, his younger son, Prince Pongnim, later known as Hyojong, came to the throne. His stepmother, Queen Changnyŏl, was then 25 years old and became *Chaŭi-taebi*, dowager queen.

Ten years later, in summer 1659, Hyojong died and was succeeded by his son Hyŏnjong, aged eighteen. There was a question as to how long the Dowager Queen should wear mourning for Hyojong, her stepson. On the advice of the ruling Western **faction**, led by **Song Siyŏl**, she began to observe one year in mourning dress, as prescribed by the ritual textbooks, *Chuja-garye* and *Kukcho-orye-ŭi*. In the following spring, the Southern faction, led by Yu Hyu (1617–80) and Hŏ Yok (1595–1682), supported by a large group of country scholars from Kyŏngsang province, submitted a memorial saying that she ought to mourn for three years, because she had mourned three years for Hyojong's elder brother, Crown Prince Sohyŏn. The implication was that if she mourned less for a king than for a crown prince, doubt would be cast on the legitimacy of the king; but young Hyŏnjong stood by the decision already made.

In 1674 a similar question arose on the death of Hyojong's queen, Insŏn Taebi, the king's mother and Queen Changnyŏl's step-daughter-in-law. The Westerners said the Queen Dowager should mourn for nine months; but the Southerners objected, saying that the one year established for King Hyojong should be observed, implying again that doubt was being cast on the King's legitimacy. This time King Hyŏnjong, now 32, sided with the Southerners. The Westerners were purged and the Southerners came to power, having skilfully used a ritual argument for political advantage. Hyŏnjong died later that year and was succeeded by his thirteen-year-old son, **Sukchong**. The Queen Dowager lived till 1688.

DRAGON 龍

The dragon, *yong*, is the oldest mythical creature of East Asia, the supreme sign of heaven, the *yang* influence, and change. Its origin is much debated. Perhaps it was inspired by the sight of salmon leaping their way up-river during the spring rains, for the dragon that reaches the heavenly lake is said to be transformed into a fish. Korea certainly knew the dragon motif in the days of the **Lelang** commanderies. Chinese symbolism and legends came with it, especially those connected with fertility and rain, and legends of the *yŏŭi-ju*, the 'what-you-will jewel' or pearl of wisdom. The dragon became virtually a rain spirit, but also symbolised the King or Emperor. From Ming times the Chinese imperial dragon had five claws; in Korea it sometimes has seven.

DRESS

Early evidence is sparse. Mural paintings from Koguryŏ **tombs** show women dancing and men hunting on horseback in belted pyjama suits of brightly patterned cloth, but are difficult to interpret. We do not know how realistic the pictures were intended to be, and the social implications can only be guessed. While it is possible that early Korean clothing differed from that in China and **Manchuria**, it is more likely that the tradition of the whole region was homogeneous. Chinese influence was certainly strong in later periods and **Tang** court dress regulations were adopted in **Silla**. The costume of late Koryŏ times would be recognisable as Korean clothes today.

Chosŏn court dress was elaborate and made in the Office of Royal Costume (Sangŭi-wŏn). Indications of rank were provided by the Korean version of the Chinese mandarin squares (*hyungbae*), worn in panels on the chest and back, and included cranes (for civil officials) and **tigers** (for military officials). Female dress bore patterns of **phoenixes** and **flowers** and was decorated with *appliqué* gold leaf, while small jewelled **crowns** were worn on the head.

The dress worn by female dancers was distinguished by long, rainbow-banded (*saektong*) sleeves covering the wrists and hands. This style was imported from China and the sleeves were used as an integral part of **dance** movement.

What is now regarded as *hanbok* traditional dress is a simplification of the semi-formal middle-class costume of late Chosŏn. It preserves some archaic characteristics. All upper garments are open at the front, with the left front carried over the right and fastened before the right shoulder, as it was in China in earliest times. Underwear – a late development in most cultures – scarcely exists, except for thin under-trousers worn by women. The proud boast of being the 'white-clad people' suggests a conservative taste for undyed cloth, and outside officialdom there was little surface ornamentation. For festive and formal wear, gold block-printing is the commonest form of decoration on clothes for women and children.

There are no buttons: all fastenings are single-bow knots tied in strips of cloth that function as ribbons or tapes, whether attached to a garment or not. Even the Turk's-knot toggle with a loop to slip over it, much used in China, was hardly used in Korea before 1900. There is no fitted tailoring of seams or darts to follow the contours of the body, though the shapes of garment pieces may be subtly designed, especially in gored coat-skirts and shaped sleeves. Such loose clothing insulates the body well, keeping it cool in the heat and warm in the cold.

The cut gives the dress its grace, following the movements of the wearer. The distinctive hang is free but not flowing, because the fabrics used are of vegetable fibres in relatively close weaves. Until cotton was introduced in the 14th century, all clothing must have been made of hemp, linen, ramie or **silk** (*see* **textiles**). Animal fibres were only horsehair for men's hats and perhaps **felt** for some hats and shoes. Fur and silk floss padding were used in winter, but before the introduction of cotton made cheap padding possible, insulation against cold must have been achieved by layering with extra garments. Summer clothing, especially for men, even today is virtually transparent grass-cloth that depends for decency on the folds in the cloth at the joints of the body.

The essential difference between the sexes is that women wear skirts. The items of a woman's dress are thin trousers (*paji*), one or two skirts or petticoats (*chima*, oblongs of cloth gathered into a deep waistband tied above the breasts), a brief jacket (*chŏgori*, whose cut changes subtly from year to year), short stockings of cut cloth (*poson*) and slip-on shoes (*sin*) with up-turned toes. A long coat (*turumagi*) may be worn over the rest. The *chŏgori* may be decorated at the collar, wrists and under-arm side-seams. Red jacket-ties may mean a woman's husband is alive, and blue cuffs that she has a living son.

A man's trousers have a wide waist, doubled over the abdomen and secured by a cloth belt. (There is no opening at the front or crotch.) The wide leg-bottoms are gathered by strips of cloth (*taenim*) tied inside the ankles. Both belt and anklets are tied in single-bow knots, the bow of each anklet lying towards the front of the leg. Such trousers are well suited to those who have no chairs and always sit on the floor. A man's *chŏgori* is cut longer and looser than a woman's. A *chokki* and *magoja* may also be worn. The *turumagi* overcoat is worn out of doors and for formal occasions. Men's footwear is large and plainer than women's.

Children have generally worn brighter colours, especially the multi-coloured sleeves of the **saektong** *chŏgori* for festivals. Wedding dress for both groom and bride (often communally owned in villages) is based on court dress, which was heavily influenced by Chinese ritual texts. Mourning costume, too, made of coarse undyed cloth with the seams outside and worn with a huge umbrella-sized hat, is controlled by the **Confucian classics**.

Modernisation of dress went through uneven stages. In the 1920s male **students** wore black uniforms of simple military style, peaked caps and cloaks. The cloaks were soon discarded, but the uniforms lasted nearly till the end of the 20th century. Rubber slip-on shoes (*kkomu-sin*) appeared in the 1920s, became widely worn during the 1930s and remained dominant till about 1980, except in cities. The woman's *chima* has been shortened, though not in formal wear. Versions of Western bridal dress are common.

Both men and women usually wear western clothes in public, but they have by no means renounced traditional dress. Women often prefer *hanbok* for formal occasions. Young people are experimenting with adaptation of Korean styles, and national dress remains a point of national pride.

KIM KUMJA PAIK & HUH DONG-HWA, *Profusion of Colour: Korean Costumes and Wrapping Cloths of the Chosŏn Dynasty*, Seoul: Asian Art Museum of San Francisco, 1995; KIM YONG-SUK & SON KYONG-JA, *An Illustrated History of Korean Costume*, 2 vols., Seoul. Yekyong Publications Co., 1984

See also **footwear**; **headdress**; **jewellery**; **topknot**

DRINKS

Alcoholic beverages, though usually called 'wine', are strictly ales, like the 'wines' of China and Japan. They come in many varieties, from the cloudy unstrained *makkŏlli*, drunk in large bowls and reminiscent of the roughest English cider, to the clearest *ch'ŏngju*, drunk in small cups, often warmed. Traditionally popular wines flavoured with chrysanthemums, other flowers or fruit are now uncommon. *Soju* 'fired liquor' is a type of distilled vodka made since the mediaeval period, using various kinds of **rice** and millet. Drinks are usually served before, rather than during, a meal. After a meal, hot rice water (*sungnyung*) or barley tea (*porich'a*) may be served. In the 20th century lager-type beer has become popular.

See also **tea**

DRUMS

Early texts refer to processional and military music as *koch'wi* ('banging and blowing'), and it is clear that during the Three Kingdoms period drums were commonly used in both native Korean and imported Chinese **music**. Written sources record the names of a large number of standing and portable drums. Most had bodies made of wood and were covered with cowskin, though examples of pottery and metal drums are preserved.

The largest drums seen in Korea were the *kŏn'go* and *chin'go*, originally used in performances of **aak** and ceremonial *hyangak*. Both were double-headed barrel drums mounted horizontally, the former on a decorated pedestal and the latter on a four-legged frame. The body of the *kŏn'go* measured approximately 150 cms in length and was surmounted by an ornate wooden pagoda. From the corners of the two topmost storeys extended the heads of four dragons, long tassels dangling from their mouths, and on top stood a white crane. The heads of each drum were around 110 cms in diameter: early illustrations from China, whence the instruments came to Korea, show them being beaten by two players, one at each end, though there is no evidence of this in Korea.

Medium-sized single-headed barrel drums were suspended either horizontally on a four-legged cradle or vertically from the crosspiece of an upright frame. An example of the former was the *kyobanggo* used in the drum dance (*mugo*). Today, the *chwago* is still commonly seen as an example of the latter. It is often used as the principal drum in orchestral ensembles, and is banged with a single soft-headed stick.

Portable drums included the *nodo*, a ceremonial instrument consisting of two barrel drums transfixed at right angles to each other at the top of a pole. Two leather cords were fastened to the side of each body, and beat against the drumheads when the pole was rotated backwards and forwards. A much smaller but related version of a drum twirled to rattle thongs against the two sides of its head was the *togo*: it could be held by a player in one hand while in the other he held the *so* panpipes.

The most commonly seen drums today are the *puk* (also known as *yonggo*, 'dragon drum') and the *changgo* ('stick drum'). The *puk* is a small double-headed barrel drum used in rural bands and for the accompaniment of *p'ansori*. It may be hung across the shoulders for use in procession or stood on its rim in front of a seated player. The *p'ansori* accompanist beats the left head with the palm of his hand and the right head – and the wooden rim – with a stick. The *changgo*, an hour-glass drum, has been one of the most familiar drum types in East Asia for more than one and a half millennia. In Korea it exists in two versions, the heavier for orchestral use by a seated player and the lighter as a portable accompaniment to **nongak**. Larger drums may measure over 60 cms in length and have a diameter of over 30 cms; smaller ones are around a third less. On the orchestral instrument the left head, covered in cowskin, is thicker than the right and produces a dull sound when struck with the palm of the hand. The right head, or its rim, is hit or rolled with a thin stick and gives a sharper, more distinct note. It may be made of sheep- or dog-skin. The tension of this head is adjusted by moving the leather girdles that grip the strings. The smaller drum is carried on the player's left hip with a strap hung across the right shoulder. Its heads are tuned to equal tension. That on the left is struck with a round-headed mallet, that on the right with a stick, although the player will sometimes cross hands and use his mallet on the right head.

KEITH PRATT, *Korean Music, its History and its Performance*, London and Seoul: Faber Music Ltd and Jung Eum Sa, 1987

See also **musical instruments**

DU FU (K. Tu Po) 杜甫 (712–770)
A brilliant poet of both court life and exile, the most revered of Chinese poets in Korea, where he is often known as Tu Kongbu, 'Board of Works Tu', from a minor office he held for a short time; or as Tu Chami (C. Du Zimei).

DU MU (K. Tu Mok) 杜牧 (803–852)
Poet-essayist of Tang, used in Korean popular literature as a model of male attractiveness to **women**. The singing-girls mobbed his carriage with gifts of tangerines in their enthusiasm to get near him, giving rise to the expression *kyulman-ch'a*, 'tangerine-filled carriage', for a much admired young man.

DUTCH, THE *See* **Hamel, Hendrik**; **Weltevree, Jan Jansen**

DYE, WILLIAM McENTYRE (1831–99)
William Dye served as a brigadier-general of volunteers during the American Civil War. In 1873 he went to Egypt for five years to help train the Egyptian army, then served in the District of Columbia Police. In 1888 he went to Seoul as leader of a party of three to train the Korean army in modern methods. He had some success in teaching drill and discipline to the palace guard and in training NCOs, but Korean conservatism and the attitudes of the Japanese, Chinese and Russians were all against him, and he was not of the right temperament to overcome such difficulties. When the pro-Japanese party came into the ascendant he was demoted, but stayed bravely in the palace by the King during the murder of **Queen Min** (which he reported to the *New York Herald*) and thereafter until the king took refuge in the Russian Legation in February 1896. His contract expired in May, but he remained for a further three years as unofficial manager of a government farm, an example of the remarkable power of Korea and its monarchy to enlist the loyalty of westerners. He was invalided home in 1899 and died that year in America.
DONALD M. BISHOP, 'American Military Advisors in Korea 1888–1896,' *TRASKB*, LVIII, 1983

E

EARTHENWARE *See* **Pottery**

ECKARDT, ANDREAS (1884–1974)
Ludwig Otto Eckardt was born in Munich and took the name of Andreas when he became a Benedictine monk of the St Ottilien Congregation in 1905. He worked in Korea from 1908 to 1928, when he returned to Bavaria and soon left the order. After World War II he became professor of Korean Language and Culture at Munich. He wrote the first western account of Korean art, *Geschichte der Koreanische Kunst* (1929, translated as *History of Korean Art*), and an early language-book, *Koreanische Konversationsgrammatik* (1923), as well as *Koreanische Musik* (1930)* and *Koreanische Märchen and Erzählungen*, 'Korean legends and tales' (1928).
* Revised and re-issued as *Musik-Lied-Tanz in Korea*, Bonn: H. Bouvier, 1968

ECKERT, FRANZ VON (1852–1916)
This young German arrived in Tokyo at the age of eighteen to teach military music in the Japanese army. In 1900 he was invited by Emperor **Kojong** to found and train a military band in Seoul, which he did with some success, composing the music for Korea's first *aegukka*, 'national anthem', in 1902. He died in Seoul aged 64.

EDUCATION *See* **Ewha Women's University**; **examinations**; *Kukcha-gam*; **Protestants**; **schools**; *Sŏnggyun-gwan*; *sŏwŏn*; *T'aehak-kwan*; **universities**

EDUCATIONAL ASSOCIATIONS *hakhoe* 學會
Were founded during the last decade of the 19th and first decade of the 20th century as an attempt to foster a sense of Korean **nationalism** and spread interest in new knowledge from the West. Some, such as the **Korean Language Society**, had specific areas of study. Others, including the Women's Education Association (*Yŏja Kyoyukhoe*), were aimed at particular sections of society, or had provincial affiliations. Examples of the latter were Yi Kwangjong's Kyŏnggi-Ch'ungch'ŏng Educational Association (*Kiho Hŭnghakhoe*), and Yi Ch'ae's Chŏlla Educational Association (*Honam Hakhoe*). Some associations published influential periodicals.
See also **self-strengthening movement**

EIGHT SCENES [IN THE LIFE OF SAKYAMUNI] *P'al-ssang* 八像
Incidents in the life of Lord Gautama (Sakyamuni) popular in Buddhist painting. All eight may be shown in one picture, or there may be eight separate pictures. Of several different lists, the one most frequently met in Korea is:

1) *kang-Dosol-sang*; his mother's dream of his descent on a white elephant from the Tushita heaven into her womb;
2) *ch'osaeng-sang*: his birth under the asoka tree among the lotus flowers in the Lumbini gardens;
3) *samun-yugwan-sang*: his meeting with the four sights: an old man, a sick man, a funeral and a hermit;
4) *ch'ulga-sang*: his leaving home at 19, aware of the four sufferings (birth, age, sickness, death) and carried over the wall by his horse, whose feet are borne by the **four Heavenly Kings** (*sa ch'ŏnwang*);
5) *sŏngdo-sang*: his ascetic life in the mountains of snow, when he cut off his hair and sent it to his father;
6) *hangma-sang*: his enlightenment and victory over the demons under the bodhi tree at Gaya;
7) *chŏn-bŏmnyul-sang*: turning the wheel of Dharma (preaching) for the first five disciples and others in the Deer Park at Sarnath;
8) *im-nyŏlban-sang*: entering nirvana (death or parinirvana) at Kusinara in the presence of 500 disciples.

EIGHT TREASURES *p'albo* 八寶
Eight talismans against evil and ill health, a Chinese category of no great antiquity that sometimes occurs in Korean decorative art: a pearl (*zhu*, K. *chu*), a coin (*qian*, K. *chŏn*), a rhombus (*fangsheng*, K. *pangsŭng*), a mirror (*jing*, K. *kyŏng*), a stone chime (*qing*, K. *kyŏng*), two books (*jing*, K. *kyŏng*), a pair of rhinoceros-horn cups (*xijiao*, K. *sŏgak*) and an artemisia leaf (*ai*, K. *ae*). Each is usually embellished with ribbon. They probably appear mostly on Chinese artefacts, for the names are unfamiliar in Korea. The expression *p'albo* is, however, used in cookery to refer to mixed flavours or ingredients, as in the sweet rice-pudding called *p'albo-ch'ae*.

EIGHT VIEWS *p'algyŏng* 八景
The original Eight Views were landscape paintings by Song Di of the Song dynasty, showing evening light on the Xiao and Xiang rivers near the great central Chinese lake of Dongting: *Pingsha yanluo* (K. *P'yŏngsa allak*), 'Wild geese alighting on the sands'; *Yuanpu fangui* (K. *Wŏnp'o pŏmgwi*), 'Sails returning to a distant harbour'; *Shanshi qinglan* (K. *Sansi ch'ŏngnam*), 'Rain clearing over a hill village'; *Jiangtian muyun* (K.

Kangch'ŏn moun), 'Clouds in the twilight sky over a river'; *Dongting qiuyue* (K. *Tongjŏng ch'uwŏl*), 'Autumn moon at Dongting'; *Xiaoxiang yeyu* (K. *Sosang yau*), 'Night rain at Xiaoxiang'; *Yansi wanzhong* (K. *Yŏnsa manjong*), 'Evening bell of a temple in the mist'; and *Yucun xizhao* (K. *Ŏch'on sŏkcho*), 'Dusk in the fisher village'. Similar lists were made for other places, and most Korean scenic areas have them. Those for Chŏnju, Haeju, Hanyang (Seoul), **Kaesŏng**, Kwandong (Kangwŏn province), Namwŏn, **Puyŏ** and Tanyang are famous. Sometimes (as for Puyŏ) the mood titles of the original list, or variants of them, are preserved. Other lists (as for Kwandong) simply name eight beauty spots and play their part in tourism promotion.

EIGHTH ARMY, U.S.

The XXIVth Corps of the Eighth Army under Lt-General John **Hodge** was ordered from Okinawa to Korea to accept the Japanese surrender and to counter-balance the Soviet troops already entering northern Korea from **Manchuria**. After landing at **Inch'ŏn** it received Governor-General Abe Nobuyuki's surrender on 6 September 1945.
See also **American Military Government**

ELECTIONS *See* **Constitution**

EMIGRATION, KOREAN

During the protectorate and colonial period many Koreans were forced by the Japanese to leave their country. Perhaps those of them who suffered the greatest sense of shame as well as personal loss were the 'comfort women', sent to serve the military in Japan and south-east Asia and badly abused. Many others sought to escape Japanese oppression by migrating to other parts of north-east Asia where there were already Korean communities. These were principally **Manchuria**, **Siberia** (the Maritime Provinces), **Japan**, and eastern China (especially Shanghai). Estimates of Koreans living in Manchuria suggest 200,000 in 1910, 600,000 in 1919, and around 1·6 million in 1942. The Maritime Provinces were home to some 200,000 in 1919. In Japan, the total rose from around 26,000 in 1919 to approximately two million in 1945: many of these were workers who had been forcibly relocated, but they also included many **students** taking advantage of superior opportunities in Japanese colleges and universities. Both compulsory and voluntary exile were familiar concepts from earlier periods in Korean history, and served equally to strengthen the feeling of determination to recover lost rights and avenge injustice.

Following liberation in 1945 a huge number of Koreans returned to their homeland: less than a quarter of a million were left in Japan by the beginning of 1946. Korea was unable to cope with such an influx. Some went back to Japan again, but discontent among those who remained contributed to the outbreak of revolt in spring 1946 (*see* **rebellion, peasant**).

Of those who remained in China, the majority of Koreans settled in the North-East, especially in what came to be defined as the Yanbian autonomous region (*see* **Kando**). Until political tensions began to relax in the 1980s they were allowed few contacts with their homeland even in the North, and none at all with the South until the 1990s.

LEE CHAE-JIN, *China's Korean Minority: the Politics of Ethnic Education*, Boulder: Westview Press, 1986; RICHARD MITCHELL, *The Korean Minority in Japan*, Berkeley: University of California Press, 1967; OH YANG HO, 'Korean Literature in Manchuria: Exile and Immigrant Literature during the Japanese Colonial Period', *KJ*, 36/4, 1996; WAYNE PATTERSON, *The Korean Frontier in America: Immigration to Hawaii, 1896–1910*, Honolulu: University of Hawaii

Press, 1988; SUH DAE-SOOK, *Koreans in the Soviet Union*, Honolulu: University of Hawaii Press, 1987; SUH DAE-SOOK, EDWARD SHULTZ, eds., *Koreans in China*, Honolulu: University of Hawaii, 1990; MICHAEL WEINER, *Race and Migration in Imperial Japan*, London: Routledge, 1994
See also **Immigration, Japanese**

EMBASSIES *See* **Beijing, embassies to**; **tribute**

EMILLE

Emille-jong is a popular name for the huge Pongdŏk-sa **bell** now in the National Museum at **Kyŏngju**, cast in AD 771. A well-known legend tells how the bell cracked repeatedly after founding, and the casting was successful only after a woman had thrown her little daughter into the molten metal. The very long resonance of the sound of the bell is supposed to suggest a child's voice crying *Emille*, said to mean 'Mother'. The story became well-known only after 1945. An older story, recorded by **Allen** in *The Korean Repository* I.131-132 and **Hulbert** in *Korea Review* (1901, repeated in the **Royal Asiatic Society** *Transactions*, 1925), tells how when the great **curfew** bell of Seoul was being cast by King T'aejo of the Chosŏn dynasty, a witch of Anae (possibly Pyŏngch'ŏn in Ch'ungch'ŏng) gave a little boy instead of metal, intending him to be put into the metal. Only after the bell cracked several times was this sacrifice tried and success obtained. The sound of the bell was given by Allen as *Amella-a-a*.

ENNIN 圓仁 (794–864)

A Japanese Buddhist monk, disciple of Saicho, founder of the Tendai sect. He was sent to Tang China from 838 to 847 by the Japanese Emperor to study harmonising **Buddhism** and Shinto. He returned with a large collection of Buddhist books and had a lasting influence on Japanese Buddhism. While in China he met Korean communities, which he recorded in his travel diary *Nit-Tō guhō junrei gyōki* (K. *Ip Tang kubŏp sullye-haeng-gi*), 'Account of Pilgrimage entering Tang to Seek the Dharma').
EDWIN REISCHAUER, trans., *Ennin's Diary*, New York: Ronald Press, 1955; EDWIN REISCHAUER, *Ennin's Travels in T'ang China*, New York: Ronald Press, 1955

EUNUCHS *hwan'gwan* 宦官

Palace eunuchs, *hwan'gwan* or colloquially *nasi*, though there are about twenty synonyms, existed in Korea from Koryŏ days, when they were at first either congenitally or accidentally emasculated. Later, under Chinese influence, castration was introduced. They were regarded as a very low class until the Yuan emperors enforced annual levies of both nubile girls and young eunuchs, beginning from the last quarter of the 13th century. This brought some of them into contact with Chinese practice. They were then admitted to higher grades of office, but they provided the same recurrent problems of graft and bribery as in China. The *Naesi-bu* was instituted in the palace to supervise them. This office was maintained by the Chosŏn dynasty until all eunuchs were dismissed in the *kabo* **reforms** of 1894. They were the royal family's closest servants, responsible for serving meals, running messages, cleaning, domestic security, washing and laying out the dead, preparing graves and other personal functions. They were permitted to marry and to adopt sons, and although the normal adoption rules confined a man's choice of adopted son to those of his own surname, eunuchs were not thus restricted.

EVER NORMAL WAREHOUSES *sangp'yŏngch'ang* 常平倉
Economic institution introduced together with Charitable Granaries (*ŭich'ang*, 'righteous granaries') under the Koryŏ King **Sŏngjong**. They were aimed at price stabilisation, developed out of King Kwangjong (949–75)'s *chewibo* which had loaned grain and devoted the interest to poor relief. Following a concept once recommended by Mencius (IIIa.3.vii), supplies of grain and cloth were derived from the land and military taxes (*see* **taxation**) or purchased when prices were low and stored for resale at higher but regulated prices in times of scarcity. This had the advantage of discouraging profiteering. In the early Chosŏn period the warehouses also took over responsibility from the *ŭich'ang* ('charitable granaries') for the **Rice Loan System**, and a system which had been aimed at alleviating hardship among the **peasantry** later became associated with extortionate usury. *Sangp'yŏngch'ang* nevertheless survived until the 19th century, when their abuse by corrupt local officials contributed to the outbreak of peasant violence in the **Chinju Rising** of 1862.
See also **Taedongpŏp**

EWHA WOMEN'S UNIVERSITY *Ihwa Yŏja Taehakkyo* 梨花女大學校
Established in Seoul as a private liberal arts college by American missionaries in 1925. Its origins can be traced back to a Methodist missionary, Mary Scranton, who first taught a court **concubine** in 1882, and to the opening four years later of Ewha Girls' School. This marked the beginning of formal education for women in Korea. It was given **university** status in 1950.
See also **Plum blossom; Scranton, William**

EXAMINATION PAPERS *kwamun-nyukch'e* 科文六體
Examinations (*kwagŏ*) required candidates at each session to produce one or two compositions in literary Chinese. These had to be written according to strict patterns that were traditionally called *kwamun-nyukch'e*, 'the six forms of examination documents': *si* 'poems', *pu* 'rhymed prose' (written, for examination purposes, in 6-character phrases), *p'yo* 'personal memorial to the king', *ch'aek* 'policy document', *ŭi* 'exposition (of the Five **Confucian Classics**)' and *ŭi* 'explanation (of the Four Books)'. These are general terms. In detail, the *saengwŏn* examination required one *ŭi* 'exposition' and one *ŭi* 'explanation', while the *chinsa* examination required a *pu* and either a *kosi* 'old-style poem' (in which the tones of the characters did not matter), *myŏng* 'inscription' (commemorative or hortatory) or *cham* 'admonition'.

In *taekwa ch'osi* there were three sessions. The first required two essays on the nine classics; the second a *pu, myŏng, cham* or *ki* 'record of historic remains or scenery', together with a *p'yo* or *chŏnmun* 'memorial to the king on some great occasion or crisis'. The third session required a *taech'aek*, 'policy document requested by the king'. *Taekwa poksi* required an essay on the classics at the first session; a *pu, p'yo* or *chŏnmun* at the second; and a *taech'aek* at the third. The *chŏnsi* required a *taech'aek, p'yo, chŏnmun, song* 'eulogy', or *cho* 'royal edict'.

Regulations about these required documents became fossilised in stultifying rigidity, which was criticised by scholars as early as *Chibong yusŏl* (1614).

EXAMINATIONS *kwagŏ* 科擧
In the 7th century the National University (*Kukhak*) allocated its graduates after nine years' study into one of three classes according to their knowledge of the **Confucian Classics**. They were all members of the aristocracy, and were then appointed to administrative posts. In 788 a revised system known as *Sambun-gwa* allowed lower

members of the nobility to take the exams without attending the University, now called the *Taehakkam*.

In 958 a Chinese envoy from the court of the Later Zhou dynasty, Shuang Ji (K. Ssang Ki), stayed on in **Kaesŏng** and advised King Kwangjong on the establishment of a Chinese-style civil service examination system. This opened up the bureaucracy to a wider social range and number of entrants. Two classes led directly into higher administrative posts, one (*chinsa* or *chesul*) testing skill in Chinese literary forms, the other (*myŏnggyŏng*) a knowledge of five **Confucian Classics** (The *Book of Songs*, *Book of History*, *Book of Changes*, *Book of Rites* and *Spring and Autumn Annals*). A third category (*chapkwa*) examined practical accomplishments such as **law**, mathematics, **medicine**, *p'ungsu* and **divination**, and was mainly taken by members of the *chungin* class. A separate examination system existed for the Buddhist clergy until it was ended as part of the 15th century suppression of Buddhism (*see* **Examinations, Buddhist**).

In 1369 **Yi Saek** introduced the Yuan pattern of three successive grades: local, provincial, and metropolitan. By 1390 there were military as well as civil examinations. The Chosŏn leadership continued and elaborated upon the Koryŏ examination system, and modelled it closely on that being administered in China. In theory candidature was open to all men who were free from criminal record or criminal descent and were the legitimate sons of primary wives; in fact, *yangban* monopolised the system. Examinations were held every three years, augmented by additional occasions to celebrate special events which increased as time went on. The **examination papers** were written tests in literary Chinese, but the *baguwen* 'eight-legged essay' that was so important in China was not used in Korea. Nor were the entrants secluded in separate cells as in China. They sat on the ground in the open, under sunshades, with visitors walking among them. At all stages the number of successes was a fixed quota.

There were five stages. The first two constituted *sokwa*, 'the lesser examination'. (1) *Ch'osi*, 'first test', was taken locally in Seoul or one of the eight provincial centres in the autumn. In the following spring successful candidates took (2) *poksi*, 'repeat test', at the Board of Rites in the capital. Those who succeeded in the *poksi* were given a certificate on white paper (*paekp'ae*) and were entitled to study further at state institutions such as the **Sŏnggyun-gwan**. If they had been examined in the classics, they became *saengwŏn* 'recognised scholar'; if they had been examined in literary composition they became *chinsa* 'advancing scholar'. The same two titles (C. *shengyuan* and *jinshi*) were used in China, but had different connotations there.

In due time the more ambitious *saengwŏn* and *chinsa* would present themselves for *taekwa*, 'major examination', often called *munkwa*, 'civil service examination'. Again they took (3) *ch'osi* and (4) *poksi*. The 33 who passed went on to (5) *chŏnsi* 'palace examination'. The king was present, sitting behind a fence of spears stuck into the ground by his guards. Candidates threw their finished papers over the fence of spears and two panels of assessors decided the final placing. Those who passed were now eligible for appointment to government office. The first laureate, *changwŏn*, was admitted to 6th **grade** in the civil service. Two others received 1st class honours (*kap*) and 7th grade, seven received 2nd class honours (*ŭl*) and 8th grade, while the remaining 23 received 3rd class honours (*pyŏng*) and 9th grade. Their certificates were on red paper (*hongp'ae*). Each man was capped with two sprays of paper flowers (*ŏsŏhwa*), set on a pony and led through the streets by a band of musicians on a lap of honour that was marked by much horseplay.

A parallel three-honours system was used for the *mugwa*, 'military examinations', It too culminated in a palace test before the king. Its syllabus was more practical and included martial arts and military science as well as the Confucian Classics.

As in the Koryŏ period, a class of practical subjects was also examined to select the nation's specialists in astrology (*ŭmyangkwa*), medicine (*ŭikwa*), law (*yulkwa*), geography and foreign languages (*yŏkkwa*, conducted in Chinese, Japanese, Mongolian and Manchu), all accomplishments which the literati might scorn but depended upon. The *chupkwa*, 'miscellaneous examinations', were held at licentiate and metropolitan levels but did not offer the royal test and conveyed nothing like the esteem accorded to *munkwa* and *mugwa*. All examinations were subject to cheating and corruption of various kinds, especially in the course of factional struggles. The whole system was abolished in the *kabo* **reforms** of 1894, and replaced by a new range of options emphasising more modern studies, including international relations, science and technology.

YONG-HO CH'OE, *The Civil Examinations and the Social Structure in the Early Yi Dynasty Korea, 1392–1600*, Seoul: Korea Research Center, 1987; EDWARD WAGNER, 'The Recommendation Examination of 1519: its Place in Early Yi Dynasty History', *Chōsen Gakuho* 15, 1960; EDWARD WAGNER, 'The Ladder of Success in Yi Dynasty Korea', *Occasional Papers on Korea* 1, 1974; EDWARD WAGNER, 'The Civil Examination Process as Social Leaven – The Case of the Northern Provinces in the Yi Dynasty,' *KJ*, 17/1, 1977; YI SONG-MU, '*Kwagŏ* System and its Characteristics,' *KJ*, 21/7, 1981
*See also **sama-si**; schools*

EXAMINATIONS, BUDDHIST *sŭnggwa* 僧科

Official Buddhist examinations began in the mid-10th century, for **Sŏn** monks at Kwangnyŏng-sa and for *Kyo* monks at Wangnyun-sa. They were later established at three-yearly intervals and gave grades that qualified the candidates for appointment to administrative and national responsibilities. Early Chosŏn kings maintained the system: under **Sejong** the syllabus for *Sŏn* monks was *Chŏndŭng-nok* 'lamp anthology' and Hyesim's *Sŏnmun-yŏmsong-jip*, for *Kyo* monks *Sipchi-ron* and the **Hwaŏm** Sutra. The examinations were abolished by **Prince Yŏnsan** in 1502, but reinstated under **Pou** in 1552, then finally abolished in 1566 after the death of Queen Munjŏng.

EXTRA-TERRITORIALITY

Was claimed by Japanese citizens residing in Japanese settlements in Korea under the terms of the **Kanghwa Treaty** (1876), by Americans under those of the Chemulp'o **(Shufeldt) Treaty** (1882), and by other western governments under the **Unequal Treaties** of 1883 (Great Britain, Germany), 1884 (Russia, Italy), and 1886 (France).

F

FACTIONS *tang, tangjaeng* 黨爭

Political factions undermined the rule of mid-Chosŏn kings and impaired their ability to achieve balanced government. Although this problem is often ascribed to too many men being qualified for a limited number of official posts, factionalism is inevitable in any absolute monarchy governing through a bureaucracy. The intensity of Korean factionalism derives primarily from neo-Confucian ethics. Loyalty to ancestors was sacrosanct: men were born into factions from which they could not escape, factions that were not divided by ideologies, but on the application of a single ideology held by all concerned. Divisions occurred because the lack of objective laws about succession to the throne weakened the monarchy at source, while the pressure of the bureaucracy was constantly debilitating. Added to all this was the influence of the queens and subsidiary royal wives. Their jealousies and the greed of their families motivated some of the bloodiest purges in three and a half centuries of *tangjaeng*.

Although seeds had been set in the reign of **Sejo**, factional strife is generally reckoned to begin from rivalry in 1574 over official appointments, between supporters of Sim Ŭigyŏm and Kim Hyowŏn, known from the location of their homes in Seoul as Westerners (*Sŏin*), who included **Yi I**, and Easterners (*Tongin*), who honoured the teachings of **Yi Hwang** (T'oegye). The two factions shared political control for about ten years, until in 1589 they quarrelled about the Westerner **Chŏng Ch'ŏl**'s suggestion for the appointment of the Crown Prince. The Easterners took power, but soon split into moderate Southerners (*Namin*), loyal to T'oegye's philosophy, and adamant Northerners (*Pugin*), violently opposed to Chŏng's suggestion and preferring the philosophy of **Cho Sik**.

For five years the Northerners held power, then for five years power went back and forth. In 1599, on the occasion of an appointment to the Inspectorate-General, the Northerners split again into Greater Northerners (*Taebuk*), who supported Hong Yŏsun, and Lesser Northerners (*Sobuk*), who supported Nam Igong (1565–1640).

At the accession of **Prince Kwanghae** in 1608 the Greater Northerners came into power, but soon split into three groups: Bone Northerners (*Kolbuk*), led by Hong Yŏsun (1547–1609); Flesh Northerners (*Yukpuk*), led by Yi Sanhae (1538–1609); and Central Northerners (*Chungbuk*), led by Chŏng On (1569–1641) and Yu Mongin (1559–1623). The Lesser Northerners split into Moderate Lesser Northerners (*T'aksobuk*) around Yu Yŏnggyŏng (1560–1608), and Hardline Lesser Northerners (*Ch'ŏngsobuk*) around Nam Igong. All five groups enjoyed some degree of power, but when Kwanghae-gun was deposed in favour of King Injo in 1623, the Lesser Northerners barely managed to survive, whereas the Greater Northerners disappeared.

The Westerners then entered upon a period of influence, but they split into Meritorious Westerners (*Kongsŏ*), who had supported Injo, and Hardline Westerners (*Ch'ŏngsŏ*), who had been inactive. The Hardline Westerners were briefly split into a Han (Hanyang or Seoul) faction (*Handang*) and a Mountain faction (*Sandang*). The Meritorious Westerners split into Elder Westerners (*Nosŏ*) and Younger Westerners (*Sosŏ*), then during the 1640s the Elder Westerners split into the Nak faction (*Naktang*) led by Kim Chajŏm (d. 1651), who held the title *Nakhung-buwŏn'gun*, and the Wŏn faction (*Wŏndang*) led by Wŏn Tup'yo (1593–1664). With the end of the reign, the Meritorious faction petered out, though Hardline Westerners remained in power until 1674.

Factionalism reached a new peak in King **Sukchong**'s reign (1674–1720). There was another dispute about the appointment of a Crown Prince in 1674. **Song Siyŏl**, leader of the Westerners, lost the argument, and the Southerners split into Hardline Southerners (*Ch'ŏngnam*), who wanted Song executed, and Moderate Southerners (*T'angnam*), who were prepared to spare him. He was spared, and in 1680 came back to power. In 1683 his Westerners divided into the Elder Teaching (*Noron*), led by Song, and the New Teaching (*Soron*), led by Yun Chung. Thus were created the 'Four Colours' (*sasaek*): Noron, Soron, Southerners and Lesser Northerners. They all survived till the end, though the Westerners (Noron or Soron) were never again dislodged from power.

CHOSŎN DYNASTY FACTION LINEAGES
This diagram shows only the occasion of each split, and does not show the periods of power for each faction.

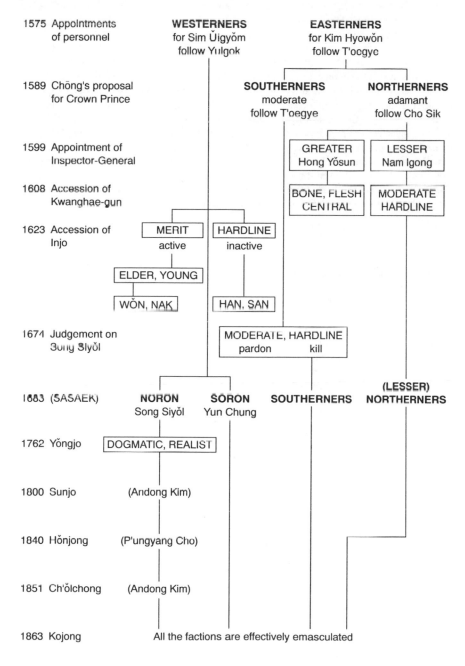

1575 Appointments of personnel	**WESTERNERS** for Sim Ŭigyŏm follow Yulgok	**EASTERNERS** for Kim Hyowŏn follow T'oegye	
1589 Chŏng's proposal for Crown Prince		**SOUTHERNERS** moderate follow T'oegye	**NORTHERNERS** adamant follow Cho Sik
1599 Appointment of Inspector-General		GREATER Hong Yŏsun	LESSER Nam Igong
1608 Accession of Kwanghae-gun		BONE, FLESH CENTRAL	MODERATE HARDLINE
1623 Accession of Injo	MERIT active	HARDLINE inactive	
	ELDER, YOUNG		
	WŎN, NAK	HAN, SAN	
1674 Judgement on Song Siyŏl		MODERATE, HARDLINE pardon kill	
1683 (SASAEK)	**NORON** Song Siyŏl	**SORON** Yun Chung	**SOUTHERNERS** **(LESSER) NORTHERNERS**
1762 Yŏngjo	DOGMATIC, REALIST		
1800 Sunjo	(Andong Kim)		
1840 Hŏnjong	(P'ungyang Cho)		
1851 Ch'ŏlchong	(Andong Kim)		
1863 Kojong	All the factions are effectively emasculated		

117

Under Sukchong's successor **Yŏngjo** (r. 1724–1776), power passed permanently to the Noron, but the suffocation of Prince **Changhŏn** in a rice chest in 1762 split them into Dogmatists (*Pyŏkp'a*), who thought the king had been too indulgent with the prince, and Realists (*Sip'a*), who sympathised with the Prince. This split ran across the other divisions: most Southerners joined the Realists, and when the Prince's son, later called **Chŏngjo**, came to the throne in 1776, he naturally favoured the Realists, who included Southerners and Catholics. The persecution of Catholics after his death in 1801 was partly due to the fall of the Realists from favour under the next king, Sunjo.

Early in the 19th century a French missionary wrote that a Noron would have the pick of the feast, while a Soron waited obsequiously upon him, a Lesser Northerner sat quietly apart, and the ragged Southerner stood at the back, nursing his anger. The backlash finally came when the *Sirhak* **movement** aimed at political advancement for deserving officials regardless of factional allegiance, and the strong control of the Regent, Hŭngsŏn **Taewŏn-gun**, put this policy (*tangp'yŏngch'aek*) into practice after 1864.

The table on page 117 gives only a very broad outline of factional history. It does not convey details of power-sharing, tensions between groups or the processes of power change. Most changes were immediate, but some were gradual. The dates given below are of significant events related in various ways to power changes listed in the chart.

1574	Division between Eastern and Western factions
1584	Death of **Yi I**
1589	Division of Easterners into Northern and Southern factions
1592	Japanese invasions (***Imjin***-*waeran*)
1599	Appointment of Inspector-General
1608	Division of Northerners into five groups
1623	Accession of Injo
1649	Accession of Hyojong
1674	2nd **Dowager Queen** mourning rites controversy
1680	Purge of Southerners
1683	Division of Westerners into Noron and Soron
1689	Deposition of **Queen Min**
1694	Restoration of Queen Min
1701	Death of Lady Chang
1721	Accession of **Kyŏngjong**
1725	Accession of **Yŏngjo**
1728	Rebellion of Yi Injwa
1755	Naju graffiti incident
1762	Death of Crown Prince **Changhŏn**
1800	Accession of **Sunjo**
1851	Accession of **Ch'ŏlchong**
1863	Accession of **Kojong**

OVERVIEW OF FACTIONS IN POWER

1575–1584 EASTERNERS & WESTERNERS IN TENSION

1584–1623 EASTERNERS (South and North) IN TENSION
        1584–1589 Joint Easterners
        1589–1592 Northerners
        1592–1598 Southerners

1598–1608 Five Group Northerners
1608–1623 Great Northerners

1623–1674 WESTERNERS
    1623–1649 Meritorious Westerners
    1649–1674 Hardline Westerners

1674–1694 WESTERNERS and SOUTHERNERS IN TENSION
    1674–1680 Southerners
    1680–1683 Hardline Westerners
    1683–1689 Divided Westerners
    1689–1694 Southerners

1694–1725 WESTERNERS (NORON/SORON) IN TENSION
    1694–1701 Westerners
    1701–1721 Westerners (Noron)
    1721–1725 Westerners (Soron)

1725–1800 NORON
    1725–1728 Noron
    1728–1755 Noron-Soron tension
    1755–1762 Noron
    1762–1800 Dogmatic and Realist tension

1800–1895 (NORON) Queens' families
    1800–1840 Andong Kim
    1840–1851 P'ungyang Cho
    1851–1863 Andong Kim
    1863–1895 Yŏhŭng Min

FAIRIES *See* **Immortals**

FAITHFUL WIDOW GATE *yŏllyŏ-mun* 烈女門
A **banner gate** (*chŏngmun*) in memory of a widow who remained unmarried.

FANS
Korean fans (*puch'ae*) have been classified into seventy or so categories. Two broad categories are *tansŏn* 'spatulate' and *hapchuk* or *chwil-puch'ae* 'folded'. The earliest fans were probably large leaves, which were later imitated in wicker and other vegetable matter to create spatulate fans. Folded fans came later, invented perhaps in Japan. They were known in Korea by the beginning of the 10th century and passed from Korea to China in the mid-11th century.
    Although most Korean spatulate fans are now made of **paper** pasted over a frame of split **bamboo** and have a wooden handle, the names of some shapes are still derived from leaves: banana-leaf, lotus-leaf, lotus-petal, paulownia-leaf. There are also circular (*yunsŏn*) fans. Others are categorised by decoration, *t'aegŭk*, **wheel of bliss**, magpie-wing (parti-coloured), or by the shape of the handle, such as monk's-head, snake's-head or fish-head. Spatulate fans are used by both sexes indoors and were carried by **women** in palanquins, but men did not use them outside the home.
    In the street men used folding fans, usually lacqered black (*ch'ilch'ŏp*). Otherwise the white paper fan (*paekch'ŏp*) was normal. Mourners always used white fans. At a

wedding the groom had a blue fan and the bride a red one, for shading their faces from the sun.

Folding fans as gifts often used to be painted with **Diamond Mountains** landscapes, but other subjects, especially orchids and **calligraphy** have become popular. The peculiar problems of pictorial composition on the segmental fan-shape intrigue the connoisseur, and unmounted fan paintings are collected in albums, but the painting is more esteemed if it is done after the paper has been mounted on the bamboo struts. Special fans may be made with struts of mottled bamboo. The highest quality of fanwork comes from Naju, Namp'yŏng and Chŏnju. Wooden or bamboo parts are often decorated with pokerwork (*nakchuk*).

Mudang use their own very large type of folding fan, with black struts and brightly coloured paintings, often floral. *Namsadang* used large white folding fans for tight-rope walking and acrobatics. Feather fans and large floral fans are used in some *kisaeng* dances. Some palace fans were spatulate, decorated with pearls and inlay. Ceremonial fans on long poles formed part of the royal insignia.
See also pul

FELT *tam* 毯

Felt-making was an ancient skill of the **Mongols** and Manchus. Although sheepswool makes the best felt, other animal fibres will also serve. In Korea felt was used chiefly for making military headgear and apparently came from the Mongol tradition in the 14th century. The fashion for the soldier's round felt hat with a brim (*pŏnggŏji*) was adopted by the upper classes, especially senior army officers, after the 17th-century **Manchu invasions**. In the last years of Chosŏn only servants and agricultural workers wore such headwear. The *pŏnggŏji* is now typical of farmers' bands (*nongak-tae*).

FENGSHUI 風水 *See P'ungsu*

FÉRON, STANISLAS (b. 1827)
A French priest who arrived in Korea in 1857 and worked in the Ch'ŏnan-Chinch'ŏn district. In 1866 he sent Felix-Clair **Ridel** to China and himself went to **Kanghwa**, hoping to meet Roze. He was forced to flee via Zhifu to Shanghai and never returned to Korea.
See also **Oppert, Ernest**

FERRÉOL, JEAN-JOSEPH (1808–53)
Ferréol arrived at Macao in 1840 as a priest of the Paris Foreign Missions, destined for Korea. He reached Shenyang and tried unsuccessfully to cross the **Yalu**. In 1843 he was appointed to succeed **Imbert** as third bishop in Korea, but still had to wait in **Manchuria**. Because the local people were afraid of harbouring a foreigner, he had to remain in hiding at Bajiazi, a sympathetic Catholic hamlet north of Shenyang. Unable to cross the Yalu, he went to Shanghai, where he waited until, with **Kim Taegŏn** and Fr **Daveluy**, he crossed to Kanggyŏng near Ŭnjin in October 1845. He reached Seoul and worked there for four years, secretly and in relative peace. In 1849 he visited Macao and returned with Fr Thomas Ch'oe Yangŏp, Andrew Kim's fellow-student. Four years later he fell ill and died in Seoul at the age of 45.

FESTIVALS
Have been important to upper and lower classes of society since ancient times as opportunities for communal worship and communication with the spirit world (*see*

shamanism), and as markers of seasonal progression in the year. They were accompanied by **music**, **dance** and feasting. Some festivals were national, others limited to regional or occupational observance, and individual village tutelary gods (*sŏnang*) were regularly invoked. Spirits of mountains, rivers, and great trees were worshipped, and villages near rivers or the sea would pay homage to the dragon king. The most widely practised festivals were those associated with the harvest and spring sowing, and with the **new year** (when, for example, the sun and moon were worshipped in the kingdom of **Silla**). In ancient times they included the late autumn rites known as *Much'ŏn* ('Dance to heaven', associated with the Eastern **Ye** people in modern South Hamgyŏng province), *Tongmaeng* ('Founder allegiance', a **Koguryŏ** festival), and *Yŏnggo* ('Welcoming drums', associated with the people of the south-west). In the mediaeval period the **P'algwanhoe** harvest festival and **Yŏndŭnghoe** (Lantern festival) were kept as occasions for national celebrations, and the Koryŏ court, which was observant of many shamanist as well as Buddhist rites, also sponsored ceremonies on four great mountains, Paegak, Tŏkchŏk, Songak and Mongmyŏk. Communal and religious festivals have continued to be widely observed to the present day, especially in rural areas. Village rites are led by shamans, generally accompanied by musicians playing farmers' music (*nongak*). The annual festival of Buddha's birthday (*see Ch'op'ail*) is observed on a national scale: processions pass through streets gaily decorated with streamers and paper lanterns, and crowded temples, packed with worshippers, resound to the hum of incantation, stallholders' patter, and entertainment.

Competitive games (such as **tug-of-war**, *ssirŭm* **wrestling**, and **swing** competitions), **masked dance** dramas, **dance**, and performances by *kwangdae* entertainers were traditionally associated with festivals, which provided working people with welcome opportunities to relax and give vent to their emotions.

CHOE SANG-SU, *Annual Customs of Korea*, Seoul: Seomun-dang, 1983

See also **Children's Day**; **Chungyang**; **Ch'usŏk**; **Ch'ilsŏk**; **Hansik**; **New Year's Day**; **Paekchang**; **rites and ceremonies**; **Tano**; **Taeborŭm-nal**

FICTION, TRADITIONAL *See Kodae sosŏl*

FILIAL CHILDREN, TWENTY-FOUR *isipsa hyo* 二十四孝
Ershısı xıao by the Yuan writer Guo Jujing provided popular moral examples for Chosŏn in 24 examples of filial piety that were much anthologised.
1 The mythical Shun (K. U Sun) was chosen as emperor because of his filial devotion. 2 Emperor Wendi of Han (K. Ham Munje) did not leave his mother's side or change his clothes during her three-year illness. 3 Cen Can (K. Chŭng Ch'am), disciple of Confucius, out cutting firewood, felt a sympathetic twinge when his mother bit her finger. 4 Min Sun (K. Min Son), when his stepmother gave him only leaves for clothing, said 'Better one son suffer cold than three go motherless.' 5 Zhong You (K. Chung Yu), disciple of Confucius, said 'I peddled ice to support my parents when I was young and would do so again if I could call them back to life'. 6 Dong Yong (K. Tong Yŏng) borrowed money for his father's funeral on the security of his own person as a bond-slave. 7 Yan Zi (K. Yŏm Cha) put on a deerskin and waited in the woods till he got the doe's milk his parents asked for. 8 Jiang Ge (K. Kang Hyŏk) rescued his mother from brigands, carrying her on his back. 9 Lu Ji (K. Yuk Chŏk) was freed from prison because of his devotion to his mother. 10 The woman Tang, née Cui (K. Tang Buin), suckled her aged mother at her own breasts. 11 Wu Meng (K. O Maeng) refused to drive away mosquitoes for fear of annoying his parents. 12

Wang Xiang (K. Wang Sang) lay on a frozen river till his body-heat melted the ice, because his stepmother wanted fresh fish in winter. 13 Guo Ju (K. Kwak Kŏ) was ready to bury his baby in order to provide for his mother. 14 Yang Xiang (K. Yang Hyang) was killed at the age of 14, rescuing his father from a tiger. 15 Zhu Shouchang (K. Chu Such'ang) spent fifty years finding his lost mother. 16 You Qianlou (K. Yu Kŏmnu) nursed his sick father. 17 Lao Laizi (K. No Naeja) at the age of 70 put on fancy dress and danced to please his senile parents. 18 Cai Shun (K. Ch'ae Sun) in a famine gave his mother ripe berries while he ate green ones himself, and refused to leave her funeral when told his house was on fire. 19 Huang Xiang (K. Hwang Hyang), having lost his mother at the age of seven, ever afterward fanned his father's pillow in summer and lay in his bed to warm it in winter. 20 Jiang Shi (K. Kang Si) walked daily to a distant river to get drinking water and fish for his mother. 21 Wang Pou (K. Wang P'o) visited his mother's grave to comfort her during thunderstorms and refused to recite Ode 202 *Liao e* about dead parents. 22 Zheng Lan (K. Chŏng Nan) beat a man who struck a statue of Zheng's dead mother. 23 Meng Zong (K. Maeng Chong) went through the woods in winter to find bamboo shoots for his mother's whim. 24 Huang Tingjian (K. Hwang Chŏnggyŏn, 1045–1105) was the famously filial poet, a friend of Su Dongpo.

FILIAL PIETY CLASSIC (C. *Xiaojing*, K. *Hyogyŏng*) 孝經

A short book in the form of conversations between Confucius and his disciple Zengzi (K. Chŭngja) about proper behaviour and attitudes to superiors, especially parents and rulers (themes found in *Liji*). It is counted as one of the Thirteen **Confucian Classics** and probably antedates the 3rd century BC. Some modern scholars regard it as partly based on genuine sayings of Confucius.

FILIAL SON GATE *hyoja-mun* 孝子門

A **banner gate** (*chŏng-mun*) to honour an outstanding example of filial piety.
See **Five Relationships**

FINGERS POINTING AT THE MOON *chiwŏl* 指月

Zhiyue lu (K. *Chiwŏl-lok*) 'Records of Fingers Pointing at the Moon' is a bulky thesaurus of *Chan* (K. **Sŏn**) biographies by Qu Ruji (1602). ('A finger pointing at the moon' is a metaphor from the Surangama **Sutra** that came to mean a teacher guiding one to buddhahood.)

FIVE BLESSINGS *o-bok* 五福

A late Chinese classification that has provided material for Korean decorative art: *su* 'long life', *pu* 'riches', *kangnyŏng* 'health', *yuhodŏk* 'acquiring desirable virtue' and *kojongmyŏng* 'peaceful death in old age'. The five are often represented by five **bats**; if only four characters are required, the first two may be used, with *kangnyŏng* divided into *kang* 'health' and *yŏng* 'peace'. In popular use *tanam* 'having many sons' is associated with these four characters as the fifth blessing.

FIVE CLOUDS *o-un* or *osaeg-un* 五雲

The five mythical clouds in decorative art are portents: *ch'ŏng* blue, for plagues of insects; *paek* white, mourning; *chŏk* red, war; *hŭk* black, floods; *hwang* yellow, abundance.

FIVE COMMANDMENTS FOR LAYMEN *Sesog-ogye* 世俗五戒
According to **Samguk sagi** and **Samguk yusa**, two youths of Silla named Kwisan and Ch'wihang were given a rule of life for laymen by the monk Wŏn'gwang (d. c.630), who had returned from study in China. The rules are of mixed Confucian and Buddhist content: (1) Serve the king loyally; (2) Serve your parents devotedly; (3) Treat friends with sincerity; (4) Never flee the field of battle; (4) Use discrimination in killing. Nothing in the texts connects this story with **hwarang**.

FIVE DIRECTIONS GENERALS *O-bang Changgun* 五方將軍
Also known as *O-bang Sinjangmu*; important rulers of the spirit world and guardians, like the **Four Heavenly Kings**, of the cardinal directions. They were,

East	*Ch'ŏngje changgun* ('Azure general')
South	*Chŏche changgun* ('Scarlet general')
West	*Paekche changgun* ('White general')
North	*Hŭkche changgun* ('Black general')
Centre	*Hwangje changgun* ('Yellow general')

See also **Changsŭng**; **Five Phases**; **Four Spirits**

FIVE ELEMENTS *See* **Five Phases**

FIVE FAMILIES SYSTEM *O-ga-t'ong* 五家統
Local administrative structure organised for political control and tax collection in the Chosŏn period; also known as *o-ga-jakt'ong* ('five families guarantee system'). It was first introduced in the mid-15th century following the rebellions of Yi Chingok (1453) and Yi Siae (1467), and was based on the Chinese system of organising families into groups of five (*oga*) for purposes of mutual surveillance. Five families formed a *t'ong* and were led by a headman (*t'ongju*), five *t'ong* constituted a *ri* under an *yang*. *Ri* were grouped into districts (*myŏn*).
See also **hyangyak**

FIVE MILITARY COMMANDS *o-wi* 五衛
The five commands for the military forces were set up in 1450, but after the Japanese invasions of 1592 (*see* **Imjin Wars**) they became nominal organisations until a new system was created in 1882. The Central Command, for Kyŏnggi, Ch'ungch'ŏng, Kangwŏn and Hwanghae provinces, was called *Ŭihŭng*, 'righteous rising'. The Command of the Left, for Kyŏngsang province, was *Yongyang*, 'dragons leaping'; the Command of the Right, for P'yŏngan province, was *Hobun*, 'tigers rearing'; the Forward Command for Chŏlla province was *Ch'ungjwa*, 'loyal helpers'; and the Rear Command, for Hamgyŏng province, was *Ch'ungmu* 'loyal warriors'.

FIVE PEAKS OF KOREA *o-ak* 五嶽
Just as China was symbolised by five peaks at the cardinal points of the compass, Korea was typified by the **Diamond Mountains** in the east, Myohyang-san (north P'yŏngan) in the west, Chiri-san in the south, **Paektu-san** in the north and Samgak-san near Seoul in the centre.

FIVE PHASES (Five Elements) *o-haeng* 五行
The doctrine of Five Phases or Processes (wood, fire, earth, metal and water) dates from the 4th and 3rd centuries BC and became popular in Korea through the spread of

123

neo-Confucian ideas. Though often called Five Elements, this is not chemical theory, but a theory of metaphysics as a process. The phases relate in two cycles: *sangsaeng*, 'generative', in which wood burns as fire, fire makes earth (ash), earth yields metal, metal melts into liquid, water nourishes wood; and *sanggŭk*, 'obstructive', in which water puts out fire, fire melts metal, metal cuts wood, wood digs earth, earth dams water. The following are the correspondences most commonly found in Korea. Asterisked lines either do not follow the normal order of these processes or can also be found with the items differently distributed.

	Lesser Yang	*YANG*	*Neutral*	*Lesser Yin*	*YIN*
phases	wood	fire	earth	metal	water
yang	pine	burning	mountain	weapons	waves
yin	bamboo	lamplight	plain	pans	streams
qualities	flexible	rising	receiving	malleable	falling
natures	mild	fiery	moist	cool	frigid
colours	blue/green	red	yellow	white	black
seasons	spring	summer	(midyear)	autumn	winter
compass	east	south	(centre)	west	north
*notes	*kak* (mi)	*ch'i* (sol)	*kung* (do)	*sang* (re)	*u* (la)
quadrant	Dragon	Phoenix	(centre)	Tiger	Tortoise
planets	Jupiter	Mars	Saturn	Venus	Mercury
*weather	wind	heat	thunder	sunshine	rain
metals	tin	copper	gold	silver	iron
*grain	barley	millet	rice	broomcorn	pulse
animals	scaled	feathered	naked	furry	shelled
sacrifices	sheep	fowl	ox	dog	pig
organs	muscles	blood	flesh	pelt	bones
*viscera	liver	heart	lungs	stomach	kidneys
tastes	sour	bitter	sweet	peppery	salty
smells	musky	scorched	fragrant	rancid	mouldy
senses	sight	taste	touch	smell	hearing
feelings	anger	joy	thought	sorrow	fear
virtues	benevolence	propriety	sincerity	justice	wisdom
*dynasties	Xia	Zhou	Huangdi	Shang	Qin
fortunes	infestation	war	abundance	mourning	floods
government	people	affairs	ruler	ministers	objects
ministries	Agriculture	War	Capital	Justice	Works
consonants	palatal	lingual	guttural	dental	labial
Ten Stems	*kap*	*pyŏng*	*mu*	*kyŏng*	*im*
	ŭl	*chŏng*	*ki*	*sin*	*kye*
*numbers	9	7	5	8	6

FIVE RELATIONSHIPS *o-ryun* 五倫

Also known as *o-sang*, the central relationships of **Confucian** ethics and social behaviour, described in *Mencius* IIIa.4.viii: affection between father and son, justice between ruler and subject, complementarity between husband and wife, precedence between elder and younger, trust between friends.

FIVE RITES O-rye 五禮

Classification of state rituals drawn up on the orders of Kings **T'aejong** and **Sejong** by Hŏ Cho (1369–1439), Chŏng Ch'ŏk (1390–1475) and Pyŏn Hyomun (b. 1396). Hŏ Cho's work on sacrificial rites was completed in 1415, that of Chŏng and Pyŏn in 1451, and all three based their research on imperial Chinese precedent. The results are to be found in chapters 128–135 of the *Sejong sillok*. The five rites are those of sacrifices (*killye*, or *chesa*), congratulatory festivities (*karye*), receptions for state guests (*pillye*), military occasions (*kullye*) and mourning (*hyungnye*). All apart from the latter were accompanied by music and dance (*see* **music, court**). Sin Sukchu's *Kukcho oryeŭi* ('Rubrics for the Five Rites of State') was published in 1474.

ROBERT C. PROVINE, *Essays on Sino-Korean Musicology: Early Sources for Korean Ritual Music*, Seoul: Il Ji Sa, 1988

FIVE SAGES OF KOREA O-hyŏn 五賢

The Five Sages of Korea are sometimes thought of as a Korean imitation of the **Five Sages of Song**, but are in fact the five men whose canonisation in the *Sŏnggyun-gwan* in 1610 marked the permanent triumph of neo-Confucian philosophy as the state orthodoxy of the Chosŏn period. They are **Kim Koengp'il, Yi Hwang, Yi Ŏnjŏk, Chŏng Yŏch'ang** and **Cho Kwangjo**.

FIVE (or SIX) SAGES OF SONG C. *Wuzi, Liuzi*; K. *o-ja, yukcha* 五(六)子

The six founders of neo-Confucianism in China, key authors of Confucian orthodoxy in Korea, are canonised in the *Sŏnggyun-gwan*. Five of them were friends, deeply interested in the *Book of Changes*, who lived just before the end of Song rule over all China. Three were of the same generation: Shao Yong (K. So Ong, 1012–1077), a numerologist who studied the structure of the hexagrams; Zhou Dunyi (K. Chu Toni or Yŏmgye Sŏnsaeng, 1017–1072), who opened up the metaphysical meanings of *taiji* (K. *t'aegŭk*) and *yin-yang* (K. *ŭmyang*) in the Great Treatise of the *Book of Changes*, and Zhang Zai (K. Chang Chae, 1020–1077), also called Zhang Hengqu (K. Chang Hoenggŏ) or Changja, who identified *taiji* with *qi* (K. *ki*, material force). Zhang's nephews, Cheng Hao (K. Chŏng Ho, or Myŏngdo Sŏnsaeng, 1032–1085) and his younger brother Cheng Yi (K. Chŏng I, or Ich'ŏn Sŏnsaeng, 1033–1108) carried these principles into the investigation of *xing* (K. *sŏng*, human nature). Cheng Yi also wrote a commentary on the Changes and began treating the Four Books (*Lunyu, Mengzi, Daxue* and *Zhong yong*), rather than the pre-Confucian classics, as the fundamental scriptures of Confucianism. Four generations later, when Song rule was restricted to the southern part of China, the great **Zhu Xi** (K. Chu Hŭi, or Chuja) synthesised all neo-Confucian learning in commentaries on all the classics, and became the teacher par excellence for Korean orthodoxy.

See also **Confucian Classics**

FIVE TEACHINGS O-gyo 五教

The five principal schools of *Kyo* or doctrinal **Buddhism** in **Silla**, set against the **nine mountain schools** of *Sŏn*. The categorisation seems to be late. All were founded in the 7th century, and all but (5) below with plain Chinese inspiration: (1) *Yŏlban-jong* 'Nirvana-**sutra** school', later called *Sihŭng-jong*, was founded in **Koguryŏ** by Podŏk and taken up by King **Muyŏl** of **Silla**; (2) *Yul-jong* or *Kyeyul-jong* 'Vinaya school', the school of the rule or discipline, later called *Namsan-jong* 'south mountain school', founded by **Chajang**; (3) *Wŏnyung-jong* or *Hwaŏm-jong* 'Avatamsaka-sutra school', later called *Haedong-jong* 'Korean school', founded by **Ŭisang**; (4) *Pŏpsang-jong*

'Dharmata school', later called *Chaŭn-jong* after the Tang monk Ci'en (K. Chaŭn, founder of the Dharmata school, 632–682), founded in mid-8th century Silla by Chinp'yo; (5) *Pŏpsŏng-jong* 'Dharmalakshana school', later called *Chungdo-jong* 'middle way school', founded by **Wŏnhyo** and exemplified in his *Simmun hwajaeng-non*, 'Harmonising the Debates between the Ten Schools'.

LEWIS R. LANCASTER, *Assimilation of Buddhism in Korea, Religious Maturity and Innovation in the Silla Dynasty,* Berkeley: Asian Humanities Press, 1991

FIVE TONES *o-ŭm* 五音

The Chinese early realized that sounds had a cosmic aspect. Their concepts of life and breath had an obvious connection with playing bamboo pipes, and they discovered the ratios between the size of bamboo tubes and the notes they produced. The pentatonic scale, common in the early development of music all over the world, has been known in China for longer than anyone would dare to guess. Korean neo-Confucianism ensured that these theories became entrenched in relation to *aak*, the formal music of sacrifices and court ceremonies (*see also* **music, court**), and knowledge of musical theory was part of every scholar's education.

The five notes of the scale were roughly equivalent to the western 'tonic solfa' system. The commonest scale was *kung, sang, kak, ch'i, u* (fa, sol, la, doh, re; C. *gong, shang, jie, zhi, yu*). As in Western solmisation, they were not of fixed pitch.

Pitch within the octave (which has never been tempered) was defined, probably during Zhou times (c. 1000–221 BC), when names were given to the twelve semitones (*sibi yullyŏ*) of a chromatic octave. Six were regarded as *yang* and called *yul* (C. *l ü*), the other six regarded as *yin* and called *yŏ* (C. *lü*). The names are given here in Korean pronunciation. Some of them are very obscure. In Korea since the 15th century *hwangjong*, the lowest pitch, has been Middle C.

	Korean	*Chinese*	*'translation'*	
C	*hwangjong*	*huangzhong*	yellow bell	*yul*
C sharp	*taeryŏ*	*dalü*	great pipe	*yŏ*
D	*t'aeju*	*taicu*	great frame	*yul*
D sharp	*hyŏpchong*	*jiazhong*	pressed bell	*yŏ*
E	*kosŏn*	*guxian*	old purified	*yul*
F	*chungnyŏ*	*zhonglü*	median pipe	*yŏ*
F sharp	*yubin*	*ruibin*	luxuriant guest	*yul*
G	*imjong*	*linzhong*	forest pipe	*yŏ*
G sharp	*ich'ik*	*yize*	equalised	*yul*
A	*namnyŏ*	*nanlü*	southern pipe	*yŏ*
A sharp	*muyŏk*	*wuyi*	unceasing	*yul*
B	*ŭngjong*	*yingzhong*	resonant bell	*yŏ*

FIVE TRAITORS *o-jŏk* 五賊

The five ministers who accepted the Japanese **Protectorate Treaty** in 1905: Yi Chiyong (b. 1870), Home Minister; Pak Chesun (1858–1916), Foreign Minister; Yi Kŭnt'aek (1865–1919), War Minister; **Yi Wanyong** (1858–1926), Education Minister; Kwŏn Chunghyŏn (1854–1934), Agriculture, Trade and Industry Minister.

FIVE WATCHES OF THE NIGHT *o-gyŏng* 五更

The night hours were divided into five watches that are referred to in three ways: (1) number + *-gyŏng* 'watch'; (2) **sixty-fold cycle** stem + *-ya* 'night [watch]; (3) branch + *-si* 'hour'. Each watch was divided into five *kyŏngchŏm* 'watch points'.

1900-2059	*Ch'ogyŏng*	KABYA	*Sulsi*
	1st watch	1st of night	Dog hour
2100-2259	*Igyŏng*	ŬRYA	*Haesi*
	2nd watch	2nd of night	Pig hour
2300-0059	*Samgyŏng*	PYŎNGYA	*Chasi*
	3rd watch	3rd of night	Rat hour
0100-0259	*Sagyŏng*	CHŎNGYA	*Ch'uksi*
	4th watch	4th of night	Ox hour
0300-0459	*Ogyŏng*	MUYA	*Insi*
	5th watch	5th of night	Tiger hour

See also **Hours of the day**

FLAG, NATIONAL *T'aegŭk-ki* 太極旗

The Korean national flag bears symbols beloved by orthodox neo-Confucians. Korea had been asked to use a variant of the Chinese dragon flag, when, at the end of his voyage to Kobe in October 1882 (*see Imo* **Incident**), **Pak Yŏnghyo** produced a sketch of the *t'aegŭk*, a **roundel** composed of a red above a blue or black comma (*yang* and *ŭm*, the ultimate limit of being, next to the primal monad), surrounded by the eight **trigrams**, the next stage of development into the '10,000 entities'. A Briton (probably William George **Aston**, HBM Consul-General) advised using only the four **trigrams** that are vertically symmetrical, keeping the eight-trigram version as the royal standard. This was decreed by the King in March 1883, and soon became popular, especially later in the century with the **Independence Club**. These four trigrams have many meanings, but are usually interpreted as heaven-earth-sun-moon, father-mother-daughter-son, or benevolence-justice-propriety-wisdom. The placing of the trigrams and tilt of the *t'aegŭk* were fixed by the Ministry of Education in 1949.

FLAGS, MILITARY *kun'gi* 軍旗

In the Chosŏn dynasty a commander's flag, *yŏng-gi*, was a square blue flag bearing the Chinese character *yŏng* (C. *ling*) and adorned with tiny bells.

Each army division had 38 positional flags (*taegich'i*): 5 *koch'ogi*, 'high signal flags', bearing the eight **trigrams**, one in each of the five colours bordered with the appropriate colour in the order of mutual production of the **five phases** theory (red on the blue flag, black on the white, yellow on the red, blue on the black, and white on the yellow); 5 large directional flags (*tae-obang-gi*), also in the colours of the four cardinal points of the compass, set at the outer gates of the camp and carrying the **four spirits** (*chujak-ki, ch'ŏngnyong-gi, paekho-gi, hyŏnmu-gi*), with *tŭngsa-gi*, 'rearing snake flag', yellow with a snake on it, in the camp centre; 10 smaller directional flags (*chung-obang-gi* or *sin-gi*, 'spirit flags', abolished in 1869), two in each of the five colours, with a picture of a spirit-general on a winged horse; 10 square 'gate-flags', *mun-ki*, two in each of the five colours, all bordered in yellow and carrying a picture of a winged **tiger**; and eight square corner flags, *kak-ki* (reduced to four in 1869).

The division also had 2 triangular pathfinder flags, blue with a red border, inscribed with the characters *ch'ŏngdo*, 'clear way' in black; 2 triangular military band flags in yellow watered silk with red border, inscribed with black characters *kŭmgo*, 'golden drum'; and, until 1869, 1 *p'yomi-gi*, with a drawing of two 'leopards' tails' intertwined, used for marking forbidden areas.

The Palace Guard (*Kŭmgun-ch'ŏng*, called *Yongho-yŏng*, 'dragon and tiger division', from 1755), had only 18 flags: 2 *ch'ŏngdo-gi*, 2 *kŭmgo-gi*, 2 *mun-ki* (both yellow), 4 *kak-ki*, and 8 square commandants' flags, *Kŭmgun-ch'ŏng in-gi*. These eight were yellow for the commander; yellow with blue border, with white border and with yellow border; blue with blue border and with white border; and white with blue border and with white border.

FLAGS, PROCESSIONAL *ŭijang-gi* 儀仗旗

When the king went out in procession (*kŏdong*), his entourage carried **insignia** including an array of flags, mostly triangular. After the **Great Han Empire** was declared in 1897 their number was increased and the emperor was followed by a moving forest of small flags. Some bore mythical creatures: *kaktan-gi* (the Chinese *jiaoduan*), a unicorn that runs 18,000 *li* in a day; *paekt'aek-ki* (the Chinese *paize*), that talks with men; *yurin-gi*, the wandering *qilin* or griffin (often called a unicorn); *ŭibong-gi*, the royal **phoenix**, and *sangnan-gi*, a soaring phoenix; *ch'ŏllok-ki*, heavenly **deer**, the one-horned Chinese *taoba*; *ch'ŏnma-gi*, the heavenly horse ridden by the Supreme God; *hwach'ung-gi*, the 'millefleurs creature', a pheasant said by *Shujing* to have been put on royal robes by Shun; *chŏgo-gi*, a red crow from a legend of King Wu of Zhou; *chillo-gi*, 'white egrets', title of Ode 278 in *Shijing*, meaning representatives of Xia and Shang at a sacrifice by the Zhou king. Ch'ŏngnyong-gi was another blue **dragon** pennon; *chujak-ki* was the Red Bird of the South; *myŏngyŏn-gi* the crying kite; *unhak-ki* the clouds and crane; *sunsa-gi* the tame lion; *sŏu-gi* the rhinoceros; *hwangnyong taeduk* a yellow dragon from the Qing flag; *paekch'i-gi* a white pheasant; *kongjak-ki* the peacock; *chŏgung-gi* a red bear; *hwangung-gi* a 'yellow bear' that was really a three-legged turtle; *hwanggok-ki* a 'golden goose' that was a kind of roc.

Auspicious emblems were *kamu-gi*, seasonal rains; *pŏksa-gi* the (C.) *pixie*, a mythic beast that chases evil away, as its name suggests; and *oun-gi*, **five clouds** of different colours, for predicting weather and luck. Ch'wihwa-gi was a 'kingfisher feather flag'.

A cosmic sense of the realm was proclaimed by *p'alp'ung-gi,* the eight winds (S, SE, to W, SW); *oroe-gi*, the five thunders used in *p'ungsu*; *osaek-ki* five colours; flags for the **four spirits**; *oak-ki* **five peaks of Korea**; *sadok-ki* **four rivers of Korea**; *il-gi*, the sun, *wŏl-gi*, the moon, and *osŏng-gi*, the five planets. The 28 pennons, the *yŏlsuk-ki*, one named after each of the **lunar mansions**: *Kaksŏng-gi, Hangsŏng-gi, Chŏsŏng-gi* and so on, each bearing the diagram of the mansion, were just as they are described as being used by **Zhuge Liang** around his army camp before the battle of the Red Cliffs in *The Romance of the Three Kingdoms*, chapter 49. There was also a *ch'ŏngso-gi*, 'plain blue flag'.

Other flags bore black Chinese characters: *ipp'il-gi* 'entry to the royal halting place', *ch'ulgyŏng-gi* 'coming out to admonish'; and two square flags: the red *kumja-gi* with the word *kŭm* 'metal'; and the white *kunwang-ch'ŏnse-gi*, with red, blue, yellow and white borders, bearing the words 'May the king reign 1,000 years'. A very large square 'paired dragons' flag, *kyoryong-gi*, yellow with dragons and a red border, was the sign of the king as commander of the army. High-ranking military officers in procession carried *sugi*, small hand-flags, varying in size and colour according to the officer's rank.

FLOWER AND BIRD PAINTING *hwajo-hwa* 花鳥畫

Despite its name subjects in this category also include animals, insects, fish, fruit, vegetables, and other elements of the natural world such as rocks and trees. It was practised on scrolls and fans in the Koryŏ dynasty, but achieved its greatest popularity in the Chosŏn period, both among literati and folk artists. The symbolism of elements from the countryside provided popular decorative themes in the home: the **lotus** was admired as a symbol of purity and for its Buddhist associations; the peony stood for wealth, the orchid for feminine fragrance; rocks and pines indicated venerability and old age, the chrysanthemum endurance; magpies were the harbingers of good news, mandarin ducks of marital bliss; butterflies and flowers suggested the combination of *ŭm-yang*; the list was endless. Many famous painters practised flowers and **birds**, including **Chŏng Sŏn** and **Kim Hongdo**, and many good examples of their work survive. Some specialised: **Pyŏn Sangbyŏk** (Hwaje), for example, is known for his paintings of **cats**, a symbol of happiness. Stylistically, both infilled outline and 'boneless' techniques were employed. Some artists depicted the structure and texture of their subjects, such as leaves, petals and fur, in great detail: **Sim Sajŏng**'s monochrome study of peonies skilfully emphasized the soft and velvety feel of the flower head in contrast with the darker and harder surface of the leaves.[1] Others veered towards the more 'minimalist' approach of *Sŏn* art: **Kim Chŏnghŭi**'s *Orchid*, simple though it is, is renowned as the epitome of this class of painting and for the perfect balance between the leaves of the plant and the strokes of the **calligraphy** surrounding it.[2] As in the case of bamboo painting, balance was an essential quality of the flower and bird picture. Brushwork and texture were important, but without good compositional use of line and space the harmonious effect of the whole would be lost.

Among modern artists, **Yi Chungsŏp** is known for his paintings of fish, crabs, and fighting cocks and bulls. The latter expressed his passion and anger at the Japanese ill-treatment of Korea, but when asked about the symbolism of his fish and crabs, he replied that it was probably that he had eaten so many of them as a refugee after the **Korean War** that he must have felt sorry for them.

(1) KEITH PRATT, *Korean Painting*, Hong Kong: Oxford University Press, 1995
(2) CHOI SUNU, *5000 Years of Korean Art*, Seoul: Hyonam Publishing Co., 1979
See also **folk painting**; *genre* **painting**; **landscape painting**; **painting**

FLOWER, NATIONAL *Kukhwa* 國花

The concept of a national flower is modern and romantic. Only during the 20th century was the wild Korean hibiscus *Hibiscus syriacus* popularly and informally adopted in this rôle. References in *Shanhai jing* and a thin trickle of other sources, including *Chibong yusŏl*, suggest that the Chinese have long thought of Korea as a country where hibiscus flourishes. In 1937 **Ch'oe Namsŏn** recorded *Kŭnyŏk*, 'hibiscus territory', as a sobriquet for Korea, but the first example he could find was **O Sech'ang**'s book on Korean **calligraphy** and **painting** called *Kŭnyŏk sŏhwa-jing*, published in 1928. There had been a **women**'s group among the nationalist **students** called *Kŭnu-hoe*, 'Friends of the hibiscus', in 1927. In 1933 the Presbyterian journalist and patriot Namgung Ŏk (1863–1939), who grew hibiscus, was imprisoned by the Japanese for writing a song *Mugunghwa tongsan*, 'Hibiscus Garden', for his school at Hongch'ŏn. The present national anthem (*Aegguka*), in which Korea is called 'Three thousand leagues of hibiscus flowers' was already circulating.

In the 12th century **Yi Kyubo** wrote a poem about the paradoxical names of the flower: *sun* or *ilmol* 'die in a day', and *mugunghwa* 'undying flower' (found in *Sasŏng t'onghae* (1517) and now the popular Korean name). The latter is thought to be a corruption of *mokkŭnhwa*, 'shrubby mallow flower'. The common variety is mauve with a crimson centre, but the red-hearted white is much esteemed. It is called *paek-tansim*, 'red-hearted white', an expression that echoes **Chŏng Mongju**'s famous song of loyalty.

FLOWERS, GARDEN

The cultivated man's approach to flowers is epitomised by the **Four Gentlemen**; but Confucian prejudice against exotic animals did not extend to exotic plants. The three-coloured peach, bearing red, pink and white flowers on one tree, was being grown in the 15th century; and when Chŏng Tuwŏn came back from Beijing in 1631 with a purple *mokhwa* (probably a magnolia) given him by the Portuguese Jesuit Fr João Rodriguez (1561–1633), it was thought worthy of entry in the royal *sillok*.

Common garden flowers include the scarlet cockscomb, *maendurami* (*Celosia*) of South China, sometimes used instead of red **pepper** in *kimch'i*. It occurs in *Gaiziyuan huazhuan*, the Chinese 'Mustard-seed Garden painting manual' first published in 1679. The first mention in Korea is in a 12th-century poem by **Yi Kyubo**. *Mirabilis jalapa*, the 'Four-o-clock' from Peru that opens its flowers in the afternoon and has a powdery white endosperm, said to have been used as face powder, may have come in the 18th century, for it is called *pun-kkot* 'powder flower'. *Portulaca* (*chaesonghwa*) from Brazil probably arrived later, because it has no name in native Korean. Nor has the zinnia from Mexico, called *paegilch'o* because it blooms for about a hundred days. The poppy, despite having a Sino-Korean name, *Yanggwibi* (*see* **Yang Kwibi**), is an import from southern Europe. The queen of Korean flowers, the **lotus**, was imported from India.

The *pongsŏnhwa* 'balsam' (*Impatiens balsamina*), whose petals little girls crush with salt or alum to make red stain for their finger-nails, is indigenous. So too are *Hibiscus syriacus*, the **national flower**; *paegilhong* 'hundred-day-red'; the crape-myrtle, *Lagerstromia indica*; the yellow kerria; the tree peony, symbol of the married woman and of prosperity; and *suguk*, the hydrangea. The wild crimson *rugosa* roses of the east coast beaches are famous everywhere (*See Myŏngsa-simni*).
See also **Horticulture**

FLOWERS, WILD

Some wild flowers have made their way into the minds of modern poets who find their subject matter in rural life, especially the dog-rose (*tchille-kkot*) and the abundant cosmos that covers the verges and banks along country roads, though cosmos is an exotic, native to Mexico, that became widespread during the colonial period. In literary culture these are successors to the wild flowers that appear in **folk songs** and tales, like the little purple anemone *halmi-kkot*, 'grandmother flower', whose seed-head looks like a mop of wispy grey hairs; the white flowers (*pakkot*) coming out at evening on gourds climbing over thatched roofs; the bell-flower (*toraji*) of the campanula family, renowned for its edible roots, and theme of a famous love-song; the violet (*chebi-kkot*), lily-of-the-valley (*ŭnbangul-kkot*), and wild pink (*p'aeraengi-kkot*).

Among useful wild plants the kudzu vine (*Pueraria*) continued to be used in the mid-20th century much as was described nearly 4,000 years earlier in *Shijing*, for making country-folk's shoes and repairing the shoulder-straps of *chige*. **Ginseng**, the precious root that tastes of earth, an ancient panacea and aphrodisiac, is now largely a cultivated plant.

FLORENCE CRANE, *Flowers and Folk-lore from Far Korea*, Tokyo: Sanseido, 1931; Seoul: Sahm-bo, 1969

FOLK PAINTING *minhwa* 民畫

Folk artists imitated the classes of painting preferred by their literati superiors, including **landscapes** and religious images. In particular, their views of the **Diamond Mountains** were often sparkling in their uninhibited joy at the jagged peaks and tumbling waterfalls. Their deities included many derived from the Buddhist pantheon, as well as those of **shamanism** and folk religion. Prominent among these were the Mountain God *Sansin* and deified military heroes, worshipped as protectors of the local community. Sansin might be accompanied by his messengers, a **tiger** and a magpie, and the tiger was also a favourite subject on its own. **Flower and bird** paintings provided numerous symbols of hope and inspiration: mandarin ducks represented long marital harmony, and the carp success in child-bearing. The **Ten Symbols of Longevity** and the eight Chinese characters (*p'altŏk*) proclaiming auspicious social virtues (*hyo* filial piety, *che* brotherly love, *ch'ung* loyalty, *sin* trustworthiness, *ye* respectfulness, *ŭi* righteousness, *in* broadmindedness, and *chi* a sense of shame) stemmed respectively from the traditions of popular **Daoism** and **Confucianism**. 'Book-pile scenery' (*see* **ch'aekkŏri**) showed the respect that folk artists had for the education of the literati, or perhaps the result of a profitable commission from the landlord's estate.

Some members of the literati imitated styles and categories of folk painting, but as its name suggests, this type of painting belonged principally to the less self-conscious artists of the lower classes. They enjoyed it as a means of expressing their beliefs and hopes. They demonstrated their interest in the natural and spirit worlds and their sense of humour. Less concerned than literati artists about verisimilitude, some of their pictures were so imaginary as to verge on the surreal. They employed bright and decorative colour schemes, frequently reflecting preference for the Five Colours: black, white, red, blue and yellow. Though they used poorer quality materials than professional and scholar artists and did not sign their names, their work now finds a place in museums and collections as a demonstration of distinctively Korean culture.

CHO CHA-YONG, *Guardians of Happiness – Shamanistic Tradition in Korean Folk Painting*, Seoul: Royal Asiatic Society, Korean Branch, 1982; ROBERT MOES, *Auspicious Spirits, Korean Folk Paintings and Related Objects*, Washington D.C., 1983; JANE PORTAL, 'Korean Shaman Paintings,' *OA*, XLI/1, 1995; ZO ZAYONG, *The Flavor of Korean Folk Painting*, Seoul: Emillle Museum, 1972, repr. 1981

FOLK SONG *minyo* 民謠

Korea has a large corpus of folk songs with a great variety of tempo, mood and subject matter. They include work songs, love songs, and songs to accompany games and entertainments, and express all kinds of emotions and spiritual feelings. The titles of some can be traced back to the Three Kingdoms period, though no tunes of such antiquity have survived. Those that share features with Buddhist chant (*see* **pŏmp'ae**) may have the earliest origins. Rhythmic patterns are relatively simple (12:4, 12:8, or a slow 6 beats), but rules governing the choice of words are more complicated. They are repeated according to fixed patterns, and the refrain, which may be sung by the chorus in answer to the soloist's verse, may include nonsense syllables. The most popular songs have regional and even village-to-village variations, corresponding to some extent with spoken **dialect** areas. In the 18th and 19th centuries folk song tunes were woven into the pattern of instrumental music through the *sanjo* form, but during the colonial period the Japanese discouraged them because they expressed nationalist sentiment. Others have since become casualties of the modern tendency towards cultural standardisation, and the effect of economic progress on the life of the countryside has reduced still further the corpus of *minyo* in authentic use. However, the **minjung** movement has recognised their value to communal life and Korean culture, and has encouraged their preservation.

HAHN MANYOUNG, trans. I.Paek and K.Howard, *Kugak: Studies in Korean Traditional Music*, Seoul: Tamgu Dang 1990; KEITH HOWARD, *Bands, Songs and Shamanistic Rituals: Folk Music in Korean Society*, Seoul: Royal Asiatic Society Korean Branch, rev. ed. 1990
See also Arirang; Nongak

FOOD

Since the economy was wholly agrarian, Korean diet has been mainly vegetarian. Dairy products were virtually unknown until the colonial period. Edible wild plants (**namul**) and fungi are still used in profusion, but some of today's more important food plants were introduced from other countries. Millet and buckwheat are native, but **rice** originated in China. Soya and red bean, scallion and chives, some brassicas and top fruits (apricot, persimmon, plum, and pear) are probably indigenous. Soya beans are cooked with rice, but used also in soy sauce, bean-curd (*tubu*) and fermented pastes and sauces, all of which are first mentioned in Song China. Plants indigenous to south and west Asia, such as broad beans, sesame, garlic, onions, melons, walnuts, spinach, aubergines, cucumbers, ginger, peas, barley, wheat and sorghum have entered Korea at different times. They were all present before the inflow of American species between 1550 and 1850, when maize (known in China before 1555), **potatoes** (in Korea about 1840), sweet potatoes (in China by 1594, Korea 1763), chilli **peppers** (in Korea possibly by the 17th century), peanuts (in China 1538) and tomatoes (in China before 1600, Korea perhaps after 1800) arrived by way of Europe, the Philippines and China.

Until the rapid introduction of western food after 1980, kitchens scarcely changed from the Three Kingdoms period. Cooking was limited to what could be done with a rice cauldron embedded in the earthen kitchen-range (smaller pots for cooking other things can be placed on the cauldron), and charcoal braziers. There were no ovens, hence no baking and little roasting, and yeast cookery did not develop, though some cakes (*ttŏk*) were leavened with wine or *makkŏlli* (cloudy rice-beer). Meat was grilled, stewed, boiled, broiled or braised. Grilling slices of beef (*pulgogi*) on metal plates over fire was perhaps learnt from the **Mongols**, and was not practised by the lower classes. Most cooking is quick and uses fuel economically.

Men and women traditionally eat separately, the men forbidden to speak at table, owing to a fundamentalist interpretation of *Analects* x.10. All meals consist of a large helping of *pap* (boiled grain), with *panch'an* (numbers of side-dishes of vegetables, fish and meat) and a bowl of soup. Dipping sauces are much used.

The distinction between *pap*, the essential part of the meal, and *panch'an* preserves the ancient distinction between carbohydrates and other foods that is traditional in China. Carbohydrates include noodles (*myŏn*) and other confections of finely milled flour (which was developed in China in the last century BC). The two elements can be combined in one-dish meals, *yori*, such as stuffed dumplings (*mandu*, which originated in central Asia); or cold vegetables, minced meat and cold rice, all wrapped in seaweed (*kimbap*). Other *yori*, such as braised spare-ribs of beef cooked with vegetables and jujubes (*kalbi-tchim*), grilled beef slices (*pulgogi*) or, for a special occasion, a *sinsŏllo* chafing-dish in which choice ingredients are cooked over charcoal on the meal-table, may be served instead of *panch'an*. Some of today's *yori*, stews such as *sŏllŏng-t'ang* or risottos such as *pibim-pap* and *pokkum-pap*, are former peasant dishes adapted as inexpensive eating-house meals.

There are few sweet dishes beyond a preparation of diced fruit in honeyed water (*hwach'ae*) or a compôte of dried persimmons (*sujŏnggwa*). Coloured rice-cakes, dried fruit and other sweets are piled high on a special table for New Year and other ceremonies, in displays that resemble sacrificial offerings. As in pre-Qin China, malt was used for sweetening, as it still is for making *yakpap* (sweet rice). There was little bee-keeping: most honey came from wild bees. Cane sugar became important in Song China. Pine-pollen is much used (*see* **trees**).

The impression that all Korean food tastes of garlic, chilli and salt is false, derived partly from experience of Korean populations in northern China, partly from fleeting experience by foreign visitors. Most food is strongly flavoured, but the range of flavours is wide, and some dishes, such as wild vegetables, are fragrantly delicate.

Food preservation consists of drying (fish, seaweed, fruit and vegetables); salting (fish, meat and vegetables); and fermentation (vegetables). Vegetables cured by lactic acid fermentation in brine or salt make **kimch'i**, the single most typical Korean food, which may go back to **neolithic** times. Refrigerating fruit and vegetables in subterranean chambers packed with ice cut from frozen rivers was known from Silla times. Cold dishes, including iced noodles, are served in winter.

Meat (chicken, pork and beef) is used sparingly. Sheep or goat flesh is reserved for medicinal use; horseflesh is not eaten, and **dog** meat in highly spiced stew (*posin-t'ang*), at least since late Chosŏn, is eaten during the hottest weather by men only. Fish and seaweed are eaten throughout the year.

The colonial period had little influence on the Korean table, though it contributed to portable snacks in the Japanese *bento* (now called **tosirak**). Traditional snacks also survive, varying from the spit-roast sparrows and toasted silk-worm larva-cases of winter street-vendors to the toasted garlic cloves in honey of the gentleman-scholar.

Modern industrial food-processing has brought changes, but the national tradition shows great power for survival. Even wild plants and fungi are now cultivated for an expanding market.

See also **drinks**; **tea**

FOOTWEAR

Before the introduction of western boots and shoes Korean footwear was of simple design, save for the ingenious design of the twined shoes of the common folk. All shoes slipped on without fastenings or ties, except certain royal shoes. **Felt**, hemp, hides and cloth were used, even *papier mâché* for indoor wear. Men's ceremonial shoes were made of deerskin. The twined shoes were boat-shaped, clinging to the foot, cleverly made of twined and knotted straw, bast or twisted paper strips. Wealthy women wore indoor shoes of **silk** cloth, painted or decorated (often in *tangch'o* **pattern**). Women's shoes generally had upturned toes, even the chopines carved out of wood for negotiating muddy passages.

See also **dress**

FORTRESSES *sŏng* 城

Walled settlements from early periods of Korean history protected against attack by earthen or stone ramparts. They were often centres of civil and military administration (*see for example* **Hansŏng**). Surviving examples of fortresses are the **Koguryŏ** site of Mt. Taesŏng, outside P'yŏngyang, the **Paekche** fortress of **Wiryesŏng** in south-east Seoul (3rd–4th century), the **Wŏlsŏng** fortress outside **Kyŏngju** (6th–7th century), and the late Koryŏ Nagan fortress at Sunch'ŏn (southern Chŏlla province), built as defence against Japanese invasions. The modern town of **Puyŏ** (southern Ch'ungch'ŏng province) overlies the walls of the Paekche fortress of Sabisŏng. The early Chosŏn authorities built two mountain castles to protect their new capital city of Seoul (*see* **Namhan sansŏng**; **Pukhan sansŏng**). The last to be built, Hwasŏng fortress at **Suwon**, was constructed for King **Chŏngjo** between 1794 and 1797. Recently restored, it has been designated a UNESCO World Heritage Site.

W.D.BACON, 'Fortresses of Kyŏnggi-do,' *TRASKB*, XXXVII, 1961; GINA BARNES, 'Walled Sites in Three Kingdoms Settlement Patterns,' *Papers of the 5th International Conference on Korean Studies I*, Songnam: Academy of Korean Studies, 1988

FORTY-NINTH DAY PRAYERS *sasipku-il-jae, ch'ilch'il-jae* 四十九日齋(七七齋)
Buddhists say a departed soul transmigrates to a new body on the 49th day (7 x 7 days) after death. This period, known as *chungŭm*, was observed with prayers, frugality and special services.

FOUNDATION MYTHS
The mixed tribal origins and early formation of separate states in north-eastern **Manchuria** and the Korean peninsula encouraged the emergence of a variety of claims and counter-claims to divine authority. Geographical locations and topographical features were important in these, and helped to underline both the Korean sense of the country's separateness from its continental neighbour China, and the need to claim some early participation in its culture. The principal stories are related in *Samguk yusa*. The legitimation of ruling clans by appeal to divine origin was evidently accepted as important even by the hard-headed scholars of the early Chosŏn court, for the compilers of the *Koryŏ-sa* prefaced their history with a patently fictitious account of **Wang Kŏn**'s antecedents. (*See below.*)

OLD CHOSŎN
This, the most ancient of the early states mentioned here, can claim possession of the most ancient foundation myth, and the one which still arouses interest and even pride among some modern Koreans. In the time of the mythical Chinese Emperor Yao (reputedly around 2,333 BC), the supreme deity Hwanin allowed his son, Hwanung, to descend to earth, which he did at T'aebaek-san near modern P'yŏngyang. There, so one version of the story goes, he turned a female bear into a woman (Ungnyŏ, 'Bear woman') and married her. Their son, **Tan'gun**, was born, who created the state of Chosŏn with its capital at P'yŏngyang. Old Chosŏn is therefore sometimes known as Tan'gun Chosŏn. The Chinese King Wu, one of the idealised founders of the Zhou dynasty, is said to have enfeoffed **Kija** as first king of Chosŏn.

JAMES GRAYSON, 'The Myth of Tan'gun: a dramatic structural analysis of a Korean foundation myth', *KJ* 37/1, 1997.

WIMAN CHOSŎN
Is traditionally said to have been founded in 190 BC by Wei Man, a refugee from the state of Yan in the north-east of Han China, who usurped the throne of his adopted ruler in Old Chosŏn. He is reputed to have driven Kijun south from the area of P'yŏngyang (*infra*, MAHAN).

SARO (later SILLA)
King Hyŏkkŏse was said to have been miraculously born of heavenly will from an egg at the foot of Yangsan in 69 BC. He was raised with a girl also divinely born near

Saryangni in a palace on Namsan, and became king in 57 BC, the first of the Pak line. Separate myths existed concerning the divine origins of other royal and aristocratic Silla clans, including the Sŏk and Kim.

MAHAN

Is said to have been founded by a king, Kijun, fleeing from Wei Man (*supra*)'s attack on the region of modern P'yŏngyang. He established his capital in Iksan in 194 BC.

PUYŎ

The son of the supreme deity of ancient China, Shangdi, took human form in 59 BC, claimed the name Hae Mosu, and founded Northern Puyŏ; later he followed divine instructions and moved to Cholbonju to establish Eastern Puyŏ. Its king Tongmyŏng (or Chumong) became the founder of Koguryŏ (*infra*). The story is found in the *Qian Han Shu*.

KOGURYŎ

The legendary founder was Chumong (traditionally 59–19 BC), also known as King Tongmyŏng, 'Eastern light'. He was born from a miraculous egg to Yuhwa, daughter of Habaek, after her meeting with the son of the Lord of Heaven Hae Mosu near Bear Spirit Mountain (Ungsin-san) on the **Yalu** River. The legends about Tongmyŏng are doubtless a mythopoesis of emigration combined with the royal avian progenitor theme. He was a skilful archer and horse trainer, and took the surname Ko before founding Koguryŏ in 37 BC. Versions of the myth appear in *Samguk sagi* and *Samguk yusa*, with a translation of the latter in **Gale**'s *History of the Korean People*. **Yi Kyubo**'s valuable poem on Chumong is in *SKC* I, pp. 25–30.

PAEKCHE

The founder of Paekche is supposed to have been a prince of Koguryŏ, Onjo (traditionally reigned 18 BC – 28 AD). He was the younger son of Chumong (*supra*), who moved south of the **Han** River and formed the Mahan tribes into a kingdom. His story is in *Samguk sagi*.

SILLA

Samguk sagi begins with a man named Sobŏl hearing a horse squeal in a forest. The horse, which was kneeling by a huge egg that looked like a gourd, soon vanished; a boy was born from the egg. He was named Pak, 'gourd', and Hyŏkkŏse, 'Light in the world'. Later Pak Hyŏkkŏse (traditional dates 69 BC – AD 4) was elected chief of six villages and first king of Silla. This myth is taken to explain the totem animals of early communities (**horse** and domestic **fowl**), the origin of Silla kingship in the election of village-group chiefs, and an origin for the Pak surname. *Samguk yusa* has a variant of the story. (Avian descent for founder kings was claimed in ancient China too, but Pak is a purely Korean name.)

KORYŎ

Wang Kŏn's antecedents are traced in *Koryŏ-sa*, citing at length a book entitled *P'yŏnnyŏn t'ongnok* by Kim Kwanŭi. According to this account, he was descended from a man named Hogyŏng who came from **Paektu-san**. Hogyŏng, having reached the vicinity of the later city of **Kaesŏng**, settled there and married, but he and his wife remained childless. One day he confronted a **tiger** on P'yŏngna-san. It disappeared without harming him, but when he offered thanks to the spirit of the mountain she took him away in marriage. When he subsequently returned to his widow in dreams she became pregnant and bore his son. The text gives details of succeeding generations and recounts how Wang Kŏn's father, Yong, learned from an expert in *p'ungsu* of the particular advantages of Kaesŏng as a capital site.

MICHAEL ROGERS, '*P'yŏnnyŏn T'ongnok*: the Foundation Legend of the Koryŏ State', *JKS*, 4, 1982–3.

FOUR BRANCHES OF BIBLIOGRAPHY *sago* 四庫

As early as AD 264 Xun Xu, royal librarian of Jin, was using a four-part bibliographical classification; *jing* (K. *kyŏng*) 'classics', *zi* (K. *cha*) 'philosophers' – i.e. 'arts and sciences', *shi* (K. *sa*) 'records' and *ji* (K. *chip*) 'belles lettres'. A century later, the order was changed to *jing/shi/zi/ji*. This order was used in 1772–1782 for *Siku quanshu* 'All the books of the four storehouses', a monumental collection of Chinese texts made by order of the Qianlong Emperor. *Siku quanshu* provided the model for the colonial **Government General**'s catalogue of Korean books, *Chōsen Sōtokufu kotosho mokuroku* (1921), and the 'four branches' are still used for historical purposes.

There are traditional, though historically fluctuating, divisions within each of the four divisions.

Kyŏng includes editions of all the **Confucian classics** with their commentaries, anthologies and general studies on them; other books regarded as minor classics, such as the '*Filial Piety Classic*'; books on **music**; and **dictionaries** of Chinese characters.

Sa includes official records (dynastic histories, reign-histories, government department diaries); records of specific events; other records; privately compiled records; government and law (digests of departmental work, decrees, minutes, all state papers); registers and manuals; geography; metal and stone inscriptions; genealogies and chronological biographies; chronologies; bibliographies and catalogues.

Cha includes **Confucianism**, **Daoism**, **Buddhism**; military arts (including veterinary science); **agriculture**; **medicine**; **astronomy** (including calendrical science and mathematics); **divination**, *fengshui* (K. *p'ungsu*) and astrology; foreign languages; encyclopaedic works; miscellaneous notes and essays; fine arts; and fiction.

Chip includes personal collections; anthologies; literary criticism; songs; national examination documents.

FOUR GENTLEMEN *sa-gunja* 四君子

The four flower-paintings, one for each of the four seasons, highly esteemed by calligraphers and literati painters of the Chosŏn dynasty. They usually appear, especially on **screens**, as a set of four pictures, though many calligraphers specialised in one of them. *Maehwa*, the winter-flowering *Prunus mume*, is usually called '**plum-blossom**' or 'Japanese apricot'. It is a true apricot with sessile flowers and downy fruit, symbolising purity and courage, that blooms in the snow on gnarled branches with slender twigs. *Nanch'o*, the spring-flowering terrestrial orchid *Cymbidium virescens*, is symbolic of frugality, modesty and refinement because of its shady habitat, long elegant foliage and sweet fragrance. It is Korea's favourite, a small woodland plant of dry places and has greenish-white flowers tipped with red or purple. *Chuk*, the **bamboo** of summer, symbolises fortitude by its durability and greenness in the frost. *Kukhwa*, the chrysanthemum of autumn, has been a symbol of a retired and honourable life-style since it figured in the poems of **Tao Qian**. All four are ideally suited to **painting** in Chinese ink with quasi-calligraphic strokes. Though ink painting of flowers came to Koryŏ from Song China, the vogue for the quartet seems to have been inspired by the *Meilan zhuju pu* 'Apricot-orchid-bamboo-and-chrysanthemum Album' of the Ming calligrapher Chen Jiru (1558–1639) and the 'four gentlemen' epithet is distinctively Korean. A similar set, known also in China, is the *sam u* 'three friends [of the cold season]': pine, bamboo and apricot. Ink paintings of *moran*, the tree peony, were less popular in Korea than in China.

KUMJA PAIK KIM, 'Nineteenth-Century Korean Painters of the "Four Gentlemen",' *OA*, XLI/4, 1995/6

FOUR GREAT CALLIGRAPHERS *sa tae-sŏye-ga* 四大書藝家
The four great calligraphers of early Chosŏn were Prince Anp'yŏng (**Yi Yong**), **Kim Ku**, Yang Saŏn (1517–84) and **Han Ho** (Han Sŏkpong).

FOUR GREAT MASTERS OF CHINESE WRITING *Hanmun sa-daega* 漢文四大家
From the reign of Sŏnjo till the accession of Injo there a was a great flowering of *hanmun* (literary Chinese). Four men came to be regarded as representatives of the period: Sin Hŭm (brush-name Sangch'on, 1566–1628), Yi Chŏnggwi (Wŏlsa, 1564–1635), Chang Yu (Kyegok 1587–1638) and Yi Sik (T'aektang, 1584–1647). They are sometimes referred to jointly by the first characters of their literary names as Sang-wŏl-gye-t'aek, 'image-moon-valley-lake'. They were esteemed, despite inevitable criticism, both as elegant imitators of Tang and Song writers and as distinguished neo-Confucian statesmen.

FOUR GREAT RIVERS *sa-dok* 四瀆
China reckoned four great rivers, the Yellow River, Yangzi, Huai and Ji. Korea, as Sohwa, 'Little China', used the same term for the Naktong flowing into the east sea, **Han** to the south, **Taedong** to the west and Yonghŭng to the north.

FOUR HEAVENLY KINGS *Sa-ch'ŏnwang* 四天工
Lokapala, Hindu deities who were adopted into Buddhist cosmology. They live on the four sides of Mount Sumeru (K. Sumi-san), the centre of the universe, as officers in a complex series of heavens, and are associated with the four cardinal points. After being introduced into China, possibly in the 8th century, as guardians of the Buddha-world, and therefore of temples, they were partly sinified. They are often found as enormous statues in temple gatehouses, either fierce or smiling. They also appear in paintings, even behind the main Buddha images. Their iconography is variable, but generally:

East, Dhrtarastra (K. Chiguk 'keeping a country'), predominant colour blue/green, has a lute; South, Virudhaka (K. Chungjang 'increasing and growing'), red, a parasol; West, Virapaksa (K. Kwangmok 'huge eyes') white, a sword; North, Vaisravana (K. Tamun 'much hearing'), black (or yellow), a pearl or a miniature pagoda.

They wait upon Buddha and supervise the lowest of the series of **Thirty-three heavens**, where those already on the path to Nirvana await rebirth, and with assistance from squadrons of lesser spirits they command the four elements, fire, air, water and earth.

See also apsara; **Buddhism**; **Five Directions Generals**

FOUR RITES *sa-rye* 四禮
The four domestic observances by which, according to neo-Confucian protocol as it was particularly observed in the Chosŏn period, correct etiquette was maintained. They were **capping, marriage, mourning**, and **ancestral rites**.

See also Chuja-garye; **five rites**; *Kwan-hon-sang-je*; **ritual studies**

FOUR SEASONS 四時

Traditional Korean culture is a clear example of a culture conditioned by climate. The country lies in the same latitude as Portugal, Virginia and northern California, but its climate is extreme. Four clearly differentiated seasons have influenced domestic and public manners, **dress**, **food**, **reading** habits, writing and festivities.

Spring is ecstatic but very short, a few weeks between the end of March and early May, typified by the end of severe frosts and the appearance of blossom on the trees. Winter clothes are put away, summer clothes brought out and laundered for wear. Wind-borne Mongolian dust produces a blue haze in the bright sunshine until spring rains arrive, important, but not heavy. Rural people often suffered spring famine after the winter's grain and *kimch'i* had all been eaten. As soon as the first winter-sown barley ripened and appeared on the market (*pori kogae*, 'the barley pass'), the price of foodstuffs began to fall.

Summer begins hot and soon turns wet. Field work rises to a peak with the transplanting of **rice**. The monsoon rains (*changma*) are unpredictable, but come between June and September, spasmodic, yet disruptive of all work and causing poets to speak of 'ropes of moving water' cascading off the eaves. Catastrophic floods occur every few years. Administration becomes sluggish. The sweltering heat discourages mental effort, and in the *sŏdang* **schools**, boys used to turn to poetry for less taxing reading.

Autumn is the longest season, traditionally thought to start in the early days of August, though the intense heat lasts for another month. In September the heavy work of harvest is compensated by plentiful foodstuffs. This is the time for weddings and the great harvest festival *Ch'usŏk*, when the summer's rank herbage is mown on the graves. It was also a peak time for executions (justice was associated with autumn). The nights are cool, becoming cold, but the days remain sunny and mild well into November – it is the time of *ch'ŏn'go-mabi*, 'skies cloudless, horses plump'. Brilliant autumn foliage shines red, purple and gold. New clothes are bought and aired in the sunshine along with the books that are dank with summer humidity (*see* **airing of books and clothes**). For people who live in relatively crowded conditions with small **paper**-covered windows, this is the season for reading, because now it is pleasant to read outdoors. **Book** sales flourish.

The difference in length between summer and winter days is no more than two hours at either end, but winter cold is bitter. Ice and snow are everywhere, though from December to February the typical weather pattern is *samhan-saon*, 'three days cold, four days warm' – an alternating pattern caused by high pressure bringing cold air from Siberia, inducing low pressure over China to bring warm southerly winds. Padded clothing is brought out and worn. Everyone expects to stay indoors, and winter work is indoor work. The lunar **New Year** festival, towards the end of winter, used to be two weeks of relief and feasting, looking forward to spring.

FOUR-SEVEN DEBATE *sach'il-lon* 四七論 *See* **Yi Hwang**; **Yi I**

MICHAEL KALTON, *The Four-Seven Debate, an Annotated Translation of the Most Famous Controversy in Korean Neo-Confucian Thought*, State University of New York Press, 1994

FOUR SPIRITS *Sa-sin* 四神

The four creatures representing the divine guardian spirits of the universe, belonging to an early animistic belief system inherited from China. Together with their associated directions and colours they were:

East	The Dragon	Blue (not distinguished from Green)
South	The Phoenix	Red
West	The Tiger	White
North	The Tortoise	Black.

A well preserved and well known series of paintings depicts them on the walls of the Great Tomb of Kangso, Maesan, South P'yŏngan province, North Korea (early 7th century).
See also **Animals, mythic; Four Heavenly Kings; tombs**

FOUR TREASURES (or FRIENDS) *munbang-sabo* or *-sau* 文房四寶(友)
The four friends of the writing table are **paper,** writing-brushes, ink and inkstone (K. *chongi, put, mŏk, pyŏru*; Sino-Korean *chi-p'il-mug-yŏn*). All were objects of connoisseurship. Paper was made in Korea in many qualities; brushes in many sizes and qualities, *hwangsŏ-p'il* made of the gold-yellow hair of the weasel being especially prized, the coarser hair of the racoon-dog less so. Koreans claimed that the famous Huizhou ink of China was based on the method of making **Koguryŏ's** finest *songhyŏn-muk,* 'pine-soot ink'. (The oldest extant inkstick is dated to the Koryŏ period.) Perhaps the greatest affection was reserved for the scholar's inkstone, on which he meditatively ground the inkstick with water while preparing himself mentally for doing **calligraphy.** Inkstones were carved in many ways, the simplest often being most esteemed. Closely associated were the *yŏnjŏk* or water-dropper, usually of **ceramic,** frequently in the form of a **peach,** monkey, or mandarin duck; and the paperweight *munjin* or *sŏjin,* often in the form of a simple slab, but sometimes sculpted, of wood, stone or ceramic. Both objects can be of great, if usually restrained, beauty. The cult of the Four Friends came from China at least as early as Koryŏ, for it is mentioned in *P'ahan-jip.*

FOWL, DOMESTIC
Domestic fowl have been found in **neolithic** village sites, and they figure in the **Kyerim** legend. According to *Samguk Yusa,* 'Kwich'uk chesa' section, Silla was famous in India for wearing cock's feathers and venerating a divine fowl. Cock-fighting was a popular sport before World War II. Most cocks show variations on the red, gold and black feathering of the basic south Asian stock. This handsome colouring has made the cock a favourite subject in decorative painting. 4-foot tail feathers are mentioned, but have not received the attention of breeders. Korean poets, like those in most of the rest of the world, believed that cocks crow only at dawn. (In fact they crow at all hours, but are noticed at dawn.)

FOX
The Korean fox is the common Eurasian red species. It has a firm place in folklore and literature as a crafty animal, as likely as the **tiger** to change into human form.

FRANCE, RELATIONS WITH
First developed in the context of the Catholic missionary effort. Despite the proscription of Christianity, French missionaries entered Korea illegally, sometimes transferring from Chinese junks to Korean fishing boats at sea, and by 1863 there were estimated to be 23,000 Korean Catholics. Korean Catholics proposed that French aid should be sought to counter the perceived Russian threat in the mid-19th century, but this was rejected and in 1866 the **Taewŏn'gun** ordered the persecution

of Christians. Of twelve French missionaries nine, including two bishops, were martyred, in retaliation for which a French squadron of warships commanded by Admiral Roze was sent from northern China. It inflicted severe damage on **Kanghwa Island**, but an expeditionary force advancing on Seoul was repelled. It was not until 1886 that France signed a Treaty of Amity and Commerce with Korea, the last western nation to do so.

WOO CHUL-KOO, 'Centenary of Korean-French Relations,' *KJ*, 26/6, 1986

See also **Berneux; Cécille; Martyrs, Catholic; Nam Chongsam; Roman Catholic Church**

FURNITURE

Was reserved mainly for use at court until the 17th century, the majority of the population sitting, eating and sleeping on floors (*see ondol*). Then, as the court could no longer afford to maintain the **craftsmen** previously employed by the government office in charge of furniture in the aftermath of the **Imjin Wars**, they dispersed with their skills across the countryside and out into lower levels of society. Literary and pictorial evidence shows that in the earlier periods furniture included short-legged tables and beds, with occasional higher tables and chairs reserved for ceremonial use. In the late Chosŏn period the principal types of furniture in the male quarters of the household comprised low tables (*sŏan*) used for reading, writing, and accommodating smoking accessories and the **chess** board; an armrest next to the scholar's cushion; chests for the storage of writing equipment (*yŏn'gap*); bookcases (*ch'aek-t'akcha*; *see also ch'aekkŏri*); and display shelves for luxury items and other treasured possessions. There might also be a ***paduk*** board. The female quarters were furnished with wardrobes (*mŏritchang*); low chests (*nong*) and front-opening boxes (*pandaji*) for the storage of textiles, bedding, clothing, and scrolls; cabinets with drawers for medical herbs (*yakchang*); reading tables; and a sewing box. Furniture was usually made of **bamboo** or hardwoods (*see* **trees**). Though some was lacquered (*see* **lacquer**) and decorated with mother-of-pearl inlay or painted oxhorn (***hwagak***), the preference was for the grain of the unadorned wood to speak for itself, or to be enhanced with metal fittings (*changsŏk*).

Folding **screens** were used as room dividers or protection against draughts, and were decorated with ornamental **calligraphy** or embroidered or painted pictures.

EDWARD WRIGHT & PAI MAN SILL, *Korean Furniture: Elegance and Tradition*, Tokyo & New York: Kodansha International, 1984; YOON BOKCHA, CHI SOON, PARK YOUNGSOON, *Korean Furniture and Culture*, Seoul: Shinkwang Publishing Co., 1988

See also **pillows**

G

GALE, JAMES SCARTH 奇一 (Ki Il, 1863–1937)
A Scottish-Canadian Presbyterian missionary from Ontario, who arrived in Korea in 1884 and was in his lifetime the foremost interpreter of Korean culture to English-speakers. In 1891 he was posted to Wŏnsan, where he began writing about the language and got to know **Yun Ch'iho**. He was later pastor of Yŏnmot-kol (Yŏnji-dong) church in Seoul until he retired to Bath, England, in 1927. His most important works were *A Korean-English Dictionary* (1897, 3rd edition 1931), which remained standard until the 1960s; *The Cloud Dream of the Nine* (1922), a translation of ***Kuunmong***; *Ch'ŏllo yŏkchŏng* (1895), a translation of Bunyan's *Pilgrim's Progress*, done in collaboration with his wife; and *The History of the Korean People* (1927, an anecdotal

approach). He was an industrious translator of English texts for Korean students and of Korean poems and essays into English; a mainstay of *The Korean Repository*, *The Korea Magazine* and various Christian Korean-language journals; made his own translation of the Bible into Korean; and contributed significant papers on language and history to the *Transactions* of the Korea Branch of the **Royal Asiatic Society**.

RICHARD RUTT, *A Biography of James Scarth Gale and his 'History of the Korean People'*, Seoul: Royal Asiatic Society, 1972

GAMES *See* **backgammon; chess; dice; dominoes; hide-and-seek; jacks; *kawi-bawi-bo*; *konjil*; *konu*; *omok*; *paduk*; playing cards; seesaw; shuttlecocks; *sŭnggyŏng-do*; toys, children's; tug-o'-war; *yut***

STEWART CULIN, *Games of the Orient*, Tokyo: Tuttle, 1958, a reprint of *Korean Games*, Pennsylvania, 1895

GANDHARVA kŏndalp'a 乾達婆

Attendant spirits of the sky-god **Indra**, who lived in the first six of the **thirty-three heavens**. Because they ate incense, they emitted beautiful fragrance. They were symbolic of erotic love. Their city, Kŏndal-sŏng, gives a word for 'mirage'. They were spouses of the *apsaras*.

GARDENS *See* **Flowers, garden; horticulture**

GENEALOGIES *chokpo* 族譜

Because both social status and proper performance of **ancestral rites** depended so heavily on membership of the male line of a family, the study (*pohak*) of one's own ancestry and that of other people became of paramount importance for the educated classes in a neo-Confucian state. From the 15th century onwards, clan genealogies were increasingly published, as essential documents for maintaining this system. The oldest extant example is the Andong Kwŏn genealogy of 1476, though there is evidence of the Munhwa Yu genealogy being printed in 1423. Many more were published during the next three centuries. The earliest sections of a genealogy will have been reconstructed more or less imaginatively, but most are reasonably reliable for late Koryŏ times onward. The prefaces are of great interest, expressing such concerns as the wish to include as many daughters as possible. Genealogies are still a source of great pride to modern Koreans.

MARTINA DEUCHLER, *The Confucian Transformation of Korea: A Study of Society and Ideology*, Cambridge, Mass.: Harvard University Press, 1992; EDWARD WAGNER, 'The Korean Chokpo as a Historical Source', in SPENCER J. PALMER, *Studies in Asian Genealogy*, Provo: Brigham Young University Press, 1972

GENERAL SHERMAN

Armed American merchant steamship which sailed up the **Taedong** River as far as P'yŏngyang in 1866 in an attempt to open trading relations. On board also was **R. J. Thomas**, who had joined the vessel with Bibles and Christian tracts. It ran aground and all on board were killed by local people. The refusal by the Korean government to give compensation prompted an American naval expedition in May 1871 under Admiral Rodgers. Fighting around **Kanghwa Island** resulted in heavy Korean casualties but no satisfaction for the Americans as far the opening of relations was concerned. The **Taewŏn'gun**'s policy of isolationism appeared to be holding firm.

See also **America, relations with**

GENEVA CONFERENCE (1954)

On Korea and Indo-China. It was held as part of the South Korean President Syngman Rhee (**Yi Sŭngman**)'s agreement to sign the **Armistice Agreement** halting the **Korean War**, and was the first international conference in which South Korea participated as a sovereign state. Fifteen countries took part. The American delegation was headed by Bedell Smith, that of the Soviet Union by Andrei Molotov, the British by Anthony Eden and the Chinese by Zhou Enlai. Foreign minister Pyŏn Yŏngt'ae led the South Korean team. The aim was to plan the withdrawal of foreign troops from the peninsula and initiate moves towards its peaceful reunification, but the result was merely to reconfirm the stalemate of the Armistice. Talks took place from 28 April to 15 June 1954. They were adjourned without resolution of the conflict between the American proposal for UN-supervised elections across the whole country, and the counter-demand from the communists that a neutral commission should take charge of them. The Chinese played a prominent part in the talks, which gave them a new rôle in international diplomacy. However, against the background of China's own economic difficulties, they accepted the need for coexistence between the two Korean states.

See also **People's Republic of China, relations with**

GENRE PAINTING *sokhwa, p'ungsok-hwa* 俗畫, 風俗畫

Depicted social activities among both lower and upper classes. Earliest examples appear among the **tomb** murals of the Three Kingdoms period, showing **dancing**, **wrestling** (*ssirŭm*), **hunting**, music-making, and **food** preparation. These pictures were painted by folk artists, who probably also assisted Buddhist monks in decorating temple walls. From the 18th century onwards a particular class of picture sometimes appears on a wall of the main hall in a Buddhist temple showing scenes of daily social life. Generally classified as *t'aenghwa* but technically known as *kamno-jŏng* 'sweet dew paintings' or 'nectar paintings' (from the 'sweet dew' of Buddha's law that according to the Lotus **Sutra** pervades all life), they are unique to Korea. Centred on 'sweet dew rituals' for the dead, they show ordinary social events for the first time in Buddhist art, and for that reason are also referred to as *p'yŏngsaengdo* ('daily life pictures'). Properly, however, *p'yŏngsaengdo* describes the series of pictures, often on screen panels, showing the auspicious events in a man's life. They may include such things as scenes of family life, of a man with grandchildren, and even of a sixtieth wedding anniversary. This kind of documentary and honorific art represents a Confucian outlook and tradition but was nevertheless practised by folk artists as well as the literati. When literati painters painted stylised pictures of scholars pursuing activities particular to their refined way of life it is debatable whether this may properly be called *genre* painting, but *p'yŏngsaengdo* frequently contain so many details of behaviour among the bystanders and onlookers as well as the main subjects as to qualify without question. Just as folk artists practised artistic styles and subjects derived from the sinicised outlook of the gentry, so too in the 18th and 19th centuries did professional court artists show their sense of Koreanness by painting members of lower as well as upper classes performing daily tasks. The two greatest exponents of *genre* painting were **Kim Hongdo** (Tanwon) and **Sin Yunbok** (Hyewŏn), but others who were interested in depicting the activities of, for example, farmers and **women** were Cho Yŏngsŏk (1686–176) and Yun Tusŏ (1668–1715). Kim Hongdo is renowned for his lively pictures of ordinary people performing daily tasks such as tiling a roof, ploughing a field, and washing clothes. Sin Yunbok found his subjects more among the activities of the *yangban*, and showed them in realistic and

humorous situations. Some of his best known pictures poke fun at scholars in sexually compromising situations with *kisaeng*. In the late 19th century the painter **Kim Chun'gŭn** (Kisan) produced large numbers of detailed, but naïve, *genre* studies of people's occupational and recreational pursuits, invaluable as records for social history.
See also **Kim Tŭksin**
KANG WOO-BANG & KIM SEUNG-HEE, *The World of Nectar Ritual Painting*, Seoul: Yekyong Pub. Co., 1995; KUMJA PAIK KIM, 'Tanwon and the Development of Korean Genre Painting,' *KC*, vol.4 pt.2, 1983

'GENTLEMEN'S SIGHTSEEING GROUP' (1881)   *See Sinsa yuramdan*

GENTRY, THE
Did not comprise a defined social or political class, though in reference to the Chosŏn period the term is sometimes used almost interchangeably with *yangban*. It included those élite families whose power was derived from blood-relationship with a dynastic **lineage**, those who were rewarded with land or rank by the court for military or political service, and those whose authority rested on their ownership of landed estates, whether inherited or newly acquired. In the Unified Silla period the bone-rank system (*see **Kolp'um***) formed a blood-related aristocracy which defined the composition of the ruling class at court. It could not, however, comprise all those powerful families who, through descent, inherited regional powers, or military and economic roles, exercised actual authority across the country. The court expected allegiance, too, from its *sŏngju* ('castle lords'), leaders of local communities which they surrounded with protective walls and defended with private armies as potentially *de facto* warlords. **Chang Pogo** maintained a garrison of this kind on Chŏnghae Island.
     Castle lords survived actively through the **Later Three Kingdoms** period until King Kwangjong (949–75) asserted royal authority over them and a system of promotion by merit was instituted (*see* **examinations**). King Sŏngjong extended the rôle of educated men into local government and further challenged the power of the landed gentry, encouraging them to become educated. Successful sons of gentry households could then gain promotion from local government into central administration, but officials sent to take over positions in the countryside still depended on support from the local knowledge and established authority of the gentry. The early Koryŏ rulers also extended the court-related aristocracy by marriage and strengthened the position of its constituent families in the political process. Such families accumulated large estates. Under the **Ch'oe dictatorship** and the Mongol overlordship the number of powerful landlords grew still further as a result of land given as political reward, and absentee landlordism was common. But the power of the blood-related aristocracy then declined, and the late Koryŏ saw a rise in the number of educated men content to live on their rural estates, as well as of those striving to enter government service.
See also **land tenure; merit subjects**

GEOMANCY *See p'ungsu*

GERMANY, RELATIONS WITH
The first Korean acquaintance with Germans came with the unwelcome behaviour of Karl **Gützlaff** in 1832 and Ernest **Oppert** in 1867. More propitious was the service

143

afforded to the court by Paul-Georg **von Möllendorff**, who took up his post of adviser to King **Kojong** in 1882. In the same year a Treaty of Amity and Commerce was drafted and signed on 30 June by the German minister to Beijing, Max von Brandt, and the Koreans **Kim Hongjip** and Cho Yŏngha. Chinese consent had been obtained and the signing took place in the presence of the Chinese envoys Ma Jianzhong and Ding Ruchang. The agreement was not ratified, however, because of German government dissatisfaction with the tariff clauses, but after a visit to Seoul in the following year by the German Consul in Yokohama, Eduard Zappe, a revised version was signed on 26 November 1883 and ratified by the Reichstag in 1884. Although the Treaty opened Korean ports to German shipping, it did not lead to any significant volume of trade. German diplomacy in East Asia led to a joint protest with Russia and France in 1895 against Japan's acquisition of the Liaodong peninsula under the **Treaty of Shimonoseki**, a move which encouraged Koreans to see Russia as a potential ally against the Japanese threat to Korea. Following Japan's victory in the **Russo-Japanese War**, however, Germany, like all the Western powers, acknowledged the establishment, first, of the **Protectorate** and subsequently of the colonial government.

WERNER SASSE, 'The Historical Development of Korean-German Relations,' *KJ*, 23/11, 1983; THOMAS VOGTHERR, 'The Development of German-Korean Relations up to 1910,' *KJ*, 19/6, 1979

See also **Eckardt, Franz**; **Eckert, Andreas**

GINSENG *insam* 人參

A perennial mountain plant (*Panax schinseng*) of the ivy family, whose sun-dried root is used worldwide as a panacea, aphrodisiac and prophylactic (*paeksam* 'white ginseng'). Korea is the main source of supply. The earliest recorded mention is of a present made to the **Silla** king in 795. Korean exports to China are recorded from Tang times, often as a form of **tribute**, also commercially to China and Japan. Supplies were limited and unpredictable as long as wild plants were the only source, and the trade had sometimes to be controlled. Cultivation began in the mountains of Kyŏngsang about 1770 and soon spread to Chŏlla. Within twenty years, red ginseng (*hongsam*) was produced (by steaming, drying, rehydrating and pressing), which was popular in China and stimulated the trade. Shortly after 1800 cultivation began in the **Kaesŏng** district, which became the chief centre. After the division of the country in 1945 the low matsheds that simulate forest shade for the plants began to be seen throughout south Korea. Wild *sansam* is extremely expensive, but even cultivated *kasam* of high grade is not cheap.

C. T. COLLYER, 'The culture and preparation of ginseng in Korea', *TKBRAS*, III, 1903, pp. 10–18.

GLASS

Early remains found in Korea fall into three categories and chronological periods. (1) From the 2nd century BC coloured glass beads were popular. They were probably indicators of social status and were exchanged as currency. Their original importation from China led to the beginning of glass manufacture on the peninsula, from where examples were exported to Japan. A pair of fine blue glass earrings was found in the tomb of an official in the **Lelang** capital near P'yŏngyang. (2) Glass vessels date from the beginning of the 4th century, and include pieces of Roman Empire origin as well as local products. Evidence suggests that Korean craftsmen were the first to make glass of barium-free lead. During the Three Kingdoms period glass jewellery was used in **Silla**, **Kaya**, and **Paekche**, including *kogok* and bracelets. The preponderance of finds from sites in the vicinity of **Kyŏngju**, including a 5th century cup of Iranian style, indicates the rapid development of Silla and the rôle of international trade in it. A glass figurine of a boy found in the tomb of the Paekche King **Muryŏng** is unique. (3) The third category comprises fine glass *sarīra* containers of the 7th and later centuries. Glass manufacture continued into the Koryŏ period, when quality was already in decline, and disappeared altogether in the early Chosŏn.

GOLD CROWN TOMB *Kŭmgwan-ch'ong* 金冠冢
Wood-lined chamber **tomb** of the 5th–6th century AD surmounted by a stone mound, discovered in **Kyŏngju** in 1921. It contained over 40,000 artefacts, including the first **gold crown** to be found in Korea, gold, silver and bronze vessels, gold and silver weapons, gilt-bronze plate **armour**, stoneware vessels, and horse fittings.

GOLD CROWNS
Probably the most distinctive symbol of Korean royalty during the Three Kingdoms and Unified Silla periods. Examples have been found in Paekche and Silla **tombs**, with a stylistically complementary example in gilt bronze from a Koguryŏ tomb of the 6th 7th century from Ch'ongam-dong, near P'yŏngyang. The latter is not unlike Northern Wei dynasty examples from China, such as that found in 1981 at Damaoqi, Inner Mongolia. The earliest known example comes from Hwangnam-dong, Kyŏngju, and dates from the mid-5th century. Though the techniques of goldworking may have been inherited from China through the **Lelang** commandery, the surviving crowns are unique to the peninsula. Made of thin sheet gold, they consisted of three sections. Worn on the top of the head was a roughly conical cap of delicately decorated openwork metal, into which might be fitted a forward-pointing ornament of wing or butterfly shape. Circumventing these around the brow and sides of the head was a diadem, a band of gold from which arose five or six cut-outs, those in front like trees with U-shaped branches and those to the sides and rear like antlers. The three parts may have fitted together or may have been worn individually, as suggested by the fact that in *Ch'ŏnma-ch'ong* they were found in separate areas of the tomb. A stylistic connection has also been noted between these and shaman crowns from Siberia, suggesting a line of cultural influence between the steppe and Silla, and that – as in Shang dynasty China – early Korean royalty assumed supreme religious as well as political functions. Wired to the trees and antlers by gold thread were gold and jade jewels which must have tinkled and shimmered with movement like leaves. Two strings of golden spangles dangled from the band itself and would have hung between the eyes and ears. Complemented by sumptuously decorated gold earrings and a gold girdle, such a crown would undoubtedly have enhanced the wearer's aura of authority. On the other hand such exceptional pieces may have been worn only on special ritual occasions, or even made solely for funerary purposes.
LISA BAILEY, 'Crowning Glory: headdresses of the Three Kingdoms period', *PBAKS*, 5, 1994; KANG DUK-HEE, 'Gold Crowns of Shibarghan in Afghanistan and of the Three Kingdoms Period of Korea,' *KJ*, 23/6, 1983
See also **Gold Crown Tomb**; *kogok*; **Muryŏng, King**

GOVERNMENT, CENTRAL
From the Three Kingdoms period until 1910 Korea was ruled by a monarchy in which the king was advised and served by a number of institutions (*maŭl*). This system was completed in the Koryŏ period, when Tang models were taken and men who were successful in the state **examinations** were eligible for appointment.

THREE KINGDOMS

In each kingdom the top levels of government were drawn from the aristocracy, and offices were divided into a hierarchy of ranks, thus establishing the tradition of a centralised bureaucracy. The supreme council selected its chief minister. In **Silla** the council was known as the *Hwabaek*. Six departments of government already seem to have existed with specialised functions such as taxation, rites and ceremonies, law and order, and military affairs. The political organisation comprised sixteen office-holding ranks, most senior of which were held by the ministers, *chwap'yŏng*, who headed the six departments.

UNIFIED SILLA

The organisation of central government was continued and further modelled on Chinese lines when King **Munmu** added a **Censorate** (*Ŏsadae*) to the six departments, but in 651 the Chancellery (*Chipsabu*), headed by the *Chungsi* (Secretary General), succeeded the *Hwabaek* as the top council of government.

KORYŎ

The Privy Council (*Chaech'u*) took the most important decisions of state. It combined the members of the Central Council (*Chungch'u-wŏn* or *Ch'umir-wŏn*), which dealt with royal edicts and military affairs, and the Ministerial Office (*Chaebu*). The latter superintended the Secretariat (*Sangsŏ-sŏng*), which in turn controlled the six boards or departments, namely Rites, Personnel, Taxation, Punishments, Public Works, and Military Affairs. The Censorate operated on a level equal to that of the Central Council and Ministerial Office. Titles and functions of certain offices changed under the **Ch'oe dictatorship** which, despite accepting royal authority, governed by ignoring it. The senior council was the Directorate of Decrees (*Kyojŏng Togam*), headed by a military leader, and government appointments were made through a Political Office (*Chungbang*). During the period of Mongol domination the power of central Korean authority was weakened. The Central Council was abolished and a new State Council created. Reforms to the **Six Boards** included the merging of Rites and Personnel and the closure of Public Works.

EARLY CHOSŎN

Chosŏn adapted the Koryŏ system. A supreme Council of State (*Ŭijŏng-bu*) of three Councillors acted as a deliberative forum and advised the king, and a central secretariat (*Sŭngjŏng-wŏn*) managed communications to and from the state council, and gained considerable power from its direct access to the king. It passed decisions to the Six Boards (*Yukcho*), which were the same as those under the early Koryŏ dynasty but now with enhanced authority. Review bodies or 'censorates' (*Samsa*, 'Three Offices') acted as checks on bad government. They combined the Offices of Special Advisers (*Hongmun-gwan*), Inspectors (*Sahonbu*) and Censors (*Saganwŏn*), and were intended to act as a further brake on royal autocracy. However, both Kings T'aejong and **Sejong** sought to strengthen the power of the monarchy in relation to that of the bureaucracy, and under them the Council of State lost its power to advise on policy.

The king, though counselled and admonished according to Confucian theory, was supposedly an absolute monarch; but the monarchy had inbuilt weaknesses. There were no clear rules for succession to the throne and no international royal bloodlines that could sustain the mystique of a royal caste. Kings married their own subjects, thus bringing other family interests into the palace. As a result, the king was little more than the highest *yangban* in the land. His position was further weakened by the activities of the councils. The struggle between the throne and its Confucian officials resulted in the so-called 'literati purges' (*see also* **sahwa**). In early Chosŏn civil officials were known as the Eastern Ranks (*Tongban*) and military ones as the Western Ranks (*Sŏban*), the two together forming the *yangban*, although with a heavy imbalance in favour of the civil. Military influence increased, however, with the establishment of an Office of Frontier Security (*Pibyŏn-sa*) in 1555 to counter the activities of **pirates**, and in the era after the **Imjin Wars**, which showed the need for more effective central control but plunged the country into ever more divisive political **factionalism**, Pihyŏn-sa became for nearly two centuries the most powerful organ of government.

LATE CHOSŎN (*see also* Government organs of the Chosŏn dynasty)
From the beginning of the 19th century a succession of young monarchs led to the domination of the throne by the most powerful clans related to them by marriage, Andong Kim and P'ungyang Cho (*see* **sedo-jŏngch'i**). This process came to a head with the accession of the 12-year-old **Kojong** and the regency of his father, the **T'aewŏn'gun** in 1864. In 1865 the *Pibyŏn-sa* was abolished, the *Ŭijŏng-bu* again became the most powerful political body, and the Office of Three Armies (*Samgun-bu*) – an old-fashioned body dating from the times of King T'aejo – was restored as the main military command. The T'aewŏn'gun's aim was to restore the authority of the throne over the bureaucracy, but his reactionary response to rapidly declining and unprecedented conditions, if comprehensible from the point of view of the traditional Korean respect for the past and sense of self-sufficiency, helped to throw government into turmoil. Consequently, changes to the organs of government in the late Chosŏn reflect both internal political and economic decay and foreign pressure for reform. Political reforms began in 1881 with the opening of the *T'ongni-gimu amun* on a par with the Council of State, but were only approached with any sense of commitment in 1894, and even then reflected Japanese advice. Following the recommendations of the 17-member Reform Council (*Kun'guk Kimuch'ŏ*), the power of the king was reduced and the cabinet structure of his government made more powerful. The Council of State was reorganised under a Prime Minister, with representatives from eight Boards (the original six with the addition of Foreign Affairs and Agriculture & Commerce). Four months later the Cabinet (*Naegak*) was divided into seven modern ministries, including Education & Finance. Court business was separated from government and put in the charge of the Royal Household Deparment (*Kungnae-bu*).

COLONIAL PERIOD
Under the Japanese, government was in the hands of the **Government-General**. The **Governor-General** was nominated by the Japanese Prime Minister and was advised by a Central Advisory Council. The higher administrative offices were the Bureaux of Land Survey, Police, Investigation, Monopolies, Communications, and Railways, to which in 1912 were added General Affairs, External Affairs, Education, and Building. The initial Departments of General Affairs, Internal Affairs, Justice, Finance, and Agriculture/Commerce/Industry (ACI) were soon modified by the abolition of General Affairs, the division of ACI into Agriculture/Forestry and Production, and the creation of Security. All senior posts were held by Japanese.

REPUBLIC OF KOREA
The system of government inaugurated in South Korea in 1948 comprised a president, a cabinet of senior ministers (State Affairs Council), and a National Assembly comprising a House of Representatives and (from 1960) an upper House of Councillors. Political parties were to play an active part in democratic elections to the National Assembly, which acted as an electoral college in selecting the president

(*see* **South Korea: political parties**). In 1963, following a two-year period of military rule (*see* **military junta**), democracy was outwardly enhanced by the introduction of popular presidential elections, although Park Chung Hee (**Pak Chŏnghŭi**) managed to preserve a strongly autocratic tradition of rule (*see* **Third Republic**), and under the *Yusin* **Constitution** of 1972 had himself re-elected by a new nominating college and gained the right to appoint one third of the National Assembly members. Despite the dismantling of the *Yusin* Constitution after 1980, government continued to be militaristic and authoritarian under President Chun Doo Hwan (**Chŏn Tuhwan**), and political opposition within the National Assembly and through the country led to the restoration of popular presidential elections under Roh Tae Woo (**No Taeu**) in 1988.

DEMOCRATIC PEOPLE'S REPUBLIC OF KOREA
The Supreme People's Assembly (SPA) was created in August 1948 as the highest official forum of government in the **Democratic People's Republic of Korea** (DPRK). It comprised representatives of the people elected for periods of four years and nominally had wide powers over the **constitution**, the economy, and foreign and domestic policy. It elected the chairman, effectively the head of state, and the members of its Standing Committee, which had legislative powers to act between sessions of the SPA. Similar Assemblies were established at provincial, county, and urban levels. People's Assemblies had been the first elected bodies inaugurated by the communists in both south and north Korea in 1947. In 1948, 572 persons were elected to the first SPA, supposedly including representatives from south Korea.

Government is defined in terms of the 'dictatorship of the proletariat' but is more accurately described as a Marxist-Leninist system of democratic centralism. Despite the popular election of the SPA and theoretical provision for popular participation in political affairs at local and national level, power and policy making after 1948 remained consistently in the hands of a caucus of senior communist party and military leaders, and adhered to the lines laid down by Chairman, later President, **Kim Ilsŏng**. The highest government body under the president was the Central People's Committee, superintending also the work of the Administration Council and the National Defence Commission. Kim Ilsŏng's death led to speculation about possible changes of government structure and policy, largely because of the uncertain nature of his son **Kim Chŏngil**'s support. However, despite an intense economic crisis in the mid-1990s and increased political pressure from abroad, there were few signs of either popular or military revolt against the political system.
YANG SUNG CHUL, *The North and South Korean Political Systems: a Comparative Analysis*, Boulder: Westview Press, 1994
See also **grades, government**

GOVERNMENT-GENERAL, JAPANESE *Chōsen Sōtokufu* 朝鮮總督府, 1910–45
Title adopted by the Japanese government of Korea (renamed Chōsen) during the colonial period from 1910 to 1945. As a senior member of the Japanese government drawn from high military rank the Governor-General (*Sōtoku*) was responsible to the emperor, the prime minister and the cabinet in Tokyo. Within Korea, however, his authority was supreme, and he exercised full legislative, executive, judiciary and military rights. There were nine occupants of this post from 1910 to 1945 (see page 83), the first being General Terauchi Masatake. Central government in Keijō (Seoul) was initially divided into a number of departments and bureaux, modified in 1920 to bureaux only. These covered such areas as Finance, Land Survey, Agriculture and Forestry, Security, Education, Monopolies, Construction, Internal Affairs, External

Affairs, and Railways (established 1925). The military police system, upon which the administration relied heavily for the enforcement of law and order, came directly under the control of central government. Provincial administration divided the country into thirteen provinces, subdivided according to the traditional pattern into prefectures, counties, towns and hamlets. Although a small number of collaborating Koreans were appointed to the Central Advisory Council, the majority of all posts in both central and provincial government were held by non-Korean-speaking Japanese.
See also **colonial period**; **police system, Japanese**

GOVERNMENT, LOCAL See **Provincial administration**

GOVERNMENT ORGANS OF THE CHOSŎN DYNASTY
The later history of government institutions was complex. Though most existed in **Ming dynasty** China, Chinese models were not followed slavishly. Their names and functions were frequently changed. The information given below describes the system as it existed in ideal at the peak of the Chosŏn dynasty, before 1894.

The *maŭl* had names with suffixes, often derived from the buildings in the palace where the original groups had worked, that suggest the dignity of each institute.

Pu originally meant a treasure house or store, later coming to mean 'palace' or 'prefecture', but here translated as 'council'. It was used for the groups of highest status (*Ŭijong-bu*, *Sahŏn-bu*, *Ŭigŭm-bu*), including those that were of high rank but little influence (*Chungch'u-bu*, *Chongch'in-bu*, *Tollyŏng-bu*). The president was usually a man of the 1st grade.

Cho ('servants') was used only for the **Six Boards** (*yukcho*).

Kwan ('hall' or 'lodge') usually had a president of the 1st **grade** and was concerned with scholarship and writing (*Sŏnggyun-gwan*, *Hongmun-gwan*, *Ch'unch'u-gwan*, *Yemun-gwan*, *T'ongmun-gwan*).

Wŏn, originally a courtyard or building with a courtyard, here translated 'office', was widely used for groups of varying importance (*Sagan-wŏn*, *Sejasigang-wŏn*, *Sŭngmun-wŏn*, *Sŭngjŏng-wŏn*, *Changnye-wŏn*), with presidents usually of the 3rd grade. Most of them were linked to *pu* or *cho*.

The names of the minor *maŭl* included -*si*, originally a hall or public office, as in *Saboksi*, the Royal Stables Office (though the same character, pronounced *sa*, was the common word for a Buddhist temple and came from an early Buddhist office in a royal palace); -*sŏ*, an office, coming to mean *yamen*; -*ch'ang* and -*ko*, a storehouse or granary; and -*kam*, an inspectorate or gaol. The common prefix *Sa*- means 'to be in charge of'.

Officials of each *maŭl* had distinctive titles that were many and varied. A degree of coordination between offices was ensured by certain posts being held concurrently by the same men.

The **grade** of the presiding officer is given in the right-hand column. Sr = Senior (*chŏng*), Jr = Junior (*chong*).

Royal Councils

CHONGCH'IN-BU: Royal Family affairs	1 Sr
CH'UNGHUN-BU: Affairs of **Meritorious Subjects**	1 Sr
ŬIBIN-BU: Affairs of Royal Sons-in-Law	1 Sr
TOLLYŎNG-BU: Affairs of royal relations by blood and marriage	1 Sr
PONGJO-HA: Ceremonial duties of noble pensioners	3 Sr

Central government and **censorate**
ŬIJŎNG-BU: State council | 1 Sr
ŬIGŬM-BU: Royal inquisition | 1 Jr
SAHŎN-BU: Government censorate | 2 Jr
SŬNGJŎNG-WŎN: Receipt and issue of decrees | 3 Sr
SAGAN-WŎN: Royal censorate | 3 Sr
KYŎNGYŎN: Royal lectures | *1 Sr

City governments
HANSŎNG-BU: The capital city | 2 Sr
KAESŎNG-BU: The former capital city | 2 Jr

Sŏban: the western class
CHUNGCH'U-BU: Advisers without office | *1 Sr
OWI-TOCH'ONG-BU: **The Five Military Commands** council | 2 Sr
KYŎMSA-BOK: A palace guard unit | 2 Jr
NAE-GŬMWI: A palace guard unit | 2 Jr

YUKCHO: the Six Boards

IJO Board of Personnel | 2 Sr
CHUNGIK-BU: Affairs of Junior Meritorious Subjects | 3 Sr
SANGSŎ-WŎN: Seals, tags, passes, **flags**, ceremonial emblems | 3 Sr
CHONGBU-SI: Royal family tree, royal etiquette | 3 Sr
SAONG-WŎN: Royal food | 3 Sr
NAESU-SA: Grain, cloth, **slaves** | 5 Sr
NAESI-BU: Meals, errands, door-keeping, cleaning (**eunuch** work) | 2 Sr
AEKCHŎNG-SŎ: Visits to **tombs**, temples and palaces; opening of
    private areas; keys; writing-brushes and inkstones | 6 Sr

HOJO Board of Revenue | 2 Sr
NAEJA-SI: Palace foodstuffs and weaving necessities | 3 Sr
NAESŎM-SI: Palace wines and entertainment of foreign envoys | 3 Sr
SADO-SI: Royal rice, soy sauce, mustard, etc | 3 Sr
SASŎM-SI: Hempen cloth and currency paper | 3 Sr
KUNJA-GAM: Military supplies | 3 Sr
CHEYONG-GAM: Gifts of clothing and **ginseng** to the King; doles of
    clothing, **silk** and gauze; dyeing and weaving cloth | 3 Sr
SAJAE-GAM: Meat, fish, salt, firewood and charcoal | 3 Sr
CHŎNJŎ-CH'ANG: Grain, pulse and **paper** | 4 Sr
KWANGHŬNG-CH'ANG: Salaries | 4 Sr
CHŎNHAM-SA: Boats outside Seoul | 4 Jr
P'YŎNGSI-SŎ: **Market** prices, weights and measures | 5 Sr
SAON-SŎ: Ales and vodkas ('wines') | 5 Sr
ŬIYŎNG-GO: Oil, honey, beeswax, **peppers** | 5 Sr
CHANGHŬNG-GO: Reed mats and oiled paper for flooring | 5 Jr
SAP'O-SŎ: Vegetables | 6 Sr
YANGHYŎN-GO: Food for *Sŏnggyun-gwan* students | 6 Jr
OBU: Five departments of the capital city, N E S W and Centre | 6 Jr

YEJO Board of Rites | 2 Sr
HONGMUN-GWAN: Reviewing documents | *1 Sr
YEMUN-GWAN: Drafting office | *1 Sr

SŎNGGYUN-GWAN: National Confucian College   *2 Sr
CH'UNCH'U-GWAN: State archives   *1 Sr
SŬNGMUN-WŎN: Diplomatic correspondence   *1 Sr
T'ONGNYE-WŎN: Ceremonial   3 Sr
PONGSANG-SI: Sacrifices; **temple names**   3 Sr
KYOSŎ-GWAN: **Printing** classics; providing incense and prayer
    texts; designing seals   3 Sr
NAEŬI-WŎN: Preparing medicaments   3 Sr
YEBIN-SI: Banquets for guests, royal relations and officers of 1st and 2nd grade   3 Sr
CHANGAG-WŎN: Care of **musical instruments**   3 Sr
KWANSANG-GAM: Astronomical and meteorological observation
    and records; calendar; water-clocks   *1 Sr
CHŎNŬI-GAM: Distribution of **medicines**   3 Sr
SAYŎG-WŎN: Office of translators   3 Sr
SEJA-SIGANG-WŎN: Instruction of the Crown Prince   *1 Sr
CHONGHAK: Instruction of the royal family   4 Sr
SOGYŎK-SŎ: Sacrifices to Heaven, Earth and stars   5 Jr
CHONGMYO-SŎ: Royal tablet house   5 Jr
SAJIK-SŎ: **Sajik** Altars   5 Jr
PINGGO: Ice-houses   5 Jr
CHŎNSAENG-SŎ: Sacrificial sheep, pigs, etc.   6 Jr
SACH'UK-SŎ: Cattle and larger animals   6 Jr
HYEMIN-SŎ: Medical relief for the people   6 Jr
TOHWA-SŎ: Paintings   6 Jr
HWARIN-SŎ: Medical relief in Seoul   6 Jr
KWIHU-SŎ: Coffins and funerals   6 Jr
SAHAK: The four colleges of Seoul   6 Jr

PYŎNGJO Board of War   2 Sr
    †OWI: The Five Commands   2 Jr
    †HULLYŎN-WŎN: Military training   3 Sr
    SABOK-SI: **Horses** and stables   3 Sr
    KUN'GI-SI: Weaponry   3 Sr
    CHŎNSŎL-SA: Tents   4 Jr
    *SEJA-IGWI-SA: Guards of the Crown Prince   5 Sr

HYŎNGJO Board of Punishments   2 Sr
    CHANGNYE-WŎN: Register and freeing of slaves   3 Sr
    CHŎGOK-SŎ: Prisons   3 Sr

KONGJO Board of Works   2 Sr
    SANGŬI-WŎN: Clothing and **jewellery**   3 Sr
    SŎN'GONG-GAM: Earth and wood (construction work)   3 Sr
    SUSŎNG-KŬMHWA-SA: **Wall** repair and fire precautions   4 Sr
    CHŎNYŎN-SA: **Palace** buildings repair   4 Sr
    CHANGWŎN-SŎ: Parks and gardens, **flowers** and fruit   6 Sr
    CHOJI-SŎ: Paper-making   6 Jr
    WA-SŎ: Making tiles and bricks   6 Jr

* A superintendent holding another appointment concurrently. Some other minor *maŭl* had superintendents of less significance.

† *Sŏban* (western or military class).

GRADES, GOVERNMENT *p'umgy* 品階, *kwan'gye p'umjil wigye*
From Koryŏ onwards government officials, both civil and military, were graded in imitation of Chinese usage, said to have been invented by Cao Cao (*see Romance of the Three Kingdoms*). The grades are sometimes called 'ranks', but 'rank' is better reserved for titled ranks such as *kun, taebu, nang,* etc. (*see* **princely titles**), given according to the numbered grades. The highest was *chŏngil-p'um* '1st grade senior' and the lowest *chonggu-p'um* '9th grade junior'. Each level was further divided into *sang* 'upper' and *ha* 'lower' divisions.
See also **Taebu**

GREAT BRITAIN, RELATIONS WITH
The first known British reference to Korea occurs in the trading charter granted to Sir Edward Michelbourne in 1604. Nothing came of that. In 1797, Captain **Broughton** of the Royal Navy visited the **Pusan** area, but again this isolated event led to no further links. In succeeding years, however, both Royal Navy and merchant ships began to visit Korean waters. Britain's first treaty with Korea was signed in 1882. It was a copy of the first American treaty of the same year (*see* **Shufeldt Treaty**), and was regarded as unsatisfactory. Consequently it was soon replaced, and from 1884 Britain had diplomatic relations with the Kingdom of Korea. Korea was something of a backwater, and while there was a British consul-general in Seoul from 1884 (*see* **Aston, William George**), formally the British minister in Beijing was accredited to Seoul. There was some British trading interest in Korea, which led to the British naval occupation of **Kŏmun-do** (Port Hamilton) off the south coast of Korea between 1885 and 1887. This move was designed to dissuade the Russians from occupying a Korean port, and when satisfactory assurances to this effect were received from Moscow, the British withdrew. More peaceable was the English Church Mission, established in Seoul in 1890 (*see* **Anglicans**).

In 1900, Great Britain appointed a resident minister to Seoul, but the **Anglo-Japanese Alliance** of 1902, renewed in 1905, paved the way for the Japanese **annexation** of Korea in 1910. Britain maintained a consular post in Seoul during the colonial period, and there was some small-scale trade. In 1919 the British government protested at Japanese brutality in suppressing the **March First movement**, but in general British interest in Korea during this period was minimal. As war approached in 1941, pressure on the small British community increased, and most had withdrawn by the time of Pearl Harbour.

After 1945, the British slowly returned, and diplomatic relations were established with the new **Republic of Korea** in 1949. On the outbreak of the **Korean War**, Britain hoped to avoid too great an involvement, mainly because of widespread commitments elsewhere. But a wish to keep alongside the USA, and a belief that the war was an important stand against communism, led to the commitment of British naval forces from July 1950, while the first British ground forces arrived in Pusan in August 1950. Thereafter, British forces were involved in all stages of the fighting. Koreans particularly remember the valiant fighting of the Gloucester Regiment at Sŏlma-ri near the Imjin in April 1951. At the end of the war in 1953, British casualties were 1109 killed and 2674 wounded.

Britain played an important part in South Korea's post-war reconstruction and in the economic development of the 1960s and 1970s. British know-how and finance were particularly valuable in both the automobile and shipbuilding industries, while British equipment was bought by the textile, petro-chemical, power generating and mining industries. Britain also helped in the establishment of the Ulsan Institute of Technology, later the University of Ulsan, South Korea's first higher education technical institution.

Diplomatic relations with South Korea were raised to ambassadorial level in 1957. Britain was a prominent supporter of South Korea's campaign to enter the **United Nations Organisation** in the 1970s, and in other ways too supported South Korea internationally. Although Britain recognised North Korea on its admission to the United Nations in 1992, no diplomatic relations were established between the two countries. However, low-level political dialogue began, culminating in the first visit to P'yŏngyang by British officials in 1997.

JAMES E. HOARE, 'The Centenary of Korean-British Diplomatic Relations: Aspects of British Interest and Involvement in Korea, 1600–1983', *TRASKB*, LVIII, 1983; BRIAN BRIDGES, *Korea and the West*, London and New York: Routledge and Kegan Paul, 1986
See also **Bethell, Ernest; Bird, Isabella; Brown, John MacLeavey; Corfe, Charles John; Harding, J. R.; Scott, James; Thomas, R. J.; Trollope, Mark**

GREAT HAN EMPIRE 大韓帝國

As part of the 1895 reform programme (*see Kabo* **reforms**) King **Kojong** decreed the inauguration of a new system of single-reign naming, beginning with the immediate adoption of the title *Kŏnyang* ('Establishment of the *yang*'). In 1897 this was ceremonially changed to *Kwangmu* ('Glorious Warrior'; *see* **reign titles**). An **Altar of Heaven** (*Wŏngu-dan*) was built near the **Tŏksu Palace**, where the King had taken up residence to be close to the protection of the British, Russian and Japanese embassies, and there, to equate himself with the rulers of China and Japan, he now took for the first time the title of Emperor (*hwangje*) and proclaimed the foundation of the Great Han Empire (*Taehan-cheguk*).

GRIFFIS, WILLIAM ELLIOT (1843–1928)

Born in Philadelphia, he was invited to Japan as a science teacher in 1870. In 1871 he visited Tsuruga, where he gazed over the sea towards Korea and was moved to write its history. He returned to America in 1874 and the book was published in 1882: *Corea; the Hermit Nation* (9th edition 1911). He used Japanese and Chinese sources, giving Korean names in Japanese pronunciation. Constantly revised and enlarged, it remained a standard work for thirty years and popularised 'hermit nation' as a **name for Korea**.

GUAN YU 關羽 (d. AD 219)

Known as the 'God of War' (though this Western title begs theological questions), Guan Yu (K. Kwan U) was a much-revered Chinese hero of *The Romance of Three Kingdoms*, given various honorific titles from the 12th century onwards. In 1582 the Wanli Emperor Shenzong raised him to 'helper of Heaven, great emperor' (*Xietian dadi, di* being the highest rank for departed spirits) and protector of the country. Ten years later, Shenzong sent Chinese troops to help the Koreans against Hideyoshi's army (*see* **Imjin Wars**). Their general, Li Rusong, built a temple near the south gate of Seoul in honour of Guandi, who was said to have appeared over the city with a heavenly army. In 1602 the emperor had a bigger temple, Tong-Gwanwang-myo, erected outside the East Gate for the Chinese who fell during the war. West, north and central temples followed, but only Tongmyo remains, the sole example of Chinese temple architecture in Seoul. It is a centre for Chinese residents.

GUTZLAFF, KARL FRIEDRICH AUGUST (1803–51)

A colourful Prussian who went to Batavia in 1827, serving the Netherlands Missionary Society. On tract-distributing journeys, he worked as an interpreter on opium ships up and down the China coast. In 1832 he visited Hongch'ŏn on the *Lord Amherst*, an East

India Company vessel seeking trading opportunities, and spent some weeks at Monggŭmp'o in Hwanghae, where he distributed Protestant tracts (perplexing the local Catholics) and taught Koreans to grow **potatoes**, not knowing they were already being grown in the country. He wrote of his experience in *Journal of Three Voyages along the Coast of China* (London 1834).

H

HAEDONG CHEGUK-KI 海東諸國紀 'Record of all lands to the east of the sea'
A comprehensive survey of Korean relations with Japan, the Japanese islands, including **Tsushima**, and the Ryukyu Islands, compiled by **Sin Sukchu** in 1471. It contains maps printed from woodblocks.
See also **cartography**

HAEDONG KOSŬNG-JŎN 海東高僧傳 'Lives of Eminent Korean Monks'
Only the two first books (*kwŏn*) remain from this collection of Buddhist biographies compiled by the monk Kakhun in 1215. The first contains lives from the first generations of Korean **Buddhism**: **Sundo**, Mangmyŏng, Ŭiyŏn and Tamsi of **Koguryŏ**; **Malananda** of **Paekche**; and **Ado**, Pŏpkong (King Pŏphŭng) and Pŏbun (King Chinhŭng) of **Silla**. The second book, mostly quoting from other works, deals with 6th- and 7th-century monks of Silla who studied in China, some of whom also went to India: Kaktŏk, Chimyŏng, Wŏn'gwang, Anham, Arinabalma, Hyeŏp, Hyeryun, Hyŏn'gak, Hyŏnyu, and Hyŏndaebŏm.
PETER H. LEE, *Lives of Eminent Korean Monks*, Cambridge, Mass.: Harvard University Press, 1969

HAEDONG YŎKSA 海東繹史 'Unravelled Chronicles of East of the Sea'
A compendium of history, edited by Han Ch'iyun (b.1765), a *sirhak* scholar who drew on some 550 earlier works, including Chinese and Japanese sources. It was not printed until 1911. The 16 historical books deal with **Tan'gun** to Koryŏ. The 54 other books, corresponding to the monographs and biographies of traditional histories, include a section (Book 60) on the **Suksin** (C. Sushen) peoples. Han's nephew Han Chinsŏ added 15 supplementary books on Korean geography.

HAEGŬM 奚琴
The two-stringed fiddle. It was of central Asian origin and had reached Korea by the 13th century, where it quickly became a favourite instrument in both court and popular ensembles. The soundbox may be of hollowed out **bamboo** or of hardwood, and is open at the rear. It has a long, curved neck, and the two strings of twisted **silk** are stretched across the soundbox and tuned a fifth apart by means of large wooden pegs. In modern instruments these are near the top of the neck, though older illustrations show them half way up. There is no fingerboard, the strings being pulled with the fingers of the left hand. The bow, of loosely woven horse hair, is threaded between the two strings. The player holds the instrument vertically, resting the soundbox on his left knee, and bows the strings horizontally. The *haegŭm* produces a rather harsh sound but is nevertheless capable of expressive tone, and is one of the most indispensable instruments in almost any ensemble.

HAEIN-SA 海印寺
Buddhist temple on Kaya-san, near **Taegu**, Kyŏngsang province, founded in AD 802. It is renowned as the repository of the unique Koryŏ dynasty printing set of the *Tripitaka Koreana* on 81,258 wooden blocks. It had been begun in 1236 on **Kanghwa-do** by the court in exile and completed in 1251. Like an earlier set carved in the hope of protecting Korea against **Khitan** conquest but destroyed by the **Mongols** in 1254, it also failed to save the country from foreign subjugation, but was itself preserved and moved to Haein-sa in 1398. In 1488 a special library was constructed for it consisting of two cleverly designed storage halls with wooden slatted walls, which protect it against the extreme ravages of the summer and winter climate. Here the blocks are kept to the present day,

Haein-sa was home of the great poet **Ch'oe Ch'iwŏn** after his return from China, and the temple to which the famous soldier-monk **Samyŏng** retired after fighting the Japanese in the 1590s (*see* **Imjin Wars**).
SUSAN LAUSTER, 'A Guide to Haeinsa,' *TRASKB*, XLVII, 1972

HAESŎ INCIDENTS (1902 3) 海西事件
Examples of civil disorder in Hwanghae (Haesŏ) immediately before the **Russo-Japanese War**, resulting in six court actions between Protestants and Catholics. There were faults on both sides. After the French priest Joseph Wilhelm began working there in 1895, many Protestants in the Chaeryŏng area became Catholics, partly because they hoped for French protection. At Changyŏn in 1900 a Protestant local official was accused of embezzlement; in 1902 there was fighting at Sinhwan-p'o when Catholics used pretended governmental authority to compel Protestants to contribute to building a Catholic church. The situation was resolved by the tact of the French Legation in 1903.
YUN KYUNGNO, 'The Relationship between Korean Catholics and Korean Protestants in the Early Mission Period,' in YU CHAI-SHIN, ed., *Korea and Christianity*, Seoul, Berkeley, Toronto, 1996

HAET'AE 獬豸
A mythical animal (C. *xiezhai*) that occurs among the stone animals lined up before royal tombs. Known to Chinese writers since Han times, it was said to be a plump one-horned deer or mountain goat that devoured the wicked, because it was able to tell right from wrong. Because *hai* suggests 'sea' in Korean pronunciation, it was wrongly thought of in Korea as a marine creature. It would also eat fire, even suicidally. For this reason, a pair of *haet'ae* statues was erected in front of the **Kyŏngbok Palace**, glaring defensively at Anak-san, the mountain that stood south of the **Han River** in line with the north-south axis of the palace. *P'ungsu* experts declared that the influence of Anak-san was responsible for the fires that frequently broke out in the palace buildings.

HAGUE PEACE CONFERENCE (1907)
The Second International Peace Conference, held in 1907, was secretly attended by envoys sent by King **Kojong** to state Korea's claim to independence and objections to the Japanese **protectorate**. Two Koreans, Yi Sangsŏl and **Yi Chun**, were accompanied by the American missionary **Homer Hulbert** and travelled via Russia where they were joined by a diplomat from St Petersburg, Yi Wijong. Refused permission to take part in the official proceedings, they nevertheless solicited sympathetic international publicity when they spoke to the press. The Japanese, however, gained revenge by using Kojong's duplicity to add pressure for his abdication.

HALL, BASIL (1788–1844)

After accompanying Lord Amherst on his embassy to China, Captain Basil Hall RN visited Korea with HMS *Alceste* and HMS *Lyra* in 1816, surveying the coast from Hwanghae province to the southwestern islands. He memorably visited the local magistrate during a stay of several days off Maryangjin, South Ch'ungch'ŏng. His books were highly popular, not least *An Account of a voyage of discovery to the West Coast of Korea* (London 1818).

HALLIM 翰林

An honorific title for certain royal secretaries. The sign of office was a huge document case (*hallimgwe* or *nŏl*), about the size of a coffin, which the *hallim* was allowed to retain when he retired. In Silla and Koryŏ the word *hallim* was used as it was in China, to mean the royal academy of scholars. In both countries the title was held in great honour.

HALLYANG 閑良

(1) Class of lower military officers in the Koryŏ and early Chosŏn periods. In the latter they qualified for hereditary grants of military land (*kunjŏn*) in return for distinguished service, and also obtained sinecure posts in the lower ranks of the bureaucracy.
See also **Military systems**

(2) A youth of later Chosŏn who had not taken his military or professional examinations. Practising **archery** was a principal requirement for military candidates and they spent much time at the butts in established peer-groups. Since this was an enjoyable way of life, the term *hallyang* came to applied to any young layabout.

HAMEL, HENDRIK (1630–92)

Hamel was the ship's writer of the *Sperwer*, a Dutch vessel sailing from Taiwan to Nagasaki that was wrecked off **Cheju-do** in August 1653. There were 36 survivors. After being interviewed by **Jan Weltevree**, they were transferred to Seoul in January 1654 and became musketeers in the royal guard. Two years later they were sent to Chŏlla province, where they were kept in various places until eight of them escaped by boat to the Dutch settlement at Nagasaki in September 1666, leaving seven others behind. The seven were sent to Nagasaki at Japanese request in 1668. By 1669 all fifteeen were back in Holland. Hamel's account of their adventures (the first account of Korea in a Western language) was published in Dutch in 1668, in French in 1670, and in English in 1704 (*An Account of the Shipwreck of a Dutch Vessel off the Coast of Quelpaert, together with a Description of the Kingdom of Corea*).
HENDRIK HAMEL, trans. Br. J-P Buys, *Hamel's Journal and a Description of the Kingdom of Korea, 1653–1666*, Seoul: Royal Asiatic Society, Korea Branch, 1994; GARI LEDYARD, *The Dutch Come to Korea*, Seoul: Royal Asiatic Society, Korea Branch, 1971. A website devoted to the story of Hamel may be found at http://www.henny.savenije.demon.nl

HAMHŬNG CH'ASA 咸興差使 'Hamhŭng messenger'

After Yi T'aejo, founder of the Chosŏn dynasty, had abdicated in 1402 and retired for a while to his old home at Hamhŭng, his son, King T'aejong, sent emissaries to improve his relations with his father. The old man slew some and imprisoned others. Hence the proverbial 'messenger to Hamhŭng', meaning a messenger who does not return or is unreasonably delayed.

HAN DYNASTY 漢朝 (China, 206 BC – AD 220)

Following years of confrontation between the early rulers of Han China and **Wiman Chosŏn** Emperor Han Wudi's armies established the first of several Chinese **commanderies** in **Manchuria** and northern Korea in 108 BC. The most enduring was that of **Lelang**, from which Chinese influence spread across the peninsula. Han historians classified Koreans among what they called the 'Eastern Barbarians' (*dong yi*), though the term *junzi zhi guo* ('Country of Gentlemen') had already been coined (it appears in the 2nd century BC *Huainanzi*), indicating a measure of respect for the Middle Kingdom's neighbours. The most important of these were **Koguryŏ** (whose armies clashed with those of Wang Mang in AD 12 and those of the Later Han dynasty under King T'aejo), **Chin**, and the Manchurian state of **Puyŏ**.

HAN HO *See* **Han Sŏkpong**

HAN RIVER 漢江

The principal river of modern South Korea. The downstream body of the river, already crossed by 16 bridges at Seoul with others under construction, is formed by the confluence of two upper courses, the Northern Han (Pukhan) and Southern Han. Both rise in the mountains near the east coast, but far apart in North and South Korea respectively. At its mouth, in the Han-Imjin estuary, lies the strategic island of Kanghwa (**Kanghwa-do**).

Archaeological discoveries show that the Han basin has been a centre of civilisation since the **neolithic period**. In historical times it has more than once played a strategic rôle as a political dividing line. It marked the northern limit of **Chin** territory in the last quarter of the first millennium BC and of **Mahan** territory in the early **Samhan** period. Its basin was the centre for the rise of **Paekche** as an integrated and expansionist state in the 4th century and the river separated the kingdom from that of **Koguryŏ** when the latter struck back under King **Kwanggaet'o**. **Silla** armies captured the South Han and lower Han basin in the 6th century in their drive against Paekche and Koguryŏ. In 676 Silla victories over Chinese armies in the Han and Imjin basins destroyed Tang hopes of establishing a protectorate on the peninsula. The Han held up the **Mongol** invasion of Korea in 1232, saw a major defeat for Japanese armies at Haengju in 1592, and was the site of famous resistance to the forcible entry of the Americans in 1871 (*see* **General Sherman**; **America, relations with**).
See also **commerce; merchants**

HAN SŎKPONG (Han Ho) 韓石峰 (Sŏkpong, 1543–1605)

Although he is usually known by his brush name 'stone peak', his official name was Han Ho. As a boy he was encouraged to practise **calligraphy** by his mother, copying the Chinese giants Wang Xizhi (K.Wang Hŭiji, 303–379) and Yan Zhenqing (K. An Chin'gyŏng, 709–785). He eventually gave up imitating Chinese masters in order to develop his own style. Working his way up through country prefectures, he became known in China through embassies. He is now regarded as one of the top three calligraphers of the Chosŏn dynasty in *yesŏ*, *haengsŏ*, and *ch'osŏ* styles (*see also* **Yi Yong**; **Kim Chŏnghŭi**). He had a prolific output, many examples of which are extant, and was in charge of writing official documents, including letters to China and Japan during the **Imjin Wars**. His *Sŏkpong-sŏppŏp* and *Sŏkpong Ch'ŏnja-mun* have become copybooks in their own right. Together with many rubbings of his work, all repeatedly re-published, they provide the most esteemed models for formal style, even in the 20th century.

HAN YONGUN 韓龍雲 (Manhae, 1879–1944)
Original name Han Pongwan. Born at Hongsŏng in south Ch'ungch'ŏng, and educated in the traditional manner at home, he was involved in the **Tonghak** rising. After it failed, he went to study **Buddhism** at a monastery in Sŏrak-san. Becoming a monk at Paektam-sa near Inje, he took the name Yongun, 'dragon cloud'. He visited Japan in 1908; and in 1910, after the **annexation** of Korea, travelled to China and visited an **Independence Army** training school. Returning through **Siberia** and **Manchuria** to Seoul, in 1913 he began writing *Pulgyo sajŏn* (Buddhist Dictionary). In 1919 he was imprisoned as one of the **33 signatories** of the **Declaration of Independence**. His 1926 poem *Nimŭi ch'immuk*, 'Silence of the Beloved', was a parable of patriotism in terms of Buddhism and romantic love. From 1931 he edited the magazine *Pulgyo*, 'Buddhism'. His novel *Hŭkp'ung* 'Black Wind' appeared in 1935. He continued to write, educating Buddhists and hoping for national independence, till he died of a stroke at the age of 65.

HAN YU 韓愈 (K. Han Yu; 768–824)
The great statesman, poet, and Confucian philosopher of Tang, a doughty opponent of **Buddhism**, was highly regarded in Chosŏn, where he was usually referred to as Han T'oeji (C. Tuizhi) or Ch'angnyŏ (C. Changli).

HAN'GUK INDEPENDENCE PARTY ARMY *See Ŭibyŏng*

HAN'GŬL 'Korean writing'
Han'gŭl is a true alphabet or system of letters that represent phonemes (units of sound that distinguish meanings), published as *Hunmin chŏngŭm* at the end of 1443 or beginning of 1444 by King **Sejong**, who saw the value of being able to write Korean rather than keep all records in Chinese. The phonetic theory involved was learnt from Ming studies such as *Hongwu zhengyun* (1375), which owed much to Sanskrit phonetics. The alphabetic principle and the square form of the letters were probably inspired by '**Phags-pa script**, which was well known in Korea at the time. *Han'gŭl* was largely Sejong's own invention and was used to print *Yongbi-ŏch'ŏn-ga* and other works before it was described in *Hunmin chŏngŭm*. This brief document was accompanied in 1446 by a commentary, *Hunmin chŏngum-haerye*, much of which aimed to show that the new letters were in harmony with orthodox neo-Confucian doctrine.

This failed to convince many of the literati who, aware of their intellectual and social investment in Chinese writing, deplored the new invention. Ch'oe Malli had presented a memorial to this effect in 1444, calling the new letters *ŏnmun* 'vulgar writing', and few scholars deigned to use them, in spite of Chinese-character dictionaries and royal editions of the **Confucian classics** with *ŏnmun* cribs and annotations. Though not used in government or in scholarship, *ŏnmun* began to play a significant part in the national culture. It was used by **women** and writers of popular fiction and vernacular songs, and was so useful for disseminating information among the uneducated that the paranoid **Prince Yŏnsan** decreed in 1504, two years before he died, that it should not be taught or studied. Later, *sirhak* scholars like **Hong Yangho** studied it carefully and Yu Hŭi (1773–1837) wrote a monograph, *Ŏnmun-ji* (1824).

As *ŏnmun* passed into use by less educated people, who spelt by ear, spelling became very irregular and a word was often spelt in several different ways in one text.

Towards the end of the 19th century, progressive thinkers, who urged wider use of *ŏnmun*, saw the need for unified spelling and standardised language. Early **newspapers** proved their point.

The colonial government instructed elementary schools in 1912 that *arae a* should be used only in Sino-Korean words; reinforced consonants should be written *sk*, *st*, *sp* and *sch* (now written *kk*, *tt*, *pp* and *chch*); and the only syllabic-final consonants should be *k*, *n*, *l*, *m*, *p*, *s*, *ng*, *lk*, *lm* and *lp*. A dot to the left of a syllable was to mark a long vowel, but this was dropped in 1921. In 1930 the government's *Ŏnmun ch'ŏlcha-ppŏp* 'Rules for Spelling *Ŏnmun*' abolished *arae a* completely; moved towards morphophonemic spelling by using *t*, *th*, *ch*, *ch'*, *p'*, *kk*, *kch*, *nch*, *lth*, *lp'*, and *ps* as syllabic final consonants; ordered that *sai siot* should be written alone when it occurred between nouns; abolished palatalised vowels after *t*, *ch*, *ch'* and *s* in Chinese words (so that, for example, the old *chyu* 'red' was to be written as *chu* and *syong* 'pinetree' as *song*); and ordered double consonants (now called *hapsŏng-jamo*, *toen-sori* or *ssang-ssori*) for the reinforced sounds *kk*, *tt*, *pp*, *ss* and *chch*. At the same time the practice of writing *i* without an initial *iŭng* as a nominative suffix after a noun ending in a vowel was dropped and -*ga* was written instead. (In speech -*ga* had been used in this way for more than a hundred years.)

About 1912 **Chu Sigyŏng** invented the term *Han'gŭl*, 'Great script', which was later seen as a pun on 'Korean script'. He founded the society eventually called *Han'gŭl Hakhoe* (**Han'gŭl Society**). *Han'gŭl matchumpŏp-t'ongiran*, the Society's guide to orthography and standard usage, appeared in 1933, changing *han'gŭl* from a phonemic to a morphophonemic system by writing each etymological element always in the same way and distinguishing words of the same sound but different meanings, such as *pis* 'comb', *pich* 'debt' and *pich'* 'light', all pronounced *pit*. (There is evidence that Sejong himself preferred morphophonemic spelling, for it was used in his *Yongbi-ŏch'ŏn-ga* and the first printing of *Wŏrin ch'ŏn'gang-ji-gok*.) Persecution of *Han'gŭl Hakhoe* by the Japanese colonial government undoubtedly helped to unity the nation in accepting the new spelling rules.

The definitive edition of *Han'gŭl t'ongiran* ('Unified spelling standards') was published in 1946, but minor spelling changes have since been recommended by government committees in South Korea. A major dispute, *Han'gŭl-kansohwa-p'adong* 'Hangŭl simplification movement', was started by Syngman Rhee (**Yi Sŭngman**)'s directive of April 1953 that would have gone back on the principles of *T'ongiran* and effectively re-established the colonial government rules of 1921, but reaction was so strong that the directive was withdrawn in September 1955. North Korea retains the old name *Chosŏn muncha* and has reinstated (and pronounces) initial *r*, mainly in Korean words and Chinese-derived proper names beginning with *l*.

YOUNG-KEY KIM-RENAUD, *The Korean Alphabet: its History and Structure*, Honolulu: University of Hawaii Press, 1997

See also **Han'gŭl**, **alphabetical order**; *Hangŭl* **letter names**; *Han'gŭl*, **lost letters**; *Hang'ŭl* **punctuation**; *hyang ch'al*; *idu*; *kugyol*; **romanisation**

HAN'GŬL ALPHABETICAL ORDER *han'gŭl chamo paeyŏl sunsŏ* 字母排列順序

The order of the alphabet in *Hunmin chŏngŭm* followed the *Hongwu zhengyun* tradition: *k*, *k'*, *ng*, *t*, *t'*, *n*, *p*, *p'*, *m*, *ch*, *ch'*, *s*, *h*, zero initial, [glottal stop,] *l/r*, *z* and vowels (*ă*, *ŭ*, *i*, *o*, *a*, *u*, *ŏ*, *yo*, *ya*, *yu*, *yŏ*). Ch'oe Sejin, in *Hunmong chahoe* 'Collection of Chinese Characters for Teaching Children' (1527), omitted the glottal-stop letter and modified the order by dividing the letters into eight initial-and-finals *k*, *n*, *t*, *r/l*, *m*, *p*, *s*, *ng*; eight initial-not-finals *k'*, *t'*, *p'*, *ts*, *ts'*, *z*, zero-initial and h; and eleven vowels in a new order *a, ya, ŏ, yŏ, o, yo, u, yu, ŭ, i, ă*. Thus he laid the foundation of the slightly different *Ka-Na-Da* sequence called **Panjŏl ponmun**, wherein the vowels are inserted after *ng*, which had come to serve also as the zero-initial, and reordered the initial-not-finals. In 1933 the **Han'gŭl Society** standardised this in the present *k, n, t, l/r, m, p, s*, zero with vowels, *ch, ch', k', t', p', h*.

HAN'GŬL LETTER NAMES

The **han'gŭl** letters were first given names by Ch'oe Sejin in **Hunmong chahoe** (1527). He took the sound for each of the eight initial-and-final letters in initial position and joined it by *-iŭ-*, the 'Man' and 'Earth' vowels, to the sound of the same letter in final position, producing *Kiyŏk, Niŭn, Tigŭt, Riŭl, Miŭm, Piŭp, Sios* (pronounced *siot*) and *Iŭng*. Because sounds had to be expressed in Chinese characters, none of which are pronounced *ŭk, ŭt* or *ŭs*, he used a character pronounced *yŏk* in *Kiyŏk*; one meaning *gŭt* 'end' in *Tigŭt*; and one meaning *ot* 'clothes' in *Siot*. He called the eight initial-only consonants *K'i, T'i, P'i, Chi, Ch'i, Zi, I* and *Hi*; and because there was no Chinese character pronounced *K'i*, he used one whose meaning was 'a winnowing basket', which is *k'i* in Korean. The vowels he named by their sounds: *A, Ya, Ŏ, Yŏ* and so on. In 1933 the **Han'gŭl Society** altered the names of the initial-only consonants to *Chiŭt, Ch'iŭt, K'iŭk, T'iŭt, P'iŭp* and *Hiŭt*.

HAN'GŬL: LOST LETTERS

Four of the original **Hunmin chŏngŭm** letters have ceased to be used, leaving only 24 of the original 28 symbols.

(1) The sound of *pan siot* 'half *siot*', the triangular character *z*, disappeared or became assimilated with that of *siot* during the 16th century.

(2) In the central dialect the vowel *arae a* (*ă*) had come to be pronounced *ŭ* in non-initial syllables before the end of the 16th century. In initial syllables it usually became *a*, though occasionally *ŏ* or *o* and even *ŭ* in *hŭk* 'soil'. Though said to survive to this day in the **dialect** of **Cheju**, it was elsewhere replaced by other letters during the first two decades of the 20th century, to accord with these changes in pronunciation.

The laryngeal letters and their double forms were designed chiefly for Chinese words and were never easy to distinguish. Only two of them have survived: *iŭng* and *hiŭt*.

Iŭng	Ssang-niŭng	Yen-niŭng	Toen-niŭng	Hiŭt	Ssang-hiŭt
O	∞	Ó	Ō	ㆆ	ㆅ

(3) *Yen-niŭng*, pronounced *ng*, was used as an initial and as a final, but ceased being pronounced as an initial by the 1490s. *Iŭng*, the zero-consonant, was used to mark the lack of a consonant at the beginning of any syllable and at the end of a Chinese syllable that ended with a vowel (see examples on page 175); but ceased being pronounced as a final in the early 1500s. Since by the middle of the 16th century there was no initial *ng* and no final zero-consonant, *yen-niŭng* was discarded and *iŭng* was used for both zero-initial and final *-ng*.

(4) *Toen-niŭng*, the glottal stop, was used in Chinese words to mark the strength of an initial *i, w*, or *y*. By the 1490s it had become indistinguishable from the zero-initial.

Two reduplications were also lost. *Ssang-niŭng* (double-zero) was a slight pause between a verb-root with syllable-final *i* and a suffix with syllabic initial *i* or *y*. It was dropped about 1480. *Ssang-hiŭt* (*hh*), a voiced or breathy *h* in some Chinese words and the Korean verb-root *hhyŏ-* 'to pull', disappeared about 1480.

HAN'GŬL PUNCTUATION *kudu-ppŏp* 口讀法
Han'gŭl was originally written in vertical columns read downwards from right to left, with no spacing between words and no punctuation; but since 1945 horizontal lines read from left to right have increasingly found favour. Spacing was introduced by the newspaper *Tongnip Sinmun* in 1896 and there has been an increasing tendency to separate items which can be treated as separate words, especially since the 1970s, but no precise rules have been devised. Though circles were very occasionally used to separate sections in a text, especially in dictionary-style presentation, as early as the 15th century, proper punctuation marks did not appear until about 1900 and have never been standardised. In general, modern punctuation follows English principles, but colons are rare and semicolons rarer. There is a tendency to use a dash in some places where English uses a colon. Various devices replace capitalisation and italics: quotations, book-titles and other proper names may be put within quotation marks, brackets, parentheses, French guillemets, or right-angle marks (as in China and Japan, above at the beginning and below at the end in horizontal script; to the right at the top and the left at the end in vertical script); sidelining, either straight or wavy, may be seen, especially in vertical script.

HAN'GŬL SOCIETY *Han'gŭl Hakhoe*
Nationalist society established to preserve the Korean language in the face of Japanese attempts to suppress Korean culture and of continued scholarly preference for the Chinese script. Research into *han'gŭl* had been carried on since the late 19th century, inspired particularly by **Chu Sigyŏng**, and in 1907 the Ministry of Education set up a Korean Language Institute. The Society was founded on 3 December 1921 in Hwimun School, Seoul, at a meeting of Chu's disciples, including Chang Chiyŏn and Sin Myŏnggyun, who called themselves *Chosŏn-ŏnŏ-yŏn'gu-hoe* 'Korean language research society' (changed to *Chosŏnŏ-hakhoe* 'Korean language society' in 1931). In 1927 they began publishing an academic journal, *Han'gŭl*, which, despite interruptions, still continues. Their objective was to promote the study of Korean linguistics and grammar and standardisation in the use of the script. 1933 saw the first edition of *Han'gŭl matchumpŏp-t'ongiran*, a guide to standardised spelling; *Sajŏnghan p'yojun-mal* 'Agreed Standard Vocabulary' followed in 1936 and *Oerae-ŏ p'yogi-ppŏp*, 'Transcription of Foreign Words' in 1940. Work was begun on a major dictionary, but in October 1942, when the colonial government was growing anxious about internal security after Japan's entry into World War II, Pak T'aejin (1903–1952), a member of the dictionary committee who was teaching at a girls' schoool in Hamhŭng, was arrested for disloyal activities. Further members of the Society were arrested and 13 of them, including Ch'oe Hyŏnbae, Yi Hŭisŭng and Pak T'aejin, sentenced to imprisonment in Hamhŭng, where Yi Yunjae (1888–1943) and Han Ching (1886–1944) died. Many others were questioned and maltreated; dictionary materials were lost, the magazine suspended and the society disbanded. The survivors were freed in 1945, the society resumed activity and the great dictionary *K'ŭn sajŏn* was finally published.

***HAN'GŬL*, UNILINEAR** *han'gŭl karo ssŭgi*

The idea of unravelling ***han'gŭl*** syllables and writing all the letters in a straight line was bound to arise when western typesetting and typewriting were introduced to Korea. **Chu Sigyŏng** was favourable to unilinear *han'gŭl* as early as 1908 and he published suggestions in *Marŭi sori* (1914). In March–June 1914 *Taehan-in Chŏnggyo-bo*, the 'Orthodox Church [monthly] magazine for Koreans' published at Chita in **Siberia**, printed several pages in unilinear script, with proposed cursive forms. The magazine ceased publication later that year.

The subject was taken up again after 1920 as part of the nationalists' concern for their language. Kim Tubong, who had published his grammar *Chosŏn malbŏn* in 1916, had to flee to Shanghai. When he published a second edition of the book there in 1923, he used it to advocate unilinear writing. In 1929 Ch'oe Hyŏnbae proposed combining *puro ssŭgi* (unravelling the syllables) and *karo ssŭgi* (horizontal writing). His final proposals, called simply *karo ssŭgi*, were published in *Kŭlchaŭi hyŏngmyŏng*, 'Revolution in Writing' (1947), and re-issued after the **Korean War**, notably in *Han'gŭl karo-kŭlssi tokpon* (1963). His suggested letter-forms resembled roman and cyrillic. Meanwhile Kim Tubong had become a political force in communist North Korea, where he urged the adoption of unilinear script until he was purged in 1958. **Kim Ilsŏng** was still talking about it in 1980. Such is Korean pride in *han'gŭl* that all their ideas won little support. The recent revolution in printing technology has nullified arguments for unilinear script.

ROSS KING 'Experimentation with Han'gŭl in Russia and the USSR 1914–1937' in Young-key Kim-Renaud *The Korean alphabet* University of Hawaii 1997

1 Standard *han'gŭl*: *Uri kŭrŭi karo ssŭnŭn ikhim* 'The practice of writing our letters in one line'.

우리 글의 가로 쓰는 익힘

2 As given by Chu Sigyŏng:

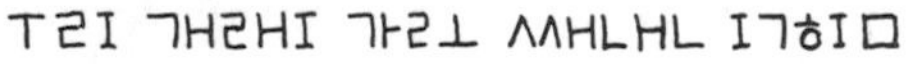

3 In the system of the Chita *Chŏnggyo-bo* (1914):

(a) printed

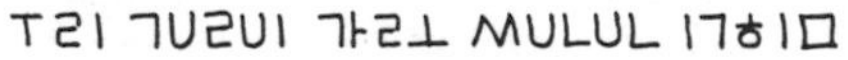

(b) cursive

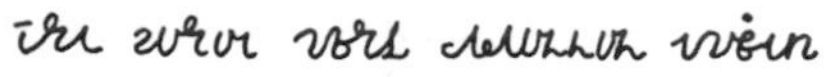

4 In the system of Ch'oe Hyŏnbae:

(a) printed

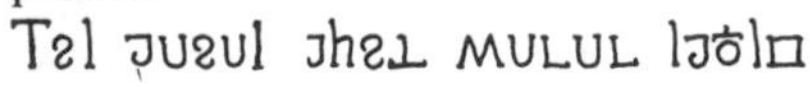

(b) cursive

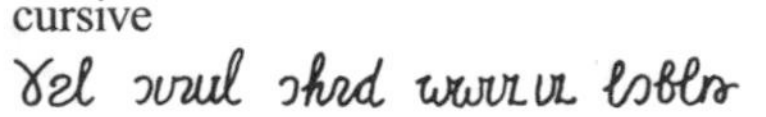

HANJUNG-NOK 閑中錄 'Record Made at Leisure'

Some believe the title originally meant 'record made in bitterness'. The book is an autobiographical account written in ***han'gŭl*** towards the end of her life by Lady Hong of the Hyegyŏng Palace (1735–1815), wife of the Crown Prince **Changhŏn** or Sado, who was executed by his father, King **Yŏngjo**, by being shut in a rice-box in 1762. There are several manuscripts and modern printed versions. *See* **Palace Literature**

JAHYUN KIM HABOUSH, *The Memoirs of Lady Hyegyŏng: the Autobiographical Writings of a Crown Princess of Eighteenth Century Korea*, Berkeley: University of California Press, 1996

HANMUN 漢文 'Chinese writing'
Hanmun is writing in Chinese characters with Chinese literary grammar. The term can be applied to all Chinese writing, but is especially used to distinguish Chinese written by Koreans from the Korean language written in *han'gŭl*. It became a major division among Korean literary *genres*. Chinese characters in themselves are described as *Hancha* 'Chinese letters'.
RICHARD RUTT, 'Hanmun – Korean Literature in Chinese,' *KJ*, 13/3, 1973
See also Hansi; Tang-style regulated verse

HANSAN 漢山
(also known as Hansŏng; modern Kwangju, Kyŏnggi province). Second capital of the tribe of **Paekche** which rose to prominence among the **Mahan** tribal federation and developed by the 3rd century AD into a state on a par with that of **Koguryŏ** to its north. Rivalry between the two led to warfare in which the Paekche king, Kaero, was killed, Hansan sacked, and the capital moved south to **Ungjin** (AD 475).

HANSI 漢詩 'Chinese poetry'
Many millions of poems in Chinese must have been written by Koreans. For six or seven centuries, every educated man was expected to be able to turn a polished stanza, and his best *Hansi* would be printed at the front of his posthumous collected works (*chip* or *munjip*). Poetry was a pastime and a social grace as well as a creative art. Meetings at which everyone wrote poems to the same rhymes thrived beyond the middle of the 20th century.
     The prosody was that of the Chinese masters – even to the use of the classic rhymes – and every verse-form was practised, especially *sa* (C. *ci*), *pu* (C. *fu*) (*see* **Poetry, Chinese**) and the highly disciplined stanzas of 7- or 5-syllable verses perfected by the Tang. Even though Koreans did not pronounce the Chinese tones that are the basis of Tang prosody, they knew the tones of all characters and observed the Chinese prosodic rules meticulously (*see* **Tang-style regulated verse**). The most esteemed Chinese models were **Tao Qian**, **Li Bai**, **Du Fu**, **Bai Zhuyi** and Su Dongpo (1037–1101); but Koreans insisted that good poetry must spring from personal experience, not fall into pastiche. (They did not, for instance, imitate Chinese lake poems, because they saw no lakes in Korea.) The content of *Hansi* was far richer and more varied than that of Korean-language verses, partly because all Korean verses were songs to be sung before an audience. *Hansi* were indeed recited by chanting, but without instrumental accompaniment and not normally before large audiences. The favourite subjects were love, loyalty and fine scenery, but they extended to self-mockery, reflections on personal experience, even looking forward to dying.
     The most esteemed of Korean poets in Chinese include **Ch'oe Ch'iwŏn**, **Yi Kyubo**, **Yi Chehyŏn**, **Yi Saek** and **Chŏng Mongju**, all from the pre-Chosŏn period. As in China itself, the art of poetry never surpassed what was done before 1500, but two groups of later poets are of special interest: Buddhist monks like Sŏsan (1520–1604), and women like **Sin Saimdang**, **Hŏ Nansŏrhŏn** and Yi Okpong (late 16th century).
     Poetry criticism flourished in the form of anecdotes and brief essays called *sihwa* 'poetry talks'. These are not afraid to criticise the Chinese masters, insist that poetry can spring only from experience, and examine technique in great detail, while maintaining that meaning is primary, diction second.
KIM JONG-GIL, *Slow Chrysanthemums*, London, 1987; RICHARD RUTT, 'Traditional poetry criticism', *TRASKB*, XLVII, 1972

HANSIK 寒食 'cold food'

The 105th day after the winter solstice, falling on 4 or 5 April, often coinciding with the **solar term** *Ch'ŏngmyŏng*. No fires are lit in houses, cold food is eaten and graves are visited, partly to tidy them after the ravages of winter. The festival is said to be in memory of Jie Zitui of the Jin dynasty (3rd or 4th century) who lost his life in a bush fire, but more probably there was an ancient spring **festival** at which a new fire was lit. Evidence from **Silla** is inconclusive, but the day was observed in Koryŏ, perhaps in imitation of Chinese custom. With *Tano*, *Ch'usŏk* and **New Year's Day**, it was one of the four major feasts of the Chosŏn period.

HANSŎNG 漢城

Regional capital of the northern kingdom of **Koguryŏ**; located in the upper tributaries of the Chaeryŏng River in Chaeryŏng County, Hwanghae province. Archaeologists have found remains of mountain **fortresses** and stone burial chambers in the vicinity of modern Ayang-ni and Wŏltang-ni which indicate its importance as a centre of military and civil administration after the transfer of the capital from **Kungnaesŏng** to P'yŏngyang in AD 427. It was known as Hansŏng and Siksŏng in the Koguryŏ period. In the Koryŏ dynasty the name was changed to Anju, and in the early Chosŏn to Chaeryŏng.

N.B. Distinguish Hansŏng, Kyŏnggi province, one of the many names by which the city of Seoul was formerly known.

HANSŎNG SUNBO 漢城旬報

The first **newspaper** published wholly in Korean, established in 1883 by the Office of Information and Culture (*see* **Independence Party**). It was published three times monthly in Chinese characters and its articles reflected modernisation and reform themes. It was closed in 1885 after the failure of the *Kapsin* **Coup**.

HANSŎNG (SEOUL), TREATY OF *See Kapsin* Coup

HANYANG 漢陽 *See* Seoul

HARDING, JOHN REGINALD (1858–1921)

A Welsh architect and engineer who was Engineer-in-Chief of the Chinese Imperial Customs Service under Robert Hart. In 1899 he visited Korea, where he worked with John McLeavey **Brown**, advising on lighthouses and developing the harbour at Mokp'o. In 1903 he was appointed consultant engineer to the Korea Lighthouse Board, toured the country and selected sites for 29 lighthouses, preparing designs and specifications. He designed the western-style Sŏkcho-jŏn in the **Tŏksu Palace**.

HARES

As in China, *t'okki*, often called 'rabbits', are really hares that do not burrow or live in warrens (*Lepus sinensis, Lepus mandshuricus*). The Chinese tale of a hare in the moon with a pestle and mortar is well loved, and folk tales like *Sugung-ga* tell of the hare as a schemer and trickster. Hares were hunted with dogs.

HARP SONG *Konghu-in* 箜篌引|

Also called *Kongmudoha-ga*, 'song of husband not crossing the river'. Claimed by some as the oldest Korean song (*see also* **Orioles' Song**; **Tortoise Incantation**), though no Korean text is known. A Chinese version (4 four-character lines in one stanza) appears in *Haedong yŏksa* 22, where it is quoted from the Jin writer Cui Bao's *Gujinzhu* (c. 4th century AD) as a story of **Old Chosŏn**. The song was supposedly sung to a harp accompaniment by Yŏok, wife of a ferryman, for a woman who drowned herself after seeing her husband drown.

My husband did not get across the river;
My husband has indeed crossed the river:
He went under and was drowned.
What about my husband now?

There are many views about these lines. Some writers hold that they are not even Korean in origin.

HEADDRESS
In Koryŏ and Chosŏn, men grew their hair long and wore it twisted into a queue, often caught up at one side of the headband or hat, until they married. At the capping ceremony the hair was put up in a **topknot**, held in place with a tight horsehair band *munggŏn* round the forehead (a torture in hot weather) and covered by a stiff gauze cap called *t'anggŏn*. The broad-brimmed black hat *kat*, whose brim was made of finely split **bamboo**, lacquered like the horsehair, was assumed at the same time. It is thought to have originated in 1367 when Mongol fashions were rejected and the supposedly 'ancient' black hat was adopted, with buttons of jade or crystal (according to rank) where the chin-strings were attached. For informal wear it could be replaced by a variety of softer hats. There were also many forms of court headgear and special hats for certain jobs and for the lowest classes. Some of these were made of **felt**.

The coiffure of upper class **women** was bulky and elaborate, making use of false hair-pieces or, for court wear in later Chosŏn, huge wooden imitations (*k'ŭnmŏri*) of loops of braided hair fixed into the coiffure. The only women who regularly wore hats were **kisaeng** and **mudang**, though there were jewelled caps for court and bridal wear, tiny warm caps for the elderly, and veils for outdoor wear. In the street women used a green coat (*changot*), thrown over the head without putting the arms in the sleeves.
See also **dress; jewellery**

HEAD-RANK ARISTOCRACY *tup'um* 頭品 *See Kolp'um*

HEAVENLY HORSE TOMB *Ch'ŏnma-ch'ong* 天馬冢
Tomb of an unknown 5th–6th century king of the kingdom of **Silla** excavated at **Kyŏngju** in 1973. It was timber-lined and surmounted by a stone mound, following the fashion seen at Pazyryk in Kazakhstan. Among its numerous and rich contents were many items of gold and jade, notably a **gold crown** embellished with 58 carved jade pendants (*kogok*) and a gold girdle hung with thirteen. The girdle measured 125 cms and the longest pendant 73·5 cms. Similarities between this girdle and those found in the **Gold Crown Tomb** and the tomb of the **Paekche** King **Muryŏng** include the carving of **dragons** on the square plates that help to make up these ceremonial items. The placing of the gold cap, ornament, and diadem in different parts of the tomb suggests that the three constitute separate items of headgear, and not necessarily three sections of a single crown, as had previously been thought. The tomb derives its name from the winged, galloping white horse painted on a birchbark saddle flap, part of the trappings of a horse sacrificed with the king and emblematic

of his shaman's role. On others of the six saddle flaps found in the tomb are painted horsemen and a **phoenix**.

HIDE-AND-SEEK *sullae-japki* or *sumpakkokchil*

Sullae, the word for 'It', the person chosen as seeker in Hide-and-seek or the blindfolded one in *kamakchapki* 'Blind Man's Buff', is possibly derived from *sulla*, the officer who policed the streets during the hours of **curfew**. The one to be 'It' was chosen by counting out the children present with a jingle of mangled numbers and nonsense words in which a beggar and a field-marshal play the parts of the English 'rich man, poor man, beggar-man, thief': *hanalttae, tualttae, samajung, nalttae, yungnang, kŏji, p'alttae, changgun, kodŭrae, ppyong* (or *pping*)! *Kodŭrae-ppyong* is used as an exclamation of satisfaction as the final touch is put to the completion of any work.

HIDEYOSHI TOYOTOMI 豐臣秀吉 *See* **Imjin Wars**

HŎ HŎN 許憲

Radical chairman of the Central Committee of the **New Shoot Society**. He was sent to conferences in Europe in 1927 to speak for Korean independence. After involvement in anti-Japanese agitation in 1929 (*see* **Kwangju Incident**) he was arrested early the next year as part of the suppression of the Society. He became a lawyer, and was deeply involved with the communist cause if not actually a member of the **Korean Communist Party**. In September 1945 he replaced the more moderate **An Chaehong** on the Preparatory Committee for Building the Country, and was appointed prime minister of the hastily proclaimed **Korean People's Republic** (KPR). In a critical meeting on 27 November, he failed to persuade the newly returned leaders of the **Provisional Government in Exile**, **Kim Ku** and **Kim Kyusik**, to unite it with the KPR government. As the prospect of political coalition faded through 1946, Hŏ and **Yŏ Unhyŏng** were identified with the pro-Soviet line. In November Hŏ was nominated to the leadership of the newly formed South Korean Workers' Party (SKWP), and both he and Yŏ were presidents of the left-wing Democratic National Front. In 1948, the SKWP helped to 'elect' the South Korean delegates to the Supreme People's Assembly of the **Democratic People's Republic** set up in P'yŏngyang. Hŏ was the chairman of its First Congress (1948–57), and a member of the Political Committee.

HŎ KYUN 許筠 *See HONG-GILTONG-JŎN*

HŎ NANSŎRHŎN 許蘭雪軒 (1563–89)

Nansŏrhŏn is perhaps Korea's most famous woman poet. 214 poems of hers survive. Born at Kangnŭng, she was married at the age of about fifteen to Kim Sŏngnip (1562–92), who when he died at the age of 30 was an 8th **grade** official of the *Hongmungwan*. They lived near **Kwangju** in Kyŏnggi province. She lost a son and a daughter in infancy and herself died at the age of 26. Her husband is said to have been unfaithful. He died during the Japanese invasion of 1592 and his body was never recovered.

Nansŏrhŏn's poetry is modelled on Tang work and is full of concern for the world of the **immortals**. It is not original, but it is feminine in the manner of her time and has a graceful charm. Sometimes it reflects her worries during her husband's absences, but it is most affecting when she mourns for her dead children.

HŎ PAENGNYŎN 許百鍊 (Ŭijae, 1891–1977)

A widely admired calligrapher and landscape artist of the Southern School, an amateur of the ancient Daoist classics, and connoisseur of Korean **tea**. In his later years he had a charity school for boys on the slopes of Mudŭng-san, near **Kwangju** (South Chŏlla), where he lived in the style of **Tao Qian** and taught the boys to grow tea. His brush name means 'Resolute studio'.

*See also **Tongyŏnsa***

HODGE, LIEUTENANT GENERAL JOHN R. (1893–1963)

Commander of the United States Army XXIV Corps, a force of 72,000 men which landed at **Inch'ŏn** on 8 September 1945 with a threefold task: to disarm and receive the surrender of the Japanese; to restore and maintain order and to establish the basis of democratic government and an operating economy; and to train the Korean people for eventual self-rule. American suspicion of the communists on one hand and distrust of arch-conservatives such as Syngman Rhee (**Yi Sŭngman**) on the other meant that Hodge was cast, at least temporarily, in the rôle of policy-maker and day to day leader of south Korea, a part for which he had no political training, no local knowledge, and no desire. He is infamous for his comment that Koreans and Japanese 'are all the same breed of cats'. He set up a Korean Advisory Council to assist the **American Military Government** (AMG) and an interim government to work with the AMG under **An Chaehong** in May 1947, but his efforts to promote synarchy were undermined by general Korean opposition to the spectre of **trusteeship** adopted by the **Moscow Conference Agreement**, by US-Soviet rivalry for domination of Korean politics, and by the personal antipathy between Hodge and Yi Sŭngman. Despite his desire to prevent the spread of communism in the south he was also wary of the right-wing nationalism of **Kim Ku**. When **UNTCOK** took over the attempt to organise national elections in 1948, Hodge clashed with it over the record of the AMG and the timetable for an American withdrawal.

HOMOSEXUALITY *tongsŏng yŏnae* 同性戀愛

Since neo-Confucianism had little moral concern with sexual purity, there was little or no discussion of male homoeroticism and no suggestion that there was such a thing as a homosexual orientation. Yet the vocabulary applied was disparaging (*kyegan* 'cockerel copulation' (*piyŏk* in native Korean); *myŏn, totchaengi* and *midongaji* for catamites). In later Chosŏn *namsadang* troupes lived homosexually and provided prostitutes, but they were *ch'ŏnmin*. A young widower might be known to have a favourite, at least in provincial society, but neither of the two would be regarded as marked for life. Anecdote collections contain occasional stories of earthy humour. Nevertheless, accusations of homosexuality were levelled at enemies, as they were by Chosŏn historians against the last kings of Koryŏ. It is often hard to distinguish between homoeroticism and favouritism. The classic Chinese expression *Yongyang-ji-ch'ong*, 'favour for Prince Longyang', used against the Koryŏ kings, refers to a story in *Zhanguoce* that has more to do with favouritism than with eroticism. The subject is also complicated by the intensity of male friendships in neo-Confucian society, which regarded marriage and procreation as primary social duties, but restricted the sharing of emotional life to the same sex. Female homosexuality is the subject of oral history about the many palace women.

HONG KUGYŎNG 洪國榮 (1748–81)

A kinsman of the Kyŏnggŭi-gung (titled Queen Kyŏnghŭi in 1899). She was the reputed authoress of *Hanjung-nok*, wife of the suffocated Crown Prince **Changhŏn**, and mother of the Crown Prince who became **King Chŏngjo**. Hong Kugyŏng was only 23, three years older than Chŏngjo, when he was appointed his tutor in 1771. He schemed against the dogmatist **faction** and succeeded in having his pupil made king in 1777. Hong then effectively controlled the government through the young king, and is reckoned as the first example of *sedo-jŏngch'i*. Three years later there were further plots in which the palace women played key rôles. Hong was sent off in disgrace, and died in Kangnŭng at the age of 33.

HONG KYŎNGNAE 洪景來 (1780–1812)

A disaffected *yangban* who smarted under the discrimination against men from P'yŏngan province. Disappointed at his failure to enter government service, he retired to the hills to study for a while. During this period he began to gather a reputation as a charismatic leader. He met men who shared his disaffection and they began preparing for action. After the bad harvests of 1811 they marched on Kasan in January 1812. Their rebellion was not finally crushed until five months later, when Chŏngju was captured from the rebels by government troops. Hong was killed in the fighting. This was the first of the uprisings that occurred throughout the 19th century.

HONG YANGHO 洪良浩 (Igye, 1724–1802)

From his early twenties onward he lived peacefully in government service, mostly employed in posts connected with learning (at the *Sŏnggyun-gwan*) or in the provinces. In 1777, when **Hong Kugyŏng** was in power, he was virtually banished from court by being appointed to Kyŏnghŭng on the **Tumen** River, but in 1781 he was on his first embassage to Qing. He went again in 1794. In China he met Ji Yun (Ji Xiaolan) and other scholars of the *kaozheng* 'empirical research' tendency, which he did much to promote in Korea. His interests were wide and practical, inspiring what were later called *sirhak* concerns. As a provincial official he became expert in forestry and in 1764 introduced Japanese flowering cherry seedlings. He was a gifted writer and poet, called upon by **King Chŏngjo** to edit the manuscripts of **Ch'a Ch'ŏllo** as well as *Yŏngjo sillok* and *Kukcho pogam*. His *Haedong myŏngjang-jŏn* 'Lives of Famous Generals East of the Sea' (1794) gives biographies of 55 Korean military leaders from Silla to Chosŏn, centred on defence of the realm and showing partiality to Ming in accounts of the **Manchu invasions**. His *Puksaek kiryak* 'Sketch of the Northern Border' contains interesting studies of Hamhŭng **dialect**.

HONG-GILTONG-JŎN 洪吉童傳 'Biography of Hong Kiltong'

The so-called 'first Korean novel', probably written about 1640, and said to owe much to the famous Chinese novel *Shuihu zhuan*. It tells of the difficulties of Hong Kiltong, both at home and in his public career, which arise from the fact that, though he is of upper class birth, he is illegitimate. He narrowly escapes death, forms a band like Robin Hood's and eventually becomes king of a utopian state. The story is full of miracles and magic. There is an underlying theme of protest against injustices in Korean politics and society, which has added to the book's value for 20th-century critics; but there are many problems. It is not known whether it was first written in Chinese or in Korean; no edition earlier than the 1880s has been traced; its origin and authorship have not been verified. The author is usually thought to have been Hŏ Kyun (1569–1618), illegitimate son of a government minister. Hŏ was a learned man, who held office through the period of the Japanese invasions. He belonged to the faction that brought Prince **Kwanghae** to the throne in 1608, but was executed ten years later on a charge of treason against the same king. (*See* **illegitimate sons** and *Kodae sosŏl*).

PETER H. LEE, *Anthology of Korean Literature*, Honolulu: University of Hawaii Press, 1981

HONGMUN 紅門 'red gate'

A '**banner gate**' (*chŏngmun*) or '**red arrow gate**' (*hongsal-mun*).

HONGMUN-GWAN 弘文館 'Hall of Extensive Writings'

One of the *Samsa*, a review body of learned scholars named after an institute of Tang and Ming China. Established by King **Sejo** in 1463 as a successor to the *Chiphyŏn-jŏn* Academy and concerned with historical precedents, it drafted major documents, and came to be influential in advising and admonishing the king. *Hongmun-gwan* maintained an excellent library, badly damaged in the **Imjin Wars,** and like the *Chiphyŏn-jŏn* published many books reflecting the neo-Confucian priorities of the early Chosŏn leadership, especially on history and government. The twenty officials were led by a 1st **grade** senior.

See also **censorate; government, central; names, temple;** *Sahwa*

HONGSAL-MUN See **red arrow gate**

HŎNJONG, KING 顯宗 (1827–49, r. 1834–49)

Ikchong's son, appointed to the throne at the age of seven by his grandmother, the Dowager Queen Sunwŏn (1789–1857), widow of **Sunjo**, a woman of the Andong Kim clan. She ruled through the screen (*suryŏm-ch'ŏngjŏng*) for seven years and had Hŏnjong married to another Andong Kim (later known as Queen Hyohyŏn, 1828–1843). The P'ungyang Cho (his mother's clan) resumed power, but this did not help the desperate economic and political situation inherited from the reign of Sunjo. Persecution of **Catholics** was renewed: among the **martyrs** were Bishop Laurent **Imbert** and two French priests in 1835 and St Andrew **Kim Taegŏn** in 1846. Hŏnjong assumed rule personally in 1841. His queen died in 1843 and in 1844 he married one of the Hong clan, later known as Queen Hyŏnjong (1831–1904). The country was still in dire condition when he died at the age of 22. He did, however, initiate the compilation of *Tongguk munhŏn pigo*.

HORAK-HONGJO 湖洛鴻爪 'Footprints of a wild goose [in the snow]'

A lyrical description of Korean scenery written in 1850 by a woman poet, Kumwŏn (b. 1816), and published by **Ch'oe Namsŏn** in *Ch'ŏngch'un* 1917–8. The title is from the Song poet Su Dongpo (1037–1101), but Kumwŏn preferred *Hodong-sŏrak-ki* 'From eastern provinces to western capital'. It tells how at the age of thirteen she was dressed as a boy and taken from her home in Wŏnju on a tour of central and eastern Korea, including the **Diamond Mountains** and the **Eight Views** of the East Coast, then to Seoul. In 1830 she became the secondary wife of Kim Tŏkhui (b. 1800), whom she accompanied to Ŭiju on the **Yalu** River when he was appointed governor there in 1845. They retired to Seoul, where she lived at Yongsan, reading and writing poetry with congenial women friends.

HOROSCOPES *See Saju-p'alcha*

HORSES

The horse probably came from China, perhaps even before 1000 BC. By the 4th century AD, Korean miniature horses were famous. They were called *kwaha*, 'under fruit', horses, suggesting they could pass below fruit-tree branches, though the word is possibly a transliteration of some non-Chinese word. They were renowned in **Paekche** and are thought to have been the same as a tiny island race in **Cheju**.

Riding was primarily a military skill. The king owned large numbers of choice animals kept in large enclosed pastures. They were esteemed, as they were in ancient China, for their appearance, fleetness and valour. By late Chosŏn, horses had also become the principal beasts of burden for long hauls and were used to draw carts; but travellers might ride the same horses, using high wooden saddles. Horses were not used in **agriculture**.

HORTICULTURAL INTRODUCTIONS TO BRITAIN

Most Korean plants in British gardens were introduced through nurseries in Japan. The Chelsea horticulturalist John Gould Veitch (1839–1870) collected *Pinus koraiensis* (*chat-namu*) when he visited Japan in 1861. His employee Charles Maries (d. 1902) sent *toraji* (*Platycodon grandiflorum mariesii*) from Japan in 1879. William Richard Carles (1848–1929), the first British consul in Korea (**Chemulp'o**, 1883–6), sent a specimen of *Viburnum* (or *Solenolantana*) *carlesii* from Korea in 1885, but the plant was not introduced until 1902. Veitch's son, James Herbert Veitch (1868–1907) visited Korea in spring 1892. He was impressed by the intense blue of *toraji* flowers on the hills around Seoul and declared Korean **rice** had no equal in the Far East, but found the flora generally unsuitable for British soils and climate. He obtained *Rhododendron schlippenbachii* (*chŏltchuk*) and *Physalis francheti* (the 'Chinese lantern', *kkwari*), but from Japan. Seeds of *kusang namu*, the Korean fir (*Abies koreana*), whose pretty blue cones are capped with tiny purple flowers, were brought by Ernest Henry Wilson (1876–1930) in 1917. The early-flowering *Forsythia koreana* (syn. *ovata*) reached England in 1918, and the delightful *misŏn-namu* 'round-fan shrub' (*Abeliophyllum distichum*), endemic to only two parishes in North Ch'ungch'ŏng (Yongjŏng-ni in Chinch'ŏn-gun and Songdŏng-ni in Koesan-gun), in 1928. Of the Turk's-head lilies, *Lilium hansonii*, common throughout Korea as *sŏm mal-lari*, is said to have come from an island (Ullŭng-do?) by 1871; *amabile* (*t'ŏlchung-nari*) in 1912; and *cernuum* (*sollari*, endemic to Korea and Manchuria) in 1934. The Tiger Lily (*ch'am-nari*), though common in Korea, came from China or Japan. The so-called 'Korean chrysanthemum' is an American hybrid introduced after World War II.

HORTICULTURE

Horticulture has been practised at least since Koryŏ times, but garden design has been virtually a royal prerogative. The 'Secret Garden' (*see* **Piwŏn**) of the **Ch'angdŏk palace** means strictly a 'private park' with landscaping of pools, lakes, trees and elegant buildings. Yet many Koreans have been devoted to plants that could be grown in courtyards, near houses and in temple precincts. Country folk were usually content with a vegetable patch.

An early book on growing plants and flowers is *Yanghwa-rok*, 'Account of Flower-growing' (1440) by **Kang Hŭian**, which includes a chapter on bonsai. The *sirhak* writers gave attention to horticulture and forestry in their encyclopaedic compilations at a later date. Interest in **garden flowers** has increased during the 20th century.

For a thousand years poets have said that spring is the season for colour. In spring the hills are covered with purple azaleas, the villages full of golden forsythia-hedges

and pale apricot blossom, white pear blossom and the deep rose-purple of peach flowers. (**Peach**-blossom has a canonised place in literature derived from **Tao Qian**'s 4th-century utopia, *Taohuayuan ji* 'Peach-blossom spring', as well as being an emblem of brides and matrons derived from *Shijing*, the ancient Chinese *Book of Odes*.) Summer is the green season, enlivened with the scarlet flowers of the pomegranate, which certainly goes back to the days of Koryŏ. Colour returns in autumn with the red and gold of maple leaves.
See also **bamboo**

HOURS OF THE DAY

The twelve hours of the calendar day, each equal to two hours of the 24-hour day, were named after the 12 branches of the **sixty-fold cycle**. The hours of darkness were known as the **Five Watches**. They all had alternative names, shown here.

2300-0059	CHASI	*yaban*	3rd watch
	Rat hour	midnight	
0100-1259	CH'UKSI	*hyemyŏng*	4th watch
	Ox hour	cockcrow	
0300-0459	INSI	*p'yŏngdan*	5th watch
	Tiger hour	dawn	
0500-0659	MYOSI	*ilch'ul*	
	Hare hour	sunrise	
0700-0859	CHINSI	*siksi*	
	Dragon hour	breakfast	
0900-1059	SASI	*ujung*	
	Snake hour	mid-morning	
1100-1259	OSI	*illam*	
	Horse hour	sun due south	
1300-1459	MISI	*ilch'ŭk*	
	Sheep hour	slanting sun	
1500-1659	SINSI	*p'osi*	
	Monkey hour	evening	
1700-1859	YUSI	*irip*	
	Fowl hour	sunset	
1900-2059	SULSI	*hwanghon*	1st watch
	Dog hour	dusk	
2100-2259	HAESI	*injŏng*	2nd watch
	Pig hour	curfew	

HUAINANZI 淮南子 (K. *Hoenamja*)
A Chinese Daoist compilation covering topography, **astronomy**, government and philosophy, dating from the 2nd century BC. It is occasionally quoted by Korean writers.

HULBERT, HOMER BEZALEEL 轄甫 (1863–1949)
Hulbert was born at New Haven, Connecticut, and arrived in Korea in 1886 as a Methodist missionary to teach English at the Royal College. Though hampered by a distaste for Chinese, he was an early student of Korean history and language, who occasionally published eccentric material, such as a theory that Korean was related to

Dravidian languages. From 1901 to 1905 he published a monthly magazine in Seoul, *The Korea Review*, most of which he wrote. He probably supervised the writing of *Taedong Kinyŏn*, a history of the Chosôn dynasty printed in Shanghai in 1903. His *History of Korea* (1905), originally published serially in the *Review*, is an uninspired account based on *Tongsa gangmok* and *Taedong kinyŏng*, but *The Passing of Korea* (New York 1906) is a useful account of contemporary affairs. When the Japanese **protectorate** was set up in 1905, he changed from favouring Japanese influence to working against it, and went as a secret amateur diplomat for Korea to the Second International Peace Conference at the Hague in 1907 (*see* **Hague Peace Conference**). As a result he had to leave the country, but in 1949, aged 86, he returned as a national guest, honoured for his efforts for independence. He was taken ill and died while in Seoul, where he is buried.

HŬMCH'I-GYO 吽哆教
A 20th-century '**new religion**', also called *Chŭngsan-gyo*.

HUNDRED AND FIVE, THE CASE OF THE *Paego-in sakkŏn* 百五人事件 (1912)
On 28 December 1910, a meeting between the American missionary George McCune and Governor-General Terauchi at Sŏnch'ŏn, North P'yŏngan province, was said by the Japanese authorities to have been the occasion for an abortive attempt by An Myŏnggŭn to assassinate the Governor-General. The Japanese military police made many arrests, the estimated numbers ranging from 600 to an improbable 50,000. They included leaders of the *Sinminhoe* ('**New People's Association**') such as **Kim Ku** and **Yun Ch'iho**. World-wide attention was drawn to the subsequent trial, which began on 28 June 1912. The 123 defendants were accused of treason on the basis of falsified evidence and had been tortured. Nine were exiled and Yun Ch'iho and five others sentenced to prison terms. The support given to the Korean independence movement by the Christian church prompted the Japanese to try to discredit it, and the faith of Kim Ku and many of his co-defendants gave this case its alternative title, 'Christian Conspiracy Case'. The trial was denounced by British officials in Seoul and Tokyo as a grave miscarriage of justice, and on appeal in April 1913 the majority were freed. The condemnation to hard labour during 1911 and 1912 of 105 men convicted of complicity in the affair gives it the title *paego-in sakkŏn*, '105 men incident'. It is also referred to as the 'Korean conspiracy case.'

HŬNGBU-JŎN 興夫傳
A *kodae sosŏl* also known in *p'ansori* form. Hŭngbu is the virtuous younger brother of greedy and selfish Nolbu, who treats him cruelly. Hŭngbu finds a swallow with a broken wing, which he mends. The bird rewards him with a seed that grows and produces gourds full of treasure. Nolbu is envious, catches another swallow, breaks its wing and mends it. The second bird brings a seed to Nolbu, but the gourds it produces are full of trouble. Modern commentators have interpreted this simple fable on the universal younger-brother theme as a political and social satire.

HUNGSŎN TAEWŎN'GUN 興宣大院君 *See* **Taewŏn'gun, The**

HUNMIN CHŎNGŬM 訓民正音 'Correct Sounds to be Taught to the People'
The *han'gŭl* alphabet was published by King **Sejong** under this title between 21 December 1443 and 19 January 1444. An explanatory document, *Hunmin chŏngŭm haerye*, appeared in 1446.

CONSONANTS were given in the order found in *Hongwu zhengyun*, 'The Hongwu Emperor's Complete Rhymes', a Ming work of 1375, where consonants are classified according to place of articulation in the vocal tract as it was then perceived and described. velar, lingual, labial and laryngeal. A semi-lingual and a semi-dental completed the list. They were also classified in terms of the **clear-and-cloudy** dichotomy as 'completely clear' (unvoiced); 'partly clear' (aspirates); 'completely clouded' (voiced); and 'neither-clear-nor-cloudy' (nasal and liquid sonants). This table docs not show the original order.

	not clear not cloudy: sonant		completely clear: unvoiced		partly clear: aspirate		completely cloudy: voiced*	
velar	ㆁ	ng	ㄱ	k	ㅋ	k'	ㄲ	g
lingual	ㄴ	n	ㄷ	t	ㅌ	t'	ㄸ	d
semi-lingual	ㄹ	r/l	-		-		-	
bilabial	ㅁ	m	ㅂ	p	ㅍ	p'	ㅃ	b
dental		-	ㅅ	s	ㅈ	ts†	ㅊ	ts'†	ㅉ ㅆ	dz† ss
semi-dental	ㅿ		-		-		-	
laryngeal	ㅇ	zero initial	ㆆ	glottal stop	ㅎ	h	ㆀ ㆅ	zero-zero hh

* Voiced initials occurred only in Chinese words. Double letters were not used for reinforced sounds until the 20th century.
† These sounds became *ch, ch'*, and *j* after the 15th century.

The sonant letters were designed as diagrams of the speech organs articulating the sounds of each group. Lingual *n* depicted a tongue touching the roof of the mouth; labial *m*, pursed lips as a quadilateral; dental *s*, a tooth; and the laryngeal zero-initial, a circular throat. Each diagram was reinforced with one stroke for its unvoiced form, and with a second stroke for the aspirated form. In the velar group the sonant was not taken as basic, because its laryngeal quality demanded a circle: unvoiced *k*, depicting the root of a tongue blocking the throat, was taken as basic and reinforced with an extra stroke for the aspirate *k'*. Labial *m* was reinforced to make *p* and *p'* without destroying the basic square. A curled tongue is shown in semi-lingual *l/r*, based on lingual *n*; and a tooth in semi-dental *z*, based on dental *s*.

Kabyŏun piŭp	*Kabyŏun* piŭp	*Kabyŏun* ssangbiŭp	*Kabyŏun* miŭm
ㅸ	ㆄ	ㅹ	ㅱ

The labial consonants *p, p', pp* and *m*, had *kabyŏun* 'light' forms, written with *iŭng* below. In practice, only *kabyŏun piŭp*, pronounced *w*, was much used. It survived till about 1520. All the consonants in a cluster were probably pronounced (*ns, nz, nch, nh, ks, lk, lks, lm, lp, ls, lz, lt', lp', lh, mk, ms, pk, ps, pt, psk, pst, pch, pt', sk, st, sp, ss, and sch*).

173

In neo-Confucian apologetic, the five consonant groups were related to the **Five Phases**, five seasons, five points of the compass and five notes of the pentatonic scale (**Five Tones**).

velar	wood	spring	east	*kak* = la
lingual	fire	summer	south	*ch'i* = do
labial	earth	late summer	centre	*kung* = fa
dental	metal	autumn	west	*sang* = sol
laryngeal	water	winter	north	*u* = re

VOWELS also depicted the speech organs, and were explained according to neo-Confucian ideas, derived from the ***Book of Changes***, about *samjae*, the 'Three Powers' (Heaven, Earth and Man).

· ă	— ŭ		i
heaven	earth	man

The far back vowel, romanised here as *ă* (sounding rather like the English exclamation *uh*), was a dot whose roundness typified Heaven. It was later called *arae a* 'lower *a*', because it was written under a preceding consonant. The central vowel *ŭ* (as in English *book*) was a horizontal line depicting the flattened tongue and flat Earth; and the front vowel *i* (as in English *pique*) was a vertical line depicting the raised tongue and upright Man.

yang (heaven above and right)		yin (heaven below and left)	
⸬ o	⊦ a	⸗ u	⊣ ŏ
⸬ yo	⊧ ya	⸗ yu	⊨ yŏ

These three fundamental vowels combined to form eight other vowels, typifying the generation of all entities by Heaven interacting with Earth and Man. The horizontal line with one dot above gave *o* and with two dots above it gave *yo*; one dot below it gave *u*, and two dots below it gave *yu*. The vertical line with one dot to the right gave *a*, and with two dots to the right it gave *ya*; one dot to the left gave *ŏ*, and two dots to the left gave *yŏ*. The dots were very soon changed into short strokes, vertical on the horizontal lines and horizontal on the vertical lines (*see* pages 15, 162).

SPELLING was phonemic, each syllable consisting of an initial consonant, a medial vowel, and, when necessary, a final consonant, all written within a square space, like that occupied by a Chinese character. A vowel with a vertical main stroke was written to the right of the initial consonant, while *arae a* (*ă*) or a vowel with a horizontal main stroke was written beneath the initial consonant. A vowel combination with both vertical and horizontal main strokes was written below and to the right of the initial consonant. The final consonant was put at the bottom. Every Chinese syllable (marked below with C) had to be written with a final consonant: if it was open it had a final zero.

even		high		rising		falling
쟝	돌ㄱ	·양	·ㅉ·	:용	:감·	·법
chyang (C)	tolk	.ya (C)	.pcha	:ngo (C)	:kam	.pŏp (C)
worker	stone	night	weave	five	persimmon	law

TONES (lexically significant combinations of vowel length and pitch) have not entirely disappeared from Korean, at least in **dialect**. In the 15th century three probably existed, though there were four in literary Chinese (not the same as in modern Chinese). In *Hunmin chŏngŭm* tones were shown by *pangchŏm* 'side-dots', placed to the left of the syllable. The even tone *pingsheng* (K. *p'yŏngsŏng*, short-and-low) had no dots; the 'going' tone *qusheng* (K. *kŏsŏng*, high) had one dot; the 'rising' tone *shangsheng* (K. *sangsŏng*, long-and-rising) had two dots. The 'entering' or falling tone *rusheng* (K. *ipsŏng*) belonged to any syllable ending with -*k*, -*l* or -*p* and therefore needed no special mark. Tone dots were abandoned by about 1700.
See also Han'gŭl: lost letters

HUNMIN CHŎNGŬM HAERYE 訓民正音解例 'Explanation and Examples of *Hunmin chŏngŭm*'
Hunmin chŏngŭm haerye (1446), a brief commentary on *Hunmin chŏngŭm* was prepared by a royal commission in which Chŏng Inji, Minister of Personnel and Rector of the **Sŏnggyun-gwan**, directed **Kang Hŭian** of the Royal Household Department and six men in their late twenties from the **Chiphyŏn-jŏn**: Ch'oe Hang, Pak P'aengnyŏn, **Sin Sukchu**, **Sŏng Sammun**, Yi Kae and Yi Sŏllo. The work contains seven sections: (1) *Cheja-hae* 'explanation of the letter-shapes', showing that they harmonised with neo-Confucian doctrine, *yin-yang* (**ŭm-yang**) theory, the **five phases** and **clear-and-cloudy** dichotomy; (2) *Ch'osŏng-hae* 'explanation of initial consonants'; (3) *Chungsŏng-hae* 'explanation of medial sounds' (vowels and tones); (4) *Chongsŏng-hae* 'explanation of final consonants'; (5) *Hapcha-hae* 'explanation of combined letters' (syllable groups, consonant clusters and the double letters *ss* and *hh*); (6) *Yongja-rye* 'examples of letters in use' (90 words); and (7) postface by Chŏng Inji.

HUNMONG CHAHOE 訓蒙字會 'Collection of Characters for Teaching the People'
A textbook for boys, compiled by Ch'oe Sejin in 1527 and designed to replace already obsolete traditional texts such as **Ch'ŏnja-mun** (*The Thousand Character Classic*). It contains 3,353 characters with pronunciation and explanations in **han'gŭl**. They are arranged sixteen to a page according to a logical classification, developed from the rudimentary system in *Ch'ŏnja-mun* (**astronomy**, geography, flora, fauna, humanity and so on, finishing with abstract words). The most valuable part of the work for linguistic history is an introductory essay on *han'gŭl*, *Ŏnmun chamo*, which deals with 27 letters (*toen-niŭng* being disregarded), gives the first indications we have of the present alphabetical order and letter-names, and discusses spelling and 'tone dots'.

HUNTING *sanyang*
Little is known about hunting in early Korea, although Three Kingdoms paintings show men hunting on horseback with bow-and-arrow. Until about the 16th century, hunting remained the sport of kings, but under pressure of strict Confucian advice it was abandoned by both monarchs and **gentry**. It became the occupation of professionals, many of whom were **ch'ŏnmin**. They hunted on foot. Those who hunted

with matchlock rifles were known as *p'osu* 'gun hands', and they were the only hunters who tackled leopards and **tigers**. In Hamgyŏng and Kangwŏn-do they were sometimes called upon to resist bandits who crossed from **Manchuria**. They were called upon to help resist the foreign attacks on **Kanghwa** in 1866. During the American attack, 51 of them were killed, together with two regular officers who led them under a 'Twin Tigers' banner. Foreigners referred to them as 'tiger-hunters'. Angus Hamilton, who hunted with them in Hamgyŏng in 1901, describes their costume as a blue canvas shirt with necklets and bandoliers of beads and seed-beans. A blue or green headcloth entwined with coloured beads was coiled into the hair so that a frayed end hung over the forehead.

ANGUS HAMILTON, *Korea*, London, 1904
See also **deer**

'HUNTING MEMORIALS' *sunsu-bi* 巡狩碑

After King Chinhŭng of Silla extended the boundaries of his realm, he made tours of inspection. In some places he erected memorial stones that are now known as *sunsu-bi*, 'inspection tour stones'. Because *su* can mean 'winter hunting', they have often been erroneously called 'hunting memorials'. The sites of four of these stelae are known. Two are in south Hamgyŏng province (Maun-nyŏng and Hwangch'o) and another in South Kyŏngsang at Ch'aryŏng; but the most famous was close to Seoul, behind the North Mountain (Pugak-san) near Sŭngga-sa monastery. It had about 250 characters on it, of which about seventy were deciphered by **Kim Chŏnghŭi**, the famous calligrapher, in 1816 and 1817. The stone has now been moved to the National Museum.

HUNYO SIPCHO 訓要十條 *See* **Ten Injunctions**

HWABAEK 和白

Council of nobles formed by the leaders of the six tribes under the **Chinhan** and early **Silla** federation. Its meetings were held at four sacred locations around the capital **Kŭmsŏng**. Following a decision by King Pŏphŭng in 531 one chieftain held the presidency (*sangdaedŭng*), and unanimous agreement was necessary on important matters, such as declarations of war and major political appointments. It was the *Hwabaek* that took the decision to adopt **Buddhism** in 527. In the Unified Silla period its responsibilities were gradually rivalled by the *Chipsabu* until it was eventually abolished in 651.

WERNER SASSE, 'The Shilla Stone Inscription from Naengsu-ri, Yŏngil-gun,' *KJ*, 31/3, 1991

HWAGAK 華角 'decorated horn'

In the later Chosŏn period, small wooden objects such as document-cases, jewel-boxes, pillow-ends and miniature chests were coated with thin sheets of prettily painted ox horn, about 3 mm thick and not more than 12 cm across. The decoration was outlined on the horn in black and then coloured with earth pigments mixed in fish glue. The **ten symbols of longevity**, **flowers**, **tigers**, mandarin ducks and other auspicious symbols were the usual motifs, mostly on a red background. The painted surface was glued to the wood, completely covering the object with horn. The outside surface was given a glassy polish. The decoration would not fade or rub off.

HWANDO 丸都 *See* **Kungnaesŏng**

HWANG CHINI 黃眞伊

Hwang Chini was probably a *kisaeng* (professional entertainer) of **Kaesŏng** at the beginning of the 16th century. Half a dozen highly esteemed *sijo* lyrics are traditionally attributed to her. They are beautiful but essentially simple love-songs that have led to her personality being treated over-confidently by some writers. Despite some colourful anecdotes, nothing certain is known about her life.

HWANG HYŎN 黃玹 (Maech'ŏn, 1855–1910)

Born at Kwangyang in south Chŏlla and educated in Seoul, he was disgusted by corruption in the state **examinations**. Persuaded to persist, he became *saengwŏn* at the age of 33, withdrew to Kurye in his home province to read and teach, and stayed there through the **Tonghak rebellion**, coming to despair for Korea. After the Japanese **protectorate** was declared in 1905, he planned to go to China, but did not leave before the **annexation** of 1910, when he committed suicide by drinking **poison**. He was a fine poet in Chinese. His verse was published in China in 1912–13 under the brush-name 'apricot-blossom spring'; his journal *Maech'ŏn yarok*, a valuable historical source, came to light in 1945.

HWANG YŎNGYŎP 黃用燁 (Yihwang, b. 1931)

He was born in P'yŏngyang and enrolled between 1948 and 1950 in the P'yŏngyang Fine Art College. Resenting the ideological education he had experienced under both the Japanese and the communist régime, he fought on the South Korean side during the **Korean War** and was wounded. After the War he completed his artistic training at Hongik University, Seoul, where he studied under **Kim Hwan'gi** (Kim Whan Ki) and graduated from the Department of Western Art in 1957. His first work was painting portraits for American servicemen at bases around Seoul. For many years, his work showed the deep sense of despair and persecution instilled in him by his own experiences and his sympathy for the countless broken families across the whole country, including his own. A devotee of abstract expressionism, he developed a personal style in which the *leitmotif* consisted of human beings – represented either in surrealist shapes or as grotesque and emaciated figures – struggling hopelessly to free themselves from entangling networks of lines and shapes. In the tortured melancholy of Hwang's mind, man was born to suffer the incarcerating constraints of both natural and man-made forces. Through the 1980s, however, his style reflected a more positive approach to Korean cultural traditions and was characterised by brighter colours and more balanced composition. By the end of the decade the sense of suffering in his pictures had given way to a guarded optimism.

BARBICAN CENTRE, *Flow from the Far East: Aspects of Modern Korean Art*, London, 1992

HWAN'GAP 還甲 'return to birth-year number'

Also called *hwagap* 'flowery number' and *hoegap* 'returning number'. On one's sixtieth birthday the year number in the **sixty-fold cycle** is the same as for one's year of birth. (Anyone born in the year of the Blue Ox will be 60 in the next year of the Blue Ox. Koreans tend to call this the 61st birthday, because they reckon their **age** by the year begun on the birth date rather than by the year completed.) The occasion is celebrated with great festivity by the family. Formal poems may be composed and recited and, if the sexagenarian is renowned, a *Festschrift* may be planned. In some families the eldest son is expected to emulate the filial piety of Lao Laizi and dance before his parents. (*See* **Filial children, twenty-four**)

HWANGSŎNG SINMUN 皇城新聞 'Imperial Capital News'
Newspaper representing the views of some of the more conservative members of the
Independence Club; successor to the *Kyŏngsŏng Sinmun* ('Seoul News'). Founded in
1898 by Namgung Ŏk under the editorship of Pak Ŭnsik, it was published in a mixture
of *han'gŭl* and Chinese characters and advocated reform along Confucian lines. It
stood out particularly against Japanese oppression, and was closed down in 1905 when
the editor Chang Chiyŏn wrote bitterly against the **Protectorate Treaty**.

HWAŎM 華嚴
Sect of **Buddhism** prominent in the Unified Silla period. It was founded by the monk
Ŭisang in the 7th century following his study of the *Huayanjing* (S. *Avatamsakasutra*) in
China, and taught the unity of principle and matter within the mind of Buddha (*see* **Sutra**).
Among the temples founded by this sect were Hwaŏm-sa, Pusŏk-sa, and **Haein-sa**.

HWARANG 花郎 'Flower boys' or 'Elite youth'
Groups of teenage boys in **Silla**, apparently religious in origin, who banded together to
sing and dance in famous scenic places. Their ideal was called *p'ungwŏlto* ('way of
wind and moon'), the original meaning of which is not clear. They are recorded in AD
596, but the date is problematical and they probably existed earlier. Mutually
irreconcilable legends in *Samguk sagi* and *Samguk yusa* say that the first groups were
female. Their purpose was evidently educational. They received instruction in morals
and **music** and visited famous mountains. **Ch'oe Ch'iwŏn** said their teaching
combined Confucian, Buddhist and Daoist elements. *Samguk yusa* says they learned
the **Five Relationships**, the Six Arts, the Three Scholarly Occupations, and the Six
Ways of Government Service. Nothing is known of their organisation, except that their
leader was called *kuksŏn* ('national immortal'). They painted their faces and wore
jewelled shoes. They did not remain *hwarang* for life. Since 1945 (not before), it has
been commonly assumed that their primary purpose was military, though there is no
justification for this in the sources. Among about 30 *hwarang* who are named, only
five are described as soldiers in later life (*see* **Kim Yusin**; **Kwanch'ang**; **Sadaham**).
There are no records of military training or of *hwarang* as warrior groups. (Translating
hwarang as 'knight' begs further questions by introducing inappropriate concepts from
European military chivalry.) Nor were the '**Five commandments for laymen**' (*Sesok
Ogye*) given by Monk Wŏn'gwang (d. c. 630) specifically intended for *hwarang*,
though they are sometimes taken to have been so.
    In the Chosŏn dynasty the word *hwarang* came to mean shaman, playboy, or
prostitute, but connections between this and the Silla institution have not been
established.
RICHARD RUTT, 'The Flower Boys of Silla', *TKBRAS*, XXXVIII, 1961; VLADIMIR
TIKHONOV, 'Hwarang organization', *KJ*, 38/2, 1998

HWAT'U 花鬪 *See* **Playing Cards**

HYANGAK 鄉樂 *See* **Music**

HYANGCH'AL 鄉札 *See Idu*

HYANGGA 鄉歌 'country songs'
Literally meaning 'country (as opposed to Chinese) songs', this is a term applied to a
heterogeneous group of poems surviving from Silla and Koryŏ and written in *idu*.

They are often called *saenaennorae* from a putative reconstruction of the Old Korean term. Only 25 are extant, fourteen in **Samguk yusa** (short songs of love, sorrow and Buddhist devotion, some connected with **hwarang**) and eleven in *Kyunyŏ-jŏn* (all Buddhist hymns; *see* **Kyunyŏ**). Many of them have a mysterious beauty, sometimes perplexingly obscure. Most of them are composed of couplets in which each line contains four syllables. The couplets are joined in quatrains, a complete song often consisting of two quatrains and a closing couplet. One of the best known is the **Song of Ch'ŏyong**. Famous composers of *hyangga* are said to include the monks **Wŏnch'ŭk**, **Wŏnhyo**, and Kyunyŏ. A 9th-century anthology by monk Taegu, *Samdaemok*, was destroyed during the **Mongol** invasions.

HYANGGYO 鄉校 'rural schools'

Local Confucian schools were set up in Koryŏ. In Chosŏn they were put under government administration and produced the candidates for local **examinations**. The centre of the institution was a modest *munmyo*, 'temple' of Confucius, where his and other worthies' tablets were installed (as in the **Sŏnggyun-gwan**) and regular sacrifices offered. There were also lecture halls and study rooms. When the **sŏwŏn** arose the *hyanggyo* declined. At the end of the 19th century they were closed, but many of the buildings have survived and have even been restored. They are often set among **trees**: places of great charm, whose rustic simplicity contrasts strongly with the colour and complexity of Buddhist temples.

HYANGNI 鄉吏

Low level officers in local government systems during the Koryŏ and Chosŏn periods.
See **provincial administration**

HYANGYAK 鄉約 'village contract'

Campaign inspired by the neo-Confucian idealism of the **yangban** to confirm their authority over rural **peasantry**, emphasizing the promotion of morality, the control of wrong-doing, the importance of social respect and mutual assistance. Widely implemented after 1520, it strengthened the power of the literati and improved administration.
See also **kye**

HYECH'O 慧超 (704–87)

A monk of **Silla** who studied in Tang China, where he met an Indian teacher. In 723 he went to India by sea, returning through Kashmir and the Pamirs to the Buddhist centre at Kucha in modern Xinjiang about 727. He compiled a record of what he had seen on his travels, called *Wang-o Ch'onch'ukkuk-chŏn*, 'Account of a Journey to the Five Lands of India'. He never returned to Korea. A substantial fragment of his book was found by Paul Pelliot in the Cave of a Thousand Buddhas at Dunhuang in 1908, and is now in Paris. It is of considerable interest, especially for Indian and Central Asian history in the 8th century.
YANG HAN-SONG et al., *The Hye Ch'o Diary*, Berkeley, n.d.

HYOJA-MUN 孝子門 *See* **Filial son gate**

HYŎRŬI NU 血淚 ('Tears of Blood')

The 'first modern Korean novel'. It was written by Yi Injik (1862–1916) and published by instalments in *Mansebo*, the newspaper of the **Ch'ŏndo-gyo** religion, in 1906. Yi had been enthused by what he learned of modern literature when he went to Japan in 1900. He wrote other novels, including *Ŭnsegye*, 'Silver World' (1908), none of them distinguished, and was involved in **Wŏn'gak-sa**. *Hyŏrŭi nu* was the first fiction of its kind, written in the spoken language of the day with a journalist's flair for narrative, and intended to foster modernising ideas.

HYUJŎNG 休靜 (1520–1604)
Also known as Grand Master Sŏsan; *Sŏn* Buddhist monk famous for his cursive and semi-cursive calligraphic script. He led one of the many bands of monks which waged guerilla warfare against the Japanese invaders during the **Imjin Wars**.

HYUNGBAE 胸背 'breast panels'
Embroidered panels or 'mandarin squares', worn on the breast and back by government officers in court **dress**. Those of third **grade** senior and above wore two cranes for a civil officer and two tigers for a military officer. Those of third grade junior down to ninth rank wore one crane or one **tiger**.

I

ICH'ADON 異次頓 (501–527)
Also called Kŏch'adon, but originally named Pak Yŏmch'ok. A high born and loyal minister of **Silla** at the time when **Buddhism** was still strongly opposed by the court establishment. In 527, at the age of 26, he devised a stratagem with the king, who wanted to promote Buddhism. Ich'adon provoked a situation in which he would have to be condemned to death because of his Buddhist activity. It is said that, when his head was cut off, his blood flowed white as milk and there were miracles involving the sun and heavenly flowers. Thereafter the opposition to Buddhism crumbled.

IDU 吏讀 'Korean written in Chinese characters'
Knowledge and use of Chinese characters must have entered Korea through the Han dynasty **commanderies** or earlier. Once they became familiar in Korea during the Three Kingdoms period, they began to be used for writing Korean words. The earliest use was for names of people and places. Rural place-names are still written in this way, as when a hamlet called Tume, 'place in the hills', is written with characters pronounced *tumae* but meaning 'Seven Stars and apricot blossom'.

The practice is complex and problematical because, apart from its meaning, a Chinese character has two sound values for a Korean reader: (1) its Sino-Korean sound and (2) the sound of a Korean word with the same meaning as the character. For example, the Chinese character *wei* 'to act' has (1) Sino-Korean pronunciation *wi*, and (2) can express the sound *ha-*, root of the Korean verb 'to act'. Either value may be used in transcribing Korean words: the character can simply mean 'to act' or it can represent the purely phonetic values *wi* or *ha-*. Thus the string of three Chinese characters *wei jia ni* means 'act add nun', which is nonsensical, but when read with two Korean sounds and one Sino-Korean sound, becomes the Korean sequential verb-ending *-hadoni*.

Whole sentences were thus clumsily transcribed in a system that dates from Silla and is preserved only in *hyangga* poetry. By Koryŏ times (1075) it was called *hyangch'al*, 'country (i.e. Korean as opposed to Chinese) writing'. In any sentence, some characters were to be read as Chinese words with Sino-Korean or Korean sounds, and others as Korean phonetics. Not all the *hyangga* can now be read with certainty.

Closely related to *hyangch'al* is *idu* (also written *it'u* or *it'o*), 'clerk's readings'. The word is first recorded in **Chewang-un'gi** (1287) and its traditional attribution to **Sŏl Ch'ong** is no longer regarded as tenable. It means Chinese characters used for *t'o*. *T'o* are the Korean grammatical endings (like *-hadoni* above) that are sometimes inserted into books and documents composed in Chinese, as a kind of punctuation to indicate the relations between groups of characters and thus help unskilled readers construe the text. In *hyangch'al* the language is wholly Korean, but *idu* means additions to a text that is purely Chinese. It is simpler to read than *hyangch'al* because there is a limited vocabulary of *t'o* and they are easily recognisable amidst the Chinese text.

Idu, also termed *kugyŏl*, *hyŏnt'o* or *sŏgŭi*, came into administrative use, notably for notices and instructions, and the *t'o* were often written in drastically simplified Chinese characters of two to four strokes each, used solely for this purpose. They were used until the end of the 18th century and later, even though, since the spread of *han'gŭl*, *t'o* have usually been written in *han'gŭl*.

ADRIAN BUZO, 'An Introduction to Early Korean Writing Systems,' *TRASKB*, LV, 1980
*See **Imun-jimnam***

IKCHONG 翼宗 (1809–30)

Although given a kingly title by his son **Hŏnjong**, Ikchong never reigned. He was son of **Sunjo** and Queen Sunwŏn of the Andong Kim clan, but his wife, later known as Queen Sinjŏng (1809–90), belonged to the P'ungyang Cho clan. In 1827 his father made him president of the state council, where he strove to have ministers appointed for their ability rather than their political loyalties, and to moderate excessive punishments; but he died aged 21, too soon to achieve anything, leaving one son, who became King Hŏnjong

ILCHINHOE 一進會 *See* **United Progress Society**

ILLEGITIMATE SONS *ch'ŏpcha, sŏja, sŏŏl* 妾子, 庶子, 庶孽

Illegitimate sons are best called secondary sons. They were not bastards in the common western sense, but sons of secondary wives, brought up and educated with the sons of the primary wife. Hence their frustrations, which have no parallel in Western culture. Their status was often debated, especially in the 15th and 16th centuries, and was in some respects dubious. They were not admitted to state **examinations** and were usually unable to undertake a son's ritual responsibilities, though **Yi I**, who had no primary sons, appointed a secondary son as his ritual heir. Discrimination against them was based not on extra-marital conception, but on the lower-class status of their mothers.

*See **Hong-Giltong-jŏn**; **Kyusa***

ILSIM-GYO 一心教 'single-minded teaching'

A sparsely recorded minor **new religion** from Iri in north Chŏlla. A tiny group existed at **Sindonae** in the 1960s, in some ways comparable to the Amish of north America. They rejected modern education and other forms of modernisation, living as though they were in the last days of Chosŏn. The boys and men did not cut their hair. Their religion, however, had 'new religion' characteristics, combining folk beliefs with **Confucianism**.

IM CHE 林悌 (1549–87)
Im Che finished his examinations in his late twenties and entered government service, but soon withdrew because of strife between the East and West **factions**. He retired to the mountains to write and drink wine, and is now remembered as a writer of stories in *hanmun*. The most famous is *Susŏng-ji*, 'Story of Grievance Castle', a satire on a world where promotion does not depend upon ability. *Hwasa*, 'Story of Flowers', was formerly attributed to him but is now believed to have been written by No Kŭng (1738–90).

IM KKŎKCHŎNG 林巨正 (d. 1562)
Between the **literati purges** and the onset of the major factional struggles of the mid-Chosŏn period, the people of the countryside were deeply unsettled and groups of bandits began to circulate. One of these was led by Im Kkŏkchŏng, a man of the *paekchŏng* class from Yangju. From about 1559 for three years his band of malcontents ranged over Hwanghae and northern Kyŏnggi provinces, robbing and murdering corrupt officials and distributing their wealth to the poor. He was finally caught and executed at Chaeryŏng in 1562. Many legends exist about him.

IM KYŎNGŎP 林慶業 (1594–1646)
Im was born in Ch'ungju and was athletic, a good rider and archer, who ascended the ladder of government through the military **examinations**. In 1624 he earned a reputation during the rebellion of **Yi Kwal**; but when the **Manchu invasions** began in 1627 he had little opportunity to shine. He was more successful in the war of 1630 and duly honoured by the king, but his loyalty to Ming left him ashamed at the Korean surrender to the Manchus at **Namhan sansŏng**. He joined those at court who thought it possible to restore the Ming. The rest of his life was a series of plots, discoveries, betrayals, captures and escapes, even a period in hiding as a Buddhist monk. After the accession of Injo he continued his quixotic devotion to the Ming and was imprisoned by Qing. The king hoped to secure his release, but further plots ended in his being clubbed to death by Qing. A violent death after a life of loyalty so rich in incident was bound, despite his lack of judgement, to be popular with posterity. His good name was reinstated fifty years after his death and stories about him circulated freely in both *hanmun* and Korean.

IMANISHI RYŪ 今西龍 (1875–1932)
Having read history at Tokyo University and graduated in 1903, he specialised in Korean history, first visiting **Kyŏngju** in 1906. While a lecturer at Kyoto University, he visited both China and Britain. In 1925 he was appointed to Keijō University in Seoul and joined the **Korean History Compilation Committee**. His most valuable work was on early Korean history, much of it published as papers and articles. Posthumous books included *Chōsen-shi no shiori*, 'Guide to Korean History' (1935), *Chōsen koshi no kenkyū*, 'Studies in Ancient Korean History' (1937) and collections of essays on Silla (1933), Paekche (1934) and Koryŏ (1944).

IMBERT, LAURENT-JOSEPH-MARIE, SAINT 範世亨 (1797–1839)
A priest of the Paris Foreign Missions, who arrived in China in 1820 and worked in Sichuan, where he became auxiliary bishop. In 1837 he was appointed second vicar-apostolic of Korea on the death of Bishop **Bruguière**, and arrived at Seoul in January 1838. He worked with Frs **Chastan** and **Maubant** for nearly two years before the severity of the persecution of Catholics led him to ask his two companions to

surrender themselves with him like good shepherds giving their lives for their sheep. He was arrested near **Suwŏn** in June 1839 and all three were executed on 21 September on the sands of Saenamt'ŏ, when Imbert was 42 years old.
See also **Capsa; martyrs, Catholic**

IMDUN 臨屯
Tribal federation on the north-east coast formed by the 4th century BC, and conquered and ruled by **Han** China from 109 to 82 BC.

IMJIN AND CHŎNGYU 壬辰丁酉 INVASIONS, LITERATURE ON
There are many contemporary and near-contemporary accounts of these invasions (1592, 1597) and the events surrounding them. Some of the more important are:

Kim Uhyŏn (1540–1603),	*Tonggang-jip*
O Hŭimun (1539–1613),	*Swaemi-rok*
Sŏng Hon (1535–1598),	*Ugye-jip*
Yi Chŏngam (1541–1600),	*Sŏjŏng-illok* and *Saryu-jae-jip*
Yi Sanhae (1539–1609),	*Agye-yugo*
Yi Sunsin (1545–1598),	*Yi Ch'ungmu-gong chŏnsŏ*
Yi Tŏkhyŏng (1561–1613),	*Hanŭm-mun'go*
Yu Sŏngnyong (1542–1607),	*Chingbi-rok* and *Sŏae Sŏnsaeng munjip*

See also ***Imjin-nok***

IMJIN WARS (1592–8) 壬辰倭亂
Name given to the wars fought against the Japanese leader Toyotomi Hideyoshi (1536–98) in 1592–3 and 1597–8 as he pursued his planned conquest of China. His first army, said to be of over 158,000 men, landed at **Pusan** in spring 1592. Benefiting from surprise, low morale amongst the Koreans, and superior weaponry which included firearms, it defeated General Sin Ip in the battle of Ch'ungju. Seoul (Hansŏng) was captured in less than three weeks. King Sŏnjo and his effete and unpopular government fled to the Chinese border and appealed for aid from their suzerain as much of the peninsula fell under Japanese control. The **Ming** government sent a force which recaptured P'yŏngyang in January 1593, and Korean resistance also rallied. The combined efforts of *yangban*, **peasants** and **slaves**, together with the inspired leadership of Admiral **Yi Sunsin**, led to three important victories at Haengju (on the Imjin River), **Chinju** and Hansan. The Japanese armies withdrew and sought peace talks. Despite the Chinese offer to enfeoff Hideyoshi as king of Japan, his grandiose ambitions were unsatisfied and negotiations dragged on fruitlessly.

A second invasion was mounted by 141,500 Japanese troops in 1597. This time they were confined to the south, and the success of Admiral Yi's 'turtle ships' disrupted Japanese control of the sea lanes between the two countries. In 1598 Admiral Yi was killed in action and Toyotomi Hideyoshi also died, whereupon the wars were broken off. The Tokugawa shogun, Ieyasu, restored peaceful relations in 1606, but the effects of Hideyoshi's campaigns were far-reaching. An estimated 126,000 Koreans were killed and their ears and noses taken back to Japan for burial in Kyoto. A further 60–70,000 were taken to Japan as prisoners. In China the costs of the relief expeditions added to the economic misfortunes of the declining Ming dynasty. In Korea the physical damage to property and cultural treasures was immense. The population of the capital, Seoul, fell from over 100,000 to less than 40,000. The disruption of the old political, social and economic order led to many changes and prompted a revaluation of the traditional reliance on China (*see* **Sadae**; **Sirhak movement**). In Japan the results were more positive: not only did the inauguration of the Tokugawa shogunate mark the beginning of a long period of stability, but society benefited from the learning and skills brought by Korean captives, who included scholars, painters, ceramic **craftsmen** and expert typecasters.

A.L.SADLER, 'The Naval Campaign in the Korea War of Hideyoshi (1592–98),' *TASJ*, second series, 14, 1937

See also **China, relations with**; **Imjin and Chŏngyu invasions, literature on**; **Japan, relations with**

IMJIN-NOK 壬辰錄 'Account of the Black Dragon Year (1592)'
Various books and manuscripts referred to by this and similar titles deal with the Hideyoshi invasion of 1592. Some are in *han'gŭl* and are treated as *kodae-sosŏl*.

IMMIGRATION, JAPANESE
Korea was a key plank in the platform for Japanese colonisation of continental East Asia, and from the **Protectorate** period onwards migrants moved to take over land and jobs in Korea. Throughout the colonial period they received preferential treatment in a variety of ways, from educational opportunities to money-raising and career openings in government, business and industry, yet their numbers remained relatively small as a proportion of the total **population**. In 1905 they totalled 42,460, in 1910 171,543 (1·28%), in 1930 501,847 (2·48%), and in 1940 707,377 (2·91%). Landowning by Japanese increased substantially, from around 3 per cent of arable land in 1910 to around 60 per cent in 1930. Japanese owned over 90 per cent of the mines and the majority of the factories. After the Japanese seizure of **Manchuria** in 1931 (*see* **Manchurian Incident**) Japanese settlements and military installations increased there too.

OH YANG HO, 'Korean Literature in Manchuria: Exile and Immigrant Literature during the Japanese Colonial Period', *KJ*, 36/4, 1996

See also **Emigration, Korean**

IMMORTALITY *See* **Longevity, ten symbols of**

IMMORTALS (*sinsŏn*) 神仙
Immortals, in both art and literature, are the equivalent of western fairies, and their paradise is really a fairyland, where there is no death but much magic. Though their origin lies in Chinese Daoist art and literature, they have virtually no religious significance in Korea. Most of them are aged sages (*sŏnin*), fairy women (*sonnyŏ*) or *sŏndong*. Young adult male immortals (*sŏllang*) are less common. All are depicted in a conventionalised version of Tang clothing.

This fairyland is often regarded as the domain of Sŏ-wangmo (C. Xiwangmu), the Queen Mother of the West, a pre-Han cosmological figure, who lives by Pearl Lake (C. Yaozhi, K. Yoji), surrounded by bluebirds (*ch'ŏngjo*) and keeping the **peaches** of immortality. In Korea the peaches are mentioned oftener than the queen herself. Her opposite, Tong-wangbu, the King Father of the East, is much less often mentioned.

See also **Daoism**

IMO INCIDENT *Imo kullan* 壬午軍亂 (1882)
Revolt in July 1882 by military units opposed to King **Kojong**'s growing support for reform and modernisation and to his request for Japanese military advice. Sometimes

known as the Military Mutiny. It was supported by the **Taewŏn'gun** who was strongly critical of the **Shufeldt Treaty** signed with the United States of America on 22 May, and who used the insurrection as a means of reasserting his control at the expense of **Queen Min**. She fled from the capital in disguise. Anti-reformist sentiment led to anti-Japanese rioting, the burning of the Japanese embassy and the return home of the Japanese Minister. Both Japanese and Chinese governments now despatched troops. The Chinese seized the Taewŏn'gun and sent him to Tianjin. Queen Min returned to the palace and the pro-China inclination of the government was reaffirmed. Under an agreement made on 4 October, China obtained preferential trade terms and nominated advisers to the Korean government, one of whom was the German Paul-Georg **von Möllendorff**. **Yuan Shikai** was appointed to train the newly established army garrisons in the capital (*Ch'in'gunyŏng*), and became the Chinese Resident-General in Korea. Japan, meanwhile, had obtained financial reparation under the Treaty of Chemulp'o (30 August 1882), with the right to station troops at its legation in Seoul and permission for its staff to travel inland. In October a mission was sent to Japan under **Pak Yŏnghyo** to try and improve relations, and between 1883 and 1886 the newly created Foreign Office (*Tongni-gimu Amun*) concluded a succession of treaties with foreign powers: Great Britain and Germany in November 1883, Italy in June 1884, Russia in July 1884, and France in June 1886. **Min Yŏngik** headed a mission to the United States in July 1883.

See also **Japan, relations with;** *Kapsin* **Coup; Kim Okkyun; Unequal treaties; United States, relations with**

IMUN-JIMNAM 吏文輯覽 'Systematic View of *idu* Writing'
An abbreviated edition of an earlier manual on the use of *idu* in administrative documents, produced by Ch'oe Sejin in 1539. It contains evidence of some 16th-century Korean colloquialisms.

INCH'ŎN 仁川
Also known as **Chemulp'o**; coastal city to the west of Seoul, the site of the first landfall of US troops sent to Korea in August 1945 following the Japanese surrender. It has become most renowned as the landing place of General MacArthur's amphibious assault force on 15 September 1950 which reversed the trend of the **Korean War** and launched the **United Nations** counter-offensive into North Korea.
PAUL EDWARDS, *The Inchon Landing, Korea, 1950: an Annotated Bibliography*, London: Greenwood Press, 1994

INDEPENDENCE ARCH *Tongnim-mun* 獨立門 *See* **Yŏngŭn-mun**

INDEPENDENCE ARMY *Tongnipkun* 獨立軍
Name given to armies and guerilla units of Korean freedom fighters operating against Japanese targets as part of the independence movement, principally in the **Kando** region of **Manchuria** (*see* **March First Movement**). Known also as the *ŭibyŏng* ('righteous armies'), it included the *Ŭiyŏltan* ('Righteous Heroes Unit'), the *Aeguktan* ('Love Country Unit'), and several larger armies, the strongest of which were the Han'guk Independence Army and the Chosŏn Independence Army. In 1919 overall command of its operations was assumed by the **Provisional Government in Exile** in Shanghai but was difficult to exercise, partly for logistic reasons and partly because of political differences between left- and right-wingers. Significant military victories were scored, as for example at **Ch'ŏngsan-ni** in 1920; terrorist attacks

included attempts at high-level assassination, as when *Aeguktan* member **Yun Ponggil** threw a bomb at senior Japanese military and government personages in Shanghai in April 1932. He was caught and executed, but shortly afterwards Chiang Kai-shek invited **Kim Ku** to send Koreans to the Chinese Military Academy for training.
KU DAE-YEOL, 'The Chientao Incident (1920) and Britain,' *TRASKB*, LV, 1980

INDEPENDENCE CLUB *Tongnip Hyŏphoe* 獨立協會

Organisation established in July 1896 by young reform advocates fired by feelings of **nationalism** and a desire for social change. Among its founding members, many of whom were past or present government officials, were **Sŏ Chaep'il**, **Yun Ch'iho**, Yi Sangjae and Syngman Rhee (**Yi Sŭngman**). Its chairman was the Foreign Minister, **Yi Wanyong**, and the president was Minister for War An Kyŏngsu. Its educational and cultural programme included discussions, talks, and the publication of the *Independent* newspaper (*see Tongnip Sinmun*), which all helped to foster a mood of interest in modernisation and democratisation among the *yangban*. Its political ambition, nevertheless, was directed towards the eradication of foreign influence in Korea and the stimulation of a **self-strengthening movement** in education and industry. Branches opened in provincial centres and admitted ordinary people as members, and business was conducted along democratic lines. The Club was publicly supported by Korean women's organisations. Among its initial goals and visible successes were the building of the Independence Gate, replacing the old *Yŏng'ŭn-mun*, and the Independence Hall, where its weekly debates were held. It promoted the **national flag** (*t'aegŭk-ki*) and national anthem (*see Aegukka*). In apparent contrast to the setback suffered by China's would-be reformers with the failure of the Hundred Days of reform in September 1898, those in Korea were encouraged by support from the throne, and in return the Club supported **Kojong**'s adoption of the title Emperor for himself and *Taehan cheguk* (**Great Han Empire**) for the country. Convinced of the need to open up the government to more popular participation, the Club tried to instigate reform from within, and pressed for consideration of democracy. Following a meeting of officials and people's representatives arranged by the Club in October, the King agreed to admit twenty five of its nominees to the Privy Council. This success was short-lived, however, for government opponents unleashed a slanderous backlash which undermined Kojong's support, and after violent fighting on the streets of Seoul the Club was proscribed at the end of November. Members were tortured and sentenced to long terms of imprisonment.
VIPAN CHANDRA, *Imperialism, Resistance, and Reform in Late Nineteenth-Century Korea: Enlightenment and the Independence Club*, Berkeley: University of California, 1988
See also Hwangsŏng Sinmun; **Russia, relations with**

INDEPENDENCE, DECLARATION OF *Chosŏn Tongnip Sŏnŏnsŏ* 朝鮮獨立宣言書 (1919)

(1) Statement inspired by President Woodrow Wilson's defence of national self-determination and composed by the writer **Yi Kwangsu** as a representative of the **Korean Youth Independence Association**. It stressed Korea's ancient history of cultural and political independence; reiterated the acknowledgement of Korean independence stated in the 1905 **Protectorate Treaty**; denounced Japanese suppression of modernisation benefits to Koreans; and underlined the importance of Korean independence to the peaceful future of Asia. The Declaration was read aloud on 8 February 1919 to students in the Korean YMCA in Tokyo, whereupon the Association's leaders were arrested.

(2) Pronouncement of Korean independence conceived in response to news of the Tokyo Declaration and of ex-Emperor **Kojong**'s death on 21 January. Following the initiative taken by a group of *Ch'ŏndo-gyo* leaders, including Kwŏn Tongjin, **O Sech'ang**, Ch'oe In and **Son Pyŏnghŭi**, it was written by **Ch'oe Namsŏn** and signed by 33 prominent members of the *Ch'ŏndo-gyo*, Christian and Buddhist churches in Seoul in February 1919 (*see* **Thirty-Three Independence Signatories**). The statement affirmed the Korean people's right to independence, release from tyrannical oppression, and participation in the establishment of peace throughout East Asia. It called for harmony and self-development. The tone of the document was firm in stressing the need for popular but non-violent action to achieve its aims. Twenty-one thousand copies were quickly printed for distribution. The signatories' intention was to proclaim the Declaration publicly in **Pagoda Park** at 2 p.m. on March 1st, but fearing disturbances prior to Kojong's funeral on 3 March, they read it instead in the morning at the nearby Myŏngwŏl-gwan restaurant, announced Korea's independence, and surrendered to the police. It was left to a teacher to make the public reading to the large crowd assembled in the afternoon, who sang the *Aegukka* and waved the Korean flag (*see* **nationalism**). Inevitably they then took to the streets, where radicals incited many to ignore the non-violence plea of the Declaration.

KIM HAN-KYO, 'The Declaration of Independence, March 1, 1919: a New Translation,' *KS*, 13, 1989

See also **March First Movement**

INDEPENDENCE PARTY *Tongniptang* 獨立黨

(1) Also known as *Kaehwa-dang* ('Progessive Party'); name given to a group of scholar officials who urged reforms from the 1870s onwards. They included **Pak Yŏnghyo**, **Kim Okkyun** and **Sŏ Kwangbŏm**. Their influence on King **Kojong** led to limited success in the drive for modernisation: the government set up an Office for Information and Culture (*Pangmun-guk*), which published the first Korean newspaper *Hansŏng Sunbo*; a post office was established; a modern army unit was formed; and students were sent to Japan for study. They urged the development of diplomatic relations with advanced countries. But the group was opposed by the conservative *Sadaedang* group of **Queen Min**'s supporters and by the Japanese, and its members' involvement in the *Kapsin* **Coup** in December 1884 forced them to flee to Japan.

See also ***Imo* Incident**

(2) Unofficial name for a group of *ŭibyŏng* units active in **Kando** from 1919 onwards.

See also **Independence Army**

INDEPENDENCE SOCIETIES

While Korea was under Japanese occupation many secret organisations at home and abroad were dedicated to the restoration of independence. Continuing the spirit of the **Independence Club**, these included the *Sinminhoe* (**'New People's Association'**), *Kwangbokhoe* ('Restoration Association'), and *Chosŏn Kungminhoe* ('Korean People's Association'). **Students** were active in these societies, and among the more politically aware were left-wing groups with socialist and communist affiliations (*see* **Korean Communist Party**; **Korean Socialist Party**). The **women's movement** was also prominent, and included the *Taehan Min'guk Aeguk Puinhoe* ('Korean Women's Patriotic Association'). Armed resistance was maintained both at home and abroad by the so-called 'justice fighters' (*ŭibyŏng*), but overseas organisations preferring to work through diplomatic and peaceful pressure included Syngman Rhee (**Yi Sŭngman**)'s *Kungminhoe* ('Nationalist Association') in Hawai'i, established in 1909, and Sin

Kyusik's *Tongjesa* ('Mutual Assistance Society'), established in Shanghai in 1912. Representatives were sent to speak at international gatherings, such as the International Socialist Congress in 1917.
See also **Provisional Government in Exile**

INDEPENDENT, THE See Tongnip Sinmun

INDRA (Ch'ŏnje or Chesŏk 天帝, 帝釋)
A Hindu sky-god who retained a place in Buddhist mythology, though as a god he was inferior to a Buddha. He is king of the Devaloka, first six of the **thirty-three heavens**, and fights demons with his adamantine sceptre, the *vajra* or 'diamond'. This has become the diamond of the Diamond **Sutra** and the **Diamond Mountains** and is a symbol of the indestructible law of the buddha.

INHYŎN WANGHU-JŎN 仁顯王后傳 'The Story of Queen Inhyŏn'
An elegantly written *han'gŭl* account of the life and sufferings of Queen Inhyŏn (1667–1701). A member of the Yŏhung Min clan, she was married to King **Sukchong** in 1681, when he was nineteen and she was fourteen. In 1689 he put her aside for a **concubine**, but in 1694, received her back. She died childless in 1701. There are many texts, and some scholars consider that the book was written by a man rather than by a woman.
RICHARD RUTT & KIM CHONG-UN Trans. in *Virtuous Women*, Seoul: Royal Asiatic Society, Korea Branch, 1974
See **Palace literature**

INMOK, QUEEN 仁穆王后 (1584–1632)
Mother of Sŏnjo's second son, Prince Yŏngch'ang. When **Prince Kwanghae** exiled the boy to **Kanghwa**, he sent her with him. Yŏngch'ang was killed in 1614. Queen Inmok was kept in punitive seclusion until the accession of Injo in 1623, when her titles were restored. She is also remembered as a competent calligrapher.
See also Kyech'ug-ilgi

INSIGNIA, PROCESSIONAL *ŭijang-gi* 儀仗
When **processional flags** were used in the *kŏdong* a number of insignia mounted on red staves were carried with them, near or behind the emperor's chair: **fans**, banners, lanterns, parasols, umbrellas and emblems such as *kŭm-dŭngja* (an inverted golden stirrup), the *hoenggwa* and *ipgwa* (wooden melons, some gold, some silver, some recumbent, some upright). Others were descended from the ancient ox-tail banners of China (possibly originally fly-whisks), like the *mojŏl* or 'yak-tail', a swinging cord ornamented with five tufts of brindled ox-hair; and there were weapons, racks of arrows on staves, a precious sword and several axes, single and double-headed.

IRON / IRON AGE
Korea's Iron Age dates from approximately 400 BC. It was probably initiated through contacts with the state of Yan in north-east China, and was later developed through the Chinese **commandery** in Lelang. The period has been divided into Iron Age I (400 BC – AD 1) and Iron Age II (Late Iron Age or Proto-Three Kingdoms Period, AD 1 – 300). Agricultural implements and weapons were made of iron and played a significant part in the development of improved food production in the **Samhan** (*see* **agriculture**), as well as in the warfare between them. Iron manufacture took place

along the **Han** and Naktong Rivers, and its widespread use is shown by the discovery of iron artefacts in an Iron Age I tomb of the 1st century BC at **Kyŏngju** and an Iron Age II shellmound of the 3rd century AD at **Kimhae**, west of modern **Pusan**. The former include four iron swords, and the body was laid to rest on a 'mattress' of seventy iron plates, possibly intended as a medium of exchange as the deceased entered his next existence. The south became the centre for iron production, both **Pyŏnhan** and **Kaya** sending iron as tribute to **Lelang** and Daifang (*see* **Chinbŏn**), and trading it commercially to the north-east (**Tongye**) and to Japan (**Wa**). Iron **armour** has been found in Kaya sites.

CHOI SUNGRAK, 'The Iron Age Culture in Southern Korea and its Chinese Connection', *KJ*, 36/4, 1996; SARAH TAYLOR, *Ploughshares into Swords: the Iron Industry and Social Development in Protohistoric Korea and Japan*, PhD Thesis, University of Cambridge, 1990

IRYŎN 一然 *See SAMGUK YUSA*

ISAGŬM See **Silla kingly titles**

ISLAM *Hoehoe-gyo* 回回教
Islam reached China in Tang times as the faith of the Hui people (after whom it is named in both Chinese and Korean), some of whom appear to have lived in Koryŏ. It did not re-enter Korea until some men were converted under the influence of Turkish soldiers in the UN Forces stationed in Korea during the 1950s. It has grown slowly, though in Yongsan, Seoul, there is an impressive mosque, built with funds from Saudi Arabia.

ITŌ HIROBUMI 伊藤博文 (1841–1909)
Japanese nobleman and statesman who played a prominent part in the establishment of the **Protectorate** over Korea. In 1885, following the **Imo Incident** (1882) and the *Kapsin* Coup (1884) he signed the Treaty of Tianjin with **Li Hongzhang**. Affirming Korean independence, this weakened China's traditional rôle as suzerain in Korea but strengthened Japan's position with regard to sending troops to the peninsula, an opportunity that they were both to exploit in 1895 (*see* **Tonghak Rebellion**). He served as Prime Minister in 1892–6, 1897–8, and 1900–01. Following the **Sino-Japanese War** he signed the Treaty of **Shimonoseki** in 1895 with Li Hongzhang. In 1901 he paid a fruitless visit to Moscow to negotiate an understanding with Russia over Korea. In 1905 he helped to force the conclusion of the **Protectorate Treaty**, and then became the first **Resident General** in Korea. As such he was responsible for the conclusion of the second **Korea-Japan Protocol** of 1907. He was widely excoriated for disbanding the Korean army, and for the Japanese soldiery's merciless treatment of those of its former members who joined the *ŭibyŏng*. One of his key advisers was the American **Durham Stevens**. Itō did not himself approve the plan for the annexation of Korea, and resigned as Resident General on 15 June 1909. On 26 October, while on his way to discuss Russian-Japanese relations in the context of his government's determined action, he was assassinated in Harbin by a *ŭibyŏng* member and ex-Tonghak leader, **An Chunggŭn**.

GEORGE LADD, *In Korea with Marquis Ito*, New York, 1908

J

JACKS *konggi*
The virtually universal children's game played with five small pebbles or nuts, which are picked up in one hand, thrown in the air and caught in the same hand, starting with one pebble and progressing to five, with various refinements of gesture. The simplest operation is called *al-lak'i*, 'laying the eggs'. *Alp'umki* 'setting the eggs' and *alkkagi* 'hatching the eggs' follow. A similar game played with old-fashioned cash was called *tonjigi*.

JAPAN, BUDDHIST MISSIONARIES TO
In 588 three nuns from Japan arrived to spend three years studying in **Paekche**. Korean Buddhist missionaries went to Japan. Hyeja (d. 623), who was in Japan from 595 to 615; Hyegwan, who went in 625 and lived to be 90; and Todŭng, who was there from 629 to 646, were all from **Koguryŏ**. Hyech'ong, who went with Hyeja in 595, and Kwallŭk (from 602 to 624) were from Paekche.

JAPAN, RELATIONS WITH
The earliest economic links between the Korean peninsula and 'Japan' (probably the island of Kyushu, known to the Chinese as **Wa** (K. *Wae*)) were probably formed during the **Samhan** period, when Chinese historical sources record the sending of envoys with tribute to **Lelang** and Daifang (*see* **Chinbŏn**). The female ruler of the state of Yamatai also sent tribute to the Chinese court of Wei via Daifang in AD 238. Through the Three Kingdoms period, **Koguryŏ**, **Paekche**, **Silla** and **Kaya** all maintained contact with Japan, where signs of cultural influence include the building of Paekche-style horizontal tomb chambers in the 5th century. Artists from Koguryŏ and Paekche worked in Yamato, and writing is said to have been transmitted by Buddhist monks from Paekche in AD 405, only a few years after an attack by a joint Paekche-Kaya-Yamato force on Silla had brought a powerful army to its rescue under King **Kwanggaet'o**. The **iron** armour and weaponry found on both sides of the straits have so far failed to establish whether it was southern Korea that exported military culture to Yamato, or whether, as some Japanese historians claim, the influence was in the reverse direction. Some Koreans have interpreted the archaeological evidence from Kyushu and Chinese literary evidence as showing that Yamato was a vassal state of Paekche, ruled by designated *tamno* kings (*see* **Paekche**).

Trade flourished during the Unified Silla period, and temples and museums in Japan today bear witness to the work that Korean Buddhist artists and **craftsmen** did there during the Koryŏ dynasty. However, the population of the peninsula suffered badly as a result of the **Mongols'** vain ambition to extend their empire to Japan, when Koreans were forced to build and sail the ships for the ill-fated invasions in 1274 and 1281. Japanese **pirates** became a serious menace around the Korean coastline in the 14th century, and in 1419 King T'aejong, having recently abdicated, led a successful attack on their base on **Tsushima** Island. Legitimate trade was then profitably developed and was confirmed by the Treaty of **Kyehae** in 1443, though piracy continued spasmodically.

In 1590 the Chosŏn court rejected Toyotomi Hideyoshi's demand for tributary submission, though it did recognise his successful reunification of his country. Despite having sent an ambassador, Hwang Yun'gil, to Japan in 1589 and being informed of Hideyoshi's proposed attack on China by way of Korea, the Korean government persisted in treating him as little more than a pirate. In the end, his imperial ambitions wrought enormous devastation across much of Korea (*see* **Imjin Wars**). Much art from earlier dynasties was destroyed in the fierce fighting, and many **craftsmen** were taken to Japan among the prisoners of war. China's intervention on Korea's behalf failed to prevent a subsequent revaluation of Korea's tributary relationship with the Middle Kingdom (*see* **Sirhak movement**) and the entire political and social systems of the kingdom underwent a shake-up. Although diplomatic relations with Japan were soon restored, and twelve Korean cultural missions were sent via Tsushima between 1607 and 1811 to celebrate the accession of new shoguns, Korea now entered a period of isolationism out of which Japan only began to force it after the beginning of the Meiji Restoration (*see* **Kanghwa Treaty**).

As the court became embroiled in the politics of modernisation, King **Kojong** recognised the opportunities of learning from Japan and sent missions there in search of ideas and financial support (*see* **Kim Hongjip; Kim Okkyun**). The **Taewŏn'gun**, on the other hand, headed the reactionary opposition, and this bitter rivalry led to violent events such as the *Imo* **Incident** (1882), and the involvement of Japanese troops in destructive and murderous attacks on the **Kyŏngbok Palace** (*see* **Queen Min**). Korea became the focus of growing hostility between Japan and China, and, after both countries had responded with troops to the **Tonghak Rebellion**, played unwilling host to the **Sino-Japanese War**.

The attention of the Japanese Prime Minister **Itō Hirobumi** was by now firmly fixed on Korea. Although the growing number of Koreans working and studying in Japan contributed to the late Chosŏn **self-strengthening movement**, Korea's ability to maintain its independence was further undermined by the results of the **Russo-Japanese War** and the backing of the western powers for Japan's establishment of the **protectorate** in 1905. Whilst still asserting a concern for Korean benefit, the Japanese assumed control of key sectors of public and financial organisation, forced the abdication of King Kojong and disbanded the Korean army. **Annexation** in 1910 maintained the fiction that Japan sought Korea's best interests. During the **colonial period** (1910–45) the Japanese brought an unprecedented level of administrative efficiency to Korea, and economic investment assisted the modernisation of its industries, but it was at the cost of much suffering by the Korean population, who were treated as an inferior and subject race by their colonisers. Korea was to be the industrial base for the expansion of the Japanese empire through east and south-east Asia. Korean **nationalism** was stirred, especially among Korean communities in Japan, but resistance was fragmented and only reinforced the ruthlessness of Japanese control.

Following liberation in 1945 Japan itself served as a base for American involvement in the **Korean War**, after the ending of which American policy rebuilt the economy and promoted the development of democratic government both there and in South Korea. President Park Chung Hee (**Pak Chŏnghŭi**) led the move towards rapprochement with Japan in the 1960s as part of his own drive for industrial modernisation and international investment. A goodwill treaty was concluded in June 1965 (*see* **Korea-Japan Treaty**) and a second in April 1970 which led to the return of considerable Japanese influence over the South Korean economy and society. However, in contrast to the United States, which pursued a hard line of opposition to the communist régime in North Korea, Japan had to take account of the fact that its own Korean population had strong affiliations with both South and North. Therefore, while the government in Tokyo developed good relations with Seoul, it also experienced political pressure from P'yŏngyang, and refused to tread the hard anti-communist line advocated by Washington. North Koreans in Japan were involved in terrorist operations against the South and helped to raise badly needed funds and supplies for the hard-pressed DPRK economy. On the other hand, Park Chung Hee's **Korean Central Intelligence Agency** used Japan as a base for the kidnapping of the opposition leader **Kim Taejung**. In the 1990s Japan's preference for a balanced foreign policy was seen in its caution over supporting proposed sanctions against North Korea because of its nuclear programme (*see* **North Korean nuclear programme**). The difficulty for both peoples in resolving their deep-seated antagonism continued to be seen in argument over issues as far apart as the interpretation of ancient peninsular history, the naming of the Eastern Sea (Sea of Japan), and the use of Korean 'comfort women' by Japanese troops in the colonial period. In January 1992 the Japanese Prime Minister, Kiichi Miyazawa, visited Seoul and apologised for actions against the Korean people during the Japanese occupation, but many Koreans remained unsatisfied.

HILARY CONROY, *The Japanese Seizure of Korea 1868–1910: A Study of Realism and Idealism in International Relations*, Philadelphia, 1960; PETER DUUS, *The Abacus and the Sword: the Japanese Penetration of Korea, 1895–1910*, Berkeley: University of California Press, 1995; WILLIAM WAYNE FERRIS, 'Ancient Japan's Korean Connection,' *KS*, 20, 1996; KIM HYUN-KOO, 'A Study of Korea-Japan Relations in Ancient Times: Centering on the Taika Reforms and Formation of Cooperation among Shilla, Japan, and Tang China,' *KJ*, 29/10, 1989; LEE CHONG-SIK, *Japan and Korea: the Political Dimension*, California: Hoover Institution Press, 1985; RONALD P. TOBY, *State and Diplomacy in Early Modern Japan: Asia in the Development of the Tokugawa Bakufu*, Princeton University Press, 1984

See also **Japan, Buddhist missionaries to**; *Kabo* **reforms**; **Stevens, Durham**

JEWEL MOUNTAINS *mani-san*

Several mountains in Korea are known as *Mari-san* or *Mani-san*. The most famous, on **Kanghwa** Island, is crowned with an ancient rectangular altar about 3·5 x 5 metres, built of large stones and attributed to **Tan'gun**. The altar is called *Ch'amsŏng-dan*, 'moat-star-altar'. (The first character was also read *ch'ŏm*, which might mean 'worship' and makes better sense, as in *Ch'ŏmsŏngdae* at **Kyŏngju**). The Kanghwa altar name is recorded from Koryŏ times, but the site has been repaired so often that it is now impossible to guess its history or the original shape of the structure.

Mani 'jewel' is a Buddhist term, short for Sanskrit *cintramani*, meaning the *yŏŭi-ju* jewel, and often changed to '*mari*'. Even Mai-san, 'horse-ears mountain', near Chinan in North Chŏlla, despite its twin peaks, may really be a 'jewel mountain'.

JEWELLERY

Gemstones have been little used. **Silla** used *kogok*, curved comma-shaped beads of jade or turquoise, suspended on crowns by wire links so that they would shimmer with movement of the head. Jade, amber, coral, turquoise, nacre and pearls have since been the staple materials of jewellery. **Women** wore such jewels in hairpins and as *norigae* 'trinkets', often embellished with silken tassels, on the knot of the jacket tie. Heavy earrings were worn in Silla and earrings have never quite disappeared. Finger-rings, often made too large to wear, have been worn on garment ties.

JIN DYNASTY 金代 (Manchuria and Northern China, 1115–1234)

Empire founded by the **Jurchen** leader Wanyan Aguda (1068–1123), who assumed the imperial prerogative of worshipping heaven in 1115. Since the Koryŏ court was known to have contacts with the Jurchen, the Song Emperor Huizong tried to influence the situation by proposing to King **Yejong** that he should help to bring a Jurchen delegation to Kaifeng to discuss mutual co-operation against the **Liao** kingdom. The

Korean court tried to keep its options open. Yejong refused Huizong's request and despatched a mission of his own to the Jin capital in 1116. In 1119 he sent an anti-Jurchen message to Kaifeng, but his successor King Injong refused to join an alliance with Song in 1123 and the next year sent envoys to both Chinese and Jurchen capitals. Finally, in 1126, the court pledged submission to Jin, King Injong evidently accepting that from a pragmatic point of view this was the current interpretation of 'serving the great' (*sadae*). Jin armies had overrun the Liao capital in Shenyang in 1125 and went on to drive the Song court from Kaifeng. When the emperor and his heir apparent, Qinzong, were captured along with 3,000 courtiers in 1127 the government sought Korean help to obtain their release, but King Injong would not compromise his own fragile peace with Jin, and refused.

HOK-LAM CHAN, *Legitimation in Imperial China: Discussions under the Jurchen Chin Dynasty*, Seattle, University of Washington Press, 1984; MICHAEL ROGERS, 'The Regularization of Koryŏ-Chin Relations (1116–1131),' *CAJ*, 5/3, 1960; MICHAEL ROGERS, 'The Chinese World Order and its Transmural Extension: the Case of Chin and Koryŏ,' *KSF*, 4, 1978

JUCHE See Chuch'e

JUNE TENTH INCIDENT *Yuksip manse undong* (1926) 六十萬歲運動

Mass demonstration against Japanese imperialism which followed the funeral in Seoul on 10 June 1926 of the last emperor, **Sunjong**. **Students** were prominent in the movement, which was reminiscent of the **March First Movement** and was organised by members of the *Ch'ŏndo-gyo* and the **Korean Communist Party**. Many were arrested.

See also **Kwangju Incident**

JURCHEN, THE 女真

Descendants of the Tungus **Malgal** and former inhabitants of the Manchurian kingdom of **Parhae**. In the early 11th century semi-independent Jurchen tribes poured into northern Korea to seek protection from the **Khitan**. One of them was Hanpu, the first ancestor of the subsequent **Jin dynasty**. In 1103 they revolted against Koryŏ and in 1109 defeated its army (*see* **Pyŏlmuban**), and for a long time they controlled the northern provinces of Korea, where they were known as *Yain*. Trading relations between Jurchen and Koreans flourished at designated centres such as Kyŏngsŏng and Kyŏngwŏn, and the Koreans tried to settle their nomadic neighbours down by granting their chieftains titles and small official posts. Many Jurchen did settle permanently in Korea, but their leaders had grander aspirations and led the campaigns against both **Liao** and **Song** China. Against this background, the decision by King Injong in 1126 to acknowledge the Jin claim to imperial legitimacy is politically understandable.

Early in the 13th century the **Mongols** broke Jurchen control across north-east Asia. After they themselves had been ousted from China and Korea in the late 14th century the Chosŏn General Kim Chongsŏ (1390–1453) fortified the **Tumen Yalu** frontier. But Jurchen border raids continued through the 15th century, and the Koreans sent expeditionary forces against Jurchen tribes in 1434, 1437, 1460, and 1467. The final act in this on-going Tungus-Korean rivalry came in 1636, when the descendants of the Jurchen, now generally known as the Manchus, overran Korea.

HERBERT FRANKE, 'The Forest Peoples of Manchuria: Kitans and Jurchens,' *in* DENIS SINOR, ed., *The Cambridge History of Early Inner Asia*, Cambridge University Press, 1990; ULRIKE JUGEL, *Studien zur Geschichte der Wu-liang-ha im 15. Jh.*, Wiesbaden, 1982;

KENNETH ROBINSON, 'From Raiders to Traders: Border Security and Border Control in Early Chosŏn, 1392–1450,' *KS*, 16, 1992; JING-SHEN TAO, *The Jurchen in Twelfth Century China: A Study of Sinicization*, Seattle: University of Washington Press, 1977
See also **Manchu invasions**

K

KABO **REFORMS** *Kabo kyŏngjang* 甲午更張 (1894)
Series of radical reforms initiated by the Korean government in the context of the **Sino-Japanese War** and at the instigation of the Japanese authorities in Seoul, notably their Minister Inoue Kaoru. The name *Kabo* refers to the year, 1894, in which they began to be introduced. The measures were taken from July onwards by a new Advisory Council headed by **Kim Hongjip**. Perhaps because their modernising intent was not out of keeping with the nation's needs at the end of the 19th century, some modern Korean historians now dispute the earlier view that they were forced on a wholly unwilling and recalcitrant court by the imperialistic Japanese. Certainly, the reforms could later be seen as a significant part of the **Self-strengthening** and Independence Movements, though their purpose in Japanese eyes was to tighten their grip on Korean administration. They were strongly opposed by the **Taewŏn'gun**, who vainly sought Chinese help to overturn the reforms and even oust the king. Nevertheless, **Kojong** offered the new plans to his ancestors at an oath-taking ceremony on 7 January 1895. Anti-Japanese feeling increased following the murder of **Queen Min** in October and Kim Hongjip's insensitive introduction of a second round of reforms, which included the compulsory cutting off of the **topknot** by men. Like the 1898 Reform Movement in China, however, the immediate effect of the *Kabo* programme proved to be short-lived, even though the changes to the monetary system could be said to have brought longer term benefit to the Japanese. As a result of international pressure the Japanese were forced to return the Liaodong peninsula, which they had acquired under the Treaty of **Shimonoseki**, to China, and the majority of the reforms lapsed. Members of the reform group of politicians joined the **Independence Club**. Fearing Japanese reprisals, the King took refuge in the Russian Embassy.

The principal reform provisions were:

1) Revision of the highest levels of government organisation, including the reform of the Council of State (*Ŭijŏng-bu*) as *naegak* (Cabinet) and the creation of eight ministries (*amun*); reduction of the king's financial powers and rights of political appointment, now to reflect merit based on success in
2) a revised examination system including subjects such as mathematics, international relations, and Chinese and Korean language, replacing the traditional Confucian **examinations**; expansion of the **school** system and introduction of modern textbooks under the newly created Ministry of Education;
3) reorganisation of the local government map, abolishing the eight provinces and creating 23 prefectures and 336 counties;
4) a new monetary system based on silver; official salaries to be paid wholly in cash; collection of taxes in cash instead of kind; modernisation of weights and measures on western lines;
5) the establishment of an hierarchical system of higher and lower law courts independent of the government;
6) military reorganisation to include better training, equipment and deployment between the capital and regions;

7) promotion of greater social fluidity with the abolition of traditional distinctions, giving the *yangban* the right to engage in trade; abolition of **slavery**; ending of child marriage and the neo-Confucian prohibition on widow remarriage; a ban on the torture of suspected criminals; promotion of more practical, western-style dress.

LEW YOUNG-ICK, *The Kabo Reform Movement: Korean and Japanese Reform Efforts in Korea, 1894*, PhD dissertation, Harvard University, 1972
See also **Pak Yŏnghyo**

KAEGYŎNG 開京 *See* **Kaesŏng**

KAEHWA SASANG 開化思想 'Enlightenment thought'
Term used to describe the spirit of intellectual enquiry in the latter half of the Chosŏn dynasty that brought about the *Sirhak* **movement** and the **self-strengthening movement**.

KAEHWADANG 'Progressive Party' 開化黨 *See* **Independence Party**

KAESŎNG 開城
Created from the two districts of Songak and Kaesŏng in 919 and called Kaeju, the city was renamed Kaegyŏng in 959 and Kaesŏng in 995. It was the home region and power base of the family of **Wang Kŏn**, who followed advice on *p'ungsu* and established it as capital of the Koryŏ dynasty. The **Altars of Earth and Harvest** (*Sajik*) were set up in 991 and it became both an administrative and educational centre. Much of the life-style of the court and aristocracy imitated that of their Chinese neighbours, and admiration for Kaifeng was reflected in the grand architectural scale of the palaces, official buildings, temples, and broad streets. The city had a population of over 130,000 and greatly impressed the Chinese envoy Xu Jing, who visited it in 1123 and described it in his *Xuanhe fengshi Gaoli tujing* (K. *Koryŏ Togyŏng*).

After the city suffered heavy damage from invading **Khitan** forces in 1010 an outer city wall was built in 1029 with 25 gates (*see also* **walls**). Other defensive measures initiated by the court included the carving of **printing** blocks for the *Tripitaka Koreana* (*see also* **Haein-sa**). The perceived threat to the dynasty and its heritage also prompted the compilation of historical records. The threat from within, however, proved to be just as serious as that from abroad, and in 1126 the rebel minister **Yi Chagyŏm** burned the palace. In the 1190s the **slaves** of Kaesŏng took part in the popular revolts which erupted across the country against the financial and *corvée* exactions of the aristocracy. Further troubles occurred in 1232, when the court fled Kaesŏng to **Kanghwa** Island in face of the **Mongol** invasion. It did not return until accommodation had been reached with the occupiers in 1270 (*see also* **Sambyŏlch'o**). The capital was again captured, albeit temporarily, by foreign troops during the revolt of the **Red Turbans** in 1361, and by then its days of royal glory were numbered. In 1388 **Yi Sŏnggye** occupied it and overthrew the last Koryŏ king. Seven years later he transferred his court to Hanyang (Seoul).

OH SUNG, 'Family Structure in Kaesŏng at the End of the Chosŏn Dynasty', *KJ*, 36/4, 1996

KAGOK 歌曲
Long lyric songs composed in stanzas of five lines of irregular length, usually accompanied by a small instrumental ensemble. They are in *u* and *kyemyŏn* modes and are characterised by difficult melismatic vocal lines that require long training, similar to the *chissori* tradition in *pŏmp'ae*.
See also **kasa**; **music**

KAJAE YŎNHAENG-NOK 稼齋燕行錄
The diary of Nogajae 'old farmer', Kim Ch'angŏp (1658–1721), younger brother of Kim Ch'angjip (1648–1722), written during the annual embassy to Beijing for the celebration of the emperor's official birthday on New Year's Day, 30 November 1712 to 10 February 1713 (Gregorian reckoning). Despite many longueurs, a vivid account in simple style by a vain and inquisitive, yet likeable, man, devoted to the **Ming dynasty**. His father, **Kim Suhang**, a leading Noron politician, died in **factional struggles**, as did his brother Ch'angjip.
See also **Beijing, embassies to**

KAMSA 監司 'inspector' or 'provincial governor'
There are two readily confused words, with different Chinese characters, each denoting a person of distinction. Both occur in folk literature where no Chinese characters are used. The context generally indicates if an inspector is intended, while a distinguished husband is more likely to be a provincial governor.

KAMŬN-SA 感恩寺 'Temple of gratitude'
Near **Kyŏngju**, begun by King **Munmu** and completed by his son King **Sinmun** in 682 as an invocation of divine help against Japanese **pirates**. Excavation of the site began in 1979. Its unique feature is its underfloor chamber and corridor opening eastwards from beneath the main hall, intended as an entrance for the spirit of the 'Dragon King', Munmu, who was believed to dwell on **Taewang-am** following his cremation. The main stone stairway seems to have served as a model for that at **Pulguk-sa**. The twin three-storey **pagodas**, 14·5 metres tall and undecorated, were each found to contain a **sarira** casket. That from the west pagoda, a richly decorated bronze box, enclosed a small crystal bottle for the remains of a Buddhist priest.

KANDO 間島
Historically, Kando (C. Jiandao) means the eastern part of Jilin province in **Manchuria**, centred on Yanji (K. Yŏn'gil). In a wider use, it stretches from the headwaters of the **Yalu River** along the whole of the north bank of the **Tumen**. From the 18th century onwards Koreans fled or migrated into this region in response to adverse economic or political conditions at home, establishing substantial Korean communities there with schools and a flourishing press. The territory was sometimes disputed, but was formally surrendered to China by the Japanese in 1909. In the early 20th century Korea resistance fighters (*see* **Ŭibyŏng**) based in Kando entered Korea to harrass the Japanese, especially after the beginning of the **March First Movement**, while Korean military volunteers clashed with Japanese army units within the Kando region. After their occupation of Manchuria in 1931 (*see* **Manchurian Incident**), the Japanese strove to re-educate the population as Japanese.

Today the region is known as the Yanbian Chaoxianzu Zizhizhou (Yanbian Korean Autonomous Prefecture), created on 8 August 1952. Its capital is Yanji City. In 1982, ethnic Koreans constituted 62·5 per cent of the population of Jilin province.
HONG I-SUP, 'Facts about Kando or Chient'ao,' *KJ*, 9/5, 1969; KU DAEYEOL, 'The Chientao Incident (1920) and Britain,' *TRASKB* LV, 1980; CHAE-JIN LEE, *China's Korean Minority, the Politics of Ethnic Education*, Boulder and London: Westview Press, 1986

KANG HŬIAN 姜希顔 (Injae, 1419–64)
A senior official and member of the *Chiphyŏn-jŏn*, skilled in **horticulture**, **painting**, **poetry** and **calligraphy**. He travelled to China three times, the first as leader of a

mission in 1455, and met artists there. Though tending to be self-deprecatory about his artistic skill, he had a strong influence on others, and his brushwork is notable for its boldness. In *Sage Resting on a Rock* (National Museum of Korea)[1] the sparseness of line describing the figure of the monk and the tendrils of the vegetation hanging behind him are reminiscent of *Sŏn* painting style.

(1) CHOI SUNU, *5000 Years of Korean Art*, Seoul: Hyonam Publishing Co., 1979

KUMJA PAIK KIM, 'Two Stylistic Trends in Mid-15th Century Korean Painting,' *OA*, XXIX/4, 1983/4

See also **Hunmin chŏngŭm haerye**

KANG ILSUN 姜一淳 (1871–1909)

A farmer's son and herb-doctor of the Chŏngŭp district in North Chŏlla, founder of a **new religion** called *Chŭngsan-gyo*. (Chŭngsan, 'bowl mountain', was a local place-name he adopted as a brush-name.) He became a **Tonghak** adherent in his early twenties and followed Chŏn Pongjun's army to Ch'ŏngju, but rejected the idea of armed struggle. For three years from the age of 26 he wandered the country, seeking enlightenment and gaining a reputation for madness. After returning home he received enlightenment during a thunderstorm at Taewŏn-sa near Chŏnju in 1901. In 1902 he began preaching an amalgam of Confucian, Buddhist, and Protestant elements with home-made mantras, healing rites and paper charms and amulets. His group was nicknamed *Hŭmch'i-gyo*, from the first words of his favourite **mantra**, but also because *hŭmch'i-gyo* was a pun on 'thieving religion'. The magistrates distrusted him. In 1908 he was arrested as a potential disturber of the peace and detained for forty days. His followers, never many nor loyal, lost heart, and few attended his funeral in 1909. His *Chŭngsan-gyo* teachings survived in various splinter groups.

KANG KAMCH'AN 姜邯贊 (948–1031)

Koryŏ general who led the defence against **Liao** invaders in 1010 and 1018. His birthplace at Naksŏngdae ('Falling star terrace'), on the southern outskirts of modern Seoul adjacent to Seoul National University, is marked by a three-storey **pagoda**.

KANG P'IRHYO 姜必孝 (Hacŭn, 1764–1848)

A famous neo-Confucian philosopher, born at Andong, South Kyŏngsang. He was nominated to public office in 1800 on the recommendation of a Secret Royal Inspector, but resigned early from his first two appointments. Later he held several middle-rank posts in various places, ending up in the royal household; but he is remembered chiefly for his collected writings, *Haeŭn yugo*. His brush name means 'Sea recluse'.

KANG SEHWANG 姜世晃 (P'yoam, 1713–91)

Scholar painter and calligrapher with a reputation as a prominent art connoisseur. Despite not entering government service until he was 61 years old, he was sent on a mission to China ten years later (*see* **Beijing, missions to**). He painted *genre* subjects and portraits, including self-portraits, but his landscapes are now best known. Having followed the Chinese Southern School tradition, he helped to develop the 'true view' (*chin'gyŏng*) style of landscape painting primarily associated with **Chŏng Sŏn**. Most remarkable of his extant works are the 16 album leaves entitled *Scenic spots of Sŏngdo* (Seoul National Museum)[1]. His use of dots may be reminiscent of Mi Fei (1052–1107), but the bold overlapping outlines of rocks and colourful shading wash create an effect that is novel in both China and Korea. He was a teacher of **Kim Hongdo**, whose work shows Kang's innovative influence.

(1) SUSAN COX, 'An Unusual Album by a Korean Painter, Kang Se-hwang', *OA* XIX/2, 1973

KANG WANSUK, COLUMBA 姜完淑 (1759–1801)

Kang Wansuk was born at Tŏksan in South Ch'ungch'ŏng and married as secondary wife to Hong Chiyŏng, who divorced her because of her Catholicism. When she was about 42 she went to Seoul with her daughter, mother-in-law and stepson, all Catholics. She clearly had financial resources of her own, for she took a leading part in arranging and paying for the arrival in Seoul of the Chinese priest **Zhou Wenmo** in 1795. So long as he was in Korea, he lived in Columba's house in Seoul. He baptized her and appointed her *yŏ-hoejang*, 'woman catechist', in charge of all female Catholics, choosing and training the women workers. She instructed Princess Song, wife of **Chŏngjo**'s brother Prince Ŭnŏn, and the princess's daughter-in-law Sin, in the faith while they were under house arrest during Ŭnŏn's exile in **Kanghwa**. (Both princesses were martyred in 1801.) Columba alone knew the whereabouts of Fr Zhou during his travels. She therefore had great power in the Church. When he was arrested and executed, she and four of her helpers were tortured before being killed on 3 July 1801. Paucity of documentation explains why she has not yet been canonised, but her cause is now being promoted.
See **martyrs, Catholic**

KANGDONG 江東

Fortress outside P'yŏngyang where a joint siege by **Mongol** and Koryŏ armies destroyed a force of **Khitan** invaders of northern Korea in 1219.

KANGGANG-SUWŎLLAE 'round and round'

A ring **dance** of southern Chŏlla, danced by **women** in the moonlight at *Ch'usŏk*, while a singer sings a song with an attractive refrain, '*Kanggang suwŏllae*', in which all join. Legend connects the custom with a ruse used during the Hideyoshi invasions (*see* **Imjin Wars**) to dissuade Japanese soldiers from attempting to land. Another legend interprets the refrain as a poem about rivers, water and moonlight; but the dance is older than Hideyoshi, more likely part of an old harvest festival, and the words mean 'Here we go round and round' in local **dialect**.

KANGHWA TREATY *Pyŏngja suho choyak* 丙子修好條約 (1876)

The conclusion of the so-called *Unyō-kan* Incident of September 1875, in which three Japanese ships, one of them the *Unyō-kan*, attacked **Kanghwa-do**. Having killed 35 Koreans and injured more, they then sailed for **Tongnae**, where further clashes with Korean troops occurred. The Japanese government saw this as an opportunity to obtain the entry to Korea it had been seeking. It therefore sent a heavily armed flotilla to Kanghwa to demand an apology and a treaty. After negotiations with the Korean official Sin Hŏn, the Japanese General Kuroda Kiyotaka and minister Inoue Kaoru concluded the Treaty of Kanghwa on 26 February 1876. It began by recognising Korean freedom from its traditional Chinese suzerainty. It then went on effectively to end the **Taewŏn'gun**'s policy of isolationism and to place Korea potentially under the commercial domination of Japan by granting the Japanese **extraterritoriality**, the right to use their own currency in Korean ports, exemption from import taxes, the posting of Japanese consuls in trading ports, and the mutual right to establish diplomatic missions in Seoul and Tokyo. The latter was first implemented by an exchange of ministers in 1879.

KANGHWA-DO Kanghwa Island 江華島

Island at the mouth of the **Han** and **Imjin** River estuary with many historical associations. The mythical Korean founder **Tan'gun** (*see also* **foundation myths**) is said to have worshipped at the stone shrine preserved on Mount Mani. As authentic evidence of its ancient occupation it has a prehistoric **dolmen**. It is the site of one of the oldest surviving Buddhist temples in Korea, Ch'ŏndŭng-sa (formerly Chinjong-sa), built in AD 381, and of a **Silla** naval garrison. It was the seat of exile between 1232 and 1270 to which the Koryŏ court fled in the face of **Mongol** invasion, and where the *Tripitaka Koreana* was carved. In 1636 women of the Chosŏn court also took refuge here, but were captured by the Manchus.

In modern times the history of Kanghwa has again been associated with conflict. An attacking French force was driven away in 1866 (*see* **France, relations with**) and an American one with more difficulty in 1871 (*see* **General Sherman**). Japanese sailors from the ship *Unyō-kan* killed 35 Koreans here in 1875 in an incident which led to the **Kanghwa Treaty** in February 1876, the opening of modern Japanese involvement in Korean affairs. In 1907 the Korean military garrison of Yu Myŏnggyu defeated Japanese forces in a battle here (*see* ***Ŭibyŏng***).
See also **hunting; Jewel mountains**

KANGJIN 康津

Rural district near the south-western tip of South Chŏlla province which was the more important of the two centres for **celadon** production in Korea between the mid-9th century and late 14th century. Its natural advantages included fine clay, abundant sources of timber for fuel, running water, good communications by sea, and surrounding hills protecting the location and its climate. The discovery of Koryŏ pottery remains there began in 1913 and has continued in every decade until the present. Hundreds of historic **kilns** have been mapped. Finds demonstrate that China provided the source of inspiration for the early potters, but that native aesthetic and technical mastery had developed by the 11th and 12th centuries.
See also **ceramics**

KANSONG 澗松 MUSEUM *See* **Chŏn Hyŏngp'il**

KAPCHA CHARACTERS (the Sixty-fold Cycle) 甲子

Two series of very ancient Chinese characters are used for dates. The so-called 'Ten Heavenly Stems' (*ch'ŏn'gan*),

KAP, ŬL, PYŎNG, CHŎ'NG, MU, KI, KYŎNG, SIN, IM, KYE,

were used for the days of the 10-day 'week'. The 'Twelve Earthly Branches' (*chiji*),

CHA, CH'UK, IN, MYO, CHIN, SA, O, MI, SIN, YU, SUL, HAE,

were used for the 12 moons of the year and later for the 12 hours of the solar day (each equal to two hours of the western 24-hour day). When the two series are listed side-by-side, six repeats of the stems and five of the branches complete a cycle of 60 stem-and-branch pairs (*kapcha*: KAPCHA, ŬLCH'UK, PYŎNGIN, etc) that has been repeated continuously since the 14th century BC for numbering days, and since the 1st century BC for numbering years. The yearly sequence was given a fictional starting point in 2637 BC, the 61st year of the reign of Huangdi (K. Hwangje), the legendary Yellow Emperor, and the 78th cycle began in 1984. (*See* ***Saju-p'alcha***)

In dating Korean historical events, the *kapcha* for a year are prefixed by a king's name (or an emperor's reign title) and the number of the year within the reign, as in *Sejong O Kyemyo* 'Sejong 5[th year] Black Hare' (1423) (*see* **Dates of Kings**). After 1644 some Koreans used **Ming loyalist dating**.

Neo-Confucian **Five Phases** theory emphasised the Five Colours as alternatives for the stems:

KAP,	ŬL	=	*CH'ŎNG*	blue	PYŎNG,	CHŎNG	=	*CHŎK*	red
MU,	KI	=	*HWANG*	yellow	KYŎNG,	SIN	=	*PAEK*	white
IM,	KYE	=	*HŬK*	black.					

Zodiac animals for the branches were known as early as Silla:

		Sino-Korean		Korean			Sino-Korean		Korean
CHA	=	*SŎ*	rat	*chwi*	O	=	*MA*	horse	*mal*
CH'UK	=	*U*	ox	*so*	MI	=	*YANG*	sheep	*yang*
IN	=	*HO*	tiger	*horangi*	SIN	=	*HU*	monkey	*wŏnsungi*
MYO	=	*T'O*	hare	*t'okki*	YU	=	*KYE*	fowl	*tak*
CHIN	=	*YONG*	dragon	*yong*	SUL	=	*KYŎN*	dog	*kae*
SA	=	*SA*	snake	*paem*	HAE	=	*CHO*	pig	*twaeji*

Thus *HŬKHO* 'Black Tiger' = IMIN; *CH'ŎNGNYONG* 'Blue Dragon' = KAPCHIN; *PAENGMA* 'White Horse' = KYŎNGO.

The zodiacal animal is referred to in Korean as *tti* 'band', as in *sotti* for one born in the year of the ox, *yangtti* for the year of the sheep and so forth.

THE CYCLE OF SIXTY

1 KAPCHA	Blue Rat	31 KABO	Blue Horse
2 ŬLCH'UK	Blue Ox	32 ŬLMI	Blue Sheep
3 PYŎNGIN	Red Tiger	33 PYŎNGSIN	Red Monkey
4 CHŎNGMYO	Red Hare	34 CHŎNGYU	Red Fowl
5 MUJIN	Yellow Dragon	35 MUSUL	Yellow Dog
6 KISA	Yellow Snake	36 KIHAE	Yellow Pig
7 KYŎNGO	White Horse	37 KYŎNGJA	White Rat
8 SINMI	White Sheep	38 SINCH'UK	White Ox
9 IMSIN	Black Monkey	39 IMIN	Black Tiger
10 KYEYU	Black Fowl	40 KYEMYO	Black Hare
11 KAPSUL	Blue Dog	41 KAPCHIN	Blue Dragon
12 ŬRHAE	Blue Pig	42 ŬLSA	Blue Snake
13 PYŎNGJA	Red Rat	43 PYŎNGO	Red Horse
14 CHŎNGCH'UK	Red Ox	44 CHŎNGMI	Red Sheep
15 MUIN	Yellow Tiger	45 MUSIN	Yellow Monkey
16 KIMYO	Yellow Hare	46 KIYU	Yellow Fowl
17 KYŎNGJIN	White Dragon	47 KYŎNGSUL	White Dog
18 SINSA	White Snake	48 SINHAE	White Pig
19 IMO	Black Horse	49 IMJA	Black Rat
20 KYEMI	Black Sheep	50 KYECH'UK	Black Ox
21 KAPSIN	Blue Monkey	51 KABIN	Blue Tiger
22 ŬRYU	Blue Fowl	52 ŬLMYO	Blue Hare
23 PYŎNGSUL	Red Dog	53 PYŎNGJIN	Red Dragon
24 CHŎNGHAE	Red Pig	54 CHŎNGSA	Red Snake
25 MUJA	Yellow Rat	55 MUO	Yellow Horse
26 KICH'UK	Yellow Ox	56 KIMI	Yellow Sheep
27 KYŎNGIN	White Tiger	57 KYŎNGSIN	White Monkey
28 SINMYO	White Hare	58 SINYU	White Fowl
29 IMJIN	Black Dragon	59 IMSUL	Black Dog
30 KYESA	Black Snake	60 KYEHAE	Black Pig

THE 68TH – 77TH CYCLES WITH WESTERN DATES
FOR THE PERIOD OF THE CHOSŎN DYNASTY

Western and Chinese years do not precisely coincide. Since AD1, the Chinese year has begun between 13 January and 20 February of the western year. Thus the first two to eight weeks of a Western year fall in the previous Chinese year, and the last 12 to 50 days of a Chinese year fall in the following Western year. The table shows the cyclical character for the lunar years that begin in January or February of the solar years listed. *See* **Dates, Concordance of Lunar and Solar**

KAPCHA	1384	1444	1504	1564	1624	1684	1744	1804	1864	1924
ŬLCH'UK	1385	1445	1505	1565	1625	1685	1745	1805	1865	1925
PYŎNGIN	1386	1446	1506	1566	1626	1686	1746	1806	1866	1926
CHŎNGMYO	1387	1447	1507	1567	1627	1687	1747	1807	1867	1927
MUJIN	1388	1448	1508	1568	1628	1688	1748	1808	1868	1928
KISA	1389	1449	1509	1569	1629	1689	1749	1809	1869	1929
KYŎNGO	1390	1450	1510	1570	1630	1690	1750	1810	1870	1930
SINMI	1391	1451	1511	1571	1631	1691	1751	1811	1871	1931
IMSIN	1392	1452	1512	1572	1632	1692	1752	1812	1872	1932
KYEYU	1393	1453	1513	1573	1633	1693	1753	1813	1873	1933
KAPSUL	1394	1454	1514	1574	1634	1694	1754	1814	1874	1934
ŬRHAE	1395	1455	1515	1575	1635	1695	1755	1815	1875	1935
PYŎNGJA	1396	1456	1516	1576	1636	1696	1756	1816	1876	1936
CHŎNGCH'UK	1397	1457	1517	1577	1637	1697	1757	1817	1877	1937
MUIN	1398	1458	1518	1578	1638	1698	1758	1818	1878	1938
KIMYO	1399	1459	1519	1579	1639	1699	1759	1819	1879	1939
KYŎNGJIN	1400	1460	1520	1580	1640	1700	1760	1820	1880	1940
SINSA	1401	1461	1521	1581	1641	1701	1760	1821	1881	1941
IMU	1402	1462	1522	1582	1642	1702	1762	1822	1882	1942
KYEMI	1403	1463	1523	1583	1643	1703	1763	1823	1883	1943
KAPSIN	1404	1464	1524	1584	1644	1704	1764	1824	1884	1944
ŬRYU	1405	1465	1525	1585	1645	1705	1765	1825	1885	1945
PYŎNGSUL	1406	1466	1526	1586	1646	1706	1766	1826	1886	1946
CHŎNGHAE	1407	1467	1527	1587	1647	1707	1767	1827	1887	1947
MUJA	1408	1468	1528	1588	1648	1708	1768	1828	1888	1948
KICH'UK	1409	1469	1529	1589	1649	1709	1769	1829	1889	1949
KYŎNGIN	1410	1470	1530	1590	1650	1710	1770	1830	1890	1950
SINMYO	1411	1471	1531	1591	1651	1711	1771	1831	1891	1951
IMJIN	1412	1472	1532	1592	1652	1712	1772	1832	1892	1952
KYESA	1413	1473	1533	1593	1653	1713	1773	1833	1893	1953
KABO	1414	1474	1534	1594	1654	1714	1774	1834	1894	1954
ŬLMI	1415	1475	1535	1595	1655	1715	1775	1835	1895	1955
PYŎNGSIN	1416	1476	1536	1596	1656	1716	1776	1836	1896	1956
CHŎNGYU	1417	1477	1537	1597	1657	1717	1777	1837	1897	1957
MUSUL	1418	1478	1538	1598	1658	1718	1778	1838	1898	1958
KIHAE	1419	1479	1539	1599	1659	1719	1779	1839	1899	1959
KYŎNGJA	1420	1480	1540	1600	1660	1720	1780	1840	1900	1960
SINCH'UK	1421	1481	1541	1601	1661	1721	1781	1841	1901	1961
IMIN	1422	1482	1542	1602	1662	1722	1782	1842	1902	1962
KYEMYO	1423	1483	1543	1603	1663	1723	1783	1843	1903	1963

KAPCHIN	1424	1484	1544	1604	1664	1724	1784	1844	1904	1964
ŬLSA	1425	1485	1545	1605	1665	1725	1785	1845	1905	1965
PYŎNGO	1426	1486	1546	1606	1666	1726	1786	1846	1906	1966
CHŎNGMI	1427	1487	1547	1607	1667	1727	1787	1847	1907	1967
MUSIN	1428	1488	1548	1608	1668	1728	1788	1848	1908	1968
KIYU	1429	1489	1549	1609	1669	1729	1789	1849	1909	1969
KYŎNGSUL	1430	1490	1550	1610	1670	1730	1790	1850	1910	1970
SINHAE	1431	1491	1551	1611	1671	1731	1791	1851	1911	1971
IMJA	1432	1492	1552	1612	1672	1732	1792	1852	1912	1972
KYECH'UK	1433	1493	1553	1613	1673	1733	1793	1853	1913	1973
KABIN	1434	1494	1554	1614	1674	1734	1794	1854	1914	1974
ŬLMYO	1435	1495	1555	1615	1675	1735	1795	1855	1915	1975
PYŎNGJIN	1436	1496	1556	1616	1676	1736	1796	1856	1916	1976
CHŎNGSA	1437	1497	1557	1617	1677	1737	1797	1857	1917	1977
MUO	1438	1498	1558	1618	1678	1738	1798	1858	1918	1978
KIMI	1439	1499	1559	1619	1679	1739	1799	1859	1919	1979
KYŎNGSIN	1440	1500	1560	1620	1680	1740	1800	1860	1920	1980
SINYU	1441	1501	1561	1621	1681	1741	1801	1861	1921	1981
IMSUL	1442	1502	1562	1622	1682	1742	1802	1862	1922	1982
KYEHAE	1443	1503	1563	1623	1683	1743	1803	1863	1923	1983

KAPCHA YEAR NUMBERS, EVENTS KNOWN BY

Korean historians customarily refer to certain historical events as 'disturbance', 'plot', 'treaty', or the like, preceded by the cyclical characters of the year of the event. The following is a list of the most frequently encountered examples. *See also* **literati purges** and *sahwa*.

1170	*Kyŏngil-lan*	Rebellion of **Chŏng Chungbu**
1173	*Kyesa-ran*	Kim Podang's attempt to restore Ŭijong
1398	*Muin-jŏngsa*	Rebellion of Yi Pangwŏn
1443	**Kyehae**-*joyak*	**Tsushima** agreement
1453	*Kyeyu-jŏngnan*	Usurpation of **Sejo**
1455	*Pyŏngja sahwa*	Plot to restore **Tanjong**
1460	*Kyŏngjin-bukchŏng*	Control of the **Jurchen** at the **Tumen**
1467	*Chŏnghae-sŏjo'ng*	Control of the Jurchen at the **Yalu**
1498	*Muo-sahwa*	Prince **Yŏnsan**'s 'history purge'
1509	*Kapcha-sahwa*	Insult to Prince Yŏnsan's mother
1510	*Kyo'ngo-ran*	Japanese riots at three ports
1512	*Imsin-yakcho*	Tsushima agreement
1519	*Kimyo-sahwa*	Death of **Cho Kwangjo**
1520	*Ŭlsin-yakcho*	Tsushima agreement
1521	*Sinsa-muok*	Accusation against An Ch'ŏgyŏm
1531	*Sinmyo-samgan*	Three traitors: Sim Chŏng, Yi Hang, Kim Kŭkpok
1531	*Chŏngyu-samhyung*	Overthrow of Kim Allo and his companions
1544	*Kapchin-byŏn*	Japanese riots at Saryang-jin
1545	*Ŭlsa-sahwa*	Purge at accession of Myŏngjong
1547	*Chŏngmi-sahwa*	Purge after Yangjae graffiti
1547	*Chŏngmi-yakcho*	Reopening ports to Japan
1549	*Kiyu-sahwa*	Yi Hongyun affair
1555	*Ŭlmyo-waebyŏn*	Japanese raid

1589	Kich'ungnyŏnŭi-ch'amo	Trouble with **Chŏng-Gam-nok**
1589	Kich'ug-oksa	Rebellion of **Chŏng Yŏrip**
1592	**Imjin**-waeran	Hideyoshi invasion
1597	Chŏngyu-jaerun	Second Japanese invasion
1609	Kiyu-joyak	Tsushima agreement
1613	Kyuch'uk-hwaok	Death of **Prince Yŏngch'ang**
1627	Chŏngmyo-horan	**Manchu invasion**
1636	Pyŏngja-horan	Second Manchu invasion
1680	Kyŏngsin-daech'ulch'ŏk	Purge of Southerners
1689	Kisa-hwan'guk	Purge of Noron on appointment of Crown Prince
1694	Kapsur-oksa	Restoration of **Queen Min**
1699	Kimyo-hwaok	Cheating at examinations
1721–2	Sinim-oksa (or sahwa)	Accession of **King Kyŏngjong**
1722	Imin-ok	Another name for Sinim-sahwa (1721-2 above)
1727	Chŏngmi-hwan'guk	End of factionalism
1755	Ŭrhae-saok	Naju graffiti incident
1762	Imo-ok	Death of Crown Prince Sado (**Changhon**)
1791	Sinhae-saok	**Catholic** persecution in Chinsan
1791	Sinhae-t'onggong	Commercial equalisation enactment
1800	Kyŏngsin-nyŏndo-hoegye	Annual audit
1801	Sinyu-saok (or -gyoran)	Catholic persecution
1810	Kyŏngo-nyŏndo-hoegye	Annual audit
1839	Kihae-saok (or -bakhae)	Catholic persecution
1846	Pyŏngo-bakhae	Catholic persecution
1862	Imsul-ijŏngch'ŏng-dŭngnok	Record of provincial troubles
1866	Pyŏngin-saok	Catholic persecution
1866	Pyŏngin-yangyo	Repulse of French at **Kanghwa**
1871	Sinmi-yangyo	Repulse of Americans at Kanghwa
1876	Pyŏngja-suho-joyak	Treaty with Japan (Kanghwa)
1882	**Imo-gullan**	Soldiers' mutiny
1884	**Kapsin**-jŏngbyŏn	Post Office coup
1894	**Kabo**-gaehyŏk (-gyŏngbyŏn or gyŏngjang)	Reforms
1895	Ŭlmi-sabyŏn	Assassination of **Queen Min**
1900	Kyŏngja-mogye-sakkŏn	Abortive plot by **Pak Yŏnghyo**
1905	Ŭlsa-boho-joyak	**Protectorate Treaty**
1905	Ŭlsa-ojŏk	**Five traitors**
1907	Chŏngmi-ch'il-choyak	Korean-Japanese Agreement
1909	Kimyo-gaksŏ	Japanese takeover of justice and prisons
1919	Kimi-dongnip-undong	**March First Independence Movement**
1919	Muo-dongnip-sŏnŏn-sŏ	Declaration of Independence in **Manchuria** and the Soviet Far East

KAPSIN COUP Kapsin Chŏngbyŏn 甲申政變 (1884)
An attempt by a group of modernisation supporters, known as the **Kaehwadang** ('Progressive Party'), to seize power and overturn foreign influence at the court of King **Kojong**, especially that of China and Russia. Leaders of the group included **Kim Okkyun** and **Sŏ Chaep'il**. The coup occurred on 4 December 1884 (the Kapsin year) and is sometimes known as the December 4th Incident. It took place at a dinner party marking the opening of the Korean post office. The plotters attacked

conservative supporters of **Queen Min**, who were opposed to over-rapid change, killing members of her family. At Kim's instigation the King took refuge in the Japanese embassy, where the minister Takezoe Shin'ichirō had advance warning and apparently condoned the plot. The next day a new government of reformers assumed power, issuing a list of reform demands aimed at freeing Korea from Chinese domination, ending *yangban* domination of the government, improving the financial, military and police systems, reforming education, promoting *han'gŭl*, and improving the conditions of the lower classes. They also demanded the return of the **Taewŏn'gun** from China (*see Imo* **Incident**), where his stay was symbolic of China's suzerainty over Korea. But only two days later Chinese troops, acting on orders from the Resident General **Yuan Shikai**, returned Kojong to the palace and abruptly ended the coup. Some of the plotters died, but Kim and Sŏ escaped to Japan. Because they had already visited it and admired its modernisation, and because their aims were later reflected in the *Kabo* **reforms** of 1894, the plotters are sometimes described as being pro-Japanese, but this obscures their sense of **nationalism**. They have also been seen as inheritors of the *sirhak* tradition of seeking the best for Korea's own interests.

In the wake of the coup, Japan demanded that Korea sign the Treaty of Hansŏng (Seoul), compensating the Japanese victims and paying for repairs to the damaged Japanese embassy. The bid to boost Russian interests in Korea was led by the court's German adviser, Paul-Georg **von Möllendorff**, and was regarded with suspicion by the Chinese, the Japanese, and the British. The coup, however, only enhanced Kojong's trust in Russian support, which in turn led the suspicious British to seize the **Kŏmundo** Islands. In April 1885 the Chinese and Japanese concluded the Treaty of Tianjin, also known as the Li-Itō Agreement after its main signatories **Li Hongzhang** and **Itō Hirobumi**. Both powers pledged to withdraw their troops from Korea except in the event of future trouble. China's position in Korea, however, was little weakened by the coup. It retained its Resident General in Seoul, who now had the King firmly in his grip, and the Min faction was again in control and able to slow down the country's rate of development.

YONG-HO CH'OE, 'The Kapsin Coup of 1884: A Reassessment,' *KS*, 6, 1982; HAROLD COOK, *Korea's 1884 Incident: Its Background and Kim Okkyun's Elusive Dream*, Seoul: Royal Asiatic Society Korean Branch, 1972; SHIN KI-SUK, 'International Relations with Respect to the Coup d'Etat of 1884,' *KJ*, 24/12, 1984; SHIN YONG-HA, 'The Coup d'Etat of 1884 and the Pukch'ŏng Army of the Progressive Party,' *KJ*, 33/2, 1993

See also **Independence Party**; **Min Yŏngik**

KARAK 駕洛 *See* **Kaya**

KASA 歌辭 'sung lyrics'
A form of long poem, intended to be sung, and designed for use with previously extant melodies. A *kasa* line consists of two groups of four syllables, and the lines are arranged in pairs that are mostly parallel couplets. There is no division into stanzas. The subject matter is commonly rural life and scenery, or loyalty to the king parabolised as the song of a faithful wife or lover. The tone is discursive, though often passionate, and there may be lists and Chinese literary allusions that resemble the Chinese *fu*. The literary form was perfected in the 16th and 17th centuries. Typical works are **Chŏng Ch'ŏl**'s *Kwandong-byŏlgok* (1580) about the Eight Views of the **Diamond Mountains**, and **Pak Illo**'s *T'aep'yŏng-sa*, a war poem about the Japanese invasion of 1592–3 (*see* **Imjin Wars**). In the 18th century, anonymous *kasa* by **women**

began to sing of daily life (comparable to the *sasŏl sijo*). There are also travel diaries of envoys to Tokyo and Beijing in *kasa* form.

PETER LEE, 'The *Songgang kasa* of Chŏng Ch'ŏl', *TP*, XLIX, 1961; PETER LEE, 'The *Kasa* Poems of Pak In-no', *OE*, X, 1963; DAVID McCANN, 'Between Literary and Folk: The Art of the Twelve Kasa Songs,' *KJ*, 14/9, 1974

KASA S. *kasaya* 袈裟 (Buddhist monk's formal robe)

For daily wear and travel a Buddhist monk wears old-fashioned peasant clothes (jacket and baggy trousers with leggings) made of grey cloth. For formal gatherings and worship he dons *changsam*, a long robe with very wide sleeves, also grey. Over the *changsam* he wears a *kasa* (S. *kasaya*), a rectangular toga-like garment made of dark brown cloth, draped over one shoulder – a stylised form of the monastic robe still worn in south-east Asia. It is constructed of a patchwork of twenty five pieces 'like tilled fields'. Old examples kept in some monasteries are made of rich and brilliant scraps. Married monks wear a red *kasa* (*see* **T'aego**). Novices wear a miniature square *kasa*, dating from Japanese colonial days and called *ojo-gasa*, made of five pieces of cloth hung round the neck and worn like a breastplate.

KAWI-BAWI-BO 'scissors, stone, cloth'

A universal game for settling precedence. Each player simultaneously thrusts one hand forward with the index and middle fingers spread (scissors), clenched fist (stone) or open palm (cloth). Scissors lose to stone (blunted), stone loses to cloth (wrapped) and cloth loses to scissors (cut).

KAYA 加耶

Early federation of six tribes established out of twelve Pyŏnhan tribes previously living to the south of Mount Kaya and the west of the Naktong River; also known as Karak. Most powerful were the Kuya tribe, later known as Pon ('Original') Kaya, and the Tae ('Great') Kaya. The date of its formation is generally thought to have been by the 1st century AD, and discoveries in a prehistoric cemetery at **Kimhae** suggest a possible date of two centuries earlier. A shell-mound pit also contained Chinese coins dating from the reign of Wang Mang (AD 9–23). In 1985 the location of more than one thousand **tombs** helped to identify Kimhae as the capital of Pon Kaya. Its **craftsmen** used gold and silver, and made grey **pottery**, stoneware, and **iron** products which were exported to China (via **Lelang**), the north-east (**Tongye**), and Japan. By the 5th century Kaya settlers had established **kilns** in Yamato. The flourishing trade across the straits has prompted disputes among modern Korean and Japanese historians over which people taught skills to which. The finding of pieces of Yamato **armour** in southern Korea has been taken to support the suggestion of the *Nihon Shoki* that Kaya was a colony of Yamato, but the Kaya region was a source of raw materials for the iron industry and produced armour of its own, and the evidence is far from conclusive. Moreover, the 'horse-rider theory' proposed by some archaeologists sees Kaya as the point of departure for continental conquerors of southern Japan.

Pon Kaya was destroyed by **Silla** in 532 and Tae Kaya in 562, giving Silla control of the Naktong river basin.

The name of the state is perpetuated to the present day in that of the *kayagŭm*, Korea's most famous native **musical instrument**.

J. RUSSELL KIRKLAND, 'The 'Horscriders' in Korea: a Critical Evaluation of a Historical Theory,' *KS*, 5, 1981

See also **Japan, relations with**; **Wa**

KAYAGŬM 加耶琴 'zither of Kaya'
Ancient **musical instrument** of Korea widely used to the present day. It is said to have been invented by King Kasil of **Kaya** on the model of the Chinese *zheng*, and to have been carried to **Silla** in 552 by his minister U Rŭk, fleeing his state's imminent annihilation. It is a half-tube zither, widely used in ensembles and to accompany song, and is the commonest instrument to play the distinctive sonata form, *sanjo*. It is thought of as having *yin* characteristics that complement the *yang* of the six-stringed *kŏmun'go*. It has twelve strings of twisted **silk** stretched over moveable bridges and tied at the bottom end in an elaborate knot. They are tuned differently for court and folk music, and are plucked with the right hand while the left twists and depresses them to the left of the bridges to create a wide range of effects. The instrument is widely regarded as the archetypal representation of traditional Korean culture. Performance traditions have been passed down orally by teacher to pupil to the present, thus preserving the best of earlier techniques and tunes, but in modern times musicologists have devised a transcription system for *kayagŭm* music which has encouraged the composition of new pieces for the instrument.
KEITH HOWARD, 'The Making of a Korean Musical Instrument', *PBAKS*, 5, 1994

KEIJŌ IMPERIAL UNIVERSITY *See* **Universities**

KHITAN, THE 契丹
Mongolian inhabitants of south-east **Manchuria** who were incorporated into the **Parhae** empire in the 7th century. Under the leadership of Yehlu Abaoji (872–926) they overthrew Parhae in 926 and established their own powerful **Liao** dynasty. Between 983 and 985 they conquered the **Jurchen** people along the **Yalu River**. Korean reaction showed anxiety at the new threat from the north. The fourth of **Wang Kŏn**'s influential **Ten Injunctions** said: 'Do not respect or imitate the Khitan: theirs is an animal kingdom; their habits and speech are different.' But contemporary polemics mask the fact that the sinicised Liao court had adopted many Chinese customs, and after its military superiority had been established over northern Korea in 994 and northern China by the Treaty of Shanyuan (1005), the multi-ethnic mix of Manchuria lived in tolerable racial harmony through much of the 11th century.
HERBERT FRANKE, 'The Forest Peoples of Manchuria: Kitans and Jurchens,' *in* DENIS SINOR, ed., *The Cambridge History of Early Inner Asia*, Cambridge University Press, 1990

KI, EMPRESS 奇皇后 (14th century)
A girl of Koryŏ, youngest daughter of Ki Chaö, was sent to the palace harem of Shundi, the last Yuan emperor. She attracted his attention and tried to become empress in 1335, but was foiled by the opposition of Mongol ministers. In 1339 she bore Shundi a son and was named secondary empress. Although she played a powerful and conspiratorial role in Yuan politics for nearly 30 years, while her father did much the same in Korea, she was not named Empress until 1365. Within two years she fled from Beijing before the approaching Ming forces and is believed to have disappeared into the Manchurian marches of Mongolia.

KIHO SCHOOL 畿湖學派 *See* **Kim Changsaeng**

KIHWA 己和 (1376–1433)
A Ch'ungju man who received a Confucian education, but became a Buddhist monk at the age of twenty. He spent some time at Hoeam-sa, studying under **Muhak**. He was a

devoted *Sŏn* practitioner and a distinguished teacher and writer, favoured by King Sejong. He strove to reconcile **Buddhism** with **Confucianism**.

KIJA CHOSŎN 箕子朝鮮

The second of the states traditionally said to have ruled ancient Korea. Kija (C. Jizi), 'Viscount of Ji', is mentioned in the *Book of Changes* (Hexagram 36) and reputed by the Chinese historian Sima Qian (145–c 86 BC, *Shiji* 3 and 4) to have been a virtuous man of the decadent kingdom of Shang who fled at the time of the Zhou conquest and reported to King Wu of Zhou. The *Hongfan* section of the classic *Book of Documents (see* **Confucian Classics**) purports to be the text of Jizi's report. Zhou became proverbial for good government, the historical fount of the Chinese empire. Jizi is nevertheless said to have remained conscientiously loyal to Shang, declined to remain in China under the Zhou, and moved to Korea. Modern Korean historians believe this is legendary. Kija's tomb at P'yŏngyang is thought to date from the beginning of the 12th century AD.
JAMES LEGGE, *Shoo King*, xxxxx, 1892, page 8 (The Texts of Confucianism Pt. 1. Sacred Books of the East III, Oxford: Clarendon Press, 1895)
See also **foundation myths; Old Chosŏn; Wiman Chosŏn**

KIL CHAE 吉再 (Yaŭn, 1353–1419)

One of the Samŭn, **'Three Recluses'** of the last years of Koryŏ. Born in Sŏnsan, north Kyŏngsang province, he was a friend of Yi Pangwŏn (later King T'aejong) from boyhood. After entering government service he was posted to the Confucian College in 1387. Two years later he retired, ostensibly for family reasons, but really because he foresaw the coming troubles in which the dynasty would end. He went back to Sŏnsan and taught local boys. After the change of dynasty, he accepted office in 1400, but quickly found his conscience uneasy, asserted his loyalty to the last Koryŏ king and returned home to the countryside. His students formed the beginning of a tradition in neo-Confucianism that produced, among others, **Cho Kwangjo**. The meaning of his brush name is 'Smelter Recluse'.

KILNS

In the late **Iron Age**, primitive open pit or trench kilns were superseded by climbing tunnel-kilns built up hillsides at an angle of about thirty degrees. Examples at Chinch'ŏn, North Ch'ungch'ŏng province, have been dated to the 4th century AD. The floor of the trench was covered in sand and the sides built up with clay or brick and roofed with thatch, allowing the smoke and hot air from the lower end of the kiln to rise and be put to good use rather than going to waste. Timber was inserted as fuel at the base and at points up the shaft of the tunnel where the fire could also be stoked. This achieved a breakthrough of the critical temperature level of 1000 degrees Celsius above which hard-fired stoneware is produced. Sloping kilns of this sort spread across the country from the south (*see* **Kimhae**) and became standard. In the Koryŏ period they were improved by the introduction of divisions along the tunnel, thus forming separate chambers with their own flues in which temperatures could be more easily controlled. A refinement in the Chosŏn dynasty arched the tunnel sections into domed chambers and allowed the conditions within to be monitored still more precisely. Use of various types of timber resulted in heavy carbon production and the loss of oxygen known as reduction firing. This was used by Koryŏ potters to make their distinctive green celadons and copper- and iron-oxide inlay of red and brown. The government kiln centre for the production of celadons in the Koryŏ dynasty was **Kangjin** in South Chŏlla, that for white porcelain in the early and mid-Chosŏn dynasty at **Kwangju**

(Kyŏnggi province). The potters employed there struggled on low pay to meet high official quotas for their products. Their occupation was hereditary and they were members of the *chungin* class, employed by the *Wa-sŏ* Office under the Board of Works. Widespread destruction of kilns occurred during the **Imjin Wars**, sometimes known as the 'Pottery Wars' because of the capture of so many potters by the Japanese, but the diffusion of skills by refugee **craftsmen** assisted in the subsequent spread of kilns into other rural areas. During the 18th century, economic and social changes permitted potters to develop private enterprise as an additional means of supplementing their income.

See also **celadon; ceramics; pottery**

KIM AN'GUK 金安國 (Mojae, 1478–1543)

A disciple of **Kim Koengp'il**, he adopted the brush name 'Longing for study' and served under Prince **Yŏnsan**, becoming governor of Kyŏngsang in 1517. He escaped the **literati purge** of 1519 because he was then living in Chŏlla, but retired to live in Ich'ŏn. Later he returned for another spell in office. An energetic neo-Confucian, he prepared and published *han'gŭl* versions of a number of Chinese books, including titles on **medicine**, **agriculture** and sericulture as well as classic texts and ethical treatises. His brother, Kim Chŏngguk (1485–1541), has a similar reputation.

KIM CHANGSAENG 金長生 (Sagye, 1548–1631)

A disciple of **Song Ikp'il** and **Yi I**, he is regarded as the father of the **Ritual Studies** school of neo-Confucianism. He qualified for office in 1578 and gave distinguished service during the Japanese invasion of 1592. In 1613 he escaped involvement in the Kyech'uk affair, when Queen Inmok and her son were persecuted (*see* **Kyech'ug-ilgi**), but he left office until the accession of King Injong in 1623. After a short break he was back in government at the **Manchu invasion** of 1627, during which he resisted opening peace negotiations. In 1628 he retired to study and write. His brush name Sagye means 'Sandy Valley'. Perhaps the most widely influential of his writings was *Karye chimnam*, 'Exposition of family rites', a commentary on **Zhu Xi**'s directions, especially for funerals and ancestral sacrifices (*see* **ancestral worship**), which were at that time perfunctorily performed by most Koreans. His son **Kim Chip** carried these studies further. They and like-thinking Westerners thus started what became known as the Kiho (Kyŏnggi-Ch'ungch'ŏng) school of Confucian thought, as opposed to the Yŏngnam (Kyŏngsang) school that stemmed from **Yi Hwang**'s tradition. Kim Changsaeng was canonised in 1717.

KIM CHE / SI 金禔 (Yangsongdang, 1524–93)

An artist who was highly regarded during his life time, and who held a senior post in the *Tohwa-sŏ*. Most of his work perished during the **Imjin Wars**, and he is best known today for his picture of a *Boy Pulling a Donkey* (Hoam Art Museum).[1] His surviving pictures show a suggestion of influence in the Chinese Zhe tradition (*see* **landscape painting**), interpreted in Korean style. This was continued by his grandson Kim Sik (1579–1662).

(1) CHOI SUNU, *5000 Years of Korean Art*, Seoul: Hyonam Publishing Co, 1979

KIM CHIP 金集 (Sindokchae, 1574–1656)

A son of **Kim Changsaeng** who carried on and developed his father's **ritual studies**. Graduating at 17 in 1591, he entered government service, but retired in 1610 to avoid the turmoils of Prince **Kwanghae**'s rule. His brush name means 'Careful Solitary Study'.

When Kwanghae was replaced by Injo in 1623, Kim returned to office, but retired again when the Meritorious Westerners' **faction** attained power. Hyojong's accession in 1649 brought the Clear Westerners to power, and Kim returned to government. He was forced to retire once more when he argued against attacking the Manchus, but came back yet again and died in office. Discussions about his canonisation began in 1759, but did not end until 1883. He was the last Korean to be canonised.

KIM CHŎNGHO 金正浩 (d. 1864)
Born in Hwanghae but reared in Seoul, he managed to be well educated despite an impecunious family background. After thirty years travelling throughout the land he produced a remarkable map of Korea, called *Ch'ŏnggu-do* 'Map of the Green Hills' (*see* **Korea, names for**), in 1834. Dissatisfied with it, he spent the next 25 years in further perambulations before bringing out a revision, *Taedong yŏji-do*, in 1861. He presented a copy to the Hŭngsŏn **Taewŏn-gun**, and was imprisoned for having revealed too much to Korea's enemies. He is said to have died in prison, but in truth almost the whole of his biography is a matter of aural tradition. The quality of his **cartography** gives him his historical stature. His maps were not printed, but circulated as hand-drawn copies.

KIM CHŎNGHŬI 金正喜 (Ch'usa; Wandang, 1786–1856)
One of the greatest painters and calligraphers of the late Chosŏn period, renowned as a scholar-aesthete of outstanding taste. His influence on art at the end of the 19th century was profound. He himself was influenced by the work of 18th century Chinese calligraphers which he had seen on a mission to Beijing in 1809. He practised varied styles of **calligraphy**, but showed especially his admiration for the contrasting forceful strokework of early Chinese epigraphy in clerical style (*ye*) and the vitality of grass script (*ch'ŏ*). He entered the civil service by examination in the **Confucian Classics**. His painting shows the Wu School tendency of the scholar to individual self-expression, or even to the minimalist *Sŏn* tradition of sparse but tightly controlled brushwork. This is seen in his most famous painting, *Orchid*,[1] in which the simplicity of the single bloom blends in perfection with the calligraphic inscriptions that surround it. His most productive period as an artist, amply demonstrating his individuality, came during the last ten years of his life which were spent in exile on the southern island of **Cheju**.

(1) CHOI SUNU, *5000 Years of Korean Art*, Seoul: Hyonam Publishing Co., 1979
CHUN HAE-JONG, 'Kim, Chŏng-hŭi – Master Calligrapher and Epigraphist,' *KJ*, 13/4, 1973;
CH'OE WAN-SU, 'A Study of Kim Ch'ŏng-hŭi,' *KJ*, 26/11, 1986

KIM CHŎNGIL 金正 (b.1942 (?1941))
Succeeded his father, **Kim Ilsŏng**, as 'Dear Leader' (*Kyŏngaehanŭn chido tongji*) of the **Democratic People's Republic of Korea** (North Korea) in July 1994. Although he had long been groomed as the successor, he did not at first take either of his father's formal rôles as president of the state or as secretary-general of the **Korean Workers' Party** (KWP). His only formal title was commander-in-chief of the armed forces. His supremacy was confirmed on 5 September 1998, when his re-election as chairman of the National Defence Commission indicated that this was the highest office of state.

According to North Korean accounts, his birth took place in an anti-Japanese guerilla camp on **Paektu-san**, the sacred mountain on the Sino-Korean border, on 15 February 1942, sixty days before his father's 30th birthday. In reality, he was probably born less auspiciously in 1941 in the Soviet Union, where his father lived from 1941 to

1945. During the **Korean War** he was sent to north-east China for safety. He was educated at an East German pilots' college and at Kim Il Sŏng University in P'yŏngyang, graduating in 1964. He then worked in the secretariat of the KWP, eventually becoming his father's secretary and assisting him in the 1967 purges. In 1973, he became party secretary in charge of organisation and propaganda; from then until he was formally acknowledged as his father's successor in 1980 he was not named, but referred to as 'the party centre'. In February 1974 he was elected to the Politburo; North Korean accounts say that at this time he was selected to succeed his father.

South Korean sources have tended to demonize him as a hard-drinking playboy and often attribute to him some of the more aggressive policies followed by North Korea since the 1970s. In fact, not a great deal is known about his rôle or his abilities, apart from a well-established interest in films and film-making. After his father's death, he spent much time with the military, leading to speculation that he was dependent on them for support. He continued to promote his father's proposals for Korean reunification, and remained equally hostile to better relations with South Korea.

TAI-SUNG AN, *North Korea in Transition, from Dictatorship to Dynasty*, Westport, Conn. & London: Greenwood Press, 1983; KIM JŎNG IL, *On the Juche Idea*, Pyŏngyang: Foreign Languages Publishing House, 1989

KIM CHONGJIK 金宗直 (1431–92)

Born at Miryang in south Kyŏngsang, he was educated in the tradition of **Kil Chae**, a strict neo-Confucian, loyal to *sŏngni-hak*, but even more deeply attached to the moral principles of loyalty and filial piety. He became the forefather of the *sallim*, 'forest and mountain scholars' of scrupulous morality who were opposed to the **meritorious subject** groups. As chief royal lecturer (*kyŏngyŏn*) to the young King **Sŏngjong**, who was equally devoted to the same Confucian principles, he encouraged the promotion of men of his own school and province to high office in the **censorate** and royal lectureships. *Muo-sahwa* was a reaction after his death, in the course of which his body was exhumed and dishonoured. He took part in work on *Tongguk yŏji-sŭngnam* and was a renowned calligrapher and painter.

KIM CHŎNGP'IL 金鐘泌 (b. 1926)

Was born in South Ch'ungch'ŏng province on 7 January 1926. He attended Seoul National University, but dropped out and joined the Korean Military Academy in 1948. He was linked by marriage to Park Chung Hee (**Pak Chonghŭi**), and was one of the chief architects of the 1961 coup (*see* **Military junta**). He organised and became the first head of the **Korean Central Intelligence Agency** (KCIA), helped found Park's **Democratic Republican Party** (DLP), and was its chairman from 1964 to 1968. He was prime minister from 1971 to 1975. Elected president of the DLP in November 1979 after Park's assassination, he and his brother were among those purged in 1981 by **Chŏn Tuhwan** (Chun Doo Hwan). From 1984 to 1986 he lived in the United States, returning in 1986 when the political ban was lifted. He then formed the New Democratic Liberal Party, and was its presidential candidate in the 1987 elections. He did not do very well, but his political rehabilitation was complete, and the party did better in subsequent local and national elections. In a deal with **No Taeu** (Roh Tae Woo) and **Kim Yŏngsam** (Kim Young Sam), he joined the ruling **Democratic Liberal Party**, becoming co-leader in May 1990, and then chairman, in an arrangement which allowed Kim Yŏngsam to become the party's presidential candidate. However, Kim Yŏngsam ousted him, and Kim Chŏngp'il formed the United Liberal Democrats, based on his home province. The party did reasonably well in the 1996 general election, and in 1997 Kim joined the veteran opposition leader – and his own old opponent under Park – **Kim Taejung**, in the latter's successful bid for the presidency. His reward was a return to the premiership when Kim Taejung assumed office in February 1998.

KIM CHUN'GŬN 金俊根 (Kisan; 2nd half, 19th century)
A late 19th-century *genre* artist whose sketches of daily life were used by several foreigners as book illustrations, including **Gale** (*Pilgrim's Progress* in Korean, 1893) W. R. Carles (*Life in Corea*, 1888), and Stewart Culin (*Korean Games*, 1895). The Korea Foundation's *Korean Relics in Western Europe* (*Yurŏp pangmulgwan sojang*, Han'guk munhwajae, [1992]) lists over 800 drawings attributed to Kisan in museums throughout the world. Nothing is known of his life except that in 1886 and 1895 he was reported as living at Ch'oryang near **Pusan**, and that he went to Wŏnsan in 1890.

KIM CH'UNCH'U 金春秋 (d. 661)
Member of the **Silla** aristocracy who achieved prominence as a travelling diplomat. In 642 he was sent to try and persuade Yŏn Kaesomun of **Koguryŏ** to break his alliance with **Paekche** and side with Silla instead. Yŏn's terms proved too high, and Kim was threatened with being kept hostage until rescued by a military force headed by his brother-in-law **Kim Yusin**. Undeterred by personal risk, he crossed the sea to Yamato in 647, and in 648 went to China to seek aid from Emperor Tang Taizong. This time his plea was heard, but remained unanswered because of Taizong's death in 649. In 650 his son, Pŏmmin, was sent to reiterate the request to the new Emperor Gaozong. Ch'unch'u was second cousin of Queen Chindŏk, and when she died childless in 654, he took the throne and was later known as King **Muyŏl**. Following further Paekche attacks on Silla in 655 a Chinese force was despatched in 660.
See also **Tang dynasty**

KIM HŎNCH'ANG 金憲昌 (d. 822)
Son of Kim Chuwŏn, whose rightful claim to the Silla throne on the death of **Sŏndŏk** in 785 had been set aside by Wŏnsŏng. Hŏnch'ang nursed his grievance. In 822, at a time of famine, the south-west had been called on to send a large army to China. Hŏnch'ang, governor of Ungju (modern **Kongju**), raised a rebellion and proclaimed a new state (called Changan), which for a time won support over a wide area of southern and central Korea. When it was suppressed he committed suicide.

KIM HONGDO 金弘道 (Tanwŏn, 1745–post-1814)
Perhaps the best known and loved of all painters in Korea. He was a pupil of **Kang Sehwang**, on whose recommendation he became a member of the *Tohwa-sŏ*. A successful portrait of King **Chŏngjo** gained him an official post as a county magistrate, where he came into contact with ordinary people whose daily activities inspired the *genre* **paintings** that comprise some of his greatest work. In particular, his series of album leaves showing boys in a schoolroom, onlookers watching a wrestling match, and a dancer gyrating to the tunes of a band of musicians[1], all demonstrate his sense of compositional balance and fine brushwork. They and other scenes from the lives of ordinary people performing everyday tasks, such as a roofer re-tiling a house[2] or a farmer ploughing a field[3], reveal a surprising interest for a *yangban* in the work of the lower classes.

But Kim Hongdo's greatness is not dependent on his *genre* paintings alone, and is reflected in his eclecticism. He painted the Daoist **Immortals** on screens and album leaves, Buddhist figures on altars, official Confucianist receptions (for example *Festival at Manwŏltae* (1804)[4], **flower and bird** studies, and superb **landscapes**. He could paint in both Northern- and Southern-School Chinese manner, but like **Chŏng Sŏn** and as a true Korean scholar of the *Sirhak* persuasion he preferred to depict actual scenes from the Korean mountains in his own native style, and the court gave him commissions to do so.

(1) ROGER GOEPPER & RODERICK WHITFIELD, *Treasures from Korea*, London: British Museum Publications, 1984

(2)(3) KEITH PRATT, *Korean Painting*, Hong Kong: Oxford University Press, 1995

(4) CHOI SUNU, *5000 Years of Korean Art*, Seoul: Hyonam Publishing Co., 1979

KUMJA PAIK KIM, 'A Yi Dynasty Court Painter, Kim Hong-do (1745– before 1818): Seen through the *Tanwŏn yumuk* and his Landscape Paintings,' *OA*, XXXII/1, 1986

KIM HONGJIP 金弘集 (1842–96)

Reformist minister sent to Japan by King **Kojong** in 1880. He returned convinced by the arguments of the Chinese minister in Tokyo, He Ruzhang, and the counsellor, Huang Zunxian, that in the interests of modernisation Korea should develop alliances with China and Japan, and with the United States as a counter-balance to the rising force of Russia. After the Japanese occupation of the **Kyŏngbŏk Palace** on 23 July 1894 he was put in charge of the new Advisory Council formed at Japanese insistence to repudiate Chinese claims to suzerainty over Korea and to implement the so-called *Kabo* **reforms**. In December the Advisory Council was superseded by the *Chungch'u-wŏn* Privy Council. In January 1895 the king swore to his ancestors to uphold Korean independence. Kim took charge of the newly named cabinet (*naegak*) which succeeded the Council of State. Following the murder of **Queen Min** in October 1895 he became prime minister of another new cabinet, and being convinced of the need for continuing reform defied the prevailing anti-Japanese mood by introducing a further round of reforms in December. These included the order that men should cut off their **topknots** (*sangt'u*). In the resulting pandemonium King Kojong took refuge in the Russian embassy (see **Russia, relations with**). There he ordered the arrest of the pro-Japanese ministers, but Kim was assassinated by an angry mob before this could be carried out.

KIM HŬMCH'UN 金欽春 (7th century AD)

Also known as Kim Hŭmsun. According to *Samguk sagi* he was a **Silla** man of noble birth, who was a *hwarang* in his youth. Some thirty years later, he became chief minister to **King Munmu** (r. 661–681). In 660 he went with **Kim Yusin** to assist the Tang army against **Paekche**. At the battle of Hwangsan he encouraged his son Pan'gul to go into the thick of the fighting, where Pan'gul was killed. Hŭmch'un went on to fight for Silla against **Koguryŏ** and to visit China as a diplomat in 669.

KIM HWAN'GI (Kim Whan Ki) 金煥基 (Suhwa, 1913–74)

Leading Korean experimenter with abstract art. He was educated and received his artistic training in Japan, where he became familiar with the works of western expressionism and cubism. His best known painting, *Rondo* (1938; National Museum for Contemporary Art, Seoul),[1] reflects his admiration for Picasso at this time. But neither Japanese nor western influences could diminish his sense of Korean identity. He returned to Korea in 1937 and after the war worked hard to promote art through exhibitions and in education. In the 1950s he developed an individual style for portraying well-loved Korean themes based on circles, straight and curved lines, and dots. If *Rondo* had indicated an attraction to the West in the 1930s, the titles of his later

works, such as *Moonlight in summer*, *Mountain moon*, and *Pine with crane*, show the depth of his native cultural roots. He spent his later years in New York, where he died.
(1) YOUNG ICK LEW, ed., *Korean Art Tradition*, Seoul: Korea Foundation, 1993
OH KWANG-SU, 'The Art of Kim Whanki and the Whanki Museum,' *Koreana*, VII/4, 1993
See also **Pak Sŏbo**

KIM ILSŎNG 金日成 (1912–94)

Kim Sŏngju was born near P'yŏngyang in 1912 and taken by his parents to **Manchuria** in 1925. There he joined the **Korean Communist Party** in 1931, took part in guerilla actions against the Japanese, and later claimed he had founded a **Korean People's Revolutionary Army** and served in the remote Kapsan area of the Changbaek Mountains. He attracted Russian notice and was taken to Russia for training, during which he adopted the name of a legendary anti-Japanese guerila, Kim Ilsŏng. During World War II he commanded a Korean contingent in the Red Army. In 1945 he was sent back to Korea to establish a provisional government in the Russian sector, becoming first premier of the **Democratic People's Republic of Korea** in 1948. With Russian support, he invaded the South in 1950, but failed in his attempt to reunify the country. In 1953 the border between North and South was left much as it had been in 1945, and Kim, having eliminated all rivals in his Communist Party, became absolute ruler of the North, fostering a lavish personality cult for himself. In 1972 he was elected president and in 1980 he named his son **Kim Chŏngil** as his political heir. In September 1998 the Supreme People's Assembly abolished the political office of president and bestowed the title upon Kim Ilsŏng in perpetuity.
LIM UM (pseud.), *The Founding of a Dynasty in North Korea: An Authentic Biography of Kim Il-sung*, Tokyo: Jiyūsha, 1982; SUH DAE-SOOK, *Kim Il Sung: the North Korean Leader*, New York: Columbia University Press, 1988
See also **Korean War; Korean Workers' Party**

KIM INHU 金麟厚 (Hasŏ, 1510–60)

A disciple of **Kim An'guk**, he studied together with **Yi Hwang** at the *Sŏnggyun-gwan*, entering government service in 1540. In the **literati purge** of 1545 he retired to study neo-Confucian philosophy in the country at Changsŏng. He declined government appointments several times, but took an active part in the debate about *i* and *ki*. He was also interested in practical matters: **astronomy**, geography, **medicine** and calendrical science. His brush name means 'West of the River'. He was canonised in 1796.

KIM KOENGP'IL 金宏弼 (Hanhwŏn-dang, 1454–1504)

Born in Seoul, he became a disciple of **Kim Chongjik** and a keen promoter of the neo-Confucian philosophical tradition, especially expert in the compendium known as *Sohak* 'lesser learning'. His brush name means 'Cold and warm hall'. He qualified early but did not take government office until he was forty, only to be exiled during the **literati purge** of 1498 to Hŭich'ŏn near the northern border, then to Sunch'ŏn in the far southwest. At the age of fifty he was executed by **poison** during the purge of 1504. **Cho Kwangjo** and **Kim An'guk** were his disciples. He was one of the five canonised in 1610.

KIM KU 金九 (Paekpŏm, 1876–1949)

A leader of the Independence Movement, born in Haeju, where after the usual study of Chinese letters, he joined the **Tonghak** at 17 and played a leading rôle in the uprising at Haeju. To escape the Japanese he fled to **Manchuria**, where he joined the volunteer army that raided Kanggye. In 1896 he returned home intending to avenge the death of **Queen Min**, and shot (some sources say strangled) a Japanese army lieutenant in a wine shop near Anak in Hwanghae. He was tried and his death sentence was commuted to imprisonment. On release in 1898 he spent a year as a Buddhist monk at Magok-sa near Kongju. Returning home he worked as a school teacher at Anak, becoming a Protestant Christian in 1903. He was implicated in the murder of Prince **Itō Hirobumi** by **An Chŭnggŭn** in 1909 and in 1911 imprisoned after the *Paego-in* affair (*see* **Hundred and Five, Case of the**). On release in 1914 he devoted himself to the agricultural enlightenment movement until the **Declaration of Independence** demonstration of 1919, after which he fled to Shanghai and helped to found the **Provisional Government in Exile** (PGE). After forming a party of his own in 1922 (an association of Korean workers and soldiers) he became leader of the PGE in 1926. He later took to terrorism and provided bombs in 1932 for **Yun Ponggil** in Kongkou Park and **Yi Pongch'ang** in Tokyo, and then had to flee to Jiaxing in northern Zhejiang. In 1933 he met Jiang Jieshi (Chiang Kai-shek) at Nanjing and established a Korean section in the Guomindang military academy. He was by now a right-wing leader among Koreans and in 1935 founded the *Han'guk Kongmindang* on Jiang's model. In 1940 he organised the move of the PGE from Shanghai to Zhongqing, and in 1944 became its chairman. In 1945 he returned to Korea and was active on the outer right, but the American authorities favoured Syngman Rhee (**Yi Sŭngman**)'s claim to lead the nation. In 1948 Kim went to P'yŏngyang for fruitless talks about unification of the north and south. When the ROK government was established, he remained out of office as leader of the centre right. In 1949 he was shot in his home by Lieutenant An Tuhŭi, doubtless in the service of Yi Sŭngman. This act was avenged nearly fifty years later, when An was shot in his own home in 1996.

KIM KU 金緱 (1488–1534)
One of the **Four Great Calligraphers**. He was involved in the *Kimyo sahwa* with **Cho Kwangjo** and exiled to Namhae. Later allowed home to Yesan, he died there of an illness.

KIM KU 金玖 (711–91) *See* **Kim Saeng**

KIM KYUJIN 金奎鎮 (Haegang, 1868–1933)
A famous calligrapher and painter of orchid and **bamboo**. He was also skilled in **landscape** and **flower and bird** painting. He began studying **calligraphy** at the age of 6/7, and went to China at the age of 15/16, staying there for ten years studying antiquities and calligraphy. He contributed much to the development of the arts in Korea through exhibitions. He is reported to have been one of the first Koreans to be interested in fine photography, which he studied in Japan about 1895. He was appointed a teacher of the Crown Prince and is said to have been the first official court photographer. His brush name means 'sea ridge'.

KIM KYUSIK 金奎植 (1881–1950)
Was raised as an orphan by the American missionary **Horace Underwood**. After going to the United States and completing his higher education at Princeton University he returned to teach in Korea in 1905, but was exiled to China in 1913. He subsequently moved to Paris, and was there when the Shanghai **Provisional Government in Exile** nominated him as foreign minister in 1919 and ordered him to

the **Paris Peace Conference** to present the Korean case for independence. Thereafter he was sent to Washington as director of the newly opened Korean Commission. This was closed in 1923 because of Kim's left-wing affiliations and he returned to Shanghai, where he struggled to hold together a united front between those of more extreme views. A moderate nationalist, he helped to found the **Korean National Revolutionary Party** in 1935. He returned to Korea from China in November 1945, as vice-president of **Kim Ku**'s Provisional Government in Exile, and was nominated to a cabinet place in the **Korean People's Republic** (KPR), but as a political neutral he was suspicious of its left-wing inclinations and refused it. Unlike the right-wing Syngman Rhee (**Yi Sŭngman**) he found it possible to work with General **Hodge**. After the suspension of the KPR he accepted the chairmanship of the South Korean Interim Legislative Assembly and held it from December 1946 until March 1948, when he resigned over the **United Nations**' declaration of elections in South Korea. He and Kim Ku were united in pledging the need for north-south unification, and approached **Kim Ilsŏng** about the formation of a national government. Both took part in the resulting conference in P'yŏngyang in April 1948, and returned convinced of the sincerity of Kim Ilsŏng's plans for reunification and opposed to separate elections. But they were betrayed: on 1 May the P'yŏngyang Supreme People's Assembly unilaterally adopted a 'national' **constitution**, and soon afterwards North Korea cut off electricity supplies to the South. Kim Kyusik was forced to accept the inevitability of the United Nations plan.

See also **An Chaehong; Pak Hŏnyŏng; Yŏ Unhyŏng**

KIM MANJUNG 金萬重 *See Kuunmong*

KIM OKKYUN 金玉均 (1851–94)

Born in Kongju as a scion of the powerful Andong Kim clan. He entered government service at the age of twenty and soon grew discouraged by the politics of the time and the misery of the country. He was first identified as an advocate of reform in the mid-1870s, and was sent to Japan by King **Kojong** in 1881 to study its modernisation. On his return he was given a post in the reshaped government of 1882 and promptly sent as an adviser to **Pak Yŏnghyo** on his voyage of observation to Japan later that year. Kim tried to obtain Japanese help for his modernisation dreams, but was only partially successful. The immediate fruits of the trip were the establishment of a postal service and the publication of the *Hansŏng Sunbo*. In 1883 he made a third trip, but on that occasion his objective of obtaining a Japanese loan of three million yen was unsuccessful. He was impressed by the Japanese moderniser Fukuzawa Yukichi, who despatched technical advisers to Korea, and in his enthusiasm for modernisation Kim is accused by modern Korean historians of being disingenuous in failing to see the true nature of Japanese intentions towards his country. He became a leader of the *Kaehwadang* (see **Independence Party**), and was one of the plotters who carried out the *Kapsin* **coup** in December 1884. He afterwards fled to Japan, where he spent ten years, continuing to urge Japanese support for change in Korea. In 1894 he was inveigled into visiting Shanghai, where he was assassinated by Hong Chongu for the conservative faction. His body was returned to Korea, where it was divided and the parts sent to the eight provinces as a grisly warning to traitors. His reputation was reinstated in 1910.

HAROLD F. COOK, *Korea's 1884 Incident: its Background and Kim Okkyun's Elusive Dream*, Seoul: Taewon, 1972; ANDREW NAHM, 'Kim, Ok-kyun and the Reform Movement of the Progressives,' *KJ*, 24/12, 1984

KIM PŎMU 金範禹 (d. 1787)
A translator of Chinese in the *Sayŏg-wŏn*, who joined **Yi Pyŏk**'s students of Catholicism at Kwangju about 1784. They met at Kim Pŏmu's house in Seoul on the plot where the **Myŏngdong Cathedral** now stands, and were discovered at prayer there by the authorities. The names of the *yangban* in the group were not published, but the *chungin* Kim was exiled to Tanyang in north Ch'ungch'ŏng province. On the way there he died of injuries he had sustained when he was questioned, and so is reckoned the first of the **martyrs**. From that time onwards Catholicism was proscribed.

KIM SAENG 金生 (Chiso, 711–91)
Also known as Kim Ku, noted as a calligrapher in the *ye*, *ch'o*, and *haeng* styles (*see* **calligraphy**). No original examples of his work survive. A stele preserved in the **Kyŏngbŏk Palace** bears an inscription carved in the style of his running script. It was dedicated by Tamnok to his fellow monk Nanggong in 954.

KIM SATKAT (SAKKAT) 金笠 (Kim Nip, 1807–63)
Both Korean and Chinese forms of his given name mean 'a mourner's wide reed hat'. His real name was Kim Pyŏngnyŏn. Born of a disgraced and impoverished family in Hamgyŏng-do, he married and had two sons, but from the age of twenty adopted the *satkat* and took to the roads as a vagabond, often composing poems to earn his supper and night's lodging. He died at Tongbok in Chŏlla-do. His eccentric poetry and witticisms, collected during the 1930s by Yi Ŭngsu, may include folk material that has become attributed to Kim Satkat. He shows delight in scenery and compassion for unfortunates, but much of his output, full of lexical virtuosity and metrical skill, is word-play in which Chinese characters have to be read as Korean puns, creating earthy fun and grotesque insults. The general effect is of bohemian nihilism, which has made him hugely popular, but is more interesting as folk humour than as literature.
RICHARD RUTT, 'Kim Sakkat: vagabond poet', *TKBRAS*, XLI, 1964

KIM SISŬP 金時習 *See **Kŭmo Sinhwa***

KIM SŎKSIN 金碩臣 (Ch'owŏn, 1758–?)
Professional artist employed in the ***Tohwa-sŏ***; nephew of the court landscape artist Kim Ŭnghwan (1742–89) and younger brother of **Kim Tŭksin**. The influence of **Chŏng Sŏn** can be seen in his *Mount Tobong*[1], especially in the use of black ink wash emphasising heavy rock formations, horizontal axe-cut strokes for the mountain-top vegetation and treetops, and sharp angular lines depicting the distant peaks of the **Diamond Mountains**. The two boatloads of musicians being poled past the rocky outcrop in *Pipes and Drums in Mid-stream* are more detailed[2], but the brushwork of this picture shows the same distinctive characteristics.
(1) R.GOEPPER & R.WHITFIELD, eds., *Treasures from Korea*, London: British Museum, 1984
(2) CHOI SUNU, *5000 Years of Korean Art*, Seoul: Hyonam Publishing Co., 1979

KIM SŎNGSU 金性洙 (1891–1955)
A prominent industrialist and political figure during the first half of the 20th century. He was born into the rich landowning Kim clan of Koch'ang county, North Chŏlla province, and whilst admiring the spirit of the Meiji era he resented Japanese exploitation of his country during the **Protectorate**. After six years' study in Japan he returned to Korea, where he supported the **March First Movement** in 1919 and was an opponent of the Japanese colonial rule. He used his wealth to invest in educational

ventures, including Kobu (Chŏlla) School and Posŏng College (later Korea University), and the *Tonga Ilbo* newspaper, which he helped to found in 1920 and which had a history of outspoken criticism against the colonial authorities. However, Kim's principal venture was the formation of the Kyŏngsŏng Spinning and Weaving Company (*Kyŏngbang*) in 1919, which developed as a major cooperative Korean-Japanese business conglomerate, the first *chaebŏl*. The company's collaboration with the Japanese authorities, adherence to their manufacturing and export policies, pursuit of profit, and treatment of its Korean workforce have been severely criticised.

After liberation in 1945, Kim was one of the leaders nominated to **Yŏ Unhyŏng**'s **Korean People's Republic**. He was a leading figure in the formation of the **Korea Democratic Party** (*Han'guk Minjudang*), and was nominated by General John **Hodge** as head of the Democratic Advisory Council to work with the **American Military Government** in Korea. In 1949 he became a leader of the **Democratic Nationalist Party**. As a leading opposition figure under the Republic of Korea he was Vice-President under Syngman Rhee (**Yi Sŭngman**) in 1951–2.

CARTER J. ECKERT, *Offspring of Empire: The Koch'ang Kims and the Colonial Origins of Korean Capitalism 1876–1945*, Seattle: University of Washington Press, 1991, KIM CHOONG-SOON, *A Korean Nationalist Entrepreneur: A Life History of Kim Songsu, 1891–1955*, New York: SUNY Press, 1998

KIM SOWŎL 金素月 (1903–1934)

Real name Kim Chŏngsik. The most popular lyric poet of the 20th century. He was born of well-to-do farming stock at Kusŏng in the far north-east, and educated at the famous **Osan School**, where he was taught by Kim Ŏk (1893–?1950). His first published poem, *Chindallae-kkot* (Azaleas), appeared in the **literary magazine** *Kaehyŏk* in 1921. The rest of his poems were written before he was twenty-two. He failed to enter commercial college in Tokyo and returned home to his beloved wife in 1924. Various business efforts failed and he struggled along as a local reporter for the newspaper *Tonga Ilbo* until he killed himself with opium in 1934. His verses, many of them with a folk-song quality, have a deceptive simplicity of diction and a striking limpidity of image.

KIM SUCH'ŎL 金秀哲 (Puksan, 19th c.)

Painter who studied under **Kim Chŏnghŭi** and is best known for his landscapes and flower paintings. In the manner of Southern School artists he allowed his work to express his personality, and his brushwork was bold and uninhibited. He made expressive use of ink wash, with strikingly contrasting areas of light and shade, and enhanced his colours with gold and silver leaf.

KIM SUHANG 金壽恒 (Mun'gok, 1629–89)

A distinguished writer (his brush-name means 'literary vale') and minister of the pro-Ming Western **faction** who became a member of the **Noron**. The highest point of a career much interrupted by factional dispute and exile was his appointment as *Yŏngŭijŏng* in 1680. He sided with **Song Siyŏl** in the disputes about the **Dowager Queen's mourning** duties in 1660 and 1674. His career and his life ended in 1689 when he and Song Siyŏl failed in the dispute over the appointment of the Crown Prince. The Southerners took power. Song and Kim were both ordered to drink **poison**. He had six famous sons:

1) Ch'angjip (1642–1722). Brush-name Mongwa, 'dream hut'. *Yŏngŭijŏng* 1717. Executed during the *sahwa* of 1722.

2) Ch'anghyŏp (1651–1708). Brush-name Nongam, 'farmer rock'. Retired from political service in disgust.
3) Ch'anghŭp (1653–1722). Brush-name Samyŏn, 'three pools'. The least distinguished of the six, but a competent poet.
4) Ch'angŏp (1658–1721) Brush-name Noga-jae, 'old farmer studio'. Spent his life on his country estate. Wrote a Beijing travel diary *Kajae Yŏnhaeng-nok*.
5) Ch'angjŭp (1662–1713). Brush-name P'oŭm, 'vegetable-garden shade'. A life-long scholar.
6) Ch'angnip (1666–1683). Brush-name **T'aekchae**, 'favoured studio'. A remarkable teenage poet.

KIM TAEGŎN, SAINT ANDREW 金大建 (1822–46)

The first Korean Catholic priest and most venerated of the **martyrs**. Born near Tangjin in south Ch'ungch'ŏng, he was chosen by Fr **Maubant** as a candidate for priesthood and sent in 1836 to study in Macao, whence he twice had to take refuge in Manila from local disturbances. In 1842, after serving as interpreter to the French admiral **Cécille**, he entered Korea across the frozen **Yalu**, but was unable to reach Seoul and withdrew to Bajiazi in **Manchuria**, where his bishop, **Ferréol**, was living. After another abortive attempt to enter Korea across the Yalu in 1843, Andrew reached Seoul at his third attempt in 1845. Hoping to open contact with China by sea, he bought a small boat at **Chemulp'o** and with an amateur crew in dangerous storms, reached Shanghai, where a British consul helped him and he met Bishop Ferréol and Fr **Daveluy**. He was ordained priest on 17 August. In October 1845 he and the two Frenchmen entered Korea by sea, landing at Kanggyŏng. Next summer he went by sea to contact the Chinese boats that came every spring to fishing grounds off Hwanghae, and was arrested at Sunwi Island, near Ongjin, on 14 June. Showing great courage throughout his trials and tortures, he was executed at Seoul on 16 September 1846, aged 24, a priest of one year.

KIM TAEGONG 金大恭 (d. c.771)

Initiator of a power struggle against the rule of King Hyegong in AD 768. It lasted three years and was unsuccessful, but it seriously weakened the authority of the royal line of descent through King **Muyŏl** (654–661). Beginning with Sŏndŏk (780–5), Hyegong's successors claimed *their* descent from King Naemul (356–402) through a different lineage.

KIM TAEJUNG 金大中 (b. 1924)

Leading South Korean politician, long known for his opposition to successive presidents from Syngman Rhee (**Yi Sŭngman**) to **Kim Yŏngsam**. Taejung was elected president in December 1997, at his fourth attempt. He was born in South Chŏlla province on 6 January 1924. He graduated from high school in 1943, and became a clerk in a Japanese-owned company in the shipping port of Mokp'o. At the end of the war in 1945 he took over the company, and was also associated with a local newspaper. During the **Korean War**, he was captured by North Korean forces and sentenced to death, but escaped. After several attempts, he entered the National Assembly in 1960 as an opposition member. In 1971, he was the **New Democratic Party**'s candidate against President Park Chung Hee (**Pak Chŏnghŭi**) in the presidential election, losing by a narrow margin. From then on, he became a bitter critic of Park, alleging in particular that he used the 'threat from the North' to justify repression in South Korea. Park's government regarded him as one of its most dangerous opponents, and during a visit to Japan in 1973, he was kidnapped by agents of the **Korean Central Intelligence Agency** (KCIA) and brought back to Seoul. Kim claimed that the KCIA intended to kill him, but that he was saved by US intervention. In the next six years, he remained a stringent critic of Park, frequently arrested for anti-government activities. After Chun Doo Hwan (**Chŏn Tuhwan**) seized power in 1979, Kim was again arrested. Although in jail, he was accused of responsibility for the **Kwangju Massacre** in May 1980, and sentenced to death after a court martial. Government sources also implied that he was a communist, and sympathetic to North Korea. This last accusation was based on alleged similarities between Kim's proposals on reunification and those from the North. Following US pressure, the sentence was commuted, first to life imprisonment and later to twenty years. In December 1982, he was permitted to go to the US for medical treatment. He spent two years studying, speaking and writing, until he was allowed to return to South Korea in February 1985. In theory still banned from politics and under house arrest, in reality he was very much involved, with Kim Yŏngsam, first as an adviser to the Council for the Promotion for Democracy, and later as a member of the Reunification Democratic Party. He and Kim Yŏngsam fell out over the 1987 presidential election. Both stood, allowing the ruling party candidate, Roh Tae Woo (**No Taeu**), to win. In the 1992 presidential election, Taejung lost again, this time to Kim Yŏngsam, who had in the meantime thrown in his lot with Roh and the ruling party. Kim then announced his retirement from politics, and spent some time in Britain.

On his return to Seoul, however, he resumed his political career, founding the National Council for New Politics. In 1997, he joined another veteran political leader, **Kim Chŏngp'il**, to fight the presidential election. The ruling party split, and Taejung won by a tiny margin. Despite this, his victory had great symbolic significance, since it marked the first time that power had passed out of the hands of the government party since 1948. Athough some conservative South Koreans claimed that the North would welcome Kim Taejung as president, the first reactions from P'yŏngyang were cautious. Kim, for his part, began his presidency having to cope with the most serious economic and financial crisis ever experienced in South Korea.

KIM DAE JUNG, *Building Peace and Democracy: Philosophy and Dialogues*, New York: Korean Independent Monitor, 1987; KIM DAE JUNG, trans. Choi Sung'il and David McCann, *Prison Writings*, Berkeley: University of California Press, 1987

KIM TAESŎNG 金大城 *See* **Pulguk-sa**; **Sŏkkuram**

KIM TONGIN 金東仁 (1900–1951)

A prolific short-story writer, born in P'yŏngyang and brought up as a Presbyterian. After studying in Tokyo, he returned to Korea and in 1919 founded the **literary magazine** *Ch'angjo*, 'Creation' (1919–1921), which stood for modernisation of the language and for literature as pure art, in distinction from **Yi Kwangsu**'s literature as enlightenment. *Kamja*, 'Potato' (1925) and *Kwangnyŏm Sonat'a*, 'Madness Sonata' (1930) are representative works, Wildean in their passionate despair. He also wrote historical novels, such as *Unhyŏn-gungŭi pom*, 'Spring in the Unhyŏn Palace' (1933), and the biographical *Ŭlchi Mundŏk* (1946). He died at home of meningitis.

A translation of *Potato* is in PETER H. LEE, *Flowers of Fire*, Hawaii, 1974

KIM TONGNI 金東里 (1913–)

Real name Kim Sijong. He was born at **Kyŏngju** where he largely educated himself. In 1933 he went to Seoul, became a friend of the budding poet, **Sŏ Chŏngju**, and tried his hand at verse. In 1935 he won a newspaper prize for his *Hwarangŭi huye* 'Heir of the hwarang', which set him on course as a short-story writer, and provided his expenses for visits to the Buddhist monasteries of Tasol-sa (on the eastern slopes of Chiri-san, near Chinju) and **Haein-sa**. In 1936 he published *Munyŏ-do* 'The Mudang's Picture', about the confrontation of **shamanism** and Christianity. Its dark view of the supernatural and the forces of nature is typical of his work. To escape the Japanese presence in Seoul, he went to **Manchuria** in 1940, but by 1945 was back in South Kyŏngsang, shedding his leftist leanings and moving towards art for art's sake. He moved to Seoul and began to interest himself in national issues. His later work is less esteemed, though he retained his place as a leader in literary circles.

AHN JUNGHYO trans., *Ulhwa the Shaman*, Larchmont, N.Y.: Larchmont Press, 1979

KIM TŬKSIN 金得臣 (Kungjae, 1754–1822)

One of the principal exponents of Korean *genre* **painting**, but trained in the *Tohwa-sŏ* and also a successful painter of **landscape** in the Southern tradition, **flower and bird** painting, and **portraiture**. The composition of his *Playing Music for Guo Fenyang*[1] is reminiscent of the kind of complex horizontal scroll paintings imitated by Chinese artists as a training exercise, such as Zhang Ziduan's *Going up the River at Qingming*. The formality of its draughtsmanship is quite different from the informality and vigour seen in a *genre* picture such as *Shattering the Stillness* (Kansong Museum)[2], in which a woman has dropped her weaving and a man uses his pipe to chase a cat away from a mother hen and her chicks.

(1) KEITH PRATT, *Korean Music, its History and its Performance*, London & Seoul: Faber Music and Jeung Eum Sa, 1987

(2) CHOI SUNU, *5000 Years of Korean Art*, Seoul: Hyonam Publishing Co., 1979

KIM TURYANG 金斗樑 (Namni, Unch'ŏn, 1696–1763)

Artist who, as a member of the *Tohwa-sŏ*, combined eclectic skills and interests in all major categories of painting, but is best known for his animals, human subjects, and **landscapes**. His style not only embraced both Northern and Southern School traditions but also on occasion showed the influence of western art entering Korea from the Jesuit missionaries now working in China. His ability to convey atmosphere in conjunction with the detail associated with the Northern School can be seen in the wistful, almost eerie effect created in his *Moonlit Landscape* (1744, National Museum of Korea)[1], and his use of western shading techniques in *Black Dog* (National Museum of Korea)[2]. In *Dog Scratching*[3] he combines a detailed realism in his treatment of the animal with a boneless form for the background tree in a manner reminiscent of **Cho Sok**'s *Magpies*.

(1)(2) KIM WONYONG, CHOI SUN'U, IM CHANGSOON, *The Arts of Korea*, Vol. 2, Seoul, 1979

(3) CHOI SUNU, *5000 Years of Korean Painting*, Seoul: Hyonam Publishing Co., 1979

KIM ŬNHO 金殷鎬 (Idang, 1892–1979)

The leading Korean portrait painter of early modern times (*see* **portraiture**), known especially for his pictures of Chosŏn kings including **Sunjong**. Critics also remarked that he was obsessed with painting large and meticulously detailed pictures of women in traditional palace costume. Nevertheless, he continued to paint marvellously lively birds and fish almost until he died. He studied in the Painting and Calligraphy Institute (*Sŏhwa Misurwŏn*) in Seoul and spent three years in Japan during the 1920s. As a senior establishment figure in artistic circles after 1945 he was a judge for the *Kukchŏn* National Exhibition.

KIM YANGGI 金良驥 (Kŭngwŏn, late18th– early 19th century)
Son of **Kim Hongdo** who continued his father's tradition of *genre* painting, landscape, and **flowers and birds**. His best known extant work is *Sparse Grove of Old Trees* (National Museum of Korea)[1]. His *Immortal Playing a Mouthorgan* (National Museum of Korea)[2] is a fine example showing koreanised treatment of a Chinese-style subject.
(1) KIM WONYONG, CHOI SUNU, IM CHANGSOON, *The Arts of Korea*, Vol. 2, Seoul, 1979
(2) KEITH PRATT, *Korean Music, its History and its Performance,* Seoul: Jeung Eum Sa, 1987

KIM YŎNGSAM 金泳三 (Kim Young Sam, b.1927)
President of South Korea from 1993 to 1998, the first elected non-military president since Syngman Rhee (**Yi Sŭngman**) in 1960. He was born in Kŏje island in South Kyŏngsang province, and graduated from Seoul National University in 1951. He may have spent a short time in the army, but he was soon working as a secretary to the premier, before entering the National Assembly in 1954 as a member of the ruling **Liberal Party**. Before long, he switched to the opposition benches and was to remain a prominent figure in opposition circles until 1990. In 1971, he lost to **Kim Taejung** in the opposition's selection of a presidential candidate, but continued to play a prominent rôle in opposition politics, becoming leader of the **New Democratic Party** in 1974. He was expelled from the National Assembly in 1979, during the political crisis that eventually led to the death of President Park Chung Hee (**Pak Chŏnghŭi**). Following Chun Doo Hwan (**Chŏn Tuhwan**)'s military coup, he was arrested in May 1980. He was later held under house arrest, and like most prominent politicians from the Park era, he was banned from political activity. In May 1983, he went on hunger strike for 23 days in protest at political oppression. Although technically still banned from politics, he became a co-chairman of the Council for the Promotion of Democracy on its establishment in 1984, and like Kim Taejung, adviser to the **New Korea Democratic Party** in 1986. The following year, however, as the presidential **election** approached, he set up his own party, the Reunification Democratic Party, and ran as its presidential candidate against Roh Tae Woo (**No Taeu**) and Kim Taejung. He lost, but in February 1990 he merged his party with the ruling **Democratic Justice Party** and the smaller **New Democratic Republican Party** to form a new government party, the **Democratic Liberal Party** (DLP). Kim became Executive Chairman of the DLP, and was its successful candidate for the 1992 presidential election.
As president he began well, with a series of reforming measures. Before long, however, he was faced with the problem of the North Korean nuclear crisis and domestic pressure to re-open enquiries into the 1980 **Kwangju Massacre**. In his dealings with the North, Kim Yŏngsam seemed to lack the skills or the interest of his predecessor, and to swing between concern and bravado. His refusal to send condolences to the North following the death of **Kim Ilsŏng** in July 1994, although he had been actively preparing to meet him at a summit meeting, led to much hostile comment from the North and a refusal to re-open direct dialogue with the South. Even though he eventually authorised the trials of Roh Tae Woo and Chun Doo Hwan, he gained little political benefit since he was felt to have agreed only under pressure. In 1997, his last months in office were marred by scandal over his son's alleged corruption and tax evasion, a massive financial and economic crisis, and his attempts to prevent the election of Kim Taejung as his successor.
Crusader for Democracy: the Life and Times of Kim Young Sam, Seoul: Yonhap News Agency, 1993; HAKKYU SOHN, *Authoritarianism and Opposition in South Korea,* London and New York: Routledge, 1989

KIM YUNSIK 金允植 (1835–1922)

Senior official associated with the **self-strengthening movement** of the late 19th century. In 1880 **Kim Hongjip** had brought back from Japan a proposal from the Chinese counsellor in Tokyo, Huang Zunxian, recommending that Korea should forge stronger ties with the United States and China, and should adopt western technology. In January 1882 Kim Yunsik was despatched to Tianjin with a party of young technicians to study modern armaments. **Li Hongzhang** confirmed his diplomat's advice, and through Kim urged Seoul to make friendly agreements with foreign powers whilst they still had the chance (*see* '**Unequal' treaties**). While the Koreans were in China the **Shufeldt Treaty** was signed in Chemulp'o, but a reactionary response directed against the increase of both American and Japanese influence led to the *Imo* **Incident** (July 1882). Li approved Kim's urgent request for Chinese troops to be sent to Korea to counter the increasing Japanese military presence. A force of 4,500 men was sent under Wu Changqing, Ma Jianzhong and **Yuan Shikai**, and the **Taewŏn'gun** was seized and taken to Tianjin.

Appointed foreign minister, Kim maintained his pro-Chinese line. In 1885, following the British occupation of **Kŏmundo**, he persuaded King **Kojong** to reject Russian overtures brokered by **von Möllendorff**, and Li Hongzhang's influence over Korean government policy was strengthened. In 1894, in response to the Japanese minister Ōtori's demand for a pledge of Korean independence, Kim defended the Korean request to China for soldiers to help against the **Tonghak** rebels, and the consequent arrival of Japanese troops precipitated the **Sino-Japanese War**. Nevertheless, Kim was reconfirmed as foreign minister in the new but short-lived cabinet which accompanied the *Kabo* **reforms** of 1894–5.

KIM YUSIN 金庾信 (595–673)

A great **Silla** general. Descended from the royal house of **Kaya**, he became a *hwarang* at 14, and attractive stories are told of his spirituality and nobility of character. He was a friend of **Kim Ch'unch'u**, whose sister he married, and whom he eventually helped to succeed to the throne in 653 (now known as King **Muyŏl**). Before that Ch'unch'u was a successful diplomat for Silla in the years before the whole peninsula was unified under Silla rule. This involved alliance with Tang, with whose general Su Dingfang the two Kims co-operated in the subjection of **Paekche**. Yusin organised a remarkable relief of the Tang army, moving huge loads of **rice** to P'yŏngyang in winter 661, but was too old and ill to lead the war against **Koguryŏ** that completed the unification.

KIMCH'I

Root vegetables preserved in salt are recorded by **Yi Kyubo**, and some archaeologists believe there are prehistoric signs of such pickling for lactic acid fermentation, but Korea's most famous **food** in its present form is a comparatively recent development. Chinese cabbage *paech'u* (C. *song*), its principal ingredient, is a southern plant that from Tang times onwards replaced mallow, the chief green vegetable of early north China, and possibly did not come to Korea until Koryŏ times. Red **pepper**, now an essential ingredient of *kimch'i*, did not arrive in Korea before the 17th century. There are many kinds of *kimch'i*, made with various vegetables and spices, according to the season. The cooperative labour in which the women of several households combine to lay down winter *kimch'i* in late autumn is called *kimjang*.

KIMHAE 金海

County near Pusan in South Kyŏngsang province where archaeological discoveries at sites along the Naktong River have shed light on the ancient history of the **Kaya** region. The first to be found was a shell mound excavated in 1907 by the Japanese archaeologist Imanishi Ryū. The people lived on **rice** and barley, and by hunting animals and marine life. They may have been involved in early **commerce** with China, exchanging local **iron** goods for **pottery**. The district gives its name to a pottery style which indicates the beginnings of hard-fired stoneware on the Korean peninsula, a technique which may have been imported from the mainland (but *cf.* **Wasil**) and involved improvements in **kiln** design.

Of particular importance is a cemetery excavated between 1990 and 1996 at the village of Kagok, Yangdong-ni, which was used for some five hundred years between the 1st century BC and 4th century AD. A total of 562 **tomb** sites show the development of burial styles from wooden coffins to vertical stone chamber tombs. Artefacts found include bronze **mirrors** from **Han dynasty** China with local imitations and a rare inscribed Chinese bronze pot. Many of the iron objects, including weapons, **armour**, helmets and horse trappings, are in styles indicating Kaya's connections with the Japanese island of Kyushu (*see* **Wa**). Some fine items of personal **jewellery** include crystal and **glass** coloured beads, many in the *kogok* shape which became fashionable in the 3rd century AD. The site proves the rôle of Kaya as an important maritime state playing a profitable part in trading between China and Japan.

KIRYŎ-SUP'IL 騎驢隨筆 'Donkey-rider's notes'

Less correctly called *Kiro-sup'il*. Song Sangdo (1871–1946) took his brush-name, Kiryŏja 'donkey-rider', from a Ming writer Qilü Daozi (K. Kiryŏ-doja), who wrote a book on Chinese patriots. Song, born at Yŏngju in North Kyŏngsang, was trained as a traditional neo-Confucian. He travelled throughout the country collecting information about Korean patriots, beginning with Yi Siwŏn, who died in the engagement with the French in 1866 (*see* **France, relations with**). The book includes events (such as the **Kwangju Incident** of 1928 and setting up the **Provisional Government** in Shanghai) as well as individuals: 239 subjects in all. Much of the information is of primary historical value.

KISAENG 妓生 'skilled women'

Courtesans, often the daughters of *kisaeng* mothers; professional girls trained in special skills of **music**, **dance**, **poetry** and conversation, with which they entertained upper-class men at banquets. Some specialised in particular types of song or recitation. Many could read and write Chinese to some extent, and some wrote poems which are still admired. Others were trained in horsemanship, archery or sword-dancing, and gave displays at parties of the highest rank. They served food, drink and more personal favours, but were not to be hired loosely in the manner of prostitutes. Despite their low social standing (they were members of the *ch'ŏnmin*), an individual attachment to a single patron might offer the chance of becoming a **concubine** with a permanent place in his household, and some became secondary wives of the **gentry**. The institution of court entertainment by *kisaeng* was established by the Koryŏ period. They performed at ceremonial banquets, although Confucian-inspired argument at the Chosŏn court about the appropriateness of having girls perform before male spectators led to their dancing being restricted to the Inner [female] Quarters under Kings **Sukchong** (1674–1720) and **Yŏngjo** (1724–76). In the Chosŏn royal palace there were also **medical** *kisaeng*. The beauty of the most famous girls was legendary. Probably the most

renowned was **Non'gae**, who is said to have dragged one of Hideyoshi's invading officers to his death over a cliff at **Chinju** in 1592, sacrificing her own life on the eve of her wedding.
DAVID McCANN, 'Traditional World of Kisaeng,' *KJ*, 14/2, 1974

KITE FLYING *yŏn nalligi*

Chinese studies of the atmosphere, 'proto-aeronautics', carried out largely because of Daoist spiritual interest in the extent and nature of the atmosphere, may have led to the creation of kites as early as the 4th century BC. There are stories of 6th-century experiments with manned kites, but they do not prove such devices were ever perfected. The military value of kites for getting messages over enemy lines or barricades was recognised later.

Korean kites are first recorded in **Silla**, used by the army. It is said that in the 18th century King **Yŏngjo** encouraged kite-flying, and the custom of New Year kite-flying stems from that time. In later Chosŏn, men and boys of all ages flew kites from the 1st to the 15th of the 1st moon. Anyone who flew kites after that was called *kori-baekchang*, 'wicker-worker', lowest of the low. A favourite sport was *yŏn-ŏulligi*, covering the kite-string with a mixture of glue and powdered porcelain or glass (a process called *kaemi*), and then trying to cross strings with another kite in the air, manipulating a sawing motion until one of the two strings was severed. Four or five strings might be crossed at one time and the contest be prolonged. A fallen kite could be claimed by whoever picked it up. At the end of the season a kite with *songaek* ('away with evil') or *songaeg-yŏngbok* ('away with evil, welcome good luck') written on it would be flown and cut loose to bear away the year's bad luck.

Fancy kites like Chinese and Japanese bird and fish kites were not used. Korean kites (*yŏnji* '**paper** kites') are of severely practical design with high ergonomic efficiency. Six bamboo struts form the top (about 42·5 cm) and two sides (about 50 cm) of a rectangle, two diagonals and a central vertical strut. There is no bottom-edge strut. The frame is covered with white *ch'angho-ji* 'window-paper', and a round hole (diameter about 20 cm) is cut in the middle where the vertical and diagonal struts cross. The unfixed lower edge allows enough give in the paper for the dihedral effect that is necessary if a flat kite is to have self-righting balance. The central hole prevents the paper from being destroyed by strong wind. Small triangular paper tabs (*kalgae-bal* 'jackdaw feet') at the bottom corners are all that is needed as tail to offer wind resistance. The most expensive part is the silken string (*yŏnchul*), often coloured, attached to four shorter strings that are tied to the four corners of the kite. The square or hexagonal box-frame reel (*ŏllae*) is built on a spindle that may be 75 cm long.

Decoration is simple. A red or black **roundel** (*kkokchi*), 10 cm across, or a 20 cm half-moon with its straight edge flush with the top strut, is often pasted above the central hole. The bottom half may be coloured with a black, red, blue or purple *ch'ima* 'skirt'. Three horizontal stripes of the **saektong** type make a *samdong-ch'ima*; eight make a *p'algwae-nyŏn* (*see* **trigrams**)and usually have a black *kkokchi*. A magpie kite has the two side triangles created by the diagonal struts painted black. All-over decoration, such as fish scales or chequering, is sometimes used.

KKOKTUK-KAKSI See **Puppet play**

KNOTTING *maedŭp*

A form of macrame, elaborate ornamental knotting with silk cord (often red or blue) was used as a decoration on women's bodices in conjuction with *norigae*. The simplest knots were *pyŏl* the star and *p'ari* the fly, *maehwa* the apricot flower and *nabi* the butterfly. Complicated flat lozenges, *ch'amae*, and even more complex patterns were also used. Multi-coloured tassels depended from the knots.

KO HŬIDONG 高羲東 (Ch'un'guk, 1886–1965)

Leading figure in the history of modern Korean painting. He learned traditional styles in Seoul from the *Sŏhwa Misurwŏn* ('Calligraphy and Painting Fine Art Society') during the **Protectorate**, but went to Tokyo in 1909 in search of modern western training. After returning to Korea in 1915 he established the *Sŏhwa Hyŏphoe* ('Calligraphy and Painting Study Association') to promote westernised art techniques including the use of oils and charcoal, but his own self-portrait[1], the first to be done by a Korean in oils, earned him considerable criticism from those still wedded to traditional Confucian and nationalistic ideas of what **portraiture** should be. Under the influence of the nationalist movement during the colonial period Ko returned to traditional Korean painting, now trying to achieve a new style of synthesis between East and West. After liberation he held senior posts in organisations devoted to the restoration of Korean art, including the Korean Arts Exhibition.

(1) YOUNG ICK LEW, ed., *Korean Art Tradition*, Seoul: Korea Foundation, 1993

KO UN 高雲 (Hach'ŏn, 1495–?)

An official of the early Chosŏn court who earned a reputation as a calligrapher and amateur artist. He was linked especially with **tiger** paintings. Two such works attributed to him survive, but neither can be firmly authenticated.

KODAE SOSŎL 古代小說 'old time fiction'

This term covers all fiction written without influence from western novels. William Skillend lists 531 examples, counting some known only by title, but excluding minor variants and alternative titles[1]. Most are written in *han'gŭl*; a few exist also in **hanmun**. The content is varied: stories, fables, legends, historical anecdotes, biographies, autobiographies, diaries and memoirs. Many of the stories are Chinese, others are Korean. Some are hortatory, some are romances, some are merely intended to entertain or edify. Very few texts are known that certainly date from earlier than the middle of the 19th century, though the content must often be very much older. Surviving wood-block editions were printed in Seoul (*Kyŏngp'an*), Ansŏng (*Ansŏngp'an*) or Chŏnju (*Wanp'an*). 20th-century paperback brochure editions with gaudy covers are commoner, known from about 1911 onwards as *yukchŏn sosŏl* 'sixpenny fiction', but more often as *iyagi-ch'aek* 'story-books' or *ttakchi sosŏl* 'pulp novels'. They form a mine of language and a mirror of popular culture.

(1) WILLIAM E. SKILLEND, *Kodae Sosol: a Survey of Korean Traditional Style Popular Novels*, London: SOAS, 1968

See **Changkki-jŏn**; **Ch'unhyang-jŏn**; **Hanjung-nok**; **Hong-Giltong-jŏn**; **Hŭngbu-jŏn**; **Kuunmong**; **Kyech'uk ilgi**; **Myŏngsa-simni**; **Ongnu-mong**; **Pyŏngja-rok**; **Sim-Ch'ŏng-jŏn**; **Romance of the Three Kingdoms**; **T'okki-jŏn**.

KOGOK 曲玉

Small, comma-shaped pendants made of jade, other hardstone, or **glass**. From the early **Bronze Age** to the Unified Silla period they were extensively used as ornaments on jewellery and accessories on crowns, to which they were attached by wire links. The style in **Paekche** was shorter, thicker and more curved than in **Silla**, where they were extensively used on necklaces and belts, as well as on crowns. There is a suggestion that they were modelled on bears' claws or teeth, the **bear** being an animal of mystic, if not totemic, significance. They are often called *magatama* in Japanese.

KOGURYŎ 高句麗

The most northerly of the three kingdoms into which the Korean peninsula was divided between the 4th and 7th centuries AD. Its heartland was situated in the upper reaches of the **Yalu** and **Tumen** Rivers, south of the Sungari (*see also* **Paektusan**), the former location of the **Yemaek** tribes. Its warlike people were descended from a league of five tribes, of which the Sono and Kyeru were successively the most dominant, and came into early contact with the north-eastern expansion of the Chinese **Han** Empire, forcing the removal of its **commandery** in **Xuantu**. The traditional date for the foundation of the state of Koguryŏ is 37 BC and its founder is said to have been a refugee from **Puyŏ**, Ko Chumong, but although territorial expansion to east and west of the heartland, including the capture of the Chinese commandery **Lintun**, took place under a 'king', T'aejo (53–146), there is no evidence of consolidated political organisation as early as this. In AD 12 its armies clashed with those of the Chinese ruler Wang Mang. Centralised authority was extended under King Kogukch'ŏn (179–96). It was in the 4th century AD that its major achievements were won: in 313 the last and greatest Chinese commandery of **Lelang** was overrun, and in 370 the Xianbei threat fom the north was extinguished. Strife was to continue with both China and the neighbouring southern kingdom of **Paekche**, but under King **Kwanggaet'o** and his successor Changsu, Koguryŏ attained its greatest dominance: over most of the northern half of the peninsula and much of **Manchuria**. In 427 Changsu moved the capital from **Kungnaesŏng** to P'yŏngyang, and Puyŏ was annexed in 494.

Despite regular military friction with China, Koguryŏ paid tribute to the courts of the Northern and Southern Dynasties and its civilisation was strongly influenced by the Middle Kingdom. Both **Confucianism** and **Buddhism** were adopted, along with their associated cultural traditions and the Chinese writing system. **Tombs** built and furnished in Chinese style provide evidence for the quality of élite culture.

Relations with Paekche and **Silla** were founded upon self-interest and competition, and involved China as the suzerain of all three states. Alliances were formed first by Koguryŏ with Silla against Paekche (late 4th century AD), then between Silla and Paekche against Koguryŏ (AD 434), and later by Koguryŏ and Paekche against Silla (late 6th century). The latter had seized Koguryŏ territory in the **Han** River valley and was looking for Chinese support from across the sea, but in 598 Koguryŏ mounted a pre-emptive strike on **Sui** territory beyond the Liao River (*see* **Liaodong**). Emperor Wendi's armed response and that of his son Yangdi in 612 resulted in huge Chinese losses, especially at the hands of General **Ŭlchi Mundŏk** in the battle of the **Salsu** River. A long defensive **wall** was then built by General Yŏn Kaesomun along the Liao River, but the new **Tang** rulers in China still failed to appreciate the rôle played by Koguryŏ in the downfall of their predecessors. They mounted a land and naval invasion in 644 which again proved costly and unsuccessful, followed by further vain attacks in 647, 648 and 655. A fresh alliance with Koguryŏ led Paekche to mount new attacks on Silla in 655, and in response to the latter's appeal for help Tang joined in an offensive which this time led not only to the elimination of Paekche but ultimately to the fall of Koguryŏ also. The forces ranged against it were too strong and its energy and resources depleted. It was politically weakened by the death of Yŏn Kaesomun, now senior minister, in 666, and in 668 King Pojang surrendered the capital and was taken hostage to China. China took over Koguryŏ, as it had Paekche, as a province of the Middle Kingdom.

KINGS:

Tongmyŏng	37–19 BC	Mich'ŏn	300–331
Yuri	19 BC – AD 18	Kogugwŏn	331–371
Taemusin	18–44	Sosurim	371–384
Minjung	44–48	Kogugyang	384–391
Mobon	48–53	Kwanggaet'o	391–413
T'aejo	53–146	Changsu	413–491
Ch'adae	146–165	Munja	491–519
Sindae	165–179	Anjang	519–531
Kogukch'ŏn	179–197	Anwŏn	531–545
Sansang	197–227	Yangwŏn	545–559
Tongch'ŏn	227–248	P'yŏngwŏn	559–590
Chungch'ŏn	248–270	Yŏngyang	590–618
Sŏch'ŏn	270–292	Yŏngnyu	618–642
Pongsang	292–300	Pojang	642–668

LI OGG, *Recherche sur l'Antiquité Coréenne, I, Ethnie et Société de Koguryŏ*, Paris: Collège de France, 1980

KOJONG, KING 高宗 (1852–1919, r. 1864–1907)

When Ch'ŏlchong died sonless in 1864, the Dowager Queen Sinjŏng appointed Yi Myŏngbok (now known as Kojong), 11-year-old son of Hŭngsŏn-gun, as the next king. His father became Hŭngsŏn Taewŏn-gun (now commonly known as **'the Taewŏn'gun**) and dominated the young king, but the king's marriage to a member of the Yŏhŭng Min clan brought another strong character into the palace. Kojong lived in the midst of tension between his queen and his father for thirty years. The Taewŏn-gun withdrew from court in 1873. This was the period of the opening of Korea to world powers, treaties being concluded with Japan (1876); Germany and the USA (1882); Britain, Italy and Russia (1884); and France (1886). Soon China, Russia and Japan were locked in struggles for domination of the peninsula. No one in Korea was equipped to cope with the successive crises. In 1884 the opening of a modern postal service was the occasion of the Post Office *émeute* (*see* **Kapsin coup**), an attempt by young progressives to seize power, and its failure led to strengthening of the Min family hold on government. Modernisation began to reach within the palace when electric lighting was installed in 1887. In 1894 the **Tonghak** rebellion led to Japanese intervention, which provoked the short, but for Korea destructive, **Sino-Japanese War**. In the following year Kojong's beloved **Queen Min** was assassinated in a Japanese plot. In 1896 he fled with his secondary wife, Lady Ŏm (later called Sunhŏn Hwanggwibi; *see* **Ŏm-bi**) and the Crown Prince (later **Sunjong**) to the Russian legation, where they remained for several months. This event was a contributory cause of the **Russo-Japanese war**, which finally put an end to Russia's designs in Korea. In 1897 Kojong took up residence in the **Tŏksu Palace**, safely between the British and American legations, declared Korea's independence of China, and was himself crowned as the Emperor of **Great Han** (Taehan Hwangje), with the **reign title** Kwangmu 'shining warrior'. His son **Yi Ŭn** was born in the same year. The Japanese moved steadily towards their objective, signing a treaty that gave them virtual control of Korea in 1904. Kojong made an attempt to assert his independence and expose Japanese intentions at the **Hague Peace Conference** in 1907; but the western world was generally in line with Japan, which forced Kojong to abdicate in favour of his son. Kojong became known as T'aehwangje, 'great emperor'. In 1910 he was reduced to Yi T'aewang, 'great king Yi'. He lived on, lonely and sad, in the Tŏksu Palace until he died in 1919, a kindly man who, though shrewder than he often appeared to be, was bound to be dominated by others. It was almost inevitable that rumour should claim he was poisoned. Three sons and a daughter survived him: **Sunjong**, **Yi Ŭn**, **Yi Kang** and Princess Tŏkhye. Five other sons and a daughter died in childhood. Princess Tŏkhye (1912–89) was married in 1931 to the Lord of **Tsushima**, Sō Takeshi. She returned to Korea in 1962.

For a contemporary portrait of the King, done by the Dutch American artist Hubert Voss, see K.O.I.S., *Korean Art Guide*, Seoul: Yekyong Publications Co., 1987.

KOLP'UM 骨品 'bone-rank'

System of political and social stratification employed in **Silla**, based on lines of descent. There were three principal classes, *sŏnggol* ('sacred bone'), *chin'gol* ('true bone'), and *tup'um* ('head rank'). Kings bore *sŏnggol* status. They were drawn from the original royal **lineage** of Pak, its successors the Kims and the royal Kims of **Kaya** incorporated into Silla in 532. The Pak lineage continued to provide royal consorts. *Sŏnggol* disappeared in the mid-7th century, after which all royalty belonged to the *chin'gol*.

Tup'um were divided into six classes, of which numbers six, five and four comprised the aristocracy, and three, two and one the ordinary people. 'Head rank' status was an essential consideration in appointment to civil and military posts of responsibility (*see* **government, central**). It was also the basis of strict sumptuary regulations indicating a person's social status, including the style of his housing, dress, means of transportation, and numbers of servants.

C. S. KIM, 'The *Kolp'um* System: Basis for Sillan Social Stratification,' *JKS*, 1.1, 1971
See also **class system**; **foundation myths**

KŎMUN-DO 巨文島 (Port Hamilton)

The small group of islands known as Kŏmun-do in Korean and Port Hamilton in English lies between the mainland and **Cheju** Island. The nearest port on the mainland is Yŏsu, and the journey can take as long as four and a half to six hours, depending on the type of craft used. The islands' main claim to fame is that for a brief period between 1885 and 1887 they were occupied by the British Royal Navy. The Navy had coveted the islands since Captain **Belcher** had visited them in HMS *Samarang* in 1854 and gave them their English name. In the mid-1870s Sir Harry Parkes, the British Minister in Japan, proposed that they should be occupied by Britain, but the government in London turned down the idea. It was revived in the 1880s, as a means of bringing pressure on Russia, which was thought to have designs on a Korean port, and on 1 April 1885 the Royal Navy established a base on the islands. They proved to be a poor harbour, difficult to defend and with strong currents which tore away both defensive booms and submarine cables. The occupation also caused concern to the Japanese, Chinese and Korean governments, none of which had been consulted about British plans. When the Russians indicated that they had no intention of occupying a Korean port, the British withdrew in February 1887, though their naval vessels continued to call at the islands for many years afterwards. In the colonial period, the islands served as a Japanese naval base, and since 1948 they have been an outpost for the South Korean navy. A British graveyard from the 1880s survives, as does a lighthouse with British equipment built about 1906.

JAMES HOARE, 'Komundo-Port Hamilton,' *AA*, 17, no.3, 1986
See also **Li Hongzhang**; **Russia, relations with**

KŎMUN'GO (*hyŏn'gŭm*) 玄琴
A native Korean long zither, probably invented in **Koguryŏ** in the Three Kingdoms period. It is highly respected as the *yang* instrument which complements the *yin* *kayagŭm*, and in the traditional Korean orchestra of today, its player is often the most senior member of the ensemble. It is slightly tapered in width, and like the *kayagŭm* it is laid on the floor to the left of the player with its narrower end on his knees. It has six strings of twisted silk and varying thickness. The second, third and fourth are stretched across sixteen fixed wooden bridges and are tuned by circular pegs underneath the bottom end of the instrument. The three remaining strings are tuned by adjusting single, moveable bridges shaped like the claw of a bird. With his right hand the player plucks the strings with a short wooden plectrum, *sultae*, or strikes them against a leather band covering the top end of the sounding board. The left hand pushes the two most important strings for melodic performance, numbers two and three, to produce vibrato and slur.
SONG BANG-SONG, *The Sanjo Tradition of Korean Kŏmun'go Music*, Seoul: Jung Eum Sa, 1986
See also **music; musical instruments**

KOMUN-JINBO 古文眞寶 'True Treasures of Old Literature'
Korean printings of *Xiangshuo guwen zhenbao daquan*, first issued in 1472, copying a 15th-century Chinese edition. Both the Chinese text and Korean editions have been through several recensions. Popular Korean editions are abridged. In the full version, Part I contains poetry from Qu Yuan to **Zhu Xi**, Part II contains *fu* and prose from the same period. Selection was based on moral content as well as literary style.

KONGAN (C. *gongan*, J *koan*) 公案 'proposed case'
Also called *hwadu* or *koch'ŭk*: a fragment of conversation from a revered teacher, containing a logical absurdity that can be proposed for meditation by **Sŏn** Buddhists. This meditation is called *kanhwa*, 'looking at the *hwadu* or crux [of the *kongan*]'. This crux is not to be logically analysed or intellectually ruminated, but continually savoured until the absurdity resolves into a sense of stillness and doubt. A monk may use the same *hwadu* for many years, and although 'enlightenment' may be sudden, it will still be a long time before he dares to become a teacher.

The favourite *kongan* among Korean monks, now as for **Chinul** and **T'aego**, is *Choju-mucha*, 'Zhaozhou's negative' (otherwise *Kuja-bulsŏng*, 'a dog's buddha-nature'), the reply given by the Chinese monk Zhaozhou (778–897) when asked 'Has a dog buddha-nature?' He answered 'No' (K. *Mu*; C. *Wu*). This 'No' is the *hwadu* of the *kongan*. In terms of Mahayana teaching, it is a nonsensical denial of the truth, for everything has buddha-nature; yet to controvert this *hwadu* would be to deny one's own buddha-nature, and this No is not the denial of existence nor the No of true nothingness. The meditator strives to enter into Zhaozhou's mind at the point just before he said 'No,' thus uniting himself with the universal buddha-mind.

Kongan collections form an important part of *Sŏn* literature.

KONGAN COLLECTIONS *kongan-jip* 公案集
Kongan are collected in many books. *Piyan lu* 'Blue Cliff Record' (K. *Pyŏgam-nok*), compiled by Xuedou Chongxian (980–1052), treasured by the **Linji** school, exists now only in a Yuan period recension. It is connected with *Jingde chuandeng lu* (K. *Kyŏngdŏk Chŏndŭng-nok*) 'Record of Transmission of the Lamp: compiled in the Jingde period' by Dao Yuan (AD 1006). There are other 'lamp anthologies' that

combine *kongan* with hagiography. *Wumen guan* (K. *Mumun-gwan*) 'The Doorless Gate' is a small *kongan* anthology by Wumen Huikai (1184–1260). The Koryŏ monk Hyesim (1178–1234) collected 1,127 Korean *kongan* in *Sŏnmun-yŏmsong-jip* 'Collection of *Kongan* of the *Sŏn* School', which was expanded to 1,472 by Kugok (otherwise Kagun), a learned follower of **T'aego**, in the mid-14th century.

KONGJA-GAŎ (C. *Kongzi jiayu*) 孔子家語 'Sayings of the Confucian School'
A collection of traditions about Confucius current in early Han as additional to the Analects, apparently interspersed with a smaller number of pieces added by An Su (195–256) in the 3rd century AD. The general emphasis is on ethics and ritual, much of the material being available from other sources. In Korea it was a source of Confucian apocrypha, but does not seem to have been widely read.

KONGSINJŎN 'Meritorious subject lands' 功臣田 *See* **Meritorious subjects**

KONGSŎ-PA *See **Sinsŏ-pa***

KONJIL
Also called *konjil-konu* or *yŏltu-bat konu* '12-field *konu*', a game popular throughout Europe in the 14th century under the name 'merels' and now known as 'Fox-and-geese' or 'Nine-men's-morris'. The board is marked with three concentric squares with two lines from side to side and two diagonals (which do not appear across the central square), making 24 intersections. Two players have nine pieces (*mal*) each, which they set on the intersections. The object is to get three pieces standing in a straight line.

KONU

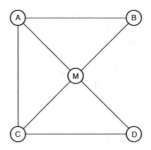

A simple game of the ***paduk*** family. A grid (*malpat*) is drawn on paper or scratched on the ground. In the form called *umul konu*, 'well konu', the grid is a square with one side missing (the 'well'), but with diagonals. The two players each have two counters (*tol* or *mal*): pebbles (black for one player, white for the other), bits of wood, paper, or leaves. The game is set either by placing the black counters at B and D and the white ones at A and C, or by the two players putting counters down alternately. Black moves first. Thereafter each player in turn moves a counter along a line to the unoccupied corner or centre. When black occupies M and A, with white at C and D (or black occupies M and C, with white at A and B), white cannot move and has been defeated.

Umul konu has an inbuilt disadvantage, perhaps not always understood by the children and labourers who used to play it so much: the player who makes the first move (black) always wins. Hence the proverbial *umul konu ch'ŏssu*, 'first move in *umul konu*', for anyone who knows only one way to approach a problem or for a ruthless way of winning anything.

More complicated forms of *konu* exist, played with more counters. There are similar games in China and Japan.

KŎNYANG 建陽 'Establishing *yang*'
Reign title adopted by Emperor **Kojong** in 1896. In 1897 it was changed to *Kwangmu* 'Glorious warrior'.
See *Kabo* **reforms**

KOREA DAILY NEWS See **Bethell, Ernest**; *Taehan Maeil Sinbo*; **Yang Kit'aek**

KOREA-JAPAN PROTOCOL *Hanil ŭijŏngsŏ* 韓日議定書 (1904)
Alliance signed under duress by the Korean government on 23 February 1904, in the course of the **Russo-Japanese War**, constituting the first diplomatic step towards the **Protectorate** and colonial annexation. On the pretext of offering Korea help to protect its independence, the Japanese gained the right to maintain troops at key positions on Korean soil. Under the terms of a second Protocol (22 August 1904) Korea acceded to a Japanese demand to be allowed to appoint advisers to the Korean government on financial policy and foreign affairs. Later the same year additional, unstipulated, Japanese advisers began to take charge of matters related to defence, justice, education, and the royal household.
See also **Protectorate Treaty**; **Stevens, Durham**

KOREA-JAPAN TREATY 韓日協定 (1965)
Treaty of 'Basic Relations' signed on 22 June 1965 after protracted negotiations which rectified diplomatic relations and established embassies in the respective capitals. It was ratified by the National Assembly in Seoul on 14 August, but its expression of apology from Japan for its past ill-treatment of Korea was not judged adequate in Korea, and was met with widespread hostile reaction in both countries. South Korean **students**, in particular, had to be quelled by troops when they vented their anger on the streets. The Treaty was a key factor in President Park Chung Hee (**Pak Chŏnghŭi**)'s attempt to make South Korea less exclusively dependent on the United States. Japan agreed to pay Korea US$300 million and to make loans worth a further $500 million; the rights of Koreans living in Japan to residency permits and education were guaranteed; and coastal fishing limits of 12 miles were agreed (but failed to clarify the situation around the island of **Tokto** sufficiently to avoid trouble in the 1990s). Korea agreed not to press future compensation claims for offences committed during the Japanese occupation. Japan maintained its right to maintain non-diplomatic links with North Korea, including trade.

A subsequent treaty in April 1970 awarded Japan preferential terms for industrial investment in South Korea.
KIM KWAN BONG, *The Korea-Japan Treaty Crisis and the Political Instability of the Korean Political System*, New York: Praeger Books, 1971

KOREA MAGAZINE, THE
A monthly magazine on Korean culture and education, intended chiefly for missionaries, printed by the YMCA Press, and first published in January 1917. The editorial board consisted of S. A. Beck of the American Bible Society, the Methodists

Willard G. Cram and W. Arthur Noble, and Presbyterian **J. S. Gale**. Gale, using several pseudonyms, did most of the writing, including a translation of **Yi Haejo**'s *Okchunghwa*. The last issue was in April 1919, when Gale went on furlough.

KOREA MISSION FIELD, THE

A monthly magazine published in Seoul by the General Council of the Evangelical Missions in Korea from 1904 to 1941. Most of the content was missionary-related, but articles on Korean culture and history also appeared in it. **Gale**'s *History* appeared from July 1924 to September 1927.

KOREA, NAMES FOR

The first native name for the whole peninsula was **Silla**, earlier called Saro, Sŏbul or Sŏrabŏl – probably *idu* spellings of a native name meaning 'eastern capital', which may also have given 'Seoul'. Silla was succeeded by **Koryŏ**, 'high and beautiful', an abbreviation of **Koguryŏ** (possibly a native word meaning 'high fortress'), whose military tradition Koryŏ hoped to restore.

In 1392 the Hongwu Emperor was asked to name the new dynasty and given two suggestions: Hwanyŏng, another name for Yŏnghŭng, **Yi Sŏnggye**'s birthplace, and **Chosŏn**, which appeared in 5th-century Chinese records as the first legendary Korean state. He chose Chosŏn. The Chinese characters *chaoxian* suggest 'dynastic freshness' or a land where 'morning is fresh' – the sunrise direction, east of China – but may be a transliteration of a tribal name, such as Suchen (*see* **Suksin**). The quaint translation 'Land of Morning Calm' first appears in *Chosŏn* by the American Percival Lowell in 1885, and probably derives from **Dallet**'s use of *Sérénité du Matin* in 1874.

Koryŏ remained the familiar name for the country in China (as *Gaoli*) and Japan (as *Korai*) and was thus the name first heard by western voyagers. The earliest known western reference is to 'Caule' in chapter 29 of William of Rubruck's account of his visit to Mongolia in 1253. This becomes 'Cauli' in Marco Polo's story of Nayan's revolt against Kublai Khan. Cartographers begin to reflect Japanese contacts in the latter part of the 16th century, as when the Fleming Peter Plancius notices 'Corai' in 1593 and Jan Huygen van Linschoten 'Corea' in 1596. English 'Coray' appeared in Hakluyt (1600), apparently learnt through Portuguese. 'Corea' (1613) soon became normal, but 'Korea' appears as early as 1738 and was generally accepted in the 19th century, though 'Corea' lingered as a rarity until 1940. The sobriquet 'Hermit Kingdom' was first used in an article 'Corea, last of the Hermit Nations' in *The Independent*, New York, May 1878. (The modern Korean equivalent of 'hermit nation' is *swaeguk* 'locked country' or *tun'guk* 'recluse country'.)

'Chosŏn' (J. Chōsen) did not pass into international use until the Japanese **annexation** of 1910. It was retained after 1945 in Chosŏn Inmin Konghwaguk by the Communist state in the north; but in 1948 the Republic restored the name of the short-lived Korean Empire of 1895–1910: Taehan 'Land of the Han', after the Han tribes (**Samhan**) who preceded the Three Kingdoms.

Sobriquets for the country included *Dongyi* (K. *Tongi*), 'eastern barbarians', and *Junzi zhi guo* (K. *Kunja-ji-guk*), 'country of gentlemen' (from *Shanhai jing*). Koreans preferred references to their location east of China: *Haedong* 'east of the sea', *Tongguk* 'east country', *Taedong* 'great east', *Tongt'o* 'eastern land', *Chindan* 'eastern rule' (*chin* – C. *chen* – being the **trigram** for the east in the 'King Wen order' and -*dan* possibly a transliteration of -*tan* in 'Turkestan' and the like) and *Ch'ŏnggu* 'blue or green hills' (found in *Shanhai jing*; *ch'ŏng* was the colour of the east). *Sohwa* 'lesser flower' or 'Little China', and *Kyerim* 'cock forest' were used in the Chosŏn dynasty.

Asadal (perhaps an ancient non-Chinese word for Chosŏn), *Kunyŏk* 'hibiscus land' (*see* **flower, national**), *Chejam* 'flatfish ridges' and *Chŏbyŏk* or *Cheyŏk* 'plaice land' (referring to the fish of Korean seas or to the map of the country with its mountain spine) are recorded by **Ch'oe Namsŏn**, apparently as modern names.
See also **Chōsen**

KOREA PRESERVATION SOCIETY (*Poanhoe* 保安會)

Founded in 1904 by Song Suman (b.1857) and subsequently led by Yi Sangsŏl (1871–1917), one of many brief-lived societies that filled the vacuum left by the **Independence Club**. Its initial aim was to resist Japanese seizure of Korean land.

KOREA REVIEW, THE

A monthly magazine (January 1901 – December 1905) published by the Methodist Mission, planned as a record of current affairs with a general 'notes and queries' department and intended as successor to *The Korean Repository*. Edited and almost entirely written by **H. B. Hulbert**, it ceased publication without warning when he became politically active. Some contributors with Korean names were probably foreigners using pseudonyms.

KOREA-U.S.A. TREATY (1882) *See* **Shufeldt Treaty**

KOREAN CENTRAL INTELLIGENCE AGENCY/ AGENCY FOR NATIONAL SECURITY PLANNING *Chungang Chŏngboguk* 中央情報局 */Kukka Anjŏn Kihoekpu* 國家安全企劃部

The (South) Korean Central Intelligence Agency (KCIA) was established in June 1961. **Kim Chŏngp'il**, one of the architects of the 1961 military coup (*see* **Military junta**), was its first head. It was loosely modelled on the United States' Central Intelligence Agency. Its main task was to gather and assess information about North Korea, but it also had a domestic function, helping to support Park Chung Hee (**Pak Chŏnghŭi**)'s autocratic rule and the *Yusin* **constitution**. It became widely hated for its secrecy and use of censorship, intimidation and terror. It suffered an eclipse when its director, Kim Chaegyu, killed President Park in 1979, but was renamed the Agency for National Security Planning in 1980 and resumed its former rôle. President **Kim Taejung**, who was frequently one of its targets in the past, promised far reaching reforms of the organisation after his election in 1997.

KOREAN COMMUNIST PARTY (KCP) *Chosŏn Kongsandang* 朝鮮共產黨

Established in Seoul in April 1925 by Cho Pongam (1898–1959) and **Pak Hŏnyŏng**, recently returned from study in Moscow, with support from the Irkutsk faction of **Yi Tonghwi**'s **Koryŏ Communist Party**. Its beginning was inauspicious. Almost destroyed by the so-called **Sinŭiju Incident** in November, it was re-formed in December only to collapse again with the arrest of members in the **June Tenth Incident**. Further attempts at reorganisation between 1928 and 1930 were scotched by the Japanese, and Pak himself was arrested. Some members went abroad, and of those who remained some radical left-wing activists joined the **New Shoot Society** (*Sin'ganhoe*). In May 1936 **Kim Ilsŏng** became chairman of the united front Association for the Restoration of the Fatherland, set up in **Manchuria**. It liaised with the *Ch'ŏndo-gyo* sect in northern Korea and with Chinese communists in the north-east, but it was not itself a communist front organisation. When the Japanese responded to guerilla activities in Manchuria in 1939–40 its members fled to **Siberia**.

Communism first gained popular support in Korea after the Japanese surrender. Under the terms of the **Moscow Conference** Agreement the Soviet Union occupied northern Korea and accepted the aim of four-power **trusteeship**. Korean communists returned from abroad late in 1945 to join those already there, one of whom was the man who quickly assumed the mantle of leadership, **Pak Hŏnyŏng**. Despite Soviet influence in the north, Seoul was recognised as the centre of communist authority, but the party was riven by disunity from the very beginning. Pak proclaimed the formation of a new, united front, KCP, on 11 September. A conference of northern communists took place from 10 to 13 October 1945 in P'yŏngyang, and set up a North Korea Bureau of the KCP, of which it is possible that **Kim Ilsŏng** was appointed Secretary. Kim was as yet little known in Korea, but already had strong Soviet backing.

Though members of the KCP played an active part in promoting the **Korean People's Republic**, it extended its power by suppressing nationalists such as **Cho Mansik** and members of *Ch'ŏndo-gyo*. In the south, it was one of the parties on the Korean Advisory Council appointed to assist the **American Military Government**, but in May 1946 its leaders were arrested for forging currency, and many more were punished after the ensuing rioting. Pak escaped to P'yŏngyang, where in 1948 he became vice-premier of the Supreme People's Assembly. In the north, the KCP embarked on its path towards totalitarian rule. By 1947 it had a membership of 680,000 (in contrast to the estimated 30–40,000 members in the south), and when elections to local **People's Committees** were held in November 1947 the Democratic National United Front, a mainly communist bloc, obtained 97 per cent of the votes. Meanwhile communist sympathisers in the south helped to organise the **Cheju Rebellion** in 1948, after which a purge effectively destroyed the party.

ROBERT A. SCALAPINO & CHONG-SIK LEE, Communism in Korea, Part I: the Movement, Part II: the Society, Berkeley: University of California Press, 1972; SUH DAE-SOOK, Documents of Korean Communism: 1918–1948, Princeton University Press, 1970; SUH DAE-SOOK, The Korean Communist Movement, 1918–1948, Princeton University Press, 1967

See also **Communist Youth League**

KOREAN CONSPIRACY TRIAL (1912) *See* **Hundred and Five, the Case of the**

KOREAN DECLARATION OF INDEPENDENCE (1919) *See* **Independence, Declaration of; March First Movement**

KOREAN DEMOCRATIC PARTY *Chosŏn Minjudang* 朝鮮民主黨
North Korean middle-ground nationalist party founded in 1945 by **Cho Mansik** supported by intellectuals, students, Christians and small landowners. Under its second leader, the communist Ch'oe Yonggŏn, its democratic ideals were subverted and it was sacrificed to the political consolidation of the North under **Kim Ilsŏng**.

KOREAN DEMOCRATIC PARTY (KDP) *Han'guk Minjudang* 韓國民主黨
Right-wing party formed on 16 September 1945 to counter the proclamation of the **Korean People's Republic** (KPR) by **Yŏ Unhyŏng**. Its founders, who had only recently created smaller right-wing groups such as the Chosŏn Minjok Party and the Han'guk Kungmin Party, included Song Chinu (b.1889), **Kim Sŏngsu**, Kim Pyŏngno (1887–1964), Yi In, Pak Namhun, Hŏ Chŏng, and Chang Tŏksu (b.1895). Syngman Rhee (**Yi Sŭngman**), **Kim Ku** and **Sŏ Chaep'il** were elected to its leadership, although they had not yet returned to Korea and their support had not been obtained. The membership included a broad spectrum of intellectuals, landowners, businessmen

and industrialists. Some had been former members of the **New Shoot Society** (*Sin'ganhoe*), and on 24 October the leaders gained the support of a group of **Korean Communist Party** members who were disaffected with the policies of **Pak Hŏnyŏng** and now committed themselves to support for the **Provisional Government**, still in Chongqing, and its swift return to Seoul. The KDP manifesto was not dissimilar to that of its rival KPR. It called for **land reform**, guaranteed freedom of speech, and improved standards of industrial management, education, and health care. It anticipated a gradual transition to democracy. Its members had influence within the **American Military Government**, which supported it rather than the leftist KPR. However, they were disappointed by the refusal of General **Hodge** to recognise the Korean Provisional Government in the reestablishment of independent Korean politics.

Song Chinu was assassinated in December 1945 and Chang Tŏksu in December 1947, reputedly by supporters of Kim Ku. In 1948, under Kim Sŏngsu, the Party won 29 of the 198 seats filled by the 10 May elections to the first South Korean version of the National Assembly, but was awarded no cabinet places. In 1949 it merged with other parties to form the Democratic Nationalist Party.

See also **Republic of Korea; UNTCOK**

KOREAN HISTORY COMPILATION COMMITTEE / SOCIETY *Chōsenshi Henshū-kai* 朝鮮史編修會

Body established by the Japanese **Government General** in 1922 to rewrite the history of Korea from earliest times to 1894, interpreting it as one of dependence on Japan rather than as that of an independent state, and justifying the colonial occupation. It completed its publication of *Chōsen-shi* in 37 volumes in 1938. The formation of the Committee, renamed Society in 1925, has been seen as a response to the work of Pak Ŭnsik (1859–1926), formerly editor of *Taehan Maeil Sinbo*, who during his years in exile in **Siberia** and Shanghai between 1919 and 1926 wrote books denouncing the Japanese seizure of his country. **Nationalism** continued to influence studies of Korean history by Japanese and Korean historians alike into the second half of the century. It cannot, however, hide the remarkable achievements of Japanese archaeologists and engineers during the Colonial Period. The former were responsible for the first discoveries, of the utmost consequence, of the earliest remains from **Lelang, Koguryŏ, Kaya, Paekche** and **Silla**. Their findings were published in, *inter alia*, *Koseki Chōsa Hōkoku* ('Reports on the Investigation of Ancient Sites', 19 volumes, 1918–1937), *Chōsen Koseki Zufu* ('Record of Ancient Sites and Monuments in Korea', 5 volumes, 1915–1935), and *Koseki Chōsa Tokubetsu Hōkoku* ('Special Reports on Investigation of Ancient Sites', 7 volumes, 1919–1930). The latter prompted the enormous task of repairing and restoring important buildings and monuments after centuries of neglect.

KOREAN INDEPENDENCE PARTY *Han'guk tongnip-dang* 韓國獨立黨

Party formed in **Manchuria** in 1930. It moved to Shanghai and under **Kim Ku** helped to breathe fresh vigour into the **Provisional Government in Exile**. It was members of this Party who attempted to assassinate the Japanese emperor in 1932 and who attacked senior Japanese officials in Shanghai later the same year. Members of its military branch, the Korean Independence Army, received training at Chiang Kaishek's Luoyang Military Academy, but Japanese pressure reduced the effectiveness of this programme after 1933. In 1937 the Independence Party allied with the Korean Nationalist Party and was re-formed under Kim Ku in Chongqing in 1940 in an attempt to reunite the divided nationalist groups. It co-operated with Chiang Kai-shek's government, and organised the **Restoration Army**. After Kim's return to Korea in 1945 he re-formed and used the Party to oppose **trusteeship** and the move towards separate governments in south and north Korea (*see* **Moscow Conference**). Consequently the Party boycotted the election on 10 May 1948 from which Syngman Rhee (**Yi Sŭngman**) subsequently gained the presidency of the **First Republic**.

KOREAN LANGUAGE *See* **Language, Korean**

KOREAN LANGUAGE [RESEARCH] INSTITUTE / SOCIETY *Han'gŭl Hakhoe, Chosŏnŏ Hakhoe* 朝鮮語學會 *See Han'gŭl* **Society**

KOREAN MARITIME CUSTOMS SERVICE *See* **Maritime Customs Service**

KOREAN NATIONAL REVOLUTIONARY PARTY *Minjok Hyŏngmyŏngdang* 民主革命黨
Grouping of left-wing Korean nationalist parties formed in Shanghai in 1935, with a military front dedicated to the ending of Japanese imperialism. Its organisers included **Kim Kyusik**, Kim Wŏnbong (*see Ŭibyŏng*) and Cho Soang. In response to its formation, **Kim Ku** established his **Korean Nationalist Party**.

KOREAN NATIONALIST PARTY *Kungmindang* 韓國國民黨
Formed by **Kim Ku** in 1936 following the effective demise of the **Korean Independence Party** in the mid-1930s. Cho Soang (1887–?1950) revived the latter in 1937, and the Marco Polo Bridge Incident and Japanese aggression in China had the effect of reuniting the two Parties under Kim.

KOREAN PEOPLE'S ARMY (KPA) *Chosŏn inmin-gun* 朝鮮人民軍
The army of the **Democratic People's Republic of Korea** (DPRK), founded in February 1948 and including resistance fighters returned from Yan'an, north-east China and **Siberia**. The bulk of its strength was drawn from conscripts, described as volunteers, as it built up its resources to prepare for the reunification of the country by force if necessary. It received training and weapons from Russian and Chinese communists, and was under the overall command of **Kim Ilsŏng**. Some 56,000 Koreans who had fought with the Chinese People's Liberation Army (PLA) in the Chinese Civil War returned to North Korea after 1 October 1949. By the outbreak of the **Korean War**, it is estimated that the army comprised 100,000 men, the tank brigade 8,800, the navy 15,000 and the air force 2,300. Weaponry and equipment received from the Soviet Union included 258 tanks. The KPA launched its attack on the South on the night of 24 June 1950 and made rapid progress against numerically inferior opponents. Despite post-War propaganda from the South and the United States, the evidence suggests that KPA treatment of the population in captured towns and territory throughout the War was less brutal than that meted out by South Korean commanders and politicians.

Since the ending of the Korean War the DPRK has become a military dictatorship in which the KPA has ruthlessly carried out the policies of the ruling communist hierarchy. It is controlled by the Military Committee of the **Korean Workers' Party** (KWP) and the Military Commission of the Central People's Committee. As in China, the Communist Party commands the gun, though reaction to power changes since the death of Kim Ilsŏng, coupled with the effects of famine, may have strained KPA loyalty. Indeed, if the KWP commands the gun, it is no less true to say that in inheriting his father's mantle as national leader, **Kim Chŏngil** is dependent upon the support of the KPA. With an estimated strength of up to 1·1 millions, it has been the chief beneficiary of an increasingly overstretched economy, although despite fears of the country's nuclear capacity it is doubtful how modern its equipment generally is. Conscription begins at the age of sixteen, and there are extensive reserve and militia units. Though North Korea spends much time in a state of heightened military alert and concentrates substantial forces along the **DMZ**, units of the KPA – like the Chinese PLA – also have a rôle in construction and other tasks assisting the civilian population. South Korean defence forces have apprehended or killed a significant number of its members sent to carry out spying and subversion raids.

KOREAN PEOPLE'S PARTY *Inmin-dang* 人民黨
Left-wing political party founded by **Yŏ Unhyŏng** in November 1945. General **Hodge** sought to involve it in a coalition Council of centre and leftist politicians, but despite Yŏ's professed readiness to collaborate with **Kim Kyusik** he remained deeply involved with the affairs of the more extreme **Korean Communist Party**, and continued to contend with **Pak Hŏnyŏng** for the allegiance of the communists in South Korea.

KOREAN PEOPLE'S REPRESENTATIVE ASSEMBLY *Minju-ŭiwŏn* 民主議院
Meeting of 1500 representatives from north and south Korea convened in March 1947 by **Kim Ku**. Kim sought approval for the declaration of a Provisional Republic of Korea, but his proposal was rejected. When he then resigned as chairman of the **Provisional Government in** [former] **Exile**, Syngman Rhee (**Yi Sŭngman**) urged the delegates to disband the Assembly.
See also **American Military Government**

KOREAN PEOPLE'S REPUBLIC *Chosŏn Inmin Konghwa-guk* (KPR) 朝鮮人民共和國
Body formed in Seoul on 6 September 1945 by representatives of **Yŏ Unhyŏng**'s Preparatory Committee for Building the Country (*Kŏn'guk Chunbi Wiwŏnhoe*), in readiness for government after the unexpectedly sudden Japanese surrender. Yŏ's objective was to form a united front, and 600 delegates met to choose a cabinet and draft a constitution. Syngman Rhee (**Yi Sŭngman**) was nominated as president, Yŏ himself vice-president, and **Hŏ Hŏn** prime minister. Among the cabinet members were **Kim Ku** (Minister for the Interior), **Kim Kyusik** (Foreign Minister), **Cho Mansik** (Finance Minister), and **Kim Sŏngsu** (Education Minister). But Cho and Kim Sŏngsu were not present and had not agreed to their nomination, while Syngman Rhee, Kim Kyusik and Kim Ku had not yet returned to Korea. Its manifesto anticipated **land reform** and the nationalisation of large companies, and it organised the establishment of **People's Committees** throughout the country. On 12 November, Yŏ resigned and founded the **Korean People's Party**, leaving the communists **Pak Hŏnyŏng** and Hŏ Hŏn effectively in control. Kim Ku and Kim Kyusik returned to Seoul on 23 November, but Hŏ failed to persuade them to join the KPR. Because of its left-wing orientation it was accepted in the Soviet-backed north, where Cho Mansik became head of the People's Committee for North Korea, but in the south it failed to gain recognition from General **Hodge**'s **American Military Government** and prompted the counter-formation of the right-wing nationalist **Korea Democratic Party** (KDP), which itself elected Syngman Rhee and Kim Ku to its Central Committee. The American Military Government preferred to deal with the KDP rather than the KPR, which was proscribed by General Hodge on 12 December 1945.

KOREAN PEOPLE'S REVOLUTIONARY ARMY

Military wing of the **Korean Revolutionary Party**. The Anti-Japanese People's Guerilla Army collaborated with Chinese communist military organisations in **Manchuria**, and together they achieved a joint victory over Japanese forces at Xingjing in October 1933. Among the Koreans who were recruited into the Sino-Korean North-East People's Revolutionary Army, formed in 1933, was one who became known as a hero, **Kim Ilsŏng**. The name was subsequently claimed by four anti-Japanese guerillas, including the one who would later become leader of the **Democratic People's Korean Republic**, and it is now claimed that he was the founder of the KPRA in March 1934. In the first half of the 1930s KPRA units undertook missions through Manchuria and northern Korea, not only harrassing the Japanese but also educating local people with resistance and communist propaganda. The Japanese gained the upper hand through the late thirties, but the KPRA was again active in northern Korea before the Japanese surrender in 1945.
See also **Korean People's Army**

KOREAN PEOPLE'S SOCIALIST PARTY (KPSP) *Hanin Sahoedang* 韓人社會黨

Party formed in Khabarovsk, **Siberia**, in June 1918 by **Yi Tonghwi** with the help of Russian Bolsheviks. Other left-wing Korean organisations in eastern Russia included the Korean section of the Irkutsk Communist Party. Military groups had considerable resources at their command, some supplied by Soviet sympathisers, and Yi was reported by the Japanese to have set up a Korean military training academy. On 25 April 1919, following the outbreak of the **March First Movement** in Korea, the KPSP organised a joint conference of pro-Bolshevik Korean groups at Vladivostok in an attempt to coordinate socialist activities in the Russian Far East. A delegation was sent to Moscow and was successful in soliciting funds. However, by the time it returned to Siberia in September, Yi Tonghwi had left for Shanghai. The Irkutsk Korean communists then claimed to have superseded the KPSP as leaders of the Korean independence movement in Siberia, and took the title **Koryŏ Communist Party** (*Koryŏ Kongsandang*).
ROBERT A. SCALAPINO & CHONG-SIK LEE, *Communism in Korea, Part I: the Movement*, Berkeley: University of California Press, 1972
See also **Provisional Government in Exile**

KOREAN PROVISIONAL GOVERNMENT *Taehan Min'guk Imsi Chŏngbu* 大韓民國臨時政府 *See* **Provisional Government in Exile**

KOREAN REPOSITORY, THE

A monthly magazine for expatriates, published January to December 1892 by the Methodist Mission Press with Franklin Ohlinger as editor, and January 1895 to December 1898 by the Trilingual Press at Paejae School with the Methodists Henry Gerhard **Appenzeller** and George Heber Jones as editors. It was the most readable of the missionary magazines published in Seoul, and contained articles on current affairs as well as culture and language. Some of **J. S. Gale**'s first **sijo** translations appeared in it and some articles on language by 'Yi Ikseup', who was probably a foreigner using a pseudonym. When the Methodist Mission was depleted by furloughs during 1899, publication was suspended and was never resumed; but the *Repository* had prepared the way for the **Royal Asiatic Society**.

KOREAN REVOLUTIONARY PARTY *Han'guk hyŏngmyŏng-dang* 韓國革命黨
Also known as the National Centre; united front of nationalists and communists formed in **Manchuria** in April 1929, aimed at coordinating the anti-Japanese efforts of Koreans across the North-East and the establishment of a socialist republic in Korea. Those who refused to collaborate with the communists formed the **Korean Independence Party** in 1930.

KOREAN SOCIALIST PARTY *Chosŏn Sahoedang* 朝鮮社會黨
Said to have been formed by Sin Kyusik (1879–1922) in Shanghai in August 1917 as part of the incipient nationalist movement abroad. Its aims represented the ideals of young Koreans abroad dedicated to the restoration of Korean independence, and it may have sought to send an appeal to the International Socialist Conference in Stockholm, but its activities were quickly subsumed in events following the arrival of **Yi Tonghwi** from Khabarovsk in September 1919.
See also **Koryŏ Communist Party; Provisional Government in Exile**

KOREAN TEMPORARY SECURITY ORDINANCE (1940)
Measure passed by the **Government-General** on 26 December 1940 in order to further limit freedom of speech by Koreans and to deter them from the anticipation of Japanese defeat. The Ordinance resulted in the imprisonment of suspected spies and the arrest of many people accused of spreading sedition.

KOREAN WAR *Yugio tongnan* 六二五動亂 (1950 3)
Following the division of Korea in 1945 and the establishment of separate states north and south of the **Thirty-Eighth Parallel** in 1948, both claimed the allegiance of all Koreans and called for the reunification of the peninsula. There was considerable tension along the parallel and much fighting between the two sides, with each engaging in armed excursions and artillery attacks against the other. Such incidents increased after the withdrawal of Soviet forces from the North in 1948, and US forces from the South the following year. However, the two sides were not evenly matched militarily, for the departing Soviet troops had laid the foundations of a proper army, which was reinforced after the end of the Chinese civil war in 1949 by the return of Koreans who had been fighting with the victorious communist forces. The North may have had some 100,000 men in combat divisions, though estimates vary from 89,000 to 139,000 against the South's 65,000. The Soviet Union had also supplied more and better equipment to Koreans in the North than the United States did to those in the South. In June 1950, with Soviet and Chinese agreement, **Kim Ilsŏng** began an attempt to reunify the country by force. He himself assumed the job of commander-in-chief of the armed forces. His chief of staff was Lt. General Kang Kon and the deputy chief of staff Yi Sangjo. The chief of the operations directorate was Lt. General Yu Sŏngchŏl. The First Corps was commanded by Lt. General Kim Ŭng, and the Second by Major General Kim Kwanghyŏp, with General Kim Ch'aek as overall 'Front Commander'. The South Korean army was organised in three Corps, with Major General Ch'ae Pyŏngdŏk as chief of staff and General Kim Paegil as his deputy.

The Korean War erupted on the Ongjin Peninsula at 0400 hours on Sunday 25 June 1950, following which North Korean guns opened up eastwards along the 38th parallel. The artillery attack was followed by an armoured advance, which met little resistance. Within three days, the North Korean armies occupied Seoul. As the advance carried on south, the South Korean government retreated to Taejŏn, then to **Taegu**, and finally to the port of **Pusan**.

Although the United States had declared in 1949 that Korea lay outside its area of defence interests, President Truman now decided that the North Korean attack was a challenge by international communism to the free world which could not be ignored. The US sent a small contingent of troops to try to shore up the South Korean resistance, without success. It also mobilised the United Nations Security Council, in the absence of the Soviet Union, to agree to a series of resolutions between 25 June and 7 July 1950. These demanded an immediate end to hostilities, the withdrawal of North Korean forces, recommended that member states should assist South Korea, and established a Unified Command under a US-designated commander to resist the North Korean forces. On 7 July Truman appointed General Douglas MacArthur, then Supreme Allied Commander in Japan, as the head of the Command. Sixteen nations – Australia, Belgium, Canada, Colombia, Ethiopia, France, Greece, Luxembourg, the Netherlands, New Zealand, the Philippines, South Africa, Thailand, Turkey, the United Kingdom, and the US – supplied contingents to serve under him. The US Eighth Army was headed by Lt. General Walton Walker, who also assumed command of UN ground forces. A number of other countries sent medical assistance.

As indicated above, the North had profited from prior Soviet military assistance, and it continued to do so even though no Russian combat troops were sent openly to the war. Senior military experts served as advisers to Kim Ilsŏng, notably Lt-General Vasilyeyev and Major-General Vostnikov. After the Chinese entry into the war, the deputy chief of staff in the Soviet army, General Zakharov, was assigned as head of the military adviser group to the People's Liberation Army general staff. Moreover, in the virtual absence of any North Korean air force, Russian pilots under the command of Lt. General Lobov dressed in Chinese uniforms and flew MiGs against UN aircraft. Throughout the war, the Soviet Union supplied the greater part of the arms and ammunition used by the communist side – for which it later required recompense from North Korea and China.

By early September 1950 North Korean soldiers occupied most of the peninsula, while the South Korean government was confined to the far south-east in an area known as the 'Pusan perimeter'. However, in early September MacArthur launched an ambitious amphibious operation against **Inch'ŏn**, the port of Seoul. Both Mao Zedong and Stalin had warned Kim Ilsŏng that this would be the most likely place for the start of a United Nations counter-offensive, but Kim had disregarded the advice. Using Japanese naval personnel to guide his forces through the sandbanks on 15 September, MacArthur achieved a major victory. Inch'ŏn was taken, and Seoul soon recaptured. Meanwhile, UN forces began a breakout from Pusan, driving the North Koreans back towards the 38th parallel. MacArthur's view was that there should be no stopping there, a position endorsed by a further UN Security Council resolution on 7 October. P'yŏngyang, capital of the Democratic People's Republic, fell on 19 October, and the UN armies pushed on towards the **Yalu River**. North Korea virtually ceased to exist as a functioning state, and the end of the war seemed in sight.

On 1 October, Kim Ilsŏng had appealed to Mao Zedong for help. As the United Nations penetrated further into North Korea, the Chinese government expressed its concern to diplomats in Beijing, hinting that unless the foreign forces stopped their advance, China would intervene. The warnings were discounted by MacArthur and the UN command, as were initial contacts with small groups of Chinese troops, who had crossed the Yalu River on 19 October. They fired their first shots on 25 October, and the floodgates quickly opened. As large numbers of Chinese troops, thinly disguised as **'Chinese People's Volunteers'**, were thrown at the UN soldiers by the end of the month, it was no longer possible to ignore them. Chinese and Soviet pilots in MiG-15s fought an air battle over Sinŭiju on 8 November. MacArthur panicked and ordered a retreat south, a retreat which soon became a rout, known as the 'bug out'. In December, General Walker died and was succeeded by General Matthew Bunker Ridgway.

The Chinese swept across the 38th parallel, capturing Seoul for the second time on 4 January 1951. They were commanded by Peng Dehuai, with Deng Hua as his deputy and Xie Fang as chief of staff. Their main force was the XIII Army Corps, though the III and IX Army Corps also took part in the war. The United Nations regrouped south of Seoul, and from there launched a counter-offensive in February. Extended supply lines soon told on the Chinese forces. Seoul was retaken on 15 March, and UN forces again crossed the 38th parallel in April. This time there was no attempt to push further north, and the war settled down into a stalemate. The Chinese launched a major retaliation later the same month, but while they inflicted heavy casualties, they failed to penetrate the UN lines. On the UN side, 11 April 1951 saw President Truman's dismissal of General MacArthur, who was replaced by General Ridgway. Command of UN ground forces passed to Lt-General James van Fleet.

The war now became one of attrition, similar to the First World War. Following a Soviet initiative, supported by the Chinese, suggesting talks about a cease-fire, the United Nations responded positively, and negotiations began on 10 July 1951 at **Kaesŏng**, behind North Korean lines. They were suspended in August after alleged Chinese and North Korean violations of the area's neutrality; they resumed at a new venue, **P'anmunjŏm**, on 25 October 1951.

These meetings continued until the summer of 1953, with intermittent fighting, sometimes heavy, continuing at the same time. The death of the Soviet leader, Joseph Stalin, in March 1953 seemed to improve the atmosphere and to speed up the dialogue. After much discussion, sick and wounded prisoners were exchanged between 20 April and 3 May. At the same time, diplomats and other civilian detainees held in North Korea since 1950 were released via the Soviet Union. However, in an attempt to sabotage the truce negotiations, South Korean President Syngman Rhee (**Yi Sŭngman**) set free on 18 June some 25,000 prisoners of war who did not want to return to the communist North. Despite this and continued fighting along the front almost to the last minute, an **armistice** was finally signed at 10.00 Korean time on 27 July 1953, coming into force at 22.00. As well as setting up a Military Armistice Commission to supervise the cease-fire, the agreement called for a political conference to address the issue of Korean reunification. Although Korea was a main item on the agenda of the 1954 **Geneva Conference**, no agreement was reached there, and the armistice remains in force.

The cost of the war was great. Estimates of casualties vary greatly, but all attest to its devastating legacy. Some four million were killed, wounded and left missing, of whom three million were Koreans. 50,000 Americans may have died in battle or as a result of wounds, and perhaps ten times as many Chinese. An additional ten million Koreans saw their families broken up by the war; most remain divided to the present day, with little or no news of their relatives. South Korea claims that up to 5,000 prisoners of war may still be detained in the North. Physical damage was equally horrendous, as huge areas of the peninsula had been bombed or damaged by the movement of the armies. Both North and South Korea lost most of the economic gains made since independence in 1945, and both were left heavily dependent on outside support, which confirmed Korea's deep involvement in the Cold War between East and West. There was also a political price to pay domestically: in the North, Kim Ilsŏng moved fast to create a dictatorship. In the South, the war had both reinforced Rhee's autocratic tendencies and paved the way for nearly three decades of military dominance and repression.

CHEN JIAN, *China's Road to the Korean War: the Making of the Sino-American Confrontation*, New York: Columbia University Press, 1994; KOH BYUNG CHOL, 'The war's impact on the Korean peninsula', in WILLIAM J. WILLIAMS, ed., *A Revolutionary War: Korea and the Transformation of the Post-War World*, Chicago: Imprint Publications, 1993; BRUCE CUMINGS, *The Origins of the Korean War*, Princeton University Press, 2 vols. 1981, 1988; MAX HASTINGS, *The Korean War*, London: Michael Joseph, 1987; PETER LOWE, *The Origins of the Korean War*, London & New York: Longman & Co., 2nd ed. 1997; JOHN MERRILL, *Korea: The Peninsular Origins of the War*, Newark, N.J.: University of Delaware Press, 1989; WILLIAM STUECK, *The Korean War: an International History*, Princeton University Press, 1997; ZHANG SHU GUANG, *Mao's Military Romanticism: China and the Korean War, 1950-1953*, Lawrence: University Press of Kansas, 1995

KOREAN WOMEN'S PATRIOTIC SOCIETY *Taehan Min'guk Aeguk Pŭinhoe*
大韓民國愛國婦人會 *See* **Women's movement**

KOREAN WORKERS' PARTY (KWP) *Chosŏn Nodong-dang* 朝鮮勞動黨
The main organ of communist power in North Korea, founded in August 1946 and quickly dominated by **Kim Ilsŏng**. In establishing his own authority, and that of the Kapsan faction of members returned from **Manchuria**, he outdid the leader of the communists in the south, **Pak Hŏnyŏng**. Kim became chairman of the Party and Pak his deputy until his purge in 1953.

The KWP National Party Congress should take place every five years but in fact meets irregularly. It elects a Central Committee of some 250 members, which together with the Politburo and the Standing Committee directs the Party. The leader of the Standing Committee is the General Secretary, a post held by Kim Ilsŏng alone until his death and then inherited by his son **Kim Chŏngil**. The Central Committee supervises a Political Committee, a Military Committee, a Control Committee, and the mass organisations which help to control the population. These organisations include the Socialist Working Youth League, the Young Pioneer Corps, the Democratic Women's League, and professional organisations for artists, scientists, medical, agricultural and industrial workers, and others. KWP is pledged to uphold *Chuch'e* ideology and to oppose 'capitalism, feudalistic Confucianism, revisionism, dogmatism, flunkeyism, factionalism, provincialism and nepotism'. In reality, it was called on to enforce the will of its demagogue Great Leader until his death in 1994. Its Military Committee part-controls the **Korean People's Army**.
LEE CHONGSIK, *The Korean Workers' Party*, Stanford: Hoover Institution Press, 1978

KOREAN YOUTH INDEPENDENCE ASSOCIATION *Chosŏn Ch'ŏngnyŏn Tongniptan* 朝鮮青年獨立團
Organisation of Korean youth in Japan, founded in January 1919. It was outspoken in calling for Korean independence, and in February its leaders, under the guidance of **Yi Kwangsu**, prepared a printed Declaration of Independence which was distributed widely to the Japanese government and press, as well as to the **Government-General** in Seoul. Many of its members were arrested.
KENNETH WELLS, 'Background to the March First Movement: Koreans in Japan, 1905–1919,' *KS* 13, 1989
See **Independence, Declaration of**

KORYŎ CHANGGYŎNG 高麗藏經 'Great Canon of Koryŏ'
Printed compilation of Korean Buddhist scriptures in 5,048 *kwŏn*. Begun on the orders of King Hyŏnjong in 1009 it took some forty years to complete, but was destroyed

during the **Mongol** invasions. A supplement in 4,874 *kwŏn, Sok Changgyŏng*, was prepared under King Sukchong (r. 1095–1105) but lost at the same time.
See also **Tripitaka Koreana**

KORYŎ COMMUNIST PARTY *Koryŏ Kongsandang* 高麗共產黨
Name adopted by **Yi Tonghwi**'s political party, formerly known as the **Korean People's Socialist Party**, following his move to Shanghai in 1919. The new party's date of inauguration is uncertain, and may have been in May 1920 or January 1921. Because the Irkutsk Korean communists had already assumed this title, there is some feeling that the term *Chosŏn Kongsandang* might have been used in Shanghai. Certainly, rivalry now developed between the factions in the two centres, not least because Moscow recognised Yi's party as the legitimate successor to the Korean People's Socialist Party and the rightful organisation to promote Korean independence outside Siberia. Moreover, it sent further financial support to the Party in Shanghai. Yi's use of these funds caused controversy within the **Provisional Government in Exile**, where other members claimed they were intended for non-partisan use. Factionalism within Yi's party and antagonism between the parties in Shanghai and Irkutsk escalated. The Irkutsk party established its own China centre in Peking and even recruited members within Shanghai, one of whom was **Yŏ Unhyŏng**. By mid-1921, it is estimated that the membership of Yi's party was c.6,000, that of the Irkutsk party c.4,500. Within both, tensions were apparent between Korean nationalist imperatives and the supra-nationalist expectations of the Comintern. Following the failure of a conference organised from Moscow at Verkhneudinsk (now Ulan Ude) on 20 October 1922 to resolve the differences between the warring factions, the Comintern ordered the dissolution of both parties, and their replacement by a Far East Area Committee, Korean Bureau, in Vladivostok.
ROBERT A. SCALAPINO & CHONG-SIK LEE, *Communism in Korea, Part I: the Movement*, Berkeley: University of California Press, 1972.

KORYŎ DYNASTY 高麗 (918–1392)
By adopting a name ('High and beautiful') derived from that of **Koguryŏ**, the founder of this dynasty, **Wang Kŏn** not only made a claim for historical legitimacy but, perhaps unwittingly, presaged the continuation of some of the characteristics of that great northern kingdom. These included reliance upon **Buddhism** and **Confucianism** as well as the native rites of **shamanism**, acknowledgement of the indispensibility of both education and military strength to the ruling classes, and an ambivalent attitude towards neighbouring **China** and **Japan** that veered from willing emulation to staunch independence. It was a long period of marked intellectual, cultural and technical progress, marred by political strife and foreign invasion.

Early Koryŏ maintained many of the institutions of Unified Silla, but its government benefited from the expansion of the aristocratic clan base from which leaders were drawn. Opportunities developed for lower members of these clans to move into the ranks of government through the **examination system**, establishing a combination of birth, landownership and education that evolved into the *yangban* system of the Chosŏn period. But social mobility was not free for all. Jealously guarded and widely resented aristocratic privileges prompted a crisis in the mid-12th century. **Myoch'ŏng**'s attempt to overthrow the dynasty in 1135 failed, but opened the way for military leaders to depose King Ŭijong in 1170 (*see* ***Chunghang***). They then proceeded to govern, or to misgovern, in the name of their puppet King Myŏngjong until brought to order by Ch'oe Ch'unghŏn (*see* **Ch'oe dictatorship**).

Admiration for China strengthened the position of the literati in government, and the basis of state education was implementation of the teachings of the **Confucian Classics** in both public and private life (*see* **An Hyang**). But the effects of the neo-Confucian renaissance in China took time to travel and were not yet strongly felt in Korea. Early Koryŏ had inherited the Silla period's widespread belief in Buddhism. Wang Kŏn's '**Ten Injunctions**' (*Sip hunyo*) established the ruling clan's reliance on the faith, and the court also maintained shamans to look after its own and the nation's interests (*see P'algwanhoe*).

At the beginning of the dynasty the boundary between Korea and **Manchuria** was fixed for the first time along the **Tumen** and **Yalu** Rivers, incorporating the southern provinces of the former **Parhae** kingdom. This was the cause of ongoing dispute with the new **Khitan** rulers of Manchuria, whose **Liao** state formed a triangular relationship with **Song** China and Koryŏ on the basis of military confrontation as well as peaceful diplomacy and commerce. A similar pattern of enmity and accommodation followed in the 12th century when the Khitan were ousted from Manchuria by the **Jurchen**. In both 11th and 12th centuries the Koryŏ royal family vainly invoked Buddhist and shamanistic rites as defence against attack, but after military defeats they came to terms with their neighbours, paying tribute to Liao and **Jin** rather than to Song China. More serious were the effects on the country's morale, economy and institutions of **Mongol** conquest and occupation between 1270 and 1392.

Regardless of the country's diplomatic or military fortunes, Korean **merchants** enjoyed notable success in international trade by land and sea during the Koryŏ period. In particular, the 11th century saw flourishing **commerce** with China and Manchuria. A record of the shipping and **market** systems was left by the Chinese envoy Xu Jing after his visit to the capital **Kaesŏng** in 1124 (*see Xuanhe fengshi Gaoli tujing*).

Koryŏ's position at the centre of international exchange, whether peaceful or hostile, is reflected in its outstanding cultural achievements, notably in ceramic technology, **painting**, **poetry**, **printing**, and **sculpture**. It was a period when Korean **craftsmen** responded imaginatively to many stimuli from outside. They imitated, adapted and in some fields even enhanced the best that China had to offer, and exported their own skills to Japan.

The subservience of the Korean kings to the Mongols was underlined after 1274 by the omission of the suffix -*jong* ('progenitor') from their titles and its replacement by the inferior form *Ch'ung x-wang*, 'loyal king x'. By the mid-14th century, however, the evident decline in the conquerors' authority encouraged King Kongmin to drop the 'loyalty' from his title, and by the time of his death in 1374 the Mongol Empire in East Asia had been shattered. The power vacuum which followed under the last three ineffectual Koryŏ rulers was marked by fierce rivalry between literati, soldiers, neo-Confucians and Buddhists, until General **Yi Sŏnggye** finally assumed the throne and established the new, Chosŏn, dynasty.

KINGS:

T'aejo	918–943	Chŏngjong	1034–46
Hyejong	943–5	Munjong	1046–83
Chŏngjong	945–9	Sunjong	1083
Kwangjong	949–975	Sŏnjong	1083–94
Kyŏngjong	975–981	Hŏnjong	1094–5
Sŏngjong	981–997	Sukchong	1095–1105
Mokchong	997–1009	Yejong	1105–1122
Hyŏnjong	1009–1031	Injong	1122–46
Tŏkchong	1031–4	Ŭijong	1146–70

Myŏngjong	1170–97	Ch'ungsuk Wang	1313–30, 1332–9
Sinjong	1197–1204	Ch'unghye Wang	1330–2, 1339–44
Hŭijong	1204–1211	Ch'ungmok Wang	1344–8
Kangjong	1211–3	Ch'ungjŏng Wang	1348–51
Kojong	1213–59	Kongmin Wang	1351–74
Wŏnjong	1259–74	U Wang	1374–88
Ch'ungyŏl Wang	1274–1308	Ch'ang Wang	1388–9
Ch'ungsŏn Wang	1308–1313	Kongyang Wang	1389–92

KIM UI GYU, 'Consciousness of Inheriting History in the Early Koryŏ Period,' KJ, 23/7, 1983
See also **ceramics**; **foundation myths**; **Sambyŏlch'o Resistance**; **Ŭich'ŏn**

KORYŎ-JANG 高麗葬 'Koryŏ funerals'

Koreans of the Three Kingdoms and Koryŏ periods impressed the Chinese with the richness of their grave goods, which made 'Korean funerals' proverbial. 20th-century Koreans say *Koryŏ-jang* means men of Koryŏ (or Koguryŏ) took weak and aged relatives to **tombs** where they enclosed them with food, leaving them to die. This notion is not supported by archaeological or literary evidence. It appears to be based on misunderstanding the purpose of food-vessels found in chamber-tombs.

KORYŎ-SA 高麗史 'History of Koryŏ'

The official history of the Koryŏ dynasty (918–1392). After Yi T'aejo founded the Chosŏn dynasty in 1392 he set about compiling the history of the previous dynasty according to the *sillok* procedure, entrusting the work to **Chŏng Tojŏn** and others, who finished *Koryŏ-guksa*, 'National History of Koryŏ', in 37 books by 1395. This proved unsatisfactory, partly because it recorded the use of imperial titles and pronouns for Koryŏ kings, which was considered insulting to Ming. A new draft was made, but this too proved inadequate, and another, *Sugyo Koryŏ-sa*, 'Corrected History of Koryŏ', was ordered by **Sejong** in 1424. The imperial vocabulary was restored, but the book still did not please the king. When an enlarged version, under the direction of Kwŏn Che, was printed in 1448, Kwŏn was found to have tampered with the facts and the book was destroyed. Kim Chongsŏ was entrusted with a fresh revision, planned on the lines of Sima Qian's great *Shiji* with fifty books of *sega* 'annals'; 39 of *chi* 'monographs' on **astronomy, music, dress**, finance, criminal justice and the like; two of *yŏnp'yo* 'year-tables' and fifty of *yŏlchŏn* 'biographies' of distinguished and notorious people. It was finished in 1451, but not printed till **Sejo** had usurped the throne, when the names of Kim Chongsŏ and other editors who had supported King **Tanjong** were removed from the preface. The work is designed to justify the 1392 change of dynasty, but remains the fundamental document for study of Koryŏ.

KORYŎ-SA CHŎRYO 高麗史節要 'Chronological Summary of Koryŏ History'

A history of the Koryŏ dynasty, setting all the material out in chronological order, printed in 1453, but virtually lost until it was republished in 1932. It was compiled by Kim Chongsŏ (1390–1453) and others, using *Sugyo Koryŏ-sa*, an early draft of *Koryŏ-sa* that no longer exists. *Koryŏ-sa chŏryo* is shorter than *Koryŏ-sa*, but contains some matter not in that work.

KORYŎ TOGYONG 高麗圖經 See *Xuanhe fengshi Gaoli tujing*

245

KOSA 告祀

The biggest of the sacrifices made to household spirits, usually in the autumn, to pray for good fortune and drive out evil.

Although *p'ansu* might be invited or *mudang* asked to dance and bring their music, the lady of the house presided. She bathed in preparation for the ceremony. In the evening straw tabu ropes were set up with pine-branches before the door of the yard, and yellow earth was scattered on the threshold. No one was allowed to go in or out. A sacrificial offering of food was prepared and **mantras** or prayers recited to the *t'ŏju* and the spirits of each room, gatehouse, storeroom and outhouse, including the *ch'ŭksin* and the spirits of pigstyes and cowsheds. In the morning the family joined in eating the sacrificial food.

See also **festivals; rites and ceremonies; shamanism**

KUGU-P'YO 九九表 'nine nines table'

Also known as *kugu-ppŏp*. Traditional Chinese multiplication table of 45 phrases giving all multiples of single digits. It consists of numbers only, the first two in each line giving the remainder of the line when multiplied together.

1-1-1	4-4-16	4-6-24	7-7-49	1-9-9
1-2-2	1-5-5	5-6-30	1-8-8	2-9-18
2-2-4	2-5-10	6-6-36	2-8-16	3-9-27
1-3-3	3-5-15	1-7-7	3-8-24	4-9-36
2-3-6	4-5-20	2-7-14	4-8-32	5-9-45
3-3-9	5-5-25	3-7-21	5-8-40	6-9-54
1-4-4	1-6-6	4-7-28	6-8-48	7-9-63
2-4-8	2-6-12	5-7-35	7-8-56	8-9-72
3-4-12	3-6-18	6-7-42	8-8-64	9-9-81

Kugwi-ga, 'division song', is a mnemonic for *kugwi-ppŏp* or *kugwije-ppŏp*, 'division of single digits by larger digits'. It consists of 45 5-character lines of varying grammatical form and is more useful and more memorable than it appears to be in translation. The answers are calculated in tenths.

1 into 1: 10/10 = 1
2 into 1: 5/10
2 into 2: 10/10 = 1
3 into 1: 3/10; 1/10 over
3 into 2: 6/10; 2/10 over
3 into 3: 10/10
4 into 1: 2/10; 2/10 over
4 into 2: 5/10
4 into 3: 7/10; 2/10 over
4 into 4: 10/10 = 1
5 into 1: 2/10
5 into 2: 4/10
5 into 3: 6/10
5 into 4: 8/10
5 into 5: 10/10 = 1
6 into 1: 1/10; 4/10 over
6 into 2: 3/10; 2/10 over
6 into 3: 5/10

7 into 3: 4/10; 2/10 over
7 into 4: 5/10; 5/10 over
7 into 5: 7/10; 1/10 over
7 into 6: 8/10; 4/10 over
7 into 7: 10/10 = 1
8 into 1: 1/10; 2/10 over
8 into 2: 2/10; 4/10 over
8 into 3: 3/10; 6/10 over
8 into 4: 5/10
8 into 5: 6/10; 2/10 over
8 into 6: 7/10; 4/10 over
8 into 7: 8/10; 6/10 over
8 into 8: 10/10 = 1
9 into 1: 1/10; 1/10 over
9 into 2: 2/10; 2/10 over
9 into 3: 3/10; 3/10 over
9 into 4: 4/10; 4/10 over
9 into 5: 5/10; 5/10 over

6 into 4: 6/10; 4/10 over
6 into 5: 8/10; 2/10 over
6 into 6: 10/10 = 1
7 into 1: 1/10, 3/10 over
7 into 2: 2/10; 6/10 over

9 into 6: 6/10; 6/10 over
9 into 7: 7/10; 7/10 over
9 into 8: 8/10; 8/10 over
9 into 9: 10/10 = 1

KUGUNG 九宮 *See* nine palaces divination

KUGYŎL 口訣
System of Korean phonetic symbols used during the Unified Silla dynasty to facilitate the reading of texts in Chinese characters. Its invention has been attributed to Su Ch'ŏl (817–893), but this suggestion is now discredited.
See also *idu*

KUIN-HOE 九人會 The Club of Nine Men, 1933–7
The members were all writers of between 25 and 30: **Yi T'aejun, Chŏng Chiyong** (b. 1903), Kim Kirim (b.1908) and Yi Muyŏng (1908–1960), Yi Hyoŏk, Yi Chongmyŏng and Kim Yuyŏng – early replaced by Pak T'aewŏn (b.1909), **Yi Sang** and Pak P'aryang (b.1905); Cho Yongman (b.1909) and Yu Ch'ijin (b.1905) – later replaced by Kim Yujŏng (1908–1937) and Kim Hwant'ae (1908–1944). In reaction against KAPF (*see* **K'ap'ŭ**), they were non-aggressive and stood for literature as pure art, but they disbanded early because they lacked a single strong ideology.

KUKCHA-GAM 國子監
National Academy, predecessor of **Sŏnggyun-gwan**, founded in 992 by King **Sŏngjong** at **Kaesŏng**. Under King Injong (r. 1122–46) it was expanded to comprise six colleges in an attempt to revive the reputation of the Academy in face of competition from private academies (*see* *sŏwŏn*). These were:

Kukchahak	for sons of officials of **grades** 1-3;	teaching the **Confucian Classics** and Chinese literature
T'aehak	for sons of officials of grades 4-5;	teaching the Confucian Classics and Chinese literature
Samunhak	for sons of officials of grades 6-7;	teaching the Confucian Classics and Chinese literature
Yurhak	for sons of officials of grades 8-9;	teaching law
Sŏhak	for sons of officials of grades 8-9;	teaching calligraphy
Sanhak	for sons of officials of grades 8-9;	teaching mathematics and accountancy.

See also **examinations**; **schools**; *T'aehakkam*

KUKCHO POGAM 國朝寶鑒 'Mirror of the Dynasty'
An anthology of the achievements of the Chosŏn dynasty. **Sejong** planned an encomium of his father and grandfather, but died before it was finished. **Sejo** had the work continued (as far as the reign of Munjong, but stopping before **Tanjong**) by **Sin Sukchu** and others, and printed in 1458. Supplements were added from time to time until a full new edition appeared in 1848. This was revised and reprinted in 1908, bringing the record up to 1863 and treating T'aejo, Changjo, **Chŏngjo**, **Sunjo** and Munjong as emperors (with titles accorded them in 1899), while removing evidence of vassalage to China.

KUKCHŎN 國展
Competitive annual art exhibition organised by the South Korean government between 1949 and 1981 (*see also **Sŏnjŏn***). In 1957 *avant garde* artists broke free of the conservative rules imposed by the government for the submission of work and inaugurated the Modern Artists' Invitational Exhibition series, the modern equivalent of a rebellion by Southern School literati painters against the style preferred by the official ***Tohwa-sŏ***.

KUKHAK 國學 'National College' *See **T'aehak-kwan***

KUKHAK 國學 'National learning' *See **Sirhak** movement*

KUKSADANG 國師(祀)堂 'national shrine'
This shrine to the spirit of Seoul's south mountain seems to have been erected on Namsan early in the Chosŏn dynasty. Though sometimes described as a shrine to **Muhak**, this was probably not its original purpose. It came to be the informal national centre for ***mudang***. In 1925 it was moved by the colonial government to make way for the central Shinto shrine (*see* **Shrine question**). Its collection of religious folk paintings is in the replacement shrine built on the west slope of Inwang-san, Seoul's western mountain.

KUMARAJIVA 鳩摩羅什 (K. Kumarasŭp, 343–413)
Kumarajiva was an Indian of Kashmiri stock, born in the city of Kucha in the Tarim Basin (now in Xinjiang). He was trained as a Buddhist in north India, but captured and taken to China when the Eastern Jin dynasty subdued Kucha in 383. In 401 he was taken to Chang'an and put in charge of a translation bureau, many of whose **sutras** are still used in Korea.

KŬMGANG-SAN 金剛山 *See* **Diamond Mountains**

KŬMHO-MUN **INCIDENT** *Kŭmho-mun sakkŏn* 金虎門事件
In April 1926 Song Haksŏn (1893–1927) attempted to assassinate Governor-General Saitō as he entered the **Ch'angdŏk Palace** by the Kŭmho-mun ('golden tiger gate') during funeral ceremonies for the Emperor **Sunjong**. The attempt failed, though others in the Japanese party were killed and injured. The fleeing assassin was quickly caught and eventually executed. Ripples of disturbance spread throughout the country.

KŬMO SINHWA 金鰲神話 'New Golden Tortoise Stories'
The book contains five stories of the supernatural, owing much to *Jiandeng xinhua* by Qu Tou (1341–1427), though with Korean settings. It was written in Chinese by Kim Sisŭp (1435–93), one of the *Saeng-yuksin*, '**six surviving subjects**' of King **Tanjong**. He refused to serve the usurper **Sejo** and became a wandering Buddhist monk, settling at Kŭmo-san, 'golden tortoise mountain', near **Kyŏngju** at the age of 30. He returned to Seoul when Sejo died, but remained out of government.

KŬMSŎNG 金城 *See* **Kyŏngju**

KUNDIKA (K. *chŏngbyŏng*) 淨瓶
A Buddhist container for holy water patterned after Indian and Chinese models. It has a slender spout at the top, from which the water was sprinkled, and a lidded mouth on the

shoulder through which it was filled. It was usually made of metal or porcelain. Fine inlaid examples date especially from the Koryŏ dynasty, when court patronage of **Buddhism** encouraged their manufacture for aesthetic appreciation as well as practical use.

KUNGHAP 宮合 'union of palaces'
A table expressing in terms of the **five phases** the relationship between the *saju p'alcha* of a boy and girl for whom **marriage** has been proposed. Soothsayers use it, together with the *Nabŭm* table, to determine the prospects of the marriage. All the oracles are equivocal and variant forms are found.

Earth boy + Earth girl:	Get sons, riches, honour: bursting blossoms cover branches.
Earth boy + Water girl:	Riches, honour, long life: wine-drinking, sad singing.
Earth boy + Wood girl:	Short life, half misfortune: withered trees welcome autumn.
Earth boy + Fire girl:	Long life, riches, honour: fish changes into dragon.
Earth boy + Metal girl:	Clothing, food, more than needed: small birds turn into falcons.
Wood boy + Wood girl:	Half fortunate, half unfortunate: gnat turns into dragon.
Wood boy + Metal girl:	Poverty, hardship, great misfortune: resting ox laden with hay.
Wood boy + Water girl:	Many sons, riches, honour: small birds turn into falcons.
Wood boy + Fire girl:	Possessions, descendants: three summers welcome fans.
Wood boy + Earth girl:	Disease and death: when winter comes, make clothing
Fire boy + Fire girl:	Death, great misfortune: dragon turns into fish.
Fire boy + Water girl:	Life divides, death separates: old feet crossing bridges.
Fire boy + Earth girl:	Heavenly income, long life: men turn into immortals.
Fire boy + Metal girl:	No sons, half unfortunate: dragon loses bright gem.
Fire boy + Wood girl:	Good luck, income, descendants: bird turns into crane.
Water boy + Water girl:	Poor, bitter, most unfortunate: sick horse welcomes needle.
Water boy + Earth girl:	Long life, clothing, food: all things welcome frost.
Water boy + Wood girl:	Official post, possessions, income: gnat turns into dragon.
Water boy + Fire girl:	Clothes, food, office, long life: falling blossoms welcome heat.

Water boy + Metal girl:	Affairs, great good fortune: three guests welcome cousin.
Metal boy + Metal girl:	No sons, no clothing: dragon turns into fish.
Metal boy + Water girl:	Poor, bitter, and unfortunate: chariot horse bears a burden.
Metal boy + Fire girl:	Descendants, loyalty, filial piety: scraggy horse heavily loaded.
Metal boy + Wood girl:	Half unfortunate, half happy: lively fish lacks water.
Metal boy + Earth girl:	Husband and wife rejoice: immortals live on earth.

KUNGMIN ŬIHOE 國民義會 *See Ŭibyŏng*

KUNGMINBU *See Ŭibyŏng*

KUNGNAESŎNG 國內城
Also known as Hwandosŏng; modern Tonggou, Ji'an, in China's Jilin province, on the northern bank of the **Yalu** River. It was the site of the second capital of the **Koguryŏ** kingdom from AD 3, from where attacks were launched against lines of communication between China and its **Lelang** commandery. This brought an attack and temporary capture by armies of the Wei dynasty in AD 244, and the capital was further sacked by the Xianbei Former Yan dynasty in 342. The capital was later moved to **Wanggŏmsŏng** (P'yŏngyang), but Kungnaesŏng's continued importance as an urban centre is shown by **tombs** such as the 6th century *Muyong-ch'ong* ('Tomb of the Dancers') and *Kakchŏ-ch'ong* ('Tomb of the Wrestlers').
KIM JOO-YOUNG, 'Jian, Vestiges of the Koguryŏ Spirit', *Koreana*,10/1, 1996
See also **Kwanggaet'o**

KUNGYE 弓裔 (d.918)
A young aristocrat who joined Yanggil in his rebellion against the Silla government, killed him in 897, and set up his own capital at Songak (**Kaesŏng**), proclaiming the kingdom of Later Koguryŏ. He was supported by the powerful Wang clan, a merchant family who dominated the east coast from their base on **Kanghwa-do**. His Buddhist faith eventually turned into religious mania and paranoia. After recognising himself as a living Buddha he had a new capital built at Ch'ŏrwŏn, in Kangwŏn province, and renamed his state T'aebong, but much of his military success was due to his first minister **Wang Kŏn**, who rebelled against him in 918.
See also **Kyŏn Hwŏn**

KUT *See* **shamanism**

KUUNMONG 九雲夢 'Nine Cloud Dream'
The best of old Korean book-length stories, written in *Hanmun* by Kim Manjung (1637–1692) about 1687. Kim was bought up by his widowed mother in a very strict Confucian household, where he learned poetry from an early age. From the age of 28 he was in government service, during a period of constant factional struggle, much of which centred on the influence wielded by the women in King **Sukchong**'s palace.

(Kim also wrote *Sa-ssi namjŏn-gi*, 'The Dismissal of Lady Xie', a shorter story, thought to be about royal marriage problems.) In 1687 he was banished to Sŏnch'ŏn in north P'yŏngan, and in 1689 again to the island of Namhae off the south coast. *Kuunmong* was probably written in Sŏnch'ŏn. The textual history of the book is complex. The oldest printed edition is from 1725; slightly abbreviated versions and several Korean translations are known. The story, set in Tang China, tells of a young Buddhist monk who dreams that he is reborn to meet and marry eight women in succession, including the emperor's daughter, during a highly successful worldly career. In the last chapter he awakes to find himself a young monk again. Much of the interest of the novel lies in the romances, but also in the problems the author sets for himself to resolve about matters of court ceremonial. In this and other ways the book is profoundly Confucian, though the overall message is Buddhist.

RICHARD RUTT, *Virtuous Women*, Seoul: Royal Asiatic Society, 1974

KWAGO 科擧 *See* **Examinations**

KWAJŎNPŎP 科田法 'Rank land law'
Land reform law introduced by King T'aejo in 1390. As applied in parts of Kyŏnggi province it confiscated lands from the Koryŏ nobility and Buddhist monks and redistributed it to officials and former officials according to their rank. Elsewhere it broke up large estates and reclaimed land for the state. It thus created a fresh economic foundation for the new Chosŏn dynasty. Lands were not supposed to be held by the recipients' families in perpetuity, though there was a tendency for them to be so. Other beneficiaries of the redistribution were government agencies, **schools**, and Confucian shrines.
See also **Meritorious subjects**

KWAK YŎ 郭輿 (1038–1130)
After a distinguished official career, he withdrew early to live in rural simplicity at Kŭmju. In 1105 he was recalled after the accession of **King Yejong** and became a royal tutor. When he retired for the second time, the king built him a house in the hills to the east of **Kaesŏng**, and would visit him, so that they could recite poems together.

KWANCH'ANG 官昌 (d. AD 660)
Also known as Kwanjang, a **Silla** youth who was a *hwarang* in his boyhood. He fought alongside **Kim Hŭmch'un** and Pan'gul at Hwangsan in 660 and was captured. When the **Paekche** commander saw Kwanch'ang was only a teenager, he sent him back to his own side. Pausing only to drink a cup of water, the lad returned to the fray and was killed. His head was sent back on a horse. The tragic anecdote is given a Confucian twist by *Samguk sagi*, which records that his father did not grieve, because his son had died for the king.

KWANGDAE
Wandering male entertainers of the Chosŏn period who performed **masked dramas** (*sandae-togam*), **puppet plays** (*kkoktu-gaksi*), tumbling and tightrope-walking, or sang the long poetic tales called *p'ansori*. There were also known as *chaein*, 'skilled men'. Like other entertainers, they belonged to the lowest social class, *ch'ŏnmin*.
SONG BANG-SONG, 'Korean Kwangdae Musicians and their Musical Traditions,' *KJ*, 14/9, 1974

KWANGGAET'O, KING 廣開土王 (375–413)

Posthumous name ('Broad enlarger of territory') of Tamdŏk, King of **Koguryŏ** from 391 to 412. His exploits are recorded in *Samguk sagi*, and carved in 18,000 Chinese seal (*yesŏ*) script characters on a 24-foot stele by his tomb at Tonggou, on the bank of the **Yalu** River near Ji'an in Manchuria. It was erected by his son King Changsu in 414, near the site of the second Koguryŏ capital of **Kungnaesŏng**. The inscription begins with the legend of Chumong (*see* **foundation myths**) and quotes *Shujing* (*see* **Confucian Classics**). Kwanggaet'o is given a Chinese **reign title** (*Yŏngnak*) and a posthumous personal title: warring against China did not prevent the adoption of Chinese culture. The stele tells how, at his death, Koguryŏ covered nearly two-thirds of the peninsula and most of **Manchuria** as far as the Sungari River. Coming to the throne at 19, he occupied **Liaodong**, annexed the Sushen tribal area in the north-east, took land from **Paekche** in the **Han River** basin, and in AD 400 sent troops to help **Silla** repel **Wa** raiders from Japan who were in league with Paekche. The controversial stele was lost for many centuries and rediscovered in the early 1880s. A rubbing was taken by a Japanese soldier in 1883, and has been interpreted by Japanese historians as indicating that Yamato maintained a colony in south-eastern Korea from AD 365 to 561. On the other hand, the section describing Kwanggaet'o's defeat of the Japanese has since been defaced, possibly during the colonial period. A bronze bowl from the Tomb of the Bowl (*Houch'ong*) at **Kyŏngju** is inscribed with a dedicatory inscription to Kwanggaet'o, also in *yesŏ*: it is not known how it came to be placed in a **tomb** in the neighbouring kingdom of **Silla**.

TAKAHASHI HATADA, trans. V. Dixon Morris, 'An Interpretation of the King Kwanggaet'o Inscription,' *KS*, 3, 1979

KWANGHAE, PRINCE 光海君 (Kwanghae-gun; 1575–1641, r. as king 1608–23)

One of the two Chosŏn kings who were refused posthumous kingly titles (the other was **Prince Yŏnsan**). Prince Kwanghae was the second son of King Sŏnjo, who installed him as Crown Prince at P'yŏngyang during the Japanese invasions of 1592–3. He came to the throne at the age of 33, supported by Great Northerners **faction**. The Lesser Northerners supported his seven-year-old half-brother, Prince Yŏngch'ang. He proved a capable ruler, sponsoring the **printing** of **books**, restoring the office of royal archives, reviving the use of identification tags (*hop'ae*) for officials, refurbishing the army and the border defences. He was a realist who, although he had to act in loyalty to the fading **Ming dynasty**, instructed his officers to take a neutral stance when it became clear that the Manchus were winning. Largely for this he was forced to abdicate in 1623 by the pro-Ming Westerners faction, whose policies provoked the **Manchu invasions** of 1627. He lived in island exile for his last nineteen years, first on **Kanghwa** and then on **Cheju**. Modern historians generally see him as a good king ruined by intransigeant factionalism, but pre-modern writers vilified him as lacking in loyalty, a coarse man addicted to **tobacco**, whom they held responsible for the death of his little half-brother by suffocation in an overheated room.

See also **Kyech'ug-ilgi**

KWANGHYE-WŎN 廣惠院 'office of abundant favour'

Korea's first modern hospital, founded by royal patronage in 1885 after Horace N. **Allen** had demonstrated the value of western **medicine** in the aftermath of the *Kapsin* **coup** of 1884. Renamed Chejung-wŏn 'office for relief of the masses' in 1886, *Kwanghye-wŏn* came under the *T'ongni Kyobo T'ongsang Samu Amun*, Korea's

incipient Foreign Office advised by **von Möllendorff**, and included Korea's first medical school for training doctors and nurses.
See **Avison, Oliver**; *T'ongni Kimu Amun*

KWANGJU (1) 光州 (2) 廣州

(1) Provincial capital of Chŏlla Namdo. Former capital of the United Silla province of Muju. In 892 it was captured by the rebel **Kyŏn Hwŏn** prior to his proclamation of the **Later Paekche** kingdom.

In November 1929 fighting erupted here between Korean and Japanese students, sparking a nationwide student protest movement against Japanese colonialism (*see* **Kwangju Incident**).

Kwangju students again led a widespread political upheaval on 18 May 1980 which led to the fall of President Ch'oe Kyuha and the assumption of power by Chun Doo Hwan (**Chŏn Tuhwan**) (*see* **Kwangju Massacre**).

(2) (Kyŏnggi province) A place on the **Han River** 25 miles south-east of Seoul which was the **kiln** centre for the production of fine white porcelain in the early Chosŏn dynasty (*see* **ceramics**).

KWANGJU INCIDENT *Kwangju haksaeng undong* 光州學生運動 (1929)

Serious outbreak of fighting between Korean and Japanese **students** in October-November 1929 following insults to three Korean girls from three male Japanese students in Kwangju, South Chŏlla. The trouble broadened into a nationwide denunciation by Korean high school and college students of Japanese colonial education policy. This provided better facilities in schools for Japanese students and poor teaching in Korean schools, with inadequate teaching of Korean language and history. Resentment had been simmering since the previous period of demonstrations in 1926 (*see* **June Tenth Incident**), and was fostered by *Sin'ganhoe* ('New Shoot Society'). Many hundreds of students were expelled or arrested and imprisoned, their campuses invaded by the police, and societies closed down.

KWANGJU MASSACRE (1980)

In the spring of 1980, there were large-scale demonstrations in Seoul protesting at the increasingly dominant rôle of the military in the government under Major Chun Doo Hwan (**Chŏn Tuhwan**). A massive **student** demonstration on 14 May was followed by the extension to the whole country of martial law (in force in the capital since the assassination of President Park Chung Hee (**Pak Chŏnghŭi**) in October 1979); a number of leading politicians were arrested, including **Kim Taejung**. When news of this reached **Kwangju**, the capital of Kim's home province, South Chŏlla, there were violent protests, involving attacks on the police and public buildings. In order to suppress these protests, Chun despatched paratroop Special Warfare Commandos, trained to handle North Korean infiltrators. Although these forces used considerable brutality, in the course of which large numbers of people were killed and injured, they proved unable to recapture the city. Instead, they withdrew to the outskirts, sealing Kwangju off from the rest of the country from 22 May. On 27 May, regular army units, together with some special forces in regular uniforms, launched an attack on the city at three in the morning and succeeded in restoring order. Official figures gave the total number of dead as 170. This was revised in 1985 to 240, but it is widely believed that many more died, though not perhaps as many as the two thousand claimed by some of the student groups involved.

The events of Kwangju cast an early shadow over Chun's presidency, and as political controls relaxed, there were regular demands that the matter be reopened.

There were also regular claims that the US was involved in the massacre, since there had been no attempt to prevent Chun from withdrawing troops from the control of the joint US-Republic of Korea command. A Ministry of National Defense enquiry in 1985 satisfied nobody outside the military, and in 1988, after Chun left office, the National Assembly conducted another enquiry. This led Roh Tae Woo (**No Taeu**)'s **Sixth Republic** to reclassify the Kwangju rising as a stage in the development of democracy. An apology was issued to those who had suffered, compensation paid, and a monument erected. Later, when both Roh and Chun were under investigation for fraud and other matters in 1995–6, Kwangju again featured in the charges against them, and in Chun's case was one of the reasons why he was sentenced to death. Only with the election of Kim Taejung as president in December 1997 did the way seem to be open for the removing of Kwangju from the political agenda.

DONALD N. CLARK, ed., *The Kwangju Uprising: Shadows over the Regime in South Korea*, Boulder, Colorado: Westview Press, 1988; TIM WARNBERG, 'The Kwangju Uprising: An Inside View,' *KS*, 11, 1987

KWANGJU STUDENT MOVEMENT *See* **Kwangju Incident**

KWAN-HON-SANG-JE 冠婚喪祭
The necessary domestic rites that bound the family into society as defined by the neo-Confucians. They comprised **capping** (signified by the tying up of the hair into a **topknot** (*sangt'u*) or chignon), **marriage**, funerary obsequies, and worship of ancestors. All were marked by elaborate ceremonies.
See also **ancestor worship; Four Rites; lineages; mourning**

KWANSEŬM 観世音 'He who regards the world's sounds'
Kwanseŭm is Avalokitesvara, the bodhisattva of compassion, most popular of all **bodhisattvas**. He usually has a **Buddha** painted or carved in the front panel of his crown, and holds a **lotus** flower in his right hand, but he has many manifestations. He may be *Ch'ŏnsu* 'thousand-handed' (actually showing only 40 hands but with 27 faces). As *Yŏŭi-ryun Kwanseŭm* he has six hands and carries the *yŏŭi* jewel, a rosary, a lotus and a golden wheel; as eleven-faced Ekhadasamukha, he is crowned with ten heads, has four arms and a lotus flower; in the rare *madu-gwanŭm* he has a horse's head, a buddha crown, a lotus and an axe; as *paegŭi-gwanŭm* 'white-clad' he sits on a lotus, holds a lotus, and grants all prayers; as *yangyu-gwanŭm*, he bears a willow-branch; as *suwŏl-gwanŭm*, a form common in early paintings, he contemplates the sea [of this world] in the moonlight; as *oram-gwanŭm* he carries a fisherman's creel for the souls he saves. He may float on a lotus-flower or lotus-leaf, ride a **dragon**, be dressed in leaves, or study a **book**. In popular religion he is effectively a buddha and a god. In Pure Land teaching, constant repetition of his name *Kwanseŭm-posal* is an effective way to salvation.

In China and Japan he has become a 'goddess of mercy' (C. Guanyin, J. Kwannon). Some Koreans have adopted this idea during the second half of the 20th century, but it is not part of the Korean heritage. The sex-change seems to have arisen in 12th-century China as a result of earlier devotion to Kwanseŭm as *songzi boshi*, 'the boddhisattva who sends children', who appeared in pictures as an androgynous figure holding a child.

KWANSŎNG-GYO 關聖教 'teaching of Guan the holy one'
This name was given to a number of 20th-century **new religions** that were devoted to **Guan Yu** (K. Kwan Yu) of *The Romance of the Three Kingdoms*. One of them,

founded in 1921 by Pak Kihong and Kim Yŏngsik, was centred on Tongmyo, 'eastern temple' outside the Great East Gate (**Tongdae-mun**) of Seoul. Tongmyo was a temple of Guan Yu erected in 1602 with money from the Wanli Emperor in memory of the Ming soldiers who died defending Korea during the Japanese invasion of 1592 (*see* **Imjin Wars**).

KWŎN KŬN 權近 (Yangch'on, 1352–1409)

He held high office in the government during the last years of Koryŏ and was employed as an envoy to Yüan. In 1375 he joined **Chŏng Mongju** and others in a pro-Ming stance, which led to a period of disfavour and exile. (His brush-name, 'willow village', has particular significance in this context.) He returned to office, later serving under the new government of **Yi Sŏnggye**, and being made a **Meritorious Subject** by T'aejong. A strong and thoughtful neo-Confucian, he supervised editions of the **Confucian Classics**, wrote much good poetry and distinguished prose. His writings came to influence the great **Yi Hwang**.

KYE 契

Voluntary rural organisations active between the 16th and 19th centuries, mostly comprising **peasantry** but with some *yangban* involvement. Their original purpose was economic self-help through the sharing of tools, animals and other resources, especially as a means of meeting the **military cloth tax**. Occupational groupings included a *kye* for the collectors of *kongin* **tribute** goods, and other branches assumed purely social or religious functions. Later in the Chosŏn dynasty some branches became secret societies waging anti-government activities. In modern times, *kye* have continued to function as 'rotating-credit associations', offering social and economic cooperation and assistance to members, especially in rural areas. Recent *kye* were nearly all arranged and administered by **women**, who sometimes covered great distances in looking after them and not infrequently found themselves in financial distress as a result. A subsidiary type was the club of village women who contributed an agreed amount of food for the wedding feasts of members' sons.

GERARD KENNEDY, 'The Korean *Kye*: Maintaining Human Scale in a Modernizing Society,' *KS*, 1, 1977

KYECH'UG-ILGI 癸丑日記 'Diary of Black Ox Year (1613)'

Also known as *Sŏgung-nok*, 'Record of the Western Palace'. An artless and unpolished account of events in the palace between 1602 and 1621, written in *han'gŭl*, apparently by a servant of the Queen Mother Inmok (1584–1632), widow of King Sŏnjo. It tells of the tragic ill treatment of the queen and her son Yŏngch'ang-gun by **Prince Kwanghae**. No woodblock editions or manuscripts survive. Opinions vary as to its historical value.

See **Palace literature**

KYEHAE TREATY 癸亥約條 (1443)

Agreement made between the government of King **Sejong** and the Ashikaga shogunate, as a means of controlling Japanese piracy and legitimate trade between the island of **Tsushima** and the Korean ports of **Tongnae**, Ungch'ŏn and Ulsan. The Sō *daimyo* (feudal lords) of **Tsushima** were granted monopolistic rights to conduct trade with Korea in fifty ships *per annum*, in exchange for sending **tribute** to Seoul. The treaty was abrogated following Japanese disturbances in the three ports in 1510 and

restored on more limited terms in 1512. The treaty of Chŏngmi (1547) gave the *daimyo* the right to send 25 trading ships a year, subsequently increased to thirty.
See also **commerce; pirates; Sin Sukchu**

KYEMONG-P'YŎN 啓蒙篇

The second primer of the schoolboy in later Chosŏn, tackled when *Ch'ŏnja-mun* had been memorised. It was his introduction to simple Chinese syntax (printed with Korean grammatical aids or *idu*, called *t'o*) and to the vocabulary of neo-Confucianism. The sections are: Heaven (planets, **lunar mansions**, earthly branches and heavenly stems – *see kapcha* – the calendar); Earth (weather, seasons, seas, mountains, the **five phases**); things (**animals, domestic** and **mythical**, crops, measurement units); and Man (human relationships, morals, deportment and study). The author and date are unknown, but may belong to the 19th century. There are several versions.

KYERIM 雞林 'Cock forest'

The legend of a white cock that crew in a forest to draw attention to a gold box from which emerged a beautiful boy who later became king of **Silla** and founder of the Kim 'gold' line of kings is probably a myth to explain why the royal house of Silla passed between the Pak, Kim and Sŏk clans. It comes in *Samguk sagi* and *Samguk yusa* under the heading of King T'arhae, where the Sŏk clan also is given an egg-born ancestor (*see* **foundation myths**).

The name Kyerim was given to the principal **commandery** created by Tang China as its intended means of re-establishing imperial authority over the Korean peninsula after 668. It covered the territory formerly occupied by **Silla**, whose King, **Munmu**, was nominated governor-general. Further commanderies were designated in the former kingdoms of **Koguryŏ** and **Paekche**. Munmu, however, refused to accept the rôle assigned by Emperor Gaozong either to him or his state, drove the Chinese back into **Liaodong**, and reaffirmed his own nationwide authority. The name Kyerim was still recognised by educated Chinese in the early 12th century, when the secretary to a Chinese embassy, Sun Mu, compiled a glossary of Korean words appended to a book entitled *Kyerim yusa.*[1]

(1) Werner Sasse, *Das Glossar Koryŏ-pangŏn im Kyerim-yusa*, Wiesbaden: Otto Harrassowitz, 1976
See also **China, relations with; Tang dynasty**

KYEWŎL 桂月 (18th century)

'Cinnamon moon', a famous *kisaeng* of P'yŏngyang, favourite of the scholar-official Yi Kwangdŏk (1699–1748), who was exiled to the north during factional struggles in 1742. She was reputed to be a good poet.

KYŎN HWŎN 甄萱 (867?–936)

A man of late Silla, a successful commander against marauders from Japan, who during the turmoil of the collapsing state, took the city of Wansanju (Chŏnju) and declared himself ruler of Hubaekche (**Later Paekche**) in 900. For nearly thirty years he maintained his position against **Kungye** and his successor **Wang Kŏn**, rulers of Hugoguryŏ (Later Koguryŏ), even opening diplomatic relations with China. His armies attacked Silla, whose King Kyŏngmyŏng called on Wang Kŏn for help in 920 and 924. In 926 Kyŏn attacked **Kyŏngju**, killed Kyŏngmyŏng's successor, Kyŏngjae, at **P'osŏk-chŏng** and installed Kim Pu in Kyŏngjae's place, but in 929 he was defeated by Wang Kŏn at Koch'ang, and by 934 was losing both territory and supporters. When he appointed his fourth son, Kŭmgang, as his successor, Kŭmgang's elder brother, Sin'gŏm, rebelled and imprisoned his father at Kŭmsan-sa. In 935 Kyŏn submitted to Wang Kŏn, asking for Sin'gŏm to be punished. In 936 he commanded an army against his son which destroyed his own former state, thereby contributing significantly to the reunification of the peninsula under Wang. Kyŏn is said to have died of a spinal abscess exacerbated by his rage at Sin'gŏm's escape.

KYŎNGBANG 京紡 (*Kyŏngsŏng Pangjik-hoesa* 京城紡織會社)
The Kyŏngsŏng Spinning and Weaving Company. It was founded at Yŏngdŭngp'o by **Kim Sŏngsu** in 1919, and though his initial aim was to strengthen his own country in the face of Japanese colonialism, the company was a co-operative venture of Korean and Japanese stockholders. It took advantage of financial subsidies from the **Government-General**, loans from the Chōsen Industrial Bank, and machinery imported from Japan. It developed its operations according to Japanese terms of economic collaboration, not only in Korea but also in Japan, **Manchuria**, and China, and the bulk of its products were exported to Japan. Conditions in its factories for Korean workers were appalling, but strikes in 1925 and 1931 failed to gain any concessions from the management. The company operations extended into a wide range of other manufacturing, financial and service industries, including **railways**, and it became the first example of a Korean business conglomerate (*chaebŏl*). In 1935 **Pak Yŏnghyo** was succeeded as president by Kim Sŏngsu's brother Yŏnsu, and as soon as the Japanese were defeated in 1945 the workers again went on strike, denouncing him as an 'imperialist lackey'.
CARTER ECKERT, *Offspring of Empire: the Koch'ang Kims and the Colonial Origins of Korean Capitalism, 1876–1945*, Seattle: University of Washington Press, 1991

KYŎNGBOK 'Shining blessings' **PALACE** 景福宮
The name 'shining blessings' is an expression that occurs at least seven times in the classic *Book of Odes* (e.g. 207, 239, 281), always as a prayer, usually interpreted as being for a ruler.
   The palace was built as the principal royal residence and centre of government administration for the early Chosŏn period following **Yi Sŏnggye**'s coronation in **Kaesŏng**. The sites for the new capital (initially known as Hanyang) and this, the most important of its four palaces, were chosen according to the rules of *p'ungsu*, and occupied the location of a former Koryŏ dynasty government centre. Building was begun in 1394 under architect and **meritorious subject Chŏng Tojŏn** and his associate Sim Tŏkpu. It was Chŏng who chose the name Kyŏngbok, and the new palace epitomised the peak of Korean architectural skill and tradition in the 14th century. Its many buildings included the Kŭnjŏng throne hall, the main ceremonial and audience hall, Sajŏng, and royal residential quarters. Its main entrance was the Kwanghwa Gate in the south wall. T'aejo's successor King Chŏngjong temporarily moved the capital back to Kaesŏng in 1399, and thereafter Kyŏngbok remained unoccupied until it was destroyed during the **Imjin Wars**. Its rebuilding was begun at the behest of the Dowager Queen Cho and the **Taewŏn'gun** in 1865, and completed with over two hundred buildings in 1867 at great cost to the government and tax-payer. On 8 October 1895 Japanese soldiers ransacked the palace, killed **Queen Min**, and captured King **Kojong**. After **annexation** in 1910 most of its buildings were destroyed, only the *Kŭnjŏng-jŏn* and banqueting centre *Kyŏnghoe-ru* remaining of the former main halls. In 1923 the Japanese erected the Capitol Building in front of the palace and removed the Kwanghwa Gate. The gate was rebuilt in its original position in 1968, but the palace did not become

properly visible again until 1997, when the South Korean government demolished the Capitol Building. As a demonstration of nationalist sentiment the government then embarked on a project to restore the palace to its earlier glory.

EDWARD B. ADAMS, *Palaces of Seoul: Yi Dynasty Palaces in Korea's Capital*, Seoul: Taewon, 1972, repr. 1982

KYŎNGDŎK, KING 景德 (r. 742–65)

Ruler under whom the culture of the Unified Silla state reached its apogee. It is best represented today by **Pulguk-sa** and **Sŏkkuram**, which were built during his reign. As an admirer of Chinese government methods he tried to institute a system of regional government through centrally appointed officers, but was thwarted by the opposition of the *chin'gol* aristocracy.

KYŎNGGI-CH'E KA 景幾體歌 "'how-about-that?" style songs'

A form of *changga*, also called *pyŏlgok* ('vernacular song'), written chiefly in the 13th and 14th centuries, though a 19th-century example is known. The basic form is 5 to 8 stanzas, each comprising 6 verses of 3 or 4 'feet', and each 'foot' containing 3 or 4 syllables. The content is scholar's material, usually delighting in mountain scenery or Confucian studies. The language is Chinese words in Korean syntactical order, and the stanza falls into two parts, with a refrain typically beginning with '*Kyŏnggi*', a Chinese locution meaning 'How about that?'. The best known include *Hallim pyŏlgok* 'scholars' vernacular song', *Kwandong pyŏlgok* 'vernacular song of the **Diamond Mountains**' and *Chukkye pyŏlgok* 'vernacular song of the bamboo glen'.

KYŎNGGUK TAEJŎN 經國大典 *See* **Law**

KYŎNGJONG 景宗 (1688–1724; r. 1720–1724)

Son of **Sukchong** by a secondary wife, he was made Crown Prince in 1690 under **Soron** influence, but because of his physical weakness and presumed infertility, in 1717 the **Noron** *yŏngŭijŏng* Kim Ch'angjip had Prince Yŏnging, Sukchong's son by another secondary wife, made Crown Prince instead. When Sukchong died in 1720, this became the cause of a struggle between the **factions**, called *Imin-oksa*, in which Kim Ch'angjip was executed. Kyŏngjong ascended the throne but lived only four years before he died and was succeeded by Prince Yŏnging, who was later called **Yŏngjo**.

KYŎNGJU 慶州

Capital of North Kyŏngsang province, famous for its profusion of rich archaeological and religious sites. Known in the **Chinhan** and early Silla periods as Saro, it was the capital of the Kingdom of **Silla** and of the Unified Silla dynasty. Its contemporary name of Kŭmsŏng ('Golden City') draws attention to the opulence of its élite lifestyle (*see* **gold crowns**). The original palace was inside the **Wŏlsŏng** fortress, where further palace buildings were erected in the 6th and 7th centuries. After the unification of the country in 668 under King **Munmu**, a new city was laid out in east-west and north-south grid formation in imitation of the Chinese capital of Chang'an. It was situated to the north of Wŏlsŏng and divided into 55 wards; in the late 9th century these contained nearly 180,000 households with a population estimated at over one million people. New palaces were built, and all the buildings in the city are believed to have beeen roofed with tiles rather than the more commonplace thatch. Evidence of life at court has been found at **Anap-chi**, and the rôle of Kyŏngju as a leading centre of the Buddhist faith is demonstrated by its numerous temple sites, **pagodas** and relics, notably at **Pulguk-sa** But all sections of society also practised **shamanism**, and the grassy tomb-mounds that rise amid the modern city streets and loom over the surrounding countryside indicate the people's strong belief in an afterlife, and the need to go to it well prepared. Of the **tombs** that have been excavated, the most famous is that of *Ch'ŏnma-ch'ong*. Other sites of major historical importance in Kyŏngju include the 7th century observatory *Ch'ŏmsŏngdae*.

EDWARD B. ADAMS, *Korea's Golden Age: Cultural Spirit of Silla in Kyongju*, Seoul: Seoul International Tourist Publishing Co., 1991; KIM WON-YONG, 'Kyŏngju: The Homeland of Korean Culture,' *KJ*, 25/12, 1985; KOREAN NATIONAL COMMISSION FOR UNESCO, *Kyongju, City of Millennial History*, Elizabeth, NJ & Seoul: Hollym International, 1998

KYŎNGYŎN 經筵 'Classics mat'
Originally a government department for instructing the king in the **Confucian classics**, formed by Koryŏ in 1116 on a **Han dynasty** model, and given this name in 1390. It became a place for general discussion of government by the king and the 24 appointed officials. Because of the king's presence, the president was a 1st **grade** senior.

KYUHAP CH'ONGSŎ 閨閣叢書 'Miscellany for the Women's Quarters'
A little book in *han'gŭl* about cookery, making wine and sauces, dyeing, and making and caring for clothes, written by Yi-ssi Pinhŏgak (1759–1824), daughter of Yi Ch'angsu and wife of Sŏ Yubon. The earliest known edition is of 1869. Her mother was an aunt of Yu Hŭi, author of *Ŏnmun-ji*. She was therefore in the *sirhak* tradition. Neither *kimch'i* nor red **pepper** are mentioned in the book.

KYUJANG-GAK 奎章閣
Library established by King **Chŏngjo** within the **Kyŏngbok Palace** as part of the promotion of practical studies inspired by the *sirhak* **movement**. It took its name from that of the spirit that presides over literature and study, the spirit of the Kyu star, one of those named in the twenty-eight **lunar mansions**. Scholars were appointed to it regardless of **lineage** as part of the policy of playing down differences between **factions** and reducing the power of the **Noron** clique. Abolition of the Library was one of the measures proposed in the manifesto of the *Kapsin* **Coup** conspirators.

KYUNYŎ 均如 (923–973)
He began his Buddhist studies at the age of fourteen and became an eager teacher of the dharma, with a deep concern about unifying the various schools of thought. His work as supervisor of the monks' *kwagŏ* examinations (*see* **Examinations, Buddhist**) from 958 put him in a position to encourage leadership in others. In 963 the king built the monastery of Kwibŏp-sa for Kyunyŏ to become its abbot. He wrote much, especially **sutra** commentaries, but his best-known legacy is a series of *hyangga* songs for teaching Buddhist devotion, *Pohyŏn sibwŏn-ga* 'Pohyŏn's ten vow songs', which appear in the compendium published by his followers in 1075: *Tae-hwaŏm-sujwa wŏnt'ong yungjung taesa Kyunyŏ chon*, usually called *Kyunyŏ-jŏn*.

KYUNYŎK-PŎP 均役法 'Equal Tax Law'
Measure introduced in 1750 by King **Yŏngjo** in an effort to improve the living conditions of his subjects. The **Military Cloth Tax** was halved, with additional revenue being raised by a surcharge on the land tax and new levies on fishing, salt, and ships. The effects were minimal.
See also **taxation**

KYUSA 葵史 'Records of Mallow Plants'
A collection of brief biographical accounts of good men who were **illegitimate sons** (*sŏŏl*), published by a group of scholars in **Taegu** in 1858. They were disqualified from obtaining high office and good salaries. The title comes from a metaphor: 'Mallow plants are humble greens that strain toward the sun, but cannot choose the trees they grow under. A subject may want to give loyal service, but how can illegitimate birth be put right?' The subjects range from Koryŏ times to Yi Tŏngmu (1741–93).

K'AP'Ŭ (KAPF): *Chosŏn P'ŭro[llet'aria]* (or *Musan Kyegŭp*) *Yesul Tongmaeng,* 'Korean Proletarian Artists Federation'
A group formed in 1925 and at one time claiming 200 members, of writers who regarded literature as a weapon in the class struggle. They turned communist in 1927, and after trouble with the Japanese authorities became a Tokyo-based underground group until they disbanded in 1935. Of their early members, Yi Hyosŏk left to join the **Kuin-hoe** in 1933; while Yi Kiyŏng (b. 1895), the journalist Han Sŏrya (b. 1900) and Cho Kich'ŏn (1913–1951), a poet who lived in **Siberia** and Kazakhstan until 1945, both continued to write after 1950 in North Korea.

K'ONGJWI P'ATCHWI
A folk tale extant in *han'gŭl* only, but said to be related to a Tang story. It concerns two step-sisters. K'ongjwi, 'Soybean-mouse', daughter of the first wife, is cruelly mistreated by the second wife and her daughter, P'atchwi, 'Red-bean mouse'. K'ongjwi is eventually married to a *kamsa*, but is drowned in a lotus-pond by her step-sister. Their father learns the truth from a fairy (*sŏnnyŏ*); K'ongjwi is restored to life and avenged. Much has been made of partial similarities to the Cinderella story.

L

LACQUER *ch'il* 漆
The lacquer tree *Rhus vernicifera* grows across wide areas of Korea and produces high quality lacquer sap. Its decorative use was first introduced by the Chinese, and the oldest extant traces date from the 3rd century BC. Archaeological remains from the **Lelang** commandery in the early AD era include lacquered vessels, containers, pillows, footwear, **armour** and coffins. Lacquered objects have survived in **tombs** from the kingdoms of **Koguryŏ**, **Paekche** (*see* **Muryŏng, King**) and **Silla**, and especially in those of the Unified Silla period and from the site of the **Anap-chi** complex. In that period lacquer production was under the control of a government department, *Ch'ilchŏn*. Black, yellow and red lacquer was applied to bases of wood, metal, leather, **bamboo**, **paper** and horsehair. Some objects also bore brightly painted decorations, but it was the development of inlay, first seen on pieces so decorated with gold and silver found at Anap-chi, that came to distinguish Korean craftsmanship from Chinese. Artisans in the Koryŏ period produced outstanding examples inlaid with mother of pearl, from large objects such as carriages and sedan chairs to small ones such as cosmetic boxes. A wide variety of inlaid lacquered Buddhist objects included cases for scriptures, rosary beads, and incense sticks. Decorative subjects were similar to those seen on inlaid **celadons** of the same period, namely, trees, flowers, vines and ducks. Lacquer was then a preserve of the upper classes, but as the taste of the neo-Confucian literati grew more austere during the Chosŏn period and the resources of the Buddhist monasteries diminished, so the social restrictions on its use relaxed and

craftsmen sought other outlets for their work. Lacquered goods were adopted by the lower classes for everyday use, including **furniture**, hats and **fans**, and standards of design and quality declined.

CHOI SUN-U, 'Lacquer Ware and Ornaments,' *KJ*, 19/4, 1979

LAND REFORM *nongji kaehyŏk* 農地改革

Though Koreans sometimes expressed interest in and admiration for the ancient Chinese 'well-field' land system, advocated as a reform ideal by Mencius and others, the country never experienced a comprehensive programme of land confiscation and redistribution. Partial attempts, however, were made. At the beginning of the Unified Silla period the aristocracy of all three former kingdoms owned large estates, including 'stipend villages' (*nogŭp*) from which they collected taxes and recruited *corvée* labour. In 689, a new system called *kwallyo-jŏn* deprived them of their lands and their proprietary rights over the **peasantry** but recompensed them with the income from 'office lands' (*chikchŏn*) measured in grain. In 722 the *chŏngjŏnje* was introduced, which allocated lands at regular intervals on the basis of adult male occupancy and was accompanied for tax assessment purposes by the institution of **census registers**. By 757 both systems were defunct and the aristocracy had recovered their lands.

The early Koryŏ kings also endeavoured to limit the powers of the aristocrats. Lands were allocated to subjects who had helped in the reunification, and in 976 and 998 – under the Land Stipend Law (*chŏnsi-gwa*) – to post-holders according to their rank. Lands were returned to the throne at the end of an official's tenure of his post. 'Merit privilege lands' (*kongŭm jŏn*) continued to be awarded in heredity to senior officials. *Chŏnsi-gwa* was replaced in 1271 by a new system, *nokkwa-jŏn* ('salary rank land'), which granted lands to post-holders around the capital **Kaesŏng**, but by then the powerful families were building up their estates by other means.

In the late Koryŏ disregard for the traditional ideal of fair land distribution among tillers had become blatant. After a land survey in 1389, **Chŏng Tojŏn** complained at the injustice of land accumulation by the rich and lack of return for those who worked it. He proposed nationalisation and redistribution measures to **Yi Sŏnggye**, which led to the *kwajŏn* reforms of 1390. Though perhaps not implemented effectively on a national scale, these reforms evidently improved conditions for some time. In 1466 they were replaced by King **Sejo**'s *chikchŏn* ('office land') system, which lasted until 1556 and was intended to prevent the hereditary accumulation of land. Once again officials were only rewarded with rents from land during their period of office tenure. Nevertheless continuing estate accumulation meant an increasing shortage of land for use in this way. Proposals for comprehensive land redistribution according to the Chinese 'well-field' system were made in the 17th and 18th centuries but not implemented, and despite popular uprisings through the 19th century (*see* **rebellions, peasant and slave**) the call for reform had still been unanswered by the time of the **Tonghak Rebellion**.

Between 1910 and 1918 the Japanese **Government General** instituted a major Land Survey. All land owned by Koreans had to be reported to the Land Survey Bureau; any that was not reported was confiscated, along with land that formerly belonged to the Chosŏn government and Yi royal household. When its initial findings were implemented as law in 1912, approximately 40 per cent of Korean land passed into Japanese hands, although some rich Korean landowners also succeeded in increasing their holdings.

Following liberation in 1945 all privately-owned estate lands, together with those belonging to temples and churches, were confiscated by the communists in North Korea and allocated to working farmers under the Land Reform Law (5 March 1946).

It is estimated that 70 per cent of peasant households benefited from this redistribution. Collectivisation of land, however, began after the **Korean War**. In the South, the **American Military Government** proposed the sale of former Japanese-owned land to its tenants in March 1948, following which the government of Syngman Rhee (**Yi Sŭngman**) passed a Land Reform Act in June 1949 which redistributed 29 per cent of cultivated land and resulted in many poor farmers acquiring small plots. Figures show that by 1957, tenancy had dwindled to only 12 per cent of the rural population, while the great majority of peasants were the owners of small farms.

WHANG IN-JOUNG, 'Administration of Land Reform in Korea, 1949-52,' *KJ*, 24/10, 1984
See also **land tenure**; *Saemaŭl undong*

LAND TENURE
Korea has a long tradition of free land ownership dating back to the **Samhan** period, when farmers also contributed to work on communal village land. At the same time, the view that all land ultimately belongs to the state had an equally early origin, underlying the recurrent habits in subsequent dynasties of kings both making grants of and laying claim to land.

THREE KINGDOMS
In addition to the small farms of ordinary freemen all three states saw the rise of royal household and aristocratic estates, aided by hereditary grants of land (*sajŏn*) by the king. **Silla** also introduced the practice of granting salary lands to officials during their periods of office. Tenancy resulted from the inability of freemen to pay taxes. The practice of communal labour activities continued.

UNIFIED SILLA
Under the *nogŭp* ('stipend villages') or 'office lands' (*chikchŏn*) system aristocratic wealth was swollen by hereditary awards of villages and land in recognition of services to the crown. One such beneficiary was **Kim Yusin**. Recipients of these villages and their local administrators were awarded grain income, and probably other agricultural produce, from them.

KORYŎ
Land was owned by (1) the royal family; (2) members of the aristocracy ('merit privilege land', *kongŭm-jŏn*); (3) government officials and military leaders who received the income from hereditary allotments of land in recognition of services towards the establishment of the new régime ('stipend land', *see **Chŏnsi-gwa***); (4) former 'castle lords' of the Silla and **Later Paekche** régimes reappointed as local magistrates; (5) government departments ('public land', *kongjŏn*) and local officials; (6) Buddhist monasteries; and (7) free farmers on 'people's land'. The aristocracy built up large estates of privately owned land (*nongjang*), on which rents charged to tenant farmers far exceeded those on public lands or taxes on 'people's land'. After the Mongol conquest, the estates of absentee landlords who benefited from collaboration with the foreigners grew enormous, and government income from land correspondingly diminished. **Yi Sŏnggye** promulgated a programme of land nationalisation and redistribution which destroyed the power of the old-established landed aristocracy (*see* **land reform**).

CHOSŎN
The new system reiterated the concept that all land belonged to the king, but the reforms did little more than tinker with the Koryŏ pattern of land tenure and income. The chief beneficiaries of King T'aejo's reforms – and consequent landowners – were the royal

household, senior *yangban* families in and around the capital, recipients of 'merit lands' and 'military lands', local government offices, Confucian shrines, **schools**, military posts and temples. Private estates belonging to the *yangban* continued to increase and to provide employment for tenant farmers. Dispersed across the country, some supported private academies (*sŏwŏn*). Surveys of land holdings were supposed to be held every twenty years as a guard against excessive estate expansion, but were ineffectual.

After the **Imjin Wars** the royal household took possession of many fallow lands and some lands previously owned by provincial *yangban* families. The latter expanded their income-deriving activities into manufacturing and **commerce**, and economic diversification through the 17th and 18th centuries also prompted agricultural developments involving improved irrigation, and new crops, techniques and technology. *Yangban* landlords, free **peasants**, and even some tenants benefited. Rich peasants hired labour and became landlords themselves, and a new type of tenant-landlord relationship emerged which gave the tenant more independence to farm as he wished in return for a pre-determined rent, rather than a proportion of the harvest. But fundamental change in land tenure arrangements would have meant revolution and was never envisaged. Through the 19th century the familiar pattern of injustice resulting from the traditional social hierarchy, frequently witnessed in extortionate landlordism, was evident, and among the demands of the **Tonghak** rebels in 1894 were land redistribution and the abolition of illegal tax exactions.

COLONIAL PERIOD
The Japanese took possession of large amounts of land, especially after the Land Survey of 1910–18 (*see* **land reform**). More than three quarters of households surveyed in 1916 worked either wholly or in part as tenants, either for the Japanese or *yangban* landowners. Their plight deteriorated and was accompanied by growing unrest through the 1920s and 1930s. In 1938 only 19 per cent of Korean farming families owned their land. 63 per cent of these owned less than the average of one *chŏngbo* (2·45 acres). The Japanese government sought higher **rice** output to benefit its own people, and more land was irrigated and brought into production. In 1934, in an attempt to counter food shortages during the depression years, Governor General Ugaki Kazushige launched a Rural Revival Movement aimed at diversifying peasants' productive activities. But Japanese companies owned much of the fertile land (*see* **Oriental Development Company**), landlord-tenant relations were abysmal, farmers starved because of excessive taxes, and a combination of absentee landlords, rising mobilisation on labour projects, abandonment of land, and emigration led to a slump in land use. Large numbers of peasants became migrants and worked on 'fire fields' (*hwajŏn*), waste land on which they burned the vegetation before planting subsistence crops for their own survival.

EDWIN H.GRAGERT, *Landownership under Colonial Rule, Korea's Japanese Experience 1900–1935*, Honolulu: University of Hawaii Press 1994; JAMES PALAIS, 'Land Tenure in Korea, Tenth to Twelfth Centuries', *JKS*, 4, 1975; PARK BYOUNG-HO, 'The Legal Nature of Land Ownership in the Yi Dynasty,' *KJ*, 15/10, 1975; SUSAN SHIN, 'Some Aspects of Landlord-Tenant Relations in Yi Dynasty Korea', *Occasional Papers on Korea* 1, 1974; SHIN YONG-IIA, 'Landlordism in the Late Yi Dynasty, I and II,' *KJ*, 18/6, 18/7, 1978; CLARK SORENSEN, 'Land Tenure and Class Relations in Colonial Korea', *JKS*, 7, 1990
See also **agriculture**; **class system**; **gentry**; **taxation**

LANDIS, ELI BARR 南得時 (1865–98)
Korean name Nam Tŭksi. An American Mennonite from Pennsylvania who became an Episcopalian while studying medicine at the University of Pennsylvania and joined the

Church of England Mission to Korea in 1890. He founded a hospital at **Inch'ŏn**, but died of typhoid fever at the age of 33. He was in his day a respected Koreanologist, publishing papers on folklore, history, pharmacy, *p'ungsu*, **Buddhism** and Confucian **rites**.
RICHARD RUTT, 'Eli Barr Landis', *TRASKB*, LV, 1979

LANDSCAPE PAINTING *sansu-hwa* 山水畫

The beginnings of landscape painting in Korea may be seen in the depiction of trees and mountains in **tomb** mural decorations, including the Tomb of the Wrestlers (5th–6th century) and Tomb of the Dancers (6th century) at **Kungnaesŏng**, and the Great Tomb (*T'aemyo*) of Kansŏng (late 6th century; Sammyo, South P'yŏngan province). Literary evidence shows that landscape painting was practised in the Unified Silla and Koryŏ periods, but no examples have survived.

In the early Chosŏn period artists had little direct contact with fellow painters in China, but admired and imitated the styles of Chinese masters from the Five Dynasties and Song periods such as Li Cheng, Guo Xi, Mi Fu, Ma Yuan and Xia Gui (*see* **An Kyŏn**). Later, they also came to appreciate the work of the Yuan, Ming and early Qing masters, especially the Four Masters of the Late Yuan; Shen Zhou, Dong Qichang, Shi Tao; and the Four Wangs. In China, painters of the Imperial Academy concentrated on techniques of precise brushwork and careful depiction of detail, and are identified with the so-called Northern or Zhe[jiang] traditions, while amateur scholar-artists favoured the use of bold outline and ink-washes aimed at a more impressionistic conveyance of atmosphere. They saw this type of painting as a vehicle for self-expression, and their work acquired the self-laudatory epithet of *wenren hua* ('scholars' paintings'). They were also known as the Southern, or Wu, school. In Korea, professional and literati painters alike admired and imitated both styles, so that the term 'Southern School' does not identify an artist as an amateur, but as one who followed the style of the great Chinese amateurs. Some artists, such as **Sim Sajŏng**, **Kim Che**, and **Yi Chŏng**, produced fine landscapes in both traditions.

It was in the post-**Imjin Wars** period that Koreans, though trained in Chinese skills, also began to develop a distinctive approach of their own to landscape painting. Individualism was, after all, encouraged by the Southern School tradition. Foremost in this respect was **Chŏng Sŏn**, whose *chin'gyŏng* ('true view') style perfectly represented the nature of Korean mountains and expressed the growing national consciousness of artists through the period of the *sirhak* **movement**. Famous painters such as Sim Sajŏng, **Kang Sehwang**, **Yi Insang** and **Yi Inmun** carried forward Chŏng Sŏn's style, though Yi Inmun is also known for his *Mountains and Rivers without End*, the longest traditional Korean landscape still in existence (8·5 metres). This was inspired by Song dynasty horizontal scrolls and, though it clearly demonstrates his individual genius, indicates the continuing appreciation of the Chinese Zhe tradition. Even **Kim Hongdo**, whose *genre* **paintings** are the epitome of Korean self-expression, painted landscapes that remained rooted in Chinese style. By the middle of the 19th century independent inspiration seemed to have deserted Korean landscape artists, though folk artists continued to depict the **Diamond Mountains** in their own impressionistic manner, free from Chinese stylistic preconceptions (*see* **folk painting**). 20th century painters struggled to reconcile the **nationalism** inspired by love of their native countryside with, on the one hand, an instinctive feeling for the whole East Asian artistic heritage and, on the other, the new approach and techniques of art learned from the West. One who achieved considerable success in combining these sometimes contradictory forces was **Yi Sangbŏm**.

AN HWI-JUN, 'Korean Landscape Painting of the Early and Middle Chosŏn Period,' *KJ*, 27/3, 1987; BURGLIND JUNGMANN, *Die koreanische Landschaftsmalerei und die chinesische Che-Schule vom späten 15. bis zum 17. Jahrhundert*, Stuttgart, 1992; KUMJA PAIK KIM, 'The Introduction of the Southern School Painting Tradition to Korea,' *OA*, XXXVI/4, 1990/1
See also **Kukchŏn**

LANGUAGE, THE KOREAN
Korean has similarities, some of them deceptive, to most of the languages that surround it in north-east Asia: Chinese, Japanese and the Altaic family. They all lack definite and indefinite articles, grammatical number and gender. They use pronouns with reluctance and are often vague about the subject and tense of a verb. Korean resembles Japanese in grammar, though the sounds of the two languages are quite different; there are many Chinese words in Korean, though its grammar is entirely unlike Chinese. **G. J. Ramstedt** showed that Korean has deep resemblances in phonology and grammar to the Altaic family (Mongol, Manchu-Tungus, and Turkic), but evidence of any historical relationship – which must be remote – is not conclusive.

HISTORY The history of a language can be known only from the time of its earliest decipherable records. Before the creation of *han'gŭl* in the 15th century the only records of Korean are poems, place-names and a few phrases, transcribed in *idu* or *hyangch'al*, using Chinese characters whose phonological value is far from clear. It is therefore impossible to make any reliable periodisation for the development of Korean before the 15th century or to be certain of relationships between ancient languages spoken in different parts of the peninsula. These languages are nevertheless usually regarded as one, called Old Korean.

The language of the first *han'gŭl* texts is called Middle Korean. The pivot period in the ensuing changes into Modern Korean is usually taken to have been the time of the Japanese and **Manchu invasions** early in the 17th century. There have been further major developments during the 20th century, especially since the *Han'gŭl* **Society** decided in 1936 to take the language of the Seoul middle class as the national standard.

Though lexical counts show that most modern Korean words are of Chinese origin, in ordinary conversation Sino-Korean words are less frequent than this would suggest. They are usually treated as nouns, often turned into adjectives or verbs by suffixed particles. In literary style this may be done with Chinese phrases several words long. Sino-Korean expressions function much as Latin- and Greek-derived words do in English: they are more frequent in formal style and in technical vocabulary. Modern usage more often accords with Sino-Japanese than with mainland Chinese. A text otherwise written in *han'gŭl* may have Sino-Korean words written in Chinese characters, though this practice was abandoned in North Korea from 1949. Many English loan-words are now coming in, generally based on American pronunciation.

The most distinctive characteristic of Korean phonology is the way in which consonants in morphemic elements are modified by contiguous sounds. Some account of this will be found under **Romanisation** and *Hunmin chŏngŭm*. Within agglutinative words there are also features of '**vowel harmony**' that may hint at an Altaic relationship.

GRAMMAR In general, any modifier precedes what it modifies. Adjectives modify nouns, nouns modify verbs, adverbs modify verbs. Subsidiary clauses modify the main clause, whose verb ends the sentence.

A verb can be a complete sentence. The grammatical ending of a verb shows whether that verb is the end of a sentence or stands in some relation (conditional, causative and so on) to the next clause in the sentence. The grammatical form of the verb also reflects the speaker's relationship both to those addressed and those who are spoken about, using agglutinative syllables to express at least nine degrees of respect or familiarity. There are two 'tense-indicators' that can be inserted into a verb: (1) *-ŏss-* (often pronounced *-ŏt-*, because of a following consonant) for what has taken place, which can be doubled to *-ŏssŏss-* or *-ŏssŏt-*, for what happened earlier than some other event that is mentioned or implied; and (2) *-kess-* (or *-ket-*), for what has not yet taken place. These two indicators can be combined to form *-ŏtkess-* (or *-ŏtket-*) for what will (*or* may *or* must) have happened; and even *-ŏssŏtkess-* (or *-ŏssŏtket-*) for what probably happened earlier than some other event mentioned or implied. Further agglutinative syllables refine the speaker's intentions and conviction or hesitation as to the truth of what he says. *Hasiŏssŏtketchiman* politely says 'Although I think he (a person I respect) must have acted [before something else we know about], . . .'

Nouns take suffixed particles that have an effect comparable to Latin and Greek case endings. There is also a particle (*-nŭn*, or *-ŭn* after a consonant) that sets the noun outside the rest of the sentence, as a theme or background. This particle can also follow phrases and clauses.

Many adjectives, even colour adjectives, are formed like verbs. For example, *chŏlmŭn* 'young', is the attributive form of the verb *chŏmta* 'to be young', which also gives *chŏlmŏtta* 'was young' and *chŏlmŏjin* 'which has grown younger'. *P'urŭn*, 'green', is part of the verb *p'urŭda* 'to be green'.

HYUN BOK LEE, *Korean Grammar*, Oxford University Press, 1989; SAMUEL E. MARTIN, *A Reference Grammar of Korean*, Rutland, Vermont, and Tokyo: Charles E Tuttle Co, 1992

LATER PAEKCHE/ LATER THREE KINGDOMS *See* **Three Kingdoms, Later**

LATTICEWORK *ch'angho ŭijang* 窗戶意匠
Korean designs for lattice (*munsal*) in doors and windows are distinctive. They may cover the frame with an **all-over pattern**, but typically they have large panes symmetrically arranged. The finer lattices (*sessal*) may be arranged in a simple grid pattern, called *chŏngcha-mun*, 'well-character pattern' (diagram F) or, if arranged so as to emphasise grouping into six panes, *yongcha-mun* from the Chinese character *yong*, meaning 'to use'. When the horizontal lattice-work forms bands at the top or bottom of the panel, or across the middle, it is called *ttissal* 'belt latticing' (F).

More complex vertical and horizontal lattices are of two kinds. One is *wancha-mun* (A, B), based on regularly placed swastikas or part-swastikas, which are usually easy to discern. The other is called *atcha-mun* (C) from the general resemblance of its shapes to the Chinese character *a* 'second' (nowadays familiar as meaning 'Asia'), in which all spaces are rectangular. *Atcha-mun* is composed of quadrilateral spaces without swastikas in the lattice-work.

Diagonal lattices are called *pissal* 'slanting lattice' and are often used in octagonal window-panels. When vertical lattices, or both vertical and horizontal lattices, are introduced into *pissal*, the resulting pattern is called *sosŭl-pissal*, in which all the interstices are triangular. This is seen in palaces and temples, where heavy lattices may be carved in relief and have floral emblems at the intersections of the lattice (D). *Sosŭl-kkossal*, 'floral lattice with uprights' (E), is distinguished from *pitkkotsal*, 'diagonal floral lattice', which has no vertical or horizontal lines in it. Floral lattice is normally polychromed in *tanch'ŏng*.

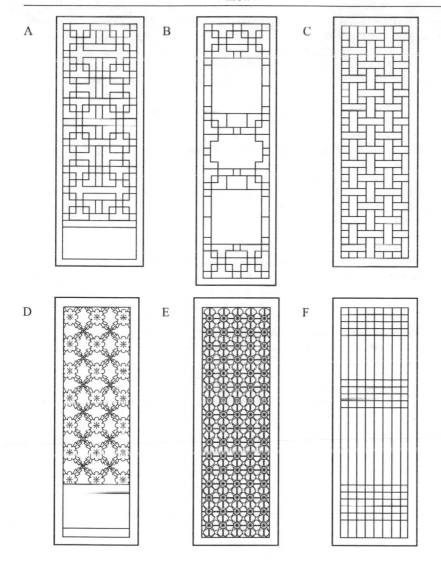

LAW

Law codes were instituted by **Koguryŏ** under King Sosurim (371–84) and by **Silla** in 520. The Koryŏ court adopted a code modelled on that of **Tang** China, consisting of laws and supplementary statutes, and under King Injong (1122–46) a Law College was established for the sons of lower grade officials and commoners. Scholars in the early Chosŏn also studied Chinese forms and precedents. The **Ming** criminal code was translated into *idu* in 1395 and adopted for use in Korea. Attempts were made to codify all the edicts and laws of the late Koryŏ period in the *Kyŏngje yukchŏn* ('Six Codes of Government', 1397); *Sok Yukchŏn* ('Supplement to the Six Codes', 1413); and further recensions made under Kings **Sejong** and **Sejo**. In 1470 King **Sŏngjong** promulgated a revision of the first comprehensive National Code (*Kyŏngguk Taejŏn*), compiled by the **Chiphyŏn-jŏn** and enshrining Confucian rituals and principles for social organisation promoted by the government. For example, a law of 1413 required a girl's parents to arrange her **marriage** at the appropriate age. Both the Six Codes and the National Code were arranged in six sections according to the **Six Boards** of government (*yukcho*). A Supplement to the National Code was issued in 1746, and a new code, *Taejŏn hoet'ong*, in 1865.

CHOI CHONGKO, 'The Reception of Western Law in Korea,' *KJ*, 20/5, 1980; CHOI CHONGKO, 'Traditional Korean Law and its Modernization,' *TRASKB*, LXIV, 1989; CHUN BONG-DUCK, *Traditional Korean Legal Attitudes*, Berkeley: Institute of East Asian Studies, 1980; HAHM PYONG-CHOON, *The Korean Political Tradition and Law*, Seoul: Royal Asiatic Society, Korean Branch, 1971; KIM CHIN, 'Legal Privileges under the Early Yi Dynasty Criminal Codes, I and II, *KJ*, 15/4, 15/5, 1975; PARK BYOUNG-HO, 'Characteristics of Traditional Korean Law,' *KJ*, 16/7, 1976; WILLIAM SHAW, *Legal Norms in a Confucian State*, Berkeley: Institute of East Asian Studies, 1981

LEFT AND RIGHT *chwa-u* 左右

The superiority of left over right in neo-Confucian practice was all-pervasive. In the *Uijŏng-bu*, the senior deputy was the left-hand minister, showing the priority of left over right. In relations between the sexes, *namjwa-yŏu* 'man left, woman right' was proverbial. In early formal photographs a man stood or sat to the left of his wife; his pulse was taken from the left wrist first, hers from the right; a palmist looked first at a man's left hand, but a woman's right. In a simple way of divining by the *Book of Changes*, the hexagram was chosen by picking swatches of pine-needles, a man starting with his left hand, a woman with her right.

This principle depends on *yin-yang* (K. *ŭm-yang*) theory. The seat of a ruler faces south, direction of major *yang* influence. The east is *yang* (whence the great *Yang* or sun rises) and to his left, which is therefore the correct place for a male. To his right is the *yin* west, appropriate for the female.

See also **Music, court**.

LELANG 樂浪 (K. Nangnang)

One of four Chinese commanderies in Korea established in 108 BC when armies sent by Emperor Han Wudi overthrew **Wiman Chosŏn**. It ruled the north-west of the peninsula through Chinese administrators and was divided into prefectures with its Chinese-style capital at Wanggŏmsŏng (modern T'osŏngni south-west of P'yŏngyang). It survived the fall of Wang Mang's régime and the Later **Han dynasty** only with difficulty and during the Chinese Three Kingdoms period was under the control of the state of Wei. It fell to **Koguryŏ** in AD 313, but had been instrumental in the economic development of the region and the spread of Chinese civilisation through the local Chosŏn nobility and into the southern Korean **Han** states.

H. IKEUCHI, 'A Study of Lo-lang and Tai-fang, Ancient Chinese Prefectures in Korean Peninsula,' *MRDTB*, 5, 1930; HYUNG IL PAI, 'Culture Contact and Culture Change: the Korean Peninsula and its Relations with the Han Dynasty Commandery of Lelang,' *WA* 23.3, 1992

See also **Chinbŏn**; **Lintun**; **Xuantu**

LI BAI (K. Yi Paek) 李白 (701–762)

The great Tang poet of wine. He was much admired in Korea, where he was more often called Yi T'aebaek, from his *cha* (familiar name), Taibai.

LI HONGZHANG 李鴻章 (1823–1901)
China's greatest statesman of the 19th century. He played a prominent part in trying to save China's place in the rapidly changing world, but while he recognised the need to develop relations with western countries on a footing which lay outside China's traditional view of her international position, he could not make such a radical break wth the past when it came to dealing with Japan and Korea. He first assumed responsibility for defining Korean policy when he became Governor General of Zhili and Imperial Commissioner for the Northern Ports in 1879. In the same year Japan annexed the Ryukyu Islands, and Li recognised the danger of losing Korea as well. His policy on Korea was therefore dedicated to re-enacting China's age-old suzerainty over the peninsular kingdom, to supporting the more conservative elements around the court in Seoul – especially the **Queen Min** faction, which favoured the China link – and to encouraging the anti-Japanese forces. Following the Military Mutiny of 1882 (*see Imo* **Incident**) and the subsequent Chinese capture of the **Taewŏn'gun**, he sent General **Yuan Shikai** to train the new military units formed in the capital, and Ma Jianzhong and the influential Paul-Georg **von Möllendorff** as advisers to the Korean government. He encouraged Korea to make treaties with western countries as a way of countering Japanese influence. After the *Kapsin* **Coup** of 1884 he and his Japanese opposite number **Itō Hirobumi** signed the **Treaty of Tianjin** in 1885, but Chinese influence remained stronger than Japanese, and Li's promotion of Yuan Shikai to be China's Resident-General in Seoul marked a quasi-colonial appointment which had not been attempted since the beginning of the Unified Silla dynasty. However, the **Tonghak Rebellion** led to the ruin of Li's foreign policy in East Asia. Failing to recognise the likelihood of Japanese retaliation, he sent troops to Korea as requested in June 1894, a course that ended with comprehensive defeat in the **Sino-Japanese War** and utter humiliation in the Treaty of **Shimonoseki**.
ARTHUR HUMMEL, *Eminent Chinese of the Ch'ing Period*, Washington 1943; KIM KEY-HIUK, 'The Aims of Li's Policies towards Japan and Korea 1870–1882,' *CSH*, 24/4, 1991; LIN MING-TE, 'Li's Suzerain Policy Toward Korea 1882–1894,' *CSH*, 24/4, 1991; T.C.LIN, 'Li Hung-chang: His Korean Policies,' *CSPSR*, XIX, 1935

LIANCOURT ROCKS *See* **Tokdo**

LIAO DYNASTY 遼代 (Manchuria, 907–1122)
Empire of the **Khitan** people in **Manchuria** and northern China founded by Yehlu Abaoji, who took the title of Emperor Taizu. It was contemporaneous with the Five Dynasties and Northern Song periods in China and the first half of the Koryŏ dynasty in Korea. It overcame the kingdom of **Parhae** in 926, and in 938 gained control of sixteen commanderies inside the Great Wall. It ruled its extensive territories from four regional capitals, of which the nearest to Korea was the 'Eastern Capital', Dongjing (near modern Shenyang). Some of its officials were Han natives of northern China and its courts practised Chinese rites and ceremonies, but the invasion of Korea as far as the **Ch'ŏngch'ŏn River** in 994 brought home to the Koreans their neighbours' independence, and by the 11th century Liao had destroyed the Middle Kingdom's traditional assumption of superiority in north-east Asia and forced both China and Korea to pay it **tribute**. The Koryŏ court tried to play safe. It adopted the Liao calendar, sent students to Shenyang to learn the Khitan language, and included maps among its tribute in 1002; it acknowledged that the best editions of the Buddhist scriptures were Liao as well as Song; nevertheless it also sent six official missions to China between 994 and 1003. In 1005 King Mokchong congratulated Liao on its

recent victory over Song, which had led to the Treaty of Shanyuan, but when he was assassinated in 1009 a large Liao army invaded Korea in revenge and drove as far south as **Kaesŏng**. Further battles took place on Korean soil in 1018, after which a triangular balance of political power developed around the Gulf of Bohai (*see* **Liaodong**), and regular commercial intercourse was carried on by **merchants** of China, Manchuria and Korea. The Liao empire fell to its own northern rivals, the **Jurchen**, in 1122. In part this was due to the poor political judgement of Song Emperor Huizong, who would have done better to align with his nearer and more familiar neighbours rather than to seek in vain an alliance with the Jurchen against them; but the collapse was mainly due to unquestionable Jurchen military supremacy.

NAOMI STANDEN, *Frontier Crossings from China to Liao, c.900–1005*, PhD thesis, University of Durham, 1994; K.WITTFOGEL & C.S.FENG, *History of Chinese Society: Liao 907–1125*, New York: American Philosophical Society, 1949

LIAODONG 遼東

Region of south-eastern **Manchuria** lying between the Liao River in modern northeast China (Jilin Province) and the **Yalu River**. In ancient and mediaeval times no attempt was made to fix or observe national borders precisely, and Liaodong was contested and controlled by **Koguryŏ** and its Chinese neighbours before being incorporated into the kingdom of **Parhae** in the late 7th century. Local inhabitants assumed command of the region with the rise of the **Khitan** empire of **Liao** in 926, but they were ousted by the **Jurchen** and they in turn by the **Mongols**, before Liaodong was once more incorporated into the Chinese empire under the Manchu **Qing dynasty**.

The significance of Liaodong to Korea lay in the threat its rulers might pose to the peninsular kingdom, and conversely the opportunities it offered the Korean people for migration and agricultural settlement, overland trade, and communication with continental China. For century after century ships followed the sea routes between the two countries, but the direct course from the Shandong Peninsula to the west coast of Korea was rough and dangerous, and those hugging the coast past Liaodong were frequently attacked by **pirates**.

See also **Shenyang, King of**

LIBERAL PARTY *Chayudang* 自由黨

Party formed by Syngman Rhee (**Yi Sŭngman**) in December 1951, which ensured his presidential re-election in 1952 through reforms to the **constitution**, passed by the National Assembly on 5 July 1952 under martial law. In 1954 it gained a sweeping victory in the general election through widespread intimidation of voters and opposition workers, and two years later ensured Rhee's re-election as president. Following a better showing by opposition parties in the 1958 National Assembly elections it amended the **National Security Law** (18 November 1958) limiting democratic activity, and in 1960 it again used corrupt methods to win his third re-election. Popular resentment erupted into the **April 19th Student Uprising** that year which led to Rhee's resignation, and in the July elections to the two newly constituted houses of parliament the Party was all but eradicated.

See also **South Korea: political parties**

LI–ITŌ AGREEMENT *See* **Tianjin, Treaty of**

LINEAGES *chong* 宗

Korean society attached great importance to ancestry and descent. Clan names had been first adopted following Chinese example in the **Proto-Three Kingdoms Period**. Chinese immigrants brought new names with them, and others were given as rewards for service by the leaders of the three kingdoms. By the early 15th century, 298 **surnames** were recorded. Aristocratic privilege was pronounced in the Three Kingdoms, Silla and Koryŏ periods: the lineages that comprised the Silla true-bone and head-rank leadership (*see kolp'um*) broadened into a wider but still exclusive class of nobility in the Koryŏ. When clans split, they were commonly known by their name and regional affiliation, such as the Ansan Kim clan of the 11th century, or the Andong Kim clan of the 19th. In the Chosŏn dynasty, membership of the *yangban* class as a whole, and at times of the **factions** and parties within it, conveyed political, economic and social power. Membership of the *yangban* was dependent upon belonging to an established lineage. In the Koryŏ era descent groups were broadly based and both patrilinear and matrilinear in construction; in the Chosŏn patrilineage alone counted. The neo-Confucian clan placed great store by the **genealogy** (*chokpo*) tracing its descent from a common male ancestor, and **ancestral worship** was an important element in lineage ritual. In time, primogeniture came to convey authority and privilege to the detriment of second and successive sons.

CHUNG SEUNG-MO, '*Chokpo*: Clan Genealogies', *Korean Cultural Heritage*, vol. IV, Seoul: Korea Foundation, 1998; KAWASHIMA FUJIYA, 'Lineage Elite and Bureacracy in Early-Yi to Mid-Yi Dynasty Korea', *Occasional Papers on Korea* 5, Seattle, 1977; MARK A. PETERSON, *Korean Adoption and Inheritance, Case Studies in the Creation of a Classic Confucian Society*, New York: Cornell East Asia Series, 1996; SHIMA MUTSUHIKO, 'In Quest of Social Recognition: a Retrospective View on the Development of Korean Lineage Organisation,' *HJAS*, 50: 1990
See also **class system**

LINJI BUDDHISM *Imje-gyo* 臨濟宗

A form of *Sŏn* Buddhism established in the Tang dynasty by Linji (K. Imje, J. Rinzai, d. 867), otherwise known as Yixuan (K. Ŭihyŏn). It emphasised the use of *kongan* and introduced shock tactics of beating and shouting into meditation training. This severe approach appealed to samurai culture and accounts for the importance of the Rinzai school in Japan. It was introduced into Korea in less extreme form by **Chinul** and **T'aego**.

LINTUN (K. Imdun) 臨屯

Chinese commandery established by **Han** armies in 108 BC over the native state of Imdun which had formed part of the **Wiman Chosŏn** kingdom. It was absorbed into **Xuantu** Commandery in 82 BC and finally into **Lelang** in 75 BC. It covered territory along the north-east seaboard in modern South Hamgyŏng province, and was taken by **Koguryŏ** in the 2nd century AD.
See also **Okchŏ**

LION DANCE *sajach'um*

There are two traditions. In one, *saja-norŭm* 'lion game', two men with lion masks visit the houses of the village in a simple exorcism drama, usually on *Taeborŭm-nal*. In the other, *sajach'um* 'lion dance', there are two lions again, but each lion is made up of two men in one simulated lion-skin, usually performing in association with **masked drama**. The 'skins' are suits covered with strips of cloth. This custom seems to have come through Tang from Central Asia. There was once a court version.
See also **dance**

LITERARY MAGAZINES 1919–22

The 1919 Independence Movement happened when a new generation of Koreans educated in Japan was mature enough to gather its forces in both literary and political fields. Their emotions found expression in a series of literary magazines published by groups of friends, mostly in their twenties, who were generally interested in writing as art rather than as enlightenment. The most important of these magazines were of lasting influence in the development of modern Korean literature. *Ch'angjo*, 'Creation', was produced by a group of Korean students in Japan in February 1919 and issued 9 numbers. *Kaebyŏk*, 'Dawning', starting in June 1920 with the backing of the **Ch'ŏndo-gyo** religion, lasted for 72 numbers and was politically outspoken enough to be fined and suspended several times by the Japanese government. *P'yehŏ*, 'Ruins', which appeared in July 1920 and issued only two numbers, intended to promise new life from the ruins of the Korean state and its culture, but was marked by a tendency to decadent imagery. *Changmi-ch'on*, 'Rose Village', of May 1921, a poetry magazine with a romantic bent, was one of many that did not run to a second number. *Paekcho*, 'White Tide', in January 1922 declared 'What is not beautiful is not true' and rejected decadence, but was inclined to romanticism. It ran to three issues, and like some others was published under the auspices of a foreigner (W. E. Billings, a Methodist missionary) to avoid government action.

PETER H. LEE, *Korean Literature: Topics and Themes*, Tucson: University of Arizona Press, 1965

See also **March First Movement**

LITERATI PURGES, TWELVE *sibi sahwa* 十二士禍

The traditional count of *sahwa* between 1453 and 1722 comprises:

1453 *KYEYU-JŎNGDAN*. Prince Suyang (later King **Sejo**) killed the regents for the boy-king **Tanjong**.

1455 *PYŎNGJA-SAHWA*. A plan to assassinate Sejo and restore King Tanjong was betrayed. 70 or so were executed.

1498 *MUO-SAHWA*. **Yŏnsan-gun**'s 'history purge'. *See Sahwa*.

1504 *KAPCHA-SAHWA*. Insult to Yŏnsan-gun's mother. *See Sahwa*.

1519 *KIMYO-SAHWA*. Death of **Cho Kwangjo**. *See Sahwa*.

1521 *SINSA-MUOK*. Song Saryŏn (1496–1578) made a false accusation of treason against An Ch'ŏgyŏm (1486–1521), who was executed.

1545 *ŬLSA-SAHWA*. Accession of King Myŏngjong. *See Sahwa*.

1547 *CHŎNGMI-SAHWA*. Seditious graffiti were found at Yangjae post-station near Kwangju, Kyŏnggi-do. Executions followed.

1549 *KIYU-SAHWA*. Yi Hongnam (b. 1515) accused his younger brother Hongyun of plotting treason. Hongyun and others were executed.

1613 *KYECH'UG-OKSA*. The Lesser Northerners were accused of banditry to finance putting Prince Yŏngch'ang on the throne.

1689 *KISA-HWAN'GUK*. Westerners opposed the appointment of a young Crown Prince. They lost the argument; **Song Siyŏl** was executed.

1721–1722 *SINIM-SAHWA*, (1721 *Sin*[*ch'uk*] – 1722 *Im*[*in*]). The Soron opposed making the Crown Prince regent when King Kyŏngjong was ill. Kim Ch'angjip and the **Noron**, who preferred the prince who later became King **Yŏngjo**, were accused of treason and persecuted.

LITERATURE *See changga; hanmun; hansi; hyangga; kasa; Kodae sosŏl;* **Palace literature;** *P'aegwan* **literature;** poetry; *sihwa; sijo;* **Tang-style regulated verse**
KICHUNG KIM, *An Introduction to Classical Korean Literature, from Hyangga to P'ansori,* New York and London: M.E. Sharpe, 1996; KIM HUNGGYU, *Understanding Korean Literature,* New York and London: M.E. Sharpe, 1997; PETER H. LEE, ed., *Anthology of Korean Literature, from Early Times to the Nineteenth Century,* Honolulu: University of Hawaii Press, 1981

LONDON, JACK (1879–1916)
The American adventurer and writer who used this pseudonym visited Korea in 1904 as correspondent for the *San Francisco Examiner* during the **Russo-Japanese War**. In 1914 he published *The Star Rover* (in England, *The Jacket*), a novel telling of six former incarnations of the narrator. One of the stories was based on the experiences of **Hamel** in 1665 and **Oppert** in 1867. It is a tale of violence and fantasy, full of garbled information about Korean history, largely miscopied from the writings of **H. B. Hulbert**.

LONGEVITY, THE TEN SYMBOLS OF *Sip changsaeng* 十長生
A series of ten auspicious symbols much used in domestic decorative work during the Chosŏn dynasty, mentioned by **Yi Suck** and apparently a Korean notion to comfort the elderly. They were painted on **screens** (notably one used at New Year in the royal palace), **fans, pillow** ends, jewel-boxes and other furnishings. Their history is not recorded, though obsession with long life was typical of Daoist thinking. The ten are usually given as sun, mountains, flowing water, rocks, clouds, pine-trees, longevity fungus (*Ganosperma lucidum*), turtles, cranes and spotted **deer**. Often some of them are omitted, while **peaches**, peonies, **lotus** or **bamboo** may be added.
AKIBA TAKASHI, 'A study of Korean folkways', *Folklore Studies* (Tokyo), XVI, 1957

LORD AMHERST
Ship of the British East India Company which visited the west coast of Korea in 1832 in search of a trade treaty and protestant missionary openings. It was forced away, but Karl **Gützlaff** succeeded in distributing some Bibles.

LOTUS *yŏnkkot* 蓮花
The lotus (*Nelumbo nucifera,* S. *pundarika* or *padma*) is not native to Korea, but is a cultivated plant from China, grown in pools of water, where in summer the long-stemmed white or pinkish flowers and broad blue-green leaves have a characteristic beauty and a pleasant faint scent. Every part of the plant is said to be edible and the underwater stems, called 'roots' (*yŏn'gŭn*), are a much loved delicacy. They have large air passages in them and slices look like spoked wheels. The same stems can be milled to fine flour and used to make a nourishing gruel. While thought of as a Buddhist symbol of purity springing unsullied from the mud, the lotus also means immortality, health, good fortune, long life, and honour. Lotus flowers and leaves are therefore frequent motifs in decorative art. They were made respectable for neo-Confucians by a

famous miniature essay, 'Love of the Lotus' *Ailianshuo* (K. *Aeryŏn-sŏl*), by Zhou Dunyi, one of the **Five Sages of Song**, included in ***Komun-jinbo***.

LUNAR MANSIONS *isip-p'al su* 二十八宿

Long before Han times the Chinese divided the celestial sphere into 28 *su* (C. *xiu*) 'mansions' or 'lodges', unequal segments, each named after a prominent asterism in it. In Korea the diagrams of the asterisms, showing from 2 to 22 stars as little circles joined by straight lines (*see examples below*), were used in ceremonial **flags** and occasionally in decorative art. The translations of *su* names given here are probable early meanings.

East blue/green		North black		West white		South red	
Kak	horn	*Tu*	dipper	*Kyu*	astride	*Chŏng*	well
Hang	neck	U	ox	*Nu*	bond	*Kwi*	ghost
Chŏ	root	*Yŏ*	girl	*Wi*	stomach	*Yu*	willow
Pang	room	*Hŏ*	void	*Myo*	Pleiades	*Sŏng*	7 stars
Sim	heart	*Wi*	roof	*P'il*	net	*Chang*	bow
Mi	tail	*Sil*	house	*Cha*	turtle	*Ik*	wing
Ki	winnower	*Sam*	triad	*Pyŏk*	wall	*Chin*	chariot

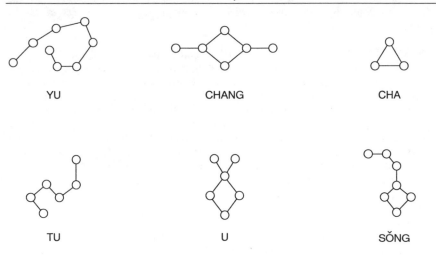

YU   CHANG   CHA

TU   U   SŎNG

M

MAEIL SINMUN 每日新聞 'Daily News'
Korea's first daily **newspaper**, written partly in Korean and partly in English. It was established in February 1898. One of its founder-editors, Syngman Rhee (**Yi Sŭngman**), used its columns to campaign for democratic and social reforms. Its fervent anti-government editorial policy caused it to be closed down late the same year.

MAEMA KYŌSAKU 前間恭作 (1868–1942)

A native of **Tsushima**, where he learned Korean as a schoolboy. In 1894 he went to Korea for further study, working at the **Inch'ŏn** consulate. After a year out in Australia he joined the Seoul Legation staff in 1901. In 1910 he became chief translator for the **Government General**, but retired in 1911 with a huge library on which he continued to work. Among his books the most important are *Kosen zuppu*, 'Old Korean Booklist', and *Senzatsu meidai*, 'Famous Korean Book Titles'. His collection is now in the Tōyō Bunko, 'Oriental Library', in Tokyo.

MAGOJA

A collarless jacket for informal wear, fastened at the throat with a single large loop and toggle (often a piece of amber), worn by men over the *chokki* and frequently made of figured **silk**. It is said to be a version of the Manchu *maguazi*, originally a riding jacket, introduced by the Hŭngsŏn **Taewŏn-gun** after he returned from detention in China in 1884.
See also **dress**

MAGYŎNG-ŎNHAE 馬經諺解 'Book of the Horse, with Korean translation'

A book of veterinary science, also called *Magyŏng-ch'ojip ŏnhae*, written by Yi Sŏ (1580–1637) and published about 1630. It is a pastiche from Korean and Chinese sources, discussing equine diseases, with lyric passages and anatomical drawings. Yi Sŏ was a military *yangban*, a **meritorious subject** who had helped instal Injo as king. He served as *kwanch'alsa* of Kyŏnggi province, rose to be *p'ansŏ* of the Board of Works, and died of illness shortly after the **Manchu invasion** of 1636.

MAHAN 馬韓

One of three federations of tribes (collectively known as **Samhan**) which ruled the southern half of the peninsula after the decline of **Chin** authority. Located on the western side of central south Korea, its strongest clan eventually formed the independent state of **Paekche**, which under King Kŭn Ch'ogo is said to have conquered Mahan in 369. But the stone burial chamber of a Mahan leader discovered in 1996 at Naju, Chŏlla Namdo, and dated to the 6th century AD, indicates that the state continued to exist until that time in the shadow of Paekche.
KIM JUNG-BAE, 'Characteristics of Mahan in Ancient Korean Society,' *KJ*, 14/6, 1974

MALANANDA 摩羅難陀 (4th century)

Malananda (K. Maranant'a) is believed to have been an Indian or Serindian monk from the Eastern Jin state in the Yangzi valley. He entered **Paekche** in 384 and was welcomed there as the teacher of **Buddhism**.

MALGAL 靺鞨

Nomadic Tungusic tribespeople of eastern **Manchuria** ancestrally related to the **Jurchen** and Manchus. They formed part of the population of **Koguryŏ** mobilised to fight the **Sui** and **Tang** Chinese between 598 and 668. In the 8th century they comprised the greater part of the population of the **Parhae** kingdom, and some also served in the armies of **Unified Silla**. They became subject to **Khitan** rule following the fall of Parhae in 926, but established their own **Jin** dynasty in the 11th century.
See also **Liaodong; Puyŏ**

MANCHU INVASIONS *Chŏngmyo, Pyŏngja Horan* 丁卯，丙子胡亂
The Manchus who invaded Korea in 1627 and 1636 were descendants of the **Jurchen** people. Anxious to remove any threat from Korea to their flank as they prepared to attack China, they found an opportunity in response to a request for aid from Korean dissidents involved in **Yi Kwal's** unsuccessful revolt (1624) against King Injo. They captured P'yŏngyang, the King escaped to **Kanghwa-do**, and to obtain their withdrawal the court recognised the supremacy of the Later Jin régime. The second invasion came when Injo refused to acknowledge Abahai (Emperor Taizong)'s self-styled **Qing** state. The Manchu leader himself led a force which caused devastation across northern Korea and drained it of many resources. This time the queen and other members of the royal family fled to Kanghwa-do, where they were captured, and the King to the fortress of Namhan-san (**Namhan sansŏng**). Here he too eventually surrendered. Two of his sons were taken to **Manchuria** as hostages and Korea was compelled to support its new suzerain in its attack on **Ming** China. The princes were later returned, and as King Hyojong one of them, Pongnim, planned an unfulfilled revenge attack on Manchuria.
See also **Samjŏn-do hanbi**; **Sohyŏn, Crown Prince**

MANCHU LANGUAGE TEXTS
Apart from *Ch'ŏngŏ nogŏltae* (1703) there was a small library of books about Manchu. *Samyŏk ch'onghae* was published in the same year, and *Hanch'ŏng mun'gam* in 1779. Earlier, in the reign of Injo, two storybooks had been written, which were several times re-issued: *P'alse-a*, 'Eight-year-old child' (telling of a little boy from a poor family who could answer the emperor's difficult questions) and *Soa-ron*, 'Discourse of a little child' (a similar account of a boy of three).

MANCHURIA 滿洲
Region of three north-eastern provinces of modern China first incorporated into the Chinese Empire by the Manchus following their establishment of the **Qing dynasty** in 1644. It was previously the domain of the **Malgal**, the **Jurchen**, the **Khitan** and the **Mongols**. The present border between Korea and China defined by the **Yalu** and **Tumen** Rivers was not always an agreed political frontier, and from ancient to early modern times territory to the west and north was frequently contested and occupied by Koreans, especially in the fertile Liao River basin (*see* **Liaodong**). The mediaeval kingdom of **Parhae** was created in central Manchuria by former natives of **Koguryŏ**, recalling the early origins of their ancestors in the same region.

In 1881 the Qing government first accepted legitimate Korean settlers, of whom some acquired land deeds and others went to work as tenant farmers. By 1908 the Korean population was estimated at 323,000, and by 1920 that of **Kando**, swollen by refugees from the Japanese occupation, as approximately 600,000. Many of them engaged in anti-Japanese activities (*see* **Korean Independence Army**; **Ŭibyŏng**; **Yi Tŏnghwi**). After the creation of the Japanese puppet state of Manzhouguo in 1935 Koreans were forcibly removed there as farm and factory labourers. By 1943 the Korean population is estimated to have been 1·4 million. Encouraged by the Chinese Communist Party, Koreans in Manchuria were among the supporters of the communist régime in North Korea and fought in the **Korean War**.

GEORGE LENSON, ed., *Korea and Manchuria between Russia and Japan: the Observations of Sir Ernest Satow, British Minister Plenipotentiary to Japan (1895–1900) and China (1900–06)*, Tokyo: Sophia University, 1966; GEORGE LENSEN, *Balance of Intrigue: International Rivalry in Korea and Manchuria, 1884–1899* (2 volumes),

Tallahassee: University Presses of Florida, 1982; C. WALTER YOUNG, *The International Relations of Manchuria*, Chicago, 1929

MANCHURIAN INCIDENT 滿洲事變 (1931)
Also known as the Mukden Incident. On 18 September 1931 the leaders of the Japanese Guandong Army in **Manchuria** took advantage of a trumped-up incident in the **South Manchuria Railway** Zone the harmless explosion of a small bomb on the track outside Mukden (Shenyang) – and used it as an excuse to launch an armed invasion of the North-East. It was the beginning of the phase of Japanese territorial expansion on the mainland which would shortly lead to the creation of the puppet state of Manzhouguo (J. Manchukuo) (1935), the outbreak of the Chinese anti-Japanese War (1937–45), and the Japanese occupation of south-east Asia. It thus played a critical part in the path to World War Two in the Far East. Korean resistance units in Manchuria joined Chinese in the struggle against the conquerors. In Korea itself, people quickly experienced the repercussions of the Incident, which marked the beginning of a new stage in Japan's policy towards its colonial base. Living and working conditions plummeted as production of raw materials and manufactured goods, especially munitions, took priority. Workers were forced away from the land into factories and agricultural output declined. At the same time, educational and cultural indoctrination was intensified to force home an awareness of Japanese-ness and to diminish appreciation of Korean heritage. Ironically, increased repression led to enhanced determination by Korean patriots to resist.
CHRISTOPHER THORNE, *The Limits of Foreign Policy: the West, the League of Nations, and the Far Eastern Crisis of 1931–1933*, London: Hamish Hamilton Ltd., 1972
See also **Colonial period**

MANCHUS, THE *See* **Manchu invasions**

MANI-SAN 摩尼山 *See* **Jewel mountains**

MANTRA
Namu Amit'abul, 'Hail **Amida** Buddha', is the most popular Buddhist prayer in Korea. If recited sufficiently often, it is reckoned an adequate means of getting to the Pure Land paradise at death. The names *Sŏkkamoni-bul* (*see* **Buddhas**) and *Kwanseŭm-bosal* are often repeated in much the same way. The mystic Sanskrit syllable *om* is known but not much used.

MAP'AE 馬牌 'horse tokens'
The *Sangsŏ-wŏn* (*see* **Government organs**) issued copper discs to officials who were entitled to receive **horses** at the post-stations throughout the country. The number of horses allowed, varying from one to ten, was shown by an engraving of that number of horses on the obverse. The reverse showed the *Sangsŏ-wŏn* seal, a serial number from **Ch'ŏnja-mun** and the date of issue. The same token was carried by an *amhaeng-ŏsa* or secret inspector, who displayed it when he disclosed his identity.

MAPS *See* **Cartography**

MARCH FIRST MOVEMENT *Samil-undong* 三一運動
Also known as the *Manse* ('Long live [Korea]') Revolution, after the cry used by its demonstrators. Encouraged by news from Shanghai and Tokyo of Korean student

organisations calling for Korean independence and by prospects for the recovery of national sovereignty at the Paris Peace Conference, but suspicious of possible Japanese involvement in the death of the former Emperor **Kojong** on 21 January 1919, a group of *Ch'ŏndo-gyo*, Christian and Buddhist leaders composed a **Declaration of Independence**. Though it was intended as an incitement of non-violent resistance to the Japanese occupation the signatories were immediately arrested. **Students** fanned the flames of nationalist protest and the popular mood became threatening as demonstrations spread quickly across the country, involving all levels of society. Attacks took place on Japanese military and civilians. The Japanese army reacted with brutal force, killing at their own estimate 7,509 and almost certainly more, wounding nearly sixteen thousand, arresting some twenty thousand, destroying property, banning demonstrations and assemblies, and closing down markets. Order was restored by May 1919 and the independence movement seemed to have been crushed, but its effects were more long-lasting. Realising the depth of Korean antagonism and apprehensive of hostile world-wide publicity, the Japanese government now adopted an apparently more accommodating approach to its colony (*see* **Colonial period**). Korean resistance was stimulated, although like the demonstrations of the March First Movement it was uncoordinated and its success less marked than it might have been.

KO SEONG KYUN, 'The March First Movement: A Study of the Rise of Korean Nationalism under the Japanese Colonialism,' *KQ*, XIV, 1972; KU DAE-YEOL, *Korea under Colonialism: the March First Movement and Anglo-Japanese Relations*, Seoul: Royal Asiatic Society Korea Branch, 1985; KENNETH WELLS, 'Background to the March First Movement: Koreans in Japan, 1905–1919,' *KS*, 13, 1989
See also **Provisional Government in Exile**; **Thirty-three Independence Signatories**; **Yi Kwangsu**; **Yu Kwangsun**

MARIPKAN 麻立干 *See* **Silla kingly titles**

MARITIME CUSTOMS SERVICE *Haegwanse suse ŏmmu* 海關稅收稅業務
Established in 1883 as part of **Li Hongzhang**'s policy for exerting Chinese control in Korea, and initially advised by a German member of Li's staff, Paul-Georg **von Möllendorff**. Until 1905, its senior staff were Chinese government appointees. Like the Chinese Imperial Maritime Customs Service, of which it was independent, it was a synarchic organisation of foreigners and nationals, whose job was to collect tariffs on behalf of the government and to regulate the growing quantity of international trade. Among its foreign officers who also acted as advisers to the Korean government was the Irishman McLeavey **Brown**, who worked with the Ministry of Finance (*T'akchibu*) from 1892 to 1905. He played a key rôle in the modernisation of the capital after 1896, including the creation of **Pagoda Park**. The Service was taken over by a Japanese director in 1904 under the terms of the **Korea-Japan Protocol**.
YURBOK LEE, 'Robert Hart and Chinese Domination of Korea: a Study of Misguided Imperialism', *PBAKS*, 4, 1993

MARKETS
Were important as centres for the bartered exchange of goods in a predominantly agrarian economy from earliest times to the 20th century. Three markets had existed in **Kyŏngju** by the end of the 5th century AD, controlled by the government office *sijŏn*. In the Koryŏ period markets were known as *hyangshi*; the central market in **Kaesŏng** was managed by the *Kyŏngsi-sŏ*, which fixed prices, opening hours, and rules of

operation Xu Jing commented favourably on them in his *Xuunhe fengshi Gaoli tujing* (K. *Koryŏ To'gyŏng*). Despite initial opposition from the government, permanent markets developed through the mid-Chosŏn period, especially in the capital. Six specialised markets (*yug-ŭijŏn*) were officially recognised in Seoul and situated in the central district (*see* **six licensed shops**), and shops were authorised in Kaesŏng and P'yŏngyang; in provincial centres a wholesale market industry began to supply goods to travelling pedlars (*pobusang*) in the 18th century, and guilds were formed (*see* **Pedlars' guild**). Periodic markets were held across the country every five days and were an essential way of distributing craft manufactures (*see* **craftsmen**) and imported wares, as well as regional food produce. They were served by *pobusang*, who also participated in seasonal fairs specialising in particular goods such as medicinal products, animals and birds. The more successful transported their goods by cart or boat.

JUNG CHANG-YOUNG *et al., Economic Life in Korea*, Seoul: Sisa Yongosa, 1982; LEE HYOUN-YOUNG, 'A Geographic Study of the Korean Periodic Markets,' *KJ*, 15/8, 1975; PAK WON-SON, 'The Market in Korea: A Historical Survey,' *KJ*, 29/6, 1989

See also **coinage**; **commerce**; **merchants**

MARRIAGE

In the Chosŏn period, the chief purpose of marriage was to ensure the continuance of **ancestral rites**. It was seen as a union of two families, with economic and political effects, class-endogamous (within the same social stratum) and clan-exogamous (the spouses must have different surnames), though marriage between spouses from different descent-groups (*pon'gwan*) of the same **surname** was never fully eradicated. Match-makers were employed. Apart from status, health and divinatory indications, the controlling considerations were political. The groom was supposed to be at least 16 and the bride 14, but exceptions for marriage as early as 12 were often invoked. Marriage was the sign of adulthood.

Chinese Confucian **rites** were never accepted in full detail, though they were used by **Sejong** at the wedding of the Crown Prince (later King Munjong) in 1427 and generally adopted by the upper classes in the 16th century. The Koryŏ system by which the groom went to live in the bride's house left lingering traces.

The wedding ritual, allowing for local and class variation, began with the betrothal, in which the matchmaker (*chungmae*) might take part. The bridegroom's *saju* (sexagenary characters of his birth year, month, day and hour) would be sent to the bride's parents with gifts of a wild goose (normally wooden), cloth, thread, and symbols of fertility (such as ears of grain and **peppers**), and the marriage contract in a lacquered box. Once this had been accepted the marriage was regarded as legally binding. On the appointed day the bridegroom, wearing court robes and in a palanquin or riding a horse, was escorted by friends to the bride's house. They would be met by friends of the bride, usually with horseplay that might be brutal (hinting at resistance to ancient marriage by abduction). Groom and bride would meet for the first time when she emerged into the awning-covered courtyard, splendidly dressed and wearing a tiny crown. He would stand to the east and she to the west of a table, laden with food symbolic of fecundity and decorated with pine and **bamboo**. An attendant stood by holding a live **fowl**. The couple performed formal bows and shared cups of wine. The bride then withdrew and the guests sat down to a banquet. When the couple retired for the night there was more teasing, with women and children wetting their finger-tips to puncture spy-holes in the paper windows of the bridal chamber, until the candles were blown out. The groom was supposed to undress the bride. Neither should have smiled throughout the day.

After a period, during which the groom might go away at times, the couple went to the bridegroom's home, taking gifts to the groom's parents. With more bowing the bride was introduced to her parents-in-law and to the ancestral shrine. She then joined the women of the family as a junior member.

LAUREL KENDALL, *Getting Married in Korea: of Gender, Morality and Modernity*, Berkeley: University of California Press, 1996

MARTYRS, CATHOLIC *Ch'ŏnju-gyo sun'gyoja* 天主教殉教者

The persecutions are the core of the early history of the **Catholic** Church in Korea. The number of martyrs between **Kim Pŏmu** in 1787 and the last in 1868 cannot be told, though the names of 1,746 are known. In 1984, at Saenam-t'ŏ Church, above the sands by the **Han River** west of Seoul, where many of them were executed, Pope John Paul II canonised 103 of those martyred in 1839, 1854–6 and 1866. The number was limited to those for whom detailed documentation could be assessed, and many regret that no names from the earliest persecutions could be included in the list. Ten were French: Bishops **Imbert, Berneux** and **Daveluy**, Fathers **Maubant, Chastan**, Simon Marie-Antoine-Just Ranfer de Bretenières (1838–66), Pierre-Henri Dorie (1837–66), Bernard-Louis Beaulieu (1840–66), Martin-Luc Huin (1836–66) and Pierre Aumaître (1837–66). Marie-Alexandre Petitnicolas (1828–66) and Charles-Antoine Pourthié (1830–66) were also martyred, but not canonised.

Of the 93 Koreans, **Kim Taegŏn** was a priest; 45 were lay men, headed by **Chŏng Hasang**. The youngest, 12-year-old Peter Yu Taech'ŏl, gave himself up after his father's martyrdom in 1839; the oldest, Mark Chŏng Ŭibae, executed in 1866, was 72.

Just over half the Koreans (47) were women: Lucy Kim 'the hunchback' was a widow aged 71; two sisters in their twenties, Columba Kim Hyoim and Agnes Kim Hyoju, executed in 1839, intended to live as virgins, and so were both stripped and put for the night in the prison of common thieves, who left them unmolested; Barbara Yi was fifteen. Women like these and **Kang Wansuk** (who was not canonised) were largely responsible for the spread of catholicism. It says much for the importance accorded to **women** in Chosŏn that they were thought worth executing in such numbers.

The martyrs' feast day is 20 September. The process for canonisation of 17 more, including **Zhou Wenmo** and Kang Wansuk, has begun.

ADRIEN LAUNAY, *Martyrs Français et Coréens 1838–1846*, Paris: Tequis, 1925

MASAN DEMONSTRATION (1960)   *See* **April 19th Student Uprising**
See also **New Democratic Party**; **Second Republic**

MASKED DANCE / DRAMA *t'alchum*; *kamyŏn-gŭk* 假面劇

A form of cultural expression with many regional forms, incorporating **music, dance** and acrobatics. The early history of masked plays is extremely obscure. It is tempting to over-interpret the exiguous references to drama in the Three Kingdoms Period, but there is little doubt that it was originally associated with **shamanism** and popular religious observances. In Koryŏ and early Chosŏn, dance-dramas were also produced at court. Neo-Confucian solemnity ensured that they disappeared, as they did in 1634, when the closure of the responsible office dispersed performers into urban and rural areas.

After that, drama was a provincial and largely rural affair. Villagers or travelling players (*kwangdae*) acted the plays (*t'allori, sandi-nori, tŏtpogi* or *t'alch'um*) at **New Year**, Buddha's birthday (*see* ***Ch'op'a-il***), ***Tano*** or ***Ch'usŏk***, in time of drought and on other special occasions.

Performances were given at night by the light of flares, and sometimes lasted until dawn. The arena was a circle of bare ground out of doors. The musicians sat to one side. A dressing room was improvised in a tent or nearby house. All the actors were men. The dialogue was repeated verbatim from year to year, with occasional ad-libbing, earthy and intentionally humorous.

Most of the plays fell into desuetude under the Colonial government in the 1920s, but Korean folklorists have been successful in recording several sets of dialogue from surviving participants. The best known are from Pongsan in Hwanghae, Yangju in Kyŏnggi, T'ongyŏng and Kosŏng in south Kyŏngnam (the *Ogwangdae* plays), Pukch'ŏng in North Korea and Hahoe near Andong. A few plays have been revived, but in partially sanitised form, performed within a proscenium or in daylight. A few **women** may take part – perhaps because younger men have been reluctant to perform in recent years. The old boisterousness and earthiness have been diluted.

The masks (*t'al*), made of wood or of gourds, are the outstanding feature. All are grotesque and garishly painted in red, black, white, blue and yellow. Sometimes they were burned after the performance. In other places they were stored in a special shrine outside the village.

Folklorists have classified the plays in various ways, but the main outline is the same in all areas. There is no unifying theme or plot. The show starts with a dancing monk and one or two companions, in racy dialogue with a girl called a young *mudang*. This scene is followed by one or two scenes with larger numbers of monks, some of them with **drums**, or by a female impersonator performing a drum **dance**. The third element consists of incidents involving a senior monk, and perhaps a renegade monk (*ttaengch'u*), a shoe-vendor and a wastrel. In some places a **lion dance** is then inserted. (At Pongsan the lion dance is thought to date only from 1890.) The fourth element sees *yangban* being caricatured as ignorant, lascivious and pompous. There may be a scene of a **dragon** or serpent being driven away. The final turn is domestic, involving an old married couple, and often ending in the wife's funeral. A **puppet play** may be added.

Modern commentators are tempted to interpret all this in terms of 20th-century preoccupations, as vigorous political protest and religious satire, and in the **Republic of Korea** masked drama has voiced popular opposition to military dictatorship (*see Minjung* **movement**). In their palmy days the plays were primarily fun. Fun for **peasants** always means joking about landlords, and people always joke about their religion. It is possible to be over-serious about masked plays.

The Hahoe play, near Andong in north Kyŏngsang, is associated with a ten-yearly religious ceremony called *pyŏlsin-kut* and has retained much of its religious character. The Hahoe masks are notable in that they are hinged at the jaw. The Korea Mask Art Museum at Hahoe has information on nearly four hundred different masks.

Closely related to the masked drama are the simpler religious observances, chiefly exorcisms, that involve masks or animal costumes. The finest of these is the *Ch'ŏyong* **dance**, a revival of an ancient exorcism performed by five masked men.

CHO OK-KUN, '*Ogwangdae*: A Traditional Mask-dance Theatre of South Kyŏngsang Province,' *KJ*, 21/7, 1981; CHO OK KUN, 'The Mask-dance Theatre from Hwanghae Province,' *KJ*, 22/5, 1982; CHO OK-KUN, trans., *Traditional Korean Theatre*, Seoul: Asian Humanities Press, 1988; HYUNG-A KIM VAN LEEST, 'Political Satire in Yangju Pyŏlsandae Mask Drama,' *KJ*, 31/1, 1991

MAUBANT, PIERRE PHILIBERT, SAINT 羅伯多祿 (1803–39)

The first western missionary to enter Korea, Fr Maubant met Bishop **Bruguière** in Sichuan and joined him on the journey through **Manchuria**. After the bishop died at

Majiazi, Maubant, helped by **Chŏng Sahang**, crossed the frozen **Yalu** in January 1836. The Chinese priest Yu Hengde (Pacificus), who had volunteered for Korea while studying in Naples, was already there. Working in secret, mostly in south Ch'ungch'ŏng province, Maubant noticed the ability of 13-year-old **Kim Taegŏn** and arranged for him and two other lads to be taken to Macao by Fr Yu, who did not return to Korea. On receiving a letter from Bishop **Imbert**, Maubant surrendered to the authorities at Hongju and was beheaded with the bishop and Fr Chastan at Saenamt'ŏ in 1839.

McCUNE-REISCHAUER ROMANISATION SYSTEM *See pages xiii–xvii*

MEDICAL *KISAENG* *ŭinyŏ* 醫女

During the Chosŏn dynasty, because it was impossible for a male doctor to examine a woman, a trained group of *kisaeng* was maintained to care for the women of the royal household. The first proposal for appointing them to feel pulses and give acupuncture was recorded for 1406. The most arduous part of their training was learning enough Chinese to read medical textbooks, and they were regularly examined as to their knowledge and skills. Individuals were appointed to wait upon particular queens and princesses. Some became skilled in particular problems, such as toothache, headache or eye troubles; some were trained as apothecaries; but they were rarely allowed to prescribe **medicine**. The *kisaeng* would examine her patient behind a screen and describe the symptoms for a male doctor who attended on the other side of the screen. He would prescribe any medicines needed. Medical *kisaeng* also acted as custodians for noble ladies under arrest, carried out searches of the **women**'s quarters when incriminating evidence was being sought, and delivered the hemlock to queens and other ladies who were ordered to commit suicide (*see* **poison**). They survived till the last days of the dynasty and were doubtless the 'palace women' who were assigned to work in the first government hospital, opened by Horace N. **Allen** in the 1880s.

MEDICINE

Traditional Korean medicine was based on systems learned from Chinese texts and doctors, and leant heavily on herbal and other natural pharmacology. Medicines were exchanged between China, Korea and Japan as **tribute** and commercial commodities. It was a subject for specialist academic study in the early Koryŏ capital and was promoted across the countryside by order of King **Sŏngjong**, and independent Korean research and publication was carried on through this and the early Chosŏn periods. A request from King Munjong to the Chinese court for doctors in 1078 resulted in a big Chinese medical expedition the following year, and more were sent at the request of King **Yejong** in 1122, after which an official medical office was opened. As a profession, medicine was a preserve of the *chungin* class, and could be taken as a subject in the *chapkwa* **examination**. The oldest surviving Korean medical text is the *Hyangyak kugŭppang* ('Folk Medicine Emergency Remedies') of 1236. King **Sejong** instigated the research and publication of two encyclopaedias: in 1433 the *Hyangyak chipsŏngbang* ('Compendium of Native Korean Prescriptions') appeared, and in 1445 the *Ŭibang yuch'wi* ('Classified Collection of Medical Prescriptions'). Important as they were, neither could compare in usefulness with the *Tongŭi pogam* ('Exemplar of Korean Medicine') of 1610. The compiler of the latter, Hŏ Chun (d. 1615), stressed both the medicinal value and dangers of alcohol. Another widely used beverage to which many healing properties were credited was made from the root *insam*, better known in the West as **ginseng**. The 19th century saw the development of Yi Chema (1837–1900)'s *sasang ŭihak* ('four types of medical study'), a holistic approach to the integrated health of mind and body based on an interpretation of *ŭm-yang* philosophy.

DONALD BAKER, 'Sirhak Medicine: Measles, Smallpox and Chŏng Tasan,' *KS*, 14, 1990; DONALD BAKER, 'Monks, Medicine and Miracles: Health and Healing in the History of Korean Buddhism,' *KS*, 19, 1994; GIL SOO HAN, 'The Rise of Western Medicine and Revival of Traditional Medicine in Korea: a Brief History,' *KS*, 21, 1997; GRANT S. LEE, 'The Growth of Medicine and Protestantism under Persecution: The Korean Experience,' *KJ*, 29/1, 1989; DOROTHEA SICH, 'Some Aspects of Traditional Medicine and Illness Behavior in Korea,' *KJ*, 18/3, 1978

MENCIUS'S MOTHER 孟母

Maengmo samch'ŏn, 'Mencius's mother moved three times.' A favourite moral example from Liu Xiang (80–9 BC)'s *Lienu zhuan*, 'Stories of Great Women'. After Mencius's father died, his mother took the little boy to live near a cemetery, but he began playing at funerals. She moved to a house near a market, where he began playing at shops. She then moved near a school, where he began imitating the polite behaviour of the scholars.

MERCHANTS

Overseas **commerce** dates back to the **Proto-Three Kingdoms Period**, and probably brought foreign merchants to the peninsular courts from early times. Trade with China was carried on both by overland routes, via **Liaodong**, and by sea, either from the Shandong peninsula to the west coast of Korea or from the ports of south-east China to the south-west corner of the peninsula. Archaeological evidence shows that in the early **Iron Age** the south coast was involved in trade with both China and Japan, and that the east coast maintained links with Siberia. In the Unified Silla period, Korean shipowners and merchants continued to play a profitable part in international commerce (*see* **Chung Pogo**). The founders of the Koryo dynasty, the Wang clan, came from merchant stock and it is no surprise that trade was encouraged in **Kaesŏng**. Official hostels were opened for the large numbers of Chinese merchants visiting the capital, and Muslim traders were among the many foreigners received at the court. Nevertheless, the mediaeval Korean economy remained so firmly circumscribed by the limited needs of the *yangban* aristocracy, most of which were supplied by the tribute tax (*see* **taxation**) and by the localised outlook of the rural **peasantry**, that no distinctive Korean merchant class developed. It was the replacement of tribute tax by a uniform land tax through the 17th century that brought into being government-sponsored merchants (*kongin*, 'tribute men') authorised to obtain supplies of specific manufactured goods required by the *yangban* in return for cash payment (*see also* **coinage**). This had the effect of stimulating handicraft production (*see* **craftsmen**), private distribution of manufactured goods, and profit making by makers and distributors alike. The merchants of Seoul and Kaesŏng were particularly active, especially in the **Han River** estuary. Some expanded into complementary areas such as boatbuilding and **ginseng**-farming. Some financed the manufacture of craft goods and operated as wholesale distributors to small shopkeepers or itinerant pedlars. As intermediaries in the delivery of goods between the provinces and metropolitan areas through inland and coastal **markets**, known respectively as *kaekchu* ('guest lords') and *yŏgak* ('travellers' counsellors'), they began to offer allied services such as money-lending, warehousing, and inn-keeping. Guilds (*kye*) were formed of both *kongin* and private traders, and even the *yangban* themselves began to engage in trade, enabling merchants to flout the law against commoners wearing horsehair hats. By the end of the 18th century, however, developing capitalist forces and the economic problems of the government brought an end to the government's regulation of monopolistic production and distribution of goods, and competition increased as unlicensed commerce was allowed to spread. In the 19th century the *yŏgak* and *kaekchu* found a new rôle as compradors, middlemen for foreign traders who were not allowed to move outside the treaty ports. Some diverted their resultant fortunes into the traditional form of investment, landholding; but others moved into new areas of economic activity such as **banking**, trading corporations and industry. *See also* **Pedlars' Guild**

KANG MAN-GIL, 'Research on Han River Merchants,' *KJ*, 19/1, 1979; MARK PETERSON, 'Merchants and *Hyangban* in Kaesŏng,' *KJ*, 18/10, 1978; YU WONDONG, *Le Déclin des Marchands Privilégiés en Corée*, Paris: Collège de France, 1984

MERITORIOUS SUBJECT TITLES

Twenty-five times during the Chosŏn dynasty, kings gave awards of land and honorary titles to men who had served and saved them during crises. They were known as *kongsin*, '**meritorious subjects**', and sometimes formed significant political groups. Asterisks in the following list indicate awards that were later abrogated. In the titles, *sa* 'altars', *kuk* 'realm' or *sŏng* 'sacred one' mean the dynasty.

Date	King	Title granted	Occasion	Grants
1392	T'aejo	Kaeguk 'Founding Dynasty'	Establishing dynasty	52
1398	Chŏngjong	Chŏngsa 'Helping the altars'	Yi Pangwŏn rebellion	29
1401	T'aejong	Chwamyŏng 'Saving Mandate'	Accession of T'aejong	47
1453	Tanjong	Chŏngnan 'Calming trouble'	**Kyeyu-jŏngsin**	43
1455	Sejo	Chwaik 'Helping, protecting'	**Sejo**'s usurpation	44
1467		Chŏkkae 'Overcoming envy'	Rebellion of Yi Siae	45
1468	Yejong	Iktae 'Aiding the Crown'	Treason of Kang Sun	40
1471	Sŏngjong	Chwari 'Aiding the right'	Accession of **Sŏngjong**	73
1506	Chungjong	Chŏgguk 'Calming the realm'	Accession of **Chungjong**	105
1507		Chŏngnan 'Calming trouble'	Rebellion of Yi Kwa	22
1545	Myŏngjong	Wisa 'Guarding the altars'	Accession of Myŏngjong	28
1590	Sŏnjo	P'yŏngnan 'Pacifying trouble'	**Chŏng Yŏrip** affair	22
1590		Kwangguk 'Glorifying the realm'	**Chonggye-byŏnmu**	19
1604		Sŏnmu 'Renowned Warrior'	Japanese invasion 1592	18
1604		Hosŏng 'Attending the sacred'	Guarding Sŏnjo 1592	86

1604		*Ch'ŏngnan* 'Clarifying trouble'	Yi Monghak affair 1596	5
1613	Kwanghae	*Wisŏng* 'Guarding the sacred'	Guarding prince 1592	80
		Iksa 'Aiding the altars'	Yŏch'ang-gun affair	48
		Chŏngun 'Correcting affairs'	Yu Yŏnggyŏng affair	11
		Hyŏngnan 'Success in trouble'	Kim Sikchae affair	24
1623	Injo	*Chŏngsa* 'Calming the altars'	Accession of Injo	53
1624		*Chinmu* 'Restorer Warrior'	**Yi Kwal rebellion**	32
1627		*Somu* 'Brilliant Warrior'	Yi In'gŏ rebellion	6
1628		*Yŏngsa* 'Pacifying the altars'	Yu Hyurip plot	12
1644		*Yŏngguk* 'Quieting the realm'	Sim Kiwŏn rebellion	7
1680	Sukchong	*Posa* 'Protecting the altars'	Purge of Southerners	8
1722	Kyŏngjong	*Pusa* 'Supporting the altars'	Sinim **sahwa**	3
1728	Yŏngjo	*Punmu* 'Courageous Warrior'	Yi Injwa affair	15

MERITORIOUS SUBJECTS *kongsin* 功臣

Powerful members of aristocratic and military families who were rewarded by dynastic leaders for their support with hereditary, taxable lands, the income from them, and **slaves** to work them. The grants were known as merit lands (*kongŭm-jŏn* in the Koryŏ dynasty and *kongsin-jŏn* in the Chosŏn) and were usually located in Kyŏnggi province. In the early Chosŏn period meritorious subjects wielded political power as members of the king's close consultative council, *Top'yŏngŭi-sasa*. Their daughters were favoured for royal marriages and court service. In the 15th century they were strongly criticised by neo-Confucian members of the **Sarim**. In 1466 they lost the right to hand the lands on to their descendants, and in 1556 the distinction was replaced by one of salary alone.

Yi T'aejo created about one thousand junior *kongsin* (*wŏnjong-gongsin* 'subsidiary to the original meritorious subjects') after the inception of the Chosŏn dynasty. Their privileges extended to sons and sons-in-law. The Chinese character *wŏn* 'original' that was first used became tabu, because it occurred in the personal name of the first Ming emperor. *Wŏn* meaning 'source' was substituted.

DONALD CLARK, 'Chosŏn's Founding Fathers: a Study of Merit Subjects in the Early Yi Dynasty,' *KS*, 6, 1982

MILITARY CLOTH TAX *kunp'o* 軍布

Levy payable by peasant farmers of 16–60 years of age to support the army in lieu of **military service** during the later Chosŏn period. It formed one of the principal sources of fiscal income for the government. The rate of two bolts of cloth *per annum* was a

substantial burden and was halved in 1750 under the *Kyunyŏkpŏp*. Evasion was widely practised, exacerbating the plight of those who could not escape the tax. In 1870 the **Taewŏn'gun** replaced it by a new military tax on every household.
See also **taxation**

MILITARY EXAMINATIONS *Mukwa* 武科

Were first introduced towards the end of the Koryŏ dynasty and continued in the Chosŏn. Though initially confined to the selection of officers from the *yangban* class, they eventually came to be taken even by *ch'ŏnmin*. Like civil examinations they were set at three levels, the first in provincial towns and the second in the capital. The quota of 28 who were successful in this, the *sŏndal* degree, were then eligible to undertake a further test in the palace, grading them into three classes. The literary syllabus included the **Confucian Classics** and military texts, but practical skills were also examined, including horse-riding and archery.

MILITARY JUNTA *Kunsa Hyŏngmyŏng Wiwŏnhoe* 軍事革命委員會 (1961–3)

On 16 May 1961 soldiers of the South Korean army staged a political coup against President **Yun Posŏn** and the **Second Republic**. They acted on the orders of a small group of young officers, headed by Major-General Park Chung Hee (**Pak Chŏnghŭi**), who had unsuccessfully tried to instigate a purge of corrupt senior military leaders. The cabal established a Military Revolutionary Committee, later renamed the Supreme Council for National Reconstruction, under the chairmanship of the Chief of Staff General Chang Toyŏng. It arrested Prime Minister Chang Myŏn and nearly two thousand politicians, dissolved the National Assembly, suspended the **constitution** and conducted a widespread purge of government and military officials, yet managed to persuade President Yun to stay in office for another ten months. This, and the assurance that it would work towards the restoration of democratic civilian rule, helped to avoid outright condemnation by the United States government. Yet factionalism threatened the military junta as it had the Second Republic. Chang Toyŏng himself was convicted of plotting to assassinate Vice-Chairman Park Chung Hee and exiled to America. Park assumed the leadership of the junta. A **Korean Central Intelligence Agency** was established under the command of Colonel **Kim Chŏngp'il**. Strong action was taken against corrupt bureaucrats and leftist politicians, and there were widespread arrests. The first Five Year Economic Development Plan was announced for 1962–6; the Political Activities Purification Law (16 March 1962) barred many former politicians from further activity and brought about President Yun's resignation; many newspapers were closed down; plans were announced for the restoration of a modified constitution, which came into being on 26 December 1962, and for new elections to be held in May 1963. Park Chung Hee succeeded Yun Posŏn as acting President, and the new constitution afforded greater powers to the future president, who was to be elected by popular franchise. As a result of continuing disagreements between military junta and civilian politicians the elections were postponed, but on 15 October 1963 Park, now a self-declared civilian, narrowly defeated his rival Yun, and in the National Assembly elections on 26 November his **Democratic Republican Party** gained a substantial majority under the chairmanship of Kim Chŏngp'il.
See also **South Korea: constitutional changes; Third Republic**

MILITARY MUTINY (1882) *See Imo* **Incident**

MILITARY POLICE, JAPANESE *See* **Police system, Japanese**

MILITARY SERVICE

In addition to **taxation** the traditional Korean state made heavy demands on farmers in the form of time and labour required for *corvée* and military service. Compulsory military service was enforced in **Koguryŏ**, **Paekche** and **Silla** (*see also hwarang*) and in all subsequent periods. In the Koryŏ and early Chosŏn periods all *sangmin* males between fifteen and sixty, with the exception of government officials and students in Confucian *schools*, were obliged to become ordinary soldiers (*pubyŏng*), but commutation became so common that the standard rate, two bolts of cloth *per annum*, came to constitute a form of tax (*see* **military cloth tax**), and by the time of the Japanese invasions (*see* **Imjin Wars**) the Korean army was a negligible force.

In the colonial period, the Japanese began conscripting Korean men into the Japanese army in 1943.

See also **military system**

MILITARY SYSTEM

Military organisation in each of the Three Kingdoms matched and worked in conjunction with civilian administrative structures, with élite professional units serving in the capital and provincial centres under the supreme command of the king. In **Silla**, this meant that each of the six provinces was guarded by a garrison (*chŏng*) commanded by officers of true-bone status (*see* **kolp'um**). The youth of **Koguryŏ** received training in the **Confucian Classics** and archery in local institutions known as *kyŏngdang*.

Under the Unified Silla military system, nine regiments (*sŏdang*) were stationed in the capital **Kyŏngju** and ten garrisons (*sip chŏng*) across the remainder of the kingdom, two in the frontier province of Hanju and one in each of the remaining eight provinces. As a gesture of reunification the capital's *sŏdang* comprised Koguryŏ, **Paekche** and **Malgal** soldiers as well as native men of Silla.

The threat from the **Khitan** forced the Koryŏ government to update and strengthen the defensive system. Some 45,000 men defended the capital (*kyŏnggi*) and the borders, organised into two guard armies and six divisions. They were professional soldiers from hereditary military families, whom the government rewarded — though more in theory than in actual practice — with grants of land known as 'soldiers' fields' (*kunin-jŏn*). The two border regions (Pukkye and Tonggye) were military zones in which battle-ready armies were stationed, while the five circuits (*to*) were served by units that undertook a greater variety of duties. Military affairs played a prominent part in the second half of the Koryŏ dynasty, involving the seizure of power by Ch'oe Ch'unghŏn's military dictatorship (*see* **Ch'oe Dictatorship**; *Chungbang*), the Mongol invasions and the *Sambyŏlch'o* **Rebellion**, but neither the court, the military régime nor the **Mongols** succeeded in setting up a new military system. Rather, new armies were raised to cope with successive threats as they occurred.

Chosŏn put civil administration back in control but did not fail to recognise the need for military organisation. The Board of War (*Pyŏngjo*) constituted one of the **Six Boards**. Other important agencies for military supervision were the *Chungch'u-wŏn* (*see* **Chungch'u-bu**) and (after 1555) the *Pibyŏn-sa* ('Frontier Defence Office'). Defence of the new capital was initially in the hands of the Three Righteous Armies Command (*Ŭihŭng samgun-bu*), centralised under tighter royal control after 1464 in the Five Guards Central Command (*Owi toch'ong-bu*). Its five armies, garrisoned in the centre, north, south, east and west of Seoul, comprised conscripted men led by professional officers. Each of the eight provinces had separate Army and Navy Commands with army and naval garrisons.

As a result of experience during the **Imjin Wars** the *Owi* were reorganised as Five Army Garrisons (*Ogunyŏng*). In 1865 the **Taewŏn'gun** abolished the *Pibyŏn-sa* and in 1868 command of all military installations was given over to the *Samgun-bu*. No further changes were made until 1882, when as part of King **Kojong**'s planned military modernisation the Five Garrisons were re-formed as two, *Muwi-yŏng* and *Changŏ-yŏng*, and a Special Skills Force (*Pyŏlgi-gun*) formed with Japanese instructors. The measure was rescinded by the Taewŏn'gun as part of the Military Mutiny (*see Imo* **Incident**). In turn, however, the capital's forces were again re-constituted after his removal, this time under Chinese command (*see* **Yuan Shikai**) as the *Ch'in'gun-yŏng* ('Capital Army Command'). The 1894 *Kabo* **reforms** created a new Military Affairs Ministry and two new armies, one guarding the capital and the other provincial centres, but failed to introduce serious changes or modernisation in the military system. When the Japanese disbanded the Korean army in 1907 it numbered less than nine thousand men, four thousand of whom were in the capital.

Following liberation, the communist régime in the North moved quicker to develop a new army, taking full advantage of Soviet and Chinese advice. Its **Korean People's Army** was formed in February 1948. Rapid conscription took place into the army, navy and air force, creating a total force of over 150,000 men by June 1950. By contrast, the **American Military Government** in the South neither built up a Korean army nor made any effort to train Koreans for future military leadership. When it handed over power to Syngman Rhee (**Yi Sŭngman**)'s **Republic of Korea**, the new country's army, founded in November 1948, comprised 50,000 ill-trained and poorly equipped former members of the National Constabulary, and its fledgling navy 3,000 members of the Coast Guard. Organisation and training measures were swiftly introduced and an air force formed in October 1949. Conscription was introduced in August 1949 for men between 20 and 40 years of age. By June 1950 the Republic had some 67,000 men under arms.

KONSTANTIN AZMOLOV, 'The System of Military Activity of Koguryŏ,' *KJ*, 32/2, 1992; BENJAMIN HAZARD, 'The Creation of the Korean Navy during the Koryŏ Period,' *TRASKB*, XLVII, 1973; W.E.HENTHORN, 'Some Notes on Koryŏ Military Units,' *TKBRAS*, XXXV, 1959

MIN, PRINCESS *Pudae-buin Min-ssi* 府大夫人閔氏 (1818–98)
Mother of King **Kojong** and wife of Hŭngsŏn **Taewŏn'gun**. The choice of a member of her own clan as wife for the king was due to her influence and was the source of the *sedo* power of the Yŏhŭng Min clan in the mid-19th century. As a convert to Catholicism, studying doctrine and learning prayers, she became involved with **Nam Chongsam** in the events of 1866. Bishop Mutel baptized her thirty years later, secretly in a house near her **Unhyŏn Palace** after dark on 11 October 1896. She died on 8 January 1898, six weeks before her husband.

MIN, QUEEN 閔妃 (仁顯王后) (1667–1701) *See Inhyŏng Wanghu-jŏn*

MIN, QUEEN 閔妃 (明成皇后) (1851–95)
An impoverished member of the Yŏhŭng Min clan, married to **Kojong** as his queen in 1866. She was recommended to Hŭngsŏn **Taewŏn'gun** by his own wife, who belonged to the same clan. Kojong was at the time much fonder of a secondary wife named Yi who bore him a son, the Wanhwa-gung (1868–1880), in 1868. Queen Min, who was already in opposition to the Taewŏn'gun, set about winning the king's affections and in 1871 bore him a son, the Wanja, who died after five months. It was

rumoured that the Taewŏn'gun had provided poisoned **ginseng**. (Her second son became the Emperor **Sunjong**; another son and a daughter died in infancy.) She got the Min clan into power, diligently marshalled supporters and persuaded Ch'oe Ikhyŏn to present a memorial to the throne indicting the Taewŏn'gun's misdemeanours. The prince fought back, but had to withdraw from court in 1873. During the 'soldiers' riot' of 1882 (*see Imo* **Incident**), the queen had to flee and took refuge at Changho-wŏn near Ch'ungju. While she was there in hiding, the Taewŏn'gun circulated news of her death. Chinese help was sought, the Taewŏn'gun was removed and the Queen returned to the palace. Her reliance on *mudang* dates from this time. She became increasingly extravagant, and the Min family more and more corrupt. In 1884 she was victorious over the progressives in the Post Office *émeute* (*see Kapsin* **coup**), but she had become the arch-enemy of the Japanese, who engineered her assassination in October 1895. She was repeatedly stabbed by agents who entered her quarters, and her body was at once taken out and burned in the courtyard. She was posthumously and promptly demoted to commoner status, but on the declaration of the Empire in 1897 was entitled Myŏngsŏng-hwanghu, 'Empress Myŏngsŏng'. Her finger, the only remaining fragment of her body, was given a full imperial funeral.
TATIANA SIMBIRTSEVA, 'Queen Min of Korea: Coming to Power,' *TRASKB*, LXXI, 1996
See **Chillyŏng-gun**

MIN T'AEHO 閔台鎬 (1834–84)
Minister of Rites, a conservative whose daughter was married to Crown Prince **Sunjong** in 1883 as a means of cementing the power of **Queen Min**'s clan. Both were children, and she is now known as Sunmyŏnghyo Hwanghu (1872–1904). Min T'aeho was the father of **Min Yŏngik** and a famous calligrapher. He was killed on 4 December 1884 in the *Kapsin* **coup**.

MIN YŎNGHWAN 閔泳煥 (1861–1905)
A nephew of both **Queen Min** and **Princess Min**, therefore well placed to gain a position of power, he was also a man of great ability, reaching high office in his late twenties. The Queen's murder in 1895 temporarily interrupted his career, but in 1896 he represented Korea at the coronation of Tsar Nicholas II in Moscow, and in 1897 visited several European countries, also representing Korea at the Diamond Jubilee of Queen Victoria. He is said to have been the first Korean to wear a western suit. His travels turned him into a moderniser and he became an adviser to the **Independence Club**, but had to withdraw because of family pressure. Decorated by the Emperor, he became Prime Minister, but was reduced to royal aide-de-camp. Firmly opposed to the plans of the Japanese for Korea, at the time of the 1905 **Protectorate Treaty** he did his best to reverse the tide, but failed. On 30 November he committed suicide, leaving impassioned letters for the nation. A green **bamboo**, the famed *hyŏlchuk* 'blood bamboo', is said to have grown through the floor boards of the room where his blood-stained clothes were placed.

His *siho* is Ch'ungjŏng, 'loyal and upright', and his writings were collected in *Min Ch'unjŏng-gong yugo*. They include *Ch'ŏil-ch'aek*, 'One in a thousand suggestions' (named from the proverbial *uja-ch'onnyŏ p'iryu ildŭk*, 'among a fool's thousand plans, one is bound to be useful') about policies necessary for restoring the Korean nation; *Haech'ŏn-ch'ubŏm*, 'Sea and sky, autumn sailing', an account of his journey to Japan, New York, London, Berlin, St Petersburg, Moscow and Vladivostok between April and October 1896 – the first round-the-world journey by a Korean; and *Sagu-sokch'o*, 'Continuing writing of an envoy to Europe' telling of the following year's journey to

Shanghai, Nagasaki, Hong Kong, Singapore, Suez, Odessa, St Petersburg and London for the jubilee, but ending before his visits to mainland Europe.

MIN YŎNGIK 閔泳翊 (1860–1914)

Nephew of **Queen Min** and son of **Min T'aeho**. He became head of the Min clan in 1874 when his adoptive father Min Sŭngho was killed by a bomb. Following the **Shufeldt Treaty** he was sent to the United States as head of a major exploratory diplomatic mission, which toured the country from May to September 1883. He sought American advisers for his government, as a result of which President Arthur designated George Foulk to return to Korea with the mission in the USS *Trenton*. After visiting London, Paris and Rome the mission arrived back in Chemulp'o a year after its departure. Though convinced of the need for reforms, Min was associated with the pro-Chinese *Sadaedang* rather than the **Independence Party**. He was the chief target of the *Kapsin* coup plotters, but escaped the massacre badly injured after being rescued by Dr **Horace Allen**. He subsequently spent two further periods of exile in Hong Kong, and died in exile in Shanghai. He was a distinguished calligrapher in the *haengsŏ* style and a famous painter of orchids.

MING DYNASTY 明朝 (K. Myŏngjo, China, 1368–1644)

Chinese régime established by Zhu Yuanzhang (the Hongwu Emperor) after the expulsion of the **Mongols**. Their Confucian persuasion, as well as a sense of political strategy, led the founders of the Chosŏn dynasty to seek immediate Chinese approval for their own new authority and its title ('Dynastic Freshness', *see* **Korea, names for**). Both countries were relieved at the prospect of restoring good relations after a long period of political upheaval in north-east Asia, and the exchange of Korean **tribute** for Chinese recognition quickly began. In Korea the study of Chinese political and social rites was allied with strong criticism of **Buddhism** and its effects under the previous dynasty. The Ming law code was adopted by the end of the 14th century, and though both institutional **law** and neo-Confucian *mores* were adapted to Korean circumstances, the literati nonetheless accepted and admired Ming models.

In 1592 the Japanese *daimyo* Toyotomi Hideyoshi embarked on an ambitious plan to invade China by way of the Korean peninsula (*see* **Imjin Wars**). The Ming government responded by sending an army of 50,000 soldiers under General Li Rusong. Hideyoshi withdrew to negotiate, but in 1595 the Ming court rebuffed his claims, which included a bid for Korean territory, a Korean prince as a hostage, and the marriage of a Ming princess to the Japanese emperor. When the war was resumed in 1597 the Chinese again sent an army and a naval force, but the threat of further serious escalation disappeared with Hideyoshi's death in the summer of 1598. The cost to China of this rare acknowledgement of its suzerain obligations – albeit in its own perceived interest – was enormous, and not only contributed to the economic difficulties of the late Ming régime but also afforded encouragement to the rising ambitions of the Manchus. In 1616 the earlier Sino-Korean rôles were reversed when China asked for Korean aid in securing the northern frontiers against Nurhachi. A force of 10,000 men was sent under Kang Hongnip (1560–1627) and joined with Chinese troops, but the Koreans surrendered without fighting in the hope of protecting their own kingdom. Their success was only temporary (*see* **Manchu invasions**).

DONALD CLARK, 'The Ming Connection: Notes on Korea's Experience in the Chinese Tributary System,' *TRASKB*, LVIII, 1983; DAVID MASON, 'The *Sam Hwangje Paehyang* (Sacrificial Ceremony for Three Emperors): Korea's Link to the Ming Dynasty,' *KJ*, 31/3, 1991

MING LOYALIST DATES

The last Ming emperor's reign title was Chongzhen (K. Sungjŏng, 1628–44). Although he died in the 17th year of his reign, 1644 (year of the Blue Monkey), some Koreans continued to date documents as if he were still alive. For them 1652 was *Sungjŏng 25 nyŏn*, '25th year of Chongzhen', though he had died eight years earlier. Or they continued to use the **cyclical** year names, calling 1665, 11 years after his death, *Sungjŏng ŭlsa* 'The Blue Snake year of Chongzhen'. Then they counted the 60-year cycles. 1725 was *Sungjŏng-hu chaedo Ŭlsa*, 'Second Blue Snake year after Chongzhen'; and as late as 1904 the year was given as '5th Blue Dragon (*kapchin*) of Sŭngjŏng'. Alternatively, they would count from his last year, *Sungjŏng kapsin* 'Chongzhen Blue Monkey' (1644), so that 1742 was *Sungjŏng kapsin-hu 98nyŏn* '98th year after the Blue Monkey year of Chongzhen'.

Another method was to count years after Yongle (K. Yŏngnak, 1403–24), reign title of the great Ming emperor Chengzu. Thus 1765 became *Yŏngnak-hu yukto ŭryu* '6th Blue Cock after Yongle'.

MINJUNG (People's) **MOVEMENT** 民衆運動

A movement aimed at earning respect for the views and culture of ordinary Koreans, expressed in political, religious, literary and artistic form from the Japanese colonial period to the **Sixth Republic** of South Korea. In its wider sense it may be seen as the Korean equivalent of the Chinese people 'standing up' in 1949, an expression of **nationalism**, culturalism and populism which over many decades struggled against the sinicised culture of the old aristocratic élite, the oppressive measures of alien conquerors, and the corrupt government of military dictatorship. It was not an expression solely of class anger: like China's May Fourth Movement it united intellectuals – including **students** – and workers. Some of its elements were consciously arranged and promoted, some were spontaneous eruptions of emotional feeling; others developed gradually and were only definable subsequently as contributions to a diffuse but nonetheless powerful trend. Its outspoken exponents were labelled dissidents by the authorities, but thousands of ordinary and peace-loving Koreans unwittingly aided its development through changing practices in their daily lives. Examples of its manifestation include the rise of Korea's syncretic religion *Ch'ŏndo-gyo* and its involvement, along with that of other churches and religions, in social and political protest throughout the century; the growth of **Christianity** and a *minjung* Christian theology reminiscent of Latin American liberation theology; the promotion, albeit briefly in the 1970s, of **shamanism** as a distinctive Korean philosophy with universal application; the revival of interest in traditional story-telling forms such as *p'ansori* and **masked dance** drama; a surge in *minjung* literature in the 1970s and *minjung* art (*minjung misul*) in the 1980s drawing attention to the suffering of the working classes; the **Kwangju Massacre** of 1980 and its aftermath; the move towards openness in politics and the economy in the late 1980s and the trial of ex-Presidents Roh Tae Woo (**No Taeu**) and Chun Doo Hwan (**Chŏn Tuhwan**) in 1996. Violence was often associated with the *minjung* movement, yet it was not iconoclastic, for underlying it may be recognised a strong sense of patriotism and a developing concept of loyalty to the nation-state.

NANCY ABELMANN, *Echoes of the Past, Epics of Dissent: a South Korean Social Movement*, Berkeley: University of California Press, 1996; CHO HUNG-YOUN, 'The Characteristics of Korean *Minjung* Culture,' *KJ*, 27/11, 1987; KENNETH M.WELLS, ed., *South Korea's Minjung Movement, the Culture and Politics of Dissidence*, Honolulu: University of Hawai'i Press, 1995

MIRRORS
Bronze mirrors were made in the style of those common in China from the **Han dynasty** onwards, with a smooth reflecting obverse and an often richly decorated reverse with a raised handling knob at the centre. In some instances the knob is replaced in Korea by a small pair of looped handles through which a cord may be threaded for suspension. Occasionally a bronze carrying handle forms part of the design. Mirrors are often round, but may also be square (with sharp or rounded corners), petal-shaped, or bell-shaped. Decorative patterns include flowers, fish, dragonflies, **dragons**, mythical scenes, and the animals of the Four Quarters (*see* **Four Spirits**).

MIRŬK Maitreya 彌勒
Mirŭk (Maitreya) is sometimes regarded as a Buddha, the one who is to come in the future. He is now in the Tushita Heaven, where he is associated with the *naga-puspa* 'dragon-flower tree'. Sometimes he is dressed like a **bodhisattva**, sometimes like a buddha, standing or seated on a stool with one foot over the other knee and his chin resting on his hand – the typically Korean *asana* of 'half-lotus meditation'. His name is given to the monumental rock figures found in many places. often carved in living rock, whose history is obscure – they may be pre-Buddhist. Maitreya's cult was particularly strong in the Three Kingdoms Period and Unified Silla, when he was much honoured by the *hwarang*.
LEWIS LANCASTER, 'Maitreya in Korea', *KJ* 29/11, 1989

MO YUNSUK 毛允淑 (1910–90)
Born at Anju in North P'yŏngan, she was brought up in Hamhŭng, went to school in **Kaesŏng**, then graduated from the English Literature department of **Ewha** College before becoming a schoolteacher in **Kando** and Seoul. Her first poetry was published in *Pinnanŭn chiyŏk* 'The Shining Land' (1933), which included attractive accounts of rural life. As her thought matured, she maintained her limpid romanticism in further collections of poetry in 1947 and 1949, and her deeply felt view of life became a typical expression of Korean **women**'s attitudes. At the peak of the **Korean War** of 1950–53 she wrote a moving account of refugee life in *P'ungnang* 'Wind and Wave'(1951). She continued to publish verse in Seoul after the war, when she became a leading figure in the literary and cultural life of the capital.
PETER HYUN & KO CHANG-SOO trans. *Wren's elegy*, Larchmont N.Y.: Larchmont Publications, 1980

MOFFETT, SAMUEL AUSTIN 馬富悅 (Ma Puyŏl, 1864–1939)
Samuel Moffett arrived in Korea on his 26th birthday in 1890. In 1893 he was stationed in P'yŏngyang and began his work as the primary planner of Presbyterian expansion in the northern part of the country. He soon began training Korean catechists in an establishment that turned into the P'yŏngyang seminary, of which he became president in 1907. In the same year he was elected moderator of the first presbytery of the Presbyterian Church of Korea, uniting the first four Presbyterian missions (Northern and Southern American, Australian and Canadian). He was prominent in the *Paego-in* incident of 1911 (*see* **Hundred and Five, Case of the**), when he and other missionaries made the world outside Korea aware of Japanese activities. In 1918 he became principal of Sungsil School. He was again prominent in the **Shrine Question** of the 1930s. He retired to the United States in 1936.

MOHADANG 慕夏堂 (Kim Ch'ungsŏn, 1571–1642)
'Scholar who yearns for Xia', brush name of a Japanese whose name is usually read as Sayaga, the most distinguished of the Japanese who stayed in Korea after the Hideyoshi invasion (see **Imjin Wars**) and were assimilated into Korean life. Brought up in Kumamoto, he early learned that Korea had preserved the most ancient customs of classical China (Xia), including white clothing. In 1592, when twenty years old, he enrolled in Katō Kiyomasa's army and came as a commander of the advance force to **Tongnae**. Within a week of landing he had changed sides. He taught the Koreans to use small arms and explosives, won battle honours and corresponded with **Yi Sunsin**. He was eventually enrolled by King Sŏnjo into the Kŭmhae Kim clan and given the name Kim Ch'ungsŏn. After the Japanese left he spent nearly ten years with the troops on the northern borders; took a command in the suppression of the revolt of **Yi Kwal** in 1624; and triumphed over the Manchus at Ssanggogae near **Kwangju**, Kyŏnggi province, in 1636, when he was over sixty (see **Manchu invasions**). In disgust at the surrender of Namhan Mountain **Fortress** (**Namhan Sansŏng**) soon afterwards, he retired to the estate he had been given at Urok-ch'ŏn, twenty miles south of **Taegu**, where he died at the age of seventy. His descendants live there still and preserve the woodblocks of his collected writings, *Mohadang munjip*.

MÖLLENDORFF, PAUL-GEORG VON (1847–1901)
Was born in Brandenburg, went to school in Goerlitz and studied Oriental Languages at Halle. Joining the German consular service, he went to China in 1869. Together with his brother Franz Otto, he wrote a *Manual of Chinese Bibliography* (1876: it was quickly superseded by Cordier's *Bibliotheca Sinica*, 1878–1895). In 1882 **Li Hongzhang** sent him to Korea to supervise diplomatic affairs and the **Maritime Customs Service**. He started the royal English school in Seoul, oversaw the British and German treaties with Korea in 1883, and was thought to have supported Russia in preparing the Russian Treaty of 1884. He returned to China in 1885 and died at Ningbo in 1901. He also wrote a Manchu grammar (Shanghai 1892).
LEE YUR-BOK, *West Goes East: Paul Georg von Mollendorf and Great Power Imperialism in Late Yi Korea*, Honolulu: University of Hawaii Press, 1988; WALTER LIEFER, 'Paul-Georg von Mollendorff – Scholar and Statesman,' *TRASKB*, LVII, 1982; WALTER LEIFER, *Paul-Georg von Möllendorff – ein deutscher Staatsmann in Korea*, Saarbrücken: Homo et Religio, 1988

MOMIL-KKOT P'IL MURYŎP
'When the buckwheat comes in bloom', Korea's favourite modern short story, was written by Yi Hyosŏk (1907–1942) in 1936, when he belonged to the **Kuin-hoe**. The massed white blossoms of the buckwheat fields of North Ch'ungch'ŏng province are most beautiful in the moonlight; two itinerant market traders, one old, lonely and pock-marked, the other young and brash, pass through the moonlit fields. The older man recalls his one night of love, but he does not know who the woman was. The younger man is an orphan. He never knew his father and has long parted from his mother. He might be the older man's son . . . A warmly affectionate tale of fate at work in the lives of the lowly, while the deprivations of country folk unfold against the beauty of the rural setting.
Translated in HONG MYOUNG-HEE, *Korean Short Stories*, Seoul, 1975, and in P. H. LEE, *Flowers of Fire*, Hawaii, 1974

MONGOLS, THE

The first Mongol invasion of Korea took place in 1231, during the period of Ch'oe U (d.1249)'s military rule (*see* **Ch'oe Dictatorship**). After accepting the costly terms of subjugation the court fled to **Kanghwa-do** the following year. This prompted a second invasion in December 1232. An attack on Kanghwa was repulsed but **Kaesŏng** was soon taken, and the stoutest resistance inland came from the **peasant** and **slave** classes. When the Mongol commander Sartaq was killed his army again retreated. A third invasion in 1235 caused great destruction as far south as **Kyŏngju**, which was sacked. During a period of truce the court tried to secure its defence by having a set of the Buddhist *Tripitaka* carved, but in 1254 the enemy returned and the campaign was resumed until 1259. Then, following the assassination of Ch'oe Ŭi in 1258, King Kojong (r. 1213–59) was free to submit. In 1269 an attempt by the Koryŏ military under Im Yŏn to thwart compliance was defeated, the court returned to Kaesŏng, and when one last gesture of defiance was overcome in 1273 (*see* **Sambyŏlch'o resistance**), Mongol suzerainty was secure.

It was a costly period of subjection, reinforced by the fact of Kublai Khan's conquest of China. The subservience of the Korean court was emphasized in all titles and forms of communication. Tributary demands were heavy. The Koryŏ crown prince was taken to Cambaluq (modern Beijing); Korean princes were obliged to wed Mongol princesses, and Korean girls to enter the Mongol court (*see* **Ki, Empress**). The system of government was reformed and its responsibilities diminished. Mongols involved themselves in Korean politics and economic development (*see* **Shenyang, King of**). Social divisions became more marked as the growth of private estates belonging to wealthy collaborators drove peasants into slavery. Ordinary Koreans suffered heavy human and economic losses through their forced involvement in the two abortive Mongol naval attacks on Japan in 1274 and 1281. According to *Koryŏ-sa*, 14,600 Koreans took part in the first of these, along with Mongols and Chinese.

As political, social and economic problems afflicted the Mongols in China and led to popular rebellion against them (*see also* **Red Turbans**), King Kongmin (r. 1351–74) initiated Korean resistance. Ironically, however, it was the Chinese overthrow of the Yuan dynasty that rescued Korea from its subjugation, while Kongmin's anti-Mongol policies involved him in confrontation with the powerful clans among his own upper classes who had prospered from alien occupation.

W.E.HENTHORN, *Korea: the Mongol Invasions*, Leiden: E.J.Brill, 1963
See also **Cheju-do**; **Koryŏ dynasty**

MONOCYCLE *ch'ohŏn* 輶軒

A carriage for one, shaped like an armchair on a small platform with one wheel beneath it. A long pole extended before and behind to be held by the footmen who propelled and balanced the vehicle. It was used by officials of 2nd **grade** senior and above.

MORNING CALM

A name for **Korea** used for the magazine of the English Church Mission, published in London monthly from July 1889 to December 1895; quarterly 1896 to July 1939, then September 1946 to November 1989. The earlier years are of most general interest.

MOSCOW CONFERENCE (1945)

Meeting of Russian, American and British Foreign Ministers held in December 1945, culminating in an agreement signed on the 27th. The establishment of a five-year joint

.international **trusteeship** over Korea was approved, to work with an elected provisional Korean government in preparation for independence. The trustees were to be representatives of the United States, the Soviet Union, Great Britain, and the Chinese Republic, and planning for the election of the government was to be in the hands of a **US-Soviet Joint Commission**. This held its first meeting in Seoul in January 1946. The agreement was not welcomed by right-wing politicians in Korea, who realised they had little chance of winning elections, but gained the grudging support of the left. Post-War politics rendered trusteeship inoperable, not only because of growing distrust between the two super-powers but also because of the Chinese civil war, and the outcome of the **Yalta** and Moscow Conferences was the partition of Korea into North and South.

See also **American Military Government; Hodge, General John; Kim Ku; Korean Independence Party; Korean People's Republic**

MOURNING

Mourning was the subject of many disputes about ritual. The rules were complex and many books were published about details of who should mourn for whom and how long. The longest period was three years for a father and the shortest three months for certain cousins. During the whole period a man had to wear mourning weeds of hemp, abstain from meat, wine and spices, avoid the company of **women**, eschew convivial parties and spend his time in a simple hut by the grave. He could not arrange a **marriage** or sit an **examination**. He had to withdraw from official life. Such a period could mean a welcome sabbatical for a statesman or the gratifying rustication of a political enemy. The periods were in practice normally shortened. Three years' mourning usually lasted 27 months.

See also **Dowager Queen Changnyŏl's mourning rites**

MUDANG

Often translated as 'sorceress' or 'witch', but better as 'shamaness', for *mudang*, though often written with Chinese characters, is a Korean word resembling some of the words used for shamans in Siberian languages. *Mudang* are women, often psychotics, of the lowest social class, who perform shaman functions. They are usually either daughters or adopted daughters of *mudang*, and generally begin to practise after a strange illness or experience of a visionary journey – a widespread feature of north east Asian **shamanism**. They are traditionally without any organisation, though they were widely patronised by the Koryŏ court and their influence persisted at the Chosŏn court. Queens have on occasion resorted to them, and **Queen Min** made much of one called **Chillyŏng-gun** in the 1890s. Men, called *paksu*, who perform the same function are far less common.

Mudang claim a special relationship with spirits, who possess them during the ceremonies (*kut*) at which they conduct intercessions for private, communal and national purposes. The Korean shaman, unlike those in some parts of the world, retains self-control and may conduct a dialogue between the humans and spirit present. Their **rites** range from those of general importance, as at lunar **new year**, to the more particular, such as the worship of local folk heroes, invocation of blessings (on threatened crops, for example, or for rescue from sickness), and exorcism. They may also celebrate blessings that have been received. A family may hire a shaman to seek the pacification of a soul denied the proper burial rites by accidental death.

Details of shaman practices vary between regions, but common features include the use of pictures of popular deities, the offering of gifts (food and drink, money, cigarettes, paper models of physical objects needed in the afterlife) to the spirits on an altar with some characteristics of Buddhist or Confucian rites, and the induction of the shaman through **music** and **dance** into a trance state where communication with the spirit takes place. The *mudang* dresses in the clothes of the opposite sex, often with **iron** ornaments. She dances simple steps while a small band of **drum** and pipes plays incessantly, and she clangs a large cymbal as she sings and declaims. The noise may continue from sunset to dawn, with the *mudang* changing her costume according to the spirit in whose possession she claims to be. There may be a symbolic chasing away of evil spirits; and the climax may be a balancing act (a pig's head on the point of a large knife induced to stand on the tip of its handle) or the *mudang* walking barefoot and unharmed up a short ladder of knife-edges, either feat proving her spiritual powers.

The prayers and incantations uttered are made up by the *mudang*. They often include Buddhist and Daoist elements. Various styles of patter, reminiscent of those used by *kwangdae* and *sadangp'ae*, are used to persuade those present to offer more money. At the end there is general feasting, giving rise to the **proverb** *kut mot pogo, ttŏgŭl mŏngnŭnda*, 'eating the cakes without attending the ceremony'.

A *kut* may take place in the courtyard of a house, and a householder's wife may perform shamanistic functions. Specific spirits are invoked for blessings on family business in particular quarters, such as the courtyard, hearth and **privy**, while those with greater overall powers include the house guardian Sŏngju and the childbirth protectress Halmoni (*See* **Kosa**).

LAUREL KENDALL, *The Life and Hard Times of a Korean Shaman*, Honolulu: University of Hawaii Press, 1988
See also p'ansu

MUDRA *insang* 印相
Positions for the hands, of interest in Korea for their appearance in Buddhist iconography. The whole vocabulary of mudra is rich and complex. This note outlines a few common forms.

Vairocana has two distinctive mudra. *Chigwŏn-in*, 'wisdom fists', shows the left hand with the fingers clenched and held toward the breast, the right hand similarly clenched below it, and the right index-finger alone extended and clasped by the left hand. *Musobuji-in*, 'nowhere not reached', has both hands placed palm-to-palm, but with each thumb-tip touching the tip of the index-finger of the same hand.

Pŏpkye-jŏng-in, 'dharma-boundary-fixing', the gesture of dhyana or meditation, is more widely used. The two hands rest on the lap, right over left, palms upward, with the thumb-tips touching each other. In *simuoe-in*, 'granting fearlessness' or granting protection, the right hand is raised, palm outwards, with finger-tips pointing upwards. *Yŏwŏn-in*, 'granting wishes', shows the right hand with palm outwards, wrist above and fingers pointing down.

Ch'okchi-in, 'calling earth to witness [his enlightenment]', is especially associated with Sakyamuni: the right hand, palm held inward, touches the ground. *Chŏn-bŏmnyun-in*, 'turning the dharma wheel', or 'teaching', is used for Sakyamuni and for others. It has many forms, all characterised by each thumb-tip touching the tip of the index-finger or middle-finger in both hands. All the fingers are slightly curved, and the position of the hands suggests they are turning an imaginary small wheel in front of the breast and away from it. The right hand is held with palm facing outwards or downwards (turning the top of the wheel away from the body), the left hand lower, with the palm facing inwards or upwards (turning the bottom of the wheel toward the body).

Images of **Amida** Buddha show what appear to be variants of *pŏpkye-jŏng-in* but are actually his own *kup'um-in* 'mudra of the nine stages of Paradise', the different stages being expressed by different contacts between thumb and finger tips.
See also **Buddhas; Buddhism**

MUHAK (1327–1405) 無學

Son of a Koryŏ government officer, Pak Inil, he became a monk at the age of 18. From 1353 to 1356 he studied at Yanjing (Beijing). He was a well known man of learning, respected by **Yi Sŏnggye** (later T'aejo), who relied on Muhak for advice, in particular the choice of site for his new capital when he founded the Chosŏn dynasty in 1392. Having considered both Kyeryong-san and Hanyang, Muhak decided on Hanyang, the present Seoul. In 1402 he withdrew to Kŭmjang-am in the **Diamond Mountains**, where he finished his days. There is a wealth of legend about his rôle in the foundation of Seoul, much of it related to his use of *p'ungsu*.

MUJARI

Also known as *yangsuch'ok* or *such'ok* ('water carriers' or perhaps a Sino-transliteration of *mujari*) and sometimes called the gypsies of Korea. Ethnologically, they may have been late entrants into the peninsula, possibly descended from remnants of foreign groups defeated within the northern boundaries. Early Koryŏ marked their largest numbers. They were hunters and wicker-workers who peddled their wares, forebears of the *kwangdae*, *kisaeng* and *paekchŏng* of the Chosŏn period.

MUKHOJA *See* ADO

MULBERRY PALACE *Kyŏnghŭi-gung* 慶熙宮

A detached royal palace built in 1616 by **Prince Kwanghae** as part of the restoration of Seoul after the Hideyoshi invasion (*see* **Imjin Wars**). It was originally called *Kyŏngdŏk-gung* and was unusual in that it faced east rather than south. It was much used as a royal family residence. King **Sukchong** was born there. It suffered several fires during the 19th century and was slowly dismantled under the colonial administration, finally disappearing in 1922. Foreign residents named it 'the Mulberry Palace' after A. Maertens planted mulberry trees in the compound in 1884 as part of a sericulture venture that failed. The trees were still there in 1895, but their subsequent fate is unrecorded.

MUMUN 無文

Late neolithic 'unpatterned' (*mumun*) pottery of generally hard-fired earthenware produced from the middle of the second millennium BC until the **Proto-Three Kingdoms Period**. It is uncertain whether it originated within the **Chŭlmun** culture zone or was the result of influence from the mainland through the **Liaodong** region. Regional variations appeared throughout the **Bronze Age**. *Mumun* communities were sited in upland areas away from the coast, where they cultivated grain.
SARAH NELSON, '*Mumunt'ogi* and Megalithic Monuments: a Reconsideration of the Dating', *PBAKS*, 3, 1992

MUNAN-P'AE 問安牌 ('gate-peace token')

A wooden disc bearing the characters *munan*, with *taejŏn* 'great palace' on the reverse, used for passing through palace gates.

MUNJIP 文集 *See Chip*

MUNMU, KING 文武王 (r. 661–81)

Silla king who achieved the unification of the country in 668. He rejected China's nomination as its Governor-General of a new province, evicted the Tang armies and established the Unified Silla dynasty. In 674 he commissioned the laying out of the Imhae-jŏn detached palace complex later known as **Anap-chi**, and before his death he began the construction of **Kamŭn-sa** temple. He ordered that to save expense he should be cremated and his ashes buried at sea, so that his spirit could protect his kingdom. An underwater tomb was therefore built at **Taewang-am**, and he was known posthumously as the Dragon King.

See also **Song of Ch'ŏyong; Tang dynasty**

MURYŎNG*, KING 武寧王 (r. 501–23)

Personal name Sama; he is said to have been born on an island off Kyushu to the sister-in-law of Kongji, **Paekche** *tamno* king of **Wa**. Having served himself as a *tamno* king, he became the 25th King of **Paekche**. He died in May 523 and was entombed with his queen in August 525. His tomb, outside modern Kongju, was discovered intact in 1971. It comprised a rectangular chamber lined with bricks decorated with a **lotus** pattern, entered through an arched access. Stone inscriptions in *haesŏ* **calligraphy** recorded the date of the royal burial. Among its contents were gilt-bronze crowns and spiked shoes, a silver wine cup with a decorated cover, gold and silver decorated bracelets and earrings (one bearing the name of the silversmith Tari), a gold hairpin in the style of a flying bird, bronze **mirrors**, **iron** goods including a sword, jade pendants, and a unique **glass** figurine of a boy. The coffin itself was lacquered and contained a lacquered pillow and footrest. Many of the tomb's treasures, including the crown, shoes and **jewellery**, are matched by similar pieces from southern Japanese tombs, and are taken by Korean historians to show the political relationship between Paekche and Wa.

Note: The romanisation Munyŏng is commonly met.

HONGNAM KIM, 'China's Earliest Datable White Stonewares from the Tomb of King Muryong (d. AD 523), Paekche, Korea,' *OA*, XXXVII/1, 1991; PAIK SYEUNG-GIL, 'Excavation of the Tomb of Paekche King Muryŏng,' *KJ*, 11/8, 1971

MUSIC

Korea has a long and distinctive musical history, the first mention of which occurs in Chinese writing from the **Han dynasty**. Korea's own written and archaeological sources show that music already formed an important part of life at court and at popular levels across the peninsula during the Three Kingdoms period. It also accompanied military operations. Bands of musicians and dancers from **Koguryŏ** and **Paekche** were kept at the Sui and Tang courts in China, and it is clear that musical teachers and performers came and went between the Middle Kingdom and its tributary states. **Musical instruments** formed part of official gifts in both directions.

Chinese music was known to the sinicised élite in Korea as *tangak* ('music of Tang'). Modern scholars have retrieved examples of **Song dynasty** *zi* tunes from the music surviving in Korea for the pieces *Nagyangch'un* ('Spring in Luoyang') and *Pohŏja* ('Walking in the Void'). Korean forms and tunes were different, and were naturally popular among the literati and ordinary people alike. They were known as *hyangak* ('country music'), a term which paradoxically included other foreign, but non-Chinese, music. As Chinese tunes were koreanised, the distinction between *tangak* and *hyangak* sometimes became blurred, even at court. *Hyangak* was used for the rites to the royal ancestors of the Chosŏn dynasty at the **Chongmyo Shrine**. In its present form, it dates from 1463, when King **Sejo** selected and adapted two suites, *Pot'aep'yŏng* and *Chŏngdaeŏp*, with texts praising the achievements of his ancestors, which had first been arranged by his father **Sejong** for use at banquets.

Music accompanied court **rites and ceremonies** (*see aak*; *music, court*), military occasions, farmers' work and relaxation (*see nongak*), popular entertainment including games, **masked dance** drama (*t'alch'um*) and public storytelling (*see p'ansori*), and religious ceremonies of both shaman and Buddhist tradition. New and distinctive forms evolved in both song (*see kagok*) and instrumental music (*see sanjo*) during the Chosŏn period, creating a tradition with the highest levels of originality and virtuosity. Even so, after the fall of the monarchy, modernisation and colonial conditions between 1910 and 1945 caused the appreciation of native music to wane, until it revived strongly in the last quarter of the 20th century, to some extent under the influence of the *minjung* movement. Modern Korean musicians have also sought to accommodate their own traditions with those of Western music, forming ensembles of Korean and Western instruments and writing new music for Korean instruments. Korean musicality has, however, become most familiar through the success of Korean performers playing Western classical music on the international concert circuit.

See also **Akhak kwebŏm**; **bells**; *chŏngak*; **folk song**; **nabŭm**; *pŏmp'ae*; **Yŏngsan hoesang**
JONATHAN CONDIT, *Music of the Korean Renaissance: Songs and Dances of the Fifteenth Century*, Cambridge University Press, 1984; HAHN MANYOUNG, trans. I.Paek and K.Howard, *Kugak: Studies in Korean Traditional Music*, Seoul: Tamgu Dang, 1990; ANDREW KILLICK, 'Nationalism and Internationalism in New Music for Korean Instruments,' *KJ*, 31/3, 1991, *KOREANA*, *Korean Cultural Heritage*, vol. III, *Performing Arts*, Seoul: Korea Foundation, 1997; LEE HYE-KU, 'Sung Dynasty Music Preserved in Korea and China,' *KS*, 10, 1986; LEE HYE-KU, trans. Robert C. Provine, *Essays on Korean Traditional Music*, Seoul: Royal Asiatic Society, 1981; KEITH PRATT, *Korean Music, its History and its Performance*, Seoul and London: Jung Eum Sa and Faber Music Ltd., 1987

MUSIC, COURT

Music and **dance** accompanied all but one of the **Five Rites** performed at court. Only mourning was unaccompanied, thereby according with ancient Chinese tradition recorded in the *Analects* of Confucius.

Government offices charged with training musicians and organising musical performance in the early dynasties were the *Ŭmsŏng-sŏ* ('Music Office') in the Unified Silla and *Taeak-sŏ* ('Great Music Office') and *Chŏnak-sŏ* ('Ritual Music Office') in the Koryŏ. With the determined restoration of Confucian ceremonial at the early Chosŏn court, especially under King **Sejong**, a number of offices were responsible for the work of a large number of musicians and dancers, including the *Chŏnak-sŏ*, *Aak-sŏ* ('Ritual Music Office'), *Changag-wŏn* ('Court Music Bureau', established in 1458), *Pongsang-si* ('Respect and Constancy Office'), *Kwansŭp Togam* ('Genuine Learning Inspectorate') and *Akhak Togam* ('Music Studies Inspectorate'). A total of 971 musicians is recorded in the late 15th century. Those of *ch'ŏnmin* class, the majority, were called *akkong*, while those of the middle class, *chungin*, origin were referred to as *aksaeng*. They played Music of the Left (i.e. that of Chinese origin, *aak* and *tangak*) and Music of the Right (native music). (*See* **Left and right**)

The trauma of the **Manchu invasions** meant an interruption to regular court music between 1637 and 1646, and when it was restored it was on a more modest scale. An Office for Manufacturing Musical Instruments (*Akki Chosŏngch'ŏng*) was set up in 1682. Music of the Left continued to be that played for the sacrifices, but *tangak* joined *hyangak* as Music of the Right, and as before, the number of players of this category were greatly in the majority. The *Changak-sŏ* ('Control of Music Office') employed 688 performers, but the number had crept up to 722 in the *Kyobang-sa* ('[Music] Teaching Office') of 1897. According to Chinese protocol, King **Kojong**'s assumption of the title of Emperor in that year gave him the right to employ 64 dancers to perform at the imperial rites. In 1907, however, Japanese pressure led to this Office being renamed the *Changag-wŏn*, and by the following year its staff was scaled down to 270. Under the Japanese **Government General** the Music Department of the Yi Household (*Yiwangjik Aakpu*) was set up, and in 1911 the *Changag-wŏn* was renamed *Aaktae* ('Sacrificial Music Unit'). The number of musicians declined to 57 in 1917 and 30 in 1945. In 1950 the *Kungnip Kugag-wŏn* ('National Classical Music Institute') was established to revive the tradition of music for state purposes. The scope and scale of its activities developed, and it was later renamed the National Center for Korean Traditional Performing Arts.

See also Akchang; Akhak kwebŏm; Five Tones; Pak Yŏn

MUSICAL INSTRUMENTS

The oldest surviving musical instrument found in Korea is claimed to be a bone flute of the **Bronze Age**, with nine holes on its upper face and a notch at the blowing end. It was found at Kalp'o-ri in Northern Hamgyŏng province, and is now in the Central Historical Museum at P'yŏngyang. In 1997 the remains of a zither were discovered at an archaeological site in Shinch'ang-dong, Kwangju, and are also believed to be of the Bronze Age. Few other early instruments still exist, though the National Museum of Korea possesses pottery **drums** of the Koryŏ period and jade flutes of the Chosŏn. Plentiful literary and pictorial evidence, however, describes the large traditional Korean instrumentarium, which was divided into eight categories, or 'eight sounds' (*p'arŭm*). These were defined according to the distinctive timbres resulting from the use of particular materials in their manufacture. Together with their principal constituents they were:

1) *metal*: bronze bells (in sets, known as *p'yŏnjong* and singly, as *t'ŭkchong*), **iron** chimes (*panghyang*)

2) *stone*: jade and other hardstone chimes (in sets, known as *p'yŏn'gyŏng* and singly, as *t'ŭkkyŏng*)

3) *silk*: the zithers *kŏmun'go*, *kayagŭm*, *ajaeng*; the vertical two-stringed fiddle *haegŭm*; and the dulcimer, *yanggŭm*

4) *bamboo*: the flute family, including the long transverse *taegŭm* and the short vertical *tanso*; the double-reed oboe family, *p'iri*; and the *so* panpipes

5) *gourd*: the *saenghwang* mouth organ

6) *pottery*: the *hun* ocarina

7) *wood*: the *t'aep'yŏngso*, a double-reed oboe ; the *pak* clappers, a percussion instrument used by the 'conductor' of an ensemble to indicate the beginning and end of musical sections and pieces

8) *skin*: a variety of vertical and horizontal, single- and double-headed drums. The most versatile and commonest of these was the hourglass drum *changgo* ('stick drum').

The majority of these instruments were introduced into Korea from China, and were in turn passed on from the peninsula to the islands of Japan. Some favourite Chinese instruments never achieved the same popularity in Korea: the *konghu* harp seems to have had only a brief existence there (*see* **Harp Song**), while even the important *pip'a* lute family, despite frequent appearances in the hands of musicians in pictures and sculptures from the Chosŏn period and earlier, had died out of common use by the 20th century. Others were incorporated into all levels of musical performance, from **court music** to *nongak*, and in time underwent local development and modification just as they did in China. Comparatively late arrivals were the family of bowed fiddles, received as part of the mediaeval Mongol heritage, and the dulcimer (*yanggŭm*), brought to East Asia by the Jesuit missionaries in the 17th century.
KEITH HOWARD, *Korean Musical Instruments*, Hong Kong: Oxford University Press, 1988; STANLEY SADIE, ed., *New Grove Dictionary of Musical Instruments*, London: Macmillan & Co., 1985

MUTUAL DEFENSE TREATY (1953)
Signed between the United States of America and the **Republic of Korea** on 1 October 1953. It was accepted by the South Korean President, Syngman Rhee (**Yi Sŭngman**), in return for his somewhat unwilling signing of the **Armistice Agreement**. The preamble to the Treaty referred to the need for 'regional security in the Pacific area'. It pledged that in the event of any future attack on South Korea the United States would respond to defend it in accordance with constitutional procedures, and was accompanied by offers of US financial and military support, and the promise of American participation in the diplomatic search for reunification of the peninsula. This led to the **Geneva Conference** of 1954 and the Geneva Agreement which could do no better than acknowledge the stalemate in which the **Korean War** had ended.

MUYŎL, KING 武烈王 (r. 654–61)
Born **Kim Ch'unch'u**, a nephew of Queen Sŏndŏk and second cousin of Queen Chindŏk. (*See* **Silla queens**.) As a **Silla** diplomat he was sent to **Koguryŏ**, Yamato, and China, and became king despite the challenge from two *sangdaedŭng*, Pidam and Alch'ŏn. His political credentials as a ruler were therefore impressive. His second son Kim Inmun, a renowned calligrapher, served as Korean representative at the Tang court. He was succeeded by his eldest son, Pŏmmin (*see* **Munmu**), and his great-grandson King **Sŏngdŏk** erected the temple of Pongdŏk-sa in his memory.

MYOCH'ŎNG REBELLION 妙清 (1135–6)
Rising led by the monk Myoch'ŏng against the court of King Injong (r.1122–46). Myoch'ŏng took advantage of the overthrow of **Yi Chagyŏm** and his supporters to argue the case for P'yŏngyang as capital in succession to **Kaesŏng** and an increase in influence for its officials. He also tried to persuade Injong to attack the **Jin** state. When Injong rejected both suggestions, Myoch'ŏng raised his rebellion in the north-west in 1135. He set up his self-styled kingdom of Taewi in P'yŏngyang, but it was crushed by troops under **Kim Pusik** early in 1136. Myoch'ŏng was assassinated by his own collaborator Cho Kwang.

MYOJI 墓誌 'tomb epitaph'
Important graves were provided with an inscription giving the place of the **tomb**, dates of birth, death and burial, name, rank, achievements, and descendants of the departed. A eulogy or *myŏng* in prose might be appended. The *myoji* or *kwangji* was carved on

stones or written in blue on glazed white ceramic tiles (perhaps twenty in number) and buried beside the coffin. Sometimes it was engraved on the coffin.

MYŎNG-DONG CATHEDRAL 明洞大聖堂

In 1892, all restrictions on Christian missionary activity having been removed, Bishop Gustave Charles Marie Mutel (1854–1933) began to build Korea's first cathedral at the former home of **Kim Pŏmu**, in the Gothic style, though in red brick. Chinese brickmakers were imported to make the bricks on a site near the **Han River**. Dedicated to the Immaculate Conception in 1898, the cathedral was first known as Chonghyŏn Sŏngdang ('Bell Hill Church') and for fifty years dominated the city before multi-storey buildings began to proliferate. It is now best known as Myŏng-dong Taesŏngdang, the name it acquired in 1945. It survived the bombing of Seoul in 1950, and in 1961 a modern hospital (St Mary's) was built on the same site. Between 1960 and 1990 the cathedral was several times the scene of political activity. In 1984, Pope John Paul II canonised 103 Korean **Catholic martyrs** in a ceremony at the Cathedral.

MYŎNGHWAL SANSŎNG 明活山城

Walled mountain **fortress** to the east of **Kyŏngju**. According to *Samguk sagi* it was unsuccessfully attacked by a **Wa** army in AD 405, and repaired and occupied by King Chabi (r. 458–79) after 473, when **Silla** was threatened by the southward expansion of **Koguryŏ** under King Changsu (413–91). During the reign of Queen Sŏndok (632–46) it was briefly held by the rebel force under Pidam, but was recaptured by General **Kim Yusin**.

MYŎNGSA-SIMNI 明沙十里 '10 *li* of shining sand'

A famous beach on the east coast near Wŏnsan, made more beautiful by the plentiful crimson *haedanghwa* 'rugosa roses' growing above the water line. *Myŏngsa-simni* is also a poetic cliché, used as the title of a novel generally regarded as an early 20th-century rewrite of an older tale called *Posim-nok*, 'Record of Guarding the Heart'. This is a complicated romance in *han'gŭl*, heavy with moralising. The earliest text is from 1912.

MYŎNGSIM POGAM 明心寶鑒 'Precious Mirror of the Enlightened Heart'

A collection of Chinese sayings and quotations, some of them spurious, which attained great popularity in Korea and was frequently reprinted. It is unreliably attributed to the Koryŏ scholar-statesman Ch'u Chŏk (whose brush name was Nodang 'dew hall'), at the end of the 13th century. A preface and postface spuriously attributed to **Yi I** are printed in some editions. The extracts come from about 35 authors from Confucius to **Zhu Xi** and include such unorthodox writers as Zhuangzi, but no Buddhists. The material is divided into Confucian moral categories.

N

NA SŎKCHU 羅錫疇 (1892–1926)

Born at Chaeryŏng in Hwanghae, he attended Myŏngsin School. At 23 he went for four years to **Manchuria** to train as an independence fighter. After that he collected and sent funds to the **Provisional Government in Exile** in Shanghai, while doing his best to obstruct the Japanese in Korea. After he had shot and killed a policeman and the town chairman at a country office in P'yŏngsan County, Hwanghae, he fled to China, received further military training and served in the Chinese army before joining **Kim Ku**'s terrorists. He returned to Korea and on 28 December 1926 broke into three Japanese offices in Seoul, including the **Oriental Development Company**, shooting Japanese but failing to explode his bombs. He was chased through the centre of the city, where he killed more Japanese police before shooting himself.

NA TOHYANG 羅稻香 (1902–1927)

Real name Na Kyŏngson; also known as Na Pin. Tohyang means 'Fragrance of growing rice'. The son of a Seoul pharmacist, after taking first steps in a medical education, he went in 1919 to Waseda University, Tokyo, to study English literature. For lack of financial support, he returned to Korea without graduating, and almost at once published his first story in the **literary magazine** *Paekcho* (1921). After a year as a schoolteacher in Andong, he spent his days in Seoul, drinking and wandering aimlessly through the streets, writing and publishing stories. He was the foremost exponent of romanticism. His masterpiece, *Pŏngŏri Samnyong* 'Samnyong the mute', was made into a film by **Na Un'gyu**. Drinking ruined his health, and he died of tuberculosis.

NA UN'GYU 羅雲奎 (1902–37)

Korea's first film-star and film producer. He was born at Hoeryŏng in North Hamgyŏng, but spent much of his boyhood moving from place to place in **Siberia**. In 1920 he entered Hong Pŏmdo's **Independence Army** for a while before going to Seoul, where he was in trouble with the Japanese police for his nationalist activities, and served a spell in prison. He visited **Manchuria** again, then joined a Japanese film company and in 1923 appeared in *Unyŏng-jŏn* ('The Ch'unhyang story'; *see also* *Ch'unhyang-jŏn*)). In 1926 he directed and took the lead in *Arirang*, a film later seen as symbolic of Korean national aspirations. During the next ten years he was connected with 26 films, for at least 15 of which he wrote the script, directed the production and played the male lead. *Pŏngŏri Samnyong*, 'Samnyong the mute' (*see* **Na Tohyang**), was probably the peak of his achievement. In 1936 he introduced sound-recording to Korea with *Arirang 3*. His commercial ventures in film-making were unsuccessful.
See also **cinema**

NABŬM 納音 'contained notes'

A table of Chinese origin (C. *nayin*, used by Guan Lu, 210–256) that shows the correspondence of the sixty **cyclical characters** with the theoretical sixty scales of classical Chinese **music**. The scale of five notes (K. *kung, sang, kak, ch'i* and *u*; *see* **five tones**) can be based on any of the twelve pitches. The lower six pitches (*yul*) are *yang* and the upper six (*yŏ*) are *yin*. The sixty scales are listed in *yin-yang* (*ŭm-yang*) pairs, distributed to the sixty cyclical characters and related to the **five phases**, which appear in the same order in both halves (*) of the table. *Nabŭm* is concerned with musical sounds purely in their cosmic aspect, not with musical performance. The oracular phrases (*sang*) were probably added in late Song times. The table is used in Korea together with the **Nine Palaces** table when divining the prospects for a proposed **marriage**, especially when choosing the day for the wedding. The *saju-p'alcha* of the couple provide eight *nabŭm* oracles to be considered.

cyclical characters		phase	oracle
yang	yin		
kapcha	ŭlch'uk	METAL*	in sea
pyŏngin	chŏngmyo	FIRE	in brazier
mujin	kisa	WOOD	great forest
kyŏngo	sinmi	EARTH	roadside
imsin	kyeyu	METAL	sword tip
kapsul	ŭrhae	FIRE	atop mountain
pyŏngja	ch'ŏngch'uk	WATER	under torrents
muin	kimyo	EARTH	atop fortress
kyŏngjin	sinsa	METAL	white wax
imo	kyemi	WOOD	willow tree
kapsin	ŭlmu	WATER	in a spring
pyŏngsul	chŏnghae	EARTH	atop house
muja	kich'uk	FIRE	thunder
kyŏngin	sinmyo	WOOD	pinetree
imjin	kyesa	WATER	far-flowing
kabo	ŭlmi	METAL*	in sand
yŏngsin	chŏngyu	FIRE	below mountain
musul	kihae	WOOD	flat land
kyŏngja	sinch'uk	EARTH	atop cliff
imin	kyemyo	METAL	gold leaf
kapchin	ŭlsa	FIRE	covered lamp
pyŏngo	chŏngmi	WATER	Milky Way
musin	kiyu	EARTH	great post-station
kyŏngsul	sinhae	METAL	brooch & bangle
imja	kyech'uk	WOOD	mulberry tree
kabin	ŭlmyo	WATER	big brook
pyŏngjin	chŏngsa	EARTH	in sand
muo	kimi	FIRE	over heaven
kyŏngsin	sinyu	WOOD	pomegranate tree
imsul	kyehae	WATER	great sea

NAEBANG KASA 內房歌辭 'songs of the women's quarters'
Also called *kyubang kasa*. From the 17th century onwards a *genre* of **kasa** came into being that was of particular interest to **women**, though not always composed by women. The subject matter was largely domestic.

NAGYANG-CH'UN 洛陽春 'Spring in Luoyang'
A poem by the Chinese poet Ouyang Xiu (1000–72) set to music and preserved in Korea as one of two extant pieces of *tangak* (the other being **Pohŏja**). The tune no longer bears any strong similiarity to its Chinese original, and even the sound of the orchestra which may once have accompanied its singing at court entertainments has changed, the bells and chimes of **aak** having taken the place of the iron slabs (*panghyang*), and the *pip'a* lute and *sheng* mouth organ having disappeared.
JONATHAN CONDIT, *Music of the Korean Renaissance*, Cambridge University Press, 1983; KEITH PRATT, *Korean Music: Its History and its Performance*, London and Seoul: Faber Music and Jung Eum Sa, 1987. *See also* **music**; **musical instruments**

NAHAN 羅漢 'a worthy one'
In Hinayana **Buddhism** there are no **bodhisattvas**. Their place is taken by *nahan* (C. *lohan*, S. *arhat*), 'enlightened ones', regarded as historical. Mahayana Buddhism retains *nahan* with a vaguely defined status, chiefly as distinguished disciples of Sakyamuni. They are portrayed as monks, without the distinctive head-shape and hair-style of buddhas. Four disciples of Sakyamuni who often appear in paintings and statues are: the young Ananda (K. Anant'a) and older Kasyapa (K. Kasŏp); and Sariputra (K. Saribul) and Maudgalyayana (K. Mokkŏllyŏn or Mongnyŏn). They may be seated beside Sakyamuni, or two of them outside a buddha and two bodhisattvas in a row of five images. Groups of 500 or 16 *nahan* are common.

NAKSŎ 洛書 (C. *luoshu*) 'Luo River Chart'

4	9	2
3	5	7
8	1	6

A magic square with the numbers 1 to 9 arranged to give a sum of 15 when read horizontally, vertically or diagonally. It is mentioned in the ***Book of Changes*** Taejŏn, written about 200 BC. The present form was long thought to be a reconstruction by 12th-century neo-Confucians, but its discovery in 1977 in the grave of the Marquis of Ruyin at Fuyang, Anhui, proved that it dates back at least to the earliest years of Han, before 150 BC. It is much used in Korean fortune-telling, especially in **Nine Palaces divination**.

NAM CHONGSAM 南鍾三 (1817–66)
Nam passed in the 3rd grade at the palace **examination** of 1838 and was given a post educating the royal children. He became a Catholic and was well acquainted with Bishop **Berneux**. When a group of Catholics had been encouraged by Catholic women and sympathisers in the Hŭngsŏn **Taewŏn'gun**'s household (his wife, **Princess Min**; his eldest daughter, wife of Cho Kijin; and **Kojong**'s wet-nurse, Martha Pak) to suggest a treaty with Britain and France in order to withstand Russia's intentions, Nam became chief intermediary with the regent, who asked to meet Berneux. The meeting never took place, perhaps because the Catholics were too slow in organising it, perhaps because the regent never intended that it should. Probably reports of French aggressiveness in China, the presence of American vessels off shore, the *General Sherman* incident, and his political need to please the dowager queen Cho, who had made his son king (Kojong), led him suddenly to take the opposite course, affirming a 'Hermit Kingdom' policy and the persecution of Catholics. Nam was executed in 1866, on the same day as Berneux, but on a different execution ground. He was canonised in 1984 as Saint John-Baptist Nam.
See also **martyrs, Catholic**

NAM HYOON 南孝溫 (Ch'ugang, 1454–92)
One of the **six surviving subjects** of King **Tanjong**, a disciple of **Kim Chongjik** and friend of Kim Sisŭp (*see **Kŭmo sinhwa***). He joined the *ch'ŏngdam* ('pure conversation')

305

neo-Confucian group and led a retired life, but died at the age of 38. Both his poetry and his *hanmun* prose are highly esteemed. His brush-name means 'autumn-river' and gives the title to his collected works *Ch'ugang-jip*.

NAM PYŎNGCH'ŎL 南秉哲 (1817–63)
He and his brother **Nam Sanggil** were the most distinguished astronomers and mathematicians of late Chosŏn. They were allies of the Andong Kim clan. Having been *pansŏ* of the Board of Rites in 1856, Pyŏngch'ŏl ended his career as *taejehak*. His works include *Haĕgyŏng sech'o-hae* (1861) on the properties of the right angle and astronomical calculations, *Ch'ubo sokhae* (1862) on the movements of heavenly bodies, and *Ŭigi chipsŏl* on astronomical instruments.

NAM SANGGIL 南相吉 (1820–69)
Also known as Nam Pyŏnggil. Brother of **Nam Pyŏngch'ŏl**. His political career was slightly less distinguished than his brother's, though he became *ch'ampan* of the Board of Appointments. His many writings include *Suhak chŏngŭi* on mathematics, *Chipko yŏndan* (1860: algebraic solutions to Wang Xiaotong's 7th-century problems), *Sihŏn kiyo* (calendrical principles), *Sŏnggyŏng* (uranographical mirror) and *Chungsŏng sinp'yo* (1853, new tables of the stellar mansions, revised in 1864 as *Chungsu chungsŏng p'yo*). He was a friend of the calligrapher **Kim Chŏnghŭi**.

NAMDAE-MUN 南大門 'Great South Gate'
National Treasure No.1. Built in 1398, the former main entrance gate to the city of Seoul was officially known by its colloquial name Namdae-mun ('Great South Gate') during the Japanese colonial period but had its original title of Sungnye-mun ('Gate of Noble Ceremony') officially reasserted in 1996.
See also **Tongdae-mun; walls**

NAME CREATION ORDER *Ch'angssi chedo* 創氏制度 (1940)
After 1937 the Japanese colonial government introduced a general policy for the assimilation of Koreans into the Japanese nation. Japanese became the language of education. Koreans were encouraged to take Japanese names from about 1938, and an enforcement order was issued in February 1940. Each name had to be registered. It might include characters from the Korean name or other references, such as characters from the sept name, but had to be approved by Japanese authority. These names disappeared naturally at the Liberation in 1945.

NAME TABU *p'ihwi* 避諱 'avoiding personal name'
Tabu on the name used during his lifetime by a man who has died is recorded for emperors in Qin (3rd century BC). The first examples in Korea are for the Three Kingdoms period. The rules have varied, but became stricter, even to being observed within non-royal families. Either the name-character or its sound might have to be avoided. The effects were widespread. A place-name might be changed because the death of a king made part of it tabu; and the personal name given to a Chosŏn prince tended to be a very rare character, because if he were to become king, it might give much trouble by becoming tabu for later generations.

There were two principal methods of keeping the tabu in mind for readers. One was to write the tabu character with another character of similar meaning but different sound; the other, called *kyŏlp'il* 'defective brushwork', was to leave out some strokes of the tabu character so as to leave a character of different sound. Both methods were combined when *tan* 'morning' (the sun character above a horizontal stroke) became tabu during the Chosŏn dynasty, because it was the personal name of Yi T'aejo, founder of the dynasty. The character *cho* 'morning' was usually substituted; but when *tan* ocurred in Couplet 68 of the *Thousand Character Classic* (*Ch'ŏnja-mun*), in which no character could be repeated and this *cho* character already appeared, another *cho* 'morning', that also happened to be the name of a marine turtle, was written instead. Unfortunately the top element in the turtle character was the tabu character *tan*. Therefore the horizontal stroke in that element was left out, even though the resulting character did not otherwise exist.

See also **names, kings'; names, personal; surnames**

NAMES, CHRISTIAN

Baptismal names are given by **Catholics, Russian Orthodox** and **Anglicans**. They are usually koreanised versions of Latin, French, Russian or English names, respectively. **Protestants** do not give new names at baptism, but some, especially writers, have adopted Christian names, as much, it appears, for stylishness as for devotion. The names of early Catholics may be difficult to read. Some of them, particularly names from the Bible and the great religious orders, are in forms derived from the Portuguese and Italian names used by early China missionaries, like Bundo for Benedict (Portuguese *Bentao*) and Pangjigŏ (*Francisco*) for Francis. Many more are derived from obscure saints and martyrs in the pre-1969 Latin Calendar: Kŭrisando (Chrysanthus), Pibiana (Bibiana), Uborosina (Euphrosyne).

NAMES, FOREIGNERS'

When westerners first arrived in the 19th century, since all formal writing was in Chinese script, Sino-Korean names were needed for them. Those who had lived in China continued to use their Chinese names, but with Korean pronunciation. Thus **Jacques Chastan**, called Zheng Yagebo (Yagebo – Jacobus = James) in China, was called Chŏng Yagŏbo in Korea. Others were often given approximations to their western names; **H. N. Allen** became An Yŏn ('peace', 'lotus', pronounced Allyŏn) and **H. G. Underwood** Wŏn Tuü. These names, usually devised by Korean friends, vary in elegance according to who makes them. Though they are less necessary today, they are still given. Foreigners delight in them. Koreans find them convenient partly because of difficulty in pronouncing foreign names and partly because of the Korean custom of using only the first syllable of a name, as when Prime Minister Harold Macmillan was referred to as *Maek Susang*.

NAMES, KINGS'

Chosŏn dynasty kings had:

1) *Myoho*, the temple name given after death. The second syllable of a temple name is *-cho* for kings who performed great feats, did not come peacefully to the throne, or who lived through great wars; *-chong* for 'kings of virtue'. *Chong* could be upgraded to *-cho* (Yŏngjong became **Yŏngjo** and Chŏngjong became **Chŏngjo** in 1899). Deposed or disgraced kings were termed as (5) below.

2) *Hwi*, a personal name given early in life, but after accession treated as tabu till the end of the dynasty (*see also* **name tabu**).

3) *Cha*, a familiar name, given at marriage.

4) *Ho*, a brush-name.

5) A princely title, a real or symbolic geographical name prefixed to *-kun* 'prince' and used before accession. (*See* **princely titles**)

6) *Chonho*, an honorific name created or changed by a special government department during the king's lifetime for use on seals and inscriptions. It might have up to 58 characters.

7) *Siho*, a posthumous honorific title given by the **Ming** court.

The name of a Chosŏn king as recorded in *Sŏnwŏn-gyebo* (*see* **Sŏnwŏn poryak**) contains all the names and honorifics given after he ascended the throne. The longest is that of Yŏngjo (r. 1724–1776) with 58 syllables. **Sejong** (lived 1397–1450) has 14: *Sejong Changhŏn Yŏngmun-yemu-insŏng-myŏngho Taewang. Sejong* is his *myoho* 'temple-name', given after death. *Changhŏn* 'good and respected' is a *siho* bestowed after Sejong's death by the Chinese emperor. *Yŏngmun-yemu-insŏng-muŏngho* 'florescent scholar, sagacious warrior, benevolent sage, resplendently filial son' is the honorific *chonho* given by the Korean Board of Rites after his reign ended. Beside all this, his *hwi* or personal name was To 'blissful (or sleeve-cuff)'. Since this was tabu, *Hyul* 'sleeve' was written in its place. His *cha* 'familiar name' was Wŏnjŏng, 'fundamentally upright', but, unlike many kings, he apparently never used a *ho* 'brush-name'. His princely title Ch'ungnyŏng-gun, given in 1408, was raised to Ch'ungnyŏng Taegun in 1413. He was made *seja* Crown Prince in 1418, a few weeks before he acceded to the throne.

See also **Names, personal; names, temple; posthumous king titles; reign titles**

NAMES, PERSONAL 名, 號

During the Chosŏn dynasty a Korean male received an *amyŏng* 'baby name' or a *yumyŏng* 'milk name', which was temporary. When studying, he might have a *hangmyŏng* or *sŏmyŏng* 'school name'. At some point he would receive a *myŏng* or *kwanmyŏng*, a name used for official purposes; but it was *hwi*, partially tabu, and until recently was not used without circumspection. There is usually an aura of nobility about the *myŏng*.

Although some individuals and certain families, such as Hŏ and those with **two-character surnames**, prefer single character names (*tanmyŏng*), a *myŏng* usually consists of two characters. One of these (*tollim-cha* or *haengnyŏl-cha*) is a generation character, given to all the boys of one generation; the other is the personal character given to one individual alone. Generation characters, decided in advance by the clan council, follow a sequence that usually shows the generative order of the **Five Phases**. Thus one generation with *chong* 'bell' (a character containing the metal radical), may be followed by one with *ku* 'seek' (water radical), followed by *yŏng* 'glory' (tree radical), *hwan* 'shining' (fire radical) and *ki* 'foundation' (earth radical). This character takes first or second place alternately in successive generations: T'aekchong and P'ilchong's sons, for example, might be Kuho and Kuin, their grandsons Siyŏng and Changyŏng, great-grandsons Hwanjin and Hwansu, great-great-grandsons Pyŏkki and Sŏpki. In some lineages the generation characters are not derived from the Five Phases, but from other sources, such as the *Book of Changes*, the *Thousand Character Classic* (*Ch'ŏnja-mun*) or the Ten Heavenly Stems (*see* **Kapcha characters**).

The personal character is sometimes chosen to create a set for uterine brothers, as when *ha*, *ŭn* (or *sang*) and *chu*, names of the classic dynasties (Xia, Yin/Shang and Zhou) are given to three brothers in that order. Or all the brothers may have characters with the same radical element, such as *ch'un* 'springtime', *ho* 'dawn' and *min* 'sky', which all have the sun radical.

When a man was capped or married he received a *cha* 'familiar name', for use by his equals. The *cha* was plainer than the *myŏng* and often contained a male epithet, such as *cha* 'son', *kyŏng* 'gentleman', or *suk* 'elder brother', or it might refer to the *myŏng*, as when a man with the *myŏng* Pongnae, 'phoenixes come', had as *cha* Sunso, 'summoned by [the music of] the Emperor Shun'.

More important historically is the brush-name or *ho*, also called *pyŏrho* 'special name', *aho* 'elegant name', or *tangho* 'studio name'. It might be chosen by teacher or friends, or by the man himself; and was normally used for the title of his posthumously published collected works (*chip*). It included a literary or poetic element, and was frequently derived from the man's studio, having *-tang* 'hall', *-am* 'hermitage' or *-chae* 'study-retreat' for its second element, as in Sŏltang 'snow hall', P'ungam 'maple hermitage' or Yŏmjae 'studio of recollection'.

Buddhist monks have a *pŏphwi* or *pŏmmyŏng* 'dharma name'.

Women were rarely given personal names outside **yangban** families, though there have long been educated women with *ho*. **Kisaeng** had poetic names.

In modern times men's and women's names have become assimilated, though women's tend to have a gentle or flowery aura (favourite characters include *-sun* 'gentle', *-suk* 'pure', *-ja* 'child' and *-hŭi* 'princess'). Professional aliases and pen names (*p'irho*) of the western kind became popular during the 20th century, notably for film stars. **Christian names** are also taken, especially by Catholics. The *cha* and *siho* have virtually disappeared, but the *ho* remains popular. **Name tabu** has been lost, but Koreans still prefer to address and refer to others by relational terms (Elder Sister, Teacher, etc) or titles (Chairman, Headmaster, etc).

NAMES, TEMPLE 諡號
Distinguished men were given a posthumous *siho* 'temple name' for use in the Confucian sacrificial system. Though a few monks of Koryŏ have four characters, a *siho* usually consists of two characters selected from a list of some 120 with solemn Confucian meanings. The first was often *mu* 'warrior', *mun* 'literary', *chŏng* 'faithful', *ch'ung* 'loyal', *ik* 'profound thinking' or *hyo* 'pious'. In practice the *siho* is suffixed with the posthumous honorific *kong*, originally meaning 'Duke' or 'Lord', but later used as a general honorific. Thus the temple name of **Yi Sunsin** is Ch'ungmu-gong and **Yi Hwang** is Munsu-gong.

The earliest recorded *siho* is for King Chijung of Silla in 514, but further evidence is incomplete before the end of Koryŏ. In Chosŏn the posthumous name was granted on petition from the dead man's family and decided by a joint process involving the **Hongmun-gwan** and a group from the Board of Rites called **Pongsang-si**. Originally restricted to men of 2nd **grade** and above, it was later more widely distributed. The same *siho* could be given to many men. At least 85 received Munjŏng-gong 'Literary and Loyal Lord', including **Song Siyŏl** and **Yi Ik**.

NAMHAN SANSŎNG 南漢山城
Fortified mountain castle protecting the southern approach to the Chosŏn capital Seoul. In face of the second **Manchu invasion** in 1636 the body of the court fled to **Kanghwa** Island, but King Injo and the Crown Prince **Sohyŏn**, unable to escape, took refuge here and were surrounded for more than five weeks before finally capitulating. *See also* **fortresses; Mohadang; Pukhan sansŏng; *Samjŏn-do hanbi***

NAMJU-BUKPYŎN 南酒北餅 'in the south, wine; in the north, cakes'
In the southern part of Seoul people were generally poorer, and drowned their worries in wine; in the north they were wealthier and could afford festal food. This probably applied to the **yangban** of the Noron **faction** during their long years of power.

NAMSADANG 南寺黨

Namsadang 'male-temple-players', both men and boys, banded in itinerant groups (*namsadang-p'ae*) of low-class entertainers who performed in the villages during spring and autumn. Their leader was called *mogap* or *kkoktusoe*. They probably originated in groups of begging monks, and a group might maintain links with a particular monastery. During the day they would perform simple religious **rites** for villagers. Their entertainments were given at night by the light of flares; standing, lying or sitting, jumping and dancing on a tight-rope (*chul-t'agi* or, in their jargon, *ŏrum*), balancing with a huge **fan**; performing acrobatic feats on the ground (*ddang-jaeju* or *salp'an*); and spinning dishes (*taejŏp-tolligi* or *pŏna*) – all accompanied by patter and banter with the audience. They gave displays of drumming, danced and played percussion and wind instruments in **music** (*p'ungmul-lori*) like that of farmers' bands. There might also be a performer, often masked, on the village *sottae*. The boys (*midong*) were dressed as girls. At the climax of the show a man would balance a boy on each hip while a third boy stood on his shoulders. A fourth boy, called *sami* 'novice monk' and wearing a monk's cornette, would be thrown in an upward somersault to stand on the shoulders of the top boy. They also performed **masked dance** drama (*kamyŏn-guk* or *totpogi*) and concluded with a **puppet play** (*inhyŏng-guk* or *tolmi*). The sophisticated *Samullori* (Samul Nori) drumming that became internationally famous in the 1990s was developed by Kim Tŏksu (b. 1952), son of a Namsadang *mogap*.
See also **Nongak**

NAMUL fresh greens and wild vegetables
Perhaps the most distinctive and delicately flavoured of all Korean foods: fresh leaves, shoots and roots. They are simply washed and wilted, scalded, dipped in cold water to preserve the colour, and served with a simple dressing of soy sauce, sesame oil and vinegar, which may or may not be spiced with red **pepper**, garlic and fresh ginger. Most of them are restricted to Korea, and they are more characteristic of good Korean cooking than any *kimch'i* or meats. They have long been eaten by all social classes and they have their own place in poetry.

Among the roots are *tŏdŏk* (*Codonopsis lanceolata*), *toraji* Chinese bellflower (*Platycodon glaucum*), *naengi* Shepherd's Purse (*Capsella bursa-pastoris*), *uŏng* Burdock (*Arctium edule*) and *ssŭbagwi* Milkweed (*Ixeris dentata*). Shoots include two ferns that are eaten when the crosiers are very young: *kosari* Bracken (*Pteridium aquilinum*) and *kobi* Royal Fern (*Osmunda japonica*). *Turŭp* is the shoot of the Angelica Tree (*Aralia elata*), sold in long straw plaits. *Minari*, an aquatic plant of the Evening Primrose family (*Oenanthe stolonifera*) has an aromatic, smokey flavour. The common mallow *auk* (*Malva verticillata)* has been cultivated and valued as food in China and Korea for many centuries. *Wŏnch'uri* are the young shoots of the Day Lily (*Haemerocallis aurantiaca*). Many delicious fungi are prepared in much the same way.

NANGNANG 樂浪郡 *See* **Lelang**

NAONG 懶翁 (1320–76)
'Lazy old man', also known as Hyegun 'wise, diligent'. Monk adviser to King Kongmin of Koryŏ. Moved by the death of a friend when he was twenty, he entered a monastery and was enlightened four years later. He visited **Chigong** in Beijing, returning to Korea two years later and receiving the robe. He visited Beijing again before beginning a distinguished teaching career throughout the Korean monasteries.

In 1371 he was invited to the palace and appointed *kuksa*, 'national teacher'. He died at Sillŭk-sa near Yoju and **Yi Saek** wrote his epitaph there. His portrait appears in temples with those of his contemporaries, **Chigong** and **Muhak**.

NATIONAL ANTHEM *See Aegukka*

NATIONAL CONFERENCE FOR UNIFICATION *See Yusin* **Constitution**

NATIONALISM
Asian states from India to Japan have experienced and expressed nationalism in a variety of peaceful and non-peaceful ways since the age of western imperialism. In East Asia the situation was complicated by Japan's own imperialist behaviour and China's revived assumption of its traditional regional supremacy. In Korea, resentment at Chinese and Japanese possessiveness was stronger than concern at western intrusion, though the latter was by no means absent, and the independence movement in the late 19th century, symbolised by newly felt pride in *han'gŭl*, had the potential to link upper and lower classes in powerful ethnic harmony. Japanese politics, however, moved too fast and proved too strong for nascent Korean nationalism, and through the colonial period its expression was limited to uncoordinated indications of patriotic fervour delivered more in the manner of protest than as indication of positive optimism (*see Ŭibyŏng*). Korean nationalism, despite being keenly felt by many under Japanese occupation, played little part in the Japanese defeat in 1945, and seemed to have been hopelessly compromised by the disunity displayed in the **Korean War**. It has therefore been since the rebuilding of the country began in 1953 that it has been most noticeable.

In the **Democratic People's Republic of Korea** (DPRK), commitment to Marxism-Leninism may seem to have surrendered the cause to international socialism, yet **Kim Ilsŏng**'s balancing of rival Soviet and Chinese bids for influence and his efforts to build an independent communist state may be interpreted as nationalism presented in ideological guise. Though its form and language may be foreign and belong to the 20th century, neither in style nor purpose does DPRK government differ greatly from that of its traditional predecessors, which also tried to identify a safe Korean middle path between two powerful neighbours.

So too in the **Republic of Korea** (ROK), the uncompromising political behaviour of its early leaders represented a continuation of Korea's own traditions in the face of pressure from abroad for swift and unfamiliar changes to politics and society. Here, however, in contrast to the North, self-confidence returned with the astonishing economic revival through the 1970s and 1980s. Not only did this encourage experimentation with new systems such as democracy, it also paid for the grandiose demonstration of keenly felt national pride. Sometimes this took wholly positive form, such as the opening of the majestic Sejong Cultural Centre in Seoul in 1978, boasting the largest pipe organ in Asia. Sometimes, as in the decision in 1996 to demolish the Capitol Building, to reconstruct the **Kyŏngbok Palace** once again on its site, and to replace it as the headquarters of the National Museum with an enormous new building, it showed the need to destroy symbols of foreign oppression and replace them with reminders of Korea's past and present greatness.

In the past, Korean men regarded their **topknots** (*sangt'u*) as a sign of their national identity, and many resented the order to cut them off as a sign of reform in 1895. In modern Korea, both North and South, **Mount Paektu** and even its associated foundation myth of **Tan'gun** are often cited as powerful symbols of Koreanness. So too are **tigers**, no longer extant on the peninsula but chosen as a happy and appropriate

311

pan-Korean mascot for the 1988 Seoul **Olympic Games**. It was, ironically, from Japan that Korea learned the value of a **national flag** and national anthem (*see Aegukka*), as well as the system of enhancing national cultural pride through the nomination of National Treasures, National Living Treasures, and Important Intangible Cultural Properties. These include, for example, pieces of outstanding **celadon** from the Koryŏ dynasty, performers such as the great *p'ansori* singer Kim Sohŭi, and cultural forms such as the Hahoe **Masked Dance** drama.

Both in the DPRK and ROK politicians have worked hard to foster pride in their own nation. To all Koreans, however, the division of the country into two hostile states evokes the strongest possible feelings of nationalism. Both in South and North, when future priorities are assessed the necessity for reunification outdoes all others.

CHUNG CHONG-SHIK & RO JAE-BONG, *Nationalism in Korea*, Seoul: Research Center for Peace and Unification, 1979; DANIEL JUHN, 'Nationalism and Korean Businessmen under Japanese Colonial Rule,' *KJ* 17/1, 1977; LEE CHONG-SIK, *The Politics of Korean Nationalism*, Berkeley: University of California Press, 1963; MICHAEL ROBINSON, *Cultural Nationalism in Colonial Korea, 1920–1925*, Seattle: University of Washington Press, 1988; MICHAEL ROBINSON, 'Narrative Politics, Nationalism and Korean History', *PBAKS*, 6, 1996; SHIN YONG-HA, *Formation and Development of Modern Korean Nationalism*, Seoul: Dae Kwang Munhwa Sa, 1990; KENNETH WELLS, *New God, New Nation: Protestants and Self-Reconstruction Nationalism in Korea 1896–1937*, Sydney: Allen & Unwin, 1990
See also **March First movement; *Minjung* movement; National flower**

NATIONAL SECURITY LAW *Kukka poan-pŏp* 國家保安法 (1948)

Measure passed by the administration of Syngman Rhee (**Yi Sŭngman**) in December 1948 in the wake of the **Cheju Rebellion** and **Yŏsu-Sunch'ŏn Rising**. Directed against the threat of communist sedition, it quickly functioned as an essential weapon in the armoury of successive autocratic presidents. Forbidding the formation of groups devoted to activities which could be interpreted as hostile to the state, it has been estimated to have led to the arrest of 188,621 people within a year, including the future president Park Chung Hee (**Pak Chŏnghŭi**). Revised and strengthened several times, it was extended in December 1958 to cover a wider range of less precisely defined activities, including the dissemination of 'false information' and publishing attacks on the president. It was retained by Park Chung Hee and widely exploited by the **Korean Central Intelligence Agency** in support of its politically repressive policies. Subsequent presidents, especially Roh Tae Woo (**No Taeu**), also took full advantage of its ban on 'anti-state activities' to arrest numerous dissidents and deny complete freedom of political expression.

PARK WON-SOON, *The National Security Law*, Los Angeles: Korea NGO Network for the UN Conference on Human Rights, 1993

NEO-CONFUCIAN GROUPS

From the time of King **Sejo**, neo-Confucians were divided into four kinds, loosely called parties, though they were not politically organised. They were the *Hun'gu-p'a*, 'meritorious old-timers', who remained in government office and were rewarded for loyalty to the king; *Chŏrŭi-p'a*, 'faithful loyalists' like Kim Sisŭp (*see Kŭmo Sinhwa*) who lived as outcasts; *Ch'ŏngdam-p'a*, 'pure conversationalists' like **Nam Hyoŏn**, who lived as rural hedonists, drinking, chatting and writing about anything but politics; and *Sarim'p'a*, 'forest scholars' like **Cho Kwangjo**, who devoted themselves to the classics and neo-Confucian philosophy. The terms fell out of use in mid-Chosŏn.
See also **factions; *sarim***

NEO-CONFUCIANISM *See* **Confucianism; Yi Hwang; Yi I; Zhu Xi**
THEODORE DE BARY & JAHYUN KIM HABOUSH, eds., *The Rise of Neo-Confucianism in Korea*, New York: Columbia University Press, 1985; HAECHANG CHOUNG & HAN HYONG-JO, eds., *Confucian Philosophy in Korea*, Seoul: The Academy of Korean Studies, 1996; MARTINA DEUCHLER, *The Confucian Transformation of Korea, a Study of Society and Ideology*, Cambridge, Mass: Harvard University Press, 1992

NEOLITHIC PERIOD, THE
Is associated on the Korean peninsula with the ***Chŭlmun*** and ***Mumun*** pottery cultures. Rough dating is from 6000 BC to 700 BC, by which time **rice** cultivation may have arrived from the Chinese mainland. For the greater part of the period the population subsisted on hunting, fishing and gathering, the transition to **agriculture** occurring around the end of the 2nd millennium BC. Evidence suggests cultural links between early neolithic culture in north-west and north-east Korea and the Laioxi and **Liaodong** regions of China.
IM HYO-JAI, 'Korean Neolithic Chronology: a Tentative Model,' *KJ*, 24/9, 1984; IM HYO-JAI, 'The Korean Neolithic Age and its Cultural Relationship to Northeast China', *KJ*, 36/4, 1996; SARAH NELSON, *The Archaeology of Korea*, Cambridge University Press, 1993

NEVIUS METHOD
A missionary policy often regarded as vital in the success of Protestant missions in Korea. John Livingston Nevius (1829–93), an American Presbyterian missionary in China, who wrote *The Planting and Development of Missionary Churches* (Shanghai 1866), was invited to expound his ideas to a joint meeting of Presbyterian missions in Seoul in 1890. His method, designed for the first stages of a missionary venture, is usually described as self-government, self-propagation and self-support by the native church, but equally important was his insistence on the Bible as fundamental to all teaching and decision-making. Nevius ideals were first applied by the Southern Presbyterian mission in 1893, when it also agreed to concentrate on **schools** and teacher-training, on the lower rather than the upper social classes, and on **women**'s work; to use the native language and alphabet (not ***hanmun***); and to expect medical missionaries to do evangelistic work.
KIM YONG-JAE, 'A Re-evaluation of the Mission Policies of Nevius,' *in* YU CHAI-SHIN, ed., *Korea and Christianity*, Seoul, Berkeley, Toronto, 1996
See also **Protestants**

NEW CULTURE MOVEMENT *Sin munhwa undong* 新文化運動
Nationalist movement aimed at preserving and regenerating Korean cultural identity under Japanese occupation. It involved writers, dramatists, artists, musicians, dancers, and film-makers. It was to be seen in the formation of clubs and societies, such as the left-wing Torch Society, the establishment of fine arts institutes, the composition of new songs and music, the increased use of ***han'gŭl*** as a medium of vernacular communication, the promotion of literacy, the publication of books, **literary magazines**, and journals, and the output of a new literary movement. Many of its participants were plainly anti-Japanese and thereby risked attack, but others took refuge in the arts for their own sake, exploring novel forms of personal self-expression, and in introducing western literature and drama to Korean audiences. New writing included poetry, novels, and short stories, much of it portraying the stresses of

contemporary life and pride in Korea's rich and independent history. Painters and calligraphers were encouraged by the **Government General** to contribute to its annual Chōsen Art Exhibition, instituted in 1922, but more expressive works went on show at the rival exhibitions of the *Sŏhwa Hyŏphoe*.
See also **newspapers; Yi Sangbŏm**

NEW DEMOCRATIC PARTY (NDP) *Sinminju-dang* 新民主黨

Formed by Kim Toyŏn and other discontented members of the ruling **Democratic Party** in October 1960 to enhance the move towards parliamentary democracy in South Korea. It fared badly in the 1967 election, but its candidate in the 1971 presidential election, **Kim Taejung**, was only narrowly defeated and it became the strongest party in opposition to the ruling **Democratic Republican Party** (DRP). In 1973 (*see* **Yusin Constitution**) it obtained 52 National Assembly seats to the DRP's 73. Relations between the two parties were soured by the kidnapping and imprisonment of Kim Taejung. The response of President Park Chung Hee (**Pak Chŏnghŭi**) to the growing demands for constitutional reform was to intensify his personal grip on the political machine and his reliance on the secret activities of the widely hated **Korean Central Intelligence Agency**. In 1978, following the rigged re-election of Park as president, a majority of voters turned to the NDP, whose 61 members combined with independents to outnumber the DRP. The DRP nevertheless continued to form the government. In June 1979 **Kim Yŏngsam** was elected leader of the NDP, but he and his members encountered frequent violence. In return, **students** played a prominent part in widespread opposition to the government, and demonstrations spread during the autumn. Political events moved swiftly following the assassination of Park Chung Hee on 26 October. Martial law was imposed and Acting President Ch'oe Kyuha promised a new **constitution** for 1980; but opposition leaders – notably Kim Yŏngsam and Kim Taejung – were unable to work together to seize their opportunity, and under the new President Chun Doo Hwan (**Chŏn Tuhwan**) military dictatorship continued. Popular unrest grew and broke out in further demonstrations. The climax of the disturbances was reached in May 1980 (*see* **Kwangju Massacre**) and suppressed by the army. In October all political parties were proscribed pending new National Assembly elections. By the time they were called in 1982, Kim Yŏngsam, along with **Kim Chŏngp'il** and Kim Taejung, had been banned from political activity. The Party was re-formed as the New Korea Democratic Party in January 1985, and became the Reunification Democratic Party in May 1987. In February 1990 it became part of the ruling coalition Democratic Liberal Party.
See also **South Korea: political parties; Third Republic**

NEW KOREA YOUTH PARTY *Sinhan Ch'ŏngnyŏndang* 新韓青年黨

Association of young Korean patriots formed in Shanghai in 1919. It sent members to Korea, Japan, the United States and **Siberia** to promote independence activities. In particular, it delegated **Kim Kyusik** to go to Paris to represent claims for Korean freedom at the post-War Peace Conference.
See also **Provisional Government in Exile**

NEW PEOPLE'S ASSOCIATION *Sinminhoe* 新民會

Party founded in 1907 by **An Ch'angho** as part of the nationalist movement advocating self-strengthening, continuing the work of the **Independence Club** (*see* **Self-strengthening Movement**). Its membership included intellectuals and Christians and it promoted patriotic education through secondary schools and bookshops. In 1908 it opened a school of its own, Taesŏng, in P'yŏngyang and funded it with profits from the P'yŏngyang Ceramic Company. (The school was closed by the Japanese in 1913.) Early in 1911 many of the Association's members were arrested on suspicion of plotting to assassinate Governor-General Terauchi (*see* **Hundred and Five, Case of the**). In January 1913 the Association's leaders, including **Kim Ku**, were also arrested and it was dissolved.

NEW PEOPLE'S PARTY *Sinmindang* 新民黨
Name adopted by the former Korean Independence League. Its founder and chairman was Kim Tubong, who had been with Mao Zedong in Yan'an. It comprised some 22,000 Koreans who had also been in the Chinese North West Soviet. In 1945 they were disarmed and returned to Korea, mainly in the North. In 1946 it merged with **Kim Ilsŏng**'s **Korean Communist Party** (North Korean Branch) to form the [North] **Korean Workers' Party**.

NEW SHOOT SOCIETY *Sin'ganhoe* 新幹會
Founded on 15 February 1927 to create a broad leftist organisation of nationalists and socialists. Its founders included the Christian nationalist Yi Sangjae (1850–1927), owner of the *Chosŏn Ilbo* newspaper, and the socialist Hong Myŏnghŭi, and it quickly attracted a widespread membership of around 35,000. On 18 December a branch was formed in Tokyo, and in March 1928 a parallel organisation for women, the *Kŭnuhoe* ('Helping Friends Society', also known as the Korean Women's League), was established (*see* **women's movement**). Though the Society's objectives included the pursuit of Korean independence, the Japanese tolerated it, believing that close supervision would enable them to keep a check on political developments. The Society was strongly critical of Japanese policies. It called for a strengthening of Korean cultural education including a return to teaching the Korean language; the right to study Marxism Leninism; an end to discriminatory anti-Korean laws such as restrictions on freedom of speech and assembly; an end to policies encouraging Korean emigration to **Manchuria**; and an end to the exploitation of Korean people and resources through the closure of companies such as the **Oriental Development Company**. In 1927 it sent representatives, including the socialist **Hŏ Hŏn**, to international conferences in Brussels and Cologne to denounce Japanese colonialism. Among Korean **students** it played an active part in fomenting the **Kwangju Incident** in 1929 and used it to protest vigorously against Japanese oppression. Though communist influence made its outlook increasingly radical, prompting some nationalists to desert it, it was not offensive enough for the Comintern. When the Japanese authorities arrested 44 of its left-wing leaders, including Hŏ Hŏn, in January 1930, right-wing nationalists endeavoured to take it over, but the communists forced its closure on 16 May 1931.
KANG MAN-GIL, 'Significance of the Shin'gan-hoe Society Movement in the History of the Korean National Movements,' *KJ*, 27/9, 1987; KIM CH'ANG-SUN, 'How the Shin'gan-hoe Society Came to be Dissolved,' *KJ*, 27/9, 1987; YI KYUN-YONG, 'Inauguration of the Shin'gan-hoe Society and Establishment of its Chapters,' *KJ*, 27/9, 1987

NEW YEAR / NEW YEAR'S DAY *sŏllal*
Each family celebrates New Year's day with a morning *ch'arye* before the family spirit tablets. Young people don new clothes (*sŏlbim*) and visit their elders, beginning with parents, to make a deep bow, called, for this occasion, *sebae*. Those who bow are rewarded with titbits or small gifts of money. Much *yut* is played, **kites** are flown and

ttŏkkuk (a savoury soup with large disks of white *ttŏk* 'rice cake' in it) is eaten. The holiday traditionally lasted until *Taeborum-nal*, a fortnight later.
See also **Ancestral worship; festivals**

NEWSPAPERS

The first Korean newspapers appeared in the 1880s. They were the *Chōsen Shimpo* (1881), *Hansŏng Sunbo* (1883) and *Hansŏng Chubo* (1886). All were produced with some Japanese help and can be associated with the **self-strengthening movement** of that decade. All printed Korean in a mixture of *han'gŭl* and Chinese characters and were short-lived. **Sŏ Chaep'il**'s *Tongnip Sinmun*, first published in 1896, was the organ of the **Independence Club**. The theme of **nationalism** was taken up by others such as *Hwangsŏng Sinmun* ('Capital Gazette'), *Mansebo* ('Independence News'), *Taehan Maeil Sinbo* ('Korean Daily News'), and *Taehan Minbo* ('Korean People's Report'), which spread anti-Japanese propaganda until most were closed down by the Residency General in 1908. After 1910 only one Korean-language newspaper (*Taehan Maeil Sinbo*) and one English-language paper (*see* **Bethell**) were permitted to publish in addition to those in Japanese, all of them acting as official Japanese organs. The **March First Movement**, however, forced a change in the approach of the **Government General**, which in 1920 permitted the reintroduction of a number of papers, including the right-wing *Tonga Ilbo*, the left-wing *Chungang Ilbo*, and the *Chosŏn Ilbo*. All were subject to tight censorship, but managed to promote Korean interests and pursue anti-Japanese editorial policies despite being subject to cuts and suspensions. When Son Kijŏng won the marathon in the 1936 **Olympic Games** the *Chungang Ilbo* and *Tonga Ilbo* printed his photograph with the Japanese flag erased from his vest, and were suspended for ten months as a result. In August 1940 all Korean newspapers were closed down except for the *Maeil Sinbo*, which became an organ for Japanese propaganda. Publication recommenced under the **American Military Government**, and by 1947 21 daily papers were on sale, representing a spread of political opinion. Under the **First Republic** they were prevented from expressing their views freely and reporters and editors were continually harrassed. The revised **constitution** of 1960 promised freedom of the press and many more papers appeared, but the dictatorship of Park Chung Hee (**Pak Chŏnghŭi**) stifled any opportunity for them to engage in political debate, especially as evidence accumulated of growing opposition from politicians, intellectuals and **students**. Government control over the press was relaxed after 1980, although fear of communist subversion continued to deny publishers the right of unimpeded freedom of expression.
KIM BONG-GI, *Brief History of the Korean Press*, Seoul: Korean Information Service, 1965; LEE KWANGRIN, 'Newspaper Publication in the Late Yi Dynasty,' *KS*, 12, 1988; OH IN-HWAN, 'Journalism in Korea: a Short History of the Korean Press,' *TRASKB*, LI, 1976

NINE MOUNTAIN SCHOOLS *ku-san-mun* 九山[禪]門

Towards the end of Unified Silla *Sŏn* Buddhist teaching was based on nine important monasteries, founded by Korean monks who studied in Tang China and became leaders of Korean **Buddhism** on their return: (1) *Silsang-sanmun*, the first, was founded by Hongch'ŏk early in the 9th century at Silsang-sa near Namwŏn; (2) *Kaji-sanmun* by Pojo (804–880) at Porim-sa, near Changhŭng, south Chŏlla; (3) *Sagul-sanmun* at Kulsan-sa, Kangnŭng, by Pŏmil (810–889); (4) *Tongni-sanmun* by Hyech'ŏl (785–861) at T'aean-sa, Koksŏng, south Chŏlla; (5) *Sŏngju-sanmun* by Muyŏm (801–888) at Sŏngju-sa, Poryŏng, south Ch'ungch'ŏng; (6) *Saja-sanmun* by

Toyun (798–868) at Ssangbong-sa in south Chŏlla; (7) *Hŭiyang-sanmun* by Chisŏn (824–882) at Pongam-sa, Mun'gyŏng, north Kyŏngsang; (8) *Pongnim-sanmun* by Hyŏnuk (787–868) at Pongnim-sa, Ch'angwŏn, south Kyŏngsang; and (9) *Sumi-sanmun* by Iŏm (866 932), at the behest of **Wang Kŏn**, at Kwangjo-sa near Haeju. They provided the basis on which **Ŭisang**, **Chinul** and **T'aego** worked for unity with *Kyo* schools (*O-gyo; see* **Five Teachings**).

NINE PALACES DIVINATION *kugung* 九宮

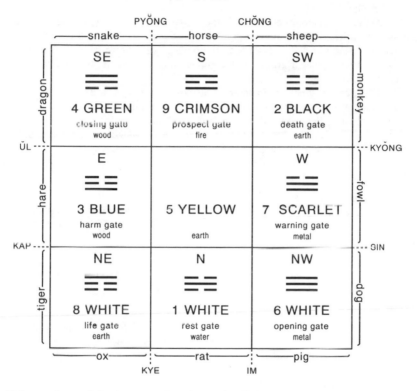

A Chinese chart of the heavens, found now in **Ch'ŏn'gi-daeyo**, and much used by fortune-tellers for choosing lucky days, deciding the depth of a burial and other purposes. The material in it has several historical layers, but little has been done as yet to clarify them.

The basis is *Luoshu* (K. *Naksŏ*), the magic square of 3, taken as a chart of the heavens. This dates at least from early Han. The four cardinal points and their intermediary points are indicated by the eight **trigrams** in their 'later than heaven' sequence. The centre is added to express the ancient cosmological value of the figure 9. This has been attributed to the astronomer Zhang Heng (AD 78–120).

By Tang times each square had been given a colour. These are the Five Colours, but two of them are given in two shades each (two reds and two blue/green) and white is given three times. Hence the nine palaces are called *ilbaek* '1 white', *ihŭk* '2 black', *sambyŏk* '3 blue', *sarok* '4 green', *ohwang* '5 yellow', *yukpaek* '6 white', *ch'ilchŏk* '7 scarlet', *p'albae* '8 white' and *kuja* '9 crimson'.

The *p'al mun* 'eight gates' of *tun'gap* (C. *dunjia*), 'hidden **kapcha characters**', (a numerological technique for reading fates) were also introduced by Tang times. The gates consist of two complementary sets of four: *hyumun* and *kyŏngmun* 'gates of rest and of prospect', *saengmun* and *samun* 'gates of life and of death', *sangmun* and *kyŏngmun* 'gates of harm and of warning', *tumun* and *kaemun* 'gates of closure and of opening'. The white ones (rest, life and opening) are auspicious; the other five are inauspicious. In Korea the eight gates are best known from their appearance in the **Romance of the Three Kingdoms** (chapter 84), where they are connected with the name of **Zhuge Liang**.

The twelve palace-edges are given to the animals of the **zodiac**, perhaps inserted as late as Song times, when the correspondence of the palaces and the **twelve hours** of the day was established. The **twenty-four hours** or directions are accommodated by adding the four corner-trigrams and eight stem-characters to the twelve zodiacal animals round the edges.

The **five phases** appear with their usual compass points and trigrams, but with wood and metal doubled and with earth stretched diagonally across the centre. They may originally have been entered as names of the planets.

Since Tang times the whole diagram has been understood as being annually transformed. Every year the numbers are all changed, each being decreased by 1 for men and increased by 1 for women. Nine transformations cover a cycle of nine years (given here for 1964–1972).

Man:

8 4 6	7 3 5	6 2 4	5 1 3	4 9 2	3 8 1	2 7 9	1 6 8	9 5 7
7 9 2	6 8 1	5 7 9	4 6 8	3 5 7	2 4 6	1 3 5	9 2 4	8 1 3
3 5 1	2 4 9	1 3 8	9 2 7	8 1 6	7 9 5	6 8 4	5 7 3	4 6 2

Woman:

5 1 3	6 2 4	7 3 5	8 4 6	9 5 7	1 6 8	2 7 9	3 8 1	4 9 2
4 6 8	5 7 9	6 8 1	7 9 2	8 1 3	9 2 4	1 3 5	2 4 6	3 5 7
9 2 7	1 3 8	2 4 9	3 5 1	4 6 2	5 7 3	6 8 4	7 9 5	8 1 6

The colours, phases and gates change to match the number; but the compass points, trigrams and *kapcha* references all remain fixed. The sequence is described by giving each transformation the number of the figure in the central square of the diagram – making 5 the number of the standard form, which alone is a magic square. (5 is the central number between 1 and 9.) Transformation 3 occurs in the same year for both sexes.

In Korea the base year for calculation is 1684. This was probably chosen as convenient when the current edition of *Ch'ŏn'gi-daeyo* was published. 1684 was the first year of a 180-year cycle which begins when the *kugung* transformation for a man is 1 and the year is *kapcha*, the first in a sexagenary cycle. The transformations for the years 1964–1972 were:

Year	Man	Woman	Year	Man	Woman	Year	Man	Woman
1964	9	6	1967	6	9	1970	3	3
1965	8	7	1968	5	1	1971	2	4
1966	7	8	1969	4	2	1972	1	5

There was much alarm in 1966, a Year of the Horse (of the Red Horse in ordinary **saju-p'alcha** numbering), which *kugung* diviners said was also a 'white horse-year' for women, because it was a Year of the Horse in which the *kugung* transformation for women was '8 white'. This was widely believed to presage exceedingly bad luck for women and especially for babies born during the year. Such a 'white horse year' occurs every 36 years. The distress of 1930, when many women aborted their babies, was recalled and similar distress was forecast for 2002. Popular superstition held that women's bad luck in 1966 could be reversed by wearing red petticoats, which had phenomenally high sales in autumn 1965.

The ramifications of *kugung* are complex. The nine transformations are matched with the 12 months in a cycle of 36 that covers three years. Further calculations relate to days and hours. The astrologer must then refer to much other material for assistance in interpreting how all this affects his client.

NO CH'ŎNMYŎNG 盧天命 (1913–57)

Perhaps the first significant modern woman poet. Born at Changyŏn in Hwanghae, graduating in English Literature from **Ewha** College in 1934, she started writing poetry in her student days. Later working chiefly as a journalist, she published her first poem in *Siwŏn* 'Garden of verse' magazine in 1935. Her romantic love for a school-teacher made an impression on the women of her day, as did her poetry, which was lyrical and sentimental. During the invasion of 1950 she remained in Seoul. After the few months of communist occupation of the city she was imprisoned for having supposedly collaborated with them as a writer, but was released at the pleading of other writers in spring 1951. She became a Catholic in 1951, taking the name Veronica, and thereafter turned to religion in some of her poetry. In later years she stressed solitary frugal living, and is remembered for her severe dress of white Korean jacket and black skirt, as well as her predilection for minor antiques. Her principal works include the collections *Sanho-rim* 'Coral forest' (1938), which includes the poem *Sasŭm* 'Deer', so celebrated as to become her trademark; *Ch'angbyŏn* 'Glass wall' (1945); *Santtalgi* 'Wild Strawberries' (1948), and the posthumous collection *Sasŭmŭi norae* 'Song of a Deer' (1958).

NO PAENGNIN 盧伯麟 (1875–1926)

Pioneer aviator. He was educated in Japan and returned to Korea to work in the royal military school. In 1907 he worked with **An Ch'angho** and others, founding the *Sinminhoe*, **'New People's Association'**, to work for Korea's freedom. In 1914 he went to Hawaii, where he joined Pak Yongman (1881–1928) in founding the *Kungmin-gundang*, 'People's Army' (*see* **ŭibyŏng**). Travelling by way of California he went to Shanghai and became the armed forces commander of the **Provisional Government in Exile**. In 1920 he was in California again, founding a Korean aviation school. After a visit to Vladivostok to work with those struggling against Japanese domination, he returned to Shanghai, where he fell ill and died.

NO SASIN 盧思慎 (Pojin-jae, 1427–98)

After steady progress through the **examinations** and government ranks, at the end of his career he reached senior posts in the State Council. Under **Sejo** he edited the *Hojŏn* section of *Kyŏngguk taejŏn*, the compendium of laws. Under **Sŏngjong** he joined **Sŏ Kŏjŏng** in preparing the *han'gŭl* versions of *Hyangyak chipsŏngbang* and assisted in editing the gazetteer *Yŏji sŭngnam*. In 1471 he compiled the *Samguksa chŏryo*, 'Essentials of Three Kingdoms History'; in 1478 he helped edit the royally sponsored *Tongmun-sŏn*, 'Anthology of Korean Writings'. In 1498, as a member of the Hun'gong (conservative old guard), he saved the lives of many of the *sarim* who were persecuted in the **literati purges**. His brush name Pojin-jae means 'Nurturing truth study'.
See Sinjŭng Tŏngguk Yŏji-sungnam.

NO SUSIN 盧守慎 (Sojae, 1515–1590)

He had a long education in the classics and passed first in a national **examination** of 1543. Two years later he was exiled in the **literati purge** of 1545. For the next nineteen years he was in exile, mostly on the south-western island of **Chindo**, where he wrote prolifically, sending letters and poems to many scholars. He corresponded with **Yi Hwang** and other neo-Confucians, becoming identified with the *Hallim* or philosophers' party, and taking a lively part in the Four-Seven debate. After the accession of Sŏnjo in 1564 he was recalled to office, eventually becoming prime minister; but in 1580 he had to retire. Confucian purists regarded him as suspiciously sympathetic to Wang Yangming, **Daoism** and **Buddhism**. Only a small proportion of his literary output, written with the brush name 'refreshed scholar', has survived.

NO TAEU 盧泰愚 (Roh Tae Woo, b.1932)

Was born in the village of Talsŏng, near **Taegu** in North Kyŏngsang province, where his father was a minor local official. He attended local schools and then joined the army. In 1951, he transferred from the military police to the Korean Military Academy, graduating in 1955. He attended the US Special Warfare School in North Carolina in 1959, and in 1968 he graduated from the (South) Korean Army War College. He then served in Vietnam.

On returning to Seoul, he was promoted to Brigadier-General and in 1974 became commander of the Airborne Special Warfare Brigade, a post he held until early 1979. He then became commander of the 9th Infantry Division and later in the year, commander of the Capital Security Command. He played an important part in the coup d'état which brought his close associate, Chun Doo Hwan (**Chŏn Tuhwan**), to power in December 1979. Following the coup, Roh succeeded Chun as commander of the Defence Security Command in August 1980.

In July 1981, he was appointed full General and retired from the army to become Minister of State for Political and Security Affairs. From then on, he was widely seen as Chun's choice of successor. In March 1982 he became Minister for Sport, and Minister for Home Affairs the following month. In July 1983, he became president of the Seoul Olympic Organising Committee, a post he held until 1986 concurrently with the presidency of the Amateur Sports Association and the (South) Korean Olympic Committee.

Further signs of his rôle as Chun's successor included his election to the National Assembly and as President of the ruling Democratic Justice Party (DJP) in 1985. In June 1987, his selection as the DJP candidate for the presidential elections led to widespread demonstrations which were only ended when he announced on 29 June that he would not stand unless a series of reforms were introduced. These included direct election of the president and an amnesty for the veteran opposition leader, **Kim Taejung**. Chun reluctantly accepted these proposals, and Roh became president of the DJP in August 1987.

In the December 1987 election, Roh won by two million votes, with 36·6% of the vote. His presidency was notable for the successful Seoul **Olympic Games** in the summer of 1988, and for his achievements in establishing relations with communist countries, known as *Nordpolitik*. The same policy also led to a series of agreements with North Korea in 1991–2, but these remained largely unimplemented by the time Roh left office in early 1993. His domestic policies, which saw a more liberal approach in some areas such as press freedom, were overall deemed to have failed to redress the injustices of the past. In 1990, he concluded an alliance with **Kim Yŏngsam**, which brought that veteran opposition leader into the government party.

After leaving office, he found himself, like Chun Doo Hwan, under constant attack from those who wished to see the question of responsibility for the 1980 **Kwangju massacre** reopened. In 1993, former General Chŏng Sŏnghwa brought a case of mutiny to the courts against both Chun and Roh. The prosecution agreed that the 1979 incident was a mutiny, but declined to take action. However, popular protest continued and in December 1995 both Chun and Roh were arrested on charges of bribery and corruption, to which treason and mutiny were soon added. Both men were convicted in 1996, with Roh sentenced to twenty two years and six months' imprisonment and fined. His sentence was reduced to seventeen years on appeal. Following the 1997 presidential election, President Kim Yŏngsam, with the approval of the incoming president, Kim Taejung, released both Roh and Chun from prison, though the heavy fines still stood.

ROBERT E. BEDESKI, *The Transformation of South Korea: Reform and Reconstruction in the Sixth Republic under Roh Tae Woo, 1987–1992*, London: Routledge, 1992; JAMES COTTON, ed., *Korea under Roh Tae-woo: Democratization, Northern Policy and Inter-Korean Relations*, St Leonards, New South Wales: Allen & Unwin, 1993; ROH TAE WOO, *Korea, a Nation Transformed: Selected Speeches*, Oxford: Pergamon Press, 1990; CHRISTOPHER J. SIGUR, ed., *Democracy in Korea: the Roh Tae Woo Years*, New York: Carnegie Council on Ethics and International Affairs, 1992

NOGŎLTAE 老乞大

The standard textbook on spoken Chinese, officially published by the *Sayŏg-wŏn* or *T'ongmun-gwan*, a valued source for Korean linguistic history. It was possibly first written in the 14th century. *Chunggan Nogŏltae* 'Revised Nogŏltae', published in 1763, was reprinted in 1795. The book contains conversations by a horse dealer working between Seoul and Beijing. *Nogŏltae* literally means 'old man asks great man', but has been reconstructed as 'an old Chinese' or 'Mr Chinaman', *kŏltae* being taken as a form of *Kitai*. The title became generic. Yi Ch'oedae's *Mongŏ Nogŏltae* (1741) deals with Mongol, and Ch'oe Hutaek's *Ch'ŏngŏ Nogŏltae* (1703) with Manchu. *Inŏ taebang* 'General Method for the Neighbour Tongue' (1790) is a Japanese textbook.

NONG CH'ŎNHA-JI-BON (C. *nong tianxia zhi ben*) 農天下之本

A motto often written on the great white banner with dagged red or blue edges that is carried before the *ture*, cooperative band of field workers, when accompanied by their musicians. It means '**Agriculture** is the basis of the empire (*or* society)' and is quoted from a decree of the Han emperor Wendi (r. 179–156 BC) as recorded in *Shiji* 10. The grammar is often made clearer by inserting two extra characters, so that the sentence reads: *Nongja ch'ŏnha-ji-daebon. Sinnong-ssi yuŏp*, 'the heritage of the Divine Husbandman', is another motto sometimes seen on the banner.

NON'GAE 論介 (d. 1593)

A *yamen* **kisaeng** of Chinju in Kyŏngsang province, a favourite of the magistrate Ch'oe Kyŏnghoe. When the Japanese invaders of Hideyoshi's army took the town in 1593, they held a victory banquet in Ch'ŏsong-nu, 'pavilion of clustered rocks'. Non'gae enticed a Japanese officer into her arms and threw herself over the parapet into the South River below, killing them both. A memorial stone to her courage and patriotism was erected on the site, and a **banner gate** at Changsu, where she was born. *See also* **Imjin Wars**

NONGAK 農樂 'Farmers' music'

During the heavy work season of the 6th and 7th moons, the farmers went to the fields in procession, playing **musical instruments** including gongs (*kkwaenggwari*, *ching*), cymbals, **drums** (*changgo*, *puk*, *sogo*), flutes, a horn (*nabal*), and the principal melodic instrument, the double-reed oboe with a wooden pipe and conical metal bell, the *t'aep'yŏngso*. One man carried a huge banner marked *Nong ch'ŏnha-ji-bon*. One or two of the younger and good-looking ones would continue to play and dance while the others worked under the searing sun throughout the day. Their music encouraged the workers and lightened their labour. Often they would play and dance in the dusk at the end of the day in the village square. A skilled dancer might then entertain them with *sangmo tolligi*, twirling a long paper streamer attached to his hat.

Bands of itinerant performers helped to spread popular folk tunes and occupational songs from one province to another, but distinctive regional variations developed, some of which are still preserved. Being used mainly out of doors, one of the chief characteristics of *nongak* was its exuberance and loud volume. Another was its rhythmic complexity.

The chief purposes of *nongak* were to lighten the strain on workers in the fields and to invoke the blessing of the spirits on the village crops and the health of its inhabitants. As an aid to its preservation in the latter part of the 20th century, it has been deliberately encouraged in festivals and competitions, while the troupe Samul Nori (*Samullori*) has acquired an international reputation for its vibrant performances of music based on agricultural music and drumming. The sound of *nongak* remains the most evocative sound of old-style village life, music akin to that of *mudang* and *sadangp'ae*, treasured today as a stirring heritage, and associated in the 1990s with political demonstrations.

KEITH HOWARD, *Bands, Songs and Shamanistic Rituals: Folk Music in Korean Society*, Seoul: Royal Asiatic Society Korea Branch, rev. ed. 1990; KIM YANG-KON, 'Farmers' Music and Dance,' *KJ*, 7/10, 1967

See also **folk song**; **masked dance**; *namsadang*

NONGSA-JIKSŎL 農事直說 'Plain Words on Agriculture'

The first Korean treatise on **agriculture** was written in 1429 by Chŏng Ch'o (d. 1434) on the basis of information obtained from all over the country, under **Sejong**'s policy of encouraging rural improvements. It was included in Sin Sok's *Nongga-jipsŏng* (1665).

NORIGAE

Trinkets, usually on silken cord loops with *maedŭp* work (*see* **knotting**) and tassels attached, used to decorate the bow on a woman's *chŏguri* (*see* **dress**), or hung at the waist. They may be of gold, jade, coral, crystal, amber or other material. There are many designs. A famous one for the rich is the *samjak*, 'three workmanships', in which a yellow cord and tassel hang from a little *pulssu* 'Buddha's finger' (a curiously shaped citrus fruit called bergamot) of *mirhwa* (amber with milky streaks), a blue tassel from a pair of *ong-nabi* ('jade butterflies' of bluish nephrite, *ch'ŏnggang-sŏk*, decorated with gilt) and a red one from *sanho-gaji* 'a twig of coral'. Very different is the tiny case of gold, silver, amber or tortoise-shell enclosing a sharp *changdo(-kkal)* 'cosmetic knife'. There were also tiny medicine flasks (*horobyŏng*) and tasselled gilt lockets containing scented powder or paste (*kŭmsa-hyanggap*).

NORON 老論 'Old reasoning'
Political **faction** of the late 17th and early 18th centuries associated with **Song Siyŏl**.

NORTH KOREAN NUCLEAR PROGRAMME

North Korea began to develop nuclear power for civilian purposes in the 1950s, with assistance from the Soviet Union. Such a programme made sense because of the limited fuel resources of the Korean peninsula, and the fact that North Korea has indigenous supplies of uranium and graphite, both required for nuclear plants. North Koreans received technical training in the Soviet Union, and in 1965 the Soviet Union supplied an experimental reactor, built at Yŏngbyŏn. At Soviet insistence, this was registered with the International Atomic Energy Agency (IAEA) in 1977, and subject to IAEA inspection. In 1985, again on Soviet insistence, North Korea joined the Nuclear Non-proliferation Treaty (NPT). Despite this, it refused to sign the required safeguards agreement, or to submit a full list of nuclear facilities to the IAEA. In the meantime, following a South Korean declaration that there were no nuclear weapons in South Korea, the two Koreas signed a non-nuclear agreement in December 1991.

In 1992, North Korea finally signed the safeguards agreement. By that stage, satellite photography had indicated that there were more facilities than the reactor at Yŏngbyŏn, and the list supplied by the North Koreans to the IAEA confirmed this. One of the facilities, claimed to be a radiochemical laboratory, appeared to be a spent nuclear-fuel reprocessing plant. Such a plant would allow the extraction of plutonium, required for the making of nuclear weapons. When the IAEA insisted on inspecting this and all other nuclear facilities, North Korea announced in May 1993 that it was withdrawing from the NPT. There was considerable international concern, led by the United States, at the implications for the whole non-proliferation system, and much pressure was put on North Korea, including the threat of United Nations' sanctions, not to withdraw. Eventually, the North Koreans were persuaded to suspend their withdrawal, and following the visit of former US President Jimmy Carter to North Korea in June 1994, negotiations began which eventually led to an agreement in October 1994 between the US and North Korea for the supply of two less dangerous light water reactors to North Korea by the Korean Peninsula Economic Development Organisation (KEDO). KEDO was established in 1995, and the ground-breaking ceremony for the reactors took place in 1997. South Korea was to supply the reactors and most of the staff for the work, and North Korea was to halt work on its nuclear weapons programme. Under the terms of the 1994 agreement, the IAEA would not investigate further until the completion of the light water reactor project. Tension rose again in 1998 as spy satellites detected the excavation of a deep bunker at Kŭmchang-ni, 25 miles north west of Yŏngbyŏn, which the United States suspected of serving nuclear purposes. P'yŏngyang refused to admit international inspectors, until an agreement was reached in Washington on 16 March 1999 promising them future access to the site. This was implemented in May 1999.
MICHAEL J. MAZAAR, *North Korea and the Bomb: a Case Study in Non-proliferation*, New York: St Martin's Press, 1995; LEON V. SIGAL, *Disarming Strangers: Nuclear Diplomacy with North Korea*, Princeton University Press, 1998

NORTHERN LEARNING 北學 *See Pukhak*

O

O SANGSUN 吳相淳 (Kongch'o, 1897–1963)

Born in Seoul, he studied religion and philosophy before becoming a school-teacher in Seoul. In 1920 he published poetry in the **literary magazine** *P'yehŏ*, 'Ruins', which he helped to found. About 1926 he spent two years at Pŏmŏ-sa, studying **Buddhism**. From then onwards he lived a vagabond life. He never married. After the **Korean War** he could be found daily in tea-rooms near Chogye-sa, the main Buddhist temple in Seoul, chain-smoking and talking. He died of high blood-pressure and pneumonia in the Red Cross Hospital. At the funeral his friends made offerings of packets of cigarettes. His pen name, 'Transcendent Void', was a pun on 'cigarette-end'.

O SECH'ANG 吳世昌 (Wich'ang, 1864–1953)

In 1884 'Reed lake' became a clerk in the government information department and a writer for the newspaper *Hansŏng Sunbo*. In the interim administration of 1884 he had charge of postal services. He spent a year in Tokyo teaching Korean for the Japanese government, and returned to Tokyo as a refugee in 1902 when he fled because his involvement with progressives put him in danger. There he met **Son Pyŏnghui** and joined *Ch'ŏndo-gyo*. Five years later he returned to Korea and took charge of the **newspapers** *Mansebo* and *Taehan Minbo*. Yet in 1919 he was one of the **thirty-three signatories** of the **Declaration of Independence**. After being imprisoned for three years he devoted himself to **calligraphy**, of which he was a great connoisseur, himself skilled in the seal scripts. He published *Kŭnyŏk sŏhwa-jing*, 'Gleanings on Calligraphy and Painting in the Land of Hibiscus', in 1928. After 1945 he was honorary director of *Maeil Sinbo* and *Seoul Sinmun*. He died at **Taegu** as a refugee during the **Korean War**.

ŎAP 御押 ('royal seal')

A seal on which was cut a facsimile of the king's *sugyŏl* 'personal signature' – a virtually illegible monogram.

'OCTOBER INCIDENT' (1895) *See* **Min, Queen**

OGAT'ONG 五家統 *See* **Five families system**

O-GYO 五教 *See* **Five teachings**

OGYŎNG-BAEKP'YŎN 五經百編 'A Hundred Excerpts from the Five Classics'

A famous compilation, published by order of **King Chŏngjo** in 1798, of one hundred excerpts from each of the Five **Confucian Classics**. In a 5-volume woodblock edition, the classical quotations were printed in large characters, 3 cm high. It is not known for certain whether the king did this because his own eyesight was failing.

OKCHŎ 沃沮

Ancient tribal territory and people lying to the south-east of **Koguryŏ** and the north of **Tongye** from the 4th century BC to approximately the 2nd century AD. As a walled town state it formed part of the Chinese commandery of **Lintun** (modern South Hamgyŏng province), after which it enjoyed a brief period of independence before being incorporated into Koguryŏ by King T'aejo (53–?146). Its land was mountainous but sea fishing was profitable. Its people traded with Tongye and Koguryŏ, and its society was controlled by a legal system.

OLD CHOSŎN

State with walled communities which evolved in the **Taedong** River basin in the middle of the first millennium BC (*see* **Bronze Age**), controlling territory as far north as the Liao River. Its ruler adopted the title of king (*wang*) from its neighbouring Chinese state of Yan. Its civilisation was more advanced than that of its contemporary polities, **Puyŏ, Yemaek, Imdun** and **Chinbŏn**. It was succeeded by **Wiman Chosŏn**.

LEE KI-DONG, 'Ancient Korean Historical Research in North Korea: Its Progress and Problems,' *KJ*, 32/2, 1992; YOON NAU-HYUN, 'True Understanding of Old Chosŏn,' *KJ*, 27/12, 1987

OLIVE TREE CHURCH *Chŏndogwan, Kamnam Kyohoe* 傳道館

A **new religion** based on Protestant Christianity. Pak Taesŏn, born at Tŏkch'ŏn in south P'yŏngan, was brought up in straitened circumstances, but managed to get to school in Tokyo. He ran a little precision tool factory at Kurata, but returned to Korea in 1944 and set up a small engineering company in Seoul. In 1955, as a Presbyterian elder at an evangelistic meeting in Namsan Park, Seoul, he claimed to have received a transfusion of the blood of Christ and to have performed a miracle of healing. He said he could transmit the blood of Christ to others by a form of massage called 'laying on of hands' and could change water into the blood by blessing it. His followers, who soon numbered some hundreds of thousands, declared that he was the Olive Tree of Revelation 11.4, that he was the Second Advent of Christ and that Korea would save the world. In the following year he was disowned by the Presbyterian Church as heretical. In 1957 he founded a new town with several factories near Sosa, between Seoul and **Inch'ŏn**, which was followed in 1962 by another at Tŏkso and later a third near **Pusan**. These towns were remarkably successful both socially and economically. Worship in his temples was based on the Presbyterian model with ecstatic elements. He was highly authoritarian and generally regarded as politically powerful and at one time imprisoned. In 1960 his angry followers invaded the *Tonga Ilbo* newspaper office and wrecked it because the paper had declared some of his miracles were faked.

OLYMPIC GAMES

Two sessions of the Olympic Games stand out in Korean history. On 9 August 1936 Son Kijŏng won the gold medal for the marathon in Berlin, establishing a world record of 2 hours, 29 minutes, 2 seconds. The bronze medal in the same race was won by Nam Sŭngnyong. Both ran under the Japanese emblem. Nationalists in Korea invoked Japanese ire by lauding a Korean victory. On 29 August *Tonga Ilbo* published a picture of Son's victory in which the Japanese emblem on his singlet had been obliterated. The paper was suspended by the colonial government until 2 June 1937. Son's feat and its significance were recalled in 1992 when a Korean runner, Hwang Yŏngcho, beat a Japanese into second place in the marathon at the Barcelona Games.

The 1988 Olympic Games were held in Seoul and in terms of spectacle and organisation proved to be a great success. Early plans to share them between the South and the North failed, but politics played a prominent part in the preparation for the sporting jamboree. Widespread opposition to the military *junta* of President Chun Doo Hwan (**Chŏn Tuhwan**) threatened the disruption of the Games and compelled him to accede in 1987 to demands for a new **constitution**, presidential elections (*see* **No Taeu**), and the freeing of political prisoners such as **Kim Taejung** and **Kim Yŏngsam**.

ŎM-BI 嚴妃 (1854–1911)
Lady Ŏm entered the palace to serve on the queen's staff, but after the queen was murdered in 1895 her status as the king's consort was gradually enhanced until after the birth of her son **Yi Ŭn** in 1897 she was named Sunhŏn Hwang-guibi, 'imperial concubine Sunhŏn'. She made generous contributions to the establishment of several modern **schools** for girls.

OMOK 五目 'five places'
A game like noughts-and-crosses played on a *paduk* board by two players with 100 pebbles each. Placing one pebble on the board at a time, turn by turn, each tries to set five pebbles in a straight line, vertically, horizontally or diagonally, and at the same time to prevent his opponent from doing so. The game is won when one player succeeds in making the line of five.

ONDAL 溫達 (d. 590)
Samguk sagi contains a charming legendary account of a poor boy called 'Silly Ondal', who marries a princess and is groomed by her for a life of higher social standing. The historical Ondal was a **Paekche** general who died in a battle against **Silla** in 590.

ONDOL
The typical Korean system of heating a house by flues passing under the floor is first clearly recorded in the Chinese *Jiu Tang shu* history, which describes *ondol* in **Koguryŏ** in the early 7th century. It seems probable that **Silla** and **Paekche** domestic architecture was not suitable for *ondol* heating, but the system was in use throughout the peninsula by late Koryŏ. It was also known north of the **Yalu**, and is related to the Chinese *kang*. It is economical: the fire for the morning meal heats the room for the day and the fire for the evening meal heats the room for the night; but it is suitable only for a life-style in which people sit on the floor. The upper air of the room remains cool.
WARREN VIESSMAN, 'Ondol Radiant Heat in Korea,' *TKBRAS*, XXXI, 1948–9; FRANCIS MACOUIN, 'Aux origines de l'hypocauste coréen,' *AAS*, XLII, 1987

ONGNU-MONG 玉樓夢 'Dreams of the Jade Pavilion'
A bulky *kodae sosŏl*, with another version called *Ongnyŏn-mong* 'Dreams of Jade Lotuses'. Both are sometimes attributed to Nam Yŏngno (or Ongnyŏnja, 'jade lotus child') and dated to 1840. The original may have been written in *hanmun*. It opens with a scene at the White Lotus Pavilion (*Paengnyŏn-nu*) in heaven, where an immortal and five star-fairies enjoy a picnic among the lotus flowers, for which they have to atone by being born in the flesh as a man with two wives and five **concubines**. The story was surely inspired by *Kuunmong*, but lacks *Kuunmong*'s spiritual content and proposes nothing beyond the joys of this world.

ONJO 溫祚 *See* **foundation myths**

ŎNMUN-JI 諺文志 'Notes on the Vulgar Script'
A short essay on Korean language by Yu Hŭi (1773–1837), a poor but learned man, of whose writings only three pieces are known to have survived. In *Ŏnmun-ji* he categorises the sounds of Korean as 25 initials, 16 medials and 7 finals. This analysis represents a significant stage in the study of Korean, though his perceptions were still influenced by Chinese linguistic theories.

OPPERT, ERNEST JACOB (b. 1832)
Oppert was a Prussian Jewish merchant adventurer based on Shanghai. He made three attempts in 1866–8 to establish trading relations with Korea, all unsuccessful. His last attempt was helped by Catholics led by Fr **Féron**. They sailed to Haemi on the west coast of Ch'ungch'ŏng province, with over a hundred men, left a guard on the magistracy at Tŏksan and went inland to rob the tomb of Prince Namyŏn, father of the **Taewŏn'gun**, in a deliberate act of sacrilege designed to avenge the Catholic **martyrs** and to force Korea to open its borders. They failed to open the tomb before they had to leave in order to catch the tide. As a result, Korea's anti-foreign policy and the oppression of Catholics were intensified.
ERNEST OPPERT, *A Forbidden Land; Voyages to the Corea*, London, 1880

ORIENTAL DEVELOPMENT COMPANY *Tōyō takushoku kabushiki kaisha*
東洋拓殖株式會社
A large semi-official Japanese company formed in 1908 to exploit Korean resources in Japanese interest. Its presidency was awarded to retired military leaders. It began by claiming unused state land, and by 1918 had sponsored the migration to Korea of 380,000 Japanese colonisers, rising to 752,000 by 1942. In the early 1930s it was one of the largest controllers of agricultural property and tenants, and a major issuer of usurious loans to impoverished farmers. Under the **American Military Government** it was revived as the New Korea Company.

ORIOLES' SONG *Hwangjo-ga* 黃鳥歌
Sometimes declared to be the oldest Korean lyric verse (*see also* **Harp Song**; **Tortoise Incantation**), though it is known only in a Chinese version of 4-character lines, appearing in *Samguk sagi* under Year 3 of King Yuri of **Koguryŏ**. There it is given as a song of affection for his wife when they are separated, but scholars have many theories about its true origin. (*See* **birds**)

> Flutter, flutter, orioles,
> male and female, always together!
> Sadly I am all alone . . .
> To whom can I turn?

O-RYUN 五倫 *See* **Five Relationships**

ORYUN HAENGSIL-TO 五倫行實圖 'Pictures of the Five Relationships in Practice'
A book, published by royal authority, containing 120 stories of notable examples of the **Five Relationships** of Confucianism, published in 1797 (and several times re-issued), with remarkable illustrations thought by some to have been drawn by **Kim Hongdo**. The stories deal with *hyoja* filial children, *ch'ungsin* loyal subjects, *yŏllyŏ* virtuous wives, *hyŏngje* loving brothers, *pungu* faithful friends and *sasaeng* faithful disciples. Only seventeen stories tell of Koreans; the rest are all Chinese, including many of the Twenty-four **Filial Children**. The text is in both Chinese and Korean.

This book had two forerunners: *Samgang haengsil-to*, published in 1434, of which no copy remains, dealing with the first three relationships only; and *Iryun haengsil-to* (1518), on the remaining two relationships, which was based on palace lectures by **Kim An'guk**. These two books were combined and edited to make *Oryun haengsil-to*.

In 1433 a similar work containing only Korean examples was prepared: *Tongguk sinsok Samgang-haengsil*. The history of the text is complex. It was eventually

327

published during the reign of **Prince Kwanghae**, after the wars of the Japanese invasions (**Imjin Wars**).

OSAN SCHOOL *Osan Hakkyo* 五山學校 'Five Hills School'
A **school** founded in 1907 at Chŏngju, North P'yŏngan province, by Yi Sŭnghun (1864–1930), notable as an early school founded entirely by Koreans. Many of its staff and pupils became famous in the independence movement and as poets and writers. Yi Sŭnghun was a local man who became a Presbyterian in 1910 and was arrested and imprisoned after the attempt on the life of Terauchi Masatake, the new Japanese Governor-General, in 1911 (*see* **Hundred and Five, Case of the**). He became a Presbyterian minister and was the leader of Protestant Christians among the 33 men of the 1919 independence demonstration. Retiring to Chŏngju, he died there in 1930.
See also **Independence, Declaration of; Thirty-three Independence Signatories**

ŎŬM
A promissory note. The sum owed or promised is written down the centre of a sheet of paper which is then torn down the middle of the column of characters, so that both debtor and creditor can each keep half. The left-hand piece, kept by the creditor, also bears the debtor's name and signature (*sugyŏl*) or seal.

OX
Before the introduction of Western stock, Korean oxen were of one breed, an ancient yellow ox that was spread across **Manchuria** and North China, rarely much taller than 1·5 metres. Its horns were short and forward-pointed. The colour varied from light yellow-brown through chestnut to a darker brown. Some specimens showed black shading like that of Jersey cattle, and occasional black beasts occurred. Bulls were docile and were used to draw carts without being castrated. Cows did most of the ploughing, especially in flooded paddy-fields. The calf would play on the field, gambolling round its mother as she worked. Ox-fodder, including herbage, was traditionally boiled before being fed to the animals. The colonial government forbade this practice, but many farmers re-introduced it after 1945, an expression of their traditional sympathy for the hard-working beasts.

P

PADUK the pebble game
Korea's most esteemed board game, also called *wigi* or *hyŏkki* (C. *weiqi, yiqi*); sometimes called 'Korean chequers', though it is not of Korean origin and is not a form of chequers or chess. *Go* is its Japanese name. *Paduk* is a highly sophisticated form of noughts-and-crosses, concerned with establishing territory, not with moving pieces. It calls for great skill and is played throughout East Asia, especially by the educated. Today's world-wide organisation of the game centres on Japan. The first Chinese mention is in Eastern Zhou (*Zuo zhuan*, Duke Xiang 25) and Korea has known it since Silla, but the present design of the board was fixed after Tang.

The board (*paduk-p'an*) is square, marked with a squared grid of 19 lines vertically and 19 lines horizontally, giving 361 intersections (*chip* or 'nests'). The traditional Korean board has the lines cut in the top of a small table about 28 cm high. The sides of the table are deep, reaching down to the four stubby feet – a design that creates a sounding chamber for the wire that is strung across the underside of the table and vibrates to a musical note when a pebble is set down on the top.

Each of two players keeps small round pebbles (*tol*), 181 black and 180 white, at his side in a spherical pot with a lid. These pebbles are placed on the *chip* (not in the squares) one at a time by the two players in turn, black being played first and white allotted to the stronger player. Each player attempts to surround areas of the board with continuous lines of pebbles, at the same time preventing the opponent from doing so. Lines of pebbles must be vertical or horizontal (i.e. connected by lines marked on the board), not diagonally across squares. Once a pebble has been put on the board it cannot be moved, unless it is surrounded by opponent's pebbles on all sides, when it is removed from play. A game ends when one player can surround no further territory. The other player is then allowed to continue until no further ground can be gained. When the pebbles that have been removed and the *chip* that have been surrounded by each player are counted, the winner is the one with the larger score.

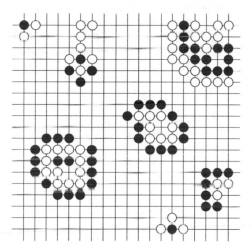

PAEBAENGI-GUT

An entertainment from Hwanghae and south P'yŏngan in which one person performs all the rôles and actions in song and dance. Paebaengi is an only daughter with no brothers, who fails to win the heart of the monk she loves, and dies at the early age of 18 to become a *ttŭn sin* (wandering spirit). The recital begins with her mother's dream during pregnancy, then works through her life, love, death and funeral. It ends with a parody of a *kut* (*see* **shamanism**), held to call up her soul, and a scene in a wineshop.

PAEGILCHANG 白日場 'white sunshine ground'

An outdoor competition, based on the *kwagŏ* **examination** procedure, in which a large number of men write poems on a given theme. The winner is called *changwŏn* and is given prizes. In earlier times he had a banquet. It seems that King **Yejong** held the first *paegilchang* at the *Sŏnggyun-gwan* in 1111. The tradition deteriorated as *paegilchang* were held in smaller communities and ghost-writing became common, but it survives in modernised form as an enjoyable way of fostering literary skills.

PAEGO-IN SAKKŎN 百五人事件 '105 men incident' *See* **Hundred and Five, Case of the**

PAEJAE 培材 DEBATING SOCIETY

Formed by **Sŏ Chaep'il** in 1896, meeting in an American Methodist school in Seoul, *Paejae Haktang*. Its purpose was to hold debates on subjects related to the democratic system and to demonstrate to the State Council the advantages of parliamentary debate and voting. Among those who gained experience of political argument here were **An Ch'angho** and **Yi Sŭngman** (Syngman Rhee). It was closely connected with the **Independence Club**.

PAEKCHA 白磁 *See* ceramics

PAEKCHA-DO/PAEKCHADONG 百子圖 'hundred children pictures'

Pictures of many children at play, often used for **screens** or paired hanging scrolls.

PAEKCHANG / PAEKCHŎNG

Executioners, butchers, grave-diggers, leather-workers, tanners, and wicker-workers were regarded as outcasts in Koryŏ times. Attempts were made to assimilate them to other commoners under the Chosŏn dynasty, treating them as *paekchŏng*, a Koryŏ name for commoners; but the title came to be transferred to those in the outcast trades, who continued to live in segregated hamlets. They were officially relieved of the obligation to wear the *p'aeraengi* (or *pyŏngnyang-nip*) 'butcher's hat' in 1894; but even a century later traces of prejudice against *paekchŏng* ancestry still remain. *See also* **class system**

PAEKCHE 百濟

One of the Three Kingdoms which ruled the peninsula in the period between that of the **Samhan** and the Unified Silla. Its leaders are said to have been descended from one of the tribes of **Puyŏ** who migrated south to the region of modern **Kwangju** and then formed part of the **Mahan** tribal federation.

The process and date of its evolution into a centralised state are obscure, but much credit for this is traditionally given to King Koi (234–86), under whom it rivalled **Koguryŏ**, and soon afterwards it absorbed Daifang commandery (*see* **Chinbŏn**) at approximately the same time as Koguryŏ was conquering **Lelang** (AD 313). King Kŭn Ch'ogo (346–75) is said to have destroyed the remainder of the Mahan tribes and to have killed the Koguryŏ King Kogugwŏn in an attack on P'yŏngyang in 371. He also established contacts with the Southern Chinese dynasty of Eastern Jin and with the **Wa** people in southern Japan. The pattern was thus set for later Paekche history, combining rivalry with its neighbours and culturally and commercially advantageous overseas links to west and south-east. Korean historians believe that both archaeological evidence and written Chinese records show that Wa was a feudal state of Paekche in the 5th-early 6th centuries, ruled by Paekche royalty invested as *tamno* kings (*see* **Muryŏng, King**: *Tamno* was a subsidiary area.).

At its furthest extent Paekche territory stretched from modern Hwanghae province down the western side of the country to the south coast, but it could not long resist pressure from the more belligerent Koguryŏ. Despite paying tribute to the Northern Wei court and seeking its help, King Kaero was killed and his capital evacuated from Hansŏng (modern Kwangju) to **Ungjin** (modern Kongju) in 475. In 538 it was transferred south again, for strategic reasons, to **Sabi** (modern Puyŏ). Thereafter the state was mainly confined to the south-west. 120 years of alliance with **Silla** ended in 553 when the latter seized Paekche territory in the lower **Han River** valley, and in subsequent fighting the great King Sŏng (523–54) was killed.

Koguryŏ and Paekche united against Silla, while both southern kingdoms also tried to invoke support from Japan. When Paekche attacked Silla in 655 the latter called on its suzerain China for help. Both **Sui** and **Tang** China had failed in attempts to exert their dominion over the peninsula by invading Koguryŏ, but now a two-pronged land and naval campaign launched by Silla (its army commanded by General **Kim Yusin**) and Tang was more successful, and in 660 Sabi fell. King Ŭija was sent to China as a prisoner, and an administration was set up to govern Paekche as a Chinese province.

The Paekche court had first adopted **Buddhism** in 384. The new religion flourished and was fostered by good relations with China, especially from the territories of the Southern Dynasties. Buddhism coloured many aspects of Paekche society and culture, rendering it less belligerent than that of Koguryŏ and more sophisticated than that of Silla, and many aspects of Chinese literati culture were imported. Migrants from all three Korean kingdoms crossed the sea to Japan, but teachers from Paekche were most prominent in transmitting religion, arts and crafts.

KINGS:

Onjo	18 BC – AD 28	Asin	392–405
Taru	28–77	Chŏnji	405–420
Kiru	77–128	Kuisin	420–427
Kaeru	128–166	Piyu	427–455
Ch'ogo	166–214	Kaero	455–475
Kusu	214–234	Munju	475–477
Saban	234	Samgŭn	477–479
Koi	234–286	Tongsŏng	479–501
Ch'aekkye	286–298	Muryŏng	501–523
Punsŏ	298–304	Sŏng	523–554
Piryu	304–344	Widŏk	554–598
Kye	344–346	Hye	598–599
Kŭn Ch'ogo	346–375	Pŏp	599–600
Kŭngusu	375–384	Mu	600–641
Ch'imnyu	384–385	Ŭija	641–660
Chinsa	385–392		

JONATHAN BEST, 'Diplomatic and Cultural Contacts between Paekche and China,' *HJAS*, 42: 1982; JONATHAN BEST, 'Tales of Three Paekche Monks Who Travelled Afar in Search of the Law,' *HJAS*, 51: 1991; HONG WONTAEK, *Paekche of Korea and the Origins of Yamato Japan*, Seoul: Kudara International, 1994; HWANG SU-YOUNG, 'Paekche Remains in Iksan,' *KJ*, 30/11, 1990

PAEKCHE, LATER *See* **Three Kingdoms, Later**

PAEKCHONGIL / PAEKCHUNGIL 百種日 'hundred seeds day' or 'mid-century day'
A summer festival on the 15th of the 7th moon when outdoor parties were held with singing and **wrestling**. In origin it was almost certainly a harvest festival, though in Koryŏ it was called *uranbun-je* and was a Buddhist commemoration.

PAEKPAEK-KYO 白白教 'white, white teaching'
Paekpaek-kyo was a **new religion** descended eventually from the **Tonghak** movement. In 1912 Chŏn Chŏngun set up *Paekto-gyo*, 'the doctrine of the white way', at Kŭmhwa. After his death in 1919 the group divided and in 1923 Ch'a Pyŏnggan set up

Paekpaek-kyo at Kap'yŏng, Kyŏnggi province, teaching a mixture of Confucian, Buddhist and Daoist ideas. The cult became increasingly corrupt. Devotees were defrauded of their property and women were sexually abused. The discovery of female bodies buried under one of the buildings led to the suicide of the leader, Chŏn Haeryong, in 1937 and the execution of 14 other officials in 1940, when *Paekpaek-kyo* had ceased to exist.

PAEKP'AL PŎNNOE 百八煩惱 '108 Passions and Delusions'
A Buddhist category also described as the 108 karmaic bonds (*kyŏrŏp*), used by **Ch'oe Namsŏn** as the title of the first collection of modern *sijo*, written by him in 1926. The number of 4×3^3 is variously explained. It is the number of beads in the Buddhist **rosary**, the number for tolling the **bell** in a monastery at dawn and dusk, and the number of *chon*, 'honourable ones', in the Vajradhatu 'spiritual realm of perfect enlightenment'.

PAEKSU-PAEKPOK 百壽百福
Writing the Chinese characters *su* 'long life' and *pok* 'blessings' in many different styles of **calligraphy**; done in ink on paper scrolls and **screens**, but also in embroidery for screens. If two panels are made the left-hand one is *su*, the right-hand one *pok*. Larger screens may show different arrangements, in which the two characters alternate or mingle in other ways.

PAEKTU-SAN 百頭山 'White headed mountain'
Korea's highest peak (2,750 metres), a volcano situated in the Changbaek ('Always white') mountain range on the present Korean-Chinese border in North Hamgyŏng province; the source of both **Yalu** and **Tumen** Rivers. Its eruption in the first half of the 11th century, when it was situated in **Jurchen** territory, may have been the largest ever volcanic explosion in the northern hemisphere and may have contributed to the climatic changes that affected north-east Asia at that time. The mountain was reputed to have outstanding *p'ungsu* properties and is associated with the **foundation myth** of **Tang'un**, the rise of **Wang Kŏn**, and in modern times the quasi-divine powers of **Kim Ilsŏng**. In 1712 a stone monument was erected at its base marking the boundary between Korea and China.

PAGODA *t'ap* 塔
Form of monument designed as a repository for Buddhist relics or sacred texts, often sited in temple courtyards. The first examples date from the 6th century, and by Unified Silla pagodas had become an advanced form of architectural and sculptural art. Conceptually, they represent the cosmos in architectural form. They were built of granite, wood, brick, stone or metal, and consisted of two or three storeys or, in later periods, as many as ten. Silla pagodas were generally square, in imitation of the larger Chinese buildings on which they were modelled. Later styles had as many as eight faces on some of the storeys, on which were carved *apsaras*, **Buddhas**, animals of the **zodiac**, guardian deities and other auspicious figures. The complementary pair of pagodas at **Pulguk-sa** in **Kyŏngju** are judged to be among the finest examples of Silla artistry (*see Tabot'ap*), while the ten-storeyed 15th-century marble pagoda in **Pagoda Park**, Seoul, is one of the most elaborately decorated.
HWANG SU-YOUNG, 'The Pagoda as an Art Form and Object of Faith in the Three Kingdoms Period,' *KJ*, 6/4, 1966
See also sarira **containers**; **stupa**

PAGODA PARK *T'apkol kongwŏn*
Public park on Chongno, central Seoul, developed in 1898 as part of Emperor **Kojong**'s programme of urban revival, on the site of Wŏn'guk-su, a temple originally built by King **Sejo** but destroyed by Prince **Yŏnsan** in 1504. The ten-storey marble **pagoda**, on a three-tiered base, dates from 1467 and was built in imitation of one of the most beautiful in Korea, the 14th-century Koryŏ pagoda at Kyŏngch'ŏn-sa. It was here that the **Declaration of Independence**, previously signed by thirty-three representatives of *Ch'ŏndo-gyo*, Christian and Buddhist organisations, was read aloud to a large crowd at 2 p.m. on 1st March 1919 (*see also* **March First Movement**).
See also **Brown, McLeavey; thirty-three independence signatories**

PAINTING
Earliest surviving examples of painting in Korea are found on the walls of **tombs** from the kingdoms of **Koguryŏ** and **Paekche** and the Chinese commandery of **Lelang**. They date from the 4th century AD and include scenes of ceremonial occasions, entertainments and portraits, as well as religious motifs and elements belonging both to **Buddhism** and to animistic belief systems (*see* **Four Spirits**). Artists painted in imitation of Chinese subjects and styles, as they would continue to do until the 20th century, but not exclusively and not without achieving high standards of their own. From the Unified Silla dynasty comes a unique painting of a flying horse on a saddle guard (*see* *Ch'ŏnma-ch'ong*). In the Koryŏ period the work of Korean painters was much appreciated and collected in Japan, especially in temples. Surviving examples which have long been believed to be Japanese in origin are now being re-attributed to immigrant Korean artists. Buddhist paintings are known as *t'aenghwa*, a term that embraces elaborate mural decorations, hanging scrolls both large and small, and handscroll illumination. Some fine illustrations of Buddhist **sutras** in gold and silver on blue paper dating from this period were preserved in Japanese and Korean temples.
   In early Chosŏn, painters were strongly influenced by Chinese precedents, and their work reflects both the Northern (or Zhe) and Southern (or Wu) Schools, representing the [Chinese] Academy and literati traditions respectively. Aesthetic purists valued painting in ink more highly than with colour, stressing the affinity of such work, especially bamboo subjects, with the 'senior' art of **calligraphy**, and likening the dualism to that of the pure and ethereal (*yin*) and the complex and worldly (*yang*), or to the moon and the sun. In keeping with Chinese attitudes, the literati rated the self-expressive potential of calligraphy, bamboo and **landscape** painting more highly than the representational priorities of **flower and bird**, human and even religious subjects, Buddhism no longer being so widely accepted among the literati. The true spirit of the universe flowed through the scholar's brush onto silk or paper, while **craftsmen** were employed to carry out the more mundane tasks of decorating screens or walls.
   After the **Imjin Wars** doubt arose about the need for exclusive imitation of the Chinese (*see* *Sirhak* movement), and the great artist **Chŏng Sŏn** developed his own Korean landscape style. Others followed his example. **Kim Hongdo** and **Sin Yunbok** excelled at portraying characteristics of Korean people and society (*see* **genre painting**). By the early 20th century Korean painters were subject to western as well as Chinese artistic influence. The first self-portrait in oils was painted by **Ko Hŭidong**, completed after he had entered the Tokyo Art School in 1909,[1] and the first nude by an alumnus of the same institution, Kim Kwanho (1854–1923).[2] During the colonial period the Japanese encouraged Koreans to study subjects deemed to be politically harmless at art schools in Japan, such as landscape and flowers and birds, or modern western styles such as cubism. Nevertheless painters such as **Kim Hwan'gi** and **Yi**

Chungsŏp used their art to express powerful feelings of resentment at their national humiliation. Like religion, art has involved itself in and been used as a vehicle in pursuit of political aims in the 20th century. During the colonial period both independent nationalists and the Japanese authorities organised national exhibitions (*Hyŏpchŏn*, *Sŏnjŏn*), and these were resumed by the new government in South Korea following liberation (**Kukchŏn**). In North Korea, the communist régime has encouraged art in the socialist realist vein as a means of political propaganda. Anguish at the suffering caused by the **Korean War** was commonplace in South Korean paintings of the 1950s and 1960s, but subsequent artists have cast off many of their restraints and have experimented both with the avant garde as well as with the properties of traditional Korean materials such as mulberry paper.

Many painters and calligraphers signed their work with brush-names (*ho*) in preference to their given names, and are commonly known by them today. In entries devoted to individual artists in this Dictionary, brush-names are shown in brackets after given names.

(1)(2) YOUNG ICK LEW, ed., *Korean Art Tradition*, Seoul: Korea Foundation, 1993 KWON YOUNG-PIL, 'Ancient Korean Art and Central Asia: Non-Buddhist Art Prior to the Tenth Century,' *KJ*, 31/2, 1991; LEE KYUNG-SUNG, 'The Modern Art Movement in Korea,' *AOA*, 11/4, 1981; PAIK SYEUNG-GIL, *Modern Korean Painting*, Seoul: Korean National Commission for UNESCO, 1971; KEITH PRATT, *Korean Painting*, Hong Kong: Oxford University Press, 1995; D. SECKEL, 'Some Characteristics of Korean Art: ii, Preliminary Remarks on Yi Dynasty Painting,' *OA*, XXVI/1, 1975; H. H. SØRENSEN, *The Iconography of Korean Buddhist Painting*, Leiden: E.J.Brill, 1989
See also **Names, personal**; **portraiture**; *Tohwa-sŏ*

PAK CHEGA 朴齊家 (1750–1815)
Calligrapher in the cursive and semi-cursive style, and since he was a *Pukhak* enthusiast his painting shows signs of western influence. He became tutor to **Kim Chŏnghŭi**, but although he was sent with a mission to Beijing in 1790 his official career was hampered by his illegitimacy.
KIM YONG-DOK, 'The Life and Thought of Pak Che-ga,' *KJ*, 12/7, 1972

PAK CHIWON 朴趾源 *See Yŏrha Ilgi*

PAK CHŎNGHŬI 朴正熙 (1917–79)
Pak Chŏnghŭi (Park Chung Hee), president of the **Republic of Korea** (ROK) from 1962 until his assassination in 1979, was born in North Kyŏngsang province in 1917, the son of a poor farmer. After study at Taegu Normal School, he became a primary school teacher in 1937. Soon afterwards he moved to the Japanese puppet state of Manzhouguo and enrolled in its Military Academy. Later he also attended the Japanese Military Academy, graduating as a second lieutenant in 1944. At the end of the Pacific War he returned to Korea, completed a short course at the US-established Military Academy, and became a captain in the newly-organised Korean Constabulary in 1946.

Following the outbreak of the **Korean War** in 1950, Pak joined the new ROK army. By 1953 he was a brigadier general, and he became a major general in 1958 after studying at the War College. In 1960 he was engaged in planning a coup. Along with other officers of his generation he was concerned at the growing corruption of the Syngman Rhee (**Yi Sŭngman**) régime, but there were also complaints about military corruption and the paucity of promotions. The 1960 plans were put on hold following the **April 19th student uprising** and the overthrow of Rhee. However, in May 1961, the plotters re-launched their plan and seized power. Although President **Yun Posŏn** was unhappy about the coup, he remained in office long enough to give it the appearance of legality. Having seized power, Pak banned all political activity and purged allegedly corrupt politicians and businessmen. Yun resigned in 1962 and Pak, hitherto the chairman of the Supreme Council for National Reconstruction, became acting president. He retired from the army in 1963 as a lieutenant general, and was elected president of the **Third Republic**.

He was re-elected president in 1967, 1971, 1972 and 1978. Despite later claims, there is no evidence that he had a particular plan for his country when he seized power. Once in power, and after a few false starts, he set out to develop a strong economy for protection against the North. For this purpose he began a series of five year plans, and by the mid-1970s was well on the way to transforming South Korea, which had been one of the world's poorest economies in 1961, into a leading developing country.

This was not achieved without cost. Pak emphasized the 'threat from the North' to justify restrictions on labour rights and civil liberties. He worked hard to ensure US support for South Korea, sending ROK units to the Vietnam War. Following the opening of contacts between the US and China in the early 1970s, he began a limited opening with the North, while remaining staunchly anti-communist. The North-South dialogue, however, ultimately petered out with little benefit to either side. The alleged danger which such contacts posed to South Korea was used to justify the introduction of a new and more restrictive constitution, the *Yusin* **Constitution**, in 1972, designed to allow Pak to remain president as long as he wished.

After 1972 he grew steadily more aloof and suspicious, especially after the assassination of his wife in 1974. At the same time, the 1970s witnessed a steady increase in authoritarianism. Anti-government demonstrations also increased, as did the use of draconian measures to suppress them. Faced with widespread protests in the summer of 1979, the government reacted by expelling the opposition leader **Kim Yŏngsam** from the National Assembly and declaring martial law in the southern city of **Pusan**. There then followed a split between those who favoured a compromise, such as the head of the **Korean Central Intelligence Agency** (KCIA), Kim Chaegyu, and others, including Pak himself, who preferred continued repression. While this was in progress, Pak accepted an invitation to dinner at a KCIA restaurant on 26 October 1979. A quarrel developed and Kim Chaegyu shot and killed the president, thus setting in motion the events which brought General **Chŏn Tuhwan** (Chun Doo Hwan) to power.

Pak was widely seen as personally incorruptible, and many believed that, for all his authoritarian ways, he acted with the best interests of the country at heart. But while there can be no doubt that real economic gains were made between 1961 and 1979, it was at considerable cost: Pak's political legacy was much more dubious, and had a continued influence on South Korean politics long after his death.

C.I. EUGENE KIM, 'Korea at the Crossroads: the Birth of the Fourth Republic,' *PA* 46, 1973; PARK CHUNG HEE, *The Country, the Revolution and I*, Seoul: Hollym Corporation, 2nd ed., 1970; PARK CHUNG HEE, *Korea Reborn, a Model for Development*, Englewood Cliffs, New Jersey: Prentice-Hall Inc., 1979; SOHN HAK-KYU, *Authoritarianism and Opposition in South Korea*, London & New York: Routledge, 1991; WOO JUNG EN, *Race to the Swift: State and Finance in Korean Industrialisation*, New York: Columbia University Press, 1991; NAM KOON WOO, *South Korean Politics: The Search for Political Consensus and Stability*, New York & London: University Presses of America, 1989

See also **Korea-Japan Treaty**; *Saemaŭl Undong*

PAK HŎNYŎNG 朴憲永 (d. 1955)
One of the founders of the **Korean Communist Party** in Seoul in April 1925 after a period of training at university in Russia. During the troubled early years of the Party he was arrested in April 1928. His later career was marked by radical nationalism. He took part in collaboration with the Chinese communists over wartime resistance to the Japanese, and became chairman of **Yŏ Unhyŏng**'s Workers' Party. As leader of the more extreme communist movement in southern Korea he reorganised the Korean Communist Party there in September 1945, but fled to the north in October 1946 when General **Hodge** tried to suppress it. In July 1946 Stalin met both Pak and **Kim Ilsŏng** in Moscow to determine which of them should receive his mandate as Korean leader. Kim won, but on the formation of the People's Assembly in North Korea in 1948 Pak was elected vice-premier and foreign minister. When the two leaders again met Stalin in April 1950 to debate the invasion of the south, Pak spoke of the readiness of people there to rise up in support of the communists. Kim, however, perceived Pak's potential support in the south as a threat and had him executed at the end of the **Korean War**.

PAK HYŎKKŎSE 朴赫居世 *See* **foundation myths**

PAK ILLO 朴仁老 (Nogye, 1561–1643)
His brush name means 'Rushy Valley'. He was a military commander during the Hideyoshi invasions, but after 1605 went into retirement, where he wrote *sijo* and *kasa* that show his Confucian doctrine, his devotion to frugal living and his love of the countryside.
PETER H. LEE, 'The *Kasa* Poems of Pak In-no', *OE*, X, 1963

PAK SECH'AE 朴世采 (Namgye, 1631–95)
A Seoul man (brush name 'South Valley') who created an impression when he entered the *Sŏnggyun-gwan* at 18 and attacked those who opposed the canonisation of **Yi I** and **Sŏng Hon**. He was taught by Kim Sanghŏn (1570–1652) and much influenced by **Song Siyŏl**, devoting himself to the study of neo-Confucian philosophy. In 1659 he sided with the victorious Western **faction** over the **Dowager Queen Changnyŏl's mourning rites**. From 1674 to 1680 his faction was out of power; then in 1683 when the Westerners split into the Noron and Soron factions, he became leader of the Soron. Though much involved in factional politics, he did his best to calm the strife. He wrote in many fields of Confucianism, but was most deeply interested in **ritual studies**. He was canonised in 1764.

PAK SŎBO 朴棲甫 (b. 1931)
Graduated from Hong Ik University, Seoul, in 1954. Like **Hwang Yŏngyŏp**, Pak was initially moved to express his personal experience of war and suffering through his art. Inspired by trends in Western painting, he became a leading artist in the *Art Informel* movement of the late 1950s, and his participation in international events from 1957, when he exhibited in New York, into the 1960s hastened the modernisation of Korean art. Paradoxically, however, it was his exploration of concepts and materials within the East Asian philosophic and artistic tradition through the 1980s and 1990s that produced his most significant work. Showing the strong influence of the Confucian literati and Daoist naturalist heritage, his calligraphic *Ecriture* series[1] investigated the special qualities of traditional Korean **paper**, *Hanji*. The results were abstract compositions showing distinctive properties of line, texture and colour that blend the traditions of Western and Eastern art.

(1) YOUNG ICK LEW, ed., *Korean Art Tradition*, Seoul: Korea Foundation, 1993
TATE GALLERY, *Working with Nature: Traditional Thought in Contemporary Art from Korea*, Liverpool, n.d. (c. 1992)

PAK T'ONGSA ŎNHAE 朴通事 'Korean version of Interpreter Pak'
A translation of a textbook of Chinese language, first published by Ch'oe Sejin, but re-edited by Kwŏn T'aewŏn and Pak Sehwa in 1677.

PAK YŎL 朴烈 (b. 1902)
Born at Mun'gyŏng in North Kyŏngsang province, originally named Pak Chunsik. At fifteen he went to school in Seoul, but was dismissed on suspicion of nationalist activities and went to Japan in 1919. There he became an anarchist and founded the secret Black Wave Society, *Hŭkto-hoe*, and met Kaneko Fumiko (1902–26), another anarchist, daughter of a businessman who had been brought up in Kimch'ŏn. They planned to assassinate Emperor Hirohito, but the plot was discovered and they were both imprisoned for life. They married in prison, where Kaneko committed suicide in 1926. Pak was released in 1945 and returned to Korea in 1948, still politically active, but was taken to North Korea in 1950.

PAK YŎN 朴燕 (1378–1458)
Musical reformer under King **Sejong**. In 1426, as a 5th **grade** junior official in the Pongsang-si (*see* **Government organs**), he was commissioned to make new sets of stone chimes (*p'yŏn'gyŏng*), tune them and the rest of the orchestra to pitches in accordance with imported Chinese chimes, and to try to restore pure Chinese **music** for ritual use (*see aak*). He worked on the new recensions with his superior, **Chŏng Inji**, and based them on Chinese tunes by the Song scholar **Zhu Xi** and the Yuan musicologist Lin Yu. The results, though certainly not a genuine revival of ancient Chinese tunes, were found acceptable when the first performance was given in 1433, and Pak was promoted. His desire to purify ritual and ceremonial music became obsessive, and over the last thirty years of his life the *Sejong sillok* records more than forty proposals from him, many of them to do with the manufacture and use of **musical instruments** and all but a few approved by the king. In keeping with the strongly Confucian ethos of the court he memorialised against the use of girls as dancers at banqueting rites. He had more boy dancers recruited and new costumes designed for them. Most important of all, he continued to work on the compilation of purified ceremonial music, including new versions of *Yŏmillak* and *Pot'aep'yŏng* ('Protecting the peace'), a song lauding the dynastic ancestors, and he assisted in the creation of the song cycle *Yongbi-ŏch'ŏn-ga* ('Song of Dragons Flying in Heaven'), published in 1447. In 1445 Pak held the 2nd grade senior post of Senior Magistrate in the provincial administration, and his career continued to prosper until 1453, when his son Kyeu's involvement in the succession crisis (*see* **Tanjong, King**) led to his dismissal. Many of his reforms were undone as 'modernists' reasserted the priorities of contemporary taste over the deliberate archaism of his style, but his reputation improved again in the 18th century, and his writings were published in 1822.
See also Akhak kwebŏm

PAK YŎNGHYO 朴泳孝 (1861–1939)
A progressive *yangban* who promoted the cause of modernisation and reform in the late 1870s and headed the post-*Imo* **Incident** restitution mission to Japan in 1882 with **Kim Okkyun** and Sŏ Kwangbŏm; a member of the *Kaehwadang* (*see* **Independence**

337

Party) and an adviser to King **Kojong**. He escaped to Japan after the *Kapsin* **coup** in 1884 and visited the United States, but continued to press King Kojong for reforms, and was called back to Korea to assist **Kim Hongjip** in leading the new Kabo cabinet, as Home Minister, in December 1894. Once again his success was short lived: accused by the pro-Russian faction of plotting against **Queen Min**, he fled back to Japan before her murder in 1895. During the **Protectorate** he served in **Yi Wanyong**'s cabinet, and was made a marquis by the Japanese in 1910. Pak was a Korean director of the Chōsen Industrial Bank from 1918 to 1930. In 1919 he became president of the Kyŏngsŏng Spinning and Weaving Company (*Kyŏngbang*), the first major example of Korean industrial capitalism.

LEW YOUNG-ICK, 'The Reform Efforts and Ideas of Pak Yŏng-hyo, 1894–5,' *KS*, 1, 1977

PAKSU

Paksu, male *mudang*, have been very rare indeed, at least since Chosŏn times, and perhaps no longer exist. Like the *mudang* they were of the lowest social class. Their activities appear to have been indistinguishable from those of *mudang*, except that they wore women's clothing as *mudang* wore men's clothing. There have been suggestions of sexual inversion in some cases.

See also p'ansu; **shamanism**

PALACE DIALECT *kungjung-ŏ* 宮中語

The language spoken within royal palaces of Chosŏn was distinctive, with special and partly archaic honorifics. Royal meals, for instance, were *sura*, the midday meal *nassura*, socks *chokkŏn*. Members of the royal family were addressed with the honorific *mama*, as in *Sanggam-mama* 'highest one' for the king, *Tonggung-mama* 'eastern palace' for the crown prince, and *Chungjŏn-mama* 'central palace' for the queen. Some words were euphemisms, such as *maehwa* 'apricot-blossoms' for the contents of the chamber-pot.

PALACE LITERATURE *kungjŏng-munhak* 宮殿文學

Three works, **Hanjung-nok**, **Kyech'ug-ilgi**, and **Inhyŏn Wanghu-jŏn** are often classified together as 'palace literature'. All they have in common is their subject matter: dramatic and historic events within the royal palace, which of necessity set **women** in leading rôles. *Hanjung-nok* is a memoir, possibly autobiographical; *Kyech'ug-ilgi* may be an eye-witness record, but is naïvely, even obscurely, written; *Inhyŏn Wanghu-jŏn* is an elegant and well crafted narrative, probably written by a man. All three show relatively little interest in the politics behind the events they describe.

PALACES, ROYAL *See* **Ch'angdŏk Palace**; **Kyŏngbok Palace**; **Mulberry Palace**; **Tŏksu Palace**; **Unhyŏn Palace**

PETER BARTHOLOMEW, 'Chosŏn Dynasty Royal Compounds – Windows to a Lost Culture,' *TRASKB*, LXVIII, 1993; YOUL HWA DANG EDITORIAL DEPARTMENT, *Ancient Korean Palaces*, Seoul: Youl Hwa Dang Publishing Co., 1988; MICHAEL WICKMAN, 'The Palaces of Seoul,' *AOA*, 11/4, 1981

PALAEOLITHIC PERIOD, THE

Relatively few sites have been discovered on the Korean peninsula. Among those that have, dates of strata have been estimated at between 400,000 and 20,000 years old. They include Sangwŏn (South P'yŏngan province), which may be the oldest, Turubong (North Ch'ungch'ŏng province), Sŏkchang-ni (South Ch'ungch'ŏng province), Kulp'o (North Hamgyŏng province), and Chŏn'gok (Kyŏnggi province). An excavated dwelling site from Sŏkchang-ni shows evidence of human habitation including a hearth and post holes, but no human bones have been found. Stone hand-axes have been found at Chŏn'gok. Representations in rock art appear to be of deer and reindeer, and subsistence apparently depended on hunting, fishing, and supplies of uncultivated fruit. Kitchen tools have been found at Turu-bong, and bone sculpted figures include human faces, animals, birds, and fish.

LEE YUNG-JO, 'Paleolithic and Mesolithic Cultures in Korea: An Overview,' *KJ*, 22/3, 1982; LEE YUNG-JO, 'Progress Report on the Paleolithic Culture of Turubong No. 2 Cave at Ch'ŏngwŏn,' *KJ*, 23/8, 1983; SARAH NELSON, *The Archaeology of Korea*, Cambridge University Press, 1993; POW-KEY SOHN, 'Paleolithic Culture of Korea,' *KJ*, 14/4, 1974

PALKWAE 八卦 *See* **Trigrams**

PANGSAENG 放生 'releasing living creatures'

A Buddhist custom of setting free birds, fish and other animals that have been caught by others and offered for sale. Groups called *palsaenggye* arrange for *palsaenghoe* ceremonies, at which very large crowds may gather, usually in secluded places on the 3rd day of the 3rd moon or the 15th of the 8th, though other dates may be chosen.

PANGSANG-SSI 方相氏

A grotesquely masked exorcist dressed in red and black who appeared in a small wheel-chair drawn by another man, at royal processions and funerals in Chosŏn times. He wore a huge circular mask surrounded by a fringe of bearskin and carried a spear and shield. The mask had four golden eyes. The details were all copied from the Chinese classic *Zhouli*.

PAN'GUDAE 盤龜台 *See* **Rock art**

PAN'GYE SUROK 磻溪隨錄 'Essays of Panqi'

Pan'gye (C. Panqi), name of the secluded valley where the legendary councillor Jiang Taigong was fishing when he was discovered by King Wen of Zhou, was adopted by Yu Hyŏngwŏn (1622–73), who declined to accept public office and spent his life among farmers near Puan in north Chŏlla. At the age of 48 he finished his *surok*, which dealt with land distribution, tax and management; education and the state **examinations**; government appointments and salaries; **military service**; language, ritual, and custom. He was a precursor of *sirhak*, fiercely critical of the current state of affairs, envisioning an independent agricultural system, which required vigorous fiscal reform. His work was not printed until 1700 and remained little known until the 20th century.

PANJŎL 反切 (C. *fanqie*) 'cutting, turning'

A method of showing the pronunciation of Chinese characters, probably conceived during the **Han dynasty** and regularised in the Chinese Three Kingdoms period. Two characters whose pronunciation is presumed to be common knowledge are used, one having the same initial consonant as the character being described, and the other the same rhyme (vowel and final consonant, if there is one, and tone). *Fanqie* for one historical period may not be correct for another, and a Chinese *fanqie* may not be accurate for Sino-Korean.

Panjŏl was sometimes used as a name for *han'gŭl* after 1500, occurring, for instance, in *Hunmong chahoe* (1527) and *Oju-yŏnmun changjŏn-san'go* (19th century) and in *Panjŏl ponmun*.

PANJŎL PONMUN 反切本文

A syllabary using the *fanqie* (K. *panjŏl*) method (or using *panjŏl* as a name for the Korean alphabet), formerly used for teaching the alphabet to children: *Ka, gya, gŏ, gyŏ, go, gyo, gu, gyu, gŭ, gi, gă*. This string of vowels is repeated with each initial letter of the alphabet in order as far as *hu, hyu, hŭ, hi, ha*. Then *kwa, gwŏ, nwa, nwŏ* . . . is added as far as *p'wa, p'wŏ, hwa, hwŏ*; and finally *kak, gan, gal, gam, gap, gat, gang* and *gae*.
See also **Language, the Korean**

PAPER

Was probably introduced to Korea through the Chinese **commandery** in **Lelang** and manufactured during the Three Kingdoms period. The high level of literary sophistication by the Unified Silla period (*see* **books**; **calligraphy**) and the fact that **Tang dynasty** China admired and imported Korean ink implies that paper quality must also have been highly prized then. High quality paper was made from mulberry trees (*tak*) and exported to China during the Koryŏ dynasty. It was still requested as a tributary product in the Chosŏn dynasty, so that King **Sejong** encouraged production from a greater variety of plant materials, including **bamboo**. Within Korea, paper was a local **tribute** (*kong*) item during the Koryŏ and early Chosŏn periods. Government requirements were supervised by the *Chŏnjŏ-ch'ang* (*see* **Government, central**); official workshops were situated in the capital and at five provincial centres in Kyŏngsang, Chŏlla, Ch'ungch'ŏng, Hwanghae, and Kangwŏn.

Everyday uses for paper included window, floor- (*see ondol*) and lantern-coverings, **screens**, umbrellas, **kites**, and **fans**. **Armour** might be made of multiple layers of compressed paper.
See also **printing**

PARHAE 渤海

Manchurian kingdom founded in 698 by the **Malgal** General Tae Ch'oyŏng. He gathered together remnants of the population of **Koguryŏ** defeated by the Silla-Tang alliance in 668 and established his kingdom on the southern side of Taebaek-san (modern Changbaishan, Jilin province, China). Its first capital was near present-day Tunhua, but through the 8th century five larger cities were built along Chinese lines to succeed it. In 794 the Supreme Capital (Shangjing) was permanently established on the fertile plain of the Hurkha River. The boundary between Parhae and Korea followed the course of the Yunghŭng and **Taedong** Rivers, from the vicinity of modern Wŏnsan in the east to that of P'yŏngyang in the west. Parhae pursued a strong foreign policy acknowledging China as its suzerain but not shrinking from independent, even hostile action on occasions. Trade and diplomacy was skilfully pursued with China, Silla and Japan. In letters to the Japanese emperors, the kings of Parhae refer to themselves as heirs and successors of the kings of Koguryŏ. The height of their power was reached in the 9th century under King Tae Insu. His territory extended across the whole of **Manchuria**, and the threat it posed to Silla was lamented by the courtier **Ch'oe Ch'iwŏn**. Silla may have claimed to have united the country, but its northern neighbours were substantially Korean too, and Parhae-Silla coexistence is sometimes referred to as the period of North-South division (*Nambuk sidae*).

The end came unexpectedly quickly, when the kingdom was swept away by the Mongolian **Khitan** in 926. Soon afterwards Silla too fell, to the founders of the Koryŏ dynasty, who saw themselves as the new heirs of Koguryŏ and incorporated the southern provinces of Parhae into their kingdom. Many Malgal refugees fled south from the Khitan into Korea.

Literary evidence for Parhae culture is sparse, but archaeological material reveals an advanced civilisation in a mixed Korean-Chinese tradition. Its system of five capitals was imitated by the Khitan and **Jurchen** rulers of Manchuria.

KINGS:
[The titles of all the kings of Parhae are not known. The following list therefore supplements them with personal names.]

Kings	Ko	Tae Ch'oyŏng	698–719
	Mu	Tae Muye	719–737
	Mun	Tae Hŭmmu	737–793
	P'ye	Tae Wŏnŭi	793
	Sŏng	Tae Hwayŏ	793–4
	Kang	Tae Sungnin	794–809
	Chŏng	Tae Wŏnyu	809–812
	Hŭi	Tae Ŏnŭi	812–818
	Kan	Tae Myŏngch'ung	818
	Sŏn	Tae Insu	818–830
	?	Tae Ijin	830–857
	?	Tae Kŏnhwang	857–? 871
	?	Tae Hyŏnsŏk	? 871–? 894
	?	Tae Wihae	? 894 –? 907
	?	Tae Insŏn	? 907–926

NORBERT ADAMI, *Bibliography on Parhae: A Mediaeval State in the Far East*, Wiesbaden, 1994; E.H.HENDERSON, 'Some Notes on Parhae,' *TRBRAS*, XXXVIII, 1961; JOHANNES RECKEL, *Bohai – Geschichte und Kultur eines mandschurisch-koreanischen Königreiches der Tang-Zeit*, Wiesbaden: Aetas Manjurica 5, 1995; SONG KI-HO, 'Several Questions in Studies of the History of Palhae,' *KJ*, 30/6, 1990

PARIS PEACE CONFERENCE (1919)
Was attended in May 1919 by a delegation from the Korean Provisional Government (KPG) in Shanghai (*see* **Provisional Government in Exile**), headed by Foreign Minister **Kim Kyusik**. Korean hopes of independence had been raised by President Wilson's Fourteen Points, but were dashed when the delegation was not officially recognised, only two months after the **Declaration of Independence** in Seoul. Three months later, however, the International Socialist Party Congress in Switzerland heard a speech from another KPG representative from Shanghai and passed a resolution calling for Korean independence.

PATTERNS, ALL-OVER SURFACE
Most of the all-over surface patterns traditionally used for **furniture**, decorative painting, embossed yellow book-cover **paper**, **textiles**, embroidery, **ceramics**, mother-of-pearl inlay in **lacquer** and other crafts are also found in China, but they represent Korean taste. Though their history has been little studied, few of them can be traced before the Chosŏn period.

Wancha-mun, 'swastika pattern' (i), showing structure (at top) and two treatments.

Wancha-mun, 'swastika pattern' (i)

Wancha-mun, 'swastika pattern' (ii)

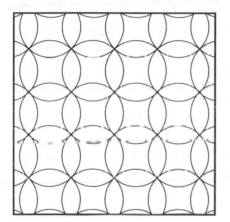

Sabanwŏn-mun, 'quartered circles'

Ŏrŭm-mun, 'ice pattern'

Tangch'o-mun, 'Chinese plant pattern'

Wancha-mun, '**swastika** pattern': Many patterns made of straight lines are based on regularly spaced swastikas. In one common form (ii) rows of swastikas, alternately clockwise and anti-clockwise (the direction has no religious significance) are each connected to four others by four additional arms. The interstices appear as double crosses. Another classic pattern (i), sometimes called 'weaving pattern', uses swastikas as the essential link in large interlocking H-forms, usually set diagonally.

Noe-mun, 'thunder patterns', or *pŏn'gae-mun*, 'lightning patterns', are classic scrolls akin to 'Greek key' or 'Greek fret' and are almost universal. They are essentially frieze or border patterns, but can be adapted as all-over diapering. In Korea they are often used on rush-mats, bamboo blinds, pottery, furniture and inlaid lacquer.

Sŏksoe-mun, 'grid-iron', is a graticulation with oblong interstices. A square grid is called *chŏngcha*, from the Chinese character for a well (two pairs of parallel lines crossed to make a central square). These grids and *pyŏktol-mun*, 'brickwork' (bicolour oblong check), are probably very recent introductions. A square check is called *padukp'an*, '*paduk*-board'.

Sabanwŏn-mun, 'quartered circles', is composed of rows of circles, both vertically and horizontally symmetrical, in which each circle is overlapped by four others to create crossing horizontal and vertical rows of lentoid motifs. It can be found on old book-covers.

Kwigam-mun, 'tortoise-shell', appeared first on very early Chinese **bronzes** and appears on Korean book-cover papers in the 16th century. It is a hexagonal honeycomb pattern, often used in mother-of-pearl inlay. An asterisk or other motif may be drawn in each hexagon.

Pinŭl-mun, 'fish-scale pattern', may also be relatively recent. Equidistant lines are drawn horizontally and in both directions diagonally, producing an all-over pattern of triangles. The inverted triangles are coloured with one hue and the others with a second hue.

Nŭnghwa-mun, 'diapered flowers', has the surface covered by diagonal lines or groups of parallel lines, making a diaper of lozenges. Each lozenge contains *nŭnghwa*, a water-chestnut flower of four lentoid petals, such as is used to decorate the folded edge of a printed page. The *nŭnghwa* may be replaced by swastikas, or the two motifs may be alternated row by row horizontally. *Nŭnghwa* motifs also occur in 8- and 12-petalled forms, the petals growing thinner as their number increases, and are used with a variety of backgrounds, some of which date from the 15th century.

Ŏrŭm-mun, 'ice pattern', was possibly derived from underglaze crazing in ceramics, though it is much used in plaster on walls in royal palace grounds and on *pojagi*. The surface is covered with lines that break it into exaggeratedly irregular polygonal shapes like cracked sheet-ice. All the lines may be straight or some may be curved. Other motifs may be superimposed.

Sŏsŏl-mun, 'auspicious snow patterns', appear on book-covers of the 15th to 18th centuries. They make use of six-pointed motifs or groups of six dots, usually on a ground of irregular broken flowing lines. (Koreans were aware of the hexagonal structure of snowflake at least from the 12th century. It is clearly visible to the naked eye in the dry winter atmosphere.)

Kurŭm-mun or *un-mun*, 'cloud pattern', is known from Koryŏ ceramics: regularly repeated small clouds, usually three-topped cumuli with wispy tails.

Other motifs may be superimposed on most all-over patterns, favourites being **phoenix**, **dragon**, chrysanthemum (usually seen as circular, but sometimes from the side as *hojŏp-kukhwa* 'butterfly chrysanthemum'), *yŏnhwa* 'lotus flowers', *maehwa* 'apricot blossom', and *ihwa* '**plum blossom**'. The pattern may then be described by such names as *wanja un-mun* 'cloud and swastika', *unhang-mun* 'cloud and crane', or *unnyong-mun* 'cloud and dragon'.

Tangch'o-mun, 'Chinese plant pattern', sometimes translated 'arabesque', appears on embroidery, ceramics, painted borders and mother-of-pearl inlaid in lacquer. It began to appear in 14th-century China and Koryŏ, on ceramics and book-cover paper. The pattern is based on regularly spaced flowers that grow on the tips of long slender tendrils that curl from edge to edge of the surface, often curving into almost complete circles. They bear leaves that tend to be smaller in later examples. There is some confusion about the version called *posanghwa-mun*. *Posanghwa* (S. *ratnaketu*) 'precious likeness flower' refers to the lotus as an image of buddhahood. On circular **roof-tiles** from Silla and later, as well as silk **sutra** covers from Koryŏ, it is a many-petalled lotus rosette. It can appear in this form in *Tangch'o-mun*, but some writers use *posanghwa-mun* for *Tangch'o-mun* with flowers (not always obviously lotus) shown in profile rather than as rosettes. Some describe this form as 'honeysuckle' and take it as another symbol of Buddha, the *udumbara* flower (K. *udam*), a tree that fruits every year but flowers only once in 3,000 years – one of the fig family, whose flowers are contained within the 'fruit'.

Chongja-mun, 'small bowl pattern', is named after the table-ware sauce-bowls (*chongja* or *chongji*) on which it is frequently used. The two Chinese characters *su* and *bok* (as in **paeksu-paekpok**), often each contained in its own circular medallion, are repeated over the surface.

For *Tangch'o-mun*, see *The Korean Relics in Western Europe*, Seoul: Korea Foundation, 1992, pp. 35 and 157. There is a rich collection of book-cover papers in CHŎNG PYŎNGWAN, *Han'gugŭi ch'aekp'an munyang*, Seoul: National Central Library, 1980.

PEACH *poksunga*

There are four primary sources for the symbolism of the peach. The blossom is emblematic of brides because it occurs in a wedding song in the *Book of Odes* 6; and more generally of contentment because it is the main feature of **Tao Qian**'s Shangri-la story of the Peach-blossom Spring (K. *Tohwa-wŏn-gi*). The fruit is also a sign of immortality, frequently mentioned by Korean poets as associated with the Queen Mother of the West, ruler of the Daoist **immortals**. Finally, it was in a peach orchard that the three heroes of *The Romance of the Three Kingdoms* made their oath of friendship.

PEASANTS

In the Three Kingdoms the majority of peasant farmers may have been freemen, with only a minority working as tenants. They lived in villages under village headmen, paid grain and cloth taxes levied on their households, and performed *corvée* labour. Under the Unified Silla dynasty a greater number of families were unable to pay their dues, and as the size and power of the aristocracy grew, so too did the proportion of the population sinking into **slavery**. Doubtless, however, some of those abandoning farming as a profession did so to join the ranks of the **craftsmen** who produced ever-increasing quantities of fine goods in stone, clay, metal, wood, cloth, **paper** and paint for the court, Buddhist temples, and upper class households.

In the Koryŏ period all land belonged to the state, which nominally retained ownership while distributing it in grants to **meritorious subjects**, government officials and institutions, Buddhist temples and certain other deserving categories (*see* **land tenure**). In practice, this meant that the powerful aristocracy were able to build up large estates and to employ many peasants as their tenant farmers. Free farmers were able to rent 'people's land' from the state, and were liable in addition to a tribute tax of cloth or other goods as well as to *corvée*. By the 12th century their conditions had become so intolerable that a succession of peasant **rebellions** broke out.

By the early Chosŏn period peasants benefited from developments in **agriculture**, and King **Sejong** took a personal interest in improving the quality of their food and clothing. Free commoners (*sangmin*) either worked small farms of their own or tilled the lands of the *yangban*. They were in a bound occupation, and were obliged to wear wooden or metal identification tags (*hop'ae*) to prevent them from absconding and to facilitate their call-up for periods of labour service. Taxes included the land tax and a tribute tax (*see* **taxation**), as well as dues demanded by the landlord, and the combination of these brought suffering to many families. The cost of buying exemption from rising demands for military and *corvée* services went up. High rates of usury resulted from the abuse of the **ever normal warehouses** (*sangp'yŏngch'ang*) system. Peasant families sought to improve their livelihood through cottage industries such as weaving and making and repairing tools, and with the development of a monetary economy in the 17th century (*see* **coinage**) more peasants were tempted to engage in **commerce**.

At the beginning of the 19th century weak government caused income from its principal fiscal sources (the land tax, military tax and **rice loan system**) to fall, and inevitably it was the peasantry who were on the receiving end of escalating tax and rent demands. Rates of tenancy varied considerably, from 5 per cent of a village's lands to over 80 per cent. Though some tenant farms were large and provided a minority of farmers with the opportunity to become farm managers, subletting land to tenants of their own, the majority were small and uneconomic, and eventually intolerable pressures led to the greatest peasant uprising in Korean history, the **Tonghak Rebellion**.

In the Japanese colonial period things were no better. Though the Land Survey (*see* **Land Reform**) succeeded in redistributing former royal and unallocated lands, peasant farmers did not benefit. Absentee Japanese landlordism was common, and some of the best farming land was taken over by immigrant Japanese farmers. Almost half of Korean farms were worked by tenants who paid half or more of their annual crop to their landlord as rent, and were then confronted by the land tax, further expenses for fertilisers etc., and labour dues. Whilst **rice** production and levels of land cultivation rose through the 1920s as a result of official policy, the peasantry reaped no advantage. Statistics showed that 75 per cent were in debt in 1930. After 1931 investment in agricultural development by the **Government General** decreased. Starvation increased, and many peasants migrated to **Manchuria** or Japan, where they were forced into poorly paid industrial occupations. In the 1930s levels of tenant-occupancy averaged over 60 per cent of all farmed land across Korea and was even higher near urban centres. The Tenant Arbitration Ordinance (1932) and the Agricultural Lands Ordinance (1934) appeared to afford tenants some protection against landlordism, but a growing number were driven to become so-called 'fire-field people' (*hwajŏnmin*). These tried to subsist by burning off the cover on uninhabited land, usually in poor hilly areas, tilling small plots of it for a brief period, and then moving on to do the same elsewhere. In 1936 nearly 1·5 million *hwajŏnmin* were recorded. Marxist propaganda circulated among the peasantry and the Peasants' Union was one of many rural revolutionary organisations which attempted to stimulate the cause of independence in the late 1920s and early 1930s.

VINCENT BRANDT, *A Korean Village*, Cambridge, Mass.: Harvard University Press, 1971; SHIN GI-WOOK, *Peasant Protest and Social Change in Colonial Korea*, Seattle: University of Washington Press, 1996

See also **class system**

PEDLARS' GUILD *Pobu-sangdan* 褓負商團
A guild of itinerant traders who carried their wares in wrapping-cloths (*potchim* or *po*) or on their backs (*tŭngchim* or *pu*), peddling them at **markets** throughout the country. The history of the organisation is obscure, but some early 17th-century records may be relevant. The guild was used by the conservative Imperial Club (*Hwangguk-hyŏphoe*) to attack the **Independence Club** (*Tongnip-hyŏphoe*) on the streets of Seoul in autumn 1898.

PEOPLE'S ASSEMBLIES *See* **Government, central** (Democratic People's Republic of Korea)

PEOPLE'S COMMITTEES *inmin wiwŏnhoe* 人民委員會
Local organisations formed spontaneously in summer 1945 to restore native government in towns and villages formerly controlled by the Japanese. They were originally branches of the Preparatory Committee for Building the Country, encouraged by **Yŏ Unhyŏng** and the **Korean People's Republic** which succeeded it. They included prominent local figures as well as hitherto unknown intellectuals, anxious to play a part in the running of their country. Although they contained not a few leftist members, they were generally anxious to achieve decisions in line with local interest and popular consensus. The **American Military Government**, however, wrongly suspected them of having predetermined communist goals. In southern Korea, therefore, they were refused official recognition and many of their members were purged and imprisoned in 1945–6, provoking widespread and serious civil unrest in late 1946 known as the 'autumn harvest uprising'. The Committees failed to preserve any political power, but resentment at their rejection and the substitution of a second foreign Power's control for that of the hated first simmered on, eventually breaking out into the **Cheju Rebellion** of 1948. In the same year leaders of the **Yŏsu-Sunch'ŏn Uprising** attempted to revive People's Committees in their area.

American apprehension was not unnaturally heightened by what was happening in the north: there, a Five-Province Administrative Bureau had been created by the Russians in October 1945 under the nominal control of the People's Committee in P'yŏngyang. In February 1946 a People's Assembly renamed it the Provisional People's Committee for North Korea, under **Cho Mansik**, and a year later it became the People's Committee for North Korea, effectively the forerunner of the state government. In November 1946 elections to People's Committees at municipal, prefectural and provincial level were held, resulting in almost total success for the leadership's approved candidates. In February and March 1947 the inhabitants of villages and townships similarly selected, or endorsed, nominees acceptable to the communists (though not all were members of communist parties, for like Mao Zedong in China, **Kim Ilsŏng** was currently advocating the virtues of a united front approach). Meanwhile, as Kim Ilsŏng increasingly used the People's Committee system to exercise tight communist control over the behaviour and minds of people in the north, the communist press in the south urged the replacement of American rule by that of the People's Committees as precursors of democratic government. Except, however, for a brief period in 1950 when North Koreans quickly established Committees in regions conquered during early stages of the War, they would never enjoy any official recognition as part of the governmental system in South Korea.
ROBERT A. SCALAPINO & CHONG-SIK LEE, *Communism in Korea*, Part I: *The Movement*, Berkeley: University of California Press, 1972

PEOPLE'S REPUBLIC OF CHINA (PRC), RELATIONS WITH

In 1949 the political outlook in both Korea and China was uncertain. The unsatisfactory and possibly temporary division of the peninsula had recently led to the formation of two separate governments with totally differing ideological outlook, while the success of the communists in the Chinese civil war left Korean and American officials alike in a state of indecision about possible PRC policy and behaviour. In effect, China's foreign policy conformed to guidance from Moscow, and soon led to its involvement in the **Korean War**. Though Mao Zedong may initially have had doubts about this, the threat posed to China's national security by the advance of United Nations forces on the **Yalu River** made intervention inevitable. Thereafter the pattern of Sino-Korean relations for years to come was determined by the outcome of the War and the reaction of the United States and its allies to it. China's unexpected military successes took the world by surprise, gave the PRC a natural place at the **Geneva Conference** in 1954, and strengthened **Kim Ilsŏng**'s respect for his great neighbour. At the same time South Korea and its American allies developed a military dictatorship which justified its tough, undemocratic rule as being essential to confront the communist threat from the north. While the PRC withdrew its troops from North Korea in accordance with Geneva aims, the USA felt unable to relinquish its defensive responsibilities to the South by reciprocating. The weak post-War Chinese economy was itself dependent on Soviet aid, and PRC support for North Korea was more moral and propagandist than material, but was nonetheless valuable to P'yŏngyang, especially as it attempted to sit on the fence when the Sino-Soviet split widened in the early 1960s. The Cultural Revolution, however, harmed China's image in North Korea while confirming Southern fears about its hostile unpredictability.

Zhou Enlai's visit to P'yŏngyang in 1970 improved relations with the North, and through the 1970s the DPRK inclined towards China rather than the Soviet Union. Despite the rapprochement between China and the USA, the continued confrontation between the DPRK and ROK confirmed the great powers in their support for one or other of the two Korean sides. Change only came when, from 1985 onwards, shifts in policy became noticeable in China and the Soviet Union, signalling the triumph of economic considerations over ideological ones. Both powers now needed to benefit from trade with South Korea, and rejecting criticism from the North, both took part in the 1988 Seoul **Olympic Games**. Full diplomatic relations were established between Beijing and Seoul in 1992, after which China showed some skill in handling diplomatic tensions over the growing numbers of North Koreans seeking asylum at the South Korean embassy, notably the senior official Hwang Changyŏp in 1997. China remained concerned about the impact of developments on the peninsula. It advised P'yŏngyang to cooperate with the international inspection of its nuclear installations, and, fearing the effects of uncontrolled collapse, it continued to supply food and oil to the North, while urging its leaders to soften their stance against gradual reconciliation with the South.

ZHANG SHU GUANG, *Mao's Military Romanticism: China and the Korean War, 1950–1953*, Lawrence: University Press of Kansas, 1995

PEPPER

The traditional pepper (*pundi*) of east Asia, including Korea, is fagara (the word is Portuguese), otherwise called Sichuan pepper or Japanese pepper. It comes from *Zanthoxyla*, indigenous plants of the Rue family. Black pepper (*huch'u*) is the untreated seed of a vine of the Pepper family, which can be washed and traded as white pepper. Black and white peppers spread to China from India during the Tang dynasty, arriving in Korea at least by Koryŏ times. Their powder is still used as a condiment for meat. For pickling and cooking vegetables, both fagara and pepper have been largely superseded by Capsicum, known as Red or Chilli Pepper. This member of the Nightshade family from equatorial America arrived in Europe at the end of the 16th century. Green Chilli fruits are used fresh. Red Chilli is dried and may be used whole, powdered or shredded. It has become a distinctive ingredient of Korean cookery. **Hamel**'s companion Eibocken gives the word *koch'u* for 'pepper' in his vocabulary but does not describe the fruit. Some writers doubt whether chilli arrived so early. More chilli is used by poorer people – a fact that may reflect the lower social standing of the more recent arrival as well as the power of red pepper to kill subtler flavours.

'PHAGS-PA SCRIPT *P'alsap'a muncha* 八思巴文字

'Phags-pa Lama, 'Exalted One', was the title given to a Tibetan monk (1235–1280) who was taken to Mongolia at the age of twelve and later became the confidant of Kublai Khan, the first Yuan emperor. 'Phags-pa Lama was appointed *guoshi*, 'grand lama', and together they worked out a *modus vivendi* for **Buddhism** in the Mongol state. The emperor asked him to devise an alphabet that could be used for all the languages of the empire; and in 1269 he produced the 'Phags-pa script, an alphabet of 42 letters, based on Tibetan script, but written from top to bottom and right to left in the Chinese way. Because of the letter-shapes, it was dubbed *panghyŏng-muncha* 'square letters'. The first documents written in it to reach Korea arrived in 1273. The script is mentioned in *Koryŏ-sa* as late as 1385, but it was cumbrous and fell out of use after the end of Yuan in 1368. Books about it were still kept by the *Sayŏg-wŏn* in 1469.

When he designed *han'gŭl*, **Sejong** undoubtedly gained a degree of inspiration from 'Phags-pa's alphabetic principles, using the same letter for both initial and final consonants – an idea foreign to Chinese linguists at the time. Four basic letters of *han'gŭl* also closely resemble 'Phags-pa letters for the same sound-groups. Sejong's recorded attention to *-gu-jŏnja*, often understood as 'Old Seal Chinese characters', more probably refers to *Monggu-jŏnja* 'Mongol seal letters', i.e.'Phags-pa script.

'PHAGSPA SCRIPT AND HAN'GŬL
(Basic shapes of consonant groups)

	Han'gŭl	'Phagspa
Velar	ㄱ	石
Lingual	ㄷ	ㄷ
Semi-lingual	ㄹ	린
Bilabial	ㅁ,ㅂ	근
Dental	ㅈ,ㅅ	지

A full account of the question can be found in GARI LEDYARD, 'The international linguistic background of the Correct Sounds for the Instruction of the People', *in* Y-K KIM-RENAUD, *The Korean Alphabet*, Honolulu: University of Hawaii Press, 1997, pp.31–87.

PHOENIX, THE 鳳凰

The *ponghwang* 'phoenix' image appeared in China later than the **dragon** (probably during the Warring States period, for it is mentioned in the *Analects*), and must have come to Korea with Chinese script. Originally a sun-related bird, among the *sasin* (**Four Spirits**) it is the Red Bird of the South quadrant. In pictorial form it has long combined the dancing crane of north-east Asia with the peacock or some species of pheasant from the south. It is a bird of good omen that heralds the arrival of sages, dances for rulers and married couples, and is frequently depicted above the royal throne, very often shown as a pair (*pong* has come to mean the male and *hwang* the female). The only tree on which it will perch is the *pyŏg-odong* (Chinese parasol tree, *Firmiana simplex*), which has a bright green bark. When a husband went on a long journey, his wife might plant a *pyŏg-odong*, for the phoenix to bring him safely back. A promising son is called a soaring phoenix and when depicted over the royal throne, the phoenix may imply that the Korean king has the Chinese emperor as father.

PIBYŎN-SA 備邊司 'Frontier Defence Office' *See* **Military system**

PIGYŎK-CHINCH'ŎLLOE 飛撃震天雷 'Flying striker, heaven-shaking thunder'
A missile invented by the gunmaker Yi Changson and used to great effect during the Japanese invasion of 1592 (*see* **Imjin Wars**). It was an iron ball containing gunpowder, shrapnel and a detonator, fired from a cannon.

PILLOWS
Although pillows made of wood or ceramic have various shapes, soft Korean pillows are cylindrical.The ends, called *pyegae mok*, may be made of wood – carved, inlaid or lacquered – or of needlework that provides some stiffness. Favourite decorations are long-life symbols and mandarin ducks (the latter especially on double-length conjugal pillows). The *chat-pegae*, 'pine-cone pillow', has needlework ends decorated with the folded patchwork known in the West as 'prairie point'. This technique makes a fabric that resembles the surface of a pine-cone, covered with triangular scales of folded silk. Various patterns are produced by arranging the colours of the 'scales' in circles covering the round surface.

PIRATES *waegu* 倭寇
Whether Chinese or Japanese (or local Koreans), pirates were a frequent source of trouble to coastal traders and authorities. The Unified Silla government built military garrisons at strategic points down the west coast as defence against Chinese pirates (*see* **Chang Pogo**). In the early Koryŏ period merchants sometimes preferred to brave the rough crossing from the Shandong peninsula to the shores of Chŏlla province rather than risk the pirates operating around the coast of **Manchuria**, and at the same time the east coast was being ravaged by **Jurchen** pirates. As legitimate Chinese trade with Korea declined through the 12th century, so did piracy increase, but Koreans have traditionally blamed the Japanese for the most serious growth in organised raiding on their coasts, which began during the reign of King Kojong (1213–59). The problem became acute in the mid-14th century, with fleets of hundreds of ships using **Tsushima** Island as a base and attacking targets as far north as **Kanghwa** Island. The Korean government, which had acquired the secret of gunpowder from the Mongols, set up an Office of Armaments in 1377 and built ships armed with cannon to repel them. **Ch'oe Musŏn** earned a reputation for his success in naval battle.

Harrassment continued in the early Chosŏn period, prompting a major counter-attack against Tsushima under Yi Chongmu (1360–1425) in 1419. But despite the Treaty of **Kyehae** (1443) the problem was not solved, and through the 16th century China as well as Korea suffered badly from marauding fleets. Both blamed the

Japanese, calling them (K.) *waegu* or (C.) *wakou*, but in reality they came from bases in Taiwan as well as Japan, and were joined by Portuguese adventurers. The inhabitants of the south coast of Korea in particular were at risk of being seized and taken as **slaves** to Japan, where some were sold to Portuguese slave-traders. In 1589 the Chosŏn government executed two of its citizens as collaborators with pirates.
See also **commerce; merchants**

PIWŎN 秘園 'Secret garden'
The private park for the Chosŏn kings and royal family to the north-east of the main hall in the **Ch'angdŏk Palace** in Seoul. Within its extensive walled enclosure it observed the principles of *p'ungsu* in a layout that recreated the varied beauties of the natural countryside in the city centre. Pavilions and arbours were tucked into the folds of hills and valleys in a landscape watered by running streams feeding into a lotus pond. The choice of trees and flowers ensured a sequence of colour throughout the seasons and blended harmoniously with the decoration of the wooden buildings. The garden was stocked with animals and birds for the further enjoyment of visitors.
See also **horticulture**

PLACENTA BURIAL *t'aebong* 胎封
The after-birth of the king's offspring was put into a *t'ae-hangari*, a small vase with a narrow neck. The lid was sealed and the vase deposited in a *t'aesil* 'placenta chamber' or *t'aebong* 'placenta sealing' built of stone. The official in charge of this procedure, *ant'ae-sa* 'reposing placenta officer', was appointed for the occasion. He had to choose the site and superintend the burial. Most of the known examples of *t'ae-hangari* are in *punch'ŏng* ware and date from the 15th and 16th centuries.

PLAYING CARDS
Before the advent of western playing cards, Korean cards were *t'ujŏn*, 'contest slips', strips of thick oiled **paper**, about as wide as a finger (190 x 6–12 mm). They are thought to have been imported by the Ming troops during Hideyoshi's invasion of 1592 (*see* **Imjin Wars**), and are now uncommon. Numerical values 1–10 were shown by peculiar narrow black ink-figures; suits by similar drawings of people, **animals**, Chinese characters or verses. The suits were *saram* 'man', *mulkogi* 'fish', *kamagwi* 'crow', *kkwŏng* 'pheasant', *noru* 'roe-**deer**', *pyŏl* 'star', *t'okki* '**hare**' and *mal* '**horse**'. A pack might contain 80 or 60 cards, but 40 was most popular. The various forms of game included *t'ujŏn*, *yŏt-pangmangi* and *tongdang-jigi*.
     The garishly coloured little *hwat'u* 'flower contest' cards that came from Japan in the 19th century are still popular. The usual size is 4·5 x 3 cm. A pack has 48 cards in 12 suits: *sol* 'pine and crane'*, *maejo* 'apricot-blossom and bush-warbler', *pŏt-kkot* 'cherry-blossom and curtain'*, *hŭkssari* 'lespedeza printed in black and cuckoo', *nanch'o* 'orchid and firefly', *moran* 'peony and butterfly', *hongssari* 'lespedeza printed in red and wild boar', *kongsan* 'bare mountain and wild goose' or with moon*, *kukhwa* 'chrysanthemum and wine-cup', *tanp'ung* 'maple and deer', *odong* 'paulownia and **phoenix***, and *pi* 'rain and swallow' (or with willow*). The simple picture of the plant or mountain is worth 1 point. Adding a drawing of writing-tablet makes the card worth 5 points; adding the secondary symbol makes it worth 10 or, in the suits asterisked above, 20 points. There are two 1-point cards to each suit save the paulownia, which has three, and the rain, which has only one. The bare mountain and paulownia suits lack 5-point cards. There are several forms of game.

PLUM BLOSSOM

This confusing term is used for *maehwa*, 'winter-flowering apricot', one of the **Four Gentlemen**, and for *ihwa*, the true plum blossom, emblem of the Yi, ruling family of the Chosŏn dynasty. *Ihwa* may also mean 'pear blossom', quaintly romanised as *Ewha* in the name of the famous university for women at Seoul. In decorative art the three are virtually indistinguishable, unless it is clear that *maehwa* sits on the branch, while the other two have stalks.

POCH'ŎN-GYO 普天教

A schismatic group of *Chŭngsan-gyo*.

POEMS, EARLIEST *See* Harp Song; Orioles' Song; Tortoise Incantation

POETRY

In traditional Korea, poetry was either written in Chinese language and literary forms (*see* **poetry, Chinese**) or in native forms appropriate to the Korean language (*see changga*; *hyangga*; *kasa*; *sijo*). As one of the principal intellectual achievements of the Confucian and Buddhist literati, it expressed the refined loyalties and emotions of the educated élite, but as the means for ordinary Koreans of all classes to exult in or lament their fortunes it displayed a nationalist sentiment that distinguished it from simple imitation of Chinese models (*see* **Sirhak movement**). Suffering during the Japanese colonial period was the inspiration for much poetry of sorrow and protest.
See also **Tang-style regulated verse**; **Tortoise Incantation**

POETRY, CHINESE, WRITTEN IN KOREA *Hansi* 漢詩

The distinction between poetry and prose, assumed as self-evident in the West, is subtler in China and Korea, where the two forms blend more readily. For Korea the fundamental reference is to *Yao dian*, in the classic *Shujing*: *si ŏn ji, ka yŏng ŏn*; *sŏng ŭi yŏng, yul hwa sŏng* (Sino-Korean transliteration), understood as: 'Poetry speaks of meaning, song has prolonged (chanted) words; tones (or notes) depend on chanting, metre harmonizes tones.' Although *yul* originally meant 'pitchpipes' rather than 'metre', this fairly interprets the passage, which formed the basis of Korean critical theory and gave the term *yŏngŏn*, meaning 'song'. Poetry is inseparable from song and is essentially the art of lyric.

The Chinese classic *Book of Odes* is divided into *p'ung*, *ya* and *song*; folksongs, lyric odes and solemn odes or hymns, written in various stanza forms, using assonance and rhyme, with a marked preference for a four-syllable line. These forms were imitated by Korean writers, but all three words usually referred to poems in the *Book of Odes*.

Longer and more varied lyric forms of two kinds, not always easy to distinguish formally, were called *sa* (C. *ci*), using a different Chinese character for each kind. Both used lines of varying length and developed considerably over the centuries. Koreans used the two words *sa* in reference to the Chinese authors who were imitated. The first *sa*, developed in China long before Han, was named after the ancient *Qusi* (K. *Ch'osa*) poems, which led to the development of the Chinese *fu* (K. *pu*). The other, later, *sa* was based on songs for professional singers and had its Chinese peak in the Song dynasty.

Pu, called 'prose-poem' or 'rhapsody' in English, is usually a long composition, using parallelism and rhyme, typically descriptive and tending to indulge in litanical lists – a form that was readily imitated in Korean vernacular poetry. *Pu* continued to be written by Koreans until the end of Chosŏn. The relation of poetry and song was emphasised in the development of *ka*, poems written to the tunes of popular songs. All these forms were popular in Koryŏ, and from time to time required in **examinations**.

From Han times onwards the Chinese developed the shorter verse forms in 2, 4 and 8 lines. The favoured length of line was 5 or 7 syllables. When described as *kuch'e* 'old style', they had rhyme but no prosodic pattern of tones (which corresponds to the western prosodic patterns of stress); when called *kŭnch'e* 'recent style', they had strict tonal prosody as well as rhyme. Tang poets developed strict metrical rules in **Tang-style regulated poems** *yulsi*. These became the chief concern of Korean writers in the Chosŏn period, so that the mention of *si* 'poetry' was often assumed to mean *yulsi*.

Although clearly distinguished from Korean vernacular poetry, Chinese poetics influenced Korean poetry profoundly.
See also ***changga*** ; ***sijo***

POHŎJA 步虚子 'Walking in the Void'
One of two surviving pieces of Chinese **music**, *tangak*, which entered Korea during the Koryŏ period from Song China. By the Chosŏn period it had become so koreanised that it was classified as native Korean music (*hyangak*) in the score book *Taeak hubo* of 1759.
See also ***Nagyangch'un; Yŏmillak***

POISON, EXECUTION BY *sayak* 賜藥 'bestowal of medicine'
Although there is no mention of the practice in the law-codes, members of the royal family and high-ranking subjects who were condemned to death were sent a dose of poison by the king. By drinking it they legally committed suicide. This form of execution was much used during the the factional struggles of Chosŏn dynasty. The poison used was called *chimnyak* 'snake-eagle medicine', from a southern Chinese snake-eating eagle (C. *zhen*) that was presumed to have a poison of its own stronger than any snake's. In practice gold or mercury were used, but the commonest poisons administered were arsenic and concoctions of roots from plants of the aconite family (*puja* or *pagot*).

POJAGI 'wrapping cloths'
A rectangular wrapping cloth is the traditional and still popular container for items to be carried or stored. Diagonally opposed corners are usually tied in two reef knots over the contents. *Pojagi* were made in various sizes, sometimes elaborately ornamented or made of fine patchwork.
HUH DONG HWA & SHEILA MIDDLETON, *Traditional Korean Wrapping Cloths*, Cambridge: Fitzwilliam Museum, 1990

POLICE SYSTEM, JAPANESE
Throughout the **Protectorate** Japanese military police (often known as the gendarmerie) and civil police had assumed authority over their Korean counterparts and used it to exercise racial oppression, though it was not until the Agreement of 1907 that the Japanese formally assumed law enforcement powers. Under the **Government General** the Police Bureau was one of six within the Secretariat, and the police force, under the command of a major-general, functioned as an an army of occupation with police stations in all towns and villages. The abolition of the

military police by Governor-General Saitō Makoto in 1920, following the **March First Movement**, was a cosmetic exercise. Numbers of civilian police increased dramatically, including a small percentage of Koreans from 1921 onwards. The Japanese did not read or speak Korean, but the importance of censorship made the employment of native collaborators necessary. Estimates vary, but the rate of growth is suggestive of the vital rôle of the police in suppressing Korean nationalist activity. In 1910 their total number was around 6,000; by 1920, around 20,000 (out of a combined Korean and Japanese population of 17·76 millions). They played a leading part in the suppression of demonstrations such as the **June Tenth Movement** and **Kwangju Incident**.

POLO *kyŏkku/t'agu* 擊毬
Polo is a game of the Central Asian steppe riders. It seems to have arrived in Korea during the Three Kingdoms period, reaching the height of its popularity in the 12th century AD, when it was played specially at *Tano*. By the end of Chosŏn it had become a military skill and a subject for the military **examinations**, performed with some ceremony, preceded by *kisaeng* dancing and requiring equestrian acrobatics. Some believe that *t'agu* was a less formal game than *kyŏkku*. There is said also to have been an unmounted form, a kind of hockey.

PŎMP'AE 梵唄
Buddhist **music** said to have reached Korea from **Tang dynasty** China during the Unified Silla period. *Pŏmp'ae* is used to refer generally to all Buddhist chant, but applies more properly to one of three types of Buddhist vocal music. These are (1) *pŏmp'ae*, long, complex chants consisting of *hossori* and *chissori*, only performed by highly trained singers. *Hossori* includes non-rhythmic monophonic recitation of the **sutras**. *Chissori* comprises difficult melismatic music and is infrequently performed in modern times. (2) *Yŏmbul*, the recitation of **sutras**. This is performable by any monk. (3) *Hwach'ŏng*, folksong-style songs with Buddhist content.

Over the centuries, elements of Korean Buddhist chant have been derived from China, Tibet and Central Asia, as well as from native folk song. The principal percussive sources are the hollow wooden clapper, *mokt'ak*, the flat iron gong, *unp'an*, and the drum. *Pŏmp'ae* **dances** are among the most dramatic in the repertoire of both professional and amateur performers and are frequently seen on the stage and the open-air performance ground. They include the butterfly dance (*nabich'um*), the cymbal dance (*parach'um*) and the **drum** dance (*pŏpkuch'um*).
BYONG WON LEE, *Buddhist Music of Korea*, Seoul: Jung Eum Sa, 1987
*See also **Sŭngmu**; **Yŏngsan hoesang***

PONGSA 奉事
A minor official (8th **grade** junior) in certain less important government departments.
See also **Government, central**; **provincial administration**

PŎPSANG 法相
A Buddhist sect. *See* **Five teachings**

POPULATION
Detailed figures were not recorded until the 20th century. The following figures include pre-modern estimates extrapolated from household **census registers**.

11th century	2·1 million (m)	
1392	5·5 m	
1511	10 m	
1591	14 m	
1657	2,290,083	
1675	4,703,505	
1768	7,006,248	
1807	7·5 m	
1832	8·75 m	
1910	14,766,000	
1920	17,764,000	
1930	20,438,000	
1935	22,208,000	
1944	25,133,352	
	North (millions)	South (millions)
1945	9·170	15·944
1949	9·62	20·189
1953	8·49	
1955		21·5
1956	9·359	
1960	10·789	
1961		25·7
1966		29·2
1970		31·5
1976		35·9
1980		38·2
1983	19·185	
1985		40·466
1989		42·380
1995	23·487	45·553

In 1950, approximately 75 per cent of Koreans lived in the countryside. In the 1990s, an estimated two thirds of North Koreans and four fifths of South Koreans lived in towns and cities. While North Korea's rural population remained numerically constant at around 8·4 million, that of South Korea had halved to approximately 9·6 million. The population density in South Korea, 435 per square kilometre, was one of the highest in the world.
KWON TAEHWAN, *Demography of Korea: Population Change and its Components, 1925–66*, Seoul National University Press, 1977; KWON TAEHWAN & SIN YONGHA, 'On Population Estimates of the Yi Dynasty, 1392–1910,' *Tonga munhwa* 14, 1977; NICHOLAS EBERSTADT & JUDITH BANISTER, *The Population of North Korea*, Berkeley. Institute of East Asian Studies, 1992

PORT HAMILTON, *see* Kŏmun-do

PORT LAZAREV
A name used by the Russians during the 19th century for Yŏnghŭng-man, the big bay on the north-east coast on whose southern side stands Wŏnsan.

PORTRAITURE
Rare examples survive from the Three Kingdoms period, including a fine wall painting from Anak No. 3 **tomb** in Hwanghae province of the Chinese official Dong Shou and

his wife. From historical records it is known that portraits of Buddhist monks were also done during this period, of kings in Unified Silla, and of kings and queens in Koryŏ times. It is under the Chosŏn dynasty, however, when the widespread adoption of neo-Confucianism put emphasis on family records (*see* **genealogies**) and the honouring of ancestors (*see* **ancestral worship**), that the practice flourished most strongly; and most examples have survived from that time. Royal portraits (*ujin*) were regularly produced, along with those of deserving '**meritorious subjects**'. The honouring of distinguished officials with feasts and entertainments on occasions such as their 60th birthdays was a duty taken seriously by many Chosŏn kings. In 1394 King T'aejo founded the Office of the Venerable Aged, *Kiroso* (*Kisa* for short) to show respect for officials of second **grade** senior who had attained the age of 70. Portraits were made of those who became members. In similar vein, both Confucian academies and family ancestral halls preserved portraits of scholars who had attained distinction and seniority in their organisations. In such circumstances the painting of the picture was a serious matter. As in China, from where the custom was inherited, the initial purpose was to record a physical likeness, and early examples make no attempt to suggest the personality of a living person. Only from the 18th century did the introduction of shading techniques allow artists to create more of a three-dimensional effect and encourage them to depict the character of their subject, but even then, the Confucian sense of respect for seniority gave most portraits a deferential air. Self-portraiture was not unknown before modern times, an example being that by Yun Tusŏ (early 18th century)[1], but the first modern example in oils was done in the Tokyo Art School by **Ko Hŭidong** in 1915. Two versions of this survive, one at the Tokyo Fine Arts School,[2] the other in the National Museum for Contemporary Art at Kwach'ŏn.[3]

(1)(3) YOUNG ICK LEW, ed., *Korean Art Tradition*, Seoul: Korea Foundation, 1993
(2) K.O.I.S., *Korean Art Guide*, Seoul: Yekyong Publications Co., 1987
See also **painting**

PORTSMOUTH, TREATY OF (1905)

Treaty concluded at Portsmouth, New Hampshire, in September 1905 terminating the **Russo-Japanese War**. Though it officially recognised the independence of Korea, the Treaty also acknowledged Japan's paramount political, economic and military authority there, exercised through its right to offer 'guidance' to the Korean government. The Treaty also transferred Russian concessions in Port Arthur and Dalian to Japan and granted Japanese commercial development rights in **Manchuria**.

POSSAM

A custom that grew up at some time after the early 15th century, when the remarriage of widows began to have legal effects to the disadvantage of the sons of their second marriages. When the *saju-p'alcha* divination for the daughter of an upper-class family indicated that she would be married more than once, in order to avoid this bad luck a bachelor (easily identified by his hair-style) would be kidnapped at night, bound up (*ssam*) in cloth (*po*) and put to bed with her, and then killed or quietly sent away, so that her family could confidently present her for marriage to a suitable husband. (If the divination indicated a third or fourth **marriage**, two or three men would be so treated.)

'POST OFFICE *ÉMEUTE*' (1884) *See Kapsin* **Coup**

POSTHUMOUS KING TITLES (ch'ujŏn wangho) 追尊王號

Just as **Yi Sŏnggye** gave posthumous kingly honours to four generations of his ancestors, so any other Chosŏn king whose father had not reigned might give him a posthumous royal title. Thus Tŏkchong (1438–57) was honoured by **Sŏngjong**; Wŏnjong (1580–1619) by Injo; Chinjong (1719–28) by his adopted son **Chŏngjo**; Changjo (**Prince Changhŏn**, 1735–62) by his great-great-grandson **Kojong; Ikchong** (1809–30) by **Hŏnjong**.

POTATOES

Several species of yam (*ma*) are native to Korea. Their stem tubers are edible and are eaten, but they have never become a significant part of the food supply. The sweet potato eaten in Korea, though called a yam, is a root tuber of the Convolvulus family, native to tropical America. It was known in China from the mid-17th century, but did not arrive in Korea until seeds were brought from **Tsushima** in 1763 by Cho Ŏm, on his way back from a diplomatic journey to Japan. The new tuber attracted notice as a crop to help solve famine; but it is not easy to grow in Korea and has remained a secondary food.

The true 'white' or 'Irish' potato is a stem tuber of the Nightshade family, native to the Andes. It was introduced to Europe in the late 16th century, to China by the Dutch in the 17th century, and to Korea from China about 1840. Like the sweet potato, it was proposed as a food for the poor, but it remains a seasonal food, and has not entered classic cuisine.

The sweet potato was first called *kamjŏ* 'sweet yam', and later *nam-gamjŏ* 'southern sweet yam', but is now called *koguma*. The true potato was called *puk-kamjŏ* 'northern sweet yam' (and sometimes *maryŏng-sŏ* 'horse-bell yam'), but is now called *kamja*.

POTSDAM CONFERENCE (1945)

Held in Berlin between Winston Churchill, Harry Truman and Joseph Stalin from 16 July to 2 August 1945. Churchill was succeeded by Clement Attlee on 28 July. Unlike those at **Cairo, Yalta** and **Moscow**, this Conference did not discuss the future of Korea specifically, simply reiterating the reference made at Cairo to its eventual independence. However, the Declaration of 26 July calling on Japan to surrender and the entry of the Soviet Union into the war against Japan on 8 August precipitated the arrival of Soviet troops in northern Korea, and advanced the looming partition. A meeting of military chiefs of staff approved the adoption of the **Thirty-Eighth Parallel** as a temporary demarcation line separating Soviet from American military operations against the Japanese.

POTTERY

The earliest examples of Korean pottery date from the **neolithic period** and are associated with the *yunggi-mun* ('raised pattern') and *chŭlmun* traditions of c. 6000 to 1500 BC. Storage and cooking pots were decorated with incised and stamped lines forming geometric patterns. The succeeding pottery culture, the *mumun*, merged into the earliest **Bronze Age** civilisation in the early part of the first millennium BC. Cultural sub-regions include those associated with Misŏng-ni pottery stretching from western Liaoning province in modern China to the **Ch'ŏngch'ŏn River** valley. Misong-ni pottery is flat-bottomed and characterised by Z-shaped or parallel line patterns and horizontal handles. Between the Ch'ŏngch'ŏn and **Han River** valleys the distinctive regional culture was in the style of Sihŭng-dong. Vessels taper more sharply towards the bottom and have double rims at the top. A pottery style marked by a number of holes beneath the rim occurs between the Han and Kŭm Rivers, and in the south-west that named after a 5th-century BC site at Songgung-ni, South Ch'ungchŏng province, was widespread. It is a round-bodied, red burnished pottery. The introduction of stoneware, fired at a higher temperature, is associated with **Iron** Age sites at **Kimhae** (near **Pusan**) of the 1st century BC to 3rd century AD (*see wajil*). It was exported from **Kaya** to Japan. Regional variations in the sophistication of pottery manufacture and decoration may be seen in the pattern of **roof tiles** from the Three Kingdoms, those of **Paekche** being the most refined and those of **Silla** the least. An earthenware model of a rowing boat of the 4th–5th century from the Kaya kingdom is sufficiently detailed to provide information about methods of boat construction and propulsion. Crudely decorated earthenware jars and figurines (*t'ou*) from Silla continue to have a naïve charm well into the 6th century, but a finely modelled stoneware horseman from the Golden Bell Tomb shows that the potters of **Kŭmsŏng** were capable of making more elaborate pieces.

Korean potters migrated to Japan from Paekche and Kaya. Later, as a result of the **Imjin Wars**, a community of Korean potters settled in Kyushu where they founded the tradition of Satsuma ware. The wars are sometimes known as the 'Pottery Wars'.

EDWARD ADAMS, *Korea's Pottery Heritage*, 2 vols., Seoul International Publishing House, 1986; GINA BARNES, 'The Development of Stoneware Technology in Southern Korea,' *in* C.M.AIKENS & S.N.RHEE, eds., *Pacific Northeast Asia in Prehistory*, Washington State University Press, 1992; KIM WON-YOUNG, 'Clay Figurines of Old Silla,' *KJ*, 8/4, 1968

See also **celadon**; **ceramics**

POU 普愚 (1515–65)

Pou entered a monastery at the age of 14, studied both *Sŏn* and *Kyo* **Buddhism**, and became a distinguished teacher. During the regency of Munjŏng Wanghu, mother of King Myŏngjong, from 1545 to 1553, he was in favour with the queen, and much of the anti-Buddhist policy of **Sŏngjong** and **Prince Yŏnsan** was reversed. The Buddhist *kwagŏ* (*see* **examinations, Buddhist**) was restored and thousands of new monks recruited. After the queen died in 1565 there was a strong neo-Confucian reaction in which the Buddhist advantages were lost again. Pou was exiled to **Cheju**, where he was beheaded by the governor.

PREZHEVALSKY, NIKOLAI MIKHAILOVITCH (1839–88)

One of the first Russians to enter Korea in modern times was the great explorer, Nikolai Prezhevalsky, famous for discovering the Mongolian wild horse in 1879. While exploring the Ussuri region in summer 1867 he was impressed by the thousands of Korean immigrants in **Kando**, many of whom had become Orthodox Christians (*see* **Russian Orthodox Mission**). He crossed the **Tumen** to the Korean town of Kyŏnghŭng and met the governor, Yun Hyŏp. Yun had a number of such encounters, and later, as governor of Inch'ŏn, took part in negotiations for the **Treaty of Kanghwa** (1876).

DONALD RAYFIELD, *The Dream of Lhasa*, London: Elek, 1976

PRINCELY TITLES

During the Chosŏn dynasty, titles of honour were given to members of the royal family and **meritorious subjects**. The title was normally prefixed by a two-character real or putative place-name, often the presumed origin of the man's clan or sept.

1) *Kun* for deposed kings (*see* **Tanjong**; Prince **Kwanghae**; Prince **Yŏnsan**); sons of the king's secondary wives; eldest sons and eldest grandsons of *taegun* (see (2) below), borne by principal wives; all sons and grandsons of a Crown Prince; and meritorious subjects of the first and second classes.
2) *Taegun* for the sons of a queen.
3) *Puwŏn'gun* for the king's father-in-law and honoured ministers of the first rank.
4) *Taewŏn'gun* for the father of a king appointed from a collateral branch of the succession because the previous king had left no son to succeed him. There were three of these: Sŏnjo's father, Tŏkhŭng Taewŏn'gun; **Ch'ŏlchong**'s father, Chŏn'gye Taewŏn'gun; and **Kojong**'s father, Hŭngsŏn Taewŏn'gun. The latter is almost universally referred to as 'the Taewŏn'gun'.

See also **Names, kings'**

PRINCES' REBELLIONS *See* **Yi Sŏngye**

PRINCESSES' TITLES
During the Chosŏn dynasty a daughter of a king by his queen was entitled *kongju*. A king's daughter by a woman of lesser rank was called *ongju*.

PRINTING
A sheet of the Pure Light Dharani **Sutra** (*Muju-jŏnggwang tae-darani-gyŏng*), printed some time early in the 8th century and enclosed within a stone **pagoda** at **Pulguk-sa** in AD 751 (*see* **Tabot'ap**), is the world's oldest extant example of block printing. In the Chosŏn capital, printing from woodblocks was supervised by the *Kyosŏ-gwan* and the Astronomy Bureau *Sŏun-gwan* (*see* **Government, central**), while in the provinces it was in the charge of local magistrates and Buddhist monasteries. Movable type printing may have been introduced to Korea from China as early as the 13th century: references by **Yi Kyubo** suggest that *Sangjŏng kogŭm yemun*, 'Old and new ritual texts', was cast in movable metal type in 1234. No examples of this survive, and the oldest extant book produced in this way is the *Sŏn* treatise *Pulcho-jikchi simch'e-yojŏl* (1377). Printed seventy years earlier than Gutenberg's Bible at Hŭngdŏk sa, near Ch'ŏngju, North Ch'ungchŏng, it is now in the Bibliothèque Nationale in Paris. Such work was probably carried on in monasteries, which cast the pieces, *chuja* ('cast characters'), in their own foundries, until in 1392 the government took charge of metal type printing through the *Sŏjŏg-wŏn*. At first the quality was undistinguished compared with the fine block printing of the Koryŏ period, which may be seen in surviving examples of **sutras** printed in gold and silver on dark blue or white paper and in the 13th century set of blocks for the **Tripitaka**, carved by royal command in hope of protection against the **Mongols**. But in 1403 King **T'aejong** established the type casting office *Chuja-so*, and as its work continued into the reign of King **Sejong** with the fresh inspiration derived from the need to increase the output of neo-Confucian texts, the quality of movable type rapidly improved, using pieces made of **bronze**, **iron** and wood. Three fonts were produced, known as *kyemija* (1403), *kyŏngjaja* (1420), and *kabinja* (1434). The British Library has an edition of the Chinese history *Shiji* (K. *Sagi*), printed with *kyŏngjaja* at Kyŏngju-sa in 1425, which includes double commentary lines and in which the print is well adjusted; but the *kabinja* type face was the most attractive, and it was re-cast seven times throughout the Chosŏn dynasty. In 1436 a lead font (*pyŏngjinja*) was cast to print larger editions of books for elderly readers with poor eyesight. Despite these advances, fine woodblock printing continued to be practised and

appreciated, especially for books with anticipated long print runs such as *Hunmin chŏngŭm*. Woodblocks were economical in time and cost for printing large editions, while movable type, which had to be tied into its forme, was dislodged by every impression taken. Hence it was reserved for books produced in smaller numbers.

JEON SANG-WOON, 'Korean Printing with Movable Metal Types,' *KJ*, 11/4, 1971; SOHN POW-KEY (intr.), *Early Korean Printing*, London: Victoria & Albert Museum, 1984

See also **books**; **Haein-sa**

PRIVY, SPIRIT OF THE *ch'ŭksin* 厠神

A small bundle of paper strips and rags hung under the roof of the privy is a nest for the *ch'ŭksin*. This spirit is regarded as female and carries out errands for the *sŏngju* or *t'ŏju*, especially administering punishments.

PROGRESSIVE PARTY *Kaehwadang* 開化黨 *See* **Independence Party**

PROTECTORATE (1905–1910)

Five-year period following the **Protectorate Treaty** and culminating in the Treaty of **Annexation** and the inauguration of the Japanese colonial period. It was marked by the tightening of the Japanese grip on all aspects of Korean life, including financial and postal services, publishing and education. Emperor **Kojong** was forced to abdicate on 22 June 1907, having failed in an attempt to awaken international condemnation of Japan at the **Hague Peace Conference**. He was succeeded by his son **Sunjong**, who was too young to resist manipulation by the Japanese. An agreement of 24 July 1907 gave the **Resident-General** supreme authority over the Korean government, with power to make and veto laws and appointments. Nationalistic feeling was stimulated and seen in the opening of new **schools**, the publication of pro-Korean books and **newspapers**, the formation of patriotic societies, and outbreaks of armed struggle led by the *ŭibyŏng* ('justice fighters'). But the Japanese responded by proscribing such books, closing schools and newspapers, disbanding the official Korean army and ordering the confiscation of arms and ammunition in Korean hands. Law and order were harshly enforced through the Japanese military police and Japanese-administered courts.

Nevertheless Korean patriots exacted a price for their subjugation. The pro-Japanese American 'adviser' to the Korean government, **Durham Stevens**, was assassinated by Korean students in San Francisco in March 1908; **Itō Hirobumi** was killed by **An Chunggŭn** in Harbin on 26 October 1909, four months after his resignation; and Prime Minister **Yi Wanyong** was knifed by a would-be assassin the following December.

After such acts of resistance the third Resident-General, Terauchi Masatake, clamped down even more harshly on expressions of Korean independence, banning meetings and the publication of any critical writing, arresting critics of the régime, and increasing military control. On 16 August 1910 he put forward his Treaty of Annexation for the approval of the Korean government. Since it had been drafted in collusion with the quisling Yi Wanyong the result was a foregone conclusion.

See also **police system, Japanese**; **United Progress Society**

PROTECTORATE TREATY (1905)

Document signed on 17 November 1905 by Korean Foreign Minister Pak Chesun (*see* **Five Traitors**) and the Japanese Minister Hayashi Gonsuke, after armed Japanese troops had confined Emperor **Kojong** for two days. The Treaty was not signed by either Korean or Japanese emperor and was legally incomplete. Though its five clauses were all concerned with aspects of foreign policy and diplomatic affairs, it gave Japan almost unlimited control over the Korean government and people. The Japanese, victorious in the **Russo-Japanese War**, had persuaded President Theodore Roosevelt that their tutelage was essential to the peaceful modernisation of Korea (*see* **Taft-Katsura Memorandum**), and Kojong's final appeal to the State Department to save his country's independence, carried by **Homer Hulbert**, was ignored. The US government accepted the Japanese claim that the Treaty had been signed voluntarily, and that Korea would regain its freedom at some unspecified future date "when Korea is strong enough and wealthy enough" (Homer Hulbert). **Itō Hirobumi** became the first Resident-General in Seoul. Kojong's military adviser Min Yŏnghwan and a number of officials committed suicide in protest. On 24 July 1907 the Treaty was superseded by a new Agreement forbidding any legal or administrative action or any appointments or dismissals by the Korean government without the approval of the Resident-General.

MICHAEL FINCH, 'German Diplomatic Documents on the 1905 Japan-Korea Protectorate Treaty,' *KS*, 20, 1996

See also **Colonial period**; **Korea-Japan Protocol**; **Seven Traitors**; **Stevens, Durham**; **United Progress Society**

PROTESTANTS *Kidok-kyo*, *Yesu-gyo* 基督教

Apart from the casual visit of Karl **Gützlaff** in 1832 and the *General Sherman* incident of 1866, the first Korean contact with Protestantism seems to have been made by John **Ross**, the Scottish Presbyterian Bible translator in **Manchuria**, whose convert colleague, **Sŏ Sangnyun**, started Korea's first protestant church at his home village of Sorae in Hwanghae province about 1880.

The first foreign missionary was **Horace N. Allen**, sent to Seoul by the US Northern Presbyterian Church as doctor to the American Legation in 1884. The Presbyterian H. G. **Underwood** and the Methodist Episcopal H. G. **Appenzeller** arrived in 1885. They quickly established stations in **Pusan**, Chŏnju, P'yŏngyang and Wŏnsan, spending much energy on **medicine** and education. Later groups included Canadian and Australian Presbyterians, but all the Presbyterian missions worked to found a single Korean Presbyterian Church. The Holiness Church (*Sŏnggyŏl Kyohoe*), founded by Americans in Japan in 1901, came in 1907. All combined in the work of the British and Foreign Bible Society from 1895, replaced by the Korean Bible Society after World War II.

Although the denominations remained structurally separate, theological differences were minimal. Most of the missionaries were theologically conservative and most adopted the **Nevius Method**. There was an early strand of premillenarianism, and much use of 'revival missions' as a method of evangelism, which bequeathed a certain charismatic heritage. Protestant missionaries emphasised Bible reading and translated American and English hymns. A few, such as **J. S. Gale** and H. G. Underwood, were notable scholars of Korean history and language. Like others in East Asia, they had to face the 'term question'. They opted for the native word *Hananim* as the word for God rather than *Ch'ŏnju*, the Riccian Chinese used by Catholics. (After the Second Vatican Council, Catholics began to use *Hanŭnim* – an etymologically preferable spelling.)

Protestant missions did much for the modernisation of Korea, especially in education. Their use of the Korean alphabet (*han'gŭl*) encouraged the advancement of literacy, especially among women. Yŏnsei and **Ewha Universities**, some of the leading high schools and the biggest hospitals, including **Avison**'s Severance, were of missionary origin. Protestant Church structures also introduced Koreans to practical democracy, which influenced the development of political consciousness. Many Koreans gained their first experience of joint decision-making in the **Young Men's Christian Association**. Half the activators of the Independence Movement of 1919 and many members of the **Independence Club** were Protestants.

After the Second World War, because Syngman Rhee (**Yi Sŭngman**) was a Methodist, Protestants tended to be identified with reactionary politics; but from the 1960s onwards their political attitudes became more varied as students trained in America introduced less conservative theological ideas. Protestantism also brought Korea a work ethic which contributed to the 'miracle' economic development of 1975–1990.

Today Protestants, claiming to number 35 per cent of the total population of the Republic, form the majority of Korean Christians.

ALLEN CLARK, *History of the Korean Church*, Seoul, 1971; GEORGE L. PAIK, *The History of Protestant Missions in Korea 1832–1910*, P'yŏngyang, 1929; KENNETH WELLS, *New God, New Nation: Protestants and Self-reconstruction Nationalism in Korea, 1896–1937*, Sydney: Allen & Unwin, 1990
See also **Baird, W. M.**; **Bible in Korea, the**; **Hulbert, Homer**; **Moffett, Samuel**; **Scranton, W. B.**

PROTO-THREE KINGDOMS PERIOD
Name sometimes applied to the Late **Iron Age**, corresponding to the period of the Chinese **commanderies** on the Korean peninsula and the **Samhan**, or the first three centuries AD. It covered the transition from the ancient states of **Wiman Chosŏn** and **Yemaek** to the establishment of the three kingdoms of **Koguryŏ**, **Paekche**, and **Silla**.
K.H.B. GARDINER, *The Early History of Korea: the Historical Development of the Peninsula up to the Introduction of Buddhism in the Fourth Century A.D.*, Honolulu: University of Hawaii Press, 1969

PROVERBS *soktam* 俗談
Proverbs are pithy sayings using stock epithets, similes and metaphors to express commonplace experience or advice. They include maxims, adages, saws, aphorisms, numerical categories and mottoes. Their 'wisdom' is often trite and is virtually the same in all languages. In Korean they are called *soktam* 'folk sayings', *kŭmŏn* 'golden words', *kyŏgŏn* 'wise maxims', *iŏn* 'common sayings' or *sŏngŏ* 'set phrases'. Like proverbs worldwide, they are frequently bipartite, containing two propositions in balanced syntax and rhythm, as in *Iyŏl ch'iyŏl, inaeng ch'inaeng*, 'Control heat with heat, control cold with cold' (a medical maxim leading to hot drinks in summer and iced food in winter); or *Yong kanŭnde, kurŭm kanda*, 'As the dragon goes, so will the cloud' (a predictable grouping). Korean prefers ironic statement to exhortation and eschews the negative advice common in English proverbs. Thus an equivalent of 'Don't count your chickens before they are hatched' is *Nŏguri kul pogo, p'imul ton naeŏ ssŭnda*, 'On seeing a racoon-dog's lair, straightway spending the price of its skin.'

Both form and content may be universal, as in *Yŏ ri pakpal*, 'Like walking on thin ice', or *Purhaeng chung tahaengira*, 'In the midst of misfortune, good fortune'; but distinctively Korean references are common, as in *Purip hohyŏl, an tŭk hoja*, 'How can one take the tiger's child without entering the tiger's den?' Provincial attitudes are reflected in *Sŏul nomŭn piman omyŏn p'ungnyŏn iranda*, 'A Seoul man feels a spot of rain and predicts a good harvest' Secluded Buddhist monasteries provide *San kkamagwi yŏmbul anda*, 'Mountain ravens know the mantras', while village **shamanism** gives *Kut mot pogo, ttŏgul mŏngnŭnda*, 'Missing the rite, but eating the feast'

Kwŏnhak 'urging study' proverbs, such as *Iril pu toksŏ, kujung saeng hyŏnggŭk*, 'Miss one day's reading and thorns will grow in the mouth,' form a distinctive group showing neo-Confucian earnestness. The same proverbial purpose shows in learned Chinese clichés like *hyugyu-gyup'o*, 'never noticing the mallow-plot' (like Dong Zhongshu, who studied so hard for three years that he never noticed the vegetable garden outside his window) and *sŏran-hyŏngch'ang*, 'snow-desk and glow-worm net' (from two boys who were too poor to buy oil: in winter Sun Kang read by the glare from snow, in summer Che Yun lit his desk with a gauze bag full of glow-worms).

Weather sayings too are often Chinese, like the hackneyed autumn saw *Ch'ŏn-go ma-bi*, 'The sky is high (clear) and horses fat', and the winter observation *samhan-saon*, 'three [days] cold, four warm', that neatly describes the alternation of high pressure from Siberia and low pressure from China from December to February.

Rhythmic rules, like *Ch'un pul ch'ul, ha pul il; ch'u pul kŏn, tong pul sŭp*, 'In spring not outside, in summer not in the sun; in autumn not dry, in winter not wet,' for growing orchids in one's study, are mnemonic. So are 'numerical categories' like the Three Points of Pride (*sam kyo*): *pan, mun, pu*, 'social class, literary skill and wealth'. Earthy proverbs raise no giggles: *Kaettongdo yage ssŭryŏmyŏn, madange ŏpta*, 'When you want dog-dung for medicine, there's none in the yard.'

Many proverbs are current in both Chinese and Korean form. *Tŭngha pulmyŏng* comes in native Korean as *Tŭngjan mit'i ŏdupta*, 'It is darkest under the lamp.' Korean forms may preserve archaic words, like *kumk* in *Nŏgurido tŭl-gumk nal-gumgŭl p'anda*, 'Even a racoon-dog digs a hole to go in by and a hole to go out by',

Records begin with traces of proverbs in *Samguk yusa*. **Chŏng Yagyong** collected 200 examples in *Idam sokch'an* and translated them into rhymed couplets of four-character verse; but the best collection, Yi Kimun's *Soktam sajŏn* (1962, containing 7,000 examples), is far from complete, and production continues in phrases like *plhaengi t'aeunda*, 'to take for an aeroplane ride' (to overpraise).

BRUCE GRANT, *Korean Proverbs*, Salt Lake City: Moth House, 1982

PROVINCES *to* 道

The thirteen provinces of the 20th century (if we disregard communist divisions in the north) were established in principle in 1402 when the Chosŏn kingdom created eight. (*See* map, p. xix). Most of them had existed before in some form as political or administrative areas. Following the configuration of mountain ranges and other natural demarcations, they evoke strong loyalties in their inhabitants (*see* **provincial stereotypes**). In the list below, the provinces asterisked are those that were divided into North and South provinces in 1896, when the number was increased from eight to thirteen. The years when the present names were first used are shown in the second column. (Apart from Kyŏnggi, each name is composed of the first syllables of two of the major towns.) In the 3rd column, W or N indicates that the northern or western part of the province was the *udo* in the five provinces that were divided into *chwado* and *udo*, left and right provinces, from mid-Chosŏn times until 1896. The 4th column shows the single-syllable poetic names that were also applied to the provincial military commands, with the meaning of each in the 5th column. The last column shows the Chosŏn period provincial capitals.

Kyŏnggi	1402	N	Ki	'royal domain'	Seoul
P'yŏngan*	1413	–	Ki	'**Kija**' (reputed founder)	P'yŏngyang
Hamgyŏng*	1473	–	Ham	'united'	Hamhŭng
Kangwŏn	1311	–	Wŏn	'source'	Wŏnju
Hwanghae	1407	W	Hae	'sea'	Haeju
Ch'ungch'ŏng*	1356	W	Kŭm	'embroidered' (river name)	Kongju
Chŏlla*	1018	W	Wan	'whole'	Chŏnju
Kyŏngsang*	1314	W	Yŏng	'mountain pass'	**Taegu**

Alternative names, some of them ancient, are found in literary and popular use. Two refer to the Kŭm River, also known as the Ho River: Honam for Chŏlla, Hosŏ for Ch'ungch'ŏng. The rest refer to mountain passes. Yŏngnam or Kyonam ('south of the ridge'), for Kyŏngsang, means 'south of the pass', referring to Choryŏng or Saejae, the 'Bird Pass' that took the main road from Koesan in Ch'ungch'ŏng to Mun'gyŏng in Kyŏngsang. *Yŏng* for mountain pass is also used in Yŏngsŏ and Yŏngdong, meaning the western mountains and eastern coastal strip of Kangwŏn province, the pass in question being Taegwallyŏng near Kangnŭng.

Kwan, meaning a border post and hence often a pass, gives Kwannam and Kwanbuk ('south or north of the pass') in Hamgyŏng, where the border is at Mach'ŏl-lyŏng near Sŏngjin; but the *kwan* in Kwandong and Kwansŏ ('east or west of the pass'), meaning Kangwŏn and P'yŏngan, has not been identified.

Two new cities have become provincial capitals. Taejŏn, which replaced Kongju for South Ch'ungch'ŏng in 1914, was before that date a hamlet called Hanbat. The Japanese wrote that name in Chinese characters and gave it to the nodal railway junction. **Pusan,** the old harbour for **Tongnae**, became a treaty port in 1876 and the provincial capital of South Kyŏngnam was moved there from Chinju in 1925.

YI CHUNGHWAN (1690–1756), trans. CHOI INSHIL, *Yi Chung-hwan's T'aengniji, the Korean Classic for Choosing Settlements*, University of Sydney Press, 1998

PROVINCIAL ADMINISTRATION *oegwanjik* 外官職

Under the Chosŏn dynasty, officials (K. *suryŏng*), usually called 'governors' and 'magistrates' in English, were appointed by the king for the whole country. There was a *kwanch'alsa* 'inspector' or *kamsa* 'governor', a man of 2nd **grade** junior, for each of the eight **provinces**. He was appointed for one year only, lest he should build up a local power-base. Each province also had an office, *kyŏngjaeso*, in Seoul.

Within a province larger cities such as **Kaesŏng**, **Kanghwa** and **Suwŏn** ranked as *pu* 'city', headed by a *puyun* 'city overseer' or 'mayor' of 2nd grade junior. The capital was governed by *Hansŏng-bu* 'Hansŏng council' of 9 members, with a *p'anyun* 'judge-and-overseer' of 2nd grade senior for mayor, independent of the provincial arrangements.

The rest of the province was divided into areas of different rank, all independent of one another, conventionally termed prefectures. The 20 most important prefectures in the land were *mok*, cities of some size, governed by *moksa*, 'pastoral deputy', of 3rd grade senior. The 82 prefectures of the next grade were *kun* 'prefectures', headed by *kunsu* 'prefects' of 4th grade junior. Then there were 26 *hyŏn*, 'larger counties', the third size of prefecture, governed by *hyŏllyŏng* 'district commanders' of 5th grade junior; and 138 smaller *hyŏn* 'districts', the smallest administrative areas, under *hyŏn'gam* 'district supervisors', of 6th grade junior.

These officials were responsible for the prosperity of their areas, collecting **taxes** and organising **corvée** labour. They were assisted by *yukpang*, 'six chambers', named after the **Six Boards** of the central goverment and fulfilling the same functions at local level. The **yamen** was staffed by minor local officials called *ajŏn* 'yamen front', meaning 'subordinates'. The *ajŏn* were all *chungin*, and were classed as *sŏri* 'writer', *sŏwŏn* 'clerk' or *yŏngni* 'garrison clerk'. Hereditary *ajŏn* were called *hyangni* 'local scribes' or, if they had come from another place, *kurl* 'incomer scribes'.

There were also 360 local institutions called *hyangch'ŏng* 'rural offices' or advisory groups organised by local landowners, an institution that was sporadically abolished and restored by the central government. They could become fulcrums of power for the local *yangban*.

PROVINCIAL STEREOTYPES *P'alto-insim-p'yŏng* 八道人心評
Four-character phrases stereotyping the inhabitants of the eight **provinces** were popular in late Chosŏn. They say much for the cultural arrogance of the central region, but they are historically important, reflecting *Weizhi dongyizhuan* (*see* **Wei, histories of**) and *Hunyo sipcho* (**Wang Kŏn's Ten Injunctions**). The following versions are typical:

Kyŏnggi:	Handsome face in a mirror	*kyŏngjung miin*
Kangwŏn:	Old Buddha under a rock	*amha nobul*
P'yŏngan:	Fierce tiger out of the forest	*maengho ch'ullim*
Hamgyŏng:	Dogs fighting in a muddy field	*ijŏn t'ugu*
Hwanghae:	Ox ploughing a stony field	*sŏkchŏn kyŏngu*
Ch'ungch'ŏng:	Clear breeze and bright moon	*ch'ŏngp'ung myŏngwŏl*
Chŏlla:	Slender bamboo before the wind	*p'ungjŏn seryu*
Kyŏngnam:	High peaks and sheer cliffs	*chunam chŏlbyŏk*

PROVISIONAL GOVERNMENT IN EXILE *Imsi chŏngbu* 臨時政府
Also known as the Korean Provisional Government (KPG); established in Shanghai by around 1,000 Korean nationalists on 10–11 April 1919. It was the first government in Korean history to claim to be democratically entitled to represent the Korean people. It passed a constitution providing for an elected president and legislative assembly, with an independent judiciary. Its chosen leaders themselves were mostly not in Shanghai. Its premier, Syngman Rhee (**Yi Sŭngman**) was in the United States. **Yi Tonghwi** arrived from Siberia in early September. **Kim Kyusik** was in Paris, and one of KPG's first acts was to nominate him as foreign minister and send him to the **Paris Peace Conference**. Thereafter he headed its Commission in Washington. KPG published the ***Tongnip Sinmun***, liaised with the independence movement in Korea, and directed military operations by *ŭibyŏng* in **Manchuria** and **Siberia**. It opened an officers' training school in Shanghai, and set up a historical commission to gather materials that would convince the world of the Korean right to independence. In the United States Syngman Rhee assumed the initial premiership and later the [self-appointed] presidency, though amid frequent disagreements between radical and moderate nationalists, socialists and communists his leadership was not unquestioned and the work of the government was less effective than it might have been. Throughout the 1920s and 1930s a plethora of political societies, more or less radical, were active among overseas Koreans, and the work of KPG continued to be hampered by factionalism and disagreements over policy as well as by financial difficulties. Among its best known sometime leaders were Yi Tonghwi (who succeeded Syngman Rhee as premier in 1919), **An Ch'angho**, Kim Kyusik, **Yŏ Unhyŏng**, and **Kim Ku**, but friction led to the resignation of the first four of these. Rhee himself remained in Shanghai for little more than a year in 1920–2 before returning to the United States. Under Kim Ku's leadership in the 1930s the

organisation engaged in more terrorist activities, including an ill-fated attempt on the life of the Japanese emperor in 1932 (*see* **Yi Pongch'ang**).

In order to avoid Japanese surveillance the Government moved regularly, to Nanking in 1932, Jinjiang in 1935, Changsha in 1937 and Chongqing in 1940. From here it declared war on Japan in 1942 and directed the operations of the **Restoration Army**. Following the Japanese surrender Kim Ku and Kim Kyusik returned to Seoul in November 1945, a month after Syngman Rhee. They found a situation which was already politically divided between left- and right-wing nationalist leaders, headed by Yŏ Unhyŏng and Song Chinu respectively. KPG leaders were resentful of the American refusal to afford it political recognition, and at the frustration of their efforts to guide the establishment of Korean government under the **American Military Government**, but the Americans were suspicious of Rhee's excessive right-wing **nationalism** and had always been alarmed by disunity within the KPG. They were therefore unwilling to deal with it in the formation of the new provisional government in Korea.

Kim Ku resigned as President following the defeat of his proposal to set up a **Korean People's Representative Assembly** in March 1947.

CHONG-SIK LEE, *The Politics of Korean Nationalism*, Berkeley: Institute of East Asian Studies, 1963

See also **Korean Communist Party**; **Korean Democratic Party**; **Korean People's Republic**

PUJŎK 符籍

Also called *pujak* or *puja*. A paper charm inscribed with a mystic diagram, prayer or motto, often unintelligible, that is stuck on a house, boat, or other possession, or carried on the person as a prophylactic against bad luck, curses, demons and the like. Pieces of animal bone, horn or tooth, pebbles, clods of earth, items of food and dolls of various kinds may be used for the same purpose.

PUKHAK 北學 'Northern learning'

Name given in the 18th century to *Sirhak* **movement** scholars in favour of adopting practical elements of Chinese and Western learning. They had encountered new ideas on manufacturing and **commerce** while in China and saw their possible benefits to the Korean people. In particular they urged the introduction of new technology and an end to the reactionary outlook of the dominant *yangban* class in Korea. **Pak Chega** had even advocated trade with Japan and the West.

See **Yŏrha ilgi**

PUKHAN SANSŎNG 北漢山城

The northern **fortress** positioned astride the Pukhan mountains to protect the city of Seoul. Early fortifications had been built in the period when **Paekche** dominated the **Han River** valley. Around 555 the region fell under control of **Silla**, whose King Chinhŭng made a tour of inspection commemorated by an inscribed stone monument ('**Hunting memorial**') erected on the mountain. In the mid-17th century, King Hyojong, faced with the Manchu threat, repaired both Pukhan and Namhan fortresses, and in 1711 King **Sukchong** built the more elaborate castle battlements of Pukhan whose ruins survive today.

See also **Namhan sansŏng**

PUL

A symbol painted on the side of a coffin near the head and on a *pulsap* or placard carried on a pole in the procession to the grave, explained as turning the back on evil and facing the good. It is often confused with the character *a* 'Asia', though it lacks the central third of the top and bottom strokes of *a*. An old form of *anil pul*, the Chinese negative particle, it has been understood since Han times as the symbol called *pul* or *pobul*, one of the **twelve ornaments** for imperial robes. It can also be found repeated in double rows round the edge of uncoloured circular **fans** – perhaps intended for use by mourners.

PULGUK-SA 佛國寺 'Buddha Land Temple'
Buddhist temple constructed at **Kyŏngju** in AD 751 on an earlier **Paekche** foundation. It represents the highest achievement of Unified Silla architecture, craftsmanship and aesthetic appreciation. Its designer is reputed to have been the Chief Minister Kim Taesŏng (701–74). Nestling into the wooded hillside of Toham-san, many of its timber buildings were destroyed in the **Imjin War**. Rebuildings in Chosŏn and modern times according to contemporary descriptions have recreated a complex much smaller than the Silla temple, but evocative of its beauty and peace. Its surviving stone **pagodas** (*see Tabot'ap*) and staircases display superb artistry and sense of symmetry and proportion. *See also* **bronze**; **Buddhas**; **Sŏkkuram**

PUNCH'ŎNG 粉青 'light blue/green'
A class of utilitarian **pottery** that developed and became popular in the early Chosŏn period. It went into widespread production at **kilns** across central and southern Korea, and is characterised by its unpretentious style and an exhilarating boldness in decoration. It was made of grey clay containing **iron**, and was thickly covered with white slip before glazing. Its transparent glaze gave it a powder blue quality, and painting with underglaze iron oxide provided a distinctive and pleasant brown and bluish-cream colour combination. Designs were generally simple and even humorous in the manner of folk art rather than refined artistry, but frequently display a high sense of compositional balance and rhythm. Subjects include flowers, fish, butterflies, and birds, as well as calligraphic and abstract patterns and overall geometric designs, and were painted, inlaid, incised, and stamped.
See also **ceramics**

PUNHONG-BANG 粉紅榜 'pink roster'
A satirical expression from 1378, when very young sons of powerful men, 'still smelling of milk and wearing red clothes', were passed in the state **examinations**.

PUPPET PLAY *kkoktuk-kaksi*
The traditional Korean puppet play is performed outdoors at night in the light of flares, by *namsadang* (who call it *tŏlmi*) using wooden puppets with jointed limbs, mounted on sticks so that the puppeteer can be hidden below the stage, as in the English Punch and Judy. All the puppets are caricatures. The puppeteers speak the dialogue; *sanbaji*, a member of the troupe standing or sitting in front of the stage, comments and conducts conversations with the puppets during the performance. The words vary with each

performance, but there is only one play. Its content has much in common with **masked drama** and is equally earthy, though the incidents are linked by two characters who appear throughout. The chief character is an old *yangban* with a huge beard, called Pak **Ch'ŏmji**, who gets into all sorts of trouble and consorts with disreputable people. He is supported by Hong **Tongji**, a naked ithyphallic man painted red, given to horseplay, but puckishly helpful. Supporting cast includes Pak's wife, called Kkokktuk-kaksi, a stupid Governor of P'yŏngan (*P'yŏngan kamsa*), a **concubine**, dancing girls, amorous Buddhist monks, and a man-eating snake. Incidents include the monks dallying with the girls, a pheasant hunt (in which the pheasant flies on wires), the snake terrorising the village and a funeral procession with banners – at which Hong Tongji causes uproar by appearing naked as a pall-bearer. The finale is a transformation scene in which a brightly coloured and gilded Buddhist temple hall is built on the stage. As they leave, the spectators make offerings to this shrine.

The history of this theatre is obscure, but there were puppets in **Koguryŏ** and a continental, perhaps central Asian, origin has been surmised. Earlier plays may have expressed Buddhist devotion. The present story, poking fun at the gentry and monks, bears marks of the Chosŏn dynasty. It was probably intended more as entertainment than as social protest.

PURE LAND *See Ch'ŏntae-jong*

PURGES, LITERATI 士禍 *See* **literati purges**; *Sahwa*

PUSAN 釜山 'Cauldron Hill'
The harbour for **Tongnae**, from which it was approximately five miles distant, and the main port for trade between Japan and Korea. It was officially opened for residence by Japanese merchants in the reign of King T'aejong, confirmed by treaties in 1443 and 1512. In 1592 it was the landfall for Admiral Hideyoshi's invasion at the start of the **Imjin War**, and in 1875 the scene of a clash between Japanese marines and local troops. The following year it was opened to foreigners as a Treaty Port under the **Kanghwa Treaty**. By the end of the century Japanese merchants had heavy investments in the port, and in 1898 the Japanese were granted a concession to build a **railway** line between Seoul and Pusan, to be managed jointly by the Korean and Japanese governments. It was begun in 1904. As part of the nationwide unrest of workers at Japanese exploitation in the early colonial period, Pusan dockworkers went on strike in 1921. In August 1950 South Korean and American forces staged their last stand around Pusan (the 'Pusan perimeter') and fought off the North Korean aggressors (*see* **Korean War**).
PAUL EDWARDS, *The Pusan Perimeter, Korea, 1950: an Annotated Bibliography*, London: Greenwood Press, 1993; PUSAN HISTORY COMPILATION COMMITTEE, *The History and Culture of Pusan*, City of Pusan, 1993

PUYŎ 扶餘
(1) Agricultural kingdom located in the Sungari River basin of north-eastern **Manchuria**; its capital was at Nong'an, near modern Jilin. It originated some time before the 4th century BC and maintained friendly tributary relations with China in the Later **Han dynasty**. Frequently threatened, it suffered defeat by the nomadic Xianbei from the east in AD 285 and 346 and also lost territory to its southern neighbour **Koguryŏ**. Finally, after invasion from the north by a new Tunguistic tribe, **Malgal**, its royal family sought asylum in Koguryŏ in 494.

PAK YANGJIN, 'Archaeological Evidence of Puyŏ Society in Northeast China', *KJ*, 36/4, 1996
See also **Chumong**; **Parhae**
(2) City in South Ch'ungch'ŏng province. It was the capital of the kingdom of **Paekche** from 538 to 660, known as **Sabi**. Substantial historical remains of this period have been found and are housed in the Puyŏ branch of the National Musuem, built in Paekche architectural style.

PYŎGWI-P'YŎN 闢衛編 'Documents of Exposition and Defence'
Also called *Pyŏgwi-hwip'yŏn*. A collection of official documents and other material about the treatment of Catholics from 1785 to 1839, containing some Catholic texts and material on foreign relations and **factions**. Originally made by Yi Kigyŏng (1756–1819), an acquaintance of **Yi Pyŏk** who became a critic of Catholicism, it was expanded by his fourth-generation descendant, Yi Manjae, and printed in 1931.

PYŎLMUBAN 別武班 'Extraordinary Military Division'
Special army formed by King Sukchong (r. 1095–1105) to confront the **Jurchen** threat. It consisted of three sections, cavalry drawn from the aristocracy, infantry made up of **peasants**, and – reflecting the religious orientation of the court – a unit of Buddhist monks, *hangmagun* ('Exorcise demons army'), who not only had an established reputation for fighting, but might help to bring supra-human powers to bear in the battle. Under the leadership of Yun Kwan it attacked the Jurchen in 1107 and occupied and fortified a region between modern Wŏnsan and Hŭngnam (Kangwŏn province).

PYŎN KWANSIK 卞寬植 (Sojong, 1899–1976)
Leading participant in artistic relations between Korea and Japan in the 20th century and contributor to the development of modern Korean landscape painting. He studied at the *Sohwa Misurhoe* and exhibited in the Korean Art Exhibition (*see Sŏnjŏn*) in 1922. In 1922, together with **Yi Sangbŏm**, he founded the *Tongyŏnsa* ('Joint Research Society'). After further study in Japan between 1925 and 1929 he returned as Secretary General of the *Shōwa Hyŏphoe*. In 1954 he became a judge in the National Art Exhibition (*Kukchŏn*), but resigned in 1957. His own landscape style, developed in the **Diamond Mountains** after 1937, used layers of Chinese ink and wavy lines, and took a bird's eye view of a scene. Examples of his work are *Farmhouse* (National Museum for Contemporary Art) and *Lone house by a riverside village* (National Museum for Contemporary Art).

PYŎN SANGBYŎK 卞相璧 (Hwaje, 18th century)
Professional artist and a member of the *Tohwa-sŏ*. He painted portraits and animals, and was most renowned for his pictures of cats, hens and chicks, which earned him the nickname Pyŏn the Cat, Pyŏn Koeyang (literally 'wondrous form' but a pun on *koyangi*, 'cat'). His close observation of animal behaviour and meticulous care for detailed depiction of their fur and feathers can be seen in *Cats and sparrows* (National Museum of Korea).[1]
(1) ROGER GOEPPER & RODERICK WHITFIELD, *Treasures from Korea*, London: British Museum Publications, 1984

PYŎNGJA-ROK 丙子綠 'Records of the Red Rat Year (1636)'
The title sometimes given to various books about the **Manchu invasions** of 1636–7. Some of the stories may come from *han'gŭl* translations and expansions of a book of similar title, a genuine diary by Na Man'gap (1592–1642).

PYŎNHAN 弁韓
One of the three proto-states (*see* **Samhan**) which covered much of southern Korea from the 1st to the 3rd century AD (the **Proto-Three Kingdoms Period**). It was located in the central southern part of the peninsula with its walled capital at Kuya (modern **Kimhae**). Unlike **Chinhan** and **Mahan** it did not evolve into one of the three kingdoms of the succeeding era, but was the forerunner of the later **Kaya** federation. It served as a centre for **iron** distribution northwards to **Lelang** and **Ye** and outwards to **Wa** (Japan).

P'AEGWAN LITERATURE 稗官文學
P'aegwan munhak is a vague term first used by Kim T'aejun in *Chosŏn sosŏl sa*, 'History of Korean Fiction' (1933), referring to late Koryŏ writing. It has since been used in various ways, but is generally applied to oral and anecdotal literature, *p'aegwan* having been an official sent out by the king to learn from the common people's talk what their opinions were.

P'AHAN-JIP 破閑集 'Collection [written] to dispose of leisure'
Yi Illo (1150–1220) was a gifted poet. During the **Chŏng Chungbu** rebellion he spent some time as a Buddhist monk, but later became leader of the **Seven Worthies** club. Early in his career he visited China, where his poetry was admired, but *P'ahan-jip* is all that remains of his writings. It is not a *chip* in the commoner sense, meaning a collection of his whole works, but a small volume of poems by himself and others, many of which he feared might get lost. It is reckoned the oldest of Korean *sihwa*.

P'ALGWANHOE 八關會 'Eight Vows Festival'
Festival in commemoration of departed spirits, derived from a **Koguryŏ** village festival, *Tongmaeng*. The first record of its observance occurs in AD 572. It was maintained through the Unified Silla and was specially commended in the **Ten Injunctions** (*Sip Hunyo*) of **Wang Kŏn**. During the Koryŏ dynasty it was celebrated as a national festival on the 15th day of the 11th moon. Its rites were drawn from both **Buddhism** and **animism** and enjoyed by Koreans of all classes. The Ten Injunctions said, 'It is with the *p'algwan* that we serve the Heavenly Spirits, the Five Sacred Mountains, the Famous Mountains, the Great Rivers, and the Dragon Spirits.' At court Chinese elements such as the stately ball-throwing game *p'ogurak* were introduced into this formal entertainment and were observed by visiting Chinese envoys and **merchants**. In the countryside it was associated with the harvest and was characterised by the raucous fun of farmers' music, *nongak*. It was not observed by the Chosŏn dynasty.
See also ***Yŏndŭnghoe***

P'ALGYŎNG 八景 *See* **Eight Views**

P'AL-SSANG 八相 *See* **Eight scenes [in the life of Sakyamuni]**

P'ANMUNJŎM 板門店 *See* **DMZ**

P'ANSA 判事
A title given to the president of the ***Ŭigŭm-bu*** and to the second officer of the ***Tollyŏng-bu*** and ***Chungch'u-bu*** (posts of 1st **grade** junior), though in the early years of the Chosŏn dynasty it was used more widely for posts of 1st to 3rd grades. Variously translated as 'chief magistrate' or 'director'.

P'ANSŎ 判書
The title for the presiding officer of each of the **Six Boards**, held by a 2nd **grade** senior. Often translated as 'minister'.

P'ANSORI 'open-air singing'
Korea has no operatic tradition, but *p'ansori* preserves a form of outdoor public story-telling which, together with **masked dance drama**, is its nearest equivalent. It is a sung narrative, performed by a *kwangdae*, which probably emerged in Ch'ungch'ŏng and Chŏlla provinces during the 18th century, though neither the origin of the *genre* nor the meaning of *p'an* are generally agreed. Some scholars have suggested a link with **shamanism**. The earliest account is in *Kwanuhŭi*, 'at the performance', a Chinese poem by Song Manjae (1769–1847), listing twelve titles, of which five texts survive. The **Sirhak movement** gave impetus to *p'ansori*, and it enjoyed particular development and popularity in the 19th century. During the 20th century *ch'anggŭk* was developed from *p'ansori*. After languishing under Japanese colonial rule it has again thrived under the influence of the *minjung* **movement** in the late 20th century.

P'ansori is performed by a single singer, using only a fan and a handkerchief as props, with an accompanist on the *puk* or *changgo* **drum**. The stories are well known to audiences as adaptations of old vernacular novels. The best-known examples deal with such popular themes as *Ch'unhyang, Sim Ch'ŏng, Hungbu-jŏn, Sugung-ga*, and *Chŏkpyŏk-ka*. The singer employs an unnatural and strong form of voice production which requires long and arduous training. The sung parts, which are a mixture of elegance and popular satire, are linked by spoken passages called *aniri*. The performer may ad lib and entertain the listeners with satirical comments attacking the leaders of local society, and engages in repartee with the accompanist and the audience. The complete performance of a single story may last eight hours, but abbreviated versions are normal.

MARSHALL PIHL, 'Dramatic Structure and Narrative Technique in the Korean Oral Narrative, P'ansori,' *KJ*, 24/11, 1984; MARSHALL PIHL, *The Korean Singer of Tales*, Cambridge, Mass.: Harvard University Press, 1994

P'ANSU
A type of male shaman, to be distinguished from both *mudang* and *paksu*. A *p'ansu* does not use the paraphernalia, trances and dramatic dancing of a *mudang*, nor keep a spirit shrine. He is usually blind and functions in the hours of darkness, as a rule in his clients' houses. His chief purpose is healing, which he performs by reciting incantations and spells taken from printed **books**. These books are said often to be imports from China. He also divines the future with a kind of metal **dice**, coins or Chinese characters. On occasions he will perform exorcisms or instal domestic spirit nests (*see t'ŏju*). There are very few sighted *p'ansu* and even fewer women *p'ansu*. The blind masseurs who walk the streets at night crying out for clients are not *p'ansu*.
See also **divination; shamanism**

P'IRI 觱篥
Four double reed oboes are known in Korea. One, the *t'aep'yŏngso*, is unique in the Korean instrumentarium. The other three are related to each other. *Hyangp'iri* ('native oboe') is the largest of them, and because of its powerful and expressive dynamic range it often leads orchestral ensembles in the announcement of the tune. Its tone may be warm and mellow or strident and piercing, and strong vibrato is produced by movement of the lips and control of the air in the cheeks. Its double reed is bound by a

copper band and inserted into the upper end of the bamboo pipe at a slight downward angle. The pipe has eight finger holes, the first of which is on the reverse. The *sep'iri* is a more slender instrument producing a softer tone, and the *tangp'iri* ('Chinese oboe') a shorter, fatter version used in *tangak* pieces. Despite their names all three probably originated in central Asia and the first of them arrived on the Korean peninsula during the Koguryŏ dynasty.
See also **musical instruments**

P'OSŎK-CHŎNG 鮑石亭 'Abalone Stones Pavilion'
A Silla palace site at **Kyŏngju**. The pavilion has long since disappeared, but the 'abalone stones (*yusang-goksu* 'winding stream for floating cups')' remain: a narrow runnel made of carved stones, set out on the ground roughly in the shape of an abalone shell. It was used for party games, when wine-cups were floated on the water of the runnel in some form of poetry competition. The floor of the pavilion was originally built level with the top of the runnel, as at Lanting, the 'orchid pavilion' of the great calligrapher Wang Xizhi (321–379) at Shaojing, Zhejiang, and other Chinese examples. P'osŏk-chŏng is famous because in 926, during the death throes of Silla, **Kyŏn Hwŏn** and his men burst in on a party there and slaughtered King Kyŏngae and his courtiers.

P'UNGSU 風水 (C. *fengshui*) 'wind and water'
The art of choosing good sites for settlements, buildings and graves is usually called 'geomancy', but this word is increasingly criticised, because *p'ungsu* is not a mantic method and does not use earth as geomancers do. It must originally have been a simple and rational art, easily learned in the climate and terrain of northern China and Korea, and correctly, if quaintly, called 'ubication'. The placing of most Korean villages is typical: on the south side of a hill, to catch the winter sun; well above flood level, with water further south, sheltering spurs to east and west, and curving approach roads to hinder intruders. This art was possibly regarded as a distinct skill even before *yin-yang* theory began to flourish in China during the 3rd or 2nd century BC. By the 2nd or 3rd century AD, while **Daoism** was becoming an organised religion, though not as part of Daoism, a pseudo-science (now K. *p'ungsu-jiri-sŏl* 'wind-and-water theory of land principles') evolved, giving *fengshui* a philosophic substructure.

Life-forces were posited in geology, and their relationship to human prosperity was discerned. Technical terms were introduced from other sciences, especially **astronomy**. An eastern spur became *chwa-ch'ŏngnyong*, a blue/green **dragon** on the left, with *yang* power; a western spur *u-baekho*, a white **tiger** on the right, with *yin* power. A grave site needed *naeryong* 'approaching dragon' (a ridge of small peaks) which was best if it were *hoeryong-gojo* 'a curled dragon looking to its ancestor' (a curving ridge where the lowest point faced the highest). The *chwahyang* '[southern] prospect from the seat' became important, and there must be no *kyubong* (overlooking peak), however distant. Recipes were found for curing poor *p'ungsu* by erecting **pagodas** and digging lakes. The subject became occult, but began to permeate society and to be used politically.

The founder of *p'ungsu* in Korea is said to have been **Tosŏn** in the 10th century. Traces in such Three Kingdoms tales as that of King T'arhae of Silla are ambivalent, but **Wang Kŏn**'s trust in Tosŏn was expressed in his **Ten Injunctions**. It influenced the location of his capital at **Kaesŏng** and the creation of western, eastern and southern capitals at P'yŏngyang, **Kyŏngju**, and Seoul. Soon King **Chŏngjong** (r. 945–9) and later the monk-rebel **Myoch'ŏng** (in 1127) tried to move the capital on *p'ungsu* principles. In 1392 **Yi Sŏnggye** built his new capital of Hanyang on a site that is still visibly a perfect *p'ungsu* choice. Early in the Ch'osŏn dynasty the Confucian officials in the Department of Astronomy and Meteorology (*Sŏun-gwan*, later Kwansang-gam) used Chinese *fengshui* books in an attempt to control the spread of Buddhist burial practices.

P'ungsu theory was eventually enshrined in *Ch'ŏn'gi-daeyo*, which remains in use. A *chigwan* 'siting expert' is called in with his *yundo*, a compass marked with the 24 directions and other signs (more even than the *kugung*), to investigate proposed sites for industrial complexes as well as humble homes and graves. The *yundo* played a vital part in the Chinese development of the magnetic compass.

CHOI CHANG-JO, '*P'ungsu*, the Korean Traditional Geographic Thoughts,' *KJ*, 26/5, 1986; ERNEST EITEL, *Fengshui*, London: Trubner, 1873 and various reprints, including Singapore: Brash, 1995; YI CHUNGHWAN, trans. CHOI INSHIL, *Yi Chung-hwan's T'aengniji, the Korean Classic for Choosing Settlements*, University of Sydney Press, 1998

P'YŎNGYANG 平壤

The capital of modern North Korea and a city with ancient historical associations; situated on the **Taedong River** and sometimes known as the 'willow capital' (*yugyŏng*). Its seaport is the city of Namp'o. Reputedly chosen by **Tan'gun** (*see* **foundation myths**) as his capital on earth, as **Wanggŏmsŏng** it was the capital of **Wiman Chosŏn** and later as T'osŏngni the centre of the Chinese commandery of **Lelang**. From 427 to 668 it was the [third] capital of the kingdom of **Koguryŏ**. Here, in 668, China set up a regional centre (**Kyerim**) from which it hoped to direct the newly unified peninsula as a Chinese protectorate (*see* **Tang dynasty**). Having declined through the Unified Silla period it was strategically redeveloped by King T'aejo in the Koryŏ dynasty and designated the Western Capital, and in 1135 it was briefly taken over by the **Myoch'ŏng** rebels as their headquarters. It continued to entice attack, being occupied subsequently by the **Mongols** (1232), the **Red Turbans** (1359), the Japanese (1593, *see* **Imjin War**), and the Manchus (1627, *see* **Manchu invasions**). The armies of Japan defeated those of China at P'yŏngyang in the course of the **Sino-Japanese War** (1895). In the first half of the 20th century its inhabitants were active in resistance to the Japanese and as adherents of Christianity. In 1945 the city became *de facto* capital of the north Korean zone under Soviet control, and **Kim Ilsŏng** was put in charge of the communist administration. As subsequent capital of the **Democratic People's Republic of Korea** it has remained the largest city in the country, with an estimated population in 1986 of around two million inhabitants.

P'YŎN'GYŎNG 編磬

One of the most important musical instruments in ancient China, officially transmitted to Korea for the first time with the gift of *aak* in 1116, although written sources suggest that it had already been made in Korea in the previous century. It comprised sixteen stones hung in two ranks of eight on a decorated wooden frame, and represented the *ŭm* equivalent of the [*yang*] *p'yŏnjong* bells, with which it played in unison. The stones, similar in shape to a capital 'L', were suspended by a cord threaded through a hole near the point of the right angle, so that their longer sides hung lower. The player, seated before them on the ground, struck them near the bottom edge with a hammer made of horn. The pitches of the stones could be adjusted by varying the respective lengths of the longer and shorter arms. The instrument was played in both *aak* and *tangak*, and had been adopted for *hyangak* use by the early Chosŏn dynasty.

See also **musical instruments**

P'YŎNJONG 編鐘

One of the largest instruments used in traditional Korean musical ensembles. It is closely matched by the *p'yŏn'gyŏng*, with which it was paired as *yang* to *ŭm*, the two frequently playing in unison. Twenty examples were received from China in 1116 for the performance of *aak* (*see* **Yejong, King**). Ten consisted of twelve **bronze** bells and ten of sixteen. Today, only the sixteen-bell version is used. Two ranks of eight bells are suspended on a decorated wooden frame. At the base of the two uprights are a pair of lions, giving the instrument its military feel in contrast to the civil tone imparted by the ducks in the same position on the *p'yŏn'gyŏng*. The bells are elliptical in cross-section and all of the same size, differences in thickness determining their pitch. The player, seated on the ground, uses a hammer made of horn to strike the bottom rim of the bell at a point indicated on it by a circle. Though originally reserved for use in Confucian ritual the bells also came to be used in other court ceremonies. They are still played at the **Sŏnggyun-gwan** and the **Chongmyo** Shrine, and may also be heard in performances of *Nagyang-ch'un*, *Pohŏja*, and *Yŏmillak*.
See also **musical instruments**

Q

QING DYNASTY 清朝 (K. Ch'ŏngjo, China, 1644–1911)

Relations with China under its Manchu rulers could have been fatally compromised by the **Manchu invasions** of Korea in 1627 and 1636. However, both China and Korea had known and survived foreign overlordship before, the sense of sinocentrism among the Korean neo-Confucian literati was strong, and the Korean court was anxious not to prompt further Manchu displeasure by withholding its traditional show of allegiance to the Middle Kingdom. Consequently, **tribute** was sent to the foreign Sons of Heaven both before and after their occupation of Beijing in 1644. Though Korea's dependence on China was called into question by scholars contributing to the *sirhak* **movement** through the 17th and 18th centuries, this did not hinder the flow of Koreans travelling to China for all kinds of purposes, and though a growing mood of intellectual self-sufficiency encouraged political isolationism in the early 19th century, there was no suggestion that diplomatic ties with China should or could be cut. The **Taewŏn'gun** was no lover of China but accepted that it was the one foreign country to which Korean doors must be kept open. However, the growing interest in Korea shown by Japan and the western powers, including **Russia**, put China's traditional influence at risk, and following King **Kojong**'s assumption of authority in 1873, the court at Beijing had to take more positive steps to try to preserve its special relationship. The chief architect of its policies was **Li Hongzhang**, who sent **Yuan Shikai** to Seoul after the *Imo* **Incident**. There Yuan not only took charge of Sino-Korean Trade Regulations but also of the Korean army. In 1884 he commanded the Chinese troops who crushed the pro-Japanese plotters of the *Kapsin* **coup**, and strengthened the position of the pro-Chinese Queen **Min**. When he became Chinese Resident-General in Seoul the following year he was not only, in the eyes of some, the most powerful man in Korea, but was also the first man since the 7th century to be entrusted by the Chinese court with such a responsibility (*see* **Tang dynasty**). China had little international influence in the late 19th century and was not going to let Korea slip without a struggle. Koreans, however, were resentful at Yuan's interference in their affairs, and the Japanese also objected to the growth of Chinese exports to Korea, which came about despite the preferential trading position enjoyed by Japan since the **Kanghwa Treaty**. In 1894 the success of the **Tonghak** rebels led to the government's request for Chinese aid, the last occasion on which Korea would recognise its tributary relationship with the Middle Kingdom. In a re-run of 1592 (**Imjin Wars**) the result was military confrontation between Chinese and Japanese soldiers on Korean soil. The effect, as it had been in the late Ming, was to drive a nail into the coffin of the ruling dynasty in Beijing.

FREDERICK FOO CHIEN, *The Opening of Korea: a Study of Chinese Diplomacy 1876–85*, Hamden, Conn.: Shoe String Press, 1967; HAE JONG CHUN, 'Sino-Korean Tributary Relations in the Ch'ing Period', in FAIRBANK, J.K., ed., *The Chinese World Order: Traditional China's Foreign Relations*, Cambridge, Mass.: Harvard University Press 1968; KIM KEY-HUICK, *The Last Phase of the East Asian World Order: Korea, Japan, and the Chinese Empire, 1860–82*, Berkeley: University of California Press, 1980; MARY WRIGHT, 'The Adaptability of Ch'ing Diplomacy: the Case of Korea,' *JAS*, XVII, 1958

See also **Sino-Japanese War**

QUEEN CHINDŎK'S POEM *T'aep'yŏng-si* 太平頌

A 'song in praise of prosperity', supposedly the oldest extant Korean poem. The text is preserved in several places, notably *Samguk sagi* and the 18th-century Chinese *Quan tang shi*. **Yi Kyubo** considered it as good as the work of early Tang poets and better than **Ŭlchi Mundŏk's** famous quatrain. It was sent to the Tang emperor in AD 650 with a report of the decisive **Silla** victory over **Paekche** in 649, the diplomatic purpose being to cultivate the friendship of the relatively new but powerful **Tang dynasty**. The poem is an ode of fulsome praise in twenty old-style 5-character verses on a single rhyme, replete with classical quotations, and probably not written by Queen Chindŏk (r. 647–54) herself.

> When great Tang began its glorious work
> And the plans of the eminent emperor prospered,
> Fighting stopped and men donned robes of peace,
> Civil rule resumed the heritage of earlier kings.
>
> Heaven was constrained to bestow precious rain,
> The earth put in order and all things made bright.
> Now high imperial goodness shines like the sun and moon,
> The peace and prosperity of Yao and Shun have returned.
>
> How brilliant his streamer banners,
> How thunderous his gongs and drums!
> Outer barbarians who oppose his commands
> Suffer Heaven's displeasure and fall by the sword;
>
> Gentle manners prevail in private and public,
> While happy omens vie with each other, far and near;
> The four seasons are balanced in perfect harmony,
> The seven planets swing through their full courses;
>
> The hills bring forth great ministers,
> The emperor employs the loyal and good.
> The Three Sovereigns and Five Rulers combine in one man
> To adorn the imperial house of Tang.

QUELPAERT
This name for **Cheju-do** (Cheju Island, which was earlier called by the Portuguese name Ilha dos Ladrones, 'isle of robbers') is first found in 1648, in Netherlands East India Company records. In Dutch *quelpert* or *quelpaert* means a shallow-draft two-masted vessel such as began to be used in the China Seas about that time, though why this should have been chosen as the name for the island – if indeed this is its explanation – is not clear. Quelpaert became the usual European name for Cheju and remained in use until the opening of Korea to the West.

R

RAILWAYS
The question of building railways in Korea was first raised and rights allocated to the Japanese in the Provisional Agreement concluded on 20 August 1894 by Foreign Minister **Kim Yunsik** and the Japanese Minister Ōtori Keisuke. This concession was soon revoked, but before the end of the century Japan had acquired the partially completed Seoul-Sinŭiju and Seoul-Inch'ŏn lines from French and American constructors in 1896 and 1899 respectively. For financial reasons small Korean companies and the Korean government alike failed in their attempts to build railways around the turn of the century. The outbreak of the **Russo-Japanese War** encouraged Japanese plans for the exploitation of Korea as its protectorate, including the development of its railway system. The Seoul-Pusan and Seoul-Sinŭiju lines, linking the south coast with the northern border on the **Yalu River**, were important to the war effort and were taken over and finished in 1905. In the process, a large number of Koryŏ tombs were disturbed in the vicinity of **Kaesŏng**, revealing a substantial quantity of high quality **celadon** wares. Guerillas of the Korean resistance made attacks on railway lines and installations, but after the Japanese **annexation** in 1910 further lines were built under the control of the **South Manchurian Railway** Company. Between the 1920s and 1940s the rail network was greatly expanded as part of the economic base for Japanese continental expansion, linking the south coast with Manchuria. It was built by Korean labour and operated by the **Government-General**, and was used predominantly by the Japanese and their industries. Nevertheless it opened up rural areas for new economic development and led to the creation of many new towns. By 1945, Korea had around 4,000 miles of single and double track railway, but much of this system was destroyed in the **Korean War**. In the South, this mileage had been restored and modernised by 1980.

RAIN-GAUGE *ch'ŭgu-gi* 測雨器
King **Sejong** planned rain-gauges in 1441, but did not succeed in producing them until the following year. At first they were made of **iron**, with the main cylinder 43cm high and 17cm in diameter. Subsequently copper was used. **Ceramic** versions in the provinces may have been patterns for making metal gauges. Although these have been claimed as the first rain-gauges ever made, Qin Jiushao discussed mathematical problems involved in making them in China two centuries earlier (*Shushu jiuzhang*, 1247). In both China and Korea they were set up throughout the provinces. The western rain-gauge was devised by Benedetto Castelli, disciple of Galileo, in 1639.

RAMSTEDT, GUSTAF JOHAN (1873–1950)
Finnish linguist, who studied Finno-Ugrian languages at Helsinki university. After graduating in 1895 he spent twenty years travelling in central Asia, collecting Turkic

and Mongol language materials. In Kazan about 1899 he met his first Korean and became interested in the Korean language. In 1917 he was appointed minister to China, Japan and Thailand, residing in Tokyo, where he became interested in the relationship of Japanese and Korean to other languages. Returning to Finland in 1930 he became honorary professor of Altaic Languages, continuing to study and publish. Ramstedt's work is the basis of an emergent consensus linking the Korean language with the Altaic group. His principal works on the subject are *A Korean Grammar* (1939), *Studies in Korean Etymology* (I 1949, II 1953) and *Einführung in die Altaische Sprachwissenschaft* (published by his pupil Pennte Aalto: I 1952, II 1957, III 1966).

RANKS, GOVERNMENT *See* Grades, government

RATS

'Rats' traditionally meant vermin, but the now universal brown rat is a fairly recent arrival. The ancient east Asian pillager of grain-stores and crops is the Great Grey Hamster or Korean Grey Rat (*Cricetulus triton*), a solitary, fierce rodent that lies on its back and screams when threatened, but because of its connection with grain-stores, in the **zodiac** it was considered a sign of wealth.

READING

Until the end of the 19th century few **women** were taught to read Chinese characters and *ch'ŏnmin* were rarely able to read much. Few readers read silently as a matter of course. The sound of reading was a chant-like hum, if not a clear verbalisation. Winter, when days were short, was not a good time for reading, because privacy was rare and lamps gave wretched light. Summer was too hot for reading, indoors or out. The best season for reading was autumn, when the weather was good and sitting out of doors was pleasant. Through the 20th century, autumn was the season when most books were bought. At the end of the monsoon, all books were brought outside and **aired** in the sunshine. This neither discoloured mulberry-bark **paper** nor faded printing ink.

REBELLIONS, COUPS D'ETAT *See* Chŏng Yŏrip; Ch'oe Ch'unghŏn; Hong Kyŏngnae; *Kapsin* Coup; Kim Hŏnch'ang; Kim Taegong; Myoch'ŏng; Rebellions, peasant; Tonghak Rebellion; Yi Chagyŏm

REBELLIONS, PEASANT AND / OR SLAVE

Broke out in 889 around the provincial capital of Sangju as a result of the excessive dual burden of **taxation** and *corvée*, and spread throughout the country. The resulting struggle between rival leaders **Kyŏn Hwŏn** and **Kŭngye** divided the country into three competing kingdoms (*see* **Three Kingdoms, Later**) and brought about the downfall of the Unified Silla dynasty. The following Koryŏ period, however, was rarely free from political violence, resulting either from the ambition of members of the aristocracy or the sufferings of the lower classes. In 1172 low class soldiers rose against their leaders in the Pukkye Northern Border Region. A slave rebellion broke out in 1176, briefly captured Kongju and Yesan (southern Ch'ungch'ŏng province), and advanced on the capital **Kaesŏng**. It was suppressed, but further uprisings were staged by peasants in Sŏgye, P'yŏngan province (1177–9), and **slaves** and soldiers in Chŏnju (1182). Worse was to come for the government in 1193, when rebel armies led by Kim Sami and Hyosim combined into a large force in northern Kyŏngsang, and were only put down with heavy losses in a battle at Miryang. In 1198 the entire slave population of Kaesŏng, headed by one of Ch'oe Ch'unghŏn's slaves, Manjŏk, plotted a revolt but was discovered. Next year peasants rebelled in Kangnŭng and Kyŏngju; in 1200 in Chinju and Hapch'ŏn; and in 1202 at Kyŏngju and neighbouring regions. Peasants and slaves struggled bravely against the **Mongol** invasions, and many were captured or killed, especially in 1254, but popular resentment increased against the court for its failure to resist the foreign challenge.

The early Chosŏn rulers had to face rebellions instigated by military and political challengers, but the first expression of peasant discontent was in 1562, when **Im Kkŏkchŏng** led an uprising against absentee landlords in Hwanghae province. There then followed a long period when peasant resistance was channelled principally against the Japanese and Manchu invaders. The 18th-century Kings **Yŏngjo** and **Chŏngjo** did their best to alleviate the hardships of the peasantry, though not with complete success *(see kyunyŏk-pŏp)*, and in the 19th century their sufferings were greatly intensified through a combination of natural disasters, maladministration, and corrupt landlordism. Peasant uprisings began in 1811 in P'yŏngan province, under a discontented member of the *yangban*, **Hong Kyŏngnae**, and continued in 1813 on **Cheju** Island and again in 1816. The most serious rebellion took place in 1862 (*see* **Chinju Rebellion**) and was followed by widespread uprisings across the southern provinces and Cheju. This was the fertile ground in which were sown the seeds of **Ch'oe Cheu**'s new socio-religious Tonghak movement, which would lead eventually to the outbreak of the disastrous **Tonghak Rebellion** in 1894.

In the first half of the 20th century peasant discontent was directed mainly against the Japanese. Large-scale armed resistance took place between 1906 and 1908, involving peasants, *yangban*, and soldiers whose army was officially disbanded in 1907. When their force was crushed as it advanced on Seoul in January 1908 they turned to guerilla warfare. After **annexation** the Japanese military police prevented any widespread peasant revolt, and armed protest was maintained by the *ŭibyŏng*, mostly operating from **Manchuria**. However, frequent disputes between tenants and landlords erupted through the 1920s and 1930s, and resulted in legislation by the **Government-General** aimed at safeguarding tenants, the Tenant Arbitration Ordinance (1932) and Agricultural Lands Ordinance (1934).

Liberation in 1945 brought a continuation of dictatorial government in North Korea and of autocracy in the South. Sweeping **land reform** in the north in 1946 appeared to bode well for peasant interests, but thereafter any expression of popular discontent was effectively suppressed in the **Democratic People's Republic of Korea**. In the south trouble broke out in 1946 among urban workers in Seoul, **Pusan** and **Taegu**, and quickly spread across the countryside, involving an estimated 2·3 million people. They were protesting against corrupt and oppressive local administration, landlordism, repressive police, and food shortages exacerbated by the high level of sudden immigration from Manchuria and Japan. The uprisings were crushed by the **American Military Government**, but led to land reform measures. The extent of communist involvement in the 1946 movement has been disputed, but communists were prominent in the 1948 **Cheju Rebellion**. Subsequent peasant dissatisfaction in the **Republic of Korea** has found expression in the *minjung* movement rather than in open rebellion and has been discouraged by improvements in economic conditions.

GI-WOOK SHIN, *The Politics of Popular Protest: the Roots and Legacy of Peasant Activism in Twentieth Century Korea*, Seattle: University of Washington Press, 1996

RED ARROW GATE *Hongsal-mun*

Also called *hongjŏn-mun*, *-jŏn* being Sino-Korean for the native Korean *sal* 'arrow'. Two red poles with a row of upright arrow-like pieces of wood set on a bar across the top, forming a gate without a roof, a square 'arch' over the road. It was set over the approach to a royal **tomb**, a **palace** or a **yamen**.

RED CLIFFS, SONG OF THE See *Chŏkpyŏk-ka*

RED TURBANS *Honggŏn-jŏk* 紅巾賊
Chinese rebel forces who invaded Korea in 1359 and 1361 after their defeat by the **Mongols** in **Liaodong**. Though their incursions were brief, they succeeded in occupying the capital **Kaesŏng**, and forced the court to flee temporarily south to Andong. In the second attack the gift of **musical instruments** made by Emperor Huizong to King **Yejong** in 1116 was destroyed. **Yi Sŏnggye** established his reputation in helping to repulse the rebels, thereby strengthening his own dynastic ambitions.

REFORM MOVEMENT, THE *kaehwa undong* 開化運動
Really began with the *Sirhak* **movement** in the 18th century, though its immediate effects were insufficient to overcome the combined weight of tradition, political factionalism, ethnocentrism and self-interest among the *yangban*. Consequently, Korea had taken no fundamental reforming steps to face the need for modernisation by the second half of the 19th century, when it was confronted by the challenge of economic collapse and foreign intervention. Only after the end of the **Taewŏn'gun**'s regency in December 1873 and the conclusion of the **Kanghwa Treaty** did the early admirers of Japan, such as **Kim Hongjip**, become the first to revive 18th-century calls for change. Those who sought to open up the country to outside influence included **Kim Yunsik**, Pak Kyusu, **Kim Okkyun**, and a monk, **Yi Tongin**, whom **King Kojong** sent on a mission to Japan with the object of gaining acquaintance with Americans and their ideas. The modernisers were rewarded in 1881 by the opening of the *T'ongni-gimu Amun*.

The reform movement was deeply embroiled in the struggle between China and Japan for influence in Korea and the consequent growth of the independence movement (*see* **Independence Club**; **Independence Party**). While the forces of conservatism were ranged principally behind the Taewŏn'gun, the reformers were successful in persuading King **Kojong** of the need for reform. The call for reform underlay the *Kapsin* **coup** in December 1884, but it was not until 1894 that serious changes were decreed, in the form of the proposals put forward by Kim Hongjip's Reform Council (*Kun'guk Kimuch'ŏ*) and approved by the King (*see* **Kabo reforms**). Advocates of reform included **Yun Ch'iho, Sŏ Chaep'il**, and **Yi Sŭngman** (Syngman Rhee). The Korean reform movement proved to be more enduring than its equivalent in China after the failure there of the Hundred Days' reform period of 1895, but was nevertheless hampered by Japanese determination to control Korea's future. Consequently, the energy of activists became associated with **nationalism** and cultural identity, and thoughts of revolutionary initiative were blunted by pride in Korean tradition. When fundamental reforms came, they were in unwelcome form, at the hands of the Japanese under the **Protectorate** and colonial **Government-General**.

REIGN TITLES *yŏnho* (C. *nianhao*) 年號
Korean historians have numbered years by counting from the accession of each king, using his posthumous honorific name, as in '5th year of Kojong' (1869)(*see* **Dates of kings**). From 140 BC China used a special title for the period of each emperor's reign, usually of two characters with an auspicious meaning or classical reference. Thus the reign of the Qing emperor Shengzu, 1662–1722, is called Kangxi 'Peace and

Splendour', and 1715, for example, is called '54th year of Kangxi'. Similar titles were used in **Silla** from 536 to 650 AD. Thereafter Silla and its successors, following a policy of *sadae*, regarded reign titles as an imperial privilege, not to be used by mere kings. **Kwanggaet'o** of **Koguryŏ** had adopted a reign title and the rulers of **Parhae** also did so, as did the short rebellion of Kim Hŏnch'ang in 822, while **Kŭngye** used four between 904 and 917. **Wang Kŏn** asserted his independence by using the reign title Ch'ŏnsu 'Heaven's gift' (918–933) when he established the Koryŏ dynasty, and his son Kwangjong, coming to the throne in 950, when China was in dynastic turmoil, called himself *hwangje* 'emperor'. He used the reign title Kwangdŏk, 'shining power', for nearly two years, after which he accepted Later Zhou as the imperial house. Finally when the Empire of **Great Han** (Taehan) was proclaimed in 1896, Kŏnyang 'establishment of the yang (as in **ŭm-yang**) principle' was used for the first year, then changed to Kwangmu 'glorious warrior' (recalling the legendary dynastic restorer, the Emperor Guangwu of Han, r. AD 25–57). The reign of **Sunjong** (1907–10) was Yunghŭi 'noble splendour'.

RELIGIONS, NEW *sinhŭng chonggyo* 新興宗教

Religions founded in Korea after the rise of **Ch'ŏndo-gyo** in 1860 were called *yusa chonggyo* 'pseudo-religions' until about 1960, when the term *sinhŭng chonggyo* 'new religions' came to be preferred. Like similar phenomena in other countries, new religions have appeared in Korea at times of political instability and dissatisfaction with established religions, resulting in a strong desire for visible fruits of faith, especially healing and prosperity. A charismatic leader, who carries ultimate power within his group, can at such times readily gain followers and bond them into close communities, usually exclusive of others. Morals may be either revolutionary (especially in sexual matters) or, more likely in Korea, strict. If the nation is at the time in some sense emergent, the new religion is likely to promise an earthly paradise and identify the salvation of the world with the national destiny. Doctrine is liable to syncretise elements of other faiths.

Fifty or so such religions sprang up in Korea in the 20th century, including **Chŭngsan-gyo**, **Hŭmch'i-gyo**, **Ilsim-gyo**, **Kwansŏng-gyo**, **Olive Tree Church**, **Paekpaek-kyo**, **Poch'ŏn-gyo**, **Sich'ŏn-gyo**, **Taejong-gyo**, **Tan'gun-gyo**, **Unification Church** and **Wŏn Buddhism**. A noted centre for new religions is **Sindonae**.

Murayama Chijun, *Chōsen no ruiji shūkyō*, 'Pseudo-religions of Korea' (1935), is a valuable illustrated record.

SPENCER J. PALMER, 'The New Religions of Korea,' *TKBRAS*, XLIII (1967 2nd ed., Seoul, *TRASKB* undated)

REPUBLIC OF KOREA (ROK) *Taehan min'guk* 大韓民國

Title adopted by the new state established in south Korea by the elections held on 10 May 1948. The elections had been organised by the **United Nations Temporary Commission on Korea** (UNTCOK), despite opposition from the USSR, Canada and Australia, following the breakdown of talks between the United States and the Soviet Union in the summer of 1947 on the future of the peninsula (*see* **trusteeship**; **US-Soviet Joint Commission**). They represented an American attempt to influence Korea's political future amid the post-World War Two cold war climate. Though the elections purported to choose delegates to a nationwide assembly, the communist north refused to participate and organised its own elections on 25 August (*see* **Democratic People's Republic of Korea**). The fact that the elections were neither free nor well supported by an electorate that had no previous experience of democracy did not prevent the 198 chosen representatives from forming a 'national' assembly in Seoul and installing Syngman Rhee (**Yi Sŭngman**) as first President of the Republic of Korea. The legitimacy of the assembly to form the government of the new Republic was then recognised by the United States and the United Nations. One of its first moves was to pass a National Security Law (December 1948) clamping down on left-wing political activity. Rhee's opponents were purged. The people of Cheju, however, rebelled against the new régime, prompting a military campaign which foreshadowed future displays of repression of the southern Korean people by their rulers (*see* **Cheju Rebellion**).

As a result of the **Korean War** the ROK developed a high level of military, economic and political dependency on the USA which had not been anticipated or desired by either side in the first years after Liberation. The continuing communist threat from the North helped to perpetuate a series of military governments paying only lip service to democratic reforms before 1988, although the rate of economic growth from the 1970s until 1997 earned the ROK the reputation as one of East Asia's 'little tigers'. This was associated with a rapid expansion in higher education, but accompanied also by embarrassment to successive governments by **student** agitation for social and political reforms and for reunification with the North. For approximately two years prior to the financial crisis in late 1997, government intellectuals had linked the nation's success with the modern Korean interpretation of neo-Confucianism in an apparent bid to establish ideological hegemony over the rising economic fortunes of the East Asian region. In doing so, they laid claim to leadership in reviving an ancient and respected socio-philosophical tradition, and implicitly challenged the failure of the North Korean *chuch'e* ideal.

PRESIDENTS:

First Republic	Yi Sŭngman	1948–60
Second Republic	Yun Posŏn	1960–61
[Military junta	Pak Chŏnghŭi	1961–3]
Third Republic	Pak Chŏnghŭi	1963–72
Fourth Republic	Pak Chŏnghŭi	1972–79
[Interim period	Ch'oe Kyuha	1979–80
	Chŏn Tuhwan	1980–81]
Fifth Republic	Chŏn Tuhwan	1981–88
Sixth Republic	No Taeu	1988–93
	Kim Yŏngsam	1993–98
	Kim Taejung	1998–

SOHN HAK-KYU, *Authoritarianism and Opposition in South Korea*, London: Routledge, 1989, repr. 1991; DAVID STEINBERG, *The Republic of Korea: Economic Transformation and Social Change*, Boulder: Westview Press, 1989; NAM KOON WOO, *South Korean Politics: The Search for Political Consensus and Stability*, London: University Presses of America, 1989

See also **American Military Government**; **Constitution**; **Military junta**; *Minjung* **movement**; **Second Republic**; **Sixth Republic**; **South Korea: constitutional changes**; **students**; **Third Republic**; **United Nations Organisation**

RESIDENT-GENERAL J. *Tōkan* 統監
Title of the senior Japanese minister who was effective ruler of Korea under the Japanese **Protectorate** (1905–10). The post was first established in February 1906 and taken up by **Itō Hirobumi**. When he resigned in June 1909 he was succeeded by Sone

Arasuke (1849–1910). When he too resigned, in May 1910, Terauchi Masatake (1852–1919) became the last holder of the post before becoming the first Governor-General.

RESTORATION ARMY *Kwangbokkun* 光復軍
Korean nationalist force set up by **Kim Ku** in Chongqing for the **Provisional Government in Exile** on 17 September 1940. It was commanded by Yi Pŏmsŏk, and fought the Japanese alongside Chinese units in China and in Burma.

RHEE, SYNGMAN *See* **YI SŬNGMAN**

RICE
The early history of rice in Korea is far from clear. The native grain was millet. Rice came through China, where it had been grown and eaten since perhaps 5000 BC. It probably arrived in the peninsula late in the 2nd millennium BC and was at first sown and grown in wet fields. Dry-field cultivation developed in mediaeval times. During the Song period rice came to dominate Chinese diet, ousting millet and buckwheat from the tables of the ruling classes. This was about the time better varieties were produced and the art of transplanting seedlings from the seedbeds to the paddies (larger wetfields) was perfected. This skill was learned in Korea around the end of Koryŏ, but was not widely adopted until the beginning of the 17th century, after which rice became more dominant in the national diet, though millet remained important in the northern regions. The traditional broad classification of rice varieties was into *maepssal* for ordinary eating and *chapssal*, which is stickier when cooked. (The stickiness is due to a high content of starch amylose, for there is no gluten in rice.) Both kinds were divided into paddy-field rice and dry-field rice. Some regions are famous for good rice and Koreans are very discerning about its quality and flavour. They have a penchant for round grains that adhere to each other when cooked. The usual method of cooking is virtually unchanged since 2000 BC. *Maepssal* is also used for porridge and gruel, as well as paste for sticking **paper**. *Chapssal* is less digestible, and though cooked in small quantities for special occasions, is used chiefly for brewing, and for making steamed cakes (*ttŏk*).
LEE KWANG-KYU, 'Socio-Cultural Aspects of Rice Cultivation,' *KJ*, 27/1, 1987; SARAH NELSON *et al.*, 'The Origins of Rice Agriculture in Korea: a Symposium,' *JAS*, 41.3, 1982

RICE LOAN SYSTEM *hwan'gok* 還穀
Early Chosŏn system, dating back to Koryŏ and Koguryŏ precedents, of making free loans of seed to farmers in times of hardship. Loans were made in spring and repayment required in produce after the autumn harvest. The system was administered through Charitable Granaries (*ŭich'ang*), first established in the late 10th century. Gradually, rapacious officials levied interest of ten per cent or more, and it came to be one of the principal sources of government tax income.
See also **Ever Normal Warehouses; taxation**

RIDEL, FÉLIX-CLAIR 李福明 (1830–1884)
A French priest who entered Korea in 1861. When nine of the twelve missionaries were martyred in 1866 (*see* **Martyrs, Catholic**) he fled to Tianjin. His reports to the French community in China led to his accompanying Admiral Roze to the sack of **Kanghwa** later that year. In 1870 he was made sixth bishop for Korea, but did not enter the country until 1877, when he was promptly banished. He went to Beijing and

later to Japan to work on the missionaries' grammar (*Han-Bul-munjŏn*) and dictionary (*Han-Bul-sajŏn*). He died in France.

'RIGHTEOUS ARMIES' See *Ŭibyŏng*

RITES AND CEREMONIES

Were important to rulers as a means of regulating behaviour and expressing and reinforcing their authority, and to the rural classes as a way of contacting the spirits to ensure protection, rescue from trouble, and future blessings. In traditional times they were propagated by **Confucianism**, **Buddhism**, and **shamanism**, as they had been by animistic societies of ancient times; and in the modern era they have continued to play an essential part in the political control of the North Korean population by the communist régime, and in the public affairs of South Korean politicians.

A survival of early worship of totemistic deities can be seen in the protective *sottae* and *changsŭng* spirit posts still to be seen on approach paths to villages. Village rites reflected the inhabitants' routine needs and anxieties, about fertility, weather, crops, sickness, and defence against animal and human predators. They were conducted by shamans, and made use *inter alia* of crude clay figurines (*t'ou*), images of horses, stone effigies, and wooden phalli. Worship was offered to heaven on **Paektu-san** and T'aebaek-san (*see also* **Five Peaks**), to rocks on **Cheju** Island, to the spirits of natural features such as trees, rivers and mountains (especially the generalised mountain spirit *Sansin*), to deities with particular local connections, such as the dragon king at Igyŏndae near **Kyŏngju** (*see* **Munmu, King**), and to animals including **tigers** and **horses**. In the home, household rites were performed in honour of the **spirits** of the hearth, the kitchen, the roof, the well, and the **privy**.

Buddhist rites were more individualistic than communal, although some annual **festivals** such as the *P'algwanhoe* and Buddha's Birthday (*ch'op'a-il*) were widely observed with elaborate ceremonial. To many, the expression of their faith was made through prostration before the figure on the altar, the chanting of **sutras**, circumambulation of a **pagoda**, telling rosary beads, and lighting incense sticks.

Confucianism, adopted as the state political and social philosophy in the Chosŏn period, made maximum use of rites among the literati. Court ceremonial followed carefully prescribed patterns, described in writing and picture in *ŭigwe*; complex and formal ceremonial accompanied the worship of clan ancestors (*see* **ancestral worship**); and although actual practice varied from time to time and place to place, observance of correct forms of social relationships was precisely defined according to the Korean interpretation of **Zhu Xi** (K. Chuja)'s regulations for family life given in his *Jiali* (K. *Chuja-garye*) (*see kwan-hon-sang-je*; **marriage**; **mourning**).

In modern Korea, leaders continue to make maximum political use of rites and ceremonies. In the North, everyone from schoolchildren to factory workers is drilled to express reverence to the 'Dear Leader' or the 'Great Leader' (*Kyŏngaehanŭn Chidoja* or *Widaehan Suryŏng*), and crowds are trained to take part in elaborate ceremonies demonstrating allegiance to their communist idols. Such patterns of conformist behaviour deny the right to any show of any individualism. The South uses ceremonial in a more sophisticated way to advance the social and moral values espoused by its leaders, but continues in modern guise many of the rites of royal times, including formal presentations to honour men of achievement, elaborate official openings of national shrines and monuments, and well publicised participation by government figures in homage to parents, national tree-planting days, and other occasions emphasising family and public service.

CHOE SANG-SU, *Annual Customs of Korea*, Seoul: Seomun-dang, 1983; LAUREL KENDALL & GRIFFIN DIX, eds., *Religion and Ritual in Korean Society*, Berkeley: Institute of East Asian Studies, 1987; DAVID MASON, 'The *Sam Hwangje Paehyang* (Sacrificial Ceremony for Three Emperors): Korea's Link to the Ming Dynasty,' *KJ*, 31/3, 1991; ROBERT C. PROVINE, 'The Sacrifice to Confucius in Korea and its Music,' *TRASKB*, L, 1975

RITES CONTROVERSY

During the late 16th century the earliest Jesuit missionaries to China adopted a policy of 'accommodation' that permitted their converts to take part in Confucian ancestral rites. From 1632 onwards they were opposed by Franciscan and Dominican missionaries. The popes were inclined to follow the Jesuits, but controversy persisted until Benedict XIV issued the bull 'Ex Quo Singulari' in 1742, which finally ruled against them. (Many now think the bull was a tragic mistake, though its principle was later adopted by all Protestant missions.) Seeing the direction in which Rome was moving, the Qianlong Emperor had already virtually proscribed Christianity. In Korea, King **Chŏngjo** followed suit with a destruction of books, when the matter of **Kim Pŏmu** came to light and Christianity was proscribed in 1785. A small Catholic community survived the rest of the century, but persecution became severe in 1801 and recurred sporadically until 1867, producing thousands of **Catholic martyrs**.

The **Shrine Question** of the 1930s brought a second rites controversy, when schools were ordered to observe Japanese Shinto rites. This time the content of the ceremonies was non-sacrificial, and anti-Japanese feeling affected the issue. Though many – but not all – Protestants went to prison rather than attend the ceremonies, the Vatican permitted Catholics to take part if they could regard them simply as civil patriotic rites.

DONALD BAKER, 'The Martyrdom of Paul Yun: Western Religion and Eastern Ritual in Eighteenth Century Korea,' *TRASKB*, LIV, 1979; ANDREW ROSS, *A Vision Betrayed*, Edinburgh University Press, 1994
See also **Shrine question**

RITUAL STUDIES 禮學

Study of the purpose and details of family rites for the departed was the absorbing interest of upper-class Koreans during the 17th century. The groundwork for this development was laid by **Song Ikp'il** in the 16th century, and the 'great luminary' of the school was his pupil **Kim Changsaeng**. The basic text was **Zhu Xi**'s *Jiali* (K. *Chuja-garye*), but much attention was paid to Korean traditions and how they should be included. The vast literature that developed was concerned not only with ritual correctness, but also with the value and purpose of ritual in the Confucian scheme of living.

ROCK ART

Discoveries of significant examples of ancient Korean rock art, dating from the **neolithic period** or **Bronze Age**, have been made almost entirely in south-east Korea, though similarities in style with comparable pictures in Siberia suggest a possible wider link. An earlier, **palaeolithic**, date cannot be ruled out for some examples. The pictures were drawn with stone or metal tools, using pecking, grinding and engraving techniques. Engraving seems to date from a later period. Designs include pictures of humans and animals, geometric patterns, and variations on an abstract theme which may represent masks. The most important site is at Pan'gu-dae, near Ŏnyang, in South

Kyŏngsang province, where subjects are seen from the side and include land and sea animals, human beings, and scenes of hunting and fishing.[1]
(1) CHOI SUNU, *Five Thousand Years of Korean Art*, Seoul 1979
WERNER SASSE, 'Prehistoric Rock Art in Korea: Pan'gudae', *KJ*, 36/2, 1996

ROH TAE WOO *See* **No Taeu**

ROMAN CATHOLIC CHURCH *Ch'ŏnju-gyo* 天主教
The Japan Jesuits dreamed of a mission to Korea as early as 1556. A Spanish Jesuit, Gregorio de Cespedes (1551?–1611), sent as pastor to Japanese Catholics in Hideyoshi's army, was in the fort at Ungch'ŏn near **Tongnae** from the last days of 1593 until February 1595. Other Japan Jesuits followed him, but, apart from baptising some abandoned infants, failed to contact Koreans. Some of the many Koreans deported to Japan were baptised there. Several, like Vincent **Caoun**, were martyred. Others may have returned to Korea, where from 1585 some knowledge of Catholicism was obtained from literature that trickled in from China. Prince **Sohyŏn** brought Catholic books from Beijing in 1644. Some members of the Southern **faction** in particular were drawn to the political implications of Catholic teaching; others were interested in European sciences.

A group of these young Southerners, including **Chŏng Yagyong** and **Yi Pyŏk**, held a crucial conference at Ch'ŏnjin-am and Chuŏ-sa, Buddhist monasteries near **Kwangju**, south of Seoul, in 1777. In 1784 they arranged for **Yi Sŭnghun**, one of the group, to join the winter **embassy** to Beijing. He contacted the French missionaries there and was baptized. Having studied the books he brought back, the group set up a church in 1785 at the house of **Kim Pŏmu**. In 1787 the group appointed clergy and concocted liturgies. After a few months, further study made some members become dubious about this and they suspended their 'hierarchy'. The Bishop of Beijing confirmed their doubts and in 1790 wrote telling them to renounce Confucian **rites**, to dismantle their impromptu priesthood and wait for a priest to be sent. In 1791 **Yun Chich'ung** was executed in the 'Chinsan incident'. There was no general persecution, and Catholics continued in secrecy. A Chinese priest, **Zhou Wenmo**, entered Korea at the end of 1794 and began working secretly from the house of **Kang Wansuk** in Seoul.

Sunjo came to the throne in 1800, when a factional struggle put Southerners at disadvantage and therefore Catholics at risk. In October a letter written on silk by Hwang Sayŏng (1755–1801) to the Bishop of Beijing, asking the pope for military assistance, was intercepted. Hwang, Yi Sŭnghun, Fr Zhou and the scholarly Chŏng Yakchong were among the 300 **martyrs** of that year (*Sinyu-saok*). The 10,000 or so Catholics stayed underground, though persecution eased because the King married into the Andong Kim clan, which was sympathetic to Southerners. In 1829 the Vatican made Korea a Vicariate Apostolic ('pro-diocese'), entrusted to the Paris Foreign Missions Society. The first bishop, **Bruguière**, failed to enter the country. The second, **Imbert**, and two French priests entered the country secretly after 1835, but when **Hŏnjong** had come to the throne in 1834, political power had passed to the P'ungyang Cho clan, which harried Catholics as a way of attacking the Andong Kim. The many martyrs in 1839 (*Sinhae-saok*) included the three Frenchmen and **Chŏng Hasang**. **Kim Taegŏn**, the first Korean priest, was martyred in 1846.

On **Ch'ŏlchong**'s accession in 1849, the Andong Kim returned to power. Catholics had some respite under Bishops **Ferréol** and **Berneux**. In 1865 the

Hŭngsŏn **Taewŏn'gun** became regent. Some of the women in his family were Catholics, and he was initially in contact with the Church through **Nam Chongsam**, but he soon became anxious about threats of foreign invasion and was led into the worst of the Catholic persecutions (*Pyŏngin-saok*). Probably 8,000 of the 23,000 Catholics were killed during the next few years, including two French bishops (Berneux and **Daveluy**) and seven priests in 1866. Catholics lived in hiding, many of them becoming itinerant potters, moving from place to place searching for clay and peddling their wares. Potters remained a notable Catholic group into the second half of the 20th century. Persecution ended after 1868, but Catholics only slowly came out of hiding, even though they were legally able to do so after the Korean-French treaty of 1886. The cathedral in Seoul was begun in 1892 (*see* **Myŏng-dong Cathedral**).

Partly because of the Paris Missions' policy of restricting themselves to strictly evangelistic and pastoral work, Catholic missions, unlike Protestant missions, made little contribution to the modernisation of Korea. The tradition of the martyrs, 103 of whom have been canonised, remains strong and Catholics have tended to be associated with the political opposition, especially after 1953.

Bavarian Benedictines of St Ottilien arrived in 1909 and soon took over Hamgyŏng-do and **Kando**. The Irish Columban Fathers and American Maryknoll Fathers arrived in the 1920s. Since 1954 other religious orders have become established. Sŏgang University was founded in Seoul by Jesuits in 1960. The first Korean bishop was No Kinam (Paul Rho, 1901–84), consecrated as Vicar Apostolic of Seoul in 1942, later archbishop of Seoul (1972). The first Korean Cardinal was Kim Suhwan (Stephen, 1969). In 1998 there were 15 dioceses in the Republic of Korea, containing 3·5 million Catholics (about 10% of the total population) and 3,000 priests. In the two dioceses of North Korea few Catholics have survived the communist régime.

ANDREAS CHOE, *L'Erection du premier vicariat apostolique en Korée. . . 1592–1837*, Rome, 1961; CHARLES DALLET, *Histoire de l'Eglise de Corée*, Paris, 1874; JUAN RUIZ-DE-MEDINA, *Origines de la Iglesia Catolica Coreana*, Rome, 1987; *ibid.*, trans. JOHN BRIDGES, *The Catholic Church in Korea: its Origins 1586–1784*, Rome: Istituto Storico SI, 1991; YU CHAI-SHIN, ed., *The Founding of the Catholic Tradition in Korea*, University of Toronto Press, 1996
See also **Féron**, **Stanislas**; **Ridel**, **Félix-Clair**

ROMANCE OF THE THREE KINGDOMS, THE Sanguozhi yanyi, K. Samguk-chi yŏnŭi 三國志演義

Usually referred to in Korean as *Samguk-chi* (C. *Sanguozhi*), though this is strictly the title of an official history of the same period (*see* **Wei, histories**). The romance, described as 'the most popular prose work in East Asia', is a Chinese book of stories about the collapse of the Han dynasty in AD 220 and the struggles (AD 168–280) between the three states into which it was divided: Wei (north), Wu (south) and Shu or Shu-Han (west). The present Chinese text probably dates from the 15th century and has long been a favourite book in Korea, esteemed for its tales of chivalry, wisdom and loyalty. The heroes are Liu Bei (K. Yu Pi), a seller of straw shoes who became ruler of Shu; **Guan Yu** (Kwan U), the beancurd-seller who became a great general supporting Liu, and was later canonised as God of War; Zhang Fei (Chang Pi), a butcher and wine-seller who became a general; and **Zhuge Liang** (Chegal Yang), a wise strategist with mysterious powers, who helped Liu Bei. The villain is Cao Cao (Cho Cho), a Han general who became ruler of Wei. The stories most loved by Koreans include an oath

of mutual fidelity sworn by Liu, Guan and Zhang, known as the 'Oath in the Peach Orchard' (*towŏn kyŏrŭi*: Chapter 1) and the decisive Battle of the Red Cliffs, fought on the Yangzi in 208, when Cao Cao was defeated by Wu and Shu (Chapters 49 50: also the subject of songs called *Chokpyŏk-ka*, 'Song of the Red Cliffs').
MOSS ROBERTS, trans., *Three Kingdoms*, Berkeley: University of California Press, 1991

ROMANISATION: FRENCH SYSTEM
A system devised by French missionaries has survived in the Catholic Church and is found in much 19th-century writing. It is a phonemic transliteration, using French sound values and fixed equivalents for each *han'gŭl* letter, without regard to euphonic change. The *han'gŭl* alphabet becomes: *k, kk, n, t, tt, r/l, m, p, pp, s/t, ss, ng, tj, ttj, tch, hk, ht, hp, h; a, ya, e, ye, o, yo, ou, you, eu, i; ai, yai, ei, yei, oa, oai, oue, ouei, oui, eui.*
In the 19th century, palatalised vowels were common, as in *Tjyen-tjyou* (Chŏnju). Hyphens were used liberally, as in *Sai-nam-hte* Saenamt'ŏ. Personal names were given as one word: *Tjyeng-hoak-yeng* (Chŏng Hwagyŏng), *Pak-heui-syoun* (Pak Hŭisun), *Ryou-tji-kil* (Yu Chigil). Reinforcements might be expressed or not, as in the village names *Hkeun-sal-ni-mout-kol* (K'ŭn Sallimutkol) and *Neu-ri-kol* (Nŭritkol).

ROMANISATION: KOREAN SYSTEMS *Roma-ja p'yogi-ppŏp* 羅馬字表記法
In view of their justifiable pride in *han'gŭl*, it is not surprising that many Koreans prefer a romanisation system that is phonemic, transliterating *han'gŭl* spelling. They are also impressed by the freedom from breathing signs and diacritics in Chinese Pinyin (though it is often forgotten that Pinyin is incomplete without its full complement of diacritics). A Korean romanisation system with some of these advantages was planned by the Korean Phonetic Society (*Chosŏn Ŭmsŏng Hakhoe*) in the mid-1930s. Variant forms have been devised by others and one form was approved by the Ministry of Education in Seoul in 1959, though later replaced by **McCune-Reischauer** (*see* page xiii) with minor unscientific alterations.

The underlying principle of these forms is that the *han'gŭl* alphabet is transliterated by consonants *g, gg, n, d, dd, r/l, m, h, hh, s, ss, ng, z* or *j, zz* or *jj, cs* or *ch, k, t, p, h*; vowels *a, ya, eo, yeo, o, yo, u, yu, eu, i; ae, yae, e, ye, wa, oe, wae, weo, we, wi, eui.* In final position *s, z* or *j, cz* or *ch*, and *t* are replaced by *d*. Reinforced consonants may be marked by a preceding apostrophe; epenthetic *n* is optional. A child is asked its age with *Neo ddeog-gug myeod geureud meog-eod-neunya?* (in McCune-Reischauer, *Nŏ ttŏkkuk myŏt kŭrŭt mŏgŏnnŭnya?*).

For Koreans transliterating their own language into roman script this is much easier that the subtler McCune-Reischauer transcription of sounds. They have no prejudices about the aesthetic effect of roman letters and may even feel that a letter-for-letter transliteration is a more reliable guide to correct pronunciation; but such a system does not win favour with English speakers because to them it suggests mispronunciations and is aesthetically displeasing: 'Mrs Pak' becomes Mrs Bag, 'independence' *dogrib*, 'honeyed rice' *yag-bab*, 'blessings' *bog* and 'place' *god*.

ROMANISATION, McCUNE-REISCHAUER SYSTEM *see* page xiii

ROMANISATION, YALE SYSTEM
A romanisation system used by Samuel E. Martin in *Korean Morphophonemics* (1954) and described in his *(New) Korean-English Dictionary* (1967) and *Reference Grammar of Korean* (1992): a transliteration of the morphophonemic spelling of *han'gŭl*, with

indications for reading it as a phonemic transcription. Though it can be written on any typewriter, it is most commonly used for linguistic work. It gives more information than McCune-Reischauer (*see* page xiii), but assumes readers have some knowledge of Korean phonology. Contractions, where one or more letters are omitted, are shown by an apostrophe. Hyphens are used to help identify words and parts of words. The macron may be used for long vowels.

The vowels are *a, ay, ya, yay, e, ey, ye, yey, o, wa, way, oy, yo, wu* (shortened to *u* after labials and *y*), *we, wey, wi, yu, u, uy,* and *i*. The consonants are *k, kk, n, t, tt, l, m, p, pp, s, ss, ng, c, cc, ch, kh, th, ph* and *h*. Reinforcement of a following consonant is shown by *q*. Superscript ^{h}, ^{l}, ^{n}, ^{s} and ^{y} show P'yŏngyang spelling; superscript ^{y} also shows Seoul spelling in words like *ph^{y}ey* 'lungs'. A full point within a word indicates that: (1) morphological divisions are at variance with the spoken word, as in *iss.ess.e*, pronounced *i-sse-sse*; (2) *y*, as in *o.yat*, is not the second letter of a digraph (though the point is omitted after a palatalised vowel, as in *yoyuk*); (3) reinforcement occurs after a verb root, as in *sin.ko* (pronounced *sinkko*); or (4) there is automatic sound change, as in *coh.ta* (pronounced *cotha*) and *ilk.nunta* (pronounced *ingnunta*).

These examples are from the *Reference Grammar*:

Ku nun an^{h}ay eykey cocha allici anh.ko cip ul na-kass.^{s}up.ni.ta. 'He left home without telling even his wife.' Ani 'n key ani 'la ku ^{n}yeca ka miin iess.ta. 'Without question she was a beautiful woman.' Canq ^{l}yen khaylye 'ta ka kwulk.unq ^{l}yenq iph tachilq sey 'la. 'You may damage the big leaves when trying to gather small lotus.'

The system can be used for Middle Korean if *wo* is used for *o*; *z* for *pan siot*; *o* for *arae a*; *q* for *yen-niung*; *W* for *kabyoun piup*; *G* for the zero initial *iung* when it follows syllabic final *i, y, l* or *z* and represents the lenited velar fricative consonant written with gamma in IPN; and superscript points for tone-marks. The following two examples are from the *Reference Grammar*: ·*I* ··*hhwuw* ·*qilq-*·*quk* ·*so-chyen na·mon* ·*hoy* ·*yey* ·*za* ·*stwo Mi·luk* ·*ppwulq* ·*i isi·l i* ·'*la*. 'It will be 100,004,000 years before Maitreya Buddha comes again.' ··*Cywong towoy Ge ci·la* ·*hono·ta*. 'He says he wants to become a slave.'

ROOF TILES

The common form of roofing in traditional Korea was thatch, but following Chinese custom introduced in the **Proto-Three Kingdoms Period**, sloping roofs of more important buildings or upper class households were protected with overlapping lines of convex (male) and concave (female) pottery tiles (K. *wŏnang kihwa,* 'mandarin duck tiles'). The outward-facing lower end-tiles were frequently decorated with moulded patterns, or were faced with decorated disc-shaped tiles to finish off the downward ridge sequences. Patterns included floral and geometrical designs, and human faces. The style of decoration favoured in each of the three kingdoms was varied and reflected something of their geographical situation as well as cultural preference. In **Koguryŏ** it included frightening mask faces, showing the bold, even fierce, outlook of a border people toughened by a harsh climate, rough terrain and frequent military clashes. **Paekche**, which enjoyed a slightly less tempestuous development and embraced **Buddhism** more unreservedly as its experience of Chinese influence, allowed it to imbue its art with a gentler nature: here the lotus pattern was the most common form of end-tile decoration. **Silla** was the most remote from Chinese influence and the least advanced artistically. Tile decorations of the pre-unification period are more naïve, though those of the Unified Silla dynasty attain much higher levels of complexity and sophistication.

The last word in the luxurious decoration of roof tiles came in the 12th century, when the hedonistic King Üijong (1146–70) ordered a new octagonal pavilion (*Yŏngt'ae-jŏn*) beside an ornamental lake in his palace to be roofed entirely with celadon tiles from the royal **kilns** at **Kangjin**.

YONG BUM CHO, 'The Traditional Korean Roof,' *KC*, 14/2, 1993
See also **Chapsang**

ROSARY CLASSIC 木患子經
The **sutra** of which **Landis** gave a slightly confused version under this name in *The Korean Repository* for 1898 is *Mukhwanja-gyŏng* (C. *Muhuanzi jing*) 'soapberry seed sutra'. The seeds of the soapberry *Koelreuteria paniculata* are used for making rosaries in China and in Korea, where the tree is grown in temple precincts. The sutra is a single paragraph explaining a method of using the rosary by dedicating each bead to a **buddha**, **bodhisattva**, **heavenly king**, deva-guardian, one of the **thirty-three heavens**, the avoidance of one of twenty hells, a *paramita* (way of salvation), a benefactor (parents or superiors) or the person using the beads. These dedications are inscribed on a chart of the string of 108 beads (not 110, as Landis counted) that surrounds the sutra text.

The rosary can also be used to count recitations of the **mantra** *Namu Amit'abul*; but 108 refers to the 108 anxieties (*paekp'al pŏnnoe*) that afflict us. Smaller rosaries may be used as **worry beads**.

Both the Buddhist and the Catholic rosary are called *yŏmju*, 'invocation beads', but the Catholic rosary prayers are called *maegoe-sin'gong* or *maegoe-gyŏng*, from Chinese *meigui*, the red *Rosa rugosa* (K. *haedanghwa*).

ROSS, JOHN (1841–1915)
A Scottish Presbyterian missionary in Mukden (Shenyang) between 1872 and 1910, who met there Sŏ Sangnyun, a 27-year-old itinerant **ginseng** pedlar from Sorae, Hwanghae province. Sŏ had been baptized in Newchwang (Yingkou) In **Manchuria**. Together they did the first Korean Bible translation, printing St Luke's Gospel in 1883 and the whole New Testament in 1887. Using sources available in China, Ross also wrote *Corean Primer* (1877), *The Corean Language* (1878) and the first history of Korea in English: *History of Corea, Ancient and Modern, Manners and Customs, Language and Geography* (1880, reprinted London 1891), including interesting material on his own time.

See also **Bible in Korean, the**

ROUNDELS
Three roundels, none of them known from earlier dates, are constant features of Chosŏn period decorative art. The *t'aeguk* is the favourite neo-Confucian cosmogonic symbol of *ŭm-yang* (C. *yin-yang*) metaphysics. The '**wheel of bliss**' is used in non-religious decoration. A third very common form that appears in brass-work and lacquerware, symmetrical in two planes, is usually explained as a fanciful version of the character *su* 'longevity': but its real origin may be connected with the **swastika** or *pok* blessing and have no strong symbolic value. *Su* has other circular forms. (*See* diagrams, page 390.)

Roundels

ROYAL ASIATIC SOCIETY, KOREA BRANCH
For much of the 20th century, the *Transactions* of the Royal Asiatic Society, Korea Branch, were the most important Western-language source on Korean culture.* In 1900 American missionaries G. H. Jones, H. G. **Appenzeller** and H. B. **Hulbert**, with the Canadian J. S. **Gale** (all of whom had worked on *The Korean Repository*) and Britons A. B. Turner (later Bishop), Alexander Kenmure (Scottish agent of the British and Foreign Bible Society in Korea 1895–1905) and J. McLeavey **Brown** founded a branch of the Royal Asiatic Society of London in Seoul. *Transactions* appeared annually till 1904, then lapsed until the return of Bishop **Trollope** to Korea in 1911, when work revived and continued until World War II interrupted it in 1941. Work resumed in 1947, led by H. H. **Underwood** and the Anglican Fr Charles Hunt; but was stopped by the **Korean War** of 1950, though the 1951 *Transactions* were printed in Hong Kong. In January 1956 the British diplomat Dugald Malcolm stimulated the

three surviving councillors (George L. Paik, H. G. Underwood and Marcus Sherbacher) to revive the branch yet again. Since then *Transactions* have appeared annually, the title being changed from TKBRAS to TRASKB with Volume 45 in 1969. The logotype *Kŭnyŏk chŏngu*, adopted in 1966, combines a name for Korea (*Kŭnyŏk*) with words from *Shijing* Ode 176 meaning 'abundant artemisia plants', a standard literary allusion to fostering scholarship.
*An index of papers is given in *TRASKB LIX*, 1984.

RURAL REVIVAL MOVEMENT (1934) *See* **Land reform**

RUSSIA, RELATIONS WITH

After Russia and Korea first came into regular contact, with Russia's acquisition of the Maritime Province under the Treaty of Aigun (1860), their relations were rarely unhampered by diplomatic or commercial rivalry, usually involving other countries, and were frequently tense. The Chinese-nominated adviser to the Korean court, Paul-Georg **von Möllendorff**, first tried to foster good relations with Russia to counter the growth of Japanese influence in the early 1880s. A treaty was signed between Korea and Russia in 1884 which resulted in the posting of the first Russian minister to Seoul, Karl Wacber. International tension grew and Russian interests were threatened when Great Britain occupied **Kŏmun** Island in 1882, which it only surrendered in 1887 in return for a guarantee that Russia would not occupy any part of Korea. Amid the international competition to gain advantage in Seoul, however, nothing came of resulting suggestions that Korea should be neutralised. In 1888 a trade treaty gave Russians extraterritoriality in the border town of Kyŏnghŭng and the right to sail up the **Tumen River** (*see also* **Prezhevalsky, Nikolai**).

When Alexis de Speyer arrived to succeed Waeber as minister in Seoul in January 1896, he made plain Russia's intention of countering Japanese pressure on the court. Five weeks later King **Kojong** and his son were smuggled from the **Kyŏngbok Palace** into the Russian embassy. There they stayed for one year, as Russian influence grew and that of Japan temporarily waned, until the conclusion of the **Russo-Japanese Protocol** allowed them to emerge in safety. The result, however, was only to emphasise Korea's rôle as a focus for international rivalry, which it was to remain for almost the next century. Not until the development of post-Cold War ties in the 1990s could Seoul again feel confident of Moscow's intentions. In between, Korea suffered from antagonism respectively between Russia and Japan, the Soviet Union and the United States of America, and the Soviet Union and the PRC.

Manchuria often figured in these rivalries, either as cause or contributory factor. In the late 19th century, as Russia sought to develop trade through Vladivostok, it eyed both Manchuria and Korea as possible spheres of influence, and thereby came into conflict with Chinese and Japanese interests. Through the 1890s Manchuria was tacitly recognised as a Russian sphere of influence by the western powers in China, and in 1898 the Japanese Foreign Minister Nishi Tokujirō unsuccessfully proposed to formalise this in exchange for the Russian recognition of his country's special position in Korea. Their failure to agree led to the **Russo-Japanese War** of 1904–5, fought largely on Korean soil. Victory for Japan was a major step on the way towards its **annexation** of Korea, and throughout the colonial period Korea had no power to conduct its own relations. However, the Korean population in **Siberia** was swollen by refugees from the peninsula, and anti-Japanese operations by Korean patriots from Siberia and Manchuria caused the Japanese considerable embarrassment and anger (*see* **Korean Communist Party**; *ŭibyŏng*).

ANDREW MALOZEMOFF, *Russian Far Eastern Policy, 1881–1904*, Berkeley, 1958; ANDREW NAHM, 'Russia's Policy Toward Korea, 1854–1904, A Re-examination,' *JSSH* 64, 1986; M.N. PAK & WAYNE PATTERSON, 'Russian Policy toward Korea before and during the Sino-Japanese War of 1894–95,' *JKS*, 5, 1984; SYNN SEUNG KWON, *The Russo-Japanese Rivalry over Korea, 1876–1904*, Seoul: Yuk Phub Sa, 1981
See also **Soviet Union, relations with**

RUSSIAN ORTHODOX MISSION *Chŏnggyo-hoe* 正教會

Some Korean immigrants to eastern **Siberia** and **Manchuria** who had been baptised in the Russian Orthodox Church returned to Korea after the **Sino-Japanese War** in 1895, when Russia's political influence in Korea was at its height. The Holy Synod in Moscow established a Korean Mission and Archimandrite Chrysanth Shchetkovsky arrived at Seoul in 1900. Liturgical texts were prepared in Korean and a church was dedicated in 1903. Kang Hant'ak (John, 1877–1939), the first Korean priest, was ordained in Tokyo in 1912, and the Korean parish seems to have passed into the control of the Church in Japan. Five outstations opened between Seoul and Munsan were all abandoned by 1930, but from 1929 to 1939 there was a small congregation in P'yŏngyang. Russian priests served in Seoul until 1947, when a Korean priest took over. After the **Korean War** of 1950–3 the mission passed to the jurisdiction of the Greek Orthodox Church of North America, and is now within the province of New Zealand.
THEODISIUS PEREVALOV, *Rossiiskaya dukhovnaya missiya v Kore*, Harbin, 1926; RICHARD RUTT, 'The Orthodox Church in Korea', *Sobornost*, Series 3 no. 21, London, 1957

RUSSO-JAPANESE AGREEMENT (1898)

Despite the existence of the **Russo-Japanese Protocol** signed in June 1896, the Russian government approved fresh aid to Korea in the second half of 1896 and continued to enjoy beneficial relations with the government in Seoul. Japan was naturally incensed. But when King **Kojong** left the Russian embassy after his period of sanctuary and initiated reform measures from the **Tŏksu Palace**, the **Independence Club** took the lead in demanding an end to Russian influence and privileges. By the end of March 1898 the downturn in its fortunes was noticeable, symbolised by the closure of the Russo-Korean Bank after less than one month's trading. Russian interests in East Asia were nevertheless enhanced by the lease of the **Liaodong** Peninsula from China on 27 March, and seeing its prospects in Korea thwarted, Russia once again turned to Japan, with whom an end to confrontation would be desirable. On 25 April 1898 the Russian Minister in Tokyo, Roman Rosen, signed a new agreement with Foreign Minister Nishi Tokujirō, which reiterated Korean independence, agreed that the two countries would agree jointly in future on any plan to provide military or financial advice to Korea, and specified that Russia would not interfere in Japanese commercial or industrial developments in Korea.
See also **Russia, relations with**

RUSSO-JAPANESE PROTOCOL (1896)

Pressure in the aftermath of the murder of **Queen Min** forced King **Kojong** to take refuge in the Russian embassy on 11 February 1896, where he stayed until 21 February 1897. The Japanese were anxious to prevent his falling too much under Russian influence, and began negotiations with their rivals. On 14 May 1896 the Japanese Minister Komura Jutarō and Russian *Chargé d'Affaires* Karl Waeber signed an agreement on the stationing of equal numbers of troops in Korea until such time as the Korean government could guarantee the safety of their nationals and property, including the Japanese telegraph between Seoul and **Pusan**. On 9 June a Protocol was concluded in Moscow between General Yamagata Aritomo and the Russian Foreign Minister Aleksei Lobanov-Rostovsky pledging their joint willingness to advise and assist the Korean government on economic matters, and promising not to interfere in its maintenance of law and order unless the safety of their nationals required the presence of foreign troops, in which case action would be agreed jointly and might involve the military partition of the country between them. The Japanese were to retain ownership of the telegraph. The Protocol was made despite a concurrent Korean request to Lobanov-Rostovsky for Russian aid, accompanied by a warning against any alliance with Japan. Superficially the Protocol gave the two countries equal rights to exploit opportunities to extend their influence in Korea, while asserting their recognition of its independence. In practice neither would have any qualms about seeking unilateral advantage at the expense of the other or of Korea.

IAN NISH, *The Origins of the Russo-Japanese War*, London. Longman Group, 1985
*See also **Kabo** reforms; **Russia, relations with***

RUSSO-JAPANESE WAR (1904–5) *Noil-chŏnjaeng* 露日戰爭
Rivalry between Japan and Russia for influence in north-east Asia accelerated through the late 19th century and in 1902 precipitated the **Anglo-Japanese Alliance**, an admission of Japan's hopes for exclusive influence on the Korean peninsula. Further evidence of Russian expansionist plans, including land acquisition at Yongamp'o on the **Yalu River**, construction of the **South Manchurian Railway**, and continued failure to withdraw troops from **Manchuria**, prompted Japan to begin negotiations in August 1903. In return, Russia challenged Japan's ambitions in Korea, and no agreement was reached. On 21 January 1904 the Korean government proclaimed its neutrality in the dispute.

On 9 February Japanese warships attacked the Russian fleet in Port Arthur and Japanese soldiers entered Seoul. Next day Japan declared war on Russia. On 23 February the Japanese Minister in Seoul compelled the Koreans to sign the first of two agreements (*see* **Korea-Japan Protocol**) which led to the establishment of the Japanese **protectorate** over Korea on 17 November 1905. In the meantime, Korean government appeals for help to the United States were rejected (*see* **Taft-Katsura Memorandum**).

The war inflicted huge losses on both sides in land battles, especially at Shenyang in March 1905. Off **Tsushima** the Japanese achieved a shattering victory over the Russian Baltic fleet in May. Fighting was concluded by the **Treaty of Portsmouth**. The ease of the Japanese success surprised the world. Long-term effects were experienced in Russia, where the terminal decline of the *ancien régime* was hastened; in Korea, where **annexation** came a step closer; and in China, where the next step proclaiming Japanese imperialist ambitions on the mainland came with the presentation of the Twenty-One Demands in January 1915. Yet for the time being, Japan claimed that thanks to its victory, 'sovereign power over Manchuria and Mongolia was restored to China,' and there was no reason why it should be suspected of any sinister design. Outside East Asia the implications were not appreciated for a long time to come. Both Great Britain and the United States accepted the Japanese claim that Japan acted to promote peace in the region and modernisation in Korea.

SYNN SEOUNG KWON, *The Russo-Japanese Rivalry over Korea, 1876–1904*, Seoul: Yuk Phub Sa, 1981, repr. 1983; IAN NISH, *The Origins of the Russo-Japanese War*, London: Longman Group, 1985
See also **Brown, Miss Emily**; **London, Jack**; **Russia, relations with**; **United Progress Society**

S

SABI 泗沘
Modern **Puyŏ**, South Ch'ungch'ŏng province; capital of **Paekche** in succession to **Ungjin** from AD 538, when pressure from **Koguryŏ** compelled King Sŏng to move his court down the Kŭm River to a town which had the advantage of good access to the south-western farmland and the sea. For over a hundred years it was a centre for the highest quality Korean and Chinese craftsmanship, especially in the Buddhist arts, many of which can still be seen in and around the city. It was attacked by both **Silla** and **Tang** Chinese forces in 660, and the kingdom fell.
H.B.CHAPIN, 'Puyo: One of Korea's Ancient Capitals,' *TKBRAS*, XXIII, 1951

SACRIFICES *See* **Altar of Heaven**; **Altars of Earth and Harvest**

SADAE / SADAEJUŬI 事大/ 主義 'serving the great'
A phrase first used in ancient Chinese political philosophy based on the mutual responsibilities between son and father, defining the parallel relationship between smaller, tributary states, and the larger, suzerain state of China. Its clearest statement is in *Mencius* Ib.3, where it is recognised that if serving the great (C. *shida*) is the pragmatic policy of the principled ruler of a small state, it should be reciprocated by the neighbourliness (*jiaolin*, K. *kyorin*) of the benevolent (*ren*, K. *in*) ruler of the large kingdom. In Korea, the legitimacy of this concept was recognised from the Three Kingdoms period to 1897 (*see* **Great Han Empire**), even though it was not always thought necessary to implement it scrupulously. Korean politicians were quite capable of weighing up the merits of independence against tributary submission (*see* ***Sirhak*** **movement**), but when pragmatism determined that independence could not realistically be sustained, the definition of which 'great' neighbouring power should be served in Korea's best interests was not always to China's satisfaction. Thus from time to time during the Koryŏ period the court paid tribute to **Liao** and **Jin** rather than to their rival Chinese claimants in Kaifeng or Hangzhou. Korea, on the other hand, saw itself as superior to other neighbours such as **Parhae**, Japan and Ryukyu, and exercised *kyorin* by receiving their embassies as tribute-bearers.

In modern times defenders of those who collaborated with the Japanese during the colonial period have sometimes claimed that they were acting in similar vein, cooperating with the current 'great' as a means of defending Korean interests in the longer term. Since 1945, North Korea has criticised what it terms 'flunkeyism' (*sadaejuŭi*) in the South, though its own policies towards either the Soviet Union or the People's Republic of China, or both, may also be interpreted as an up-to-date form of a basically empirical foreign policy.
MICHAEL ROBINSON, 'National Identity and the Thought of Shin Ch'ae-ho: *Sadaejuŭi* and *Chuch'e* in History and Politics,' *JKS* 5, 1984
See also **China, relations with**; ***Sadaedang***; ***yangban***

SADAEBU 士大夫 'Scholarly and great officers'
Classical Chinese term (*shi dafu*) for the ruling bureaucrats, most commonly encountered in the Chosŏn period; sometimes used interchangeably with the term *yangban*, though the latter also included non-office-holding landed **gentry**. *Sa* were officials of **grades** nine to five, *dae* those of four and above. Members of the class were defined by patrilineal descent groups, and adhered closely to the teachings of the **Confucian Classics** as interpreted according to both Chinese and Korean neo-Confucian writers for guidance on social and political morality.
See also **rites and ceremonies**

SADAEDANG 事大黨 ''Serve the Great' Party'
Relatively conservative pro-Chinese political group headed by **Queen Min**. It included members of her clan such as **Min Yŏngik**, and opposed the Progressive Party (*Kaehwadang*) which instituted the *Kapsin* **Coup** in 1884.

SADAHAM 斯多含 (d. 562)
A young hero of **Silla**. He was of high birth and became a *hwarang*, said to have been the leader of one thousand. In AD 562, at the age of about fifteen, he was allowed to command an attack on **Kaya** in which his men were successful. As a result, he was given 300 prisoners for his own, but he set them all free. Shortly afterwards, when he was about sixteen, his friend Mugwan, with whom he had sworn they would die together, died of illness. Sadaham died seven days later. His story, with its clear elements of romance and exaggeration, is contained in *Samguk sagi*.

SADANG 寺黨 'temple troupes'
Wandering female entertainers, presumed to have descended from Buddhist **women**'s groups of later Koryŏ. In Chosŏn times they danced, singly rather than in groups, and sang to entertain villagers. The woman usually had a husband (*kosa*) who acted as her manager and accompanied her performance on an hour-glass **drum** (*changgo*). Many writers accept that *sadang* were prostitutes. Like other entertainers, they were of the lowest social stratum.
See also **namsadang**

SAEKTONG 'coloured bands'
The bright multi-coloured banding on the sleeves of children's clothes and bridal dresses was derived from the sewing together of bands of variously coloured material. Cloth with the colours woven into it is a product of industrial weaving. Today's colours also are recent, especially the lurid pink and green of aniline dyes. A typical modern pattern has equal bands of deep green, crimson, yellow, pink, deep blue, white, light green and scarlet. The hues of older examples are more restrained.

SAEMAŬL UNDONG 'New Village / Community Movement'
Campaign launched in 1971 by President Park Chung Hee (**Pak Chŏnghŭi**) with the aim of revitalising the countryside, modernising its conservative outlook and practices, improving living conditions, and increasing agricultural output. It was also intended to encourage initiative and self-reliance, supported with government funding and expertise. The programme ran for many years and achieved significant success, even being exported in principle to some Third World countries. Agriculturally, it promoted better plant varieties and land-use techniques, educated peasants in the cultivation of cash crops, increased use of fertilisers and machinery, improved cultivation and

harvesting methods, and extended irrigation and land reclamation schemes. It introduced new industries to the countryside and gave fresh encouragement to traditional cottage industries such as weaving. New roads and houses were built, sanitation and medical services were improved, and electricity and telephones brought to rural areas. The value of co-operative enterprise was emphasised and banks appeared in villages for the first time to teach the virtues of thrift and long-term planning. New schools and leadership training centres were opened as the government endeavoured to instil a sense of idealism in the population. The deeply ingrained Confucian appreciation of mutual responsibility and community welfare predisposed conservative country people to accept the underlying philosophy of the movement. There were some, wary perhaps of the example in the North, who objected to the concept of excessive state direction, and traditionalists lamented the loss of rural features such as thatched roofs, replaced with brightly coloured corrugated iron as a fire precaution measure. But living standards improved and rural incomes rose, and with them for a while the President's appeal to the voters. The economic imbalance between town and country began to be righted. Park Chung Hee himself played an active part in *Saemaŭl undong* activities, often presenting medals and sashes of honour to those responsible for conspicuous successes. But public enthusiasm for the government-inspired programme waned from 1976 as inflation rose and corruption spread, and pressure to reinvest profits was resented. Those who became rich on the land preferred to spend their money – and the educated young to seek their fortunes – in the only city to offer real glamour in the 1970s and 80s: Seoul.

OH MYUNG-SEOK, 'Peasant Culture and Modernization in Korea: Cultural Implications of the Saemaŭl Movement in the 1970s', *KJ* 38/3, 1998; WHANG IN-JOUNG, *Management of Rural Change in Korea: the* Saemaŭl Undong, Seoul National University Press, 1981

SAENGHWANG 笙簧

The mouth organ. Its Korean form is similar to the Chinese and Japanese, and is related to the much larger mouth organs of south east Asia. Its wind-chest was once made of a gourd but is now of wood or metal. Seventeen pipes of varying length are inserted vertically into the top of the wind-chest and a short mouthpiece into the side. One of the pipes is mute; the remainder produce one note each by the stopping of the hole at the base of the pipe, so that when the instrument is played, air is directed across a metal tongue which vibrates inside the tube. The instrument can play clusters of notes but in Korean music does not do so. It is less popular than it used to be, and is now confined mostly to performances of ritual music and a chamber duet with the *tanso* flute.
See also **musical instruments**

SAGAN-WŎN 司諫院 'Office in charge of admonitions'

One of the *samsa*, often called the '**censorate**'. A body of some 54 men that could criticise the decisions of the king, led by a 2nd **grade** senior. Its literary name was *Miwŏn*, 'rose-tree office' or 'pear-tree office', from a tree by the *Zhongshusheng*, an equivalent office in the Tang dynasty.

SAGES, KOREAN *See* **Canonised Sages**

SAHŎN-BU 司憲府 'Council in charge of officials'

One of the *samsa*. A body of thirty officials that could criticise the work of all other government bodies. Partly in order to make it more independent, it was led by a 2nd

grade junior. It was also known as *Sangdae*, 'frost terrace', because it delivered punishments, and punishment is connected with autumn, the season of frosts.

SAHWA 士禍 'Scholars' disasters'
Twelve [bloody] purges of the literati took place at court between 1453 and 1722. Those between 1494 and about 1550 are best known.

Most of those purged were *sarim*, 'country scholars', descended by blood or doctrine from the loyalists of Koryŏ who retired to the provinces when the Chosŏn dynasty was founded in 1392. They venerated the teachings of **Kim Chongjik**. They were puritanical neo-Confucians, devoted to study of the Classics and to philosophical and moral issues. They were critical of the *hun'gu*, older men led by **Meritorious Subjects** (men rewarded with influence and money for their service to the king), who paid more attention to literary skills than to philosophy. King **Sŏngjong** (r. 1469–1494) appointed young *sarim* to newly created **'censorate'** posts for drafting documents and commenting on policies by way of check and balance.

1498 *MUO SAHWA*. The 'history purge'. When **Prince Yŏnsan** came to the throne in 1494, intent on asserting royal power, he hoped to use the *sarim* for controlling the *hun'gu*. In 1498 the older men, who were compiling the *sillok* for the reign of King Sŏngjong, responded by bringing to light criticism of the usurper King **Sejo** emanating from Kim Chongjik and his followers, thus accusing the *sarim* of disloyalty. Yŏnsan'gun reacted with a ruthless programme of executions and banishments (including men from both sides) and had Kim Chongjik's corpse exhumed and decapitated.

1504 *KAPCHA SAHWA*. In 1504 Yŏnsan'gun learned about his mother's persecution and execution by **poison**, of which he had been kept in ignorance, since he was only three when she died. His rage was vented in another bloody purge of both groups. Shortly afterwards he was deposed and succeeded by **Chungjong** (r. 1504–44).

1519 *KIMYO SAHWA*. Chungjong restored the censorate and brought some *sarim* back to power. He favoured **Cho Kwangjo**, a man in his thirties who tactlessly effected some drastic reforms, and at the peak of his power attacked the Meritorious Subjects, most of whom lost their titles. They fought back and the king was forced to purge many of the *sarim*. Cho and some others were executed. This broke the ascendancy of the neo-Confucian philosophers for a while.

1545 *ÜLSA SAHWA*. When Chungjong died in 1544, he was succeeded by his son Injong, whose mother belonged to the P'ap'yŏng Yun clan, which was already bitterly divided within itself. Her brother Yun Im, an orthodox *sarim*, with his Greater Yun faction (*Taeyun*), came to the fore and began to restore Cho Kwangjo's ideals; but Injong died within eight months and was succeeded by Myŏngjong, aged eleven, son of Chungjong's third wife, another P'ap'yŏng Yun. Her brother Yun Wŏnhyŏng, leader of the Lesser Yun (*Soyun*), instituted a purge of *sarim* that lasted several years.

As a result of these four *sahwa* the *sarim* withdrew again to the countryside, where they established *sŏwŏn*, local schools in which they reinforced their philosophy and classical education and from which they eventually recovered their ascendancy throughout the land. The purges had also laid the foundations on which the **factions** of the mid-Chosŏn period were based.
EDWARD WAGNER, *The Literati Purges: Political Conflict in Early Yi Korea*, Cambridge, Mass.: Harvard University Press, 1974
See also **kapcha characters; literati purges**

SAJIK-TAN 社稷壇 *See* **Altars of Earth and Harvest**

SAJU-P'ALCHA 四柱八字 'eight characters in four pillars'
For horoscope purposes the time of a birth can be fixed by its 'four pillars'. These are the two-character combinations in the **sixty-fold cycle** that apply to the lunar year, moon, day and hour respectively, making eight characters in all. Thus the 1st hour of the 9th day of the 7th moon of Ŭlch'uk year in the 77th cycle was *Ŭlch'uk-kapsin-sinch'uk-muja*, 'Blue Ox year, Blue Monkey moon, White Ox day, Yellow Rat hour' – in western terms, the hour after midnight on 27 August 1925. Sixty years later by the lunar calendar, the same time on the 9th of the 7th moon in Ŭlch'uk year of the 78th cycle (24 August 1985) was *Ŭlch'uk-kapsin-ŭlmi-pyŏngja*, 'Blue Ox, Blue Monkey, Blue Sheep, Red Rat'.

For the yearly and daily cycles and for western equivalent dates, a Chinese perpetual calendar is needed; but the *kapcha* of moons and hours have a regular relationship to the *kapcha* of the years and days, tabulated below.

The monthly cycle begins in the 11th moon of *MU-* and *KYE-* years.

Year stem	KAP	ŬL	PYŎNG	CHŎNG	MU
moon	KI	KYŎNG	SIN	IM	KYE
1st	PYŎNGIN	MUIN	KYŎNGIN	IMIN	KABIN
2nd	CHŎNGMYO	KIMYO	SINMYO	KYEMYO	ŬLMYO
3rd	MUJIN	KYŎNGJIN	IMJIN	KAPCHIN	PYŎNGJIN
4th	KISA	SINSA	KYESA	ŬLSA	CHŎNGSA
5th	KYŎNGO	IMO	KABO	PYŎNGO	MUO
6th	SINMI	KYEMI	ŬLMI	CHŎNGMI	KIMI
7th	IMSIN	KAPSIN	PYŎNGSIN	MUSIN	KYŎNGSIN
8th	KYEYU	ŬRYU	CHŎNGYU	KIYU	SINHAE
9th	KAPSUL	PYŎNGSUL	MUSUL	KYŎNGSUL	IMSUL
10th	ŬRHAE	CHŎNGHAE	KIHAE	SINHAE	KYEHAE
11th	PYŎNGJA	MUJA	KYŎNGJA	IMJA	KAPCHA
12th	CHŎNGCH'UK	KICH'UK	SINCHUK	KYECH'UK	ULCH'UK

The hourly cycle begins with the 1st hour of *KAP-* and *KI-* days.

Year stem	KAP	ŬL	PYŎNG	CHŎNG	MU
Hour	KI	KYŎNG	SIN	IM	KYE
2300–0059 1st hour	KAPCHA	PYŎNGJA	MUJA	KYŎNGJA	IMJA
0100–0259 2nd hour	ŬLCH'UK	CH'ŎNGCH'UK	KICH'UK	SINCH'UK	KYECH'UK
0300–0459 3rd hour	PYŎNGIN	MUIN	KYŎNGIN	IMIN	KABIN
0500–0659 4th hour	CHŎNGMYO	KIMYO	SINMYO	KYEMYO	ŬLMYO
0700–0859 5th hour	MUJIN	KYŎNGJIN	IMJIN	KAPCHIN	PYŎNGJIN

Year stem	KAP	ÜL	PYŎNG	CHŎNG	MU
Hour \	KI	KYŎNG	SIN	IM	KYE
0900–1059 6th hour	KISA	SINSA	KYESA	ÜLSA	CHŎNGSA
1100–1259 7th hour	KYŎNGO	IMO	KABO	PYŎNGO	MUO
1300–1459 8th hour	SINMI	KYEMI	ÜLMI	CHŎNGMI	KIMI
1500–1659 9th hour	IMSIN	KAPSIN	PYŎNGSIN	MUSIN	KYŎNGSIN
1700–1859 10th hour	KYEYU	ÜRYU	CHŎNGYU	KIYU	SINYU
1900–2059 11th hour	KAPSUL	PYŎNGSUL	MUSUL	KYŎNGSUL	IMSUL
2100–2259 12th hour	ÜRHAE	CHŎNGHAE	KIHAE	SINHAE	KYEHAE

Horoscopes are read by consulting oracle-lists such as **Kunghap** and **Nabŭm**, and noting the correspondences of the stems and branches to *yang* and *yin* (two *yang* may sometimes become *yin* and two *yin* become *yang*) and to the **Five Phases** (in both *sangsaeng* 'generative' and *sangguk* 'obstructive' relationships) as shown in the following tables.

KAP	ÜL	PYŎNG	CHŎNG	MU	KI	KYŎNG	SIN	IM	HAE
yang	yin	yang	yin	yang	yin	yang	yin	yang	yin
wood		fire		earth		metal		water	

CHA	CH'UK	IN	MYO	CHIN	SA	O	MI	SIN	YU	SUL	HAE
yang	yin	yang	yin	yang	yin	yang	yin	yang	yin	yang	yin
water	earth	wood		earth	fire		earth	metal		earth	water

Informal prediction made by year animal alone (a rat will be busy, an ox hard-worked, a pig rich, a dragon successful, and so on) is taken less seriously and forms part of genial teasing.

SALLIM 山林 *See **Sarim***

SALSU RIVER 薩水 *See* **Chŏngchŏn River**

SAMA-SI 司馬試 'master-of-the-horse examination'
A name given to the *sokwa* **examination**. The ancient Chinese term 'Master of the horse' had come to be used for local government officials in general.

SAMBOK 三伏 'three oppressions'
Three days, fixed by **solar terms**, that mark the 'oppressive days' of high summer, when the *yin* principle is held to 'oppress' the *yang* principle. They were named in China from Qin times, but their history in Korea is scarcely known. *Ch'obok* the 'first **dog** day' is the 3rd *kyŏng* day, according to the **sixty-fold cycle**, after the summer solstice (21 June); *chungbok* the 'middle dog day' is the 4th *kyŏng* day after the solstice; and *malbok* is the *kyŏng* day next after the beginning of autumn (8 August).

The period lasts from twenty to thirty days, falling between 20 July and 18 August, the dates varying with the year. This is regarded as the hottest part of summer. Red-bean porridge (*p'atchuk*) is eaten and it is a time for picnics, especially by mountain streams. Young men eat dog-meat stew, called *posint'ang*, 'prophylactic dish'. In English *pogil* are called 'dog days', but they do not exactly coincide with the western dog days, which depend on the heliacal rising of the Dog Star, Sirius.

SAMBYŎLCH'O 三別抄 'Three Elite Patrols'
Loyalist campaign led by the private armies of the former **Ch'oe dictatorship** against the **Mongol** invasion and Koryŏ submission to it in 1252. Having failed to hold **Kanghwa** for King Wŏnjong (r. 1259–74), they moved to **Chindo** island under the command of Pae Chungson when the court returned to **Kaesŏng** in 1270, and there set up their own king and government. After defeat by combined Koryŏ and Mongol troops in mid-1271 they evacuated to **Cheju** island, where they were again crushed in 1273.
W. E. HENTHORN, *Korea: the Mongol Invasions*, Leiden: E.J.Brill, 1963

SAMDŎK-KYO 三德教 'Three Virtues Doctrine'
A 20th-century '**new religion**', offshoot of *Chŭngsan'gyo*.

SAMGANG ORYUN 三綱五倫 *See* **Three Bonds and Five Relationships**

SAMGUK SAGI 三國史記 'Records of the Three Kingdoms'
The first official history of Korea, compiled by the Confucian scholar-offical Kim Pusik (1075–1151) and others on the orders of King Injong of Koryŏ and presented to him in 1145. Their work was modelled on the Chinese dynastic history format invented by Sima Qian in his *Shiji* (K. *Sagi*). First come three sections of *benji* (K. *pon'gi*), chronological annals for each kingdom, **Silla**, **Koguryŏ** and **Paekche**; then chronological tables, followed by *zhi* (K. *chi*), monographs on such subjects as **sacrifices**, **music**, dress, and geography; finally 50 *liezhuan* (K. *yŏlchŏn*), biographies of distinguished persons. The compilers used earlier documents which have been lost, presenting the material objectively, but not impartially: there is Confucian bias both in selection and editing. The Chinese transliterations of place-names in *Samguk sagi* are valuable in the study of linguistic history.

SAMGUK YUSA 三國遺事 'Additional Material on the Three Kingdoms'
This work was compiled about 1285 by the Buddhist monk Iryŏn (original name Kim Kyŏnmyŏng, 1206–1289), who lived through the **Khitan** and **Mongol** invasions of Koryŏ. There is one insertion by his disciple, Mugŭk. The history of the text before 1512 is obscure.

Though the title refers to the Three Kingdoms, 95 per cent of the text is a collection of Buddhist legends from **Silla**. The commonly accepted translation of *yusa* as 'memorabilia' (meaning either 'important matters' or 'keepsakes') is misleading. *Yusa* (C. *yishi*) is a term for unofficial records or remnants added to records already published. The author, who is nowhere explicit about his purpose, knew the official *Samguk sagi* (published 140 years earlier) and presumably intended to supplement that official Confucian record with Buddhist material. Two chronological tables are prefixed to the main text. They cover **Koguryŏ**, **Paekche**, **Kaya** and Silla, concentrating on the royal successions. The relation of these tables to the text is not clear. They may have been added in a second stage of composition.

Some 45 per cent of the main material is headed 'Strange Events'; 'The Coming of Buddhism', '**Pagodas** and Statues' and 'Famous Teachers' make about 35 per cent; and shorter collections on 'Exorcisms', 'Graces', 'Hermits' and 'Filial Devotion' comprise the remaining 20 per cent. The first fifteen paragraphs of 'Strange Events', mostly taken from other works, some of which are now lost, are not about wonders but briefly identify the peoples or states known as Ancient Chosŏn (*see* **Old Chosŏn**), **Wiman Chosŏn**, **Lelang**, the Three Han (*see* **Samhan**), **Puyŏ**, Kaya, **Parhae**, Paekche, Koguryŏ and six lesser tribes. Two longer paragraphs contain the myth of King Tongmyŏng, founder of Koguryŏ (*see* **foundation myths**), and our oldest version of the **Tan'gun** myth. 'The Rise of Buddhism' has one paragraph each for the first missionaries to Koguryŏ and Paekche, and one of the 'Pagodas' was in Koguryŏ. All the rest is folk material from Silla, including myths of dynastic origins, making a rich store of legends full of the fantastic (and beautiful) imagery of popular Buddhism.

Samguk yusa contains fourteen *hyangga* songs, many of them as eulogies at the end of biographical entries. It is possible that they are not all of Silla date.

Sifting the historical value of *Samguk yusa* is a delicate operation in discernment of folklore and myth.

HA TAE-HUNG & GRAFTON K. MINTZ, trans., *Samguk Yusa* (Legends and History of the Three Kingdoms of Ancient Korea), Seoul: Yŏnsei University Press, 1972

SAMHAN 三韓 'Three Han'

The three federations of tribes which dominated the southern half of the peninsula from the 1st to the 3rd centuries AD (the **Proto-Three Kingdoms Period**). **Mahan**, comprising 54 tribes, occupied territory south of the **Han River** on the western side of the country, **Chinhan** (12 tribes) the south-east, and **Pyŏnhan** (12 tribes) the central south. Each 'state', or polity, was centred on walled towns from where the political élite ruled the subsidiary lineages and outlying agricultural villages, but the centralised hierarchies of the future Three Kingdoms had not yet evolved. The tribes were composed of **lineage** clans and their leaders constituted the ruling council of each federation. Religious leaders, distinct from political rulers, practised **shamanism**.
See also **Chin**; **Kaya**

SAMIN: SA-NONG-GONG-SANG 四民：士農工商 'four peoples: scholar, farmer, artisan, merchant'

A traditional social classification from top to bottom, much honoured in the snobbery of Chosŏn Korea. It comes from the *Guliang zhuan*, a commentary on the **Confucian classic** *Chunqiu* (Duke Cheng, Year 1), where, however, the merchant was placed before the artisan. *Sa*, which came to mean a scholar, doubtless originally meant a knight or soldier.
See also **class system**

SAMJŎN-DO HANBI 三田渡汗碑 'Three Fields Ferry stone of shame'

A stele, some 3·5 metres tall, inscribed in Chinese and Manchu, erected at the end of 1638 by the River **Han** near **Kwangju** to commemorate the submission of King Injo and his Crown Prince, kneeling in the snow, to the Qing emperor at the end of the siege of **Namhan sansŏng** in the early days of 1637 (*see* **Manchu invasions**). During the presidency of **Yi Sŭngman** (Syngman Rhee) orders were given for its destruction, but the Ministry of Culture demurred and the stone was buried. After 1960 it was disinterred and re-erected about a kilometre from the riverside, near the village of Sonp'a-ri.

SAMSA 三司 'Three authorities'
The three bodies which reviewed and censured the work of the government: **Sahŏn-bu**, **Sagan-wŏn**, **Hongmun-gwan**.

SAMSIN 'womb spirit'
A woman anxious to conceive a child may pray to Samsin. This spirit's nest is a gourd or paper bag containing a little **rice** and a few *pujŏk*, hung in a cosy corner of the living room. A food offering, especially the *miyŏkkuk* – 'brown-seaweed soup' rich in iron and iodine, with which mothers are fed immediately after giving birth – may be set before this nest, or placed before a bitch suckling her pups. The bitch eats the food, but the sacrifice is made to the spirit that produces her pups rather than to her. Samsin is also the guardian spirit for babies and tiny children. Although the name is often taken to mean 'three spirits', it must be derived from the Korean word *sam* 'afterbirth'.

SAMUL NORI samullori See **Namsadang**; **nongak**

SAMŬN 三隱 *See* **Three Recluses**

SANDS, WILLIAM FRANKLIN (1874–1946)
Sands was a member of the United States foreign service in Tokyo who was sent to the Seoul legation in 1898. In 1900 he was adviser to the Emperor **Kojong**. He remained in that post until February 1904, generally seeing the situation through Korean eyes, at odds with the official American view. After serving in Central American countries until 1910, he resigned and went into business. His memoirs of the period were published in 1930 as *Undiplomatic Memoirs* (reissued in 1987 as *At the Court of Korea*) in which he claimed to have been responsible for producing *Ch'unhyang* at **Won'gak-sa**.
W. F. SANDS, *At the Court of Korea*, London: Century Hutchinson Ltd., 1987

SANGA / HANGA 嫦娥 (C. Change / Henge)
In Chinese legend, wife of the mythic archer, Hou Yi, from whom she stole the elixir of immortality and took it to the moon, where she lives still, some say in the form of a frog – a literary alternative to the hare that lives in the moon of both Chinese and Korean folklore.

SANGDAEDŬNG 上大等 'Senior great rank'
Leading member of the **Silla** aristocracy and prime minister at the head of the **Hwabaek**. The office was created in AD 531 by King Pŏphŭng and preserved under the Unified Silla, when its power was eroded by that of the head of the **Chipsabu**, the *Chungsi*.

SANGGYŎNG 上京 'Superior Capital'
The capital of the kingdom of **Parhae**. It was situated in the vicinity of modern Dongjingcheng, Heilongjiang province, China.

SANGMIN 常民 'common people'
Also known as *yangin* ('good people'), *sŏin* ('multitudinous people'), and *p'yŏngmin* ('ordinary people'); members of the class of freeborn commoners ranked beneath the *yangban* and *chungin* and above the *ch'ŏnmin*. Upward social mobility was theoretically possible in the Koryŏ dynasty, when *sangmin* were eligible to take the

examinations, but was not actually attainable until the 17th century, when despite their lack of **lineage**, the chance of rising into *chungin* occupations improved. The majority of *sangmin*, however, remained **peasants**, and worked either as independent or tenant farmers. They were liable for **taxation**, *corvée*, and **military service**.
YOO SEUNG-WON, 'The Status System in the Early Chosŏn Period,' *SJKS* 1, 1988
See also **class system**

SANGMO TOLLIGI 'hat-streamer twirling'

Synchronised twirling of the tassel attached to the crown of each dancer's felt hat is part of any *nongak* performance. The climax may be a demonstration of virtuoso twirling by a talented dancer who puts on a tight cap with a paper streamer of enormous length. Traditionally it measures 12 *pal* (22 metres). He twirls it in figures of eight, sideways and forwards in magnificent circles, while he dances, sits down, stands up, skips over the streamer, always beating a small hand-drum. This is thought to be a military skill from the continent, which has found a place to survive with the farmers' wild music. The felt hat is certainly military, and not worn for normal agricultural work.

SANGP'YŎNGCH'ANG See **Ever normal warehouses**

SANGSURI 上守吏

Form of labour service devised in the early Unified Silla period for locally powerful members of élite families from newly unified provincial regions. In order to prevent their remaining or becoming over-mighty they were required to spend time in the capital undertaking service duties.

SANGT'U See **Topknot**

SANJO 散調 'Scattered tunes'

A musical suite of continuous movements played by a single melodic instrument to the accompaniment of the *changgo* drum. It probably evolved from folk tunes in south-western Korea and may have been associated with the musical traditions of **shamanism**, its characteristic being a slow beginning and gradual increase in varied tempi and rhythmic complexity leading to a fast and exciting conclusion. It was developed as a form in the 19th century by virtuosi such as Kim Ch'angjo (1865–1920), whose students preserved the *sanjo* of their great teachers by aural transmission. For the *kayagŭm*, the most frequently used *sanjo* instrument, fewer than ten *sanjo* are in common use today.
SONG BANG-SONG, *The Sanjo Tradition of Korean Kŏmun'go Music*, Seoul: Jung Eum Sa, 1986

SANKAJI / SUTKAJI See **Counting rods**

SANSIN 山神 'mountain spirit'

One of the most important deities of folk religion and **shamanism**, *Sansin* or *Sansillyŏng* 'mountain spirit' is the spirit of the hill or mountain to the north of most settlements, large and small. For a town or city he might be called *chinho-sin* 'guardian spirit'; but mountain shrines are also found far from any dwellings and were once frequented by travellers and herb-gatherers. This spirit was probably worshipped as far back as the 1st century AD and is associated with **Tan'gun** (*see* **foundation myths**). With the arrival of **Buddhism** he acquired the status of a **bodhisattva**, and in addition

to his place on village altars he was to be found on shrines inside Buddhist temples. He was particularly invoked by women wanting a son, and was powerful in averting natural disasters of all kinds. Formal worship used to be offered at the **New Year**, and at mid-spring and mid-autumn. Personal offerings of fruit, flowers or water might be made privately at any time. The spirit never appears in statuary form but only in paintings, where he is represented by a picture of a **tiger**, or an old man with white beard and high forehead (like a Daoist **immortal**), or an immortal riding on or attended by a tiger.
EDWARD KANDA, 'The Korean Mountain Spirit,' *KJ*, 20/9, 1980

SANSU 山水 'Mountains and water' *See* **Landscape painting**

SARIM 士林 'country scholars' / *SALLIM* 山林 'mountain scholars'
Two words often used interchangeably, especially by foreign writers. Both include -*lim*, a polite suffix found in *Hanlin* (K. *Hallim* 'writing-brushes forest'), the highest literary degree in China, and in *yurim* 'forest of learned men', a general term for Confucians. *Sarim*, short for *Sarim-p'a*, refers to a scholarly neo-Confucian element in the governing classes of the 15th–16th centuries that withstood the aristocracy created by awards to **Meritorious Subjects**. Some formed communities of scholars dedicated to the upholding of high standards of public morals and showing support for the rural **peasantry**. They were first inspired to keep alive the tradition of faithfulness exemplified by **Chŏng Mongju** and **Kil Chae**, and then by the **Six Martyred Subjects** who had died at the hands of King **Sejo** on behalf of his predecessor Tanjong. Their title was earned by their preferring to eschew office and pursue their studies in mountain retreats, but when they did show a readiness to enter government, in the time of King **Sŏngjong** (1469–94), they were obvious candidates for appointment to the **censorate**. One of their most outspoken and self-sacrificing representatives was **Cho Kwangjo**. Their chief political opponents were the *hun'gu* ('meritorious and conservative') faction, who owed their power to inherited **lineage** influence and court contacts.

  Sallim is a more general term, applied from the 17th century onwards to rural scholars who did not take office in government, especially those involved in *sŏwŏn*.
LEE WOO-SUNG, 'Confucian Politics in Chosŏn Period and the Existence of *Sallim*,' *KJ*, 23/4, 1983
See also **literati purges**; *Sahwa*; *yangban*

SARIRA / *SARIRA* CONTAINERS
This Sanskrit name was originally given to relics of a Buddha's body, but has long been used chiefly for gemlike objects found in the ashes after the cremation of a holy person – usually vitrified gallstones and similar mattter.

  The relics were placed in elaborately crafted containers and stored in **stupas** or **pagodas** for veneration. Later, copies of the scriptures were also enshrined in this way. *Sarira* containers were made of **glass**, gold, silver or **bronze**. Two outstanding examples of bronze *sarira* containers survived at **Kamŭn-sa** and Songnim-sa from the early Unified Silla period, shaped like a funeral palanquin and a pavilion respectively, decorated with ornate canopies and surmounted with guardian figures, musicians and dancers.[1]
(1) ROGER GOEPPER & RODERICK WHITFIELD, *Treasures from Korea*, London: British Museum Publications, 1984

SARO 斯盧 *See* **Kyŏngju**

SASAEK 四色 'four colours'
An expression used to describe the remaining four Chosŏn dynasty **factions** that had to accept the *t'angp'yŏng-ch'aek* of **King Yŏngjo**: Southerners, Lesser Northerners, Noron and Soron. Offices were to be distributed without regard to party loyalty. There was a remarkable degree of success, but the old tensions did not disappear. The situation was only partly masked by the appearance of *sedo-jŏngch'i*. Bloodshed was divorced from factional strife, though the factions cast their shadows over the treatment of **Catholics**.

SASIN 四神 *See* **Animals, mythic**

SASŎNG T'ONGHAE 四聲通解 'Complete Explanation of the Four Tones'
A rhyming dictionary of Chinese characters compiled by Ch'oe Sejin in 1517, containing 13,000 head-characters, arranged according to the four classic Chinese tones, annotated in Chinese. Pronunciations used in China and in Korea are given in *han'gŭl* and described in some detail, distinguishing the theoretically correct from the colloquial and recent ('recent' generally meaning Yuan dynasty). This is an important document for the study of 16th-century Korean phonology.

SA-SSI NAMJŎNG-GI 謝氏南征記 'Lady Xie's Journey to the South'
A story about 16th-century China, existing in both *hanmun* and *han'gŭl* versions. It tells how Lady Xie was set aside by her husband in favour of a **concubine**. She left home for a while, but was later reconciled to her husband. The book is attributed to Kim Manjung (1637–92), author of *Kuunmong*, and often said to be an allegory of King **Sukchong**'s treatment of Queen Inhyŏn.

SAYŎG-WŎN 司譯院 'Office in charge of translation'
Office that succeeded the *T'ongmun-gwan* from late Koryŏ. Presided over by a 3rd **grade** senior, its 23 members (later reduced to 19) dealt with Chinese, Mongol, Japanese and Manchu translation. It was also known as *Sŏrwŏn* 'office of tongues'.

SCHOOLS

Buddhist and Confucian education was promoted in the Three Kingdoms for the training of future officials, and the Unified Silla had a government department in charge of it. Many scholars travelled to China to study either in the Imperial Academy or in monasteries, and levels of scholarship among the Korean literati élite were highly respected in China. Twelve private academies (*sŏwŏn*) existed in **Kaesŏng** in the early Koryŏ dynasty, and during the reign of King Injong (1122–46) more government schools were opened in the capital (*kyŏnghak*) and rural areas (*hyanghak*) with the intention of spreading literacy and selecting talent more widely for future official service. The Chosŏn dynasty, with its enthusiasm for neo-Confucianism, extended the system. Small private elementary schools (*sŏdang*) prepared the sons of *yangban* for entry at the age of fifteen to one of the Four Schools (*sahak* or *haktang*) in Seoul or a country school (*hyanggyo*), where they studied for the licentiate **examination**.

In the 1890s and 1900s Korean modernisers and foreign missions opened nearly 200 private elementary and secondary schools (*see* **Osan School**), extending the syllabus and opening up more opportunities for girls. But Japanese rule introduced fresh restrictions. Many private schools were closed. Despite the policy of extending education for Koreans, percentages of Korean children receiving primary, secondary and college education remained low. Teaching in government schools emphasised Japanese language and interests at the expense of Korean, and loyalty to Japan became of paramount concern. A fresh generation of privately-run *sŏdang* sprang up to preserve Korean culture. By 1945, only about 35 per cent of children attended primary school and 77 per cent of the adult population were illiterate.

Primary and secondary schooling have been emphasised in both North and South Korea since Liberation. Literacy rates have greatly improved in both states, and emphasis has been laid on political education, science and technology, mathematics and physical training. In the South, the New Community Movement (*Saemaŭl Undong*) of 1971 and the *Yusin* **Constitution** of 1972 put education at the forefront of their programmes to stimulate patriotism and modernisation. More schooling was extended to rural areas. As in the past, state education continued to be complemented by a strong private sector. In the North, a 1976 law made pre-school education compulsory and the *chuch'e* philosophy formed the foundation of education at all levels. Vocational training took precedence over the humanities.

SCOTT, JAMES (1850–1920)
Son of an Aberdeenshire farmer, he joined the British Consular Service in China in 1872, when he was 21. Though he retired from the senior post of Consul-General at Canton in 1906, he never lost his Scottish brogue and rustic manners. In 1887–1892 he spent much time in the consulate at **Chemulp'o**. His *A Corean Manual, with Introductory Grammar* (1887, 1893) and *English-Corean Dictionary* (1891) are quarries for the spoken language of those times.

SCRANTON, WILLIAM BENTON (1856–1922)
A physician from Connecticut who in 1885 arrived in Seoul with his mother Mary (1834–1909), as a medical missionary of the Northern Methodist Church. Within twelve months he built a hospital with the goodwill of King **Kojong**. In 1895 he and Oliver **Avison** were active in combating the cholera epidemic. He was chairman of the Bible Translation Committee until he returned to medical work in 1907. He died in Kobe. His mother founded Ihwa Haktang for women, forerunner of **Ewha University**.
See also **Protestants**

SCREENS *pyŏngp'ung* 屏風
Indoor draught-excluding screens are recorded in China from Han times and in Korea from the 7th century AD, though no extant examples are earlier than Chosŏn. They are made of two to twelve panels of **paper** or cloth stretched and pasted on wooden frames, joined so that they will fold together. In size they range from the low *ch'imbyŏng* that protects a sleeper's **pillow** and is usually a *karigae* or *kokpyŏng* (two-panelled screen), to screens five feet or more high. Large screens form ritual backdrops, especially for domestic occasions such as *hwan'gap*. They may be decorated with **calligraphy** or with paintings in ink, watercolour, or tempera; or they may be embroidered. Designs include some specially designed for screens (*ch'aekkŏri*, *paeksu-paekpok*, ancient Chinese bronzes and others); the **Eight Views** (*p'algyŏng*); matching sets of orchids, bamboo and the like; or illustrations of famous stories. Screens were removed to storage on *Ch'unbun* (spring equinox) and brought out on *Ch'ubun* (autumn equinox) (*see* **twenty four solar terms**).
EVELYN McCUNE, *The Inner Art – Korean Screens*, Seoul: Po Chin Chai Printing Co., 1983

SCULPTURE

Small earthenware figurines of humans, animals and reptiles dating from the Three Kingdoms period are unsophisticated and may have been used as fertility symbols (see *t'ou*). On the other hand a tiny (3 cm) metal openwork figure of a deva playing a flute, discovered at **Anap-chi** and now in Kyŏngju National Museum, shows that early artists were already capable of fine craftsmanship in miniature.[1] From the same site were excavated a gilt-bronze phoenix, dragon heads and monster mask door handles. Fearsome guardian deities looked down from end **roof tiles**. On a larger scale came stoneware warriors mounted on horseback from **Kaya** (5th century) and **Silla** (6th century),[2] and stone figures of the **zodiac** sculpted in the round and in relief (Unified Silla dynasty).[3] Lions supported **pagodas** and turtles carried memorial stelae. Sculptors worked in metal, stone, and doubtless wood, although no early examples of the latter have survived; they produced pieces for palaces, households, **tombs** and temples, ranging in size from the minute to the monumental.

It was, however, **Buddhism** that provided the Korean sculptor with his greatest opportunities, and the flourishing of the art coincides with the dynasties in which it was most widely patronised, the Unified Silla and Koryŏ. The figure of Sakyamuni from **Sŏkkuram** at **Pulguk-sa, Kyŏngju** (8th century) is part of a UNESCO World Heritage Site and stands out as the best known example of Korean Buddhist sculpture. But all three kingdoms of the pre-unification age had earlier produced many fine statues of the historical **Buddha, Mirŭk** and **Amida** in stone and gilt-bronze. China provided the models for standing and seated figures, of the meditating Maitreya with one leg crossed over the other, and of the **lotus** leaf seat and surrounding halo, or mandorla. Early Korean sculptors managed to combine a greater feeling for naturalness without forsaking a sense of otherworldliness, and local styles developed and continued through succeeding periods, when artists also added gold, granite and iron to the materials in which they worked. Fine examples of **bronze** plaques decorated in filigree and of standing and seated Buddhas have come from Anap-chi. A seated triad (27 cm) is outstanding for its decoration and sense of proportion and balance.[4] Metal sculptures were produced by the *cire perdue* process, and large pieces were cast in section-moulds. Although Buddhist sculpture was widespread across the entire peninsula, the capital area around Kyŏngju saw the greatest concentration of temples and monuments, and Kyŏngju branch of the National Museum has an outstanding collection of statuary.

In contrast, while temples in many regions preserve fine Buddhas from the Koryŏ dynasty (for example, the gilded wood and clay altar figure in the main hall at Pusŏk-sa, Yŏngju, north Kyŏngsang province, 10th–11th century;[5] and the 14th century gilt-bronze statue of Bhaisajyaguru at Changgŏk-sa, southern Ch'ungch'ŏng province),[6] and while many sculptures of the period are still to be found carved on rock faces in the open air, the National Museum in Seoul displays the greatest indoor collection of Koryŏ religious art. An example is a 2·88-metre cast iron seated Buddha of the 10th century.[7] Foreign influence continued to enter Korea by way of the Chinese, **Khitans, Jurchen** and **Mongols**, especially towards the end of the dynasty, and Korean **craftsmen** added decorative details of their own, such as local **jewellery**, to their statues. Regional styles of sculpture displayed lower levels of artistic sophistication, while preserving the essential Buddhist aura of spirituality.

After such a long period of inspired artistry it was perhaps inevitable that decline should set in during the Chosŏn period, especially when specialist craftsmen were deprived of official sponsorship for Buddhist works of art. Instead it was folk artists who preserved the tradition. They used cheaper and more easily obtainable materials such as wood, clay and stone, and the results of their work were smaller, less varied in style, and of generally lower quality. Exceptions occur, however, notably a gilded wooden statue of the Bodhisattva **Kwanseŭm** (Avalokitesvara) from Kirim-sa, near Kyŏngju (late 15th-early 16th century).[8]

(1)(3) KEITH PRATT, *Korean Music, its History and its Performance*, London and Seoul: Faber Music and Jung Eum Sa, 1987

(2)(4)(5) CHOI SUNU, *5000 Years of Korean Art*, Seoul: Hyonam Publishing Co., 1979

(6)(7) R.WHITFIELD & PAK Y.S., eds, *Korean Art Treasures*, Seoul: Yekyong Publications Co., 1986

(8) HWANG SU YONG, ed., *Arts of Korea: Buddhist Art*, Seoul: Dong Hwa Publishing Co., 1974

AHN KYE-HYON, 'Buddha Images in Korean Tradition,' *KJ*, 10/3, 1970; CHIN HONG-SUP, 'Silla Sculpture,' *KJ*, 5/5, 1965; CHIN HONG-SUP, 'Sculptural Art in the Three Kingdoms,' *KJ*, 6/4, 1966; LENA KIM LEE, 'Buddhist Sculptures of Korea,' *AOA*, 11/4, 1981

SECOND REPUBLIC (1960–61) *Che-i konghwaguk* 第二共和國
Public discontent at the corrupt and oppressive government of the First Republic reached a peak in March 1960, when Syngman Rhee (**Yi Sŭngman**) was unconstitutionally returned for a fourth term of office. Following the **April 19th Student Rising** he was forced to stand down. With heavy reliance on American advice and support, the National Assembly, under the temporary leadership of Hŏ Chŏng, published an amended constitution. The introduction of a cabinet system with an executive prime minister (Chang Myŏn was the first holder of this post) implied a move away from the absolutist presidential power of the First Republic towards greater democracy. When elections were held on 29 July 1960 the **Democratic Party** won majorities in both upper and lower houses of the National Assembly and chose **Yun Posŏn** as President, but some discontented members broke away to form the **New Democratic Party**. The split within the majority ruling party seriously weakened it and it was unable to eradicate corrupt and factional practices. Radicals urged the punishment of ex-President Rhee's associates, the expulsion of foreign troops, and moves towards reunification with North Korea. As a purge of criminal elements in government and the police failed to prevent a rising crime rate, and the government failed to cope with growing economic problems, confidence in the new democracy ebbed and a political crisis developed. On 16 May 1961 troops under the command of General Park Chung Hee (**Pak Chŏnghŭi**) occupied key locations in Seoul and staged a political coup (*see* **Military junta**).
See also **South Korea: constitutional changes; South Korea: political parties**

SEDO-JŎNGCH'I 勢道政治 'rule by the queens' clans'
The word *sedo* can be written with two different Chinese characters for the first syllable: *se* meaning 'world, people' so as to mean 'the way [of ruling] the people' or *se* meaning 'power' so as to mean 'the way of power'. The former was used in the 15th century as a technical term in Confucian discussion of kingship, the latter became confused with this when *sedo* was later used to describe the power of the royal affine families emasculating royal authority. This kind of *sedo* began in 1776 when the young king **Chŏngjo** was dominated by **Hong Kugyŏng**, a relative of Chŏngjo's mother. During the 19th century the reigns of three kings (**Sunjo**, **Hŏnjong**, and **Ch'ŏlchong**) appointed by dowager queens, who thus empowered their own clans, cover the period 1800–1863, during which power oscillated between the Andong Kim and P'ungyang Cho clans. On the marriage of **Kojong** in 1866 the Yŏhŭng Min, the new Queen's

clan, assumed *sedo* in a somewhat milder form until 1905; but the effects of the system were consistently bad for the country throughout the century.
See also **Min, Queen; Taewŏn'gun, The**

SEESAW *nŏlttwigi*
A game associated with **New Year**, enjoyed mostly by women and children. A board about 3·5 m by 50 cm is laid across a bag of **rice** or other suitable fulcrum, over which a small boy is usually persuaded to squat in order to steady the board. One player stands on each end of the board. By jumping alternately they can send each other very high. Some skill is needed if the body is not to be jarred unmercifully. The practice was known in Koryŏ but nothing is known of its earlier history. The suggestion that it formed part of military training is unconvincing.

SEJA-SIGANG-WŎN 世子侍講院 'Office of tutors to the Crown Prince'
Although called -*wŏn*, rather than *pu*, this *maŭl* of twelve members was presided over by a 1st **grade** senior, because of its personal connection with the royal family.

SEJO, KING 世祖 (b. 1417; r. 1455–68)
Sejong's second son, Prince Suyang. Having assassinated his nephew **Tanjong** after usurping the throne in 1455, Sejo could never quieten his conscience. He was an effective king, though dictatorial, consistently bypassing censors and advisers in his idealistic pursuit of just government. Personally proficient in archery and other military skills, he reorganised the army and strengthened the northern border defences. He encouraged literature, having the *Kukcho pogam*, 'Precious Mirror of the Royal Court' (a record of the achievements of kings of the current dynasty), edited by **Sin Sukchu** in 1477; made **No Susin** and Ch'oe Hang compile the code of laws *Kyŏngguk taejŏn* (*see* **law**), and started work on *Tongguk t'onggam*, though it was not completed before his death. He encouraged the use of his father's Korean alphabet, having Chinese books translated and printed in Korean. Like his father, he found comfort in personal Buddhist faith and built **Wŏn'gak-sa**, a large monastery in central Seoul: the pagoda he erected still stands in **Pagoda Park**. As Crown Prince he had *Sŏkpo sangjŏl*, a life of Sakyamuni, compiled from the Lotus **Sutra** and other works. When he became king he established an office for printing Korean translations (*ŏnhae*) of Buddhist texts.

SEJONG, KING 世宗 (1397–1450; r. 1418–50)
The fourth monarch of the Chosŏn Dynasty, a grandson of T'aejo, the founder. No Korean king had a greater personal influence on the country's culture. While he fostered the development of a Confucian state, he took great interest in **Buddhism**. His finest inspirations were the devising of the native alphabet now known as *han'gŭl* and the revival of *Chiphyŏn-jŏn*, to a department of which he entrusted the presentation and justification of the new alphabet in *Hunmin chŏngŭm*. He encouraged developments in **printing**; personally supervised the development of **music** and the provision of guidance for performing Confucian rituals in both home and state; ordered the preparation of important publications such as *Yongbi-ŏch'ŏn-ga*, *Tongguk chŏngun* (a **dictionary** of Chinese characters) and *Wŏrin-ch'ŏn'gang-ji-gok*; began keeping records of rainfall and encouraged improvement of **agriculture** and the raising of silk worms. In his Observatory, the construction of eighteen astronomical instruments and the carving of a new star map are further evidence of the breadth of his scientific interest. He exemplified the Confucian ideal of the ruler who governs by virtue and personal example.

YOUNG-KEY KIM-RENAUD, ed., *King Sejong the Great: the Light of Fifteenth Century Korea*, Washington: The International Circle of Korean Linguists, 1992
See also **astronomy**; **Pak Yŏn**

SEKINO TADASHI 關野貞 (1867–1935)
The scholar who wrote the first important works on Korean art. He studied architecture at Tokyo University, where he eventually became a professor, retiring in 1928. In 1902 he visited Korea and China, making the first survey of Korean antiquities. His principal work on Korea is in Volumes I, IV and V of *Koseki chōsa tokubetsu hōkoku* (Seoul, 1919 and 1927) on the **Lelang** period; and *Chōsen bijutsu-shi*, 'History of Korean Art' (1932).

SELF-STRENGTHENING MOVEMENT *chagang undong* 自強運動
Name given to the attempts made by elements of the Korean court and government to modernise their country in accordance with lessons learned from China, Japan and the West. Choosing the most appropriate source of inspiration, however, bitterly divided them, and the growing sense of **nationalism** in the late 19th century acted both as an incentive and a deterrent to change. While the **T'aewŏn'gun** struggled to maintain the pattern of relative isolationism that had characterised Korea's international rôle in the 18th century, **King Kojong** and **Queen Min** were manipulated by rival supporters of Japan and China, while Western missionaries – in contrast to their more patronising approach in China – encouraged the ambitions of those who sought change while preserving Korean independence.

The movement, which suffered from this lack of agreed goals and policies and from lack of strategic co-ordination, may be dated from the late 1870s and early 1880s, coincidental with Korea's series of unprecedented treaties with foreign countries (*see* **Unequal Treaties**). In 1876 Kim Kisu was sent on a diplomatic and fact-finding mission to Japan, and in 1879 reforms were advocated by a group of scholars known as *Kaehwadang* ('Progressive Party') (*see also* **Independence Party**) which included **Kim Okkyun** and **Sŏ Chaep'il**. A new government department was opened in January 1881 (*T'ongni-gimu Amun*) which was to become the first Foreign Office; the next month Pak Chŏngyang and Kim Okkyun were sent with a second mission to Japan to study the economic and military reform measures undertaken there (*see Sinsa yuramdan*); and at the beginning of 1882 students arrived in China in an ultimately abortive attempt to undertake practical studies. After the settlement of the *Imo* **Incident**, **Pak Yŏnghyo** was sent on a goodwill mission to Japan, where he obtained financial loans to back reform projects. Kim Okkyun returned to Japan with other reformers in 1882 and 1883. Also in 1883 **Min Yŏngik**, Hong Yŏngsik, Sŏ Kwangbŏm and a group of reformers were sent to the United States of America with the first Korean embassy there. They returned with proposals for modernisation of **agriculture**, industry, and the political and social systems, and the King sought American advisers for his government.

At this stage, however, the reform and modernisation movement turned into a more violent struggle between its strongest advocates (largely pro-Japanese), those associated with Queen Min and her clan, and the reactionaries who looked to the Taewŏn'gun for support. The *Kapsin* **Coup** illustrates the strength of opposition faced by the reformers despite their King's support. Those who fled to Japan and the United States after its failure, including Sŏ Kwangbom, Pak Yŏnghyo and Sŏ Chaep'il, continued to memorialise Kojong about the need for modernisation and reform.

Though fundamental change remained unattainable, exchanges with foreign countries, and the growing number of foreigners in Korea, brought about some advances: **medicine** and education benefited from the work of Christian missionaries; the first **newspapers** appeared in the early 1880s; a national post office was established in April 1884; and the telegraph was introduced, linking Korea with China and Japan (1883–5). However, the effect of these innovations across the nation as a whole was slight, and as the predominantly rural population and agricultural economy of Korea suffered more and more from foreign incursions in the 1890s and 1900s, the need for self-strengthening took on a more desperate note. Nationalist societies were formed, dedicated to survival through both modernisation and stress on Korean culture. They included Chang Chiyŏn's Self-strengthening Society (*Taehan Chaganghoe*), established in 1906, and **An Ch'angho's New People's Association** (*Sinminhoe*), formed in 1907.

HAROLD NOBLE, 'The Korean Mission to the United States in 1883,' *TRASKB*, XVIII, 1929

SEOUL

The present capital of South Korea stands on the **Han River** 39 kilometres upstream from **Inch'ŏn**. The city has borne several titles, including Hansŏng 'fortress on the Han' and Hanyang 'north bank of the Han'. Maps from the Chosŏn period refer to it by almost twenty different names, composed of Chinese characters. Seoul (K. Sŏul) is of relatively modern usage, though it had been the colloquial way of referring to the capital for centuries. It means 'capital city' and was not strictly a proper name until after World War II. It probably derives ultimately from a Silla name for **Kyŏngju**, **sŏrabul*, which may have meant 'eastern city'. The accepted romanised form 'Seoul' was inherited from the French missionaries, who rendered *sŏ* as *se* and *ul* as *oul*. It has always been the customary name used by foreigners, and is the only city name in the country that is not Chinese. Seoul is known to the Chinese as Hancheng and the Japanese as Kanjo (both K. Hansŏng).

The city was already important in the Three Kingdoms period. It was situated in **Koguryŏ** until captured by **Silla** in 569. It became the 'Southern capital' (*Mongmyŏngyang*) of the early Koryŏ dynasty in succession to Kyŏngju. On the fall of Koryŏ, geomantic investigations by the Buddhist monk **Muhak** led to its approval as an appropriate site for the new capital by King T'aejo in 1392. It was then also referred to as Hansŏng (not to be confused with **Hansan**, which was also sometimes known by this name). Under T'aejo the city was laid out according to the ancient Chinese pattern with streets running north-south and east-west. Defended on the north by the conical Pukhan-san and to the south by the Han River, it was ringed by a city wall. Entrance was provided through four massive gates, of which the ancient south gate (Sungnye-mun, also known as **Namdae-mun**) and east gate (Hŭngin-ji-mun, also known as **Tongdae-mun**) survive. Inside, the chief axes consisted of the east-west Unjong-no and the main street north from the south gate, called T'aep'yŏng-no, because the T'aep'yŏng-gwan ('Hall of great peace') guest house for Chinese imperial envoys, was situated there. Lesser roads divided the city into sectors, districts and wards. The splendid **Kyŏngbok, Ch'angdŏk**, Ch'anggyŏng and Kyŏngun (or **Tŏksu**) Palaces were built and walled off out of sight of the general populace. The city was synonymous with privilege, power and wealth, and was the centre of political, economic and commercial opportunity. It had the highest concentration of *yangban* households in the country. Its inhabitants numbered around 100,000 at the end of the Koryŏ dynasty and 194,000 by 1669. Though the rich built spacious, tiled-roof houses, the majority occupied small, tiled or thatched single-storey buildings, crowded closely together, and through the remainder of the Chosŏn dynasty neither the size of the population nor its living conditions changed very much. According to the census register of 1789, 112,371 lived within the walls and 76,782 outside, and by 1807 the figure had broken through the 200,000 barrier. Foreigners familiar with western cities in the late 19th century found it backward, dirty, and entirely lacking in modern facilities until an urban redevelopment programme was initiated in 1896 with advice from McLeavey **Brown**, a British employee of the **Maritime Customs Service**.

In the colonial period the city's name became Keijō (K. Kyŏngsŏng 'capital fortress'), and through the 20th century its transformation has been remarkable. From 218,225 in 1907, the population rose to around 700,000 in 1945. Many new and large buildings were erected under Japanese rule, yet most of its housing, shops and amenities still lagged far behind those of the developed world in 1950, and the widespread destruction caused by the **Korean War** had the eventual advantage of clearing ground for modern reconstruction. The economic development of the **Republic of Korea** turned Seoul into a magnet for many socially aspiring rural dwellers, and until the 1990s governments failed to distribute investment away from the capital into the provinces. As a result, the population had grown to 10·612 million in 1990, making it the tenth largest metropolis in the world.

The present city has expanded far to the south of the Han River, which is crossed by 16 bridges with more under construction. Among its important dormitory towns is Kwach'ŏn, the location of the National Museum for Contemporary Art and the site of the new National Museum of Korea. To the west of the city, Kimp'o Airport served as a military airfield during the Korean War, and the enormous growth of air traffic during the 1990s led to a second airport for the capital being started at **Inch'ŏn**.

EDWARD ADAMS, *Through Gates of Seoul*, Seoul: volume I 1974, volume II 1977; A. D. CLARK & D. N. CLARK, *Seoul Past and Present: a Guide to Yi T'aejo's Capital*, Seoul, 1969; HUR YOUNG-HWAN, 'Chosŏn Dynasty Maps of Seoul,' *KJ*, 30/6, 1990; KIM WŎN, 'Histoire de l'urbanisme à Seoul et perspectives', *Revue de Corée* 13.1, 1981; YON-UNG KWON, 'Seoul: Founding the New Capital,' *TRASKB*, LXVIII, 1993; YI TAE-JIN, 'The Nature of Seoul's Modern Urban Development during the 18th and 19th Centuries,' *KJ*, 35/3, 1995

See also **census**; **land tenure**; **slavery**

SEVEN STARS *See* **Ch'ilsŏng-sin**

SEVEN TRAITORS *ch'ilchŏk* 七賊
Pejorative term used for the group of senior ministers who accepted the **Protectorate Treaty** of 1905: Prime Minister **Yi Wanyong**; Home Minister Im Sŏnjun (b. 1860); Justice Minister Cho Chungǔng (1860–1919); Agriculture and Industry Minister Song Pyŏngjun (1858–1925); Education Minister Yi Chaegon; War Minister Yi Pyŏngmu (b. 1864); and Finance Minister Ko Yŏnghǔi (b. 1849).
See also **Five traitors**

SEVEN TREASURES *ch'ilbo* 七寶
The seven treasures mentioned in Buddhist **sutras** are precious materials without symbolic meanings. Most Korean references are probably to the Lotus **Sutra** list: *kǔm* 'gold', *ǔn* 'silver', *yuri* 'lapis lazuli', *kŏgŏ* 'giant clam-shell', *mano* 'agate', *chinju* 'pearl' and *maegoe* 'carnelian'. Pearl and carnelian are replaced in *Amit'a-gyŏng* by *chŏkchu* 'red pearl' and *p'ari* 'crystal'; in *Muryangsu-gyŏng* by *sanho* 'coral' and crystal; in *Panya-gyŏng* by coral and *hobak* 'amber'.

SEVEN WORTHIES *Ch'irhyŏn* 七賢

Yi Illo (1152–1220), author of ***P'ahan-jip***, gathered six friends (O Sejae, Im Ch'un, Cho Dong, Hwangbo Hang, Ham Sun and Yi Tamji), all little known otherwise, and spent his time with them at wine-drinking poetry picnics in order to avoid the strife-ridden court life of the day. **Yi Kyubo** wrote two essays (*Paegun-sosŏl*; *Ch'irhyŏn-sŏl*) about them. The seven were called *Chungnim kohoe*, 'High gathering in the bamboo forests' or *Haejwa Ch'irhyŏn*, 'Seven worthies to the Left (i.e. East) of the Sea', meaning 'seven worthies of Korea'. This was in imitation of *Zhulin qixian*, 'Seven worthies of the Bamboo Groves', also known as *Jiangzuo qixian*, 'Seven worthies to the Left of the River (i.e. East of the Yangzi)', who were renowned for their political protest in similar style in 4th-century China.

SHAMANISM *Musok* 巫俗

Although 'shaman' is now used for describing religion in many parts of the world, the word strictly refers to north-east Asian and other sub-Arctic and Arctic cultures. Shamanism is not a religion in the sense that **Buddhism** is, nor does it have many of the quasi-religious aspects of **Confucianism**. Most religious systems evolve and appoint leaders, but shamanism consists wholly of self-selected specialists. They have no hierarchy, no teaching rôle, indeed no dogma to teach; they can exist only in a matrix of animism. Animism is, however, to be distinguished from shamanism.

Shamans have no institutionalised social or communal responsibility, but claim they can contact spirits of all kinds, both good and bad, and use this skill to help others in crises. This spirit contact is effected by falling into trance, brought on by dancing and drumming. The trance may induce possession by a spirit, though a Korean shaman often has a conversation in which there is recurrent possession, her own words alternating with those of the spirit.

There is little doubt of the fundamental identity of Korean and Siberian shamans. The theory (based partly on the comparison of **gold crowns** from the Three Kingdoms period with others found in Siberia) that there were ancient shaman-rulers remains hypothetical. During Koryŏ, shamans were marginalised, but there were traces of a state cult. During the Chosŏn period shamans were excluded from court by neo-Confucianism, but were recurrently invoked by queens and remained important in the life of ordinary people. **Queen Min** made much use of one called **Chillyŏng-gun** in the 1890s. Shamanism influenced **dance** and **music**, especially the **Ch'oyŏng** dance and instrumental *sanjo*, while some tunes and rhythms of *nongak* are virtually the same as those in shaman music.

Most Korean shamans are female (*mudang*), though there are male *paksu* and *p'ansu*. Initiation is entirely self-authenticated and typically occurs after an illness during which a spirit journey is experienced in a dream or trance. Daughters of *mudang* are especially susceptible to this initiation.

Shamanism is in no way exclusive. Those who employ shamans will also ask the prayers of Buddhist monks and of *namsadang*, offer their own *kosa*, make their own offerings in **spirit worship** shrines and attend community sacrifices at *sŏnang-dang*. The power of shamans resides in the psychological value of their performance. They have a highly personal culture-bound ministry, and for this reason attempts to give Korean shamanism a universal philosophic value are bound to be unsuccessful.

Koreans describe shamanism as *misin*, 'superstition'.

KEITH HOWARD, *Korean Shamanism: Revivals, Survivals, and Change*, Seoul: Royal Asiatic Society, Korea Branch, 1998; H.P. HUHM, *Korean Shaman Rituals*, New York: Hollym International Corp., 1980, LAUREL KENDALL, *Shamans, Housewives, and Other*

Restless Spirits, Honolulu: University of Hawaii Press, 1985; BOUDEWIJN WALRAVEN, *Songs of the Shaman: the Ritual Chants of the Korean* Mudang, London: Kegan Paul International, 1994
See also **ancestral worship**; *mudang*

SHANHAI JING (K. *Sanhae-gyŏng*) 山海經 'Classic of Mountains and Seas'
A fantastic world description, including wonders and prodigies, written in Han dynasty China, but traditionally regarded as much older. It was thought to mention Korea under the name of Qingqiu (K. Ch'ŏnggu) 'blue/green hills', and is the source of other legendary place-names on early Korean world-maps.
See also **cartography; flower, national; Korea, names for**

SHENYANG, KING OF 沈陽王
Title bestowed by the **Mongols** on members of the Koryŏ royal family resident at Shenyang in **Manchuria** in the 13th–14th centuries, giving them authority over Koreans in the region. The Mongol intention was also partly to establish a rival power base to the king in **Kaesŏng** as a means of extending their own control over the peninsula.

SHIMONOSEKI, TREATY OF (1895)
Treaty marking the end of the **Sino-Japanese War** signed by **Li Hongzhang** and **Itō Hirobumi** on 17 April 1895. Its specific affirmation of the independence of Korea was no more than a Japanese device to end China's claim to suzerainty over its former tribute vassal (*see* **China, relations with**). In May Korea greeted with relief Japan's enforced surrender of the **Liaodong** Peninsula lease, granted to it under the Treaty, by the so-called 'Triple Intervention' of Russia, France and Germany, but if anything it reinforced Japanese efforts to exert control over affairs in Seoul, whilst at the same time encouraging Russian interest in **Manchuria** and Korea. In due course, this led to the outbreak of the **Russo-Japanese War**.
See also ***Kabo* reforms; Tonghak Rebellion**

SHINTO 神道 *See* **Shrine question**

SHRINE QUESTION *sinsa ch'ambae* 神社參拜 (1935)
Under its policy of making Korea part of Japan, the colonial government built Shinto shrines throughout the country, opening the Seoul shrine in 1925. In 1932 all schools in P'yŏngyang were asked to attend a Shinto ritual. Mission schools were alarmed and the Presbyterian Church tried to negotiate with the **Government-General**, but without success. In November 1935 the schools of P'yŏngyang were again required to take part in Shinto rites. George Shannon McCune (father of the author of the **McCune-Reischauer** romanisation system), the leading Presbyterian school head in the area, resisted. Teaching licences were withdrawn from him and Miss Snook, head of the girls' school, in January 1936. They left Korea in March.
   The Japanese sometimes claimed the rites were not religious but purely secular. Catholics, **Anglicans**, Methodists and Canadian Presbyterians accepted this interpretation. In 1938 the Presbyterian General Assembly was suborned by the police into accepting the rites, though many of its schools were closed. Some Korean Presbyterians resisted the order and were imprisoned after being held without trial until early in 1945. About fifty of them died in prison; the rest were freed after 15 August. Division over the Shrine Question underlay Presbyterian schisms in the 1950s.

KIM YANGSON, 'Compulsory Shintō Shrine Worship and Persecution,' in YU CHAI-SHIN, *Korea and Christianity*, Seoul, Berkeley, Toronto, 1996
See also **Rites Controversy**

SHUFELDT TREATY (1882)

Treaty of Amity and Commerce between Korea and the United States of America signed on 22 May 1882. It had been brokered by **Li Hongzhang** in the hope that America would then support China's suzerainty over Korea. Commodore Robert W. Shufeldt (1822–1895), who had been involved in the follow-up to the *General Sherman* incident and was anxious to end Korean isolationism, concluded the agreement at Chemulp'o (**Inch'ŏn**) with the Korean envoy to China, Sin Hŏn. Among privileges gained by America under the Treaty were **extraterritoriality**, low tariffs, and the right to open a legation. However, the popular outcry against the Treaty was a factor in provoking the *Imo* **Incident** two months later.

LEW YOUNG-ICK, 'The Shufeldt Treaty and Early Korean-American relations,' in HAN SUNGJOO, ed., *After One Hundred Years: Continuity and Change in Korean-American Relations*, Seoul: Asiatic Research Center, Korea University, 1982
See also **United States, relations with**

SHUTTLECOCKS *chegi*

Shuttlecocks, made by twisting coins in paper, or tying dried scallions with their leaves on, or knotting rags, or even by fixing feathers to a little bag of ash, are kept in the air by kicking with the instep. A single player may try to go on as long as possible without letting the shuttlecock fall to the ground. In *semjegi* two or more may compete to see who can kick the shuttlecock most times before it falls. This is also called *Chongno-jegi*, because it was played by shopkeepers in Chongno, the main street of Seoul, to keep warm in cold weather. They also played *sabang-jegi*, in which four men kicked the shuttlecock from one to the other.

SIBERIA, KOREANS IN

Koreans suffering from agricultural poverty in north Korea began to emigrate from Hamgyŏng province to Irkutsk during the famine of 1864. Others followed in increasing numbers (415 in 1871 alone). A new settlement, Sinhan-ch'on 'new Korea village', with a Korean school and church (presumably Russian Orthodox), was established in Siberia in 1874. By 1880 these immigrants were sending students to Moscow. The Sikhote Alin littoral to the north of Vladivostok attracted many. 32,000 were living there by 1902 and 100,000 by 1910. Among them were armed bands who made forays against the Japanese in Hamgyŏng. Two anti-Japanese Korean newspapers were suppressed there in 1909, but one, *Taedong Kongbo*, managed to reappear. By 1910 there was a large and strongly anti-Japanese Korean community in the city of Chita, where an Orthodox Church monthly, *Taehan-in Chŏngyo-bo*, was published in 1913–14. By 1919 there were 500,000 Koreans in Siberia. 3,000 of them joined Russian communists withstanding Japanese efforts to take over the Trans-Siberian Railway through the Sikhote Alin after the Russian revolution of 1917.
See also **Emigration, Korean**

SICH'ŎN-GYO 侍天教 'doctrine of serving Heaven'

When **Son Pyŏnghŭi**, the **Tonghak** leader, went to Japan in 1894, Yi Yonggu (1868–1912), a Tonghak staff member, took the opportunity to establish a pro-Japanese party within the Tonghak movement. When Son returned in 1906 and renamed the movement **Ch'ŏndo-gyo**, he expelled Yi's group from the cult. In 1907 the dissidents were constituted as *Sich'ŏn-gyo* with Yi at their head. For a while they had influence with **Yi Wanyong**, but on Yi Yonggu's death in 1912 they began to split up and shortly faded away. Doctrinally indistinguishable from *Ch'ŏndo-gyo*, they were differentiated only by their pro-Japanese political stance.

SIGŬP 食邑

Estates built up in the Three Kingdoms period by members of aristocratic clans with land awarded to them for meritorious service to their rulers. They were allowed to benefit from the income from these lands.

SIHWA 詩話 'poetry criticism'

Literary criticism of poetry has existed in China since late Tang, in Korea since late Koryŏ, when Yi Illo's *P'ahan-jip* was written. It usually takes the form of short notes, anecdotes, letters and prefaces, which are excerpted and collected in books called *mallok*, *yasa*, *chapki*, *swaerok*, *ch'onghwa* and other titles for collectanea. *Sihwa*, often rather clumsily translated as 'poetry talk', is the commonest general name for the individual pieces. The criticism sometimes applies to poetic technique, sometimes to the genuineness of the poet's experience and emotion. Korean critics tend to disparage poems that are mere imitations of Chinese work: they want evidence of Korean experience in both imagery and meaning. The *sihwa* material available is vast and fascinating.
RICHARD RUTT, 'Traditional poetry criticism', *TRASKB*, XLVII, 1972

SIJO 時調 'Period tunes'

The word *sijo*, meaning a poem of a particular metre, first appeared in **Choe Namsŏn**'s anthology *Kagok-sŏn* (1913); the earlier word was *tan'ga* 'short song'. *Sijo* is a musical term, and the form was originally intended to be sung. The lyric is usually about love, loyalty, virtue or lovely scenery, ending with an implied question or lingering doubt. Its origin is endlessly debatable, but the form cannot certainly be traced earlier than the middle of the 16th century. It was written in *han'gŭl* and developed as an art form mainly by men of the *yangban* class, and became a favourite way of expressing their emotions and their response to nature. *Sijo* were also written by *kisaeng*.

The standard form (*p'yŏng sijo*) consists of three lines, each constructed of groups of 3 or 4 syllables – such groups are the building blocks of all pre-modern Korean poetry – averaging 45 syllables for the whole poem. The first group in the third line is always a three-syllable exclamation, and is followed by a group of five or more syllables; while the final group of the whole poem is an otiose grammatical conclusion that is omitted when the *sijo* is sung.

Normative syllable count

1st line:	3	4,	3–4	4;
2nd line:	3	4,	3–4	4.
3rd line:	3!	5+,	4	(3).

The melodies used are related to those still used for recitation of Chinese quatrains in the strict Tang style, based on three notes (A flat, B flat and the E flat below) and sung very slowly to the accompaniment of an hour-glass **drum**. Another connection with Tang quatrains is that the first two lines of a *sijo* correspond to the first two lines (theme and development) of a quatrain; the first syllable-group of the third line corresponds to the third line (twist or counter-theme) of the Tang quatrain; and the rest of the *sijo* to the last line (conclusion) of the quatrain.

Divorce of the lyric poem from sung performance began when retired statesmen of the 16th century onwards had *sijo* words printed in their collected works. Scholars' *sijo* were frequently composed in cycles of up to forty poems, on linked themes, such as the joys of rural retirement. Later *sijo* anthologies remained the province of professional singers, who composed new poems and sometimes adapted Chinese poems by famous men, who came to be regarded as the authors of the *sijo* – which may explain the attribution of *sijo* to pre-Chosŏn writers. There are also many anonymous *sijo*, some of high quality. The most famous anthologies are *Ch'ŏnggu yŏngŏn*, 'Drawn-out Words of the Green Hills' (1728, i.e. Songs from Korea, *yŏngŏn* being a definition of song in *Shujing*), *Haedong kayo*, 'Songs from beyond the Eastern Sea' (i.e. Korea, 1761) and *Kagok wŏllyu*, 'Source and Flow of Songs' (1876). Since 1970 there have been several modern compendia of texts in diplomatic editions.

From the 18th century onwards expanded forms, *ŏssijo* 'altered sijo' and *sasŏl sijo* 'discursive sijo', were written, using demotic language. They often dealt with daily life in rural households, but were still intended to be sung.

Sijo are now written by people in all walks of life, but more often intended for reading than for singing, almost as though *sijo* were the Korean equivalent of the Japanese *haiku*. Modern examples often have something in common with the western epigram, increasingly unlike the traditional song-words. Meanwhile literary scholarship tends to emphasise the musical aspect of the *sijo*'s nature and history.

RICHARD RUTT, *The Bamboo Grove: an Introduction to Sijo*, Berkeley: University of California Press 1971; and University of Michigan Press, 1998

SIJO MELODIES

By the 18th century *sijo* were sung to *kagok* melodies, and then to a simpler tune said to have been composed by the singer Yi Sech'un. It was this 'new tune', now known as *p'yŏng sijo*, that gave both the music and the poetic form its present name. In turn, it gave rise to a limited number of additional simple tunes, to which were – and are – sung any number of *sijo* poems. Simpler though they may be than *kagok*, their wide range of dynamics and heavy vibrato similarly demand great breath control. There are stylistic differences between *sijo* of the capital region (*kyŏngje*) and those of the provinces (*hyangje*). The latter principally comprise *Yŏngje* (from South Kyŏngsang province), *Wanje* (North Chŏlla), and *Naep'oje* (South Ch'ungch'ŏng). *Hyangje* are sung slowly to the accompaniment of the hour-glass **drum** *changgo* alone, but melodic instruments may be used for *kyŏngje*.

SILK

Was the traditional material of upper class clothing, and features prominently in lists of **tribute** goods exchanged between Korea and China. Silk probably first entered Korea from China in the **Proto-Three Kingdoms Period**, and historical texts and wall paintings show that fine silks were worn by the aristocracy in the first centuries AD, when Korea stood at the end of the Silk Road between the Roman and Han Chinese empires. The earliest extant examples of Korean silk are fragments found in the 6th-century **Heavenly Horse Tomb** in **Kyŏngju**. In the early Chosŏn period silk was supplied by one of the **Six Licensed Shops** in the capital, and was manufactured for court use under the aegis of a government office. Sumptuary laws restricted the wearing of highly decorated silk garments to senior members of the aristocracy.

KWON YUN-HUI, *Symbolic and Decorative Motifs of Korean Silk*, Seoul: Il Ji Sa, 1988
See also **textiles**

SILLA 新羅 (before AD 668)
State which developed from the **Chinhan** tribal confederacy in south-eastern Korea (*see also* **Samhan**). It was one of the three kingdoms which developed in parallel and frequently in rivalry between the 4th and 7th centuries, and established unified rule across the peninsula for the first time in AD 668 (*see* **Unified Silla**). The founder of the state is said to have been **Pak Hyŏkkŏse**. Its capital was at Saro, the site of the walled town which was the centre of authority of the dominant Chinhan clans, and which later became known as Kŭmsŏng (modern **Kyŏngju**). Although *Samguk sagi* affords Silla the earliest date of state formation (57 BC), it was actually the last of the three kingdoms to assume the title of King for its ruler (*see* **Silla, kingly titles**). In 503 the name of the state was changed from Saro to Silla by King Pŏphŭng, who also strengthened the centralised political authority of the state. It was during his reign that the 'bone-rank' system (*kolp'um*) was instituted, and that the Chinese practice of naming **reign titles** was adopted.

Though the most remote of the three kingdoms from the Middle Kingdom and culturally the most under-developed, Silla paid **tribute** to China in the late 4th century and received envoys in return, and soon became embroiled in international as well as inter-state politics. The first alliance was made with **Koguryŏ**, whose king **Kwanggaet'o** helped to expel a Japanese invasion force supporting **Paekche** in 400. But Koguryŏ's subsequent expansion frightened Paekche into a new agreement with Silla. This lasted from 434 to 553. It ended when Paekche, having recovered some territory from Koguryŏ in the upper **Han River** valley in 551, soon lost it to Silla. Not satisfied with this, Silla went on to take more land belonging to Paekche in the lower Han valley, thus opening a route from the south-east through to the west coast, and direct lines of contact with China. Paekche fought back, but King Sŏng was killed in battle at Kwansansŏng (modern Okch'ŏn), and the unstoppable Silla armies claimed further dominion over the south by overrunning the state of **Kaya** in 562.

Sui and **Tang dynasty** emperors harboured hopes of restoring direct Chinese rule over the peninsula, but failed with land invasions (*see* **Koguryŏ**). When Paekche, with Koguryŏ support, attacked Silla in 641, Silla appealed to China for aid (*see* **Kim Ch'unch'u**). Both states tried to enlist Japanese help, but in the end it was the Tang court that seized its opportunity. After further Paekche provocation in 655 the Chinese mounted an expeditionary force. In 660 a fleet carrying 130,000 men sailed up the Paek (modern Kŭm) River, mounted a pincer operation on the Paekche capital **Sabi** in conjunction with 50,000 Silla soldiers under their general **Kim Yusin**, and destroyed the state.

The allies then turned north against Koguryŏ. An attack on P'yŏngyang was repulsed in 661, but resistance was weakened by attrition and by dissension among the Koguryŏ military dictatorship, and the northern kingdom succumbed to further campaigns in 668. Having captured the rulers of two of the three kingdoms, no doubt Emperor Gaozong anticipated the imminent submission of Silla to Chinese rule. But his plans were to be thwarted (*see* **Unified Silla**).

RULERS:

Pak clan	Hyŏkkŏse	57 BC – AD 4		Ilsŏng	134–54
	Namhae	4–24		Adalla	154–84
	Yuri	24–57	*Sŏk clan*	Pŏrhyu	184–96
Sŏk clan	T'arhae	57–80		Naehae	196–230
Pak clan	P'asa	80–112		Chobun	230–47
	Chima	112–34		Ch'ŏmhae	247–61

Kim clan	Mich'u	262–84		Chijŭng	500–14
Sŏk clan	Yurye	284–97		Pŏphŭng	514–540
	Kirim	298–309		Chinhŭng	540–76
	Hŭrhae	310–55		Chinji	576–9
Kim clan	Naemul	356–402		Chinp'yŏng	579–632
	Silsŏng	402–17		[Queen] Sŏndŏk	632–47
	Nulchi	417–58		[Queen] Chindŏk	647–54
	Chabi	458–79		Muyŏl	654–61
	Soji	479–500			

KIM WON-YOUNG, 'Clay Figurines of Old Silla,' *KJ*, 8/4, 1968; WERNER SASSE, 'The Shilla Stone Inscription from Naengsu-ri, Yŏngil-gun,' *KJ*, 31/3, 1991; ELLEN UNRUH, 'Reflections on the Fall of Silla,' *KJ*, 15/5, 1975
See also **Ch'ŏmsongdae**; *hwarang*; **Silla kingly titles; Silla, Queens of**

SILLA (post-668) *See* **Unified Silla**

SILLA KINGLY TITLES

The records do not refer to the rulers of **Silla** by the Chinese word *wang* 'king' until the reign of Chijŭng, who took office in AD 500. The founder of Silla rule, Hyŏkkŏse (*see* **foundation myths**), has *kŏsŏgan* suffixed to his name. *Kŏsŏgan* is interpreted as 'great man' or 'chief'. His successor Namhae is called *ch'ach'aung*, taken to be a shaman title. From AD 24 to 356 the title is recorded as *isagŭm*, thought to mean 'successor prince'. From the accession of Naemul in 356 until Chijŭng in 500 the title is *maripkan*, 'ridge' or 'high place'. Chijŭng is the first recorded as using the Chinese *wang* and giving the kingdom a name: **Saro**. These titles may reflect the development of the Silla people from a local group to a centralised kingdom adopting Chinese ideals; but the real significance of the records and the meanings of the words are probably beyond discovery.

SILLA, QUEENS OF

Korea had three women who were sovereigns in their own right. All ruled Silla. They are referred to in *Samguk sagi* simply as *wang*, like male sovereigns. 20th-century historians distinguish them as *yŏwang*, 'queens'. The first two, Sŏndŏk (r. 632–47) and Chindŏk (647–54), ruled at the end of the Three Kingdoms period; Chinsŏng (887–98) at the end of Unified Silla.

In 632, after a reign of 53 years, King Chinp'yŏng died leaving no male heir. His eldest daughter, later known as Sŏndŏk, was chosen (possibly at his suggestion) to succeed him and was recognised by Tang in 635. During her reign **Buddhism** became more fully established, and the **Ch'ŏmsŏngdae** observatory and other major building works were completed. There were constant border struggles with **Paekche** and **Koguryŏ**, in which she was well served by **Kim Yusin** and **Kim Ch'unch'u**.

When Sŏndŏk died in 647, she was succeeded by her cousin (daughter of Chinp'yŏng's uterine brother), later known as Chindŏk. Chindŏk carried on with the same loyal officers and strengthened the relationship with Tang China (*see* **Queen Chindŏk's poem**). When she died in 654, Kim Ch'unch'u, who was a grandson of Chinp'yŏng through another daughter, succeeded her. He is now known as King **Muyŏl**. Both queens' reigns contributed to the process of unifying the whole peninsula under Silla rule.

The story of Chinsŏng, two hundred years later, belongs to the time when Unified Silla was in decline, attacked by such as **Kyŏn Hwŏn** and **Kŭngye**. She succeeded her brother Chŏnggang, who died a few months after his accession. As he was dying he recalled Queens Sŏndŏk and Chindŏk and recommended that his sister should succeed him. She has been accused of bad government and many misdemeanours that added to the troubles of the times. After ten years she abdicated in favour of her nephew Hyogong. She died very soon afterwards. Twenty years later, Silla had given way to Koryŏ.

SILLOK See Chosŏn Wangjo Sillok

SILTAM MUNCHA 悉曇文字

Siddham or Siddhamatrka. An ancient script for Sanskrit, out of which Devanagari evolved. It came from India to East Asia with **Buddhism** and is found in Korean manuscripts and printed books. It consists of 16 vowels and 35 consonants, sometimes counted as 50 letters and called *Pŏmŏ osip cha*. There is no connecting line between syllables as in Devanagari. Because the letters are written in syllabic clusters they are often shown in Korea as equivalents of *han'gŭl* syllables.

SIM SAJŎNG 沈師正 (Hyŏnjae, 1707–69)

Scholar-artist who studied under **Chŏng Sŏn** in the 1720s while the latter was still practising in his Chinese style. Sim himself painted almost entirely in the Wu, or Southern manner, before turning later to the Zhe (*see* **landscape painting**). It was said that his landscapes were on a par with those of the best contemporary Northern School artists in China, although they now evoke some criticism from Korean art historians for their imaginary quality at a time when other great artists were painting real Korean landscape scenes in the *chin'gyŏng* style. *Immortal Playing with a Toad* (Kansong Museum)[1] is an amusing example of his figure painting, which was reputed not to be his *forte*, but the *Tiger* (National Museum of Korea) attributed to him is a meticulously brushed and outstanding depiction of a threatening beast.[2]

(1), (2) CHOI SUNU, *Five Thousand Years of Korean Art*, Seoul: Hyonam Pub. Co., 1979

SIM-CH'ŎNG-JŎN 沈清傳

An old story, recorded both as *p'ansori* and as *kodae sosŏl*. The baby girl, Sim Ch'ŏng, loses her mother when she is only seven days old. She grows up caring for her father, Sim Pongsa (*pongsa* means both a minor official and a blind man) with intense devotion, making great sacrifices for him, but after she is drowned in a river, he takes up with a low woman. His daughter has in fact been taken into the Crystal Palace under water, and she reappears above the surface as a **lotus** flower. The flower is taken to the king's palace, where Sim Ch'ŏng is transformed into an empress. She holds a banquet for the blind at which her father is restored to sight and virtuous living. The tale has an intriguing blend of Buddhist and Confucian motifs, and is second only to *Ch'unhyang-jŏn* in popularity.

SIN SAIMDANG 申師任堂 (1504–51)

Korea's most famous female artist, renowned as a painter, calligrapher, poet, and embroiderer. When only seven years old she was said to have copied **An Kyŏn**'s pictures successfully. As a **flower and bird** painter she excelled at portraying insects and plants (for example, *Grapevine* (Kansong Museum)[1]), and as a calligrapher she practised a fine cursive script. She was married into the royal Yi clan and was the mother of the reformist neo-Confucian minister **Yi I**.

(1) CHOI SUNU, *Five Thousand Years of Korean Art*, Seoul: Hyonam Pub. Co., 1979

SIN SUKCHU 申叔舟 (Pohan-jae, 1417–75)
A favourite of **King Sejong**, he was appointed to the **Chiphyŏn-jŏn** in 1441 and took part in the work on the new alphabet. Several times with **Sŏng Sammun** he visited the Chinese scholar Huang Zan in Liaodong to discuss Chinese phonetics. In 1443 he went as an envoy to Japan, pausing on the homeward trip to visit **Tsushima** and conclude the treaty known as *Kyehae-yakcho* **Kyehae Treaty**. He accompanied Prince Suyang (**Sejo**) on an embassy to the Ming court in 1452. During the reign of **Tanjong** he supported Sejo in his successive coups, thus surviving when his friend Sŏng Sammun was killed. Climbing the ladder of government, he finally reached the post of *yŏng-ŭijŏng*. Although he was a famous scholar, served under six kings with great distinction, and was a gifted poet and astute statesman, his reputation has suffered in posterity because he shifted his loyalty from Tanjong to Sejo. He was the author of a book on the geography of Japan, the Ryukyus and Tsushima entitled *Haedong cheguk-ki* 'Record of lands to the east of the sea' (1471).

SIN TON 辛旽 (P'yŏnjo, d. 1371)
Sin Ton was an obscure Buddhist monk when he was chosen by the Koryŏ King Kongmin about 1365 as an adviser independent of the court cliques. Sin Ton was persuaded to become a layman and appointed regulator of land and **slaves**. In this post he freed many slaves and returned much misappropriated land to its rightful owners, thus becoming a saint to many but an enemy to others. The king eventually made him Prime Minister Plenipotentiary. Their friendship appears to have had an obsessive quality, though Chosŏn dynasty accounts, on which we must rely, are hardly impartial. He was accused of corruption and sexual misdemeanours. The king was forced to banish him to **Suwŏn**, where he was beheaded as a traitor in 1371.

SIN WI 申緯 (Chaha, 1769–1847)
Scholar official sent to China with an embassy in 1813, who was critical of factionalism in politics. He was exiled in 1830 but later recalled. A participant in the **Sirhak** movement, he was famous for achievements in all **Three Perfections**. His painting shows the influence of his teacher **Kang Sehwang**, and he was also a disciple of **Yun Sun**. He is reckoned to be one of the greatest painters of **bamboo**, and his simple but effective **landscape** style, modelled on the Chinese Southern School, showed his individuality. The same was true of his **calligraphy**, in which he took Su Shi (1036–1101) and Dong Qichang (1555–1638) as his masters, but interpreted them with a boldness of his own. His brush-name means 'mauve mist'.

SIN YUNBOK 申潤福 (Hyewŏn, 1758–c.1820)
One of the most famous Korean artists, a *Tohwa-sŏ* professional specialising in *genre* scenes and some **landscapes**. Unlike **Kim Hongdo**, however, with whom he is often bracketed as representing the true Korean life-style of the 18th century, Hyewŏn confined himself mostly to *yangban* subjects. It is for his light-hearted, informal pictures that he is best known, showing his preoccupation with *kisaeng* girls and their activities. *Portrait of a Girl* (Kansong Museum)[1] is a respectful, carefully executed study of female beauty, hair style and **dress**. *Girl by a Lotus Pond* (National Museum of Korea)[2] is a relaxed, sketch-like study of a girl sitting on her doorstep holding a pipe and a mouth organ (*saenghwang*), in which the bold brushwork and light colour-wash are an essential complement to the casual nature of the scene. In contrast, *Sword Dance* (Kansong Museum)[3] is more deliberately constructed and drawn, and makes a colourful and lively picture of two dancers performing to a band of seven musicians,

watched by a mixed group of men and girls. There is no hint of impropriety here, but in other pictures Hyewŏn pokes fun at his fellow gentlemen for taking sexual liberties with *kisaeng*, as in *Boating Scene* (Kansong Museum)[4] and *Picnic by a Lotus Pond* (Kansong Museum).[5] And in *Women on Tano Day* (Kansong Museum)[6] he verges on the semi-erotic, as two young Buddhist monks watch a group of girls bathing in a stream. To the sensitivities of 18th-century Confucian society these were unprecedented and rather offensive subjects.

(1), (2) CHOI SUNU, *Five Thousand Years of Korean Art*, Seoul: Hyonam Pub. Co., 1979
(3) W.Y.KIM, S.U.CHOI, C.S.IM, eds., *Arts of Korea*, vol. 2, *Paintings*, Seoul: Dong Hwa Publishing Co., 1974
(4), (5), (6) CHOI, op. cit.

SINAN 新安

Site off the south-west coast of Chŏlla where a Chinese merchant ship, carrying a large cargo of Chinese porcelain, sank around the year 1323. It was probably *en route* from China to Japan and had been blown off course. Evidence suggests that its crew was multi-national and included Koreans. Since 1976, archaeologists have recovered over twenty thousand pieces of **celadon**, white, and blue and white ware from the underwater wreck, and around one million coins from the seabed. A museum has been built to exhibit the materials, which include just three Korean vessels: a *meiping* vase of the first half, 12th century; an inlaid celadon vase of the mid-12th century; and an inlaid celadon cup tray of the first half, 13th century.

D.H.KEITH & H.E.KIM, 'Yellow Sea Yields Shipwreck Trove: a 14th-Century Cargo Makes Port at Last,' *National Geographic*, August 1979; PAK SONG-GIL, *The Treasure of the Sinan Seabed*, Seoul: Dong Hwa Publishing Co., 1983

SINAWI

An instrumental piece of folk music. It is played by an ensemble which may include the *kŏmun'go*, *kayagŭm*, *ajaeng*, *p'iri*, *taegŭm*, *haegŭm*, and perhaps the double-reed oboe *t'aep'yŏngso*, and percussion instruments drawn from the *changgo*, *puk* (*see* **drums**), *ching* (large gong), *kkwaenggwari* (small gong) and *para* (cymbals). The players have opportunities between the ensemble passages for solo extemporisation rather as they do in western jazz, enabling each to display his skill in a free and melodic way. The result is a performance brimming over with energy and passion, perhaps evocative of the **shaman** ceremony from which it is thought to have been derived. In its turn, it may have been one of the sources of inspiration for *sanjo*, both of them originating in the south-western province of Chŏlla. A version for solo instrument alone, with drum accompaniment, is confined to the *kutkŏri* and faster rhythmic patterns.
See also **nongak**

SINDONAE 新都内

Sindo, 'new capital', is a small group of villages (2 km x 3 km) in the mountain area of Kyeryong-san, near Nonsan in south Ch'ungch'ŏng. It was here that Yi T'aejo began to build his new capital in 1392 before he decided on the site at Hanyang (Seoul). Shortly before the First World War (after the death of **Kang Ilsun**) the area proved a magnet for members of the **new religions**, such as *Ilsim-gyo*, drawn there by the prophecies in *Chŏng-gam-nok*.

SIN'GANHOE 新幹會 *See* **New Shoot Society**

SINJŬNG TONGGUK YŎJI-SŬNGNAM 新增東國輿地勝覽 'Newly Enlarged Geographical Survey of Korea'

The great gazetteer *Tongguk yŏji-sŭngnam*, intended as an aid in national administration, was completed by a group led by **No Sasin** in 1486, revised in 1499 and 1530, and finally printed with the prefix *sinjŭng* 'newly enlarged' in 1612. Original copies are rare, but there are several facsimile editions. Influences from the Song dynasty *Fangyu shenglan* (K. *Pangyŏ sŭngnam*) by Zhu Mu, whose title was borrowed, and *Da Ming yitongzhi*, 'Unified Description of Great Ming' (K. *Tae-Myŏng ilt'ong-ji*) are detectable. The first four books deal with Seoul and **Kaesŏng**, after which each prefecture is described, giving its position, historic names, local surnames, customs, scenery, products, **fortresses**, **beacons**, pavilions, **schools**, post-stations, **yamens**, bridges, Buddhist establishments, Confucian shrines and institutes, royal **tombs**, biographies of local worthies and appropriate poems.

SINMINHOE 新民會 *See* **New People's Association**

SINMUN, KING 神武王 (681-92)

Second king of the Unified Silla dynasty. He purged his opponents, including the *sangdaedŭng* Kun'gwan, and took steps to establish the authority of the throne over the *kolp'um* aristocracy. Military reforms based on the creation of nine regiments (*sŏdang*) and ten garrisons (*sip chŏng*) established a national army, and the consolidation of peace permitted the development of a system of provincial government directed from five regional capitals. These were situated in Kŭmgwan (modern **Kimhae**), Sŏwŏn (modern Ch'ŏngju), Chungwŏn (modern Ch'ungju), Pukwŏn (modern Wŏnju), and Namwŏn. The country was divided into nine provinces (*chu*), subdivided into commanderies (*kun*) and counties (*hyŏn*). A **land reform** measure introduced in 689, though ultimately rescinded, further attempted to curb the power of the landed aristocracy by abolishing the system of stipend villages which gave them rights over the **peasantry**. In keeping with the Chinese inspiration for his reform measures, Sinmun founded the *Kukhak* (National [Confucian] Academy) in 682. Intended to strengthen the position of families below *chin'gol* status, this taught the **Confucian Classics** to students of head-rank six, and art and handicrafts to lower classes.

SINMUN'GO 申聞鼓 'petitioner's drum'

In 1402 a drum was set up at the palace gate so that those who could not get justice through the normal channels could signal to the king, who would act directly. The system was open to abuse, and strict limits had to be put on the kind of case that could be dealt with in this manner. **Prince Yŏnsan** abolished the custom, but it was restored by **Yŏngjo** in 1777. In later years petitioners were allowed to strike a gong (*kyŏkchaeng*) when the king passed in the public procession called *kŏdong*.

SINO-JAPANESE WAR (1894-5) *Ch'ŏngil chŏnjaeng* 清日戰爭

The last, and psychologically and militarily perhaps the worst, of all China's 19th century defeats by foreign powers. The underlying *casus belli* was the long-standing rivalry between the two countries, fuelled by the impetus of modernisation and exacerbated by the imperialist rôle of the Western nations in East Asia. In China, this was predominantly met with resentment at perceived exploitation and damage to tradition; in Meiji Japan, with greater readiness to seize the opportunities offered by modernisation; in Korea, with an awakening of **nationalism** directed against the Chinese and Japanese as well as western interference in their country.

Against a background of growing Sino-Japanese competition for influence in Seoul (*see* **Tianjin, Treaty of**), the Korean government had appealed to its traditional suzerain, China, for assistance against the **Tonghak** rebels. 3,000 soldiers arrived on 8 June 1894, only to be followed a week later by a counter-force of over twice as many Japanese marines in seven warships. Both China and Korea called on Russia, the United States and European powers to intercede against the Japanese invasion, but the West was unwilling to become positively involved. Half-hearted attempts by Russia and Britain to achieve negotiations on a joint withdrawal were unsuccessful. When the Korean government rejected a Japanese list of demands for far-reaching political, financial and social reforms, Japanese troops occupied the **Kyŏngbok Palace** on 23 July and restored the **Taewŏn'gun**. On 25 July, the Japanese navy sank the British steamer *Kowshing*, one of three ships carrying Chinese soldiers to Korea, with the loss of 950 lives. War was formally declared on 1st August. A new cabinet under **Kim Hongjip** signed an agreement with Japan on 6 August affirming Korean independence and leading immediately to the **Kabo** reforms. But it was not sufficient to end the Japanese military presence.

The turning of the Tonghak rebels against the Japanese was insufficient to check the drive that now began against China. On 17 September Japanese ships inflicted a severe defeat on the superior Chinese fleet off the mouth of the **Yalu River**; on land, a major battle was fought and won against the Chinese at P'yŏngyang; in November a newly landed Japanese force occupied Dalian and Port Arthur; and in February 1895 the Japanese landed on the Shandong peninsula and captured Weihaiwei. The war was concluded by the Treaty of **Shimonoseki**, and marked a personal tragedy for the principal Chinese politician involved, **Li Hongzhang**, as well as a decisive stage in the Japanese advance towards the occupation of Korea, **Manchuria**, and ultimately China.

MUTSU MUNEMITSU, ed. and trans. by GORDON MARK BERGER, *Kenkenroku: a Diplomatic Record of the Sino-Japanese War 1894–5*, University of Tokyo Press, 1982

SINO-KOREAN CHARACTERS ENDEMIC TO KOREA *Han'guk sokcha*
韓國俗字

About 100 Chinese characters are peculiar to Korea, either because they have been invented in Korea, or because they are standard characters used with peculiarly Korean sounds or meanings. In many dictionaries they are identified as *kukcha* 'national characters', but *kukcha* also means *han'gŭl*. The list given by **Ch'oe Namsŏn** in *Sin chajŏn* (1915) is headed *Chosŏn sokcha* 'Korean vulgar characters'. Most of them derive from the practice of local clerks who refused to use *han'gŭl* in any way. Some relate to crops, like *tang* 'maize'(the grain radical combined with *tang* meaning 'sweet'); or *so*, usually meaning 'to call', used to mean 'jujubes'. Land records provide *tap* 'paddy'(written as *su* 'water' over *chŏn* 'dry-field'); and *tae* 'house-site', (*tae* 'a generation' written over *t'o* 'earth'). Military records use *pak*, (usually meaning 'to bind') for 'pock-marked'; and *soe* (a simplified form of *ch'ŏl* 'iron') for 'not pockmarked'. In vernacular names for **slaves** and children, special characters are used for purely Korean syllables that do not occur in Sino-Korean, such as *tol* (written with *sŏk* 'stone' over the **cyclical character** *ŭl*). Some of these characters occur in place-names, like *ki* (the heart radical beside *chi* 'only') in 'Kijŏ-san' (a name for the **Diamond Mountains**); and the character *kwan* 'to skewer' (K. *kotta*) used for the Korean word *kot* 'promontory'. Of special interest are *Kwŏk*, a Korean surname based on an old form of *pong* 'phoenix', and *sa* 'the game of *yut*', written with the tree radical beside *sa* 'four', a rare character that in Chinese usage means a spoon used in funeral **rites**.

424

SINSA YURAMDAN 紳士游覽團 'Gentlemen's sightseeing group', 1881
Name given to a mission to Japan authorised by **King Kojong** following receipt of the report by **Kim Hongjip** on his own exploratory visit (1880). Its twelve members, all senior officials with an average age of 30, were Pak Chǒngyang, Ǒm Seyǒng, Cho Chunyǒng, Cho Pyǒngjik, Min Chongmuk, Kang Munhyǒng, Yi Hǒnyǒng, Sim Sanghak, Hong Yǒngsik, Yi Wǒnhoe, Ǒ Yunjung, and Kim Yongwǒn. Including interpreters and servants, the total strength of the party came to 62. The party left Korea quietly in February 1881 on board a Japanese ship, and arrived at Yokohama in May. Its members were assigned particular fields of investigation, including trade and economics, industry, military systems, education, medicine, law and order, and they met Japanese officials and the reform advocate Fukuzawa Yukichi. They remained in the country until August, and on their return to Seoul reported to the King in October. They spoke in favour of self-strengthening through reform, but not of over-dependence on Japan, of whose ambitions they remained wary. Four of their number were then appointed to the newly established *T'ongni-gimu Amun*; Cho Pyǒngjik was made superintendent of the developing Treaty Port at **Chemulp'o (Inch'ǒn)**.

The mission should be seen as part of the self-strengthening movement. Concurrently with it, **Yi Tongin** was also sent to Japan in March 1881, where he evidently linked up with Yi Wǒnhoe, whose particular brief was to examine military organisation. Later the same year a further visit by **Kim Okkyun** was approved, and in November, **Kim Yunsik** was despatched to Tianjin in China (where he arrived in January 1882), again for military study.

SINSǑ-P'A 信西派 /*KONGSǑ-P'A* 恐西派
As interest in Western learning burgeoned in the late 18th century, the Southern faction was divided into *Sinsǒ-p'a*, those favourable to western learning (including Catholicism) and those who rejected it, *Kongsǒ-p'a*. Most Southerners at this time belonged to the *Sip'u* or Realist school of thought.

SINǓIJU INCIDENT (1925)
The arrest in November 1925 of Kim Kyǒngsǒ and Tokko Chǒn, two agents of the newly and secretly formed **Korean Communist Party** (KCP), following a fight with a Japanese policeman at the town of Sinǔiju (North P'yǒngan province) on the Manchurian border. They had been carrying messages from **Pak Hǒnyǒng** in Seoul to a leading Korean nationalist in Shanghai, **Yo Unhyǒng**. It signalled the beginning of a period in which the Japanese authorities arrested many leading communist figures, including Pak, and in which the KCP had to struggle hard to survive.
See also **June Tenth Incident**

SIP CHǑNG 十停 'Ten Garrisons' *See* **Military systems**

SIP HUNYO 十訓要 (*or Hunyo Sipcho*) *See* **Ten Injunctions**

SIRHAK 實學 ('Practical learning') **MOVEMENT**
Intellectual movement by scholars in the 17th–19th centuries to revaluate the sources of political and intellectual guidance, regardless of origin, that would be most valuable to their country. It resulted in part from disillusionment with China after the **Imjin Wars** and the **Manchu invasions**, when the value of support from Korea's traditional suzerain power was questioned; and in part from the political **factionalism** which barred some of those with a genuine desire to serve the country from positions of

influence. They began to adopt a fresh approach to public life. The value, they believed, of all information and arguments should be judged on its practical effect. Instead of accepting the traditional assumption that Korean outlook and methods should naturally follow the Chinese, they were prepared to consider habits, ideas and knowledge from their native traditions, as well as from China and even from the West. In the former respect writers gave attention to the possibilities of using the Korean alphabet *han'gŭl*; artists followed **Chŏng Sŏn**'s development of distinctive Korean styles (*see also* **Kim Hongdo**); musicians explored the potential of *kasa* and *kagok*; poets used *sijo* to express their emotions on a wide range of subjects related to daily life. Interest was shown in ideas on possible political, economic and social reforms and for alleviating the suffering of the lower classes (*see* **Yi Ik**). Satirical writings appeared, attacking traditional *yangban* values and social habits; vernacular novels criticised social inequities. Many of these scholars gave fresh thought to the re-interpretation of traditional moral values in terms of current Korean needs. Some, therefore, became interested in Christianity, which they had encountered for the first time from Jesuit missionaries in China (*see* **An Chŏngbok**; **Chŏng Yagyong**). Others were attracted by the ideas of the Chinese neo-Confucian philosopher Wang Yangming (1472–1528) as an alternative to the standard teachings of **Zhu Xi** (*see* **Chŏng Chedu**). The movement stimulated fresh studies of history (*see* **Chibong yusŏl**; **Tongsa gangmok**), geography, agriculture (*see* **Pan'gye surok**), education, military affairs, **medicine** and **commerce**. Its most encyclopaedic publication was the *Tongguk munhŏn pigo*, commissioned by King **Yŏngjo** and completed in 1770, and as a further stimulus to practical study King **Chŏngjo** established the *Kyujang-gak* research centre.

HABOUSH, JAHYUN KIM, 'The Sirhak Movement of the Late Yi Dynasty,' *KC*, 8/2, 1987; MICHAEL KALTON, 'An Introduction to Sirhak,' *KJ*, 15/5, 1975; KIM YONG-SOP, 'Two Sirhak Scholars' Agricultural Reform Theories,' *KJ*, 14/10, 1974; PARK SEONG-RAE, 'Western Science and Shilhak Scholars,' *KJ*, 26/3, 1986
See also **Haedong yŏksa; pukak; sohak**

SISA SINMUN 時事新聞 'Current Events Newspaper'
A **newspaper** founded in Seoul in 1920 by Min Wŏnsik for his pro-Japanese society, *Kungmin-hyŏphoe*. It collapsed the following year when Min was murdered in a Tokyo hotel by the nationalist Yang Kŭnhwan.

SIX BOARDS *yukcho* 六曹
The government administrative boards or 'ministries', first fully established in the Koryŏ period on Tang models. All six had the same constitution; in Chosŏn times the head of the board was *p'ansŏ* (2nd **grade** senior), his deputy was *ch'amp'an* (2nd grade junior), and the third officer *ch'amŭi* (3rd grade senior). They were each supported by six other officials. Their satellite minor *maŭl* did not represent the division of the whole responsibility of each board. The satellites were chiefly concerned with palace affairs, but the boards had wider remits. *Ijo* and *Pyŏngjo* were *chŏnjo* 'selection (or appointment) boards'.

The idea of six boards goes back to *Zhouli* (*see* **Confucian Classics**), but their names are those used by the Song dynasty. Korean alternative names are taken from *Zhouli*, which is why they do not completely conform with the **Five Phases** theory, developed after the *Zhouli* was written.

Ijo, 'Civil Service Board' or 'Board of Personnel', dealt with civil service appointments, promotion, demotion and censure. Hence it was often called *Tongjŏn* 'Eastern (or civil) Selection', *Sŏnbu* 'Selection Council', or *Taegwan* 'Great Office'.

Hojo, 'Board of Revenue', dealt with **population**, censuses, taxes and liens, levies and duties, currency and grain. It was known in Koryŏ by older Chinese titles that survived as sobriquets in Chosŏn, *Minjo* 'People's Board' or *Nongjo* 'Agriculture Board'. It was also called *Chijo* 'Earth Board'.

Yejo, 'Board of Rites', dealt with protocol, ritual **music**, **sacrifices**, banquets, embassies (*see* **Beijing, embassies to**), **schools** and state **examinations**. Its alternative name from *Zhouli* was Ch'un'gwan 'Springtime Office'. It was also called *Namgwan* 'South Office'.

Pyŏngjo, 'Board of War', dealt with all military matters, including appointments, training, conscription, **armour**, weapons and ammunition, military bands, ceremonial escorts, the post system and post-stations. It was also called *Sŏjŏn* 'Western (or Military) Selection Office' and *Hagwan* 'Summer Office', because ancient warfare was a summer activity and the name is given in *Zhouli*.

Hyŏngjo, 'Board of Punishments', dealt with **law**, litigation, penalties, prisons and **slaves**. It was called *Sŏgwan* 'West Office' and *Ch'ugwan* 'Autumn Office', because autumn was the *Zhouli* season for administering punishments.

Kongjo, 'Board of Works', was responsible for mountains, forests and rivers, buildings, civil engineering, buildings and **pottery**. It was called *Tonggwan* 'Winter Office' and *Subu* 'Water Council', irrigation being the chief ancient concern of Chinese civil engineering.

See also **Government, central; provincial administration**

SIX DOMESTIC ANIMALS 六畜 *See* Zodiac

SIX LICENSED SHOPS *yug-ŭijŏn / yuk-chubijŏn* 六矣廛
Early in the Chosŏn dynasty six official shops or **markets** were established in central Seoul, centred on Chong-no and leased to **merchants** who paid rent in goods supplied on demand. The six were called *sonjon* (for thread), *myŏnp'o-jŏn* (cotton cloth), *myŏnju-jŏn* (**silk**), *chijŏn* (**paper**), *chŏp'o-jŏn* (ramie-cloth) and *nae-ŏmul-chŏn* (an inner fish-market; there was also a *oe-ŏmul-chŏn* 'outer fish-market' beyond the West Gate). With some changes over the centuries, the system lasted until 1894.

See also **coinage; commerce**

SIX MARTYRED SUBJECTS *Sa-yuksin* 死六臣
Six who lost their lives in the plot to restore **Tanjong** to the throne in 1456: **Sŏng Sammun**, Pak P'aengnyŏn (b. 1417), Ha Wiji (b. 1387), Yi Kae (b. 1417), Yu Ŭngbu and Yu Sŏngwŏn.

SIX SURVIVING SUBJECTS *Saeng-yuksin* 生六臣
Six men who refused to accept public office after the deposition of King **Tanjong**: **Kim Sisŭp**, Wŏn Ho, Yi Maengjŏn, Cho Yŏ (1420–89), Sŏng Tamsu (d. 1456) and **Nam Hyoŏn**.

SIXTH REPUBLIC (1988–) *Cheryuk konghwaguk* 第六共和國
Inaugurated in February 1988 following the December 1987 election of Roh Tae Woo (**No Taeu**) as president in succession to Chun Doo Hwan (**Chŏn Tuhwan**). The **constitution** had been revised on Roh's instructions in October 1987, and this was the first direct presidential election since 1972. In a declaration on 29 June 1987 Roh had pledged himself to the restoration of democratic rule, but his ruling Democratic Justice Party (DJP) could not command a majority in the new National Assembly, and the

election results gave encouragement to the veteran opposition politicians **Kim Taejung** (Party for Peace and Democracy), **Kim Yŏngsam** (Reunification Democratic Party), and **Kim Chŏngp'il** (Democratic Republican Party). Roh quickly took steps to try and distance himself from his predecessor and former patron Chun. Late in 1988 he was arraigned for corrupt government and responsibility in the **Kwangju Massacre** in 1980. His televised apology and internal exile failed to defuse criticism of Roh for his own implication, and **student** demonstrations continued to plague the government. Shrewdly, or because he had no choice, Roh responded by allying with some of his principal opponents. In May 1990 the DJP merged with the PPD and DRP and was reformed as the **Democratic Liberal Party** (DLP), giving posts to Kim Yŏngsam and Kim Chŏngp'il. This left Kim Taejung as principal opposition leader, and after local elections in 1991 his PPD joined with members of other smaller parties as the new **Democratic Party** (DP). The main candidates in the December 1992 presidential elections were Kim Yŏngsam (DLP), Kim Taejung (DP), and chairman of the Hyundai *chaebŏl* Chŏng Chuyong (United People's Party). Kim Yŏngsam gained over 42 per cent of the poll, winning the most genuinely free election in Korean history. Pledged to the support of democratic principles, the clean-up of politics and business, and justice for the victims of the Kwangju massacre, he refused to spare his predecessors Chun and Roh from trial and long prison sentences. Fresh evidence of a new approach to public responsibility by those holding high office came in April 1997 with the trial for corruption of the former president of the Hanbo Iron and Steel Company. Ironically, however, the country's economic collapse in late 1997 brought charges of financial irregularity and incompetence against companies and government alike. The presidential election in December 1997 was narrowly won by the veteran politician Kim Taejung, but his victory was achieved against a crisis of international confidence in South Korea's political and commercial maturity.

ROBERT BEDESKI, *The Transformation of South Korea: Reform and Reconstruction in the Sixth Republic under Roh Tae Woo 1987–92*, London: Routledge, 1994
See also **South Korea: constitutional changes**

SIXTY-FOLD CYCLE (SEXAGENARY CYCLICAL CHARACTERS) *See kapcha*

SLAVES *nobi* 奴婢
Hereditary members of the *ch'ŏnmin* ('despised people'), the lowest order of society. They probably existed from very early times, but are clearly attested only from the Koryŏ period. Male slaves were *no*, female slaves *bi*. Estimates of total numbers vary, but in contrast to China and Japan, where slavery was of no statistical significance in early modern times, between twenty and thirty percent of the Korean population may have been enslaved in the 16th century, falling to fewer than half as many, or less than 200,000, in the mid-17th century.

Slaves were either public or private. Public slaves were kept in temples, government offices, **schools** and posting stations. Their jobs varied from craft worker to prostitute, those of private slaves from farmer to household retainer. Female slaves were sometimes taken as **secondary wives** by their masters (*see* **concubines**), though, since slave status derived from their mother, irrespective of the rank of the father, their children ranked as slaves. Men, enslaved either after military defeat or as a result of criminal conviction, might be awarded by the government to landowners to work their estates, and could be bought and sold. Frequently ill-treated, they joined with soldiers and peasants in uprisings against the military leadership of the Koryŏ period (*see* **Ch'oe Dictatorship**) and in resistance against the **Mongol** invasions. Many were pressed into military service against the Japanese in 1592 (*see* **Imjin Wars**) and gained their freedom amid the bureaucratic chaos that ensued. Moreover, the effect of post-war economic and social changes was to blur the distinction between slaves and *sangmin*, and increasingly to allow slaves to farm as free peasants. Some held slaves of their own and some were able to commute their service into fees and, since they could hold land, lived much as freemen of the poorest class. Efforts to abolish slavery resulted in the destruction of all records of slave status within the royal household in 1801, but the institution was not fully suppressed until the modernisation reforms of 1894 (*see Kabo* **reforms**).

JAMES B. PALAIS, 'Slavery and Slave Society in the Koryŏ Period,' *JKS*, 5, 1984; MARK PETERSON, 'Slaves and Owners, or Servants and Masters? A Preliminary Examination of Slavery in Traditional Korea,' *TRASKB*, LX, 1985; ELLEN UNRUH, 'The Landowning Slave: A Korean Phenomenon,' *KJ*, 16/4, 1976
See also **class system**

SŎ CHAEP'IL 徐載弼 (1866–1951)

Born at Posŏng in South Chŏlla, he studied Chinese letters in Seoul from the age of six. From twelve onwards he associated with **Kim Okkyun** and other progressives. In 1883 he went to Tokyo Army Cadet School. Back in Seoul in 1884 he was one of the young men involved in the Post Office *émeute* (*see Kapsin* **Coup**). When it failed he fled to Japan, leaving his family to be arrested. Several of them committed suicide and his baby son died of starvation. He went to America, where he called himself Philip Jaisohn, qualified as a medical doctor, took United States citizenship and married an American. In 1896 when the Min family lost power he returned to Korea and founded the newspaper *Tongnip Sinmun*, written in pure *han'gŭl* with one page in English, and published on alternate days. He was a founder member of the **Independence Club** and inspired the changes at the *Yŏng'ŭn-mun* and the Mohwa-gwan pavilion on the Peking Pass just north of Seoul, where Chinese embassies had been greeted. The pavilion became an independence movement centre and the gate was replaced by the Independence Arch. His activities frustrated pro-Japanese elements, and foreigners were partly responsible for the pressure that led to his return to America in 1898. He spent the rest of his life practising medicine and encouraging Koreans in America to support the independence movement. In 1947 he was brought back to Korea as principal adviser to the **American Military Government**. The following year he returned to America and died three years later.

VIPAN CHANDRA, 'The Concept of Popular Sovereignty: The Case of Sŏ Chae-p'il and Yun Ch'i-ho,' *KJ*, 21/4, 1981; LEE KWANG-RIN, 'On the Publication of *The Independent* by Suh Jae-pil (Philip Jaisohn),' *JSSH*, 43, June 1976

SŎ CHŎNGJU 徐廷柱 (1915–)

Born at Puan in North Chŏlla, he learned Chinese letters in his home village before attending high school in Puan and Seoul. In 1931 he started towards becoming a Buddhist monk by studying under the distinguished monk, Chŏngho (Pak Hanyŏng 1870–1948), at the Buddhist academy Chŏngho had founded at Taewŏn-am, near the East Gate of Seoul. Sŏ became a teacher in the academy, and in 1936 won a newspaper prize for poetry. He married in 1938, but did not settle down, spending time in **Manchuria**, then returning to Korea, oscillating between Puan and Seoul. After 1945 he was a college teacher and journalist in Seoul, with an established reputation as a poet. He fled to Chŏnju as a refugee during the two invasions of 1950 and 1951. A spiritual darkness began to overtake him, but he later became a teacher at Tongguk

(Buddhist) University in the capital. He continued to write poetry during his fifties, deeply influenced by Buddhist phenomenology and Daoist philosophy. As a lucid poet with great delicacy in handling words, he is notably accessible to foreign readers of Korean.

DAVID R. McCANN, *Selected poems of Sŏ Chôngju*, New York: Columbia University Press, 1989

SŎ KŎJŎNG 徐居正 (1420–88)

This gifted and learned man spent 45 years in government office, chiefly during the reigns of **Sejo** and **Sŏngjong**, and was the greatest writer of the early Chosŏn period. He worked as editor or compiler (with others) on *Koryŏ-sa* (1448), the first edition of *Tongmun-sŏn* (1478), *Tongguk yŏji-sŭngnam* (1481), and *Tongguk t'onggam* (1484); and excelled as a writer of short stories (as in *T'aep'yŏng hanhwa*, 'Leisured Tales for Times of Peace') and essays (as in *P'irwŏn chapki*, 'Mélanges from Writing-brush Meadows').

SŎ SANGNYUN 徐相崙 (1849–1926)

A **ginseng**-pedlar from Ŭiju who in 1876 met the Scottish missionary John **Ross** in Shenyang, was baptized and worked with Ross at translating the New Testament into Korean, using the Chinese Bible known as the Delegates' Version (1853). When the gospels were complete in 1883, Sŏ Sangnyun himself went off as a colporteur in **Kando**, where he ran into danger with the authorities. In 1884 he returned to Korea, gathering converts in Ŭiju to form the first Korean prayer-meeting. Under pressure for his contacts with foreigners, he withdrew to Sorae village in Hwanghae province, where in 1887 he founded Songch'ŏn (Sorae) Church, Korea's first Protestant church. *See also* **Bible in Korean, the**

SOCIAL CLASSES *See* **class system**; *Samin*

SOCIALIST MOVEMENT *sahoe-juŭi undong* 社會主義運動

In the second decade of the 20th century young intellectuals in East Asia were influenced by western socialist principles, and the example of the apparently successful revolution in Russia encouraged some of the lower classes to question their traditional social subjugation. Furthermore, the unprecedented show of solidarity between students and workers in China's May Fourth Movement (1919) inspired Koreans in the aftermath of their own **March First Movement** as they struggled against Japanese colonisers and their own outdated **class system**. The Shanghai Bureau of the Comintern, formed in 1919 to recruit young Chinese communists, also trained Koreans, and the next decade saw a proliferation of left-wing Korean societies active in China, **Manchuria**, **Siberia**, Korea and Japan. Some were socialist, some professedly communist, and in their shared determination to recover their country they even attempted to form a united front with more right-wing nationalists (*see* **New Shoot Society**). Women played a more active rôle in political affairs than they did in China, and had several left-wing organisations of their own, such as the *Kŭnuhoe*, the Proletarian Women's League, and the Society for the Promotion of Korean Women's Education (*see* **Women's movement**). However, even communists and socialists found it hard to agree common ideology and strategy, with the result that the Japanese police had little difficulty in suppressing their demonstrations. Fragmented and politically inept though it may have been, the socialist movement was kept alive by support from abroad and by hatred of the conqueror. When the colonial occupation ended, left-wing

politicians gained considerable popular support in southern as well as northern Korea, and it was the prospect that free nationwide elections might return a communist régime that led the United States to accept the return of Syngman Rhee (**Yi Sŭngman**) as its favoured presidential candidate (*see* **Korean People's Republic**). Events after the **Korean War** appeared to polarise political feeling and practice into neatly separated left- and right-wing convictions in North and South Korea respectively. The reality was more complex. Its early spontaneous enthusiasm for communism long since past, the North became one of the world's most remarkable examples of a forcibly socialised state, and it was impossible to estimate the degree of popular support for the ideology developed by **Kim Ilsŏng** (*see* **Chuch'e**). The **Republic of Korea** was ruled by a series of non-democratic, right wing governments whose antipathy to socialism was understandably coloured by their threatening neighbours in the North. The socialist movement, however, survived native autocracy as well as it did Japanese colonialism and was nurtured particularly by **students**, who again linked it to nationalistic calls for reunification.
*See also **Minjung** movement*

SŎDANG 書堂 *See* schools

SŎDONG 薯童 (Mattung)
A single-stanza *hyangga* recorded in *Samguk yusa* tells of a **Paekche** boy called Sŏdong ('yam boy', possibly *idu* for a Korean name 'Mattung') who teaches street-children a song about a princess having an affair with a boy called Mattung. The princess is disgraced, Mattung meets her, marries her, and eventually becomes King Mu of Paekche (AD 600–641). The story may be a mangled memory of the marriage of the Paekche King Tongsŏng to a **Silla** princess in 493.

SŎGAM-NI 石巖里
Site at T'osŏngni, near modern P'yŏngyang, containing almost 1,500 **tombs** from a graveyard outside the military headquarters of the Chinese **commandery** of **Lelang**. It was discovered by Japanese archaeologists in 1934–5. Tomb 212 is an example of a Chinese-style wooden chamber tomb dating from the first century BC. It contained the coffins of a man and wife, richly dressed and well furnished with mortuary goods of wood, **bronze**, **iron** and **pottery**. The woman's hair had been remarkably preserved with its adornments still in place.

SŎHAK 西學 'Western learning'
Korean name by which Catholicism became known in the 18th century.
See **Roman Catholic Church**; *Sinsŏ-p'a*

SOHAK (C. *Xiaoxue*) 小學 'Young Studies'
Xiaoxue is a Confucian florilegium edited by Liu Zicheng with a preface by **Zhu Xi** in 1187. It was much used in Korea as a textbook for young boys. There are several *ŏnmun* editions (*see* **han'gŭl**), including one by **Yi I** revised in 1666, and a royal edition, *Ŏje Sohak ŏnhae*, of 1744.

SO-HAKSA-JŎN 蘇學士傳 'Story of Minister Su'
A story of 15th-century China. Su Wei is killed by a pirate, who later adopts his son Yunjing. Yunjing rises to high office and avenges his father's death. The tale exists in both *han'gŭl* and *hanmun*.

SŎHWA HYŎPHOE 書畫研會 'Calligraphy and Painting Association'
Founded by **Ko Hŭidong** and others in 1918 to promote modern artistic concepts and theories. In 1919 the presidency was filled by Cho Sŏkchin (*see Sŏhwa Misulwŏn*). It held annual exhibitions (*hyŏpchŏn*) between 1921 and 1936, when it was closed down by the **Government-General**, and replaced by the rival Chōsen Art Exhibitions organised by the Japanese authorities from 1922 onwards. Some of its members contributed to the **New Culture Movement**, using their arts to proclaim Korean cultural independence.
See also **Tongyŏnsa**

SŎHWA MISURWŎN 書畫美術院 'Calligraphy and Painting Fine Art School'
Also known as *Sŏhwa Misulhoe Kangsupsŏ*. This was the first modern art school in Korea, founded in 1911 by Yun Yŏnggi, An Chungsik, and Cho Sŏkchin, and staffed by leading artists. It succeeded the *Tohwa-sŏ*, which was closed down following the Japanese **annexation**. Cho Sŏkchin had been the Tohwa-sŏ's last entrant, and having modelled himself on the work of **Chang Sŭngŏp**, served as a link between tradition and innovation in artistic institutions. Among the alumni of the Misurwŏn were **Ko Hŭidong**, **Yi Sangbŏm**, and **Kim Ŭnho**. It was closed down itself in 1919, but had already done valuable work in maintaining artistic education and initiating the transition between traditional and modern art in Korea.

SŎHWA YŎN'GUHOE 書畫研究會 'Calligraphy and Painting Research Society'
Founded in 1915 by leading artists including **Kim Kyujin**, a noted calligrapher and bamboo painter. Together with the *Sŏhwa Misurwŏn* it formed the main source of art education in Korea in the late 1910s.

SOHYŎN, CROWN PRINCE 昭顯世子 (1612–45)
Eldest son of Injo, he became Crown Prince in 1625. On the surrender of the king to the Manchus in 1636 (*see* **Manchu invasions**), he and his younger brother Pongnim (later Hyojong; *see* **Dowager Queen Changnyŏl**) were taken to Shenyang as hostages. Later they went to Beijing, whence Sohyŏn returned in 1644 with books on Western learning, including Catholic literature obtained when he met the Jesuit Adam Schall von Bell (1592–1666). Two months after his return to Seoul he fell ill and died. There is suspicion that he may have been poisoned.

SŎKKURAM 石窟庵 'Stone cave hermitage'
Cave temple built high above **Pulguk-sa** at **Kyŏngju**. The 'cave', or grotto, was built artifically of stone blocks by Kim Taesŏng (701–74), designer of Pulguk-sa, at a remote point on the mountainside where it faces the Eastern Sea and catches the first rays of dawn sunlight. It was reconstructed by the Japanese early in the 20th century, and not everyone is convinced that the present restructuring is entirely authentic. The temple comprises a square ante-chamber and a circular image hall, richly decorated with superbly sculpted stone images of human and divine guardian figures. But Sŏkkuram is most renowned for the perfection of its 17-foot white granite statue of the **Buddha**,[1] the advanced geometrical proportions of its ground plan, and the construction of its domed ceiling. Designated as National Treasure no. 24, Sŏkkuram is also a UNESCO World Heritage Site.
(1) RODERICK WHITFIELD & PAK YOUNG-SOOK, eds., *Korean Art Treasures*, Seoul: Yekyong Publications Co., 1986
See also **sculpture**

SŎKPO SANGJŎL 釋譜詳節 'Life of Sakyamuni in Detailed Sections'
A life of Sakyamuni, first written in Chinese and later rendered into Korean by Prince Suyang (**Sejo**) at the request of his father, **Sejong**, to comfort him on the death of Queen Sohŏn (1395–1446). It was used by Sejong in writing *Wŏrin-ch'ŏn'gang-ji-gok*. Like all writings of this period that are in Korean letters, it is invaluable in historico-linguistic studies.

SŎL CH'ONG 薛聰 (c. 660–730)
Sŏl Ch'ong is recorded as having been the son born out of wedlock to the great monk **Wŏnhyo** and a widowed **Silla** princess. He became a trusted royal adviser, giving his attention to Confucian rather than Buddhist teachings. He taught the Nine **Confucian Classics** to the young. The story that he invented *idu* script is now rejected, because it is known to have been used before his time. It is possible that he codified it in some degree. His *Hwawang-gye*, 'Story of the flower king', is Korea's earliest recorded parable. It tells how the peony, king of **flowers**, seeking a companion, was asked to choose between the showy rose and the dowdy pasque-flower; after some hesitation he chose the grey pasque flower - a Confucian decision.

SOLAR TERMS 二十四節氣 *See* **Twenty four solar terms**

SŎN 禪 (S. *Dhyana*, C. *Chan*, J. *Zen*)
Sŏn is a broad division of **Buddhism** that emphasizes the meditative element, claiming that meditation is the surest course to enlightenment. The opposite view, emphasizing textual study, is known as *Kyo*. There are many schools. Some disparage books, but most *Sŏn* believers allow that intellectual study has a rôle in religious life. Fung Yu-lan, *A History of Chinese Philosophy*, vol. II (1953), lists five points on which all *Sŏn* schools agree, (1) ultimate truth is inexpressible; (2) spiritual cultivation is not possible; (3) in the last resort, nothing is gained; (4) there is nothing much in Buddhist teaching; (5) the *dao* lies in carrying water and chopping wood.

Sŏn theory arrived in China with the Indian monk **Bodhidharma** in the 6th century AD and was known in Korea as early, perhaps, as the end of the 7th century, when it began to spread in China. It established demanding patterns of training, but gained popularity in the 9th century, as did sectarianism, reflecting the division of the parental body in China into Northern and Southern Schools with their own sub-divisions. Sŏn was not influential until, in the late 9th century, the **Nine Mountain Schools** flourished, associated with particular geographical regions and the **gentry** who lived there. The Nine Schools lost strength by the 11th century with the loss of leading members to the *Ch'ŏnt'ae-jŏng*, which Sŏn regained only after **Chinul** and **T'aego** returned from China, at a time when there was concern to resolve the polarity between *Sŏn* and *Kyo* (*see Chogye-jong*). From the 12th century onwards *Sŏn* became the mainstream of Korean Buddhism, drawing on Chinese *Sŏn* **literature** and the use of *kongan* in *kanhwa*.

Today, *Sŏn* adherents constitute an élite minority of the *Chogye* Order. They must practise *kyŏ*, but they seek an understanding that cannot be adequately expressed in words and must be transmitted through the mind. They therefore tend to distance themselves from the main centres and activities of organised Buddhism.
ROBERT E. BUSWELL, *Tracing Back the Radiance: Chinul's Korean Way of Zen*, Honolulu: University of Hawaii Press, 1992; ROBERT E. BUSWELL, *The Zen Monastic Experience*, Princeton University Press, 1992; HEE SUNG KEEL, *Chinul: The Founder of the Korean Sŏn Tradition*, Berkeley: Institute of Buddhist Studies, 1984; U CHONGSANG, 'High Priest Hyujŏng: Unity of Zen and Doctrinal Buddhism,' *KJ*, 13/2, 1973

SŎN BUDDHIST LITERATURE

Sŏn teachers use some texts that are treated as ancient but are almost certainly Chinese in origin, such as *Yuanjue jing* (K. *Wŏn'gak-kyŏng*) 'Complete Enlightenment **Sutra**' supposedly transmitted by Hongren, the Fifth Patriarch (601–674); and *Dacheng qixin lun* (K. *Taesŭng-kisil-lon*) 'Mahayana Awakening of Faith', which is wrongly attributed to the Indian writer Asvaghosa (K. Magyŏng, fl. c. AD 100).

Chinese texts of later date are also used, like *Zimen jingxun* (K. *Ch'imun-gyŏnghun*) 'Admonitions to the Dark-robed School', a *Chan* compilation by Jingshan of the Ming dynasty, and ***Fingers Pointing at the Moon***. Korean writings on *Sŏn* include ***Sŏn'ga-gwigam*** and the works of **Chinul** and **T'aego**. ***Kongan*** collections may be of Chinese or Korean origin.

SON OGONG 孫悟空 (C. Son Wukong)

The 16th-century Chinese romance *Xiyou ji*, 'Record of a Journey to the West' (translated by Arthur Waley in 1942 as *Monkey*), became popular in Korea soon after it was written. Its hero is Son Houzi, a mischievous monkey spirit, known in Korea by his Buddhist religious name, Wukong 'Aware of Vacuity'. Portrayed as a monkey with a monk's hat, he is the first of the ***chapsang***, prophylactic figurines on the roof-ridges of Confucian buildings.

SON PYŎNGHŬI 孫秉熙 (1861–1921)

Ch'ŏndo-gyo leader particularly associated with the movement's pro-independence stance. As commander of the southern Tonghak rebel army from Ch'ungch'ŏng province he escaped capture in November 1894 (*see* **Tonghak Rebellion**), and was chosen to succeed Ch'oe Sihyŏng as the third Tonghak leader in 1897. He was exiled to Japan in 1901, and despite supporting Japan in the war with Russia (*see* **Russo-Japanese War**), advocated popular Korean resistance to the Japanese through non-violent measures. In 1905 he changed the name of the Tonghak sect to *Ch'ŏndo-gyo*, and in the following year helped to found the *Mansebo* ('Independence News'). In 1908 he designated Pak Inho as *Chŏndo-gyo* leader. In association with Christians and Buddhists, Son represented his religion in planning the **Declaration of Independence** in 1919 and was the first of its **thirty-three signatories**, who were subsequently imprisoned (*see* **March First movement**).

SŎNANG-DANG 'shrine of the spirit of the spot'

Sŏnang-dang is a simple shrine to the *sŏnang-sin*, the spirit of a locality or spot. It has many names in different areas, including *halmi-dang*, 'grandmother shrine', and *Ch'ŏnwang-dang*, 'heavenly king shrine'. Usually with a cairn, a tree and a tabu rope, it can be found at the top of a mountain pass, at the roadside, near a village, or at the gate of a Buddhist monastery. Sacrifices were offered at full moon, but at any time rags would be tied to the tree as votive offerings for the birth and health of children; odd straw shoes hung there as votive offerings for wealth; pieces torn from her clothes left there by a bride passing on her way to her husband's home, so that the evil spirits of her old home should be distracted from following her; tiny effigies of **horses** in brass or ceramic left by *mabu* 'horse boys'; new silk patches or salt left by **merchants** asking for success. Every traveller added a stone to the cairn or spat on it, and made a wish, silently or aloud. This was the best known of spirits and ***mudang*** frequently held their ceremonies at the *sŏnang-dang*.

SŎNDŎK, QUEEN 善德女王 (r. 632–47) *See* **Silla, Queens of**

SŎNDONG 仙童 'boy immortals'
Often called *tongja* 'children' (less justifiably 'twins'), these statues or pictures from the Chosŏn period show two small boys in what passed for Tang-style dress. Each has two **topknots**. One may carry a **peach** and the other a flask or a **tortoise**. They may have Daoist origins, representing **immortal** youth, but their presence, as wooden statuettes in shrines of mountain spirits and at weddings or engraved on charms, probably reflects the devotion of women praying for the birth of sons.

SONG CHUN'GIL 宋浚吉 (Tongch'un-dang, 1606–72)
A follower of **Yi I** and **Kim Changsaeng**, whose brush name meant 'Same spring hall'. His career was typical of a time of factional strife. In 1624, at the age of 18, he was appointed to office but withdrew for some years to continue his studies. In 1649 he was in office when he impeached Kim Chajŏm of the Meritorious Westerners **faction** and so brought his own Clear Westerners to power. He supported Hyojong's intention to attack the Manchus, but Kim Chajŏm ensured that he was forced to resign from office, and he retired to the country. Thereafter he was politically aligned with **Song Siyŏl**. They both took the same line in the debates about the **Dowager Queen Changnyŏl's mourning rites**. They won the decision, but Chun'gil retired once more. He resigned again in 1665 over the education of the Crown Prince, then again accepted appointment. He was a gifted writer, much influenced by Song Siyŏl, with whom he was canonised in 1756.

SONG DYNASTY 宋朝 (China, 960–1279)
A period during which China's mostly willing participation in foreign affairs – especially **commerce** – almost recreated the cosmopolitanism of the **Tang dynasty**, yet during which relations between the Middle Kingdom and its traditional vassal state, Korea, were complicated by the intervention of the **Khitan**, **Jurchen** and **Mongols**. The Khitan and Jurchen ruled parts of northern China from the 10th to 13th centuries (see **Liao dynasty, Jin dynasty**), while the Mongols defeated the Xi Xia (Tangut) empire in 1209 and began their military campaigns against Jin in 1211. By 1241 the north was conquered, and when the Southern Song court in Hangzhou surrendered in 1279, the world-wide Mongol empire incorporated both China and Korea. These political upheavals notwithstanding, the Song was a period in which China experienced great intellectual and cultural developments, some of which would sooner or later have a substantial impact on its neighbours in Korea.

The pattern of historical events in the two countries had not been dissimilar in the early part of the 10th century. After periods of unsettling disunity, both were relieved to be reunited under single central authorities in Kaifeng and **Kaesŏng** respectively, and the Koryŏ court initially seemed happy to send **tribute** to the Song. But by the end of the century the Liao empire in **Manchuria** was a threat to both, and self-interest determined that Koryŏ should recognise its northern neighbour, whose rulers themselves observed many familiar Chinese rites and customs. Both China and Korea suffered military defeats by Liao and were forced to pay it tribute, and from 1030 to 1071 no official missions were exchanged between Kaifeng and Kaesŏng. Trade, however, continued, and when friendly relations were restored in 1069 through the agency of a Chinese merchant, Huang Zhen, a comfortable coexistence was established between the three states. It was upset by the Jurchen, whose rise to power in northern Manchuria prompted the Chinese Emperor Huizong to see them as potential allies against the Khitan, and tried to implicate the Koryŏ court in his plotting. Instead, this only encouraged the imperial ambitions of their leader Aguda, who persuaded King **Yejong** that the current interpretation of 'serving the great' (*sadae*) meant paying tribute to him. The Koryŏ court had few scruples about the change of allegiance. The Jurchen conquest of northern China and the flight of the Song court to Hangzhou in 1126, not to mention the political problems of the Koryŏ court later in the 12th century (*see* **Ch'oe dictatorship**) and the turmoil caused by the Mongols, meant a sharp deterioration in Sino-Korean diplomatic relations. Even trade declined, as Chinese merchants looked more to south-east Asia from the ports of Zhejiang and Fujian provinces.

Enduring links between China and Korea had nevertheless been forged in this period. The export of Chinese **ceramics** in the 10th–11th centuries, especially those of Yue ware but also of Ding and later Ru, stimulated such admiration in Korea that its own potters soon learned to copy and surpass them: in particular, Korean inlaid **celadons** were unmatched in China and remain one of Korea's greatest artistic achievements. The development of pictorial art in China, notably of **landscape painting**, would create Song rôle models for Korean artists in the Chosŏn period. And it was during the Song dynasty that Chinese literati carried on the scientific and philosophical arguments of neo-Confucianism, which were eventually coordinated by **Zhu Xi** and formulated into a guide for political and social life that the Chosŏn leadership promoted as a standard for orthodox behaviour.

KEITH PRATT, 'Sung Hui Tsung's Musical Diplomacy and the Korean Response,' *BSOAS*, XLIV pt.3, 1981; MICHAEL ROGERS, 'Sung-Koryŏ Relations: Some Inhibiting Factors,' *Oriens* 11, 1958; MICHAEL ROGERS, 'Factionalism and Koryŏ Policy under the Northern Sung,' *JAOS*, 79, 1959
See also **Xuanhe fengshi Gaoli tujing**

SŎNG HON 成渾 (Ugye, 1535–98)

He began the usual career through the state examinations, but abandoned it early because of illness and took to the study of the **Confucian Classics**. In 1592, at the time of the Japanese invasion, he agreed to accept office at the age of 57, but was forced to retire for a while, because he favoured negotiating peace with the enemy. At 60 he became the principal royal lecturer. He was a friend of **Yi I**. Because he saw merit in some of **Yi Hwang**'s ideas, his six-year correspondence (1572–1578) with Yi I made a significant contribution to the **Four-Seven debate**, helping Yi I define his points. Song was also a gifted writer. He was canonised with Yi I in 1682, under the influence of the Western **faction**, but both their tablets were removed from the national shrine when the Southerners took power in 1689, only to be replaced when the Westerners returned to power in 1694.

SONG IKP'IL 宋翼弼 (Kwibong, 1534–99)

Because his grandmother was a **slave**, he was the son of a secondary wife, and therefore unable to take public office. Nevertheless, he was a friend of **Yi I** and **Sŏng Hon** and spent his life in study, writing and teaching at his home on the slopes of Kwibong-san near Koyang, northwest of Seoul. He adopted the brush name 'Tortoise peak'. Among his disciples were **Kim Changsaeng** and his son **Kim Chip**. He was one of the most famous writers of his period, expert both in the philosophy of *sŏngnihak* and in **ritual studies**. He is regarded as one of the founders of the Kiho (Kyŏnggi and Ch'ungch'ŏng) school of thought.

SONG OF CH'ŎYONG Ch'ŏyongga 處容歌

One of the *hyangga* preserved in the *Samguk yusa*. According to the song, Ch'ŏyong was the son of the Dragon King and son-in-law of Unified Silla King Hŏn'gang

(r. 876–886). Returning one night from revels in the capital, Ch'ŏyong found his wife being seduced by the Spirit of Smallpox. He forgave her attacker, and in gratitude the Spirit promised not to enter any household displaying Ch'ŏyong's portrait on the doorpost. The tale has been subjected to psychological, religious and even nationalistic analysis by modern scholars, the latter since the Japanese allowed the revival of its performance (*see Ch'ŏyong* dance) in 1923 as an example of tolerance under pressure. DAVID McCANN, 'The Story of Ch'ŏyong, a Parable of Literary Negotiation,' *KS*, 21, 1997 *See also* **Munmu, King**

SŎNG SAMMUN 成三問 (1418–1456)

One of the **Six Martyred Subjects** of Tanjong. He was a member of the *Chiphyŏnjŏn* and worked on *Hunmin chŏngŭm*. With **Sin Sukchu** he visited Huang Zan in Liaodong, making altogether thirteen visits. He was involved in the plot to reinstate Tanjong as king, for which he was executed. He is the best known of the Six Martyred Subjects because of a poignant *sijo* about loyalty, associated with the Tanjong story and attributed to Sŏng.

SONG SIYŎL 宋時烈 (Uam, 1607–89)

A great neo-Confucian, called 'second to Zhuzi' or 'the Zhuzi of Korea', and given unbounded admiration in later centuries. His brush-name was 'Another hermitage', deliberately copied from **Zhu Xi**'s name Huian (K. Hoeam), 'twilit hermitage'. Much of his interest centred on Zhu Xi's metaphysics. According to Song, *t'aegŭk* (C. *taiji*) is the essence that creates *yang* by moving and *yin* by resting. In the Four-Seven debate he followed **Yi I** rather than **Yi Hwang**, saying that *i* (C. *li*) 'principle' and *ki* (C. *qi*) 'ether/matter' are at once one and two. Yet he took an essentially monistic line: commenting on the triad of *to* (C. *dao*) 'the Way', *ki* (C. *qi*) 'objects', and *hyŏng* (C. *xing* 'shapes', described in *Dazhuan*, an appendix to the *Book of Changes*), he followed Zhu Xi to the limit, equating *to* 'the Way' with *i* 'principle', and *ki* 'matter' with *ki* 'objects'.

He was equally rigorous in politics, a member of the Western **faction**. In early years he conspired with King Hyojong in long-distance plans to overthrow the Qing and restore the Ming in China. He was also expert on Confucian **rites**, which were a fertile source of impeachments, when the court was torn apart by arguments about the moral implications of ritual decisions. In the debate about the proper procedures for Queen Cho's mourning after the death of King Hyojong in 1659 (*see* **Dowager Queen Changnyŏl's mourning rites**), the Westerners won, but at the expense of dividing into Elder (**Noron**) and Younger (**Soron**) parties. Song Siyŏl was regarded as the founder of the Noron, which maintained its ascendancy into the 19th century. In 1674 the same queen faced another decision about mourning, this time for King Hyŏnjong. This time Song lost, and the Southerners split into the **Clear** (*ch'ŏng*) or Hardline party, which wanted him executed, and the Cloudy (*t'ak*) or Moderate, which wanted him spared. Song was spared, but the new king was the boy **Sukchong**, during whose reign factional strife grew worse. Trouble recurred in 1689 over childless Queen Inhyŏn's reluctance to adopt a concubine's son in order to make him crown prince. Song Siyŏl lost his last argument. Even though he was 82, he was forced to drink hemlock (*see* **poison**). HAECHANG CHOUNG & HAN HYONG-JO, eds., *Confucian Philosophy in Korea*, Seongnam: The Academy of Korean Studies, 1996

SŎN'GA-GWIGAM 禪家龜鑑 'Tortoise Mirror of the Sŏn School'

'Tortoise mirror' is derived from the use of tortoise-shells in ancient Chinese divination, which made the tortoise a metaphor for moral guidance. This fundamental book in Korean *Sŏn* Buddhism was written by Sŏsan ('west mountain', also known as Hyujŏng 'rest and peace', 1520–1604). Born Ch'oe Yŏsin at Anju and orphaned at the age of seven/eight, he began life as a neo-Confucian, trained at the *Sŏnggyun-gwan*, but became a monk at the age of twenty. He developed into the leading teacher of his day and a major influence on later Korean **Buddhism**, continuing the tradition of **Chinul** and **T'aego** in blending the *Sŏn* and *Kyo* schools of Buddhism. Arrested during the rebellion of **Chŏng Yŏrip**, he was soon exonerated. At the time of the Hideyoshi invasions (*see* **Imjin Wars**), when he was in his seventies, he organised a volunteer force of 5,000 military monks (*ŭisŭng-byŏng*). *Sŏn'ga-gwigam* is the best known of his half-dozen extant works and is one of the most highly valued writings by a Korean Buddhist.

SŎNGAK/ SŎNGDO (Koryŏ capital) 松岳 / 松都 *See* **Kaesŏng**

SŎNGDŎK, KING 聖德王 (702–37)
Second son of King **Sinmu** and younger brother of King Hyoso. His reign marked the high point of Korean-Chinese relations. His son returned from study in China bringing portraits of Confucius and his disciples, which were deposited in the National Academy, *Kukhak*.

Korea's oldest surviving temple **bell**, that at Sangwŏn-sa, was cast during his reign in 725. He built the temple of Pongdŏk-sa in memory of his great-grandfather **Muyŏl**, and its great bell, now known as the **Emille** Bell, was cast in 771 in his honour. The inscription on its side relates that he encouraged farmers to work hard and **merchants** to deal honestly, and refers to his belief that education and skills were more valuable than gold and precious stones. On his death, the letter of condolence sent by the Chinese Emperor Xuanzong suggested true regret and respect for his achievements. His **tomb** is distinguished by its set of stone statues in the form of **zodiac** figures, with animal heads and human bodies dressed in **armour**.

SONGGUNG-NI 松菊里
Bronze Age site in South Ch'ungch'ŏng province excavated in 1975–8. It contains 33 semi-subterranean dwellings surrounded by the remains of a wooden pallisade and moat. Traces of **rice** were found on the floors. Among the **pottery** artefacts were jars with wide mouths and bulging bodies, tapering towards the bottom, and four jar coffins. Stone implements included knives, adzes, and daggers. A cist made of large flat stones contained bronze and polished stone daggerheads, stone arrowheads, and comma-shaped and tubular pieces of jade.

SŎNGGYUN-GWAN 成均館 'College of Perfection and Equalisation'
The National Confucian Academy in Seoul, incorporating the Temple to Confucius (*see* **Confucius, temple name**); its name was derived from that of a college in Zhou dynasty China (*see* **Sŏnggyun-gwan, origin of names**). A Confucian academy (*Taehak*) was first established in **Koguryŏ** in 372 and another (*T'aehakkam*) in **Kyŏngju** in 682, promoting education and examination in the **Confucian Classics**. This was succeeded in the Koryŏ period by the National University, *Kukcha-gam*, founded in 992 by King **Sŏngjong**. Neo-Confucianism was studied in Korea under the **Mongols**, and the University prospered through the 14th century (*see* **An Hyang**). In 1398 King T'aejo re-founded the Academy on its present site, where apart from the persecutions of 1498 and 1504 (*see* **Sahwa**) and the destruction of buildings in the **Imjin Wars** it continued to flourish into modern times. The rector was a 2nd **grade** senior. It offered higher education to holders of the *saengwŏn* and *chinsa* degrees in

preparation for the *taegwa* (*see* **examinations**). The syllabus included the Confucian Classics, literary studies and **calligraphy**, and encouraged debating skills. Students were allowed to express views on national issues. In modern times the College was tolerated under the Japanese occupation, and after World War II a Confucian university was established on its campus. It is the venue for the bi-annual Sacrifice to Confucius which still preserves **rites and ceremonies** and **music** of the Chosŏn dynasty.

KIM CHONGGUK & KIM CHINMAN, 'Some Notes on the Sŏnggyun'gwan,' *TKBRAS*, XXXVIII, 1961; S.J.PALMER, *Confucian Rituals in Korea*, Berkeley: Asian Humanities Press, n.d.

SŎNGGYUN-GWAN – ORIGIN OF NAMES

Sŏnggyun-gwan is the national Confucian college, named from *sŏng-gyun* (C. *chengjun*) 'perfection and equality', an expression in the ancient ritual book *Zhouli*, chapter xxii, where the Grand Director of Music is said to be in charge of young men being educated in a national institution of 'perfection and equality'.

The temple hall in which the tablet of Confucius is enshrined was earlier called *Sŏnwang-jŏn* 'Hall of the Illustrious Prince', but was changed in 1074 to *Taesŏng-jŏn* 'Hall of the Great Synthesis' – appropriately for the time when neo-Confucianism was born. Here *taesŏng* (C. *dacheng*) echoes the *Xueji* section of *Liji*, where it describes the education of students in a national college. Both names are derived from the **temple names of Confucius**.

The teaching hall of a Confucian establishment is called *Myŏngnyun-dang*, 'Hall of Polishing [the five] Relationships'.

SŎNGJONG, KING 成宗王 (r. 981–97)

Sixth king of the Koryŏ dynasty, who succeeded in firmly establishing centralised government authority. The administrative powers of local **gentry** were taken over by officials appointed from the capital. He promoted education by founding the *Kukcha-gam* and encouraging young men from the countryside to study the **Confucian Classics** and **medicine**. **Coinage** was struck in **iron**, and a government intervention system introduced into grain marketing, enabling the authorities to maintain level prices by buying stocks at harvest and releasing them when supplies ran low in the market place. He strengthened the defensive structure of the army with the formation of Two Guards and Six Divisions, comprising 45 regiments each of one thousand men. A council of military commanders, *Chungbang*, was set up. Sŏngjong was ably advised by the Confucian minister Ch'oe Sŭngno, who is famous for his policy memorial of twenty-eight points.[1] The reform of government structure was completed by his son, King Munjong (r. 1046–83), who created the Three Chancelleries (*samsŏng*, the Central Council, Ministerial office and Secretariat) and **Six Boards** (*see* **Government, central**). (1) *See SKC* I, 282 ff.

SŎNGJONG, KING 成宗王 (r. 1469–94)

Grandson of King **Sejo** and ninth king of the Chosŏn dynasty. He was a highly cultured king. He succeeded to the throne at the age of thirteen, thanks to his maternal grandmother, Sejo's Queen Yun, and at first had a period of 'rule through the screen' (*suryŏm-ch'ŏngjŏng*). His education was dominated by neo-Confucian apologists, and during his reign the proscription of **Buddhism** reached a high point. The **law** code, *Kyŏngguk taejŏn*, was promulgated in 1470. Literary projects initiated by Kings **Sejong** and **Sejo** reached a significant stage (*see Tongguk yŏji-sŭngnam*; **Sŏ Kŏjŏng**). Many of his highest advisers achieved their positions of influence as **meritorious** subjects, but in his maturity he attempted to curb the powers of the officials who, in serving his grandfather, had also advanced their own interests. He curbed their right to collect incomes personally from their state-granted estates, and promoted younger members of the so-called Southern School.

See also **Chaoxian fu**

SŎNGJU 城主 'Castle lords' *See* **Gentry**

SŎNGNI-HAK 性理學
Neo-Confucian metaphysics; *see* **Five Sages of Song**

SŎNJŎN 鮮展
Common name by which the annual Japanese-sponsored Korean Art Exhibitions (*Chosŏn Misul Chŏllamhoe*) were known during their span of 1922–44. They were divided into oriental and western art categories, and were intended to promote supposedly anodyne classes of painting, including **landscape**, **flower and bird** and still life subjects, as a means of suppressing distinctive Korean culture.
See also **Kukchŏn; Sŏhwa Hyŏphoe**

SŎNWŎN PORYAK 璿源譜略 'Genealogy of Jewel Spring'
A pedigree of the royal house of Chosŏn, compiled under various titles containing the place-name *Sŏnwŏn*, which was a name for the Tŏgwŏn area of Hamhŭng province. Yi Ansa (d. 1274), later canonised as Mokcho (*see* **Yongbi-ŏch'ŏn-ga**), was great-great-grandfather of **Yi Sŏnggye**. Mokcho lived originally at Chŏnju but moved to the north with a large band of followers and lived in the Sŏnwŏn area, where he laid the grounds of his family's later eminence, partly by controlling the local **Jurchen** tribes. Sŏnwŏn became a sobriquet for the dynasty, and name of the family portrait gallery. The genealogy was first compiled by **Sukchong** in 1679, revised with each new reign and last printed by **Kojong** in 1895. A photostat version, *Sŏnwŏn-gyebo*, appears in the Chindan Hakhoe *Han'guk-sa* (Seoul 1959), volume 7.

SŎŎL 庶孽
An alternative word for secondary or '**illegitimate**' sons and grandsons.

SORON 少論 'Young reasoning'
Political **faction** of the late 17th century associated with Yun Chŭng (1629–1711).

SŎSI 西施 (C. Xishi)
Xishi, a low-born girl in the Spring and Autumn Period of ancient China (722–481 BC), has been regarded by many Korean writers as the most beautiful woman who ever lived. She was sent by the Prince of Yue in the 5th century BC to infatuate the Prince of Wu and thus bring about his downfall. The ruse was successful. She enhanced her beauty by adopting a pitiful expression.

SOSU SŎWŎN 紹修書院 *See Sŏwŏn*

SOTTAE mast
Sottae, sacred poles or masts set up at the boundary or centre of a community area, probably date from before the Three Kingdoms Period, and their purpose is not

completely understood. Until recently they could often be found with a crude duck figure at the top, associated with *sonangdang*, *changsŭng* and tabu rope (*kŭmchul*) at village boundaries. Similar masts are found elsewhere in north-east Asia. The word *sottae* is applied to poles erected for various purposes. Farmers might erect an unpainted pole with a bag of **rice** seed hanging on it as a charm for a good harvest in the following year. A red pole with a blue/green wooden **dragon** or a blue cloth fish at the top was set up at the entrance to a village or neighbourhood when a man living there had been successful in the state **examinations**. The fish-shaped air-socket, with painted eyes and scales, was also used on a pole for other village celebrations, such as a visit by *namsadang* or *kutchung-p'ae* (begging monks). If the troupe included a *sottaejangi*, he would put on a mask, climb a plain *sottae* and perform gymnastic feats on it. Sometimes more than one would perform at one time on the same pole.

SOUTH KOREA *See* **Republic of Korea**

SOUTH KOREA: CONSTITUTIONAL CHANGES
The first **constitution** of the **Republic of Korea** (ROK) was adopted on 12 July 1948. While outwardly democratic, it gave much power to the president. Since then, the constitution has been regularly amended, usually to suit the wishes of the incumbent president. The more substantial of these changes have been regarded as creating new constitutional states.

Altogether, South Korea is deemed to have had six 'republics' since 1948. They are the first from 1948–60, which was notable for the dominance of **Yi Sŭngman** (Syngman Rhee), the second, third and fourth under Park Chung Hee (**Pak Chŏnghŭi**) from 1963 to 1980; the fifth under Chun Doo Hwan (**Chŏn Tuhwan**) from 1980 to 1988, and the sixth from 1988 onwards. In keeping with this tradition **Kim Taejung** elected in December 1997 and in office from February 1998 placed constitutional change high on his agenda.

The 'First Republic' dates from the establishment of an independent Republic of Korea under President Yi in August 1948. It ended with his resignation and exile in April 1960. The 1948 constitution bore some resemblance to the US constitution, but under Yi it was used to bolster his own authority, a process helped by the need for emergency powers during the **Korean War**. Yi controlled all aspects of the **central government**, and much of the local government as well. As the years passed, he became steadily more authoritarian, and much of the effort of the state apparatus was devoted to keeping him in power. However, widespread corruption by Yi's **Liberal Party** in the March 1960 elections for president and vice-president led to the **April 19th student uprising** and Yi's fall from power.

The '**Second Republic**', proclaimed in August 1960, moved away from an executive presidential system towards a parliamentary democracy on British lines. It also promised to introduce elected local governments, but before either system could be given a fair trial the military intervened, and South Korea reverted to authoritarian rule.

After a period of direct military rule between 1961 and 1963 (*see* **military junta**), this authoritarianism was formalised in Park Chung Hee's '**Third Republic**', which lasted until 1972. Once again, all power was concentrated in the president, who appointed the cabinet and also had total control over local government. Much of the real power lay in the presidential secretariat and in the **Korean Central Intelligence Agency**, established by one of the chief plotters of the military coup, **Kim Chŏngp'il**. Park won the 1967 presidential election with an increased share of the popular vote, but was then barred from standing again by the constitution which he had introduced.

To overcome this, he forced through a constitutional amendment allowing his re-election through the National Assembly. At the same time, the régime became still more dictatorial, imposing severe restrictions on any form of opposition.

Park was still not satisfied, and in 1972 staged a coup against his own 1962 constitution, arguing that the ROK faced new dangers in the aftermath of the Sino-US rapprochement of 1971–2 and the beginning of a dialogue between the two Koreas. This marked the start of the 'Fourth Republic'. A new constitution, the *Yusin* or revitalising constitution, allowed Park to succeed himself indefinitely, to adopt emergency powers when he considered it necessary, and to appoint one third of the National Assembly, thus giving the ruling party a permanent advantage. In addition, the president would no longer be chosen by direct vote or by the National Assembly, but by a newly constituted and theoretically non-partisan National Conference for Unification.

Yusin survived its founder by less than a year. Following Park's assassination in October 1979, the constitutional formalities were followed, with the prime minister, Ch'oe Kyuha, taking over as acting president. Ch'oe made it clear that he only intended to be an interim president, but in any case, power was already shifting again to the military. In August 1980 the martial law commander, Major General Chun Doo Hwan, left the army and became interim president. Under Chun, most political activity was banned and there were sweeping purges of politicians, academics and journalists. In October 1980, a modified version of the *Yusin* constitution was put to a referendum and accepted. Thus began the 'Fifth Republic'.

The new constitution laid down that the president could only serve a single term of seven years; otherwise most of its features represented a watered-down version of *Yusin*. The president, for example, was still indirectly elected, and retained considerable emergency powers. All former political parties were banned, and new ones emerged. In theory, these covered the political spectrum from right to (very moderate) left. The reality was that all received government funding to a greater or lesser degree, and all were subject to government control. From 1985 onwards, however, this began to change, as former political leaders such as **Kim Yŏngsam** and Kim Taejung began to return to active politics, despite being officially barred from them.

Chun's constitutional arrangements then came under criticism; in particular, there was a growing demand for direct presidential elections. Chun allowed the political parties to discuss this, but when they failed to reach agreement, announced that there would be no change until after the 1988 summer **Olympic Games** in Seoul. This, together with an increasingly tough police approach to **student** demonstrations and Chun's decision to nominate a former army colleague, Roh Tae Woo (**No Taeu**), as his successor, sparked off huge demonstrations in April and May 1987. Eventually Roh intervened, proposing a package of reforms and refusing to stand unless these were conceded. Chun agreed, and a new constitution was introduced in October 1987.

This was the basis of the '**Sixth Republic**'. It provided for direct election of the president for a five year term, gave more power to the National Assembly, and introduced more personal liberty. In December 1987, Roh became the first president elected under this constitution. He was followed in 1992 by Kim Yŏngsam and in 1997 by Kim Taejung.

HAN SUNGJOO, *The Failure of Democracy in South Korea*, Berkeley: University of California Press, 1974; C.I.EUGENE KIM, 'Korea at the Crossroads: the Birth of the Fourth Republic,' *PA* 46, 1973; YANG SUNG CHUL, *The North and South Korean Political Systems: a Comparative Analysis*, Boulder: Westview Press, 1994; YOON DAE-KYU, *Law and Political Authority in South Korea*, Boulder: Westview Press, 1990

SOUTH KOREA: POLITICAL PARTIES

Following the defeat of Japan in 1945 and the division of the peninsula at the **Thirty-Eighth parallel**, South Korea witnessed a large-scale development of political parties. They covered the whole political spectrum from extreme left to extreme right, but were often little more than interest groups, linked to a region, an organisation, or to a particular leader. As the North-South divide hardened, culminating in the establishment of separate states in 1948, so the tolerance of left-wing groups and parties diminished in the South, a process completed by the **Korean War**. Although supposedly socialist parties have surfaced in South Korea in subsequent years, they have either been persecuted by the authorities, as happened under Park Chung Hee (**Pak Chŏnghŭi**), or – as under President Chun Doo Hwan (**Chŏn Tuhwan**) – have been state creations.

In essence, since the formation of the **Liberal Party** in support of President Syngman Rhee (**Yi Sŭngman**) in 1951 during the Korean War, effective Korean political parties can be reduced to two: a Government, or ruling, Party, whose members look to the incumbent president for office and influence, and an opposition party, which has rallied around whichever current strong opposition leader is thought capable of challenging the ruling party for power. Since for much of the period from 1951 to the late 1980s, the rule of former military officers meant that it was unlikely that the opposition could win, South Korean political parties have continued to be short on ideology, placing most emphasis on loyalty to the current leader, and have tended to fragment should a leader appear unlikely to achieve success, or be challenged by a more appealing newcomer. In the National Assembly, loyalties have been equally shallow, with regular shifts between opposition and ruling parties. In such circumstances, support has generally evaporated quickly. Regional and personal loyalties continued to be more important than political platforms right up to the December 1997 election which brought the veteran opposition leader, **Kim Taejung**, to the presidency.

Although Kim Taejung relied heavily on support from his home province, South Chŏlla, and thus seemed to be in the well established tradition of South Korean politics, his victory appeared to represent a major change compared with that of **Kim Yŏngsam**, who in 1992 was the first directly elected civilian president since Syngman Rhee. In 1997, for the first time ever, the ruling party, which had traditionally enjoyed a high degree of unofficial support from local officials, especially in rural areas, as well as favourable treatment in the media, failed to win, albeit by a small margin. The long-term implications of this development for South Korean politics will remain uncertain until the first post-Kim Taejung election, but commentators noted a fundamental shift in the significance of parties as an essential part of the political system.

HAN SUNGJOO, *The Failure of Democracy in South Korea*, Berkeley: University of California Press, 1974; GREGORY HENDERSON, *Korea: the Politics of the Vortex*, Cambridge, Mass.: Harvard University Press, 1968; CHI YOUNG PAK, *Political Opposition in Korea 1945–1960*, Seoul National University Press, 1980; YANG SUNG CHUL, *The North and South Korean Political Systems: a Comparative Analysis*, Boulder: Westview Press, 1994

See also **Democratic Party**; **Democratic Nationalist Party**; **Democratic Republican Party**; **Korea Democratic Party** (*Chosŏn minjudang*); **Korea Democratic Party** (*Han'guk minjudang*); **New Democratic Party**

SOUTH MANCHURIA RAILWAY

Was constructed by the Russians in 1898 as a line connecting the Chinese Eastern Railway with Port Arthur and Dalian, newly leased to them for 25 years. A branch led to the Korean border at Sinŭiju, where it connected with the fledgling Korean rail system. The Japanese acquired control of the railway south of Shenyang in 1905 (*see* **Russo-Japanese War**), and their South Manchuria Railway Company controlled **railways** and railway development in Korea in the early part of the colonial period as an important part of the strategic exploitation of their continental foothold. The Company maintained a research department which conducted important work in Manchuria and Korea on geographical, geological, archaelogical, historical and ethnographic aspects of the region. In September 1931 it was an incident on the railway line outside Mukden (Shenyang) that initiated the Japanese invasion of north-east China (*see* **Manchurian Incident**).

JOHN YOUNG, *The Research Activities of the South Manchurian Railway Company, 1907–1945 – a History and Bibliography*, New York: Columbia University Press, 1966

SOUTHERN SCHOOL *Namjong-hwa* 南宗畫 *See* **landscape painting**

SOVIET-DPRK (NORTH KOREA) AGREEMENT (1949)

A ten-year agreement for economic and cultural cooperation signed by **Kim Ilsŏng** in Moscow on 17 March 1949. Strong Soviet influence was already exerted over the DPRK through a large mission in P'yŏngyang, which nominated advisers to the Central People's Committee (the cabinet), the National Planning Commission and the Ministry of Defence. The agreement offered North Korea trade and technical assistance worth 212 million rubles, with favourable credit arrangements, and underpinned its economic development plan of 1949–50. Soviet intercession also resolved the dispute between P'yŏngyang and Beijing over the rebuilding of the Sup'ung dam on the **Yalu River**, damaged by flooding in 1946, and the distribution of the electricity produced by it. As a result, China received some 300,000 kilowatts of electric power, despite continuing to prevent Korean trains entering China from Sinŭiju.

A simultaneous but unpublicised military agreement may also have been reached. It seems certain that Kim and Stalin discussed a possible war on the peninsula, and when Soviet troops were withdrawn from Korea in December (*see* **US-Soviet Joint Commission**) they left all their own weapons, and those seized from the Japanese, to the **Korean People's Army**. A large number of Soviet military advisers and technicians also remained behind to train the army, and in April-May 1950 Soviet tanks and artillery were delivered.

SOVIET UNION, RELATIONS WITH

In the aftermath of the Japanese defeat in 1945, the absence of an Allied plan for the restoration of Korean independence led to the division of the peninsula, which became a focus of Cold War confrontation between the Soviet Union and the United States. Soviet influence in the north, both before and after the creation of the **Democratic People's Republic of Korea** (DPRK), was strong.

The Soviet commander charged with taking over north Korea under the terms of the **Potsdam Conference** agreement was General Ivan Christiakov. Unlike his American counterpart in the south, Colonel John **Hodge**, he and his troops had some experience of Koreans and were accompanied by a large number of Korean communists returning from **Siberia**. Through the **People's Committees** they were able to establish firm Soviet control and further the interests of the Northern Bureau of the **Korean Communist Party**. Christiakov removed the independently-minded **Cho Mansik** from leadership of the People's Political Committee in December 1945 and promoted

Kim Ilsŏng in his stead. Thereafter communisation proceeded rapidly, with a programme of **land reform**, female emancipation and industrial nationalisation that brought immediate benefit to impoverished people. Russian influence quickly supplanted Japanese, through the presence of Soviet technicians and advisers, financial loans, the reorganisation of the education system along Soviet lines, the teaching of Russian language, the sending of Korean students to the Soviet Union, and the import of Marxist literature. The people of north Korea had been freed from exploitation by the Japanese only to find themselves, after a brief honeymoon period, deeply indebted to the Russians.

In December 1948 Soviet troops withdrew from North Korea, although military aid continued to arrive. Kim Ilsŏng visited Moscow twice, in March-April 1949 to sign an economic and cultural treaty (*see* **Soviet-DPRK Agreement**), and again in secrecy in February 1950. Though Stalin's influence is no longer believed to have initiated the **Korean War** which broke out on 25 June 1950, both he and Mao Zedong had given Kim Ilsŏng their advance approval, and assurance of Soviet support was no doubt important to the Korean leader.

The Soviet Union did not, however, regard its satellites as equal partners or promote their development in the way that, for all its political doubts, the United States did the **Republic of Korea**. Therefore, although Kim Ilsŏng showed his admiration for Stalinist political methods and used them to establish his own firm power base, he was shrewd enough to exploit rivalry between the Soviet Union and the People's Republic of China and to gain whatever support he could from both. After the Korean War **nationalism**, rather than ideological fraternity with either of its giant communist neighbours, drove North Korea to follow a skilful path attracting whatever support it could from each. Soviet money and advice were essential to the creation of North Korean industry and military machines, yet did not come free of interest. Though the Soviet Union (like the PRC) sold oil to North Korea at below market prices, the DPRK accumulated a heavy debt to the USSR. Refusing even to join the communist economic organisation Comecon, it pursued its own style of self-reliance (*see* **chuch'e**). Kim managed to avoid being drawn to one side or the other in the bitter Sino-Soviet dispute of the 1960s–1980s, though geographical and historical factors weighed heavily in favour of a Chinese orientation.

Nevertheless North Korean economic planning followed a familiar Soviet line, of strongly centralised planning within a succession of five-year plans and high investment in heavy industry. The results were impressive until the mid-1970s, but in the 1980s inability to adapt to changing circumstances brought the beginning of disaster. Kim Ilsŏng visited Moscow in May 1984 and acquired more advanced military systems from President Chernenko. But from 1985 onwards President Gorbachev pursued a policy of détente which began to render the North Korean emphasis on military confrontation outdated. Moreover, as its own economic picture grew darker, the Soviet Union was itelf in no state to be able to help, and Kim Ilsŏng's hard-line political obduracy proved fatal. Soviet support for P'yŏngyang dwindled as the DPRK pressed on heedlessly in outdated Soviet-style mode. By the mid-1990s a succession of bad harvests compounded excessive spending on grandiose construction schemes and military installations to produce serious famine.

Kim's dictatorial leadership style owed much to the Stalinist model, especially after Stalin's death in 1953 allowed Kim to assume centre stage and to build up his own rôle as a demagogue. It should be remembered, however, that such a performance was not out of keeping with East Asian political tradition and was not in itself a Soviet-style innovation. Neither Kim Ilsŏng nor his son **Kim Chŏngil** showed any readiness to follow the political paths of *perestroika* laid down by Michael Gorbachev, and after the collapse of the Soviet Union it was Beijing that continued to afford most ideological support for P'yŏngyang, albeit while developing its own ties with Seoul.

The Republic of Korea, meanwhile, overcame its revulsion at the shooting down of KAL flight 007 by Soviet missiles in September 1983 and responded to Gorbachev's economic advances. Trade increased and diplomatic relations were opened in 1991.

MAX BELOFF, *Soviet Policy in the Far East, 1944–1951*, Oxford University Press, 1953; CHUNG CHIN OWYEE, *Pyongyang between Peking and Moscow: North Korea's Involvement in the Sino-Soviet Dispute, 1958–75*, University of Alabama Press, 1978; KIM HAKJOON, *Korea in Soviet East Asian Policy*, Seoul: Kyunghee University, 1986
See also **North Korean nuclear programme**; **Russia, relations with**

SŎWŎN 書院 'Writing courtyards'
Private academies organised under the sponsorship of neo-Confucian scholars. They received government approval, and benefited from grants of land, **slaves**, and **books**, and from tax exemption. The first to receive royal recognition was founded by Chu Sebung in 1542 and dedicated to **An Hyang**. In 1543 King Injong accepted the proposal by **Yi Hwang** that it should be granted the title of *Sosu Sŏwŏn* ('Handed Down Cultivation Academy'). By 1600 there were around one hundred *sŏwŏn* throughout the country. They honoured past Confucian heroes, and functioned as regional centres for the promotion of neo-Confucian values and debate. But they also provided opportunities for *yangban* to develop their power and ideas away from the capital, and inevitably they became involved in the political **factionalism** of the mid-Chosŏn period. As a result, more *sŏwŏn* were established either to further factional interests or by those who wished to pursue academic study free of political considerations. Some 300 new academies were founded in the late 17th and early 18th century. Because of their economic and political threat the **Taewŏn'gun** introduced measures suppressing them in 1864, 1868 and 1871. Only 47 survived, all honouring famous Confucian scholars.

SPIRIT WORSHIP
Koreans had an ancient heritage of animistic religion of which many traces survive. The main spirits concerned are: *Ch'ilsŏng-sin*, *samsin*, *sansin*, *sŏnangsin* (*see sŏnang-dang*), the **spirit of the privy**, *tokkaebi tongsin*, *ttŭn sin, and t'ŏju*.

SSANG HŬICHA 雙喜字 'double *hŭi* character'
A square emblem of happiness made by writing the Chinese character *hŭi* meaning 'happy' twice, side by side, omitting one stroke near the base to avoid crowding the strokes. It is much used for congratulations, especially at weddings.

STAR MAPS *See* **astronomy**

STEVENS, DURHAM WHITE
An American employee of the Japanese Foreign Ministry appointed in 1905 under the terms of the **Korea-Japan Protocol** to advise the Korean government on foreign affairs. He had first gone to Korea in 1885 with the Japanese Foreign Minister Inoue Kaoru to demand reparation for Japanese losses incurred during the *Kapsin* Coup. His sympathies continued to lie with the Japanese rather than the Koreans, whom he openly despised, and he betrayed Korean trust in his professed responsibility to defend their interests. During the **Protectorate** he worked secretly for the **Resident-General**.

In 1908 he was sent to the United States by **Itō Hirobumi** to defend Japanese policy in Korea, but on 23 March he was shot and killed at Oakland railway station by two Korean Christians, Chŏn Myŏngun (b. 1884) and Chang Inhwan (1877–1930). Both were imprisoned. Chŏn was soon set free and went to join freedom fighters in Vladivostok, where he died. Chang served ten years. Stevens was posthumously awarded the Japanese Medal of the Order of the Rising Sun with Grand Seal.

ANDREW C. NAHM, 'Durham White Stevens and the Japanese Annexation of Korea', in A.C.NAHM, ed., *The United States and Korea: American-Korean Relations 1866–1976*, Kalamazoo: Western Michigan University, 1979

STONE FIGHTS *p'yŏnssam, sŏkchŏn* 石戰
Before 1910 the boys and young men of a village or town section would engage those of another community in stone-throwing battles. The participants wrapped their heads and legs in thick cloths, but this did not preclude all injuries. The team which retreated was deemed to have lost. In Koguryŏ this took place at the **New Year**, in Koryŏ and early Chosŏn at *Tano*. In later Chosŏn it returned to the New Year and the result was taken to imply which village would have the better harvest that year. Because kings are recorded as having gone to watch, some have guessed the games were intended as military training, but similar sports, often less dangerous, are provided for controlled release of young male impulses in many cultures. The Japanese colonial government abolished the custom.

STRAW RAIN-CAPE (*torongi*)
During the summer rains, men working in the rice-paddies wore very wide straw hats (*satkat*) and rice-straw capes. The cape was made of untrimmed straw with its ends overlapping one another to form a supple thatch, off which rain-water ran easily. This quaint and characteristic garb was a favourite subject for *genre* painters.

STUDENTS
There is a long tradition of political protest by students in Korea as well as in China. The whole *Sŏnggyun-gwan* would on occasion subscribe a complaint (*ch'ŏnggŭm-nok*) and march with it in procession through the streets to the palace gate. The document was sent in to the king and the petitioners sat in front of the gate – for several days, if the response was delayed. They might back the petition with strikes from refectory, dormitory or lectures, and even threaten to desert the school *en masse*. Such demonstrations were mounted in 1611 when Chŏng Inhong opposed memorial sacrifices for **Yi Hwang**; in 1631 against a **posthumous royal title** for King Injo's father; in 1650 to defend the honour of **Yi I**; in 1667 when Beijing envoys disclaimed diplomatic ineptitude; in 1780 when a gold Buddha was brought from Beijing; and again when King **Ch'ŏlchong** failed to honour the posthumous King **Ikchong** correctly.

In the 20th century students have again earned a reputation for outspokenness on political and social issues. This stems in part from the early efforts of the **Independence Club** to promote education for both boys and girls, and to link it with nationalist aims in times when Korea was increasingly affected by Japanese imperialism and colonialism. Students therefore played an active part in support for the **March First Movement**, formed branches within the **New People's Association** (*Sinminhoe*) and **Young Men's Christian Association**, and unlawfully organised many societies dedicated to the maintenance of Korean culture under Japanese occupation. Their politics were generally left-wing and they were encouraged by socialist and communist leaders, but **nationalism** was their principal motivation. They

447

protested against the inferior quality of their education compared with that provided for Japanese students, and the widespread student movement after the **Kwangju Incident** in 1929 led to harsh repression by the Japanese authorities. They joined with the *Tonga Ilbo* and *Chosŏn Ilbo* in campaigning against rural illiteracy in the late 1920s and early 1930s. Their objectives were often supported openly by their peers studying in Japan.

In post-colonial times students in the Republic of Korea continued to express their views forcefully and with political effect. The Masan Demonstration and **April 19th student uprising** brought down the government of President Syngman Rhee (**Yi Sŭngman**) in 1960. Students protested against the Treaty concluded by President Park Chung Hee (**Pak Chŏnghŭi**) with Japan in 1965 (*see* **Korea-Japan Treaty**), and through the 1960s the National Student Federation for National Unification (commonly known as *Mint'ong*) demonstrated openly in favour of reunification with the North. Even the killing of many students by the army in 1980 (*see* **Kwangju Massacre**) failed to quell their determination, still fired by a sense of nationalism. Calling for democracy, they grew more radical under the repressive measures of the Fifth Republic: they engaged in open street fighting against both the authorities and the rival student factions, and 1,275 were arrested after demonstrations at Kŏn'guk University in 1986. By now students in middle and high schools, colleges and universities, numbering over six million compared with only 90,000 in 1945, were a significant political force (*see also* **Minjung movement**). In 1987 a Pan-Korean Alliance of University Students (*Chŏndaehyŏp*) was established and backed the opposition leader **Kim Taejung** in the Presidential election campaign. The less radical *Sodaehyŏp* supported **Kim Yŏngsam**. The victory of President Roh Tae Woo (**No Taeu**), however, brought more trouble. The killing of a student activist by police in 1991 prompted a fresh wave of rioting, some of which was directed against the continued presence of American troops in South Korea and the level of American influence in the Republic. Through the mid-1990s growing numbers of students again campaigned for reunification with the North.
WILLIAM DOUGLAS, 'Korean Students and Politics,' *AS*, III/12, 1963; YANG SUNG-CHUL, 'Student Activism and Activists: A Case of the 1960 April Revolution in Korea,' *KJ*, 12/7, 1972
See also **June Tenth Incident**

STUPA *pudo* 佛台
A monument, often built of granite or stone, to a **Buddha** or a Buddhist monk in which his cremated remains might be preserved, and on which his achievements might be recorded in an inscription. The great age of stupa construction was Unified Silla, though fine examples also survive from the Koryŏ and Chosŏn dynasties. The stupa might stand on a plain octagonal base, on a **lotus** blossom, or on the back of a sculptured **tortoise**, and was sometimes topped with a stone lotus. Worship was offered by circumambulating the monument.
See also **pagoda; tombs**

SUCH'ON 手寸 'hand measure'
Also called *chwach'on* 'left [hand] measure', a mark used instead of a finger-print by **slaves** and other illiterates. A measured life-size drawing of the left middle finger between the first and second joints was used as a signature or seal. It forms a rough rectangle with lines protruding at the corners. The characters '*chwa ch'on*' may be written in the rectangle and other marks added.

SUGUNG-GA 水宮歌 'Water palace song'
A *p'ansori*, known as *T'okki-jŏn* 'Tale of a hare' when printed as a fable. The **hare** is lured to an underwater king who needs a hare's liver for **medicine**. On realising his predicament, the hare claims he has left his liver behind, asks leave to go back for it and so escapes. The story, which appears in *Samguk sagi* and *Taedong unbu-gunok*, probably reached Korea by way of Chinese translations from Buddhist jataka.

SUI DYNASTY 隋朝 (China, 589–618)
Short-lived dynasty which reunited China by ruthless military and political means after the disunion of the Northern and Southern Dynasties period. In so doing it incurred the enmity of the Turks to the north-west, with whom the kingdom of **Koguryŏ** sought an alliance. In 598 a Koguryŏ army crossed the Liao River in a pre-emptive strike into Chinese territory and halted a Sui attack. Unwisely, the new Emperor Yangdi determined on a fresh expansionist move against Koguryŏ in 612. A huge army, with naval support, vainly laid siege first to Liaoyang and then to P'yŏngyang. Its supply lines badly overstretched, it was attempting to retreat when it was ambushed and almost completely destroyed by General **Ŭlchi Mundŏk** (*see* **Anju**; **Ch'ŏngch'ŏn River**). Further Sui attacks in 613 and 614 were also unsuccessful.

SUI-JŎN 殊異傳 'Very strange stories'
A now lost collection of doubtful authorship, most often attributed to Pak Illyang of the 11th century. Thirteen extracts survive, six in *Taedong unbu-gunok*, three in *Samguk yusa*, two in *T'aep'yŏng t'ongjae* and two in *Haedong kosŭng-jŏn*. (Duplicate versions of some appear in *P'irwŏn chapki*, *Samguksa chŏryo* and *Samguk sagi*.) The stories are marked by miracles, transformation into animals and similar wonders. They include historical figures such as King T'arhae of Silla.

SUKCHONG 肅宗 (1661–1720, r. 1674–1720)
Young Sukchong came to the throne during the disputes about the **Dowager Queen Changnyŏl's mourning rites**. He was the son of Hyŏnjong, who died at the age of 33. His long reign was marred by the peak of factional fighting and his troubles with the women of the palace. He did, however, achieve much in the world of scholarship and publishing; and he restored **Tanjong** to his place in the list of kings.

SUKSIN 肅慎 (C. Sushen)
Also called Siksin or Chiksin (C. Xishen, Jishen). The first recorded inhabitants of **Manchuria**, a hunting people of eastern Manchuria, supposedly contemporary with **Old Chosŏn** (c. 1st century BC). Late in the 3rd century AD some of them submitted to **Koguryŏ**, and about AD 400 they were wholly amalgamated, though some other Manchurian tribes are thought to have been their descendants. Their name is known only in sinified forms and may have been the origin of the name Chosŏn (C. Chaoxian). *See* **Korea, names for**

SUNCH'ALSA 巡察使
A title held concurrently by the *Kwanch'alsa*, or governor, of a province, in his rôle as general inspector of the provincial administration. Also called *sun'gwan* or *sunsa*.

SUNDO 順道 (4th century)
Sundo (C. Shundao) was the first recorded Buddhist teacher to enter Korea. He was sent in AD 372, carrying **sutras** and images, with a diplomatic mission from Fu Jian,

ruler of Eastern Qin (one of the 'Sixteen Kingdoms', covering part of north-east China), who sought alliance with **Koguryŏ** against the Manchurian tribes. Sundo met with early success at the Koguryŏ court.

SŬNGGYŎNG-DO 陞卿圖 'way to rise in office'
A game of Chinese origin, also called *chonggyŏng-do*. The most elaborate of the many games, all intended to forward their knowledge of Chinese characters, played by boys in the traditional schools of Chinese literature (*sŏdang*). On a very large sheet of paper was drawn a grid with the names of ranks and offices in the government. Each boy moved his counter according to the throws of a die (*see* **dice**). This die, called *sunggyŏng-do al*, was 10–16 cm long, 2–3 cm thick and pentagonal in section, made of *paktal-lamu* or other hard wood (*see* **trees**). One to five notches, usually painted red, were cut on each of the angular longitudinal edges. The die was rolled from the hand across the floor and always came to rest with one row of notches on top, which gave the score for the throw. The end of the game might be *yŏng-ŭijŏng*. Other points of exit were *t'oe* or *p'ajik* 'retirement', *sayak* 'bestowal of medicine' (i.e. execution by **poison**) or *sa-gwejang* 'bestowal of an old man's cushion and walking-stick'.

SŬNGJI 承旨 'secretary'
Title during the Chosŏn dynasty for the six secretaries of the *Sŭngjŏng-wŏn*. Each was of third **grade** senior, and each had a distinctive prefix to the title.

SŬNGJŎNG-WŎN 承政院 'Office for carrying out government'
The Chosŏn secretariat that handled all documents going to and from the king and was called *Huwŏn* 'the throat office'. It was at the top level of administration, and hence of power, and was thus seen with the *Ŭijŏng-bu* and the *Samsa* as the third arm of government. There were six secretaries of 3rd **grade** senior and two junior officials. Another expression of its power lay in the alternative name *Ŭndae*, 'silver terrace', derived from older Chinese usage.

SŬNGMU 僧舞 'monk's dance'
A slow and graceful solo **dance**, demanding great muscular control, performed by a monk wearing a *kokkal* (cornette headdress) and the long coat called *changsam* (whose huge sleeves give the alternative name *nabi-ch'um* 'butterfly dance'). It was performed to the accompaniment of a **drum** at services during the **forty-ninth day prayers** after a death. In the 20th century it was turned into a display by a professional dancer who was also a virtuoso drummer, and is now commonly danced by a woman. This creates a very different impression from that given by a strong young man in the same costume dancing at the centre of a moving circle of praying laymen and women. The popular story that **Hwang Chini** danced it to seduce a leading *Sŏn* monk is a frivolous invention.

SŬNGMUN-WŎN 承文院 'Office for handling letters'
Chosŏn government office; fifteen officials presided over by a 3rd **grade** senior, employed in writing letters to neighbouring states.

SUNJANG 巡將 'patrol officer'
An officer of 2nd **grade** junior to 3rd grade junior, appointed by the *Chungch'u-bu* to patrol the capital at night. He carried a *sunp'ae* or disc, issued by the Board of War, bearing the character *sin*, 'faithfulness', on one side and the characters *sunjang* on the reverse.
See also **curfew**

SUNJO, KING 純祖 (1790–1834, r. 1800–34)
Second son of **Chŏngjo**. He was ten when he was chosen to be king by the senior Queen Dowager Chŏngsun (1745–1805, second wife of **Yŏngjo**) on his father's death in 1800. She belonged to the Pyŏkp'a **faction** and during her four years 'ruling through the screen' (*suryŏm-ch'ŏngjŏng*) the Pyŏkp'a used its power to purge the opposing Sip'a, attacking them in part by persecuting Catholics, with whom the Sip'a sympathised. Sunjo took over the government himself in 1804. His wife, later known as Queen Sunwŏn (1789–1857), belonged to the Andong Kim clan, which soon firmly grasped power, beginning the long period during which the country was under *sedo*, the rule of the royal in-laws. Their corrupt administration, combined with epidemics and natural disasters, led to several uprisings, notably that of **Hong Kyŏngnae** in P'yŏngan province in 1811 and another in **Cheju** in 1813. Partly in order to correct this state of affairs, Sunjo made his son, later known as **Ikchong**, president of the state council in 1827; but Ikchong died three years later and his wife's family, the P'ungyang Cho clan, regained power for the Pyŏkp'a.

SUNJONG, EMPEROR 純宗 (1874–1926, r. 1907–10)
Second son of **Kojong** and only surviving son of **Queen Min**, a weak and incapable man, made Crown Prince in 1875. In 1897 he was named Hwangt'aeja, 'Crown Prince Imperial'. When the Japanese made his father abdicate in 1907, he became the puppet emperor, Yunghŭi Hwangje, but in 1910 he was demoted to Yi Wang, 'King Yi'. His death in 1926 sparked off brief independence demonstrations and led eventually to the student uprising in 1929 (*see* **Kwangju Incident**). His second wife Queen Yun, otherwise Sunjŏnghyo Hwanghu (1894–1966), survived refugee life during the war of 1950 and ended her days as a devout Buddhist in Naksŏn-jae, a dependency of the **Changdŏk palace**.
See also **Min T'aeho**

SUNO-JI 旬五志 'A Fortnight's Jottings'
A brief collection of anecdotes and comments, some of them critical, on Korean history and literature, but including remarks on **dialect** and **proverbs**. It was dictated by Hong Manjong (c. 1643–1725, perhaps a little earlier) during fifteen sleepless nights in autumn 1678, when he lay ill at Sŏho, 'West lake' (presumably the suburban area of Seoul so called, on the **Han River** between Map'o and Sŏgang). It is a charming book, showing wide interest in religion other than **Confucianism** and a pleasing modesty in its author.

SUP'ARYŎN 水波蓮 'water-wave lotus'
A coloured paper bouquet, like those used in Buddhist temples, on a central rod that can be stuck into festal food at banquets. The paper was irregularly dyed to give a waved or watered effect. A typical central display may be based on a huge **lotus**-flower, surmounted by more lotuses and topped with a bunch of peonies, interspersed with red and green **peaches**, china-roses and imitation **longevity** fungus. Kingfishers, cranes, other birds and butterflies are introduced and as many as ten waxen figures of *sŏndong* (boy **immortals**). Among the flowers are hung gilded paper characters reading *kang-gu-yŏnwŏl su-bu-tanam*, 'busy thoroughfares and misty moon (a cliché for prosperity); long life, riches and many sons'. *Namgŭng-noin-sŏng*, the southern star of longevity, portrayed as an immortal elder (*sŏnin*), rides a **deer** at the summit.

SURNAMES
The longest lists of surnames (*sŏng* or *ssi*) contain nearly 500 names, of which fewer than a quarter are common. Most consist of a single syllable, but there are about a dozen *poksŏng* '**two-character surnames**'.

The oldest surnames go back to early Silla, including Kim and Pak, which were Korean royal names. Others have been borrowed from Chinese or brought in by Chinese immigrants. Most claim noble origin, because surnames were first used by the aristocracy, and when the lower classes assumed surnames, they often adopted the names of their overlords. As a result, the commoner surnames are more socially esteemed, a few rarer ones much less. A common list of those to be avoided in marriage-matches gives Ch'ŏn 'thousand', Pang 'room', Chi 'lake', Ch'u 'autumn', Ma 'horse', Kol 'bone' and P'i 'skin'. Some families may have been named from their occupations, P'i 'skins' being a likely example.

A surname usually covers a number of *pon'gwan* 'clans', each named after the fief of its progenitor *sijo*. Thus all those with the surname No 'black' are descended from a Chinese immigrant to late Silla, whose name was No Su (C. Lu Sui), but they are now divided into nine clans, named after the fiefs of nine of his descendants. One of these, Kyoha No-ssi, claims descent from No Kangp'il, Lord of Kyoha, northwest of Seoul, who was tutor to the first Crown Prince of Koryŏ.

A clan may be divided into *p'a*, 'septs', named after later ancestors. Kyoha No-ssi have four septs, named after four brothers of the 14th century AD. One is the Ch'angsŏnggun-p'a, named after the lord of Ch'angsŏng, a fief on the **Yalu** River.

SURNAMES, TWO-CHARACTER *poksŏng* 復姓
The two-character surnames are, in order of estimated frequency: Namgung, Sŏnu, Hwangbo, Tokko, Sagong, Chegal, Sŏmun, Tongbang, Kongsun, Sama and Yŏnggo. All exist in China (Nangong, Xianyu, Huangfu, Dugu, Sikong, Zhuge, Ximen, Dongfang, Gongsun, Sima, Linggu).

SURYŎM-CH'ŎNGJŎNG 垂簾聽政 'letting down the screen, hearing government'
When the king was a child too young to take responsibility, the senior dowager queen would act as regent and sit beside his throne, shielded by a screen so as to preserve the proprieties required in the presence of adult male subjects. This Chinese practice is first recorded in Korea for King T'aejo of **Koguryŏ** in AD 53.

SUTRA *pulgyŏng* 佛經
Mahayana sutras are regarded as canonical transmissions of the teaching of Sakyamuni. The Sanskrit word *sutra* 'thread', meaning the thread of an argument, is translated in Sino-Korean by *kyŏng*, the word used for Confucian 'classic'. Sutras are very hard to date. Most of them arrived in China through Buddhist communities in central Asia, and were translated from Indic languages (chiefly Sanskrit) into Chinese. Many of the texts used in Korea were translated into Chinese by **Kumarajiva**.

The *Prajnaparamita*, 'perfection of wisdom', school emphasised the doctrine of *sunyata*, 'emptiness of inherent existence'. Though some of its sutras are probably among the oldest, the whole group must be placed between 100 BC and AD 600. The two Korean favourites were possibly written in the 3rd century AD: *Vajracchedika-prajnaparamita-sutra* (K. *Kŭmgang-gyŏng*) the 'Diamond Sutra', which asserts a paradox of *sunyata*, that nirvana (freedom from metempsychosis) and samsara (continued transmigration) are one and the same; and *Prajnaparamita-hridaya-sutra*

(K. *Simgyŏng*) the 'Heart Sutra' that centres on **Kwanseŭm**, a short version of which is recited daily by monks and many believers.

Two works important for the Meditation or Dhyana (K. *Sŏn*, C. *Chan*, J *Zen*) school that predominates in Korean Buddhism are: *Lankavatara-sutra* (K. *Nŭnggu-gyŏng*), probably written betwen 100 BC and AD 100, which gives the Buddha's answers to 108 questions and is notably non-rational; and *Virmalikirti-sutra* (K. *Yuma-gyŏng*), which tells how Virmalikirti, a disputatious layman, is visited by the **bodhisattva** Manjusri for a conversation about meditative life for layfolk.

Parts of *Avatamsaka-sutra* (K. *Hwaŏm-gyŏng*), the 'Flower Garland sutra', were translated into Chinese by the 3rd century AD. It is the most grandiose of sutras, a composite work, even longer than the Bible, and perhaps not all written in India. Its Buddha is **Vairocana**, portrayed as the cosmic Buddha, in whom all other buddhas, indeed everything, exists. The bodhisattva Samantabhadra is a prominent character.

Saddharma-pundarika-sutra (K. *Myobŏb-yŏnhwa-gyŏng*), the 'Lotus Sutra' or 'Lotus of the Wonderful Law', holds a position among Korean Buddhists akin to that of the Bible among Christians. It is another great compilation, probably written between 100 BC and AD 100. It tells of Sakyamuni preaching to a huge congregation, including Prabhutaratna (**Tabo**), and Manjusri plays a leading rôle. Its rich store of parables includes one about rescuing children from a burning house and another about a prodigal son, both of which illustrate the doctrine of *pangp'yŏn* (S. *upaya*) 'skilful means' or adapting doctrine to suit the receptivity of the hearers.

Surangama sutra (K. *Nŭngŏm-gyŏng*, more properly *Surŭngŏm-gyŏng*, 'supreme samadhi (interior imperturbability) sutra' was probably written by Chinese. It too contains many attractive stories and similes: the man with **yŏŭi-ju** sewn in his clothes, the finger pointing at the moon, the cube of air put into a round box, and the mirror used to kindle a fire from sunlight. There is also a grand presentation by 25 bodhisattvas, culminating in Manjusri, of the means they used to reach buddahood.

Pure Land (K. *Chŏngt'o*) doctrine has three sutras. Two of them are *Sukhavati-vyuha* sutras, of which the shorter *Amit'a-gyŏng* is best known in Korea. Some think it dates from the 1st century BC and is the earlier of the two; others think the longer one, called *Muryangsu-gyŏng* in Korean, is the earlier. Both describe the western paradise as a staging-post on the way to nirvana, a blissful purgatory where **Amida** Buddha reigns. The third, *Kwan-muryangsu-gyŏng* (S. *Amitayurdhyana-sutra*), may be a 4th century AD Chinese work. *Chijang-ponwŏn-gyŏng* 'sutra of Ksitigarbha's vows', on the bodhisattva's vows to save souls, is also probably of Chinese origin.

The 'Platform Sutra', *Liuzu dashi fabao tanjing* (K. *Yukcho Taesa pŏppo-dan'gyŏng*) 'sutra preached from the podium by the Sixth Patriarch, teacher of dharma-treasure', was compiled in Chinese in 1290. It contains the teachings of the sixth Chan Patriarch, Huineng (638–713), and is called 'sutra' purely out of courtesy to him.

T. CLEARY, trans., *The Flower Ornament Scripture*, Boulder: Shambala, 1984; EDWARD CONZE, *Buddhist Wisdom Books: the Diamond Sutra and the Heart Sutra*, London: Allen & Unwin, 1975; H.H. SØRENSEN, 'The Hwaom Kyong Pyongsang to: A Yi Dynasty Buddhist Painting of the Dharma Realm,' *OA* XXXIV no.1, 1988; BURTON WATSON, trans., *The Lotus Sutra*, New York: Columbia University Press, 1993; LU K'UAN YU, *The Surangama Sutra*, London: Rider, 1966

SUWŎN 水原

Capital of southern Kyŏnggi province and an ancient city; the present city wall was built of granite, brick and timber between 1794 and 1796, and much of the original construction remains. It was constructed by King **Chŏngjo** to protect Hwasan, where the king had reburied his father, **Crown Prince Changhŏn**. Chŏngjo's plan to move the court there was later abandoned, but a detached palace was completed, where the king stayed during visits to his father's tomb. The story of Changhŏn's murder by his grandfather King **Yŏngjo** and of Chŏngjo's posthumous care for his father is known as an example of extreme filial devotion. He also established a Buddhist temple outside Suwŏn, Yŏngju-sa, which became the official headquarters of the *Chogye-jŏng* sect.

SWASTIKA 卍字 (*mancha / wancha*)
The swastika entered Korea with **Buddhism**. When drawn on Sakyamuni's breast it is called *kasŭm-man* 'the 10,000 of the breast', *pulsimin* 'seal of Buddha's heart' or *kilsang haeun* 'auspicious sea-cloud'. It is also one of the 65 signs in his footprint; but it is used in decorative art as a general good luck sign of no religious significance, and as a numeral meaning 10,000 (from being called *kilsang manbok* 'auspice of 10,000 blessings'). The anti-clockwise form seems commoner, but little attention is paid to the direction of the arms. *See also* **Latticework**; **Patterns, all-over surface**.

SWINGING *kunettwigi*
Korean swings are hung very high, often seven metres or more, in **trees** or on a tall framework for a single swing. The performer stands on the swing and attempts to rise to the point where the ropes are stretched out horizontally. *Tano* is the traditional time for swinging, which has become associated with **women**, who look pretty, soaring among the trees in billowing summer skirts. The history of the sport is obscure. In Koryŏ it was done by both sexes, and it is still most awesome when performed by strong young men. It may have originated as a strength-building exercise, as is suggested by its early association with *Tano*.

T

TABO (Prabhutaratna) 多寶
Prabhutaratna ('many treasures') is an ancient Buddha, who is never given pictorial representation. In the Lotus **Sutra**, chapter 11, though he has long been in nirvana, he is present in his **stupa** to hear Sakyamuni preach, thus showing that nirvana is not extinction. The *Tabot'ap* or 'Many Treasures Pagoda' at **Pulguk-sa** is named after him.

TABOT'AP 多寶塔 'Many treasures pagoda'
One of a pair of stone **pagodas** built in the mid-8th century at **Pulguk-sa** in **Kyŏngju**, reputedly by a master craftsman. Standing in the main courtyard to right and left of the central path approaching the main Buddha hall, *Tabot'ap* and its sister *Sŏkkat'ap* are respectively elaborate and simple in design, yet equally elegant and perfectly complementary according to concepts of *yang* and *yin* (*see* **ŭm-yang**). *Sŏkkat'ap* symbolises Sakyamuni Buddha and *Tabot'ap* the Buddha Prabhutaratna. Together they represent the summit of Unified Silla monumental art, and are designated National Treasures. A printed **sutra** discovered within *Sŏkkat'ap* in 1966 is believed to pre-date its erection in 751 (*see* **printing**). *Tabot'ap* is commonly known as *Yŏngt'ap* ('with-a-shadow pagoda') and *Sŏkkat'ap* as *Muyŏngt'ap* ('without-a-shadow pagoda'), referring to a popular belief that the stone mason's wife, in trying to see her husband's reflection in a pond near Pulguk-sa, saw only the shadow of *Tabot'ap*. She fell in and drowned.

TADŬMI 'pressing clothes'

Sometimes inaccurately called 'fulling', this process is the normal Korean way of dressing clothes and cloth after making or washing. It replaces western ironing. The clothes are folded on a smooth flat rectangular stone, made for the purpose and kept indoors. The worker then beats the cloth rhythmically with two small paddles (*pangmangi*) of hardwood (*see* **trees**) until all creases disappear and the cloth is soft and supple. If creased folds are wanted, they can be beaten into the cloth. Cloth is rolled on a wooden roller called *hongdukkae*. The sound of *tadŭmi* is nostalgically evocative of Korean life in both town and country.

See Arirang

TAEBANG (C. Daifang) *See* **Chinbŏn**

TAEBORUM-NAL 'great full-moon day'

The 15th of the 1st moon, end of the **New Year** holiday, to which many customs are attached. **Kites** are not flown after this day. It used to be customary on this night for men and boys to stage torch-fights, belabouring one another with flaming torches in all the fields of the village. Little harm resulted beyond singed hair and clothing. By the mid-20th century this had been reduced to a boys' game: after dark the hills and fields would be full of boys whirling tin cans on strings, the cans all filled with fire, flickering under the brilliance of the full moon.

TAEBU 大夫 'great man'

A title recognised in China since the Zhou dynasty (±1045–256 BC) and adopted as a rank in Koryŏ. Its value has varied slightly through the centuries. In the Chosŏn dynasty *taebu* was a rank given to men of **grades** 1 to 4. Grades 5 and below ranked as *nang*, 'gentleman'. The *taebu* title normally had a two-character attributive prefix, as in *Kasŏn Taebu*, 'great man commended for goodness', a 2nd-grade rank which was given in 1886 to **Kojong**'s Anglo-American physician, John William Heron (1856–1890). The characters in these prefixes were loosely linked to grade: 1st grades usually had *-nok* or *-dŏk*, as in *Sŏngnok taebu* for royal sons-in-law and *Hyŏllok taebu* for other royal relations.

TAEDONG 大同江

Important river rising in the mountains of central northern Korea close to the source of the **Ch'ŏngch'ŏn River** and flowing westwards to the Yellow Sea past P'yŏngyang. It was in the river basin here that **Old Chosŏn** developed as a political entity and expanded its sphere of control north to the Liao River basin, and that **Wiman Chosŏn** succeeded it. Throughout this region **bronze** and **iron** culture first entered from China, and Chinese civilisation and political authority were later extended through the **Lelang commandery**. Korean control was re-established in the Taedong basin when **Koguryŏ** overthrew the commandery in 313 and P'yŏngyang became its capital. In the 8th century the kingdom of **Parhae** extended as far south as the mouth of the Taedong. In 1866 the American merchant ship *General Sherman* sailed up the river in a vain attempt to reach P'yŏngyang and was destroyed, provoking a diplomatic incident.

TAEDONG UNBU-GUNOK 大東韻府群玉 'Great Eastern (sc. Korean) Rhyming Treasury of Assembled Jewels'

A notable encyclopaedia of Korea from **Tan'gun** to 1588, with entries in Chinese rhyme-order, modelled on Yin Shifu's *Yunfu qunyu* of the Yuan dynasty and compiled in 1588 by Kwŏn Munhae (1534–91), a disciple of **Yi Hwang** and member of the

Eastern **faction**. Much of the material under each rhyme-word is rather erratically labelled as geography, dynastic titles, **surnames**, biographies, filial sons, faithful women, magistrates, spirits, **trees**, plants and **birds**. The book contains much demotic material, especially about language, and information about pre-Hideyoshi bibliography.

TAEDONG YASŬNG 大東野乘 'Unofficial Records of the Great East (i.e.Korea)'
A huge collection of 57 items, including anecdotes, diaries and lists of personalities, published by the Chōsen Kosho Kankō-kai in 1909–1911, with a preface by **Asami Rintarō**. The latest piece was written about 1650. Among the contents are Sŏng Hyŏn (1439–1504), ***Yongjae ch'onghwa***; short works by **Sŏ Kŏjŏng**, **Nam Hyoŏn** and **Ch'a Ch'ŏllo**; Yi Yuk (1438–98), *Ch'ŏngp'a kuktam*; Hŏ Pong (1551–88), *Haedong yaŏn*; **Yi I**, *Soktam ilgi*; materials relating to the scholar **purges** of 1589, the **Imjin War**, and the reign of **Prince Kwanghae**; diaries and miscellanies of the 16th and 17th centuries.

TAEDONGPŎP 大同法 'Great Unity Law'
Tax measure proposed by Yi Wŏnik and initiated in Kyŏnggi in 1608, sometimes known as the Uniform Tax Law. It was introduced as an emergency measure following the devastation caused by the **Imjin Wars** and a series of natural disasters. The former had more than halved the population of Seoul, but the latter had driven so many starving people from the provinces into the capital that by the time of the 1648 census the city had almost returned to its former size, and had to struggle hard against post-war conditions to cope with them. In 1612 the Office of Relief Works (*Chinhyul-ch'ŏng*) was set up, managing the Board of Revenue (*Hojo*), the tax-collecting agency (the *Sŏhye-ch'ŏng*), and the **Ever Normal Warehouses** (*Sangp'yŏngch'ang*) into which the tax grain (*taedongmi*) was delivered. The new tax replaced the Tribute Tax and *corvée* dues. It was initially collected in **rice**, though cloth, **coinage** or local products required by the government were subsequently accepted as alternatives. *Corvée* obligations were replaced by a system of hired labour paid with food. *Taedongpŏp* was extended to Ch'ungch'ŏng and Chŏlla in 1623, Kyŏngsang in the mid-17th century, and Hwanghae in 1708. The measure had the effect of stimulating handicraft production, improving the lot of the **peasants** and creating a new rôle for **merchants** engaged as government intermediary 'tax men' (*kongin*).
CHOE CHING-YOUNG, 'Kim Yuk (1580–1658) and the *Taedongpŏp* Reform,' *JAS*, 23, 1963
See also **taxation**

TAEGA 大加
Wealthy and politically powerful élites of late **Puyŏ** and early **Koguryŏ**, probably members of the royal clan and queens' **lineages** whose income was derived from their landed estates.

TAEGAM 大監 'chief superintendent'
A polite reference to a government officer of 2nd **grade** senior and above. It came to be used for the guardian spirit of a site, house, tree, rock or the like, and thus to be used by ***mudang*** as a reverential title for many spirits.

TAEGAN 臺諫
An honorific title for officials of the ***Sahŏn-bu*** and ***Sagan-wŏn***.

TAEGU 大邱

Capital of North Kyŏngsang province; location of Talsŏng, the ancient **fortress** that formed one of the *sip chŏng* military garrisons in the Unified Silla period (*see* **Military systems**). It was enlarged at the end of the Mongol period in the 14th century and again in 1596 during the **Imjin War**.

On 29 September 1946, as part of a nationwide wave of communist agitation against the **American Military Government**, workers in forty Taegu factories went on strike (*Taegu p'oktong*). They were threatened with arrest, and when rioting broke out on 1 October it was suppressed with bloodshed. Violence again erupted in Taegu in 1960, when a student demonstration sparked the widespread protests that led to the downfall of President Syngman Rhee (**Yi Sŭngman**).
See also **Haein-sa**

TAEGŬM 大苓

The biggest of the native Korean transverse flute family, the *taegŭm* is used in both court and folk music ensembles. Its *sanjo* is particularly popular. It has six finger holes, a blowing hole, and an additional hole covered with a membrane, which makes a distinctive 'breathy' sound. Heavy tremolo effects are produced by moving the head and the instrument itself, rather than by the manipulation of the cheeks and lips as for the *p'iri*.
See also **music; music, court; musical instruments**

TAEHAN MAEIL SINBO 大韓每日申報 'Korea Daily News'

Korean-language partner of the *Korea Daily News*, founded by **Ernest Bethell** in February 1904. The paper was published in English and Korean (either *han'gŭl* and Chinese characters or *han'gŭl* alone) until 1 June 1908, when the English edition closed. It was resumed briefly in 1909 but ceased publication on Bethell's death on 1 May 1909. Its editorial line was strongly anti-Japanese, providing its readers *inter alia* with reports on *ŭibyŏng* activities. This brought trouble to its officials. Bethell was twice tried on orders of the Japanese authorities: in October 1907 he was bound over for six months, and in June 1908 he was imprisoned for three months. The editor **Yang Kit'ak** was arrested but freed on trial in July 1908. Shortly before **annexation** in 1910 the paper was bought by the Japanese, and as *Maeil Sinbo* from 1910 to 1920 was a mouthpiece for the **Government-General**. In January 1911 former staff of the paper were arrested and imprisoned for alleged sedition. This time Yang was sentenced to ten years' imprisonment, reduced on appeal to six years.
CHONG CHIN-SOK, *The Korean Problem in Anglo-Japanese Relations 1904–1910: Ernest Thomas Bethell and his Newspapers*, Seoul: Nanam Publishing Co., 1987

TAEHAN MIN'GUK 大韓民國 *See* **Republic of Korea**

TAEJEHAK 大提學 'president'

The title under the Chosŏn kings for the principal officers, also called *munhyŏng* and *chumun*, of **Hongmun-gwan** and **Yemun-wan**. They were of 2nd **grade** senior rank, collectively known as *yanggwan taejehak*.

TAEJŎN HOET'ONG 大典會通

The codex of national **law** published in 1865. The first such collection of laws and statutes in Chosŏn was *Kyŏngje yukchŏn* (1397), but the earliest to survive was *Kyŏngguk taejŏn* (1405). Of various revisions and supplements the most important were *Sok-taejŏn* (1744) and *Taejŏn t'ongp'yŏn* (1784). These were all superseded by *Taejŏn hoet'ong* in 1865. The material is of primary historical value and is arranged under the concerns of each of the **Six Boards**, distinguished by four single-character notations: *Wŏn* 'original' for material from *Kyŏngguk taejŏn*; *Sok* 'continued' for matter from *Sok-taejŏn*; *Chŭng* 'supplementary' for material promulgated between 1744 and 1784; and *Po* 'additional' for regulations subsequent to *Taejŏn t'ongp'yŏn*.

TAEJONG-GYO 大倧教
The 'religion of the great founding ancestor', also known as *Tan'gun-gyo* or *Han'gŏm-gyo*, a **new religion** founded in 1910 by Na Ch'ŏl. It was an attempt to revive **Tan'gun**'s own religion, believing in a triune universal God and involving ceremonies with Korean-style court robes. It attracted unfavourable attention from the Japanese government, which drove Na Ch'ŏl to commit suicide in 1916. His successor eventually took the headquarters to **Manchuria**, whence it returned to Seoul after 1945. The character *-jong-* is endemic to Korea: it is made up of 'man' (radical) and *chong* 'ancestor' (*see* **Sino-Korean characters endemic to Korea**).

TAEMADO 大馬島 *See* **Tsushima**

TAESŎNG 臺省 *See* **Government, central**

TAEWANG-AM 大王岩 'Great king rock'
King **Munmu** of Silla (r. 661–681) was cremated at his own request. His son Sinmun completed **Kamŭn-sa**, a temple Munmu had begun to build on the coast near Kyŏngju, and had his father's ashes scattered over the sea nearby. Local legend said that Munmu had become a dragon-spirit defending Silla to the east. Near the village of Taebon is the island of Taewang-am. A pool of calm water lies in its centre, where a submerged slab of rock is said to mark the place ('Underwater tomb') where the ashes were laid.

TAEWŎN'GUN 大院君 *See* **Princely titles**

TAEWŎN'GUN, THE (1820–98)
Yi Haŭng, a great-grandson of King Changjo, is properly known by his **princely title**, Hŭngsŏn-gun, or Hŭngsŏn Taewŏn'gun, but is commonly referred to as 'The Taewŏn'gun'. He was a distinguished calligrapher and painter, especially of orchids, and to avoid the attention of the Andong Kim *sedo* he let himself appear as a dilettante, although he was in fact able and ambitious (*see* **Three Orchid Painters**). He plotted with the Dowager Queen Sinjŏng, mother of **Hŏnjong**, to whom would fall the nomination of the next king, that on the death of **Ch'ŏlchong** she would name his own son Myŏngbok as king (later known as **Kojong**). This she did in 1864, when the boy was eleven. Ostensibly she ruled as regent from behind the screen for three years, but Haŭng, now Hŭngsŏn Taewŏn'gun, held the real power. He made government appointments on the basis of ability alone, balancing power between the ruling families; separated civil from military administration (1865); issued sumptuary regulations (1867) and reformed the complex tax system so as to make the privileged classes bear a fairer share of the burden; revised the legal codes (1865–7), and suppressed all but 47 of the more than 300 *sŏwŏn* (local Confucian institutes that nurtured factional attitudes) in 1871; making himself generally popular. His 1865 plan to restore the dignity of the crown by rebuilding the **Kyŏngbok Palace**, which had lain in ruins since the 16th-century Japanese invasions, was expensive and less popular.

Though he was guardedly friendly to Russia, events in China and the activities of western ships and navies around the coasts frightened him into the 'Hermit Kingdom' policy exemplified in 1866 by the *General Sherman* incident.

His wife was a Catholic; but after discussing the position of Catholics with **Nam Chungsam**, he began the severest persecution of Catholics, executing, among others, the French bishops Simeon **Berneux** and Antoine **Daveluy** together with seven French priests. In 1871 he set up *Ch'ŏkhwabi*, stones inscribed with an anti-Western slogan, throughout the country.

In 1866 the King was married to a kinswoman of the Taewŏn'gun's wife (the king's mother), a member of the Yŏhung Min clan. The new Queen had been brought up away from court and was expected to be a political nonentity; but she turned out to be astute, and her clan took up the mantle of *sedo*. The Taewŏn'gun began to treat her with contempt, provoking a memorial of protest in 1873, when he had to retire as *de facto* regent. He went to live in the country at Yangju. In the 'soldiers' mutiny' (*see Imo* **Incident**) of 1882 he seems to have been implicated in an attempt on the Queen's life. Japan and China, competing for control of Korea, were both involved, and at the subsequent **Treaty of Tianjin** in 1883 both powers agreed to withdraw their troops from Korea, but the Chinese held the Taewŏn'gun at Baoding (some 100 miles inland from Tianjin) for nearly four years (*see magoja*). The Post Office *émeute* of 1884 (*see* ***Kapsin* Coup**) destabilised the situation still further, and in 1885 he was returned to Seoul in the hope that he might strengthen feeling against Russian interest in Korea; but his activities were overshadowed first by **Yuan Shikai**, then by the Japanese, during the ***Kabo* reforms** of 1894–6. Japanese plots culminating in the assassination of **Queen Min** in 1895 led to his being forced into final retirement. Kojong refused to attend his father's funeral three years later.

CHOE CHING YOUNG, *The Rule of the Taewŏn'gun: Restoration in Yi Korea*, Cambridge, Mass.: Harvard University Press, 1972

TAFT-KATSURA MEMORANDUM/AGREEMENT (1905)

Record of a meeting in Tokyo on 27 July 1905 between Japanese Prime Minister Katsura Tarō and U.S. Secretary of State William Taft (1857–1930) in which Taft acknowledged his personal view, subsequently endorsed by President Theodore Roosevelt, that a Japanese protectorate of Korea would be justified as a means of ensuring future peace in East Asia. Taft received a written assurance from Katsura that Japan would not resist American control over the Philippines.

ANDREW NAHM, 'The Impact of the Taft-Katsura Memorandum on Korea – a Reassessment,' *KJ*, 25/10, 1985

See also **Anglo-Japanese Alliance**; **Anglo-Japanese Treaty**; **Protectorate Treaty**; **Russo-Japanese War**

TAMNO 擔魯 *See* **Paekche**

TANCH'ŎNG 丹青 'red-blue'

The traditional craft of decorating important wooden buildings in the five colours of red, blue (and green), yellow, black and white. *Tanch'ŏng* has been enriched by the skill of specialist artisans, *tanch'ŏngjang*, over the centuries and is practised to the present day. In temples, it was linked to the art of *t'aenghwa* painting. During the Three Kingdoms period the use of colours was limited according to sumptuary regulations: in **Silla**, for example, only *sŏnggol* royalty were entitled to use all five. In the early 12th century the beautiful and distinctive decoration of the royal palaces in

Kaesŏng was commented on by the Chinese traveller Xu Jing. In the Chosŏn period **craftsmen** were employed by the *Sŏn'gong-gam* department of the government to maintain official buildings (*see* **Government organs**); monks were trained in the upkeep of religious buildings. The four categories of *tanch'ŏng* are *morucho*, repeated patterns based on the **lotus**, pomegranate, feather etc.; *pyŏlchihwa*, story-telling scenes such as the life of Buddha (*see* **Eight Scenes**) and the oxherd (*see* **Ten Ox Pictures**); *pidan*, geometric designs; and *tandok*, a single animal, floral or geometric pattern.

TANG DYNASTY 唐代 (China, 618–906)

The Tang founders continued their predecessors' policies towards the three kingdoms on the peninsula (*see* **Sui dynasty**), accepting their **tribute**, maintaining troupes of their musicians and dancers at court, and engaging in military campaigns with them. Responsibility to each as their suzerain did not prevent Tang from waging war against them out of self-interest, neither did they as vassals shrink from inflicting defeat on their suzerain's armies, though the correct forms of tributary relations might still be preserved: in 647, only three years after inflicting a heavy defeat on the Tang army sent to redress a case of regicide in P'yŏngyang, King Pojang apologised and offered tribute to Chang'an. Emperor Gaozong (650–83) pleaded in vain for an end to fighting between the three kingdoms, and then became heavily involved in it. After helping **Silla** to conquer both **Paekche** and **Koguryŏ**, the Tang court anticipated that it would now be able to govern Korea in the form of old-style **commanderies** (*see* **Kyerim**). It tried to set up puppet régimes of its own in former Koguryŏ and Paekche territory, and even in Silla itself. However, King **Munmu** made it clear that he would not accept the subordinate rôle assigned to him by China. Tang armies were defeated at Maech'osŏng and Ch'ŏnsŏng and finally driven out as far as **Liaodong** in 676. Korean independence was established.

Friendly relations were then maintained and appreciated by both sides (*see* **Sŏngdŏk, King**). Both tribute and trade reinforced the high esteem in which the Tang court held Korean cultural achievements, built on the adoption of **Confucianism** and **Buddhism**, the use of the Chinese script, and observance of Chinese-style court rites and titles. Up-to-date information on the latter was collected by Korean delegations to Chang'an and Luoyang, or might be taken back to Korea by official hostages who sometimes spent long years in detention in the Chinese capital. These included persons of royal blood and high official rank, who were well treated, given education, and afforded honorary ranks and titles. They also included both male and female **slaves**, who perhaps did not fare so well but were occasionally spared by imperial decree and sent home.

Koreans served in the Chinese administration and army. Korean scholars and students studied in the Imperial Academy and in Buddhist monasteries (*see* **Hyech'o**), and returned to high acclaim to pass on their learning (*see* **Ch'oe Chiwŏn**). In 682 King **Sinmun** established a state school for the advancement of Chinese culture and political science, teaching the Confucian and Daoist classics, **calligraphy**, **poetry**, **music**, **law**, and **medicine**. For their part, Chinese poets prized Korean **paper** and ink for their high quality.

Silla admiration for the Chinese model was reflected in the layout of its capital city, **Kyŏngju**, and in much of the stone and metal craftsmanship practised in its workshops. **Ceramic** skills such as three-colour glazing were encouraged by the importation of Chinese wares. Korean **merchants** dominated seaborne trade in north-east Asia and maintained large communities in east coast Chinese towns such as Chuzhou and Lianshui.

TANGAK 唐樂 *See* **Music**

TANGGAN CHIJU 幢竿支柱 'flagmast supports'
Tall twin granite pillars, square in section, with the two outside top edges rounded, erected some 30 centimetres apart in an open space. They are the supports for the great flagmast of a Buddhist monastery that has disappeared, perhaps centuries ago. The pair in the middle of Ch'ŏngju city, once belonging to a long-lost monastery called Yongdu-sa ('dragon-head monastery'), retains a large part of the bronze mast. Local legend, recorded already in *Tongguk yŏji-sŭngnam*, has forgotten its origin and claims it was erected when Ch'ŏngju was founded, in order to give the city the stability of a ship on an even keel.

TANG-STYLE REGULATED VERSE *Tangŭm*, 唐音 'Tang sound'
Writing Chinese poems in the style developed in China during the **Tang dynasty** (*yulsi*, 'regulated verse' or *saryul*, 'four-fold regulation') has been a favourite pastime of *yangban* since mid-Koryŏ. Each poem (*su* 'head') consists of eight 5-character or 7-character lines. The poet has five points to consider.
1) The subject (*sije*). This may arise spontaneously; or be proposed by someone else, perhaps jokingly; or used by a group competitively. Choosing an object, animal or thing is called *yŏngmul* 'singing of a thing'; events produce *chŭksa* 'reaction to an event', and landscape *chŭkkyŏng* 'reaction to a view'.

2) Rhyming. *Abun* 'impressing rhymes' or *un talda* means putting *kagun* 'foot-rhymes' at the end of the even-numbered lines, all of which have to rhyme with one another. The poet may choose his own rhyme or cap rhymes that have been used by someone else; a friend may propose either all the rhyme words (*un naeda*) or a single rhyme category (*uncha-t'ong*). Every Chinese character is assigned to one of 106 classical rhyme categories (*un* or *pal*), which have never been reproduced precisely in Korean pronunciation. In poetry *ch'un* 'spring', for instance, rhymes with Sino-Korean *chin* 'true', while *kŭn* 'root' and *on* 'warm' both rhyme with *wŏn* 'primal'. Only the 30 categories assigned to the even tones are normally used in Tang poetry. Despite their artificiality, Koreans easily learn these poetic rhymes.

3) Four-part construction (*kisŭng-jŏn'gyŏl*) is obligatory. Each couplet (*yŏn'gu*) forms one part: (i) *kiryŏn* 'theme', called *kyeryŏn* in scenery poems; (ii) *sŭngnyŏn* 'development', called *kyŏngnyŏn* 'sight' in scenery poems; (iii) *chŏnnyŏn* 'twist', antitheme' or *chŏngnyŏn* 'emotion'; (iv) *kyŏllyŏn* 'ending', also called *nak* 'fall', *sa* 'thought' or *hap* 'drawing together'. *Kyŏl* is not a logical conclusion, but a hint of lingering emotion, doubt or expectation – even a question.

4) The essence of Tang prosody lies in the deployment of tones, called *p'yŏngchŭk-pŏp* 'rising and falling pattern', *kojŏ-ppŏp* 'high and low pattern', or *yŏm* 'screen'. The four tones of literary Chinese (*see* **Hunmin chŏngŭm**) are divided into two groups. Even-tone syllables are called *p'yŏng* 'even' or (in Korean) *yut'ŭn* 'low' (_) and can be used as rhymes (*r*). The other three tones are called *sang* or *nop'ŭn*, both meaning 'high', or *ch'ŭk* 'oblique' (/). None of the four tones is expressed in Korean pronunciation. Apart from the fact that all syllables ending in -*k*, -*l* or -*p* are high, tones must be checked in a **dictionary**, but Koreans are as adept with artificial tones as they are with artificial rhymes.
    The tone patterns of poetry are simple and aesthetically satisfying – somewhat like quantitative metre in Latin verse. In a line (*tchak*) of seven characters there are

grammatical breaks after the 2nd and 4th, the latter being the stronger of the two. The first six syllables have tones in alternate pairs:

$$\_\,\_\,/\,/\,\_\,\_ \quad \text{or} \quad /\,/\,\_\,\_\,/\,/.$$

Korean and Chinese poets say the rule for this is *isa pultong iyuk tae*, '2nd and 4th not the same, the 2nd and 6th correspond'. These are the crucial syllables; the 1st and 3rd need not adhere strictly to the pattern. Monotony is avoided by sometimes changing them. The 7th syllable may be of either tone but should be different from the 5th, which may have to be changed to ensure this. Thus there are four possible patterns for a line:

(A) _ _ / / _ _ /   (C) / / _ _ _ / /

(B) / / _ _ / / r   (D) _ _ / / / _ r.

(B and D rhyme (*r*), A and C do not. In line-forms A and B the 5th syllable is very occasionally given the same tone as the 7th.)

These four lines are used to create couplets (*yŏn'gu*) in which the two lines (*antchak* and *pakkatchak*) begin with different tones and the second line ends with a rhyme. The only two couplets that fill this prescription are AB and CD. The first and last couplets (*kiryŏn* and *kyŏllŏn*) of an 8-line poem must be different: if the first is AB, the last must be CD; and *vice versa*. The two middle couplets can be chosen freely, except that the 1st and 2nd may not be alike if the 3rd and 4th are also alike – stanzas ABAB-CDCD and CDCD-ABAB would fall into halves. There are therefore six possible stanza patterns, three *p'yŏnggi* 'even start' or *chŏnggyŏk* 'standard style', and three *ch'ŭkki* 'oblique start' or *p'yŏn'gyŏk* 'alternative style':

Standard	*Alternative*
AB CD AB CD	CD AB CD AB
(DB CD AB CD)	(BD AB CD AB)
AB CD CD CD	CD AB AB AB
AB AB AB CD	CD CD CD AB

In fact only the first of each style, known as *kasae yŏm* 'scissors (or criss-crossed) pattern', is much used. Since in 7-character verse the rhyme is virtually obligatory on the 1st line as well as the 2nd, 4th, 6th and 8th, the 1st couplet must take the irregular form shown in brackets. The full scheme is as follows (+ means tone optional):

```
+ _ + / / _ r          + / + _ / / r
+ / + _ / / r          + _ + / / _ r
+ / + _ _ / /          + _ + / _ _ /
+ _ + / / _ r          + / + _ / / r
+ _ + / _ _ /          + / + _ _ / /
+ / + _ / / r          + _ + / / _ r
+ / + _ _ / /          + _ + / _ _ /
+ _ + / / _ r          + / + _ / / r
```

5-character poems are written on the same patterns, omitting the first two syllables of each line. As a result, standard style 5-syllable stanzas are 'oblique start' and alternative style stanzas are 'even start'. The six 5-character patterns and six 7-character patterns together comprise the *sibi-ryŏm* 'twelve patterns'.

5) Parallelism or antithesis (*taeu*) is required in the two inner couplets (*taeryŏn*). All the characters of each line are paired with those of the other – noun for noun, adjective for adjective, number for number, verb for verb and so forth. This parallelism must be handled with care, so that it is not crude.

A quatrain (*chŏlgu*), which is a more succinct poem, consists of the first and last couplets of a *yulsi*, with the four-part structure shown in the four lines.

Four-part construction, rhymes and parallelism (but not, of course, tones) can be shown in translation. The following poem by Pyŏn Kyeryang (1369–1430) from *Tongmun-sŏn* 7 is written in standard *kasae-ryŏm* 7-character verse.

A peaceful village – piled-up peaks behind,
Some mulberry trees, two fields with furrows lined . . .
When seeking herbs, roaming the woods at ease,
When airing books, to doze in the sun resigned . . .
Through cloud-free river skies, wild geese fly home,
In moonlit bamboo groves, the nightjars grind:
It makes me sad to think of you in town,
And so I write fresh verse for you designed.

TAN'GUN 檀君

Divinity traditionally believed to have come to earth as progenitor of the Korean race (*see* **Foundation myths**). His name means 'mountain-birch ruler' (*see* **trees**) or 'altar ruler'. Early in the Japanese occupation he was worshipped as potential saviour of the nation by followers of the *Taejŏng-gyo* religious sect.

JAMES H. GRAYSON, 'The Myth of Tan'gun: A Dramatic Structural Analysis of a Korean Foundation Myth', *KJ*, 37/1, 1997

TAN'GUN ERA *Tan'gun kiwŏn* or *Tan'gi* 檀君紀元

During the Empire (1895–1910), years were sometimes numbered from the foundation of the Korean state by **Tan'gun**, which according to *Tongguk t'onggam* was in *wuchen* (K. *musin*) year of the legendary emperor Yao, identified as 2333 BC. This system was officially used by the Republic of Korea from 1948 to 1961 (Tan'gi 4281–4294).

TAN'GUN-GYO 檀君教

Another name for *Taejong-gyo*.

TANJONG, KING 端宗 (r. 1452–7)

The temple name of **Sejong**'s grandson, the boy Hongwi (1441–1457), canonised as Tanjong, hero of one of Korea's best known stories. He came to the throne in 1452, while still only ten years old. His uncle, Prince Suyang, became regent and soon usurped the throne, giving Hongwi the title *Sangwang*, 'former king'. In 1456 the men later known as *Su-yuksin*, 'Six Martyred Loyal Subjects', plotted to reinstate him, but failed. He was demoted to the rank and title of Prince Nosan (Nosan-gun) and exiled to Yŏngwŏl on the upper Han. The discovery of another plot to restore him in 1457 led to his assassination at the age of sixteen. He is buried at Yŏngwŏl. The usurper was later known as **Sejo**. The story is the subject of a novel by **Yi Kwangsu**. Much of the later **factionalism** in Korean politics stems from the aftermath of Tanjong's deposition and assassination.

See also **Six Martyred Subjects; Six Surviving Subjects**

TANO 端午 'definition of the centre'
The midsummer celebration on the 5th day of the 5th moon. The character *o* may be either the ordinary figure 5 or the 6th of the 12 branches. Both mean the central point of a series. This date may have been chosen rather than the summer solstice for the midsummer festival in order to avoid the intense solstitial heat. Yet odd-numbered days with the same number as the month have always been auspicious and the day is also called *chungo-jŏl* 'double fifth festival'. The old name *surinnal* was interpreted as 'wheel day' and flat round cakes of *ttŏk* coloured green with artemisia are still sometimes eaten. *Tano* was known in Silla. In Koryŏ it was celebrated with military sports (**polo**, **wrestling**, **swinging** and **stonefighting**). In Chosŏn times it changed into a day for washing hair, donning new summer clothes and exchanging **fans** as presents.

TAO QIAN 陶潛 (K. To Cham) (365–427)
Tao Qian was the Chinese poet best loved in Korea, where he was usually called To Chŏngjŏl (C. Tao Jingjie) or To Yŏnmyŏng (C. Yuanming), or sometimes Oryu-sŏnsaeng from the 'five willow-trees' he grew by his house. He is the archetype of the statesman who retired early from public office to cultivate his garden with wine, zither-strumming and meditation, representing 'fields and garden' (*chŏnwŏn*) poets rather than the land-scape schools. His famous *Guiqulai ci* (K. *Kwigŏrae-sa*, 'The Return') was quoted inces-santly in Korea, as was his Shangri-la story *Tohwa-wŏn-gi*, 'Record of Peach-blossom Spring'. A Korean woodblock edition of his works *To-Chŏngjŏl-chip* was issued in 1583.

TAXATION
Land constituted the principal basis for tax assessment under successive governments. Confucian unwillingness to develop **commerce** denied them the possibility of substantial regular income from this source.

THREE KINGDOMS
A heavy poll-tax was levied, principally on landowners, in grain, **textiles** and perhaps local products. A lighter burden was imposed on landless **peasants**.

UNIFIED SILLA
A land distribution system (*chŏngjŏn-je* 'able-bodied land system'), based on triennial census returns, was introduced in AD 722. It identified male family members of 20–60 years of age and provided data for tax and *corvée* registration. Taxes were payable mostly in produce, either to the government or to aristocratic landowners. As tax-exempt landed estates grew, government revenue declined, but peasants were still over-burdened. The weight of taxes contributed to the decline of central authority, rise of banditry, and eventually to the revolt that overthrew the dynasty.

KORYŎ
Tax dues on farmers were initially reduced but gradually rose again. They were assessed on land (graded into three levels of productive capacity) and adult household membership, and were mostly collected in grain. Rates varied from a quarter of the harvest, payable to the government, to as much as a half, payable to aristocratic landowners. There were also additional '**tribute**' taxes of cloth and local products (*t'ogong*), and particular levies on salt, ships and commerce.

EARLY CHOSŎN
Initial land redistribution and efforts to protect tenants against landlord extortion provided for annual land surveys (*see* **land reform**), but were never properly

implemented. Land tax was fixed at 10 per cent of the harvest, reduced in 1444 to 5 per cent when King **Sejong** introduced the Tribute Tax Law (*kongpŏp*). But the system for recording land holdings and grading their yields was open to abuse, and landlords' dues commonly increased peasants' obligations to 50 per cent. In addition, the Tribute Tax levied annual quotas of local produce and manufactured goods, and because of the corruption of tax gatherers this often proved far more onerous than the land dues. On special occasions local officials were also called on to send tribute gifts to the court. Peasants commuted their *corvée* and military service into heavy payments of cloth, while government **slaves** owed a poll-tax in lieu of their *corvée*.

LATE CHOSŎN

The *yangban* generally enjoyed tax exemption. Producers of numerous items of daily use, including salt, fish, cloth, **paper**, **ginseng**, and timber were taxed. **Merchants** paid commercial taxes. Yet despite the fact that the Japanese invasions (*see* **Imjin Wars**) severely reduced the amount of taxable land in use, and still less was correctly declared for fiscal purposes, land tax remained the principal, though declining, source of government income. In 1653 the rate was fixed at one-thirtieth of the harvest. The introduction of *Taedongpŏp* ('Uniform Tax Law') in 1608, extended through most of the country by 1708, added a surtax payable in **rice** or cloth as a replacement for the Tribute Tax. It aimed to standardise the tax system and improve revenues through a renewed emphasis on land registration. The goal of uniformity was commendable, but dues soon became commuted into cash payment, a development which had important economic and social effects as the use of **coinage** spread, but injustices and excessive demands continued to drive peasants from the land, until in 1750 King **Yŏngjo** introduced the *Kyunyŏk-pŏp* ('Equal Tax Law') in an unsuccessful attempt to ameliorate their situation. Though again well-intentioned, its effect was predictably limited because the *yangban* remained tax-exempt. A combination of the so-called *samjŏng*, 'three levies' (the land tax, the **military cloth tax**, and the **rice loan system**) and further, illegal, extortions by tax-gatherers and landlords continued to place heavy burdens on the peasantry. For centuries large areas of land belonging to the royal clan, their supporters (*see* '**Meritorious Subjects**'), private academies (*sŏwŏn*), and Buddhist temples, not to mention persons with unspecified special influence, had been exempt from taxation. In the mid-19th century the **Taewŏn'gun** endeavoured to improve fiscal revenues by bringing much of it back into assessment and by reforming the *samjŏng*. Yet any attempt to spread the load more equitably between lower and upper classes was contradicted by the introduction of additional taxes on land (*kyŏltujŏn*) and the transportation of goods through the gates of Seoul as a means of financing the rebuilding of the **Kyŏngbok Palace** in 1865. Improvements were again sought with the creation of the Ministry of Finance (*T'akchi-bu*) in 1894 (*see* **Kabo reforms**). Nevertheless, continued economic pressures on the peasantry were a major factor leading to the outbreak of the **Tonghak Rebellion**.

COLONIAL PERIOD

The Japanese introduced new taxes in every decade of the colonial period, including an income tax in 1920. Some of the growing fiscal revenue contributed to investment in Korea's economic modernisation but more went towards meeting Japanese military expenses, and the suffering of urban and rural workers alike increased.

PAK GI-HYUK, 'Chŏng Yag-yong's Economic Thought with Special Reference to Land System and Taxation,' *KJ*, 17/9, 1977

See also **Class system**; **Military service**

TEA
Tea was known in Silla, but did not become popular in China until late Song. It was soon grown and drunk by the upper classes and Buddhist monks in Korea. At the end of Koryŏ it almost disappeared, perhaps because the standing of Buddhist monks declined and most tea cultivation was in their hill-monasteries. Tea bushes are still grown in a few places in the south-western hills and famous varieties have pleasant names like *chaksŏl* 'linnets' tongues'. All are drunk as green teas.
See also **drinks; Hŏ Paengnyŏn**

TEHERAN CONFERENCE (1943)
Held in December 1943 between Franklin D. Roosevelt, Winston Churchill and Joseph Stalin. It was here that Stalin was persuaded to agree that the Soviet Union would enter the war against Japan three months after the conclusion of the war in Europe. He also accepted Roosevelt's proposition that foreign **trusteeship** over Korea should last forty years, even though the American intention was to reduce the chance of future Russian domination of the peninsula. This decision was greeted with fury by Korean leaders such as Syngman Rhee (**Yi Sŭngman**) and **Kim Ku**.

TEN GARRISONS *See* **Military systems**

TEN INJUNCTIONS *Sip Hunyo* or *Hunyo Sipcho* 十訓要
Before his death in 943, **Wang Kŏn**, later canonised as Koryŏ T'aejo, left ten exhortations to his successors.

1) The state is based on **Buddhism**: honour both *Sŏn* and *Kyo* traditions.
2) Do not allow more temples unless they accord with the *p'ungsu* principles of **Tosŏn**.
3) The eldest son should succeed to the throne. If he is unworthy choose the next. If he too is unworthy, choose the next, and so on down the list.
4) We have always followed Tang (China); do not imitate the **Khitan**.
5) The state is founded on good *p'ungsu* and the site of P'yŏngyang is crucial. Visit there every 4th year for 100 days.
6) Maintain the *P'algwan-hoe* and *Yŏndŭng-hoe* festivals.
7) Rule like the classic kings, with fairness, judiciously taking advice and not overtaxing the people. (Here Wang expresses views reminiscent of the Mencian ideals of true kingship, urging the ruler to put the interests of his people first.)
8) South of the Ch'a Pass (near Kongju) and beyond the Kŭm River the people are as difficult as the terrain. Do not give them major appointments or marry them into the royal family. (This reflects both *p'ungsu*, and the legacy of **Paekche** enmity.)
9) Practise no favouritism, pay fair emoluments, and always take care of the army.
10) Study the ancient kings (of China) and keep the classic 'No Complacency' as your motto.

The testament is now recorded in the *Koryŏ-sa*.

TEN OX PICTURES *sibudo* 十牛圖
A series of pictures of a boy and an ox, popular throughout East Asia, that appears in Korean temple murals. In books the pictures are accompanied by verses and commentary. They can be traced to the **Song dynasty**, when they were used by monks of the Chinese *Linji* school of *Chan* (*Sŏn*) **Buddhism**. At first they seem to have been sets of five or more pictures showing an ox changing progressively from a black animal

to a white one; and the last picture was an empty circle. Guoan Zhiyuan in the 12th century used what is now the best known version in Korea: (1) *simu*, seeking the ox; (2) *kyŏnjŏk*, seeing its tracks; (3) *kyŏnu*, seeing the ox; (4) *tugu*, catching the ox; (5) *mogu*, tending the ox; (6) *kiu-gwiga*, riding the ox home; (7) *mangu-jonin*, ox forgotten, man alone; (8) *inu-gumang*, man and ox both out of mind; (9) *panbon-hwanwŏn*, return to the source; (10) *ipchŏn-susu*, entering the market with open hands.

The ox, a Sanskrit rebus on Gautama, is an image of **Buddha**. Pictures 1–7 are a parable of attaining buddhahood, culminating in the empty circle of the 8th picture. Pictures 9 and 10 form an epilogue of enlightenment in mind and in daily life: 9 showing apricot blossom, mountains and streams, 10 a boy with an old hermit standing in a busy market. The 6th has made a deep impression on Korea, where the image of a boy playing a flute as he rides an ox in the twilight is an appealing symbol, used by the poet **Han Yongun** among others.

TEN SYMBOLS OF IMMORTALITY *Sip changsaeng* 十長生 *See* **Longevity, Ten symbols of**

TEXTILES
Sericulture and weaving are vouched for in the 2nd and 3rd centuries BC, but must have been known much earlier. Netting too must have been an ancient craft. **Silk**, linen, other vegetable fibres and cotton have been woven for **dress**. **Felt** may not have been known before there was cultural contact with the pastoral peoples of the north and west, and was never used in very large quantities. Nor were carpets made, not least because there was no production of wool. Hand-knitting arrived with western influence in the 20th century to be followed by machine-knitting, for which Korea now holds a leading place in the world market.
YI SONG-MI, ed., *Korean Costumes and Textiles*, New York: IBM Gallery of Science and Art, 1992

THIRD REPUBLIC (1963–72) *Chesam konghwaguk* 第三共和國
Period of elected civilian government under Park Chung Hee (**Pak Chŏnghŭi**) following two years of his own **military junta**. He held the presidency for three terms under the **constitution** adopted in December 1962, being elected first on 15 October 1963. In 1967 he was re-elected against a renewed challenge from **Yun Posŏn (New Democratic Party)** and in 1971 from the same Party's **Kim Taejung**, but his Democratic Republican Party had to amend the constitution on 14 September 1969 in order for him to stand the third time. Kim not unwarrantedly accused Park of turning South Korea into a militaristic police state, far from the democracy envisaged at the inauguration of the Third Republic. It was true that Park had clamped down on the press, **students**, and political opponents from within his own party as well as without, and that the population endured many limitations on their freedom in the name of defence against the communist threat. The activities of the **Korean Central Intelligence Agency** were widely feared, and stories of human rights and civil liberties infringements, especially in the prisons, abounded. Attempts to fire the younger generation with political idealism through the 1968 National Education Charter stirred up as much opposition as support for the régime. Yet Park's conviction that priority must be given to economic growth laid the foundations for remarkable industrial and social developments in future decades. The first two Five Year Plans (1962–6 and 1967–71) boosted productivity and exports, albeit at the cost of an underpaid workforce and imbalanced growth of metropolitan and provincial regions. Tight central control encouraged the

appearance of *chaebŏl*, powerful manufacturing conglomerates characterised by cooperation with officialdom. The *Saemaŭl Undong* ('New Community Movement') was inaugurated with the intention of raising rural living standards, promoting self-help, and stimulating agricultural productivity. Foreign relations improved and contributed to more foreign investment, on which the economic recovery depended. In 1965 a treaty was concluded with Japan (*see* **Korea-Japan Treaty**) and Korean troops were sent to Vietnam, thereby improving relations with the United States. But as well as sowing seeds for necessary change, all of these features of life under the Third Republic engendered opposition, and in 1972 heightened tension with the North. Uncertainty resulting from the Sino-American rapprochement persuaded the government that Park's powers must be tightened and his prospects of rule extended even further. On 17 October the government dissolved the National Assembly and proposed the new *Yusin* **Constitution**, bringing the Third Republic to an end.
PAK CHI YOUNG, 'The Third Republic Constitution of Korea: an Analysis,' *WPQ* XXI no.1, 1968

THIRTY-EIGHTH PARALLEL *Samsipp'al-do-sŏn* 三十八度
The 38th line of latitude north crosses the west coast of Korea at a point slightly south of Haeju, in Hwanghae province, and north of Kaesŏng, in Kyŏnggi. Passing to the north of Ch'unch'ŏn, Kangwŏn province, and through the Taebaek Mountains it reaches the east coast south of Yangyang. Following the Japanese surrender in 1945, it served the western allies as a supposedly temporary line of demarcation until the election of an independent national government could be supervised. It divided Korea into a northern zone supervised by a Soviet-backed régime and a southern zone initially administered by the **American Military Government**. National elections were never agreed, however, and it continued as an arbitrary frontier accepted by people in neither north nor south. Frequent clashes occurred along it until the outbreak of the **Korean War** on 25 June 1950. As North Korean troops crossed the line on that day, **Kim Ilsŏng** claimed that they did so in response to armed incursions from the South. There was no truth in this, but its penetration in return by United Nations forces on 9 October was one of the decisive events of the War, leading as it did to Chinese intervention.
See also **DMZ; Moscow Conference; Potsdam Conference; Yalta Conference**

THIRTY-THREE HEAVENS *samsipsam ch'ŏn* 三十三天
Though regarded in East Asia as a Buddhist cosmological concept, as well as a paradigm of the believer's progress to buddhahood, the 33 heavens are of Indian origin, and were perhaps originally based on an astronomical principle. They reflect the idea of a tripartite universe. All desires gradually diminish as one progresses through the six heavens of the world of desire (S. *devaloka*, K. *yokkye*): (1) the heaven of the **Four Kings**; (2) the heaven of **Indra**; (3) the heaven of **Yama**; (4) the Tushita Heaven of Maitreya; (5) the heaven of delight in transformation; and (6) the heaven of complete transformation. Then follow the 18 *dhyana* heavens of the world of form (S. *rupaloka*, K. *saekkye*), three groups of three heavens and one of nine. The final nine heavens are in the world without form (S. *arupaloka*, K. *musaekkye*) where one rises to the apogee of selflessness. This concept explains the 33 strokes of the end-of-**curfew** bell in Korea.

THIRTY-THREE INDEPENDENCE SIGNATORIES, THE 三十三人
The **declaration of independence** read in Seoul's **Pagoda Park** on 1 March 1919 was signed by 33 men:

1) fifteen *Ch'ŏndogyo* believers, most of whom were *Tonghak* veterans: **Son Pyŏnghui** (1861–1921), Ch'oe In (1878–?1950), **O Sech'ang** (journalist and calligrapher, 1864–1953), Im Yehwan (1865–1949), Kwŏn Pyŏngdŭk (1868–1944), Kwŏn Tongjin (1861–1947), Hong Kijo (1868–1938), Hong Pyŏnggi (1868–1941), Kim Wan'gyu (1877–1949), Na Inhyŏp (1871–1951), Na Yonghwan (1863–1936), Pak Chunsŭng (1866–1921), Yang Hanmuk (1862–1919), Yi Chonghun (1856–1935), Yi Chongil (1858–1925);

2) sixteen **Protestant** Christians: Chŏng Ch'unsu (1875–1951), Ch'oe Sŏngmo (1873–1936), Kil Sŏnju (1869–1935), Kim Ch'angjun (1889–1959), Kim Pyŏngjo (1876–1947), O Hwayŏng (1880–?1950), Pak Hŭido (1889–1951), Pak Tongwan (1885–1941), Sin Hongsik (1872–1937), Sin Sŏkku (1875–1950), Yang Chŏnbaek (1869–1923), Yi Inhwan (a.k.a. Yi Sŭnghun, 1889–1981, *see* **Osan School**), Yi Kapsŏng (1864–1930), Yi Myŏngnyong (1873–1956), Yi P'ilchu (1869–1932), and Yu Yŏdae (1878–1937);

3) two Buddhists: **Han Yongun** (1897–1944) and Paek Yongsŏng (1865–1940).

THOMAS, ROBERT JERMAIN (1840–66)

A Welsh member of the London Missionary Society who started work in Shanghai in 1863. When at Zhifu in 1865, he met Korean Catholic refugees from the Hŭngsŏn **Taewŏn'gun**'s persecution. He was inspired to evangelise Korea and immediately visited the island of Paengnyŏng-do for two months. A year later he took passage on the *General Sherman* and was killed when the ship was destroyed at P'yŏngyang, becoming Korea's first Protestant missionary martyr.

See also **Protestants**

THREE BONDS AND FIVE RELATIONSHIPS *Samgang Oryun* 三綱五倫

The basis for the Confucian definition of political and social responsibilities espoused as state philosophy during the Chosŏn dynasty (*see* **Confucianism**). The three bonds were those linking the subject to the ruler (loyalty), children to parents (filial piety), and women to men (hierarchy). The five relationships were those between the ruler and his ministers, father and son, elder brother and younger brother, husband and wife, and friend and friend. Each was conceived primarily in terms of the duties of the inferior to the superior, although the relationships were understood to be reciprocal and recognised the rulers' responsibilities towards those dependent on them.

'THREE GREAT BAMBOO PAINTERS' *sam-juk* 三竹

These were **Yi Chŏng** (T'anun, b. 1541), Yu Tŏkchang (Suun, 1694–1774) and **Sin Wi** (Chaha, 1769–1845).

THREE-JEWEL MONASTERIES, THE *Sambo-jongch'ul* 三寶宗刹

Three of the largest monasteries in Korea are traditionally regarded as representing the *triratna* '**three jewels**' **of Buddhism**. Tongdo-sa represents the Buddha (*pul*), because it holds relics of Sakyamuni in a **stupa** beyond the north wall of the main temple, which is open so that the stupa can be seen, rather than a large buddha image on the altar. This is the traditional guardian monastery of the Vinaya or discipline of the monks. **Haein-sa**, with its unique collection of **sutras** on wooden printing blocks, also kept in two halls to the north of the main temple, is the monastery of the Dharma (*pŏp*). These are both in south Kyŏngsang. The great monastery of Songgwang-sa in south Chŏlla is the representative of the Sangha, the monastic order (*sŭng*).

THREE JEWELS OF BUDDHISM *sambo* 三寶
The objects of the *trisarana* (K. *samgwi*), which is the nearest thing Buddhism has to a credal formula: 'I take refuge in the Buddha; I take refuge in the law; I take refuge in the community of monks' (K. *Kwi-ŭi-bul, kwi-ŭi-bop, kwi-ŭi-sŭng*; S.*Buddham saranam gacchami, Dharmam saranam gacchami, Sangham saranam gacchami.*)

THREE KINGDOMS *Samguk* 三國
Name given to the period prior to the establishment in AD 668 of the first dynasty to rule the whole of the Korean peninsula, the Unified Silla. The three kingdoms were those of **Paekche** (destroyed 660), **Koguryŏ** (succumbed 668) and **Silla** itself. Despite traditions cited in *Samguk sagi* ('Historical Records of the Three States') ascribing the foundation of the three kingdoms to the specific dates 18 BC, 37 BC and 57 BC respectively, their earliest establishment as sovereign states cannot be so precisely identified. However, the necessary qualifications of bureaucratic and social organisation had developed in all three by the early 4th century, and in each case influences from China and especially the adoption of **Confucianism** played an important part in progress towards the evolution of state power. Paekche and Koguryŏ adopted the Chinese title *wang* (king) for their rulers in the late 3rd century, Silla in the 6th (*see* **Silla kingly titles**). All three accepted a status and rôle as tributaries of the Middle Kingdom and sent embassies to the courts of the Northern and Southern Dynasties, and later the Sui and Tang, but their characteristics were quite different and were influenced by their geographical situations on the peninsula. Koguryŏ, with the harsher climate and terrain and the toughening experience of resisting Chinese expansion through the **Liaodong** region, was the most warlike. Paekche, less vulnerable to attack but well placed to benefit from peaceful contacts with China, Japan, and their neighbouring Koreans, was the most strongly influenced by **Buddhism** and was the gentlest in cultural forms. In Silla, more remote from the mainland than the other two, Chinese-style civilisation took longer to develop, but when it did so was turned to greatest ultimate advantage. Despite such native institutions as the bone-rank system (*see* **kolp'um**) and the Korean version of **shamanism**, the power of the Unified Silla kingdom was based squarely on the Chinese inheritance shared by all three earlier kingdoms.

Like the Warring States period in China, the Three Kingdoms saw the making and breaking of alliances without compunction and with opportunist reference to individual state interest. The same was true of the involvement of their suzerain China in peninsular politics. The principle of even-handedness among tributaries was applied only when it did not compromise Chinese national interests.

Culture in the Three Kingdoms period adopted Chinese forms in education (*see* ***T'aehakkam***), the written script, philosophy and cosmology, religious ideas, burial practices (*see* **tombs**), **music**, **painting** and **sculpture**. Some of its uniquely Korean manifestations, however, were themselves outstanding, such as the Paekche tiles finely decorated with landscape designs, and the grey stoneware warriors on horseback from Silla tombs. Moreover the **iron** crafts of the southern state of **Kaya**, contemporaneous with the Three Kingdoms, were respected far afield, and migrants from Silla, Paekche and Kaya went to southern Japan as teachers and traders.
KUNIO HIRANO, 'The Yamato State and Korea in the Fourth and Fifth Centuries,' *ACA*, 31, 1977; JOHN C. JAMIESON, *The* Samguk Sagi *and the Unification Wars*, PhD thesis, University of California, Berkeley, 1969; LEE HONG-JIK, 'Historical Transition of the Three Kingdoms,' *KJ*, 6/4, 1966

THREE KINGDOMS, LATER 後三國
Period developing before the eventual collapse of Unified Silla rule. Later Paekche (K. Hubaekje) was formed in 892 in the south-west by a peasant leader, **Kyŏn Hwŏn**, with its capital at Wansan (modern Chŏnju), and Later Koguryŏ (K. Hugoguryŏ) in 901 in the north by an aristocratic soldier-monk, **Kungye**, with its capital at Ch'ŏrwŏn. The tyrannical Kungye was assassinated and succeeded by his subordinate **Wang Kŏn** in 918, who renamed the state Koryŏ and transferred the capital to Songak (modern **Kaesŏng**). In a triangular competition all too reminiscent of the original Three Kingdoms period, Later Paekche sacked **Kyŏngju** in 927: Silla appealed to Koryŏ for help. Wang Kŏn attacked Ch'ŏrwŏn but then went on to overpower his erstwhile but brief ally, reuniting the country and inaugurating his own dynasty in 936.

'THREE ORCHID PAINTERS' *sam nan* 三蘭
The most famous painters of orchids – the most esteemed of the **'four gentlemen'** – in the modern period are Yi Haŭng, brush name Sŏkp'a 'stony bank' (the **Taewŏn'gun**), 1820–98; Kim Ŭngwŏn, brush name Soho 'little lake', 1855–1921; and **Min Yŏngik**, brush name Yunmi 'rue window', 1860–1914.

THREE PERFECTIONS *sam chŏl* 三絕
The complementary arts of **painting, calligraphy**, and **poetry**. In the sinicized traditional society of the Korean upper classes, all three were ideally not only appreciated but also practised by the true scholar. They came together when a poetic inscription was appended to a painting. Its brushwork should be in a style appropriate to that used in the picture, and the ideas it expressed should enhance the picture's visual message. The placing of the inscription was integral to the balance of the composition.
MICHAEL SULLIVAN, *The Three Perfections: Chinese Painting, Poetry, and Calligraphy*, London: Thames and Hudson, 1974

THREE RECLUSES, THE *sam ŭn* 三隱
Three Confucian scholars, all with *ŭn*, 'recluse' in their brush names, who remained loyal to Koryŏ and declined to serve the Chosŏn dynasty: P'oŭn **Chŏng Mongju** ; Mogŭn **Yi Saek**, and Toŭn **Yi Sungin**. In some lists Toŭn is replaced by Yaun **Kil Chae**.

TIANJIN, TREATY/ CONVENTION OF (1885)
Agreement signed on 18 April 1885 by **Li Hongzhang** and **Itō Hirobumi** in the aftermath of the *Kapsin* **Coup**. By agreeing to the withdrawal of both Chinese and Japanese troops it nominally acknowledged Korean independence, but in fact left Chinese influence over Korea unimpaired. It forbad either country to provide the Koreans with military training, and stipulated that in future, either country should notify the other of any intention to send troops to Korea. This clause was observed in 1894 in the context of the **Tonghak Rebellion**, when China responded to the Korean court's request for help. The Treaty is also known as the Li-Itō Agreement.
See also **China, relations with; Yuan Shikai**.

TIGERS
Probably the most popular image in Korean folk painting and decoration. The north-east Asian race of tiger, large and light-coloured, survived throughout Korea into

the early years of the 20th century, an unseen threat in the hills, a symbol of power, king of animals, able to change into human form. Because of its courage, the tiger was embroidered on the *hyungp'ae* of military officials. It was the mountain spirit (**Sansin**) in many a village shrine, the satirical image of rapacious landlords and magistrates in numberless poems and stories; yet it was thought stupid and easily outwitted by the **fox**.

T'O 吐 *See* **Idu**

TOBACCO
Tobacco seed arrived in Korea shortly before 1620 from Japan, where it had been introduced by European merchants. (It had arrived in Europe from America during the 1550s and travelled from Europe to China and Japan during the latter half of the 16th century.) In Korea it was first known as *tambago*, from the Fujian dialect pronunciation of Chinese *danbagu*, which was *tampakko*. This is clearly derived from the word 'tobacco' and was later shortened to *tambae*. The intrusive nasalisation may be from a Pacific source. The custom of not smoking before an elder or superior is said to date from an instruction given by **Prince Kwanghae**, who was deposed in 1623. Pipe-smoking spread rapidly and tobacco cultivation has ever since provided a cash-crop in central and south Korea. A profitable export trade to China was developed.

TODANG 都堂
Policy-deciding meetings of the highest level of aristocratic government in the Koryŏ period, sometimes described as a Privy Council (*Chaech'u*).
See also **Government, central**

TOHWA-SŎ 圖畫署
Office of Painting under the Chosŏn dynasty. It had been preceded in the Unified Silla period by the *Ch'aejŏn* (Office of Painting) and in the Koryŏ by the *Tohwa-wŏn* (Painting Academy). It came under the Board of Rites and originally preserved its Koryŏ title, but was downgraded to *Tohwa-sŏ* in about 1471. The number of its members, who were admitted to government service on the basis of practical tests, was increased from 15 to 30 in 1746. They were given official ranks, normally no higher than sixth **grade**, and often held minor military posts. **An Kyŏn** was promoted exceptionally to the fourth grade. Their duties were to supply works of art required by the court, but they were poorly paid. Moreover, although professional artists enjoyed more respect in Korea than they did in China, they were members of the *chungin* class, and many *Tohwa-sŏ* painters and calligraphers who are now recognised as outstanding artists were in their own day scorned by members of the *yangban* class who painted as amateurs. The Office was closed down by the Japanese in 1911. Its last appointee was Cho Sŏkchin (1853–1920), who transferred as a professor to its successor, the *Sŏhwa Misurwŏn*.

TOKKAEBI 'goblins'
Tokkaebi, goblins who appear from blood-stained clothing, and at night from rotting logs and old houses, are undoubtedly derived from phosphorescent phenomena. They are puckish: they will lead travellers astray and play jokes, but may also be helpful. *Tokkaebi* is written in Chinese as *tokkak-kwi* 'one-leg spirit', but this is a false etymology.

TOKSŎ-DANG 讀書堂 'hall for reading books'
In 1426 the principle of giving government officials sabbatical leave for study was established. In 1492 a disused Buddhist monastery at Yongsan, near the **Han River** south of Seoul, was refurbished for this purpose and called *Toksŏ-dang*. In 1777 it was absorbed into the *Kyujang-gak*.

TŎKSU 'Virtuous long life' **PALACE** 德壽宮
Was originally named Kyŏngun-gung ('Blessed fate palace'). It was built as a detached villa by King **Sŏngjong** for his elder brother, Prince Wŏlsan, who had been passed over in succession to King Yejong. It was used as the principal royal palace from 1593–1615, then became a subsidiary palace again after the rebuilding of the **Ch'angdŏk Palace**. In 1897, **King Kojong** transferred his main residence there, deriving some sense of security from its proximity to the British, Russian and American Legations following the Japanese murder of **Queen Min** and attempts to unseat him. In 1907, when Kojong was forced to abdicate, his son **Sunjong** bestowed the present name upon the palace in his honour.
   A Renaissance-style stone building, known as the *Sokcho-jŏn*, stands in one corner of the grounds. It was designed by the Welsh architect J. R. **Harding**, a member of the Imperial Maritime Customs Service in China, and built by an Englishman, H. W. Davidson. The work was completed in 1909, and the building was used after World War Two by the **US-Soviet Joint Commission** for the Reunification of Korea.
See also **Kyŏngbok Palace; Unhyŏn Palace**

TOKTO 獨島 (Toksŏm) 'Lonely isles'
Two large uninhabitable volcanic rocks with surrounding reefs, in the East Sea 50 miles east of **Ullŭng-do**. Westerners first knew them as the Liancourt Rocks, a name derived from that of a French survey vessel, but from 1855 British charts showed them as the Hornet Isles, named after a ship in the China Fleet. Japan laid claim to both Ullŭng-do and Tokto in the second half of the 17th century, but appeared to accept Korean sovereignty over them at the beginning of the Meiji period. In 1905 both Ullŭng-do and Tokto were annexed as part of the Japanese **protectorate**. Since 1952 Korea and Japan have both claimed ownership, but failed even to consider their disagreement under the **Korea-Japan Treaty** of 1965. Tokto is now guarded by the Korean navy, and a museum and research centre for Tokto was opened on Ullŭng-do in 1997.
'110th Special Issue on Tokdo,' *KO* XXVIII/3, 1997; '30th Anniversary Special Issue on Tokdo', *KO* XXIX/1, 1998

TOLLYŎNG-BU 敦寧府 'Council of the royal affines'
A Chosŏn body to care for the interests of those married into the royal family, who were called *tollyŏng* 'the regarded and respected'. Some of them sat on this council, which was led by a 1st **grade** senior and assisted by 11 officials.

TOMBS
The earliest native tombs on the Korean peninsula are **dolmens**. Evidence excavated from the stone cists, or from the chambers beneath the large covering stones, suggests that they were élite burials. They were built between the 10th and 3rd centuries BC; poorer members of society were buried in **pottery** coffin jars.
   The Three Kingdoms followed varied burial practices before each adopted Chinese tomb styles. In early **Koguryŏ** the body was placed on a stone base, surrounded with

stones, and surmounted by a rectangular platform or pyramid of large dressed stones. *Changgun-ch'ong*, 'the General's Tomb', at Ji'an, Jilin province, China, is an example of the latter kind. Discovered in 1905, it is built of 1,100 stone blocks and rises in steps to a height of eleven metres. It may be the tomb of King Changsu. **Paekche** followed the same style, and in addition buried bodies in plain wooden coffins. In **Silla**, a stone coffin was placed in a pit, but examples also survive around **Kyŏngju** of a particular form of royal and aristocratic burial. In such a case, the coffin was laid in a timber chamber, which was then surrounded by stones and buried within an earthen mound. The tomb might contain one or more chambers and be used for single or multiple burials, and could be entered through an entrance tunnel. On the Korean peninsula, this style was unique to Silla and its use continued into the Unified Silla period. But it is also found at Pazyryk in Kazakhstan (part of Siberia), which, together with design elements of the **gold crowns** found in Three Kingdoms tombs, indicates cultural influence descending from the continental mainland. Two linked mounds, each containing a single chamber, are known as 'gourd-shaped' tombs. An example of this type is *Hwangnam-daech'ong*, 'Great Hwangnam Tomb', opened in 1973–5. Other important tombs excavated at Kyŏngju have been given such descriptive titles as *Ch'ŏnma-ch'ong* (**'Heavenly Horse Tomb'**), *Hoch'on-ch'ong* ('Lotus Vase Tomb'), *Kŭmgwan-ch'ong* (**'Gold Crown Tomb'**), *Kŭmnyŏng-ch'ong* ('Gold Bell Tomb'), *Ŭnnyŏng-ch'ong* ('Silver Bell Tomb'), *Singni-ch'ong* ('Decorated Shoes Tomb'), *Pubu-ch'ong* ('Husband and Wife Tomb'), and *Sŏbong-ch'ong* ('Swedish Phoenix Tomb', so-called because the Swedish Prince Gustavus Adolphus helped to excavate it in 1926, and a gold crown found there was decorated with three phoenixes; *sŏ* also means 'auspicious', and the tomb is also known as the 'Auspicious Phoenix Tomb'). It is likely that as well as kings, members of the aristocracy were buried in such large tombs. In 1985 a group of over fifty tombs of various types of construction was discovered in the Wŏlsŏng-no district of Kyŏngju.

With the spread of Chinese civilisation, Han styles of tomb construction were gradually adopted in all three kingdoms, mainly from the 4th century onwards. These consisted of a timber- or brick-lined vault with connecting side-rooms, entered through an ante-chamber at the bottom of a downward-sloping tunnel. The whole was surmounted with a large earthen mound. An early example of this kind is that known as *Kujong-dong*, from which iron **armour** and weapons have been recovered: this may be identifiable as the tomb of King Mich'u of Silla (r. 262–84), described in the *Samguk sagi* as the 'Great Tomb'. In Koguryŏ, the style was followed in AD 357 for the burial of the Chinese émigré General Dong Shou (K. Tongsu) at Anak, Hwanghae province. In Paekche, a well-preserved example is the brick tomb of King **Muryŏng** (d. 523) at **Kongju**, constructed according to the style of the neighbouring Chinese Southern Liang dynasty although its contents are all local **Paekche** products of the highest quality.

In the far south and south-west, the discovery of a cemetery at **Yangdong-ni** in **Kimhae** has revealed the successive use between the 1st century BC and 5th century AD of wooden coffin tombs, tombs with inner and outer coffins, and finally stone chamber tombs. Meanwhile, however, the rulers of **Mahan** continued to be buried in pottery coffin jars until the 6th century, when the building of stone chambers developed and the use of jars was superseded. Twelve mound tombs with square frontages discovered in 1994 near **Kwangju**, Chŏlla Namdo, contained decorated coffin jars, and their similarity to contemporary Japanese examples is evidence for contact between southern Korea and northern Kyushu. Further suggestion of international exchange is provided by pieces of **glass** from Roman Syria, and possibly Iran, discovered in Silla tombs.

The decoration of walls and ceilings in Koguryŏ tombs indicates Chinese cultural influence. Wall paintings also provide valuable evidence of ceremonial and social activities. examples include the grand military procession in the retired Chinese official Dong Shou's tomb at Anak (*see ŭigwe*); the wrestlers from the 5th–6th century tomb of *Kakcho-ch'ong* and the dancers from *Muyŏn-ch'ong* ('Tomb of the Dancers', 6th century) at **Kungnaesŏng**, modern Tonggou, near Ji'an. The occurrence of Buddhist iconography amid the decorations is evidence of the élite interest in the religion: almost 80 per cent of painted Koguryŏ tombs contain examples of this kind. Nevertheless, the design of the gold crowns found in royal Paekche and Silla tombs suggests that **shamanism** had a strong influence on the leadership.

KIM BYUNG-MO, *Aspects of Brick and Stone Tomb Construction in China and South Korea – Ch'in to Shilla Period*, DPhil Thesis, University of Oxford, 1978; W.Y.KIM & R.PEARSON, 'Three Royal Tombs: New Discoveries in Korean Archaeology,' *Archaeology* 30/5, 1977; J.W.LEE, 'Silla Tombs in the Kyongju Basin: a Critical Review,' *JSSH*, vol. 64, 1986; SARAH NELSON, 'Protohistoric Burial Patterns in Korea', *KJ*, 36/2, 1996; HYUNG IL PAI, 'The Politics of Korea's Past: The Legacy of Japanese Colonial Archaeology in the Korean Peninsula,' *EAH*, 7, 1994; BARRY TILL, 'Tomb Statuary of Korea,' *AOA*, 22/6, 1992
See also **Koryŏ-jang Sogan-ni**; **tree-top burial**

TONGA ILBO 東亞日報 'East Asia Daily'

Newspaper founded in 1920 by Yi Sanghyŏp, **Kim Sŏngsu** and others which initially functioned as a heavily censored means of publishing Japanese-approved information in the Korean language, yet which succeeded in expressing nationalist sentiment throughout the colonial period. It supported student organisations and the anti-illiteracy campaign of 1929–34. It suffered periodic suspension for its anti-Japanese opinions, and publication was forbidden for ten months in 1936–7 after its provocative deletion of the Japanese flag from the picture of the Korean medallists in the Berlin **Olympic Games**. Along with other Korean-language **newspapers** it was shut down in 1940. It re-emerged in August 1945 to resume its support for Korean independence with a denunciation of the **Moscow Agreement**. Critics of the paper sometimes accuse Kim Sŏngsu of being a Japanese collaborator and point to the fact that as the founder of the great landlord corporation, Samyang, he and his newspaper represented bourgeois authoritarianism. They accuse the paper's ownership both for its lack of support for Korean industrial labourers demanding better treatment from their employers in the mid-1920s, and more than half a century later for its unsympathetic reporting of the Koch'ang Tenant Farmers' protest movement in 1985–7 (*see minjung* **movement**).
See also **Chosŏn Ilbo**

TONGDAE-MUN 東大門 'East Great Gate'

The great east gate of Seoul. It was built in 1399 as one of the four main entrances to the new capital through the city wall which had been constructed three years previously. When it was reconstructed in 1869 a semi-circular barbican was added in front of it. Together with the south gate (*see* **Namdae-mun**) it is one of the last remaining examples of the Chosŏn fortifications of Seoul. In 1996 the government re-asserted its formal name of Hŭngin-ji-mun 'Gate of Delight in Goodness'.

TONGGOU (near Ji'an, Jilin, China) 通講 *See* **Kongnaesŏng**; **Kwanggaet'o**

TONGGUK MUNHŎN PIGO *See* **Chŭngbo munhŏn pigo**

TONGGUK PYŎNGGAM 東國兵鑑 'Eastern Land Soldiers' Mirror'
Compiled by order of King Munjong in 1451, a description of the wars on Korea's northern borders, beginning with the creation of the **Lelang** commanderies by Han Wudi and concluding with **Yi Sŏnggye**'s campaigns to found the Chosŏn dynasty. It draws on Chinese historical sources and *Samguk sagi*.

TONGGUK T'ONGGAM 東國通鑑 'Complete Mirror of Korea'
The first history of Korea written by Koreans, completed in 1484. It was edited by a royal commission led by **Sŏ Kŏjŏng**, based on earlier official histories and *Samguk yusa*, and modelled on Sima Guang's famous *Zizhi tongjian* (1084). It gives an account of the Three Kingdoms and Koryŏ from a neo-Confucian viewpoint, including much comment by **Kwŏn Kŭn**. A preliminary extra book (*oegi*) deals with **Tan'gun** and pre-Silla history. Though popular for centuries, it is now less used.

TONGGUK YŎJI-SŬNGNAM See Sinjŭng Tongguk yŏji-sŭngnam

TONGHAK 東學 'Eastern Learning' **REBELLION** (1894–5)
Major **peasant rebellion** in which the religious ideas of **Ch'oe Cheu** played a significant part: under the title of *Ch'ŏndo* ('Heaven's Way'), these drew upon both Confucian and shamanistic traditions and proclaimed social egalitarianism stemming from the concept of God immanent in man. It reflected his resentment at official corruption, the economic and social sufferings of the **peasantry**, and foreign (both western and Chinese) intrusion in Korea. The name Tonghak implied the antithesis of western learning, *Sŏhak*, which had been brought to Korea by the Catholic church, but it also made nationalistic reference to the common name for Korea (*Tongguk*, 'Eastern country'). Ch'oe was executed in 1864, but under the leadership of his successor Ch'oe Sihyŏng (1829–1898) the network of Tonghak churches grew and the book of its scriptures, *Tonggyŏng taejŏn* ('Great Compendium of Eastern Scriptures') was compiled and disseminated.

By the early 1890s, people were suffering widely from over-taxation, lawlessness, and damage to their trade caused by foreign merchants in Korea. Conditions were particularly bad in Chŏlla and Ch'ungch'ŏng provinces. In 1892 and 1893 thousands vainly demonstrated in favour of a posthumous pardon for Ch'oe Cheu and official action against Japanese and westerners. In February 1894 the peasants of Kobu county in Chŏlla rose up against their oppressive magistrate. He was dismissed, but subsequent government recriminations against the Tonghak led to greater insurrection. The ranks of the dissidents swelled rapidly, and after defeating government troops at Changsŏng the rebels, under the leadership of Chŏn Pongjun, captured Chŏnju on 31 May. The government then offered a truce while appealing to China for military help. On 8 June 3,000 Chinese soldiers arrived to suppress the rebellion. Under the terms of the **Treaty of Tianjin**, **Li Hongzhang** had informed Japan in advance of his intentions, in response to which the Japanese also sent a force, of more than double the Chinese size. The rebels dispersed on 14 June, publishing a list of their reform demands which went beyond anything that the government could meet. They included an amnesty for Tonghak members, **land reform**, punishment of corrupt officials, selection of officials on merit, abolition of **slavery**, and the remission of farmers' debts.

The Japanese saw this as an opportunity to advance reforms in Korea which would strengthen their influence there. They invaded the **Kyŏngbok Palace**, seized the royal family, and restored the **Taewŏn'gun**. The ensuing **Sino-Japanese War** saw overwhelming military successes for the Japanese and the apparent capitulation of the Korean government to their political demands (*see Kabo* **reforms**). In October, Tonghak rebels took up arms again, this time against the Japanese as well as their own government, but they were outnumbered and outclassed. A Chŏlla army under Chŏn Pongjun and another in Ch'ungch'ŏng under **Son Pyŏnghŭi** met at Nonsan and moved towards Kongju. In their ensuing defeat Chŏn was captured and later executed; Son, together with **An Chunggŭn** and **Kim Ku**, escaped and later became prominent in the independence movement. The Tonghak movement was ended, but its members continued to play active parts in the *Ch'ŏndo-gyo* and the **United Progress Society** (*Ilchinhoe*).

SUSAN SHIN, 'The Tonghak Movement: From Enlightenment to Revolution,' *KSF*, 5, 1978–79; *KJ*, 34/4, 1994: Special issue devoted to 'The Peasant War of 1894' (8 articles)

TONGIN-JI-MUN 東人之文 'Koreans' writings'

A wood-block printed book edited by Ch'oe Hae (1287–1340), claimed as the earliest printed book of Korean poetry in Chinese. Of the three parts (four- and six-character verses; five- and seven-character verses; thousand- and hundred character compositions) only the first two have been discovered. Poetry by **Ch'oe Ch'iwŏn**, **Yi Kyubo**, **An Hyang** and O Hyŏng (1232–1314) is included.
*See also **hansi**; **printing**; **Tongmun-sŏn***

TONGJI 同知

A *Chungch'u-bu* official of 2nd **grade** junior, used as a general term for an old man without office, but also a pun on *tongji*, 'friend'.

TONGMONG SŎNSŬP 童蒙先習 'Child's early study'

A slim 'first reader' for boys, written by Pak Semu (1487–1554) early in the 16th century. The earliest known printed edition is 1670. It provides a brief account of the neo-Confucian **'five relationships'** (*o-ryun*), followed by sketchy synopses of Chinese history down to Song and of Korean history.

TONGMUN-SŎN 東文選 'Anthology of Eastern (i.e.Korean) Writings'

The major anthology of early Korean writing in Chinese, completed by **Sŏ Kŏjŏng** and others in 1478. Supplements were added in the reigns of Chungjong (1506–45) and **Sukchong** (1675–1720). The model was *Wenxuan*, made by the Liang ruler Xiao Tong (501–531) while he was still Prince Zhaoming. The earliest writer included is **Ch'oe Ch'iwŏn**. The pieces are classified according to literary *genre*: poetry, letters, prefaces, notes, decrees, memorials, essays, biographies, inscriptions and ritual pieces, both Confucian and Buddhist.

TONGNAE 東萊

Former garrison town for the port of **Pusan**, where incoming Japanese embassies were received by Korean officialdom. A ten-panel screen painted by **Chŏng Sŏn** (National Museum of Korea)[1] shows the magistrate greeting an envoy at Pusan, accompanying him to the official guest house at Tongnae, and the entertainment provided there. The distance between the two towns was approximately five miles, and they were merged into a single conurbation in 1913.

(1) KEITH PRATT, *Korean Music, its History and its Performance*, London & Seoul: Faber Music and Jung Eum Sa, 1987

TONGNIP SINMUN 獨立新聞 'The Independent News'
(1) **Newspaper** dedicated to the reform and **self-strengthening movement**, launched by **Sŏ Chaep'il** on 7 April 1896 following his return from exile in America and reflecting the views of the **Independence Club**. It was published in *han'gŭl* without the use of Chinese characters, a radical innovation, and had an English-language section which constituted the only English newspaper service in Korea at that time. It received news items from Reuter's News Agency via China, thus providing a novel source of information on events in the outside world. By 1898 it had a circulation of 3,000 and performed a valuable educational function for the less well educated. From 1897 it prompted the introduction of a number of other *han'gŭl* papers (*see Taehan Maeil Sinbo*). When Sŏ Chaep'il left for America again in May, **Yun Ch'iho** became editor and, when he was forced into writing the English language section alone, was able to continue publication until it too closed on 4 December 1899.
LEE KWANG-RIN, 'On the Publication of the *Independent* by Suh Jae-pil,' *JSSH*, June 1976
(2) Newspaper of the same name published in Shanghai by the Korean **Provisional Government in Exile**, established in 1919. Publication ceased in 1928.
See also **Hwangsŏng Sinmun**

TONGSA GANGMOK 東史綱目 'Outline of Korean History'
Zizhi tongjian 'Comprehensive Mirror of Administration', the great history of China, was written by Sima Guang (1019–86), a work in 294 volumes covering the period from 425 BC (Sima considered the evidence for earlier times unreliable) till the end of Tang. Liu Shu added an appendix (*weiji*) on those earlier times. *Zizhi tongjian* was the model for *Tongguk t'onggam* 'Comprehensive Mirror of Korea' which appeared in 1484, edited by a group led by **Sŏ Kŏjŏng**, covering history up to the end of Koryŏ. Like its model, it is interspersed with moralising essays on history from various hands, and contains an appendix (*oegi*) on very early times. Its Confucian quality is shown in such details as its coyness about the three queens of Silla (*see* **Silla, Queens of**), whom it calls simply *chu* 'ruler'; yet it differs from its Chinese model in the numbering of years. Chinese neo-Confucian practice was to give year-number 1 of each reign to the year after the death of the previous ruler: the so-called *yunyŏn-pŏp* 'following-year rule'. Korean tradition followed the *hungnyŏn-pŏp* or *pungnyŏn-pŏp* 'year of royal death rule', by which the year in which a ruler died (and his successor came to the throne) was called Year 1. *Tongguk t'onggam* retained the older Korean system.

Because *Zizhi tongjian* was such an unwieldy book, **Zhu Xi** made an abridgement, *Tongjian gangmu* 'Outline of the Comprehensive Mirror'. In 1778 **An Chŏngbok**, after twenty years' work, made a similar abridgement of *Tongguk t'onggam*, called *Tongsa gangmok* 'Outline of Korean History'. Though *Tongsa gangmok* ignores the purely Korean **Tan'gun** myth, and emphasises the China-related legend of **Kija**, it is not a slavish imitation of Zhu Xi's work, but a work in the *sirhak* manner, with critical evaluation of evidence, and contains charts, tables and maps.

TONGSIN 洞神 'village spirit'
A small shrine for the *tongsin* 'guardian spirit of the village', containing a spirit tablet or a picture of the *sansin*, may be built just outside the settlement, often with a cairn of small stones by an old zelkova or pine tree. Tabu ropes (*kŭmchul*) are put round it at the time of the *tongsin-je* sacrifice, which usually takes place on *Taeborŭm-nal*. An elder prepares himself by **bathing**, abstaining from meat for a few days, and avoiding mourners and sick people. At midnight the area is lit by flares, the village men

congregate, and the elder reads suitable prayers. A meeting about expenses is held the following day, before they feast on the food prepared for the spirit.

TONGYE 東濊 'Eastern Ye'

Name of a tribe occupying land from approximately the 4th century BC to the 2nd century AD along the north-east coast (modern Hamgyŏng province), descended from the **Ye** and thus distantly related to the tribes of **Koguryŏ**. To the north lived the more advanced **Okchŏ**, and further away in the **Yalu** River basin the peoples of the Koguryŏ federation. The Tongye practised fishing and **agriculture**, traded with Okchŏ and imported **iron** from the **Kaya** federation. They inhabited part of the Chinese **commandery** of **Lintun**, regained some independence when the latter fell, but were defeated by the armies of Koguryŏ under King T'aejo (53–146).

TONGYŎNSA 同研社 'Joint Research Society'

Name given to a group of painters formed in 1922, including **Yi Sangbŏm**, **Kim Ŭnho**, **Hŏ Paengnyŏn**, No Suhyŏn, and **Pyŏn Kwansik**, who rendered traditional subjects in Western styles, attempting to reflect both atmosphere and appearance with realism. Its slogan was 'Images for and of our own generation', looking back at Korean artistic tradition to foster a spirit of future independence. But its members' approach was also based on an assumption that westernisation was inevitable, and as such their work has been criticised by some modern Korean historians as no more than a transitional stage in the evolution of a genuinely modern Korean approach to art, a rendering of traditional subjects in a watered-down, semi-westernised manner.
See also Sŏhwa Hyŏphoe

TOPKNOT *sangt'u*

The topknot has been the male hair style of north east Asia as far back as archaeological evidence shows anything at all of men's appearance. It was possibly a looser and larger bun at some periods. The tight topknot worn at all times by men of the Chosŏn period seems to have become formalised in the Koryŏ period at the latest. **Headdress** always covered the topknot, but in later Chosŏn, miniature headdresses were made that covered the topknot only, to help keep it tidy and when no other headgear was worn in the privacy of the home. These miniatures followed the designs of other brimless caps, and were especially useful when the hair was thinning and difficult to hold in a firm knot (*see Kwan-hon-sang-je*).

One of the *Kabo* **reforms** of 1894 decreed that men should cut off their topknots as a gesture of modernisation. Some saw this as a threat to a traditional sign of their national integrity, an ironic contrast with China, where nationalists would soon begin cutting off their queues as a mark of revolt against the Manchu **Qing dynasty**.

TORTOISE

Although small turtles occur in southern Korea, and marine species are found off the coasts, the tortoise (often called 'turtle' in America, though turtles are, strictly, water tortoises) is essentially a mythical creature inherited from China. Since its reptilian cloaca was mistaken for female pudenda, it was thought to need a serpent to fertilise it and is therefore often depicted with a snake twined around it. The ancient use of tortoise-shell in divination, and the image of the cosmos conveyed by the round (and therefore heavenly) carapace set on a square (and therefore earthly) plastron with four legs gave the strange and long-lived reptile an air of mystery, symbolic of longevity and suitable as a base for a memorial stele.
See also Sasin

TORTOISE INCANTATION *Yŏng-sin'gun-ga* 迎神君歌 'song to welcome a spirit prince'
Sometimes regarded as another candidate for being the oldest Korean poem (*see also* **Harp Song**; **Orioles' Song**), this is an incantation to the Spirit of Kuji Mountain (hence sometimes called *Kwiji-ga*). It appears as Chinese 4-character verse in *Samguk yusa* 2, among the chronicles of **Kaya** (*Karak-ki*), dated to 41 AD.

> Tortoise, tortoise,
> show your head!
> If you do not put it forth,
> we shall cook and eat you.

There is much debate as to its true date and significance, complicated by the fact that the *Haega*, 'sea song', a 7-character Chinese verse (also in *Samguk yusa* 2, the story of Lady Suro, mid-8th century AD), adjuring a dragon-spirit to release a captive woman, is so similar:

> Tortoise, tortoise, free Lady Suro!
> Stealing a wife is a heinous sin.
> If you refuse to set her free,
> we shall net, cook and eat you.

TOSA 都事
An official title for various posts in the Chosŏn government, usually of 5th **grade** junior, occasionally as low as 9th grade junior, attached to the **Five Military Commands** or to the **Six Boards**. It ranked below *kamsa* and is variously translated as auditor, inspector and lieutenant.

TOSIRAK
A basket for cooked food to be taken on a journey or otherwise eaten out of doors. The basket, usually rectangular, has a high and closely fitting lid, with no handles. The word had fallen into disuse and was successfully revived by Ch'oe Hyŏnbae and his friends after World War II to replace the Japanese *bento*, meaning a snack of cold cooked **rice** and pickles in a disposable wooden punnet (a ubiquitous relic of colonialism too useful to be rejected).

TOSŎN 道詵 (827–898)
A member of a Kim clan from Yŏngam, south Chŏlla province, who became a monk at fourteen and lived till he was 71, mostly in Chŏlla monasteries, gaining favour with the last kings of **Silla**. He is regarded as the founder of *p'ungsu* in Korea and supposed to have used that art to identify all the suitable sites for monasteries and temples throughout the land. **Wang Kŏn**, whose future dynasty Tosŏn had prophesied, spoke of him with respect in his *hunyo*, exhortations to his successors (*see* **Ten injunctions**).

TOWNSEND, WALTER DAVIS (1856–1918)
One of the first American businessmen in Korea. A Bostonian, he arrived in 1884 after contacts with **Kim Okkyun**. He was a close friend of Horace N. **Allen** and lived in Inch'ŏn until his death in 1918. He is credited with having introduced to Korea the horse and dray, a water-pumping windmill and a mechanised rice-cleaning mill. During 1899 he imported a million gallons of kerosene into the country.

HAROLD COOK, 'Walter Davis Townsend: Pioneer American Businessman in Korea,' *TRASKB*, XLVIII, 1973

TOYS, CHILDREN'S
Traditional children's toys were mostly home-made. They included *p'aengi* spinning tops, much whipped in winter, made of the same hardwood as *tadŭmi* sticks and *yut* sticks; *turŭrae* paper windmills or pinwheels; *ttakch'ong* popguns or blow-guns of **bamboo**, using paper pellets; *ssŭrŭrami* cardboard and string buzzers, named after the cicada; *chungma* 'bamboo horse', a stalk of bamboo with leaves on it, used as a hobby-horse (the child straddles the other end and prances in what is called *mallorŭm-jil*); *chukpangul*, 'diabolo', a little hour-glass-shaped piece of wood, spun, thrown and caught on a thread tied between two wands held one in each hand; *ottogi* the pear-shaped self-righting doll, made of papier-maché with a weight inside (a so-called 'Kelly-doll'); *kaksi* a home-made doll, often of bamboo with grass hair; and *sokkup*, odds and ends such as small seashells, used by little girls for *sokkup-chil*, playing at serving meals.

TRADE *See* **commerce**; **markets**; **merchants**; **tribute**

TRAITORS *See* **Five Traitors**; **Seven Traitors**

TREES
Trees carry a heritage of dendrolatry in the love and superstitious fear with which very old ones may be regarded. The Pagoda tree or Scholar's Tree (*Sophora japonica*) is a legume and the Zelkova or Keyaki (*nŭt'i namu*) is an elm, but both grow to great size and they are often confused. Like ancient chestnuts, some reputed to be many centuries old, they are venerated, and a single tree in a village often serves as a shade tree under which men can meet to chat. The same function is served by giant centuries-old ginkgos in both Confucian and Buddhist temples. Ginkgos have additional fascination because they are dioecious and usually planted in pairs, one male and one female. Buddhists also cultivate the lime (*Tilia*), called *yŏmju namu* because rosaries can be made of its seeds. Stands of flowering cherry that grace both town and countryside, as do false acacias (*Robinia*), are legacies of the colonial period.

The indigenous paulownia (*Paulownia tomentosa*), named after Tsarevna Anna Pavlovna (1795–1865), is another handsome village tree, valued for its wood, often used for fine **furniture** and **musical instruments**. It might be planted when a daughter was born, to provide her wedding chest. In Korea the paulownia is called *odong*. In China this word, as *wutong*, refers to the Parasol Tree (*Firmiana*), which belongs to the cacao family, and is known in Korea as *pyŏg-odong* 'green paulownia', because its trunk remains bright green throughout its life. The Parasol Tree is the resting-place of the mythical **phoenix**.

Other culturally significant trees are the willow, a sign of rural peace, again from ancient Chinese tradition (*see* **Tao Qian**); the jujube or 'Chinese date', whose sweet fruit is dried; *Brousonnetia papyrifera*, fibre from whose inner bark is pulped to make the best 'mulberry-bark **paper**'; the poisonous **lacquer** tree *Rhus verniciflua*, whose resin is the basis of lacquer-work, a whole technique in decorative art; and the *paktal namu* (*Betula schmidtii*), a species of mountain birch whose very heavy wood is made into *honggudae* and *pangmangi*, the rollers and paddles used in *tadŭmi*, smoothing and pressing clothes by beating them. The *paktal* is more likely to be **Tan'gun**'s eponymous tree than the 'sandalwood' commonly used to translate his name. Box

(*Buxus koreana*) is the preferred wood for carving seals, *tojang*. The pine (*sollamu*) is the upright symbol of longevity.

Though cultivated apples are a 19th-century introduction, brought first by Protestant missionaries, *nŭnggŭm* (crab-apples) and *koyom*, the wild persimmon (*Diosporos lotus*), whose fruit needs bletting before it can be eaten, are native ancestors of cultivated fruit. Their own fruit also is still used. Pine-nuts (and pollen for cakes) are gathered from *chat-namu*, the wild *Pinus koraiensis*. (The flowers are cut whole and steeped in water so that the pollen floats free.)

TREE-TOP BURIAL *susang-jang* 樹上葬

Until the early 20th century, ***ch'ŏnmin***, who had no access to ground for burials, and others during outbreaks of pestilence, used to put a corpse in a box, straw bag, or large jar and fasten it in the upper branches of a tree. When the flesh had decayed away, they would bury the bones.

TRIBUTE *kong* 貢

(A) INTERNAL

In addition to the land tax and their obligation to perform periods of ***corvée*** labour, farmers in the Koryŏ and early Chosŏn periods were liable for payments of local products as internal tribute (*kong*), collected on behalf of the prefectural magistrate for the use of central or local government and the local military barracks. Commodities included **textiles**, furs, sea produce, timber, fruit, minerals, **paper**, and handicraft products. Quotas were set but demands were frequently exceeded, owing to corruption among officialdom and authorised tribute collectors (*kongin*), which greatly increased the burden on private households. Tribute tax was replaced in the 17th century by a new land surtax, ***taedongpŏp***, which led to the growing use of **coinage** in the economy.

See also **Ever normal warehouses**; **government, central**; **provincial administration**

(B) FOREIGN

As integral members of the Chinese world order, traditional Korean governments viewed official inter-state relations in terms of the exchange of envoy missions bearing symbols either of suzerain munificence or vassal tribute. This was no more than an extension of the reciprocal relationship that existed between the capital and the regions within Korea itself, and from the Three Kingdoms period to the Chosŏn no dynasty questioned the principle, even though the regularity of missions in each direction fluctuated. The principal relationship was that between the Middle Kingdom and Korea, but the Koryŏ court also formed tributary links with the **Liao** and **Jin** empires, and in its diplomatic dealings with Japan, to which it sent twelve missions between 1607 and 1811, the Chosŏn court saw its rôle as that of an elder brother addressing a younger.

Of the Three Kingdoms, **Koguryŏ** sent 173 tribute missions to the courts of both Northern and Southern Dynasties in China, **Paekche** 45, and the most remote, Silla, only nineteen. In return they received eight, six and two respectively as acknowledgement of Chinese recognition.

Unified Silla enjoyed harmonious relations with its **Tang** neighbours, the most regular period for tribute missions being the 8th century, when 63 were sent, 45 of them prior to the An Lushan rebellion (755–763). Among signs of Kyŏngju's willingness to accept nominal subordination to Chang'an and Luoyang were the occasional sending of human tribute, including serving girls, musicians and dancers, and even members of the nobility who, after heading delegations to the Chinese capital, were then detained there with full diplomatic honours. In 825 the Korean court sent twelve men with the request that they should be kept as 'hostages' and accepted as students at the Imperial Academy.

During the 10th and 11th centuries thirteen gift-bearing missions from Korea to China and seventeen from China to Korea are recorded. They carried an extensive range of luxury goods, as follows:

Korea to China: **Textiles**, clothing, gold belts, furs, rugs, furnishings, covers; gold, silver and copper objects, wine pourers; **rice**, pineseeds, **ginseng**, aromatic drugs and oils, sulphur; **horses**, saddles and fittings, one carriage, **armour**, weapons, swords and fittings, bows and arrows, military items; **screens**, scrolls, **paper**, ink, religious texts and images, **books**.

China to Korea: **Silk**, textiles, clothing, belts; gold, silver and jade articles, sacrificial and mourning items; wine warmers, bowls, teapots, candles; **tea**, wine, fruit, sheep, horses, saddles, whips, bows and arrows; medical supplies; **books**, paintings, Buddhist relics and statuary; **musical instruments** and texts.

The Mongol rulers of China, having also conquered Korea, exacted heavy tribute payments in the form of gold, silver, ginseng, hunting birds, and both male and female human hostages. Even the succeeding **Ming dynasty**, despite the restoration of a more friendly relationship, greatly increased its tributary expectations from one mission every three years under the Hongwu emperor (1368–98) to three or even four a year, not including those required on special occasions such as the accession of a new emperor. This placed a heavy burden on the ordinary Korean producers of the tribute goods, which included textiles, ginseng, horses and animal skins. Sometimes special requests were made: so beautiful had Korean white porcelain become in the early 15th century (*see* **ceramics**) that the Yongle Emperor (1403–25) asked King **Sejong** for some, and was sent two hundred pieces. Human tribute was still paid, and only formally ended in the Chosŏn period. Then, Korea sent on average three missions *per annum* to China between 1637 and 1894, the highest number (13 in 1638 and 1639) being prompted by the **Manchu invasions**. The lowest average, of less than two *per annum*, was maintained in the second half of the 18th century, when imperial embassies to Seoul also dropped to their lowest level of four in the thirty-year period 1766–95. Korean tributary goods included substantial quantities of paper, animal skins, silks, cotton goods, and rice. Hae-jong Chun has estimated that 'the value of the imperial gifts was about one tenth of that of the Korean tributary goods'.

See also **An Dao; Beijing, embassies to;** *sadae*;**Yejong, King**

HAE-JONG CHUN, 'Sino-Korean Tributary Relations in the Ch'ing Period', in FAIRBANK, J.K., ed., *The Chinese World Order: Traditional China's Foreign Relations*, Cambridge, Mass.: Harvard University Press, 1968; DONALD CLARK, 'The Ming Connection: Notes on Korea's Experience in the Chinese Tributary System,' *TRASKB*, LVIII, 1983; MORRIS ROSSABI, *China Among Equals: The Middle Kingdom and its Neighbors, 10th–14th Centuries*, Berkeley: University of California Press, 1984; RICHARD RUTT, 'James Gale's Translation of the *Yonhaeng-Nok*, an Account of the Korean Embassy to Peking, 1712-3,' *TRASKB*, XXXIX, 1974

TRIGRAMS *p'algwae*, C. *ba gua* 八卦 'eight emblems'
Trigrams consist of three parallel lines, each either whole or broken, and are created by dividing the hexagrams of the *Book of Changes*. They are first mentioned in the **Confucian classic** *Zuo zhuan* (4th century BC). The 8th Wing of the *Book of Changes* (3rd century BC or later) attributes them to 'sages' or to the mythical Fuxi, and gives

them 'temperaments', correspondences with the compass points and natural features, 'names' derived from the hexagrams that contain two identical trigrams, and other symbolic meanings that are used in interpreting *Yijing*.

The 8th Wing lists the trigrams in two different orders: the 'King Wen order', also called 'later than heaven' order, which has no obvious rationale, but gains great authority from its presumed antiquity; and what Koreans call *Wenwang chasun*, 'King Wen's second order', in which, by treating whole lines as *yang* and broken lines as *yin* (*see Ŭm-yang*), each trigram comes to denote a member of a nuclear family. (Three whole lines give father, three broken lines mother, one whole line a son and one broken a daughter.)

The Song thinker Shao Yong (1011–77) devised a third, purely mathematical, order called the 'Fuxi order' or 'earlier than heaven' order, which, through neo-Confucian influence, came to be regarded as standard in Korea. Earlier and later than Heaven are ideas derived from the 7th Wing of the *Book of Changes,* and reflect Shao Yong's belief that mathematics are in every way prior to heaven.

Trigrams appear on *T'aegŭk-ki* (**national flag**), paper charms, and as a decoration, frequently surrounding the *t'aegŭk* roundel. When set in a circle, they may occupy the compass points according to any of the three orders, usually with their tops outwards (but not always: at least one Koryŏ **mirror** has the tops of the trigrams towards the centre). They are much used as auspicious signs.

TRIGRAM CHARTS
Fuxi order
'earlier than Heaven'

1	*kŏn*	S	Heaven: strong	5	*son*	SW	wind: entering
2	*t'ae*	SE	still water: pleasing	6	*kam*	W	moving water: sinking
3	*(r)i*	E	fire: shining	7	*kan*	NW	mountain: stopping
4	*chin*	NE	thunder: moving	8	*kon*	N	Earth: compliant

King Wen order
'later than Heaven'

1	2	3	4	5	6	7	8
chin	*son*	*i*	*kon*	*t'ae*	*kŏn*	*kam*	*kan*
E	SE	S	SW	W	NW	N	NE

King Wen's 2nd order

1	2	3	4	5	6	7	8
father	mother	1st son	1st daughter	2nd son	2nd daughter	3rd son	3rd daughter
S	N	NW	SE	W	E	SW	NE

TRIPITAKA KOREANA *Koryŏ taejanggyŏng* 高麗大藏經 *samjang* 三藏
Tripitaka, 'three baskets' (K. *samjang*), means the scriptures of southern Buddhism, divided into: *sutta-pitaka* (K. *kyŏngjang*), 'teachings basket'; *vinaya-pitaka*, 'rules basket' (K. *yulchang*); and *adhidhama-pitaka*, 'treatises basket' (K. *nonjang*). Chinese scriptures were added to produce *mahapitaka* (K. *taejang*) in the 10th century. Wood-block **printing** of the *taejang* was regarded as a pious means of protecting Korea from outside attack. The first project was begun in Koryŏ in 1009, when the **Khitan** were the threat, and took around seventy years to complete. In 1090 **Ŭich'ŏn** published his list of additional indigenous texts, and they were printed as a supplement, *Sok Changgyŏng*. Nearly all the blocks were lost in the Mongol invasion of 1231. A second set of *Tripitaka* woodblocks was begun in **Kanghwa** in 1236, while the court was taking refuge there from the **Mongols**. The compilers based their edition on the best available copies of the Korean, Manchurian (**Liao**), and Chinese canons. It comprised 6,791 *kwŏn* and was carved onto 81,258 wooden blocks. Work was completed in 1251, but without Ŭich'ŏn's supplement. In 1398 the blocks were moved to **Haein-sa** in Kyŏngsang, where they are still preserved. The blocks contain 1,511 books. Each one, carved from wood of the paktal **tree**, measures 65 x 24·5 x 6·5 cm, and weighs 3·5 kg. A numerical indexing system to the *Tripitaka* was later based on the Korean version of the Chinese *Thousand Character Classic* (*Ch'ŏnja-mun*).
NAK CHOON PAIK, 'Tripitaka Koreana. Library of Woodblocks of Buddhist Classics at Haeinsa, Korea,' *TKBRAS*, XXXII, 1951
See also **Koryŏ changgyŏng**

TROLLOPE, MARK NAPIER 趙瑪珂 (1862–1930)
Educated at New College, Oxford, and ordained priest in the Church of England 1888. In 1890 he joined the nascent Anglican mission to Korea and soon became its chief scholar. Working chiefly in **Kanghwa** town, he built a Korean-style church there, now regarded as a national treasure. He returned to England in 1901 and worked in the east London slums until he was appointed bishop in Korea in 1911. A high-church socialist and forward-looking ecumenist and missionary in Anglo-Catholic style, his studies of Korean **Buddhism**, flora, books and the history of **Kanghwa** (all published by the **Royal Asiatic Society**) were outstanding in their day. He died on board ship while returning to Korea in 1930. His collection of old Korean books is now in Yonsei University Library.
CONSTANCE TROLLOPE, *Mark Napier Trollope*, London: SPCK, 1936
See also **Anglicans; Bible in Korean, the; Protestants**

TRUSTEESHIP
Plan for the supervision of interim government in Korea by three or four allied powers until the restoration of total independence after the Japanese colonial period. Its presupposition was the American view that former colonies, including Korea,

would not be capable of immediate and complete self-government, and followed an appeal made by Syngman Rhee **(Yi Sŭngman)** to President Wilson in 1919 for a League of Nations mandate over his occupied country. Nevertheless mention in 1942 by the Institute of World Affairs of a period of tutelage brought swift rejection from the **Provisional Government in Exile**, which would accept nothing but complete independence. Trusteeship was put to British Foreign Minister Anthony Eden by President Franklin D. Roosevelt early in 1943, and became part of Roosevelt's vision of post-War American influence and defence around the Pacific basin, the emphasis of which was on the containment of Soviet eastward expansion. It was not, however, a clearly thought-out strategy, and failed to distinguish between widely differing circumstances in such countries as Korea and the Philippines. It was discussed at the **Teheran** and **Yalta** Conferences, when it was agreed that the trustees should be the United States, the Soviet Union, Great Britain and China. The period of trusteeship was considered loosely to be anything up to forty years, but was in the event fixed under the terms of the **Moscow Conference** agreement as five years. News of the proposal was greeted with outrage in Korea, where leaders of the **Korean People's Republic** formed a committee to plan opposition to it and demonstrations took place throughout the country. Early in 1946, however, moderate and left-wing parties opposed to Syngman Rhee's right-wing nationalism (i.e. the **Korean Communist Party**, the **Korean Democratic Party**, the **Korean People's Party**, and the Korean Nationalist Party) came to favour the 'spirit' of trusteeship, aimed at the eventual democratisation and independence of Korea. Very soon the political polarisation of Koreans, reflecting the growing tension between the United States and Soviet Union, brought to an end the efforts of the **US-Soviet Joint Commission** to plan elections and the very concept of trusteeship. Its chief architect, Franklin Roosevelt, had died on 15 April 1945, and in August 1947 the American government abandoned it. When its call for a conference to discuss the independent government of Korea was rejected by the Soviet Union, it handed the matter over to the United Nations (*see* **UNTCOK**).

TSUSHIMA 對馬島 (K. Taema-do)
A mountainous island lying mid-way between Korea and Japan in the Korea Straits, ruled by the Japanese feudal *daimyo* of the Sō clan from the 12th to the mid-19th century. It habitually controlled much of the trade between southern Japan and **Silla**, which was well established by the 9th century, but also provided a lair for **pirates** ravaging the Korean coast. Successful counter-attacks were prompted under Pak Wi in 1389 and Yi Chongmu in 1419, after which traders from Tsushima were allowed to visit three ports including **Pusan**. The **Kyehae Treaty** of 1443 controlled cross-Straits trade but allowed Tsushima to continue to benefit from it. **Sin Sukchu** (1417–75)'s *Haedong cheguk-ki* (1471) shows a map of Tsushima as Japanese territory (*see also* **Cartography**). The island was also used as a port of call for official embassies travelling between Japan and Korea. Between 1587 and 1591 Sō Yohitoki transmitted messages from Toyotomi Hideyoshi to the Korean court proclaiming his unification of Japan, announcing his intended conquest of China, and demanding Korean recognition. In 1869 the Japanese government incorporated Tsushima into Nagasaki prefecture, and in 1895 a channel was cut across the middle of the island, dividing it in two.
KENNETH ROBINSON, 'The Tsushima Governor and Regulation of Japanese Access to Chosŏn in the Fifteenth and Sixteenth Centuries,' *KS*, 20, 1996

TTŬN SIN 'floating spirits'

The most unwelcome spirits were *son'gaksi* or *sonmalmyŏng*, the spirit of a girl who died unmarried, and *nam-sagwi*, spirit of an unmarried man. These were baleful *ttŭn sin* or *puhueng-sin*, 'floating spirits', requiring much attention and placation. It was partly for fear of these wandering *ttŭn sin* that many households went to bed early at **New Year** or *Taeborŭm*, bringing all shoes indoors and hanging a sieve near the door to discourage the spirits from coming in.

TUG-O'-WAR *chul-tarigi*

Tugs-o'-war are found in many districts, often at *Taeborŭm*, often in the 8th moon. There were tugs-o'-war in Tang China, as there were nearly everywhere else too. They are community activities, usually between east and west teams. Each side makes an immensely thick rice-straw rope by twisting heavy ropes together and splicing smaller ropes into the end for individuals to grasp. The two ropes, the east called the male (*su*, using a word reserved for animals) and the west called the female (*am*), are spliced into one. At one time only unmarried men and **women** were supposed to be present at the splicing. A tug-o'-war has always been a noisy event and could last as long as three or four days, with much drinking and betting.

TUMEN RIVER (K. Tuman-gang) 豆満江

River rising on **Paektu-san** and flowing east, thereby forming, with the westward-flowing **Yalu River**, the border between Korea and **Manchuria**. In 1991, in a project reminiscent of China's Special Economic Zones of the 1980s, it was designated as a region in which foreign investment would be welcome. The North Korean government sought private sector investment from Russia, China, South Korea and Japan, and obtained initial funding under the United Nations Development Programme.

ANDREW MARTON, TERRY McGEE, DONALD PATERSON, 'Northeast Asian Economic Cooperation and the Tumen River Area Development Project,' *P4*, 68/1, 1995

TURKISH BATHS *hanjŭngmak* 汗蒸幕

Dry and steam baths are part of northern culture throughout the sub-Artic regions, from native Canadians to the Turks and Finns. The Korean *hanjŭngmak* ('sweating tent'), used for health reasons, is a round building of stone or brick. When it is filled with pine branches and the branches are burnt, the inside of this building rises to untouchable heat. After the ash has been raked out, the floor is covered with wet straw matting, which has to be kept wet, and bathers (more strictly, 'sweaters') enter wearing wet straw cloaks to protect the skin from the fierce heat.

TURTLE SHIPS *kŏbuksŏn*

Armed warships which played a significant part in defeating Japanese naval forces in battles off the southern Korean coast during the **Imjin Wars**, cutting supply routes to the invading armies. They have ben claimed as the first ironclad battleships. Adapting an existing design which provided a concave wooden roof over the oarsmen and soldiers, Admiral **Yi Sunsin** and naval architect Na Taeyong may have used overlapping iron plates like the carapace of a turtle to give stronger protection against enemy arrows and gun shot. Cannon were placed to give all-round offensive fire, iron spikes guarded the ships against boarders, and a dragon's head at the prow blew out frightening plumes of smoke. Full details have been lost, but it is generally accepted that the boat was about 30 metres long, had 8–10 oars on each side and carried up to 160 men. All those on board were invisible to the enemy and protected from the elements. Modern estimates suggest that the ships could cover more than a hundred miles a day.

PARK YUNE-HEE, *Admiral Yi Sun-shin and his Turtle Boat Armada*, Seoul: Hanjin Publishing Co., 1973

TWELVE ORNAMENTS *sibi chang* 十二章

Twelve emblems described in the *Yiji* section of *Shujing* as ordained by the legendary Emperor Shun for use on his ministers' robes: *il* the sun, with a three-legged crow in it; *wŏl* the moon, where a hare pounds the elixir of immortality in a mortar; *sŏngsin* a diagram of three stars, as for a **lunar mansion**; *san* mountains; *yong* **dragons**; *hwach'ung* a millefleur pheasant; *chongi* two libation cups; *cho* pondweed, a rebus for literary skill; *hwa* flames; *mi* grains of **rice**; *po* an axe; and *pul* a symmetrical sign. In Korea these signs are not used together, but appear singly, as in **processional flags**.

TWENTY-FOUR DIRECTIONS / HOURS *isip-sa si* 二十四方位(時)

The *yundo* compass, used for *p'ungsu* and fortune-telling, has 24 segments, as in China. Twelve of these are named after the **zodiacal animals**. Four more are the inter-cardinal points (NE, SE, SW, NW) from the King Wen order of the **trigrams** (shown below in italic). The remaining eight segments (shown below in boldface) are filled by eight of the ten heavenly stems from the **sixty-fold cycle**, omitting the 5th and 6th. Trigrams and stems were given these compass positions in Han China by the 2nd century AD. The correspondences with *Kugung* (*see* **Nine Palaces Divination**) are clear. The same 24 names are also applied to the 24 hours of the day.

N	2400	rat	E	0600	hare	S	1200	horse	W	1800	fowl
	0100	**kye**		0700	**ul**		1300	**chong**		1900	**sin**
	0200	ox		0800	dragon		1400	sheep		2000	dog
NE	0300	*gan*	SE	0900	*son*	SW	1500	*kon*	NW	2100	*kŏn*
	0400	tiger		1000	snake		1600	monkey		2200	pig
	0500	**kap**		1100	**pyong**		1700	**kyong**		2300	**im**

See also five **watches**; **hours of the day**

TWENTY-FOUR SOLAR TERMS *isip-sa chŏlgi*

Twelve *ki* (C. *qi*) 'solar months' were marked in China before the 3rd century BC by *chŏlgi*, their 'junctures' and *chunggi*, their middle points. These 24 days, all now called *chŏlgi*, still figure in the Korean popular calendar. Since each fortnight consists of 15·218 days, the precise dates vary from year to year by one day either side of the approximate dates given here. (*See table opposite*)

T'AEGO 太古 (1301–82)

'Great antiquity', also known as Pou 'wholly stupid', perhaps the greatest Korean Buddhist leader. He began life in Chŏlla. Becoming a monk at thirteen, he achieved enlightenment in **Kaesŏng** in 1337. In 1346 he visited China, where he learned the *Linji* tradition of *Sŏn* Buddhism and the use of *kongan,* which he introduced to Korea on his return in 1348. From 1352 onwards he was much in demand as a teacher by the Koryŏ kings, twice being appointed *kuksa* 'national teacher'. During **Sin Ton**'s ascendancy he was out of favour and again visited China. On his return he was degraded and then reinstated. He gave stability to the **Chinul** tradition. Because of this key rôle in history, the central temple set up in Seoul in 1928 was called T'aego-sa, though the name was changed to Chogye-sa in 1937. After the establishment of the celibate monks as *Chogye-jong* in 1962, the married monks called themselves T'aego-jong. *T'aego hwasang ŏrok,* 'Recorded Words of the Monk T'aego' contains poems, teaching and letters, with a preface by **Yi Saek** and a postface by **Chŏng Mongju.**

Ipch'un	BEGINNING OF SPRING 4 February	Ipch'u	BEGINNING OF AUTUMN 8 August
Usu	Rainy and wet 19 February	Ch'ŏsŏ	End of heat 23 August
Kyŏngch'ip	Hibernators stir 5 March	Paengno	White dew 8 September
Ch'unbun	SPRING EQUINOX 20 March	Ch'ubun	AUTUMN EQUINOX 23 September
Ch'ŏngmyŏng	Clear and bright 5 April	Hallo	Cold dew 8 October
Kogu	Grain rain 20 April	Sanggang	Hoar frost 23 October
Ipha	BEGINNING OF SUMMER 6 May	Iptong	BEGINNING OF WINTER 7 November
Soman	Swelling grain 21 May	Sosŏl	Little snow 22 November
Mangjong	Grain in ear 6 June	Taesŏl	Great snow 7 December
Haji	SUMMER EQUINOX 21 June	Tongji	WINTER SOLSTICE 21 December
Sosŏ	Little heat 7 July	Sohan	Little cold 6 January
Taesŏ	Great heat 23 July	Taehan	Great cold 21 January

Twenty-Four Solar Terms

T'AEGŬK (C. *Taiji*) 太極 'great limit' or 'great ultimate'
The primary differentiation in the primordial monad of existence, the ***ŭm-yang*** dichotomy, first called *t'aegŭk* in the **Book of Changes** (*Xici zhuan* I.xi.5: c. 200 BC). It was much discussed by neo-Confucians, especially Zhou Dunyi (1017–72), one of the **Five Sages of Song**, who gave a circular diagram to represent it, different from the familiar two-comma **roundel** that emerged in later Song and appears in the *T'aegŭk-ki* (*see* **Flag, national**).

T'AEGŬK-KI *See* **Flag, national**

T'AEHAKKAM 太學監 National [Confucian] Academy
The successor to the National College (*Kukhak*, founded in 682 by King **Sinmun**), re-named in 750 but still known as *Kukhak* later in the same century. It came under the direction of the Board of Rites (*see* **government, central**). Its curriculum of nine years' study included the **Confucian Classics** and the Chinese literary anthology *Wenxuan*, as well as mathematics. Students graduated as *taenaema* or *naema* in one of three classes, according to the books they had mastered: top class graduates were proficient in the *Analects* of Confucius, the *Classic of Rites*, the *Spring and Autumn Annals*, the *Zuo Commentary*, and the *Classic of Filial Piety*; second class in the *Analects*, the *Classic of Filial Piety* and 'miscellaneous rites' (*ju li*); third class in the *Classic of Filial Piety* and 'miscellaneous rites' only.
See also **examinations; *hwarang*; *Kukcha-gam*; schools**

T'AEJO 太祖 (first king of Chosŏn) *see* **Yi Sŏnggye**

T'AEJONG 太宗 (**YI PANGWŎN** 李芳遠) *See* **Yi Sŏnggye**

T'AEKCHAE YUT'A 澤齋遺唾 'Remaining Dribblings of Kim Ch'angnip'
A slim volume of poems by Kim Ch'angnip (1666–84), youngest son of the *yŏngŭijŏng*, **Kim Suhang** and younger brother of **Kim Ch'angjip**, printed by his brothers in 1700. Ch'angnip had a taste for **dogs** and **horses**, and won a reputation for poetry while he was still a little boy. When his father was exiled to Puan in Chŏlla in 1675, the family went with him. Back in Seoul in 1680, Ch'angnip was given a studio of his own, which he called *Chungt'aek-chae*, 'studio of gratitude for favours'. Three years later, in spring, he wrote on the studio wall that he would die before the lunar year was out. He was married shortly afterwards, but died shortly before the new year at the age of seventeen. A daughter was born posthumously. His poems, which show a certain interest in **Buddhism**, are uncomplicated.

T'AEKKWŎN-DO 跆拳道 'Way of the foot and fist'
East Asian martial arts (unarmed self-defence skills) are clearly inter-related, but their early history is obscure. Written sources are few and of later origin. Warrior postures in ancient sculpture are suggestive but inconclusive. Certainly most forms have been much developed during the last 150 years. General Ch'oe Honghŭi states that he promulgated *T'aekkwŏn-do* in 1955, having developed it from *t'aekkyŏn*, a Korean form of leg-wrestling, and Japanese Karate. Before that date Korean self-defence was usually called *Tangsu-do*, 'way of the Chinese hand', or *T'aegyŏn*, 'kick-and-punching'. *Tangsu-do* was famous for such feats as cutting through ten clay tiles at once with the edge of the bare hand and splitting two wooden panels held cross-grained at eye-level by kicking them with the bare foot.
    T'aekkwŏn-do is now a sport of world-wide popularity with an international organisation. It is more vigorous than Chinese *Taijiquan* ('shadow boxing') and more aesthetic than Karate. Its moral ideals are fundamentally neo-Confucian, with a sub-Daoist element of *chŏng-jung-dong*, 'activity in stillness'.

T'AENGHWA 幀畫
Buddhist paintings. Their history dates back to the Three Kingdoms, though apart from surviving murals from **Koguryŏ** the earliest extant examples date only from the Koryŏ period, They fall into four categories: wall paintings, illustrations for printed **sutras**, altarpieces, and scroll paintings. Early **tomb** decoration shows links with **folk painting**, *minhwa*, but the complicated carved blockprints preserved in the illumination of Koryŏ scriptures were clearly produced by monastic experts, and through the Chosŏn dynasty great artists such as **Kim Hongdo** included Buddhist subjects among their widely varied output. Nevertheless, much Buddhist art continued to show that it represented the faith of the ordinary people, and to the present day the decoration of Buddhist temples bears witness to the artists' appreciation of colour, composition, and story-telling.
    A particular category of painting which decorated temple walls and banners in the 18th and 19th centuries was known as *kamno-jŏng* 'sweet dew pictures'. The name probably refers to the life-giving moisture described in the Lotus **Sutra** (Parable of Medicinal Plants), which also promises the 'sweet dew' of nirvana. The pictures depict three levels of existence: buddhas and bodhisattvas; Buddhist ceremonies for the dead, called 'sweet dew (or nectar) rites'; and small scenes of life on earth and in hell. These

scenes show vignettes of life around the temple, and are in effect miniature *genre* **paintings** of considerable interest.

KANG WOO-BANG, 'Ritual and Art during the Eighteenth Century', *in* KIM HONGNAM, ed., *Korean Arts of the Eighteenth Century: Splendour and Simplicity*, New York: The Asia Society Galleries, 1994; KANG WOO-BANG & KIM SEUNG-HEE, *The World of Nectar Ritual Paintings*, Seoul: Yekyoung Pub. Co., 1995; YOUNG-SOOK PAK, 'Illuminated Buddhist Manuscripts in Korea', *OA* XXXIII/4, 1987/8; PAK YOUNG-SOOK, 'Buddhist Themes in Koguryŏ Murals,' *AST*, vol. 44 no.2, 1990
See also **Painting**

T'AENGNI-JI 擇里志 'Selection of Habitat'

A human geography dating from 1714, known by several names, including *P'aryŏk-chi* 'Account of Eight Provinces'. It was compiled by Yi Chunghwan (1690–c.1750) and provides a guide to the location, means of livelihood, landscape, cultural and historical characteristics of all the regions of Korea. There are several editions. Although essentially a *sirhak* study, it includes considerations of *p'ungsu*.

CHOI INSHIL, trans., *Yi Chung-hwan's T'aengniji, the Korean Classic for Choosing Settlements*, University of Sydney Press, 1998

T'AEP'YŎNGSO 太平簫

A double-reed oboe with a wooden shaft and a conical metal bell. Its reed is shorter and narrower than that of the *p'iri*. It is closely related to the Chinese *suona*. Because of its strident tone, the *t'aep'yŏngso* is usually reserved for outdoor use, and is to be heard at all kinds of events, in traditional military bands, *nongak* ensembles, and orchestras accompanying ancestral shrine rites.

T'ANYŎN 坦然 (1070–1159)

Monk of the *Sŏn* sect renowned for his fluid style of *haengsŏ* (running style) **calligraphy**, which was imitated and developed through the later Koryŏ period.

T'ARYŎNG (a kind of singing)

The music of *p'ansori* or *chapka*. The word is used in titles of *p'ansori* pieces as an alternative to -*ka* 'song' or -*chŏn* 'story', as in *Changkki-t'aryŏng* for *Changkki-ga* or **Changkki-jŏn**.

T'OJŎNG PIGYŎL 土亭秘訣 'Earth-Pavilion Secrets'

T'ojŏng was the brush-name of Yi Chiham (1517–78), who compiled this fortune-telling manual from Chinese materials about 1550. He was a polymath disciple of **Sŏ Kŏjŏng**, much interested in mathematics. At the age of 55 he became district magistrate (*hyon'gam*) of P'och'ŏn. Five years later he was moved to Asan, where he set about providing for the poor and beggars, but died within the year. *T'ojŏng pigyŏl* is based on the identification of year, month and day by the **sixty-fold cycle** and is still popular.

T'ŎJU 'lord of the site'

Every house site had a *t'ŏju*. It lived in a small bottle or jar containing grains of **rice** and wrapped in straw, then tucked between the earthenware soy-sauce pots behind the house, or somewhere else in the backyard. More important was the *sŏngju* or *sangnyang-sin* 'ridge-pole spirit', whose nest was a small square **paper** packet containing a little rice, soaked in rice-ale and sprinkled with rice, some of which stuck to it (the more, the luckier). This nest was stuck on the mainbeam of the house in the largest room. With or without a *mudang* in attendance, the nest would be renewed with a ceremony of *sŏngju-baji*, in the 10th moon (*siwŏl-sangdal*) on a lucky day of the **sixty-fold cycle**, preferably *muo*, or at least a 'horse day' with *-o* in its name. A lower rank of spirit lived in a *kŏllip*, an old straw shoe or a bundle of selvages or rags hung indoors near the front of the building. He ran errands for the other spirits. In the kitchen was the *chowang*, who had a picture or lived in a bundle of cloths.

T'OKKI-JŎN See Sugung-ga

T'ONGJU, BATTLE OF 通州 (1010)
Confrontation which marked the beginning of the **Khitan** invasion of Korea, in modern Sŏnch'ŏn, North P'yŏngan. The Koryŏ commander Kang Cho, who had been guilty of the regicide of King Mokchong and seizing political power for himself under his protégé King Hyŏnjong, was killed. The court fled to Naju and Khitan armies captured and plundered **Kaesŏng** before withdrawing.
See also **Liao**

T'ONGMUN-GWAN 通文館 'Hall of translation'
This office of translators was established in 1276. It later became known as *Sayŏg-wŏn*. (*T'ongmun* in other contexts meant 'vast knowledge of literature'.)

T'ONGMUN-GWAN-JI 通文館志 'Records of the Hall of Translators'
An account of relations with China through the Hall of Translators, with summaries of its records from 1636. First compiled by Kim Kyŏngmun in 1720, and expanded in 1840, 1861 and 1888.

T'ONGNI-GIMU AMUN 統理機務衙門 'Office for General Management'
Government office first established in January 1881 with twelve departments, covering not only diplomatic dealings with China and other foreign countries but also such things as military affairs, foreign trade, shipbuilding, and schools for foreign languages. It represented one of Korea's first moves towards modernisation and self-strengthening (*See* **Self-strengthening movement**). In the year of its formation a request to dissolve Korea's traditional obligation to send **tribute** missions to China and to exchange resident diplomatic embassies in Beijing and Seoul was rejected by **Li Hongzhang**. In December 1882 its name was changed to *T'ongni Amun* in imitation of the Chinese *Zongli yamen*. With the advice of Paul-Georg **von Möllendorff** it was reorganised the following month and the name changed again, this time to *T'ongni Kyobo T'ongsang Samu Amun*.
See also **Kwanghye-wŏn**

T'OSŎNGNI 土城里
Location outside modern P'yŏngyang of the capital of the Chinese **commandery** of **Lelang**.

T'OU
Clay figurines, mainly associated with sites from the **Silla** and **Kaya** kingdoms. They were placed in **tombs** as burial furnishings and may also have been used for ritual purposes by the living. Subjects include human beings, animals, houses, and carts. Figures of pregnant women and men with exaggerated genitalia may have been used in

fertility rites. The best known example of a *t'ou* is that of a 23·5 cms-high mounted warrior of the 5th–6th century found in the Tomb of the Golden Bell in **Kyŏngju** (National Museum of Korea).[1]
(1) RODERICK WHITFIELD & PAK YOUNG-SOOK, eds., *Korean Art Treasures*, Seoul: Yekyong Publications Co., 1986

T'UHO 投壺 'throwing bottle'
A bottle with three round necks, used at parties as a target for two people to throw miniature arrows or darts (red for one player, blue for the other) from an agreed distance. The player who lodges most arrows in the bottle wins the game and exacts a forfeit from the other, either *pŏlchu* 'penalty-wine' to be drunk, or a song or poem to be recited. The attendant ceremonial is described at length in *Liji* 37 ('*Touhu*'). It was played at upper-class parties from the Three Kingdoms period, but fell out of use by early Koryŏ, till a gift of the toys was sent by the Song Emperor in 1116 (*see* **Yejong, King**). In Chosŏn it was played in the palace, especially by **women**, on the first 'snake' day of the year by the **sixty-fold cycle**, and at *Chungyang* during the banquet for elderly people.

T'UJŎN 鬪牋 *See* **Playing Cards**

U

ÚIBYŎNG 義兵
Often translated as 'righteous armies', a missionary-style translation for a euphemism first recorded in the **Han dynasty**. It means 'justice fighters', and is better translated as 'partisan militia' or 'volunteers'. In modern times it is particularly used to describe bands of Korean loyalists active against the Japanese in Korea, **Manchuria** and **Siberia**, the name being derived from that used by popular groups, many of them monks, who opposed Admiral Hideyoshi and the Japanese invaders during the **Imjin Wars**. The first modern manifestation of the phenomenon occurred after the murder of **Queen Min** in 1895, and following the disbandment of the Korean army in 1907 many hundreds of guerila units, consisting mainly of **peasants** and former soldiers, clashed with the Japanese army and police. After the Japanese **annexation** of Korea in 1910 the armies became better organised, but by the very nature of their dispersal across the peninsula and among widespread colonies of Koreans abroad they failed to offer co-ordinated resistance to the Japanese military machine. Yi Pŏmjin formed such an army in Siberia. In Korea the *Chosŏn Kukkwŏn Hoeboktan* ('Korean National Sovereignty Restoration Corps'), founded at a temple in **Taegu** in 1915, attacked Japanese police stations in 1919. In Manchuria, where almost one million Koreans lived, it was also possible to run large 'independence armies'. They included the West Route Army (*Sŏro Kunjŏngsŏ*) and the North Route Army (*Pungno Kunjŏngsŏ*). Among smaller groups of freedom fighters pursuing terrorist tactics from along the Manchuria-Korea border were the *Úiyŏltan*, founded in 1919 by Kim Wŏnbong, and **Kim Ku**'s *Aeguktan*. Both of these carried out high-profile attacks on prominent Japanese targets, such as offices of the **Oriental Development Company**, and on individuals: in January 1932 **Yi Pongch'ang** of the *Aeguktan* attempted to assassinate the Emperor in Tokyo.

The principal army in northern Manchuria was known as the Han'guk Independence Party Army and that in southern Manchuria as the Chosŏn Independence Party Army. These were a severe irritant to the colonial power and inflicted some significant defeats: in 1920 heavy Japanese casualties in battles with Kim Chwajin's army at Qingshanli and Fengwudong, in Jilin province, prompted a retaliatory massacre by the Japanese of Korean communities in Manchuria (the so-called Jiandao Incident). Following the **Government-General**'s agreement with the Manchurian warlord Zhang Zuolin that he should try to control the Korean armies, they merged into the *Kungmin Ŭihoe* under Kim Tongsam. After 1919 attempts were also made by the **Provisional Government in Exile** in Shanghai to co-ordinate *ŭibyŏng*, but differences of political outlook between communists, socialists, and right-wing nationalists made regular co-operation difficult. A left-wing organisation, *Kungminbu*, established in Manchuria in 1929, maintained the Korean Revolutionary Army; this merged with the Chinese First Route Army in 1933 to form the Northeast People's Revolutionary Army, which harrassed the Japanese through the 1930s.

KU DAEYEOL, 'The Chientao Incident (1920) and Britain,' *TRASKB*, LV, 1980
See also **Korean Communist Party**

ŬICH'ANG 義倉 Charity Granaries *See* **rice loan system**

ŬICH'ŎN 義天 (1055–1101)
Fourth son of King Munjong of Koryŏ, he became a monk at eleven. In 1085 he went to China for a year, trained in the *Hwaŏm* and *Ch'ŏnt'ae* schools, then returned hoping to fuse the *Sŏn* and *Kyo* schools of **Buddhism** into one. For this he revived *Ch'ŏnt'ae* teaching, which improved the standing of the *Sŏn* school and prepared the way for the work of **T'aego**. Ŭich'ŏn collected nearly 5,000 Buddhist books from China and Japan and took great interest in the **printing** of the *Tripitaka*, for which he made a supplement of indigenous treatises. An admirer of **Wŏnhyo** of **Silla**, he was made *kuksa* 'national teacher' in 1101, but died later that year, aged 46.

ŬIGŬM-BU 義禁府 'Council of righteous restraint'
A Chosŏn state council or tribunal of 32 men, led by a 1st **grade** junior, responsible for conducting inquisitions and enquiries on orders of the king.

ŬIGWE 儀軌 'Rubrics'
Sets of detailed rules for the performance of court **ceremonies** and banquets (*yŏnhyang* or *sayŏn*) published in book form and illustrated in books and on screens between 1719 and 1902. Usually entitled *Chinch'an Ŭigwe* ('Rubrics for the conduct of feasts') or *Chinjak Ŭigwe* ('Rubrics for the Conduct of Banquets') they set standards for court entertainment and secular rites over nearly two hundred years. In doing so they provided information on matters connected with the official and social life of the court, including its hierarchies, **dress**, **music**, and **dance**. The duties of concerned officials were detailed, together with instructions on the employment of **craftsmen** in the making of regalia, payments to them, etc. The precedence to be observed on such occasions, including seating arrangements, was important, as was the order of procedure in the line-up of an official procession, and artists had painted careful descriptions of these events at least since the early 17th century. The procession painted on the wall of Dong Shou (K. Tongsu)'s **tomb** of AD 357 at Anak, Hwanghae province, may be regarded as a forerunner of this kind of documentary record and prescription.*

LEE HYE-KU* (trans. R.C.Provine), 'Musical Paintings in a Fourth-Century Korean Tomb,' *KJ*, 14/3, 1974
PARK JEONG-HYE, 'The Court Music and Dance in the Royal Banquet Paintings of the Chosŏn Dynasty,' *KJ*, 37/3, 1997

ŬIJŎNG-BU 議政府 'Council of righteous government'
The state council or cabinet of twelve members which assisted the king in deciding major policies and decisions. Three officials (*samgong*) of 1st **grade** senior were *yŏng-ŭijŏng* 'prime minister', *chwa-ŭijŏng* 'minister of the left' and *u-ŭijŏng* 'minister of the right' (left taking precedence of the right in government posts). The Council was sometimes called *Hwanggak* 'yellow pavilion' from a Han dynasty council-chamber.
See **Left and right**

ŬISANG 義相 (625–702)
A man of **Silla** who became a monk at the age of 28. He set off to visit China with **Wŏnhyo** in 650, and continued the journey after Wŏnhyo had decided to abandon it. Having become devoted to the Flower Garland **Sutra** (*Hwaŏm-gyŏng*), Ŭisang returned to Silla in 670 and founded the *Hwaŏm* school, one of the **Five Schools** (*O-gyo*).

ŬIYŎLTAN 義烈團 'Righteous Heroes Unit'. *See* ***Ŭibyŏng***

ŬLCHI MUNDŎK 乙支文德 (6th–7th century)
A great national hero, though in Korean sources he is known only from one passage in *Samguk sagi* 20. When the **Sui** invaded **Koguryŏ** in AD 612, the minister Ŭlchi Mundŏk, knowing that the Sui troops were weary and hungry, lured them within sight of P'yŏngyang by pretending to lose battles and feigning surrender. They were too exhausted to take the city and withdrew to **Liaodong**, harrassed all the way by the Koreans. The peninsula was thus saved from Chinese domination. The Chinese *Sui shu* gives an admired Chinese quatrain of five-character verses with which Ŭlchi taunted the Sui commander.

ULLŬNG-DO 鬱陵島
An island in the Eastern Sea, 90 miles off the coast of North Kyŏngsang province, to which it belongs. According to *Samguk sagi* it was subjugated by **Silla** in AD 512, when it was called Usan-guk. Attempts to establish a resident population were made in Koryŏ times and early Chosŏn. During the 18th century it was a refuge for malefactors. Successful settlement was achieved in 1881–2, when a local government office was established. Though the harbour is of little strategic importance, the island is useful for fishermen and has been a bone of contention at least since diplomatic representations about Japanese claims to ownership in 1614. There were further incidents in 1693–4, when a Korean fishing boat was held by Japanese. After 1945 the Japanese ceased to make demands for Ullŭng-do, but they have not renounced claims to **Tokto**. The situation has been complicated by confusion over names. Both Ullŭng-do and Tokto have each been called Songdo (J. Matsushima) and Chukdo (J. Takeshima). The earliest European name for Ullŭng-do was Dagelet Island, said to be after the French officer who 'discovered' the island in May 1787, during a survey expedition led by the ship *La Pérouse*.

ŬMSŎ 蔭敍 '*shadow rank*'
Bureaucratic appointment system of the Koryŏ and Chosŏn periods under which the son of an official of fifth **grade** and above was entitled to a junior post. It underlined aristocratic privilege, and unscrupulous clans used it to extend their power.

ŬM-YANG 陰陽 (C. *yin-yang*)
The fundamental polarity in all reality, corresponding to negative and positive charges. The Chinese character *yin* means the shady north slope of a mountain or south side of a valley (the geographers' *ubac*), *yang* the sunny south slope of a hill or north side of a valley (*adret*); but these may not have been the original meanings of the words. *Yin* implies female, quiescent, negative, compliant, weak, dark, adversarial, heavy, large, cold; *yang* male, active, positive, forceful, strong, bright, eirenic, light, small, hot. Both develop unceasingly in all entities, underlying the generation of the manifold phenomena of the universe and needing to be held in equilibrium. Thus they are applicable to ethics, language and **medicine**, even **left and right**, as well as cosmology. Though its early history is obscure, the concept is present in late Zhou writings (5th century BC) and has its classic description in the *Book of Changes* (*Xici zhuan* section, *passim*; c. 200 BC). The neo-Confucian emblematic **roundel** of two interlocking commas, one *yin*, one *yang*, is called *t'aegŭk*.

UNCURK *See* **United Nations Commission on the Unification and Rehabilitation of Korea**

UNDERWATER TOMB *Haejung-nŭng* 海中陵 *See* **Taewang-am**

UNDERWOOD, HORACE GRANT (1859–1916) and **HORACE HORTON** (1890–1951) 元杜尤, 元漢慶
Born in London but educated in America, Horace Grant Underwood arrived in Korea as a Northern Presbyterian missionary in 1885 and taught science at *Kwanghye-wŏn*. In 1886 he founded an orphanage and in 1887 Saemunan Church. He started the Christian Literature Society in 1889, was active in Bible translation, wrote Korean-English and English-Korean dictionaries (1890), started a weekly Christian magazine *Kŭrisŭto Sinmun* (1897), and took part in founding the Korean **Young Men's Christian Association** (1900). In 1915 he started Kyŏngsin Seminary and was involved in planning the foundation of Yŏnhŭi College (now Yŏnsei University), but illness forced him to return to America, where he died in Atlantic City.

His son Horace Horton Underwood was born in Seoul and became a teacher at Kyŏngsin School in 1912. In 1917 he became principal of Chosŏn Seminary, and in 1933 principal of Yŏnhŭi College. He was active in the **Royal Asiatic Society**. Briefly imprisoned by the Japanese in 1941, he returned to America. After the war he was an adviser to the Military Government, returning to the seminary in 1949, but dying in **Pusan** after the invasion of 1950.

'UNEQUAL' TREATIES
The **Kanghwa Treaty** of 1876 forced on Korea by Japan was the first of the unequal treaties which subordinated Korea to the outside world in the late 19th century. Ironically its traditional suzerain, China, which was itself suffering from this form of imperialism at western hands, did not attempt to emulate the practice in Korea, but resorted to other diplomatic means to retain its privileged status. The first treaty signed between Korea and a western power in the 19th century was the US-Korea Treaty of Amity and Commerce, also known as the **Shufeldt Treaty** of 1882. **Li Hongzhang**, anxious to counter the growth of Japanese influence in Korea, urged Seoul to conclude other treaties with the West, and treaties followed with both Britain and Germany on 25 November 1883, Italy and Russia on 25 June 1884, France on 4 June 1886, and

subsequently with Austria, Denmark and Belgium. Though the foreign powers scarcely differentiated between these treaties and those they were making or had made with China – and indeed took advantage of assistance from Chinese officials such as Ma Jianzhong in drawing them up – and were clearly motivated by self-interest, the results are not associated with such widespread exploitation of the Korean people and their resources, for China and Japan remained the principal targets of western attention. (Indeed, it is significant that unlike the Chinese treaties made with the West in the 19th century, which are remembered in China only with grief and anger, the centenaries of those between Korea and the United States, Germany, Britain, and France were cause for mutual celebration through the 1980s in South Korea and the West.) The principal features which make the treaties 'unequal' are that they denied the Korean government tariff autonomy, fixing rates at 5–7%, and the right of jurisdiction over foreigners, putting Korea on the same footing as China and Japan regarding extraterritoriality. Two later treaties involving China, Japan and Russia did immediately have adverse effects on Korea, namely those of **Shimonoseki** (1895) and **Portsmouth** (1905). While the early treaties were mainly interested in developing commercial advantages for countries experiencing the Industrial Revolution, the two latter were also concerned with territorial rights related to the Japanese and Russian exploitation of **Manchuria** and the Korean peninsula. As far as Korea was concerned, the military, economic and political results were wholly adverse, but the longer-term cumulative effect was the stimulation of Korean **nationalism** and the **self-strengthening movement**.
H. CHUNG, *Korean Treaties*, New York: H.S. Nichols Inc., 1919; C.I. EUGENE KIM & HAN-KYO KIM, *Korea and the Politics of Imperialism, 1876–1910*, Berkeley: University of California Press, 1976

UNGJIN 熊津
Modern Kongju, Ch'ungch'ŏng Namdo province, capital of **Paekche** from 475, when **Koguryŏ** captured Hansŏng (modern **Kwangju**, near Seoul) and killed King Kaero, until 538, when the court was forced to move south to **Sabi**. The brick **tomb** of King **Muryŏng** (d. 523), which was undisturbed when opened in 1971, may be entered and is a fine example of Chinese-style burial practices. King Ŭija fled here from Sabi in face of the **Silla** and Chinese forces in 660, but was forced to surrender his kingdom.

UNHYŎN 'Cloud Hill' **PALACE** 雲峴宮
Stands midway between the **Kyŏngbok Palace** and the **Ch'angdok Palace** in Seoul. It was the birthplace of King **Kojong** and the private residence of his father the **Taewŏn'gun**, who made it the administrative centre of government during his regency. Only five buildings of the originally extensive walled complex now remain. They were rebuilt and opened to the public in 1996.

UNIFICATION CHURCH *Kidokkyo T'ongil Sillyŏng Hyŏphoe*
基督教統一神靈協會
Also known as the Holy Spirit Association for the Unification of World Christianity and the International Cultural Foundation, among other names. A **new religion** founded by Mun Sŏnmyŏng (b. 1920), a Presbyterian who set up a new church organisation in P'yŏngyang after the departure of the Japanese in 1945. He was imprisoned at times by the communists, but managed to be in Seoul by the time of the **Armistice** in 1953. He taught that although Christ had brought spiritual salvation, he, at this time known as Mun Yesu, 'Jesus Mun', had brought the necessary complementary physical salvation. He wrote a new scripture, *Wŏlli* 'The

Divine Principle', to be added to the Bible, and conducted some dramatic ceremonies, including the Marriage of the Lamb, when he took a very young new wife. He controlled every individual in his flock, conducting mass weddings of couples chosen to be spouses by himself, and instituted draconian evangelistic training for them. He was firmly anti-communist and soon established branches overseas, especially in the USA (where Mun lived after 1973 and there were 3,000 followers in 1980), preaching that full salvation came out of Korea. In 1982 he was convicted of income tax fraud. He then moved to Brazil, whence he returned to Korea in 1998. His organisation has often been accused of using brain-washing techniques. Although not large (perhaps 200,000 members), the movement is rich and international.

UNIFIED SILLA DYNASTY 統一新羅 (668–936)

The first dynasty to rule over the entire Korean peninsula. Its kingdom stretched from the **Taedong** River to the south coast, and comprised much of the territory belonging to the former states of **Silla**, **Koguryŏ**, **Paekche**, and **Kaya**. Though it quickly thwarted the expectation of its **Tang** ally by refusing to become a Chinese province after unification, it constituted the most loyal vassal state within the Middle Kingdom's tributary system, and the level of sinicisation among its educated class was the highest anywhere in the Chinese culture zone. To its north in **Manchuria** lay the kingdom of **Parhae**, a largely hostile neighbour, while political and cultural relations with southern Japan during the Nara and Heian periods were generally warm.

The capital was at **Kyŏngju**. The authority of the royal **lineage** of Kim was strengthened, especially by King **Sinmun** and his son **Sŏngdŏk**, though the bone-rank system (*see* **kolp'um**) continued to underpin the power of the aristocracy. The centralised administrative and **military systems** reflected Chinese influence, and the literate élite promoted the study and application of **Confucianism** and **Buddhism** alike. The long period of peace and stability encouraged the development of arts and crafts, and the many surviving buildings, monuments and statues attest to the interest and skill in religious art, **architecture**, **astronomy** (*see* **Ch'ŏmsŏng-dae**), mathematics and landscaping. Fine metal-working has been preserved in the form of **bells**, and may also be seen in the contents of many **tombs** excavated in modern times. The economy was based on a mixture of wet and dry farming, stock raising, forestry and trade, and the aristocratic landowners derived much of their labour and income from **slaves** and tenant farmers. Korean shipping carried much of the **commerce** between the countries around the East China Sea.

The fortunes of the dynasty started to decline in the mid-8th century, following the reign of King Kyŏngdok. Members of the aristocracy rebelled against the power of the throne, while the lower 'head-rank' nobility resented the privileges of their *chin'gol* superiors. The government began to lose control over regional 'castle lords' (*sŏngju*; *see* **gentry**) and the income from their lands, and the **peasantry** eventually rebelled against excessive demands from local and central tax-gatherers combined. Two leaders emerged to direct popular dissatisfaction into specific political ambition, resurrecting the divisions of the peninsula before unification: a peasant leader, **Kyŏn Hwŏn**, restored the kingdom of Paekche in the south-west, while a discontented aristocrat, **Kungye**, proclaimed that of Later Koguryŏ (*see* **Three Kingdoms, Later**). Both proved to be tyrants. Kungye was killed by his own people and succeeded in 918 by **Wang Kŏn**, who had a better sense of both strategy and statesmanship. He sought reconciliation with Silla, attacking Kyŏn Hwŏn after the latter had sacked Kyŏngju in 927, and the surrender of the last Silla king, Kyŏngsun, was obtained in 935 with a sense of relief at the prospect of reunification.

KINGS

a) members of the Kim clan:

Munmu	661–81	Hŭngdŏk	826–36
Sinmun	681–92	Huigang	836–7
Hyoso	692–702	Minae	838–9
Sŏngdŏk	702–37	Sinmu	839
Hyosŏng	737–42	Munsŏng	839–57
Kyŏngdŏk	742–65	Hŏn'an	857–61
Hyegong	765–80	Kyŏngmun	861–75
Sŏndŏk	780–5	Hŏn'gang	875–86
Wŏnsŏng	785–98	Chŏnggang	886–7
Sosŏng	798–800	Queen Chinsŏng	887–98
Aejang	800–809	Hyogong	898–912
Hŏndŏk	809–26		

b) members of the Pak clan:

Sindŏk	913–7	Kyŏngae	924–7
Kyŏngmyŏng	917–24		

c) member of the Kim clan:

Kyŏngsun	927–35

See also **Anap-chi; Buddhism; Chang Pogo; China, relations with; Silla, Queens; Tang dynasty**

UNIFORM TAX LAW *See Taedongpŏp*

UNITED NATIONS COMMISSION ON THE UNIFICATION AND REHABILITATION OF KOREA (UNCURK) *Kukche yŏnhap Han'guk t'ongil puhŭng wiwŏnhoe* 國際聯合韓國統一復興委員會
Successor to the **United Nations Temporary Commission on Korea** (UNTCOK), and the United Nations Commission on Korea (UNCOK) which replaced it in 1948. The latter worked in Seoul until its enforced evacuation to Tokyo on 26 June 1950. In the tense months before the outbreak of war in June 1950 its job was to try and deter both North and South Korea from igniting a general conflagration. Two United Nations military observers, the Australians Major Peach and Squadron Leader Rankin, were sent to Korea in May. They visited the **Thirty-Eighth Parallel** in mid-June and had only just returned to Seoul when war broke out on the 25th. It was on the basis of their hastily compiled report that UNCOK reported on the 26th that South Korea had been the victim of a surprise attack, and the Security Council condemned a 'well-planned, concerted and full scale invasion of South Korea'.

UNCURK, established on 7 October 1950 by the same meeting of the UN General Assembly that authorised its troops' crossing of the 38th Parallel, comprised representatives from seven member states, Australia, Chile, the Netherlands, Pakistan, the Philippines, Thailand, and Turkey, and worked in Seoul. It monitored elections in South Korea and reported annually to the United Nations General Assembly. It was never recognised by North Korea, which saw it as an agency of United States support for the South and consistently called for its dissolution. Its impartiality was particularly put in doubt by Chile's withdrawal from the Commission in 1966 and that of Pakistan in 1972. Its abolition in 1973 was a recognition of the divided nature of the peninsula, after which both North and South Korea pursued new diplomatic links with other

countries with some success. North Korea was granted equal observer status with the South at the United Nations.
BARRY GILLS, *Korea versus Korea: A Case of Contested Legitimacy*, London & New York: Routledge, 1996; LEE KWANG HO, *A Study of United Nations Commission on Unification and Rehabilitation of Korea – International System and International Organization*, PhD Thesis, University of Pittsburgh, 1974

UNITED NATIONS COMMISSION ON KOREA (UNCOK) *See* **United Nations Commission on the Unification and Rehabilitation of Korea (UNCURK)**

UNITED NATIONS ORGANISATION (UNO) *Kukche yŏnhap kigu* 國際聯合機構
Assumed responsibility for solving the problem of Korean reunification when the United States and the Soviet Union were unable to agree on the organisation of national elections called for in the **Moscow Conference** Agreement (*see* **US-Soviet Joint Commission**). It established the **United Nations Temporary Commission on Korea** and the **United Nations Commission on the Unification and Rehabilitation of Korea**, though the Soviet bloc consistently opposed its right to intervene. In practice, it was only in the south that United Nations representatives were allowed any opportunity to work and participate in the organisation of elections. Unsatisfactory as the situation was, it meant that UNO became identified with the interests of the **Republic of Korea** (ROK).

With the outbreak of the **Korean War** on 25 June 1950 the Security Council condemned the North as an aggressor, and when it refused to withdraw quickly, formed a military force from 16 nations under the command of General Douglas MacArthur. The entry of troops from the People's Republic of China, the so-called **Chinese People's Volunteers**, transformed what had begun as a local conflict into one of global proportions, and deepened the division of the United Nations into opposing American and Soviet blocs. The war resulted in the death of an estimated 14,000 soldiers of United Nations member states, not including the Americans, who bore the main brunt of the hostilities. After the 1953 **Armistice** the United Nations Command took part in regular but ineffectual meetings with North Korean military representatives at **P'anmunjŏm**. Both North and South enjoyed the benefits of access to United Nations organisations such as the World Health Organisation and UNESCO. The General Assembly debated resolutions concerning Korean issues every year until 1975, with votes consistently favouring the ROK position. Before the Korean War, US-Soviet rivalry had led to requests for dual North and South Korean membership of UNO being turned down, and after it, the North agreed to the South's regular proposal that they should seek separate membership only in November 1991. Their applications were immediately approved. In 1991 the United Nations Development Programme gave support for the **Tumen River** project. In 1994 a crisis arose following the refusal of North Korea, as a signatory to the Nuclear Non-Proliferation Treaty, to admit inspection of its nuclear facilities (*see* **North Korean nuclear programme**). The question of UN sanctions became confused by the coincidental deepening of famine conditions and the obvious need of the North Korean population for humanitarian aid.

UNITED NATIONS TEMPORARY COMMISSION ON KOREA (UNTCOK)
Kuche yŏnhap Han'guk wiwŏnhoe 國際聯合韓國委員會
Body set up by decision of the United Nations in November 1947, following the failure of the **US-Soviet Joint Commission** to arrange elections for a provisional government.

Its chairman was the Indian Dr Kumara Menon. Following the terms of the US-instigated resolution, UNTCOK was to organise national elections, whereupon American and Soviet troops were to be withdrawn. Once again, foreign nations referred to the Koreans' right to independence and self-determination, as they had ever since the late 19th century. The UNTCOK team arrived in Seoul in January 1948, but was refused entry to North Korea by the Soviet Union. Consequently, the election it arranged on 10 May 1948, to choose delegates to Korea's first independent government, selected only 198 representatives for the southern half of the country; 100 seats allocated to the northern half were left vacant. Thus was the Republic of Korea established, and recognised as the legitimate government by the United Nations on 12 December 1948. Syngman Rhee (**Yi Sŭngman**)'s National Society for Rapid Korean Independence (Tongnip Ch'oksŏng Hyŏbŭi-hoe) won the largest number of party seats, and Rhee himself was overwhelmingly elected as the first president by the new National Assembly on 20 June 1949. In the north, elections were organised on 25 August 1948 which were claimed to have chosen 572 representatives democratically from both south and north Korea to attend the Supreme People's Assembly in P'yŏngyang. They were denounced as fraudulent by **Kim Ku** and **Kim Kyusik**. In accordance with the UN resolution, both American and Soviet troops had left Korean soil by June 1949.

LEE KWANG HO, *A Study of United Nations Commission on Unification and Rehabilitation of Korea – International System and International Organization*, PhD Thesis, University of Pittsburgh, 1974
See also **United Nations Commission on the Unification and Rehabilitation of Korea**

UNITED PROGRESS SOCIETY *Ilchinhoe* 一進會

Collaborationist society formed in December 1904 by Song Pyŏngjun and Yi Yonggu. Its aim was the promotion of Korean interests through modernisation, which they believed would come through cooperation. Japan, however, used it to further its own interests before and during the **Protectorate**. The society published a newspaper, and its members, some of whom had been educated and trained in Japan, obtained jobs in administration, education and law enforcement. Song himself had spent years in Japan after fleeing the aftermath of the *Kapsin* **coup** and had worked as an interpreter in the Japanese army. With support from **Itō Hirobumi** he gained ministerial office in **Yi Wanyong**'s collaborationist government, called for Emperor **Kojong**'s abdication, and campaigned for the annexation of his country by Japan. Some of the society's members were former **Tonghak** adherents, and popular revulsion against its aims led to attacks on them and their property in 1907, but in 1910 it was the largest political party, with a reported membership of 140,000.

UNITED STATES ARMY MILITARY GOVERNMENT IN KOREA (USAMGIK)
See **American Military Government**

UNIVERSITIES

The first university to be opened in Korea was Keijō Imperial University, established in 1924. It admitted mostly Japanese students. After the Japanese defeat it was taken over by Americans and Koreans and reorganised as Seoul National University. It remained the only Korean university until 1950, when appreciation of Korea's need for higher education began the upgrading of existing colleges and foundation of new ones with university status. The latter included Han'guk University for Foreign Studies. Of the former, Yŏnsei University had been established in 1885 by American missionaries (*see* **Horace Underwood**); Korea University, founded together with its middle school for

Korean students by **Kim Sŏngsu**, was previously known as Posŏng College (*Posŏng Chŏnmun Hakkyo*); the former Confucian Academy (*Sŏnggyun-gwan*) was revived as Sŏnggyun-gwan University, and continued to teach the **Confucian Classics** as a central part of its syllabus; and **Ewha Women's University** became the first higher education institution for women. During the 1950s Korean universities benefited from American advice and aid, but as **students** became increasingly conscious of political conditions in the Republic of Korea and its relations with the outside world, they grew vocal in their attacks on their own government and the United States, and successive governments had to confront university staff and students objecting to social and political policies. In 1997 there were 136 universities in South Korea.
KIM JONG-CHOL, 'Higher Education Policies in Korea 1945–83,' *KJ*, 23/10, 1983

UNTCOK *See* **United Nations Temporary Commission on Korea**

UNYŌ-KAN INCIDENT 雲揚艦事件 *See* **Kanghwa Treaty**

ŬPCHI 邑誌 'town records'
This is a collective reference to local histories and gazetteers, some of which refer to *ŭp* 'town', but many to other administrative divisions from province downwards. They are an important source for historians. Upwards of 250 are known, mostly dating, at least in their present forms, from the 18th century and later. Examples are *Chunggyŏng-ji* (**Kaesŏng** 1830), *Tonggyŏng chapki* (**Kyŏngju**), *P'yŏngyang-ji* (1590), *Kanghwa-buji* (mid-18th century), *Suwŏn-bu ŭpchi* (late 18th century), and *Ch'ungju-gun ŭpchi* (1870).

US DEFENSE PERIMETER
First identified by Secretary of State Dean Acheson on 12 January 1950 as the line beyond which the United States would not involve itself militarily in defence of its national interests. He told the National Press Club that the line ran from the Aleutian Islands, through Japan and Okinawa, to the Philippines. Korea and Taiwan were not included within the perimeter and the State Department doubted the wisdom of trying to resist any forcible move to unite Korea from the north. The future of Korea was already in the hands of the **United Nations Organisation**. Acheson's public statement encouraged **Kim Ilsŏng** in his preparations for war. However, the North Korean invasion of the South in June 1950 led to President Truman's immediate redrawing of the line, committing American troops to support Syngman Rhee (**Yi Sŭngman**)'s régime in Korea and despatching the US Seventh Fleet to the Taiwan Straits to prevent a communist attack on the island.

US-ROK TREATY *See* **Mutual Defense Treaty**

US-SOVIET JOINT COMMISSION
Body set up under the terms of the **Moscow Conference** Agreement of December 1945. Its task was to 'assist the formation of a provisional Korean government' in consultation with 'the Korean democratic parties and social organisations', and to co-operate with the Provisional Government and other democratic organisations in working out 'measures for helping and assisting the political, economic and social progress of the Korean people, the development of democratic self-government and the establishment of the national independence of Korea.' It was thus dedicated to establishing **trusteeship** over the peninsula. The first meeting of the Commission

began in the **Tŏksu Palace** in Seoul on 16 January 1946 under Colonel Shtykov and Major General Arnold, and produced immediate disagreement over communication across the **Thirty Eighth Parallel**. Talks about the organisation of elections were broken off in May and no further meeting took place until May 1947, the main point at issue being the recognition of democratic parties and organisations. The Soviet side was only prepared to acknowledge those willing to accept trusteeship; the Americans insisted that notice must be taken of all representative parties, whether they accepted the principle or not. When the second round of talks proved equally fruitless the United States turned for help to the UNO, which voted on 14 November 1947 to establish a **United Nations Temporary Commission on Korea (UNTCOK)**.

See also **American Military Government**

V

VAIROCANA BUDDHA *Pirojana-bu* 毗盧遮那佛 or *Taeil* 大日 'great sun'
A frequent expression of buddhahood in Korean temple halls is the *samsinbul* (S. *trikaya* 'triple buddha form'): (1) in the middle sits Vairocana (K. Pirojana), essence of buddhahood and 'Great Illumination Buddha', all-penetrating, all-transforming cosmic awareness, called *pŏpsin* 'dharma-form'; (2) to his left, Locana (K. Nosana or Kwangmyŏng-bul) the blissfulness or enjoyment of buddhahood, called *posin*, the 'kharma-form'; (3) to Vairocana's right, Sakyamuni, the human transformation and historic manifestation of buddhahood in this world, called *ŭngsin* 'correspondence-form'. Vairocana has a distinctive **mudra**.

VOWEL HARMONY *moŭm-johwa* 母音調和
Vowel harmony means that all the vowels in a word are of the same general type. This is a feature of Altaic languages and is one reason why Korean is supposed by many to belong to the Altaic group. Yet *Hunmin chŏngŭm* shows that vowel harmony was already disintegrating by the 15th century. The harmonic types were called *yang* and *yin* or **clear and cloudy**. Front vowels *a*, *arae a* (*ă*) and *o* were *yang* or clear; back vowels *ŏ*, *ŭ* and *u* were *yin* or cloudy; *i* was *chungsŏng* 'neutral'. *Yang* harmonised with *yang* or neutral, *yin* with *yin* or neutral, as in *pada* 'sea', *panăl* (modern *panŭl*) 'needle', *sŏrŭ* modern (*soro*) 'mutual' and *kurŭm* 'cloud'. Accusative forms like *kurŭmŭl* and *syorăl* (modern *sorŭl*) 'cow' showed the principle applied to suffixes. Traces remain today in verb conjugations (*tŭrŏtta* 'entered' but *toratta* 'turned'); in light and heavy isotopes of adverbs such as *kkadak-kkadak* (light, *yang*) for a little boy nodding eagerly and *kkŏdŏk-kkŏdŏk* (heavy, *yin*) for an old man nodding sagely; and in contrasts like *norang* (*yang*) 'clear yellow' and *nurŏng* (*yin*) for the colour of brass or of faded leaves.

W

WA 倭 (K. colloquial *wae*)
Alliance of petty states in southern and western Japan in the early centuries of the present era, the most powerful of which was Yamato. Both tributary and commercial contacts were maintained with China and southern Korea (including **Paekche** and **Kaya**). Military attacks also took place on the Korean coast, as for example in AD 400, when a **Koguryŏ** army under King **Kwanggaet'o** came to the aid of **Silla**. Korean

historians have suggested that kings of Paekche may have sent royal relatives to Kyushu to rule there as *tamno* kings over feudal vassals (*see* **Muryŏng, King**).
MARK HUDSON, 'Ethnicity in East Asia: Approaches to the Wa,' *Archaeological Review from Cambridge* 8.1, 1989

WAJIL 瓦質
Type of hard earthenware, or stoneware, **pottery** produced during the time of the Chinese **commanderies** at the beginning of the AD era. A typical production site is at Choyang, near **Kyŏngju** (North Kyŏngsang province). Vessel types were derived from those of *Mumun* pottery, but the technology used to produce them was evidently learned from Chinese practice.

WALLS
Great defensive walls along the northern frontier were built by **Koguryŏ** in the early 7th century against the Chinese threat, by **Silla** in the early 8th century against **Parhae**, and by **Koryŏ** in 1033-44 against the **Khitan** and **Jurchen** in **Manchuria**. Walls of earth and stone formed protective ramparts around major cities, pierced by gates over which towered impressive lookout buildings. The gates were sometimes themselves defended by walled barbicans. The Great East Gate of Seoul (**Tongdaemun**) is an example. An extant section of a traditional city wall of the late 18th century can be seen at **Suwŏn**.
See also **fortresses**

WANG KŎN 王建 (reigned as King T'aejo, 918–43)
Founder of the Koryŏ dynasty. He assisted **Kungye** in the establishment of the Later Koguryŏ kingdom in 901, but overthrew him in 918. He then changed the name of the state to Koryŏ, built a new capital city at **Kaesŏng**, and reunited the country in 936 after defeating Later Paekche in battle. The king of Silla, Kyŏngsun, had surrendered the previous year, and as part of a wisely conciliatory policy T'aejo invested him and other powerful clan leaders from Silla and Later Paekche with offices and lands. Those of his own state who had assisted the reunification were rewarded as '**meritorious subjects**'. He never, however, managed to rid himself entirely of concern about the loyalty of **gentry** families, and married into several of them himself in an attempt to gain their support. He had six queens, including one from the royal clan of Silla, and twenty-three further consorts.

The political division of China and the rise of the **Khitan** in **Manchuria** made the priorities of foreign policy far from straightforward. He welcomed refugees from **Parhae**. As part of the northern defence of the country he built up P'yŏngyang as its second city, and pushed the extent of Koryŏ administration as far north as the **Ch'ŏngch'ŏn River**. To the south, he incorporated the island of T'amna (**Cheju**) into the kingdom in 938.

T'aejo was convinced of the powers of **p'ungsu** and **shamanism**. His strong belief in **Buddhism** prompted him to have ten new temples built in Kaesŏng alone, and in his famous '**Ten Injunctions**' (*Sip Hunyo*) he expressed his views on the importance of both Buddhism and *p'ungsu* to the state. Nevertheless, as a monarch T'aejo endeavoured to rule in ways that even the Confucian Mencius might have approved. **Schools** were opened in Kaesŏng and P'yŏngyang, and **agriculture** was stimulated by the reduction of **taxation** on farmers.
See also **foundation myths; Three Kingdoms, Later**

WANG SOGUN 王昭君 (C. Wang Zhaojun)
Wang Zhaojun is regarded by Koreans as the ultimate heroine of sad and lonely exile. Historically, she was a concubine of the Emperor Yuandi of Han who gave her as wife to the Khan of the Xiongnu in 33 BC. Legends have grown up around this fact. Some say she went to the Gobi desert; but the most popular says she drowned herself in the Amur and the grass on her tomb, Qingzhong (K. *Ch'ŏngch'ong*), is always green.

WANGGŎMSŎNG 王儉城
The ancient capital of **Wiman Chosŏn** near modern P'yŏngyang, captured by Han Wudi's armies in 108 BC and adopted as the capital of the Chinese **commandery** of **Lelang**. It became the capital of **Koguryŏ** in AD 427.

WANG-O-CH'ŎNCH'UKKUK-CHŎN See **Hyech'o**

WEI, HISTORIES OF 魏書(志)
After the Han empire collapsed in AD 220, China was divided into three states: Wu, Shu and Wei. Their story is fictionalised in *Sanguozhi yanyi*, '**Romance of the Three Kingdoms**', but there is also an official history, *Sanguozhi* 'Account of the Three Kingdoms', compiled by Chen Shou (233–297). The part of *Sanguozhi* that deals with Wei (the northern kingdom, which bordered on Korea) is called *Weizhi*, 'Account of Wei', and contains *Dongyi zhuan* 'Description of the Eastern Tribes' – as they were known to the Chinese of the **Lelang** commandery – written by Fu Xuan (217–278). Called *Wiji Tongi-jŏn* in Korean, it describes **Puyŏ** (Manchuria); **Koguryŏ**; Eastern Ŏkcho (NE Korea); Umnu, Ye (E Korea); the **Samhan** (Mahan, Chinhan, and Pyŏnhan) (S Korea), all of whom spoke variants of the same language. This is the earliest written account of the inhabitants of the peninsula.

A commentary on *Weizhi*, published by Pei Songzhi (360–439), cites *Weilue* (K. *Wiryak*) 'Summary of Wei' by Yu Huan, written between 280 and 289. *Weilue* refers to **Wiman Chosŏn** and the Korean Three Kingdoms.

Weishu, also called *Hou Weishu* 'Book of Later Wei', is an official history of the Wei dynasty (386–535), written by Wei Shou of the Chinese Northern Ji dynasty in 551. It includes material on Koguryŏ and **Paekche**, largely quoted from *Sanguozhi*.

Samguk yusa cites '*Weishu*' for the story of **Tan'gun**, but the reference does not occur in the *Weishu* now known.

WELL-FIELD SYSTEM *chŏngjŏn* 井田
An agricultural system described in Mencius IIIa.3. The Chinese character for 'a well' (K. *chŏng*) (two vertical lines crossed by two horizontal lines) can be imposed on a square, dividing it into nine smaller squares. When a field was divided in this way, eight families could each work one of the border squares and all could cooperate on the central square for their overlord. There is no evidence that this system was ever put into practice anywhere, but it was used as a theoretical ideal throughout history.
See **land reform**

WELTEVREE, JAN JANSE 朴燕 (b. 1595)
Weltevree was a tall blond Dutchman, born at Rijp in north Holland. He was probably engaged in piracy when he and two other Dutchmen were marooned on the east coast of Korea near **Kyŏngju** in 1627 by Chinese sailors. He was fully integrated into Korean life under the name Pak Yŏn, married to a Korean woman by whom he had a son and a daughter. His two companions died while they were all fighting for Korea

during the **Manchu invasion** of 1636. He was employed in firearms production and was responsible for other castaways (chiefly Japanese and Chinese) detained in Korea. He was still alive in 1666 when **Hamel** left Korea. He was an indirect contributor to the development of the ***Pukhak*** school of would-be practical modernisers.

GARI LEDYARD, *The Dutch Come to Korea: an Account of the Life of the First Westerners in Korea* (1653–66), Seoul: Royal Asiatic Society, Korea Branch, 1971

WHEEL OF BLISS

A decorative motif of later Chosŏn which appears to have no Korean name, a **roundel** divided into three comma-like areas of the same size and form, one red, one blue and one yellow. The lines dividing the three areas start at the centre and swirl through 180 or 360 degrees to the perimeter. In Korea it seems to have no symbolic meaning, but in Tibet it is *dga'-'kyil*, 'wheel of bliss', a symbol of primordial energy used by the Nyingma school to show the three aspects of the Buddhist path: ground, path and goal.

Koreans in the large embassies to China may have discovered the wheel in the Lama Temple at Beijing or the lamaseries at the Imperial Summer Palace in Rehe (Jehol). They used it on round objects such as hatboxes, litharge boxes and **drum**heads, on spatular **fans** and on the doors of large buildings, as well as in the corners of decorated rectangles such as box lids. Some have taken the triple form to mean heaven, earth and man, but this has not been historically justified. A form with four divisions (the fourth being green) is sometimes found on drumheads. The Japanese *mitsudomoe* 'three commas' is probably not related.

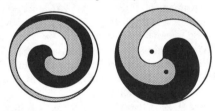

WHITE BUDDHA 白佛

Early western visitors to Seoul were impressed by a 10-foot-high rock-relief outside the North Gate. They called it 'the White Buddha', but it represents the Bodhisattva **Kwanseŭm** or Avalokitesvara, the Indian prince who over the centuries became known as the 'Goddess of Mercy', but whose sex is here made clear by his mustachios, painted green. It may be ancient, but nothing is known of its history. Even the whitewash that covers it is said to date only from the devotion shown towards it by **Queen Min**, mother of **Kojong**, in the mid-19th century.

WHITE OX SOCIETY 白牛會 *Paeguhoe*

Association of Korean artists in Tokyo, formed in 1937 (a 'white ox year' by **Nine Palaces** theory), which shunned the national exhibitions promoted by the **Government-General** in Korea. Because the ox was a symbol of self-sacrifice for many Koreans, and represented the spirit of national fortitude amid the hardships of occupation and war, the Japanese forced the Society to change its name in 1938 to the Korean Residents' Artists Association.
See also **Yi Chungsŏp**

WHITE-CLAD PEOPLE *paegŭi minjok* 白衣民族

According to *Weizhi* (*see* **Wei, histories of**), the **Puyŏ** people in the 3rd century AD wore white coats, jackets and trousers at home – a frugal taste in hemp or **silk** that is

thought to have accorded with Korean taste ever since (*see* **Mohadang**). The modernising **Kabo** decrees of 1895 required darker colours and in 1906 white clothes were forbidden; but they survived the harsh measures of the colonial government (policemen brushed black dye on white clothes worn at country markets) and after 1945 the countryside was a land of white-clothed people again. The popularity of western clothing has brought new fashions in colour, but Koreans still think of themselves as a people that prefers to wear white.
See also **Shanhai jing**

WIMAN CHOSŎN 衛滿朝鮮

Traditionally regarded as the third successive state or historical period in the ancient history of Korea. It was founded early in the 2nd century BC by Wiman (C. Wei Man), sometimes reputed to have been a refugee from the Chinese state of Yan but perhaps no more than a native of the **Liaodong** region whose power developed within the confines of **Old Chosŏn**, where he is said to have been enfeoffed by King Chun. After rebelling against the king he established his own state in place of Old Chosŏn. This posed a threat to **Han** China, especially in possible alliance with other proto-states around the north-eastern borders of China and the Xiongnu. When a pre-emptive invasion by Han Wudi's armies in 109–8 destroyed Wiman Chosŏn, then under its founder's grandson, its capital at **Wanggŏmsŏng** became the capital of the Han **commandery** of **Lelang**.

WIRYESŎNG 慰禮城

Fortress enclosing the **Paekche** capital of **Hansŏng** and its Namhan castle, surrounded by a moat. The main part of the defences, known as the Mongchon fortification, are now visible in Tunchongdong in south-east Seoul and were excavated in 1985. Evidence shows that the wall was built of stamped earth in the 3rd century AD and re-used during the Chosŏn dynasty (*see* **Namhan sansŏng**). Paekche relics included a broken bronze vessel decorated with a coin design, a five-tiered cylindrical earthenware object similar to those found in contemporary Japanese tombs, a carved wooden duck, a ceramic bowl, ironware and metal fish hooks.

Other constituent walls of the fortress were known as P'ungnap and Samsŏng. The area inside the P'ungnap fortification was excavated at P'ungnap-tong in 1997 and revealed seven semi-subterranean dwellings, with hearths, a large number of earthenware vessels, and a **kiln**, dating from the 3rd and 4th centuries AD. The largest covered approximately 83 square metres.

WŎLSAN TAEGUN 月山大君 (1454–88)

Elder brother of King **Sŏngjong**. Brought up in the palace as a favourite grandson by **Sejong**, he was made Wŏlsan-gun (Prince Wŏlsan) at six and *taegun* at 16. He was devoted to study and his verses were admired in China. Sŏngjong often visited his house and named his studio *P'ungwŏl-jŏng*, 'pavilion of wind and moon'. Wŏlsan spent much of his time in his country villa near Koyang.

WOMEN

The rôle of women in Chosŏn society was stereotyped in Confucian terms as attentive daughter-in-law, dutiful wife and wise mother. The countryside is peppered with memorials (**yŏllyŏ-mun**) to valiant women who exemplified the ideal of the chaste widow. The rôle of men was equally stereotyped: neither men nor women had any choice of career.

A girl was kept away from the company of men and boys from the age of seven, taught the domestic arts, including cooking, embroidery, sericulture, care of clothing, and the preparation of sacrificial food. *Yangban* women learned some Chinese characters, but were not usually fully literate. They read and wrote in Korean script (*see* **reading**). They were expected to be serene, chaste, complaisant, careful in speech, neat in appearance, and skilled in hospitality. They kept to the women's quarters, and out of doors rode in closed palanquins or kept their faces covered (in later days with the famous green coat worn over the head). Two important handbooks on women's ideals were *Samgang haengsilto* and *Naehun* (a florilegium composed by the mother of King **Sŏngjong** in 1475).

It was recognised that a woman's qualities would be reflected in the behaviour and achievements of her husband. On **marriage** a woman went to live in his home. She had restricted property rights, but enough to give rise to quarrels and scheming. Women were held responsible for the peace and economy of the household.

Except in *yangban* families, they often had no recorded names, but were referred to by the **surname** suffixed with *-ssi*. They were the guardians of kinship terms, which they used in addressing one another within the family. They were, however, granted honorary titles that accorded with their husbands' ranks. They did not officiate in the ancestor cult. Wives had considerable property rights. In one circumstance the power of a woman was immense, and could be of national importance. If a man died leaving an under-age son, his wife became head of the family until the son married and assumed the headship; if a man died sonless, his widow became head of the family until she personally appointed an heir: hence the number of kings who were appointed by dowager queens. (*See* **Ch'ŏlchong; Kojong; Sunjo**)

Women were usually respected and often feared by their menfolk. The reverse image of Korean womanhood comes from the jealousy and scheming that was produced by their property rights and order of dominance within the family. Relations with a mother-in-law were proverbially miserable.

Commoners strove to follow most *yangban* ideals. Shamans (*mudang*), *kisaeng* and some other women lived outside or on the fringe of this Confucian system.

LAUREL KENDALL & MARK PETERSON, eds., *Korean Women: View from the Inner Room*, New Haven: East Rock Press, 1984; KIM YUNG-CHUNG, *Women of Korea: A History from Ancient Times to 1945*, Seoul: Ewha University Press, 1977; SANDRA MATIELLI, ed., *Virtues in Conflict: Tradition and the Korean Woman Today*, Seoul: Royal Asiatic Society Korea Branch, 1977; SARAH NELSON, 'The Statuses of Women in Ko-Shilla: Evidence from Archaeology and Historic Documents,' *KJ*, 31/2, 1991; BONNIE OH, 'From Three Obediences to Patriotism and Nationalism: Women's Status in Korea up to 1945,' *KJ*, 22/7, 1982; SHIN KI-SUK, 'The Inequality of Women in the Korean Legal System,' *KJ*, 24/12, 1984

WOMEN'S MOVEMENT

Korean women played a significant part in their country's independence movement, beginning in the late 19th century and lasting into the colonial period. Organising a society for the promotion of women's education (*Ch'angyanghoe*), they ran the Sunsŏng School for girls from 1898 to 1902. Other women's societies followed, supported by the **Independence Club** and members of the Protestant churches, campaigning for recognition of equality between men and women. Some, such as Yi Ilchŏng, spoke out openly in favour of nationalism under the **Protectorate**. They demonstrated actively during the **March First Movement**, founding the Patriotic Women's Society of Korea (*Taehan Min'guk Aeguk Puinhoe*), and the wave of publications during the **New Culture Movement** included many new titles reflecting women's desire for social reform. Their outspokenness brought them suffering: the vice-chairwoman of the Patriotic Women's Society, Yi Hyegyŏng, was imprisoned for three years with hard labour in **Taegu**, one of her sisters fled abroad, and her brother was tortured.

CHOI SOOK-KYUNG, 'Formation of Women's Movements in Korea: from the Enlightenment Period to 1910,' *KJ*, 25/2, 1985

WŎN BUDDHISM *Wŏn-bulgyo* 圓佛教

Pak Chungbin (1891–1943) was a farmer's son, born at Yŏnggwang, South Chŏlla. As a little boy he did the usual Chinese studies, but at eight years old he began to doubt the purely materialistic view of nature. After studying all religions, he concluded that the truth lay in a purified and secularised form of **Buddhism**, in which personal and social behaviour follows spiritual prerogatives. He was fully enlightened in 1916 and set up a study group, based in Iksan-gun, North Chŏlla. During the 1920s he organised agricultural cooperatives and joint savings groups, advocated **women**'s rights and founded **schools**. Claiming that monastic and lay persons were spiritually equal, he rejected any need for supporting a monastic order, for temple offerings or for Buddha images. The sole object of worship was to be the *wŏn*, a circle drawn in black ink on a white ground, which had long been a symbol of the essence of buddhahood, of perfection and of enlightenment, as found in the **Ten Ox Pictures**. (The name *Wŏn-Bulgyo* was adopted in 1946.) Worship takes place at weekly meetings, based on Protestant Christian practice, but consisting of **sutra**-readings, prayers, songs and homilies. In 1972 there were 130 meeting places (*kyodang*) and 620,000 adherents. Wŏn'gwang University at Iri is the centre of the faith, which stands apart from the main line of Korean Buddhism. There are nine canonical texts, of which the founder's *Chŏngjŏn*, 'orthodox canon', is fundamental.

WŎNCH'UK 圓測 (613–696)

A very learned monk and gifted linguist, a man of royal descent who went to China while young and appears to have died there but is regarded as a distinguished example of Korean **Buddhism**.

WON'GAK-SA 圓覺社

Although the full story is not entirely clear, the first Korean theatre in Seoul (apart from an earlier Japanese one) originated in plans to celebrate the 40th anniversary of King **Kojong**'s accession. In 1902 a government agency called *Hyŏmnyul-sa*, 'co-operative troupe office', constructed a circular brick-built theatre, modelled inside on western theatres and called *Hŭidae*, 'playing place', on the site of the later Saemunan Church. **Kisaeng**, **p'ansori** singers and **kwangdae** were collected and dramatised versions of *p'ansori* (*ch'anggŭk*) were rehearsed. When the national celebrations were cancelled because of an outbreak of cholera, these players were formed into a private enterprise, whose productions, including a version of **Yi Haejo**'s *Ok-chung-hwa* (which **Sands** claimed to have mounted), responded to the entertainment needs of Seoul's emergent middle class. In 1906 performances were suspended for offending against Confucian morality, but in 1908 **Yi Injik** reopened the theatre with a dramatised version of his 'new-style novel' *Ŭn-segye*, 'Silver World'. The new venture was called *Wŏn'gak-sa*, 'Circle Company'. (*Wŏn'gak* – 'circle', a symbol of the Buddha nature, was the name of the pagoda in **Pagoda Park** as well as a reference to the shape of the theatre.) The players were disbanded in 1909. Some of them formed itinerant female *ch'anggŭk* companies that still exist. *Wŏn'gak-sa* seems to have closed down in 1910.

WŎN'GU-DAN See **Altar of Heaven**

WŎNHYO 元曉 (617–686)
The best-known name in Korean **Buddhism**. He became a monk at 28, but for some years lived an unsettled and eccentric life. Then he took to intellectual work, eager to unify the various schools of Buddhism in **Silla**. Among his more important writings were *Simmunhwajaeng-non* 'Harmonising the debates between the ten schools' and a commentary on *Mahayana-sraddhotpada-sastra*, 'The Awakening of Faith', a work attributed to the Indian writer Asvaghosa, but actually written in Chinese, that harmonised early Mahayana traditions. Later he became an itinerant teacher, declaring that the Pure Land was for everybody, not just for monks. He thus became a symbol for a Buddhism that is free of all rules, teaching that nirvana is attainable without asceticism of any kind. The story of his affair with a widowed princess of Silla, in which he became father of **Sŏl Ch'ong**, is an exceedingly popular romance (as in the novel by **Yi Kwangsu**). So also is the story from *Fingers pointing at the moon*, of how when travelling to China he slept at night in a cave and drank water from a cup he found there. In the morning he discovered the cave was a tomb and the cup was a skull. Realising that his revulsion was purely a matter of mind, he saw he had no need to study in China and returned home. His writings were highly regarded in China and Japan.
KOH IK-JIN, 'Wŏnhyo and the Foundation of Korean Buddhism,' *KJ*, 21/8, 1981
See also **Ch'ŏntae-jong**

WŎRIN-CH'ŎN'GANG-JI-GOK 月印千江之曲 'Song of the Moon Shining on a Thousand Rivers'
An epic life of Sakyamuni, written in Korean verse by **Sejong**, probably in 1447–50, the last three years of his life. It is based on *Sokpo-sangjŏl*, and was designed to be sung as *akchang*. As literature it has a distinctive cachet and is much more highly developed than *Sokpo-sangjŏl*.

WŎRIN-SOKPO 月印釋譜 'Shining Moon Biography'
A revised and combined edition of *Sokpo-sangjŏl* and *Wŏrin-ch'ŏn'gang-ji-gok*, compiled in 1459.

WORRY BEADS
A Buddhist **rosary** with fewer than 24 beads is called *tan-yŏmju*. It may be used much as worry-beads are in other cultures, but is to be distinguished from the pair of dried and polished walnuts (*hodu*), or preferably wild walnuts (*karae, Juglans mandshurica*) that older Koreans often turn in the palm of the hand. This exercise is believed to assist the circulation of the blood and maintain suppleness in the hands, especially for calligraphers.

WRESTLING *ssirŭm*
In Korean wrestling each wrestler grabs his opponent's belt and thigh band, and they strive until one is toppled, touching the floor with his body or hand. He is deemed the loser. In organised events an elimination series is played, beginning with the lighter weights. The traditional prize for the champion, usually promised but not always delivered, is a bull. The sport is universal and prehistoric. It is illustrated on the walls of a 4th-century-AD **tomb** from the kingdom of **Koguryŏ** at **Kungnaesŏng** (modern Ji'an, Jilin province, China). The tomb is popularly known as *Kakcho-ch'ong*, 'Tomb of the Wrestlers'. The earliest written record is of King Ch'unghye of Koryŏ watching

spring and autumn matches in 1344, though wrestling was then also practised at *Tano*. A military origin for the sport has been surmised, but by the Chosŏn dynasty its enjoyment as a form of folk competition had spread throughout society and was shown by **Kim Hongdo** in his *genre* painting. It is widely practised in modern Korea.

X

XUANHE FENGSHI GAOLI TUJING (K. *Sŏnhwa Pongsa Koryŏ-togyŏng*)宣和封使高麗圖經 'Picture book of the Xuanhe Emperor's Envoy to Korea'
Xu Jing (K. Sŏ Kŭng) was with the Song Emperor's embassy that spent a month in Songdo (**Kaesŏng**) in 1123. This is his account, completed a year later, of his generally favourable observations on the peculiarities of Korea and its people. The original illustrations were lost in the **Jurchen** invasions, but the work remains a valuable source for information on Koryŏ culture.
GODFREY GOMPERTZ, 'Hsü Ching's Visit to Korea in 1123,' *TOCS* 33, 1960–62
See also **bathing**, **markets**

XUANTU 玄遵 (K. Hyŏndo)
Chinese **commandery** established in succession to **Canghai** along the upper reaches of the **Yalu River** in 107 BC, transferred further to the north-west in 82 BC and finally into northern **Manchuria** in the 2nd century AD.

Y

YAKSA-YŎRAE 樂帥如來 'The healing tathagata (buddha)'
Bhaisajyaguru-vaidurya-prabhasa (K. Yaksa Yuri-gwang yŏrae), 'the tathagata (buddha) healer of gemlike light', is the Healing Buddha who appears in the Lotus **Sutra**, chapter 23. He heals diseases of body and soul, and belongs to the East. He is often attended by Ilgwang-bosal 'Sunlight Bodhisattva', and Wŏlgwang-bosal 'Moonlight Bodhisattva', but sometimes stands alone.

YALTA CONFERENCE (1945)
Conference held at Yalta in the Crimea between 3rd and 11th February 1945 in which the main participants were Joseph Stalin, Franklin D. Roosevelt and Winston Churchill. At this meeting Stalin was persuaded by the offer of rights in **Manchuria** to enter the war against Japan after the defeat of Germany. In planning future allied responsibilities and the restitution of independence to occupied territories of the axis powers, the interest of both Russia and the United States in Korea was recognised. Stalin accepted a hastily and ill thought-out American suggestion that the **Thirty-Eighth Parallel** should form a temporary dividing line between zones of Russian and American military command, and quickly launched Soviet troops against the Japanese in north Korea. But the permanent stationing of foreign troops on Korean soil was not yet formally envisaged. Roosevelt's plan that Korea should be put under a joint **trusteeship** of the United States, Russia and Chiang Kai-shek's China until it was ready to assume independence (at an estimate, anything from ten to thirty years) was discussed, but more precise arrangements were left for the forthcoming **Moscow Conference** of Foreign Ministers.
See also **Potsdam Conference**

YALU RIVER 鴨綠江

River forming two-thirds of the modern frontier between northern Korea and China. The Korean pronunciation of the name is Amnŏk. It is one of the major waterways that have played an important part in the political and economic history of the peninsula (*see also* **Ch'ŭngch'ŏng**; **Taedong**; **Tumen**; **Four Great Rivers**). It rises on **Paektu-san** and flows westwards into the Yellow Sea, and in ancient times was a route for the penetration of material culture into the peninsula from north-eastern China. Its valley was the location of the early capital **Kungnaesŏng**, and played a strategic part in military struggle for the peninsula from the early Three Kingdoms period, marking the *de facto* border of political jurisdiction between Korean states and their northern neighbours after the fall of the colony of **Lelang**. In 1592 the Chosŏn court fled to Ŭiju, near the mouth of the Yalu, as the Japanese invaders marched north as far as P'yŏngyang (*see* **Imjin War**). In 1950 the river marked the limit of the South Korean counter-offensive against the initial communist invasion, and was the location of infamous North Korean and Chinese prisoner-of-war camps during the **Korean War**.

YAMA 閻魔王, 閻邏 (K. Yŏmna or Yŏmma)

In many Buddhist temples there is a separate hall for Yama, king and judge of the underworld. He usually wears a monk's robe and carries a sceptre with a man's head on it. He may have an angry face, and possibly ride on a buffalo. He has eighteen generals and 80,000 troops under his command. It is Yama who judges the deeds of the souls of the newly dead.

YAMEN 衙門 (K. *amun*)

A term widely used as a formal equivalent of *maŭl* for any government office, and frequently used of the more important offices, especially those in the provinces.

YANG KIT'AK 梁起鐸 (1871–1938)

Born in P'yŏngyang, he early became a Presbyterian Christian and, together with his father, helped **James Gale** with the original edition of Gale's *Korean-English Dictionary*. In 1904 he joined **Ernest Bethell** in publishing *Taehan Maeil Sinbo*. A Japanese-inspired attempt to commit him to jail for embezzlement of funds failed and when Bethell died in 1908, Yang took over Bethell's newspapers. After the annexation of Korea in 1910 Yang withdrew to **Manchuria**, where he strove for Korean independence in Liuhe prefecture. In 1920 he returned to Seoul to work on the *Tonga Ilbo* newspaper and to found a religion called *T'ongch'ŏn-gyo*. He was imprisoned in the same year for anti-Japanese activity, but released early on compassionate grounds. He went back to Manchuria, where he founded another Korean newspaper and Korean schools. He was involved in various further Korean nationalist associations, dying in 1938 in Jiangsu province.

YANG KWIBI 楊貴妃 (C. Yang Guifei, 718–756)

The infamous 'Imperial Consort Yang', regarded by Koreans as the nonpareil of tragic beauty. Emperor Xuanzong of Tang was infatuated with her. He was 72 and she was 38 when they fled from Chang'an during the rebellion of An Lushan. They travelled only two or three days before the guards compelled him to have her strangled at Mawei post station, east of Xingping in Shaanxi. **Bai Juyi**'s *Changhen'ge*, 'song of lasting remorse', tells the tale. *Yanggwibi* is the Korean name for the red poppy.

YANGBAN 兩班

Name given to the élite literati class at the apex of society in the Chosŏn period; sometimes referred to loosely as *sarim / sallim*, though these terms strictly referred to 'regional' or 'country' *yangban*. The name means literally 'two classes' or 'groups'. *Pan* refers to the *panyŏl* 'ordering by classes' at the king's dawn audience, when *munban* 'civil class' stood in rows on the east side (*tongban*) of the great courtyard and *muban* 'military class' on the west side (*sŏban*). They were also called *hakpan* 'crane class' and *hoban* 'tiger class' after the signs on their *hyungbae*. A combination of civil and military powers and functions was first typified by the Ch'oe clan in the late Koryŏ period (*see* **Ch'oe dictatorship**). *Muban* was always socially inferior to *munban*, but in time the word *yanghan* came to be applied to all who were eligible for government appointment, and eventually became a polite way of referring to any gentleman.

The single most distinguishing feature of the class was its education in the **Confucian Classics** and its insistence on **examination** success as a qualification for office-holding, though rural land-holding and the resulting wealth were also inherited characteristics. Members of the class were exempt from *corvée* and **military service**. They propagated the principles of Confucian education, especially filial piety, as a means of strengthening their control over rural society and their tenants in particular. Though access to the class was difficult because it was endogamic and perpetuated itself literally as a 'class apart' from lower classes of society, it was not homogeneous. It contained many impoverished *yangban* families. Its members valued their own **lineages**, but its extent was not defined by blood ties as the Silla aristocracy had been (*see kolp'um*). Moreover, within it, rivalry based on lineage, region, office-holding and political opportunity was intense.

After the **Imjin Wars** more members of *yangban* lineages lost their paramount position in officialdom and concentrated on rural estate management instead. **Illegitimate sons** of *yangban* fathers, i.e. those born to non-*yangban* mothers, formerly excluded from office, were recognised. Meanwhile opportunities increased for those outside the class to profit from trade and skills and to acquire the education necessary to enter it. The overall effect was therefore to broaden *yangban* membership and outlook, but without threatening its élite privileges. Though admiration for China (*see* **Sadae**) remained another feature of *yangban* culture, its members also participated actively in the *Sirhak* **movement**.

See also **class system**; **factions**; **gentry**; *sadaebu*; *sahwa*; **schools**

YANGDONG-NI 良洞里 *See* **Kimhae**

YANGIN 良人 *See Sangmin*

YANGGŬM 洋琴 'Foreign zither'

The dulcimer. It was introduced to China in the late **Ming dynasty** by Jesuit missionaries and reached Korea in the 18th century, when it was incorporated into ensembles for *Yŏngsan hoesang* and the refined lyric songs. It is the only instrument in the traditional Korean orchestra to have metal strings, and the only one whose strings are hammered. There are fourteen quadruple strings, stretched alternately across one or other of the two fixed metal bridges. They are struck with a hammer of a flexible bamboo strip tipped with felt. The *yanggŭm* is not used as a solo instrument, and usually plays the tune in unison with the *kayagŭm*.

See also **musical instruments**

YE 濊

Ancient tribal state to the north of the **Yalu River**. Its acknowledgement of **Han** Chinese suzerainty in 128 BC led to the creation of the **Canghai** Commandery.

YEJONG, KING 睿宗 (r. 1105–22)

Sixteenth king of the Koryŏ dynasty, married to the daughter of one of his most powerful aristocrats, **Yi Chagyŏm**. He promoted Confucian values and education, sponsoring the study of the **Confucian Classics** and history as a guide to moral government (see *Samguk sagi*). This naturally found favour in China. In 1110 the Chinese Emperor Huizong paid Yejong the unprecedented honour of nominating him a 'true king' (C. *zhen wang*). The king was flattered, but showed a pragmatic interest nevertheless in the possibility of establishing diplomatic relations with the **Jurchen**, who threatened his country from the north. In 1114 Huizong sent him an enormous gift of 167 **musical instruments** for the performance of the new *Dasheng* music from the Chinese court, and in 1116 made an even more significant presentation of ritual Confucian music, *yayue* (see *aak*), with 428 instruments and scores. As a bribe to ensure Korean political allegiance, however, it was wasted, for Yejong died in 1122 and in 1126 his son, King Injong, accepted Yi Chagyŏm's advice that the current interpretation of 'serving the great' (*sadae*) meant sending **tribute** to the **Jin** court.
KEITH PRATT, 'Music as a Factor in Sung-Koryŏ Diplomatic Relations', *TP*, LXII 4–5, 1976; SONG HYEJIN, 'The Acceptance of *Dasheng Yayue* in Koryŏ', *PBAKS*, 3, 1992
See also **Yi Chagyŏm rebellion**

YEMAEK 濊貊

Federation of the Ye and Maek tribes located in the **Liaodong** region along the middle **Yalu River**, identified by the 4th century BC. It sought political help from China against **Wiman Chosŏn**, which led to the formation of the **Canghai** and **Xuantu** commanderies, but its allegiance to China was fickle and its leadership subsequently took part in the foundation of the kingdom of **Koguryŏ**.
See also **dolmens; Puyŏ**

YEMUN-GWAN 藝文館 'Hall of writing skills'

Chosŏn government department with thirteen officials, presided over by a 1st **grade** senior; the office where documents were composed and drafted.

YI AM 李嵒 (Kunhae, Ch'oja, 1297–1364)

One of the greatest calligraphers of the Koryŏ dynasty and a prominent central government official. He imitated the style of his Chinese contemporary Zhao Mengfu (*see also* **Yi Chehyŏn**). The only extant example of his work is on a stele inscribed to mark the opening of a new library at Ch'ŏngp'yŏng-sa, written in a version of *haengsŏ*[1] (*see* **calligraphy**).
(1) W.Y.KIM, S.U.CHOI, C.S.IM, eds., *Arts of Korea, vol.2, Paintings*, Seoul: Dong Hwa Publishing Co., 1974

YI AM 李嵒 (Tusŏngyŏng, b. 1499)

A descendant of King **Sejong**, and an important *Tohwa-sŏ* painter specialising in animals (especially cats and dogs) and birds. Only four of his pictures are known to survive, although he was so popular in Japan, where his work was widely copied, that further discoveries could be made there. His best known subject is *Dog with Puppies*,

which combines strong outline brushwork in the claws of the mother dog with equally effective boneless wash for the puppies' fur.[1]
(1) CHOI SUNU, *5000 Years of Korea Art*, Seoul: Hyonam Publishing Co., 1979

YI CHAEGWAN 李在寬 (Sodang, 1783–1839)

A self-taught artist who became a professional painter at court, known for his **portraiture**. Through his association with literati artists he was initially influenced by the Chinese Wu School, but later, as a student of **Kim Chŏnghŭi**, showed his Korean individuality. A similarity with the work of **Kim Hongdo** has been noted in his *Hermit under a Pine Tree*.[1]
(1) ROGER GOEPPER & RODERICK WHITFIELD, *Treasures from Korea*, London: British Museum Publications, 1984

YI CHAGYŎM 李資謙 REBELLION (1126)

Yi Chagyŏm inherited political power built up by his father Yi Chayŏn and strengthened it through the marriage of his daughters to Kings **Yejong** and Injong. His wealth and authority rivalled that of Injong himself, but when the King threatened to overthrow him Yi sacked the royal palace, killing most of his rivals and imprisoning Injong. Success was short-lived. His decision to recognise the new Jurchen **Jin** dynasty in northern China found little support in **Kaesŏng**, though it was approved by Kim Pusik in **Kyŏngju**, and he was exiled and died the following year, 1127.

YI CHEHYŎN 李齊賢 (Ikchae, 1287–1367)

Born in **Kyŏngju**, he passed the national **examinations** in the top **grade** at the age of fourteen. About six years later, he learned of Song neo-Confucianism from Paek Ijŏng, who had studied in Yuan China, and received the blessing of the great neo-Confucian pioneer, **An Hyang**. After King Ch'ungsŏn abdicated and went to Dadu (Beijing) in 1313, he sent for Yi to follow him and study in his new *Man'gwŏn-dang*, 'Hall of Ten Thousand Books', where Yi met such leading neo-Confucians as Yao Sui and Yuan Mingshan, and artists and calligraphers, including Zhao Mengfu. He is credited with taking back to Korea not only Zhao's highly influential calligraphic style, but also the equally important landscape painting traditions initiated by Li Cheng and Guo Xi. Among the pictures attributed to him is *Hunting Scene in Winter* (National Museum of Korea).[1]

He became an enthusiastic Confucian, though more interested in manners and government than in Song philosophy. In 1318, at Ch'ungsŏn's behest, he travelled in Sichuan; two years after that he went with the king when he was exiled to Tibet; and then visited China south of the Yangzi. During these long journeys he wrote some remarkable **poetry** about China, much of it in *sa* (C. *ci*) form. After returning to Korea he was five times chief minister. In 1344 he was in China again on diplomatic errands. At home he strove against Mongol influence within the country and helped Korea avoid becoming a province of China. He was especially successful as secretary to King Kongmin, though he was strongly opposed to **Sin Ton**. His writings include *Soakpu* ('Little Song Book', Chinese translations of vernacular songs); *Yŏgong p'aesŏl*, 'Weed-stories from an Old Man's Oak Copse' that contains some anecdotal **poetry** criticism; and *Ikchae nan'go*, 'Scattered Manuscripts of Ikchae', a collection of largely formal documents. He was a gifted poet, collector of folk material, Confucian trail-blazer, diplomat and annalist. He died aged 80, having more than fulfilled his brush-name, 'House of Profitable Study'.
(1) CHOI SUNU, *5000 Years of Korean Art*, Seoul: Hyonam Publishing Co., 1979

YI CHŎNG 李禎 (T'anun, b. 1541)
A great-grandson of King **Sejong**, and a bamboo painter in the Chinese Zhe style. He made full use of the paper, spreading out leaves in groups with a rhythmic pattern, and suggesting depth through variations in ink density. His sense of graphic design influenced the subsequent development of bamboo painting.

YI CHUN 李儁 (1858–1907)
He was an officer in the Seoul City administration when he joined **Sŏ Chaep'il**, **Yi Sŭngman** (Syngman Rhee), Yi Sangjae and others in founding the **Independence Club** and running the *Tongnip Simun* newspaper in 1896. That year, for fear of the pro-Russian lobby, he fled to Japan, where he graduated from the law department of Waseda University. Returning to Korea in 1898, he was soon active in promoting progressive Korean **nationalism** and opposing Japanese designs for his country. **Kojong** made him a secret envoy to the **Hague Peace Conference** of 1907. He picked up Yi Sangsŏl (1871–1917) in Vladivostok, as he joined the Trans-Siberian railway, and Yi Wijong, who was a diplomat in Russia, when he reached St Petersburg. After arriving in the Hague they visited the chairman of the conference, but the Japanese had little difficulty in preventing their accreditations from being accepted. Yi Chun died in the Hague very shortly afterwards, from an illness attributed to his frustration. His remains were returned to Korea in 1962.

YI CHUNGSŎP 李仲燮 (1916–56)
Painter whose work passionately expresses the grievances and frustrations of modern Korean history. He used the bull as a symbol of national fortitude amid the hardships of occupation and war in a series of studies painted between 1934 and his early death in 1956. His personal relationship with Japan was an equivocal one. As a teenager he shared his people's resentment at the attempted suppression of Korean identity, but on going to Tokyo in 1936 in search of the best training in East Asia he enjoyed the company of other artistically open-minded students such as **Kim Hwan'gi**, met the Japanese girl who was to become his wife, and experienced the first thrill of professional recognition and acclaim. He was influenced by *avant garde* western painters, and settled into his own style, a typically Korean form of expressionism characterised by bold and swift curving linear movement, which has been likened to the strong simplicity of **Koguryŏ** wall paintings and the dynamic descriptiveness of Van Gogh. Yi returned to Korea in 1943 and married in 1945, but ironically his country's liberation from Japan marked the disintegration of his life into a tragic sequence of homelessness, bereavement, separation from his beloved family, and developing schizophrenia. Nevertheless he continued to paint prolifically with emotion and not a little eroticism, whether expressing his fury at foreign interference in Korea with forceful bull or cock fights, or his agonised love for his own and all children, in whose nakedness he proclaimed unconcerned vitality but vulnerable innocence. He has been called an 'indisputable genius', whose influence helped to free other artists from the restraints of tradition to pour out their emotions at being Korean in the 20th century.
FRANK HOFFMANN, 'Yi Chung-sop's life and art', *KC* 9/4, 1988

YI HAEJO 李海朝 (1869–1927)
A journalist born at Poch'ŏn; like Yi Injik, one of the first generation of modern writers. *Hwasŏngdon-jŏn*, 'Biography of Washington' (1908), was his first novel. Others included *Pingsang-sŏl*, 'Snow on the Hair'(1908), *Moranbyŏng*, 'Peony

Screen' (1911), and *Hwaŭi hyŏl*, 'Blood of a Flower' (1911). *Okchunghwa*, 'Flower in Prison' (1912), was a version of **Ch'unhyang-jŏn**, one of his several retellings of traditional stories. Though he used current language, Yi Haejo employed essentially old-fashioned material and plot forms, with no concern for modernisation.

For *Okchunghwa*, see JAMES SCARTH GALE, 'Choon Yang' in *Korea Magazine*, September 1917 to July 1918.

YI HWANG 李滉 (T'oegye, 1501–1570)

Yi Hwang, *Han'guk Chuja* 'the **Zhu Xi** of Korea', was Korea's greatest philosopher, a genial, modest and amiable man, born in Kyŏngsang province near Andong. He studied Chinese literature as a boy, gaining an early affection for **Tao Qian**, the Chinese poet of scholarly life in rural solitude. At 19 he obtained *Xingli daquan*, a great compendium of neo-Confucianism issued by Hu Guang in 1405, and became devoted to Song thought, especially *simhak* 'psychology'.

He held twenty-nine posts in government, but had no taste for political **factions**. From 1543, when he first obtained the complete works of Zhu Xi (*Zhuzi daquan*), he longed to retire. This he did in 1549, justifying his brush name T'oegye, 'returning to the valley', by going home to Tosan near Andong. At the age of 60 he began a seven-year correspondence with 34-year-old Ki Taesŭng (Kobong, 1529–1592), in a spirit of mutual respect previously unknown between men of such disparate ages. This was the famous 'Four-Seven Discussion' (*Sach'il-lon*) about the Four Beginnings and Three Emotions, which initiated a wider debate in which **Yi I** was to take a different line. The difference much later cast its shadow over political factionalism when the Eastern **faction** followed T'oegye.

Neo-Confucian metaphysics were based on two concepts: *i* (C. *li*), the rational principle that explains individuality and activity, and *ki* (C. *qi*), the material force that concretises and energises, corresponding roughly to 'form' and 'matter' in European scholastic philosophy. Yi Hwang, emphasising personal experience and moral responsibility, thought *i* was prior to *ki*. His debate with Kobong was about the relation of this theory to two classic analyses of human nature. The 'Four Beginnings' (*sadan*, C. *si duan*) were described in *Mencius* VIa: *in* (C. *ren*) benevolence, *ŭi* (C. *yi*) righteousness, *ye* (C. *li*) propriety and *chi* (C. *ji*) wisdom. The 'Seven Emotions' (*ch'ilchŏng*, C. *qi qing*) were given in *Liji*, the *Liyun* chapter: *hŭi* (C. *xi*) joy, *no* (C. *nu*) anger, *ae* (C. *ai*) sadness, *ku* (C. *ju*) fear, *ae* (C. *ai*) love, *o* (C. *wu*) dislike, and *yŏk* (C. *yu*) liking. T'oegye's conclusion was that the Four Beginnings arose from *i* and proceeded in *ki*, while the Seven Emotions arose from *ki* and were driven by *i*. His thinking was later influential in Japan.

The 12-*sijo* cycle *Tosan-sibi-gok* celebrates his rural retreat. His major writings are to be found in *T'oegye chŏnsŏ*.

EDWARD Y. J. CHUNG, *The Korean Neo-Confucianism of Yi T'oegye and Yi Yulgok*, New York, 1995; MICHAEL KALTON, *To Become a Sage: The Ten Diagrams on Sage Learning by Yi T'oegye*, New York: Columbia University Press, 1988; MICHAEL KALTON, *The Four-Seven Debate, an Annotated Translation of the Most Famous Controversy in Korean Neo-Confucian Thought*, State University of New York Press, 1994; KIM HAT'AI, 'The Transmission of Neo-Confucianism to Japan by Kang Hang', *TKBRAS*, XXXVII (1961); TOMOEDA RYUTARŌ, 'Yi T'oegye and Chu Hsi: Differences in their Theory of Principle and Material Force,' *in* THEODORE DE BARY & JAHYUN KIM KABOUSH, eds., *The Rise of Neo-Confucianism in Korea*, New York: Columbia University Press, 1985

YI I 李珥 (Yulgok, 1536–1584)

As a philosopher, Yi I is regarded as second only to T'oegye (**Yi Hwang**), with whom his name is often coupled. He also was an original political thinker and educator. His brush-name Yulgok means 'Chestnut Valley'.

Born near Kangnŭng on the east coast, he was a precocious child scholar, educated chiefly by his widowed mother, **Sin Saimdang**, a remarkably learned woman, painter and poet. In his teens he read *Laozi* and *Zhuangzi* as well as Buddhist writings. He was only fifteen when his mother died. After completing the three years of mourning, spent in intensive reading, he went into the **Diamond Mountains**, with the intention of becoming a Buddhist. The monks he met were deeply impressed, but in 1556 he returned home for a short spell before setting off to Seoul. There he rejected **Buddhism** and took up neo-Confucian philosophy, partly because it embraced political and social activity. Four years later, at the age of 22, he spent two days with T'oegye in his retreat at Tosan. Each recognised the quality of the other, and Yi I was much encouraged by the encounter. The young man's success in public examinations was startling. He entered public office in 1559 and steadily rose in the government service, despite interruptions due to poor health. He had country properties at Sŏktam near Haeju and Yulgok near P'aju.

In 1572, shortly after the death of T'oegye, he took up the position of Ki Kobong in the Four-Seven debate, positing the primacy of *ki* in opposition to T'oegye's emphasis on *i*. He introduced into the discussion two terms from the *Damo* section of the *Book of Documents*: *tosim* (C. *daoxin*) 'dao-mind' or original goodness and *insim* (C. *renxin*) 'human-mind' or concupiscence, as corresponding to the Four Beginnings and Seven Emotions. Giving weight to experience and breadth of knowledge, he gave priority to practicality rather than to the introspection preferred by T'oegye.

In the last four years of his life, Yulgok held the highest posts in the land. He proposed new policies in **taxation**, education and defence of the realm. His advice on creating a standing army was not accepted, though ten years later the Japanese invasions proved his wisdom. He was fortunate to be at court during a period of relative factional stability, but in spring 1584 he died at the peak of his career, six weeks after his 48th birthday.

Most of his writings are printed in *Yulgok chip*. A *sijo* cycle called *Kosan kugok* 'Nine songs of Kosan' is attributed to him.

MICHAEL KALTON, *The Four-Seven Debate, an Annotated Translation of the Most Famous Controversy in Korean Neo-Confucian Thought*, State University of New York Press, 1994

YI IK 李瀷 (Sŏngho, 1681–1763)

Yi Ik never took public office but remained a private scholar all his life, taking up the mantle of Yu Hyŏngwŏn (*see **Pan'gye surok***) in starting *sirhak* trends of thought. His chief written works are the encyclopaedic *Sŏngho sasŏl*, 'Essays of Sŏngho', and *Kwagu-rok*, 'Record of Concern for the Under-privileged'. Deeply interested in the European learning now coming through Qing China and in the value of scientific historiography, he believed the object of all study was the improvement of the human lot. He urged that the **gentry** should become involved in industry and commerce, the public **examination** system should be reformed, farmers should study and scholars should plough. Many of the first generation of Catholics came from among his followers.

DONALD BAKER, 'A Confucian Confronts Catholicism: Truth Collides with Morality in Eighteenth Century Korea,' *KSF*, 6, 1979/80

YI INJIK 李人稙 *See Hyŏrŭi nu*

YI INMUN 李寅文 (Munuk; Yuch'un; Kosong Yusu Kwandoin, 1745–1821)
Eminent court artist who served Kings **Yŏngjo** and **Chŏngjo** in the *Tohwa-sŏ*, where he was a colleague of **Kim Hongdo**. Despite this he painted mostly Chinese themes and according to Northern and Southern School styles, with only a few genuine Korean landscape subjects. One of these can be seen in *Summer Landscape* (1816; National Museum of Korea).[1] He was renowned at the Chinese court. His 8·5-metre long *Mountains and Rivers without End* (National Museum of Korea)[2] was evidently inspired by a 12th-century Chinese painting. Monumental in concept, structure, and compositional detail, it follows the course of a river on a tortuous trail through mountains and valleys reminiscent of Guo Xi and **An Kyŏn**, and through the temporal sequence of four seasons. It is now the largest extant traditional landscape in Korea. His *genre* paintings include *Gathering of Four Friends* (National Museum of Korea),[3] which combines bold brushwork with fine calligraphy.
(1)(2) CHOI SUNU, *5000 Years of Korean Art*, Seoul: Hyonam Publishing Co., 1979
(3) JANE TURNER, ed., *The Dictionary of Art*, New York: Grove Inc., 1996, vol. 33

YI INSANG 李麟祥 (Nŭnghogwan, 1710–60)
An artist known for his skill in all **Three Perfections**, and for his seal-carving. Though his painting was mostly done in Chinese style, he retired early and then developed an individual style of his own (*sŏnyŏm*) which involved painting onto wet paper. The special effect created by this can be seen in his *Rocks and Pines*.[1] As a calligrapher he specialised in seal and clerical script.
(1) CHOI SUNU, *5000 Years of Korean Art*, Seoul: Hyonam Publishing Co., 1979

YI KANG (ŬI CH'INWANG) 李堈 (1877–1955)
Fifth son of King **Kojong**. His mother was the Lady Chang, and he was entitled Ŭihwa-gun 'Prince Ŭihwa' in 1891 and Ŭi Ch'inwang 'Prince Imperial Ŭi' after 1897. In 1894 he was sent to Japan to offer congratulations on victory in the **Sino-Japanese War**, and in 1895 to Russia, Britain and various other European countries. He went to study in the USA. On his return to Korea in 1905 he was made a vice-marshal of the army and president of the Korean Red Cross. After the independence demonstrations of 1919 he wanted to visit the **Provisional Government in Exile** in Shanghai, but was taken by the Japanese while travelling through Andong in **Manchuria**, disguised as a mourner. The Japanese then kept him under supervision in Japan. His reputation mingles his concern for Korean independence with his known list of fourteen wives, by whom he had at least twelve sons and nine daughters. Of his two legitimate sons, Kŏn became a Japanese citizen (Momoyama Ken'ichi) in 1947; while U was a soldier killed in the destruction of Hiroshima in 1945, leaving two sons, Ch'ŏng and Chong. The interests of those who are concerned to remember their royal **lineage** are now cared for by the Yi Dynasty Royal Family Association.

YI KWAL 李适 (1587–1624)
A military official who served as a commandant in Hamgyŏng. He was involved in the setting up of Injong as king when Prince **Kwanghae** was deposed. Although he was given recognition as a **Meritorious Subject** and a further command in strengthening the northern border defences, he was dissatisfied because he was not better rewarded and because a younger man was appointed over him. In 1624 he marched on Seoul with an army of 12,000, including some Japanese who had stayed after the Hideyoshi

war of 1592 (*see* **Imjin Wars**). Injo fled to Kongju. Yi Kwal took the capital and put another member of the royal family on the throne, but was driven out by the King's army two days later. There was bitter fighting north of the city, during which Yi was killed. Some of his followers fled to **Manchuria** and helped persuade the **Manchus** to invade Korea in 1627. Another result of the rebellion was the strengthening of the northern defences of the capital.

YI KWANGSA 李匡師 (Wŏn'gyo, 1705–77)
One of the greatest Korean calligraphers, a disciple of **Yun Sun**. Most of his life was spent in exile for political reasons, and he became a master of many calligraphic styles, eventually producing what is named after him as the 'Wŏn'gyo ('circular mountain-path') style'.

YI KWANGSU 李光洙 (b. 1892)
Born in Chŏngju county, North P'yŏngan, he was orphaned at the age of ten. After studying in Japan, he became a teacher at **Osan School** in 1910. He is regarded as Korea's first true novelist, a prolific author able to write on a grand scale. *Ŏrin pŏsege*, 'To Young Friends' (1915), criticising arranged marriages, was followed by *Mujŏng*, 'Heartless'(1917) and *Kaech'ŏkcha*, 'The Pioneer' (1918). For a while in 1918 he was a journalist with the **Provisional Government in Exile** in Shanghai, but he was in Seoul to collaborate with **Ch'oe Namsŏn** in the Independence Movement of 1919. *Hŭk*, 'Earth' (1937) showed him finding consolation in **Buddhism**. He was also inspired by Tolstoy, writing of love, enlightenment and patriotism, always regarding literature as having an educational and reforming rôle. He wrote some *sijo* cycles and a number of historical novels including *Tanjong Aesa*, 'The Sad Affair of King Tanjong' (1926), *Yi Sunsin* and *Sejo Taewang* (1931), *Ich'adonŭi sa*, 'The Death of Ich'adon' (1934) and *Wŏnhyo Taesa*, 'Master **Wŏnhyo**' (1940). He disappeared during the **Korean War**.

YI KYUBO 李奎報 (1168–1241)
Son of a minor official in local government, Yi Kyubo grew up during the military dictatorship of the **Ch'oe** family. He was a brilliant student, but avoided being drawn into the dangers of government service by feigning alcoholic irresponsibility. In quieter times he accepted appointments, and after the **Mongol** invasion became *sangguk*, the chief minister. As a poet he felt temperamentally akin to **Li Bai**, though he knew he was socially and intellectually closer to **Bai Juyi**. All his life he was a compulsive versifier, writing about everything from a new kitten and his love for his family to the major affairs of state and questions of religion. He also wrote poetry criticisms (*sihwa*) and accounts, full of acute observation and gentle humour, of his travels on duty in the provinces. His writings, including his state papers, were gathered together in *Tongguk Yi-Sangguk-chip*, 'Collected Works of Prime Minister Yi of Korea', during his lifetime by his son. After his death, the same son added his father's last poems to complete the collection.
KEVIN O'ROURKE, *Singing like a cricket, hooting like an owl*, Ithaca, N.Y.: Cornell University, 1995; RICHARD RUTT, '*Paegun sosol*: the White Cloud Essays of Yi Kyubo', *TRASKB*, LII, 1978

YI NŬNGHWA 李能和 (1868–1945)
Born at Koesan, north Ch'ungch'ŏng province, he received the usual education of a gentleman in Chinese literature and went on to study English, modern Chinese, French

and Japanese. He became head of the Foreign Languages School in 1897 and visited Japan in 1906. After the Japanese **Annexation** of 1910 he retired to collect materials on religion and folklore, which became the chief work of his life. He was active in Buddhist journalism and was a member of the Government-General's **Korean History Compilation Committee**. Many of his manuscripts were lost in the **Korean War**. Among those published are collections of material on Korean **Buddhism**; Christianity and foreign relations; **women**'s customs; **shamanism**; and **Daoism**. All are quarries for information.

YI ŎNJŎK 李彦迪 (Hoejae, 1491–1553)

A *sarim* scholar who preceded **Yi Hwang** in asserting the priority of *li* (K. *i*) over *qi* (K. *ki*). He held that the object of study was correct action. His government service from 1514 to 1530 ended with his fall from favour, and his brush name, 'Twilight studio', seemed to be justified. He went to **Kyŏngju** to spend time studying neo-Confucian philosophy until his enemies lost power in 1537. He returned to office, and in 1542 applied his Confucian principles in opposing trade with a Japanese embassage that came with a large amount of silver, which he said was an unnecessary luxury. He proposed the compromise eventually accepted, that for courtesy's sake just a third of the amount should be taken in **commerce**. His career peaked with the accession of Myŏngjong, when he retired, claiming his mother was dangerously ill. He was involved in the struggles that caused the purge of 1545 (*see* **sahwa**), and in 1547 was exiled to Kanggye on the northern border of P'yŏngan, where he died six years later. His orthodoxy earned him canonisation in 1610.

YI PONGCH'ANG 李奉昌 (1900–32)

A Seoul man who worked for a Japanese fruiterer before becoming an apprentice on the **South Manchuria Railway**. Poor health compelled him to give up and in 1924 he went to Japan, labouring in steelworks in Tokyo and Osaka. In 1931 he went to Shanghai, working in a printshop and a music shop. He joined **Kim Ku**'s terrorism campaign and returned to Tokyo in 1932 with two bombs, which he threw at Emperor Hirohito and the Manzhouguo puppet emperor, Henry Puyi, during a parade. The attempt to kill them failed. Yi was arrested and, having behaved with great courage at his secret trial, was executed in Ichigaya prison.

YI PYŎK 李蘗 (1754–86)

A relative of **Yi Sŭnghun**, Yi Pyŏk led a small group of scholars of the Southern **faction** who were interested in western learning. They met at Chuŏ-sa near **Kwangju** in Kyŏnggi province in 1777 to discuss their impressions of Catholic books. Yi Pyŏk persuaded Sŭnghun to join the embassy to Beijing in 1784 (*see* **Beijing, embassies to**) and bring back Catholic books. Sŭnghun later baptized Pyŏk as John-Baptist, but after the arrest of **Kim Pŏmu** in 1785 he was pressed by his father to abandon Catholicism. He gave in to his father and died of plague a year later. Many believe he died in the faith and honour him as the true founder of Catholicism in Korea.
See also **Roman Catholic Church**

YI SAEK 李穡 (Mogŭn, 1328–1396)

He was one of the Samŭn, the '**Three Recluses**' of the end of Koryŏ, his brush name meaning 'Pastoral Recluse'. He passed the national **examination** at the age of thirteen, then in 1348 went to Yanjing (Beijing), where his father held an official post, and studied in the *Guozigan* centre of classical studies for three years. Returning to Korea, he took the qualifying examination for sitting an examination in China. He visited Yanjing more than once and passed the examination, but returned home to enter Korean government service. In 1361 he restored the Confucian College after the disturbances caused by the **Red Turbans** rebellion, inviting teachers from China to come and lecture. He was a friend of **Yi Sŏnggye**, but remained loyal to the Koryŏ royal house and in 1392, after the change of dynasty, was banished to Hansan in south Ch'ungch'ŏng. He was in Yŏju in 1396, when at the age of 68 he died suddenly in a boat on a river outing. Often reckoned second only to **Yi Kyubo** among the writers of Koryŏ, he is a somewhat puzzling character. Although regarded as an influential neo-Confucian, the teacher of men like **Chŏng Tojŏn**, **Kwŏn Kŭn**, Pyŏn Kyeryang (1369–1430) and **Yi Sungin**, he seems to have derived much comfort from Buddhist beliefs.

YI SANG 李箱 (1910–1937)

Real name Kim Haegyŏng. A Seoul man, trained as an architect, who exhibited western-style paintings. His first poems were published when he was 21. He tried running a tea-room and a cafe, but both enterprises failed. For two years he lived in bohemian style with a *kisaeng*; but in 1936 he married. In the same year he published the short stories, *Nalgae* ('Wings') and *Chongsaeng-gi* ('The last chapter of my life'), which made him the talk of the intelligentsia. *Nalgae* was semi-autobiographical, the morbid ruminations of a man living off the earnings of his prostitute wife and spending his time in hopeless hope, toying with her trinkets and cosmetics while she was out. He went to Japan hoping to find a cure for his tuberculosis, but was arrested as a disruptive influence, and died in Tokyo University Hospital in 1937 at the age of 27. He was a member of *Kuin-hoe*.
A translation of *Wings* is in PETER H. LEE, *Flowers of Fire*, Hawaii, 1974

YI SANGBŎM 李象範 (Ch'ŏngjŏn, 1899–1978)

Painter who strove to modernise Korean art. In 1914 he entered the *Sohwa Misurwŏn* (Calligraphy and Painting Art School) in Seoul, and later joined the *Sohwa Hyŏphoe* (Calligraphy and Painting Association). For ten years he won first prize in the colonial government's Chosŏn Art Exhibition (*Chosŏn Misul Chŏllamhoe*), and was then invited to become a judge. He is best known for his horizontal landscapes, such as *Early Winter* (1926, National Museum for Contemporary Art)[1] and *Morning* (1957, National Museum for Contemporary Art),[2] using traditional ink and light colours to depict rural scenes in a realistic and atmospheric manner. In 1923, together with **Pyon Kwansik**, he founded the *Tongyŏnsa* ('Joint Research Society'), a group of artists dedicated to the study of both ancient and modern painting.
(1)(2) YOUNG ICK LEW, ed., *Korean Art Tradition*, Seoul: Korea Foundation, 1993

YI SŎNGGYE 李成桂 (1335–1408, r. as Yi T'aejo, 1392–98)

Founder of the Chosŏn dynasty. His family had moved to the northeast from the Chŏnju region several generations before he was born, the son of a military officer, at Yŏnghŭng. During his 20s and 30s, he served Koryŏ as an army leader, helping to drive out the **Red Turbans** and establish Koryŏ control in the northeast. In 1372 he was governor of Hwaryŏng. From 1377 to 1387 he was chiefly engaged in removing the menace of Japanese **pirates** from the two southernmost provinces. In 1388 he was told to move against the Ming forces in Liaoning. He saw the folly of this policy, but was finally persuaded to set out northwards. At the island of Wihwa-do in the **Yalu River** he turned back to **Kaesŏng**, where he deposed King U, replacing him by King

Ch'ang. Yi took control of the government with the support of the neo-Confucians. A year later he removed Ch'ang, claiming that like U he was a natural son of **Sin Ton**, and putting King Kongyang on the throne. In the following year he initiated a **land reform** that broke the power of the landowners, especially the rich monasteries, who had kept the failing Koryŏ dynasty alive.

In the 7th moon of 1392, Yi Sŏnggye sent King Kongyang to exile at Wŏnju, executed several members of the royal family and accepted appointment as king of a new dynasty. He sent an embassy to Ming and received the ancient name of Chosŏn for his new dynasty (*see* **Korea, names for**). With the help of *p'ungsu* experts, having first started to build in the Kyeryong-san area, he chose a new site for the capital at Hanyang (now Seoul) in 1394.

His youngest son, Pangsŏk (Ŭian-daegun, born in 1382), had been appointed Crown Prince, much to the chagrin of his able brother Pangwŏn (1367–1422). In 1398 the first Princes' Rebellion occurred, when Pangwŏn had 15-year-old Pangsŏk assassinated. Their father then abdicated in favour of another son, Panggwa (1357–1419, later canonised as Chŏngjong), who in the following spring moved the capital back to Kaesŏng. Yi Sŏnggye now became *sangwang* 'senior king'. After the bodyguard troops of Pangwŏn fought with those of another brother, Panggan (Hoean-daegun, d. 1421), in the streets of Kaesŏng in 1400 (the Second Princes' rebellion), Panggan was banished and Pangwŏn was named Crown Prince. Later that year Panggwa, having reigned just over two years, abdicated so that Pangwŏn could become king (later known as T'aejong). Their father now became *t'ae-sangwang*, 'great senior king'. Pangwŏn disbanded the princes' bodyguards and ruled for 18 years (1400–1418), defining and firmly establishing the Chosŏn dynasty's political and social systems. In 1404 the capital returned to Seoul. The golden seal denoting full recognition by the Ming Emperor did not arrive until Pangwŏn was firmly on the throne.

In 1402 the *t'aesangwang* left Seoul in dudgeon and returned to his old home in Hamhŭng (see **Hamhŭng ch'asa**), but soon returned, to spend his last years in Buddhist calm. He died in the **Ch'angdŏk Palace** in summer 1408. His canonical name, T'aejo (C. Taizu), 'great progenitor', had been used for dynastic founders in China since the beginning of the 10th century and was also used for **Wang Kŏn** of Koryŏ.

YI SŎU 李瑞雨 (b. 1633)
He passed his first **examination** at the age of 17/18 and had a distinguished career in government service, becoming *Ch'amp'an* of the Board of Works in 1693; but he fell from favour on the restoration of **Queen Min** in 1694. He was a famous poet and calligrapher.

YI SUGWANG 李睟光 (1563–1628) *See Chibong yusŏl*

YI SŬNGHUN 李昇薰 (1756–1801)
Brother-in-law of **Chŏng Yagyong**, he lived a quiet and studious life at home, interested in Catholicism. Urged by **Yi Pyŏk**'s Chuŏ-sa group, he joined the **embassy to Beijing** when his father was envoy in 1783–4, and was baptized Peter in China by ex-Jesuit Jean-Joseph Grammont. On returning to Korea he helped found the church in the house of **Kim Pŏmu**. During the ensuing troubles he wavered, but he was martyred in 1801, the first of four generations: his son Sin'gyu (Matthias) and grandson Chaeŭi (Thomas) were martyred in 1866, his great-grandsons Yŏn'gwi and Kyun'gwi in 1872. *See also* **Martyrs, Catholic**

YI SUNGIN 李崇仁 (Toŭn, 1349–92)
One of the **Three Recluses** of the last years of Koryŏ, taking the brush name 'Potter recluse'. He was born in north Kyŏngsang. As a boy he was precocious, reading *Laozi* and *Zhuangzi* as well as Confucian books. He entered the service of the state in his early twenties, and had an eventful career, on occasion imprisoned, more than once exiled, once condemned to death and pardoned – all for political reasons, though his reading of non-Confucian books was also held against him. He was always reinstated, twice sent on embassies to the Ming, and also given the task of reconstructing the national Confucian college *Sŏnggyun-gwan*. After the death of **Chŏng Mongju**, the victorious Yi faction exiled him to Sunch'ŏn in Chŏlla, where, after the accession of the Chosŏn dynasty, he was assassinated at the age of 46 by a crony of **Chŏng Tojŏn**. He is remembered as a great neo-Confucianist, poet and drafter of state documents.

YI SŬNGMAN (Syngman Rhee) 李承晚 (1875–1965)
He was born at P'yŏngsan in Hwanghae provice, but moved to Seoul as a child. After traditional instruction in Chinese, he attended the Methodist school, Paejae. He was one of the founders of the **Independence Club** in 1896, and was sentenced to life imprisonment when the club was destroyed by reactionaries in 1898. Pardoned in 1904, he went to the USA, where he gained a PhD at Princeton in 1910. He returned to Korea, but was arrested by the Japanese, and returned to the United States in 1912 as a delegate to the Methodist Conference. Until 1945 he was mostly in Washington DC or Hawaii, keeping Americans aware of the Korean independence movement. In 1919 he became president of the Korean **Provisional Government in Exile**, at Shanghai, a post he held until younger men in China ousted him in 1939. He married the Austrian Francesca Donner (b. 1900) in 1934. Since he was the Korean best known to the U S Government, he was quickly sent back to Korea in 1945. There he founded the **Liberal Party** (*Chayu-dang*) which, taking advantage of police support and assassinations of moderate politicians, won the elections in 1948 with a policy of anti-communism and reunification of the country. Yi became president, a post he retained, by juggling the **constitution**, till 1960. After the **Korean War** he successfully defied the UN Command in June 1953 by releasing 25,000 prisoners who did not wish for repatriation to north Korea. His rule was dictatorial, though with increasing age he grew out of touch. The scandalously rigged elections of 1960 brought a reaction from the **students** of Seoul, who took to the streets and were supported by the country at large (*see* **April 19th student uprising**). Yi was forced into exile in Hawaii, but received a gentle welcome on a visit to Korea before he died in Hawaii in 1965. His wife Francesca survived him and ended her days in Seoul.
ROBERT OLIVER, *Syngman Rhee: the Man behind the Myth*, London: Robert Hall Ltd., 1955; SEUNGKEUN RHEE, 'Evolution of Korean Nationalism I: The Political Views of Syngman Rhee,' *KO*, VI, 1975

YI SUNSIN 李舜臣 (1545–98)
A military *yangban*, born at Tŏksu, whose promotion was at first due to friendly connections. At the age of 46 he was made Left Admiral of Chŏlla. Rightly judging the likelihood of war with Japan and realising that mastery of the southern seas would be the clue to victory, he set about training his men and preparing his fleet.
　　This was when he took a form of covered war vessel that had been built at the beginning of the Chosŏn dynasty and developed it into the famous '**turtle ship**' (*kŏbuksŏn*). In an age when naval warfare consisted in boarding an enemy vessel and fighting hand-to-hand on the deck, the *kŏbuksŏn* required a new approach, for which

the Japanese were unprepared. Their ships could usually be destroyed by fire. It is possible that Yi had no more than five of the vessels in any engagement, but their effect was disproportionate to their numbers. It is said that he never lost any of his own ships.

He quickly established Korean mastery of the seaways, contributing significantly to the failure of the invasion. He naturally had to encroach on the territory of his neighbour, Wŏn Kyun, Right Admiral of Kyŏngsang province. When Yi was made commander-in-chief, Wŏn smarted with jealousy and was quick to seize on an accusation that Yi had failed to carry out an order from above. Yi was called to Seoul, impeached and condemned to death. Only the efforts of the elderly *chwaŭijŏng*, Chŏng T'ak (1526–1605), saved him; but he was reduced to the ranks.

When the second invasion occurred in 1597, the Koreans were distressed at their inability to defend themselves. Yi Sunsin was recalled to take command. Again he was successful, and when the Japanese withdrew on the death of Hideyoshi, he successfully harried their ships trying to get back to Japan. On the night of the 18th of the 11th moon of 1598 he was killed at sea by a stray Japanese bullet.

His story has all the elements that call forth Korean admiration. He was given the *siho* Ch'ungmu gong, 'loyal warrior'. In 1795 his collected letters, poems and other writings, including a diary of the seven years of war, *Nanjung-ilgi* 'Daily Writings during the Troubles', were published in a royal edition containing other relevant documents and laudatory notices from various hands. His tablet house, Hyŏnch'ung-sa, at Onyang in South Ch'ungch'ŏng, is a national shrine of generous proportions.
HA TAEHUNG, trans., Nanjung Ilgi, *War Diary of Admiral Yi Sun-sin*, Seoul: Yonsei University Press, 1977; HA TAEHUNG, LEE CHANG-YOUNG, trans., Imjin Changch'o: *Admiral Yi Sun-sin's Memorials to Court*, Seoul: Yonsei University Press, 1981

YI TONGHWI 李東輝 (1873–1935)
Served as head of the military garrison on **Kanghwa Island** between 1902 and 1907, and was imprisoned for two years after the disbanding of the Korean army in 1907. His release was secured by an American missionary, after which he helped to propagate Christianity. In 1911 he was imprisoned again as part of the so-called **Hundred and Five Case**. He was a member of the **New People's Association** (*Sinminhoe*). After seeking exile in **Kando** he joined with Yi Sanggol in founding the Korean Restoration Army (1914) and promoting the idea of guerilla resistance to Japanese occupation (*see ŭibyŏng*). In 1918 he founded the **Korean People's Socialist Party** (*Han'in Sahoedang*) in Khabarovsk, and sent agents to extend its operations into Korea. He then removed to Shanghai, where he became prime minister of the **Provisional Government in Exile** in October 1919. In 1920 he established the **Koryŏ Communist Party** and obtained funding for it from Soviet Russia. Critics accused him of putting Party interests before those of the Government, even of claiming that the Party *was* the Government. Following the Party's break-up in 1921 he was appointed by the Comintern as a commissar of the newly created Far East Area Committee (Korean Branch) in Vladivostok, where he lived for the rest of his life.
See also **Siberia, Koreans in**

YI TONGIN 李東仁 (19th century)
Yi was a monk of Pongwŏn-sa near Seoul, interested in progressive ideas and associated with the *Kaehwadang* (*see* **Independence Party**). He contacted the Japanese minister in Seoul, Yoshitada Hanabusa (1852–1917), learned some Japanese and was helped by **Kim Okkyun** to visit Japan in 1879. In October 1880, following **Kim Hongjip**'s visit to Japan, Yi passed on to the Chinese minister in

Tokyo, He Ruzhang, **King Kojong**'s apparently favourable reaction to his observations on the advantages of a treaty with the United States. In March 1881 Yi was again sent to Japan and linked up with a member of the *Sinsa Yuram-dan* touring party, Yi Wŏnhoe. Together they investigated Japanese military arrangements. He became an official of the Department of Extraordinary Affairs and was active on the financial side, but when the plan to buy warships ended in fiasco he disappeared.

YI T'AEJO 李太祖 *see* **Yi Sŏnggye**

YI T'AEJUN 李泰俊 (b. 1904)

A novelist and short-story writer who recorded the distress of Koreans under Japanese rule. He was born in Ch'ŏrwŏn, studied in Japan and began publishing from 1920. At first he was sympathetic to the proletarian school. Later he switched to the pure literature doctine of the *Kuin-hoe*, though he remained more socially aware than some and is described as a naturalist. Two typical short stories were *Talpam*, 'Moonlight Night', and *Poktŏkpang*, 'Estate Agent's Office'. From 1939 to 1941 he was fiction editor of the magazine *Munjang* ('Literature'). After the Liberation in 1945 he was spokesman for left-wing writers in Seoul, but he went north after 1950 and continued writing.

YI T'OEGYE 李退溪 *See* **Yi Hwang**

YI ŬN 李垠 (1897–1969)

Seventh son of King **Kojong**, and the third to reach adulthood. His mother was Queen Ŏm (*see* **Ŏm-bi**). From 1900 he was known as Yŏng Ch'inwang, 'Prince-Imperial Yŏng'. In 1907 **Sunjong** named him *Hwangt'aeja*, 'Crown Prince Imperial' rather than his elder brother **Yi Kang**, whose mother was of lower rank. He was taken to Japan at the age of ten and brought up in the Imperial court, trained at the Military Academy and given the rank of general. In 1920 he was married to a minor Japanese princess, Nashimoto Masako, known in Korea as Yi Pangja. From 1910 he was known as *wangseje*, 'royal brother-heir', and after Sunjong died in 1926 as Yi Wang. He was sent on a tour of Europe in 1927–8. After World War II he spent a short time in Hawaii, but he was allowed in 1963 to return to Korea, where he was welcomed with pride and respect. He died in Seoul in 1970. He seems to have resembled his father in character.

Pangja continued to live at Naksŏn-jae in the **Ch'angdŏk Palace** (*see* **Sunjong**), greatly respected for her interest in social work and the arts, until she died in 1989. Their only son who survived infancy, Yi Ku (b. 1931), qualified as an architect at MIT and divided his life between America, Korea and Japan. He retired to Seoul in 1996.
YI PANGJA, *The world is one*, Seoul: Taewon Publishing, 1970

YI WANYONG 李完用 (1858–1926)

Prime Minister of Korea from 1907–10. He was a graduate of the *Tongmunhak*, the first government school established under the auspices of the *T'ongni-gimu Amun*. In 1889 he headed a mission to the United States which led to Korean students being sent there. He was a close friend of **Horace Allen**, and after the murder of **Queen Min** took temporary refuge in the American embassy. As an opponent of **Kim Hongjip**'s cabinet he helped King **Kojong**'s flight to the Russian embassy in February 1896. Following Kim's assassination he became first Education Minister and then Foreign Minister in the new, pro-Russian and anti-Japanese government, and was chairman of the **Independence Club**. In 1898 he briefly succeeded An Kyŏngsu as its president, but resigned on becoming a provincial governor.

During the **Protectorate**, Yi re-appeared in September 1905 as Education Minister in Pak Chesun's government, and in May 1907 became Prime Minister. He argued that it was in Korea's interests to 'serve the [new] great', that is, Japan (*see sadae*). When King Kojong was forced to abdicate Yi's house was burned down by an angry mob, and in December 1909 he survived an assassination attempt. In August 1910 he signed the **Treaty of Annexation** prepared by General Terauchi Masatake prior to its presentation to Emperor **Sunjong**. His efforts to have the name of Korea preserved as *Han'guk* were in vain, and it was renamed *Chosŏn*. Under the **Government-General**, he served as a vice-president of the Central Council. Yi was condemned in Korea as a quisling, and became one of the so-called '**five traitors**' (or alternatively, '**seven traitors**') accused of collaborating with the Japanese.
See also **United Progress Society** (*Ilchinhoe*)

YI YONG 李瑢 (Pihaedang, 1418–53)
Third son of King **Sejong**, perhaps better known today as Prince Anp'yŏng. At the age of nineteen he served with the army on the north-eastern frontier. He was inevitably in conflict with his brother Prince Suyang (**King Sejo**) and eventually was banished to **Kanghwa**, where he finally committted suicide by royal command (*see* **poison**). He was famous as an art connoisseur whose collection of paintings included many by the Chinese artist Guo Xi, and was the patron of **An Kyŏn**. Chinese envoys delighted to receive presents of his writing. He was also a fine painter and played the *kayagŭm*. Above all, he was an outstanding calligrapher in regular and cursive style and wrote an inscription to An's *Dream Journey to Peach Blossom Spring*. He is counted as one of the **Four Great Calligraphers**.

YIJO SILLOK 李朝實錄 *See Chosŏn wangjo sillok*

YIN-YANG 陰陽 *See Ŭm-yang*

YŎ UNHYŎNG 呂運亨 (1885–1947)
Was converted to Christianity in 1910, and went to China in 1914. There he helped to organise the New Korea Youth Party. He became a member of the **Provisional Government in Exile** in Shanghai, where he had established a Korean Nationalist Youth Association. In 1919 he attended the meeting of the **Korean Youth Independence Association** in Tokyo which drafted the **Declaration of Independence**. According to some sources he joined the **Koryŏ Communist Party** in 1920, although others deny that he was ever a communist. Certainly he attended the Congress of Far Eastern Labourers in Moscow in 1921. As a moderate nationalist leader he collaborated with **An Ch'angho** in calling a major meeting of international representatives from Korean anti-Japanese organisations in Shanghai in 1923, but political views were too diverse for this to achieve significant results. He took part in the Chinese Northern Expedition in 1926 but managed to escape Chiang Kai-shek's massacre of communists in Shanghai (April 1927). Back in Korea, he served a term of imprisonment for his political activities between 1929 and 1932, and edited *Chungang Ilbo* on his release. As leader of the left-wing **Korean Workers' Party** he was active in preparing Korea for the end of the Japanese occupation in 1945. In August he headed the Preparatory Committee for Building the Country (*Kŏn'guk Chunbi Ŭiwŏnhoe*), which hurried to

forestall the arrival of American troops with the establishment of the provisional **Korean People's Republic** (KPR), in which he was to act as vice-president under Syngman Rhee (**Yi Sŭngman**). In November, however, he broke his connection with the KPR and founded the **Korean People's Party**. In 1946 he declined an invitation from General **Hodge** to serve as chairman of the mainly right-wing Democratic Advisory Council, set up in February to prepare for national elections, and continued to pursue a leftist line through contacts with communists in P'yŏngyang. Despite his search for accommodation across the political spectrum and efforts to reach understanding with the north, he was assassinated in July 1947.
See also **Pak Hŏnyŏng**

YŎLLYŎ 烈女 'faithful wife'
A wife, especially a young wife, who did not remarry after her husband's death. Such fidelity often led to the erection of a red memorial arch (*yŏllyŏ-mun*) or memorial stone (*yŏllyŏ-bi*) outside her house after her death.
See also **faithful widow gate**

YŎLLYŎ-MUN 烈女門 *See* **faithful widow gate**

YŎLLYŎ-SIL KISUL 燃藜室記述 'Glowing-Goosefoot Room Records'
Extracts from some 400 sources (memorials, diaries, letters, biographies, and anecdote collections) compiled by Yi Kŭngik (1736–1806) to make a history of the Chosŏn dynasty. It was not printed until the 20th century. Books 1–33 form a chronological account, reign by reign, 1392–1674; 34–40 contain the reign of **Sukchong** (1675–1720); 41–59 contain monographs like those in *Koryŏ-sa*. Yi's brush-name Yŏllyŏ-sil (C. Ranlishi) refers to a staff, made from the stem of a *chenopodium* or goosefoot plant, carried by a mysterious yellow-clad sage who passed a night imparting wisdom to Liu Xiang (c. 75–c. 6 BC). The old man ignited the tip of his staff and it lit the room till dawn broke.

YŎLSŎNG ŎJE 列聖御制 'Royal Writings by Successive Holy Ones (kings)'
The first collection of kings' writings printed under this or similar titles was published by Yi Kwang (Ŭich'ang-gun, 1589–1645) in 1631 and contained works from T'aejong to Sŏnjo (1392–1608). There was a special edition (*Chŏngmyo ŏje*) in the reign of **Chŏngjo** (1777–1800). The last edition, by Chŏng Wŏnyong (1783–1873), brought the collection to the reign of **Ch'ŏlchong.**

YŎM SANGSŎP 廉想涉 (1897–1963)
Yŏm Sangsŏp was born in Seoul but educated in Japan, where he studied English literature, graduating in 1918. He was briefly imprisoned for his nationalist activity, but returned to Korea, where he published his first short story *P'yobon-sirŭi ch'ŏnggaeguri*, 'Green frog in the specimen room', in the magazine *Kaebyŏk* (1921). The story begins with a specimen frog and meanders through a series of events, its interest depending on depiction of psychological conditions. His 'naturalism', said to be influenced by Zola, describes a chain of causality on which comment is unnecessary. Yŏm taught for a while at **Osan School** before going to **Manchuria**, where he edited a Korean newspaper and did some of his best writing during the 1930s. Returning to Seoul after 1945, he edited the daily *Kyŏnghyang Sinmun* and held high university posts. He died of high blood-pressure.
A translation of one of his stories is in PETER H. LEE, *Flowers of Fire*, Hawaii, 1974

YŎMILLAK 與民樂 'Pleasure with his People'
Musical setting taken from a Chinese tune and elaborated to form one of five settings for the poetic suite *Yongbi-och'ŏn-ga* ('Song of Dragons Flying in Heaven'). Its title, 'The ruler shares his] Pleasure with his People', combined praise for the Chosŏn dynasty's founder with a clear reference to the Chinese paragon of political virtue, King Wen (Mencius Ia.1). It was the only one of the five musical settings that was incomplete, consisting of only five stanzas, but it is the only one that is regularly played today. Classified as *hyangak* (*see* **music**), it became part of the very limited repertoire of tunes that accompanied court rites and entertainments.
See also **King Sejong**

YŎNDŬNGHOE 燃燈會 'Lotus Lantern Festival'
One of two major national festivals observed at all levels of society during the Koryŏ dynasty and earlier. The other was *P'algwanhoe*, and both were commended by **Wang Kŏn** in his **Ten Injunctions**. *Yŏndŭnghoe* was a Buddhist occasion and was held on the fifteenth day of the first month. It involved **music**, **dance**, and processions with lighted lanterns. In 1073 Chinese dances were incorporated into the court observances at each festival.

YONGBI-ŎCH'ŎN-GA 龍飛御天歌 'Song of Dragons Flying in Heaven'
A paean written by order of King **Sejong** to be sung at state banquets, in praise of his six paternal ancestors. The title conflates two phrases from the *Book of Changes* (Line 5 and *tuanzhuan* for Hexagram 1) in which six **dragons** flying through heaven are a sign of success. The six are the four posthumously canonised ancestors of T'aejo, founder of the Chosŏn dynasty: Mokcho (Yi Ansa, d. 1274), Ikcho (Yi Haengni), Tojo (Yi Ch'un, d. 1342) and Hwanjo (Yi Chach'u, 1315 61); T'aejo himself (**Yi Sŏnggye**); and his son T'aejong (Sejong's father, Yi Pangwŏn, 1367–1422). Two-thirds of the book praises T'aejo.
The whole work, composed in Middle Korean with a translation in Chinese, consists of 125 cantos. Each canto is composed of two stanzas, apart from the opening and closing cantos, which have only one stanza each. In 103 cantos the first stanza recalls a Chinese ruler's feats, which are paralleled by praise for one of the six Yi 'dragons' in the second.
JAMES HOYT, trans., *Songs of the Dragons Flying to Heaven: a Korean Epic*, Seoul: Royal Asiatic Society, Korea Branch, 2nd ed., 1979; PETER H. LEE, *Songs of Flying Dragons, a Critical Reading*, Cambridge, Mass.: Harvard University Press, 1975
See also *Akchang*; *Yŏmillak*

YONGDAM YUSA 龍潭遺詞 'Lyrics from the Dragon Pool'
Eight long poems expressing *Ch'ŏndo-gyo* doctrine in *kasa* form, suitable for recitation by **women** and children, written by **Ch'oe Cheu**. It was published by his successor Ch'oe Sihyŏng at Tanyang in 1881. Yongdam-jŏng, 'dragon pool pavilion', was the place in **Kyŏngju** where Ch'oe Cheu hammered out his doctrines.

YONGJAE CH'ONGHWA 慵齋叢話 'Collected talk of Idle Studio'
Yongjae, 'Idle studio', was the brush-name of Sŏng Hyŏn (1439–1504), who was at times a member of the *Yemun-gwan*, *Taejehak* and president of the Boards of Rites and Works. Much of his writing has been lost. This bulky collection of stories, biographical sketches, poems, and essays on **music**, geography, customs and other things is famous for its grace and wit.

YŎNGJO, KING 英祖 (1694–1776; r. 1724–76)
The longest reign in Korean history. He came to the throne after the *Sinim-sahwa* and early determined to rid the court of factional strife. He was largely successful in this. His reign was one of relative prosperity and he showed at least some concern about the lot of the common people. His *Kyunyŏkpŏp*, 'equalised tax law', was intended to relieve the burdens on the poor, though it did not achieve as much as he had hoped. He instituted examinations for which men over 60 years old were eligible, and encouraged scholarship and **printing**. The trend now called *sirhak* reached its peak during this reign. Although the tragedy of Prince **Changhŏn** has cast a shadow over the king's memory, he is also remembered as 'Ch'unhyang's king', for the **Ch'unhyang** story is usually set in his reign, remembered as a time of peace and plenty. His first *myoho* was Yŏngjong, but it was raised to Yŏngjo in 1899, when his son Chŏngjong was also made up to **Chŏngjo**.
JAHYUN KIM HABOUSH, *A Heritage of Kings: One Man's Monarchy in the Confucian World*, New York: Columbia University Press, 1988; JAHYUN KIM HABOUSH, *The Memoirs of Lady Hyegyŏng: the Autobiographical Writings of a Crown Princess of Eighteenth Century Korea*, Berkeley: University of California Press, 1996

YŎNGSA 領事
Title in Chosŏn for the principal officers of *Hongmun-gwan*, *Ch'unch'u-gwan*, *Yŏngyŏn*, *Tollyŏng-bu*, *Yemun-gwan*, *Chungch'u-bu* and certain other posts of 1st **grade** senior.

YŎNGSAN HOESANG 靈山會像 'Spirit Mountain Meeting'
A long suite of instrumental **music** which may have evolved from a simple Buddhist song text of the 15th century. By the 17th century the words had been dropped and the instrumental elaboration begun. It became a popular piece of performance music, or *chŏngak* ('correct music'), appreciated by the *yangban* and *chungin*. Whatever its origins, it conveyed all the qualities favoured by the Confucian **gentry**, balance, refinement, consideration, reliability, and the control of emotions. Individual sections were used to accompany court **dances**. It attained its current form in the 19th century, and is played today as a typical piece of programme music for the traditional Korean orchestra. The origins of the component sections are unknown. The first four seem to be related in the form of variations, and number seven bears the title *yŏmbul*, 'Praying to Buddha'. These five at least show some link with the original nature of the text. Other movements include popular dance tunes, while the final one, *kunak* ('military music'), clearly stems from a different *milieu* and is even in a different key from the remainder. Like much traditional Korean music, the suite begins slowly and increases in tempo and rhythmic complexity. There are no breaks between the maximum eight or nine movements. A complete performance may last as long as one hour, and selections are often made.
   The present *Yŏngsan Hoesang* exists in three versions. They are:

1) *Hyŏnak Yŏngsan* (or *Kŏmun'go Hoesang*, or *Chunggwang Hoesang*): nine movements for strings and soft wind instruments;
2) *Kwanak Yŏngsan Hoesang*: eight movements for a wind ensemble known as *samhyŏn yukkak*;
3) *P'yŏngjo Hoesang* (or *Yuch'osin-ji-gok*): eight movements for strings and loud wind instruments.

YŎNG-ŬIJŎNG 領議政 'prime minister'
The principal minister of the *Ŭijŏng-bu*, a man of 1st **grade** senior. He was the highest ranking member of the government, theoretically in charge of all the others. Though translated 'prime minister', the office was not precisely that of prime minister in a 20th-century state.

YŎNGŬN-MUN 迎恩門 'Welcoming Favours Gate'
Occasional embassies from the Chinese emperor to the king of Korea, for such purposes as announcing the succession of a new emperor, were received by the king himself, who left Seoul by the West Gate and went to the Yŏngŭn-mun at the 'Peking Pass' on the road to **Kaesŏng**. The envoy was there received in the *Mohwa-gwan*, 'hall of devotion to the Flowery [Kingdom]'. In 1896 it was demolished and replaced by the Independence Arch (*Tongnim-mun*), modelled on the Arc de Triomphe by **Sŏ Chaep'il** (*see also* **Independence Club**).

YŎNSAN, PRINCE 燕山君 (b. 1476, r. 1494–1506)
Son of King Sŏnjong, whom he succeeded at the age of eighteen. At the beginning of his reign he resolved to reassert the king's authority and was soon led by the intransigeance of politicians to set in motion the first purge of the literati, *Muo sahwa* (*see* **literati purges, twelve**). Towards the end of his reign he learned how his mother (now known as *P'yebi Yun-ssi*, 'deposed Queen Yun') had been persecuted by other women in the palace and executed by suicidal **poison** in 1482. Already ruthless, he now went beserk and started another bloody purge, *Kapcha sahwa*. He proscribed the use of **Sejong**'s national script (*han'gŭl*) and destroyed Buddhist temples such as Wŏn'gak-sa in central Seoul. He was deposed at the age of 32 and exiled to the island of Kyodong off **Kanghwa**, where he died a few weeks later, either of sickness or of poisoning. One of the two Chosŏn kings (the other was **Prince Kwanghae**) who were never given a kingly temple name, he is recorded merely by a princely title and is the more execrated of the two. He was certainly cruel, perhaps pathologically megalomaniac. The senseless factionalism of his court and the story of his mother's death must have exacerbated his condition; but the accounts of him that remain were written by his enemies. Their criticisms are suspiciously couched in conventional terms of orgy, stabling horses in temples, keeping a huge harem and loving exotic pets (the last perhaps suggesting a sympathetic side to his character, though not to a strict neo-Confucian). The whole truth is beyond recovery.
See also **Pagoda Park;** *sahwa*

YŎRHA ILGI 熱河日記
Yŏrha ilgi, 'Jehol Diary', by Pak Chiwŏn (brush-name Yŏnam, 'swallow rock', 1731–1805), is a record of the embassy that Pak accompanied to the 70th birthday celebrations of the Qianlong Emperor in his summer palace at Jehol (Rehe, now Chengde) in summer 1780. Pak also visited **Beijing** and Chengjing (modern Shenyang). The book is composite and contains digressions on religion, science and philosophy that make it a mirror of the intellectual concerns of the period. His style is plain, his thought informed by 'practical learning' (*sirhak*) and the rigorous critical methods of Qing thinkers. His satirical stories *Hojil*, 'The Tiger's Rebuke', and *Hŏ-saeng-jŏn*, 'Story of Mr Ho', are included. Like his *Yangban-jŏn*, 'Story of a Gentleman', they pillory the corruption and pretensions of the educated clesses.
PETER H. LEE, *Anthology of Korean Literature*, Honolulu: University of Hawaii Press, 1981: pp. 213–221 'The Story of Master Ho', pp. 222–7 'The Story of a Yangban'

YŎSU-SUNCH'ŎN RISING 麗順叛亂 (1948)

Mutiny led by officers of the 14th Regiment of President Syngman Rhee (**Yi Sŭngman**)'s army under Kim Chihoe, which broke out on 18 October 1948 when the regiment was ordered to subdue the **Cheju Rebellion**. A large force of armed communist sympathisers from the cities of Yŏsu and Sunch'ŏn in Chŏlla Namdo province threatened the stability of the region. The rising was crushed after eight days by soldiers of the 4th Regiment sent from **Kwangju**, but nearly 3,000 people were killed. Retribution for the mutiny included a widespread purge of suspected communists and alleged traitors, establishing the pattern of oppression which was to characterise the First Republic.

YŎŬI-JU 如意珠 'as-you-will jewel'

The magic pearl in the jaws of the **dragon**, symbolising bliss and wisdom, also called *mani*, in Sanskrit *cintramani*. It is held in both hands by Avalokitesvara (**Kwanseŭm**) when he is called *Yŏŭi-ryun Kwanŭm*, 'Kwanŭm with the *yŏŭiju* and wheel' – the bodhisattva answering all prayers. It is mentioned in the Surangama **Sutra**, in a parable about a man with a cintramani pearl sewn into his coat, who forgets all about it, thinks he is poor and goes about begging his food. When he is reminded about the pearl, all his wishes are granted and he becomes rich. Another name for the pearl is *iju* 'black [dragon's] pearl', from a story in the *Lie Yukou* section of *Zhuangzi*, about a poor boy diving in a river and finding the pearl while the black dragon was asleep.

YOUNG MEN'S CHRISTIAN ASSOCIATION (YMCA) *Kidok ch'ŏngnyŏnhoe* 基督教青年會

The Korean branch was founded in 1903 by Yi Sangjae, Namgung Ŏk and Syngman Rhee (**Yi Sŭngman**). In common with other sectors of Christian church activity it was active in fostering **nationalism** among young men, and in supporting modernisation and self-strengthening. The inaugural ceremony of the **New Shoot Society** (*Sin'ganhoe*) took place in its hall in Seoul on 15 February 1927.
See also **Self-strengthening movement; students**

YU KWANGSUN 柳寬順 (1904–20)

A heroine of Korean independence, born in the village of Pyŏngch'ŏn near Ch'ŏnan, she was a Methodist who went to Ewha school in Seoul. When the school was closed after the independence demonstration of 1 March (1st day of the 3rd solar month) 1919, she returned home and began spreading the independence message in Yŏn'gi, Ch'ŏngju and Chinch'ŏn. On 1 April (1st day of the 3rd lunar month) she organised a demonstration of some thousands in Pyŏngch'ŏn. She was sent to West Gate prison in Seoul, where she continued to urge prisoners to cry *Tongnip Mansei* 'Long live Independence'. She was tortured and died in prison the following year, aged fifteen.
See also **March First Movement**

YUAN SHIKAI 袁世凱 (1856–1916)

The Chinese politician and soldier who worked alternately for constitutional reform and for the Empress Dowager Cixi before the Chinese Republic was established. Becoming premier in 1911 and president in 1913, he declared himself emperor in 1915, shortly before his death. In 1882 **Li Hongzhang** had sent him to Korea with 3,000 men to stem Japan's increasing influence. From 1885 to 1894 he was Chinese Resident-General and Commissioner for Commerce, the most powerful man in Seoul. He was praised by the Manchus for service during the **Sino-Japanese War**.

JEROME CH'EN, *Yuan Shih-k'ai*, Stanford University Press, 1961; LEW YOUNG ICK, 'Yuan Shi-kai's Residency 1885–1894,' *JKS*, 5, 1984

YUDONG-BOSAL 儒童菩薩 'learned youth boddhisattva'
A Chinese equivalent for Sanskrit *Manavaka* (K. *Mannappakka*), meaning a young brahman, a personification of Sakyamuni as a **bodhisattva** in an earlier life. Perhaps because the first character *yu* is that used to denote Confucian scholars, he is sometimes identified, in both China and Korea, as Confucius. This identification is not universally accepted.

YUHAP 類合 'Collection of Kinds'
A textbook for students of Chinese characters, sometimes attributed to **So Kojong**, though his authorship is not certain. It is best known in its expanded form *Sinjŭng-yuhap*, containing 3,000 characters, published in 1576. Meanings and pronunciations are given in **han'gŭl**, which retains *pansiot*. The only known exemplar is in the Tōyō Bunko in Japan. Copies have been circulated in Korea.

YUKKA CHABYŎNG 六家雜詠 'Various Poems by Six Men'
A collection of poems in Chinese published in 1668. They were the work of six **chungin**, including government clerks and other professionals: Chŏng Namsu (Haengnim, 'ginkgo forest'), Ch'oe Kinam (Kwigok, 'tortoise valley'), Nam Ŭngch'im (Songp'a, 'pinetree slope'), Chŏng Yenam (Sŏju, 'west field', a physician), Kim Hyoil (Kuktam, 'chrysanthemum pool', a worker in the Royal Observatory) and Ch'oe Taerip (Ch'angae, 'green cliff'). In the reign of Sŏnjo in particular there were many non-**yangban** poets, including some of these six.

YUKSŎ SIMWŎN 六書尋源
Yuksŏ simwŏn, 'Seeking the Sources of the Six Categories of Writing', is a huge work of 8,766 pages in 31 mimeographed volumes published in 1938 by Sŏngdae 'still terrace' Kwŏn Pyŏnghun (1864–1941). It must be the longest Chinese **dictionary** ever compiled, containing entries for more than 60,000 characters, with notations probing as far as discussion of component strokes and hidden meanings. The title refers to the six categories into which Chinese characters were divided in the Han dynasty *Shuo wen*, the earliest surviving Chinese dictionary. Kwŏn was a judge in the Hamhŭng district when Japan annexed Korea in 1910. In protest at the **annexation**, he resigned and withdrew to his home at Kongju, where he spent more than twenty years studying characters. His book was published through the generosity of Ch'oe Kyudong, principal of Chungdong School in Seoul.

YUN CHICH'UNG 尹持忠 (1759–91)
A cousin of **Chŏng Yagyong**. He qualified as *chinsa* in 1783, and in 1784 went to Seoul to study under Chŏng Yagyong at the house of **Kim Pŏmu**, where he became a Catholic. He was confirmed by the bishop of Beijing in 1789 and returned home to Chinsan, south Chŏlla, where he quietly disposed of the family spirit tablets. When his mother died he had her buried without Confucian **rites**. He was arrested and executed at Chŏnju. This is known as *Chinsan sakkŏn*, 'the Chinsan incident'.

YUN CH'IHO 尹致昊 (1865–1946)
A scion of a powerful military clan, well educated in the traditional way, who at the age of 16 went as an assistant to the *Sinsa Yuram-dan* mission that visited Japan to inspect

its modernisation in 1881. Soon he was in the USA, coming back in 1883 with the American delegate Lucius Foote after the conclusion of the Korean-American (**Shufeldt**) Treaty of 1882. After the failure of the progressives' *émeute* in 1884 (*see Kapsin* **coup**) he left Korea and spent some time at the Anglo-Chinese College in Shanghai, where he was baptized in 1887. He then attended a Methodist college in the USA until 1893, before returning, with a remarkable command of English, and joining the cabinet. In the troubles after the murder of Queen **Min** in 1895 he was involved in the night-time attempt to rescue the king through the Ch'unsaeng-mun (a minor gate on the eastern side of the **Kyŏngbok Palace**). After a brief imprisonment he attended the king during his months of refuge in the Russian Legation, and went with **Min Yŏnghwan** to represent the king at the coronation of Tsar Nicholas II in Moscow. In 1896 he was a founder and chairman of the **Independence Club** and for a while editor of the *Tongnip Sinmun*, probably writing the song that in 1948 became the *aegukka*, but coming to think poorly of his own people. He declined appointment as Mayor of Seoul in 1899 but accepted the governorship of Tŏgwŏn (Hamgyŏng). In 1903 he took part in the foundation of Seoul **Young Men's Christian Association** and began to play a rôle in developing modern education, including headship of **An Ch'angho**'s Taesŏng School. He was among those arrested during the **Hundred and Five** affair, and was imprisoned for four years. Later the Japanese succeeded in compromising him as a collaborator. In 1946, aged 81 and rejected by public opinion, he died at home in Kaesŏng, allegedly having taken **poison**.

VIPAN CHANDRA, 'The Concept of Popular Sovereignty: The Case of Sŏ Chae-p'il and Yun Ch'i-ho,' *KJ*, 21/4, 1981; DONALD CLARK, 'History and Personality in the Diary of Yun Ch'i-ho,' *KJ*, 15/12, 1975; KOEN DE CEUSTER, 'From Modernization to Collaboration, the Dilemma of Korean Cultural Nationalism: the Case of Yun Ch'i-ho (1865–1945)', PhD thesis, Katholieke Universiteit, Leuven, 1994; KENNETH WELLS, 'Yun Ch'i-ho and the Quest for National Integrity,' *KJ*, 22/1, 1982; KENNETH WELLS, 'Civic Morality in the Nationalist Thought of Yun Ch'i-ho, 1881–1911,' *PFEH*, 28, 1983

YUN PONGGIL 尹奉吉 (1908–32)

Born in Yesan. His elementary education was interrupted and he studied Chinese letters alone. When he was eighteen, he went to Qingdao and worked in China as a laundry attendant and textile-factory hand. In 1932 he joined **Kim Ku**'s *Han'guk-aeguktan* (*see ŭibyŏng*) and was given bombs to throw at Japanese officials during the Emperor's birthday celebrations in Hongkou Park, Shanghai. He killed two men and injured several others. He was taken to Osaka, tried and executed.

YUN POSŎN 尹潽善 (1897–1990)

Yun Posŏn was born in Seoul of a *yangban* family, and graduated in archaeology from the University of Edinburgh. He appears to have played little part in politics before 1945, though some accounts link him with the Shanghai groups, and after 1945 he certainly became associated with the **Korean Independence Party** which had returned from China. In 1948, he was appointed mayor of Seoul, and from 1949–50 was minister of trade and industry. In 1954, he was elected to the National Assembly, and was re-elected in 1958 and 1960, becoming increasingly associated with the opposition to President Syngman Rhee (**Yi Sŭngman**). In August 1960, following the fall of Rhee, he was elected president. Following the military coup of May 1961, he was briefly under house arrest, but he then continued in office, providing some degree of legitimacy for the coup, though he resigned in March 1962 in protest at the Political Purification Law. Thereafter, he was the opposition candidate against Park Chung Hee (**Pak Chŏnghŭi**) in

1963 and 1967, but was heavily defeated on both occasions. He continued to play an active part in opposition to Park, receiving a five-year suspended sentence in 1976, and losing his civil rights. He received a further two-year sentence in 1979, but this was suspended, and his civil rights were restored on 1 March 1980. Thereafter he assumed the rôle of an elder statesman, playing no part in active politics, until his death.

YUN SŎNDO 尹善道 (Kosan, 1587–1671)

Ranked with **Pak Illo** and **Chŏng Ch'ŏl** as the greatest of Korean-language poets; his brush name means 'solitary mountain' (a place near Yangju in Kyŏnggi province). He proceeded slowly through the civil service **examinations**, but eventually took office in the bitterly factional government of his time. His career was marked by recurrent periods of self-imposed withdrawal and politically enforced exile to far places, from the Manchurian border to the islands off the south coast; but it was in exile that he wrote his best work. During the **Manchu invasions** of 1636–7 he served in the defence of **Kanghwa** Island and Namhan fortress (**Namhan Sansŏng**). Then he fell in love with the island of Pogil off the south Chŏlla coast, where he had two rural retreats, Puyong-dong, 'Lotus Vale' and Kŭmswae-dong, 'Iron Lock Valley'. Here, while banished yet again by Westerners' intrigue in 1650, he wrote the *sijo* cycle *Ŏbu-sasi-sa*, 'fisherman's songs of the four seasons', considered by many the highest achievement in all *sijo* literature. It tells of frugal living among simple folk in a beautiful place, far from the treachery of Seoul. His short *sijo* cycle *Ou-ga*, 'Song of Five Friends' (water, stone, pine, bamboo and moon), is also regarded as a masterpiece. He died on Pogil Island at the age of 84.

KIM YONG-DOK, 'Kosan, Yun Son-do (1587–1671), the Man and his Island,' *TRASKB*, LXVII, 1992; PETER LEE, 'The Life and Poetry of Yun Son-do', *MS*, XXI, 1962; RICHARD RUTT, *The Bamboo Grove*, Berkeley: University of California Press, 1972

YUN SUN 尹淳 (Packha, 1680–1741)

The most distinguished calligrapher of his times with the evocative brush-name 'Under white'. He sat the national examinations after he was thirty. In 1723 he went on an embassy to China (*see* **Beijing, embassies to**), and in 1729 had become *pansŏ* of the Board of Works. He went on to hold the same position in the Board of Rites, and then was appointed to the Crown Prince's department. In **calligraphy** he was a master of running script in the style of Mi Fu (1051–1107), called the Mi Nan'gong style, and of the *haesŏ* and *ch'osŏ* styles. There is a fine example of his work in the British Museum. **Sin Wi** was one of his disciples.

YUN TONGJU 尹東柱 (1917–45)

Born in north Kando, Tongju grew up under the influence of his Presbyterian grandfather. In 1935 he entered Sungsil School, P'yŏngyang, just before it was closed in the **Shrine Question** troubles. After he went back to **Kando** to finish his schooling at Longjing, several of his poems appeared in *K'at'ollic sonyŏn*, 'Catholic youth', a magazine published at Yanji. In 1938 he went to Yŏnhŭi College in Seoul and while there, published poems in the youth section of the newspaper *Chosŏn Ilbo*. After graduation he went to Japan in 1941 to study English, first at Rikkyo University in Tokyo, then in Kyoto. On his way home for a summer vacation he was arrested and held without trial for twelve months before being sentenced to two years' imprisonment for anti-Japanese attitudes. He died in Fukuoka prison. His family collected his manuscripts and published his poems in 1948. He has become a much loved young poet of lyrical patriotism and tragedy.

YUNŬM 綸音 'silken words'
From the time of **Yŏngjo** (r. 1724–1776) royal edicts were often published under the designation *yunŭm* (synonymous with *yunbal* and *yunji*). This expression refers to *Liji* 30, where it says: 'The prince's words are like silken threads: they come forth as cords.'

YUSIN 維新 'Revitalisation' **CONSTITUTION**
Introduced by the State Council at the behest of President Park Chung Hee (**Pak Chŏnghŭi**) on the same day (17 October 1972) as the suspension of the **constitution** of the **Third Republic** and the imposition of martial law. It followed his near defeat by **Kim Taejung** in the 1971 elections. In November it was accepted by an overwhelming majority of voters, despite the fact that it handed over their right to elect future presidents to an electoral college of 2,359 members (the National Conference for Unification). It also gave the president power to choose one third of the National Assembly, to control the activities of political parties, to pass emergency decrees, and to rule for an unlimited number of six-year terms of office. Criticism of the Constitution was a punishable offence, yet had become widespread by 1979, especially among the politically radical student body (*see* **Kwangju Massacre**). The **Korean Central Intelligence Agency** used repressive and intimidatory tactics to enforce it.
See also **Chŏn Tuhwan; Constitution; South Korea: constitutional changes**

YUT
The Korean version of a game requiring dice, counters and a board, of the same family as ludo and the Indian *pachisi*. *Yut* is suited to gambling, though more often played without stakes. Believed by some to date from Silla times, it was traditionally a game for **New Year**, when it was also used for divining the quality of the coming season's crops, but is now played at any season.

Yut sticks of standard form (*changjang-nyut* 'firewood yut'), are made by cutting two cylinders of hard wood – usually *ssari* or *paktal* (*see* **Trees**) – in halves lengthways, so as to make four pieces about 20 cm long and 3 cm thick, rounded on one side and flat on the other. *Pamnyut* 'chestnut yut' are smaller, about 2·5 cm in length. All four together are thrown in the air like dice. If they fall with only one flat side up, the score is *do* 1; two flat sides up, *kae* 2; three flat sides up, *kŏl* 3; four flat sides up, *yut* 4, and the player may cast the pieces again. If no flat side shows, the score is *mo* 5, and the player may cast again.

A *malp'an* or *yutp'an* (which may be made of paper), is a board or sheet on which is drawn a square or circle crossed by diagonals. Twenty-nine stopping points are marked on these lines: one at each corner (*mo*), one at the centre (*pang*), and four on each of the six straight lines. Each side of the square is a *pat*, 'course', named after the corner at which it ends, and the corner may be marked with a Chinese character: *appat* 'front course', marked *ip* 'enter'; *twippat* 'rear course', marked *kong* 'embrace'; *tchaelpat* 'breaking course', marked *yŏl* 'divide'; and *nalpat* 'exit course', marked *ch'ul* 'go out'. The points on the diagonals are *am-modo* and *am-mogae* 'front corner *do* and *kae*', *songnyut* and *songmo* 'inner *yut* and *mo*'; *twimmodo* and *twimmogae* 'rear corner *do* and *kae*', *saryŏ* (of doubtful meaning) and *antchi* 'inner break-point'.

On some boards the stopping points are marked with Chinese characters forming an unrhymed 7-character quatrain of which several versions are found. Each line begins at the start of a *pat* and proceeds anti-clockwise, turning in towards the centre at the next corner point.

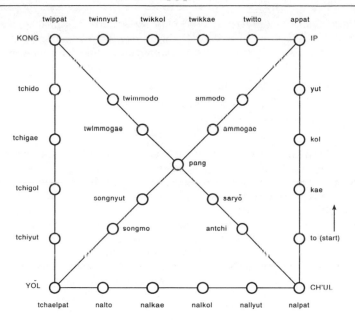

Yut diagram

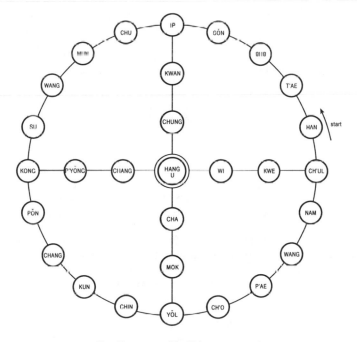

Yut diagram with Chinese quatrain

Han T'aejo sŏn IP-gwan-jung / Chu Mun-wang suGONG p'yŏng-jang / Pŏn Changgun chin-YŎL mok-cha / Ch'o P'aewang nam-CH'UL kwe-wi. (The Chinese characters naming the corners of the square were either worked into the verse or were derived from it.)

> The Founder of Han entered the frontiers,
> Like King Wen of Zhou, bringing peace and order.
> General Fan glared with bulging eyes;
> The Tyrant of Chu broke the cordon, fleeing south.

Shiji 7 tells how Xiang Yu (K. Hang U), the Tyrant of Chu, fought against Liu Bang when Liu was establishing the **Han dynasty**. While Liu was visiting Xiang, who intended to assassinate him, Liu's bodyguard, Fan Kuai, famously stared the tyrant out. Later, when Xiang made his last stand at Gaixia in Anhui in 202 BC, he had only 28 horsemen left, whom he stationed in a square round himself. This was doubtless what suggested the 28 points round the *yut* board with Xiang Yu in the centre. He was quickly forced to flee southward. The hyphenated phrases in the transcription are quoted from *Shiji*. *Sugong* is quoted from *Shujing* 'Wucheng' 10.

The game can be played by teams or individuals, each team or single player having four counters (*mal* 'horses', which may be pieces of paper). Taking turns, the players cast the sticks and place their counters on the board at the appropriate number of points from the start (*nalpat*), moving anti-clockwise. Thereafter the counters are moved from point to point through *appat*, *twippat* and *tchaelpat* according to the numbers obtained by casting the sticks; but if a *mal* comes to rest on a *mo* (corner) or *pang*, the player proceeds by a short cut along the diagonal at the next throw. If two counters belonging to different players arrive on the same point, the one that was there first is knocked out and starts again; but two counters belonging to the same player are both allowed to remain on any point. A player may use more than one counter at a time (which introduces a strategic element), but moves only one counter at each throw of the sticks. The winner is the first to get four counters to the last point (*nalpat*).

Z

ZHOU WENMO 周文謨 (d. 1801)

A Chinese from Suzhou who was married at the age of twenty. After his wife died three years later, he was baptized as a Catholic, named James, and ordained in Beijing. The Portuguese missionaries called him Jaime Vellozo, perhaps because he had a long beard. Another Chinese priest, a Macao man ordained in 1787 and now known only as Fr Wu or as João dos Remedios, was sent to Korea in 1791, but failed to get across the border and returned to Beijing, where he died in 1793. In 1794 Fr Zhou was sent to Korea in his place. While living secretly in the Seoul home of **Kang Wansuk**, first in the woodshed, later in the house, he spent nearly seven years visiting some 4,000 Catholics – *yangban*, *chungin* and farmers – in Ch'ungch'ŏng and Chŏlla provinces. He was arrested and executed in 1801. Very soon afterwards the King sent a *chujinsa*, apologetic envoy, to the Qing Emperor.

ZHU XI (K. Chu Hŭi) 朱熹 (1130–1200)

The paramount importance of Zhu Xi in Korea is shown by the fact that as Koreans habitually referred to Confucius as Kongja, 'Master Kong', so they also referred to Zhu Xi as Chuja, 'Master Zhu'. This suffix was not so freely used for any other philosopher.

Zhu Xi, also known as Yuanhui (K. Wŏnhŭi), and by his brush name Huian (K. Hŭiam), was born during the **Song dynasty** in central Fujian, while his father was serving as a magistrate there. Taught by men who were in the direct tradition of **Cheng Yi**, he passed the government examination at eighteen. He studied **Buddhism** and **Daoism**, but decided for **Confucianism** when he was about thirty. Most of his subsequent life was passed in and out of middle grade government service in Fujian and Jiangxi. He was a competent administrator, but often held sinecures that allowed him time to study and write. A large number of disciples gathered round him and he taught in many places, most famously at Bailudong (K. Paengnok-tong), 'White deer valley', in Jiangxi. His antagonism to official incompetence brought him recurrent censure and political unpopularity. Accusations of 'false learning' brought him two years of official disgrace during his late sixties, 1197–9, and he died of dysentery shortly after he regained political standing. Nearly 1,000 people attended his funeral.

Zhu Xi's great achievement was to draw together the moral and metaphysical teachings of the 11th-century neo-Confucians (*see* **Five Sages of Song**), creating the philosophic system usually known in Korea as *Sŏngni-hak*. Two generations after his death, **An Hyang** was promulgating it in Koryŏ; during the Chosŏn dynasty it became the only acceptable Confucian orthodoxy. The **Confucian Classics** were rarely read without Chuja's commentaries; his redaction of Confucian rites was the canonical basis of the **ritual studies** and controversies of the 17th and 18th centuries at the Korean court; history was understood as he had explained it in the *Tongjian gangmu* (*see* ***Tongsa gangmok***). He had views on all important subjects: he wrote about them all and they became the standards of Chosŏn orthodoxy. Constructive criticism of his thought begins in Korea with **Yi Hwang**; more radical approaches were expressed in the *sirhak* tendencies of the 18th century and later. Indeed, many believe that Zhu Xi stifled Korean thought for several centuries.

ZHUGE LIANG (K. Chegal Yang) 諸葛亮 (181–234)
Otherwise known as Gongming 'great and glorious', Wolong 'sleeping dragon' or Wuhou 'military marquess' (K. Kongmyŏng, Waryong, Muhu), an historical personage of importance in the troubled time after the demise of Later Han. In Korea he is best known as a revered hero of the ***Romance of the Three Kingdoms***. He was only 26, but already famous for wisdom, when Liu Bei found him in his thatched cottage (chap. 38). Reluctantly agreeing to become Liu's strategist and adviser, he went on to win many battles (including the Red Cliffs, chap. 49–50) and invent wonderful devices (including *mogu-yuma* 'wooden oxen and gliding horses' – best explained as sophisticated wheelbarrows – chap. 102). When Liu founded the state of Shu in 221, Zhuge became his chief minister (chap. 80). He died of illness and fatigue (chap. 104).

Chapter 117 of the *Romance of the Three Kingdoms* contains a paragraph about Zhuge's wife, Huang-shi, a plain but clever and well-read woman, who shared his studies of strategy and magic. She died shortly after him. No more is known of her, but there are Korean romances about her too (such as *Hwang-buin-jŏn*).

Chegal is one of Korea's **two-character surnames**.
See also **Red Cliffs, Song of the**

ZODIAC 獸帶 (K. *sudae*, 'animal band')
The so-called 'Chinese zodiac' consists of twelve animals: rat, ox, tiger, hare, dragon, snake, horse, sheep, monkey, fowl, dog and pig. Its origin is unclear. Some have thought that it came from Central Asia or even further west, but the arguments are

inconclusive. The list was known in China in the **Han dynasty**, and was attached to the twelve 'earthly branches' of the **sixty-fold cycle**. The 'branches' correspond to the twelve months of the year and the twelve 'hours' of the day. The annual cycle begins strongly *yin* with the rat for the first month, grows increasingly *yang* till the horse of the 7th month, then increasingly *yin* till the pig of the 12th month. The daily cycle is strongly *yin* at the beginning of the 'rat hour' 2300–0100, grows increasingly *yang* till the 'horse hour' 1100–1300, then increasingly *yin* till the 'pig hour' 2100–2300 (*see* **Twenty-four Directions/Hours**). For divinatory purposes, however, the signs are alternatively *yin* and *yang*.

The animals are not constellation names. Six of them are wild animals (Chinese in the last millennium BC believing that **dragons** really existed). The other six are the *yukch'uk* (C. *liuchu*) 'six **domestic animals**': ox, horse, sheep, fowl, dog and pig, mentioned in the 4th-century BC *Zuo zhuan* (Xi 19) as sacrificial victims. They were presumably the only domesticated animals in the culture – the cat, donkey and camel having not yet arrived. The 'zodiac' list has no value in **astronomy** but considerable value in archaeology (it is illustrated on Silla **tombs**) and ethnology. In Korean popular culture it is most mentioned when the animal of one's birth-year number in the sixty-fold cycle is supposed to preside over one's fate and influence one's choice of spouse. There is also a connection with exorcisms, in which masks of the animals (then called *sibi sin* 'the twelve spirits') have been worn.

See also **Zodiacal animals, incompatible**

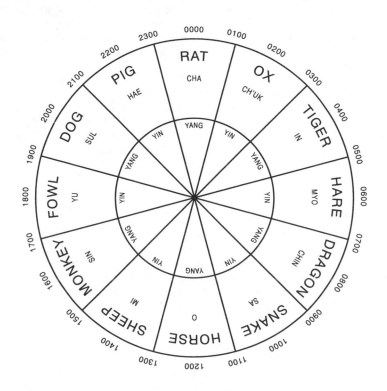

540

ZODIACAL ANIMALS, INCOMPATIBLE

Each zodiacal animal has another that is regarded as being incompatible with it. This naturally provides negative indicators in arranging marriages. Rat and sheep are inimical; so are ox and horse, tiger and fowl, hare and monkey, dragon and pig, snake and dog. Folklore gives improbable reasons for these antipathies: Rat's fear of Sheep's horns, Ox's anger at Horse's refusal to plough, Tiger's rejection of Fowl's short beak, gentle Hare's disapproval of Monkey's levity, Dragon's dislike of Pig's sooty face and Snake's fear of Dog's bark. The real rationale is less colourful. Beginning with Rat and Ox, odd-numbered signs are, for divinatory purposes, *yang* and even-numbered signs *yin*. Taking the signs in pairs, each sign is antipathetic to the sign of opposite *yin-yang* (*ŭm-yang*) nature in the pair diametrically opposite in the circular presentation of the cycle.

In Chinese almanacs other antipathies (and some compatibilities) are found, based on similar geometrical analyses of this circle.

GENERAL BIBLIOGRAPHY

Ahn Hwi-Joon, Kim Won-Yong, Lew Young-Ick, *Korean Art Tradition*, Seoul: Korea Foundation, 1993

Gina Lee Barnes, *China, Japan and Korea: the Rise of Civilization in East Asia*, London: Thames & Hudson, 1993

Byun Juna, *Early Humans in the Korean Peninsula: from the Palaeolithic Age to the Three Kingdoms Age*, Seoul: Hyŏnmunsa, 1995

Cambridge History of China, London: Cambridge University Press, 1979 –

Choi Sunu *et al., 5000 Years of Korean Art*, Seoul: Hyonam Publishing Co, 1979 (also published as René-Yvon Lefebvre d'Argence, ed., *5000 Years of Korean Art*, San Francisco: Asian Art Museum, 1979)

Bruce Cumings, *Korea's Place in the Sun, a Modern History*, New York & London: W.W.Norton & Co., 1997

Theodore de Bary & Jahyun Kim Haboush, eds., *The Rise of Neo-Confucianism in Korea*, New York: Columbia University Press, 1985

Martina Deuchler, *Confucian Gentlemen and Barbarian Envoys; the Opening of Korea, 1875–1885*, Seattle and London: University of Washington Press, 1977

Barry Gills, *Korea Versus Korea: A Case of Contested Legitimacy*, London: Routledge, 1996

James Grayson, *Korea, a Religious History*, Oxford University Press, 1989

Han Woo-Keun, *The History of Korea*, Seoul: Eul-yoo Publishing Co., 1970

James Hoare, *Korea*, World Bibliographical Series, volume 204, Oxford, Denver, Santa Barbara: Clio Press, 1997

James Hoare & Susan Pares, *Korea, an Introduction*, London: Kegan Paul International, 1988

Kim Hongnam, ed., *Korean Arts of the Eighteenth Century: Splendour and Simplicity*, New York: The Asia Society, 1994

Kim Hunggyu (trans. Robert J. Fouser), *Understanding Korean Literature*, London: M. E. Sharpe, 1997

Kim Tai-Jin, *A Bibliographical Guide to Traditional Korean Sources*, Seoul: Asiatic Research Center, Korea University, 1976

Kim Won-Yong, *Art and Archaeology of Ancient Korea*, Seoul: Taekwang Publishing Co., 1986

Kim Won-Yong, Han Byong-Sam, Chin Hong-Sop, *The Arts of Korea*, Seoul: Dong Hwa Publishing Co., 1979, 6 vols.

K.O.I.S., *Korean Art Guide*, Seoul: Yekyong Publications Co., 1987

Koreana, *Korean Culture and Heritage*, vol.1: Fine Arts, Seoul: The Korea Foundation, 1994; vol.2: Thought and Religion, 1996; vol.3: Performing Arts, 1997; vol.4: Traditional Lifestyles, 1998

Junghee Lee, *Azaleas and Golden Bells, Korean Art in the Collection of the Portland Art Museum*, Portland, 1998

Lee Ki-Baik, trans. Edward Wagner, *A New History of Korea*, Cambridge, Mass.: Harvard University Press, 1984

Peter H. Lee, ed., *Sourcebook of Korean Civilisation*, vol.1: from Early Times to the Sixteenth Century, New York: Columbia University Press, 1993; vol.2: from the Seventeenth Century to the Modern Period, New York: Columbia University Press, 1996

Stewart Lone & Gavin McCormack, *Korea since 1850*, Melbourne: Longman Cheshire, 1993

Donald MacDonald, *The Koreans, Contemporary Politics and Society*, Boulder: Westview Press, 2nd edition, 1990

Evelyn McCune, *The Arts of Korea, an Illustrated History*, Rutland, Vermont & Tokyo, 1962

Beth McKillop, *Korean Art and Design*, London: Victoria & Albert Museum, 1992

Metropolitan Museum of Art, *Arts of Korea*, New York, 1998

Andrew Nahm, *Korea: Tradition and Transformation: A History of the Korean People*, Seoul: Hollym Corporation, 1988

Andrew Nahm, *Historical Dictionary of the Republic of Korea*, Metuchen, N.J.: Scarecrow Press, 1993

Robert A. Scalapino & Chong-Sik Lee, *Communism in Korea, Part I: the Movement; Part II: the Society*, Berkeley: Univerity of California Press, 1972

Suh Daesook, *The Korean Communist Movement, 1918–1948*, Princeton University Press, 1967

Roger Tennant, *A History of Korea*, London: Kegan Paul International, 1996

Jane Turner, ed., *The Dictionary of Art*, London: Macmillan & Co., New York: Grove's Dictionaries Inc., 1996. (For the main entry on Korea, see volume 18, pp.245–385)

Roderick Whitfield, ed., *Treasures from Korea: Art through 5000 Years*, London: British Museum, 1984

Roderick Whitfield & Pak Young-Sook, eds., *Korean Art Treasures*, Seoul: Yekyong Publications Co., 1986

Michael Yahuda, *The International Politics of the Asia-Pacific, 1945–95*, London: Routledge, 1996

Further Korean bibliographies can be found at the following websites:
http://www.fas.harvard.edu/~hoffmann
http://www2.hawaii.edu/korea/table.htm

The website of the National Museum of Korea is at:
http://www.museum.go.kr/english/index.html

INDEX OF PERSONAL NAMES

INDEX OF LITERARY AND
MUSICAL TITLES